GROLIER

ENCYCLOPEDIA
OF KNOWLEDGE

Grolier Incorporated
Danbury, Connecticut

ISBN 0-7172-5300-7 (complete set)
ISBN 0-7172-5310-4 (volume 10)

Printed and manufactured in the United States of America.

This publication is an abridged version of the *Academic American Encyclopedia*.

10 9 8 7 6 5 4 3

GERMAN-GOTHIC	RUSSIAN-CYRILLIC	CLASSICAL LATIN	EARLY LATIN	ETRUSCAN	CLASSICAL GREEK	EARLY GREEK	EARLY ARAMAIC	EARLY HEBREW	PHOENICIAN

I *I/i* is the ninth letter of the English alphabet. Both the form of the letter and its position in the alphabet are derived from the Latin, which derived it from the Greek by way of the Etruscan. The Greeks, who took the form and position of the letter, along with the rest of the alphabet, from a Semitic writing system, call the letter *iota*. The Semitic name of the sign is *yodh*, and it does not represent a vowel but the consonant *y*. The Greeks used the sign to represent both the vowel *i* and the consonant *y*; this usage passed into Latin and continued into the Middle Ages. The two sounds were finally differentiated by use of the letters *I/i* and *J/j*, the latter derived from the former by the addition of a curved stroke at the bottom. In modern English pronunciation *I/i* has two basic sounds: a short *i*, as in *bit* and *lip*, and a long *i*, as in *bite* and *high*. Occasionally it has the sound of long *e*, as in *magazine*.

I Ching The *I Ching* (Pinyin form: *I Jing*), or *Book of Changes*, is one of the central texts of Confucianism and one of the earliest works of Chinese literature. It consists of 64 hexagrams, each of which is made up of six divided or undivided lines, possibly created at the end of the 2d millennium BC; a cryptic, partly unintelligible text, written at the beginning of the 1st millennium BC; and a treatise on the text, the *Ten Wings*, written at the end of the 1st millennium BC. Although rejected by the empiricist scholars of the Qing (Ch'ing) dynasty, the numerological aspects of the *I Ching* have recently been reemphasized by Westerners interested in Eastern mysticism.

Iacocca, Lee Lido Anthony Iacocca, b. Allentown, Pa., Oct. 15, 1924, is an auto-industry executive regarded by many as a U.S. "corporate folk hero." The son of Italian immigrants, he took his first job, at Ford Motor Co., in 1946 and worked his way up to Ford's presidency in 1970. In 1978, Henry Ford II discharged Iacocca, who became president and then chairman of the failing Chrysler Corp. He is widely credited with saving Chrysler from bankruptcy. As chairman of the Statue of Liberty–Ellis Island Foundation, he raised more than the $265-million goal for the landmark's rehabilitation. His autobiography, *Iacocca* (with William Novak, 1984), established sales records.

iamb see VERSIFICATION

Iamblichus [y-am'-bli-kuhs] Iamblichus, d. *c*.330, called "the divine" by Neoplatonists, was considered the authority for NEOPLATONISM for more than two centuries. His interpretation gave PLOTINUS'S and PORPHYRY'S systems of emanations (see EMANATIONISM) a mystic and religious rather than an aesthetic or logical interpretation. He differed from Plotinus in espousing a level of "ideal numbers" between The One and Mind. He differed from Porphyry in his belief that proper religious observance (theurgy) was a virtue higher than that of the intellect and could persuade the benevolent gods and repel the evil demons.

Ibadan [ee-bah'-dahn] Ibadan is the capital of Oyo state, Nigeria. It is that country's second largest city and is located about 130 km (80 mi) northeast of Lagos, near the border of the forest and savanna zones. Ibadan's population is 1,201,000 (1989 est.).

The population is primarily YORUBA. About one-third of the work force engages in agriculture on farmland located outside of the city. Cacao, cotton, corn, and palm kernels are processed and marketed in the city. Manufactures include traditional handicrafts, furniture, cigarettes, and plastics.

The University of Ibadan (1948) is located there. The date of Ibadan's founding is unknown, but its recorded history dates from 1829. The British took control of the city in 1893. It grew as a commercial center after the arrival of the railroad in 1901.

Iberian Peninsula The Iberian Peninsula, occupied by Spain and Portugal, is situated in southwestern Europe. It has an area of 580,860 km^2 (224,270 mi^2). Separated from the rest of Europe to the north by the Pyrenees Mountains, it is bounded by the Atlantic Ocean on the north and west and the Mediterranean Sea on the south and east. The southern tip of the peninsula is separated from Africa by the Strait of Gibraltar. The name Iberia, given by the Greeks, referred to an ancient people who originally lived along the Ebro (Iberus) River.

Five major rivers, of which the TAGUS is the largest, drain the peninsula. Two-thirds of the peninsula is composed of a great central plateau more than 600 m (2,000 ft) in elevation, known as the Meseta.

Ibert, Jacques [ee-bair'] The French composer Jacques Ibert, b. Aug. 15, 1890, d. Feb. 5, 1962, was a pupil of Gabriel Fauré and André Gédalge at the Paris Conservatory. Ibert served in the French Navy during World War I. Awarded the Prix de Rome in 1919 for a cantata, he later returned to Rome as director (1937–55) of the French Academy there. For two years (1955–57) he was managing director of the combined Paris Opéra and Opéra Comique. Ibert's symphonic suite *Escales* (Ports of Call), was his most successful work. First performed in 1924, it reflected Ibert's naval experiences. His other compositions include operas, symphonic poems, chamber music, and songs.

Iberville, Pierre Le Moyne, Sieur d' [dee-bair-veel', pee-air' luh-mwanh', sur] The French-Canadian explorer Pierre Le Moyne, sieur d'Iberville, b. July 1661, d. July 9, 1706, was, like his younger brother, the sieur de BIENVILLE, intimately associated with French exploration and colonization in the Gulf of Mexico. Early in his career he won distinction by his military prowess against the English in Canada, leading (1686–97) five attacks on English trading posts on Hudson Bay. He also destroyed (1696) Fort William Henry at Pemaquid, Maine, and briefly expelled (1696) the English from St. John's, Newfoundland.

In 1698, Iberville led an expedition to found a French colony at the mouth of the Mississippi River. He reached the Gulf of Mexico in 1699 and sought to establish a bastion at Pensacola. The Spaniards, however, had already fortified Pensacola, and he was forced down the coast to Massacre (present-day Dauphin) Island in Biloxi Bay. There he founded the colony of Old Biloxi. In 1706 he led an expedition that captured the West Indian island of Nevis from the English, but later in the year he succumbed to yellow fever in Havana.

ibex [y'-beks] The ibex, *Capra ibex,* is a wild goat, family Bovidae, found in mountainous areas in Europe, Asia, and North Africa. Adult males are characterized by beards and by long horns, often 75 cm (2.5 ft) and sometimes 1.2 m (4 ft) in length, that typically curve backward over the head and that have pronounced semicircular ridges spaced along their front edges. Females lack beards and have small horns, about 20 cm (8 in) long, that are straight or just slightly curved. Six subspecies, or races, of ibexes are recognized; two of these, the eastern and western Caucasian ibexes, or turs, are sometimes considered a single separate species, *C. caucasica.*

ibis [y'-bis] Ibis is the common name for various wading birds having long, curved bills and belonging to the family Threskiornithidae, which also includes the spoonbill. Ibis are found in most of the warmer areas of the world and are familiar among the hieroglyphics on ancient Egyptian monuments. The sacred ibis, *Threskiornis ae-*

The scarlet ibis of tropical South America is approximately 60 cm (24 in) long. It makes its nest in huge coastal colonies.

thiopica, of Africa was worshiped in ancient Egypt for its legendary powers. Two American species formerly confined to the extreme south have extended their ranges northward in recent years: the glossy ibis, *Plegadis falcinellus,* approximately 60 cm (24 in) in length and dark bronze blue, now reaches Maine in annual flights; and the white ibis, *Eudocimus albus,* larger and white with black wingtips, now nests in Virginia.

Ibiza [ee-bee'-thah] Ibiza, one of the BALEARIC ISLANDS, is situated in the western Mediterranean Sea, about 130 km (80 mi) east of the Spanish coast. Ibiza covers 572 km^2 (221 mi^2), and its population is 59,933 (1981). The city of Ibiza is the largest settlement. Composed of limestone outcrop, the island's rugged hills rise to 475 m (1,558 ft) at Atalayasa. Many springs and the Santa Eulalia River irrigate terraced fields of almonds, figs, olives, and potatoes. Tourism is the basis of the economy. In ancient times the island was settled in turn by the Phoenicians, Carthaginians, and Romans.

Ibn Battuta [ib'-uhn bah-too'-tah] Ibn Battuta, b. Feb. 25, 1304, d. 1368/69 or 1377, an indefatigable Arab traveler, composed the most comprehensive account of the Muslim world in the later Middle Ages. Between 1325 and 1354 he journeyed through North Africa, the Middle East, East Africa, Central Asia, India, Southeast Asia, and possibly China. Separately, he also visited southern Spain and crossed the Sahara to the Muslim lands of West Africa.

Ibn Battuta dictated an account of his travels after his

return to Morocco; the work was completed on Dec. 9, 1357. A depiction of the known world beyond Europe, the work is valuable as a major source for economic and social history.

Ibn Ezra, Abraham ben Meir [ib'-uhn ez'-ruh, ay'-bruh-ham ben mayr] Abraham ben Meir Ibn Ezra, c.1089–1164, was a Spanish Jewish scholar. His Bible commentaries combined traditional Jewish interpretation with a critical method of exegesis and emphasis on grammar; his philosophical work followed the Neoplatonic tendency (see NEOPLATONISM) in medieval thought. Ibn Ezra translated an astronomical work from the Arabic into Hebrew, creating a Hebrew prose style for scientific purposes. He was probably the model for Robert Browning's poem "Rabbi Ben Ezra."

Ibn Gabirol, Solomon ben Judah [ib'-uhn gah-bee'-rohl, sahl'-uh-muhn ben joo'-duh] Solomon ben Judah Ibn Gabirol, c.1021–c.1058, was a Jewish poet and philosopher who lived in Muslim Spain. His enormous poetic output (more than 400 extant poems) was both secular and religious. His *Keter Malkhut* (*The Kingly Crown*) is a long philosophical poem that Sephardic Jews still include in their prayer book for the Day of Atonement. Gabirol's philosophic work combined NEOPLATONISM with traditional Jewish philosophy. His ethical treatise *The Improvement of the Moral Qualities* is regarded as the first attempt to separate ethics from a purely religious framework.

Ibn Khaldun [ib'-uhn kahl-doon'] Ibn Khaldun, b. May 27, 1332, d. Mar. 16, 1406, was a famous Muslim historian, sociologist, and philosopher. Born into a distinguished Arab family in Tunis, he alternated between active involvement in the turbulent politics of North Africa and Spain and scholarly retirement. In 1382 he went to Egypt, where he became a judge and teacher of Islamic law.

Ibn Khaldun is best known for the *Muqaddimah*, an introduction to his *Kitab al-'Ibar* (Universal History). *Kitab al-'Ibar* is a valuable source for the history of North Africa, but the *Muqaddimah* is a brilliant exposition of the methodological and cultural knowledge necessary to produce a scientific history. Ibn Khaldun contended that the basic causes of historical evolution are to be sought in the economic and social structure of society.

Ibn Saud, King of Saudi Arabia [ib'-uhn sah-ood'] Abd al-Aziz ibn Abd al-Rahman, or Ibn Saud, b. c.1880, d. Nov. 9, 1953, unified much of the Arabian peninsula to create the Kingdom of Saudi Arabia, which he ruled from 1932 until his death. He was a member of the Saudi dynasty. During his youth the Saudis were eclipsed by the Ottoman-supported house of Rashid, and he spent 1891 to 1902 in exile.

In 1902, Ibn Saud spectacularly initiated the Saudi revival by retaking Riyadh, the Saudi capital, in a surprise assault. Between 1902 and 1912 he conquered central Arabia; in 1913 he expelled the Turks from eastern Arabia; between 1916 and 1922 he eliminated Rashidi power and annexed northern Arabia; between 1924 and 1926 he drove the Hashimites (see HUSAYN IBN ALI) from Mecca and western Arabia; and between 1930 and 1934 he consolidated his new borders by repulsing Yemeni incursions. His conquests were organized into the Kingdom of Saudi Arabia in 1932.

Ibn Saud carefully cultivated traditional Saudi ties with the fundamentalist Muslim sect of WAHHABISM, which provided a powerful ideological appeal. Through his Ikhwan (brotherhood) movement, he organized the settlement of many nomadic tribes in agriculturally based military colonies, providing bases from which to spearhead Saudi expansion. At the same time he displayed great diplomatic skill, especially in his dealings with Britain, which provided both weapons and money. Ibn Saud was succeeded by his son SAUD.

Ibo [ee'-boh] The Ibo (Igbo) are a major ethnic group of southeastern Nigeria. Their language is in the Kwa subfamily of Niger-Congo languages (see AFRICAN LANGUAGES), and they are estimated to number 16 million (1983). Most Ibo are subsistence farmers who grow root crops and produce palm oil for export. Local and long-distance market trade is well developed. Descent is mainly patrilineal, and marriage is polygynous, formalized by the payment of bride-price. Tribal associations are common and include title societies, groups based on age, and men's secret societies. Traditional religion centers on ancestral spirits and nature worship. Oracles are powerful and highly respected. Art forms include spectacular, painted wood carvings of human heads, masks, and figures, and doors and stools carved in geometric patterns.

Traditionally the Ibo lived in hundreds of autonomous village groups ruled by councils of elders. They practiced head-hunting and owned slaves in precolonial times. Because of the high population density of their home region, large numbers of Ibo migrated to other parts of Nigeria. Under British colonial and missionary influence, many became Christians. In 1963 the Ibo played a major part in establishing Nigerian independence. Political conflict in 1966 between the Ibo and the Muslim Hausa and Fulani of northern Nigeria led to the formation of the Ibo-supported secessionist state of BIAFRA. Thousands of Ibo were killed during the bloody civil war that followed (1967–70).

Ibsen, Henrik [ib'-suhn, hen'-rik] Henrik Johan Ibsen, b. Skien, Norway, Mar. 20, 1828, d. May 23, 1906, was a poet and dramatist whose works form the foundation of modern drama. Ibsen's lasting international reputation may be attributed to the long dramatic poems *Brand* (1866; Eng. trans., 1911) and *Peer Gynt* (1867; Eng. trans., 1907) of his middle years and to a cycle of 11 realistic plays with contemporary settings that he pro-

Henrik Ibsen, 19th-century Norwegian playwright, profoundly influenced the development of modern drama through his realistic themes and emphasis on the individual's search for meaning.

duced between 1877 and 1896, including A DOLL'S HOUSE (1879; Eng. trans., 1906), *Ghosts* (1881; Eng. trans., 1906), *The Wild Duck* (1884; Eng. trans., 1907), and *Hedda Gabler* (1890; Eng. trans., 1907).

Ibsen's childhood and youth were scarred by his father's bankruptcy in 1836 and the consequent change from affluence to relative poverty; his maturity was profoundly influenced by the oppressive and troubled aftermath of the year of revolutions, 1848. Fending for himself from age 15, he became a druggist's apprentice in Grimstad with the intention of pursuing medical studies, but failure in Greek and arithmetic on the entrance examination to the University of Christiania in 1850 closed that avenue to him. He then turned to journalism and made fledgling efforts in poetry and playwriting. The latter brought him to the attention of the celebrated Ole Bull, who in 1851 offered Ibsen an appointment as codirector and dramatic author at the newly established Norwegian Theater (later the National Stage) in Bergen.

Ibsen's tenure in Bergen (1851–57) and his appointment as artistic manager of the Christiania Norwegian Theater (1857–62) spanned 11 years, more notable for failures and frustrations than any real success. The posts nonetheless afforded him invaluable training and experience in dramaturgy and stagecraft. In 1852, on a sabbatical in Copenhagen and Dresden, Ibsen first experienced Shakespeare in performance and encountered the tradition of presenting Holberg's comedies, still strongly maintained on the Danish stage. He also studied the dramatic theory of Hermann Hettner, a professor of aesthetics at Jena University, whose programmatic essay *Das moderne Drama* (Modern Drama, 1852) was much discussed. Hettner reinforced Ibsen's awareness of the psychological truth to which drama should aspire, proceeding from the conflict and development of human character. Hettner also drew his attention to Friedrich Hebbel's bourgeois tragedy *Maria Magdalena* (1843; Eng. trans., 1914).

In 1856, Ibsen met Suzannah Thoresen, whom he married two years later. Their son and only child, Sigurd, was born in 1859. Beginning in 1864 the Ibsens lived abroad, primarily in Rome, Dresden, and Munich, on grants from the Norwegian parliament, which were awarded annually after the tremendous breakthrough that *Brand* heralded, and on the growing royalties from Ibsen's creative output. His meeting with the Danish critic George Brandes in 1871 and his reading of the first part of Brandes's *Main Currents in Nineteenth-Century Literature* (1872; Eng. trans., 1901–06) not only reinforced Ibsen's belief in the necessity of a spiritual, as opposed to a political, revolution but was also the main reason he limited his poetic vision to the sphere of contemporary life in his last 11 dramas. In 1891, as *grand seigneur* of Scandinavian letters, Ibsen returned to live in Christiania. In 1900 he suffered the first of a series of strokes that ended his literary career; he was bedridden the last 5 years of his life.

Ibsen's work as a creative writer spanned 50 years (1849–99) and yielded 25 completed plays and a sheaf of verse of consistent high quality. While his total production is remarkable for its extraordinary thematic unity—dealing chiefly with the individual human being and one's self-realization in spirit and in truth—it may be divided into two phases: an initial romantic period (1849–75), during which dramatic and nondramatic verse was his principal means of expression, and a subsequent realistic one (1875–99), when he devoted himself exclusively to the more difficult art of writing the straightforward, plain language spoken in real life, thereby laying the foundations of modern prose drama.

ibuprofen   see ANALGESIC

Icarus   see DAEDALUS (mythology)

ICBM   see ROCKETS AND MISSILES

---

ice, river and lake   Ice forms in lakes and rivers whenever the surface water supercools to 0° C (32° F) or a fraction of a degree lower. The first appearance of ice in a lake usually takes the form of spicules or platelike crystals. These grow into a network of dendrites that ultimately freeze together to form a continuous ice cover, called skim ice. This ice cover continues to thicken downward as a result of transfer of heat from the ice to the air. Such ice is generally composed of prismatic or columnar-shaped crystals oriented vertically within the ice sheet.

Freezing of lake water removes most dissolved solids; the impurities retained are usually concentrated in the crystal boundaries. During spring these impurities induce preferential melting of crystal boundaries. Such melting produces candling, or disintegration of the ice cover crystal by crystal, a major factor in its ultimate decay.

Continuous ice covers may also form on rivers that have flow velocities less than about 0.5 m/sec (1.6 ft/sec). Ice formations in more turbulent, supercooled water, however, tend to be dominated by a copious crystallization of small particles of ice, called frazil. If these particles remain suspended in the water, they may never coalesce sufficiently to form a frazil ice cover, except at obstructions in the river where bridging or damming can occur—frequently the prelude to flooding. Frazil may also clog intakes of hydroelectric plants, and accumulations can damage structures by exerting pressure.

Anchor ice may form on river bottoms. Soil and stones at the bottom may radiate enough heat on clear, cold nights to lower bottom temperature below 0° C. Solar radiation in the morning can loosen the ice and bring it quickly to the surface in large chunks.

ice ages An ice age is any part of several periods or epochs of time when glaciers, especially in the form of great ice sheets (see GLACIER AND GLACIATION), covered more of the Earth's surface than they do today. The term "ice age" has been used in two senses. First, it may refer to whole glacial epochs (the Pleistocene, for example), 1.7 million to 60 million years long, when the climate in the middle latitudes fluctuated wildly from warm to cold, and glaciation ranged from today's small polar ice caps to massive, semiglobal ice sheets. Alternatively, it may describe a single glacial stage (such as the Wisconsin or Illinoisan) within these epochs, lasting for approximately 19,000 to 100,000 years each, when glaciers covered perhaps 20% to 50% of the continents (see PALEOCLIMATOLOGY). Overall, ice ages are unusual, relatively short episodes representing only about 1% of the 4.6 billion-year span of GEOLOGIC TIME.

Evidence

The existence of five ice ages is verified by clear evidence from widely scattered parts of the Earth's surface. Evidence of the most recent ice age, which lasted more than 1.7 million years, suggests that the great ice sheets existed simultaneously on several continents. The proof of glaciation over continent-sized areas lies first in the widespread deposition of a unique kind of sediment called till (see TILL AND TILLITE) that can be observed under all glaciers today. Till and related deposits also contain a wide variety of rock types (stones and boulders called glacial erratics), such as would be derived from widely disparate areas. Third, till and erratics lie on one of the unique erosional surfaces of glaciation, such as grooved, striated, or polished bedrock pavement.

Ancient Ice Ages. Evidence for the oldest known glaciation occurs in rocks formed 2,300 to 1,700 million years ago, during Precambrian time (see EARTH, GEOLOGICAL HISTORY OF). The best tillites from this ice age occur in Canada, where they rest on striated pavement and have been dated to more than 2 billion years old (see RADIOMETRIC AGE-DATING). Three altered tillites indicate three continental ice advances. The rocks, which contain glacial erratics up to 5 m (16 ft) long, underlie a 130,000-km² (52,000-mi²) area of west central Ontario near Sudbury. Other widespread formations of the same age occur in Finland and South Africa, and a similar formation has been found in upper Michigan. These deposits were laid down when all these landmasses were at the North Pole.

Another drastic ice age occurred later in Precambrian time, 680 million years ago, and may or may not have triggered an enormous diversity of marine invertebrates whose fossil remains are found in the rocks of this time. On the west side of the Wasatch Mountains in Utah there is a 100-m-thick (330-ft) layer of sooty gray phyllite, a METAMORPHIC ROCK that was once tillite; the rock contains various erratic boulders up to 6 m (20 ft) long. In central Australia, glacial sediments of this age have been mapped in detail over an area of 250,000 km² (100,000 mi²). Tillites preserved in eastern Greenland, Scotland, and Scandinavia also date from this age.

Evidence of a major glaciation that took place at the Ordovician-Silurian boundary, about 420 million years ago, has been found in the Sahara, where a layer of sedimentary marine tillites and beautifully grooved pavement is underlain by a striated pavement of Ordovician sandstone containing TRILOBITE fossils. Central Africa was the Earth's South Pole then, and evidence of glaciation from this period extends well up through Spain and west into eastern Brazil.

The outstanding worldwide sediment record of the Pennsylvanian (Upper Carboniferous) Period shows cycles of rise and fall in sea level. It is not certain that these cycles were glacially induced, but no better explanation has been put forth. Also, the evidence for glaciation simultaneous with or just into the Permian Period (about 280 million years ago) is good. A series of marine or coal-swamp (shore) beds covered by several tillites underlie

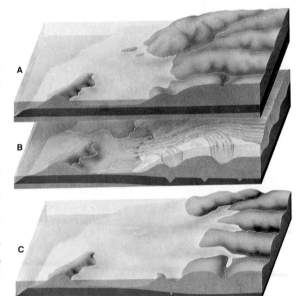

Glaciation, such as that which occurs during an ice age, leads to changes in sea level. As temperatures become lower, a land mass (A) is covered by glaciers (B), which contain much of the water originally in the ocean; thus the sea level decreases. The weight of the ice causes depression of the land that amounts to about one-third of the ice thickness. When warm conditions return and the ice melts (C), the water flows back to the ocean; an additional rise in sea levels is due to the slow recovery of the depressed land.

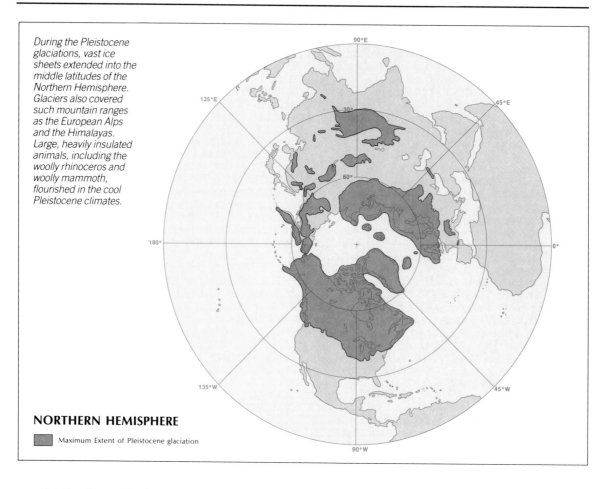

During the Pleistocene glaciations, vast ice sheets extended into the middle latitudes of the Northern Hemisphere. Glaciers also covered such mountain ranges as the European Alps and the Himalayas. Large, heavily insulated animals, including the woolly rhinoceros and woolly mammoth, flourished in the cool Pleistocene climates.

NORTHERN HEMISPHERE

▧ Maximum Extent of Pleistocene glaciation

areas totaling thousands of square kilometers in localities on five widely separated continents: Antarctica, South Africa, Brazil, India, and Australia. Although this evidence comes from far-flung parts of the globe, in Permo-Carboniferous time what are now today's continents then formed the paleocontinent Gondwanaland, which was centered about the South Pole (see PALEOGEOGRAPHY). One gigantic ice sheet may have covered 50% of Gondwanaland.

Sedimentary rocks of Permo-Carboniferous age are the first strata to show clearly the effects of an ice age on higher forms of life (see FOSSIL RECORD). Most notable were the changes in plant life that occurred worldwide, particularly EXTINCTION of species of Pennsylvanian-age trees.

Quaternary Ice Age. In the Pleistocene Epoch, beginning 1.7 million years ago, ice sheets developed on highlands in North America and Europe and spread over the northern half of North America and a quarter of Eurasia, dominating the Northern Hemisphere. As sea level fell and the ice covered more land area, glaciers spread over what is now the shallow seafloor of Hudson Bay and the Barents Sea. This glacial spread comprised 52% of the Pleistocene ice-covered area. The older Antarctic and Greenland ice sheets grew somewhat larger as well. Man-

tles of ice developed in the group of mountain ranges stretching from southern Alaska to Colorado and California, in the European Alps, in the Ural and Caucasus Mountains, and in the Himalayas. Mountain glaciers in the Southern Hemisphere (in the South American Andes, the New Zealand Alps, and western Tasmania) extended down onto the plains. Altogether the mountain glaciers made up 16% of the total ice area.

The continental glaciers became very thick. The oxygen ISOTOPES of sediments deposited on the seafloor during the colder stages of Quaternary time indicate that the thickness of the ice averaged 2,500 m (8,200 ft) much of the time.

The ice-age seas were lower than today's by 100 to 140 m (330 to 460 ft). Many wave-cut terraces and sea cliffs are found that far below today's SEA LEVEL. Elevated coral reefs and shore terraces, however, indicate that sea level was also 5 to 50 m (16 to 160 ft) higher than it is now during some interglacial intervals. By comparison, if all the Greenland and Antarctic ice melted today, sea level would rise nearly 65 m (215 ft). Ice-age sea levels are generally lower than those in the nonglacial 99% of geologic time. They certainly fluctuate wildly over the few tens of thousands of years during which the ice sheets grew and melted away. During the last ice age, sea level rose or fell over 1 to 2 m (3 to 7 ft) per century. During the same period the ice crept over the land at 50 to 150 m (160 to 490 ft) per year.

These Quaternary events occurred because of changes in CLIMATE. CIRQUES produced by local mountain glaciers that could have existed only during glacial stages are found 1,200 to 1,700 m (4,000 to 5,600 ft) lower than today's mountain glaciers; this indicates that the temperature in mid-latitude mountain ranges during these stages was 7 C degrees (13 F degrees) cooler than it is today. Most ocean surface waters at the height of the glacial stages were at least 2 to 5 C degrees (4 to 9 F degrees) cooler and slightly less saline than today. The oxygen-isotope ratios of snow falling during the last ice age indicate that on the still-remaining ice sheets (Antarctica and Greenland ice at 1,300 and 1,150 m/4,300 and 3,800 ft depth), ice-age temperatures were as much as 6 to 8 C degrees (11 to 14 F degrees) colder, and the atmosphere was ten or more times dustier than it is today.

The Quaternary ice age had great effects—far more than previous ice ages had—upon life-forms, because more-advanced life-forms and more numerous species of fauna and flora were involved. The stresses of rapidly changing temperature, precipitation, and winds must have been great.

Heavily insulated animal species—such as the woolly rhinoceros, the woolly MAMMOTH, and the MUSK-OX—developed, while slowly evolving Cenozoic species, such as the Pliocene horse and several fish, disappeared early in this ice age.

The list of extinct Pleistocene mammals is long. The large ones—the MASTODON, the great beavers, the SABER-TOOTHED CATS, the ground sloth, and the glyptodon—disappeared everywhere. Llamas, camels, tapirs, horses, yaks, and other species became extinct only in North America. Lower animal forms, such as mollusks and beetles, did not change much by adaptation, but they did migrate. River valleys became natural migratory highways; while some animal forms were frozen into extinction, others were able to escape the ice by migrating toward the equator.

Plant life changed little during the 1.7 million years of the Quaternary ice age. Plant pollen and spores, being quite hardy, are preserved in bogs between glacial layers and provide complete records of the interglacial spasms and approaching glacial stages (see POLLEN STRATIGRAPHY). Tree genuses in those times were similar to today's; although they failed to reproduce in some colder areas, they appeared and flourished anew in warmer areas as the ice slowly moved in. In North America spruce grew best 1,200 to 1,600 km (745 to 990 mi) farther south than usual—in North Carolina, Virginia, and Ohio—suggesting temperatures 7 to 10 C degrees (13 to 18 F degrees) cooler at that time. Trees lying in the path of the ice were crushed and swept up into the till. South of the ice, in temperate latitudes, a mixture of warm-climate species on hillsides facing south and cool-climate species on those facing north coexisted. The group of warmth-loving species returned in each succeeding warm interglacial time; in Europe these species were more diverse than those in America, but all the trees of that time were similar to those of today.

Today humans live in a warm interlude that, according to current theory, will end with a long-term cooling trend culminating in the next glacial stage, 23,000 years hence.

Causes of Glaciation

The only adequate source of water for such massive amounts of ice is the oceans. The creation of massive ice sheets on land thus necessarily depends on wind and weather patterns. To preserve snow from year to year, the summer climate must be cooler. There are so many ways these events could happen, and happen repeatedly, that the cause is locked into complicated OCEAN-ATMOSPHERE INTERACTIONS. It is extremely difficult to know what is cause and what is effect. For example, the STRATOSPHERE was ten times dustier during glacial times than it is today. DUST not only absorbs some radiation in the upper atmosphere but also reflects some of the Sun's heat back out, thus cooling the Earth's surface. At first this was thought to be volcanic dust, but volcanism has not been correlated with any of the glacial stages. Dust may have been raised because large areas of the CONTINENTAL SHELF were exposed around receding seas.

Evidence in SAND DUNES and LOESS blankets shows that in glacial times the wind was intensified, and the belts of WESTERLIES were pushed toward the equator. Intensified heat exchange would also produce more clouds and precipitation; the increased cloudiness would be 80% effective in reflecting solar radiation back out into space; the Earth's surface would therefore become 1 to 2 C degrees (2 to 4 F degrees) cooler.

Variations in the amount of carbon dioxide in the lower atmosphere may also have had some effect. Carbon dioxide lets in short-wave sunlight, but it also prevents long-wave heat radiation from passing out of the atmosphere (see GREENHOUSE EFFECT), thus raising the atmospheric temperature between glaciations. In glacial stages, however, surface seawater would have been 2 to 6 C degrees (4 to 11 F degrees) cooler; this cooler water could absorb more carbon dioxide from the air and thus cool the latter by 1 to 2 C degrees (2 to 4 F degrees).

When the sea level was lower, many surface OCEAN CURRENTS no longer delivered heat to the far north (or south, in earlier ice ages); this would have dropped high-latitude temperature by 2 to 4 C degrees (4 to 7 F degrees). Once it had begun to form, the snow-ice surface itself then would have cooled the AIR MASSES making contact with it by more than 5 C degrees (9 F degrees); this would have caused the further extension of sea ice that is recorded in the sandy SEDIMENTS on the ocean floor. Sea ice, like clouds, is 80% effective in reflecting the radiant energy from the Sun, thus adding to the cooling effect. This also prevents free access of moisture into the air, the principal effect behind the Ewing-Donn theory of glaciation. The ice sheets, then, begin to shrink, sea level rises correspondingly, and warm ocean currents begin to melt the sea ice. All these mechanisms are self-reinforcing, and each may contribute to the waxing of any ice age.

Continental glaciation requires either high mountain altitudes (over 4,000 m/13,000 ft) or polar land (high ground located above 60° latitude). CONTINENTAL DRIFT and shifting polar positions play a part here. Paleomagnetic analysis of ice-age sediments is now confirming the theory that today's continents were at one time united and near one pole or the other (see PALEOMAGNETISM). Also, high mountains have arisen wherever continental plates have slid into each other, as India's current collision with Asia is raising the Himalayas (see PLATE TECTONICS). Unlike the self-reinforcing mechanisms, continental drift and mountain building occur so slowly that they could contribute to only entire ice ages, not to the drastic cycling of climate characteristic of the several stages.

Some climate-altering trigger mechanism, most likely from outside the Earth or its atmosphere, seems to be necessary. Solar-energy intensities have not yet been found to vary sufficiently to have single-handedly produced an ice age, but solar activity as expressed in SUNSPOTS and MAGNETIC STORMS on an 11-year cycle has been shown to relate to short-term fluctuations in the Earth's climate. Longer cycles are currently being sought by statistical means.

Among the astronomical hypotheses, the Milankovitch theory, first proposed in 1924, has gained widest acceptance. According to this theory, the combination of a trio of orbital variations (see EARTH, MOTIONS OF)—eccentricity (a 97,000-year cycle), PRECESSION (22,000 years), and axial tilt (41,000 years)—produces effects that are large enough to cause cyclical expansion and contraction of the ice sheets. By taking the effects on climate and solar insolation of these variations and applying them to computer models of the behavior of ice sheets, scientists have succeeded in demonstrating a correlation between the cycles and the cyclic growth and decay of Pleistocene ice sheets over the past 600,000 years. COMPUTER MODELING provides a critical line of evidence by showing that combinations of orbital cycles result in lower summer insolation at 55° north latitude. Such cooler summers in high latitudes tend to preserve each winter's snowfall, and the accumulation of snow from a succession of winters induces growth of the northern ice sheets and the onset of a glacial stage.

ice cream

Ice cream is a popular frozen food made from varying mixtures of cream and milk, sweeteners, flavorings, and air. The air is beaten into the milk mixture as it freezes, making the final product light and spoonable. Other ice-cream ingredients range from the eggs used in rich French ice creams to the stabilizers and emulsifiers that are added to many commercial ice creams. Stabilizers prevent large ice crystals from forming; emulsifiers are added to smooth and fill and to render the ice-cream mixture more whippable.

The differences between ice creams are a product of the quality, richness, and freshness of the ingredients. An economy ice cream may use more dried milk products and a lower percentage of milk fats; it will often contain large amounts of stabilizers and emulsifiers and will have a higher volume of air. A high-quality ice cream is denser and less airy; it will use fresh whole products, contain 16% to 20% milk fat, and use additives sparingly, if at all. Natural ice creams avoid artificial flavorings and additives, although they do use natural products to emulsify and to stabilize.

In its standards for various frozen-milk desserts, the U.S. Food and Drug Administration requires that most ice cream contain at least 20% milk solids by weight. Ice milk must contain a minimum of 11% milk solids; sherbet, a minimum of 2%. Maximum amounts of stabilizers and emulsifiers are also regulated. Ice cream is, however, one of the few manufactured foods for which a listing of the ingredients is not required on the package label.

ice hockey

Ice hockey is a sport played by two teams of six players on a roughly rectangular surface of ice called a rink. The players, who wear ice skates, attempt to knock a circular piece of hard rubber, the puck, into one of two goals, situated at opposite ends of the rink. Players use a stick with a flat or slightly curved blade at one end to drive the puck forward at speeds that sometimes exceed 160 km/h (100 mph). Ice hockey has traditionally been a cold-weather sport, and Canada and the Soviet Union are the two nations with the greatest number of active players. Hockey is played by professionals and amateurs and is a popular spectator sport.

History

Records of early hockey games date back to mid-19th-century Canada. The first formal hockey game was played in Kingston, Ontario, in 1855, with teams drawn from the Royal Canadian Rifles, an Imperial Army troop. McGill University students played the game in the 1870s. The

Wayne Gretzky played 9 years for the Edmonton Oilers before being traded to the Los Angeles Kings in 1988. A perennial scoring champion and Most Valuable Player, he led the Oilers to 4 Stanley Cups and holds about 50 NHL records.

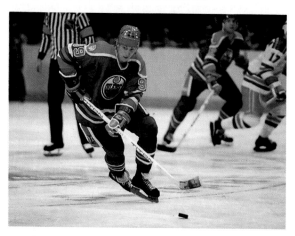

first set of hockey rules was codified by W. F. Robertson, a McGill student, who adapted the rules of field hockey for play on ice. Robertson's rules called for nine players on a side and the use of a square puck. The first amateur league was formed in 1885. In 1893 the governor general of Canada, Lord Stanley of Preston, offered a trophy (the Stanley Cup) to be awarded to the best Canadian hockey team. Today the cup is awarded annually to a professional team—the champion of the National Hockey League (NHL). In the same year (1893), hockey was first played in the United States at Yale and The Johns Hopkins universities. In 1917 several Canadian hockey teams banded together and organized the NHL. Hockey became an Olympic Games event in 1920, and in 1924 the newly founded Boston Bruins became the first professional hockey team among the previously amateur teams of the NHL. In the 1978–79 hockey season the NHL consisted of 17 professional teams in cities in the United States and Canada. The NHL was rivaled by the 6 teams of the World Hockey Association (WHA), founded in the 1972–73 season. In 1979 an agreement was reached between the two leagues to bring about the absorption of the WHA by the NHL. Beginning in the 1979–80 season the NHL had 21 teams, including 4 from the disbanded WHA.

Equipment and the Rink

Hockey rinks vary in size, although standard International Ice Hockey Federation (and NHL) dimensions specify a rink 200 ft (61 m) long and 85 ft (25.9 m) wide, with corners rounded into the arc of a circle with a 28-ft (8.5-m) radius. The rink is enclosed by 4-ft-high (1.2-m) retaining boards and is divided into three zones—two end zones and a neutral zone. The zones are marked on the ice by blue lines that extend up the sides of the boards. Two red goal lines, 2 in (5 cm) wide, run the width of the rink. There is a space of 10 ft (3.05 m) between the goal lines and the barrier boards at each end of the ice. There are two goal cages that have openings 4 ft (1.2 m) high and 6 ft (1.8 m) wide, with the posts resting on the goal lines. The backs of the goals have a netting that stops pucks shot into the goal and makes judging a score easier. Two 12-in-wide (30-cm) blue lines are marked in the center of the rink 60 ft (18.3 m) from each goal line. The blue lines also extend the width of the ice. A red line, seen only in professional ice hockey, also 12 in wide, bisects the length of the rink between the blue lines. The blue lines designate attacking and defending zones, depending on which team controls the puck.

In the center of the rink is a red spot 12 in (30 cm) in diameter, circumscribed by a line 2 in (5 cm) wide with a 10-ft (3-m) radius. There are four other spots and circles of the same size, two in each end zone. They are located halfway between each goalpost and the boards and 15 ft (4.6 m) out from the goal lines. In professional hockey four red spots of the same size are in the neutral zone midway between the boards and the center of the rink and 5 ft (1.5 m) from each blue line. The center spot is where play starts at the beginning of each period or after a goal is scored. The other spots are where play is re-

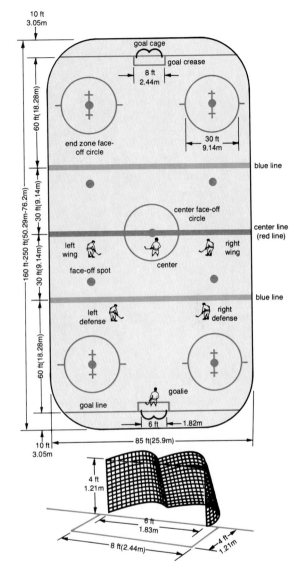

A standard hockey rink and goal appear with dimensions, markings, and players' positions. Between the blue lines lies the neutral zone, which is divided in half by a red center line. Defensive players are situated in their defending zones. Forwards are positioned behind the red line. Face-off circles and spots (in red) are places where the game is started or restarted after a referee's call.

sumed after any stop in play. Around the mouth of the goal is an area called the crease that is delineated by 2-in-wide (5-cm) red lines. The puck is a disk-shaped piece of black vulcanized rubber 3 in (7.6 cm) in diameter and 1 in (2.5 cm) thick; it weighs 5.5–6 oz (156–170 g).

Most sticks have aluminum shafts with replaceable wooden blades. The handles may be no more than 55 in

Ice hockey players require considerable protection because the game is both violent and fast-paced. Forwards and defensive players (A) wear streamlined equipment to reduce wind resistance. This gear may include a helmet with a face mask (1), chest protector and shoulder pads (2), elbow pads (3), gloves (4), hip and thigh pads (5), knee pads and shin guards (6), and skates (7). The stick (8) is smaller than that used by the goalkeeper (15). Because the goalkeeper (B) uses any part of his body to block the puck (9), his equipment must provide even more protection. He wears a special face mask (10); a mittlike glove (11), used to catch the puck; a fiberboard guard (12) to deflect the puck; bulky leg pads (13); and reinforced skates (14).

(1.4 m) long, 1.25 in (3.2 cm) wide, and 0.75 in (1.9 cm) thick. The blades may be no more than 12.5 in (32 cm) long and 3 in (7.6 cm) wide. Goaltenders' sticks may be wider and heavier. Ice hockey skates have a short blade that is slightly curved, which permits quick turns and stops. Goaltenders' skates have longer, flat blades for stability.

Players wear protective shoulder, hip, and elbow pads, knee and shin guards, and heavy leather gloves; some also wear helmets. Goaltenders wear massive leg and chest pads and a glove similar to a baseball mitt with which to catch flying pucks. Most goaltenders also wear a face mask.

Play of the Game

Each team consists of a goaltender, two defenders, and three forwards (a center and two wings). In the professional leagues play is supervised by three major officials; in amateur games two officials are used.

Play of the three 20-minute periods starts at the center spot with a face-off—the official drops the puck, and the two centers try to control it.

Actual play in hockey is frequently interrupted by one

of two infractions: offside and icing. A player is offside if he or she precedes the puck into the attacking zone. This rule prevents players from hovering by the goal when the puck is not in the attacking zone. A face-off is then held at one of the red spots in the neutral zone nearest to where the infraction was committed.

Icing is called when the puck crosses the center and goal lines without being touched by the opposition. An icing penalty warrants a face-off in the defensive zone of the penalized team and occurs at the red spot nearest to the location of the infraction.

Other infractions include tripping, holding, and hooking or spearing with the stick. For such fouls the offending player must leave the game for a period of 2 to 5 minutes. More serious infractions, such as fighting, draw 5-minute or 10-minute penalties. The penalized team must play shorthanded, while the other team, at full strength, enjoys a power-play situation. The penalized player may return if his or her team surrenders a goal.

The team that scores more goals by the end of the third period is the winner. Beginning in 1983–84, the NHL adopted a rule providing for one 5-minute sudden-death

STANLEY CUP CHAMPIONS*

1917 Seattle Metropolitans	1956 Montreal Canadiens
1918 Toronto Arenas	1957 Montreal Canadiens
1920 Ottawa Senators	1958 Montreal Canadiens
1921 Ottawa Senators	1959 Montreal Canadiens
1922 Toronto St. Patricks	1960 Montreal Canadiens
1923 Ottawa Senators	1961 Chicago Black Hawks
1924 Montreal Canadiens	1962 Toronto Maple Leafs
1925 Victoria Cougars	1963 Toronto Maple Leafs
1926 Montreal Maroons	1964 Toronto Maple Leafs
1927 Ottawa Senators	1965 Montreal Canadiens
1928 New York Rangers	1966 Montreal Canadiens
1929 Boston Bruins	1967 Toronto Maple Leafs
1930 Montreal Canadiens	1968 Montreal Canadiens
1931 Montreal Canadiens	1969 Montreal Canadiens
1932 Toronto Maple Leafs	1970 Boston Bruins
1933 New York Rangers	1971 Montreal Canadiens
1934 Chicago Black Hawks	1972 Boston Bruins
1935 Montreal Maroons	1973 Montreal Canadiens
1936 Detroit Red Wings	1974 Philadelphia Flyers
1937 Detroit Red Wings	1975 Philadelphia Flyers
1938 Chicago Black Hawks	1976 Montreal Canadiens
1939 Boston Bruins	1977 Montreal Canadiens
1940 New York Rangers	1978 Montreal Canadiens
1941 Boston Bruins	1979 Montreal Canadiens
1942 Toronto Maple Leafs	1980 New York Islanders
1943 Detroit Red Wings	1981 New York Islanders
1944 Montreal Canadiens	1982 New York Islanders
1945 Toronto Maple Leafs	1983 New York Islanders
1946 Montreal Canadiens	1984 Edmonton Oilers
1947 Toronto Maple Leafs	1985 Edmonton Oilers
1948 Toronto Maple Leafs	1986 Montreal Canadiens
1949 Toronto Maple Leafs	1987 Edmonton Oilers
1950 Detroit Red Wings	1988 Edmonton Oilers
1951 Toronto Mapel Leafs	1989 Calgary Flames
1952 Detroit Red Wings	1990 Edmonton Oilers
1953 Montreal Canadiens	1991 Pittsburgh Penguins
1954 Detroit Red Wings	
1955 Detroit Red Wings	

*The Stanley Cup (instituted 1893) was originally presented to the amateur ice hockey champion of Canada; as of 1917 it was awarded to the professional National Hockey League champion. The 1919 series was discontinued after 5 games because of an influenza epidemic.

overtime period in regular-season games. In play-off games, the sudden-death overtime continues, in 20-minute periods, until one team scores. In amateur play the first score in a 10-minute overtime period decides the outcome.

ice skating Ice skating is a sport in which people slide over a smooth ice surface on steel-bladed skates. Many millions of people skate in the United States, and millions more skate in other parts of the world wherever the winters are cold enough. Although most people ice-skate for recreation and exercise, skating for form and speed is a highly competitive international amateur sport. Ice-skating skills are also an important part of the game of ICE HOCKEY. Ice-skating shows, such as the Ice Follies and the Ice Capades, have entertained millions of spectators. These shows also provide a means for skaters to ex-

ploit their talents commercially. The increasing number of indoor rinks has made year-round ice skating possible.

History of Ice Skating

People probably skated on ice in the Scandinavian countries before the Christian era. The first skates are believed to have been sharp splinters of animal bone fitted to the bottoms of boots to ease travel over ice. Some drawings and references in literature to ice skating date from the Middle Ages. The modern word *skate* is derived from the Dutch word *schaats*, meaning "leg bone" or "shank bone."

Skating as a sport developed on the lakes of Scotland and the canals of the Netherlands. In the 13th and 14th centuries wood was substituted for bone in skate blades, and in 1572 the first iron skates were manufactured. The iron blades reduced the friction of forward motion, and their resistance to lateral slipping enabled the skater to push himself or herself ahead. Instructional books were published, and the first skate club was founded in Edinburgh in 1742.

Ice skating did not develop as an organized competitive sport until the introduction of steel skate blades permanently attached to leather boots. The earlier iron blades dulled quickly, and street shoes, to which they were tied with straps, lacked ankle support. Using the steel skates, a U.S. ballet dancer named Jackson Haines created a free-flowing skating technique that incorporated waltzlike movements. Ice speed skating, which had developed in the Netherlands in the 17th century, was given a boost by the innovations in skate construction. Figure skating became an Olympic event in 1908. Speed skating for men was part of the 1924 Olympic Games, but it was not until 1960 that women's speed skating was placed on the Olympic agenda.

Olympic champions Irina Rodnina and her husband-partner Alexandr Zaitsev of the USSR won gold medals at the 1976 and 1980 Olympic Winter games in the paired figure-skating competition.

Figure skater Katarina Witt of East Germany performs at the 1988 Winter Olympic Games. Witt, a four-time world champion, won Olympic gold medals in both 1984 and 1988.

thirds. In pairs skating, the same jumps, spins, and twirls as in the singles events are used, along with lifts and partner-assisted jumps. Ice dancing, for pairs only, differs from pairs skating: lifts are prohibited, and specific movements, based on dance, are required. The emphasis is on rhythm and steps.

Ice figure skating was popularized by Sonja HENIE, who won numerous amateur competitions before turning professional in 1936. Dick BUTTON, Peggy FLEMING, Dorothy HAMILL, and Katarina WITT also toured with ice revues after illustrious amateur careers. The typical ice show is similar to a circus on ice skates and features costumes, trick skating, and gags to entertain the audience rather than to display true figure-skating expertise.

Speed Skating. The long, narrow blades of the modern speed skate permit skaters to maintain speeds of about 48 km/h (30 mph). Formal competitions are usually held outdoors on large rinks. In major international meets, men may enter five events: 500 m (1,640 ft), 1,000 m (3,280 ft), 1,500 m (4,920 ft), 5,000 m (16,400 ft), or 10,000 m (32,800 ft). Women also may compete over five courses: 500 m, 1,000 m, 1,500 m, 3,000 m (9,840 ft), and 5,000 m. During the 1980s, men's speedskating, as traditionally, was dominated by Americans, Soviets, Scandinavians, and the Dutch. As in many other sports, however, East German women rose to clear superiority.

Sweden's Tomas Gustafson was the premier men's speed skater at the 1988 Winter Olympics. He won gold medals in the 5,000 m and 10,000 m.

iceberg   An iceberg is a large piece of ice that has broken off, or calved, from the terminus of a GLACIER into a body of water. Nearly all icebergs are found in the ocean,

Melting icebergs reveal typical features of coastal erosion: recent wave-cut notches (1), old notches cut when the iceberg was heavier and lower (2), water-runoff erosion (3), parent-glacier rock fragments (4), a water-eroded sea stack (5), and a wave-cut platform (6).

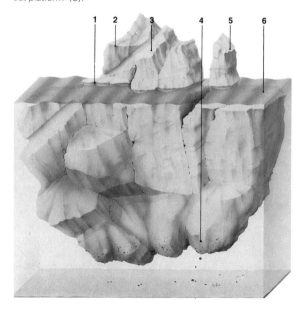

Competitive Ice Skating

Figure Skating. Figure skating is primarily a sport for amateurs. Contests are held for singles and for pairs. In the singles class there are two separate events, compulsory figures and free skating. (These two events were for many years both part of one overall figure-skating event.) The compulsory-figures event requires each skater to perform 3 or 6 repetitions of 3 figures drawn from a possible 41 patterns. All figures are based on a figure-8 pattern or variations thereof. Skaters start from a stationary position and execute the figure, with attention given to the precision of the retracing of the figure, balance, control, and gracefulness. Judges award contestants up to a maximum of 6 points for each figure executed. The free-skating event involves jumps, spins, spirals, and skating coordinated with music. For both singles and pairs, the "original program" accounts for one-third of the skater's final score, and the "long program" accounts for two-but all are composed of freshwater ice rather than frozen seawater. They are usually white, blue, or green, although some are black due to rock material incorporated in them.

The glaciers of Antarctica and Greenland are the sources of most icebergs. The largest icebergs are found in Antarctica; the U.S. Coast Guard icebreaker *Glacier* measured one that was 333 km (208 mi) long and 96 km (60 mi) wide. Icebergs may extend downward 300 m (1,000 ft) and reach a height of more than 60 m (200 ft). Icebergs float low; on the average, $6/7$ of the volume of an Arctic iceberg and $4/5$ of icebergs of Antarctic origin are submerged. The degree of submergence depends on the density, rock content, and shape.

Wind and OCEAN CURRENTS may move icebergs thousands of kilometers from their source; in 1907 and 1926 icebergs were reported as far south as Bermuda. As time passes, icebergs decrease in size, both because contact with the ocean and air melts the ice and because storm waves break off pieces. Greenland icebergs are mostly craggy and usually melt away completely by the time they are 2 years old; Antarctic icebergs are mainly tabular because of calving from ice shelves and may survive 10 years or more.

On Apr. 14, 1912, the *Titanic,* the largest ship in the world, ran into a small iceberg on its maiden voyage across the Atlantic and sank, resulting in the death of 1,503 people. Several nations have set up research stations on floating icebergs. Serious thought has been given to the possibility both of harvesting ice from icebergs and of shipping whole icebergs to arid countries for use as a source of fresh water.

iceboating

Iceboating is the sport of sailing a boat that rides on metal runners over a smooth ice surface. A modern iceboat typically has a narrow hull constructed of a rigid, light material, a forward steering runner, an outrigged runner on both sides, and a mast that supports one or two sails. Large bodies of water and low winter temperatures have made iceboating popular in the northern United States, Canada, Scandinavia, the Baltic Sea area, and the Netherlands. Iceboats are frequently used for racing, and organized clubs stage regattas. Larger craft have crews of two, whereas smaller boats are skippered by one person. The Ice Yacht Challenge Pennant of America, first run in 1881, is the sport's premier race.

The earliest record of an iceboat is a 1768 drawing of a Dutch sloop built with runners affixed to a cross plank under the hull. The Lapps and Finns, as well as the Dutch, probably had developed iceboats by the 18th century. By 1800 there were similar vessels on the Hudson River and on the waters near Red Bank, N.J. Iceboats can travel about 4 times the speed of the wind, and in 1938 a stern-steering iceboat attained a speed of 229 km/h (143 mph) on Lake Winnebago, Wis. The adoption of synthetic sail fabric, stainless-steel rigging, and fiberglass hull materials mark improvements over the boats of the last century. In the United States iceboats are classified on the basis of either adherence to the specifications of "one design" or sail area. The largest class is for boats

The pilot of a small iceboat leans to one side to stabilize the craft's runners during a race over a frozen lake. These sail-powered craft are capable of achieving speeds of up to 229 km/h (143 mph).

with more than 250 ft² (22.5 m²) of sail area. The one-design Skeeters carry 75 ft² (6.75 m²), and the most popular boat, the DN, carries 60 ft² (5.4 m²) of sail area.

icebreaker

An icebreaker is a vessel used for clearing a passage through ice-bound waters. The earliest such vessels were used on Lake Baikal and the Baltic Sea.

One of the first and most successful icebreakers was the *Ermak,* which was built for the Russian government in 1898. The vessel had a steel hull and an enormously strengthened bow that had a very gradual slope upward from below so that the ship could glide up onto the ice and use its weight to break a path from above (in what is called the continuous mode), rather than by crashing forward (the ramming mode). The *Ermak* had a displacement of over 8,700 tons and a speed of 15 knots, and its three aft screw propellers were protected from floating ice.

The first nuclear-powered surface ship was the *Lenin,* a 44,000-hp Soviet icebreaker commissioned in 1959. The USSR also operates two 75,000-hp nuclear-powered icebreakers, the *Leonid Brezhnev,* which was the first surface vessel to navigate a passage to the North Pole, and its sister ship, the *Sibir.* Nuclear icebreakers may operate for up to 20 months without refueling, and their use may bring a new era to Arctic shipping.

icefish

Icefishes are transparent or pale fishes of three families inhabiting southern polar seas and eastern Asia. The name *icefish* is sometimes applied to the glassfish, family Centropomidae, and conversely, icefishes are sometimes called glassfishes. The Asiatic icefishes, family Salangidae, are 14 species of small freshwater or freshwater-spawning (anadromous) fishes found in Japan, China, Korea, and Vietnam. They grow tc about 10 cm (4 in) in length and have elongated, transparent, scaleless or nearly scaleless bodies and flattened heads. They are neotenic, reaching sexual maturity while still retaining certain larval characteristics. The crocodile icefishes, family Chaenichthyidae or Channichthyidae, are 16 to 18 species of marine fishes with large mouths, flattened snouts, and big eyes. They inhabit the oceanic waters of Antarctica and Patagonia, South America. The largest species, *Chaenocephalus aceratus,* grows to 60 cm (2 ft) long and about 1 kg (2.5 lb) in weight. The cod icefishes, or Antarctic cods, family Nototheniidae, consist of about 59 species of marine fishes inhabiting the coastal waters of Antarctica and southern South America. They are similar in appearance to the crocodile icefishes but have extendable snouts.

The blood of certain species of marine icefishes is of biological interest because its temperature may fall below the usual freezing point of fish blood (-1° C/30° F) without freezing and because it lacks red blood cells and oxygen-carrying hemoglobin and consequently has a very low oxygen capacity. Research has indicated that marine icefishes have antifreeze in their blood in the form of glycoproteins—complex compounds containing sugars and amino acids—which presumably interfere with the formation or growth of ice crystals.

Icefish blood lacking the red pigment of hemoglobin is transparent and colorless or tinted a pale yellow. Because of this colorless blood, marine icefishes are sometimes called "bloodless." Since the oxygen-carrying capacity of blood fluid, or plasma, without hemoglobin is low, marine icefishes lacking hemoglobin must manage with a markedly reduced supply of oxygen. Studies have shown that the icefishes are able to survive this reduction by using several ecological features as well as certain physiological modifications that reduce energy expenditure and therefore oxygen consumption.

Iceland   The Republic of Iceland is the second largest island in Europe, after Great Britain. Located in the North Atlantic Ocean immediately south of the Arctic Circle, Iceland lies about 965 km (600 mi) west of Norway. REYKJAVIK, its capital, is on the southwest coast. Under the control of Denmark since the late 14th century, Iceland became fully independent in 1944.

Land

The island was formed by about 150 to 200 volcanoes, 30 of which have been active since settlement during the 9th century. Most recently (1963), the offshore island of Surtsey was created by a volcanic eruption. Only one-fourth of the country can support continuous vegetation of any type; trees, mainly birches, survive on less than 1% of the land.

The rest of Iceland is barren. Glaciers cover much of the interior. Vatnajökull, in the southeastern part of Iceland, is the largest glacier, covering approximately 8,400 km² (3,240 mi²). Waterfalls, cirques, and fjords are found throughout the island. At least two active volcanoes cause flooding by the melt flow when they erupt. Iceland has

AT A GLANCE

REPUBLIC OF ICELAND

Land: Area: 103,000 km² (39,769 mi²). Capital and largest city: Reykjavik (1988 est. pop., 95,799).

People: Population (1990 est.): 257,023. Density: 2.5 persons per km² (6.5 per mi²). Distribution (1988): 90% urban, 10% rural. Official language: Icelandic. Major religion: Evangelical Lutheranism.

Government: Type: republic. Legislature: Althing (Parliament). Political subdivisions: 23 counties.

Economy: GNP (1988): $5 billion; $20,160 per capita. Labor distribution (1987): public administration—17.6%; trade—15.7%; manufacturing—14%; fishing and fish processing— 12.7%; construction—9.3%; agriculture—5.3%; other—25.4%. Currency: 1 krona = 100 aurar.

Education and Health: Literacy (1990): 100% of adult population. Universities (1990): 1. Hospital beds (1986): 2,835. Physicians (1986): 632. Life expectancy (1990): women—80; men—75. Infant mortality (1990): 7 per 1,000 live births.

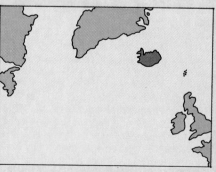

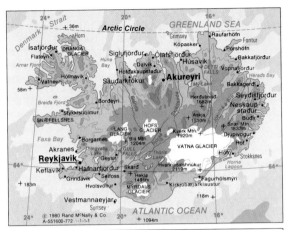

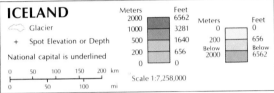

ICELAND

	Meters	Feet		Meters	Feet
	2000	6562		0	0
Glacier	1000	3281			
+ Spot Elevation or Depth	500	1640	200	656
	200	656	Below	Below
National capital is underlined	0	0	2000	6562

```
0    50   100   150   200 km
0         50        100   mi
Scale 1:7,258,000
```

benefited greatly from more than 800 thermal springs. The hot water provides home heating for Reykjavik and steam heat for a flourishing greenhouse produce industry. Iceland's rivers are unnavigable. The Hvannadalshnúkur (2,119 m/6,952 ft) is the highest point.

Although the interior of Iceland is quite cold, the perimeter experiences an even, mild temperature, averaging –1° C (31° F) in January and 11° C (52° F) in July. Rainfall, however, varies widely: 1,270–2,030 mm (50–80 in) annually on the south coast; 380–500 mm (15–20 in) on the north; and more than 3,810 mm (150 in) in the mountainous central areas.

People

Most Icelanders are of Norwegian stock, and the rest are of Celtic origin. Unaffected by large in-migration, the population is homogeneous. The Icelandic language is distinct, having evolved from Old Norse. More than 95% of the inhabitants are Evangelical Lutherans.

Demography. More than one-half of Iceland's predominantly urban population live in the Reykjavik metropolitan area along Faxa Bay. Akureyri (1988 est. pop., 13,969), the country's second largest city, is on the north coast at the head of Eyja Fjord. The only other larger cities, Hafnarfjördur and Kópavogur, are parts of Reykjavik's metropolitan area. At the beginning of the 20th century, more than 15% of the population left the island, primarily for the United States and Canada. The size of the population has increased steadily since that time.

Education and Health. Almost all educational services are provided free of charge. School attendance is compulsory for all individuals between the ages of 7 and 15. The University of Iceland, founded in 1911, is state controlled.

Public health facilities are available to all at low cost. The infant mortality rate is among the lowest and life expectancy among the highest in the world.

The Arts. The most significant literary contribution of the Icelanders is the SAGA, a historical tale of adventure. Wood carvings and woolen cloth designs are also characteristic art forms. A collection of native crafts is housed in the National Museum of Iceland (1863) in Reykjavik. The capital is the home of the National Theatre and the country's only symphony orchestra. (See ICELANDIC LITERATURE.)

Economic Activity

Iceland has a high standard of living. Produce greenhouses are important to agricultural activity. The main outdoor crop is hay, fodder for the few cattle and sheep. Potatoes and turnips are also grown.

Major industries, concentrated in Reykjavik, are fishing and fish processing (mainly cod, capelin, and herring), along with metal products, clothing, furniture, books, fertilizer, and cement. The main mineral resource is diatomite, which is used in filtration systems. Imported aluminum ore is processed for reexport as finished goods. The enormous amount of electricity required to produce aluminum is provided by the numerous hydroelectric plants and hot springs.

A general trend toward nationalization of industry, especially fishing, has been taking place. No railroad system exists, but a dense road network provides access to all inhabited areas of the island. Air transportation is important, both locally and internationally, through airports at Reykjavik and Keflavík. Radio and television broadcasting facilities are state owned.

Icelandic Airlines, or Loftleidir, contributes substantially to the economy. The nation's largest single employer, the airline uses Keflavík airport, which is maintained by the United States. The U.S. naval base there is the

Many regions of Iceland are covered by thick layers of lava. The island is one of the most volcanically active areas in the world.

country's second largest employer. Tourists, primarily Americans and Germans, are attracted to Iceland for skiing and mountaineering.

Fishing accounts for most of the export earnings, but aluminum is also significant. Machinery and transport equipment constitute nearly one-third of all imports, followed by manufactured goods and fuels. Iceland's principal trading partners are the United States, the United Kingdom, and Germany. Iceland is a member of the EUROPEAN FREE TRADE ASSOCIATION.

Iceland has suffered from the highest inflation rate in Europe in recent years. The government's policy has been to increase wages as the cost of living goes up.

Government

Iceland is a constitutional republic governed by a 60-member, 2-chamber general assembly (*Althing*). The president is popularly elected every 4 years by universal suffrage for all persons over 20 years of age. Real executive power is vested in the prime minister and the cabinet. The largest political groups are the Independence party, the Progressive party, and the People's Alliance. Local government consists of 23 counties and 14 independent towns.

History

Discovered by Irish explorers about 800, Iceland was settled by Norwegian seafarers during the late 9th century. In 930 they created a representative governing assembly (*Althing*), the oldest parliamentary body in the world. Norwegians gained control in 1263, incorporating Iceland into the Norwegian-Danish state in 1381. The steamship, invented in the 19th century, made access to the rocky, irregular coasts safer, and, along with the laying of the transoceanic cable, lessened Iceland's isolation.

In 1874, Iceland was granted a constitution and limited home rule; the subsequent Act of Union of 1918 granted full self-government under the Danish crown, with the right of either country to dissolve the union after 25 years. When Denmark fell to the Germans in 1940, Iceland was occupied by British troops to prevent a German takeover. The British were replaced in 1941 by U.S. forces, which remained throughout the war. Iceland declared its independence on June 17, 1944.

Iceland became a charter member of the NORTH ATLANTIC TREATY ORGANIZATION (NATO) in 1949, and in 1951 reluctantly signed a treaty granting the United States the right to develop and maintain an airbase at Keflavík in return for U.S. defense of the country. Iceland has no military force of its own. During the 1960s and '70s Iceland was involved in a dispute, the so-called "cod wars," with Great Britain about fishing rights in Icelandic waters. The country's economy stagnated in the 1980s. Iceland's first woman president, Vigdís Finnbogadóttir, took office in 1980 and was reelected in 1984.

Icelandic language   see GERMANIC LANGUAGES

▬

Icelandic literature [ys-lan'-dik]   Iceland was settled in the 9th and 10th centuries, but almost two centuries passed before its earliest literature was written down. This literature may be subdivided into EDDAS, that is, mythological and heroic poems; skaldic poetry (see SKALDIC LITERATURE), mostly occasional and praise poems composed by court poets; and SAGA literature, or prose works ranging from fairly solid histories to pure fiction. Among the former type of saga literature are Ari Thorgilsson's *Íslendingabók* (a history of Iceland), SNORRI STURLUSON's *Heimskringla* (about Norwegian kings), and the anonymous *Knytlinga Saga* (about Danish kings). A prime example of the fictional type is *Hrafnkel's Saga,* a short *bildungsroman*. In between fall the so-called family sagas, such as *Egil's Saga* and *Njál's Saga.* Pre-Reformation literature also includes Eysteinn Ásgrímsson's religious poem *Lilja* (14th century), a number of popular ballads, and the *rímur,* cycles of epic poetry.

The 17th century left behind the treasure of Hallgrímur Pétursson's *Passion Hymns.* Romanticism was brought to Iceland by Bjarni Thorarensen shortly after 1800 and blossomed in the poetry of Jónas Hallgrímsson and Grímur Thomsen, while the novelist Jón Thoroddsen foreshadowed realism. Writers flourishing about 1900 included the poets Stephan G. Stephansson and Einar Benediktsson. Some Icelanders began to write in Danish, such as the novelist Gunnar Gunnarsson.

After World War I, Icelandic literature experienced a renaissance, especially in the lyric poetry of Stefán frá Hvítadal, Davíð Stefánsson, and Tómas Guðmundsson. Prominent prose writers of this era included Thórbergur Thórðarson and Halldór LAXNESS. The latter won the Nobel Prize for literature in 1955. After World War II new lyric poets included Steinn Steinarr and Jón úr Vör. Among the best writers active in Iceland today are the poets Hannes Pétursson and Snorri Hjartarson and the novelists Ólafur Jóhann Sigurðsson (also a poet), Thor Vilhjálmsson, and Indriði G. Thorsteinsson.

▬

Iceman Cometh, The   The four-act drama *The Iceman Cometh,* written by American playwright Eugene O'NEILL in 1939 and first produced in 1946 (film, 1973), is one of his greatest plays. Based on a short story from 1917, the play observes the inhabitants of a seedy saloon-hotel in New York City. Goaded by a "reformed" salesman, Theodore Hickman ("Hickey"), whose arrival they had been awaiting, the barflies in turn reveal the "pipe dreams" sustaining them in their defeated lives. Hickey at last reveals that his own "conversion" is illusory, and police officers lead him away for his wife's murder, to which he has confessed. The barflies return to their pipe dreams.

▬

ichneumon fly [ik-nue'-muhn]   Ichneumon flies are parasitic wasps in the family Ichneumonidae and are found worldwide. They resemble wasps, but are slim, with long legs and often a long terminal ovipositor used to bore a hole into their hosts. Eggs are laid on or in other insects,

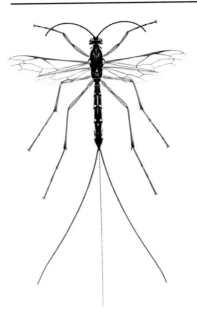

The ichneumon fly is a slender, long-legged wasp that parasitizes the horntail, Urocerus, by piercing its larva and laying an egg inside.

Ickes, Harold [ik'-eez] Harold LeClaire Ickes, b. Blair County, Pa., Mar. 15, 1874, d. Feb. 3, 1952, served as U.S. secretary of the interior in the administrations of Franklin D. Roosevelt and Harry S. Truman. Ickes earned a B.A. (1897) and a law degree (1907) from the University of Chicago.

A political activist, Ickes crusaded against corruption in Chicago and for reformers at the local and state levels. A Bull Moose party supporter of Theodore Roosevelt's presidential quest in 1912, he remained a Progressive. Ickes opposed exploitation of the nation's limited natural resources by private interests and supported federal development of electric power in the public domain.

When Franklin Roosevelt became president in 1933, he determined that a Progressive Republican should head the interior department and selected Ickes. A forceful, colorful administrator, "Honest Harold" made that department into the custodian of the nation's resources. He also headed the PUBLIC WORKS ADMINISTRATION, spending nearly $6 billion on the building of public facilities—ranging from hydroelectric dams to civic and educational facilities—and on rural electrification and military modernization projects.

and the parasitic larvae kill their host. Many ichneumon flies are specific to one species of host and are therefore valuable for biological control of certain pest insects. Adult ichneumon flies are commonly found on vegetation.

ichthyology   see FISH

Ichthyosaurus [ik-thee-uh-sohr'-uhs] *Ichthyosaurus* (Greek: *ichthys*, "fish"; *saurus*, "lizard") was one of a group of highly aquatic reptiles that inhabited the Mesozoic oceans from mid-Triassic time (about 210 million years ago) until late in the Cretaceous Period (65 million years ago). Lower Jurassic rocks (less than 190 million years old) from many parts of the world contain fossils of the creature. The name *fish lizard* is most appropriate, considering its fishlike form—sharp snout, large eyes, and streamlined head. The fin rising from the animal's back was high and sharklike; the tail was vertical, two-lobed and fishlike; and the limbs were modified into large flippers.

Ichthyosaurus *flourished about 150 million years ago. It evolved from land reptiles in much the same way that present-day seals and whales evolved from land mammals.*

icon [y'-kahn]   The icon (Greek *eikōn*, meaning "image") plays an essential part in the religious life of the Eastern ORTHODOX CHURCH. Most commonly a portrait of Christ, the Virgin, or one of the saints, an icon may also represent an episode from the Bible or from a saint's life. Icons usually were painted on wooden panels, although several miniature mosaic icons from Constantinople have survived.

The icon as a special type of sacred image developed in Byzantine art (see BYZANTINE ART AND ARCHITECTURE) in the 6th century. Veneration of the icon led to a puritani-

In Eastern Orthodox religious art, icons represent a sacred image used for veneration, as in this 16th-century Russian icon of Christ. These sacred representations are usually oil paintings on wood; mosaic, ivory, and metal have also been used. (Rublov Museum, Moscow.)

cal reaction by those who saw this practice as little removed from pagan idol worship. ICONOCLASM, the prohibition and deliberate destruction of religious images, became official Byzantine policy in AD 726. Byzantine theologians, particularly Saint JOHN DAMASCENE (d. 754), developed an elaborate defense of holy images and their place in worship; this theory led to the restoration of the icons in 843 and remains the Orthodox view to this day. John argued that the holy icon through divine grace partook of the spiritual essence of the figure it depicted, and, as the product of the emanation of its holiness, constituted the essential point of direct contact between the human and divine realms.

Icons of an established type, because of their sacred function and relationship to a heavenly prototype, changed relatively little through the centuries, although new types occasionally appeared. Thus the beautiful icon known as *Our Lady of Vladimir* (c.1130; Tretyakov Gallery, Moscow), depicting the Virgin and Child embracing, painted in Constantinople in the early 12th century, reflects with its tender lyricism a new trend toward emotional and humanistic values in Byzantine art of that period. After this icon was taken to Russia, it established a type, *Umileniye* ("merciful" or "compassionate"), reproduced there for seven centuries.

See also: RUSSIAN ART AND ARCHITECTURE.

Iconium   see KONYA

iconoclasm [y-kahn'-oh-klazm]

Iconoclasm, a Greek term that means "image-breaking," refers to the religious doctrine that forbids the veneration of images (icons) of Christ and the saints in Christian churches. Iconoclasm provoked major controversies in the BYZANTINE EMPIRE for more than a century (726–843). In 726, Emperor LEO III ordered the image of Christ at the Chalke palace in Constantinople to be destroyed. In the following years, other measures were taken to suppress the veneration of images. The veneration of images was restored in the empire during the rule of Empress IRENE, at the Second Council of Nicaea (787; see NICAEA, COUNCILS OF), but a revival of iconoclasm took place under Leo V (r. 813–20), Michael II (r. 820–29), and Theophilus (r. 829–42). The latter's widow, Empress Theodora, however, presided over the restoration of icon veneration in 843, an event still celebrated by the ORTHODOX CHURCH as the Triumph of Orthodoxy. During the second iconoclastic period, the main spokespeople for the veneration of images were the patriarch NICEPHORUS and Saint Theodore of Studios.

The iconoclastic movement was motivated by a variety of factors that possibly included Muslim influences, as well as the concern of some that the cult of icons was a form of idolatry. The essential argument of the Orthodox defenders of the images was that, since God became man in Jesus Christ, he also assumed all human characteristics, including visibility.

Iconoclasm was also a feature of the Protestant REFORMATION of the 16th century; some Protestant groups still oppose the use of religious images.

iconography [y-kuhn-ahg'-ruh-fee]

Iconography (from the Greek, *eikōn*, "image" and *graphia*, "writing") is the study of the subject matter, or content, of works of art, as opposed to their style. The content of a painting or a sculpture can convey the artist's meaning in several ways. In general, works depicting only real persons, places, and objects—that is, portraits, landscapes, still lifes, and the like—may be said to have only one level of meaning, the surface or primary level. A secondary level of meaning is added when a work contains an imagined person or a fictional or mythological scene, or when the artist attempts to render some abstract concept in concrete terms. Because these secondary levels of meaning cannot be explained in words in a painting or a sculpture, the artist must use a type of sign language—a visual shorthand, drawing on conventions and formulas that the audience will recognize. In traditional Christian art, a broken wheel placed beside the figure of a woman tells the viewer that the figure represents Saint Catherine, whereas a woman holding a bridle and reins personifies the virtue of temperance. The function of iconography is to recognize and explain images of this kind and to search literature for the origins of personages and scenes. The term *iconology* is sometimes used for the study of the way in which a work of art is related to the cultural background of its era.

In this article the word *image* denotes any portrayal of

The symbolic representation of Christ as the Good Shepherd of the biblical parable is a common iconographic type in Early Christian art. This 3d-century marble statue portrays a youthful, beardless Christ, developed from the Hellenic ideal of the beautiful and good Apollonian god. (Lateran Museum, Rome.)

an object or action that contains a secondary meaning. The word *attribute* signifies an object, such as Saint Catherine's wheel, that is associated with a human figure simply to give that figure a recognizable identity. A *symbol*, however, is an object or figure that by itself represents something else, often an abstract idea. In many 15th- and 16th-century paintings, for example, a skull is used to represent the idea of mortality—a so-called memento mori. Finally, the artist may link together individual symbols so as to convey some thematic idea or axiom; this combining of symbols into an overall pattern is known as an *allegory*. A great fondness for allegory was shown by Italian Renaissance artists, who often constructed elaborate chains of symbols. To arrive at the allegorical or overall meaning of the painting the observer must discern the symbols' interrelationships, as well as their individual meanings.

Classical Iconography. The earliest recorded images were those associated with the rites of ancient religions, especially those in which the deity had human form. To propitiate or petition the gods, worshipers offered sacrifices to statues in temples; the statue was thought to contain the actual presence of the deity, and the temple was considered to be its "house." This ANTHROPOMORPHISM of divinities was developed significantly by the great poet Homer (c.8th century BC), who organized the ancient Greek gods into a kind of family or pantheon and gave each one an individual personality and specific physical characteristics. Following Homer's lead, the classical Greek artists endowed each god with recognizable attributes: Zeus was sometimes accompanied by an eagle, the bird sacred to him; Poseidon, who ruled the sea, carried a trident; Artemis, the huntress, had a bow and quiver; and so on.

The Romans, much more than the Greeks, used art to magnify the glory of their own accomplishments. Statues of the later emperors, who regarded themselves as gods, often depicted the rulers with the appropriate divine attributes. Along with symbols and attributes, allegory was well understood by the Romans. An altar, called the Ara Pacis, built (9 BC) in honor of Emperor Augustus and dedicated to peace, shows in one panel a contented and fruitful Mother Earth holding two infants in her lap and seated amid various symbols of the abundance and prosperity that Augustus's peaceful reign had brought.

Early Christian Iconography. The plethora of symbols and attributes used by the Romans contrasted sharply to the few simple images used by the early Christians, who had to be circumspect in the face of religious persecution (see EARLY CHRISTIAN ART AND ARCHITECTURE). On sacramental cups, seals, and lamps the Holy Spirit was symbolized by a dove, and Christ by a fish (perhaps because at the time fish was one of the elements of the sacred meal) or by a shepherd carrying a sheep on his shoulders (from Luke 15:3–7). The Savior was also represented by a monogram formed by combining the Greek letters *chi* and *rho* (XP), the first two letters of the Greek word for Christ.

Byzantine Iconography. When Christianity became (4th century) the official religion of the Roman Empire, its imagery began to reflect borrowings from the emperor's

Some common Christian iconographic symbols are shown above. (1) The risen Christ is portrayed surrounded by the four evangelists: Saint Matthew as the man-angel, Saint John as the eagle, Saint Mark as the lion, and Saint Luke as the bull. (2) The passion of the crucified Christ is symbolized by the crown of thorns encircling his monogram XP (chi/rho). (3) Christ as the Lamb of God (Agnus Dei) is shown holding an unfurled banner bearing his inscriptions. (4) The dove, symbolizing the Holy Spirit, carries a lily, a symbol of purity.

court at Constantinople (see BYZANTINE ART AND ARCHITECTURE). Christ was no longer depicted as a youthful shepherd, but as an enthroned emperor and judge with a dignified beard. The Virgin Mary, whose cult developed rapidly after about 400, appeared crowned and robed like the empress, and saints dressed like courtiers approached the throne of God with veiled hands, as was the custom in the courts of Eastern monarchs.

The repertoire of symbolic subjects included scenes from the New Testament reflecting the annual cycle of the principal festivals of the Church. Subjects from the Old Testament, which earlier had served as examples of God's power to save—the Hebrews in the fiery furnace, Noah and the flood—now reflected the belief that, as part of God's plan, certain episodes in the Old Testament prefigured events in the New Testament. Jonah, who formerly symbolized the idea of salvation, now became the type—the original model—of Christ, whose death and resurrection was seemingly foreshadowed by Jonah's miraculous encounter with the great fish. Throughout the Middle Ages the Scriptures were ransacked for correspondences of this kind, which exemplify the iconographic principle of typology.

Medieval European Iconography. From about 1000 to 1300 the French monastery of Cluny (see MONASTIC ART AND ARCHITECTURE), which was founded in 910 and played a key role in the development of Romanesque and Gothic art, greatly influenced the course of Western European iconography (see ROMANESQUE ART AND ARCHITECTURE and GOTHIC ART AND ARCHITECTURE). Medieval sculpture and wall painting reflected the Cluniac monks' view that because all human activities and all creatures under heaven were part of the divine plan, they were all fit subjects for representation. Alongside more traditional subject matter now appeared such secular motifs as the 12 Labors of the Months, depicting the yearly cycle of husbandry; the birds and animals of the BESTIARY, an allegorical interpretation of natural history that was very popular in the Middle Ages; and strange humanoid monsters believed to inhabit the outer regions of the Earth.

Renaissance Iconography. The Renaissance period, which began in Italy in the 15th century, ushered in a radical shift in iconography (see RENAISSANCE ART AND AR-CHITECTURE). As artists rediscovered the forms and images of classical antiquity, the gods and goddesses of Greek and Roman mythology once more dominated Western European iconography. Ovid's *Metamorphoses* (AD 8) provided Italian artists with scenes of the amours of the gods, and French humanist artists used the pagan divinities to personify moral qualities in allegorical compositions.

Underlying this reappearance of ancient imagery was an attempt to reconcile the classical philosophy of the ancient pagan world with Christian teaching. A popular subject was the combat between Virtue and Vice in all their manifestations: Reason against Passion, for example, in which a civilized Apollo, shown with a bow or lyre, and a chaste Diana, the huntress, would be pitted against Venus, the goddess of love, and her offspring Cupid. For detailed information about the appearance of the ancient gods, and personifications in general, Renaissance artists often had to rely on contemporary handbooks and dictionaries of classical iconography, which were no less influential for being generally inaccurate. The most widely used of these source books was Cesare Ripa's (fl. 1600) *Iconologia*, the 1603 edition of which described, with illustrations, the dress, attributes, and moral symbolism of a wide range of allegorical figures.

Impact of the Reformation. Paradoxically, the Protestant reformers of the 16th century, who rejected religious imagery as blasphemous, indirectly gave religious subject matter renewed strength in Roman Catholic countries, where art became a propaganda device used to uphold specifically Roman Catholic doctrines. Roman Catholic artists depicted the Virgin Mary treading on a serpent that symbolized the Protestant heresy, as well as such specifically Roman Catholic scenes as the celebration of the Seven Sacraments and the veneration of holy relics. STILL-LIFE PAINTINGS occasionally became vehicles for allegory and at times even contained a veiled expression of Christian beliefs. Many such allegorical compositions used tokens of luxury or pleasure, such as jewels, coins, books, and musical instruments, as symbols of the transitory character of life, whose inevitable conclusion would be symbolized by a memento mori. The underlying message of the emptiness or vanity of life on Earth lent the name *vanitas paintings* to this type of work.

Modern Trends. Beginning roughly in the last part of the 17th century, the European pictorial arts were dominated by two discrete approaches to iconography. While noniconographic subject matter such as landscape, portraiture, and still life became increasingly important, widespread historicizing movements sparked the conscious revival of past artistic forms and images—NEO-CLASSICISM and ROMANTICISM in art being the principal movements. Both trends reflected the lack in early modern art of a broad-based and intrinsic cultural ethos, such as Christianity in medieval art, that could provide artists with a fund of images and symbols of contemporary value.

In the 19th century the gulf between the historicizing and the noniconographic movements widened enormously. Historicism became the keynote of so-called academic art, officially sanctioned by the political and academic establishment. Simultaneously, the trend toward nonsymbolic art led to the development of realism and impressionism. From the romantic landscapes of John Constable and J. M. W. Turner, in which humans and their works assume increasingly insignificant roles, to the series paintings of Claude Monet, in which the painter's sole object is to depict one object or group of objects under various atmospheric and lighting conditions, avant-garde artists gradually banished every trace of literary or moral meaning from their works, concentrating instead on their impressions of the exterior world.

The eventual triumph of the impressionist viewpoint

Classical myths were rediscovered by Renaissance artists and used in the development of iconographic types. In Sandro Botticelli's Mars and Venus *(1485–90) the god of war abandons his weapons for love. (National Gallery, London.)*

During the Reformation a distinctive genre emerged in still-life painting on the theme of vanitas ("vanity"). This 17th-century still life by Pieter Claesz assimilated the iconographic elements of the skull and extinguished candle, which symbolized the transitory nature of life.

over that of the academic schools resulted inevitably in the exaltation of the role of the individual artist and the rejection of any culture-based iconographic language shared by artist and audience. Almost all of the great movements that shaped 20th-century art—cubism, expressionism, surrealism, abstract art, and abstract expressionism—reflect extremely personal aesthetic visions that defy the kind of literary decoding necessary to interpret fully iconographic works. With the significant exceptions of Dadaism (see DADA) and POP ART, modern artistic movements by definition lie outside the realm of iconography.

ICSH   see HORMONE, ANIMAL; PITUITARY GLAND

Ictinus [ik-ty′-nus]   The Greek architect Ictinus, fl. 5th century BC, along with his fellow architect Callicrates, designed and built the Parthenon (447–431 BC) on the ACROPOLIS of Athens. Ictinus, in collaboration with an otherwise unknown Carpion, described the construction of the Parthenon in a lost work that fortunately was known to the Roman architect VITRUVIUS, who described it in his treatise *On Architecture* (1st century BC). Pausanias, in his *Description of Greece* (2d century AD), named Ictinus as the architect of the Temple of Apollo Epicurius (c.420 BC) at Bassae in Arcadia. The temple is highly original, incorporating engaged interior columns and the first known use in architecture of the Corinthian order (see ARCHITECTURE). Ictinus also worked (c.440 BC) in Eleusis on the Telesterion or Hall of the Mysteries, a huge hall for religious rites with a central light source in the roof.

id   see PSYCHOANALYSIS

Idaho [y′-duh-hoh]   Idaho, a Pacific Northwest state, links the Great Plains and the Northwest coast. It is bounded on the north by British Columbia, on the east by Wyoming and Montana, and on the south by Utah and Nevada. Its western border with Oregon and Washington follows, in part, the course of the SNAKE RIVER. The ROCKY MOUNTAINS dominate the entire landscape except for the Snake River plain, which cuts across the southern part of the state. Idaho's wealth of natural resources, along with its scenic attractions, forms the base of its expanding economy.

Land and Resources

The broad, arid Snake River valley arcs across the southern part of Idaho. The valley provides an access route from the Great Plains to the Pacific Northwest. Farther north, rugged mountains of the Bitterroot, Lost River, Pioneer, and Sawtooth ranges, separated by deep canyons and interrupted by occasional prairies, make up nearly all the rest of the state. Other than that portion of the GREAT BASIN rim in the southeast, all of Idaho is part of the COLUMBIA RIVER basin. Almost 64% of Idaho is owned by the U.S. government. Mountains or deserts used for forestry and grazing make up almost all these public lands.

Soils. Idaho's variation in soils is a result of elevation and climatic diversity. Most of the windblown, volcanic soils in arid parts of the Snake plain are alkaline, including about 11,100 km^2 (4,300 mi^2) of irrigated farmland. Soils receiving 279 to 356 mm (11 to 14 in) of annual precipitation are chemically neutral. Where precipitation increases to 457 mm (18 in), darker, slightly acid soils predominate. Exceptionally valuable dark, acidic windblown soils of the Palouse country near Moscow receive 432 to 635 mm (17 to 25 in) of precipitation, as do similar soils at higher elevations in southern Idaho. Mountain and forest soils, usually thin, can support only timber, although some drained mountain-basin soils yield crops.

Rivers and Lakes. Except for the Bear River in southeastern Idaho and the Kootenai, Pend Oreille, and Spokane systems to the north, the Snake River, which is more than 1,609 km (1,000 mi) long, drains virtually the entire state. The Big Wood, Blackfoot, Boise, Clearwater, Payette, and Salmon rivers flow into the Snake, along with many smaller rivers.

Idaho has four large lakes: Pend Oreille, Coeur d'Alene, Priest, and Bear. Thousands of small lakes and reservoirs contribute to the state's expanse of inland water. Idaho contains four of the National Park Service–administered wild rivers, the Clearwater, Rapid, Salmon, and Snake.

Climate. Elevation and latitude influence the diverse climate found in Idaho. The Lewiston area, in the north, has the warmest climate, while higher cities in the southeast are much cooler. Northern canyons above Lewiston average 11° C (52° F) annually; the southwestern valleys in the Boise region, averaging 1 degree cooler, are comparable. The southeastern highlands, however, are substantially colder (6° C/42° F).

Low humidity makes hot desert summers more tolerable; particularly at higher elevations, daily variation in summer temperatures often approaches 22 C degrees (72 F degrees). Precipitation ranges from 152 mm (6 in) or less in desert areas to 2,504 mm (99 in) in the mountains.

AT A GLANCE

IDAHO

Land: Area: 216,430 km² (83,564 mi²); rank: 13th. Capital and largest city: Boise (1990 pop., 125,738). Counties: 44. Elevations: highest—3,859 m (12,662 ft), at Borah Peak; lowest—216 m (710 ft), at the Snake River.

People: Population (1990): 1,011,986; rank: 42d; density: 4.7 persons per km² (12.1 per mi²). Distribution (1988 est.): 20% metropolitan, 80% nonmetropolitan. Average annual change (1980–90): +0.7%.

Government (1991): Governor: Cecil D. Andrus, Democrat. U.S. Congress: Senate—2 Republicans; House—2 Democrats. Electoral college votes: 4. State legislature: 42 senators, 84 representatives.

Economy: State personal income (1988): $12.7 billion; rank: 43d. Median family income (1979): $17,492; rank: 36th. Agriculture: income (1988)—$2.3 billion. Forestry: sawtimber volume (1987)—140.6 billion board feet. Mining: value (1987)—$269 million. Manufacturing: value added (1987)—$3.1 billion. Services: value (1987)—$2.7 billion.

Miscellany: Statehood: July 3, 1890; the 43d state. Nickname: Gem State; tree: Western white pine; motto: *Esto Perpetua* ("May it endure forever"); song: "Here We Have Idaho."

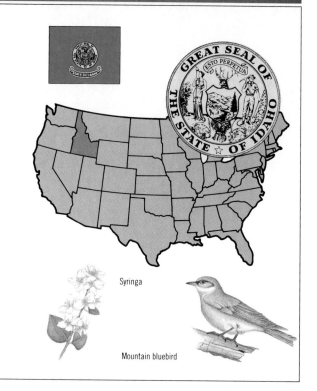

Syringa

Mountain bluebird

Vegetation and Animal Life. Coniferous forests cover about 40% of the state, while pasture and range lands constitute almost one-half of the remainder. Much of Idaho's grazing land is semiarid, and a substantial portion of the land used for farming requires irrigation.

Large indigenous animals include deer (white tailed in the extreme north, mule deer farther south), elk, moose, mountain goats, big horn sheep, antelope, cougars, and bears. A few grizzlies inhabit remote areas. A large variety of smaller animals typical of the West's mountains and deserts abound throughout the state. Wilderness-preservation efforts help to maintain the wildlife population.

Resources. In addition to abundant water for irrigation and power, Idaho's commercial minerals include extensive silver, lead, zinc, and phosphate deposits. Forest products, primarily in the north, and valuable farmland contribute to the economy. Outdoor recreation areas are found throughout the state. Along the Oregon border, Hells Canyon, the deepest gorge in the nation, is a major attraction, along with Sawtooth National Recreation Area and Bear Lake.

People

Idaho's population grew 7.2% from 1980 to 1990—an increase below the national growth rate of 10.2% and far below the state's increase of 32.4% during the previous

decade. The state's relatively rapid growth during 1970–80 took place primarily in cites and in rural communities with scenic or recreational benefits. This traditionally rural state remains sparsely populated. There are nearly 14,000 Indians and some 9,000 Asians and Pacific islanders, most of them Japanese, in Idaho. The state's southwestern area has the nation's major concentration of Basques. People of Hispanic origin make up about 5% of the state's population, but the black population has never exceeded 1%. Among religious groups, the Mormons, about 25% of the state's population, are the largest, followed by Roman Catholics and Methodists. For more than a century, Idaho has ranked second only to Utah in concentration of Mormon population.

Idaho has no large cities; most of the urban population live in small towns. BOISE, with a metropolitan area population of 205,775 in 1990, is the only place with more than 50,000 persons; POCATELLO and IDAHO FALLS in the southeast have populations exceeding 40,000, while Nampa, Lewiston, and Twin Falls have more than 25,000, and Coeur d'Alene has almost 25,000.

Education. Elementary, secondary, vocational, and higher education in Idaho have been under the jurisdiction of a single state board of education since 1912. Following a study in 1946, the legislature consolidated the state's 1,110 school districts into few more than 100.

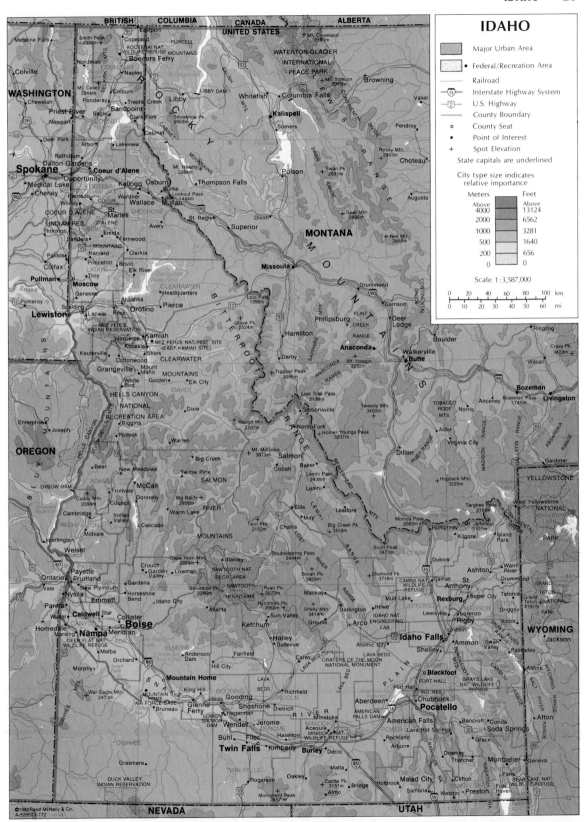

The University of Idaho was chartered in 1889 as the major state institution of higher education. Idaho State University at Pocatello (1901) and Boise State University (1932) are also 4-year state institutions that offer higher degrees.

The state's major libraries include that of the University of Idaho, complemented by the libraries of the other state universities; Idaho State Library; and Boise Public Library. Regional libraries serve the public libraries located throughout the state.

Cultural Institutions. Idaho has the State Historical Museum in Boise, the Idaho Museum of Natural History in Pocatello, and a major museum educational program at the University of Idaho in Moscow. Several symphony orchestras, including the professional Boise Philharmonic, perform in the larger communities. The Ballet Folk of Moscow and Antique Festival Theatre, based in Buhl, can be seen in performances throughout the state. The SUN VALLEY Center for the Arts and Humanities offers an extensive cultural program.

Historic Sites. Three of Idaho's places of specific historic interest are along the course of the LEWIS AND CLARK EXPEDITION. Others include Fort Hall near Pocatello, City of Rocks along the California Trail, and two important buildings—the Jesuit Coeur d'Alene Mission near Cataldo and the U.S. Assay office in Boise. Nez Percé National Historical Park has sites in northern Idaho.

Communications. The *Idaho Statesman*, the state's oldest daily newspaper, published in Boise, was established in 1864. Several other dailies and numerous weeklies also serve the state's communities. Idaho's oldest radio station dates from 1922. The state's commercial and public television stations are augmented by stations operating in neighboring states.

Economic Activity

Although originally dependent upon mining, Idaho developed farming and forestry as well. After 1940 industrial diversification broadened the state's economy, and tourism gained importance.

Agriculture. Idaho's farms dominate the state's economy. Potatoes are the most important crop, followed by wheat; barley and sugar beets are also leading crops. Although much of the state is naturally arid, extensive irrigation has enabled Idahoans to harvest valuable crops—particularly on the level river planes of southern Idaho.

Forestry and Fishing. Commercial lumber production, primarily of Douglas fir, white fir, white pine, yellow pine, and red cedar, contributes substantially to the state's income, although lumbering ranks well behind agriculture and manufacturing in value. The extent of Idaho's national forest land—much of it commercially exploited—is second to Alaska's.

In 1947 commercial rainbow-trout fish farming began near Hagerman in southern Idaho, utilizing water from Thousand Springs.

Mining. Idaho habitually ranks first nationally in the production of silver. Other commercially important metals include lead, gold, and zinc. Phosphate is also mined. Periods of increasing gold and silver prices have led to the resumption of mining in abandoned districts as well as increasing production in the Coeur d'Alene area.

Manufacturing. Most of the state's industrial development has taken place since 1940, and Idaho's manufactured products have increased in value, almost catching up with agriculture. A small population and the absence of iron and steel restricts this economic sector to agribus-

The Snake River, the largest tributary of the Columbia River, flows from east to west across southern Idaho.

Except for a period of intensive mining in the late 19th century, the greatest share of Idaho's revenue has been derived from agriculture. (Left) Sheep graze along the Salmon River, which courses across central Idaho; Idaho is a leading lamb-marketing state. (Right) The Great Basin region south of Pocatello contains some of the state's most fertile farmland. The area is noted for the growing of potatoes, wheat, and sugar beets.

inesses, and wood products, mobile-home, electronics, and construction-equipment manufacturing.

Transportation and Trade. A central mountain barrier has made railroad construction between north and south Idaho infeasible, and the first highway connecting the two sections of the state was surfaced only in 1938. As a result, Spokane, Wash., serves as commercial center for the northern counties, Salt Lake City, Utah, for the southeast, and Boise for the southwest.

Tourism. Although Idaho's mountainous topography creates serious economic problems, recreation and tourism benefit from this natural heritage. Federal financial assistance has enabled Idaho to develop areas for tourism, such as Lava Hot Springs State Resort near Pocatello. Special attractions include the nation's pioneer ski resort at Sun Valley, developed by the Union Pacific Railroad in 1936. Nez Percé National Historical Park in the north, Craters of the Moon National Monument, and YELLOWSTONE NATIONAL PARK on the Wyoming border are also popular tourist spots.

Government

Idaho's constitution was adopted in 1889, one year before statehood. It provides for a governor and seven other state officials elected to 4-year terms. A constitutional amendment enacted in 1972 called for the reorganization of the executive branch into no more than 20 departments. A 42-member senate and 84-member house of representatives form the legislature. The state supreme court, with five justices, heads the judicial branch. Two levels of trial courts (district and magistrate) serve all counties in the state. Legislators are elected to 2-year terms, judges and magistrates to 4-year terms, and su-

preme court justices to 6-year terms. All court justices are nonpartisan.

Local government consists of 44 counties and approximately 200 cities and villages.

Idaho has gained a reputation for independent voting on a national level. An almost equal number of Democratic and Republican candidates for the presidency have received the state's electoral votes since Idaho entered the Union. Statewide elections for governor have clearly favored Republicans over Democrats, however, as have elections for U.S. senators and representatives.

History

Idaho has been inhabited for more than 14,000 years. The early inhabitants hunted mammoths and other large animals now extinct. These early people migrated throughout the region. By the 18th century, Idaho was the home of six Indian tribes: KUTENAI, Pend d'Oreille (or FLATHEAD), Coeur d'Alene, and NEZ PERCÉ in the north; and Northern SHOSHONI and Northern PAIUTE (known as Bannock) to the south.

Exploration and Fur Trade. After the Lewis and Clark Expedition discovered the Salmon and Clearwater country in 1805–06, fur trappers—British and French Canadians, as well as Americans—explored the rest of Idaho in search of beaver. By 1840 trapping had almost ended, and the HUDSON'S BAY COMPANY gained control of the region. The United States acquired the southern part of the Oregon country, including all of present-day Idaho, in 1846. Hudson's Bay Company, with posts at Fort Hall and Fort Boise, continued to serve the settlers traveling to the west over the OREGON TRAIL and California Trail. Permanent white settlement began in 1860, when Mormons moved northward from Utah and miners, including Chinese, arrived from the Pacific coast.

Mining. A series of Idaho gold rushes lured many, especially after an important mineral discovery at Pierce in 1860. Idaho was then part of Washington Territory, which extended east from Puget Sound to the continental divide. By 1862, a majority of the territory's population lived in Idaho. On Mar. 4, 1863, President Abraham Lincoln approved an act of Congress establishing the Idaho Territory. Present-day Montana and nearly all of Wyoming were included in this new mining commonwealth. Despite the departure of thousands of miners, Idaho had more than 32,000 residents in the census of 1863. Population figures declined after that time. Some of Idaho's early gold camps were quickly mined out, but others continued to produce for many years. Important lead-silver discoveries in the 1880s brought permanence to Idaho's mining industry. The latter became the major lead-silver region of the United States.

Statehood. After territories were formed in Montana (1864) and Wyoming (1868), Idaho's boundaries enclosed two areas divided by mountains. For a quarter-century, North Idaho tried without success to form a new territory with eastern Washington, or, as a last resort, rejoin Washington. The U.S. Congress voted in 1886–87 to annex North Idaho to Washington Territory, but President Grover Cleveland was persuaded not to approve that change.

Although Idaho Territory had been overwhelmingly Confederate Democratic after 1864, a coalition of Republicans and anti-Mormons gained power in 1882. Idaho was made a state on July 3, 1890.

Political and Economic Unrest. A silver-price collapse (1888–92), followed by a national economic panic, severely hurt Idaho. The Populist candidate James B. Weaver received the state's votes in the presidential election of 1892, as did William Jennings Bryan in 1896. Idaho thus expressed its discontent with the federal government's economic policies. Labor battles in the Coeur d'Alene mine area attracted national attention in 1892 and 1899. Sheep ranchers and cattlemen, vying for the limited range land available, clashed during that same period.

The state developed rapidly in the early 1900s, spurred by the commercial lumber industry. National farm and forest products markets, along with large-scale mining, developed in all parts of the state, but in 1920, a severe agriculture price collapse, followed by the Depression of the 1930s, intensified the state's problems. Eventually, federal expenditures helped Idaho's economic recovery. Important military bases, including a large naval training station on Lake Pend d'Oreille, contributed to the state's economy after 1942. Idaho's largest federal installation, The National Reactor Testing Station (now the Idaho National Engineering Laboratory), located west of Idaho Falls, was the first plant to generate electricity from nuclear power (1951).

Contemporary Idaho. Issues related to maintenance of a high-quality environment and to wilderness preservation in vast mountain areas of the state have remained prominent since 1970. With extensive wilderness, and with constantly increasing pressures of economic and population growth, Idaho serves as an example for the study of contemporary environmental problems.

Idaho Falls   Idaho Falls, a city with a population of 43,929 (1990), is located on the Snake River in southeastern Idaho and is the seat of Bonneville County. Its economy depends on the processing of potatoes, sugar beets, and grain, all grown in the extensively irrigated region, augmented by diversified industry and a nearby U.S. government nuclear reactor. Settled as Eagle Rock in 1863, the city was renamed in 1890.

idealism   Idealism, the philosophical view that the mind or spirit constitutes the fundamental reality, has taken several distinct but related forms. Objective idealism accepts commonsense REALISM (the view that material objects exist) but rejects NATURALISM (according to which the mind and spiritual values have emerged from material things), whereas subjective idealism denies that material objects exist independently of human perception and thus stands opposed to both realism and naturalism.

PLATO is often considered the first idealist philosopher, because he considered the universal Idea or Form—for example, redness or goodness—more real than a particular instance of the form—a red object, a good action. According to Plato, the world of changing experience is unreal, and the Idea or Form—which does not change and which can be known only by reason—constitutes true reality.

The 18th-century epistemologist George BERKELEY was one of the major exponents of idealism. He held that the object of knowledge is an idea and that ideas can exist only in the mind; therefore, objects can exist only as objects of consciousness. Berkeley's dictum was *esse est percipi* ("to be is to be perceived"), a refutation of traditional MATERIALISM.

Johann Gottlieb FICHTE postulated a creative Ego as the ultimate source of reality, which generates all change and all knowledge. Fichte's theory was elaborated in G. W. F. HEGEL's absolute idealism. For Hegel reality is absolute Spirit or Reason, which manifests its development toward total self-consciousness in every aspect of experience from nature to human history. The English Hegelian F. H. BRADLEY argued that ordinary experience is fragmentary and contradictory and therefore appearance; reality, the Absolute, is a unified totality, which can be known only through a unique and absolute, perhaps mystical, experience.

See also: EPISTEMOLOGY; ETHICS; METAPHYSICS.

identity crisis   see ADOLESCENCE; ERIKSON, ERIK; MIDDLE AGE

ideology [y-dee-ahl'-uh-jee]   An ideology is a system of beliefs that aspires both to explain and to change the world. The concept of ideology originated in late-18th-century France, when the philosopher Destutt de Tracy coined the term to denote a science of ideas that would be based not on the discredited principles of faith and authority linked to the church and the monarchy but on knowledge gained from the senses. Today social scientists conceive of ideology as a systematic set of principles that link perceptions of the world to explicit moral values. All ideologies—CONSERVATISM, LIBERALISM, democratic SOCIALISM, COMMUNISM, FASCISM, and ANARCHISM—make certain claims or assumptions about the nature of the self, the interaction between the self and the collectivity, the relationship of the individual to the physical environment, the nature of society, and the meaning of history. Fundamental to the content of a political ideology are the ways in which the bases of political power are viewed and freedom and equality are interpreted.

The function of an ideology is to explain the key problems facing a society and to interpret key events: it gives meaning to life and history. Ideology shapes the purposes and priorities of political action, operating as a perceptual screen on the believer to make some alternatives acceptable and to filter out others. It can be used to justify policies and to mobilize human efforts behind a cause.

Ideology is an abstract, systematic set of principles rather than specific, random beliefs. People who think in terms of ideology perceive concrete events in the light of abstract ideas, such as equality for the downtrodden or freedom for the enterprising.

The most intense ideological struggles have occurred when societies were experiencing institutional disintegration, strong challenges to established authority, war, economic collapse, rapid industrialization or some combination of these. Thus, in Western Europe ideological polarization reached a peak between 1870 and 1940, as European societies faced rapid economic growth, war and depression, and challenges to long-accepted moral and governmental principles.

idiot savant Idiot savants ("learned idiots") are a small group—perhaps 3 percent of the retarded and autistic in the United States—who possess extraordinary talent in one or two fields, usually in music, chess, art, mathematics, or memory for particular types of facts. Now called the "savant syndrome," the phenomenon is nevertheless restricted to those who exhibit the classic symptoms of brain damage or autism: as small children they cannot learn to speak; they are often physically handicapped; and their IQs may fall within the lowest testing ranges. Once their talents are discovered and nurtured, however, changes in their basic abilities also frequently occur.

The talents of most savants seem to involve unusual memory capacity. A musical savant can replay music after having heard it only once; a mathematical savant can manipulate certain types of numbers in moments. Some savants are capable of creativity: they paint, sculpt, or improvise and compose music.

idol [y'-dul] Images or statues modeled after gods or goddesses that are used in worship are called idols. In ancient cultures the practice of giving tangible expression to the realm of the spiritual was widespread, and personifications of symbols of life and fertility were common. The images, usually constructed of wood, stone, and metals, were decorated, presented with food, and prayed to by their devotees. Idols remain common in many religions of the world, including Buddhism and Hinduism as well as primitive religions.

In Judaism only the one true God, who cannot be contained in forms fashioned by humans, is worthy of worship (Exod. 20:4–6; 34:17). Both Christianity and Islam maintain that prohibition on making and worshiping images.

Idomeneus [ee-dah-may-noos'] In Greek legend Idomeneus, the son of Deucalion and grandson of MINOS, was king of Crete. He was one of the major Greek leaders in the TROJAN WAR. According to Homer's *Odyssey*, he and his 80 ships returned uneventfully to Crete after the fall of Troy. In a later version of the legend, however, he was caught in a storm on the return voyage and vowed that if he reached home safely he would sacrifice to Poseidon the first creature he encountered. This proved to be his son. When Idomeneus fulfilled the vow, a plague fell on Crete and his subjects banished him. Mozart's opera *Idomeneo* was based on the legend.

Idris, King of Libya [id-rees'] Idris, b. Mar. 13, 1890, d. May 25, 1983, was the first king (1951–69) of Libya. A grandson of al-SANUSI, he became leader of the Sanusi Muslim sect in 1917 and in 1920 was recognized as emir of Cyrenaica by the Italians, who had invaded Libya in 1911. The Italian Fascists forced him into exile in 1922, but Cyrenaica was restored (1943) to him in World War II. In 1951, Idris became king of the unified Libya. Idris and the monarchy were overthrown by a military junta led by Muammar al-QADDAFI in 1969.

Idrisi, al- [id-ree'-see, ahl] Abu Abd Allah Muhammad al-Idrisi, c.1100–c.1165, was an Arab Muslim geographer employed at the court of a Christian king, Roger II of Sicily. He is chiefly known as the author of a descriptive geography, commonly called the *Kitab Rujar* (Book of Roger, 1154). This work describes the area north of the equator and is illustrated by 70 maps. Al-Idrisi, who was probably a native of Morocco, also wrote a treatise on medicine.

idyll [y'-dul] The term *idyll* originally denoted a pastoral poem, generally short, describing the innocent rustic life of shepherds. The major classical writers of idylls were the Greeks Theocritus (3d century BC), Moschus and Bion (both 2d century BC), and the Roman Vergil (70–19 BC). The English poets Edmund Spenser and John Milton were influenced by the classical idylls. Later the term lost its pastoral connotation and came to mean any composition, prose or verse, that had a country setting or merely a simple, appealing, or charming mood. Thus Alfred Tennyson's *Idylls of the King* (1859–85) contains no descriptions of rustic life, but the mood and tone are idyllic.

Ieyasu, Shogun of Japan

Ieyasu, Shogun of Japan [ee-ay'-yah-soo, shoh'-guhn] Ieyasu, or Tokugawa Ieyasu, 1542–1616, founded the TOKUGAWA shogunate that ruled Japan until 1868. The eldest son of Matsudaira Hirotada, lord (daimyo) of Okazaki castle in Mikawa province, he spent his youth as a hostage of the house of Imagawa. When freed in 1560 he formed a military alliance with the powerful NOBUNAGA. After Nobunaga's death (1582) Ieyasu competed for leadership with Nobunaga's general, HIDEYOSHI, and then allied with him during the last stages of the military unification of Japan. After the defeat of the Hojo of Odowara in 1590, he received the former Hojo territories in the Kanto, where he built a tightly organized administration, centered on Edo (later Tokyo).

When Hideyoshi died in 1598, Ieyasu was appointed a regent to his son and successor, Toyotomi Hideyori. Defeating his rivals in the Battle of Sekigahara in 1600, Ieyasu emerged as the new military leader of Japan. In 1603 he assumed the title of SHOGUN. In 1605, Ieyasu passed the office of shogun to his son Hidetada, establishing a precedent for Tokugawa succession. He eliminated Hideyoshi's successor, a threat to Tokugawa rule, in 1615.

Ieyasu initially sought to develop foreign trade and tolerated the Christian missionaries. He soon began establishing trade monopolies, however. This policy, continued by his successors, eventually led Japan into almost total isolation.

Ife

Ife [ee'-fay] The town of Ife (1983 est. pop., 214,500) in southwestern Nigeria was the seat of a powerful YORUBA kingdom from the 11th to the 17th century. It remains the sacred city of the Yoruba people where, according to tradition, the god Oduduwa created the Earth and established himself as *oni* (king). All later *oni* are traditionally believed to be descended from the mythological ruler of Ife. Ife is also known for the many magnificent art objects in copper alloy, terra-cotta, and stone excavated there. The most famous are naturalistic portrait heads of ancient kings, cast in metal by the lost-wax process, that date from the 12th to the 14th century.

Ignatius Loyola, Saint

Ignatius Loyola, Saint [ig-nay'-shuhs loy-oh'-luh] Saint Ignatius Loyola, b. 1491, d. July 31, 1556, was founder of the Society of Jesus, or JESUITS. Born into a noble Basque family, he underwent a profound change in his religious attitude in his early thirties, and while on a pilgrimage to Jerusalem he stopped at the famed Benedictine abbey of Montserrat in Catalonia, where he dedicated himself to God. He then spent nearly a year in a spiritual retreat at nearby Manresa. There he had the mystical experience that would be later developed into his method of spirituality known as the *Spiritual Exercises*.

Saint Ignatius Loyola founded the Society of Jesus (Jesuits), a Roman Catholic order devoted to missionary work and education that was highly influential during the 16th-century Counter-Reformation. (Gesù Church, Rome.)

He also discovered the orientation of his life's work. He traveled on as a poor man and beggar to Rome, to Venice, and finally to Jerusalem.

In 1528 he began his theological training at Paris. There he gathered his first associates, six in all (including Saint FRANCIS XAVIER), who together took vows of poverty and chastity at Montmartre in 1534. They were ordained in 1537.

The group wished to work in the Holy Land, but Europe's wars with Ottoman Turkey prevented them. They then offered their services to the pope. They were received (1538) by Pope PAUL III, and Ignatius drew up the rule of life for a new religious order, which was approved by Paul in 1540. Ignatius became the first general of the Society of Jesus.

By the time of Ignatius's death in 1556, the society had spread widely and had more than a thousand members. He and his order had become a major factor in the COUNTER-REFORMATION. Ignatius was canonized in 1622 and is the patron of spiritual retreats. Feast day: July 31.

Ignatius of Antioch, Saint

Ignatius of Antioch, Saint The third bishop of Antioch, Ignatius, d. *c*.107, was brought to Rome under Trajan and thrown to wild beasts. On the way to Rome he wrote letters about the virgin birth and divinity of Christ, although he stressed especially Christ's human nature. The first writer to call the church "catholic," Ignatius described it as a society of love, presided over in love by a bishop with his presbyters and deacons, and assembled "in grace, in one faith and one Jesus Christ" (Eph. 20).

Called *Theophoros* ("God-bearer"), Ignatius considered martyrdom a great honor and asked the Roman Christians not to save him. Feast day: Oct. 17 (Western); Dec. 17 (Antioch); Dec. 20 (other Eastern).

igneous rock

igneous rock [ig'-nee-uhs] Igneous rocks constitute one of the three main groups in standard rock classification, along with SEDIMENTARY ROCKS and METAMORPHIC ROCKS. Igneous rocks form from the cooling and crystallization of molten or partially molten material called MAGMA.

Long-term igneous differentiation processes, whereby lighter elements tend to become segregated from heavier

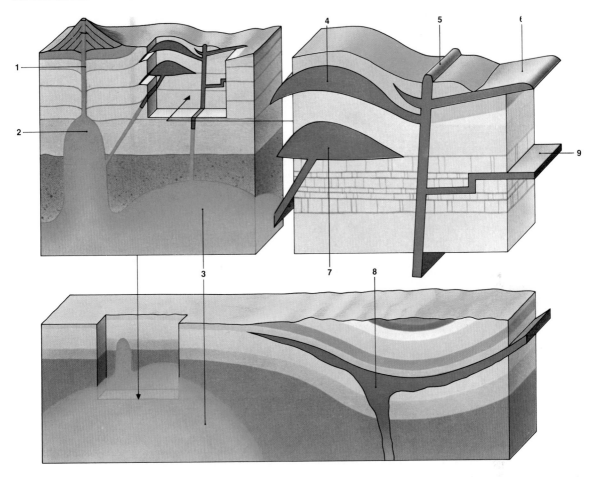

Igneous rocks are formed from solidification of magma, or molten matter from the Earth's interior. The rocks may cool as extrusive masses on the surface of the Earth or as intrusive bodies below the surface. Intrusive igneous rocks assume many different characteristic shapes. A neck (1) is solidified magma in a circular vertical feed channel of an extinct volcano. A stock (2) is a mass with a circular or elliptical shape. A batholith (3) is a huge mass, generally of granitic composition, that lies deep within the crust. Laccoliths (4, 7) are domelike masses in which the pressure of the intrusive magma has arched up the overlying sediment. A dike (5) is an inclined sheetlike body much longer than it is wide that generally occupies rock fractures and cuts across previously existing rock layers. A sill (6) is a thin band that conforms to the structural planes of the sedimentary beds around it. A lopolith (8) is a saucer-shaped mass—sometimes extremely large—that is concave upward. A transgressive sill (9) is a thin band of igneous rock that occurs in more than one horizontal plane.

ones, have been major factors in forming the Earth's chemically and mineralogically layered structure (see GEOCHEMISTRY). The wide variety of presumably igneous rocks can be explained as arising from the partial melting of many different source materials; it may also be linked to differentiation processes occurring during EROSION AND SEDIMENTATION at the Earth's surface, followed by subsequent burial and partial melting.

Types

Key variables in subdividing igneous rocks include mode of occurrence, grain size and texture, and mineralogy and chemistry. Rocks thought to be igneous may be subdivided into volcanic, subvolcanic (hypabyssal), plutonic, and pyroclastic types. Direct evidence of igneous origin is available only for extrusive (volcanic and pyroclastic) rocks, which form directly from the cooling of LAVA or other materials that flow or erupt from volcanic vents and fissures.

Volcanic. Volcanic rocks tend to be fine-grained (less than 1 mm/0.04 in), and their matrix usually contains glass as well as tiny CRYSTALS. Wholly glassy varieties are called OBSIDIAN. In porphyritic varieties (see PORPHYRY), larger crystals are embedded in a fine-grained groundmass. This texture probably results from extrusion of lava containing crystals already grown and developed under conditions of slow cooling below the Earth's surface; subsequent rapid cooling leads to crystallization of the finer-grained matrix.

The most common volcanic rocks are BASALT, ANDESITE,

Devil's Tower in Wyoming is believed to be the remains of hard igneous rock resulting from solidification of magma that filled the neck, or conduit, of an extinct volcano.

and RHYOLITE. Basalt, thought to form during partial melting of rocks in the Earth's mantle, is the most abundant volcanic rock. Andesite may form from partial melting of crustal rocks deep in fold belts. Rhyolite, composed largely of alkali FELDSPAR and free silica (see SILICA MINERALS) such as QUARTZ, forms lava flows and tuffs. Other, less common, low-silica volcanic rocks contain neither feldspar nor quartz but are rich in FELDSPATHOIDS such as leucite or nepheline. The origin of carbonatite, an unusual rock rich in CARBONATE MINERALS, was disputed until sodium carbonate lavas were observed erupting from African volcanoes.

Volcanic rocks occur in many parts of the world. A great chain of volcanoes known as the RING OF FIRE encircles the Pacific Ocean. The Mid-Atlantic Ridge is a great suboceanic chain of volcanoes, as are the East Pacific and Indian Ocean ridges (see MID-OCEANIC RIDGE). The East African Rift System is largely filled with volcanic material, as is the extension of this trough northward through the Rhine Valley and the Oslo Fjord (see RIFT VALLEY). Volcanoes rim the northern edge of the Mediterranean and cover central France. Great sheetlike flows of lava cover the Columbia River Plateau in the northwestern part of the United States and the DECCAN PLATEAU in India. Active volcanic regions appear mostly along the borders of crustal plates (see PLATE TECTONICS), with the more basaltic materials rising to the surface at divergent plate boundaries, and the more andesitic and rhyolitic materials appearing along convergent plate boundaries.

Subvolcanic. Subvolcanic rocks are fine-grained intrusive rocks occurring in DIKES or SILLS and connected directly with volcanic conduits. The discordant character of dikes and other types of forceful intrusions supports the theory that they were formed from a fluid. Some such rocks are medium-grained (1 to 5 mm/0.04 to 0.2 in), but their patterns of grain intergrowth and their compositions strongly resemble those of surface volcanics. Many subvolcanic rocks are porphyritic.

Plutonic. Plutonic rocks are coarse-grained (greater than 5 mm/0.2 in) or medium-grained and commonly occur in large masses, or batholiths, hundreds of kilometers in extent. Most common among them are rocks of the GRANITE, GABBRO, and granodiorite clans. The margins of the mineral grains in these rocks are tightly interlocking. PEGMATITES and other coarse-grained plutonic bodies appear to have formed deep within the Earth's crust, cooling and crystallizing at depths where temperatures are just below the melting point (see EARTH, HEAT FLOW IN).

Most plutonic rocks have compositional or textural equivalents among the volcanic rocks. The so-called layered igneous rocks are an exception in that they show features common in sedimentary rocks. Prominent layering in these large bodies is thought to occur because of the faster gravitational settling of larger or denser, early-formed crystals and the slower settling of smaller or less-dense crystals.

Granitic rocks, including such varieties as quartz monzonite and granodiorite, are the most abundant plutonic rocks. They may form from the partial melting of deeply buried sedimentary rocks during periods of mountain building. Varieties such as SYENITE are rich in potassium feldspar and contain no quartz.

Plutonic rocks of probable igneous origin form the cores of many of the world's great mountain ranges: the Rockies, Appalachians, Sierra Nevada, Alps, and Himalayas. In addition, the Precambrian CONTINENTAL SHIELDS—which form the central portions of all of the continents and underlie the world's sedimentary basins—contain plutonic rocks, most of which may have been formed by the melting or partial melting of other crustal rocks, followed by subsequent slow cooling and crystallization or by more active flow, injection, and intrusion.

Pyroclastic Rocks. Igneous and sedimentary processes converge in the formation of pyroclastic rocks. Tuffs, breccias, ashflows, and other fragmental rocks have many of the same characteristics as sedimentary rocks. Volcanoes erupt ash, bombs, and other clearly igneous, red-hot fragmental material into the air. When such material falls to the ground, however, it forms strata that may resemble wind deposits, such as desert SAND DUNES. When volcanic debris falls into water, it settles to the bottom and forms layers even more similar to sedimentary materials. Mineral composition may be the only feature by which pyroclastic rocks can be distinguished from more ordinary sedimentary rocks.

Some pyroclastic eruptions have been catastrophic, such as the eruptions of VESUVIUS, which buried POMPEII and HERCULANEUM, and of Mount PELÉE, which killed 35,000 people in 1902 and 1932. The great sheets of rhyolitic ash that cover wide areas in Nevada and other western states must be of similar origin.

Basic vs. Acidic. Igneous rocks are often divided into basic and acidic types. These terms relate to percentage of silica (SiO_2) rather than to hydrogen-ion content (pH). Some petrologists prefer the terms MAFIC and FELSIC. Ultrabasic (ultramafic) rocks, containing less than 45% SiO_2, include plutonic rocks such as DUNITE and PERIDOTITE, which characteristically contain OLIVINE and PYROXENE and are free of quartz and feldspars. Some contain feldspathoids. Basic rocks contain 45% to 62% SiO_2 and include gabbroic (plutonic) rocks and basaltic (volcanic) rocks. Plagioclase feldspar, olivine, and pyroxene are the key minerals in these rocks, and quartz is usually absent. Intermediate rocks (52% to 66% SiO_2) include DIORITE (plutonic) and ANDESITE (volcanic). These rocks contain hornblende (see AMPHIBOLE), pyroxene, and plagioclase feldspar. Quartz, potassium feldspar, and biotite (see MICA) may also be present. Acidic (felsic) rocks, containing more than 66% SiO_2, include the granites (plutonic) and rhyolites (volcanic). Quartz and potassium feldspar are important mineral components, along with muscovite (see MICA), biotite, and hornblende.

Economic Deposits

Rocks that are known or inferred to be of igneous origin are the sources of many economically important minerals and ORE DEPOSITS. Volcanic rocks are sources of sulfur and mercury minerals. Volcanic ash-flow deposits are sources of much of the world's copper supply—specifically the porphyry copper deposits in Chile, Nevada, and Utah. The chromium-rich mineral CHROMITE is common in layered igneous complexes such as the Stillwater Complex of Montana and the Troodos Complex on the island of Cyprus. Low-silica complexes of probable igneous origin are sources of much asbestos, as at Thetford Mines, Quebec. Precious-metal deposits of gold, silver, and platinum are related to late stages in the formation of granitic rocks. The Great Dike of Rhodesia and the Bushveld Complex of South Africa's TRANSVAAL province contain rich deposits of copper, gold, and other valuable minerals. Lead-zinc ore bodies result from late-stage concentration of these metals in cooling igneous complexes. Ores of rare-earth metals of the LANTHANIDE SERIES are found in some PEGMATITES. Many high-grade deposits of the iron mineral MAGNETITE are probably igneous, as are great nickel deposits, such as those at Sudbury, Ontario. Titanium ores occur in a plagioclase-rich gabbro called anorthosite.

Many volcanic rocks are used in various types of construction, especially as a crushed material for road building. Plutonic rocks, lavas, and tuffs are used in building construction and as decorative stone. Volcanic ash and flows (when weathered) furnish fertile soils. The cooling of igneous rocks at depth also provides sources of GEOTHERMAL ENERGY.

ignition system [ig-nish'-uhn] An INTERNAL-COMBUSTION ENGINE needs an ignition system for igniting the combustible mixture inside each cylinder at the proper

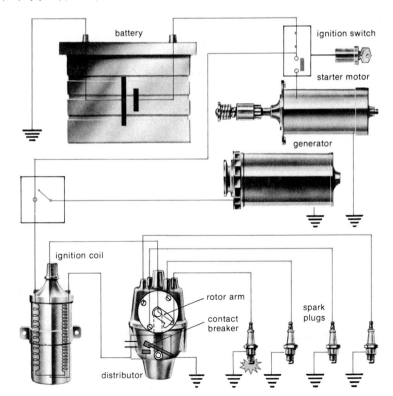

The automotive ignition system must deliver 10,000 volts up to 300 times per second in order to keep the engine running. The electrical system, which includes the ignition system, must supply a strong current to the starter motor to start the engine. When the ignition switch is turned, current flows from the battery to the starter motor and to the ignition coil. The coil produces a high-voltage pulse (10,000 volts) that is directed to the rotor arm of the distributor, and then to the spark plugs one by one. The generator is switched into the circuit to recharge the battery when the car is in normal operation.

moment. In the DIESEL ENGINE, the air inside the cylinder is compressed enough to raise the temperature above the ignition point, so that the fuel is ignited as soon as it is injected into the cylinder. This is called compression ignition. The gasoline engine, however, requires a more complex system, called spark ignition, which uses an electric spark to ignite the mixture. The two basic automotive ignition systems are the conventional breaker-point system and the newer, electronic ignition.

Breaker-Point Ignition System

The breaker-point system (see figure) consists of the source of energy (the battery), the ignition coil, distributor, ignition switch, spark plugs, and wiring. The entire electrical system includes the ignition system as a sub-

system, but contains, in addition, the GENERATOR (or a related device called an alternator), the VOLTAGE REGULATOR, the starter, and electrical lights, accessories, and gauges

Electronic Ignition

The electronic ignition system performs the same basic functions as the conventional systems but with one major difference: the battery-to-coil circuit is closed and opened electronically in the former rather than mechanically as in the breaker-point system. The cam is replaced with a rotor that has metal tips on it. As the rotor turns, the tips pass by a pickup-coil assembly. Each time a tip aligns with the assembly, a magnetic pulse is generated in the coil. These pulses are used to generate the necessary high-voltage surge.

The distributor (left) distributes the high-voltage pulse of the ignition coil to the spark plugs. The rotating camshaft turns the distributor shaft and opens the contact-breaker points once every revolution. This induces a high-voltage pulse in the coil that is fed to the high-voltage terminal of the distributor and then to the rotor arm. Timing is such that the pulse occurs every time the rotor arm is in contact with a spark-plug terminal, producing a spark at each plug. The spark plug (right) ignites the fuel in the cylinder to drive the piston. An electric pulse (blue line) from the distributor passes to the points of the plug (inner and outer electrodes) and produces an electrical spark in the spark gap, firing the fuel. The points are made of highly corrosion-resistant metal, such as platinum, and the gap must be carefully maintained at a fixed distance. The body is insulated with ceramic to prevent an electrical discharge to the engine.

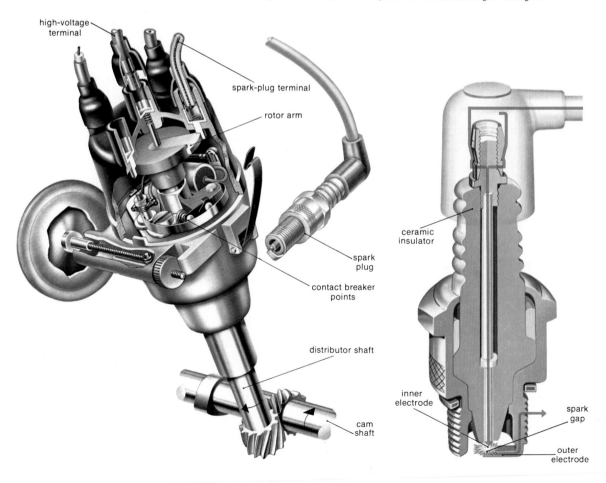

high-voltage terminal

spark-plug terminal

rotor arm

spark plug

contact breaker points

distributor shaft

cam shaft

ceramic insulator

inner electrode

spark gap

outer electrode

The common iguana, a large lizard found from central Mexico to southern South America, basks by day on a tree branch, usually over water. When danger threatens, it submerges in the water.

iguanodon [ig-wan'-uh-dahn] *Iguanodon* was a bipedal herbivorous ornithischian DINOSAUR whose fossils appear in Late Jurassic and Early Cretaceous rocks (see GEOLOGIC TIME). With massive bodies weighing more than 6 metric tons (13,200 lb), iguanodons stood up to 4.9 m (16 ft) high and were up to 9.5 m (31 ft) long. The jaws, lined with broad, flattened teeth, ended in the front with a toothless, horny beak. Armlike forelimbs had five-fingered hands with a large sharp bony spike in place of a thumb. Four-toed feet (three functional toes and a fourth very small one) produced birdlike tracks that have been preserved (see FOSSIL RECORD). The tracks suggest that iguanodons traveled in herds. Most iguanodon specimens have been found in Europe; fragmentary remains also have been found in Utah and Mongolia. *Iguanadon* was among the first dinosaurs to be discovered, in England in 1822.

The *Iguanodon,* a dinosaur with spikes on its forelimbs, flourished about 100 million years ago. Most likely the unusual spikes served as defensive weapons for jabbing into the eyes of predatory dinosaurs.

iguana [ig-wahn'-ah] The term *iguana* usually refers to the large species of typical New World lizards in the family Iguanidae. Large-bodied, with robust limbs and tails, most species of iguana live in the American tropics. Iguanas usually have compressed bodies and tails and a dorsal crest of soft spines that is more prominent in males than in females.

The common iguana, *Iguana iguana,* is widely used as food throughout its range from southern Mexico to central South America and also in the Lesser Antilles. It is an arboreal tropical-forest animal, attaining more than 1.5 m (5 ft) in total length, often found in the vicinity of rivers and streams. The common iguana eats both plants and animals, including leaves and fruit, insects, birds, and small mammals.

Large ground iguanas, genus *Cyclura,* inhabit islands of the Caribbean and attain total lengths of up to 1.2 m (4 ft). They are predators but eat vegetation as well. The marine iguana, *Amblyrhynchus cristatus,* of the Galápagos Islands, grows up to 1.5 m in length. Marine iguanas are the only lizards that regularly make use of the nearby marine environment—they usually swim close to shore and can dive to depths of more than 10.7 m (35 ft) to eat plants, particularly seaweed growing on the bottom.

A relatively small iguanid, *Dipsosaurus dorsalis,* known as the desert iguana, inhabits deserts with creosote bush in the southwestern United States. It is vegetarian and grows to little more than 30 cm (1 ft) in length. Often active during the hottest part of the day when smaller lizards are under shelter, the desert iguana runs rapidly and ascends creosote bushes to eat leaves and flowers.

Iguanas lay their eggs in burrows that they excavate themselves. Most nest individually, but marine iguanas nest communally, several females laying eggs in a single burrow.

IGY see INTERNATIONAL GEOPHYSICAL YEAR

Ihara Saikaku [ee'-hah-rah sy'-kah-koo] Ihara Saikaku, b. Osaka, 1642, d. Aug. 10, 1693, was Japan's greatest fiction writer of the Edo, or early modern, period (1603–1868). Saikaku broke new ground in creating fiction that, while not entirely realistic, was set squarely in the milieu in which he lived. In his writings he captured the zest for living and the bawdy humor of the emerging merchant class. His characters run off with their lovers and scheme to make quick commercial profit. Among his works are *The Life of an Amorous Man* (1682; Eng. trans., 1964), *The Japanese Family Storehouse* (1688; Eng. trans., 1959), and *Worldly Mental Calculations* (1692; Eng. trans., 1976).

IJsselmeer [y'-sul-mayr]   The IJsselmeer is a large freshwater lake in the north Netherlands that was once part of the Zuider Zee, a landlocked inlet of the North Sea. The lake was created when a 31-km-long (19-mi) dam, completed in 1932, was built from North Holland province to Friesland province. The IJsselmeer is 8 m (25 ft) above sea level and covers 3,440 km² (1,328 mi²). A road runs along the top of the dam, locks permit boat traffic, and sluices regulate the water flow. The dam was built as part of a drainage project in order to create new land, called polders. The first polder, the Wieringermeer, was finished in 1930. It was followed by the Northeast Polder (1945), East Flevoland (1957), and South Flevoland (1968), which became the new province of Flevoland in 1986. Concerns over rising costs and possible negative impact on the environment raised doubts about the completion of the largest polder, Markerwaard. Amsterdam is on the shore of the IJsselmeer.

Ik [ik]   The Ik (Teuso) are an African people of northern Uganda and the bordering areas of Sudan and Kenya. Once a nomadic hunter-gatherer people living in equilibrium with their environment, they now occupy barren mountaintop villages in a rocky area with only scattered patches of arable soil and an uncertain water supply. Shortly before World War II the traditional hunting ground of the Ik, the Kidepo Valley in northern Uganda, was made a national park, and hunting was forbidden. The Ik were encouraged to move to nearby mountains where their attempts to farm resulted in near starvation. Some Ik tribespeople have stayed alive by poaching in the national park or appropriating stray cattle belonging to neighboring herding peoples. Their traditional way of life has broken down almost completely. Parental support generally ends at age 3, when children must learn to fend for themselves. In 1980 the Ik population numbered fewer than 2,000. Their prospects for survival are bleak.

Île-de-France [eel-duh-frahns']   The Île-de-France is a historic region and former province of north central France dominated by PARIS and its suburbs. A fertile depression at the center of the Paris Basin, the Île-de-France is drained by the SEINE RIVER and its main tributaries, the MARNE and the Oise rivers. The region's subregions—Valois, Beauce, Brie, and Soissonais—are flat, limestone plains covered with loess. Forests, such as those of FONTAINEBLEAU and Compiègne, occupy sandy areas between the plains. Industry is concentrated in the Paris area; wheat, barley, corn, sugar beets, and dairy cattle are raised in the region.

With its capital at Paris, this duchy (then called Francia) was the nucleus around which Hugh Capet, founder of the

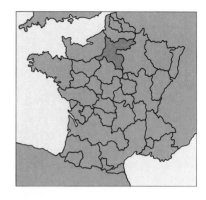

The map indicates the location of Île-de-France, a historical region of pre-Revolutionary France in the north-central portion of the country.

Capetian dynasty in 987, began the consolidation of the French state. From 1483 to 1790, when it was divided into departments, Île-de-France was a province of France.

ileitis   see ENTERITIS

ileus [il'-ee-uhs]   Ileus, or bowel obstruction, is a condition of the small or large intestine in which the passage of contents is stopped or impaired. The bowel wall becomes swollen and congested and the intestine distended; there is an increasing risk of peritonitis and death. Obstruction of the small intestine causes upper abdominal pain, vomiting, constipation, dehydration, and a drop in blood pressure. In later stages confusion and coma can result. The most common cause is mechanical blockage, which may result from surgery, inflammatory disease, or congenital factors; impacted feces or gallstones; or tumors. Paralytic ileus is the failure of normal peristalsis. Causes include interrupted blood flow due to embolism or thrombosis, peritonitis, and the effects of certain metabolic states on the nerves of the bowel wall.

Iliad [il'-ee-uhd]   The *Iliad*, an epic poem of roughly 16,000 lines in dactylic hexameter, usually ascribed to the poet HOMER, is thought to be the earliest surviving example of ancient Greek literature (see GREEK LITERATURE). Set in the tenth and last year of the TROJAN WAR, the *Iliad* deals specifically with the Greek hero ACHILLES, who leaves the battlefield in anger after the commander in chief, AGAMEMNON, confiscates his prize of war, the maid Briseis. Without Achilles' prowess the fortunes of the Greeks decline. Achilles returns to combat only after his friend Patroclus is slain by HECTOR, the Trojan prince. The final battle between Achilles and Hector, in which the Greek triumphs, presages the destruction of Troy. Achilles' vengeance ultimately yields to compassion when, in the most moving episode of the poem, Achilles returns Hector's body to his aged father, PRIAM. The *Iliad* has inspired translators from George Chapman in the 17th century and Alexander Pope in the 18th to Richmond Lattimore (1951), Robert Fitzgerald (1974), and Robert Fagles (1990) in the 20th.

Illich, Ivan [il'-ich, ee-vahn'] Ivan Illich, b. Sept. 4, 1926, is an Austrian-born American educator and social critic. In 1961 he helped found the Centro Intercultural de Documentación (CIDOC) in Cuernavaca, Mexico, to foster the teaching of the Spanish language and Latin American culture. Illich left the priesthood in 1969 when his criticism of traditional missionary activity became extremely controversial. His social targets have included ethnocentrism, paternalism, bureaucracy, and the status quo. In *Deschooling Society* (1971) he extended his radical critique to conventional schooling and compulsory education. He subsequently published *Medical Nemesis* (1975), an attack on the established medical system; and *Gender* (1982), an analysis of the position of women today.

Illinois [il-uh-noy'] Illinois is a leading agricultural, manufacturing, and urban state of the north central region of the United States. It is bordered by Wisconsin on the north, Lake Michigan on the northeast, Indiana on the east and southeast, and Kentucky on the south. The Ohio River follows its southern border, and the Mississippi in the west and southwest of the state lies along its borders with Iowa and Missouri. Illinois was explored by the French Jesuit missionary Jacques MARQUETTE and frontiersman Louis JOLLIET, who reached the area on June 20, 1673. The French changed the Indian name for the area, *Illiniwek*, meaning "the men," to Illinois. Illinois became a state on Dec. 3, 1818. Although the 24th largest state in size, its population is ranked 6th largest of all states. SPRINGFIELD became the capital in 1837. Since 1850, Illinois has been a major state in all sectors of the economy. Now it faces the problems of increasing urbanization and interregional economic competition.

Land and Resources

Illinois is composed of about 60% prairie, 30% hills with prairie, and 10% hills. The prairies cover central, northeastern, eastern, and south central Illinois; hills with prairie are found in northwestern, western, and southern Illinois; hills characterize the Driftless Area of the extreme northwest and the Shawnee Hills in the south.

Geologically, most of Illinois consists of ancient Precambrian granite overlain by sedimentary rocks of the Pennsylvanian and Mississippian periods (280–345 million years ago). These formations underlie 80% of the state in a bowl-shaped structure extending from the Shawnee Hills in the south to the Illinois River in the north. The northern fifth of the state contains bedrock from the Silurian, Ordovician, and Cambrian periods

AT A GLANCE

ILLINOIS

Land: Area: 145,933 km² (56,345 mi²); rank: 24th. Capital: Springfield (1990 pop., 105,227). Largest city: Chicago (1990 pop., 2,783,726). Counties: 102. Elevations: highest—376 m (1,235 ft), at Charles Mound; lowest—85 m (279 ft), at the Mississippi River.

People: Population (1990): 11,466,682; rank: 6th; density: 78.6 persons per km² (203.5 per mi²). Distribution (1988 est.): 82.5% metropolitan, 17.5% nonmetropolitan. Average annual change (1980–90): +0.04%.

Government (1991): Governor: Jim Edgar, Republican. U..S. Congress: Senate—2 Democrats; House—15 Democrats, 7 Republicans. Electoral college votes: 24. State legislature: 59 senators, 118 representatives.

Economy: State personal income (1988): $204.1 billion; rank: 5th. Median family income (1979): $22,746; rank: 6th. Agriculture: income (1988)—$6.5 billion. Forestry: sawtimber volume (1987)—17.5 billion board feet. Mining: value (1987)—$2.7 billion. Manufacturing: value added (1987)—$63.7 billion. Services: value (1987)—$51.7 billion.

Miscellany: Statehood: Dec. 3, 1818; the 21st state. Nickname: The Prairie State; tree: white oak; motto: State Sovereignty–National Union; song: "Illinois."

Violet

Eastern Cardinal

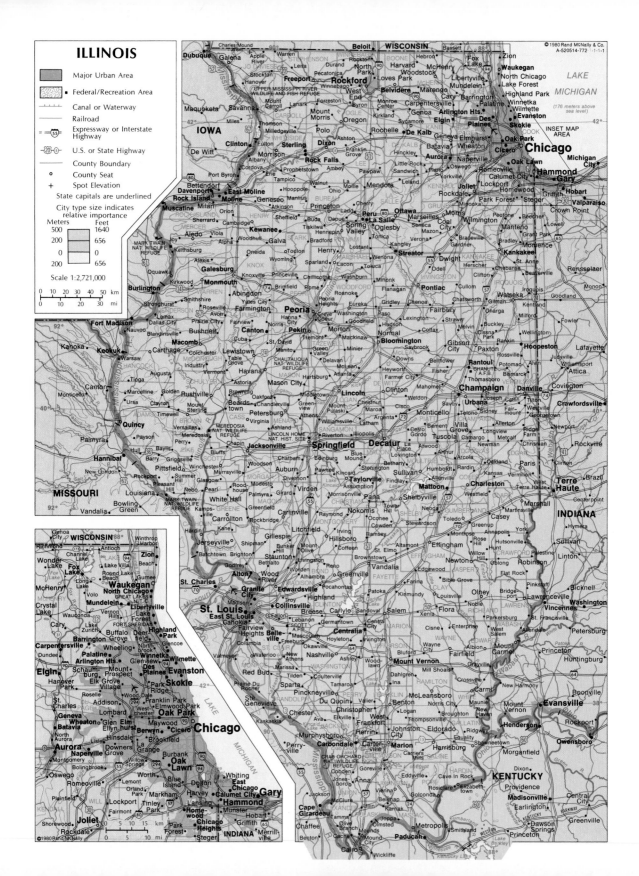

(Above) *Abraham Lincoln delivered (1858) his famous "House Divided" speech at the old state capitol in Springfield, Ill.*

(Left) *Chicago was settled during the 1830s and rapidly became a leading port. Located at the juncture of the Mississippi and St. Lawrence–Great Lakes systems, the city is a trade center for both agricultural commodities and industrial goods.*

(more than 400 million years ago). After the deposition of bedrock, four glaciers covered 90% of Illinois from 1.2 million to 13,000 years ago. Their effects are seen in glacial deposits, windblown soil (loess), and morainal ridges.

Soils. All Illinois soils are cultivable and fall into three soil groups: mollisols—a deep, highly organic, black prairie soil found in the northern two-thirds of the state; alfisols—a shallower, less organic, brown, forest-based soil dominant in the southern third of the state; and alluvium—a mixed, deep, water-deposited soil found in nearly all river valleys.

Drainage. There are more than 500 streams and rivers and 950 lakes and reservoirs in Illinois. The Illinois River is the largest river, draining about 64,750 km^2 (25,000 mi^2). Other large river basins are those of the Kankakee, Sangamon, and Fox. All of the major streams drain into either the Ohio or Mississippi rivers. The Chicago River once flowed eastward into Lake Michigan, but it is now artificially controlled by a series of locks to flow west toward the Des Plaines River. Underground aquifers, found in limestone and sandstone deposits, supply water to many northern cities. Surface water provides the rest of the state's water needs.

Climate. The climate of Illinois has distinct north-south fluctuations over the 620-km (385-mi) length of the state. Precipitation ranges from 1,130 mm (45 in) in southern Illinois to 880 mm (35 in) in northern Illinois. Most precipitation falls during late spring and early summer. Winter average temperatures are –4° C (25° F) in the north and 2° C (36° F) in the south. Summer averages are 24° C (75° F) in the north and 26° C (79° F) in the south.

Vegetation. The original vegetation cover was tall prairie grasses. Mixed deciduous forests (oak, hickory, maple, beech, sweet gum, elm, ash, cedar, pine, tamarack, fir) covered the southern third of the state and most river valleys. Virtually all this natural vegetation has been cleared

for agriculture. Wildlife includes large numbers of white-tailed deer, rabbit, squirrel, red fox, quail, and pheasant, along with several waterfowl species that fly through seasonally.

Resources. Extracted minerals include petroleum, natural gas, clay, silica, fluorspar, lead, zinc, and limestone. Illinois is a leading producer of bituminous coal in the United States. The coalfield, underlying approximately 70% of the state, yields about 60 million tons annually. Surface water is used for agriculture, industry, city water supplies, and electrical and nuclear power plants.

People

Although some areas in the state have fewer than one person per square mile, nine metropolitan areas account for 80% of the population: CHICAGO, ROCKFORD, PEORIA, Springfield, Rock Island-Moline, Metro-East Cluster (the Illinois portion of the ST. LOUIS, Mo., metropolitan area), DECATUR, CHAMPAIGN-URBANA-Rantoul, and BLOOMINGTON-Normal. Since 1950 these cities have experienced most of the state's population increase. Growth rates are highest in the many suburban cities in the Chicago area, where some communities have expanded by approximately 10,000 people in ten years.

Illinois has close ties with its neighboring states. East St. Louis, on the east bank of the Mississippi in the southwestern part of the state, is part of the St. Louis, Mo., metropolitan area. East Chicago, Hammond, and Gary, Ind., and Kenosha, Wis., are part of the Chicago consolidated statistical area. Rock Island and Moline are part of the Davenport, Iowa, metropolitan statistical area.

The largest groups of foreign-born individuals in Illinois are those of Mexican, German, Polish, Irish, and Italian extraction. Most of the foreign born live in the Chicago metropolitan area, which is also the home of the overwhelming majority of the state's black and Hispanic populations. In 1990 blacks and Hispanics constituted

14.8% and 7.9% of the population, respectively.

The largest Christian denomination in Illinois is the Roman Catholic church. That population, along with a large number of Jews, live primarily in the Chicago area. Methodist, Lutheran, Baptist, and Presbyterian congregations account for most of the state's Protestants.

Education. Under the provisions of the 1970 state constitution the state bears primary responsibility for the public school system, with each school district run locally under state provisions. Attendance is required of all children from age 7 to 16.

The University of Illinois was founded at Champaign-Urbana in 1867. Other state universities include Southern Illinois University (1869), with its main branch at Carbondale; Illinois State University (1857) at Normal; Northeastern Illinois (1961) at Chicago and Northern Illinois (1899) at De Kalb.

Culture. The Chicago Symphony is the state's largest professional orchestra. Other cultural institutions include the Lyric Opera of Chicago, the Art Institute, the Museum of Science and Industry, the Field Museum of Natural History, the Museum of Contemporary Art, the Newberry Library, and the Du Sable Museum of African-American History, all in Chicago; the Lakeview Center for the Arts and Sciences in Peoria; and the State Museum in Springfield. The Mississippi River Arts Festival in Edwardsville and the Festival of Contemporary Arts in Urbana are annual attractions. Illinois was also a laboratory for architects Louis SULLIVAN and Frank Lloyd WRIGHT; some of their buildings still stand.

Historical Sites. The heritage of Abraham LINCOLN in Illinois is preserved at Lincoln's Monument and Tomb and the Lincoln Home National Historic Site in Springfield. New Salem State Park and the Vandalia State House Memorial commemorate the beginnings of territorial settlement. CAHOKIA MOUNDS and Dickson Mounds are important relics of the state's Indian past. Other historic sites include the Stephen A. DOUGLAS Monument near Winchester, Kaskaskia Island in the Mississippi River, and the Ulysses S. Grant home in Galena.

Communications. Illinois serves as the communications center for much of the interior of the United States, with more than 300 AM and FM radio stations and nearly 40 television stations. The first Illinois newspaper, published in 1814, was the *Illinois Herald* of the territorial capital of Kaskaskia. Daily newspapers now number about 70. Chicago has become an important publishing center as well.

Economy

The industrial growth of the state was spurred by readily available natural resources, excellent transportation, and skilled laborers. The earliest large industries were directed toward the agricultural sector of the state's economy—meat-packing and farm-implements manufacturing.

Agriculture. The main crops produced in the state include corn, soybeans, wheat, hay, oats, orchard crops, and vegetables. Corn and soybeans are the leading cash commodities. Cattle and hog raising are also significant. The state's forested land, more than 40% of its area 200 years ago, has been cut back to little more than 10%.

Lumbering is a minor industry.

Fishing. The state's lakes, reservoirs, and rivers yield millions of kilograms of fish annually. Catches include carp, catfish, largemouth bass, and other species. Sport-fishing has some importance in southern Illinois and in Lake Michigan.

Manufacturing. Illinois is among the top-ranking states in the nation in value added by manufacturing. The state's leading industries include petroleum refining, nonelectrical machinery, food and food products, electrical equipment, and chemicals. The industrial center of Illinois is Chicago and its many suburbs, with smaller concentrations in Rockford, the Quad Cities (Rock Island, Moline, East Moline, and Davenport, Iowa), Peoria, and the Illinois portion of the St. Louis, Mo., metropolitan area. The Midwest Stock Exchange and Chicago Mercantile Exchange are located in Chicago, as is the Chicago Board of Trade, which has set world agricultural prices since 1848.

Tourism. An estimated contribution of several billion dollars is made annually to the gross state product by tourists attracted to the city of Chicago and to such events as the Illinois State Fair held in Springfield. Outdoor recreational facilities are plentiful. Shawnee National Forest, composed of two separate areas, is located in southern Illinois. Major sports stadiums located in Chicago include Soldier Field, Chicago Stadium, Wrigley Field, and the old (1910–90) and new (1991–) Comiskey parks.

Transportation and Trade. Illinois is a major U.S. transportation hub, with interstate highways, one of the nation's main railroad networks, the busiest airport in the world, and three major inland waterways—the Ohio, Illinois, and Mississippi rivers. The Illinois Waterway provides an access route to the Mississippi River for Great Lakes ships via the Chicago River, Chicago Sanitary and

Illinois farmlands, covering approximately 75% of the state's land area, produce crops ranging from corn and soybeans in central regions to fruit and cotton in the south.

Ship Canal, and Des Plaines and Illinois rivers. Chicago's O'Hare International Airport serves more than 100,000 passengers daily. The Chicago Port Authority handles millions of metric tons of commerce annually. Illinois is a top-ranking state in the exporting of manufactured goods. Leading exports include metals and metal products, non-electrical machinery, chemicals, electronic equipment, and transport equipment.

Energy. Illinois is one of the leading energy producers and consumers in the United States. It produces some 123.3 billion kWh of electricity annually. About 60% of the state's power production is from coal-fired plants. The state also has nuclear-power plants.

Government and Politics

Illinois was one of the five states created from the NORTHWEST TERRITORY. Its original 1818 constitution was followed by constitutions in 1848, 1870, and 1970. The 1970 constitution included protection from discrimination for women, protection for a healthy environment, and the right of suffrage for more citizens by relaxing residency requirements. The senate and house of representatives, constituting the state's general assembly, are selected from 59 districts, each represented by one senator and two at-large representatives. The executive branch includes a team-elected governor and lieutenant governor. The supreme court consists of seven judges elected from five judicial districts for 10-year terms. The appellate court judges, also elected for 10-year terms, serve each of the state's judicial districts, hearing appeals from state circuit courts, whose judges are elected for six-year terms.

Local government consists of township, county, and city governments. Cities with a population of more than 25,000 and counties with an elected chief executive have home-rule power, including the power to tax.

Illinois has been referred to as a "swing state" in national politics. On the statewide level it remained solidly Republican from the Civil War period until nearly the turn of the 20th century. Since that time, the governorship has been held by an almost equal number of Democrats and Republicans.

History

Thousands of years before the French reached Illinois, Paleo-Indians, a nomadic people, and their descendants, archaic Indians, had explored Illinois. The culture of these hunters, dated before 5000 BC, can be studied at the Modock Rock Shelter in Randolph County. Woodland Indians were their descendants. By AD 900, Middle Mississippi Indians, who succeeded the Woodland Indians, built large earthen mounds and developed complex urban areas. The descendants of the Mississippians were the Illiniwek tribes of the 17th, 18th, and 19th centuries. After years of losing land and wars to other Indian groups and European colonists, the Illiniweks were moved to a Kansas reservation.

The French controlled areas along the Mississippi River valley in the American Bottoms between Cahokia and Kaskaskia. Their occupation, from about 1675 to 1763, left few lasting marks, as did the ineffective British rule.

European control was ended by the U.S. militia of Gen. George Rogers CLARK in 1778. The area then was made a part of Virginia.

The Northwest Ordinance of 1787 charted this region, and in 1809 the Territory of Illinois was created. During the early years of settlement by fur trappers, southern Illinois was the focus of migration to the area, especially along the Mississippi River valley and the Wabash and Ohio rivers. Statehood was granted in 1818. Vandalia, along the Kaskaskia River, was chosen capital of the new state; the capital was moved to Springfield in 1839.

Early statehood problems engulfed Illinois. In the 1830s the state was near bankruptcy because of government financing of canals and railroad construction. The BLACK HAWK WAR in 1832 was fought by the Indians and newly arrived settlers over possession of Illinois land. Adherents to Mormonism, who had migrated from Missouri in 1839, were charged with many illegalities and finally driven from the state after their leader, Joseph SMITH, had been murdered in 1844.

The Civil War caused mixed loyalties among Illinoisans, many of whom were first- or second-generation Southerners. However, many took pride in the fact that the Union was led by a native son, Lincoln, and the state provided 250,000 soldiers to the Union army. It also was the weapons manufacturer, supplier of iron products, and major grain and meat supplier for the North.

By 1880, Illinois had become the fourth largest state in population. It was a leader in grain production and manufacturing. The huge migration of Europeans to Illinois provided labor to mine coal, run steel mills, and enhance the economy of the state. By 1920, Illinois was counted among the foremost states in nearly every significant growth variable—coal mining, industry, farming, urbanization, transportation, and wholesaling. Its leadership was achieved despite having suffered through the economic slumps of the 1880s, 1890s, and early 1900s; through the labor disputes in coal mining and railroading; through the Chicago fire of 1871; and through the problems caused by organized crime. World War I and World War II boosted the economy of Illinois, which soon had five ordnance depots and numerous military training camps.

The post–World War II era was a time of industrial modification to the postwar production of consumer goods. Even though meat-packing companies began to move away from Chicago and East St. Louis, in part because of obsolete physical plants, Illinois farms were being mechanized and upgraded for increased output. Post–World War II Illinois experienced rapid population growth. Migration streams of blacks from the South, Hispanics from Mexico and Puerto Rico, and whites from Appalachia reshaped neighborhoods in Chicago, its suburbs, and other large Illinois cities.

The future of Illinois appears to be one of continued consolidation of farms into huge corporate operations. The out-migration of whites and in-migration of blacks and Hispanics to Chicago will result in the state's largest city being dominated by poorer minorities while surrounded by more affluent white-dominated suburbs. The extensive railroad system is being trimmed because of financial losses, necessitating a growing dependence on interstate trucking systems. Illinois has grown phenomenally since the days of Lincoln, and its continued growth will insure its position as the "heartland" state of the nation.

Illinois (Indian tribe)   The Illinois were a large and powerful confederation of Algonquian-speaking Indian groups who dominated most of present-day Illinois, southeastern Wisconsin, and adjacent parts of Iowa and Missouri until the 1680s. The societies making up this confederacy included the Cahokia, the Kaskaskia, the Michigamea, the Moingwena, the Peoria, and the Tamaroa. Each was organized as a centralized chiefdom; to supplement their horticultural economy, they exploited extensive herds of buffalo and elk. Their name for themselves was *Ilini,* meaning simply "the people."

Illinois villages numbered about 60, and their total population probably exceeded 10,000 before 1660. They were constantly under attack from the Five Nations IRO-QUOIS, the Santee SIOUX, the FOX, the POTAWATOMI, and other tribes. Diseases of European origin contributed to the eventual depopulation of the Illinois. In addition, a Kaskaskia assassinated (1769) the great Ottawa leader PONTIAC, precipitating a bloody war which only a few Illinois survived. By 1885 they numbered only 150. Their descendants now live in Oklahoma.

illiteracy   SEE LITERACY AND ILLITERACY

illuminated manuscripts   The illuminated manuscript—a handwritten book with pictures and decoration painted or drawn in bright colors, illuminating, or lighting up, the page—was a major form of artistic expression in ancient and, more particularly, medieval times.

Illustration is the oldest type of illumination. In ancient Greece and Rome some manuscripts had the text

(Right) *The elaborate cruciform page from the Lindisfarne Gospels, one of the finest examples of Insular manuscript illumination, unites Christian symbols with decorative motifs derived from Anglo-Saxon and Celtic metalwork.* (c.697–98; British Museum, London.)

(Below) Christ Enthroned, *one of six full-page illuminations from Charlemagne's Godescalc Gospels (781–83), reflects the artist's familiarity with Lombard and Byzantine figure traditions in its full-face, seated portrait of Christ. (Bibliothèque Nationale, Paris.)*

interspersed with small paintings called miniatures, from *minium*, a red-orange lead pigment used in their execution. In the Middle Ages, illumination was further extended to the ornamentation of the text through the enlargement and decoration—sometimes lavish—of initial letters and through the framing of both text and illustrations with elaborate decorative borders.

The earliest illuminated manuscripts are Egyptian papyrus rolls from the 2d millennium BC, which include Books of the Dead with paintings of funeral and judgment scenes. The oldest surviving Greek illuminations are the drawings in an astronomical text—also on a papyrus roll—from the 2d century BC (Louvre, Paris). The principal remains of both Greek and Roman book art date from the 5th and 6th centuries AD, when the parchment codex (an early form of the modern bound book) replaced the papyrus roll.

Insular is the name used to designate the style of a series of magnificent gospel books made at monastic centers in the British Isles during the 7th and 8th centuries. Insular manuscripts are generally characterized by decorative embellishment rather than narrative illustration. The ornament is composed of spiral patterns, interlace, knotwork, and intertwined animals adopted from Anglo-Saxon and Celtic metalwork. The first masterpiece of Insular illumination was the 7th-century Irish Book of Durrow (Trinity College, Dublin); the epitome was the profusely decorated 8th-century Book of Kells (Dublin), which includes narrative illustrations and portraits.

The earliest extant work in the Carolingian style is the Godescalc Gospel book (Bibliothèque Nationale, Paris). Dated 781–83, it was written in gold and silver on purple parchment in Charlemagne's court scriptorium at Aachen, the first of a series of luxurious gospel manuscripts from the court school. Reims, the chief center of book painting under Bishop Ebbo (816–35), developed a new, emotionally charged version of late antique illusionism in the portraits of the Ebbo Gospels (Bibliothèque municipale, Épernay, France) and the drawings of the famous Utrecht Psalter (University Library, Utrecht).

The Ottonian emperors and powerful bishops were the principal patrons of the splendidly decorated gospel lectionaries and sacramentaries produced at various monasteries in Germany in the 10th and 11th centuries. Firmly delineated figures, with intense glances and gestures, were often set against brilliant gold grounds, and highly burnished gold leaf was also used for the foliate initials. The celebrated Codex Egberti (Stadtbibliothek, Trier, Germany), with 50 scenes from the life of Christ closely resembling an Early Christian model, is one of a large and distinguished group of manuscripts traditionally associated with the German abbey of Reichenau.

Anglo-Saxon book decoration in the 10th and 11th centuries is often called the Winchester school because Winchester was its first center. A variety of books were illuminated, ranging from Gospels to works of ancient authors copied from Carolingian intermediaries. The decoration was executed in a lively style: figures have animated postures, and movement dominates the ornament of the spectacular borders and initials. Two techniques were

The Limbourg brothers' Zodiac man, associating parts of the body with astrological signs, concludes the calendar illuminations of their masterpiece, the Très Riches Heures du Duc de Berry. (1413–16; Musée Condé, Chantilly, France.)

used—painting and colored-outline drawing, which was an English specialty. Both were employed in the masterpiece of the school, the magnificent Benedictional of Aethelwold (British Library).

The expansion of monasticism in Europe in the later 11th and 12th centuries (the Romanesque period of western European art) led to a great increase in the production of manuscripts by and for monastic houses. The most popular illuminated books were large Bibles and psalters (psalm books). Typical are the *Pantheon Bible* (Vatican), executed in Rome about 1125, the Bible of Stavelot Abbey (British Library), completed in 1097, and the St. Albans Psalter (St. Godehard Church, Hildesheim, Germany), written about 1120 by a monastic scribe but illustrated by a lay artist.

The Romanesque style was international, with regional variations sharing certain characteristics: the two-dimensional rendering of figures; flat backgrounds of gold-leaf or colored panels; and the emphasis on large, decorated initials—often composed of vine-scrolls inhabited by struggling men and beasts.

From the end of the 12th century when Gothic illumination first appeared, the production of decorated manuscripts increasingly shifted from monastic scriptoria to urban workshops operated by laymen. Manuscripts continued to be illuminated for the church, but the greatest demands came from individuals who wanted a Bible or BOOK OF HOURS, or illustrated histories and romances.

A more realistic style developed in the early 14th century with the fully modeled figures and perspective interiors of the miniatures by Jean Pucelle, the dominant master of the first half of the century (*The Hours of Jeanne d'Evreux*, Cloisters Collection, Metropolitan Museum of Art, New York City). The most distinctive feature of Northern Gothic decoration comprises the grotesques and drolleries—hybrid monsters, real and fantastic animals, and human figures—that invade the borders and margins of the page (for example, Queen Mary Psalter, British Library, London).

Books of hours made for aristocratic patrons were among the most lavishly decorated manuscripts of the 15th century. Miniatures opened out into broad landscape views full of naturalistic details or into deep, architectural spaces. Both are found in the celebrated *Très Riches Heures du Duc de Berry* (Musée Condé, Chantilly). Jean Fouquet of Tours was the leading French illuminator (*Hours of Étienne Chevalier*, Musée Condé). Outstanding among the Flemings was Simon Marmion, and among the Italians, Attavante of Florence. Some splendid manuscripts continued to be made in Italy, France, and Flanders in the early 16th century (for example, the *Grimani Breviary*, Biblioteca Nazionale Marciana, Venice), but they mark the end of the age of the illuminated manuscript.

___

illusion Illusions are systematic, characteristic errors in perception. They are discrepancies between the appearance of some measurable aspect of the world (such as the size, distance, location, or shape of a visible object) and the corresponding physical measures—whether of the object itself or of the light reaching the eye from the object. Illusions are different from hallucinations, in which the object is lacking or only remotely related to what is perceived. Illusions are of practical importance in environmental design and the visual arts, and of central theoretical importance to the study of PERCEPTION.

Examples of what are known as the "geometrical illusions" are shown in Figures 1 through 8. The lines labeled *i* and *ii* are equal in size in Figure 1, the Müller-Lyer illusion, and Figures 2, 3, and 4; parallel and straight in Zöllner's (Figure 5), Hering's (Figure 6), and Wundt's (Figure 7) illusions of direction; and perfectly aligned in Poggendorff's illusion (Figure 8), despite appearances to the contrary. Such phenomena have long been known to architects, who know the importance of identifying the situations that produce such illusions so they can take them into account in their designs. Figure 8, for instance, is sometimes called the plumber's illusion, for obvious reasons. Knowing that an illusion is in fact an illusion, however, does not dispel it. Even after measuring lines *i* and *ii* in Figure 1, the viewer will still perceive *i* as smaller.

Illusions also abound in color perception, notably in the phenomenon of simultaneous contrast, in which the appearance of a particular patch is greatly altered by changes in its surroundings. The color-contrast phenomena have practical importance in painting, printing, and textile

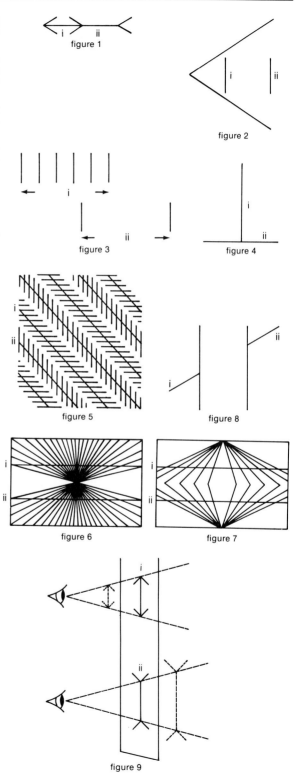

figure 1

figure 2

figure 3

figure 4

figure 5

figure 8

figure 6

figure 7

figure 9

enterprises, which frequently juxtapose different colors.

Illusions are also possible in the perception of movement, notably in the case of apparent movement, known as the phi phenomenon. In the phi phenomenon, successive stationary views of an object, even though they are located in a different place in each view, are perceived as smooth, continuous motion. This phenomenon is the basis of the motion picture and television industries.

The importance of illusions to psychology depends on which theory of illusions—and of perception—is considered. No one theory explains all illusions. Indeed, each of the stronger illusions probably results from several converging factors. To the degree that the illusions can be explained in terms of purely "local" effects, they have little general importance. In one recurrent theory, for example, the geometrical illusions are explained in terms of a filling-in of acute angles (which would shorten the free line length of *i* in Figure 1). Illusions have more often been explained in terms of confusion and contrast. The confusion explanation of Figure 1, for example, holds that the viewer compares the areas included between the diagonals and not the line lengths.

The most general theory is that illusions result from the same processes that normally produce correct perceptions and therefore reveal how those processes work. For example, because the eye most frequently encounters diagonals such as those of Figure 1 as a result of linear perspective, *i* would normally be nearer than *ii* (see Figure 9). To subtend equal angles at the eye as the lines do, *i* must be smaller than *ii*. In its strongest form, this theory holds that the illusions result from unconscious, inferencelike processes based on the erroneous application of learned depth cues.

illusionism   Illusionism comprises those painterly techniques whereby forms painted on flat planes are made to appear three-dimensional and to exist in deep space. The history of illusionism dates back to the 4th century BC in Greece; the grapes in Zeuxis's paintings were said to seem so real that birds would peck at them. Carried to this extreme, illusionism is also known as trompe l'oeil (fool the eye). The Renaissance development of one-point perspective greatly advanced illusionist technique. During the baroque period, illusionism reached its apex in the enormous ceiling paintings of various Roman churches and palaces. The vogue spread north in the succeeding rococo period and achieved fullest flower in Austria and Bavaria. The 19th-century American still-life painter William HARNETT was a master of representational illusionism, a contemporary version of which is seen in PHOTOREALISM. The OP ART of the 1960s is an abstract form of illusionism. The term *illusionism* also refers to the creation of spatial illusions in architecture and stage design.

illustration   SEE BOOK ILLUSTRATION

Illyria [ih-lir'-ee-uh]   The ancient name *Illyria* referred to the western coastal region of the Balkan Peninsula,

territory that is now included in Albania and Yugoslavia. The present-day Albanians are probably the descendants of the ancient Illyrians, an Indo-European people who originally settled there about the 10th century BC.

In the 3d century BC, Illyria asserted itself as an independent political power, but in 168–167 BC its coastal areas were conquered by the Romans, who established the colony of Illyricum there. Some of Rome's most notable emperors, such as Aurelian, Diocletian, and Constantine I, were originally from Illyria.

After an Illyrian revolt in AD 6-9, Illyria was divided into two Roman imperial provinces, Pannonia and Dalmatia. In the 4th century Illyria fell to the Byzantine Empire. The area was then successively invaded by Goths, Huns, and Slavs, and use of the name *Illyria* was dropped. It was revived by Napoleon I when he included the so-called Illyrian Provinces in his empire in 1809. From 1816 to 1849 the kingdom of Illyria was an administrative subdivision of the Austrian Empire.

See also: BALKANS.

ilmenite [il'-muhn-yt]   The iron and titanium OXIDE MINERAL ilmenite ($FeTiO_3$) is present in small amounts in basic igneous and metamorphic rocks and PLACER DEPOSITS and is the principal TITANIUM ore. It forms iron black, thick tabular or acute rhombohedral CRYSTALS (hexagonal system), as well as thin plates, compact masses, and embedded grains. Hardness is $5\frac{1}{2}$, luster is metallic to dull, and specific gravity is 4.72.

image, optical   SEE LENS; MIRROR

image and imagery   SEE FIGURES OF SPEECH

image processing   Image processing modifies pictures to improve them (enhancement, restoration), extract information (analysis, recognition), and change their structure (compression, image editing). Images can be processed by optical, photographic, and electronic means, but image processing using digital computers is the most common method because digital methods are fast, flexible, and precise. This article focuses on the use of digital computer methods.

Figure 1 represents a typical digital image processing system. The source of the image is usually visible light reflected from or transmitted through various objects in a scene. Optics gather and focus this light onto a sensor that outputs an electronic signal proportional to the received light. Images can also be formed using other sources of radiation such as infrared or ultraviolet light, X rays, radar, or sound (sonar). Images can be synthesized from spatial data by various other means, including SCANNING and computer-aided tomography.

The sensor signal is "digitized"—converted to an array of numerical values, each value representing the light intensity of a small area of the scene. The digitized values are called picture elements, or "pixels," and are stored in computer memory as a digital image. A typical size for a

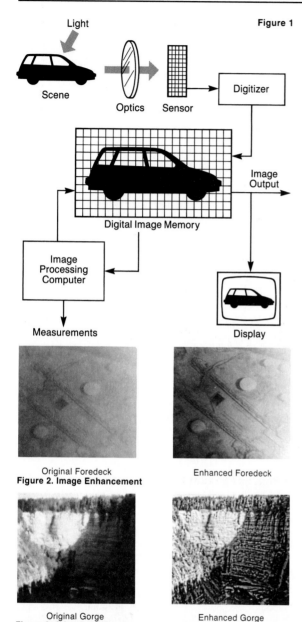

Figure 1

Light

Scene

Optics　Sensor

Digitizer

Image Output

Digital Image Memory

Image Processing Computer

Measurements

Display

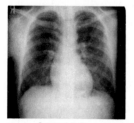

Original Foredeck
Figure 2. Image Enhancement

Enhanced Foredeck

Original Gorge
Figure 3. Adaptive Enhancement

Enhanced Gorge

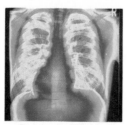

Original X-Ray
Figure 4. Pseudocolor Enhancement

Pseudocolor Enhanced

digital image is an array of 512 by 512 pixels, where each pixel has a value in the range of 0 to 255.

The digital image is processed by a computer to achieve the desired result. The sequence of processing operations is called an image-processing algorithm.

Some of the equipment and algorithms used in image processing are also used in computer graphics and scientific visualization. However, image processing is concerned with the improvement, analysis, or manipulation of existing images, whereas graphics and visualization involve the synthesis of new images. When image processing is used for automated manufacturing or inspection, it is often called "machine vision."

Image Enhancement and Restoration

Image enhancement improves the quality (clearness) of images, perhaps for human viewing or as a step in an algorithm for machine vision. Figure 2 shows an image of the foredeck of the wreck of the ship *Titanic*. This image was taken deep under water, and it is noisy, of low contrast, and somewhat blurred. The image is enhanced by reducing the noise and blurring and increasing the contrast range. In Figure 3 the original image has areas of very low and high intensity, which mask details. An adaptive enhancement algorithm reveals these details. Adaptive algorithms adjust their operation based on the image information (pixels) being processed.

Another enhancement technique assigns colors to pixel intensities, and thus makes small intensity differences more obvious to the human eye. Figure 4 illustrates the use of color to highlight details in an X-ray image. Image-enhancement operations are often used in image-processing algorithms, and are used in some digital television sets.

Image restoration improves image quality by using information beyond that in the digital image. This information might be how the image of the scene was formed and what degradations (noise, defocusing, geometric distortions, and so on) occurred in forming or transmitting the image. The license plate in Figure 5 is blurred by movement. Knowing (or estimating) this motion, one can reduce its effects. Restoration can also remove geometric distortions by changing the position of pixels within the image.

Image Analysis and Recognition

Image analysis extracts quantitative information from an image. Figure 6 shows a high-contrast image of some electronic parts. Each part is labeled with a unique color so that the position of each part is found by examining pixels of one color. Image analysis often replaces or assists human vision in inspection and machine-vision tasks.

Image-recognition algorithms attempt automatically to find and identify parts or objects within an image. For example, the two kinds of parts imaged in Figure 6 can be recognized by their size (number of pixels) and outlines. One recognition method compares images of the objects ("templates") with every area of a sample image. If a template matches some area of the sample image, the image might contain the corresponding object. Often the recognition can be made more reliable by using "feature detectors" or "matched filters" to amplify or find specific

Original

Figure 5. Image Restoration

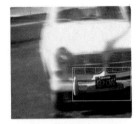

Restored

Original Airplane

"Pasted" Image

Figure 8. Image Cutting and Pasting

Original

Figure 6. Image Analysis

Positions Marked

Original

Warped Image

Figure 9. Image Warping

Original

Figure 7. Image Recognition

Edge Features

Original

Color Changed

Figure 10. Color Image Processing

image features (such as edges) or structures (such as texture or outline) that contain unique or important information about the objects. This examination might use pattern analysis (see PATTERN RECOGNITION), statistical methods, or neural net methods (see NEURAL NETWORKS) to recognize reliably the objects in the image. In Figure 7 an outdoor scene has been processed such that edges of objects are shown in color and the color represents the orientation (angle) of the edge. These edge "features" can be used for recognizing objects within the image.

Image Compression

Image compression reduces the amount of information (number of bits) required to store or transmit a digital image. Compression is called "lossless" when the original digital image can be exactly reconstructed (decompressed) from the compressed image, or "lossy" when information is lost and the original image can be only approximately reconstructed. Because pixel values are often similar to or correlated with adjacent pixel values, an image can be compressed by removing these correlations. For example, it often takes fewer bits to store the differences between pixels than the pixels themselves. Lossless and lossy image compression removes image correlations

(redundant information), but lossy compression also throws away (loses) certain information, degrading the image.

Compression is used when image storage is expensive or a large number of images must be stored, and when the image must be transmitted over a limited or expensive communication channel. For example, hospitals generate thousands of images, and the digital storage (tape, optical disk, and so forth) required for these images can be dramatically reduced by compression. Sending images from spacecraft, satellites, and other remote-sensing image sources is expensive due to the limited signal power and bandwidth. Here again, lossless compression might be used to increase the speed of image transmission. For teleconferencing, lossy compression is used to reduce the amount of information sent over standard telephone lines by a factor of 6,000 or more.

Image Editing

Image processing is used to edit images, perhaps for use in a magazine. Image editing uses many of the methods from image enhancement and restoration, such as removing image blur (or adding blur) and changing the location of pixels. For example, the airplane in Figure 8 is "cut" out, reduced in size, and inserted ("pasted") in another image. The edges of the inserted image differ in intensity and so can be seen (plane on the left). To remove this unwanted edge, the inserted image is blended (blurred) into the background by averaging pixel-intensity values across the insert edges (planes on the right). The face in Figure 9 has been edited by "warping" parts of the image. One imagines that the image is printed on a rubber sheet and the small blue crosses represent tacks that hold the sheet. The image is warped by "pulling" the rubber sheet and tacking it down.

Color digital images are composed of three (or more) images, so each pixel might have red, green, and blue intensity values. Items in the image can be selected and their color modified by changing the balance of these values. In Figure 10 the color of the flower is changed without modifying the color saturation, intensity, or background.

imaginary number   see COMPLEX NUMBER

imagism [im'-uhj-izm]

A literary movement that flourished between 1912 and 1918, imagism represents an attempt to revitalize the language of poetry and assign it a distinctive role. Ezra POUND said he first used the word to publicize the works of Hilda DOOLITTLE (H.D.), and he brought the movement to the attention of American readers in *Poetry* magazine. There F. S. Flint published these rules: "Direct treatment of the 'thing,' whether subjective or objective; to use absolutely no word that did not contribute to the presentation; as regarding rhythm: to compose in sequence of the musical phrase, not in the sequence of a metronome." Pound drew from contemporary psychology to define the image as "that which presents an intellectual and emotional complex in an instant of time." When Amy LOWELL, who edited three anthologies (1915–17) entitled *Some Imagist Poets*, entered the movement, however, Pound left, calling what remained "Amygism." The influence of the movement on modern poetry is unmistakable. Early imagist poets such as Pound, H.D., T.E. HULME, John Gould Fletcher, and Richard Aldington were the predecessors of T. S. Eliot, Wallace Stevens, and William Carlos Williams.

imam [im-ahm']

Imam is used in the Koran to mean leader, guide, model, or sign. These basic connotations are preserved in the four distinctive usages of later ISLAM. (1) The SUNNITES use imam as a title for the caliphs, the successors of Muhammad as leaders of the Muslim community (see CALIPHATE). One of the caliph's functions was to lead the community in Friday prayers. (2) A local group of Muslims may appoint an imam to lead them in the Friday prayers. Any Muslim of undisputed piety and sound knowledge of the faith and ritual can serve in this capacity. (3) For SHIITES, only a person from the clan of the Prophet can be the imam; for some of them, only a descendant from ALI, the son-in-law of Muhammad. (4) Imam is also an honorary title given to a few of the most outstanding Muslim scholars, such as al-Ghazali.

Imhotep [im-hoh'-tep]

Imhotep, an ancient Egyptian priest and vizier, served as architect and court official to King Zoser of the 3d dynasty (c.2686–2613 BC). His titles indicate that he was not of royal birth, but he was later deified—one of few nonroyals to achieve that distinction. As the chief sculptor and chief carpenter of Zoser, Imhotep is connected with Zoser's famous step PYRAMID complex at SAQQARA. This complex was, according to the late Egyptian writer Manetho, the first Egyptian building in stone.

Imhotep later came to be regarded as a sage, author of wisdom literature, and patron of scribes, and under the 26th dynasty (664–525 BC) he was deified. He was identified by the Greeks with ASCLEPIUS, the god of healing.

Immaculate Conception [im-mak'-yuh-luht]

The Immaculate Conception is a Roman Catholic doctrine asserting that MARY, the mother of Jesus, was preserved from the effects of ORIGINAL SIN from the first moment of her conception. The doctrine was defined as a dogma binding on Catholics by Pope Pius IX in the papal bull *Ineffabilis Deus* (1854). The doctrine as defined was debated by theologians during the Middle Ages and was rejected by Saint Thomas Aquinas. It is based on the biblical idea of Mary's holiness (Luke 1:28), early church teachings on Mary as the "new Eve," and the belief that Mary is the mother of God (Theotokos, or "God-bearer"), articulated at the Council of Ephesus (431). The feast of the Immaculate Conception is observed on Dec. 8.

immigration

Immigration is a form of migration that signifies the intention of a person to settle permanently in a new country. Motivating factors are generally economic, social, and political. Despite a long history in the United States and some other countries of receiving immigrants, most people who move from one country to another do not intend to leave their homelands permanently. In recent decades, millions of REFUGEES have been driven by civil war, natural disaster, and persecution to seek safety outside of their countries. Millions of others leave for temporary work.

Early U.S. Immigration. Large new countries such as Argentina, Australia, Brazil, and Canada, as well as the United States, actively recruited permanent settlers (immigrants). The United States started as a nation of immigration in the 17th century, as recruiters from different colonies urged citizens from northern and western European countries to become Americans. Of those early immigrants, a majority spoke English and became farmers. The vast majority were Protestants. Continuing waves of German immigration, however, beginning in the 17th century, made many native-born Americans nervous about the capacity of American society to absorb the foreign-speaking newcomers. Then, following large-scale Irish-Catholic immigration to the United States in the mid-19th century, Americans wondered whether or not their essentially Anglo-Protestant culture could be retained.

IMMIGRATION INTO THE UNITED STATES, 1820–THE PRESENT

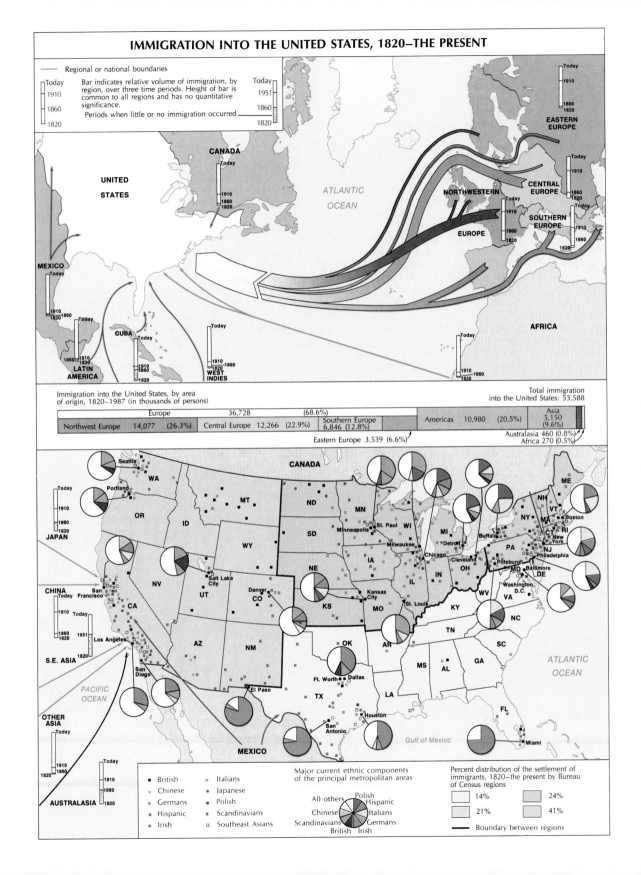

Regional or national boundaries

Bar indicates relative volume of immigration, by region, over three time periods. Height of bar is common to all regions and has no quantitative significance.

Periods when little or no immigration occurred

Immigration into the United States, by area of origin, 1820–1987 (in thousands of persons)

Total immigration into the United States: 53,588

Europe 36,728 (68.6%)			Americas 10,980 (20.5%)	Asia 5,150 (9.6%)
Northwest Europe 14,077 (26.3%)	Central Europe 12,266 (22.9%)	Southern Europe 6,846 (12.8%)		

Eastern Europe 3,539 (6.6%)

Australasia 460 (0.8%)
Africa 270 (0.5%)

Major current ethnic components of the principal metropolitan areas

- British
- Chinese
- Germans
- Hispanic
- Irish
- Italians
- Japanese
- Polish
- Scandinavians
- Southeast Asians

All others, Polish, Hispanic, Chinese, Italians, Scandinavians, Germans, British, Irish

Percent distribution of the settlement of immigrants, 1820–the present by Bureau of Census regions

- 14%
- 21%
- 24%
- 41%

Boundary between regions

By 1880, though, the great fear of German-speaking and Irish-Catholic immigrants was over. Employers who still sought worker-immigrants, and not just temporary workers, looked increasingly to southern and eastern Europe. When Italians, Greeks, Turks, Russians, Slavs, and Jews arrived in large numbers, however, new anxieties arose about making Americans of so many different kinds of strangers.

Immigration Restrictions. Employers in the West and Southwest had never found it necessary or desirable to recruit laborers as immigrants. Instead, they relied upon alien workers from Asian countries, who were made ineligible for CITIZENSHIP under U.S. NATURALIZATION laws, and, increasingly, upon sojourner migrants from Mexico, whose muscle was wanted but who were not welcome as members of American society. Prejudice against the Asians was so strong that in 1882 Congress passed the first of the CHINESE EXCLUSION ACTS preventing the importation of Chinese laborers. However, the system of sojourner Mexican workers, some of whom came lawfully and others illegally, was permitted to continue.

Immigrants, on the other hand, were encouraged to participate in American institutions. By 1917 (when a literacy test for immigrants was enacted), though, most Americans were convinced that there were too many immigrants. Their opposition to newcomers from eastern Europe particularly resulted in the passage of a law in 1924 that put a sharp limit on the number of immigrants permitted to come to the United States (154,000 annually plus the wives and minor children of U.S. citizens). This law also established national-origin quotas aimed at sharply reducing immigration from southern and eastern European countries (Asians had already been excluded in 1917).

Events following World War II caused a revision of this restrictionist policy. Congress passed several acts to admit refugees, who, under U.S. laws, could easily adjust their status to that of immigrant. By the early 1960s it was clear that the U.S. national-origins quota system of selecting immigrants was bad policy, not only because it failed to handle refugee situations, but also because it was totally inconsistent with the growing civil rights consciousness of Americans.

Amendments to the Immigration and Nationality Act in 1965 repealed the national origins provision, created an enlarged annual ceiling for immigrants from the Eastern Hemisphere with an equal limit of 20,000 for every country and a new preference system to allocate visas based primarily on admitting immigrants with close family ties in the United States (and a much smaller number who had special skills desired by the United States). For the first time a ceiling was placed on immigrants from the Western Hemisphere of 120,000. In 1976, country limitations were set for Western Hemisphere countries at 20,000, and in 1978 a worldwide ceiling was established for numerically restricted immigrants at 270,000, with the understanding that spouses and minor children of U.S. citizens would still be admitted without restriction.

Despite the passage of these amendments, immigra-tion policy continued to be a matter of national concern for two main reasons: the first was the eruption of conflicts producing large numbers of refugees, as when South Vietnam and Cambodia fell to the Communists in 1975; the second was the large inflow of illegal aliens, especially from Mexico.

The refugee issue was dealt with by the Refugee Act of 1980, which provided for the uniform admission of refugees. In 1981, Congress made several recommendations to deal with illegal immigration. These included the imposition of penalties for employers who knowingly and willfully hire illegal aliens; the legalization of a substantial number of the existing stock of illegal aliens so as to remove them from the status of an underclass of workers not fully protected by U.S. law; measures to strengthen the integrity and efficiency of the Immigration and Naturalization Service (INS); an increase in lawful immigration; and the clearance of the backlogs of immigrants waiting to come to the United States to the extent of 100,000 a year for a five-year period.

The Reform Act of 1986. The Immigration Reform and Control Act of 1986 embraced the first three of these recommendations and enlarged on the recommendation to expedite the entry of temporary workers into the United States under full protection of U.S. laws. By the end of the 1980s a wide congressional consensus supported the essential elements of U.S. immigration policy. No longer would the nation wink at the active recruitment and exploitation of illegal aliens. A special agricultural worker program invited aliens to work in the United States and provided them with the option of becoming permanent resident aliens and eventual citizens. No longer would national origins be a consideration in determining the kinds of immigrants admitted to the United States. Instead, the guiding principles of selection had become family relationships and needed skills.

Within a quarter century (1964 to 1988), U.S. immigration policy had been radically transformed. The number of immigrants admitted to the United States had more than doubled to annual levels of approximately 570,000 to 600,000. Whereas immigrants used to be overwhelmingly European, by the end of the 1980s almost half of all U.S. immigrants came from Asian countries, with at least 25% of the remainder immigrating from Spanish-speaking nations.

▬

immortality [im-mor-tal'-i-tee]   Immortality is the attribute of survival after physical death. The idea is found both in primitive religion and in the higher religions. Some philosophers have thought that whereas the physical body disintegrates in death, the human mind is not material and is indestructible. Some religions (for example, Hinduism and Buddhism) regard ultimate immortality in impersonal terms as reabsorption into the infinite. An intermediate stage of survival is reincarnation and the TRANSMIGRATION OF SOULS.

Judaism, Christianity, and Islam posit a future life, as

the survival of individual SOULS. The Christian doctrine of immortality incorporates a belief in bodily RESURRECTION, although this is usually interpreted to mean the survival of personality rather than the literal reconstitution of the old body.

See also: HEAVEN; HELL.

immunity (biology) [im-mue'-ni-tee]   The term *immunity* indicates the condition of an individual who recovers from a disease and is no longer susceptible to that disease. A broader definition of immunity includes all of the physiological mechanisms that give an organism the ability to recognize foreign substances and neutralize or degrade them, with or without injury to the organism's own tissue. Immunology is the branch of medicine concerned with the body's response to foreign substances.

History

The first step in establishing a safe procedure to prevent disease through inoculation was taken by Edward JENNER. He observed that people who caught cowpox rarely contracted smallpox. In 1796, Jenner induced a mild dose of cowpox in a young boy. A few weeks later he tried to infect the boy with smallpox but found that the immunity provoked by the cowpox viruses apparently was also effective against smallpox organisms. This is now known to occur because these two viruses are structurally and chemically very closely related.

In 1879, Louis PASTEUR discovered that neglected cultures of bacteria lose much of their ability to cause disease, but can be used to provide protection against fresh cultures. The introduction of dead or weakened bacteria, called a vaccine, into the body to develop resistance to disease is called VACCINATION. Today vaccination is used against diphtheria, measles, rabies, and many other diseases.

Until 1900 the major investigators in immunology were French or German. Two views emerged as to how the immune response functions. Paul EHRLICH proposed the humoral theory of immunity, which emphasized the role of chemical substances (ANTIBODIES) produced by cells as the major agents of immunity. Elie Metchnikoff developed the cellular theory of immunity, according to which phagocytes, the body's scavenger cells, are the major detectors of foreign material, as well as the primary defense system against infectious organisms. Today it is known that both theories are correct.

Functions of the Immune System

Under normal circumstances the immune system responds to foreign organisms by the production of antibodies and the stimulation of specialized cells, which destroy the organisms or neutralize their toxic products. When the immune system involved in this function becomes too active, however, the result may be undesirable features, such as hypersensitivity or allergic reactions. On the other hand, when the immune response is not work-

ing properly (immunodeficient), as in acquired immune deficiency syndrome (see AIDS), the individual may become more susceptible to repeated infection (see IMMUNODEFICIENCY DISEASE).

Another major function of the immune system is the removal of damaged or dying cells. This function may be misdirected, however, resulting in an immune response against the body's own cells or tissues, producing a condition known as an AUTOIMMUNE DISEASE.

The immune system is also able to recognize and eliminate the abnormal (mutant) cells that frequently arise within the body. These mutant, or cancer, cells may occur spontaneously, or they may be induced by certain viruses (oncogenic viruses) or chemicals (mutagens). An immune system that is functioning properly can usually recognize and dispose of such cancer cells by means of a process called immune surveillance. The malfunction of this process may result in the incidence of certain types of cancer.

Cells and Tissues in the Immune Response

The ability to recognize foreignness, specificity, and memory are the key characteristics of immune defense mechanisms. The immune system of the human body must be able to recognize bacteria, viruses, fungi, parasites, and foreign materials in order to locate and destroy them. Specificity means that immunity to one foreign substance or organism does not necessarily provide resistance to another foreign substance. Memory is the ability of an organism to develop an accelerated, enhanced, and long-lasting immunity after the initial attack by an infectious disease. These characteristics are invested in the lymphocyte, which is one of several types of white blood cells (see LYMPHATIC SYSTEM).

Lymphocytes are carried by the circulatory and the lymphatic systems to the site of infection. Scattered along the lymphatic vessels are small swellings known as lymph nodes, which contain large numbers of lymphocytes. These nodes become hard when packed with lymphocytes that have been stimulated by the infectious organisms to divide and produce specific antibodies against specific organisms.

There are two distinct types of lymphocyte: the T lymphocytes, or T cells, and the B lymphocytes, or B cells. Immunity provided by antibody molecules in the circulatory system (this type of immunity is called humoral immunity) is provided by the B cells, which are produced in the bone and distributed to the various lymphoid tissues of the body, such as the lymph nodes, spleen, tonsils, and Peyer's patches, which line the small intestine. T cells are involved in the rejection of transplanted tissues; in attacking certain bacteria, viruses, and fungi; in some skin reactions resulting from contact with simple chemicals (contact dermatitis); and in immunity to cancer cells. Because the immunity associated with T cells does not involve the secretion of antibodies but requires direct physical contact with antigens, it is called cell-mediated immunity. T cells originate in the thymus and also become localized in lymphoid organs.

Four kinds of T cells exist. Only one kind, the cytotoxic T cell, defends the body by destroying infected, foreign, or cancerous cells. The other three kinds regulate immune responses by secreting messenger proteins (lymphokines) or by direct contact with other cells. Helper T cells enable the other T cells and most B cells to perform their functions. It is this type of cell that is destroyed by the HIV, or HTLV-III, virus (see RETROVIRUS) in AIDS patients, resulting in a depressed immune response that allows infection by a variety of microorganisms and the growth of certain tumors. Suppressor T cells dampen the immune response of B and T cells. The fourth kind of T cell is involved in certain kinds of hypersensitivity reactions. In a normally healthy individual there is a balanced ratio of these four kinds of T cells to provide an efficient immune system for defense against all foreign substances.

Humoral Immunity

An antigen is a substance that, when introduced into an organism, induces an immune response consisting of the production of a circulating antibody. This type of immunity is called humoral immunity. Protein molecules are potent antigens. Within a few days after injection, an antigen elicits large amounts of the antibody capable of interacting with it. The interaction of an antigen with its specific antibody involves only small areas on the antigen's surface; these areas are known as antigenic determinants. Protein molecules have several antigenic determinants, each of which can be recognized by an antibody. Because they have antigenic determinants, many carbohydrates are also antigenic.

The simplest, most prevalent means by which the immune system defends the body against bacteria and viruses is by the combination of a specific antibody with the antigenic determinants located on the surface of invading organisms. An aggregate of cells, called an agglutination, is formed by antibodies bound by one of their two combining sites to one cell, and to another cell by their other site. These aggregates are then engulfed and digested by the body's wandering scavenger cells, the macrophages. Antibodies also bind to toxic molecules given off by microorganisms, forming large, insoluble aggregates (precipitates) that are also removed by macrophages. Antibodies also cover up the attachment sites of viruses and thereby prevent their ability to infect cells.

Cell-Mediated Immunity (CMI)

Several immune responses are mediated primarily or exclusively by cells through direct contact with their targets or by the effects of secreted molecules, lymphokines, from these cells. A variety of cells carry out cell-mediated reactions.

Because of their ability to engulf and digest particulate matter by the process of phagocytosis, macrophages and neutrophils are able to eliminate many foreign organisms and particulate materials that enter the body. Natural killer (NK) cells are cytotoxic to some tumor cells. This ability to kill tumor cells is enhanced by two lymphokines secreted by T cells, namely gamma INTERFERON and INTERLEUKIN-1 (IL-1).

Another cell involved in CMI is the lymphokine-activated killer (LAK) cell, which is receiving widespread attention because of its ability to kill a variety of human tumors. LAK cells are stimulated to kill tumor cells by another lymphokine, interleukin-2 (IL-2), produced by T lymphocytes.

Cytotoxic T lymphocytes destroy other cells by interacting with antigens on the cells' surfaces, such as those on grafted tissues, viral antigens on infected cells, and chemicals that have entered the body and attached to cells.

Another important lymphokine secreted by activated T cells is transfer factor, which is able to cause normal lymphocytes to release lymphokines or otherwise become activated and thus to destroy other cells. By using knowledge of the transfer ability thus gained, scientists have been able to treat individuals whose bodies cannot develop antibodies for certain bacteria, viruses, or fungi because of a hereditary defect in the cell-mediated immunity of the cells. Transfer factor is prepared from the lymphocytes of a person with good immunity to a particular disease agent and is then injected into the body of someone who is deficient in the agent. Transfer factor stimulates the lymphocytes to develop normal immunity; the body is then able to defend itself against an organism to which it was once susceptible. Cell-mediated immuni-

Lymphocytes called "helper T" cells are an essential part of the immune system, and their destruction by diseases such as AIDS leaves the body vulnerable to fatal infections. The tiny nodules seen on the cell in this micrograph are new AIDS viruses.

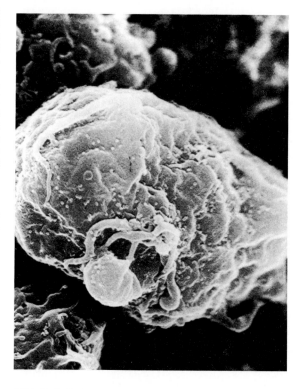

ty is also involved in contact dermatitis, a reaction against molecules such as urushiol, which is found in the sticky sap of poison ivy, poison sumac, and poison oak. Contact between urushiol and the skin causes a rash to develop within a few days.

Transplantation Immunity

When strips of skin are taken from a patient (called a donor) and grafted onto the skin of a recipient, the graft initially appears to "take"; within a few days, however, the graft becomes red, then blackens, and finally drops off or is rejected. In contrast, when skin is grafted to another part of the same patient's body, or from one identical twin to another, the graft is accepted; that is, it heals perfectly. The rejection of a graft is an immune reaction. Whether a transplant "takes" depends on preventing the organ from being rejected because of the recipient's immune response to the graft. Transplants are usually maintained by using a procedure called immunosuppression, in which the patient is given drugs designed to prevent the normal immune response. The drug that has provided the best results thus far is CYCLOSPORINE.

In recent years the success rate for organ transplants has been improved substantially by matching the tissue or histocompatibility antigens (known as the HLA system) of the donor with those of the recipient. Because of the thousands of combinations of HLA antigens on a person's cells, however, this procedure is expected to become more effective only when a large pool of potential donors is available and after the development of banks for the long-term storage of tissue.

Cancer and Immunity

If a connection exists between the failure of the immune system and the incidence of CANCER, or its growth and spread, then any substance that stimulates the immune system is likely to help destroy or at least retard the spread of the cancer. One such substance is BCG (for bacillus Calmette-Guérin), a live bacterium related to the bacillus that causes tuberculosis. In a procedure called immunotherapy, BCG has served to increase the immune response of patients suffering from various cancers. The advantage of such treatment is that it destroys every cancer cell, something no other method devised so far can do, and does not destroy normal body cells. When the tumor mass is fairly large at the time of diagnosis, however, the cancerous mass must often be removed before immunotherapy can be used effectively.

immunity (law)   Immunity is an exemption from a duty or legal punishment because of some special characteristic or status enjoyed by the person concerned. Many types of immunity exist under both criminal and civil law. In criminal law a person may be granted immunity from prosecution in return for testifying for the state. Diplomatic immunity, in international law, is enjoyed by ambassadors and certain lower-level officials, as well as by members of international organizations. This immunity allows them to be free from most local laws. Legislators, judges, and witnesses are granted official immunity (usually from libel suits) with respect to statements made in the course of their duties. Governmental bodies enjoy sovereign immunity from civil lawsuits unless they consent to be sued.

immunization   SEE VACCINATION

immunodeficiency disease [im-mue-noh-di-fish'-en-see]   Immunodeficiency diseases are characterized by failure of one or more parts of the immune system. They are usually classified as congenital or acquired, the latter being much more common. The major clinical problem associated with them is recurrent infection, ranging from mild to lethal.

Congenital. Severe combined immunodeficiency is a rare abnormality; prior to the advent of bone-marrow transplantation it was always fatal. It is characterized by a failure of the T cells and the B cells of the immune system. Very early in life its victims have severe problems with infections caused both by "low-grade" pathogens such as viruses and fungi (typical of T-cell deficiencies) and by "high-grade" bacterial pathogens such as streptococci (typical of B-cell deficiencies).

Other congenital immunodeficiencies include DiGeorge syndrome, characterized by failure in the development of the THYMUS and subsequent failure of T cells to develop and function effectively. Patients with DiGeorge syndrome have problems with viral and fungal infections. Brouton's sex-linked agammaglobulinemia is a disease of males in which the B cells do not function properly, leading to a deficiency of production of soluble ANTIBODY (immunoglobulin). Such patients characteristically are infected recurrently by bacterial pathogens. Congenital abnormalities of phagocytic cells (granulocytes and macrophages; see BLOOD), as seen in chronic granulomatous disease, also lead to recurrent infections.

Acquired. Acquired immunodeficiencies can be primary—that is, caused by a primary failure of the immune system—or secondary to some other disease, such as cancer. The most common primary disease is selective deficiency of what is called IgA immunoglobulin. This disease is frequently associated with infections of the lung. Other immunoglobulins can be absent or at very low levels in a patient with acquired common variable immunodeficiency; this can lead to clinically important problems with recurrent infections.

Up to 5 percent of all hospitalized patients have been estimated to have some form of secondary acquired immunodeficiency, often in relation to an underlying disease, such as cancer or AUTOIMMUNE DISEASE. In addition, many patients have a depressed immune system because of the therapy used to treat certain diseases, as with the corticosteroids used to treat many kinds of arthritis, and the chemotherapy used in cancer treatments. One important secondary acquired immunodeficiency that emerged in the early 1980s is AIDS, or acquired immune deficiency syndrome (see AIDS).

Treatment. The ability to treat immunodeficiency syndromes adequately has lagged behind the ability to diagnose them. Several combined immunodeficiency and congenital T-cell diseases have been successfully treated by tissue transplantation with bone marrow or, in some cases, with fetal liver and thymus transplants. Antibody deficiencies, particularly of IgG immunoglobulin, can be treated with periodic injections of human gamma globulin. This therapy does not cure the underlying cellular defect but does replace the missing cellular product (antibody), and it protects against recurrent infection. Of extreme importance, therefore, is the identification of the microorganism causing the clinical infection, as is the rapid institution of the antibiotics to which the microorganism is sensitive.

immunology   see IMMUNITY (biology)

IMP   The IMP, or Interplanetary Monitoring Platform, was a series of ten scientific satellites (part of the EXPLORER series) launched by the National Aeronautics and Space Administration (NASA) between 1963 and 1973 to probe the magnetosphere and interplanetary space during the 11-year cycle of the Sun's activity. The IMP series was the first to measure accurately the interplanetary magnetic field, the Earth's magnetospheric boundary, and the shock wave occurring when the solar wind interacts with the Earth's magnetic field.

impala [im-pal'-uh]   The impala, *Aepyceros melampus*, in the antelope and ox family, Bovidae, is a fast-running antelope of grasslands and open woodlands in central and southern Africa. A slight, graceful animal, the adult impala is about 1.5 m (5 ft) long, stands up to 1 m (3.3 ft) tall at the shoulder, and weighs up to 74.3 kg (165 lb). The coat is fawn or reddish brown above and whitish below. A black streak marks each side of the rump. The male has large, lyre-shaped horns. A powerful jumper, the impala can make leaps 9 m (30 ft) long and 3 m (10 ft) high. Impalas live in herds and feed on shrubs and grasses.

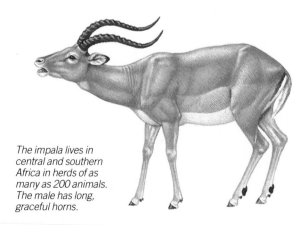

The impala lives in central and southern Africa in herds of as many as 200 animals. The male has long, graceful horns.

impasto [im-pahs'-toh]   The term *impasto* refers to the thickness of the pigment of oil and acrylic paints applied to a surface, particularly when it is thick enough to retain the mark of the painter's brush or palette knife. Rembrandt and Peter Paul Rubens used impasto for highlights, whereas Frans Hals laid the paint in more fully in slashing strokes. A heavy, swirling, overall impasto typifies the work of Vincent van Gogh. More recently, Jackson Pollock worked layers of dripped and splattered paint, sometimes with sand added for texture, into his canvases. The term does not apply to thin-surfaced painting techniques.

impeachment [im-peech'-ment]   Impeachment is the first step in the process specified in the Constitution of the United States for removing the president, vice-president, or other government official from office upon conviction of "treason, bribery, or other high crimes and misdemeanors." The House of Representatives has "the sole power of impeachment," that is, the power of bringing charges. The Senate has "the sole power to try all impeachments." A two-thirds vote is required in the Senate for conviction. When the president is to be tried, the chief justice of the United States presides. A conviction in an impeachment proceeding results only in removal from office and disqualification to hold "any office of honor, trust, or profit under the United States." A person convicted in an impeachment, however, is subject to further "indictment, trial, judgment, and punishment according to Law."

Impeachment originated in England, where the House of Commons would present articles of impeachment to the House of Lords, which then tried the case. A well-known instance was the impeachment and trial (1786–95) of Warren HASTINGS, first governor general of India.

The framers of the U.S. Constitution, although committed to a separation of powers and independence of the three branches of government from each other, believed that a means must be provided by which officers thought to be guilty of significant misconduct could be tried and removed.

Since the adoption of the Constitution, only one president, Andrew JOHNSON (1868), has been brought to trial in the Senate on charges voted by the House. The Senate failed by one vote to convict Johnson. In 1974 the House Judiciary Committee voted three charges of impeachment against President Richard M. NIXON (see WATERGATE), but he resigned from office before the charges could be voted upon by the House.

Impeachment proceedings have been brought with some frequency against federal judges. In 1804, Supreme Court justice Samuel CHASE was impeached on purely political grounds, but his acquittal (1805) effectively halted the use of impeachment to remove judges for political reasons.

Certain questions concerning the impeachment process have persisted: whether it is judicial or political in nature; how to define high crimes and misdemeanors;

and whether a conviction can be appealed to the Supreme Court. Although no conclusive answer can be given, it is safe to say that the judicial process of impeachment will always be infused with political motives; that the definition of high crimes and misdemeanors will never become entirely precise; and that once the Senate has voted to convict by a two-thirds majority, the Supreme Court is unlikely to take jurisdiction.

impedance [im-peed'-ens]

Impedance is the apparent resistance in alternating-current (AC) circuits that corresponds to true (ohmic) resistance in direct-current (DC) circuits. Symbolized by the letter Z, impedance is measured in ohms and is related to the voltage E and the current I by the relationship $Z = E/I$. This is, in effect, a generalized version of OHM'S LAW. Impedance is the inherent RESISTANCE of the circuit as well as inductive and capacitive REACTANCE. Because the value of reactance depends on the frequency of the applied voltage, so does the impedance.

Many electronic components, such as loudspeakers, radio transmitters, and generators, are rated according to their impedances. This enables the user to match impedances easily, that is, to add components with the same impedance. Maximum power is transferred when the input impedance of one device is identical to the output impedance of the other. For example, a home television installation is composed of the receiver, antenna, and lead-in cable. Optimum reception is obtained when the antenna and cable are selected to match the impedance of the receiver. When this cannot be done, an impedance-matching transformer may be inserted between components.

See also: ALTERNATING CURRENT; CIRCUIT, ELECTRIC.

Imperial Valley

The Imperial Valley, located mostly in southeastern California, is an irrigated portion of the Colorado Desert lying below sea level. Its lowest point is 71 m/232 ft below sea level. It extends south from the SALTON SEA for about 80 km (50 mi) and is about 65–100 km (40–60 mi) wide. The valley was once part of the Gulf of California, but deposits from the COLORADO RIVER gradually cut it off from the gulf. The soil is fertile, and the growing season is long, but the arid climate made agriculture impossible until the All-American Canal (130 km/80 mi), which brings water from the Colorado River, was completed in 1940. The Imperial Valley is now a profitable farming region.

imperialism

Imperialism is the policy or practice of extending national power over other states or areas of the world, often by annexing territory. Imperialism has existed in every age. The Zhou and Qin dynasties in ancient China (c.1027–206 BC) and the Maurya in India (c.321–c.185 BC) provide early examples of empire building. Attempts by Athens to establish political and military hegemony over the Greek city-states led to its ultimate defeat

The imperialist powers (left to right) England, Germany, Russia, France, and Japan divide China into spheres of influence in this cartoon from a French journal of 1898. In the background a Chinese mandarin is powerless to prevent the slicing of the pie.

in the Peloponnesian War (431–404 BC). Alexander the Great of Macedonia created an empire reaching beyond Persia in the east that signaled the end of the Greek city-state as the basic political unit of the ancient world. In the Roman Empire, policies implicit in Alexander's rule were developed further. Although Rome remained the imperial center, rights of citizenship were extended throughout the empire. From AD 395 the Roman Empire was permanently divided into eastern and western halves. In the east the Byzantine Empire remained in existence until 1453, when it finally fell victim to the expanding Ottoman (Turkish) Empire. The Roman Empire in the west collapsed in AD 476, but the imperial ideal was revived by the Frankish ruler Charlemagne, who was crowned emperor by the pope in 800. This event is sometimes taken as the founding of the Holy Roman Empire, but the imperial coronation (962) of the German king Otto I marks the beginning of that entity as a continuing institution. The Holy Roman Empire survived until 1806, although it was a weak confederation for much of the time.

In 16th-century Europe the centralization of political power in the hands of absolute monarchs was accompanied by the growth of a new social class, the bourgeoisie, or merchant class, and by the quest of European explorers for precious metals and other trade goods in the New World and the Orient. MERCANTILISM, seapower, and the establishment of powerful national armies provided impetus for a new wave of imperialism both within continental Europe and far beyond its boundaries.

The term *imperialism* is most commonly identified with 19th-century colonialism and the carving of the globe into "spheres of influence" by the European powers. One of the leading figures of 19th-century imperialism was the British financier and South African statesman Cecil Rhodes. Colonies in Asia and Africa supplied cheap labor, raw materials, and ready markets for European manufacturing, spurred on by the Industrial Revolution. They also enhanced the image of European powers.

Imperialism was also linked to concepts of racial and moral supremacy, rationalized as "the White Man's Burden"—the so-called duty to bring civilization to backward peoples. In the Western Hemisphere, much of Latin America came under the sway of commercial and financial interests in the United States. This type of expansion is called economic imperialism.

Since World War II, imperialism has taken a new form. The former colonies have become independent states, and the United States and the USSR have competed for influence over them, usually through economic and military aid to their governments. Direct military intervention is usually a last resort; certain prominent examples include American intervention in Vietnam and the Soviet invasions of Hungary and Czechoslovakia to maintain its political hegemony in those countries. Britain and France also continue to exert economic influence over some of their former colonies in Africa, and occasionally this influence is supported by military intervention. Less developed countries decry modern economic imperialism (called neoimperialism), asserting that it seriously hampers their efforts toward economic growth and independence.

See also: BRITISH EMPIRE; COLONIALISM; EMPIRE; FRENCH COLONIAL EMPIRE.

—

impotence   Impotence, or "erectile dysfunction," is a male's inability to attain a sufficiently strong erection to enable him satisfactorily to engage in sexual intercourse.

Many males experience occasional episodes of impotence due to factors such as fatigue, distress, or the effects of excessive alcoholic intake. While organic or physiological factors may cause impotence, emotional or psychogenic factors are more common.

Primary impotence is the case in which the male has never maintained an erection of long enough duration to engage in sexual intercourse. Secondary impotence is the case in which a previously potent male loses his ability to maintain an erection for sexual intercourse. Fear of failure and performance anxiety frequently are negative psychological sources that underlie impotence.

—

impressionism (art)   Impressionism, the leading development in French painting in the later 19th century and a reaction against both the academic tradition and romanticism, refers principally to the work of Claude MoNET, Pierre Auguste RENOIR, and other artists associated with them, such as Camille PISSARRO and Alfred SISLEY, who shared a common approach to the rendering of outdoor subjects. Impressionism also refers to the work of artists who participated in a series of group exhibitions in Paris, the first and most famous of which was held from April 15 to May 15, 1874, at the studio of the photographer NADAR. The artists represented at the exhibition, or in the succeeding ones held by the group between 1876 and 1886, included Paul CÉZANNE, Edgar DEGAS, Berthe MORISOT, and, after 1879, Paul GAUGUIN and the American artist Mary CASSATT.

Impression: Sunrise (1872), by Claude Monet, first shown in 1874, caused a critic to sneer: " ...since I am impressed it must contain some sort of impression." Although coined as a derogatory term, impressionism is an appropriate description of Monet's technique, which reduces solid forms to areas of pure color that dissolve into the single sensation of a glowing, hazy sunrise. (Musée Marmottan, Paris.)

In the 1890s, Monet's experiments with light led him to produce several series of paintings of the same subject seen under various atmospheric conditions. In 1892 he rented a room overlooking Rouen Cathedral and began to study the effect of light on the west facade. These two canvases (1894) depict the building at noon (left) and at sunset (below). (Louvre, Paris.)

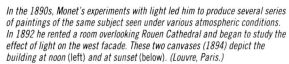

(Below) Unlike other impressionists, Auguste Renoir did not confine himself to painting landscapes. The Box (1874) brings impressionist traits to a subject that might have attracted an 18th-century baroque master. (Courtauld Institute Galleries, London.)

(Right) After experimenting with pointilism, Camille Pissarro returned to the impressionist style he had helped establish. Boulevard Montmartre (1897) displays his characteristic use of controlled color tonality to evoke atmosphere. (Hermitage, Leningrad.)

In his later work, such as Landscape with a Viaduct (c.1895) at right, Paul Cézanne invested his subjects with a geometric design that has often been regarded as a foreshadowing of abstract art. Although his membership in the impressionist group is sometimes forgotten, it was from Camille Pissarro and his colleagues that Cézanne learned to achieve naturalistic immediacy by painting directly from nature. (Metropolitan Museum of Art, New York City.)

In 1877, Mary Cassatt, an American living in Paris, was invited by Edgar Degas to exhibit her paintings with the group later called the impressionists. The Box at the Opera (1880), with its informal pose and asymmetric composition, is characteristic of her lifelong interest in social scenes. (Museum of Fine Arts, Boston.)

(Above) Ballerina Posing for a Photograph (c.1879), one of Edgar Degas's series of dancers, exemplifies the linearity and distinct form that distinguishes his work from that of the other impressionists. (Poesjkinmuseum, Moscow.)

(Left) *Paul Gauguin's* Rocks by the Sea *(1886) is typical of his early work, in which his handling of light, color, and atmosphere reflects the work of the early impressionists. He was one of the major figures of the postimpressionist movement. (Kunstmuseum, Göteborg, Sweden.)*

(Below) *Georges Seurat's* The Models *(1887–88) epitomizes the "scientific impressionism" known as pointilism, divisionism, or neoimpressionism. Tiny dots of pigment both intensify and diffuse light to create shimmering mosaics of color. (Merion, Barnes Foundation, Pa.)*

(Bottom) *Vincent van Gogh's* Small House of Vincent at Arles *(1888) exemplifies the vigorous rhythm, brilliant color, and expressive power characteristic of his late work. (Stedelijk Museum, Amsterdam.)*

(Above) *Whereas Monet had approached impressionism from his studies of nature, Manet's early painting owed much to his interest both in the flat perspectives of Japanese woodcuts and in the portraiture of Diego Velásquez.* The Balcony *(1868) resolved these disparate influences in its use of stark silhouette, large areas of color, and sharply contrasted tones. This painting reveals the influence of Spanish art on Manet's style and composition. (Louvre, Paris.)*

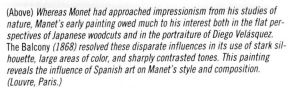

The term *impressionism* was derived from a painting by Claude Monet—*Impression: Sunrise* (1872; Musée Marmottan, Paris), a view of the port of Le Havre in the mist—and was coined for the group by the unfriendly critic Louis Leroy. Monet probably intended the title to refer to the sketchy, unfinished look of the work, similar to receiving an impression of something on the basis of an exposure that is partially obscured and incomplete in its detail. The term, however, was quickly taken up by sympathetic critics, who used it in an alternative sense to mean the impression stamped on the senses by a visual experience that is rapid and transitory, associated with a particular moment in time. Monet, Renoir, Pissarro, and Sisley were impressionists in the latter sense; beginning in the later 1860s and culminating in 1872–75, they chose to paint outdoors (*en plein air*), recording the rapidly changing conditions of light and atmosphere as well as their individual sensations before nature. They used high-key colors and a variety of brushstrokes, which allowed them to be responsive both to the material character and texture of the object in nature and to the impact of light on its surfaces.

Édouard MANET did not exhibit with the group, but works such as his *Déjeuner sur l'herbe* (1863; Musée d'Orsay, Paris) had an important influence on the younger painters during the 1860s. During the early 1870s, Manet was on friendly terms with the impressionists and adopted some of the same outdoor subjects.

Either directly or through the intermediacy of the developments of the 1880s, such as NEOIMPRESSIONISM and POSTIMPRESSIONISM, impressionism influenced modern art in such fundamental features as a loosening up of brushwork, which abolished finally the traditional distinction between the finished painting and the preliminary sketch or study; a concern for the two-dimensional surface of a painting, which is defined by the patterns and feeling of movement of the paint on the ground; and a use of pure, bright colors, often taken directly from the tube. Concurrently, the members of the original group were extending in new and highly personal directions their original commitments as impressionists and their particular pictorial concerns. These developments in the latter part of their careers do not form part of impressionism but represent a logical outgrowth, a carrying of its interests into new dimensions of technique and content.

impressionism (music)

Impressionism, a term originally applied to a style of French painting, is now used in music to refer to a style introduced by Claude DEBUSSY in the 1890s. The goal of an impressionist composer is to evoke moods and images rather than tell a story. A composition in the impressionist style typically uses short melodic fragments or motives, often derived from pentatonic (5-tone) or whole-tone scales, as opposed to the standard major and minor scales. Dissonant chords of the 7th or 9th are often left unresolved, creating an elusive, indistinct, musical structure. In impressionist piano music liberal use of the damper pedal blurs and blends harmonies still further.

Notable examples of musical impressionism include Debussy's *Prelude to the Afternoon of a Faun* (1892–94), the opera *Pelléas et Mélisande* (1902), the orchestral suite *La Mer* (1905), and several of the *Préludes* (1910–13) for piano. Another leading impressionist composer was Maurice RAVEL.

imprinting

Through the process of imprinting, an instinctive behavior pattern, the young of a species rapidly learn to recognize and follow a member of their own species, typically the mother, or another object. This phenomenon takes place early in life, within a prescribed period; if the typical object of attachment (the mother) is not present within this period, the responses are oriented toward another object, usually a living organism.

Certain birds, such as ducks, geese, chickens, and turkeys, are precocial, meaning that they are able to leave the nest soon after they are hatched. By INSTINCT they begin to follow the first object they see, most often the mother, and they continue to do so until they are almost adults. If the mother is absent during the critical period for imprinting, the chicks will follow almost any conspicuous object, such as a decoy or a human being. The variety of objects that chicks are willing to follow is extensive, although not all objects are equally effective. For example, an adult duck is more effective as an object of attachment than is another duckling. The "following" behavior is more likely to occur if exposure to the moving object occurs within some relatively restricted time period. Ducks have an imprinting period only hours in length.

Imprinting is considered to be the basis for a long-lasting dependence on the mother. Some animals, such as sheep, separate themselves from the rest of the herd when they deliver their young, ensuring that the infant will imprint on its mother rather than on another member of the flock.

If the newborn animal becomes attached to an artificial or unnatural object during this critical time, it may

The Austrian ethologist Konrad Lorenz used the term imprinting *to describe the way in which certain newly hatched birds follow the first moving object—usually the mother—they see. These greylag goslings were imprinted on Lorenz, now their mother substitute.*

not be able to respond to its own mother at a later period. For example, if a young duckling becomes imprinted to an artificial object, it will later reject the natural maternal attentions of a brood duck.

Konrad LORENZ, who studied imprinting extensively, described it as distinct from ordinary learning because imprinting can take place only during a narrow period, whereas learning is a lifelong process. He noted that once imprinted on a substitute object, the animal always responds to it as it would to another of its own species; in other words, imprinting is irreversible. Finally, Lorenz found that imprinting does not depend, as ordinary learning does, on the effects of reinforcement through rewards and punishments.

Contrary to Lorenz's assertion, other studies have shown that the irreversibility of imprinting does not always apply.

improvisational and experimental theater

Improvisational and experimental theater can be traced back at least as far as the *commedia dell'arte* productions in 16th-century Italy, although elements of improvisation no doubt occurred in primitive rain dances centuries earlier. One of the greatest experimenters of the 20th century was the Russian director Vsevolod MEYERHOLD, originally one of Stanislavsky's colleagues; he looked for innovative scenic effects, introduced circus elements, and formulated a new approach to theatrical performance that he called biomechanics. Like Meyerhold, the German Bauhaus artists in the 1920s were entranced with the image of the machine.

The French actor Antonin ARTAUD proclaimed an irrational theater, a theater of dreams and of spectacle that came to be known as the theater of cruelty. Artaud and Jerzy GROTOWSKI have been two of the most influential forces on younger experimenters. Grotowski's emphasis on the performer as a physical being, as exemplified in the work of his Polish Laboratory Theater, has sown seeds throughout Western Europe and also influenced such American groups as the LIVING THEATRE, the Open Theater, the Firehouse Theater, the Performance Group, and the Manhattan Project.

Inca

Inca [ink'-uh] The Inca were the rulers of the largest native empire of the Americas. Near the end of the 14th century the empire began to expand from its initial base in the CUZCO region of the southern Andes mountains of South America. It ended abruptly with the Spanish invasion led by Francisco PIZARRO in 1532. At the time of its demise the empire controlled an estimated 12 million people in much of what is now Peru, Ecuador, Chile, Bolivia, and Argentina.

Shaded areas indicate the expansion of the Inca empire under a progression of rulers between 1438 and 1525. Also shown are the major centers of Inca culture and the network of roads, called capac nan, *that linked them.*

Inca Empire

The Inca called their land *Tawantinsuyu,* which in QUECHUA, the Inca language, means "four parts." A land of markedly diverse terrain and climate, it included a long coastal desert strip, broken by rich irrigated valleys; the high peaks and deep fertile valleys of the Andes; and the mountainous edges of the tropical forest to the east. The term *Inca* refers to the ruler himself as well as to the people of the valley of Cuzco, the capital of the empire. Most of the dozens of smaller local kingdoms retained their identities even though politically and economically subject to the Incas. Quechua was the official language and was spoken in most of the realm by the time the Spanish arrived, but at least 20 local languages persisted in various parts of the empire.

Origins. An official version of early Incan history was told to the Spanish invaders, but it is difficult to separate actual historical events from myth and legends. The Incan empire probably started out as a small kingdom, similar to many others in the Andes during the 14th century. A powerful state centered at HUARI, in the vicinity of what is now Ayacucho, Peru, had apparently controlled the area several centuries earlier, but by the 10th century small feuding kingdoms dominated the scene. It is not known for certain whether MANCO CAPAC, listed as the founding ruler, was a historical personage.

Territorial Expansion. The Incas began their remarkable territorial expansion under PACHACUTI (r. 438–71). According to accounts set down by the Spanish, the empire achieved about two-thirds of its final size under Pachacuti. Although his reign was a long one, the conquest was achieved extremely rapidly considering the limited means of transportation and communication available to the Incas. The wheel was not employed, and the horse did not exist there.

Not all territories were brought into the realm by direct military action. Some joined in alliances with the Incas as the result of peaceful overtures from the expanding state. Others joined out of fear that military intervention would result if an invitation to peaceful alliance were rejected. About 1470 the Incas captured the rich and powerful CHIMU kingdom on the north coast of what is now Peru, and little remained to challenge Inca expansion throughout what then constituted the "civilized world" of South America. In parts of this vast territory, notably along the south coast of Peru, the price of conquest was high; great losses on both sides and the virtual extinction of local groups resulted.

Collapse of the Empire. It is theorized that, though still expanding when the Spanish arrived, the Inca empire was approaching a series of geopolitical limits that would preclude further expansion. Inca rule was predicated on a relatively stable sedentary life that provided both a system for political control and the basis around which the pro-

duction of the goods needed to sustain the state could be organized. Inca incursion into the eastern jungles and other lightly populated areas was never successful; the effort required to exert control was too great, and the resources were not sufficiently concentrated to be easily mobilized.

In 1527 the death of Huayna Capac (r. 1493–1527) plunged the Inca state into civil war. No fixed system for determining the succession of rulers appears to have been set up. His son ATAHUALPA claimed that Huayna Capac had decided to divide the kingdom, setting up a new northern capital at Quito that Atahualpa would rule. His brother Huáscar claimed to be the legitimate ruler of the entire realm. Atahualpa finally won the bloody war and was on his way to Cuzco in 1532 to claim the whole kingdom when the Spanish conquistador Francisco Pizarro arrived. The Incas allowed Pizarro and a contingent of about 150 soldiers to enter the regional capital at Cajamarca, where Atahualpa was taken captive, assuring the collapse of the empire.

Inca Culture

The sketchy 16th-century written accounts of the Incas do not provide a very complete understanding of the economic and political organization of their state. It is clear, however, that the principles of Inca economics and politics were derived from old Andean traditions.

State Organization. The Inca state was not a monolith under the absolute control of its ruler. It was an amalgam of dozens, if not hundreds, of different political, ethnic, and even linguistic groups. In some places members of the Inca elite came from Cuzco to exercise direct control over local peoples; in others the pre-Inca scheme of leadership was left relatively intact and a form of indirect rule was pursued. The threat of military force was probably always an important element in the control of the hinterlands.

An unusual characteristic of the Inca state was its ability to move people about the empire as "colonists." This custom of internal colonization allowed the Incas to place loyal groups in regions that were difficult to control. The practice also appears to have had economic aims; people could be relocated to develop new lands, new mines, or other resources.

Politics and economics were not really separate for the Incas—the exchange of many products was carried out through political channels. Leaders maintained their power by providing gifts of luxury goods and elaborate entertainment. The people returned the favors by providing their leaders with labor. Such labor provided the Inca state with its "tax" revenues. A census of the male population was held regularly in connection with labor conscription.

Perhaps the greatest achievement of the Incas lay in their efficient mobilization and organization of the state's labor force into armies of conquest, a class of bureaucrats, and attendants for the ruling class. Of greater long-term importance, however, was the planning and execution of construction projects that increased production and improved the management of resources. Most of the technologies used by the Incas were improvements on innovations

Atahualpa (left) and his brother Huáscar (right), the sons of Lord Inca Huayna Capac, plunged the empire into civil war. Atahualpa vanquished Huáscar but was himself overthrown in 1532 by the Spanish conquistador Pizarro.

(Below) *This 16th-century* kero, *a large wooden goblet used in Inca religious ceremonies, is decorated with the face of an* Orejon, *or Inca noble.*

Tambo Machay exemplifies the stonemasonry for which the Incas are admired. Even more impressive was their ability to transport huge blocks of stone without using the wheel, which the Incas apparently never invented.

dating from several centuries earlier, but the Incas wedded their organizational skills to these existing techniques and produced a series of remarkable public works.

Architecture. The Incas developed a highly functional style of public architecture distinguished above all by its superior engineering techniques and fine stonemasonry. The plan of their cities was based on a system of broad avenues intersected by smaller streets that converge on an open square lined by state buildings and temples. Structures were usually single-storied, with perfectly bonded joints of cut stone, although adobe bricks and plaster were commonly used in the coastal lowlands. For building large monuments such as the great fortress of SACSAHUAMAN near Cuzco, massive polygonal blocks were fitted together with extraordinary precision. In mountainous regions, as at the spectacularly situated Andean citadel of MACHU PICCHU, Inca architecture often reflects ingenious adaptations to the surrounding land forms. (See PRE-COLUMBIAN ART AND ARCHITECTURE.)

Road System. Approximately 20,000 km (12,000 mi) of Inca roads constituted a transportation network rivaled only by that of the Romans in the preindustrial world. Since the Incas did not utilize the wheel, the road system did not serve vehicular traffic, only pedestrians and the llamas they used to carry cargo. Levees were constructed across swamps, steps were carved into hillsides, and bridges of several types were built across rivers and streams. Two so-called royal roads were built, by which the rulers could travel the length of the empire—one near the coast and one through the Andean highland. These roads were fed by many lateral routes. As important as the roads themselves were the administrative and service centers that were built along them. On principal roads a way station was located at the end of each day's travel so that travelers could rest and get fresh supplies. On parts of the highland road, at the Peruvian sites of Tambo Colorado in the Pisco valley and at Huanuco Viejo, near modern Huanuco, several enormous administrative centers with more than 3,000 buildings each were constructed to house the bureaucracy, state manufacturing and storage facilities, and related activities.

Agricultural Production. Increases in agricultural production were achieved through the construction of large-scale terracing and irrigation systems. Many highland valleys—most notably the Urubamba, near Cuzco—were completely reshaped with terraces. Maize grew well in such irrigated areas, and maize and the beer made from it were luxury foods served by the state on ceremonial occasions. The increased production of these and other foods was important in giving the state access to an ever-increasing labor surplus, in turn leading to more craft specialization.

Storage and Recordkeeping. Storage was another technological and organizational achievement of the Incas that enabled them to maintain a stable food supply in spite of a climate that resulted in frequent crop failures, especially in the highlands. Some of the administrative centers along the roads had food storage facilities that held as much as a million bushels of grains and tubers. Some of the thousands of storehouses throughout the realm had specialized ventilation systems.

The Incas did not have writing as it is known today. But the *quipu*—a recording device by which numbers were represented in the form of knotted strings—was developed to considerable complexity. The Inca numerical system employed a base of ten. *Quipu* frequently had hundreds of strings in different colors, enabling the Incas to keep accurate account of the goods in their storehouses, census and manpower figures for various parts of the realm, and other information.

Religion. The state religion centered on the worship of the Sun. The Inca emperors were believed descended from the Sun god and were worshiped as divine beings. Gold, the symbol of the Sun god, was extensively mined for use by the rulers and members of the elite, not as a means of exchange but principally for decorative and ritual purposes.

From the Temple of the Sun in the center of Cuzco imaginary lines ran to shrines (*huacas*) in and around the city that were identified with different social groups. Religious practices included the consultation of oracles, the offering of sacrifices, religious trances, and public confessions. An annual cycle of religious festivals was regulated by the extremely accurate Inca calendar, as was the agricultural year. In this and other respects, Inca culture strongly resembled certain cultures of MESOAMERICA, such as the AZTECS and the MAYA.

Aftermath of Spanish Conquest

After the Spanish captured and killed Atahualpa, the decline of the Inca state was swift. Although resistance to the invaders continued in several places, effective native rule ceased immediately, and the fabric of the state quickly disintegrated.

Manco Inca, a half brother and enemy of Atahualpa who had collaborated with the Spanish, became a puppet ruler. He had no real power, however, and was abused by the Europeans. In 1536 he left Cuzco for Vitcos, on the edge of the jungle, where he set up a retreat inaccessible to the Spanish. There he tried to maintain the customs of the Incas and to set up a base for reconquest. After his death his son, Sayri Tupac, negotiated capitulation in exchange for personal concessions. Resistance under other Inca descendants ended in 1572 with the execution of Tupac Amaru.

Some of the Inca regional capitals along the roads were converted to Spanish towns; others were abandoned within a few years of the arrival of the Spanish. The colonial governments that replaced Tawantinsuyu were very different from that of the Incas, and much of the native population was reduced to servitude. It is easier, however, to topple a government than to alter the customs and traditions of a people. The Quechua language is today spoken by millions of Indians in the Andes region. Many native customs continued during centuries of European domination, especially in isolated parts of the Andes, and some are still maintained.

incandescent lamp [in-kan-des'-ent]   The incandescent LAMP is a device for producing light by passing an electric current through a metallic filament, thereby heating the filament to a high temperature. The filament is placed inside an evacuated bulb, which is attached to the lamp base.

Although visible light is desired, quantities of infrared and some ultraviolet are also produced, decreasing the luminous efficiency. The efficiency, in lumens per watt, may be increased by raising the temperature of the filament, since most of the output energy is transferred from the infrared to the visible spectrum. The first lamps, produced in 1880 by Thomas EDISON, used carbonized strips of bamboo for the filament. Carbon has a high melting point—3,598° C (6,510° F)—but since it evaporates or sublimates from the solid phase much below this temperature, early carbon lamps had to be operated at a lower temperature to prolong their life. Osmium and tantalum, which have higher melting points, were later used for filaments, but ductile tungsten superseded these metals when it became available in 1912. Since tungsten melts only at 3,382° C (6,120° F), it operates at a higher temperature and emits a much whiter light, attaining a luminous efficiency of about 22 lumens per watt.

incarnation   Incarnation denotes the embodiment of a deity in human form. The idea occurs frequently in mythology. In ancient times, certain people, especially kings and priests, were often believed to be divinities. In Hinduism, VISHNU is believed to have taken nine incarnations, or avatars. For Christians, the incarnation is a central dogma referring to the belief that the eternal son of God, the second person of the Trinity, became man in the person of JESUS CHRIST. The incarnation was defined as a doctrine only after long struggles by early church councils. The Council of Nicaea (325) defined the deity of Christ against ARIANISM; the Council of Constantinople (381) defined the full humanity of the incarnate Christ against Apollinarianism; the Council of Ephesus (431) defined the unity of Christ's person against NESTORIANISM; and the Council of Chalcedon (451) defined the two natures of Christ, divine and human, against EUTYCHES.

incest [in'-sest]   Incest is prohibited sexual relations between members of the same KINSHIP group. It is almost universally proscribed between unmarried members of the NUCLEAR FAMILY (between siblings or between parents and children). In many cultures the definition of incest includes other relatives also, although which ones varies from society to society.

Most social scientists believe that the primary purpose of the prohibition, often called the incest TABOO, is to protect the nuclear family from the consequences of sexual rivalry and jealousy. The taboo is linked with the rule of EXOGAMY, which requires marriage outside of one's family. Besides reinforcing the incest prohibition, this rule prevents families from becoming culturally ingrown and encapsulated through perpetual ENDOGAMY, or marriage within specified segments of a society. Marriage to relatives outside the nuclear family is common in a number of cultures, however, and it is no longer widely believed that the incest prohibition serves principally to guard against inbreeding as a negative biological consequence of incest.

Some societies permit explicit, rare exceptions to the incest prohibition for cultural reasons. Such exceptions have included brother-sister marriage among the royal families in ancient Egypt, among the INCA, and in traditional Hawaiian society. Unpermitted violations of the prohibition occur with varying frequency in all societies.

—

Inchon [in-chahn]   Inchon (Chemulpo), a city on the Yellow Sea approximately 30 km (20 mi) from Seoul, is South Korea's most important port. It has a population of 1,604,000 (1989 est.). Inchon's industries include shipping, iron and steel mills, chemical plants, a petroleum refinery, fisheries, and lumber and textile mills. Salt is manufactured on nearby tidal flats. Opened to international trade in 1883, Inchon was occupied by the Japanese from 1905 to 1945. During the KOREAN WAR, United Nations troops landed there on Sept. 15, 1950, and successfully halted the North Korean advance into the south.

—

inchworm   The inchworm, or measuring worm, is the larva of any member of the moth family, Geometridae (from the Greek "earth measurer"). The legs and prolegs are only at the front and hind ends of the larvae's slender bodies, so that crawling is accomplished by pulling the hind end forward and then extending the front in a series of vertical loops. Many species, for protection, strongly resemble twigs, and some cause serious damage to the trees they feed on.

—

income, national   National income may be defined broadly as the sum of all the incomes in an economy resulting from the production of goods and services in any given year. Estimates of the national income accounts help to provide a general picture of the operation of the economic system; they show the total value of goods and services produced within the economy and the amounts of the national income that are consumed, saved, and invested. National income accounts also show the interrelationship of households, government, and INTERNATIONAL TRADE within the national economy. This is done by dividing the economy into four sectors, each with its own income and expenditure accounts: (1) producers, (2) households, (3) government, and (4) the foreign sector. Each of these sectors represents a group of transactors— buyers and sellers; the account of each sector shows the transactors' receipts of income on the right side and their outlays and saving on the left. Every outlay by one sector is received by some other sector, and so the accounts show how the sectors are linked together.

The Production Sector. The activity of the production sector is found in the gross national income and product account. The right side of this account records the receipts from expenditures on goods and services (GROSS NATIONAL PRODUCT at market prices) that are received by producers, and the left side of the account shows how producers distribute these receipts.

On the expenditure side, government statistics provide considerable detail. Personal consumption expenditures are broken down into specific categories such as food, clothing, housing, transportation, personal services, and so on. Expenditures by the government are divided into two categories: (1) goods purchased from business (defense equipment, agricultural commodities, office supplies, and so on) and (2) wages paid to government employees. Investment expenditures (gross private domestic investment) represent investments in plant and equipment, construction of residential and commercial buildings, and the net accumulation of inventories. Finally, exports and imports include not only commodities but also purchases of services (such as freight and insurance) and payments of property income (such as dividends to and from abroad). Thus, the gross national product measures the value of the output produced by the residents of a nation, including the profits from property that they own abroad. For some purposes, however, it may be desirable to measure the output produced within the geographical area of the nation, irrespective of whether the profits belong to residents or foreign investors. This concept is called gross domestic product. Although it is not the primary measure used by the United States, it is in general use by other countries.

On the left side of the account, a distinction is made between national income, net national product, and gross national income. National income includes all payments made by producers for the use of labor and capital. These payments, which include such things as wages, interest, and profits, are referred to as factor costs. In the case of interest, only the amount of interest paid by producers that exceeds what they receive is included as net interest. The national income is valued in terms of production costs, not market prices. To convert the valuation to market prices, it is necessary to add indirect taxes (sales, excise, and property taxes), which are paid to the government; and business transfer payments, which consist of such things as charitable contributions given by business, and consumer bad debts. This concept is called net national product at market prices. It is still, however, not equal to gross national product at market prices because it excludes the capital consumption allowances that producers set aside out of their total revenues to compensate for the depreciation of their plant and equipment. It is therefore necessary to add these capital consumption allowances to net national product to arrive at gross national income, which must equal gross national product.

The Household Sector. For the household sector (which also includes nonprofit institutions, hospitals, and charities), a personal income account is drawn up that shows (1) the income households receive (on the right side) and

(2) their outlays and saving (on the left).

Households receive payments from producers, as has already been discussed in the gross national income and product account. In addition, they receive transfer payments from the government in the form of social security benefits, welfare, and unemployment payments. The total of all income received is personal income. In terms of outlays, households pay taxes to the government; their personal income minus taxes is their disposable income. From this they make consumption expenditures and pay interest on consumer debt. The income left over after all this is personal saving.

The Government Sector. The account for the government sector would indicate for federal, state, and local governments (1) the revenue they receive, on the right side, plus (2) their spending and (3) the resulting surplus or deficit, both on the left. Government revenue comes from the taxes paid by producers and households. Government spending consists of goods and services purchased from producers, compensation of government employees, and transfer and interest payments. Most of these transactions have already been recorded in the gross national income and product account or in the personal income account.

The Foreign Sector. The foreign sector account is the payments to foreigners and receipts from foreigners. If the receipts from exports are less than payments to foreigners—including interest and transfer payments—net foreign investment is used as a balancing item. A negative net foreign investment indicates that foreigners are, on balance, lending money to the United States.

Saving and Investment Account. Finally, the various saving and investment items that appeared in each of the sector accounts can be brought together to show the gross saving and investment in the economy. Because each of the saving items was determined residually, and because all entries appear twice in the accounts, saving and investment in the national accounts will always, by definition, be equal. (See SAVING AND INVESTMENT.)

---

income tax   The income tax is a levy based on the incomes of individuals, families, and corporations. The income tax is the largest source of tax revenue in advanced economies. In the United States more than half of the federal government's tax revenue comes from income taxes, with the personal income tax accounting for about 45% and the corporate income tax for another 10% of the total tax revenue. Most individual states and some local governments also levy income taxes, but income taxes are less important than other sources of state tax revenue.

Income tax revenue varies greatly from country to country. New Zealand relies heavily on income taxes, raising about 60% of its tax revenue from the personal income tax and another 7% through corporate income taxes. Canada raises 37% of its revenue from personal and 14% from corporate income taxes. The personal income tax is responsible for 32% of tax revenue in Britain, 25% in Italy, and about 15% in Germany and Sweden. Worldwide, however, countries raise an average of only 10% of revenue from income taxes because less-developed nations rely more on import and export taxes for revenue.

An income tax was first instituted in Britain on a permanent basis in 1842. The United States did not use an income tax until 1861, as a temporary measure to help finance the Civil War; that tax was repealed in 1871. When Congress tried to reinstate the income tax, the Supreme Court, in Pollock v. Farmers' Loan and Trust Co. (1895), declared that it was unconstitutional.

The 16th Amendment to the U.S. Constitution, ratified in 1913, consists of a single sentence that allows income taxation. The initial passage of the law established a progressive tax structure, which means that taxpayers are taxed at a higher percentage rate the higher their incomes are. A proportional tax would collect at the same percentage rate for all incomes, and a regressive tax collects a smaller percent of income for higher incomes. The tax structure in the United States has remained progressive since the tax was established, although specific rates have varied greatly.

One of the most significant events in the history of the U.S. income tax was the introduction of withholding during World War II. Prior to withholding, individuals were responsible for sending their tax payments to the government. Withholding, however, requires employers to deduct a part of an employee's pay and send it directly to the government to cover the employee's estimated income taxes. At the end of the year, the income earner computes the income tax due and either pays any additional amount or receives a refund from the government for payments in excess of the tax due.

The Personal Income Tax

The amount of personal income tax due is computed in several steps. First, total income from all sources is added together. Certain types of income are not included in income for tax purposes; these are called exemptions. Examples include a personal exemption for the taxpayer and for individuals who are supported by the taxpayer's income, and for employee business expenses such as the cost of travel for a traveling salesperson. Total income minus exemptions equals adjusted gross income.

Taxpayers then subtract deductions from adjusted gross income to compute taxable income. Items that can be deducted include home-mortgage interest payments and charitable contributions. In lieu of itemizing these deductions, taxpayers can choose to take a standard deduction.

The tax due is computed from taxable income according to the tax rate schedule. An important concept in income taxation is the distinction between the average and marginal rates of taxation. The average rate is the fraction of income paid in taxes. The marginal rate is the fraction of any additional income that would have to be paid in taxes. The average and marginal rates are not the same because, first, some income is not taxed—due to exemptions, deductions, and credits; and, second, the progressive tax schedule taxes lower levels of income at a lower rate than higher levels of income.

The complexities of the tax code are the result of the attempt to achieve a number of goals in its design. The first goal is fairness, and, with the income tax, fairness is generally interpreted to mean that taxpayers should be taxed in proportion to their ability to pay. In trying to implement the ability-to-pay principle, the tax code taxes single taxpayers more than married taxpayers with nonworking spouses, but taxes married couples who both work more than if they both were single. Families with children also pay less in an attempt to tax the same amount for those with equal abilities to pay. The progressive nature of the tax code implements the ability-to-pay principle by suggesting that those with more income have a more-than-proportional ability to pay. How progressive the tax code should be, however, is a matter of debate.

Historically, the tax code has also been used to further other goals by providing tax incentives. Home-mortgage interest can be deducted from taxable income, creating an incentive for home ownership. Charitable contributions can be deducted, providing an incentive for charitable giving. The use of the tax system to provide these kinds of incentives is controversial, and the Tax Reform Act of 1986 eliminated many incentives of this type.

The Corporate Income Tax

In 1960 the corporate income tax comprised 23.2% of federal tax revenues, but it made up only 6.2% of federal revenues in 1983. This decline had resulted from allowing corporations to shelter more income from taxation through credits, exemptions, and deductions. The Tax Reform Act of 1986 contained measures to reverse this trend, to oblige corporations to pay more income tax. The act reduced corporate income tax rates, but corporations must pay taxes on more of their income, since less can be deducted. This will raise the amount of corporate tax revenues collected.

One controversy regarding corporate tax rates is who actually ends up paying the tax. Corporations may raise their prices to cover the corporate income taxes they pay, which would mean that the tax is actually paid by the corporation's customers rather than by the corporation itself. If the corporation did not raise its prices to cover the tax, then the tax would lower corporate profits, so that the stockholders of the corporation would end up paying the tax. Since insurance companies and pension plans own large blocks of stock, the corporate income tax may fall heavily on those industries and their customers. Economists agree that the tax is ultimately paid from all of these groups, but there is no agreement on who pays how much.

Another controversy regarding the corporate income tax is the issue of double taxation. A tax on corporate income taxes the stockholder several times because corporations pay income tax on the money they pay out as dividends and then the recipient of the dividend must pay personal income tax on the dividend. Furthermore, stock is bought with after-tax income; then, when the stockholder is paid a dividend from the corporation or sells the stock at a profit, the income earned is taxed again. Some people argue that corporate income should not be taxed in order to avoid double taxation, whereas others argue that those who earn corporate income can best afford to pay taxes.

The Tax Reform Act of 1986

The Tax Reform Act of 1986 was designed to lower tax rates while collecting about the same amount of revenue by eliminating most deductions, credits, and exemptions and thus increasing the amount of income subject to taxation. The three main goals of the act were to increase the incentive to earn income, to simplify the tax structure, and to make the tax structure fairer. The act closed many loopholes that had allowed some people to escape taxation, and its lowered rates allow people to keep more of any additional income they earn. Both of these provisions increase the fairness of the tax structure.

See also: INTERNAL REVENUE SERVICE; TAXATION.

—

incomes policy　An incomes policy is a governmental effort to restrain INFLATION by setting limits on wage and price increases. Such a policy is usually based on an agreement by employers and labor unions to observe certain guidelines. Wage or price changes that do not exceed the guidelines are presumed to be noninflationary. The government also attempts to limit the expansion of money and credit. Actually, most incomes policies have been designed to limit the growth of inflation rather than wholly eliminate it.

—

incompetence　Incompetence, in law, is an inability, incapacity, or lack of qualification to perform an act or duty. The term applies to such situations as a person's ability to function normally, a judge's legal qualification to hear a case, and a witness's legal ability to testify, as well as to the admissibility of evidence in a judicial proceeding.

When persons are unable to understand the nature of their acts, they are considered legally incompetent. A person may be incompetent with regard to one function (such as making a will) or to many functions. If a person is unable to perform daily activities at a minimal level of proficiency, a court may appoint a guardian to oversee the incompetent's affairs or may commit the person to an institution. A court can declare invalid a will or a contract made by an incompetent.

—

incubus [in'-kue-buhs]　In medieval folklore an incubus was an evil male spirit that haunted sleeping women; it was thought to father demons and witches. The corresponding female spirit, called a succubus, seduced sleeping men. Today the word *incubus* is used to describe an oppressive person or thing. It also refers to nightmares, once believed to be caused by evil spirits.

—

incunabula [in-kue-nab'-ue-luh]　The term *incunabula* derives from the Latin for "swaddling clothes": an incunabulum, or incunable, is any BOOK, pamphlet, or broadside printed in or before the year 1500—the close of the first era of European PRINTING.

Johann GUTENBERG first used movable type in about the year 1450; by the end of the century presses had been established in over 200 communities, and as many as 40,000 different items had been printed. Books usually appeared as quartos bound between wooden boards and decorated with woodcuts. Print runs were small, averaging fewer than 500. Most 15th-century productions were religious works in Latin, the most famous being the 1455 GUTENBERG BIBLE. Although German firms remained dominant, Venice alone boasted 150 presses, and such printers as William CAXTON in England and Aldus MANUTIUS in Venice had a wide influence.

indentured service   Indentured service was a form of contract labor common in colonial North America. Because of the shortage of labor in the colonies, efforts were made to attract European workers (primarily from England and Germany) to cross the Atlantic and bind themselves by indenture, or contract, to a specified period (usually 4 to 7 years) of service in return for payment of their passage. In addition to those who voluntarily entered such an arrangement—the so-called free-willers or redemptioners—the ranks of indentured servants were swelled by those forced into servitude by kidnapping or economic or religious pressures, and by convicts deported to the colonies. The services of these involuntary immigrants were sold to the highest bidders after their arrival in the colonies, and the terms of their indenture could be harsh. The colonial courts enforced performance of the contracts.

In the 17th century indentured servants were more numerous than slaves even in the southern colonies, and they continued to outnumber slaves in the middle colonies during the 18th century. At the end of their period of indenture former servants were given clothing, a gun, and land. They were readily absorbed into the general population. In 1665 former indentured servants constituted almost half of the membership of Virginia's House of Burgesses.

Independence   Independence, a city in western Missouri, is the seat of Jackson County. It has a population of 112,301 (1990). Set in an agricultural area that grows wheat, corn, and potatoes, Independence is a commercial and industrial center. Its manufactures include petroleum products, farm and industrial machinery, food products, munitions, and construction materials. Harry S. Truman was a longtime resident of Independence and is buried on the grounds of the Harry S. Truman Library and Museum. Independence is also the world headquarters of the Reorganized Church of Jesus Christ of Latter-day Saints. Settled in 1825, the community was the starting point for pioneers following the Santa Fe, Oregon, and California trails.

Independence Day   The most important national holiday in the United States, Independence Day, July 4, celebrates the adoption of the Declaration of Independence by the Second Continental Congress on July 4, 1776. The day has always been the occasion for parades and patriotic speeches and for every variety of noisy jubilation. In fact, the firing of cannon and fireworks caused so many injuries that, by the early 1900s, ordinances forbidding private pyrotechnics were passed in many cities.

Independence Hall   Designated the State House (and before that the Province-hall) of Pennsylvania, Independence Hall in Philadelphia was the site of the proclamation (1776) of the U.S. Declaration of Independence. The Continental Congress and the Constitutional Convention met there. The Liberty Bell is on display there today.

An excellent example of colonial Georgian public architecture, the building was designed primarily by Edmund Woolley (1696–1771), a master carpenter, and by Andrew Hamilton (c.1676–1741), a lawyer. In 1828 the proportions of the building were altered by William STRICKLAND's rebuilding of the tower and steeple in the large-scale, blocky forms now visible. Various restorations of the building undertaken in the 1920s—and again in the 1950s and '60s, when it came under the National Park Service as part of Independance National Historic Park—have returned it to a pristine state.

Independent Treasury System   The Independent Treasury System was established in 1840 by an act of the U.S. Congress that withdrew all federal funds from state-chartered, private banks and placed them in government depositories located in major cities.

Intended to separate the banking system from the administration of the government's finances, the act was both a response to the bank failures that followed the Panic of 1837 and a reflection of the suspicion of banking and speculation harbored by hard-money Jacksonians. By depriving banks of federal deposits, the Independent Treasury System denied bankers the opportunity to use public funds as a basis for making loans and issuing notes.

Opposed not only by Whigs but also by conservative Democrats allied to state banking interests, the act was repealed in 1841 but reenacted in 1846. It remained in force until the passage of the National Bank Act of 1863.

Index   The Index Librorum Prohibitorum (Index of Forbidden Books) was a list formerly issued by the Roman Catholic church of published works that church members were forbidden to read without specific permission from a qualified person, usually the bishop acting through a priest-delegate.

The first official listing of forbidden books was promulgated (405) by Pope Innocent I, but a decree issued (c.496) by Pope Gelasius I has been referred to as the first formal index. In 1559 the Congregation of the Inquisition produced a long list of forbidden books, which Pope Paul IV accepted and published as an *index* (the first time the word itself was used to describe a listing of unacceptable literature). The Index went through several revisions in succeeding pontificates. Pope Leo XIII presided (1897) over the final major revision of the Index (which included, for example, all the works of the philosophers Thomas Hobbes and David Hume).

The effectiveness and appropriateness of the Index was reevaluated at the Second Vatican Council (1962–65). Soon after adjournment of the council the Index was abolished.

index An index is a list of the subjects contained in a book, magazine, computerized database, collection of audiovisual materials, encyclopedia, or other compilation of recorded information. Index entries have two parts: a heading and a locator. Headings identify the subject, usually in a word or phrase, and are arranged in a predetermined order, usually alphabetic. Locators tell where the subject is discussed. Indexes should also have a system of cross-reference: *see also* references that lead from one heading to related headings, and *see* references that lead from a heading with no locators to headings with them.

Some indexes are limited to individual books or periodicals. Others, such as the *Readers' Guide to Periodical Literature*, the *Book Review Index*, or the *Biography Index*, are limited to one kind of publication. Still others, such as the *Engineering Index* or the *Environment Index*, are limited to one subject but cover all forms of publication in that area. Today many indexes, such as the *Science Citation Index* or the BASIC index to *Biological Abstracts*, would be impracticable without the computer. Computer-stored indexes to computer-stored data also exist, such as that maintained by Dow Jones and Company to provide information on financial markets.

Experts disagree about the first index. Some say that the Alexandrian Library in Egypt maintained indexes to the papyrus rolls in its collections; others say that the first index was created in medieval times. Today the Society of Indexers in Great Britain and the American Society of Indexers in the United States have been established to improve standards and encourage education in the field.

index of refraction The index of refraction, or refractive index, n, of a substance is a measure of the extent that light is bent as it passes through the substance (see REFRACTION). The index of refraction is also the ratio of the speed of light in a vacuum (c) to its speed in the substance (v).

The index of refraction of a medium is slightly different for each color. Measurements are normally taken using the yellow light of a sodium source. If a mixture of wavelengths, such as ordinary white light, is refracted by the medium, the paths of each wavelength will be refracted to a slightly different angle, and the original beam will appear colored. This process is known as dispersion. The greater the index of refraction, the higher the dispersion.

India India, the world's second most populous nation (after China) and the seventh largest in area, is located in South Asia on the Indian subcontinent. It is about 3,000

km (1,875 mi) wide and has, because of its peninsular shape, a shoreline of about 7,000 km (4,400 mi) along the Bay of Bengal on the east and the Arabian Sea on the west. The land frontier of about 5,700 km (3,600 mi) is shared with Pakistan and a small strip of Afghanistan on the west; by China (mostly Tibet), Nepal, and Bhutan on the north; and by Bangladesh and Burma on the east. India's eighth neighbor is the island nation of Sri Lanka, located off the southern tip of the peninsula. Northeast India is virtually isolated from the rest of the nation by Bangladesh. Also part of India are the LACCADIVE ISLANDS (Lakshadweep) off the western coast and the ANDAMAN and NICOBAR islands, located in the eastern portion of the Bay of Bengal.

India and Bharat are both official names. The early settlers called their land "Bharat Varsha" or "Bharat," and during medieval times it was known as "Hind." The name India, which derives from the Indus River and was used by the ancient Greeks and Persians, came into wide usage during the colonial period.

India gained its independence from the British on Aug. 15, 1947, at which time two predominantly Muslim regions in the northwestern and northeastern corners of the subcontinent became the separate state of Pakistan. The modern country of India is a union of 25 states—Andhra Pradesh, Arunachal Pradesh, ASSAM, BIHAR, GOA, GUJARAT, HARYANA, HIMACHAL PRADESH, Jammu and Kashmir (see KASHMIR), KARNATAKA, KERALA, MADHYA PRADESH, MAHARASHTRA, Manipur, Meghalaya, Mizoram, NAGALAND, ORISSA, PUNJAB, RAJASTHAN, SIKKIM, TAMIL NADU, Tripura, Uttar Pradesh, and West Bengal—and 7 union territories—Daman and Diu, PONDICHERRY, Andaman and Nicobar Islands, Chandigarh, Dadra and Nagar Haveli, Delhi, and Lakshadweep. In 1956 the map of India was largely redrawn as provisions were made for reorganization of the states along linguistic lines, with the goal of preserving regional cultures and aspirations.

Pilgrims immerse themselves in the Ganges River as a rite of purification. The Ganges, which flows across the plains of northern India, has for thousands of years been revered as a holy river by followers of the Hindu religion.

REPUBLIC OF INDIA

Land: Area: 3,287,590 km^2 (1,269,345 mi^2). Capital: New Delhi (1981 pop., 273,026; 1985 metropolitan area est. pop., 6,993,000). Largest city: Calcutta (1981 pop., 3,288,148; 1985 metropolitan area est. pop., 10,462,000).

People: Population (1990 est.): 853,400,000. Density: 259.6 persons per km^2 (672.3 per mi^2). Distribution (1989 est.): 26% urban, 74% rural. Official language: Hindi. Major religions: Hinduism, Islam, Christianity, Sikhism, Buddhism, Jainism.

Government: Type: republic. Legislature: Parliament. Political subdivisions: 25 states, 7 union territories.

Economy: GDP (1989): $270.2 billion; $330 per capita. Labor distribution (1990): commerce and services—11%; manufacturing—20%; agriculture—52%; construction—7%; government and public authorities—7%. Foreign trade (1990 est.): imports—$26.24 billion; exports—$15.63 billion. Currency: 1 rupee = 100 piastres.

Education and Health: Literacy (1990): 36% of adult population. Universities (1987): 135. Hospital beds (1986): 695,000. Physicians (1986): 318,000. Life expectancy (1990): women—59; men—57. Infant mortality (1990): 89 per 1,000 live births.

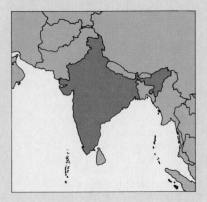

Today India ranks among the top ten industrial nations in the world. Because the huge population is growing as rapidly as the economy, however, the primarily rural population of this huge, developing nation has one of the world's lowest per-capita incomes. Despite the accompanying social and political stresses, and despite a brief period of authoritarian rule (1975–77) under Prime Minister Indira Gandhi, India remains the world's largest democracy.

Land

India can be divided into three main topographic regions; the Himalayan mountain system, on the north; the Northern Plains, drained by the Indus, Ganges, and Brahmaputra rivers in north central India; and Peninsular India, in the south.

The HIMALAYAS form parts of India's borders with Pakistan, Afghanistan, and Tibet in the west and with Nepal, Bhutan, and Tibet in the east. The region is topographically complex and divided into prominent elongated valleys and mountain ranges. The highest mountains are in the KARAKORAM RANGE, where more than 30 peaks rise above 7,300 m (24,000 ft). South of the Karakoram are the Great Himalayas, which include Nanda Devi (7,817 m/25,645 ft), the highest peak in the country. Between the two major ranges is the narrow valley of the Upper Indus River. Southwest of the Great Himalayas and between them and the lower front ranges of the mountain system is the 160-km-long (100-mi) Vale of Kashmir,

which focuses on the town of SRINAGAR. To the east, the mountains form most of Sikkim and Arunachal Pradesh.

The Northern Plains are part of a vast lowland extending across the subcontinent from Pakistan in the west to Bangladesh (formerly East Pakistan) in the east. The plains are bordered on the north by the foothills of the Himalayas; south of the Bramaputra basin are the Khasi Hills and Shillong Plateau; and south of the Indo-Gangetic Plain rise the uplands of Peninsular India. In India, this lowland has a length of about 1,600 km (1,000 mi) from east to west and a width of about 320 km (200 mi).

Peninsular India is geologically the oldest part of India. Ancient crystalline and metamorphic rocks underlie most of the region, but basaltic lavas (igneous rocks) cover parts of the DECCAN PLATEAU. Topographically, the surface of the peninsula is tilted down toward the east and north, with a belt of prominent uplands along the western edge. These uplands, reaching more than 2,500 m (8,000 ft), include the Western Ghats (see GHATS) and the Nilgiri Hills. The northern edge of the peninsula, although lower, is also prominent, forming the Aravalli Range in the west and the jungle-covered Chota Nagpur Plateau in the east. Only a very narrow coastal plain lies between the Western Ghats and the Arabian Sea; more extensive plains, including the deltas of the Cauveri, Krishna, Mahanadi, and Damodar rivers, line the east coast.

Soils. The four principal soil types in India are moun-

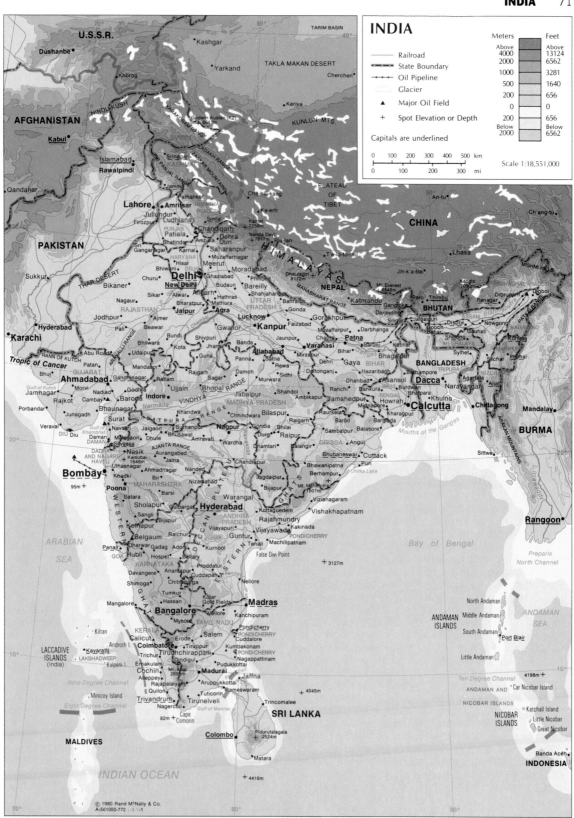

INDIA

		Meters	Feet
———	Railroad	Above 4000	Above 13124
·—·—·—	State Boundary	2000	6562
+—+—+	Oil Pipeline	1000	3281
	Glacier	500	1640
▲	Major Oil Field	200	656
		0	0
+	Spot Elevation or Depth	200	656
		Below 2000	Below 6562

Capitals are underlined

0 100 200 300 400 500 km
0 100 200 300 mi

Scale 1:18,551,000

U.S.S.R.

Dushanbe

AFGHANISTAN

Kabul

Islamabad
Rawalpindi

Qandahar

PAKISTAN

Karachi

TAKLA MAKAN DESERT

TARIM BASIN

Kashgar

Yarkand

Cherchen

Keriya

KUNLUN MTS.

PLATEAU
OF
TIBET

CHINA

Lhasa

NEPAL

Katmandu

BHUTAN

Thimbu

HIMALAYAS

Mt. Everest
8848m

BANGLADESH

Dacca

Calcutta

Chittagong

BURMA

Mandalay

Rangoon

Lahore
Amritsar
Ludhiana
Chandigarh
Simla
Patiala
Ambala
Dehra Dun
Delhi
New Delhi
Jaipur
Agra
Lucknow
Kanpur
Varanasi
Patna
Allahabad
Gaya

THAR DESERT

Bikaner

Jodhpur

RAJASTHAN

Ahmadabad

GUJARAT

Bombay

Poona

MAHARASHTRA

Hyderabad

ANDHRA
PRADESH

Bangalore

KARNATAKA

KERALA

Madras

TAMIL NADU

Cochin

Madurai

Trivandrum

Cape
Comorin

SRI LANKA

Colombo

MALDIVES

LACCADIVE
ISLANDS
(India)
LAKSHADWEEP

ARABIAN
SEA

Bay of Bengal

ANDAMAN
ISLANDS

North Andaman
Middle Andaman
South Andaman
Port Blair
Little Andaman

ANDAMAN
SEA

NICOBAR
ISLANDS

Car Nicobar Island
Katchall Island
Little Nicobar
Great Nicobar

INDONESIA
Banda Aceh

INDIAN OCEAN

Tropic of Cancer

© 1980 Rand McNally & Co.
A-561000-772

The climatic conditions of India's southern coastal regions yield fertile agricultural land and lush vegetation. The area is known for its coconut groves and spice gardens.

tain (or immature) soils, alluvial soils, regur soils, and red soils. Mountain soils are found in upland areas too steep for regular soil development. Alluvial soils cover the broad floodplains of the Indo-Gangetic valley and the Brahmaputra basin, the smaller river valleys and deltas of the peninsula, and the coastal lowlands; these soils are generally fertile. The regur soils are rich, fertile black soils found in the sections of the peninsula covered with basaltic lavas and also in some eastern and southern regions. Red soils, which cover most of the peninsula, are less fertile, as are patches of nutrient-deficient lateritic soils.

Climate. The Rajasthan Desert in northwestern India has a semiarid climate, but the majority of India has a tropical monsoonal climate associated with a wind reversal between summer and winter. The moisture-laden summer monsoon winds release heavy rainfall when they reach the coast or are forced to rise over mountains; summers (mid-June to mid-September) are accordingly wet and hot, with temperatures between 27° and 32° C (81° and 90° F). Winter in India (mid-December to mid-March) is predominantly dry and cool, with temperatures averaging 21° C (70° F). Before the summer rains, a hot and dry premonsoonal season lasts from mid-March to mid-June and is associated with temperatures between 38° and 43° C (100° and 110° F). A transitional postmonsoonal season occurs as the monsoons retreat (mid-September to mid-December) and is associated with light and sporadic rainfall and temperatures around 25° C (77° F). Cooler, more temperate conditions prevail in the Himalayas and decrease with altitude.

Precipitation ranges from almost zero in the THAR desert to 10,870 mm (428 in) annually in the Shillong Plateau, which is one of the wettest places in the world. Rainfall is generally heaviest in coastal and highland ar-

eas and diminishes inland. Amounts vary widely from year to year, especially inland, and dry years often cause widespread crop failures.

Drainage. The principal river in India is the GANGES (Ganga), which rises in the Himalayas and flows across the Northern Plains in a broad, meandering course to reach the sea at the Bay of Bengal. The major tributaries of the Ganges are the BRAHMAPUTRA, which joins the Ganges near its mouth in Bangladesh, and the YAMUNA, Gogra, Gandak, and Kosi rivers. In northern India the major drainage basin is that of the INDUS River; although most of this basin lies in Pakistan, the headwaters of the Indus and two of its major tributaries, the SUTLEJ and the Beas, are partly in India and are used heavily for irrigation. The principal rivers of Peninsular India are the Chambal, Son, Mahanadi, Godavary, Krishna, Cauveri, Narmada, and Tapi. Principal lakes include the Chilka, Kolleru, Pulicat, Lonar, Pushkar, and Wular. A coastal swamp, the Sundarban, fringes the Ganges delta. The Rann of Kutch is a saline swamp in northwestern India and southern Pakistan.

The annual regime of river flow in India is controlled by climatic conditions. Rivers flowing from the Himalayas experience two high-water seasons, one in early summer caused by snow melt in the mountains, and one in late summer caused by runoff from monsoonal rains. Other rivers experience high waters only during the monsoon, followed by periods of diminished flow, when many of the smaller rivers run dry. To counteract this marked periodicity of river flow, groundwater wells and tube wells are widely used for irrigation in the Northern Plains and peninsular delta regions; and many dams have been built on the major rivers.

Vegetation and Animal Life. Seven vegetation regions are found in continental India, although the natural cover has been modified by several millennia of human occupation. In the western Himalayas vegetation changes with altitude from temperate deciduous forests at low elevations through coniferous forests to Alpine vegetation above the tree line. The eastern Himalayas have more extensive deciduous forest cover. In northeastern India, east of Bangladesh, vegetation cover ranges from tropical evergreen in the wet lowlands to temperate deciduous forest in drier and cooler areas. The semiarid Punjab-Rajasthan-Gujarat region mainly supports scrub vegetation cover. In the heavily cultivated Ganges Plain, islands of deciduous trees and tuft grasses remain among the agricultural fields. The peninsular uplands support tropical monsoonal deciduous and scrub forest, while the wetter slopes of the Western Ghats support a tropical monsoonal deciduous forest, with an evergreen cover in some areas.

India's fauna includes about 500 species of mammals and more than 2,000 species of birds. The elephant, Indian bison, rhinoceros, and tiger live mainly in the wet, forested regions; the Himalayan markhor (ibex) and lion live in the Gir forest. Seven national parks and many wildlife sanctuaries and zoological parks are concerned with conservation.

Resources. India has a rich and varied mineral-resource base. Coal and iron ore are abundant in the Chota

Calcutta's Jain temple (above) *provides a peaceful refuge from the teeming streets* (left) *of India's largest city, a metropolis of more than 10 million people.*

Nagpur Plateau in the eastern peninsula. Manganese, lignite, copper, bauxite, kyanite, fire clays, mica, and limestone are found in large quantities. Some petroleum occurs offshore from Bombay and in Assam and Gujarat.

India also has vast land resources. Of the total land area, 20.5% is under forest; 41.6% is sown with crops; 7.6% is left fallow; 3.9% is in permanent pasture; and 1.5% supports permanent crops such as tea and fruit trees. Irrigation is of great importance to Indian farmers. India has the potential to irrigate 1.07 million km^2 (410,000 mi^2), but only 43% of this land is currently irrigated.

People

India has one of the world's most diverse populations, with most of the major races represented. Over thousands of years countless groups have migrated into the subcontinent, and many of these groups have maintained distinctive cultures down through the ages. India's tribal peoples and the large number of later migrant groups represent a wide variety of physical types and cultural traditions.

The earliest Indians may have migrated from Australia and the South Pacific islands. Most subsequent invading groups, however, entered the subcontinent through the mountain passes in the northwest. A great deal of ethnic, racial, and cultural intermingling occurred during these successive waves of migration, contributing directly to the pluralistic nature of modern Indian society. Except in the case of isolated tribal groups, linguistic and cultural practices have become far more important bases of classification than racial criteria.

Languages. More than 200 languages are spoken in India. Four major language groups are represented. The most important of these are the Indo-Aryan branch (see INDO-IRANIAN LANGUAGES) of the Indo-European group (the major linguistic family of Europe) and the DRAVIDIAN LANGUAGE group. Hindi, the fourth most widely spoken language in the world, is the language of 30% of the population and the official language of India. Hindi and the other Indo-Aryan languages—including Assamese, Bengali, Gujarati, Kashmiri, Marathi, Oriya, Punjabi, and Urdu—are spoken mainly in the northern part of the country and derive their script from ancient Sanskrit, which is no longer a spoken language. The leading Dravidian languages—Tamil, Telugu, Malayalam, and Kannada—are spoken in four southern states. SINO-TIBETAN and Austroasiatic (see SOUTHEAST ASIAN LANGUAGES) languages generally survive only in small and isolated regions.

India's state boundaries are drawn largely along linguistic lines, and the constitution recognizes 14 regional languages in addition to Hindi and English. English, although spoken by only about 3% of the population, remains important in government, education, and science.

Religion. India is the birthplace of HINDUISM, BUDDHISM, JAINISM, and Sikhism (see SIKHS). Today, it is a secular state, and its constitution guarantees religious tolerance. Hindus constitute about 83% of the population. Another 11% are followers of ISLAM, making India one of the four largest Muslim nations in the world. Christians and Sikhs each make up about 2% of the population, and Jains and Buddhists less than 1%. Aside from the Sikh concentration in the Punjab and PARSIS (who practice ZOROASTRIANISM) in the Bombay area, there is no marked regional distribution of religious groups.

The Indian CASTE system, an important facet of Hinduism, is a major social system that groups people according to birth. Although caste should not be confused with class, lower caste groups do perform much of the manual labor and fill most unskilled jobs in the economy. Harijans, formerly known as UNTOUCHABLES, have traditionally occupied the lowest rung of the social ladder. The Indian constitution prohibits discrimination on the basis of caste and reserves special quotas for Harijans (some 15% of the population) and tribal peoples (7%).

Demography. India, the second most populous nation in the world after China, will have more than a billion inhabitants before the end of the 20th century. The population doubled from the late 1940s to the late 1980s and continues to increase by nearly 15 million a year. Although the birthrate has stabilized, it remains high, and better health care has increased life expectancy.

Most of India's people live in more than 500,000 villages where the major source of livelihood is agriculture. As a result of a British policy that encouraged migration from urban to rural areas, India is more rural today than it was during the height of the Mogul empire. During the colonial period new cities based on trade became the largest cities in India. These newer cities include, in order of population, CALCUTTA, BOMBAY, Delhi (see NEW DELHI), and MADRAS. Other cities with populations exceeding one million are BANGALORE, HYDERABAD, AHMADABAD, KANPUR, NAGPUR, and POONA (Pune).

Education and Health. India's literacy rate more than doubled between 1950 and 1990. Literacy is higher among men than among women; it is also much higher in urban areas than in rural ones. Education is the responsibility of both the central and state governments, with the national government setting major policies and the states accountable for their implementation. The education system is free and open to all children through the university level. In all but two states education is compulsory for children aged 6 to 14, although not all children are able to take advantage of this opportunity.

India has the third largest university system in the world, after the United States and the Soviet Union, with more than 3.5 million students in about 125 universities. Several of India's universities, which are generally large with clusters of affiliated colleges, operate at the highest international levels of quality. A university degree is a virtual prerequisite for most white-collar jobs and is thus highly prized. The earliest universities were established by the British at Bombay, Calcutta, and Madras in 1857.

The stately government buildings of New Delhi were designed early in the 20th century by the British architect Sir Edwin Lutyens. Delhi replaced Calcutta as the capital of British India in 1912, and it retained that status after independence in 1947.

In the past two decades major epidemic diseases such as smallpox have been eliminated, and cholera is far less widespread. Inadequate sanitation and nutrition remain major public health problems. Western medicine is practiced all over India, but advanced health care is far more available in large cities.

The Arts. Independence has been accompanied by a vigorous promotion of the arts. In the visual arts a revival of Indian folk painting has occurred, along with new interest in the traditions of the Ajanta-Ellora, Rajasthan, Deccani, Mogul, and Kangra schools of painting. Indian architecture and sculpture, with magnificent ancient and medieval traditions, are finding new expressions as Western influences are combined with the old. Traditional handicrafts are being revived for the export market. For a historic survey of Indian arts, see INDIAN ART AND ARCHITECTURE.

In the performing arts a vigorous strengthening of classical Hindustani and Karnatic music has occurred (see INDIAN MUSIC). A strong revival of folk music, dance, and drama has paralleled a rise in the popularity of Western music and dance forms, radio, and television. India has the world's largest filmmaking industry, centered in Bombay and Madras.

Economic Activity

Since independence the Indian government has attempted to pursue a mixed economic policy with features of both a free market and socialist planning. Major industries such as railroads, automobile manufacturing, and banking are government run. At the same time, many consumer-goods industries and agriculture are in private hands. Despite significant economic growth since independence, however, many of India's gains have been offset by its increasing population.

Manufacturing and Mining. Under British rule industrial growth in India was inhibited. Since independence, however, the country has achieved near industrial self-sufficiency. Today India produces most of its own chemicals, automobiles, steel, textiles, and even computers and television sets. Steel production has more than doubled since 1960. India is self-sufficient in iron and coal but is heavily dependent on foreign oil.

India's chief energy sources are coal (26%), petroleum (49%), and electricity (25%). Some 156 billion kW h of electricity were generated in 1987, which is still far short of demand. Only 65% of India's villages are electrified, and electrical outages are common in urban areas.

Agriculture. The majority of Indians earn their livelihood from the land, and agriculture accounts for about 35% of national income. About half of the land is arable, and two crops a year are normal where water and climate permit. The chief summer monsoon (*kharif*) crops are rice and millet. The major winter (*rabi*) crops are wheat and pulses. India is the world's second largest rice producer and ranks fourth in wheat production. In addition to food crops, commercial crops such as cotton, jute, sugarcane, tea, coffee, oilseeds, and tobacco are grown. India is the world's leading producer of tea and sugar. Although Indian cattle are poor producers, India is the largest Asian producer of milk and butter, as well as hides.

Bombay, on the Arabian Sea, is India's second largest city and the capital of Maharashtra state.

The so-called GREEN REVOLUTION, which introduced new seed varieties and farming techniques to increase yields, has had a major impact on Indian agriculture since 1967. Total food grain production for 1986 was 150 million metric tons (168 million U.S. tons), and India remains self-sufficient in food production despite two recent monsoon failures.

Theoretically, landlordism has been abolished, and there are ceilings on land holdings in most states. Government attempts at land reform, however, have been largely circumvented by the entrenched and politically powerful landlord class created by the British. As village agriculture becomes increasingly mechanized, more small farmers will lose their land and join the millions of landless migrants already flocking to such cities as Calcutta, Bombay, and Delhi each year in a largely unsuccessful search for employment.

Forestry and Fishing. Forestry and fishing account for only about 1.3% and 0.8% of the national income but are locally important in some states. Fish production has tripled since 1947.

Transportation and Trade. The volume of railroad and road traffic has increased greatly since independence. Inland navigable waterways are also important avenues of transportation. Air services now reach most large cities, and government-owned Air India is a regularly scheduled international airline.

Major exports include cotton goods, iron, raw jute and jute products, coffee, electrical goods, leather, handicrafts, diamonds, and chemicals. India is now the world's leading importer of rough diamonds and exporter of gem diamonds. In recent years India has also exported engineers and technicians (especially to the Middle East) and thousands of medical doctors and nurses serving in hospitals in the United States and Great Britain. The country's major imports include heavy machinery, petroleum, copper, and zinc.

Government

The constitution adopted in 1950 provides for a federal system with a parliamentary form of government. Sovereignty is shared between the central government and the states, but the national government is given far greater powers. The office of president is largely ceremonial, with real authority vested in a prime minister and council of ministers responsible to Parliament. The president, however, has constitutional authority to impose president's rule should a state government appear unable to maintain order and to declare a national state of emergency and supersede parliamentary rule. President's rule was invoked in a number of states in the 1970s and 1980s, and emergency national rule was imposed in 1975 under Prime Minister Indira GANDHI.

Parliament consists of two houses, the Rajya Sabha (Council of States) and the Lok Sabha (House of the People). Real power resides in the Lok Sabha, whose members are elected directly by all eligible voters and sit for five years unless Parliament is dissolved earlier. The INDIAN NATIONAL CONGRESS, the party most identified with the Indian nationalist movement, has maintained almost unbroken power on the national level. In addition, one family provided India's prime ministers for all but five years between 1947 and 1989.

Rice, the most important food crop of India, covers almost half of Bihar's northern alluvial plain. Although the Indian government has encouraged the modernization of agriculture, change has been slow.

Jawaharlal Nehru (left) and his daughter, Indira Gandhi (right), headed the world's most populous democracy for nearly all of the three decades following independence. Nehru, a leader of the independence movement, served as prime minister from 1947 to 1964. Mrs. Gandhi was prime minister from 1966 to 1977 and again from 1980 until her assassination in 1984. She was succeeded by her elder son, Rajiv Gandhi, prime minister until 1989.

State government resembles the federal system. The governor of each state is appointed by the president. A chief minister and a council of state hold executive authority and are responsible to the state legislative assembly.

History since 1947

The history of India as a sovereign state under its own constitutional government began on Aug. 15, 1947, when the subcontinent was partitioned into the two states of India and Pakistan. The decision to partition British India and turn over power to the new nations within a period of six months left bloody turmoil in its wake. Following independence some 17 million Hindus and Muslims were uprooted and began the long march to their respective new homelands. There were at least one million casualties in the ensuing sectarian violence despite efforts to restore calm by Mahatma GANDHI, the revered father of modern India.

Nationalist leader Jawaharlal NEHRU assumed the prime ministership in 1947 and held the post until his death in 1964. The new government integrated more than 500 princely states into the new nation and finally absorbed the last vestiges of empire in 1962 by taking over Portuguese Goa, Daman, and Diu and the French territories of Pondicherry, Karikal, Mahe, and Yanam. Nehru launched India on the path of economic self-sufficiency and won it an international role far out of proportion to its power by championing a nonaligned foreign policy that was to become the model for many newly independent nations. Territorial disputes with China escalated into a brief border war in 1962, however, and the Nehru government was unable to promote cordial rela-

tions with its new neighbor, Pakistan. The struggle for Kashmir, a northern princely state with a Hindu maharaja and a largely Muslim population, led to the first (1947–49) of several armed conflicts between the two countries (see INDIA-PAKISTAN WARS).

Nehru was succeeded as prime minister by Congress party leader Lal Bahadur Shastri. In 1966, shortly after a peace treaty ending a second war with Pakistan over Kashmir was signed, Shastri died suddenly. Indira Gandhi, Nehru's daughter, emerged as a compromise candidate and became prime minister. Gandhi, a strong nationalist, continued to pursue the ideals of nonalignment while moving closer to the USSR, partly because of a 1954 U.S. decision to provide significant military assistance to Pakistan as part of cold-war strategy. Relations between India and the United States reached a low point in 1971, when India supported East Pakistan (now Bangladesh) in the Pakistani civil war. During Gandhi's first decade in office, agricultural production increased; India exploded (1974) its first nuclear weapon; and Sikkim became (1975) a state of India. After Gandhi's reelection in 1971, opposition leaders such as Jayaprakash Narayan accused her of corruption and misgovernment, staged protest marches, and threatened civil disobedience. In June 1975, Gandhi persuaded President Fakhruddin Ali Ahmed to invoke a state of emergency that gave her near dictatorial powers.

In March 1977, Gandhi suddenly called new elections, perhaps to legitimatize the powers she had taken under the emergency. Surprisingly, a coalition of parties ranging in ideology from socialists to conservative Hindus (the Janata party) won control of the Lok Sabha. Morarji

DESAI, a long-time opponent of Gandhi, became prime minister. President Ahmed died that same year, and Neelam Sanjavi Reddy was elected president. The Janata party almost immediately began to break apart, and Desai resigned as prime minister in July 1979. His successor, Charan Singh, resigned in August but headed a caretaker government until January 1980, when new elections returned Gandhi to power.

In 1982, Zail Singh was elected president, the first Sikh to serve in that office. His election occurred at a time when radical Sikh youths were attempting to win a separate Sikh state (Khalistan) in Punjab. Several years of Sikh violence culminated in the invasion of the Golden Temple at AMRITSAR by Indian troops in June 1984 and the assassination of Gandhi by her own Sikh bodyguards on Oct. 31, 1984. As the government tried to respond to the growing political crisis in Punjab, Gandhi's formerly apolitical older son, Rajiv GANDHI, was thrust into the prime ministership.

The youthful Gandhi had an auspicious beginning. His party won the December 1984 general elections by a landslide. In 1987, Ramaswami Venkataraman was elected president of India, and the country celebrated its 40th anniversary of independence. Allegations of corruption involving some of Gandhi's close associates began to grow, however, and bad monsoon years in 1987 and 1988 caused India's worst drought of the century. Gandhi's sending of peacekeeping forces to Sri Lanka in 1987 and his decision to intervene militarily to foil a coup in Maldives in 1988 were criticized by some of his neighbors. Violence by Sikh separatists continued, and ethnic groups in other parts of India were also calling for greater autonomy. Despite the central government's acquiescence in creating the new ethnic states of Nagaland and Mizoram in the northeast and a 1988 peace accord with rebels in Tripura, demands for greater cultural and ethnic political power persisted in that area. The Gurkhas of Darjeeling district won local autonomy in 1988. Tribal peoples in northeastern India were agitating for the creation of a new state of "Jharkaland," and their protest was having repercussions in Bihar, Orissa, and West Bengal. Citizens of Tamil Nadu also called for more autonomy, while tribal groups in Assam fought migrants from Bangladesh, and an often violent economic struggle between landlords and lower castes had been building for years in Andhra Pradesh and Bihar. In general the nationalistic feeling of the independence movement seemed to be giving way to communal, religious, and caste divisions.

In the November 1989 elections Congress-I decisively lost its parliamentary majority, Gandhi resigned, and the National Front, led by V. P. SINGH, formed a minority government. In regional affairs a Muslim insurgency in Jammu and Kashmir raised fears of renewed conflict between Pakistan and India. At home the coalition government was weakened by internal power struggles and communal violence. Singh resigned in November 1990, and his successor, Janata Dal dissident Chandra Shekhar, resigned in March 1991. In the midst of national elections held in May 1991, Rajiv Gandhi was assassinated.

India, history of
India, history of   This article treats the history of the Indian subcontinent before its mid-20th-century political division into the independent nations of India, Pakistan, and Bangladesh. For postindependence history, see INDIA; PAKISTAN; and BANGLADESH.

Ancient India

Because the Indian subcontinent is one of great geographical diversity, it is not surprising that at least two distinct cultures developed in ancient India. Archaeological evidence suggests that humans first migrated to the subcontinent between 400,000 and 200,000 years ago. Some of these primitive peoples probably crossed the Hindu Kush Mountains into the area that is now northern Pakistan. Others possibly sailed to southern India from regions in eastern Africa.

Indus Civilization. One of the world's oldest and greatest civilizations took shape between about 3000 and 2500 BC in the valley of the Indus River. Sites of this INDUS CIVILIZATION at Harappa and Mohenjo-daro—both in present-day Pakistan—have been extensively excavated; other sites have been uncovered in India as far east as the cities of Simla and Bikaner and as far south as the Kathiawar Peninsula and the coast of the Gujarat region. The Indus, or Harappa, civilization, one of the most advanced of ancient times, was similar in many ways to contemporary cultures in Mesopotamia.

Aryan Culture. Harappa culture thrived until about 1500 BC, when the Indus Valley was overrun by ARYAN invaders from the Iranian plateau. The seminomadic Aryans spoke an archaic form of Sanskrit (see INDO-IRANIAN LANGUAGES) and left no remains of cities, burials, arts, or crafts. What is known about the Aryans has been passed down through religious texts called the VEDAS, which describe a highly ritualistic worship with innumerable deities, a rich mythology, and an elaborate fire sacrifice. They also mention the system of *varnas*, or classes, from which evolved the CASTE system. The four *varnas* were the BRAHMINS (also known as Brahmans), or priests; the Kshatriya, political rulers or warriors; Vaishya, traders and cultivators; and Shudra, artisans. The Vedas and the caste system remain central to the Indian socioreligious system, HINDUISM. Thus the Aryans gave to India many of its basic institutions and cultural habits.

Early Cultural Cleavages. According to one theory, the Aryans, a warlike people who rode on horseback, pushed southward many of northern India's darker-skinned and shorter inhabitants, whom they called *dasas*. This theory, yet to be proven, is sometimes used to explain the origins of the division between the Aryan linguistic groups in the North and the DRAVIDIAN LANGUAGES of the South. Aryan religious texts indicate that the Aryans viewed themselves as racially and culturally superior and despised the *dasas*, who probably performed many of the unpleasant but necessary tasks in the segmented society that was developing under Aryan influence.

Challenges to Brahmin Ascendancy. Over the centuries pre-Aryan and Aryan cultures gradually fused in northern India as the Aryans expanded slowly eastward into the

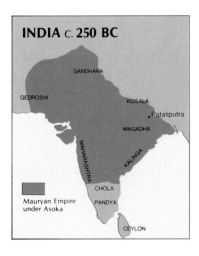

INDIA c. **250 BC**

GANDHARA
GEDROSIA
KOSALA
• Pataliputra
MAGADHA
MAHARASHTRA
KALINGA
CHOLA
PANDYA
CEYLON

Mauryan Empire
under Asoka

(Right) *This 1st-century BC Buddhist stupa, or shrine, at Sanchi was influenced by the architectural style developed during the reign of Asoka, who advocated the spread of Buddhism.*

(Left) *This map illustrates India's Mauryan Empire at its height, under the ruler Asoka (r. 273–232 BC).*

Gangetic plain, where the second of ancient India's great urban civilizations developed. In the Bihar region in the 6th century BC a wealthy merchant class began to support speculation challenging orthodox beliefs. For example, that era's UPANISHADS (scriptural texts that were part of the Vedas but attempted to go beyond them) began to challenge the traditional authority of the Brahmins. In the northeast, where Aryan influence was relatively weak, the religious systems known as JAINISM and BUDDHISM were founded around 500 BC. Both were widely supported by the merchant and landowning aristocracies of eastern India, and both can be viewed in part as revolts against Brahmanism (see BRAHMA AND BRAHMAN).

Maurya and Gupta Periods. In 326 BC, ALEXANDER THE GREAT, with his Macedonian army, invaded the Indus Valley. The subcontinent was still politically fragmented, and no Indian ruler was able to assemble a force powerful enough to stop Alexander's armies, but the vastness of the subcontinent and the discontent of his troops convinced the king to retreat.

In c.321 BC, shortly after Alexander's invasion, the great king CHANDRAGUPTA MAURYA (founder of the MAURYA dynasty) established India's first large empire, centered at Pataliputra. His grandson ASOKA ruled an empire that extended to the south of central India's Deccan Plateau and west into Baluchistan and modern Afghanistan; in the east it included the state of Kalinga, which he had conquered c.261. Asoka also attempted to create a state religion incorporating Buddhism and other faiths as well as Hinduism. A convert to Buddhism, he sent Buddhist missionaries abroad and is credited with elevating Buddhism to a world religion. Under the Mauryas and succeeding dynasties, for a period of about 800 years, India evolved a civilization that still remains fairly intact. The institution of caste was solidly implanted, and Hindu philosophy and legal codes were developed.

The era of the GUPTA dynasty (AD c.320–c.540) is generally considered to be ancient India's classic period. Indic architecture, sculpture, painting, dance, and music flourished during this time.

Medieval India

After the brilliance of the Gupta dynasty, India entered its medieval period, becoming divided politically into a number of small kingdoms. This period, which was characterized by many invasions and large-scale migrations from the northwest, was one of relative isolation from the more advanced civilizations of the Arabs and Chinese. It continued until the founding of the Mogul Empire in the 16th century.

Among the smaller states that appeared in India in the confusion of the 7th, 8th, and 9th centuries were the military aristocracies of the RAJPUTS in northern and central India. Racially, culturally, and linguistically distinct Dravidian kingdoms also flourished in southern India, where they are known to have existed from at least the 1st century BC. Most prominent were the kingdom of the Andhras, located in the areas around present-day Hyderabad, and the Tamil states of the Pandyas at the southern tip of the Indian peninsula; the Cholas, in the region that is now Madras; and the Cheras, who controlled the south-

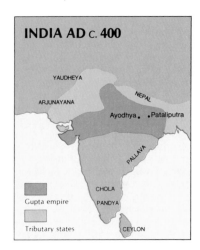

This map shows India during the Gupta Empire under the reign of Chandragupta II (r. c.380–414), who expanded his family's kingdom into a vast domain. During the reign of the Guptas—recognized as India's classical period—northern India was economically prosperous and the arts flourished.

INDIA AD c. **400**

YAUDHEYA
ARJUNAYANA
NEPAL
Ayodhya • • Pataliputra
PALLAVA
CHOLA
PANDYA
CEYLON

Gupta empire

Tributary states

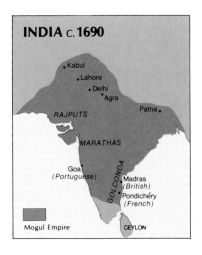

INDIA c. 1690

Kabul
Lahore
Delhi
Agra
RAJPUTS
Patna
MARATHAS
Goa
(Portuguese)
Madras
(British)
GOLCONDA
Pondichéry
(French)
Mogul Empire
CEYLON

The vast Mogul Empire expanded to include the entire Indian subcontinent except for the southern tip. At the same time that the Moguls, a Muslim people, were gaining imperial control, European merchants were establishing trading settlements along the coasts of India.

western coast. From these local kingdoms many Indian ideas and practices spread to Indonesia and other parts of Southeast Asia. The Pallava dynasty, which played a dominant role in southeast India from the 6th to the 8th century, was most likely Brahman and northern Indian in origin. Through the Pallavas, elements of Indo-Aryan Sanskritic culture were widely introduced into southern India.

Despite the fundamental unity of Indic civilization, political diversity was the rule during the medieval period. Units of government were of all sizes and types and boundaries were constantly in flux. A tradition of relative autonomy for villages helped preserve much of the stability that might otherwise have been lost in the confusion of changing boundaries and sovereigns. Cultural unity was encouraged by shrines and pilgrimage sites throughout the subcontinent, by a great body of Sanskrit oral tradition and myth, and by cooperation between Brahman religious and political leaders. The ability of Hinduism to accommodate new peoples and ideas without conceding anything fundamental to them also helped to promote civilizational continuity.

Islamic Influence

Islam first entered the Indian subcontinent in AD 711, when a young Arabian general, Muhammad ibn Qasim, fought his way into the Indus Valley. The state of Sind was added to the Arab caliphate and its people converted to Islam. In the 9th and 10th centuries, Arab traders began to convert many Hindus in port cities along the southwest coast.

The chief Muslim conquerors of India were not Arabs, however, but central Asian converts to Islam—Turks, Afghans, Persians, and Mongols—who began to enter the subcontinent around 1000. MAHMUD OF GHAZNI led (998–1030) a series of raids into the Punjab region from what is now Afghanistan, securing for the Muslims a gateway into the Indian subcontinent. The Muslims eventually converted many low-caste Hindus and Buddhists—particularly in Bengal and other eastern areas—as they

Akbar, third emperor of the Mogul dynasty, conducted military campaigns to extend his control of India. This 17th-century painting portrays his siege of Chitor, a Rajput fortress.

pushed across India. Many converts hoped that they would become part of a more egalitarian society and gain the protection of the invading armies.

The Delhi Sultanate. The first Muslim empire based in India was established in Delhi in 1206 by Qutb-ud-Din Aybak (d. 1210). This DELHI SULTANATE, a constantly expanding and contracting empire, was ruled by a line of 34 succeeding sultans. The sultanate was divided among five dynasties (the "Slave" kings, the Khaljis, the Tughluqs, the Sayyids, and the Lodis). During the Tughlug dynasty, TIMUR, the great conqueror from Samarkand, desolated (1398–99) the entire sultanate. Under the Lodi kingdom, which endured until 1526, the Delhi Sultanate stretched from the Punjab in the west to the Bihar region in the east.

Mogul Empire. The first ruler of the MOGUL dynasty was BABUR, who claimed the subcontinent as his right of inheritance because of the conquest of Delhi by his ancestor Timur. Babur (r. 1526–30), a highly cultured man from Persia, established the most glorious empire in India's history. Babur's son HUMAYUN reigned from 1530 to 1540 and again in 1555–56.

Until 1707 a series of able emperors expanded and added to the glory of the Moguls, each in his own way. The greatest of the Moguls was AKBAR (r. 1556–1605), who built the administrative machinery that forms the basis for many present-day practices in India. A tolerant man, Akbar did much to combine Hindu and Muslim motifs in palace architecture, art, literature, and music.

Akbar's son and successor, JAHANGIR, reveled in luxurious living, as did Jahangir's son SHAH JAHAN. Best known for his great building program, which culminated in the TAJ MAHAL, Shah Jahan was also instrumental in extending the Mogul Empire to the Deccan Plateau. Both Shah Jahan and his son and successor AURANGZEB were much less tolerant of Hindus than their predecessors had been. After the death (1707) of Aurangzeb, the Mogul Empire disintegrated quickly, although ineffective rulers remained on the throne at Delhi until 1858.

European Influence

Extensive European contact with India began in 1498 when Vasco da GAMA, a Portuguese navigator, landed at Calicut, on the southwest coast. Both the Portuguese and the Dutch attempted to colonize India during the 16th century, but neither proved strong enough to rival the British and French. The Portuguese, who were further handicapped by their heavy-handed policy of trying to convert Indians to Christianity by force, ended up with only a few small outposts in India, the most prominent of these being GOA on the western coast. The more tolerant Dutch concentrated on building a trading monopoly, through their Dutch East India Company (see EAST INDIA COMPANY, DUTCH). By the mid-17th century, however, they had focused their attention on Indonesia.

The British empire in India was established by a private trading firm, the East India Company (founded 1600; see EAST INDIA COMPANY, BRITISH), which governed with the consent of Parliament until 1858. The company bought a strip of sandy beach at Madras in 1639, acquired a lease to the port of Bombay from King Charles II in 1668, and in 1690 secured from the Mogul emperor Aurangzeb permission to build a settlement on a muddy flatland that eventually became Calcutta. At each of these the company erected a fort, known as a factory, from which the British conducted their trading activities.

The government-run French East India Company (established in 1664; see EAST INDIA COMPANY, FRENCH) never fostered a trade volume comparable to that of the British. In the 18th century both Britain and France sought to protect their trading interests by allying with native princes as the Mogul Empire disintegrated. As part of the War of the AUSTRIAN SUCCESSION, the two European powers came into conflict in India in 1746, when the French, under Joseph François DUPLEIX, seized Madras. However, in 1761, during the SEVEN YEARS' WAR, the French surrendered their territory of PONDICHERRY to the British, and after the 1763 peace treaty the French retained only a

few trading centers in India.

The hero of Britain's battles against the French was Robert CLIVE, whose greatest triumph came at the Battle of Plassey (1757), when he and 950 other Europeans combined with some 2,000 Indian soldiers (sepoys) to defeat a force of more than 50,000 led by a degenerate local Mogul nawab (provincial governor). Victory at Plassey led to effective political control over the vast riches of the Ganges Valley in 1765, when the nawab surrendered to Clive the right to collect land revenue for most of eastern India.

Some of the directors of the British East India Company initially demurred at the prospect of governing the eastern region, Bengal. To counter growing corruption and to reform the governance of India, Parliament passed the Regulating Act of 1773. Warren HASTINGS, governor of Bengal in 1772–73, helped to lay the administrative foundations for British rule under the provisions of this act. As India's first governor-general (1773–85), Hastings consolidated many of Clive's territorial gains. He attempted to assert the British right to interfere in the affairs of the MARATHAS, who became the leading rivals to the British after the virtual collapse of the Mogul Empire. He

The map shows the gradual British annexation of Indian territories. British expansionist plocies and insensitiviity to Indian traditions were major causes of the Indian Mutiny of 1857-58. After this revolt was suppressed, the British crown assumed governmental control from the East India Company.

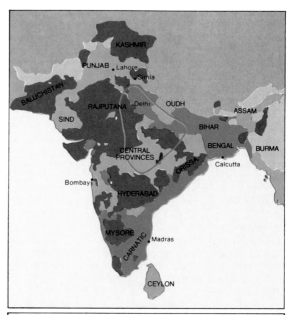

INDIA UNDER BRITISH RULE

British possessions 1805	Dependent Indian states by 1914
British acquisitions by 1858	Area of Mutiny 1857
British acquisitions by 1914	

successfully met the challenge presented by the state of Mysore and its leaders HYDER ALI and his son TIPPU SULTAN in the early 1780s.

British India

Lord CORNWALLIS, governor-general of India from 1786 to 1793, established the administrative, legal, and land-revenue codes that made British rule possible. Because of his belief that considerable corruption stemmed from contact with Indians, Cornwallis excluded people of Indian origin from higher posts of government. This policy led, during the 19th century, to a widening socioeconomic gap between the British and their Indian subjects, with British settlements taking on the character of prosperous English towns in the midst of increasingly squalid Indian slums. Poverty was encouraged by a rapid spurt in population growth that followed the establishment of peace and the adoption of public-health measures throughout the subcontinent, in addition to British unwillingness to allow large-scale industrialization within India.

Lord WELLESLEY, governor-general from 1798 to 1805, launched a policy of expansion, which culminated in the mid-19th century—when the East India Company controlled more than 60% of India, with the remaining 40% or so being run by 562 local princes who were clearly subordinates of the British raj (government). British insensitivity to Indian traditions and religious practices helped to increase tensions. Among the Indian elites resentment of British rule grew, especially during the regime (1848–56) of Lord DALHOUSIE, who attempted to modernize and westernize India. In 1857 many traditional groups, largely in north India, revolted, led by mutineers in the army. This violent and brutal INDIAN MUTINY, or Sepoy Rebellion, was put down by the British in 1858. As a direct result of the revolt, the crown took over most of the functions of the British East India Company.

The Indian Nationalist Movement

Indian nationalist sentiments found expression early in the 19th century in the writings of Rammohun Roy, a religious reformer who hoped that a modern state of India would combine the best of both Hindu and western cultures. The first organizations attempting to reform British rule were also formed early in the century. In 1885 they were welded together in the INDIAN NATIONAL CONGRESS. The Congress was originally an elitist and moderate constitutional lobby. Early in the 20th century the British made some attempts to meet its demands by widening Indian political participation. However, the extreme wing of the Congress increasingly demanded swaraj (complete independence). By 1907 the organization had split into a moderate group and a militant faction. At about the same time (1906) Muslim leaders, dissatisfied with Hindu dominance of the Congress, formed their own nationalist organization, the MUSLIM LEAGUE.

Although India's nationalist groups united temporarily in 1916 in support of Britain's World War I effort, the increasingly dominant militants were disappointed in Britain's gradual approach to self-rule for India. British prestige fell precipitously in 1919 with the passage of laws

Early in the 20th century Indian nationalist groups engaged in various campaigns to reform British rule. A militant faction was responsible for this 1913 bombing attempt on the life of British viceroy Lord Harding.

restricting political activity and with the massacre of Indian civilians by British troops at AMRITSAR. During the 1920s the Congress acquired a mass base, the support of prominent Indians, and increasing militancy under the leadership of Mahatma GANDHI, who introduced the highly successful techniques of passive resistance (satyagraha) and civil disobedience. By the end of the 1920s, however, Muslim leaders such as Muhammad IQBAL were proposing the creation of a separate Muslim state.

During World War II the Muslims, led by Muhammad Ali JINNAH, supported the British. The Congress, however, insisted that Britain leave. When Indians refused to cooperate in repelling the Japanese attack on the subcontinent in 1942, Britain arrested many leaders and outlawed the Congress. A group of extreme anti-British Indian nationalists led by Subhas Chandra BOSE even fought on the Japanese side in Burma and India.

The photograph shows Jawaharlal Nehru and Mahatma Gandhi at the All-India Congress Committee at which the "Quit India" resolution was adopted (Aug. 7, 1942.)

At the end of the war Britain agreed to self-rule for India. However, in the 1946 elections the Muslim League won most of the Muslim vote, and Gandhi was unsuccessful in preventing the partition of the subcontinent into Muslim and Hindu states. In August 1947, India and Pakistan achieved independence. Five months later Gandhi was assassinated by a Hindu fanatic. The task of governing India fell to its first prime minister, Jawaharlal NEHRU. Jinnah became governor-general of the Muslim nation of Pakistan, which was then comprised of two separate territories, East Pakistan (which became Bangladesh in 1971) and West Pakistan (now Pakistan).

India-Pakistan Wars   India and Pakistan have fought three major wars with each other since the partition of the Indian subcontinent in 1947. The first conflict was over KASHMIR in 1947–49. With independence and partition, the subcontinent's numerous princely states faced the choice of joining either Hindu India or Muslim Pakistan. Contiguous to both India and West Pakistan, Kashmir was ruled by a Hindu prince, but the majority of its population was Muslim. In 1947, Pakistani tribesmen invaded the state in support of an uprising by Muslim peasants. The maharaja fled to Delhi, where he signed papers giving Kashmir to India. Indian troops were then flown in to defend the former princely state, bringing the Pakistani army into the fray. Fighting continued in Kashmir until a United Nations commission arranged a truce in January 1949. Kashmir was then divided along the cease-fire line, with India holding about two-thirds and Pakistan the remainder. India referred the case to the UN Security Council, which has heard conflicting claims intermittently ever since; periodic fighting has broken the uneasy peace.

In April 1965 sharp fighting broke out in the Rann of Kutch, on the border between West Pakistan and India, and later spread to Kashmir and to the Punjab. India charged that Pakistani infiltrators were again invading Kashmir while Pakistan claimed that the invaders were Kashmiri freedom fighters. India seized army posts on the Pakistan side of their common border in Kashmir; Pakistan countered with tanks secured as military aid from the United States; and India dispatched planes to destroy the tanks. When Pakistan unleashed its air force—trained by the United States—and each side launched a large-scale land invasion of the other's territory in September 1965, the United Nations again intervened to bring about a cease-fire. Direct confrontation between the troops ended in January 1966, shortly after an agreement between India and Pakistan had been reached at Tashkent, USSR, through Soviet mediation.

Although neither the 1948 nor the 1965 war was conclusive, India demonstrated unquestioned military superiority over Pakistan in the third war, in December 1971, when India intervened in the civil war that had erupted between West and East Pakistan. This facilitated the secession of the latter, which became the independent state of Bangladesh. The Pakistani army and air force were severely crippled in this war.

Indian Affairs, Bureau of   The Bureau of Indian Affairs (BIA), formerly known as the Office of Indian Affairs, the Indian Department, and the Indian Service, is an agency of the U.S. Department of the Interior set up to handle Indian affairs in the nation. It is directed by the Interior Department's assistant secretary of Indian affairs, who is appointed by the president. The BIA has eight area offices that supervise its programs on reservations and in other Indian communities. Education, social services, law enforcement, mineral and water rights, and land leasing are important caretaking responsibilities assumed by the BIA on some reservations. On other reservations, these functions are now entirely or in part administered by tribal governments.

The bureau, created (1824) within the War Department, was transferred by Congress to the newly created Department of the Interior in 1849. When Indian lands west of the Mississippi were opened for white settlement in the 1850s, the bureau set aside Indian reservations and established treaties with individual tribal nations. Native Americans, however, had little or no voice in the early formulation of BIA policy and for much of its history the bureau did little to protect Indian interests. The AMERICAN INDIAN MOVEMENT and other Indian-rights groups staged protests against the bureau in the 1970s and demanded that it become more responsive to the needs of native Americans.

See also: INDIANS, AMERICAN.

Indian art and architecture   The artistic tradition of India is one of the oldest and richest in the world. Beginning with prehistoric rock paintings, which are believed to go back to the 6th millennium BC, the tradition spans about 8,000 years and comprises masterpieces in all major artistic media, including architecture, sculpture, painting, metalwork, textiles, and ceramics. The true genius of the Indian artists has manifested itself most fully in sculpture. The outstanding works of classical GUPTA and medieval sculpture are rightly regarded as supreme achievements of world art.

The most important influences on traditional Indian art were the religious ideas and institutions that inspired it—not only BUDDHISM, HINDUISM, and ISLAM, but also other cults such as JAINISM, TANTRA, and primitive fertility cults. Icons have always played such an important part in religious worship in India.

The other major influence was the extensive patronage of the arts by the various rulers and dynasties that controlled India. The Mauryan emperor ASOKA and the Kushan ruler Kanishka played a major role in the creation of Buddhist art, just as the Hindu kings sponsored the great temples of medieval times and the Mogul rulers commissioned the splendid palaces, mosques, and tombs of the Islamic period.

Art of the Indus Civilization.   The earliest artistic tradition developed in the Indus Valley, with its centers in Mohenjo-daro and Harappa, both located in present-day Pakistan. The INDUS CIVILIZATION flourished between about

The caves of Ajanta in west central India are temples and chambers carved out of rock, containing some of the finest examples of Buddhist painting and sculpture. Much of this work was executed during the Gupta period (AD c.300–600), marking the culmination of India's Buddhist art.

2500 and 1500 BC. Its most notable artistic achievements are the numerous sculptures that, although small in scale, often display superb craftsmanship. They usually represent human figures or animals and were probably religious in character. Remarkable artifacts from Mohenjo-daro include the lithe, gracefully posed copper figure of a dancing girl (National Museum, New Delhi) and the more hieratic alabaster bust of a king-priest (National Museum of Pakistan, Karachi). Steatite seals engraved with animals and inscriptions in a yet unidentified language resemble seals found in ancient Mesopotamia, which suggests possible connections between the art of the Indus Valley and Sumer; some scholars have referred to this early art as Indo-Sumerian. Other features of the Indus seals are typically Indian and foreshadow iconographic themes and artistic motifs that later figure prominently in Hindu art—the sacred animals, the mother goddess, the cult of the phallus.

Early Buddhist Art. During the middle of the 2d millennium BC, India was invaded by ARYAN nomads who destroyed Mohenjo-daro and Harappa and brought an end to the Indus civilization. The resurgence of Indian art did not occur until the 3d century BC under the powerful emperor Asoka the Great of the MAURYA dynasty (321–184 BC). Most of the art of this age is Buddhist, and technically and aesthetically, it owes much to Achaemenid Persia. Among the most important artistic monuments of this age are the great pillars topped with enormous lotus capitals and lions, of which the best-preserved example is at Lauriya Nandangarh in northern India, dated 242 BC. Other important examples of early Buddhist art are the sensually modeled sculptures of Yakshi (female) and Yaksha (male), deities associated with fertility and wealth, and the great STUPA shrine-mounds. In this early art the Buddha is mere-

ly symbolized by a wheel, a lotus flower, or by his throne. Not until the Kushan period (AD c.50–250) was the historic Buddha represented in human form.

Art of the Gupta Period. The culmination of the Bud-

A wall painting (AD c.600) from a vihara, or monk's cell, in Cave II at Ajanta, expresses in its serene expression and graceful proportion the spirituality and compassion of the Buddha.

This 7th-century relief of Shiva as Kala-bhairava, from Cave 29 at Ellora, typifies the vitality of sculpture in the Hindu medieval period.

dhist phase of Indian art occurred during the Gupta period (AD *c.*300–600), often called the classical period of Indian art. Unfortunately, almost nothing remains of the great temples and magnificent palaces of this period; the rock-cut cave temples at AJANTA, however, preserve a wealth of fresco-type wall paintings and sculptures. The images of the Buddha and Bodhisattvas show an artistic mastery and sophistication not present before that time.

Although the bulk of Gupta art was devoted to the worship of the Buddhist deities, Hindu artistic monuments include the Vishnu temple at Deogarh, with its impressive relief carvings, as well as the temples at Aihole,

which are among the earliest surviving religious edifices in India, and the rock-cut temples at Badami, both sponsored by the Chalukya dynasty (AD 550–642).

Hindu Medieval Art. Although Buddhist art continued to be produced in Bengal under the Pala dynasty (*c.*750–1100) and in Afghanistan, the dominant art of the medieval period of Indian history was Hindu, beginning in the 7th century and lasting, at least in the south, to the 17th century. Hindu monuments from the early medieval period include the magnificent rock carvings in the Shiva temple at ELEPHANTA and the great Kailasa temple at ELLORA, and the relief carvings and beautiful temples at MAHABALIPURAM.

This artistic development peaked about AD 1000 when huge temple complexes with towering *sikkharas* (spires) and elaborate sculptural decorations were erected all over India. The finest of these are at KHAJURAHO, in north central India, with its sensuous carvings of loving couples often shown in ecstatic embrace, symbolizing the union between the soul and the deity. The largest group of such temples is at BHUBANESWAR in Orissa, where no fewer than 1,000 sanctuaries were erected during this period. The most immense and ambitious is the Surya temple at KONARAK; the entire edifice takes the form of the giant horsedrawn sacred chariot associated with Surya the sun god. This colossal structure, begun *c.*1240, was never completed, and by the end of the 13th century the Muslim conquest put an end to Hindu art in northern India.

In the south, however, Hindu art continued to flourish. The huge gateways, or *gopurams*, that are covered with innumerable carvings representing the gods and goddesses and the multitude of sacred beings of the Hindu pantheon are a distinctive feature of 17th-century Madura-

The exquisite Taj Mahal (begun 1628) exemplifies the architecture produced under Islamic influence, which reached its highest expression under the Moguls.

style architecture. The other great artistic achievement of southern India is represented in the often voluptuously shaped bronze images of Hindu deities. Those made under the Chola dynasty between the 10th and 13th centuries are considered outstanding, particularly the powerful representations of SHIVA as Nataraja, the Lord of Dance.

Islamic Art of India. A very different artistic tradition, largely based on Persian and Turkish prototypes, came into existence during the 12th century, when much of northern India was conquered by Muslim invaders. Because Islam forbade the making of images, sculpture—which had been the dominant art form—declined, and architecture became the most important form of artistic expression. The first of the great edifices devoted to this faith was the Quwwat ul-Islam, or Might of Islam MOSQUE, erected (AD 1199) on the site of a Hindu temple in Delhi. Its most impressive remaining structure is the Qutb Minar, a tall MINARET.

The culmination of Indo-Islamic art occurred under the Mogul dynasty (see MOGULS), which came to power during the 16th century and ruled much of India until the British took control. It was under Mogul patronage that such architectural masterpieces as the TAJ MAHAL (begun 1628) in Agra and the great Friday mosque in Delhi were erected. Other forms of artistic expression that flourished under the Moguls were miniature painting and decorative arts, notably the making of carpets, textiles, and metalwork as well as wood, ivory, and jade carving. (See MOGUL ART AND ARCHITECTURE.)

Indian Miniature Painting. The earliest Indian miniature paintings date from the 11th century and appeared in the form of palm-leaf manuscripts illuminated with scenes from Buddhist texts. Another school, dating from a somewhat later period, was Jain in inspiration and flourished in the Gujarat region of western India. A third miniature tradition, derived from Persian sources, existed at the Mogul courts; its style was far more realistic and depicted secular themes.

Out of these various traditions evolved a new school of painting known as Rajput, because its most important centers were in Rajputana (central India). Rajput painting flourished from about 1500 to 1800. The subjects were largely Hindu; frequently illustrated were scenes from the life of the divine cowherd KRISHNA and his love for Radha. Other favorite subjects were legendary epics and the ragamalas, or musical modes. Executed in opaque pigments on paper, these pictures display striking combinations of warm, vibrant colors, which frequently carry symbolic value. The Pahari school of miniature painting, centered in the courts of the local Hindu rulers in the foothills of the Himalayas, combined elements of Rajput painting with others taken from the Mogul tradition. This school, at its best during the 18th century, continued to flourish until the middle of the 19th century.

Indian Art of the Modern Period. By the end of the 18th century both the Hindu and Mogul artistic traditions had spent themselves. By about 1850 even the Pahari school had lost its vitality. At the same time European art and artistic ideas had been introduced. Only on a folk level did traditional Indian art continue in the rural villages.

This miniature (1770) of Vishnu and his beloved on the back of his mount Garuda displays the brilliant and symbolic color characteristic of Rajput painting. (Victoria and Albert Museum, London.)

The first person to foster an integration of Indian traditions with Western styles of painting was an Englishman, E. B. Havell (1861–1934). As head of the Calcutta School of Art, he decided to base the instruction on traditional Indian models, notably the wall paintings at Ajanta and the Mogul miniatures. Although his attempts at reviving the older schools did not succeed, his ideas and writings were of great influence and helped spur the rebirth of Indian art during the 20th century. Basing their art on modern Western art and Indian folk art, such painters as Amrita Sher-Gil, Jamini Roy, and M. F. Husain have produced works that combine truly Indian qualities with the ideals of modern art. Since independence, a more abstract artistic idiom has been dominant, which nonetheless preserves much of the traditional Indian aesthetic sensibility.

Indian languages, American At the time of first European contact, probably close to 1,000 American Indian languages were spoken in North, Central, and South America. Although the number of languages in daily use has steadily declined because of persecution and pressures on the Indians to adopt Western languages and culture, more than 700 different American Indian—or, as they are sometimes called, Amerindian—languages are spoken today.

Scientific Study

American Indian languages have long been a source of fascination for both scholars and laypersons. The only transcriptions of many now-extinct languages were made by interested soldiers and explorers untrained in phonetic science; in areas of Spanish domination, the careful records of Catholic missionaries provide invaluable documentation of the way indigenous languages were spoken as many as 400 years ago.

In the United States many of the most famous linguists of the early 20th century—among them Leonard BLOOMFIELD, Franz BOAS, and Edward SAPIR—transcribed and analyzed North American Indian languages. Many descriptions of Indian languages are important in the literature of the linguistic school known as American structuralism. Today Americanists, as those who study the languages are called, hold regular scientific meetings and congresses to report on their investigations. Current research on the native languages of the Americas is published in several periodicals, notably the *International Journal of American Linguistics*.

Origins and Classification

Most scholars believe that the aboriginal inhabitants of North, Central, and South America migrated from Asia many thousands of years ago. Acceptance of this theory has led some to hypothesize that all Indian languages are genetically related—that is, that all of them can be traced back to one remote ancestor language. The great diversity of Indian languages, however, has thus far prevented proof of common origin, and most Americanists accept more conservative classifications of the languages into various distinct groups.

American Indian Historical Linguistics. Few American Indian languages have more than 100 years of written history; therefore comparative linguists must use recent recordings of native speakers' pronunciations. Following the principles of HISTORICAL LINGUISTICS, words from Indian languages believed to be related are subjected to minute comparison in a search for regular correspondences of sound and meaning. Regularity is the key; for instance, while Luiseño *paa-la*, Papago *wa-*, and Aztec *a-tl*, all meaning "water," do not immediately appear similar, the words are seen to be cognate (derived from the same word in the ancestor language) when other sets such as Luiseño *pe-t*, Papago *woog*, and Aztec *o-tli*, all meaning "road," are considered—Luiseño initial *p* and Papago initial *w* regularly correspond to the lack of an initial consonant in Aztec. When such correspondences are discovered, the languages are judged to have a historical connection, either genetic—because of descent from a common ancestor—or through language contact and the "borrowing" of words. As genetic relationships are discovered, languages are classified into families, which then are themselves compared. Related families can be classified into larger groups called phyla (singular, phy-

lum) or stocks, or into even broader groupings known as macrophyla or superstocks.

On the basis of the Luiseño, Papago, and Aztec words cited above, linguists have proposed the reconstruction of initial *p* sounds in the words for "water" and "road" in the Proto-Uto-Aztecan ancestor of the three languages. The sound systems and vocabulary of a number of different American Indian language families have been partially reconstructed by linguists. Comparison of the reconstructed protolanguages leads to more informed conjecture about earlier connections between the ancestor languages and the peoples who spoke them and may eventually support the theory that all the American Indian languages have a common origin.

Language Names. American Indian language names often seem confusing. Some names are chosen politically rather than linguistically. For instance, Chickasaw and Choctaw are mutually intelligible Muskogean languages but are traditionally treated as separate because different tribes use them. Many American Indian groups do not have a special name for themselves but call themselves simply "people"; language names sometimes translate as "my language." Often Indian groups come to be known by a foreign term, such as the English names Dogrib and Yellowknife given to Athabascan tribes in the Northwest, or the naming of coastal Californian languages for the nearest Spanish mission (Luiseño was the Uto-Aztecan language spoken around Mission San Luis Rey, for example, and the Chumash language Obispeño was named for Mission San Luis Obispo). Some designations, occasionally derogatory, originated with other Indians—like Chemehuevi, from Mojave *ʔači im-uueev-i*, "they work with fish," or Comanche, from Southern Paiute *kɨmantsɨ*, "stranger."

In some cases the same name is used for two or more languages. For instance, there are two languages in Central America called "Chontal," one Hokan and one Mayan. The names of linguistic families and stocks are usually coined by linguists, often by adding *-an* to the name of a representative language. The Yuman family, for example, is named for the language Yuma.

North American Languages. Perhaps 300 languages were spoken in North America when the first Europeans arrived, and it is estimated that 200 are still spoken by about 300,000 persons. The American explorer and ethnologist John Wesley POWELL presented the first general classification of the languages north of Mexico in 1891, dividing them into 58 families. A number of scholars have arranged Powell's families into phyla, with the most influential classification credited to Edward Sapir. C. F. and F. M. Voegelin introduced the standard modern classification of American Indian languages in 1964–65, grouping most of the languages of the United States and Canada into seven macrophyla, with a few families and language isolates left unclassified. The outline of this classification is generally accepted, though parts of it—particularly Hokan and Macro-Penutian—are still controversial.

One phylum, American Arctic-Paleosiberian, includes both Eskimo-Aleut, spoken from Alaska to Greenland, and the Chukchi-Kamchatkan family of Siberia. This phylum is the only American language family to have an accepted connection with a non-American language group.

Central American Languages. Of course language boundaries and political boundaries do not coincide. The Hokan and Aztec-Tanoan phyla of North America also include a number of Central or Meso-American languages, and it has been suggested that other Central American groups may be part of the North American phylum Macro-Penutian. An alternative proposal is a Central American Macro-Mayan stock with connections in South America. Recent estimates place the number of Central American Indian languages at about 70, with at least 3,000,000 speakers.

South American Languages. Linguistic diversity is greatest in South America, where many languages spoken in remote jungle and mountain regions remain unrecorded and unclassified. There are probably more than 500 different languages still spoken, with more than 11,000,000 speakers. The various dialects of Quechua alone have 5,000,000 speakers.

Broader classifications of the more than 80 South American language families have been proposed by Joseph Greenberg, Cestmir Loukotka, and others. Greenberg—whose suggestions were followed in the later Voegelin classification—named just three South American genetic groups, with Macro-Chibchan opposed to Andean-Equatorial, plus other smaller families, and Ge-Pano-Carib. Because these macrophyla have not as yet been documented with lists of cognate sets, they are not accepted by all specialists.

Grammatical Structure

The grammatical structure—phonology, or sound system; morphology, or word structure; and syntax, or sentence structure—of American Indian languages varies considerably, but none of the languages can be called primitive. Their organization and means of expression make them as sophisticated as English and other familiar European languages.

Phonology. Though some Indian languages have a simple phonological structure (the Arawakan language Campa, for instance, has only 17 contrastive speech sounds, or phonemes), the phonology of others is complex. Certain sounds, many articulated toward the back of the vocal tract, have been cited as characteristic of the American languages, but none of these occurs in all the languages. The glottal stop, made by briefly closing the vocal cords, as in the middle of the English word *uh-oh*, is a common sound (written ʔ). Many languages of western America, from north to south, have glottalized consonants, made with a glottal stop produced simultaneously with another consonant. For instance, Navajo *ts'in*, meaning "bone," has a glottalized *ts* sound (represented by *ts'*), while *tsin*, "tree," has a plain *ts*. Another common sound is a back *k*, normally written *q*, articulated not at the velum, like English *k*, but rather in the postvelar or uvular region. Many languages contrast *k* and *q* in words like Cahuilla (Uto-Aztecan) *nekiʔ*, "my house," beside *neqiʔ*, "by myself."

Vowel systems also vary considerably. Several American Indian languages have nasalized vowels, like those used in French. For example, Chickasaw *iyimmi*, "he thinks," is

distinct from *ĩyimmi*, "he believes him," with nasalization represented by the tilde (˜) over the *i*. The use of tonal or pitch accent systems (as in Chinese) to differentiate words is more common in the Americas than the use of contrastive stress (as found, for example, in English *impórt*, verb, beside *ímport*, noun). In the majority of American Indian languages each syllable receives equal stress.

Morphology and Syntax. The most commonly cited trait of American Indian languages is polysynthesis—the expression of complicated ideas within a single word with many separate meaningful elements. The use of verbs with attached subject and object indicators (very often prefixes) is common; in many languages adverbial and other elements may also be attached to the verb, as in Cahuilla *pe-n-taxmu-max-llew-vicu-qaʔ*, literally "him-I-sing-for-go-want-past," which means "I wanted to go sing for him," or in Mojave (Yuman) *ny-m-iyuu-mot-nti-e*, literally "me-you-see-negative-again-future," which means "you won't see me again."

Many languages use unmarked verbs for the third person. Thus Chickasaw *hiła* can mean either "dance" or "he dances." Possessive and locational indicators are often attached to nouns, as in Yup'ik Eskimo *aŋya-a-ni*, literally "boat-his-in," which means "in his boat." As in most Indo-European languages, male/female gender distinction is uncommon; but many Indian languages make a grammatically comparable distinction between animate, or living, and inanimate nouns. Alienable possession or ownership is often indicated differently from inalienable possession—as of kinship terms and body parts. Reduplication—the doubling of all or part of a word, usually to indicate plurality or intensity—is used in many languages, as in Barbareño Chumash *maʔ*, "jackrabbit," *maʔmaʔ* "jackrabbits."

The arrangement of words into sentences also varies from language to language. While the most common basic word order is subject-object-verb, subject-verb-object is frequently used, and some languages employ the rarer word orders verb-subject-object, verb-object-subject, and object-verb-subject.

Many American Indian languages make use of special syntactic patterns to differentiate several third-person participants in a sentence. Obviation (in the Algonquian languages) and the use of the so-called fourth person (in Athabascan) allow one participant to be coded as more important or interesting than another. Switch-reference is the name given to an unusual grammatical device found almost exclusively in the Americas; it allows the speaker to specify whether the subject of one clause is the same as or different from the subject of another clause. The English sentence *he knows he's fat* is ambiguous; if the first *he* is known to refer to Tom, for instance, the sentence has one meaning if the second *he* also refers to Tom ("Tom is fat, and he knows it") and another if the second *he* refers to, say, Bill ("Bill is fat, and Tom knows it"). Although the Mojave sentences *isay-k suupaw-pč* (fat—same know—perfective) and *isay-m suupaw-pč* (fat—different know—perfective) both translate as "he knows he's fat," they are not ambiguous: the first implies that the knower is fat, while the second means that someone else is.

The Whorf Hypothesis. Because of different cultural

TABLE 1: AMERICAN INDIAN LANGUAGES NORTH OF MEXICO

1. **American Arctic-Paleosiberian:**
   Eskimo-Aleut, Chuckchi-Kamchatkan

2. **Na-Dené:**
   Athabascan, Tlingit, Haida

3. **Macro-Algonkian:**
   Algonquian, Yurok, Wiyot, Muskogean, Natchez*, Atakapa*, Chitimacha*, Tunica*, Tonkawa

4. **Macro-Siouan:**
   Siouan, Catawba*, Iroquoian, Caddoan, Yuchi

5. **Hokan** (see also Table 2-1):
   Yuman, Pomo, Palaihnihan, Shastan, Yanan*, Chimariko, Washo, Esselen*, Salinan*, Karok, Chumashan*, Comecrudan*, Coahuiltecan

6. **Macro-Penutian** (see also Table 2-4):
   Yokutsan, Maiduan, Wintun, Miwok-Costanoan, Klamath-Modoc, Sahaptian, Cayuse*, Molale*, Coos, Yakonan*, Takelma*, Kalapuya, Chinookan, Tsim-shian, Zuni

7. **Aztec-Tanoan** (see also Table 2-2):
   Kiowa-Tanoan, Uto-Aztecan

Unclassified Languages of North America:
Kersan, Yukian, Beothuk*, Kutenai, Karankawa*, Chimakuan, Salish, Wakashan, Timucua*

*Extinct language or family.

TABLE 2: CENTRAL AMERICAN LANGUAGE GROUPS

1. **Hokan** (see also Table 1-5):
   Yuman, Seri, Tequistlatec Chon-tal, Jicaque

2. **Aztec-Tanoan** (see also Table 1-7):
   Uto-Aztecan

3. **Oto-Manguean:**
   Oto-Pamean, Popolucan, Mixtecan, Zapotecan, Chimantecan, Manguean*

4. **Macro-Penutian** (see also Table 1-6):
   Huave, Mixe-Zoque, Totonacan, Mayan

5. **Macro-Chibchan** (see also Table 3-A):
   Xinca, Lencan, Paya, Misumalpan

Other Central American Linguistic Groups:
Cuitlatec*, Subtiaba*-Tlapanec, Tarascan

*Extinct language or family.

TABLE 3: SELECTED SOUTH AMERICAN LANGUAGE GROUPS

A. **Major Language Families and Stocks:**
   Macro-Chibchan (see also Table 2-5), Quechumaran, Macro-Tucanoan, Arawakan, Tupian, Macro-Ge, Macro-Pano-Tacanan, Macro-Carib

B. **Additional South American Language Families:**
   Alacalufan, Araucanian, or Mapuche, Auaque, Caliana, Candoshi, Canichana, Canoe, Cariri, Catacao*, Catuquina, Cayuvava, Chiquito, Cofán, Culli*, Cunza, Guahiboan, Guaycurú-Charruan, Huarpean*, Kukura*, Lulean, Mascoy, Mataco, Mobima, Munichi, Otomaco-Taparita*, Puelche, Puinave-Maku, Salivan, Sec*, Simacu, Taruma*, Timote*, Trumai, Tuyoneiri, Yaghan*, Yuri*, Zamuco, Záparo, and others.

*Extinct language or family.

needs, American Indian vocabulary structure varies greatly, and some of the semantic concepts and sentence patterns often seem unfamiliar to those who have not grown up speaking the languages. The American linguist Benjamin Lee Whorf argued that the differences in semantic and syntactic organization of languages as diverse as English and Hopi were indicative of differences in thought processes as well. This theory, the so-called Whorf hypothesis, that language structure reflects cognitive structure, has yet to win widespread acceptance.

Language Contact

Unrelated languages whose speakers are in daily contact often come to share various grammatical traits, which can then be called areal features of the region. In the Pacific Northwest, for instance, several genetic groups are represented, but the complex phonologies of the different languages are strikingly similar. In South America many languages of the Tupian family have nasalization as an attribute, not just of vowels or consonants but of whole syllables, and this feature has been borrowed by some unrelated neighboring languages.

The study of loanwords can reveal something of the prior history of a linguistic group. Many Alaskan languages and some as far south as California have Russian loans, for in stance, dating from the time of extensive trade with Russia, and borrowings from Spanish are com-

mon in California, the Southwest, and, of course, Latin America. Borrowed words are often changed to fit the phonetic structure of the borrowing language—Spanish *cabállo*, "horse," was borrowed into Tübatulabal (Uto-Aztecan) as *kawaayú?*, for instance, because all Tübatulabal words have final stress, and the language has no bilabial *v* or *b* sound. Many Indian words have in turn been borrowed into English and Spanish. The words *moccasin*, *squash, squaw*, and *toboggan*, like the majority of Indian loans into English, are from Algonquian languages; *chocolate* from Aztec, *tobacco* from Carib, and *condor* from Quechua are examples of words that were borrowed into Spanish first, and then into English. The names of thousands of places throughout the Americas are of Indian origin.

Writing Systems

The Mayan hieroglyphic system, which has not yet been completely deciphered, was the only well-developed writing system in use in the Americas before European contact, although a number of the Central American civilizations and the Quechua used pictographic systems, primarily for religious purposes, and other groups made nonlinguistic petroglyphs. Most Indian writing systems now in use were developed by linguists or missionaries, but one exception is the syllabary devised by the Cherokee SEQUOYA, which is still used for writing the Iroquoian language. The majority of Indian languages, however, do not yet have standard orthographies.

The Future of American Indian Languages

Many American Indian languages have few speakers and are in danger of extinction, but some are increasing in both influence and number of speakers. Two nations, Greenland and Paraguay, use American Indian languages—Greenlandic Eskimo and the Tupian language Guaraní—officially. In several places elementary instruction has begun to be offered in Indian languages; for Navajo even college-level instruction is available. The recent resurgence of interest by North American Indians in their cultural heritage has led to more extensive training of native American linguists and to programs of instruction in Indian languages for older children and adults.

Indian literature   The Indian Constitution recognizes 14 official languages. Each has its regional literature, but all owe a debt to a classical culture in Sanskrit (see INDO-IRANIAN LANGUAGES). Sanskrit literature has its origins in an oral tradition that produced the Vedic holy texts (see HINDUISM) some time after 1500 BC. These homilies and hymns gave rise to many commentaries, the most famous of which are the UPANISHADS. Oral history, legend, and moral tales were later fused into the two great books of Hindu tradition, the RAMAYANA and the *Mahabharata*. Other major additions to Sanskrit literature are the *Puranas* (400 BC–AD 1400; Eng. trans., 1970) and the *Pancatantra* (AD c.450; Eng. trans., 1924).

Beginning about 400 BC, when Panini produced his Sanskrit grammar, an outpouring of literature sought to systematize all learning in the form of laws for the arts and sciences, called *shastras*, as well as devotional, epic, and lyric poetry and stylized drama. During the peak of classical poetry (7th–8th century AD) major writers such as Bhartrihari (fl. *c.*500), Mayura (fl. *c.*750), and Subhandu (fl. *c.*75) emerged. KALIDASA, a poet of note, is better known for his play *Shakuntala*. Other playwrights include Bhasa (fl. *c.*200) and Bhavabhuti (fl. *c.*700). Treatises on government, law, and love include *Arthashastra*, *Dharmashastra*, and *Kamasutra*, the last by Vatsayana (*c.*400).

By the second century AD several dialects known collectively as Prakrits were being used in literature. By 1000 they had evolved to the point of being recognizable as the forerunners of modern regional tongues. Sanskrit scholars of that time saw them as evidence of cultural decline and labeled them *Apabhramsa* ("decadence").

During the Middle Ages Sanskrit was used only by the priesthood. Bengali, Marathi, and old Gujarati were among the first Northern languages to emerge as literary vehicles. A major figure was the poet Amir Khusrou (1253–1325), who included Hindi verses among his Persian writings. In the south under the expanding Chola Empire (10th–13th centuries) the Kannada, Malayalam, and Telugu languages achieved a literary status previously held only by classical literature written in TAMIL. The best-known work of this tradition is an anthology of love lyrics, *Kuruntokai* (*c.*750).

In the 7th century two devotional sects emerged in southern India and initiated the BHAKTI Hindu revival, a mystical, personalized mode of worship that focused on the figures of Radha-Krishna and Rama-Sita and produced an abundance of poet-saints, philosophers, and hagiographers. The movement spread throughout India and reached its zenith in the 16th century. Major works include the *Gitagouinda* (*c.*1180; Eng. trans., 1940) of Jayadsua (12th century) and the *Iramavataram* (*c.*1200; Eng. trans., 1961) by Kampan (*c.*1180–1250).

In the latter part of the Middle Ages the courts of the MOGUL emperors produced Perso-Arabic writing, which inspired a literature in Urdu. The major artistic form was the *ghazal*, a stylized lyrical folk song, whose exponents include Muhammed Quli Qutb Shah (*c.*1550–1611), Vali (1668–1744), Sauda (1707–1781), Mir (1723–1810), and Mir's protégé, Ghalib (1797–1869).

The beginnings of modern Indian literature can be traced to the establishment of civil-service training schools and printing presses early in the 19th century. English became a major tool for literary expression. Pioneers such as Raja Rammohan Roy (1772–1833), Mahavir Prasad Dvivedy (1864–1938), and Arunacala Kavi (fl. *c.*1780) developed a utilitarian prose style, whereas Michael Madhusudan Dutt (1824–73) and Jayashankar Prasad (1889–1937) introduced blank verse and the sonnet. Madhusudan Dutt also wrote the first plays modeled on Western drama, and Sir Rabindranath TAGORE introduced the short story to vernacular writing. The novel was pioneered by such writers as Bankim Chandra CHATTERJEE and Hari Narayan Apte (1864–1919). The major poets include Laksminath Bezbarua (1868–1938) and Mohammed Iqbal (*c.*1876–1938).

Post-Independence writers include Sudhindranath Dutt (1901–60), Tagore, Sri AUROBINDO, R. K. Narayan, and R. Prawer JHABVALA. Leading figures in Anglo-Indian poetry are Sarojini Naidu (1879–1949), Nissim Ezekiel, P. Lal, Pritish Nandy, Kamala Das, and A. K. Ramanujan. Nonfiction includes Nirad C. Chaudhuri's *The Autobiography of an Unknown Indian* (1951), Mahatma Gandhi's *An Autobiography*, Jawaharlal NEHRU's *The Discovery of India* (1946), and works by Jayaprakash Narayan, Ved Mehta, and M. N. Roy.

Indian music   Indian music encompasses some of the richest musical traditions of the world. India's musical history begins in the second millennium BC with the advent of the Vedic period. The *Samaveda*, one of the sacred four Vedas ("four books of knowledge"), comprises

The sitar, a north Indian melody instrument, has playing strings that run over arched metal frets into a pegbox; sympathetic strings in the troughed neck run under the frets to lateral pegs.

the world's oldest notated melodies. Beginning with the second century AD, complicated theoretical systems developed, and the important raga principle was established. Islamic influences brought about the division, about 1200, of Indian music into the northern and southern systems that continue today.

The Raga. A *raga* is identified by a particular combination of musical phrases that gives it its distinctive melodic character. The pitches in a *raga* may be presented in the form of ascending and descending scales. Many of the standard phrases are so well known that the informed listener is able to tell immediately which *raga* is being performed. Regardless of whether the *raga* performance is vocal or instrumental, a drone (a sustained tone of fixed pitch) is invariably heard in the background. The drone instrument is usually the *tambura*, which has a long neck and four strings tuned to the basic tones of the *raga*. Magical powers are attributed to some *ragas*, and many *ragas* should be performed only at certain times of the day or night or during specific periods of the year. A number of *ragas* express certain moods or emotions, and some are believed to personify gods, ascetics, or devotees.

The Tala. The other basic element of Indian art music, the *tala*, is a rhythmic cycle containing a fixed number of beats. *Talas* give the rhythmic foundation of the melodic structure and are performed on drums. Within the sequence of beats the drummer plays rhythmic patterns associated with a particular *tala*. The drummer may repeat the sequence more than a hundred times in a single performance. The *tala* is divided into subsections, marked by accents on their first beat, the most important accent occurring on the very first beat of the *tala* cycle.

The North. The northern classical music (Hindustani music) usually opens with a prelude, the *alap*. Here only the soloist and the drone instrument are heard; the drum is silent, and the rhythm is free (there is no *tala*). The

purpose of the *alap* is to explore the essential features of the *raga*—the important tones and the characteristic phrases—and to establish the appropriate mood. After the *alap* a short song is sung or played, and here the drum enters for the first time with the *tala*. During the rest of the performance, improvisation is usually interspersed with recurring material from the song. The speed gradually increases, often leading to a rousing, extremely quick conclusion. The chief melody instruments are the SITAR, a stringed instrument with a body usually made of a gourd split approximately in half, a fingerboard about 1 m (3 ft) long, and seven main strings; the *sarod*, a stringed instrument about 1 m (3 ft) long, made of wood, with a metal fingerboard and six main strings; the *shahnai*, a double-reed wind instrument about 0.6 m (2 ft) long with seven finger holes; and the *sarangi*, a bowed stringed instrument used both for solo playing and for accompanying vocal music. The most common drum is the *tabla*, which is actually two small drums, each having a single head (membrane).

The South. The music of southern India (called Carnatic music, after a region in the south) is often dancelike in character. Southern *ragas* are not equivalent to those of the north, and the manner of performing them is characterized by much ornamentation. The *talas* also are different, and they are performed on a different kind of drum—the *mridanga*, a cylindrical barrel drum about 0.6 m (2 ft) long with two heads. The principal southern forms begin with a rhythmically free introduction called *alapana*, which is followed by three main sections: *pallavi*, *anupallavi*, and *carana*. The *pallavi* melody serves as a refrain throughout, intermingled with a great deal of melodic and rhythmic elaboration and improvisation. The major melody instruments of the south are the *vina*, a stringed instrument similar to the sitar of the north; the *venu*, a wooden transverse flute; the *nagasvaram*, an outdoor double-reed wind instrument with a conical bore, flared bell, and seven finger holes; and the Western violin.

Indian Mutiny   The revolt called the Indian Mutiny, or the Sepoy Rebellion, is referred to by many Indians as their first war of independence. It was initiated in Meerut on May 10, 1857, by Indian troops (sepoys) of the British Indian Army. The insurrection was triggered when the British introduced new rifle cartridges rumored to be greased with oil made from the fat of animals—and the fat of sacred cows was taboo to Hindus while Muslims were repelled by pig fat. The revolt soon spread to large sectors of the civilian population. In Meerut the sepoys killed every European that they found, and another massacre occurred at Cawnpore (KANPUR). British suppression of the mutiny quickly became barbaric.

The greased cartridges were only one factor leading to the revolt. The land policies of Lord DALHOUSIE, who served as governor-general from 1848 to 1856, and of his successor, Lord Canning, and their attempts to modernize and westernize India caused resentment. A regulation of 1856 requiring soldiers to serve overseas if needed (thus losing CASTE) intensified sepoy hostility toward the British. In addition, many discontented elements in northern India joined the revolt. Southern India was untouched by the mutiny, however, and the Sikh soldiers of the Punjab area remained loyal to the British.

The rebel troops captured Delhi and proclaimed the aged Mogul emperor Bahadur Shah II emperor of all India. No strong national leadership emerged, however, and the mutiny was quenched in March 1858; in August the British crown assumed control of India from the East India Company (see EAST INDIA COMPANY, BRITISH). After the mutiny the British became cautious and defensive about their empire, while many Indians would never trust their rulers again.

Indian National Congress   The Indian National Congress, a leading organization in India's independence movement, was the dominant political party in independent India for 30 years. Founded (1885) in Bombay, it sent petitions to the British government requesting a larger political role for Indians. In 1907 the Congress split, its moderate wing seeking eventual dominion status, while its radicals demanded immediate self-rule.

The Congress reunited in support of the British during World War I but was disappointed soon after the war when Britain restricted political activity in India. Under the leadership of Mahatma GANDHI the Congress demanded *purna swaraj* ("complete independence") and waged periodic campaigns of nonviolent civil disobedience. Although leaders of the organization were imprisoned several times, Britain made some concessions in the 1930s. During World War II the Congress was suppressed when it refused to support Britain. It had, however, proved the strength of its popular support, and Britain granted (1947) independence to India following the war. The predominately Hindu Congress reluctantly accepted the creation of Pakistan as a separate Muslim nation.

After independence the Congress party, led by Jawaharlal NEHRU and later by his daughter, Indira GANDHI, and her son, Rajiv GANDHI, dominated Indian politics; its policies were largely socialistic. Since 1969 the party has split several times. Indira Gandhi's New Congress party won the 1971 elections but was defeated in 1977 by the Janata party, a coalition that included the Old Congress party led by Morarji DESAI. In 1977, Gandhi established her own Congress (I) party, which won the 1980 elections and was ruled the official Congress party by the Supreme Court in 1981. After Mrs. Gandhi's assassination, her son Rajiv Gandhi became leader of Congress (I).

See also: INDIA; INDIA, HISTORY OF.

Indian Ocean   The Indian Ocean is the third largest body of water in the world, covering about 20% of the Earth's water surface. It is bounded on the north by southern Asia; on the west by the Arabian Peninsula and Africa; on the east by the Malay Peninsula, the Sunda Islands, and Australia; and on the south by Antarctica. It is separated from the Atlantic Ocean by the 20° east meridian south of Africa, and from the Pacific by the 147° east

meridian. The northernmost extent of the Indian Ocean is approximately 30° north latitude in the Persian Gulf. The ocean is nearly 10,000 km (6,200 mi) wide at the southern tips of Africa and Australia; its area is 73,556,000 km² (28,400,000 mi²), including the RED SEA and the PERSIAN GULF. The ocean's volume is estimated to be 292,131,000 km³ (70,086,000 mi³). Island nations within the ocean are Madagascar (formerly Malagasy Republic), the world's fourth largest island; Comoros; Seychelles; Maldives; Mauritius; and Sri Lanka. Indonesia borders it.

Environment

The African, Indian, and Antarctic crustal plates converge in the Indian Ocean. Their junctures are marked by branches of the mid-oceanic ridge forming an inverted Y, with the stem running south from the edge of the continental shelf near Bombay, India. The eastern, western, and southern basins thus formed are subdivided into smaller basins by ridges. The ocean's continental shelves are narrow, averaging 200 km (125 mi) in width, except off Australia's western coast where the shelf width exceeds 1,000 km (600 mi). The average depth of the ocean is 3,890 m (12,760 ft). Its deepest point, in the Java Trench, is estimated to be 7,450 m (24,442 ft).

Climate. The climate north of the equator is affected by a MONSOON wind system. Strong northeast winds blow from October until April; from May until October south and west winds prevail. In the ARABIAN SEA the violent monsoon brings rain to the Indian subcontinent. In the southern hemisphere the winds generally are milder. When the monsoon winds change, cyclones sometimes strike the shores of the Arabian Sea and the Bay of Bengal (see BENGAL, BAY OF).

Hydrology. Among the few large rivers flowing into the Indian Ocean are the Zambezi, Shatt-al-Arab, Indus, Ganges, Brahmaputra, and Irrawaddy. Two large circular currents, one in the northern hemisphere flowing clockwise and one south of the equator moving counterclockwise, constitute the dominant flow pattern. During the winter monsoon, however, currents in the north are reversed. Deepwater circulation is controlled primarily by inflows from the Atlantic Ocean, the Red Sea, and Antarctic currents. (See OCEAN CURRENTS.) North of 20° south latitude the minimum surface temperature is 22° C (72° F). Southward of 40° south latitude, temperatures drop quickly. Surface water salinity ranges from 32 to 37 parts per 1,000. The average northern limit of icebergs is 45° south latitude.

Economy. The warmth of the Indian Ocean keeps phytoplankton production low, except along the northern fringes and in a few scattered spots elsewhere; ocean life and consequently fishing are thus limited. The ocean's most important function has been that of trade transport. Petroleum is the area's most significant mineral, extracted primarily in the Persian Gulf.

History

The earliest known civilizations, in the valleys of the Nile, Euphrates, Tigris, and Indus rivers and in Southeast Asia,

developed near the Indian Ocean. As a transit route between Asia and Africa, the ocean has great strategic importance. The ancient peoples who lived along the ocean tried without success to control its commercial routes. Vasco da GAMA rounded the Cape of Good Hope in 1497 and sailed to India, the first European to do so. Portugal then attempted to achieve preeminence but was thwarted in the mid-1600s. The Dutch and the French sought control of trade with the East across the Indian Ocean, but Britain became the principal power, dominating the area from 1815 until World War II.

Indian Reorganization Act   The Indian Reorganization Act, a major reform of U.S. policy toward American Indians, was enacted by Congress on June 18, 1934, as a result of a decade of criticism of conditions on the reservations. It forbade the further allotment of tribal lands to individual Indians, authorized the purchase of additional lands for Indians, created a revolving-credit fund to be used for tribal enterprises, encouraged Indian groups to adopt written constitutions providing for limited self-government, gave Indians preference for positions in the Bureau of INDIAN AFFAIRS, and invoked strict conservation practices on Indian lands. The act, also known as the Wheeler-Howard Act, has been criticized by some Indians, who charge that tribal constitutions created under the act are too restrictive of tribal sovereignty.

Indian schools, American   The U.S. government, through the Bureau of Indian Affairs, provides funds for the education of Indian children living on Indian-owned or restricted trust lands. The bureau operates about 165 federal boarding and day schools for about 40,000 children and 15 dormitories for about 1,800 children attending public schools. Currently, the bureau also provides special supplemental programs for about 175,000 Indian public school students. About 80% of all Indian students attend public schools, and a small number attend private or parochial schools. The government program, which includes adult education, vocational training, and various forms of aid to higher education, applies to natives of Alaska—that is, Indians, Eskimos, and Aleuts—and to children of one-quarter degree or more of Indian blood. The bureau also operates three postsecondary schools: the Haskell Indian Junior College, in Lawrence, Kans., which famed athlete Jim THORPE, of Sauk and Fox descent, attended; the Institute of American Indian Arts in Santa Fe, N.Mex.; and Southwestern Indian Polytechnic Institute in Albuquerque, N.Mex. In 1985, Alaska took over the operation of what had been federally funded bureau schools within that state.

Indian Territory   The term *Indian Territory* was originally applied vaguely to huge areas of the western United States occupied by the American Indians. Laws passed in the 1830s, however, most notably the Indian Removal Act (1830) and the Indian Intercourse Act (1834), de-fined Indian Territory as the area of present-day Oklahoma, Kansas, Nebraska, and the Dakotas to which Indian tribes were then being forcibly moved. By creating the territories of Kansas and Nebraska, the KANSAS-NEBRASKA ACT (1854) further limited the area to the territory of the FIVE CIVILIZED TRIBES in present-day Oklahoma. Because they had allied themselves with the Confederacy, these tribes were forced by new treaties negotiated in 1866 to relinquish the western half of their territory, which became part of the Oklahoma Territory. In 1907 the remaining Indian Territory was absorbed with the Oklahoma Territory into the new state of Oklahoma.

Indian treaties   The practice of concluding treaties with the American Indians was initiated in the colonial period by the British, who employed them especially after the British victory in the French and Indian War (1754–63). During the American Revolution the U.S. government adopted the treaty system, signing its first treaty with the Delaware in 1778.

The major purposes of such treaties were to obtain land cessions from the tribes, to determine boundaries between Indian and white lands, and to regulate trade. By adopting the treaty system, the British and U.S. governments recognized the prior ownership of land by Indian tribes and in effect also acknowledged their strength and their status as independent nations. The most important of the early treaties were those of Fort Stanwix (1768 and 1784), by which the IROQUOIS LEAGUE ceded rights in the trans-Appalachian country, and the Treaty of Greenville (1795), by which 12 northern tribes surrendered the southeastern corner of the NORTHWEST TERRITORY to the United States.

By 1815 most of the Indians north of the Ohio River had been subdued, and sentiment was strong to force all Indians to settle west of the Mississippi River. Although treaties to effect this end were formally negotiated, coercion, bribery, and the use of alcohol became commonplace in wringing favorable terms from reluctant tribal leaders. In the case of the *Cherokee Nation* v. *The State of Georgia* (1831), the U.S. Supreme Court ruled that the Indians were no longer to be regarded as independent nations but rather as "dependent domestic nations," subject to regulation by the federal government. From that time until 1871, treaties became mere formalities in which terms were usually dictated by the government. Congress frequently enacted laws conflicting with the provisions of Indian treaties, and the whites frequently violated their terms, thus provoking many of the INDIAN WARS of the 19th century.

In 1871 the use of treaties was terminated by Congress, and Indians were thereafter governed by congressional legislation, executive orders, or executive agreements. On Aug. 13, 1946, Congress created the Indian Claims Commission (I.C.C.) to adjudicate Indian land claims. The I.C.C. existed until 1978, after which claims were handled first by the Court of Claims and after 1982 by the U.S. Claims Court. Claims awarded total about $1.5 billion.

Indian Wars The Indian Wars in the area of the present-day United States began in 1540 when the conquistadors of Francisco Vázquez de CORONADO clashed with ZUÑI warriors of the pueblo of Hawikuh. The wars ended three and one-half centuries later, in 1890, when U.S. cavalry troops almost wiped out Big Foot's (1825?–90) band of SIOUX at WOUNDED KNEE. These two events and the numerous clashes in between were part of the continuing struggle for possession of North America.

Colonial Indian Wars. Almost continuous Indian warfare marked the colonial experience in North America. Spain established outposts in the area of the Rio Grande early in the 17th century with a major aim of converting the PUEBLO tribes to Christianity, a program severely retarded by the Pueblo Rebellion of 1680, which drove all Spaniards from the province for 12 years. In the East, English settlers also provoked uprisings as they began to spread inland from the Atlantic Coast. A bloody outbreak in Virginia in 1622 was followed by the PEQUOT WAR in New England in 1636–37. In most of the English colonies sporadic fighting alternated with full-scale war for a century and a half. One of the most violent conflicts was KING PHILIP'S WAR of 1675–76 in New England.

Moreover, in the imperial contest between Britain and France, each power incited and led Indian allies against the other. By the middle of the 18th century this struggle had spread to the Great Lakes region and had become preeminently Indian warfare. England finally prevailed in the FRENCH AND INDIAN WAR of 1754–63, but its hold on the Great Lakes region was almost broken in 1763 with the outbreak of PONTIAC'S REBELLION. In that same year England forbade all white settlement beyond the Appalachians.

The Woodlands Wars of the Eastern United States. After the American Revolution settlers pushed west of the

The Jamestown Massacre of 1622, a surprise attack by the Powhatan Confederacy, began the intermittent warfare that was to disturb the Virginia colony for more than 20 years.

mountains, and new fighting erupted. North of the Ohio River, in 1790 and 1791, LITTLE TURTLE led warriors of the MIAMI, SHAWNEE, and other tribes to victories over U.S. troops before the Indians were crushed by Gen. "Mad Anthony" WAYNE in the Battle of Fallen Timbers in 1794. The Shawnee chief, TECUMSEH, carried on, striving to forge a grand alliance of tribes west of the mountains. His dream was shattered by the Indiana Territory governor William Henry HARRISON at the Battle of TIPPECANOE in 1811. Tecumseh fell in battle during the WAR OF 1812, fighting on the side of the British. In the South, Indian resistance collapsed after Gen. Andrew JACKSON smashed the CREEKS in 1814 at the Battle of Horseshoe Bend, located in present-day Alabama.

In the three decades following the War of 1812 the U.S. government evolved a policy of moving eastern tribes to new homes west of the Mississippi River in order to clear the way for white settlement. For the most part, Indian removal was accomplished by nonviolent though coercive measures. Notable exceptions were Florida's Seminole Wars (1817–18, 1835–42, 1856–58) and the brief BLACK HAWK WAR (1832) in Illinois and present-day Wisconsin.

The Later Indian Wars in the Western United States. In the mid-19th century the wars spread from the eastern woodlands to the plains, mountains, and deserts of the Trans-Mississippi West. The territorial acquisitions of the 1840s brought new tribes within the limits of the United States and, with the discovery of gold in California (1848), shattered the hope for a "Permanent Indian Frontier" along the eastern edge of the Great Plains. For four decades, as new mineral strikes and other economic opportunities pulled the frontier of settlement westward, armed force alternated with negotiation until, one after another, the tribes had been brought under subjection.

At first the objective of U.S. military policy was to keep the travel routes open and protect the settled areas. A system of military posts developed in response to the threat as Indian raiders, their tribal ranges invaded, attacked both travelers and settlers. In the 1850s military forces defeated rebelling tribes in the Pacific Northwest, fought the first skirmishes with the Sioux and CHEYENNE of the Great Plains, and contended indecisively with KIOWA and COMANCHE raiders along the Texas frontier and APACHE raiders in the Southwest.

During the Civil War volunteer forces conquered the NAVAJO of the Southwest and fought with the Great Plains tribes. The Minnesota Sioux outbreak of 1862 took the lives of about 800 settlers amid scenes of savagery. At the SAND CREEK MASSACRE, in Colorado Territory, volunteer troops in 1864 perpetrated barbarities on BLACK KETTLE's Cheyenne rivaling those on the Sioux in Minnesota. Heavy fighting continued into the postwar years, highlighted by the Fetterman Massacre of 1866, when a detachment from Fort Phil Kearny, Wyo., was ambushed on the BOZEMAN TRAIL and wiped out.

Treaties drawn up in the late 1860s by which many western tribes promised to settle their people on reservations did not bring peace. The wars that followed were fought to force tribes onto reservations they had supposedly already accepted and stay there.

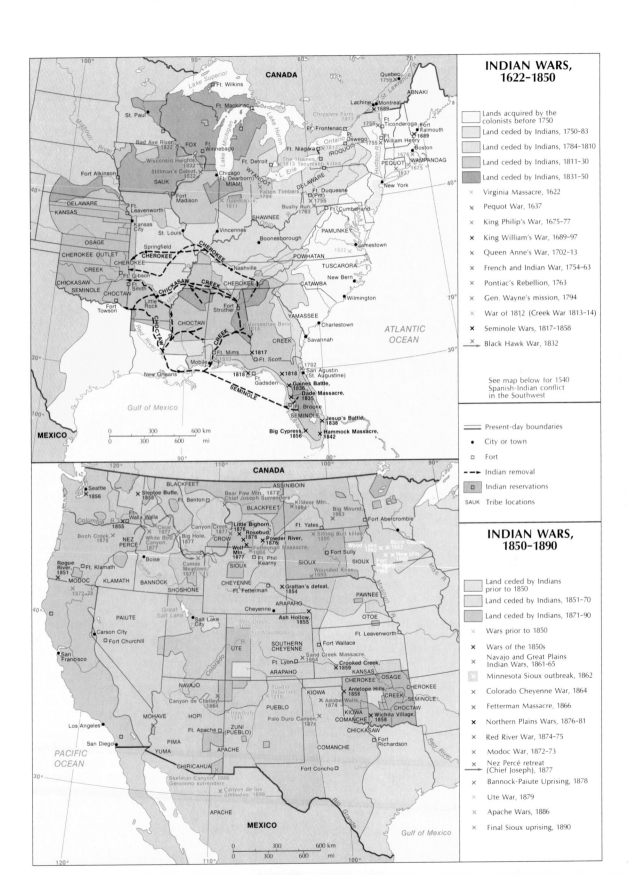

AT A GLANCE

INDIANA

Land: Area: 93,720 km² (36,185 mi²); rank: 38th.
Capital and largest city: Indianapolis (1990 pop.,
741,952). Counties: 92. Elevations: highest—383 m
(1,257 ft), in Franklin Township; lowest—98 m (320 ft),
at the Ohio River.

People: Population (1990): 5,564,228; rank; 14th;
density: 59.4 persons per km² (153.8 per mi²). Distribution (1988 est.): 68.1% metropolitan, 31.9% nonmetropolitan. Average annual change (1980–90): +0.01%.

Government (1991): Governor: Evan Bayh, Democrat.
U.S. Congress: Senate—2 Republicans; House—8 Democrats, 2 Republicans. Electoral college votes: 12. State
legislature: 50 senators, 100 representatives.

Economy: State personal income (1988): $82.9 billion;
rank: 15th. Median family income (1979): $20,535;
rank: 18th. Agriculture: income (1988)—$4.1 billion.
Forestry: sawtimber volume (1987)—19.2 billion board
feet. Mining: value (1987)—$1.3 billion. Manufacturing:
value added (1987)—$39.5 billion. Services: value
(1987)—$16.6 billion.

Miscellany: Statehood: Dec. 11, 1816; the 19th state.
Nickname: Hoosier State; tree: tulip tree (yellow poplar);
motto: The Crossroads of America; song: "On the Banks
of the Wabash, Far Away."

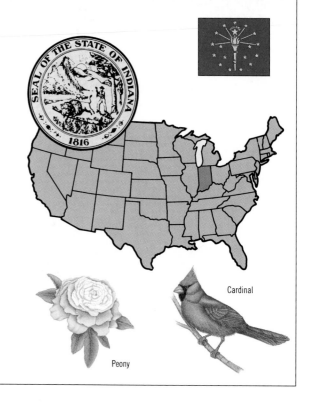

Cardinal

Peony

The most spectacular of these conflicts were those
with the Sioux and Cheyenne of the northern Plains from
1876 through 1881, notably the now legendary Custer's
Last Stand—the Battle of the LITTLE BIGHORN, in which
more than 200 men under George Armstong CUSTER perished on June 25, 1876. Sioux and Cheyenne resistance
ended with the surrender of the Sioux chief, SITTING BULL,
in 1881. The Red River War of 1874–75 finally brought
peace to the southern Plains and Texas as the Kiowa, Comanche, Cheyenne, and ARAPAHO accepted life on reservations. Other encounters were the MODOC war of 1872–
73, in the California lava beds; the dramatic flight (1877)
of Chief JOSEPH and the NEZ PERCÉ from Idaho across
more than 2,400 km (1,500 mi) of the American Northwest, almost to Canada; the Bannock-Paiute uprising of
1878 in Idaho and Oregon; and the UTE outbreak of
1879 in western Colorado. The long and bloody Apache
wars of New Mexico and Arizona closed in 1886 when
GERONIMO surrendered for the last time. Wounded Knee,
the tragic clash of reservation Sioux with U.S. troops in
1890, marked the end of the Indian Wars—in the very
year that the U.S. Census recorded the disappearance of
a frontier of settlement.

See also: FRONTIER; INDIAN TREATIES; INDIANS, AMERICAN;
articles on individual tribes.

Indiana   One of five eastern north central states, Indi-
ana is bordered on the west by Illinois, on the north by
Michigan and Lake Michigan, and on the east by Ohio.
The Ohio River follows Indiana's southern border with
Kentucky. The state is rectangular in shape; its capital,
Indianapolis, lies near its center.

Indiana was once part of the Northwest Territory; it
became a state in 1816. Its name recalls the inhabitants
at the time of first colonial exploration in 1679. The
nickname "Hoosier State" is thought to be derived from
the pioneers' greeting to strangers, "Who's yere?"

Indiana has a large, accessible market, and it is located near several important metropolitan areas in neighboring states. Its Great Lakes and Ohio River ports, along
with its major highways, provide Indiana with access to
much of the nation.

Land and Resources

Indiana has three distinct natural regions: the northern
lakes, the central plains, and the southern hills and valleys. The sand dunes along Lake Michigan are considered
by many to be the most scenic feature of the northern region. The central plains are flat or gently rolling, but tributaries of the Wabash River have dissected the western

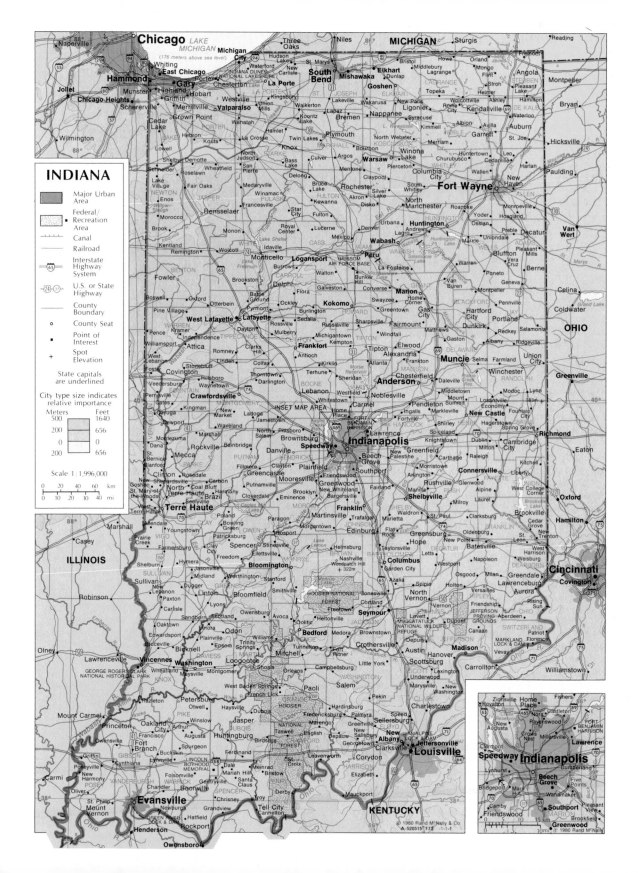

Indianapolis, the largest city of Indiana and the seat of Marion County, is located in the central portion of the state along the west fork of White River. The city has been Indiana's capital since 1825.

part of the state, creating hills and valleys. The southern hills are primarily limestone. Weathering has resulted in the formation of caves, sinkholes, underground streams, and mineral springs.

All of Indiana except the south central portion was glaciated. Deposits of clay, sand, gravel, and boulders filled the preglacial valleys, and deep and fertile soils, primarily gray brown podzols, have developed. Under the till is stratified limestone, shale, and sandstone.

Drainage. Streams eventually flowing to the Gulf of Mexico drain 97% of Indiana. The WABASH RIVER originates in west central Ohio, crosses central Indiana, and then flows southward into the OHIO RIVER, draining about two-thirds of the state. Through the lower one-third of its course, it follows the boundary between Indiana and Illinois. The principal tributary of the Wabash is the White River. The Whitewater River drains southeastern Indiana into the Ohio, while the Kankakee drains much of northwest Indiana. The Saint Joseph River, in northern Indiana, flows into Lake Michigan.

Climate. Indiana's continental climate is characterized by hot, humid summers and cold winters. January mean temperatures range from 2° C (35° F) in Evansville to −4° C (25° F) in South Bend. July temperatures at the same locations are 26° C (78° F) and 23° C (73° F), respectively.

Major temperature variations are caused by differences in latitude, elevation, terrain, and—in winter—by the lake effect. Moisture is picked up from Lake Michigan by air masses moving across it. When the moisture-laden air is forced to rise over the cold land surface, it loses its ability to hold water vapor and thus deposits the state's largest amounts of snow near the lake. Annual precipitation averages 864 mm (34 in) in the north and 1,118 mm (44 in) along the Ohio River.

Vegetation. About 20% of Indiana was originally covered with prairie grass. Dense hardwood forests covered the rest of the state but were cleared for lumber and farming. Today less than 18% remains wooded. Of the 124 native tree species, the most abundant are sycamore, maple, and beech.

Wildlife. During the early years of settlement, wilderness life was threatened by commercial hunters and farmers, who cleared the land for agriculture. Bear, buffalo, deer, and wolves disappeared from the area. Smaller game species, such as wild turkeys, prairie chickens, grouse, and pheasant, were also threatened.

During the 1880s, Indiana pioneered in the enactment of environmental-protection legislation. Deer, squirrel, and cottontail rabbit populations have been replenished; muskrat, opossum, raccoon, and fox have increased in number.

Resources. Bituminous coal, Indiana's most valuable mineral resource, lies under about 16,835 km^2 (6,500 mi^2) of the state. Indiana is one of the ten leading coal-mining states. Oil and natural gas, extracted in eastern and southwestern Indiana, are refined near Fort Wayne, Indianapolis, and Mount Vernon. Sand and gravel are found in widely scattered areas. Gypsum and clay are also mined. Abundant groundwater is found in the sand and gravel deposits of glacial till.

People

Among the 50 states, Indiana ranks 14th in population. Most of the early settlers came to Indiana from the South and were predominantly of English, Scottish, and Welsh extraction. Germans and Irish followed. Immigrants from Europe came to Indiana's cities during the period between the Civil War and the years immediately following World War I, lured by employment opportunities in the developing industries. As a result, Indiana's population grew steadily, and the state became more urbanized. Its largest cities, according to the 1990 census, are INDIANAPOLIS (741,952), FORT WAYNE (173,072), EVANSVILLE (126,272), GARY (116,646), and SOUTH BEND (105,511).

A majority of the state's population are Protestants. Roman Catholics constitute less than 15%, and Jews, less than 1%.

Education. Indiana's educational system developed gradually after the state was organized. The first kindergarten, trade school, and coeducational teaching system in the United States were founded in NEW HARMONY, Ind. Butler University (1849) was among the first institutions of higher learning to admit women.

Indiana has 74 colleges and universities (including branches). More than half of the college population attends the 4 state universities: Indiana University (1820), with the main campus at Bloomington; Purdue University (1869), with its main campus at West Lafayette; Ball State University (1918) at Muncie; and Indiana State University (1865), with campuses at Terre Haute and Evansville.

Culture. Cultural institutions include Clowes Hall in Indianapolis, home of a major symphony orchestra and theatrical touring companies. The Indianapolis Museum of Art houses collections of paintings, sculpture, ceramics, and silver.

A major sporting event is the Indianapolis 500 auto race, held annually on the Sunday preceding Memorial Day at Speedway. Basketball is the primary sporting activity for most high schools and colleges.

Indiana publishes many daily newspapers, including the Indianapolis *Star* and *News*, which have the largest circulations in the state. The state has commercial radio stations and commercial and educational television stations.

Columbus, Ind. (1990 pop., 31,802), is known for its many noteworthy buildings. In a program begun in 1957, city officials and community leaders commissioned world-famous architects, including Eero Saarinen and Harry Weese, to design buildings for the city. These structures, along with the city's pedestrian mall, have made Columbus an example of modern urban planning.

Economy

The Calumet region in extreme northwestern Indiana is the dominant industrial center in the state. Its proximity to Chicago's market, combined with its Great Lakes location, has enabled the area to maintain economic viability. The northeast's proximity to the industrial centers of Detroit, Mich., and Toledo, Ohio, fosters economic growth in such cities as Elkhart and Fort Wayne.

Agriculture. More than 70% of Indiana's land is devoted to agriculture. Corn and soybeans are the state's most valuable cash crops. Wheat, oats, tobacco, hay, rye, apples, and peaches also contribute significantly to the economy. Indiana is among the nation's leading producers of spearmint and peppermint, both of which are grown in the rich muck soils of the northern lake region. During the 1800s, Indiana was a leading producer of hardwood lumber, but land clearing sharply reduced timber production.

Mining. Extraction of bituminous coal through strip mining takes place in the southwestern quarter of Indiana. Natural gas, once abundant in the eastern part of the state, has been virtually exhausted. Building stone is quarried in the south central region. The state produces 40% of the country's building limestone.

Manufacturing. The major cities of the Calumet region—Gary, Hammond, East Chicago, and Whiting—produce iron, steel, and petroleum products. Other Indiana factories manufacture aluminum, auto parts, truck and bus bodies, cement, chemicals, brick, tile, and wood furniture. Indiana ranks first among the states in the production of pharmaceuticals and prefabricated homes and second in musical instruments.

Tourism. The state's forest land is well suited for outdoor recreation. Artificial lakes and reservoirs, primarily in central and southern Indiana, provide spawning areas for bass, bluegill, crappie, and catfish. Major fishing streams include the Kankakee, Tippecanoe, White, Wabash, Whitewater, Muscatatuck, Salomonie, and Blue rivers.

The Indiana Dunes National Lakeshore attracts visitors to the state's Lake Michigan coast. Brown County State Park is well known for its fall foliage and the artist colonies in its vicinity. Wyandotte Cave in Harrison County is one of the nation's largest. West Baden Springs near the Hoosier National Forest has mineral springs.

Indiana has 26 state parks and 15 state forests, most of them centered on a feature of natural or historical interest. Remains of a prehistoric Indian culture are preserved at Mounds State Park. Other tourist attractions include the earliest settlement by Europeans at Vincennes, Lincoln's boyhood home near Lincoln City, and the restored communal settlement at New Harmony.

Transportation. One of the first stagecoach routes, the NATIONAL ROAD, was constructed through Indiana soon after statehood. By 1840, steamboats and flatboats plied rivers and canals until the advent of the railroad. Today 10,460 km (6,500 mi) of railroad track and 147,570 km (91,700 mi) of highways cross Indiana. Five interstate routes serve the city of Indianapolis alone. Airlines fly to more than 200 airports in the state.

Huge blocks of limestone await shipment at a quarry in Lawrence County. Indiana is one of the leading states in the production of limestone used for building.

Corn is harvested in Wayne County, near Indiana's border with Ohio. Indiana's most valuable cash crop is grain corn, used for cattle feed.

Water transportation is important near Lake Michigan and the Ohio River. Burns Harbor on Lake Michigan accommodates ocean liners, and barge traffic on the Ohio stops at the ports of Jeffersonville and Mount Vernon.

Energy. Most electrical energy is generated from coal. Indiana's total power development consists of a steam plant capacity of more than 8 million kilowatts, a hydroelectric capacity of 29,155 kW, and an internal-combustion engine capacity of 26,363 kW.

Government

Structure. Indiana's original 1816 constitution was replaced in 1851 by its present one.

The general assembly consists of 50 senators and 100 representatives. Senators are elected to four-year terms and representatives to two-year terms. The state supreme court consists of five judges, appointed by the governor.

All of Indiana's 92 counties, except for Marion County in Indianapolis, are governed by a board of county commissioners. Cities operate under a mayor-council form of government: towns are governed by boards of trustees.

Politics. Politics in Indiana is a closely knit operation, resistant to outside influences or national bureaucratic interferences. Representation in the federal legislature is not dominated by one political party. The governorship, too, has passed from one party to the other.

History

Archaeologists now recognize Indian village sites and constructions in Indiana as evidence of habitation by ancient MOUND BUILDERS. Mounds State Park in Madison County preserves some remnants of their past. Most spectacular of the archaeological finds is the Angel Mound site near Evansville. Centuries of habitation by the MIAMI, POTAWATAMI, DELAWARE, and KICKAPOO Indian tribes made little change in the natural environment of Indiana.

The first European exploration of present-day Indiana was in 1679 by Robert Cavelier, Sieur de LA SALLE, who attempted to establish French military domination over the Mississippi region. French Jesuit priests founded the first permanent European settlement, VINCENNES, in 1725. The French traders bargained for furs, and the Jesuits pursued their missionary work.

Even as late as 1800 most of what is now Indiana was recognized as Indian territory. The arrival of the colonists brought on a period of violence between the settlers and the Indian inhabitants. Friendly secessions from white-occupied areas began in the late 1700s. The best known of the Indian land transfers was the New Purchase of 1818 that opened the bulk of Indiana to the whites.

Before statehood Indiana had several administrative centers. Vincennes became a French fort in 1732, about 50 years after colonial trading began. The British controlled Vincennes from 1763 until 1779, when George Rogers CLARK, financially aided by Governor Patrick Henry of Virginia, seized the fort for the Americans.

In 1784, Virginia relinquished its claim to the NORTHWEST TERRITORY. Indiana Territory was created in 1800 and included what was to become the states of Indiana, Illinois, and Wisconsin, along with parts of Michigan and Minnesota.

The Battle of TIPPECANOE in 1811 effectively broke the power of Indian tribes in the territory. Indiana was admitted to the Union in 1816, the second state formed from the Northwest Territory. Corydon, the first state capital, was superseded in 1825 by Indianapolis. Communities began to form in the territory as statehood approached. New Harmony along the Wabash was the site chosen for George Rapp's Harmony Society and by Robert OWEN for his cultural and scientific commune.

Indiana's first railroad was begun in 1834, connecting Indianapolis to the Ohio at Madison, the state's largest city in 1847. The rail line fostered economic growth and provided access to European markets for Indianapolis through the Mississippi River system. The National Road gave rise to numerous highway junctions that grew to become thriving communities.

One Confederate raid in 1863, led by Gen. John Hunt MORGAN, was the only significant incident to take place in Indiana during the Civil War. The state backed the Union efforts despite the Southern origins of many residents.

Farming, mining, and forestry developed after the Civil War. One of the oldest industries in the state produced sandstone grinding wheels and honing stones. European immigrants to Indiana provided skills that diversified the industry of the state: glassmaking, furniture manufacturing, and brick and tile making. Laborers from the industrial centers of Europe settled in the Calumet region, lured there by employment opportunities in the steel mills and foundries.

Today, Indiana maintains a diverse economy. Although farming is declining in importance relative to industry, it remains a significant sector of the economic life of the state. The state's inland location makes adequate transportation critical. Despite protests by environmentalists, Burns Harbor—the Port of Indiana—was constructed on Lake Michigan to serve oceangoing vessels, thus underscoring the priority status given to commerce in the Indiana economy.

Indiana, Robert   Robert Indiana, a leading American pop artist (see POP ART), was born Robert Clark in New Castle, Ind., Sept. 13, 1928, and later took the name of his home state. Having completed his education in 1954, he moved to New York. Indiana's early experiments with severely schematized form led in 1960 to his distinctive brand of pop painting, which combines stenciled lettering—DIE and LOVE—with clearly defined areas of bright color. Since the late 1960s he has expanded his LOVE theme to a series of sculptures, some of them monumental in size. Indiana has also designed sets and costumes for theatrical productions, most notably for the Santa Fe Opera's production (1976) of Virgil Thomson's The Mother of Us All.

Robert Indiana's Eight (1965) plays on the difference between the perception of verbal and numerical signs. (Stedelijk Museum, Amsterdam.)

Indiana University   Founded in 1820 in Bloomington, Ind., Indiana University is a liberal arts institution with a college of arts and sciences and schools of education, music, journalism, business, and law; the medical center is in Indianapolis. Other campuses of the university are located at Kokomo (founded 1945), Gary (1959), New Albany (1941), Richmond (1971), and South Bend (1922). Indiana and Purdue universities have joint campuses at Fort Wayne (1917) and Indianapolis (1969).

Indianapolis [in-dee-uhn-ap'-uh-lis]   Indianapolis is the capital and largest city of Indiana. Located in the center of the state on the unnavigable White River, the city is the seat of Marion County and has a population of 741,952 (1990). Since 1970 the city limits of Indianapolis have been coextensive with the boundaries of the county; however, four towns lying within the county (Beech Grove, Lawrence, Southport, and Speedway) do not participate in the combined city and county government, called "Unigov." The metropolitan area has a population of 1,249,822 (1990).

Indianapolis is the market center for the surrounding grain and livestock region and is an important trucking hub. Among the products manufactured in the city are pharmaceuticals, paper, furniture, transportation equipment, televisions, telephone and electrical equipment, and phonograph records. The meat-packing industry is also important.

The city's streets are laid out in a wheel pattern, with major arteries converging at Monument Circle, with the 87-m-high (285-ft) Soldiers and Sailors Monument. Nearby are the 5-block World War Memorial Plaza and the state capitol.

The Indianapolis Motor Speedway, with its annual Indianapolis 500 auto race, is to the northwest. Other places of interest are the Indianapolis Museum of Art and the Children's Museum.

Indianapolis was settled in 1820 and was designated the state capital in 1825. In 1836 it was incorporated as a town and, in 1847, as a city. The railroad arrived in 1847.

Indians, American   In 1492, when Christopher Columbus landed at the Caribbean island of Hispaniola, he believed that he had reached the East Indies. Consequently, he labeled the inhabitants of the island Indians, a misnomer still in general use referring to the indigenous peoples of North, Central, and South America. In 1735 the Swedish taxonomist Carolus Linnaeus gave formal biological recognition to the original inhabitants of the New World by labeling them the "American," or "red," race. Thus many millions of humans, in 2,000 or more different cultures, came to be lumped together under totally inappropriate racial and cultural terms. These native Americans were neither "Indians" nor "red," nor could they easily be classified under a single cultural heading because of their great variety.

Origins and Population Estimates. The ancestors of the native American people entered America from Asia more

This pre-Inca pottery vase of a warrior, dating from AD 600–800, illustrates the highly developed plastic art characteristic of the civilizations of pre-Columbian South America. (British Museum, London.)

than 20,000 years ago. Some archaeologists have suggested that this migration began much earlier—at least 40,000 years ago. The first Americans passed into the New World by way of the BERING LAND BRIDGE, an expanse of dry land that connected Siberia and Alaska during late Pleistocene times. Archaeological findings indicate that foragers and hunters were dispersed throughout North America by 17,000 years ago and had passed through to the tip of South America by 12,000 years ago. (See NORTH AMERICAN ARCHAEOLOGY.)

Little agreement exists among anthropologists on the number of people inhabiting the New World on the eve of its discovery by Europeans. Estimates have ranged from a low of 8.4 million to a high of perhaps 112 million. Scholars supporting the higher estimate have contended that new diseases (smallpox, measles, diphtheria, whooping cough, influenza, and possibly yellow fever and malaria) introduced into America through contact with newcomers may have been responsible for upward of 80 million deaths.

It is certain that for centuries after European contact, native-American populations suffered rapid decline. Only in the 20th century has the number of Indians in most countries of the Americas begun to increase, partly as the result of a declining rate of infant mortality.

Native-American Contributions to World Culture. Discovery of the New World brought about a revitalization of European culture, which would lead to the Industrial Revolution and the pursuit of raw materials and markets, which in turn would lead to worldwide European colonialism on a grand scale. The Americas' contributions to world culture included tobacco, rubber, a new form of cotton, hundreds of new plants of medicinal value, turkeys, toboggans, moccasins, snowshoes, and numerous material items of lesser significance. The domestication of previously unknown food plants, however, was perhaps the greatest of native American contributions to the Old World: of the hundreds of plant species the Indians cultivated, more than 50 are now of major significance worldwide. Maize ("Indian corn"), beans, potatoes, manioc (cassava or yucca), and sweet potatoes have become staple foodstuffs of people on all continents. Tomatoes, chili peppers, cacao, pineapples, squashes, artichokes, cashews, and maple sugar are other important plants first cultivated by native Americans.

Traditional Culture of the Native American

The history of native-American culture is sometimes divided into pre-Columbian and post-Columbian eras. Although literally meaning the periods before and after the arrival of Columbus, this chronological division is generally used to refer to the periods before and after European conquest of Indian lands. The term *pre-Columbian* is es-

The physical traits of the indigenous peoples of North, Central, and South America vary widely within a basically homogenous Mongoloid type. The Eskimo (far left) more closely resembles the Mongoloid peoples of north Asia than does this Iowa tribesman (left) of the plains.

Councils, such as the one in this painting by Seth Eastman, determined tribal policy through extensive debate; oratory was a highly developed art among many native-American groups. (Thomas Gilcrease Institute of American History and Art, Tulsa, Okla.)

pecially used in referring to cultures of the first regions to be dominated by Europeans—namely, the Caribbean area, Mexico, and Peru. Most areas of the Americas came under foreign control at a much later date, although the European presence elsewhere on the continent often affected a given area long before its actual settlement by Europeans. This sequence was especially the case in the forest regions of North America, where a European-organized fur trade flourished, and in the Great Plains, where the European introduction of the horse completely disrupted the way of life of indigenous Plains dwellers.

Social and Political Units. By far the greatest number of societies inhabiting the greatest extent of terrain in the New World before European contact consisted of nomadic bands of from 20 to 50 people who subsisted by collecting wild plant and animal foods. The culture of these simple foragers was in general characterized by a simple technology; by a system of dispersed settlement based on seasonal occupation of sites located near food resources; by consensual leadership exercised by older persons, usually males; and by weak commitment to precise territories. These band-level societies were generally peaceful most of the time.

By about 9,000 years ago certain native-American peoples had begun to domesticate plants to supplement food that was foraged. By the time of European contact maize, beans, and squash, supplemented locally by manioc, potatoes, and highland grains such as quinoa, were in wide use in areas where they could be grown. Simple slash-and-burn cultivation of such crops without the use of irrigation or other more advanced techniques was usually undertaken on small patches of land. Vegetation had to be cleared and burned before the seeds were planted by means of either a digging stick or a hoe, the two basic American horticultural tools.

Horticultural groups generally lived in tribes of about 100 to 1,000 members. These tribes tended to build relatively permanent villages, usually with leaders associated with lineage or clan organizations. Such tribal societies often had craft specialists and substantial inventories of material items for utilitarian or ritual use. Feuds, raids, and wars between tribes occurred often, in part over territory.

Only in Mexico, Central America, and the central Andes (collectively referred to as Nuclear America by anthropologists) did cultures possessing cultivation techniques—including irrigation, terracing, and fertilizing—develop sufficient surpluses to permit the formation of towns and cities. The Aztecs, Inca, and Maya attained the highest level of sociopolitical development in pre-Columbian America, characterized by chiefdoms or states with thousands to millions of citizens organized into hierarchical castes and classes. Other features of Nuclear American civilization included priest-idol-temple complexes; markets to facilitate redistribution of goods and wealth; and means to unify the labor force for public ends, including military service. War was often the focus of life. Absolutist kings, nobility of great privilege, complex state architecture for religious and civil purposes, and predatory military expansionism all mark the Nuclear American civilization as a functional equivalent of that which appeared in the Near East and from which European culture was derived.

Kin Groups. The vast majority of native-American societies were organized on the basis of kinship. Only in Nuclear America and adjacent areas did nonkinship groupings and social stratification become important. Lineages and clans existed in many culture areas of the Americas, particularly in the Eastern Woodlands of North America, among western Pueblo groups, and in Amazonia. Division of societies into reciprocating halves (moieties) for cere-

This engraving (1582) of Cuzco, the Inca capital, illustrates the magnificent organization of that civilization. The Inca empire was the largest, most powerful, and most advanced state in South America. (British Museum, London.)

monial, marriage, or competitive purposes was common.

Marriage for women usually took place in early adolescence, soon after the first menstruation and often to older men. Premarital sexuality was usually allowed and occasionally made all but mandatory. Some societies, however, such as the Cheyenne of the Great Plains, prized chastity for all the unmarried. Adultery was often harshly punished.

The incest taboo prohibited sex and marriage between close relatives and, not infrequently, between any relatives. Many societies practiced marriage with cross-cousins, usually in association with lineage or clan organizations. Marriage to a brother's widow (levirate) and to a sister's husband (sororate) were common customs.

Diet and Subsistence Methods. Few native-American cultures did more than merely supplement wild plant foods with animal products; some exceptions were the Inuit (Eskimo) and various subarctic peoples and coastal shellfish gatherers. Among the most important wild plant foods in North America were acorns, pine, walnut, hickory, and other nuts; grass and plant seeds (including amaranthus, pigweed, sunflower, and salvias); roots and bulbs (onion, Indian potato, camas, and cattail); dozens of kinds of fruits and berries; and wild rice. Desert regions of the Americas provided aloes, opuntias, and many other xerophytic plant foods. In South America palms provided fruits and nuts as well as hearts, shafts, pith, and beer. Other South American plant foods included algarroba pods, chanar fruit, and mistol seeds, as well as wild rice in swampy areas such as the upper Paraguay River. Many plant foods required complex processing in order to re-

Fish were another staple food for many native Americans. This painting (1585) by Virginia colonist John White illustrates methods used in fishing near Roanoke Island. Spears, nets, rakes, and weirs, among other devices, were employed.

move harmful substances (such as tannin from acorns or prussic acid from bitter manioc).

The most widely available animal food was shellfish, as evidenced by the remains of huge shell heaps found by archaeologists on river banks and seacoasts throughout the hemisphere. Most foragers ate larger quantities of small animal life (insects, larvae, worms, snakes, bird eggs, and rodents) than they did the more desirable but rarer large animals. In South America the primary large game were members of the camel family (llama, alpaca, guanaco, and vicuna) as well as peccaries, tapirs, monkeys, iguanas, anteaters, cats, alligators, crocodiles, and freshwater and saltwater mammals. Two or more species of deer, common in parts of South America, were the most widely hunted large game animals in North America. Also in North America were sizable regional herds of bison and caribou; smaller local herds of wapiti elk, pronghorn antelope, and mountain sheep and goats; as well as black and brown bears, badgers, raccoons, opossums, coatimundis, wolverines, and a host of other game animals.

Freshwater and saltwater fish, especially the anadromous varieties—such as salmon, alewives, steelhead trout, and striped bass—provided abundant food for peoples along the northern coasts of North America and in Amazonia. Fish were hooked, netted, trapped, or poisoned (mainly in South America) with over 50 different plant poisons. Birds also served as a source of food, particularly for peoples located on land along the migratory flyways near rookeries.

For most Indian cultures foraging enabled the population to survive in most years, to thrive in some, but in others to experience severe privation and even starvation. Bad years—particularly two or more occurring consecutively—effectively limited the population growth of most native-American societies. Marked population increases occurred in parts of Nuclear America, however, where plants had begun to be domesticated about 9,000 years ago.

By 1492 many Nuclear American peoples had become reliant on cultivation. Hundreds of species of plants were domesticated for use not only as foods, but also as raw materials (such as pima cotton), as poisons, and as hallucinogens and stimulants. Domesticated plants and agricultural techniques gradually spread to other parts of the Americas.

Hallucinogens and Stimulants. Tobacco was the most widely cultivated plant in native America, grown by some foragers who grew nothing else. It was used mainly by men in ceremonial settings by smoking, chewing, sniffing, or in enemas. Jimson weed was the next most available drug in North America; it was used mainly in the West. In Mexico and Central America peyote, mescal bean, the mushroom called teonanácatl, and a seed called ololiuqui were used. Coca, the source of cocaine, was grown in the eastern Andes, where the leaves are still chewed by the Indians.

Before the introduction of the distillation process, only beers and wines were known in the Americas. The principal types were maize beer and alcoholic beverages fermented from manioc, agave, sotol, mesquite beans, saguaro fruit, persimmons, and sea grapes.

Scouts disguised under wolfskins prepare to attack a buffalo herd in this painting (1832–33) by George Catlin. Buffalo products contributed greatly to the livelihood of the peoples of the Great Plains. (National Collection of Fine Arts, Washington, D.C.)

Hunting, Planting, and Cooking Technology. Several varieties of bows and arrows were the commonest hunting implements; thrusting lances, harpoons, atlatls (spear-throwers), clubs, bolas, and slings were also used. Blowguns with poisoned darts were used in eastern North America, the Caribbean, and Amazonia. Poisoned arrows were widely used in the tropical rain forests of South America. Woven nets, deadfalls, nooses, and dogs were also employed in the hunt.

Farmers cleared fields either by chopping trees with stone axes or by girdling trees and burning them. Sharpened sticks, simple hoes, and human labor were the means of planting. In Nuclear America complex irrigation works (with ditches and dams), terraces, and urine, potash, and guano fertilizers were developed.

Foods were prepared by boiling, roasting, broiling, or baking in preheated earth ovens. The addition of hot rocks to water and food that had been placed in either watertight baskets or stone vessels was another widely practiced cooking method ("stone boiling"). Foods were preserved by drying, smoking, salting, or packing in containers with animal lard (pemmican); in Arctic and subarctic areas foods were simply frozen in permafrost. Salt was an important item sought in trade, especially by horticultural people.

Housing and Architecture. For shelter simple foragers generally used brush windscreens or small, portable TEPEES, tents, or wigwams of poles, bark, or hides. Semisubterranean pit houses served as traditional dwellings for various Arctic and subarctic peoples. Rectangular single- or multiple-family dwellings constructed of posts and beams were used by cultivators in North and South America. Large rectangular "longhouses" accommodating entire lineages or tribes were built in Amazonia and among some tribes of northeastern North America. In the American Southwest multistory apartment houses in the form of pueblos made of stone, mud, and beams were made by the ANASAZI, possible ancestors of the Pueblo peoples.

These Arizona cliff dwellings, known as Montezuma's Castle National Monument, are typical of the complex settlements built on the mesas and into the canyons of the Southwest by the Anasazi, an advanced agricultural people.

Wigwams, as seen in this painting by Frederick Verner, were the characteristic dwellings of native Americans of the Northeast. Wigwams were built by covering poles with bark, mats, reeds, or hides. (Glenbow Foundation, Calgary, Alberta.)

The Pyramid and Temple of Inscriptions at the ancient Maya city of Palenque, in southern Mexico, is representative of the architecture of the classic period (AD 250–950) in Mayan culture.

Temple and burial mounds were built widely in Nuclear America and in the Eastern Woodlands and the southwest of North America. East of the Mississippi River are the remains of an estimated 100,000 mounds, ranging from a few feet in height to that at CAHOKIA (in Missouri), with its base of 6.5 ha (16 acres) and a height of 30 m (98 ft). The most spectacular monuments of pre-Columbian American architecture are found in Nuclear America, where entire cities with pyramids, temples, palaces, convents, civic buildings, and astronomical observatories were built in great splendor.

Clothing and Personal Adornment. Before needles became available through trade, only the Eskimo and their neighbors possessed tailored clothing. Tanned deer hide (buckskin), bison hide, and the furs of small animals were common clothing materials in North America. Feathers, bark, and various wild-plant materials were also used, especially in the Pacific Northwest and California. Woven cotton cloth was the dominant material in the American Southwest and in much of Mesoamerica, where costumes often reflected social status. Many tribes in North America wore MOCCASINS to protect their feet; sandals made of plant fibers were common in the Great Basin and the Southwest. Hide sandals made from dehaired skins were worn in Mesoamerica and in parts of South America.

Body painting and tattooing; head and tooth deformation; lip, ear, and nose plugs or rings; and bracelets, arm bands, necklaces, and head ornaments were traditionally used by many groups to enhance beauty or to indicate status.

Metallurgy, Craft, and the Arts. Beginning as early as 3000 BC raw copper was worked by simple hammering for use as weapons or as ritual objects; this process was widely practiced, particularly in the Great Lakes region of North America. By AD 500 gold, copper, and silver were being smelted and cast, soldered, gilded, and alloyed in Ecuador and elsewhere in Nuclear America; objects of copper combined with lead also appeared about this time in Mexico. Bronze was apparently in use in Bolivia by about AD 1100, but native Americans had not discovered the use of iron before European contact.

Throughout the Americas native artisans traditionally embellished tools, containers, houses, and sometimes even the human body with artistic designs and decorations. Local traditions of painting, sculpture, pottery, jewelry, tapestry weaving, and architectural decoration were well developed in various parts of North America. (See INDIANS OF NORTH AMERICA, ART OF THE.)

This 1835 portrait of Keokuk, chief of the Sauk and the Fox, was painted by the American artist George Catlin. The elaborate costume reflects the social status of the wearer. (National Collection of Fine Arts, Washington, D.C.)

(Right) This intricately crafted gold ceremonial knife, decorated with turquoise, dates from the 14th or 15th century, when the Inca empire was emerging in the Andean highlands. The Inca achieved technical mastery in metallurgy in their use of hammered metals and innovative soldering techniques.

In Nuclear America libraries of the Aztecs, Incas, and Maya contained thousands of illustrated books (called codices) with accumulated thought and knowledge about ancient ways. The invading Spaniards systematically destroyed these manuscripts, which they thought to be works of the devil. Working on walls, in the round on solid stone, in bas-relief, and with semiprecious stones (jade, turquoise, serpentine, amber, and others), artists of these and other pre-Columbian cultures produced items of both representational and abstract art ranking with the finest human productions anywhere. (See PRE-COLUMBIAN ART AND ARCHITECTURE.)

Traditional native-American music tended to be highly rhythmic and monophonic and was usually played and sung by men for either ritual or social occasions. Indian musical instruments included drums, rattles, clappers, and sticks and other percussive devices, along with flutes, whistles, and shell trumpets. (See INDIANS OF NORTH AMERICA, MUSIC AND DANCE OF THE.)

Politics and Warfare. The political complexity of most native-American societies was generally in direct relation to the mode of food production: foragers rarely had more leadership than a headman, a person respected but with little real power. Simple cultivators and, following European contact, many foraging peoples—particularly those who became horse nomads—elevated successful war leaders and SHAMANS to posts of power during war. True central government was found only in Nuclear America and adjacent areas, where privileged chiefs or kings, noble councilmen, and priests, supported by armed militia, possessed absolute power over thousands of people. War was a frequent activity in the complex political societies of Mesoamerica and the Andes. Highly organized armies of tens of thousands massed and moved under central leadership unknown elsewhere in the Americas.

Foragers were characterized by a relative peacefulness made possible by low population density, close kinship ties to neighboring peoples, and patterns of resource use that aided in avoiding conflict. Simple cultivators and horse nomads with an investment in fields, in stored foods, or in herds, engaged in frequent and often bloody conflict.

Religion and the Supernatural. The traditional way of life of native Americans was characterized by beliefs and practices stemming from an acceptance of a universe controlled by supernatural beings and forces. All cultures had beliefs in souls; in animistic spirits that occupied natural objects (rocks, trees, unusual landforms, bodies of water, or lightning); and in powerful, distant, usually diffuse creator beings. In order for a native American to succeed in life a constant balance had to be maintained between the spirit forces and human needs, a balance made difficult by the presence of evil spirits. The souls of the dead (ghosts) were often believed to be the most malignant of spirits.

Most native-American cultures possessed beliefs in a diffuse supernatural power anthropologists call MANA. This power was sought through ceremonies, vision quests, self-privation or mutilation, drugged states or dreams, or control of powerful natural entities who could then lend power, or "medicine." Taboos surrounded many commonplace events: birth, puberty, sexual relations, war, and hunting all required constant precautions.

Ceremonies. All native-American cultures possessed supernatural techniques with which to face most of life's unpredictable events. To effect cures, shamans massaged, danced, sang, smoked tobacco, or took drugs in

In this 1847 painting the Canadian artist Paul Kane recorded his experience at a medicine-man mask dance held by Clallam Indians on Vancouver Island. The Clallam believe that supernatural forces of good and evil influence health and other physical phenomena. The tribal ritual depicted here is typical of the healing rite performed by these physician-priests.

The customs and rituals of numerous American Indian tribes were captured by the 19th-century American artist George Catlin. In Catlin's Medicine Man *(1832), the magical clothing of a Blackfoot shaman includes a bearskin mask.*

order to search out the cause of ailment with the aid of spirit helpers. The source of the illness was almost always believed to be witchcraft, despite the fact that in practically no native-American cultures were there individuals who attempted to practice sorcery to harm others.

Other than those associated with curing, rites were of passage (birth, puberty, marriage, death); of crisis associated with war or rain and other natural phenomena; or of maintenance (propitiation of the sun, moon, animals, and other forces) designed to assure harmony among humans and all other elements in the universe. At death the possessions of the deceased were sometimes given away or destroyed, names forgotten, and all verbal references to the person's existence terminated.

Priests served as interpreters and intermediaries in Nuclear America's rich ceremonial complex. Public ceremonies, often conducted on top of temple-pyramids or in elaborate public buildings, were designed to provide continuing power to the leaders of the chiefdoms and states. Priests were usually drawn from the upper classes, were well educated, and served as custodians not only for formal theology and ritual but also as scholars, engineers, and scientists. As a class they were routinely slaughtered by the Spanish.

Language. Over 2,000 separate languages were spoken by native-American peoples at the time of European contact. Approximately 1,400 of these existed in South America, and roughly 200 were spoken in the territory

constituting present-day California. All American languages possessed complete sound-signaling systems (phonemes), thousands of meaning units (morphemes), and ordering systems for utterances (syntax). Only in pre-Columbian Mexico did hieroglyphic writing develop; nowhere in the Americas had phonetic-phonemic writing been invented before European contact.

Efforts continue to group the numerous American languages into families of related languages. Linguists have reduced the number of apparently unrelated language families in North America to about a dozen and as few as four for South America. (See INDIAN LANGUAGES, AMERICAN.)

Today 500 or so of America's native languages are spoken. In Paraguay, 95% of the people speak Guaraní, where it is the colegal language; native-American languages are also spoken widely in Peru (Quechua) and Greenland (Inuit). The Navajo represent the largest group north of Mexico to speak a native-American language. Navajo, along with 200 or more other native-American languages, now may be phonemically written. Many national governments are impatient with speakers of Indian languages, however, and civil administrators, teachers, and missionaries have often contributed to making European languages dominant among native-American peoples. It is highly probable that before long the number of Indian languages still being spoken will diminish to a handful.

Major Culture Areas of Native America

The original Americans came from northeast Asia tens of thousands of years ago. Southeast Asians may have reached the northwestern shore of South America (Valdivia, Ecuador) about 3600 BC; Vikings established a limited number of settlements on Newfoundland about AD 1000. Experts agree, however, that native-American culture developed indigenously, and efforts to trace its origin to these or other outside sources have proved unsuccessful.

The remains of animals hunted for food, occasionally associated with stone tools as at Folsom, N.Mex. (see FOLSOM CULTURE), provide the best evidence of paleo-Indian culture in the Americas. About 10,000 years ago more than 50 large game species began to become extinct. As available game diminished, humans came to rely more on local resources, particularly plant foods, for their subsistence. New food-processing tools—the mano and metate, mortar and pestle, and others—made new foods available, and gradually a pattern of regional adaptations developed that would characterize portions of native America until the arrival of European and American settlers. North America has been divided into the following major culture areas: the Arctic, Subarctic, Northwest Coast and Interior Plateau, Great Basin, Great Plains, Eastern Woodlands, and Southwest. The major culture areas of Latin America are Mesoamerica, the Caribbean and North Andes, the Central and South Andes, the Tropical Forest, and the Marginal Areas of South America.

Arctic and Subarctic Hunters and Fishers. The Arctic culture area comprises the longest continuous stretch of terrain occupied by any common culture and language group on Earth: it extends from southern Alaska into

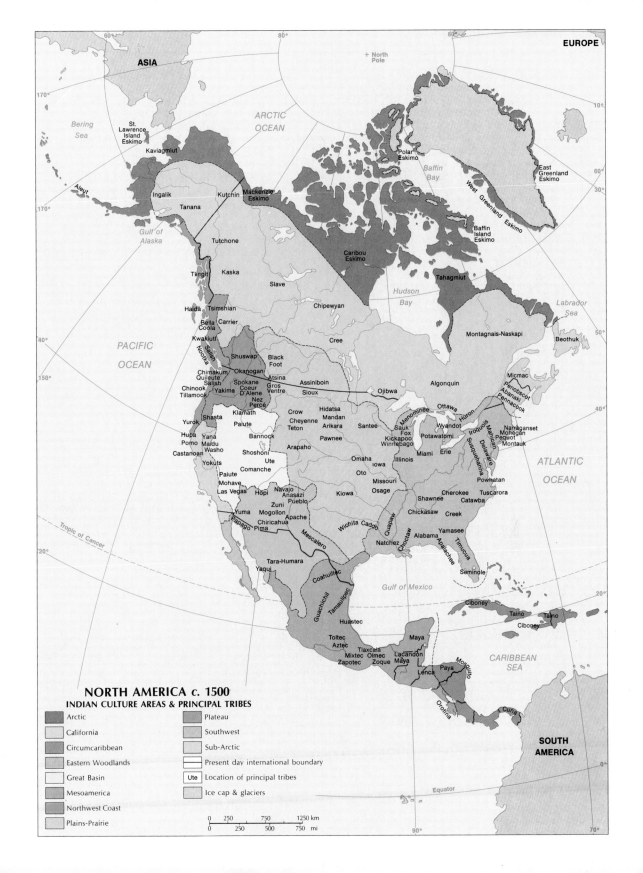

NORTH AMERICA c. 1500
INDIAN CULTURE AREAS & PRINCIPAL TRIBES

Legend:

- Arctic
- California
- Circumcaribbean
- Eastern Woodlands
- Great Basin
- Mesoamerica
- Northwest Coast
- Plains-Prairie
- Plateau
- Southwest
- Sub-Arctic
- Present day international boundary
- Ute Location of principal tribes
- Ice cap & glaciers

Scale: 0 250 750 1250 km / 0 250 500 750 mi

Regions and labels:

ASIA, EUROPE, SOUTH AMERICA

ARCTIC OCEAN, PACIFIC OCEAN, ATLANTIC OCEAN, Bering Sea, Gulf of Alaska, Baffin Bay, Hudson Bay, Labrador Sea, Gulf of Mexico, CARIBBEAN SEA

North Pole, Tropic of Cancer, Equator

Tribes (selected):
St. Lawrence Island Eskimo, Kaviagmiut, Aleut, Ingalik, Tanana, Kutchin, Mackenzie Eskimo, Polar Eskimo, West Greenland Eskimo, East Greenland Eskimo, Baffin Island Eskimo, Caribou Eskimo, Tahagmiut, Tutchone, Kaska, Slave, Chipewyan, Cree, Montagnais-Naskapi, Beothuk, Tlingit, Haida, Tsimshian, Bella Coola, Carrier, Kwakiutl, Nootka, Salish, Shuswap, Okanogan, Black Foot, Atsina, Gros Ventre, Assiniboin, Sioux, Ojibwa, Algonquin, Micmac, Penobscot, Abanaki, Pennacook, Chimakum, Quileute, Salish, Spokane, Coeur D'Alene, Nez Percé, Yakima, Chinook, Tillamook, Klamath, Crow, Cheyenne, Teton, Hidatsa, Mandan, Arikara, Santee, Menominee, Ottawa, Huron, Wyandot, Iroquois, Narraganset, Mohegan, Pequot, Montauk, Yurok, Shasta, Paiute, Bannock, Pawnee, Sauk, Fox, Kickapoo, Winnebago, Potawatomi, Erie, Delaware, Susquehanna, Hupa, Yana, Maidu, Washo, Shoshoni, Arapaho, Omaha, Iowa, Illinois, Miami, Powhatan, Pomo, Castanoan, Yokuts, Ute, Comanche, Oto, Missouri, Kiowa, Osage, Cherokee, Catawba, Tuscarora, Paiute, Mohave, Las Vegas, Navajo, Anasazi, Hopi, Pueblo, Zuni, Kiowa, Shawnee, Creek, Mogollon, Apache, Chiricahua, Wichita, Caddo, Quapaw, Chickasaw, Yamasee, Yuma, Papago, Pima, Mescalero, Choctaw, Natchez, Alabama, Apalachee, Timucua, Seminole, Tara-Humara, Yaqui, Coahuiltec, Guachichil, Tamaulipec, Huastec, Ciboney, Taino, Toltec, Aztec, Tlaxcala, Mixtec, Olmec, Zapotec, Zoque, Maya, Lacandon Maya, Lenca, Paya, Mosquito, Orotina, Cuna

northeast Siberia and around the northern rim of North America to eastern Greenland. Two primary native-American groups are found in this region: the Inuit (Eskimo) and the ALEUTS of the Aleutian Islands. For a discussion of the traditional way of life of the Arctic culture area, see ESKIMO.

The Subarctic culture area includes all of Canada, except the Northwest Coast and the Arctic margin, and south to where cultivable lands and the Great Plains begin. This cold, wet region of forests and tundra provided a harsh climate for human survival. Heavy rains in the summer, deep snows in the winter, as well as endless chains of rivers, lakes, swamps, and muskeg (waterlogged land), prohibited travel except by canoe or toboggan or with snowshoes. The hundreds of independent local

groups can be divided into two major linguistic blocks: the Athabascan speakers of western Canada and interior Alaska (CARRIER, INGALIK, Dogrib, Han, Hare, Koyukon, Kutchin, Mountain, Slave, Tanaina, Yellow-knife, and others) and the Algonquian speakers of eastern Canada (CREE, MICMAC, OJIBWA, Malecite, Montagnais, and others).

Vast migrating herds of caribou were hunted by most Subarctic peoples and along with other game (moose, bear, and deer) and fish provided a largely protein diet. Residence was in small groups, usually in hide- or bark-covered tepees or wigwams that could be easily moved. Family heads were usually the leaders; although great suspicion of one's neighbors was common, interband conflict was slight.

Religion was essentially informal, with few widely held

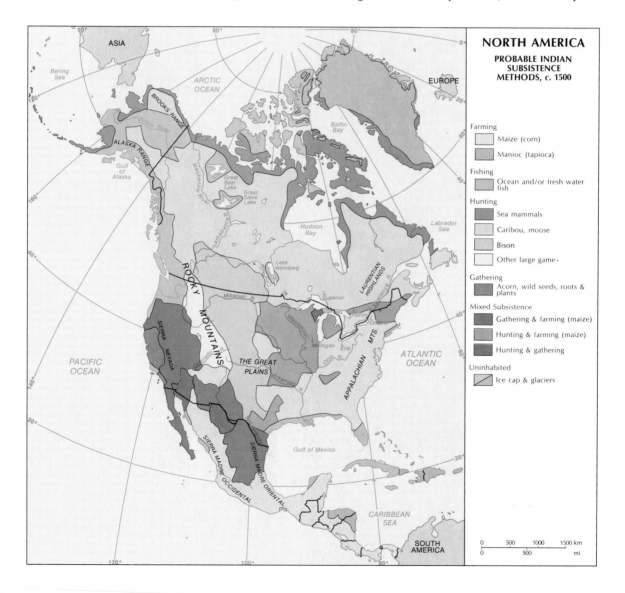

NORTH AMERICA

PROBABLE INDIAN SUBSISTENCE METHODS, c. 1500

Farming
- Maize (corn)
- Manioc (tapioca)

Fishing
- Ocean and/or fresh water fish

Hunting
- Sea mammals
- Caribou, moose
- Bison
- Other large game

Gathering
- Acorn, wild seeds, roots & plants

Mixed Subsistence
- Gathering & farming (maize)
- Hunting & farming (maize)
- Hunting & gathering

Uninhabited
- Ice cap & glaciers

This early-19th-century engraving portrays Eskimo of Melville Peninsula, in the Canadian Northwest Territories, constructing an igloo. Used in winter as a temporary shelter, the igloo is made from blocks of snow.

The Cree chief "Man Who Gives the War Whoop" is depicted in this 1848 portrait. The Cree belong to the Subarctic cultural group of Algonquian-speaking Indians from eastern Canada.

beliefs except those concerned with guardian spirits or witchcraft. Many people, particularly among the Algonquian speakers, believed that the forests harbored windigos, 9-m-tall (30-ft) monsters who could turn humans into cannibals.

The eastern Subarctic, especially the Great Lakes region, was disrupted by the fur trade in the 16th and 17th centuries. The possession of guns gave great power to the Cree, Ojibwa, and others, some of whom moved to the Great Plains to hunt bison. In the eastern and central Subarctic, little of the ancient way of life remained after about 1700. In western Canada and interior Alaska many bands were left relatively undisturbed until well into the 19th century, but disease, alcohol, missions, and other manifestations of Western influence have since brought cultural dissolution.

Northwest-Coast Fishermen. The Pacific rim of northwestern North America and the plateau drained by the Columbia and Fraser rivers formed a uniquely hospitable niche for its native-American inhabitants because of salmon-spawning streams throughout, draining into the north Pacific. From north to south important groups were the TLINGIT, HAIDA, TSIMSHIAN, KWAKIUTL, NOOTKA, SALISH, HUPA, YUROK, and Karok. Most languages spoken in the Northwest Coast culture area are of Athabascan, Penutian, or Mosan linguistic stock.

The Kwakiutl of northern Vancouver Island and adjacent British Columbia exhibited a way of life typical of Northwest Coast tribes. Heavily dependent on the sea for their livelihood, they moved seasonally from one permanent settlement to another, building rectangular, multifamily homes just above the shoreline.

A wood sculpture of a Haida woman exhibits the artistic skill of this coastal British Columbian tribe. (Pitt-Rivers Museum, Oxford, England.)

Religious practices, based mainly on faith in mythical ancestors, often took on dramatic flair in public dramas involving spirit quests and encounters. Highly stylized representations of these ancestors were everywhere, not only on TOTEM poles but also on house facades, boat prows, masks, bones, and blankets.

The Northwest Coast area, first visited (1741) by Vitus Bering, was later frequented by at least 100 foreign ships between 1774 and 1794. Disease, guns, conflict, and alcohol took a rapid toll. During these same years the decorative art for which the region is world renowned reached its greatest elaboration. By the end of the 19th century the traditional economy and culture was increasingly undermined, but the people remained on or near their ancient lands. Many, now working in forestry, have attempted to restore portions of their ancient life; there is also a strong resurgence in arts-and-crafts production.

Interior-Plateau Foragers. The Interior-Plateau culture area, located east of the Northwest Coast to the Rocky Mountains, was a high, relatively well-watered, wooded region peopled by numerous small groups of peaceful, foraging village dwellers. Some of the best-known Interior-Plateau tribes are the FLATHEAD, KUTENAI, NEZ PERCÉ, OKANOGAN, SHUSWAP, SPOKAN, YAKIMA, Coeur d'Alene, Lillooet, Thompson, and Umatilla. They subsisted on an abundance of game, fruits, and salmon harvested from the upper reaches of the Columbia and Fraser rivers and culturally resembled their Northwest Coast, Great Basin, and California neighbors. The languages of most groups were of Mosan or Penutian linguistic stock.

After horses reached the Umatilla in about 1740 and then spread northward, many plateau peoples began to participate in the great bison hunts. Fur trappers arrived during the early 19th century, followed by missionaries and tens of thousands of pioneers. Disease and bloody conflict led to loss of life, culture, and land; by 1860 lit-

Villages traditionally consisted of 100 or more related people, usually politically independent. Great variation in kinship patterns existed, but one feature was common to all: each village ranked its members according to their closeness to the headperson or chief. Only war captives and debt victims, who formed an outcast or slave category, were excluded from this strictly hierarchical ranking system.

Great emphasis was placed on individual and group wealth, measured by the enumeration of possessions such as cedar-bark blankets, dentalium shells, dried fish and fish oil, dugout canoes, coppers (native copper hammered into a shield, named, and ascribed a set value), ownership of resources, and slaves. Wealth was exchanged in reciprocal POTLATCH or gift-giving sessions. Disputes over territory, valued resources, or succession to high rank might involve bloody conflict but could also be resolved by paying indemnities.

(Below) *George Catlin's painting (1834) of a Comanche village shows women preparing bison hides, the chief material used for both clothing and shelter. (Smithsonian Institution, Washington, D.C.)* (Right) *Washakie, a chief of the Wyoming Shoshoni, consistently offered friendship and aid to peaceful settlers.*

tle remained of the traditional Plateau way of life.

Great Basin Desert Foragers. Southwest of the Interior Plateau was a vast, dry, upland expanse of mountains and basins with interior drainage and sharp extremes of temperature occurring in winter and summer. Major groups included the COMANCHE, KLAMATH, PAIUTE, SHOSHONI, UTE, WASHO, Panamint, and others. Nearly all spoke Numic (Shoshonean) languages.

Small foraging bands, sometimes a single family in size, spread over the inhospitable land with population densities as low as 1 person per 130 km^2 (50 mi^2). Brief periods of plenty and the barren winter months were times when people traditionally grouped together in larger bands, usually composed of bilaterally related people. Leadership was informal and in the hands of respected elders, usually males. Interband conflict, although rare, occasionally occurred as the result of witchcraft accusations or rivalry over females. Little existed in the way of formal religion. Powerful spirits could be known through dreams or visions; such associations were believed to bring with them the power not only to cure but also to hunt pronghorns or to gamble.

After obtaining horses in about 1680, the Ute helped to spread them north to the Comanche and to other Great Basin peoples. Thereafter, many Basin societies took to the Great Plains in pursuit of the bison herds. In 1805, Lewis and Clark became the first white explorers to cross the Great Basin; later pioneers, who used to call the Basin Indians "diggers" because they dug for roots, freely dispossessed these impoverished peoples of their lives and land. Basin culture, based upon the narrowest margins of survival, quickly succumbed.

California Foragers. The California culture area covers approximately the extent of the present state minus the southeast section along the Colorado River. Among its aboriginal population, estimated at more than 200,000

people, more than 200 independent dialects existed. Prominent groups included the MODOC, POMO, YANA, Chumash, Costano, Maidu, Miwok, Patwin, Salinan, Wintun, Yokuts, Yuki, and the so-called Mission Indians: Cahuilla, Diegueño, Gabrileño, Luiseño, and Serrano.

All Californians were primarily foragers who relied heavily upon acorns, grass seeds, cattails, and other plant foods. The single village (tribelet) of 100 or more people, bounded by its own dialect, was often the largest unit of political integration. Exogamous moieties were common, thus permitting village endogamy. In the south localized patrilineages were the common residence type. Headmanship, inherited in some groups, served to organize social and ceremonial life but carried little political power. Organized conflict between villages was rare. Drug cults and male puberty ceremonies were especially important.

Juan Rodríguez Cabrillo first explored California in 1542, followed by hundreds of boats whose impact on the native inhabitants remains unclear. The first California mission was established in 1769; within about 100 years most Mission Indians were gone. When hordes of Americans arrived in California during the Gold Rush of 1849, many Indians were ruthlessly overrun and often wantonly massacred. By 1900 fewer than 15,000 survived, and native-American cultural traditions were largely destroyed.

Plains-Prairie Bison Hunters. From the Rocky Mountains to the Mississippi River, from southern Canada to the Gulf of Mexico, the Great Plains formed the vast, undulating, sod-covered home of one of the world's great animal populations—the 60 million or more bison (American, *buffalo*) that migrated seasonally in huge herds. Three dozen or more tribes made use of the Great Plains in the early historic period (*c.*1700–1850), including the ARAPAHO, ARIKARA, BLACKFOOT, CHEYENNE, CROW, HIDATSA, IOWA, MANDAN, OSAGE, PAWNEE, SIOUX, WICHITA, Kiowa-

(Left) *George Catlin's* Buffalo Chase *(1832–33) dramatizes a Hidatsa buffalo hunt, which eliminated the herd in a matter of minutes. (National Collection of Fine Arts, Washington, D.C.)* (Right) *Rain-in-the-Face, a Hunkpapa Sioux chief, was one of the leading warriors in the defeat of General Custer at Little Bighorn.*

(Above) *Zacherie Vincent, a Huron brave, painted this self-portrait. (Musée du Séminaire de Québec.)* (Right) *The Algonquian village of Pomeioc, in North Carolina, was portrayed in 1585 by a Virginia colonist. (British Museum, London.)*

Apache, Plains Cree, and Sarci.

The Great Plains had been occupied for thousands of years by pedestrian nomads who foraged a living in its river bottoms and developed various methods of exploiting its bison herds. More than a thousand years ago peoples of the Eastern Woodlands cultural tradition established farming villages along the western tributaries of the Mississippi River. After 1600, when horses were introduced by European settlers, and by 1700, when horses became available throughout the Great Plains, the area became a melting pot of former sedentary peoples intruded upon and sometimes displaced by mounted hunter-warriors from neighboring areas.

Former foragers and farmers spent the summers based in encampments of dozens of portable tepees arranged in large circles for the purpose of bison hunting on an intensive scale. Here public ceremonials, particularly the SUN DANCE ritual, served to unite groups in common purpose. Individual power, first sought through the vision quest accompanied by self-mutilation and severe privation, was furthered by participation in raids and the counting of war honors (coups) against enemies. Warrior societies grew to be the primary war-making bodies.

Plains culture was in full flower in the 18th and early 19th centuries. With the introduction of guns and the westward movement of trappers and pioneers, the fate of the bison and Plains culture was, however, soon sealed. By 1880 bison no longer existed in sufficient numbers to permit the summer hunts, tribes were being shunted to reservations, and the Great Plains culture was essentially destroyed. The often-fierce and bloody conflicts between Plains Indians and whites culminated in 1890, when a group of Sioux followers of the revivalistic GHOST DANCE movement encountered cavalry units at WOUNDED KNEE,

S.Dak., where nearly 300 native Americans, mainly women and children, were massacred by the 7th Cavalry, George Armstrong Custer's former unit.

Although the resistance of the Plains peoples was eventually broken, many of the most powerful tribes escaped being driven outside their own territories. Indian activism in the 1970s was especially strong among the former Plains dwellers. Wounded Knee again became a symbol of native-American protest when in 1973 it was occupied by the militant AMERICAN INDIAN MOVEMENT (AIM).

Eastern Woodlands Cultivators. Many Indian cultures flourished in the great forests of the Eastern Woodlands culture area, which stretched from the Mississippi River to the Atlantic Ocean and from southern Canada to the Gulf of Mexico. The peoples of this area were descended from an ancient cultural tradition that culminated in the construction of more than 100,000 earthwork mounds and walled towns of up to 30,000 inhabitants (see MOUND BUILDERS). These mound-building cultures possessed priest-temple-idol complexes and a highly stratified set of classes and castes, all of which were in part derived from the high cultures of Mesoamerica; the southeastern portion of the woodlands is considered by some scholars to be a northern hinterland, or Chichimeca, of Mesoamerican culture.

The Northeast subsection was peopled by numerous societies that can be classified into two principal divisions: Iroquoian speakers, including the CAYUGA, ERIE, HURON, MOHAWK, ONEIDA, ONONDAGA, SENECA, TUSCARORA, and Neutral; and Algonquian speakers, including the DELAWARE, FOX, ILLINOIS, KICKAPOO, MAHICAN, MASSACHUSET, MENOMINEE, MIAMI, MOHEGAN, OTTAWA, PEQUOT, SAUK, SHAWNEE, Shinnecock, and Wampanoag.

The Iroquoian-speaking peoples were organized into

Hopi Indian priests are shown with poisonous snakes gripped between their teeth in the annual snake ceremony, a dramatic rain dance and fertility rite. The ritually bathed snakes are kept from striking by the adroit use of a feathered wand.

matrilineal villages, each governed by a council; women played a prominent role in village leadership. The Iroquois were intensely committed to raids, warfare, and the taking of captives, with torture and cannibalism inflicted upon the noblest male captives. Sometime during the 16th century the five tribes (Cayuga, Mohawk, Onondaga, Oneida, and Seneca, later joined by the Tuscarora) united into the powerful IROQUOIS LEAGUE, a military and political presence that held the balance of power in North America until the end of the 18th century.

Along the eastern seaboard, extending north and west to the Great Lakes, were the Algonquian-speaking peoples. Most lived in small, semisedentary villages. Horticultural activities were less developed along the coast, where foraging was usually excellent. Group leadership was generally weak, territory ill defined, and political organization similar to that of tribelets elsewhere. Algonquian groups were among the first native North Americans to suffer destruction at the hands of Europeans; the cultures of many effectively ended before the 18th century began.

In the Southeast prominent groups included the ALABAMA, CADDO, CHEROKEE, CHICKASAW, CHOCTAW, CREEK, NATCHEZ, QUAPAW, SEMINOLE, Biloxi, Chitimacha, Timucua, and Tunica. Many of these peoples achieved the most advanced cultural development north of Mesoamerica. Productive horticulture engaged in by both men and women and supplemented by abundant products of the forests provided the basis for large-scale settlements and political forms characteristic of chiefdoms. Villages with hundreds of inhabitants were palisaded against attack; inside they contained mounds on which were temples with perpetually burning fires, as well as residences of the highly ranked. Chiefs and kings possessed absolute political power over their noble or commoner subjects and in some cases commanded a dozen or more villages. Raids

and wars took place primarily to obtain wealth and honor but also to secure captives for slavery, sacrifice, and group cannibalism.

Disease and the effects of war destroyed many of these peoples before any but the most superficial accounts were written by European explorers and settlers. Nearly all groups to survive the period of exploration and colonization were forced by the U.S. government to move west to INDIAN TERRITORY (present-day Oklahoma) during the early 19th century.

Southwest Cultivators and Foragers. The Southwest culture area, a hot, arid region of mountains and intervening

Contemporary Navajo Indians, members of the largest native group in the United States, raise livestock on their arid reservation lands in the American Southwest.

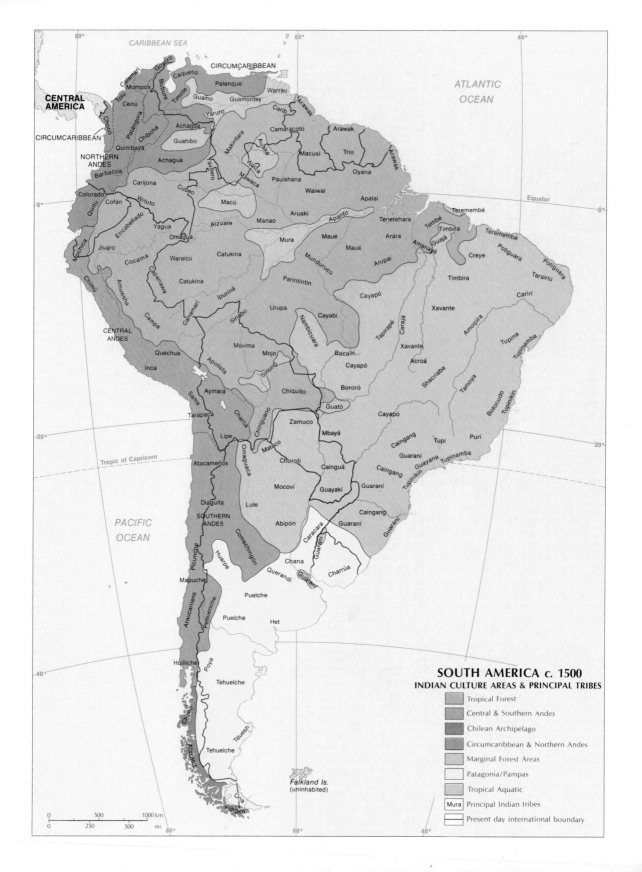

CARIBBEAN SEA

CENTRAL AMERICA

CIRCUMCARIBBEAN

NORTHERN ANDES

ATLANTIC OCEAN

CIRCUMCARIBBEAN

Equator

PACIFIC OCEAN

CENTRAL ANDES

Tropic of Capricorn

SOUTHERN ANDES

Falkland Is.
(uninhabited)

Tribes and regions (as labelled on map):

Calamari, Goajiro, Caquetío, Mompox, Tolú, Babure, Palenque, Warrau, Cenú, Timote, Guamo, Guamontey, Carib, Arawak, Chocó, Patángora, Chibcha, Yaruro, Camaracotó, Arawak, Quimbaya, Achagua, Guahibo, Makiritare, Macusi, Trio, Oyana, Achagua, Alaku, Waica, Arawak, Barbacoa, Carijona, Tavebro, Mawaca, Pauishana, Colorado, Witoto, Cubeo, Macú, Waiwai, Apalai, Quitu, Cofán, Aizuare, Manao, Aruaki, Apanto, Tenetehara, Teremembé, Mochica, Encaballado, Yagua, Mura, Maué, Arára, Tembé, Timbíra, Teremembé, Jívaro, Omagua, Catukina, Maué, Arupai, Amanayé, Guajá, Creye, Potiguara, Cocama, Capanawa, Waraicú, Catukina, Mundurucú, Cayapó, Timbira, Potiguara, Amuesha, Campa, Canamari, Ipuriná, Parintintin, Tarairiu, Quechua, Urupá, Cayabí, Tapirapé, Carajá, Xavante, Amoipira, Cariri, Inca, Móvima, Sinabo, Nambicuara, Bacairi, Xavante, Tupina, Tupinamba, Apolista, Mojo, Siriono, Cayapó, Acroá, Shacriaba, Tamoya, Botocudo, Aymará, Chiquíto, Bororó, Cayapó, Tupinikin, Siena, Charca, Chiriguano, Guató, Caingang, Tupí, Purí, Tarapacá, Zamuco, Mbayá, Guaraní, Guayana, Tupinamba, Lipe, Mataco, Choroti, Caingang, Tupinikin, Atacameños, Mocoví, Cainguá, Guayakí, Guaraní, Caingang, Omaguaca, Lule, Abipón, Guaraní, Diaguita, Caracara, Guaraní, Picunche, Huarpe, Chana, Charrúa, Mapuche, Querandí, Guaraní, Araucanians, Puelche, Pehuenche, Puelche, Het, Huilliche, Poya, Chono, Tehuelche, Téuesh, Tehuelche, Alacaluf, Ona, Yahgan

SOUTH AMERICA c. 1500
INDIAN CULTURE AREAS & PRINCIPAL TRIBES

- Tropical Forest
- Central & Southern Andes
- Chilean Archipelago
- Circumcaribbean & Northern Andes
- Marginal Forest Areas
- Patagonia/Pampas
- Tropical Aquatic
- Mura   Principal Indian tribes
- Present day international boundary

0   500   1000 km
0   250   500 mi

basins, comprises present-day Arizona, New Mexico, and portions of adjoining states and northwest Mexico. The Southwest was the homeland both of foraging peoples—including the APACHE, Havasupai, Seri, Walapai, and Yavapai—and of horticultural peoples—such as the MOJAVE, NAVAJO, PAPAGO, PIMA, PUEBLO peoples (including the HOPI and ZUÑI), YAQUI, YUMA, Cocopa, and Opata. In spite of its arid conditions the region provided substantial quantities of wild food, both plant and animal, for the foragers of the Southwest, who occupied either matrilineally or patrilineally organized settlements within a given range of territory. Raids against settled farmers in adjacent areas were common.

Maize cultivation first appeared north of Mexico in the Southwest, probably by about 200–100 BC. Introduced by the HOHOKAM, an ancient culture centered in southern Arizona, agriculture was also practiced by the Anasazi,

ancestors of the present-day Pueblo peoples, from AD 400 to 1300. When Spaniards visited the Southwest in 1540 the irrigation works, ball courts, and settlements of the Hohokam had fallen into disuse. The Pima and Papago, believed to be their descendants, lived in small, semi-independent patrilineage villages and were frequently at war with Apache bands.

The Pueblo people inhabited perhaps 90 independent villages in 1540, ranged along the Rio Grande. As village-dwelling cultivators they constructed multistory apartment houses focused around subterranean religious rooms (kivas). Political power was vested in religious organizations, and each member of Pueblo society took part in the intense ceremonial cycle that filled each year. Warrior societies existed in each village, but they were primarily oriented toward defensive actions.

The Apache-Navajo, speakers of Athabascan languag-

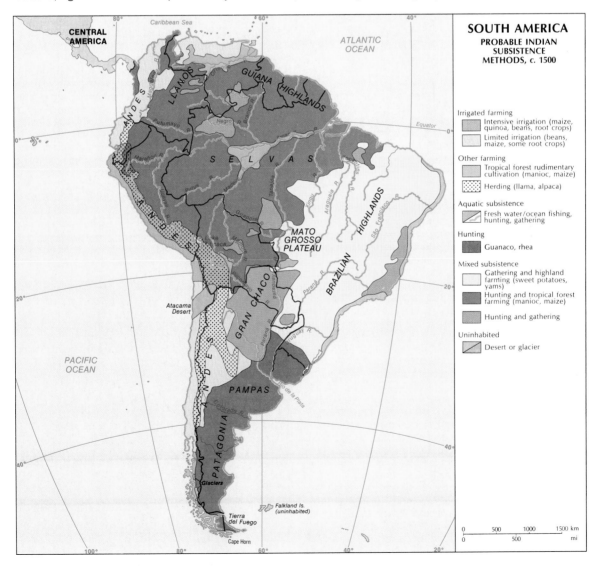

This ceramic figure, from Veracruz, Mexico, dates from AD c.600–900, the late Classic period of pre-Columbian art. (Metropolitan Museum of Art, New York.)

es closely related to those of northwest Canada, appear to have arrived in the Southwest less than 1,000 years ago. There they acquired semisedentary residence patterns, horticulture, and many cultural items borrowed from the region's more ancient inhabitants, probably the Pueblo.

From 1589 on, Spanish priests and settlers sought to control the Southwest; in 1680 the Pueblo people under POPÉ drove them out only to see them return in greater force. GERONIMO, the last Apache headman to resist, surrendered in 1886. Today the Navajo, the largest surviving body of Apacheans, constitute the largest native-American group in the United States. They and their Pueblo neighbors, the Hopi, are generally considered to possess the best-preserved traditional cultures in North America.

Mesoamerican Agriculturalists. The Mesoamerican culture area occupies present-day Guatemala, Belize, part of Honduras, and central Mexico southeast to the Yucatán Peninsula. The most famous Mesoamerican cultures were those of the MAYA and the AZTEC, but many other groups existed here also, including the HUASTEC, LENCA, MIXTEC, OLMEC, TARASCAN, ZAPOTEC, Chontal, Chorti, Jicaque, Mixe, Otomi, Totonac, Zacatec, Zoque, and others.

Cultivation of 100 or more plant species, particularly maize, beans, and squash, provided substantial food throughout this region for more than 3,000 years. Mesoamerican civilizations developed hieroglyphic writing, bark-paper books, and maps; positional mathematics and the zero concept; astronomical observatories, a highly accurate calendar, and the ability to predict eclipses; elaborate civic-ceremonial centers; and highly stratified societies with absolutist rulers.

In 1519, Hernán Cortés began his attack on the Aztecs and defeated them completely by 1521. Conquest of the Maya proved more difficult but was successful by the middle of the 16th century. Today the Maya and other Mesoamerican groups constitute the largest Indian popu-

lation of the Americas. They are chiefly subsistence farmers living in small villages, although extensive urbanization has occurred among the Indians of Mexico. Their lives are permeated by Roman Catholicism heavily mixed with native-American beliefs and ritual practices.

Circumcaribbean and North Andean Agriculturalists. The islands of the Caribbean, together with Colombia and northern Ecuador, form a zone of great climatic variation, ranging from rain forest to temperate highlands and arid desert. Two types of chiefdom traditionally existed in this culture area: those which were politically organized—including the ARAWAK, Calamari, Cenú, Mompox, Quimbaya, and Tolú—and those which were feudally organized—as were the CHIBCHA and Nicarao societies.

Villages and towns of 1,000 to 3,000 people, with both matrilineages and patrilineages, were stratified into classes of chiefs, nobles, and commoners, with captives forming a slave class. War was frequent and often either aimed at the capture of women as concubines and household workers or conducted as a search for sacrificial victims. Priests were associated with idols and temples; in some groups the chief was the high priest.

Few of the millions of native Mesoamerican inhabitants survived the first 50 years of the white man's search for gold and slaves. Today only a few of the indigenous groups remain, among them the CARIB, CUNA, and MISKITO.

Central and South Andean Agriculturalists. The Central Andean culture area occupied the Andes and the western coast of South America from southern Colombia and Peru to central Chile. This area coincides with the ancient and powerful Inca empire, which fell to Francisco Pizarro and the Spanish conquistadors in 1532 (see INCA). Today the largest Indian population in all of South America lives in this region.

These girls from Cuzco, Peru, are descendants of the Incas, founders of an Indian empire that stretched along South America's Pacific coast from Ecuador to central Chile.

A subgroup within this culture area is formed by the indigenous peoples (the Atacameños and Diaguita) of the Atacama Desert and those (the ARAUCANIANS) of the central valley of Chile. The people of the Atacama traditionally shared many cultural features with the central Andeans but because of the scarcity of water did not develop large communities or elaborate political and religious features. The southern Araucanians, especially the Huilliche and Mapuche, resisted the Spanish until the end of the 19th century. About 150,000 Araucanians remain today, living mostly in the area south of the Bío-bío River.

Tropical-Forest Culture Area. Hundreds of small horticultural cultures traditionally occupied tracts of rain forest in Amazonia and in scattered regions in the Antilles and in Central America. Tribes of this culture area included the GUARANÍ, TUPÍ, Mundurucú, Amanayé, Carajá, Guajá, Maué, Mojo, Mura, Nambicuara, Siriono, Tapirapé, and Tenetehara. The heavy rainfall of this area tends to leach nutrients from the soil; slash-and-burn cultivation provided a protein-deficient though often abundant supply of food.

Villages generally were small (100–1,000 people) and the population density low (averaging 1.3–2.6 persons per km^2/0.5–1.0 per mi^2), and the village was often the largest unit of political integration. Patrilineages, except in the Guianas and the Lesser Antilles, were the predominant form of social affiliation. In small societies leadership was exerted by the male elder; in larger groups shamans sometimes gained power through intimidation. Many men became shamans through the use of powerful hallucinogenic drugs. Puberty ceremonies for both males and females often involved whipping, scarification, and the use of drugs. Death ceremonialism in various cultures included burial, reburial, and cremation (sometimes followed by ritual consumption of the ashes in beer), as well as funerary cannibalism. Spirits of the bush and rivers were thought to be malignant and to be avoided.

A family of Araucanian Indians is portrayed against a background of Andean peaks. These peoples of southern Chile, organized as a loose confederacy of farming tribes, successfully defended their independence against the same 16th-century Spanish conquistadors who had subjugated the Incan Empire.

Tropical Forest populations declined quickly after contact with European culture—through the spread of disease and new weapons for intergroup conflict (iron knives, axes, guns) and as a result of extermination by European slavers (*bandeirantes*) and explorers.

Nomadic Foragers and Hunters of South America. Small, scattered groups of nomadic foragers and hunters traditionally occupied isolated parts of eastern and southern South America. Their cultures represented survivals of earlier, preagricultural adaptations to environmental conditions in which cultivation was not possible. These societies have been classified into the following principal

The diversity of clothing worn by the Indian tribes of Patagonia, located at the southern extreme of South America, is displayed in a French text published in 1835.

Portuguese sailors led by Amerigo Vespucci, who sailed along the Atlantic seaboard of Brazil, Uruguay, and Argentina during the early 16th century, overwhelmed a tribe of coastal Indians. (British Museum, London.)

ogy. Religion consisted of life-crisis rites, shamanism, and a belief in spirits. Feuds and raids were rare; survival for many of these societies was dependent on avoiding their more powerful, warlike neighbors. After the early Spanish explorers brought horses into the South American plains, some of the pedestrian nomads of Patagonia became gauchos (cowboys). However, most of the nomadic societies were too small and independent to serve Europeans, and many were exterminated or died out from newly introduced diseases soon after contact with Europeans.

Early Impact of European Contact

In Latin America many Indian populations succumbed completely when faced with European domination. Others were enslaved on plantations, where they intermingled with African slaves and survived mixed in race and culture. Other Indian peoples, particularly throughout the densely inhabited centers of Nuclear America, gradually entered into the economic, religious, and social life of their conquerors and became the lowest class or caste of the colonial society. Some ancient Indian communities in Mexico, Guatemala, and the Andean countries resisted domination and have managed to survive into the 20th century in ethnic enclaves that constitute what has been called a corporate peasantry.

The first Spaniards came to the New World on a quest for gold and adventure. Often they intermarried with the indigenous peoples, producing in Latin America a large, mixed class called MESTIZOS. In Canada the first French explorers were mostly trappers and traders; they, too, often intermarried with the Indians, and they maintained generally friendly relations based on cooperation and trade partnership.

The earliest Anglo-Americans generally came to North America with their families in order to set up colonies; most of them were seeking, above all, to settle the land. Because virtually all of North America was already in use

groups: the shellfish gatherers of the archipelagoes of southern Chile; nomadic hunting bands of the pampas of PATAGONIA; forest hunter-gatherers of the CHACO, the eastern Brazil highlands, and other scattered areas; and tropical aquatic nomads along certain rivers and swampy areas who traveled by means of the dugout canoe.

These groups had the lowest population density of any South American culture area and possessed only simple band organization. All shared the characteristic of low food productivity exploited by a relatively simple technol-

A sketch by Alfred Jacob Miller, titled Migration of the Pawnees, portrays a group of nomadic Plains Indians leaving their main encampment in search of more productive hunting grounds. (Yale University Library.)

by the indigenous inhabitants, conflict was inevitable. The Dutch and British began early a policy of buying land, a practice never understood by the native-American sellers, who generally believed that they were granting the newcomers rights to use rather than to own the lands occupied by the Indians.

After the American colonists won their independence from Great Britain, the U.S. government continued the British practice of treating the tribes as sovereign nations; between 1778 and 1871 a total of 389 treaties had been signed and ratified (see INDIAN TREATIES). Many of these treaties were relentlessly broken in the 19th century as large numbers of white settlers moved into Indian lands. Beginning about 1815, federal policy supported the forced removal of Indians from their traditional territories to isolated reserved areas that were administered as trusts by the U.S. government. Between 1830 and 1840 more than 70,000 highly acculturated southeastern peoples (including the Cherokee, Choctaw, Creek, and other members of the so-called FIVE CIVILIZED TRIBES) were removed to the newly established Indian Territory in Oklahoma, land already in use by other native-American peoples.

Many Indians fought bitterly against their forced resettlement on reservations (see INDIAN WARS). The doctrine of Manifest Destiny fueled the frontier people into hostile actions against even peaceful Indians, and massive slaughter of men, women, and children sometimes resulted. The spread of disease also contributed to the defeat of the Indians and the suppression of their traditional way of life. Only in the American Southwest did ancient cultures such as the Hopi, Zuñi, and Navajo manage to insulate themselves.

Indians in the Twentieth Century

In 20th-century America no single definition exists of precisely who is an Indian. To be eligible for federal Indian aid in the United States, a person must live on or near a federal reservation or be of Eskimo or Aleut descent. Persons who are listed on the rosters of state reservations or who can prove one-fourth or more Indian ancestry are generally accepted as Indians by the U.S. government. In the eastern United States some groups with mixed ancestry have claimed Indian status but have not always been granted it by the federal government.

Canada recognizes "status," or treaty, Indians (those who belong to a band with a treaty with the government) and "nonstatus," or nontreaty, Indians (those who are clearly of Indian descent but who do not have treaties). People in these categories may or may not be of unmixed Indian ancestry, but they enjoy all the rights that the government grants to Indian peoples. In some parts of Canada, primarily in Quebec Province, métis (persons of Indian and white ancestry) are accorded no special privileges under the law.

In Latin America cultural style rather than physical type or even ancestry is generally the criterion that determines whether one is deemed an Indian. Individuals or groups who speak Indian languages, wear Indian clothes, and participate in Indian cultural activities are identified as Indians.

Corpses of Sioux lie about the ruins of their camp at Wounded Knee, S.Dak., after a brief, one-sided battle with the U.S. 7th Cavalry in 1890.

In the United States. In 1990, 1,959,234 Indians, including Eskimos and Aleuts, lived in the United States. The native-American population is growing at a rate of 3.8% per year. Most native Americans live west of the Mississippi River. In 1989 an estimated 949,075 people lived on or near the some 287 federally recognized reservations. In 1990 the total land held in trust by the federal government and administered by the Bureau of INDIAN AFFAIRS was about 22 million ha (54.4 million acres).

In 1887 the Dawes Act, also called the General Allotment Act, authorized the breaking up of tribal lands into small property units of 16–65 ha (40–160 acres), to be given to individual Indians. This action, supposedly aimed at encouraging the Indians to become farmers, led instead to the widespread sale of tribal lands to whites. By 1934, when the Wheeler-Howard INDIAN REORGANIZATION ACT overturned the General Allotment Act, the land owned by Indians had dropped from about 63 million ha (155 million acres) in 1887 to about 19 million ha (47 million acres). In 1946 the Indian Claims Commission was established to settle claims of Indian groups that could prove loss of lands due to past governmental malfeasance. The commission has received several hundred claims and has so far awarded about $1.5 billion.

In the 1970s, partially stimulated by militant Indians of the American Indian Movement, many native-American groups have been more forceful in searching for their rights. Although a federal act of 1790—the Indian Trade and Intercourse Act—had prohibited sale of Indian lands without prior federal approval, vast sections of the eastern United States passed from Indian control after that time. Today many native peoples are seeking substantial recompense for these losses. In the Pacific Northwest native-American fishermen have been upheld by the Supreme Court in their claim to half of the fish in Puget Sound. In the Southwest the Apache, Paiute, Pima, and others are

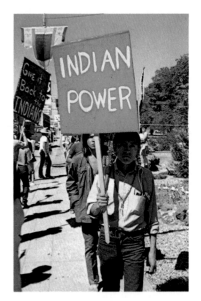

During the 1970s, various alliances of American Indians pressed for the return of their ancestral lands, using both legal means and the tactics of civil disobedience to achieve their goals.

pressing their legal claims to the increasingly valuable water rights in the region. Various western Indian groups, who control perhaps one-third of the total U.S. coal reserves, have formed a committee to ensure equitable treatment when the coal is mined.

On reservations about 50% of the population do not graduate from high school; unemployment runs at 40% or higher; birth and death rates are high; and suicides occur at twice the national rate. Beginning in the 1950s the BIA supported a relocation program for native people choosing to move to cities; more than 200,000 relocated, but most relocated Indians lacked skills useful in urban areas, and many escaped reservation poverty only to find urban poverty. Alcoholism and crime rates are extremely high among Indian communities in cities and on reservations.

Today Indians are assuming greater control of their own destiny. The BIA (of which two-thirds of the staff is now Indian) is becoming more effective in articulating Indian goals. Tens of thousands of Indians are seeking higher education, often beginning with community colleges on their own lands.

In Canada. When Europeans first arrived, Canada had an indigenous population estimated at 200,000. In 1986 the Canadian aboriginal population numbered 373,260. In the early 1990s there were about 600 separate Indian bands located on or having access to nearly 2,300 reserves.

The office of superintendent for Indian affairs in Canada was first established by the British in 1755. In 1860 control of Indian affairs passed to the Canadian government, and in 1880 a Department of Indian Affairs was established, now a part of the Department of Indian Affairs and Northern Development. All effective Indian legislation in Canada is contained in the Indian Act of 1951. All Indians are citizens of Canada; are free to elect band chiefs and councils; may leave reserves at any time; and

may participate, with representatives of the department, in running their own social and economic affairs. Indians may choose to give up band rights, become "enfranchised," and then obtain their share of any funds due the band. About 25% of Canada's Indians live in urban areas. Many of these are "nonstatus" people who suffer the same effects of economic and social poverty characteristic of urban Indian communities in the United States.

Canadian Indians historically have faced strong assimilatory pressure, which many are now resisting. Throughout the northern reaches of the country, hydroelectric power development and the exploitation of mineral resources have threatened some native peoples with displacement from their lands.

In Latin America. Today 16 countries in Latin America have sizable Indian populations. Indians are estimated to be about 30% of the population in Mexico, 45% in Peru, 55% in Bolivia, and 25% in Ecuador. Central America, Venezuela, Colombia, the Guianas, Chile, and Argentina each have several hundred thousand Indians. Brazil, Uruguay, and Paraguay also have substantial numbers.

Throughout Latin America, Indians constitute the poorest segment of the population. Their values and customs are rejected in favor of those of the Spanish-speaking white or mestizo social classes. As a result, many Indians have chosen to join the non-Indian population through cultural assimilation. This is especially true in urban, plantation, and agribusiness areas. On the frontiers of expansion, in Ecuador, Peru, Venezuela, and Brazil, many of the remaining tribal Indians have suffered persecution and displacement at the hands of large landowners and mining and forestry enterprises.

Indians of North America, art of the   North American Indian art includes many distinct traditions developed by native American peoples throughout the continent. In spite of great diversity among the traditional cultures of native American populations, several key concepts underlie the artistic expression of most groups. Primary among these is the assumption that art was to serve social purposes. It was to be used in religious and other rituals; it proclaimed class, rank, and political status; it was wealth; and it signified group solidarity.

Art objects were traditionally made from a rich variety of natural products found in the environment, ranging from shell, bone, feather, and animal skin to wood, stone, clay, colored minerals, and vegetable fibers. These materials were variously carved, abraded, engraved, modeled, baked, painted, woven, tied, twined, and braided. Later, materials of European manufacture such as glass beads and machine-made cloth were also used. Raw materials and finished art objects were sometimes traded over long distances.

Traditional styles of North American Indian art can be broadly classified according to the following culture areas.

Arctic Art. The Arctic culture area corresponds to the geographic zone inhabited by the Eskimo. A sequence of prehistoric Eskimo art that began about 2,000 years ago

(Left) *The soapstone carving of a hunter in combat with an ivory-toothed bear is representative of the stylistic refinement in modern Eskimo art. (Winnipeg Art Gallery, Manitoba, Canada.)*

Large carved totem poles, such as these of the Kitwancool of British Columbia, are commonly found in the villages of Northwest Coast Indians. Considered magical, the carvings document the lineage and social position of the patron.

can be traced in the Bering Sea region (see OKVIK); another tradition, possibly older, has been identified with the Dorset culture of central and eastern Canada. Most remaining examples of prehistoric Eskimo art are fashioned of walrus ivory, bone, antler, or stone. Carving and engraving were the principal techniques. The finely worked carvings often exhibit markedly sculptural qualities of execution, despite their tiny scale (many are small enough to be hidden in a closed hand).

Utilitarian objects such as ivory harpoon heads and other tools were often engraved, but many Eskimo sculptures have no obvious use. Game animals were favorite subjects. The 19th-century painted wooden ritual masks of the southern Alaskan Eskimo, prized by collectors of ethnographic art, are exceptionally imaginative in their lively anthropomorphic shapes and incorporation of diverse materials.

Northwest Coast. The Northwest Coast art tradition is shared by a number of different peoples living along a narrow strip of land facing the Pacific Ocean between southern Alaska and the Columbia River valley. The distinctive and elaborate tradition associated with this region is hundreds of years old and can be subdivided into two major styles. The northern style—associated primarily with HAIDA, TSIMSHIAN, and TLINGIT peoples—is characterized by precise, intellectualized art forms, often displaying great refinement and intricacy of execution. The southern style—identified with the BELLA COOLA of British Columbia and the KWAKIUTL and NOOTKA of Vancouver Island—is by contrast robust and dramatic in its use of strong colors and powerful designs.

In both of these areas art objects traditionally were used to identify rank and were displayed as symbols of wealth and status. Monumental TOTEM poles, painted house posts and canoe ornaments, feasting dishes, ceremonial dance hats and dance masks, helmets, and textiles are among the display objects that were made by professional artists throughout the region. Images were generally portrayed in curvilinear, highly conventionalized and bilaterally symmetrical modes, with great emphasis on the textural qualities of the material. In addition to wood and cedar bark, native art materials included shell, horn, and stone, the wool of mountain goats, and dog

hair, of which the Tlingit Chilkat blankets (actually capes denoting tribal rank) are woven.

California and Basin-Plateau Art. Farther south, among the Indian tribes of California, several artistic traditions flourished, in particular basketry-related arts. Twined baskets and featherwork are characteristic of northern groups such as the HUPA and YUROK, who are noted for their watertight basketry decorated with geometric patterns woven in a variety of twining techniques. Other central and southern California people, notably the POMO and Diegueño, produced coiled and twined baskets of great complexity and beauty.

The Plateau and Great Basin culture areas are situated inland between the Rocky Mountains on the east and the Cascades and Northern Sierras on the west. Parts of this region were influenced by traditions of the Plains culture area during the 19th century. Tribes of the sparsely settled Basin area produced lightweight basketry containers to hold wild foods and seeds. Handsomely styled baskets made in modern times by PAIUTE, WASHO, and other Basin people continue those traditions.

Greater variety existed in the arts of the Plateau area, where village dwellers such as the KLAMATH and Washo traditionally made hieratic, strictly frontal wooden statues. Baskets and costume arts using varied decorative techniques were made by many plateau groups; some, such as the NEZ PERCÉ, wove soft carrying bags. The beadwork of the SHOSHONI was strongly derivative of Plains designs. Rock art of great antiquity is found throughout the intermontane zone, and immense stone alignments forming patterns that often can be read from the air are located in the Basin.

Art of the Southwest. The Southwest culture area extends over present-day Arizona, New Mexico, southern Colorado, and southern Utah. Coiled baskets made at least 2,000 years ago mark the beginning of decorative traditions that continue to flourish among native American artists today.

Pottery decorated with painted motifs was made by HOHOKAM villagers of southern Arizona after about AD 200. Within a short time painted pottery became the dominant art form throughout the region. Many varieties were made by other farming groups, among them the ANASAZI and Mogollon, ancestors of today's PUEBLO peoples. Other domestic Pueblo arts include basketry, textile weaving, and shell and turquoise jewelry. Stone and wood sculpture, masks, including those used by KACHINA dancers, and impressive dry-fresco mural paintings in the underground chambers known as KIVAS are among the many traditional ritual arts. From dry materials such as sand, ocher, and

The linear decorations of this Anasazi pitcher are derived from earlier basket-making designs. The Anasazi, of the American Southwest, developed a distinctive firing technique that yielded vivid black-on-white colors. (Milwaukee Public Museum, Wisconsin.)

finely ground leaves and flower petals, the Pueblos also created sand paintings for their kivas.

The non-Pueblo NAVAJO people further elaborated the sand painting techniques, developing symbolic configurations in conjunction with the many chants used in traditional Navajo curative rites. The Navajo also developed rich styles of textile weaving and from about 1850 on have produced beautiful silver and turquoise jewelry. Other non-Pueblo southwesterners, including the PAPAGO and PIMA of southern Arizona and several bands of Apache, are famous for their coiled basketry.

Northeast, Southeast, and Subarctic Art. Small stone carvings of great subtlety were made 4,500 years ago in the Eastern Woodlands culture area, which covers much of what is now the northeastern United States. Beginning about 1000 BC people of the Adena culture built great mounds in the Ohio Valley and produced carved-stone pipes and engraved tablets associated with complicated burial rites. From about 300 BC to AD 500, artists of the Hopewell tradition built effigy mounds, sculpted naturalistic figures in clay and on stone pipes, and cut out ornaments of sheet copper and of mica.

After about 700, a vigorous tradition of stone, wood, and pottery sculpture is associated with the Mississippian mound-building cultures in the South (see MOUND BUILDERS). Carved-stone effigy pipes and masks of shell and wood are among the ritual objects that have survived. The SEMINOLE of the Southeast today produce distinctive basketry articles and cotton-cloth garments ornamented with colorful appliqué.

Articles of traditional Iroquoian culture include WAMPUM belts, composed of shell beadwork, and powerfully expressive carved masks used in religious ceremonies of the False Face Society. Silk appliqué, quillwork colored with vegetable dyes, floral beaded designs, and small containers of birchbark were traditionally made by Algonquian tribes from around the Great Lakes.

Subarctic art forms often appear to have been derived from traditions of their Plains, Woodlands, or Eskimo neighbors and later translated into a vigorous local idiom.

A Navajo artist creates a sand painting by trickling finely ground sand and mineral pigments through his fingers. The finished painting is an integral part of healing rituals, in which the power of its symbols is believed to cure an ailing person.

The Cheyenne developed a distinctive art form by decorating animal hides with dyed porcupine quills or colored glass beads. The glass beads sewn on this leather waistcoat, dating from about 1900, illustrate Indians on horseback in a typical scene from Plains life.

Plains. A Plains art tradition developed only after the European presence in the New World introduced the horse, the fur trade, and the forced westward movement of many native American groups. By about 1800 the Plains was a melting pot of displaced tribes, who invented a vigorous art style there within a remarkably short time. Prominent Plains art producers included the Blackfoot, Cheyenne, Crow, Kiowa, Pawnee, and Sioux. Art produced by women traditionally was geometric, angular, and nonfigurative. Most of it was painted or embroidered with porcupine quills, and later with glass trade beads, onto garments, moccasins, horsetrappings, parfleches (envelope-shaped satchels), and other utilitarian articles. Art produced by men was figurative, with much of it painted on robes, shields, and tepee covers. After 1875 some imprisoned Plains warriors painted nostalgic pictures of traditional life in earlier times. These depictions represent the climax of the first Pan-Indian art tradition.

North American Indian Art Today. The manufacture of art for domestic use ended in most native American communities when machine-made products replaced many indigenously made utilitarian ones. Art production for native religious and social institutions also ended wherever these were replaced by alien ones. Traditional art for religious and social ritual has been continuously produced, however, in the Southwest, where such traditional household arts as basketry, textile weaving, and pottery also became cash-producing craft industries in the 19th and 20th centuries. Ritual art production was revived during the mid-20th century among peoples of the Northwest Coast, where a high-level craft industry has long flourished. Some tribal ceremonials have also been revived among Plains peoples in recent years, and an impressive array of Pan-Indian religious and social rituals has encouraged the creation of new art traditions. Craft production has similarly become important to the economy of the Canadian and Alaskan Eskimo, who have developed distinctive styles of printmaking and soapstone sculpture.

Indians of North America, music and dance of the

The earliest known inhabitants of North America were a highly music-and-dance-oriented people who responded to their environment by creating a vast repertoire of unwritten songs and dances long before the arrival of the Europeans. These songs and dances were transmitted orally from generation to generation down to the present. Although many native Americans have been assimilated into modern society, several tribal groups are making serious efforts to preserve their traditional cultures.

Music

The music of the North American Indians is primarily vocal-monodic (single melodic line). Some songs are conceived during visionary or dreamlike states, while others are consciously created for special functions. Extemporization is rare. Musical notation is nonexistent in the traditional culture, although isolated instances of mnemonic music aids have been found. Although there is free use of microtones (intervals smaller than a semitone), melodies are based predominantly on the pentatonic (5-tone) and modal scales with intervals of the fourth and fifth being the most common. Indian music and dance range widely in character, from vigorously rhythmic to smooth and melodious. Dance is nearly always accompanied by vocal music and some kind of percussive instruments.

European forms of harmony and counterpoint are absent, although instances of incidental harmony do occur. Accompaniment is mainly percussive: drums with animal-skin heads and rattles, shakers, and scrapers made of various materials such as deer hooves, seashells, bird beaks, animal horns, and so on. Flutes, whistles, and some stringed instruments are also used. All music is

Percussive instruments, such as this gourd rattle, are an integral part of American Indian music and are frequently the only accompaniment. Gourd rattles traditionally contained pebbles or organic material, such as seeds, kernels, or grain.

functional and accompanies specific activities such as dance, work, games, prayer, harvesting, healing, hunting, whaling, burial ceremonies, etc. Chants may contain many vocables or nontranslatable vocal sounds and may have either elaborate or simple language and narrative content. Rhythms are primarily in common meter, seldom irregular, but combinations of meters do occur.

Musical forms are often related to function. For example, the war-dance songs of the Plains Indians generally have a descending contour with an introduction followed by variations of A—as in the formula AA' BA' CA'—ending with a "tail-dance" section that reiterates part of the principal section.

The increasing availability of sound recordings and ethnomusicological documentation of Indian chants has increased the musical skills and expanded the repertoire of the tribal songmakers. Moreover, in Missouri, Colorado, Arkansas, and other border areas, there are non-Indian folklorists who perform Indian dances and songs in the Indian style. Also, far afield, in Europe (Germany, France, Finland) there are non-Indian clubs of American Indian aficionados who present their folklore programs with full regalia.

Other forms of "Indian music" familiar to the public through the concert hall, the cinema, and popular music are often, at best, quasi-romantic, pseudoethnic versions of Western music that do not reflect the true Indian spirit. North American Indian music has undergone a transmutation of values in the oral-to-written process, the results of which have been intended for non-Indian audiences; tribal music has remained in its pristine state only where the Indians have remained on the periphery of American society. This will not always be the case, however, as this music comes to be understood and felt deeply by an ever-growing audience receptive to its unique artistic value. The use of Indian elements in to-day's performing arts can be a revitalizing factor in American music and music education. An excellent example of a successful ensemble is the American Indian Creative Percussion Ensemble, which performed at the National Folk Festival, Vienna, Va., to wide acclaim; the work performed was *Cacega Ayuwipi*, a tour de force for 45 Indian instruments together with standard Western percussion. Although the players donned tribal dress, the techniques used were contemporary and exemplified the best of North American Indian and Western traditions. Another group, the E-Yah-Pah-Hah Indian Chanters, was a development of the first bicultural music education program of the Bureau of Indian Affairs: it featured Indian songs, poetry, and mime within the framework of a modern choir. Also, the initial performance of the first all-Indian halftime marching band at an American football game took place at RFK Stadium in Washington, D.C., in 1977; also, 150 young Indian musicians from 80 tribes and 30 states performed a pageant called "American Indian Heroes, History and Heritage."

Dance

Dance movements derive from the dancers' concept of oneness with the earth and the natural environment. Dance styles vary; they include (1) individual free-form dances, wherein each individual is at liberty to select his or her own movements within accepted and traditional limits (examples: Plains Indian war dances, once performed prior to and after battle, that have evolved into the contest powwow dances or "fancy" dances of today; the Pacific Northwest drama-story dances, in which the dancers wear elaborate, carved masks; the Potlatch stick dances of interior-Alaska Athabascan groups; the Southwest Yaqui Pascolas-deer dances, and various Pueblo Koshare dances of Hopi, Tewa, Tiwa, and Southwest

An Ojibwa (Chippewa) snowshoe dance celebrates the season's first snowfall in this painting (c.1835) by George Catlin. (Smithsonian Institution, Washington, D.C.)

The corn dance of the southwestern Pueblo Indians is held during spring and summer to ensure a good corn harvest.

groups); (2) group free-form dances, wherein each individual selects his or her movements and follows a leader (examples: East Woodland Iroquois longhouse dances, in which a single file of male dancers performs around one or more singers seated in the middle of the room; Southwest Apache Gan, or mountain spirit, dances, wherein male dancers follow a leader around a fire while a group of male singers stands aside and accompanies with songs); and (3) group rigid-form dances, wherein each individual must adhere to uniform dance steps, movements, and formations in a choreographed fashion (examples: the special religious rituals of the Southwest Pueblo Indians, in which as many as 200 dancers, male and female, perform in formations to the accompaniment of 150 male singers and one or more drummers; the Eskimo mime dances with multiple drummers and singers and a line of female dancers; the Eastern Woodlands stomp dances, in which a leading dancer calls out a chant to be echoed by the following line of dancers, male and female, all doing a shuffle step around a wood fire, each dance sequence lasting 20 to 45 minutes during a night of festivities from sundown to dawn; and the powwow social dance known as the "two-step," in which male-female couples follow a lead couple around the dance arena, taking two steps forward and one step back, while the singers are seated around a big drum). Generally, social dances of all tribes are in the last category.

In the older traditional styles, female dancers were not allowed to be as energetic as the male dancers—for example, the old-style Plains Indian war dance, in which the female remained standing in one spot, keeping time to the music while the male dancer moved around the arena. This has changed, however, to allow more freedom

in the modern powwow. Isolated instances of all-female dances do exist (examples: the East Woodlands Penobscot pine-cone dance—group free-form—in which two concentric circles intertwine around a group of male singers seated at a big drum; the Apache girls' puberty rite—individual free-form—with one to three male singers; the Northwest Yakima butterfly dance—individual free-form; the Plateau region Colville swan dance; the Alaska Eskimo mime dance; the Eastern Woodlands sac and fox swan dance; the Plain Caddo turkey dance; the Southwest Pima basket dance; and the Plains Kiowa scalp dance—all group rigid forms.

Couple dances with and without hand contact are fairly common in the larger tribal groups and powwows and may serve exclusively social purposes or may be solely ceremonial (examples: the Eastern Woodlands Iroquois rabbit dance; the Passamoquoddy couple dance; various stomp dances of the Cherokee, Creek, Seminole, Shawnee, Eucha, and Quapaw; the Choctaw wedding and Muskogee dance; the Ute bear dance; the Southwest Pueblo corn dances; the Navajo and Apache social dances, and many others).

In the culturally rich Southwest a fairly common sight at special ceremonials is the line of dancers, all males, each holding gourd rattles, singing to their own accompaniment. If these religious society dances are seen by the public at all, viewers are prohibited from taking photos or making sketches without prior approval from tribal officials. Masked dances are done by specially initiated performers, and the music may not be recorded (the Zuni Shalako dances, performed in December; the Hopi Niman Kachina dances, performed in July; the Kiva dances, performed year-round; the Navajo Yeibichai dances, performed in winter; and healing ceremonies and masked dances of other culture areas).

Dance paraphernalia and attire vary widely; some examples are simple street clothing, as in East Woodlands stomp dances and social dances; special sash and beads, as in Plains Indian gourd dances; highly elaborate, ornate, head-to-toe special clothing, as in the Shalako dances, in which the dancer is completely hidden by the costume; a headpiece of deer tail and porcupine quills, a velvet shirt, silver armbands, leggings of broadcloth, beaded moccasins, bells, and beaded garters, as in the events of the Plains Indians Osage War Dance Society; war-dance feather outfits of the Crow, Blackfeet, Sioux, Cheyenne, Nez Percé, Cree, Arapaho; kilts, leg rattles, spruce branches, headpieces of imitation animal heads or real buffalo skin, as found in the Southwest; or simply the fur parkas worn by the Eskimo in Alaska. Generally, the male dance costume is more colorful than that of the female, although in California the women wear ornate abalone shells, feathers, and woven-basket hats.

indicator An indicator is a chemical substance that, by being able to change color, provides visual evidence of the nature of the chemical system in which it is placed. Most indicators are complicated organic molecules that exist in two different colored forms (sometimes one form is colorless) in different chemical environments, such as acidic or basic solutions. The most common acid-base indicator is litmus paper—paper that is treated with a chemical that appears red in acidic solutions (low pH) and blue in basic solutions (high pH). Acid-base indicators are available for the entire pH range. Methyl green, for example, changes from yellow to blue at pH 0.2–1.8 (acidic); alizarin changes from yellow to red at pH 5.6–7.2 (near neutral); and the common phenolphthalein changes from colorless to pink at pH 8.2–10.0 (basic).

Indicators are used mainly to signal the completion of TITRATIONS, usually by changing color at the endpoint, which is when sufficient titrant has been added to react with all the substance being analyzed in the sample solution. Ordinarily, the tiny amount of intensely colored indicator needed to impart a distinct color consumes a negligibly small volume of titrant when the color changes at the endpoint.

Most indicators can be classified according to their color-change mechanisms or kinds of titrations for which they are applicable. Acid-base indicators respond to changes in hydrogen ion concentration (see PH), oxidation-reduction indicators to changes in oxidizing strength, and metallochromic indicators (for complexation titrations) to changes in free-metal ion concentration. Indicators for precipitation titrations function by adsorbing on a precipitate surface or by forming a (colored) precipitate or colored metal complex. Occasionally, a titrant such as potassium permanganate is highly colored and serves as its own indicator. Fluorescent indicators are useful in titrating turbid or highly colored solutions.

indictment [in-dyt'-ment]

An indictment in criminal law is a formal, written accusation made by a GRAND JURY, charging someone with committing a crime. A bill of indictment is drafted by a public PROSECUTING ATTORNEY and submitted to a grand jury for its approval. Usually the prosecutor produces witnesses and evidence to support the charges, although the grand jury may conduct its own investigation. If, by a majority vote, it finds sufficient evidence to warrant a trial, the grand jury returns a true bill endorsing the bill of indictment. The indictment must, through a bill of particulars, sufficiently apprise the accused of the offense charged so that he or she can adequately prepare a defense. A grand jury may also make a formal accusation, or "presentment," without indictment by a public prosecutor; an accusation made by the prosecutor without a grand jury is called an information. The 5th Amendment to the U.S. Constitution requires presentment or indictment for serious federal crimes, whereas information may be used by state courts.

See also: CRIMINAL JUSTICE.

indigestion

Indigestion, or dyspepsia, commonly refers to general abdominal discomfort during and after meals and may be the result of specific diseases of the stomach or the intestines. The most frequently occurring symptoms are diarrhea, heartburn, abdominal cramps and pain, gas distress, and nausea. Some common caus-es of indigestion in the stomach include swallowing air in large amounts and ulcers. In the intestine, indigestion can arise from colitis, viral or bacterial infections, or chronic inflammation. Other causes include gallstones, malignant growths, and emotional tension. A physician should be consulted when the indigestion is persistent.

indigo [in'-di-goh]

Indigo is a blue vat DYE important in dyeing cotton. The dye was first obtained by fermenting leaves of various species of the tropical leguminous plant *Indigofera*. Indigo was used in India and Egypt long before the time of Christ; Marco Polo described its manufacture in the 13th century. Brought to Europe in the 16th century, *Indigofera* was introduced into South Carolina where it became (mid-18th century) the staple crop of the colony. During the 18th and 19th centuries indigo was the most widely used dye in the United States.

The first synthetic indigo was produced by Adolf von BAEYER in 1880, and today nearly all the world's production is of synthetic rather than natural indigo. In order to make the dye soluble for dyeing cotton, it must first be treated with alkali and a chemical reducing agent.

indium [in'-dee-uhm]

Indium is a relatively uncommon metallic element used in engine-bearing coatings, low-melting alloys, and solid-state electronics. Its chemical symbol is In, its atomic number is 49, and its atomic weight is 114.82. It belongs to Group IIIA in the periodic table, along with boron, aluminum, gallium, and thallium. Ferdinand Reich and H. T. Richter first isolated the element in 1863 at the Freiberg School of Mines in Germany. The name is derived from the intense indigo blue color that indium salts impart to flames; the element's presence still is detected by this method.

Indium is most commonly found in nature associated chemically in low concentration with sulfide minerals of zinc and lead. The average abundance of the element in the Earth's crust is about 0.1 ppm. Pure indium is a highly lustrous, silver white metal (m.p. $156.17°$ C, b.p. $2,070°$ C, density 7.31 g/ml) and is soft and easily deformed under pressure. The metal is a weak reducing agent comparable to copper.

Indium forms salts in the +1 and +3 oxidation states; compounds of the formula type "$InCl_2$" are really mixed +1 and +3 salts, $In(InCl_4)$. The toxicity of most indium compounds is very low. High cost restricts the use of indium and its compounds to special applications.

Indo-European languages

The Indo-European languages, spoken today on every continent and by half the world's population, descend from the speech of a single tribe that lived about 5 or 6 thousand years ago in Europe or western Asia. The surviving branches of Indo-European, the name given to the original prehistoric language, are INDO-IRANIAN, from which descend Bengali, Hindi, Persian, and several other modern languages; BALTIC, which includes modern Lithuanian and Latvian;

SLAVIC, including, among others, Russian, Polish, Czech, and Bulgarian; ARMENIAN; Albanian; GREEK; CELTIC, which includes Irish Gaelic, Scottish Gaelic, Welsh, and Breton; Italic or Romance, including LATIN and its descendants, Italian, French, Spanish, Portuguese, and Romanian; and GERMANIC, which includes German, Dutch, English, and the Scandinavian languages. At least two branches of Indo-European have died out, Anatolian and Tocharian (see LANGUAGES, EXTINCT).

The oldest written remnants of any Indo-European language date from the 17th century BC; they are in Hittite, a representative of the Anatolian branch. Records of Mycenaean, an early form of Greek, in the writing system known as LINEAR B, are nearly as old. Much Sanskrit and classical Greek also survive from well before the Christian era. Comparison of these and other languages reveals that Indo-European was a highly inflected language. Nouns, for example, were declined into eight cases, of which Latin has preserved six and Greek five. The nouns of present-day English, however, have only two cases: either no inflection or the possessive with final s. Indo-European verbs were conjugated for person, number, voice, tense, mood, and aspect.

Until nearly the end of the 18th century, false premises such as that Latin was a corrupt form of Greek prevented anyone from deducing the true relationship among the languages of Europe and Asia. In 1786, however, Sir William JONES, newly arrived in India, suggested that Sanskrit, Greek, and Latin, as well as Germanic and Celtic, descended from an earlier, extinct language; 30 years later Franz Bopp systematically demonstrated this relationship. Someday it may be as clear that Indo-European has a common source with one or more other language families. Semitic (see AFROASIATIC LANGUAGES) and Uralic (see URAL-ALTAIC LANGUAGES) are good candidates, but the evidence is inconclusive.

▬

Indo-Iranian languages [ir-ayn'-ee-uhn] Indo-Iranian, or Aryan, is a branch of the INDO-EUROPEAN family of languages. Indo-Iranian itself has three branches: Indo-Aryan, or Indic, consisting of languages spoken in India, Pakistan, Bangladesh, Nepal, and Sri Lanka by about 450 million people; Iranian, spoken in Iran, Iraq, Afghanistan, Pakistan, Turkey, and the southern USSR by about 50 million people; and Kafiri, or Nuristani, of the Hindu Kush region, spoken by an estimated 100 thousand people. Indo-Iranian's ancestral home is traced to the southern USSR, with outposts as far west as Hungary, where Ossetic was spoken. Romany, the language of the Gypsies, is descended from Indic.

Indic. Vedic (*c.*1200 BC) and the later Classical Sanskrit (see AFROASIATIC LANGUAGES) together constitute Old Indic. Middle Indic extends from Prakrit (*c.*450 BC) and Apabhramsa (AD *c.*250) to about the year 1000, when it gave way to the scores of Modern Indic languages, notably Hindi, Urdu, Bihari, Rajastani, Bengali, Assamese, Oriya, Sindhi, Nepali, Pahari, Kashmiri, Punjabi, Gujarati, Marathi, Konkani, Maldivian, and Sinhalese (see INDIAN LITERATURE).

Sanskrit is a highly inflected language, with elaborate noun, adjective, and verb morphologies. Sanskrit also has compounds, participles, and verbal nouns. Much of this complexity is absent, however, from the various present-day descendants of Sanskrit. Although Marathi and Konkani retain three grammatical genders, Hindi has only masculine and feminine; Bengali, Assamese, and Oriya do not distinguish gender at all. Dual number—the grammatical number denoting two—has been lost, and most Modern Indic languages distinguish only two cases, the nominative and oblique. The verb stem has become so regularized that tenses often must be indicated periphrastically. The simplified case system has led to subject-object-verb being the normal word order, except in Kashmiri, where the object follows the verb.

Most Indic languages are written in the Devanagari script, which has been traced to North Semitic. Urdu, Sindhi, Kashmiri, and Punjabi also employ the ARABIC alphabet.

Iranian. Ancient Iranian (600–300 BC) comprises Avestan, the language of Zoroastrian religious tradition, and Old Persian, the language of the Achaemenid rulers. Pahlavi, Manichaean, and Inscriptional Middle Persian constitute one branch of Middle Iranian (300 BC–AD 950); Parthian, Sogdian, and Saka—including the Khotanese of Buddhist literature—constitute another. In addition to Persian or Farsi, Pashto, Tadzhik, Ossetic, Kurdish, and Baluchi, all of which have literary traditions, Modern Iranian includes many lesser-known languages, such as Wakhi, Yaghnobi, and Shugni. Unlike Indic, however, Iranian lacks lineal continuity from one stage to another.

The phonology and morphology of Vedic Sanskrit and Ancient Iranian are almost identical. As with Sanskrit, simplification and loss of inflection has meant that the flexible word order of Ancient Iranian had to give way to the rigid word orders found in Modern Iranian languages.

CUNEIFORM syllabary, Aramaic, Pahlavi, Greek, and Brahmi scripts have all been used at different times for the Iranian languages. Now, however, the Arabic alphabet, of Aramaic origin, generally prevails.

Kafiri. The identification of Kafiri as a third branch of Indo Iranian is somewhat uncertain. Kafiri was once grouped with Kashmiri, Shina, Indus Kohistani, and Khowar as a Dardic language descended from Paisaci, the Prakrit dialect of northwestern India. Despite many lexical similarities, however, it is now realized that Kafiri maintains certain archaic phonological features no longer found in either Indic or Iranian.

▬

Indochina [in-doh-chy'-nuh] Indochina (French: Indochine) was the name given to France's former dependency in Southeast Asia, an area comprising the present-day states of Cambodia, Laos, and Vietnam. French rule was established between 1862 and 1893. In 1887 the French created the Union of Indochina, a federation of the colony of Cochin China (southern Vietnam) and the protectorates of Annam (central Vietnam), Tonkin (northern Vietnam), and Cambodia; the protectorate of Laos was added in 1893. French rule was interrupted by Japanese incursions during World War II. After the war France agreed to grant self-government to Vietnam, Laos, and Cambodia within the French Union. The Vietnamese nationalists rejected this arrangement, and prolonged bitter fighting culminated in the French defeat (1954) at Dien Bien Phu. France withdrew from Indochina in accordance with the terms of the GENEVA CONFERENCE of 1954.

Indochina War   see VIETNAM WAR

—

Indonesia [in-doh-nee'-zhuh]   The Republic of Indonesia is located in Southeast Asia on an archipelago of more than 13,500 islands astride the equator. SUMATRA, the westernmost major island, lies south of Burma, while IRIAN JAYA on the island of NEW GUINEA is the country's eastern extreme. The total area of the islands approximates that of Mexico. The islands command vital sea routes between Australia, Europe, and the Asian mainland and are the principal link between the Indian and Pacific oceans. The islands lie within the Java (see JAVA SEA), Flores, Banda, and Molucca seas, and are interrupted by the Strait of MALACCA, SUNDA STRAIT, and Makassar Strait. Indonesia, formerly part of the Netherlands East Indies, proclaimed its independence on Aug. 17, 1945, after more than 300 years of Dutch control.

Land and Resources

Territories on five islands make up 90% of Indonesia. The largest territory, Kalimantan, occupies the southern two-thirds of the island of BORNEO and constitutes 28% of Indonesia's total area. Second in size is the island of

Sumatra (Sumatera), with 24% of the total area. Irian Jaya forms 22% of the country; SULAWESI (Celebes), 10%; and the islands of JAVA and Madura—inhabited by 64% of the population—only 7%. Notable small islands include BALI, TIMOR, Lombok, and Sumba of the Lesser SUNDA ISLANDS (Nusa Tenggara) and Halmahera, Buru, Seram, and Ambon, parts of the MOLUCCAS (Maluku).

High mountains, some of them volcanic, extend the length of the archipelago. On Irian Jaya, Indonesia's highest mountain, Jaya, reaches 5,030 m (16,495 ft). High mountains also form the southern edge of Sumatra. They continue across the Sunda Strait, where the famous volcano KRAKATOA is located, and into Java, where they rise to 3,676 m (12,060 ft) in Semeru. On Sulawesi, the mountains rise to 3,455 m (11,335 ft) in Rantekombolo. Swampy lowlands characterize eastern Sumatra, southern Kalimantan, and southeastern Irian Jaya. As in many rainy, tropical areas, the soils are predominantly infertile in Indonesia because of leaching. The most productive are those on Java and adjacent islands.

Most islands are hot and humid throughout the year. Rain falls primarily from December to March. Only western Java and the Lesser Sunda Islands have a dry season, from June to September. Temperatures in coastal areas range from 24° C to 28° C (75° F to 85° F), while the mountains are cooler. The average annual rainfall varies from 3,040 mm (120 in) in Sumatra, Kalimantan, and Irian Jaya to 1,015 mm (40 in) in the Lesser Sundas.

Rivers are numerous, short, and important for irrigation. The longest is the Mamberamo, on Irian Jaya, navigable for 160 km (100 mi).

Tropical rain forest covers most of the islands. Indone-

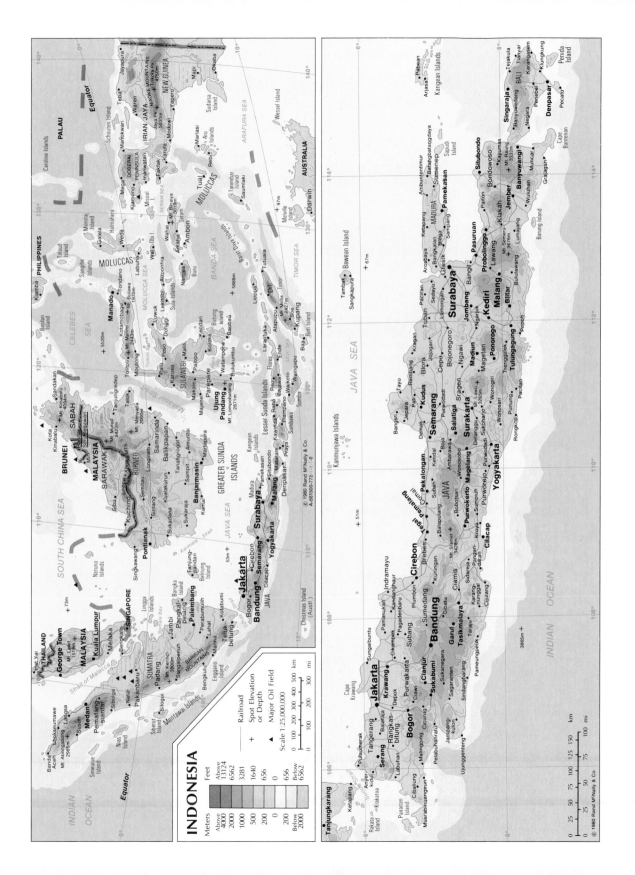

Rice terraces on the island of Bali mark the location of the small rural settlements of the mountainous interior. About 80% of all Indonesians are supported by agriculture.

sia's animals have an Asian affinity in the west and an Australian relationship in the east, suggesting the past existence of land bridges between the islands and the two continents.

Indonesia is potentially rich in mineral resources. The most important is petroleum—with associated natural gas—extracted primarily in eastern Sumatra and Kalimantan. Tin ores are found on a number of islands, as well as bauxite, nickel, coal, copper, uranium, gold, and diamonds, and large reserves of low-grade iron ore.

People

Indonesia has one of the most ethnically diverse populations in the world. More than 300 distinct groups are recognized. The largest is the Javanese, who constitute 40–50% of the total population. Sundanese make up about 15% of the population, and the Madurese an estimated 5%. Smaller, but regionally important groups of ethnic peoples include the Balinese, Batak, Dayak, Papuans, Acehnese (Achinese), and Toradja. The largest nonindigenous group is the Chinese, constituting about 3% of the total.

The official language is Bahasa Indonesia (Indonesian), which evolved from Pasar Malay, a dialect widely spoken on Sumatra and used by traders in the islands. In addition, about 25 other languages, most of Malayo-Polynesian origin, and more than 200 dialects are spoken locally.

Islam is the religion of nearly 85% of the population. Hinduism, widespread in the archipelago before the 14th century, is now practiced by only about 2% of the population, chiefly on Bali. About 8% are Christian, and many Chinese follow Buddhist-Daoist teachings. Animist religions are followed by tribes in remote areas.

Indonesia is the world's fifth most populous nation. About 64% of the population are crowded onto the island of Java. Other islands, by contrast, are sparsely populated. The largest cities are JAKARTA (the capital), BANDUNG, SURABAYA, Semarang, Malang, Surakarta, and Yogyakarta, all of which are on Java, and Medan, on Sumatra.

Compulsory elementary-school education begins at age six or seven and lasts for six years, followed by six years of secondary-school education. The University of Indonesia (1950) at Jakarta and numerous other institutions provide higher-education opportunities. Health facilities are limited, and many rural areas are grossly underserved.

The Javanese are famous for BATIK, a cloth imprinted with intricate, elaborate designs made by waxing and dyeing fabric. Indonesia is also known for SHADOW PLAYS, a popular art form used to instill moral values and for social comment. The Museum of Indonesian Culture in Jakarta houses an extensive collection of early Indonesian ceramics. (See also SOUTHEAST ASIAN ART AND ARCHITECTURE.)

Economic Activity

Indonesia's traditional subsistence and trading economy was altered radically under the rule of the Dutch. Export crops were emphasized, and for many years their growth was mandatory. A state-dominated, centralized economic system was developed after independence, but it was replaced in 1969 by the "New Order" of President Suharto, designed to build an agriculture-based economy capable of supporting simultaneous development of large-scale industrial projects and smaller consumer- and export-oriented processing industries. Economic development has been largely financed by foreign aid.

Mining and Manufacturing. Indonesia's principal mineral resource is petroleum, which accounts for more than 50% of all export earnings. Indonesia, a member of the ORGANIZATION OF PETROLEUM EXPORTING COUNTRIES since 1962, placed its oil industry under government control in 1965. Since that time refinery capacity has increased greatly.

Indonesia is the world's largest producer of liquefied natural gas. It ranks third in world tin production after Malaysia and Thailand. Bauxite is mined on Sumatra, nickel on Sulawesi, coal on Sumatra and Kalimantan, and copper on Irian Jaya.

Most manufacturing plants are on Java, where Jakarta and Surabaya are the leading industrial centers. Major industries, in addition to the processing of agricultural products, include petroleum refining and the manufacture of fertilizers, pharmaceuticals, cement, textiles, iron and steel, and plywood.

Energy. Power facilities are state owned and primarily limited to urban areas and major industrial projects. They remain inadequate despite the expansion of electrical generating capacity from 653 MW in 1966 to 11,600 MW in 1989.

Agriculture, Forestry, and Fishing. Agriculture continues to be the mainstay of the Indonesian economy, although it contributes less than 10% of export earnings. Indonesia's government was an early proponent of the GREEN REVOLUTION, and by 1984 the country had become self-sufficient in rice. Vegetables, fruits, and poultry are also raised. Cash crops, grown mostly on large estates, include rubber, palm oil, coffee, sugar, tobacco, and cocoa.

Indonesia has more than 8 million landless farmers. To open remote areas to development and provide a livelihood for the landless, the government offers free land, housing, and other assistance to those willing to move from overcrowded Java, Bali, and Madura to less-developed islands.

Indonesia has abundant forests, and wood products—especially plywood and teak—are the chief export after petroleum and natural gas. Fish are locally important, but commercial fishing is largely undeveloped.

Transportation. Despite Indonesia's rough terrain and separated commercial centers, transportation is improving. Most of the new highways are spread over Sumatra, Sulawesi, and Kalimantan; the antiquated railway system is concentrated on Java. Most of the country's imports and exports pass through Tanjung Priok (near Jakarta), Tanjung Perak (near Surabaya), Belawan (near Medan), and Padang. A new international airport in Jakarta opened in 1985.

Trade. Exports include petroleum, liquefied natural gas, timber and plywood, rubber, coffee, tin, and palm oil. The principal imports are machinery, electrical equipment, mineral fuels, chemicals, and base metals.

Government

The constitution of August 1945 was restored on July 5, 1959, in place of two provisional constitutions adopted in 1950. Executive power is vested in the president, who is elected by the People's Consultative Assembly (MPR) for a 5-year term, and in the president's appointed cabinet. Legislative power rests with the Assembly's 460-member Council of Representatives, but in effect the president rules by decree. Governors and regents appointed by the central government administer local government for 27 provinces and some 250 regencies.

History

Indonesia is thought to have been settled mainly by peoples from Malaya and Oceania, and the area was dominated from the 3d to the 13th century by the Hindu and Buddhist Indianized kingdoms of Srivijaya, Mataram, Sailendra, Kediri, and the Majapahit. Islamic influences, brought by Arabic and other traders in the 14th and 15th centuries, replaced the Indian religions in most areas except Bali. From 1602 until 1798 most of the islands were controlled by the Dutch East India Company (see EAST INDIA COMPANY, DUTCH), and from 1816 to 1949, Indonesia was regarded as a colony of the Netherlands. During World War II, Japan occupied the islands and encouraged many Indonesians in their quest for independence.

On Aug. 17, 1945, Indonesian nationalists led by SUKARNO and Muhammad Hatta proclaimed the nation independent. On Dec. 27, 1949, after much dispute, the Netherlands transferred sovereignty. West Irian became part of Indonesia in 1963, and was renamed Irian Jaya in

Jakarta, located on the northwestern coast of Java, is the capital and largest city of Indonesia. A port city and industrial and administrative center, Jakarta has experienced rapid growth since the country's independence in 1949.

1973. On July 17, 1976, the former Portuguese territory of East Timor was annexed.

Sukarno was Indonesia's first president. He ruled from 1945 to 1965. During these years, the economy declined, and Indonesia's continually closer ties with the Communist bloc stifled assistance from Western nations. At the end of September 1965, an attempted Communist coup led to an anti-Communist takeover of the government by the military under General SUHARTO. An estimated 250,000 were killed in the fighting. Sukarno continued temporarily as president, but de facto control of the nation was transferred to Suharto, who became acting president in March 1967.

Suharto looked to the West for economic aid while trying to create the internal stability that would encourage foreign investment. To unify his diverse nation he promoted *Pancasila*, a secular national ideology first enunciated by Sukarno in 1945. Raids against Malaysia, initiated by Sukarno in 1964, were ended. In 1966, Indonesia rejoined the United Nations, from which it had withdrawn in 1965; in 1967 it became a founding member of the ASEAN. Elections, held in 1968 for the first time in 13 years, gave Suharto the presidency. Despite Muslim fundamentalist opposition, a law passed in 1985 required all mass religious, cultural, and professional organizations to adopt *Pancasila*. That same year, Indonesia celebrated the 30th anniversary of the Bandung conference, a precursor of the NONALIGNED MOVEMENT. Suharto won a fifth term as president in 1988; his Golkar party won a landslide victory in the 1987 legislative elections. In 1990, Indonesia and China restored diplomatic relations, severed in 1967.

---

indri   The indri is an arboreal, lemurlike primate, *Indri indri*, formerly found in the rain forests along the eastern coast of Madagascar from sea level to mountain heights of nearly 1,800 m (6,000 ft) but now largely confined to

The largest of all lemurlike animals, the indri rarely descends from the trees. Its hands, six times as long as they are wide, are adapted for grasping branches.

a small area in the central coastal region. Its numbers are steadily dwindling due to habitat destruction (deforestation) by humans. The indri is a member of the family Indriidae, which also contains three other living species: the avahi, or woolly indri, *Avahi,* and two species of sifakas, *Propithecus,* all native to Madagascar. The indri stands about 70 cm (2.5 ft) tall and has a narrow, nearly hairless muzzle, very long hind legs, and a stumpy tail. Its coat is dense and silky and variable in pattern but often is black on the head, shoulders, back, upper arms, front of the thighs, and hands and feet, and white, gray, or pale red on the rump, the back of the legs, and the lower arms.

Indris are diurnal and feed on leaves, fruit, and flowers. They may live singly or, more commonly, in small family groups of two to five individuals. It is thought that they produce a single young after a gestation period of about 60 days. The indri has a laryngeal air sac, or throat pouch, and is able to produce very loud doglike howls.

inductance [in-duhk'-tens]   Inductance is a property of an electrical circuit in which an electromotive force (emf) is induced (see ELECTROMAGNETIC INDUCTION) by a change in current; the current change may occur either in the circuit itself or in a nearby circuit. The symbol for inductance is *L*; it is measured in units of henrys, named for Joseph Henry.

Inductance results from the interaction of the magnetic field, established by the current, with the charges inside the conductor. Inductance can be increased by winding wire into a coil to strengthen the interaction. According to LENZ'S LAW, if a changing current flows through the inductance coil, or INDUCTOR, an emf is induced that opposes the

change in the current flow. Thus, a drop in the current induces an emf in the same direction as the current, supporting the original current; if the current increases, the induced emf acts in the opposite direction, opposing it.

If a single coil is involved, the phenomenon is known as self-inductance. Two nearby coils can be linked by mutual inductance, as in a TRANSFORMER.

induction   Induction is a major kind of reasoning process (see LOGIC) in which a conclusion is drawn from particular cases. It is usually contrasted with DEDUCTION, the reasoning process in which the conclusion logically follows from the premises, and in which the conclusion has to be true if the premises are true. In inductive reasoning, on the contrary, there is no logical movement from premises to conclusion. The premises constitute good reasons for accepting the conclusion. The premises in inductive reasoning are usually based on facts or observations. There is always a possibility, though, that the premises may be true while the conclusion is false, since there is not necessarily a logical relationship between premises and conclusion. For example, a child growing up in a community where only English is spoken may wrongly conclude by induction that everyone in the world speaks English.

What is called mathematical induction is actually not a form of induction at all; rather, it is a special kind of deductive mathematical reasoning process.

inductor   An inductor is an electrical component that opposes any change in an electrical current. Also known as a coil or choke, it is composed of a coil of wire wound around a supporting core that may be magnetic or nonmagnetic. When a current running through the coil increases or decreases, the magnetic field around the coil also increases or decreases, generating (because of ELECTROMAGNETIC INDUCTION) a current in the coil opposing the original current. Because of this property, known as INDUCTANCE, an inductor is often used in an AC-to-DC power-supply filter circuit (see FILTER, ELECTRONIC) to reduce the fluctuations and smooth the current.

Another important application is in a FLUORESCENT LIGHT circuit, in which a voltage of several hundred volts is required to cause the initial current, and a much lower voltage is needed to keep the lamp lighted. A type of inductor known as a ballast serves both needs. In the preheat type of fluorescent lamp, a starter is in series with the lamp filaments and the ballast. This starter opens a few seconds after the lamp is turned on, interrupting current through the ballast. The collapse of the magnetic field induces a high voltage in the inductor, which lights the lamp. The voltage across the lamp decreases.

Because of the good magnetic properties of iron, the inductance of iron-core coils can be as high as 50–100 henries (H). Such coils are generally used at low frequencies, such as 60 or 400 Hz. Iron-core coils, however, can also be used with DC, as in the IGNITION SYSTEM of an automobile, in which two coils are wound on the same core. The primary is composed of several hundred turns of heavy wire. The secondary coil is composed of several thousand turns that produce 20 to 40 kV when the primary side is interrupted. Such an arrangement of inductors is called an induction coil, although it is actually a TRANSFORMER.

High-frequency air-core inductors are wound on a fiber, ceramic, or plastic nonmagnetic core and are used primarily in communication equipment.

indulgences [in-duhl'-jen-sez]   In the Roman Catholic church an indulgence is the remission of the punishment that remains due for SIN after sacramental absolution. This remission, which is granted by ecclesiastical authority, applies only to temporal punishment (in this world or in PURGATORY) and is, therefore, to be distinguished from divine forgiveness.

In the medieval period, punishments for breaches of church discipline could be commuted for proportionate fines. This practice was so general that the sale of indulgences was an important source of church revenue. Abuse of the system led to the protest of Martin LUTHER, whose 95 theses against the misuse of indulgences (1517) precipitated the REFORMATION in Germany. At the Council of Trent (see TRENT, COUNCIL OF) the Roman Catholic church reformed the system, which was continued only under carefully controlled conditions. A decree of Pope Pius V (1567) finally prohibited the sale of indulgences.

Indus [in'-duhs]   The Indus River, one of South Asia's longest rivers, flows for 2,900 km (1,800 mi) from its source in Tibet through northern India and then for most of its course through Pakistan. Its drainage basin covers 1,165,500 km^2 (450,000 mi^2). Its waters irrigate the arid PUNJAB plain, making it Pakistan's most productive agricultural region. Large dams have been constructed by both Pakistan and India, providing water for irrigation and hydroelectric power. Tarbela Dam, completed in 1974, is the world's largest earth-fill dam.

The river's source is the meltwater and streams of the Himalayas and the Karakoram Range. The Indus flows northwestward through the mountainous Indian state of Jammu and Kashmir, where it is a turbulent, unnavigable stream. It then turns south, entering Pakistan, and as it leaves the mountains it becomes broad and silt-laden. Here it receives its major tributary, the Punjab, with the waters of that river's five tributaries, the SUTLEJ, Chenab, Jhelum, Ravi, and Beas rivers. The Indus delta begins at Tatta, about 110 km (70 mi) from the Arabian Sea coast, where the river splits into several channels.

The Indus Valley fostered human settlement more than 70,000 years ago. Harappa and Mohenjo-daro, the great cities of the INDUS CIVILIZATION, were built along the river about 2500 BC. Until the British period the Indus formed the frontier of India. Use of the river's water has been a source of dispute between India and Pakistan during recent years.

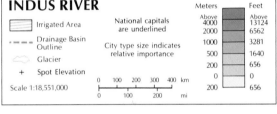

INDUS RIVER

		Meters	Feet
Irrigated Area	National capitals are underlined	Above 4000	Above 13124
Drainage Basin Outline	City type size indicates relative importance	2000	6562
Glacier		1000	3281
+ Spot Elevation		500	1640
		200	656
		0	0
Scale 1:18,551,000	0 100 200 300 400 km	200	656
	0 100 200 mi		

Indus civilization   The Indus civilization, an ancient civilization in South Asia, existed from about 2700 to 1750 BC. It is sometimes referred to as the Harappan civilization, named for the site of Harappa, one of its major centers. Geographically one of the most extensive early civilizations of the Old World, it stretched from north of the Hindu Kush down the entire length of the Indus and beyond into peninsular India; in the west, outposts that extended almost to the present-day Iranian-Pakistani border have been found along the inhospitable Makran coast. Unlike the ancient Sumerian and Egyptian civilizations, which were largely restricted to river valleys and their alluvial plains, remains of the Indus civilization have been found in diverse environmental settings. Its settlements were, however, remarkably similar in layout and material culture.

Origins. Because its script remains undeciphered, the Indus civilization is known only from archaeological evidence. Excavations at the important site of Mehrgarh, at the foot of the Bolan Pass, indicate that large settlements may have existed as early as the 7th millennium BC. Two thousand years later sites in eastern Baluchistan and the

Indus Valley were larger and more numerous; at some, like Kot Diji on the east bank of the Indus, archaeologists have found various distinctive ceramic objects, such as terra-cotta toy carts. From this evidence archaeologists speculate that there took place an early, or pre-Harappan, spread of culture from the Punjab south to the Arabian Sea. Scholars differ as to whether or not these early settlements evolved directly into the urban communities of the mature Indus civilization, but it is clear from archaeological research that by the late 4th millennium (c.3200 BC) large villages were being formed along the entire course of the Indus River.

Major Centers. During the 1920s the so-called twin capitals of Indus civilization, Mohenjo-daro and Harappa, were excavated under the direction of Sir John Marshall; other important settlements were surveyed by Sir Aurel Stein and N. G. Majumdar. The existence of a great civilization roughly contemporaneous with that of Sumer and of ancient Egypt soon was confirmed. Hundreds of smaller settlements have since been discovered. Recent archaeological investigation has been concentrated on documenting the beginnings of urban life in the area, and a

The map below illustrates the extent and major cities of the Indus civilization, which existed from about 2700 to 1750 BC in ancient India.

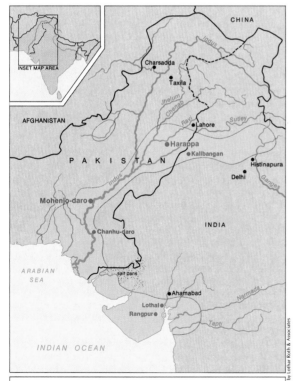

INDUS CIVILIZATION

Area of civilization
c. 2700 to 1750 B.C.

—— Modern boundaries

● Major centers of civilization

0   km   500
0   mi   300

Cartographic Production by Lothar Roth & Associates

variety of different types of sites have been excavated, including fishing villages, trading outposts, and what may have been a port.

Mohenjo-daro was situated along the west bank of the Indus River, about 320 km (200 mi) north of Karachi, Pakistan. Like most cities of the Indus civilization, it consisted of two major areas of occupation: a high citadel to the west and a lower city of domestic dwellings to the east. Careful urban planning is evident in the neat arrangement of the major buildings contained in the citadel. The lower city, which was tightly packed with residential units, was also constructed on a grid pattern. Baked-brick houses faced the street, and domestic life was centered on an enclosed courtyard. Sanitation was provided through an extensive system of covered drains running the length of the main streets and connected by chutes with most residences.

The almost identical city of Harappa, located 640 km (400 mi) northeast of Mohenjo-daro, in the Punjab of India, and the nearby but smaller site of Kalibangan, situated farther east along the banks of the now extinct Ghaggar-Hakra River, and several more cities indicate that at the height of the Indus civilization multiple regional centers may have been built according to a standard plan.

Aspects of Indus Culture. The Indus people supported themselves by irrigation-based agriculture. They grew domesticated rice, wheat, and barley, and they may have cultivated dates and cotton. Among the first people in the world known to have kept chickens, they also had dogs, buffalo, and humped cattle. They may also have domesticated pigs, horses, camels, and, possibly, elephants.

Archaeologists have long commented on the uniformity and standardization of the material remains of the Indus civilization. Except in outposts along the Makran coast and in its most remote colonies, Indus cities were all built of baked-brick blocks with a standard proportion of length to width to thickness of 4:2:1. Pottery forms and designs were also remarkably similar throughout the vast area. Few large works of art or pieces of statuary have been discovered. Spears, knives, and other objects of copper and bronze have been found, but most are of rather poor quality.

The most developed craft appears to have been the carving and drilling of square stamp seals that depict various domestic animals, such as humped bulls, rhinoceroses, and elephants. These seals, numbering in the thousands, are the major source of writings in the pictographic Indus script. Attempts to decipher these symbols have so far been unsuccessful, largely because no major inscriptions have been discovered. This lack of evidence has forced some scholars to conclude that the characters do not represent writing in the same sense as Sumerian CUNEIFORM or Egyptian HIEROGLYPHICS; instead, they may symbolize elaborate heraldic devices or standards that served to identify families and their properties from others. Three seals from Mohenjo-daro show a seated horned deity surrounded by wild animals, an image that may foreshadow the portrayal of the Hindu god SHIVA in his aspect of *Pasupati*, the Lord of Beasts. The apparent cult of the bull and the emphasis on washing, or ablutions, that are suggested by the material remains raise the fascinating if

Excavations at Mohenjo-daro, a major center of Indus civilization, have yielded rich archaeological finds. The Great Bath at Mohenjo-daro comprised bathing and robing rooms around a pool and courtyard.

unanswerable question of the influence of this early pre-Aryan civilization on Hindu practices in historic India.

Decline of Indus Civilization. The Indus civilization appears to have declined rapidly in the early 2d millennium BC. The archaeological evidence indicates that the efficient urban administration of Mohenjo-daro had deteriorated by c.1750 BC, when the construction of houses markedly declined. Evidence has also been discovered of intermittent and devastating floods from this time, and, intriguingly, the remains of 38 corpses were found apparently left unburied at the latest level of occupation.

Some scholars have postulated a final massacre, possibly by conquering ARYAN peoples whose epics refer to their conquest of walled cities. Others have attributed the decline to an ecological catastrophe that created violent and recurrent flooding along the southern course of the Indus. Still others suggest that the Indus civilization may have overextended itself, resulting in its collapse under the combined onslaught of natural disasters and barbarian incursions.

industrial arts programs   Industrial arts programs are designed to give schoolchildren a practical understanding of how things work, the materials they are made of, and the tools that are used in their construction. Programs explore aspects of technology, such as communications, power, and manufacturing. The educational pioneers John Amos COMENIUS, Maria MONTESSORI, and Johann Heinrich PESTALOZZI encouraged children to work with various materials and tools, and John DEWEY believed that manual creativity fostered both intellectual and creative development.

From kindergarten through grade six, children learn to use simple materials, assisted by hand and machine tools. Experiments with materials like clay, textiles, and wood are usually conducted in the classroom. At the secondary level, students are offered the opportunity to de-velop their creative or mechanical talents by experimenting with more sophisticated tools, materials, machines, and processes in the actual design, construction, and evaluation of industrial arts projects. Courses are given in such areas as electronics, metalworking, woodworking, mechanical drawing, textiles, and photography.

industrial design   The industrial designer creates prototypes of products for reproduction by machine. The design process often includes packaging, styling, retail displays, commercial architecture, and other devices for distribution of mass-produced goods. Industrial designers also facilitate packaging and delivery of ideas, images, and information to help manufacturers market their products.

The Beginnings of Industrial Design. Before the Industrial Revolution a single craftsperson carried out the inseparable processes of design and manufacture. After the introduction of large-scale machine production and the division of labor early in the 19th century, the role of patternmaker (designer) became independent. In Great Britain, artists found employment in such industries as textiles, ceramics, and cast iron. They provided drawings to be interpreted by shop foremen, imitating patterns and styles of traditional handicraft production. In 1849 design reformer Henry Cole began publishing the *Journal of Design*, in which he argued that true beauty implied utility, and that neither could be obtained without complete knowledge of manufacturing processes and materials. Cole promoted the Great Exhibition of 1851 at London's CRYSTAL PALACE. In the United States, as in Great Britain, 19th-century industrial design was largely a matter of surface ornamentation. In both countries, leaders of the ARTS AND CRAFTS MOVEMENT, such as William MORRIS and Gustav Stickley, denounced machine production as degrading to both worker and consumer, maintaining that only handmade goods could have real aesthetic worth. This philosophy was shared by the Wiener Werkstätte, a Viennese group founded in 1903.

The basic principle of modern industrial design was first formulated in 1901 by the American architect Frank Lloyd WRIGHT in a lecture entitled "The Art and Craft of the Machine." Rejecting handicraft production as too expensive, Wright returned to Cole's doctrine by asserting that future designers would create prototypes for machine reproduction after becoming familiar with modern techniques and materials.

German interest in design for mass production was strengthened in 1919 when Walter GROPIUS founded the BAUHAUS school at Weimar. Committed to a union of art and industry, Bauhaus leaders anticipated moral and social reform through wide distribution of mass-produced objects. Former faculty and students (including Herbert Bayer, Marcel BREUER, Ludwig MIES VAN DER ROHE, László MOHOLY-NAGY, and Wilhelm Wagenfeld) were a major influence on design after World War II.

The Emergence of the Design Profession. Despite strong traditions of design theory in Great Britain and Germany, industrial design as a full-fledged profession developed first in the United States. In the late 1920s, as a re-

Elias Howe's sewing machine (above left), patented in 1846, exemplifies the kind of functional design favored by 19th-century reformer Henry Cole. The geometric lines and stylized decoration of a 1932 radio receiver (above right) show the influence of Art Deco. Tahiti (right), a table lamp designed by Ettore Sottsass, represents the exuberant work of Memphis, a contemporary Italian design group.

cialism widened. Only after the pop-art movement of the 1960s did British design emerge from relative obscurity. In Germany the Bauhaus tradition of austerity and functional purity was revived at the Hochschule für Gestaltung (School for Design), under the direction of Max BILL and later Tomás Maldonado. Dieter Rams, who became head of design at Braun AG in the mid-1950s, was also very influential. Under his direction, Braun's small consumer appliances exhibited a restrained elegance. Two other European trends exerted a significant influence. Firmly rooted in folk traditions of craft production, Scandinavian designers such as Alvar AALTO, Arne JACOBSEN, and Kay Bojesen countered the cold precision of Bauhaus modernism. The warm biomorphic forms and textures of Scandinavian furniture, flatware, glass, and ceramics revealed a desire to go with, rather than against, the grain of nature. At the opposite extreme, urbane Italian designers playfully celebrated the artificial.

Contemporary American Design. European developments received publicity in the United States at the Museum of Modern Art (MOMA), which exhibited the work of Bauhaus refugees. MOMA sponsored design exhibits aimed at improving public taste during the 1940s and 1950s. MOMA also promoted the work of such American designers as Charles EAMES, Eero SAARINEN, and George Nelson. Critics dismissed most examples of commercial design as mere styling—"borax and chrome." However, such work comprised most of the mass-produced products sold in the United States. Dozens of young industrial designers worked on automobiles, radios, television sets, dishwashers, furniture, and other products of the postwar years.

In the 1960s social consciousness was on the rise, and industrial designers began to criticize their own commercialism. During the 1970s the profession was sharply criticized by two designers with conflicting views of the proper scale of design activities. R. Buckminster FULLER advocated a comprehensive world design science that would orchestrate the needs and resources of the entire planet (which he called "Spaceship Earth"). At the opposite extreme, Victor Papanek challenged designers to consider special problems of the aging, the handicapped, the poor, and the inhabitants of developing nations.

By the mid-1980s the gap between elite and commercial design narrowed considerably. Many products were reduced in size and had to be substantially redesigned. Computer-aided design promised to transform the way designers worked.

sponse to economic recession, American businesses began to hire industrial designers to endow products with desirability. Inspired by the Art Deco style displayed at the Paris exhibition of 1925, these new designers created cameras, radios, and other products with stylish zigzag lines, later adopting the aerodynamic forms of streamlining. Independent consultants including Walter D. TEAGUE, Norman BEL GEDDES, Raymond LOEWY, Harold Van Doren, and Henry DREYFUSS studied manufacturing processes and materials, were concerned with function as well as appearance, and soon developed large staffs of draftspersons, modelers, engineers, architects, and market researchers. By 1940, industrial design was an accepted business practice. A few companies established in-house design departments, a practice that increased after World War II. The goal of some American designers was to provide the industrial age with visual coherence and social harmony, which was shown in the futuristic exhibits of the New York World's Fair of 1939.

Postwar Europe. After World War II the gap between high-minded European design and American commer-

industrial engineering Industrial engineering, a branch both of engineering and of industrial management, is primarily concerned with the analysis of the processes of production and the design of methods for making them more efficient. An analysis of production process might include the selection of tools and materials and the design of the sequence of production operations. The industrial engineer may also design plant facilities, establish work standards through time and motion studies, develop wage scales based on an analysis of required job skill levels, and determine quality-control procedures.

industrial management Industrial management is concerned with the management of manufacturing enterprises. In its broadest sense, the term includes such specialized areas of management responsibility as INDUSTRIAL RELATIONS, MARKETING, and production management. A narrower definition restricts industrial management to the management of production processes.

A production process is a process that transforms an input of capital, labor, and raw materials into a physical product. The primary objective of industrial management is to perform this transformation as efficiently as possible.

The economics of the production process were discussed by Adam SMITH in the 18th century and by Charles BABBAGE in the 19th, but it was Frederick W. TAYLOR who popularized the basic concepts of industrial management in the early 20th century. Taylor promoted the idea of scientific management. Several fields of management evolved from his philosophy, including time and motion study.

The concept of division of labor was carried to its logical extreme in 1913 by a technological innovation—the use of a moving ASSEMBLY LINE to manufacture Ford automobiles. More recently, efforts have been made to enrich factory work by making it more varied and more challenging.

Another significant development in the early 1900s was the use of mathematical models to analyze common problems in industrial management. In 1915, F. W. Harris developed the first mathematical formula that could be used to determine an economical method for maintaining inventories. In 1931, Walter Shewhart demonstrated that statistical methods could be used to reduce the costs of the operations involved in quality control. This trend accelerated during World War II, when large mathematical models were developed to analyze problems. Mathematical modeling provided the basis for the development of the field of operations research, which now provides many of the analytical tools used in management science.

Virtually every aspect of industrial management has been affected by the use of mathematical analysis. A mathematical modeling approach known as linear programming has been applied to the problem of scheduling and allocating resources in many production systems. Theories that were developed to explain the statistical behavior of waiting lines (QUEUING THEORY) were applied to other problems as well.

Industrial management has been criticized because of its narrow definition of the notion of an efficient production process. Efforts are currently under way to enlarge the concept of efficiency to include the costs of pollution control and the social impacts of production.

industrial psychology Industrial and organizational psychology is the field of applied psychology that studies the behavior of persons in organizational work settings. Its areas of concern are personnel selection; the mapping of organizational processes; training; improvement of employee morale and working conditions; and

improvement of both individual and group productivity. ERGONOMICS and consumer psychology, once areas of industrial psychology, are now often considered fields in their own right.

Industrial psychology, on the one hand, focuses on modifying equipment, work settings, and people to maximize the productivity of the technological process itself. On the other hand, its focus on the individual rights and satisfactions of employees seems to serve the cause of employees.

Pioneers in the field included F. W. TAYLOR and Frank and Lilian GILBRETH, who originated (1911) time and motion study, and Hugo Münsterberg (1863–1916), author of *Psychology and Industrial Efficiency* (1913). In the United States, industrial psychology received impetus from psychologists' work with the military during World War I. The 1930s saw the widespread adoption of vocational guidance and counseling. Improved measurement methods and job-testing techniques were developed during and after World War II.

Industrial psychologists study worker motivation and morale, reward systems, communication processes, and working conditions as factors that may affect productivity and worker satisfaction. Many variations of Victor Vroom's expectancy theory—that performance and satisfaction are functions of employee expectancies and values—have received considerable theoretical and research attention.

Personnel selection is associated mainly with testing (see PSYCHOLOGICAL MEASUREMENT). Psychologists analyze jobs according to what employees must do to carry them out successfully, and develop tests that are helpful in evaluating individuals' qualifications for doing different jobs. Selection and job placement in an organization should meet criteria discovered in the job analysis, and should also contribute positively to each individual's own vocational fulfillment. These objectives may not always be compatible, however. It is the job of the industrial psychologist to seek, in as many ways as possible, to make them compatible. Psychological testing has sometimes been criticized for discriminating unfairly against minority groups and the economically disadvantaged. Professional guidelines have been formulated by the American Psychological Association and by government agencies to aid users in making fair and proper use of such tests.

industrial relations The field of industrial relations encompasses the formal relations between employers and employees and generally involves the work of personnel specialists, industrial engineers, psychologists, and labor-relations experts. In a large company the following activities may be considered industrial-relations functions: recruiting and selecting new employees and developing the terms and conditions of employment; classifying jobs and occupations; negotiating with unions; implementing government regulations that affect the work force; and instituting training programs.

Selecting and Evaluating Workers. When a company seeks to fill a vacant job, it may advertise the opening, promote from within, or ask an employment agency to send applicants. After interviewing, checking references, and perhaps administering a battery of tests, the company selects an employee from among the applicants. The new worker will usually require some training, which may consist of on-the-job learning or formal instruction. Many large companies formally evaluate the performance of workers, using objective standards to measure the quality and quantity of work produced. These aspects of industrial relations constitute what is usually called personnel administration or human-resources management. Much of this work requires a knowledge of INDUSTRIAL PSYCHOLOGY, PSYCHOLOGICAL MEASUREMENT, and STATISTICS.

Incentive Systems. Most workers are paid by the hour or the day. In some industries, however, payment is based on "piece rates," or a specific amount of money for each item produced. Developing a satisfactory incentive system requires that experts trained in INDUSTRIAL ENGINEERING determine what workers can reasonably be expected to produce and what can be considered equitable rates of pay for producing different amounts.

Collective Bargaining. When a company has been organized by a union, the terms and conditions of employment—wages, hours, holidays, pensions, medical benefits, insurance—are determined in negotiations between the union and the employer and are set down in a formal contract (see LABOR UNION). In addition, the union-management contract provides channels through which workers who feel their rights have been violated may seek redress. If the union and management cannot resolve the problem, it may be referred to a neutral third party for ARBITRATION (labor-management and commercial).

Industrial Revolution The term *Industrial Revolution* describes the historical transformation of traditional into modern societies by industrialization of the economy. The main defining feature of the revolution was a dramatic increase in per capita production that was made possible by the mechanization of manufacturing and other processes that were carried out in factories (see FACTORY SYSTEM). Its main social impact was that it changed an agrarian into an urban industrial society. The historical term *Industrial Revolution* can be applied to specific countries and periods of the past, but the process known as industrialization is still going on, particularly in developing countries.

The Revolution in Great Britain

Historians disagree on the exact causes of Britain's Industrial Revolution, which may be viewed as stemming from a variety of related and coincidental factors.

Britain's Advantages. Britain had certain natural advantages that help to explain why the Industrial Revolution began there. It was richly endowed with coal and iron ore, easily navigable waterways, and easily negotiated coasts. It was favorably placed at the crossroads of international trade, and internal trade was stimulated by the absence of domestic tariffs in what was, after the union of England and Scotland in 1707, the largest free-trade

area in Europe. Political liberty was guaranteed, and a relatively open social structure made upward social mobility common, thus giving an incentive to the accumulation of wealth. The principles of the Protestant NONCONFORMISTS, who were to form the backbone of the new middle class, encouraged industry and thrift. New knowledge, especially in science, was freely disseminated, breeding an inventiveness and a willingness to accept change. In short, 18th-century British society provided the framework within which could interact the effects of five fundamental sorts of change—in agriculture, population, technology, commerce, and transportation.

The Agrarian and Demographic Revolutions. Industrialization usually goes hand in hand with agrarian reform if for no other reason than that an agrarian revolution allows a relatively small agrarian labor force to feed a larger manufacturing work force. In Britain the revolution in land use, even more than improved technology, dramatically increased agricultural production. The ENCLOSURE movement of the 18th century increased the efficiency of farm lands as common pastures and fields were replaced by more compact and easily farmed private holdings. Farmers were thus motivated to experiment with new forms of husbandry—notably root crop rotation and convertibility between cultivated and pasture land—that increased productivity.

The stimulus to these agrarian changes was the increased demand for food generated by a demographic revolution—Britain's population nearly doubled in the 18th century and doubled again by 1850. Population growth tends to retard economic development in a modern developing country, but Britain was a wealthy country with a standard of living well above subsistence; thus the population explosion from 1750 on enlarged the effective demand for consumption and had a beneficial effect on economic development.

The Technological Revolution. Because British entrepreneurs were unable to meet the increased demand for goods by traditional methods of production, the domestic handicraft system of manufacture gave way beginning in the late 18th century to factory-based mechanization.

The cotton textile industry was the first to be fully mechanized. The crucial inventions were John KAY's flying shuttle (invented in 1733 but not widely used until the 1760s), James HARGREAVES's spinning jenny (1765), Richard ARKWRIGHT's water frame (1769), Samuel CROMPTON's mule (1779), and Edmund CARTWRIGHT's machine LOOM (1785).

The first factories were driven by water, but James WATT's improved Newcomen STEAM ENGINE (1769) made steam-driven machinery and modern factories possible from the 1780s. This use of steam power led, in turn, to increased demand for coal and iron. Each development spawned new technological breakthroughs, as, for example, Sir Henry BESSEMER's process for making steel (1856). Other industries such as chemicals and mining also developed rapidly.

Capital, Commerce, and Transportation. British industrialization was financed almost wholly by domestic capital. The accumulation of capital from land and overseas trade

A detail from John Ferguson Weir's Forging the Shaft: A Welding Heat *dramatizes the shaping of a massive steel shaft. The development in 1856 of the Bessemer process, the first low-cost method of producing steel, gave great impetus to heavy industry in the United States and Great Britain. (Metropolitan Museum of Art, New York City.)*

was a long-term process in which the propensity to save was crucial; thus the emergence of banking and insurance services oiled the wheels of a market economy.

For the market to respond to demand, an adequate transport system was essential, and in the 18th century British roads were improved for the first time since the Romans had withdrawn. Even more important, in the last quarter of the century a burst of CANAL building enabled raw materials to reach the factory quickly and cheaply and allowed finished goods to supply an even larger market. From 1830 on, the development of steam-driven LOCOMOTIVES brought the advent of RAILROADS, extending the transportation network.

The net effect of all these changes was a dramatic increase in production; during the 19th century the gross national product per capita in Britain increased an unprecedented 400 percent in real terms.

The Spread of Industrialization

Until well after 1850, Britain dominated the international economy. Britain itself, however, sowed the seeds of industrialization elsewhere by exporting knowledge, engineers, entrepreneurs, and, above all, capital.

Europe. In continental Europe, Belgium, rich in iron and coal, was first to embark on industrialization in the 1820s, and by the 1830s the French Industrial Revolution had begun. Prussia, much richer in essential minerals than France, developed rapidly from the 1840s; by the time of German unification in 1871, Germany was a powerful industrial nation. Those countries which industrialized most rapidly were those which established an extensive rail network—Belgium, Germany, and the United States.

The United States. American society was an ideal vehicle for industrialization. The Puritan ethic and a belief in free enterprise fostered technological innovation and economic growth, and the country had enormous natural resources. In the late 18th century Samuel SLATER, a textile worker from England, copied Arkwright's machine designs and opened a cotton mill in Rhode Island. Under the leadership of such entrepreneurs as Francis Cabot LOWELL, the New England TEXTILE INDUSTRY continued to develop. The supply of cotton fiber for the textile mills was vastly increased by Eli WHITNEY's invention (1793) of the COTTON GIN. Another major mechanical innovation in crop harvesting was Cyrus McCORMICK's reaper (1831). Labor-saving devices such as these freed workers to enter the factories, which also drew on immigrant labor.

Aided by the spread of the transportation network, the boom period in American industrialization came in the second half of the 19th century. By the turn of the century the United States had overtaken Britain in the output of iron and coal and the consumption of raw cotton. Britain, with its older plants and equipment, faced increasing economic competition from other countries. In the 20th century the United States dominated the new automobile industry, which Henry Ford (see FORD family) revolutionized by introducing a system of coordinated ASSEMBLY LINE operations. Ford's success led to the widespread adoption of mass-production techniques in industry.

Elsewhere. By 1914 other European countries such as Italy and the Netherlands had begun to industrialize, and the process had spread to Japan. There, rapid industrialization made a small island people a world power, just as it had done for the British.

The Industrial Revolution in Russia had started well before 1914, but economic development was halted by World War I and the 1917 Bolshevik Revolution. When Soviet industrialization resumed about 1930, it was no longer a response to market forces but a planned economic development by the Communist state. From the 1950s, Communist China also embarked on a planned Industrial Revolution, seeking to accomplish in a decade what had taken Britain a century.

Social Effects

The social effects of industrialization may be summed up as short-term misery for long-term gain. Factory labor was often more disciplined, tedious, and dangerous than work in agriculture or domestic industry. It exploited women and, until the introduction of child-labor laws in most countries by the early 20th century, children. People often felt that they had less control over their destiny as machines, although created by humans, seemed to become their masters.

At the same time, life in the 19th-century city was unpleasant. The environment was often polluted with filth and smoke, and housing conditions were crowded and unsanitary. Basic amenities such as water supply and sewage disposal were deficient, and as a result disease and death rates were high. For all its ill effects, however, the Industrial Revolution solved the problem of the poverty trap described by Thomas MALTHUS in *An Essay on the Principle of Population* (1798)—the cycle of low income, low consumption, low demand, and low production.

▬

industrial union   An industrial union is a LABOR UNION that admits as members all employees of a given firm or industry regardless of their jobs or skills. In the United States industrial unions began to develop in the first decade of the 20th century. They formed (1938) a national association called the Congress of Industrial Organizations (CIO). The CIO and the older, more traditional American Federation of Labor (AFL) merged in 1955 to form the AMERICAN FEDERATION OF LABOR AND CONGRESS OF INDUSTRIAL ORGANIZATIONS.

▬

Industrial Workers of the World   The Industrial Workers of the World, a revolutionary socialist industrial union, was formed in 1905 by the Western Federation of Miners and a number of other labor organizations. Its early leaders included Eugene DEBS and Daniel DE LEON. In 1908, Debs and the WFM withdrew and De Leon was forced out; leadership passed to Vincent St. John and William HAYWOOD. The Wobblies, as they were called, preached permanent class warfare against employers. As adherents of the doctrine of SYNDICALISM, they held that, ultimately, after a general strike, capitalism would be replaced by industrial democracy.

During 1909–11 the IWW tried to organize unskilled and migratory workers into industrial unions but met with strong repression by vigilantes, police, and federal troops. It had some success in textile workers' strikes in Lawrence, Mass. (1912), and Paterson, N.J. (1913), but created no lasting organization. From 1915 to 1918 the Wobblies organized blacks, metal miners, lumberjacks, dock workers, and agricultural laborers. Employers and their local allies, however, took strong countermeasures. Arizona strikers were deported into the desert; in Butte, Mont., IWW organizer Frank Little was abducted and lynched. Another IWW organizer, the folk-song writer Joe HILL, was convicted of murder on circumstantial evidence

and executed (1915) in Salt Lake City. The U.S. Department of Justice's prosecution of over 200 IWW leaders in 1917 for interfering with the war effort and for spreading antiwar propaganda brought about the organization's decline.

▬

Indy, Vincent d' [dan-dee', van-sahn']   The French composer Vincent d'Indy, b. Mar. 27, 1855, d. Dec. 1, 1931, is perhaps best known today for his Symphony on a French Mountain Air (1887) for piano and orchestra. D'Indy was an enthusiastic Wagnerite—he first met Wagner in 1873—and he visited Germany frequently. He cofounded (1894) the Schola Cantorum in Paris and saw it develop into one of the foremost music schools in the world. He traveled widely as a conductor of his own works, visiting Spain (1897), Russia (1903 and 1907), and the United States (1905 and 1921).

Like his teacher César Franck, d'Indy composed using cyclical form, in which thematic material reappears in successive movements of a large composition. Plainsong elements and baroque polyphony give his music an air of severity and reserve. His best-known works include three symphonies, the symphonic variations *Istar* (1897), and an opera (*Fervaal*, 1897). He also wrote chamber music, smaller orchestral pieces, many songs, and choral works.

▬

inert gases [in-urt']   The inert, or noble, gases are a family of gaseous elements that constitute Group 0 of the periodic table. Their physical and chemical properties are closely related. The noble gases and their atomic numbers are HELIUM (2), NEON (10), ARGON (18), KRYPTON (36), XENON (54), and RADON (86). Together they constitute just less than 1% by volume of the atmosphere near the Earth's surface. The terms *inert* and *noble* are derived from the extreme reluctance of these gases to combine chemically with other elements. Chemical stability exists because the outermost shell of each noble-gas atom is filled with eight electrons (octet), except helium, which has two. Most other chemical elements, when they react with one another, do so in order to achieve this stable octet electron configuration either by losing electrons to their reacting partners or by gaining electrons from them. Because the noble gases already have the stable electron configuration, they are relatively inert. The ability to form chemical compounds with other elements increases with atomic number. Xenon forms numerous compounds that are stable at room temperature and atmospheric pressure. Some of the compounds created since 1962—before which time chemists assumed that inert gases did not form compounds—are XeF_2, XeF_4, and XeO_3. Krypton forms KrF_2 and KrF_4, which are stable only at low temperatures.

▬

inertia [in-ur'-shuh]   The inertia of a body is its tendency to resist acceleration, or change in its velocity. The MASS of a body is a quantitative measure of its inertia. Thus, a very massive object, such as a steamship, requires a significant force acting for considerable time in order to bring it either to a stop or up to speed, whereas a relatively light object, such as a table-tennis ball, requires little effort to change its velocity.

See also: LAWS OF MOTION; MOMENT OF INERTIA; MOTION, CIRCULAR; MOTION, HARMONIC.

inertial guidance system see GUIDANCE AND CONTROL SYSTEMS

—

infallibility Infallibility means, literally, immunity from error. In Christian theology, the term is applied to the whole church, which, it is believed by many Christians, cannot err in its teaching of revealed truth because it is aided by the Holy Spirit.

Christians disagree, however, about how infallibility can be recognized. Some accept as infallible those doctrines universally taught and believed from antiquity. Others recognize as infallible the doctrinal decisions of the ecumenical councils of the church.

Roman Catholics believe that the pope can make infallible definitions on faith or morals when he speaks *ex cathedra*—as head of the church—and when he has the clear intention of binding the whole church to accept as dogma whatever he is defining. Papal infallibility was formally defined at the First VATICAN COUNCIL (1870). The doctrine was reaffirmed at the Second Vatican Council (1962–65), which also stressed that the entire body of bishops in union with the pope teach infallibly when all concur in a single viewpoint on matters of faith and morals.

—

infancy Infancy in humans is the period of life between birth and the emergence of language, at about 18 months. The most remarkable physical changes during infancy involve the shape and capacity of the body and its muscles, the complexity of the nervous system, and the growth of sensory and perceptual capacity. Infants also begin to make sense of, understand, and master objects in the world; acquire the ability to communicate in a variety of ways; form specific social bonds; and adopt characteristic personal and social styles.

Nature and Nurture

Historically, philosophers interested in epistemology (the study of where knowledge comes from and how it develops) and theologians interested in the origins and nature of moral character have looked to infancy as a kind of testing ground for different views. At one extreme have been nativists who emphasize nature—that is, biological, or internal, determinants of the origins and development of human capacities and traits. At the other extreme have been empiricists who emphasize nurture—experiential, or external, determinants. Today a transactional view has been widely adopted. It holds that at any point in the life span the effects of an experience depend on the nature of the experience, the internal characteristics of the individual, and aspects of the individual's life history.

Modern Understanding

Experimental studies and naturalistic observations carried out in homes and in psychological laboratories underpin contemporary understanding of infant development. Using measurement procedures that rely on physical abilities under the infant's control, such as looking, orienting, or sucking behaviors, scientists are able to understand more and more about biological, sensory, perceptual, cognitive, verbal, emotional, and social development in infants.

Biological Development. In the space of approximately 9 months, a single fertilized egg evolves into a neonate (newborn) with a complex, self-regulating, and differentiated nervous system that in the additional 18 months of infancy develops into a sentient child capable of intelligent feelings, thoughts, and actions. Each infant is different from every other, and each remains an individual throughout development.

Tests at the time of birth are used to assess the status of the newborn and the degree to which the newborn is prepared for life outside the womb. Although human newborns appear helpless, they are innately capable of a small number of integrated and organized—if limited—behaviors. Many of these so-called reflexes (simple, unlearned, stimulus-response sequences such as sucking) are biologically meaningful in that they appear to have survival value or adaptive significance.

Newborn behavior is not quite as random as is often thought. Close and consistent inspection reveals that infants are more or less regular in many ways and that many different internal systems are cyclical, or follow rhythms. Breathing and sucking systems constitute fast biological rhythms, and the waking and sleep states are slow rhythms.

Motor Skills. Physical and motor development in infancy are impressive because they are so evident—children begin to reach, grasp, and walk in this period—and because change is extremely rapid at this point in the life cycle. Babies pull themselves to a standing position and begin to walk at about 11 to 15 months of age. During this phase, parents must be vigilant about the possibility that the child may fall down steps, accidentally knock over something heavy, or munch on a dangerous houseplant. How parents react to a child's natural sense of exploration can affect a child's emotional development (see DEVELOPMENTAL PSYCHOLOGY).

The Senses. The sensory systems are not suddenly "switched on" at birth, for the capacities to see, hear, smell, taste, and touch all develop in the fetal period. Although infants are born in a state of sensory preparedness, their keenness of perception is poor, however. Newborns appear to seek out information in their environment, and they show distinct preferences for certain kinds of information, although they appear less capable of making very fine differentiations. Babies will systematically explore a pattern, as if trying to learn as much as possible about it. They prefer contours and edges (where visual information is rich), saturated colors, the sounds of language, sweet tastes, and pleasant odors.

Cognition. The sensory channels provide raw information to the brain. A dramatic change during infancy is in the ability to learn about and make sense of—to attribute meaning to and act upon—that raw information. In the first month of postnatal life, babies recognize mothers by voice and scent. Between the third and fifth months, babies can voluntarily focus on near or far objects, they possess the rudiments of shape and size constancies, they recognize two- or three-dimensional objects, and they discriminate complex sounds. Generally by the end of the first year, infants learn how to integrate visual information with auditory and with tactual information.

By two to three months of age, infants may be able to remember the functions of some objects for as long as one month after playing with them, even if they require some prompting to do so. During the first year, infants move from undifferentiated exploration of objects, through play related to the functions of particular objects, to pretend play with objects or even pretend play without objects.

Personality. Temperament is commonly viewed as a hereditary aspect of personality, albeit one certainly influenced by experience; and temperamental variation is already evident early in infancy. Individual differences in temperament are significant because of their potential for influencing infants' cognitive development and social interactions.

Even newborns are capable of differentiated emotional expressions that appear to be both appropriate and interpretable by adults. In the realm of social growth, the most significant changes are not simply those in the infant's ability to affect other people, however. More significant is the fact that, over a short period of time, infants come to understand the rules of social interaction and they learn to assume an intentional role in initiating, modulating, and terminating periods of social interaction. They also develop specific emotional bonds to the individuals with whom they interact most consistently.

The types of interactions that infants have with their parents appear to vary partly according to parental roles. Thus, in many families, infant-mother interactions tend to center on child-care activities, whereas infant-father interactions tend to be dominated by play. Parents' personalities and attitudes, as well as the home situation, all affect infants' experiences, but the physical and behavioral characteristics the infant brings to the situation also play a role. Families provide young infants with a richly textured array of relationships, and cultures vary with respect to the patterns of social life they encourage and support in infancy.

Language. The advent of language marks the end of infancy. Early in life, infants communicate with others by means of facial expressions, gestures, and nonverbal signals, such as crying. Eventually, the baby's repertoire expands to include gestures and a growing range of other social signals. The use of spoken language depends on the ability to segment and process auditory information, the ability to develop concepts and to represent them symbolically, the formation of social relationships with people with whom infants want to communicate, and recognition of the reciprocal basis of social interaction and internalization of the elementary rules of turn-taking and communication.

In the space of about one to two years after birth, babies begin to comprehend others and to express themselves using language. Language comprehension develops earlier than language production, and rate of word acquisition for comprehension is twice that for production. Both are increasingly shaped by the linguistic environment, reflecting infants' exquisite sensitivity to specific experiences.

See also: CHILD DEVELOPMENT.

infanticide [in-fant'-uh-syd] Infanticide (from the Latin for "child murder") is the act of killing an infant at birth. Infanticide is known to have been practiced on every continent by many different peoples. Although it is not sanctioned by any society today, it is still practiced in some areas. Religious offerings of the newborn are referred to in records of the ancient Egyptians, Greeks, and Romans. Sacrifice of the firstborn child was common among tribal groups in India until the 19th century. Eskimos and Australian Aborigines also practiced infanticide.

Many anthropologists believe that infanticide was traditionally prevalent among some primitive peoples because, along with abortion, it served as a method of controlling population size. This control was especially important for groups living in a harsh environment in which the available food supply was severely limited. Often only female children were killed, especially in hunting societies (such as that of the Eskimo) or among groups in which warriors were especially valued. In certain societies sickly or deformed children were killed at birth. Where traditionally practiced, infanticide was a socially sanctioned act, dictated for the most part by survival needs of the group, a fact recognized and accepted by those who performed it.

infantry The infantry is that part of an army consisting of armed foot soldiers, as distinguished from cavalry, air, or sea forces. Since ancient times the infantryman has been the front-line fighting soldier, bearing the brunt of offensive or defensive attack and suffering the greatest number of military casualties. Only during the feudal period and in nomad societies was the infantry's role insignificant.

Infantry appeared with the advent of organized societies in the 3d and 2d millennia BC. The most powerful early infantry were Greek and Roman foot soldiers who fought in compact groups while engaging their enemy with spear and sword. In China during the Warring States period infantry armies numbered in the hundreds of thousands. The defeat of the Roman infantry by barbarian cavalry in AD 378 heralded a thousand-year period during which infantry took second place to the cavalry.

It was not until guns began to replace swords and

(Left to right) *The Roman legionnaire's short broadsword and pilum, a type of spear, helped Rome maintain supremacy. The increased range of the long-bow enabled English archers to overwhelm the French at the Battle of Agincourt (1415), a decisive engagement of the Hundred Years' War. Standardized flintlock rifles, ammunition, and powder charges helped establish the disciplined Prussian army of Frederick the Great as the most effective fighting force of the mid-18th century. The American doughboy of World War I, who turned the tide of victory in favor of the Allies, was equipped with the U.S. Model 1903 Springfield, a reliable bolt-action rifle that remained in limited use even during World War II.In the Second World War, most American infantrymen were equiped with the M-1, a semiautomatic rifle thet held a clip containing 8 rounds.*

lances that the infantry again became the primary fighting unit. By the era of the standing or permanent army in the 17th century, foot soldiers were armed with musket and pike. The infantryman was meant to be a mindless brick in a human wall that advanced toward the enemy in a long line, firing all the while. This technique was perfected by FREDERICK II of Prussia in the mid-18th century. The method was most successful when troops had been continuously drilled and so disciplined that they could load and fire while advancing in precise formation regardless of battle conditions. In the 19th century infantry tactics were forced to change to cope with new technology. As weapons became more accurate and effective, infantry had to spread out and dig in to make itself less vulnerable. By the time of the U.S. CIVIL WAR hand grenades, barbed wire, and repeating rifles made mass attacks ineffective. Troops began to attack in waves—one wave raking the opposing troops with fire while the next scrambled toward the enemy. In spite of the many innovations in transportation, communication, and weapons during the 20th century, the foot soldier played a major role in the battles of World Wars I and II and in the Korean War, where the option of firing nuclear weapons was rejected in favor of the use of a conventionally armed infantry.

Although the range of weapons available to the present-day infantry is enormous, front-line soldiers still fight on foot. Troops and supplies, however, are likely to be transported to the battlefield by aircraft, ships, trucks, and armored personnel carriers. The helicopter, in particular, has been used extensively as the packhorse of the modern infantry.

infectious diseases [in-fek'-shohs]   All species of animals are afflicted with infections caused by a wide variety of organisms, from submicroscopic viruses to wormlike parasites. Infectious diseases range from the benign common cold to such fearsome conditions as BUBONIC PLAGUE and RABIES. Infections are usually characterized by several stages. First, the organism gains access to the patient, survives within the body, and multiplies. Next, the patient manifests symptoms of illness and, in some instances, sheds organisms that have the potential to infect other individuals. The patient may die or may recover spontaneously, or the infection may respond to specific therapy. Often, there is a postinfection IMMUNITY, which results in resistance to infection by the same organism in the future.

Some infections have a quiescent, latent period that can be measured in years. Included in this group are those infections which cause chronic destruction of the brain. Certain viral infections in animals cause cancers. A viral etiology for human cancers has not been proved but seems likely for some tumors. Evidence has been found suggesting that patients may develop diabetes following viral invasion of the pancreas with resultant destruction of the insulin-producing islet cells.

Infectious diseases have strongly influenced the course of history. The Black Death, an epidemic of bubonic plague, led to the downfall of the feudal system of medieval Europe. The outcome of major military campaigns has been influenced by outbreaks of diseases such as DYSENTERY and TYPHUS. Infectious diseases have interfered with habitation and settlement of large areas of the world. CHOLERA, MALARIA, and YELLOW FEVER have played an important role in influencing the development of society in certain regions of the Earth.

Agents of Infection

The organisms responsible for human infections are extremely variable. VIRUSES are simple life-forms consisting of nucleic acid, encoding genetic information, and surface components of protein that enable them to enter cells. Unable to multiply outside of living host cells, they are completely dependent on these cells for their continued maintenance. Viruses utilize the metabolic machinery of the cell and have the ability to interfere with, or direct in an adverse fashion, the activities of the cell. CHICKEN POX, GERMAN MEASLES, MEASLES, and MUMPS are common childhood illnesses, and the common cold is usually due to the rhinovirus. The "flu" or the "grippe" is caused by INFLUENZA viruses. HEPATITIS, an inflammation of the liver, may be the result of one of several viruses. Rabies, yellow fever, and Lassa fever are highly lethal viral diseases. Rickettsiae, small microbes that usually grow inside host cells, have a more complicated structure and metabolic makeup. Unlike viruses, they are susceptible to antibiotics. Rickettsial diseases are frequently transmitted by arthropods, and stages in the development of the pathogen often take place in ticks or lice. Examples of rickettsial diseases include Q FEVER, ROCKY MOUNTAIN SPOTTED FEVER, and typhus.

CHLAMYDIA and *Mycoplasma* are bacterialike organisms that frequently grow inside cells. Their outer cell walls are less complex than those of most bacteria. *Chlamydia* cause TRACHOMA, certain types of sexually transmitted urethritis, and PSITTACOSIS. *Mycoplasma* are commonly associated with a relatively mild type of PNEUMONIA.

Nearly all objects in the environment, including plants and animals, are associated with large numbers of bacteria. Bacterial diseases are common and include such conditions as streptococcal pharyngitis ("strep throat"), pneumococcal pneumonia, and staphylococcal boils. DIPHTHERIA, GONORRHEA, SYPHILIS, and TUBERCULOSIS are also caused by bacteria. Bacterial diseases respond to treatment with antibiotics.

Infections caused by fungi are frequently chronic and slowly destructive. Cryptococcosis, histoplasmosis, and blastomycosis may involve the lung and brain tissue. FUNGUS DISEASES may be superficial, as in RINGWORM and thrush (see CANDIDIASIS).

Parasites that commonly cause infections include protozoans and helminths, or worms. Malaria and AMEBIASIS are protozoal diseases common in the tropics. SCHISTOSOMIASIS and TRICHINOSIS are examples of helminthic diseases. Ectoparasites, organisms that live on the surface of the body, may transmit infectious diseases. For example, lice may carry epidemic typhus, and ticks may be vectors for Rocky Mountain spotted fever (see PARASITIC DISEASES).

Microbial Virulence Factors

Infectious agents cause disease in the host by several mechanisms. Most typically, microbial virulence, or the potential to cause disease, involves the ability of the pathogen to gain access to the host by surviving on mucous membranes or by being ingested or inhaled. Pili, submicroscopic hairlike structures on the surface of some bacteria, allow them to attach themselves firmly. Next, the multiplying microbe must have the capability of avoiding or counteracting the normal protective mechanisms of the host. Capsules surround some bacteria, and these structures serve to prevent the microbes from being ingested and killed by defending phagocytic cells. Other bacteria produce toxins that can destroy phagocytes. Certain highly virulent organisms produce disease in a large percentage of people whom they contact, whereas other microorganisms produce illness in only a small percentage. When a nonimmune person encounters the influenza virus, the organisms are inhaled, multiply in respiratory cells, damage these cells, and cause disease. In contrast, certain organisms produce toxins, making the patient ill without actually being invaded by the microbes. *Clostridium botulinum*, a bacterium that grows in improperly preserved foods, produces a potent toxin that when ingested may cause BOTULISM. Patients may die by ingesting products of this bacterium without actually being infected by the organism. Other organisms may produce a toxin only after infecting the patient. For example, certain strains of *Escherichia coli*, a common intestinal bacterium, produce a toxin when colonizing the intestine. This toxin, known as an enterotoxin, causes DIARRHEA.

In some instances the host's own defenses against infection may be responsible for the damage. For example, infections caused by *Mycoplasma pneumoniae* may result in inflammation of the airways and lungs. When the microbes grow in the respiratory cells, they do not damage the cells. During the host's attempt to kill foreign invaders, however, the infected cells are attacked and destroyed by immune mechanisms.

Host Defense against Infection

Because human beings exist in a veritable sea of microbes, defense against microbial attack is important for survival of the species. The skin, mucous membranes (interior of the nose, mouth, vagina, rectum), and intestines are colonized by large numbers of bacteria, called the normal flora. These organisms form a protective barrier against invasion by foreign microbes due, in part, to their metabolic products, which may be harmful to potential invaders. Also, use of essential nutrients by the normal flora may "starve" pathogenic invaders. If the normal flora are destroyed by agents such as ANTIBIOTICS, infection may become more likely. The skin and skin secretions are an effective barrier to invasion by most microorganisms. Tears and saliva have intrinsic antibacterial activity. The respiratory tract is kept clean by coughing and sneezing and by particle-trapping mucus continually transported upward by tiny cilia of the respiratory lining cells. Once microbes invade body tissues, mechanisms come into play that strive to neutralize and destroy them. These defenses may be divided into two major groups. Humoral (or fluid) mechanisms include the ANTIBODY and complement systems. Cellular mechanisms include various types of cells.

Antibodies. Antibodies are proteins produced by specialized white blood cells called lymphocytes. Antibodies have a strong chemical affinity for specific types of foreign biologic matter. ANTIGENS are components of foreign material (for example, microbes) that interact with antibodies. Thus, specific anti-influenza virus antibodies or specific antistaphylococcal antibodies may be present. The interaction of antibodies and components of microbes may serve to destroy, inactivate, or prevent the multiplication of microorganisms. In addition, when an antibody attaches to the surfaces of microorganisms, it makes these microbes more ingestible by phagocytic cells, which engulf and destroy invading microbes.

Complement. A group of proteins that constitute the complement system have the ability to destroy certain pathogens by interacting with them. This interaction may be promoted by antibodies or may take place in the absence of antibodies. Thus, blood serum from healthy individuals, lacking antibodies, will destroy many species of bacteria.

Lymphocytes. There are two major types of lymphocytes, B and T. B lymphocytes have the ability to produce antibodies directed against specific foreign antigens to which they are exposed. This is the basis for prevention of disease by immunization. For example, patients may be infected with an attenuated, or weakened, strain of polio virus (see POLIOMYELITIS). The B lymphocytes will then make antibodies against the polio virus, which will also be active against wild type, fully virulent organisms. Thus, when patients come in contact with these organisms, they are now immune. T lymphocytes respond to foreign antigens by releasing control substances that help or suppress the function of B lymphocytes and phagocytic macrophages (see Phagocytic Cells section below). Certain T lymphoctyes have the ability to kill infected cells.

Inflammation. INFLAMMATION is the phenomenon by which the body responds to an irritant or to an infection. Small blood vessels dilate and leak fluid, producing swelling, redness, and warmth. Phagocytic white blood cells enter the area, adhere to the lining of the blood vessels, and migrate into the tissue to attack microbial invaders. Fever, or elevation of the normal body temperature, is a common response to many infections. Fever appears to aid the host in fighting infection by enhancing the immune response. Fever results when products of phagocytic cells known as endogenous pyrogens act on a thermostatlike area (hypothalamus) of the brain.

Phagocytic Cells. Phagocytic cells kill organisms by engulfing them and enclosing them in a pouch called a phagosome. This pouch then becomes bathed with active metabolites of oxygen and various enzymes found in the phagocytic cell. Most microbes are rapidly killed by these cells. Three major types of phagocytic cells are involved in protecting human beings against infection. The polymorphonuclear neutrophil is a motile phagocytic cell that

can engulf and destroy pathogens. Ingestion is more efficient when the pathogens have been coated with antibodies or complement or both. Neutrophils, the cells that constitute pus, migrate rapidly to the site of trauma or infection in an attempt to destroy microbes. Macrophages are larger, slower-moving phagocytic cells that have the special capability of killing organisms that can survive ingestion by polymorphonuclear neutrophils. Thus, such organisms as *Mycobacterium tuberculosis* (the agent that causes tuberculosis) are not destroyed by polymorphonuclear neutrophils but are destroyed by macrophages, whose activity is increased by substances produced by T lymphocytes. Macrophages are found in the liver, spleen, lungs, and bone marrow. The eosinophil is a cell that has special potential for killing multicellular microbes such as helminths. Patients with infections such as trichinosis caused by a helminth will frequently have a high eosinophil count in the blood.

Immunity. Humans have a natural or inherent immunity to many infections. Intact barriers such as skin and mucous membrane secretions and normal function of the humoral and cellular systems help prevent infection. Recovery from infection most often results in acquired immunity. In addition to production of specific antibodies, the body may induce a state of cellular immunity whereby macrophages and T lymphocytes become able to destroy invaders more efficiently. Immunity may be passed from mother to fetus via the placenta. Thus, newborn infants are protected against many infectious diseases for the first few months of life. Evidence indicates that breast milk also contains antibodies that may be protective during this early period.

Routes and Modes of Infection

Respiratory Route. Pathogenic organisms may be inhaled. This mechanism by which infection is spread is especially significant in many respiratory diseases and is responsible for large epidemic outbreaks. Viral influenza is spread by tiny, airborne particles that can reach the lower airways of the lungs. Tuberculosis, smallpox, and measles are spread by contamination of the air by infected patients. In contrast, fungal diseases such as histoplasmosis and coccidioidomycosis are acquired by inhaling infectious particles derived from soil harboring the organisms, and LEGIONNAIRES' DISEASE is spread by contaminated water droplets.

Gastrointestinal Route. Infections may be acquired by ingestion of the causative organism. Infectious hepatitis, poliomyelitis, and typhoid fever are transmitted by this means. The infecting dose varies with the disease. In some conditions one or two organisms can initiate infection; in others as many as a million organisms may be required. Certain features of the person encountering the organisms may potentiate their effects. For example, *Salmonella typhi* is the causative organism of typhoid fever; persons who have a lack of acid production in their stomachs can be infected by far fewer of these organisms than can persons with normal acid production.

Direct Contact. Mucous membranes may be a portal of entry for many infections. The venereal diseases gonorrhea and syphilis are transmitted by direct contact of mucous membrane to mucous membrane. Although the skin is an impenetrable barrier for these and most infections, certain organisms may break through. For example, staphylococci may cause boils on skin that is normal or has only a trivial irritation. Streptococci may cause cellulitis (a spreading inflammation) or impetigo (a crusting lesion) on skin that is intact.

Mother to Child. It is possible for a fetus to become infected while in the uterus. Therefore, infections that the mother acquires during pregnancy may damage the fetus. Some of the most dangerous of these include rubella (German measles), cytomegalovirus disease, and toxoplasmosis. All these conditions produce mild disease in the pregnant woman but may result in devastating damage to the developing fetus. In addition, infants may be infected at birth during passage through an infected birth canal. This can result in congenital (present since the time of birth) gonorrhea, syphilis, herpes viral infections, or streptococcal infections.

Relationship of Environment to Infection

The ecology of infection is complex and involves interactions with climate, food and water supply, arthropod vectors, animal contacts, and other human beings. Many of the great scourges of humankind, such as tuberculosis, cholera, malaria, and typhoid fever, were markedly decreased in incidence by changes in the environment. These changes anteceded development of effective vaccines and therapeutic agents. The greatest danger to *Homo sapiens*, regarding the spread of infection, is other *Homo sapiens*.

Organisms may spread from one person to another by direct contact, by the airborne route, or by oral ingestion of contaminated food or water. Food and water supplies may become contaminated with microbes derived from humans or animals or from the environment. For example, unpasteurized milk may serve to transmit disease if it is contaminated with organisms from an infected cow (for example, brucellosis) or from an infected dairy person (for example, streptococci emanating from a skin lesion).

Density of population directly affects the spread of certain communicable diseases. Major epidemics have occurred in boarding schools and military barracks, where the environment yields close contact among members. When people are confined to enclosed places, airborne pathogens tend to spread more readily. Patients interacting with animals may have special problems. For example, butchers and meat packers have the highest incidence of BRUCELLOSIS; hunters may contract TULAREMIA through handling rabbit pelts.

Insects are significant in the transmission of many infections. The malaria parasite is transmitted from one human to another, or from an animal to a human being, by the bite of the anopheles mosquito. Because this mosquito cannot survive in cold climates, malaria has never been a problem in countries where the climate is temperate. Schistosomiasis is a parasitic disease caused by an organism that spends part of its life cycle in a snail. If the snail does not have the proper water conditions to survive, the disease will not be found.

The Impaired Host

It is clear that some people are more susceptible to infections than others. Sometimes the cause of the increased susceptibility is obvious. A severely burned person, for example, lacks the normal protective features of intact skin and suffers from infections as a result. Patients with IMMUNODEFICIENCY DISEASES that impair the function of the immune system frequently have severe and fatal infections. Persons with LEUKEMIA (cancer of the white blood cells) also frequently die of infections. In addition, drugs that interfere with normal host defenses may make the patient vulnerable to infection; thus, patients with cancer often have suppressed phagocytic cell function because the drugs used to treat them also kill healthy cells. Infection is also a serious potential complication of surgery; drugs given to organ-transplant patients to prevent rejection of the transplant also impair defenses, making the patients susceptible to infection. Finally, malnutrition increases susceptibility to certain forms of infection, due to impaired functioning of lymphocytes and macrophages.

Infected Body Systems

Every part of the human body may be involved in infection. Infectious nervous-system diseases (see NERVOUS SYSTEM, DISEASES OF THE), for example, include viral encephalitis, which damages the brain, and poliomyelitis, an infection of the spinal cord. GASTROINTESTINAL TRACT DISEASES may be caused by ingestion of a preformed toxin such as in some kinds of FOOD POISONING, or illness may be due to a true infection, as in viral or bacterial gastroenteritis. VENERAL DISEASES, which are transmitted by sexual contact, may infect not only the reproductive organs but numerous other parts of the body.

The most common RESPIRATORY SYSTEM DISORDERS are viral infections of the upper respiratory tract; the common cold (see COLD, COMMON), viral pharyngitis, and BRONCHITIS are annoying, but rarely serious, illnesses. Occasionally, however, bacterial infections may supervene, and the illness may become more severe. More serious respiratory system disorders involve the lungs. Bacterial pneumonias are common and serious diseases. Tuberculosis and the fungal diseases such as histoplasmosis and coccidioidomycosis may also involve the lungs. Infections of the lungs may damage tissue and cause chronic scarring and impairment of respiratory activity. In acute infections, death may result.

Infectious SKIN DISEASES may primarily involve the skin and mucous membranes, or skin lesions may indicate infection elsewhere. The most common bacterial skin diseases include those caused by staphylococci and streptococci. Measles, a systemic infection, is characterized by a generalized skin rash. Shingles, or herpes zoster, is an infection of the nerves supplying a specific area. Small mites and other parasites may invade the skin. Fungal skin diseases include ringworm, athlete's foot, and thrush.

Prevention

Prevention is much more efficient than is treating infectious diseases. Prevention may involve general improvements in sanitation and the nutritional state of the population or more specific maneuvers such as immunization. Toxoids, or altered toxins, are used to immunize against tetanus and diphtheria, two diseases where the major damage is done by the toxin rather than by invasion by the microbe. Attenuated, or weakened, live viruses are used to immunize against poliomyelitis and rubella (German measles). Killed organisms or fractions of organisms are the immunizing agents for influenza and typhoid fever. Immunization with a related virus has been effective in eliminating smallpox as a threat to humans.

Patients who may spread highly contagious diseases to other patients may have to be isolated while they are undergoing treatment. Thus, before chemotherapy for tuberculosis was available, patients with this disease were separated from the rest of society in sanitoriums. Now, because therapy is so effective, these patients may be treated in general hospitals or even in their own homes. Infections that may be acquired in a hospital can be eliminated or reduced by strict attention to cleanliness and avoidance of cross-contamination from one person to another.

Therapy of Infectious Diseases

Most infections are self-limited and require no therapy. Appropriate therapy, however, is effective in shortening the course of illness, reducing the risk of transmission to other patients, and, in the case of severe infections, reducing mortality. No truly effective agents for the therapy of infection were available until the 1930s, when sulfonamides were developed. These agents interfere with steps in the metabolism of bacteria and are effective therapy for certain bacterial diseases. Penicillin, the first antibiotic, became available in the 1940s. Antibiotics have a specific spectrum of action; thus, some agents are more effective for certain infections. Several nonantibiotic drugs are also effective against bacterial infections. Fungal infections will respond to chemotherapy, and drugs effective against a few viral infections have been developed. The vast majority of viral infections, however, remain unaffected by any known therapeutic agents.

Infections continue to afflict millions of people each year and are still a significant cause of discomfort, severe illness, and death. New methods of prevention and therapy must be developed. As cancer therapy and other medical treatments advance, large numbers of patients with severely impaired defenses as a result of such treatments are acquiring frequent and severe infections. Also, some chronic diseases that have been previously thought to be noninfectious may in fact be related to infectious organisms.

inferiority complex   see COMPLEX (psychology)

infinitesimal [in-fin-i-tes'-i-mul]   An infinitesimal is a quantity that can be made arbitrarily small (close to zero). For example, the function $f(x) = 1/x$ can be made smaller than any preassigned positive number by making x sufficiently large. This idea is expressed by saying that the LIMIT of $1/x$ as x exceeds all bounds (or approaches infinity) is zero. Because DIFFERENTIAL CALCULUS and INTEGRAL CALCULUS deal with limits and infinitesimal quantities, they are sometimes called infinitesimal calculus.

infinity [in-fin'-i-tee]   *Infinity,* as used in mathematics, denotes a quantity that increases without bound, in contrast to a finite quantity. Infinity is greater than any number that can be specified. The word is often encountered in the study of LIMITS. For example, one can consider the limit of $1/x$ as x approaches infinity, that is, as x increases without bound. The symbol ∞ is used for the word *infinity*, and $\lim_{x \to \infty} 1/x$ is written where $\overset{\lim}{\to}$ stands for *limit* and $\to$ means *approaches*. Now, $1/x$ gets closer to 0 as x gets larger. As larger and larger values of x are taken, the quantity $1/x$ can be made arbitrarily close to 0; this means that $\lim_{x \to \infty} 1/x = 0$, which is read "The limit of $1/x$ as x approaches infinity is zero."

Infinity is not a number; any number, no matter how large, is finite. The expression $\lim_{x \to \infty} 1/x^2 = \infty$ means that, by taking x closer and closer to 0, the quantity $1/x^2$ can be made larger and larger without bound.

The concept of infinity, which was studied by Georg CANTOR, is basic to a number of scientific disciplines. For example, applying RELATIVITY to COSMOLOGY, it is assumed in the big bang theory that when the universe was created the density of matter was extremely high, perhaps infinite. In CALCULUS, as mentioned above, the concept of a limit involves quantities that approach infinitely large and infinitesimally small values. In ANALYTIC GEOMETRY a curve may approach a line called an asymptote as a variable approaches infinity. In mathematics a SEQUENCE or a SERIES may have an infinite number of terms.

inflammation   The process of inflammation occurs to the tissues of the body in response to an injury, such as a sunburn, an insect bite, a wound, or an infection (see INFECTIOUS DISEASES). Despite the wide range of causative agents, this process is basically the same in all organisms. Inflammation is characterized by four physical signs: warmth, redness, swelling, and pain. Warmth and redness result from dilation of the small blood vessels in the injured area and increased local blood flow. Because blood vessels become more permeable during inflammation, protein-rich fluid (exudate) escapes from blood plasma to the damaged tissue and causes swelling. Pain is believed to result from such chemical substances as serotonin or from tension of tissue over the inflamed area, as the skin over a boil.

The series of events that constitute inflammation are controlled by chemical mediators and white blood cells.

During simple, acute inflammation in response to tissue damage, the small blood vessels in the area initially contract and then dilate. Blood circulation tends to slow down; the blood may even clot. White blood cells (leukocytes) move toward and adhere to the vessel walls. Such white blood cells as neutrophils pass into the tissue and form an exudate with the fluid that had escaped from the tissue. As a result the vessel walls lose their impermeability to protein, which escapes along with water from tissue cells. Fibrinogen, a plasma protein, also escapes and is acted on by thrombin to form fibrin. Strands of fibrin eventually wall the inflamed area off, preventing spread of infection.

Gamma globulin, a plasma substance that contains antibodies, also enters the tissue and accelerates the engulfment of bacteria by cells known as phagocytes. White blood cells called granulocytes are capable of phagocytosis. Such granulocytes as neutrophils and eosinophils are also attracted to the site of tissue damage. There, the neutrophils function through the release of lysozome, an enzyme that destroys bacteria, and the eosinophils act to control allergic reactions. Monocytes, called macrophages in the tissue, play a role in phagocytosis and in processing antigens. Lymphocytes take part in antibody production and immunity. Pus is formed from dead tissue, neutrophils, and monocytes.

Chemical mediators are classified into two groups. The first group consists of proteins that constitute an enzyme, the complement, which modulates inflammation through its ability to direct migration of phagocytic cells to the tissue. The second group consists of chemical substances, such as histamine, that have low molecular weight. These chemicals are released during allergic reactions and result in the attraction of white blood cells to the site of the injury.

Treatment of inflammation is aimed at its cause. When the cause is unknown, such anti-inflammatory drugs as cortisone and aspirin are used. When the cause is known, nonsteroidal drugs are commonly used.

---

inflation   Inflation is a process in which the average level of prices increases at a substantial rate over a considerable period of time. In short, more money is required to buy a given amount of goods and services. One can measure the rate of inflation as the annual percentage rate either of increase in the average price level or of decrease in the value of money.

Inflation properly refers only to episodes in which the rate of inflation is substantially positive over a considerable time period. What is meant by substantially positive may depend on recent experiences. In the United States during the mid-1960s an inflation rate of 3% per year aroused great alarm, but some countries' governments have proclaimed victory over inflation by bringing the rate down from 50% or even 200% per year to only 10%. A number of countries have experienced hyperinflations when prices increased at a rate of more than (often much more than) 50% per month—an inflation rate of more than 12,975% per year. A deflation is the opposite of an inflation: a period of substantially falling prices and rising value of money.

Explanations of Inflation

Explanations of inflation run along two lines: the general, or monetary, explanation and various special-factor explanations. The monetary explanation views inflation as always and everywhere the result of an excessive growth rate of money and so focuses on the roots of that monetary growth. Special-factor explanations relate each specific inflation to particular economic conditions that happen to occur before or during the inflation.

The monetary explanation starts with the observation that rising prices are the same thing as a falling value of money. The more money there is, relative to the goods and services to be bought, the less valuable is each dollar. A period of increasing prices occurs when the quantity of money grows faster than real demand for it, measured in terms of the goods and services the money buys. Thus, an inflation requires either a rapid growth in the money supply or a persistently falling real demand for money.

Rapid money-supply growth may occur for a number of reasons, depending on the type of money used in a country. When money consisted of gold coins or paper exchangeable for gold, inflations would occur after major gold discoveries. In the modern United States and most other countries money is not convertible to a precious metal but is either bank notes printed by the government or checking deposits exchangeable only for paper money. Rapid monetary growth can occur when the government sells securities to help finance a war or pay for other government programs, thus expanding the money supply through deficit spending; in concert with the central bank, the government may encourage growth of the money supply through an expansionary MONETARY POLICY that increases bank reserves, and thus loanable funds. Countries may also increase their money supply to maintain a stable domestic price for an inflating foreign currency, such as the U.S. dollar.

Monetarist economists believe that unusual events may decrease the growth rate of real-money demand in any particular year, but that over any considerable period of time these events average out. As a result the average growth rate of real-money demand measured in terms of the goods or services to be bought is quite stable, and sustained inflations arise only from rapid money-supply growth. It is here that the special-factor explanations differ.

Special-factor explanations focus on particular events or sequences of events—not necessarily directly related to the money supply—to explain an episode of inflation. An example of this approach observes that a large increase in the price of imported oil would tend to make the consuming nation poorer and so reduce its purchasing power and raise prices. Similarly, the introduction of substitutes for money, such as credit cards, which reduce the average amount of money people must hold to buy a given amount of goods, would tend to increase prices. A whole sequence of such events—and the absence of offsetting conditions (such as increased output) tending to increase real-money demand—may be used to explain a given inflation. Responding, the monetarist posits that over periods of four or five years there is very little variation in the growth of real money measured in terms of purchasing power.

A hybrid explanation of inflation begins with some special factor as the start of the process. If the initial cause relates to the costs of producing goods and services, some economists have termed the process *cost-push inflation*. If, for example, the price of oil increases, the resulting increase in prices results in higher wage demands by workers who want to maintain their current standards of living. Producers may try to pass wage increases along to the consumer through higher prices; producers could meet increased wage demands by increased borrowing, which the central bank can accommodate through larger bank reserves, which increase the money supply. The government fears the temporary increase in unemployment that would result if the demands are frustrated. Thus, the argument goes, the government increases money-supply growth, which leads to further price increases and starts the whole process over again. This sort of price-cost-money vicious circle—or the so-called wage-price spiral—converts what might otherwise be a temporary increase in the rate of inflation into a substantial and sustained one.

Solutions to Inflation

Simple acceptance of inflation is in many ways the most appealing solution. Unexpected increases in inflation benefit debtors and hurt creditors by reducing the purchasing power of contracted payments, but a constant, expected inflation rate has no such effect. Interest rates are adjusted to account for the expected decrease in the value of money, and therefore neither side benefits. Nor is there any evidence that any particular income group is disproportionately harmed by a steady, expected inflation. Many economists believe that creeping inflation is a permanent feature of the U.S. economy. There are real costs, however, to wage indexing of contracts, marking up prices, conserving on money balances, and all of the other ways of living with inflation, so it may well be less costly in the long run to eliminate the inflation even at the cost of temporarily higher unemployment.

The election of Ronald Reagan as president in 1980 was interpreted as a mandate to reduce the high inflation rates that had emerged in the 1970s, partly as a result of deficit spending for the Vietnam War and partly as a result of large price increases for imported oil. Under Reagan, the executive branch encouraged Federal Reserve efforts to reduce the money supply, even at the cost of the major 1981–82 recession. Inflation rates came down sharply, and a period of growth in output and employment followed.

The deficits and tight credit policies of the Reagan years helped to provoke the 1991 recession faced by the Bush administration. Intense political pressure on the Federal Reserve under Alan GREENSPAN resulted in moves to lower interest rates, but inflation rates began to rise, demonstrating the fine line authorities must tread. The inflation problem is further complicated by the volatility of oil prices and the value of the dollar overseas, especially during times of crisis, such as the Gulf war.

inflationary theory The inflationary model of the events involved in the rapid expansion of the universe in its first moments of creation, as depicted in the BIG BANG THEORY, was developed by American physicist Alan H. Guth in the early 1980s. It is the first successful and comprehensive attempt to correlate particle physics with COSMOLOGY.

The work of British physicist Stephen HAWKING had already shown that the law of conservation of energy does not apply at the so-called event horizon in an intense gravitational field, such as that due to a BLACK HOLE, and that quantum fluctuation can in fact cause the creation of a universe in otherwise empty space. At the high densities that would exist at that time, all the possible particle interactions would come into play. A theory that would correlate all of these FUNDAMENTAL INTERACTIONS is therefore required. Theories attempting to unify at least three of the interactions—the weak, strong, and electromagnetic forces—have been developed and are known as GRAND UNIFICATION THEORIES (GUT). Taking a simplified version of GUT, it was found that right after its creation a protouniverse could eventually expand into the kind of universe observed today. According to GUT, however, so-called magnetic monopoles should also be created (see MONOPOLE, MAGNETIC), and their very large mass would cause the universe to evolve to this present state in only 30,000 years.

In order to eliminate such inconsistencies, Guth developed his inflationary model. He introduced phase transitions during which rapid cooling took place in the very early universe, thereby eliminating certain difficulties of the big bang model. One such difficulty is the high degree of homogeneity and isotropy of the present universe. Conventional big bang theory had the early universe expanding so rapidly that homogenization would be impossible. In the inflationary model, the universe is much more compact in its earliest stage, allowing a high degree of homogeneity and isotropy to be achieved. The creation of monopoles is also avoided during successive phase transitions, thus allowing for the subsequent evolution of the universe at a rate in line with actual observation. The inflationary theory is still in skeleton form, but it does make definite predictions, such as of the ultimate decay of PROTONS. The theory continues to be refined by Guth and others, who also try to respond to further problems—such as the discovery of extremely large-scale features comprising many millions of galaxies—that have been presented by observational astronomy.

influenza [in-floo-en'-zuh] Influenza is an infectious disease of the respiratory tract caused by the influenza virus. It is probably the last remaining pandemic (worldwide) infection of humans. Periodically, when new strains of influenza virus are introduced, they spread rapidly all over the world, infecting millions of people and causing significant increases in mortality.

Although many different viral and nonviral respiratory and nonrespiratory illnesses are commonly called influenza or "flu" for lack of more exact diagnosis, influenza is an infectious respiratory disease caused by a specific virus of the genus *Orthomyxovirus*. The disease, which generally lasts 3 to 7 days, is characterized by fever, cough, and considerable muscle aching (myalgia) and is sometimes complicated by secondary bacterial pneumonia. Flu starts abruptly, usually with a fever up to 39.4° C (103° F) in adults and higher in children. The illness may be followed by a period of weakness and depression. Bed rest, aspirin, and plenty of fluids constitute the best treatment. Flu victims 50 years old or older, however, may be given antibiotics to prevent pneumonia. Persistent fever or worsening symptoms may indicate one of three types of the pneumonia form of influenza. The first is sudden, severe, and often fatal and is present from onset; the second, less severe, appears a few days after onset; and the third, also less severe, appears after apparent recovery.

Flu Prevention. An attack of influenza produces a temporary immunity, but unfortunately the protection is against only the type of virus causing the influenza. The disease is produced by any one of three types (A, B, and C), with many strains. Vaccines have been developed that have been found to be 70 to 90 percent effective for at least 6 months against either A or B types, and a genetically engineered live-virus vaccine is under development. Vaccination is considered especially important for older people, patients with cardiac or respiratory diseases, and pregnant women. In 1984 the Centers for Disease Control added to this list the physicians, nurses, and other medical personnel who have extensive contact with high-risk patients, and endorsed the dispensation of vaccine to members of the general public desiring such protection. The 1984 and successive statements also recommended the use of amantadine hydrochloride for therapy and as an adjunct to immunization for high-risk patients; amantadine hydrochloride is effective against type-A influenza infections but not type B.

Epidemiology. The name *influenza* was derived from an observation made more than 400 years ago that epidemics of cough and fever occurred more frequently at certain times of the year. At the time the conclusion was drawn that such epidemics occurred under the *influence* of particular constellations of planets. Even today the seasonal factors in influenza remain poorly understood. In northern temperate zones influenza epidemics generally begin late in December and usually end by the end of March. Although chilling and low humidity may play a role in such areas, seasonal differences in the incidence of influenza have also been observed in tropical areas. The incidence of infection is highest among school-age children, partly because of their lack of previous exposure to antigenically related strains. Infection is probably transmitted as a small-particle aerosol. A high proportion of infected individuals do not develop symptoms but are probably capable of transmitting infection to others. Deaths from influenza have been linked, in some patients, with TOXIC SHOCK SYNDROME.

Pandemic Influenza. Approximately every 10 years, influenza pandemics have been caused by new strains of type-A virus. The pandemic of 1918–19 is estimated to have killed 21–22 million people worldwide. Changes in influenza A virus have been responsible for such pandemics as the so-called Asian flu (1957) and Hong Kong flu (1968). Two characteristics, called antigens, are so different in later strains from those of previous strains that many people have little or no immunity to the later ones. Currently, the origin of the pandemic strains of the virus in humans cannot be explained satisfactorily.

----

information science   Information science is the study of the ways in which organisms process information. It embraces such disparate topics as the means of genetic information processing in cells, the individual's use of information concerning the environment, and the methods of human learning and information generation. The dominant emphasis of information science today, however, is the last of these. Information science integrates parts of other disciplines, such as biology, physics, computer science, sociology, psychology, and librarianship.

In the theoretical sense, information science tries to increase understanding of the ways in which information is generated, stored, made available, and used. In the practical sense it undertakes specific actions to try to improve these same functions of information science. The information scientist may compare alternative means of making information available, as by indexing (see INDEX), to determine which means work most satisfactorily, or the scientist may devise tools and methods for improving the transfer of information. One of the earliest of these tools was Keyword in Context (KWIC) indexing, first introduced in 1959 and developed by Hans Peter Luhn and his colleagues at IBM. In a KWIC index the computer is used to generate entries from title words, saving the time and cost of human indexing but losing the benefits of human understanding of the document. In Selective Dissemination of Information (SDI) a list, or profile, of topics of continuing interest to a user is prepared. This is then compared to the index terms of particular documents in the current literature on an ongoing basis, and the user is notified of those which match the profile.

The concept on which these and other new methods of disseminating information depend is that of the DATABASE, which is a body of information, usually computer-stored, that can be searched and manipulated for a variety of needs. Databases have grown out of computer-based publishing, in which the material is keyboarded for computer typesetting; once this process is completed, the information can be reused for other purposes. A sophisticated database technology based on magnetic tapes, drums, and disks has developed for information storage and retrieval and for data processing. When large quantities of information on printed pages must be stored, microforms are usually used (see MICROFILM). These permit maintenance of many documents in an extremely small space. Various systems that permit viewers to have interactive access to databases via their computers or television sets are called VIDEOTEX or TELETEXT.

---

information storage and retrieval

In modern society the task of the storage and retrieval of vast amounts of information has been taken over almost entirely by COMPUTER systems. No longer a tool exclusively for mathematical computation, the computer now handles large collections of information called DATABASES. Government agencies such as the Internal Revenue Service and the National Crime Information Center maintain databases, as do private industry (personnel records) and other organizations (medical records). Computer access to such stored information raises important questions: How accurate is the information, and how can inaccuracies be corrected? Who has access to the information? How is improper or illegal access prevented? These questions are currently under study.

Information is stored on various devices interfaced to computers. This storage is considered secondary, as opposed to the primary, internal COMPUTER MEMORY. Secondary memory has greater capacity than primary, but access is slower. Computer access to secondary memory may take thousandths of a second up to several seconds, in contrast to primary memory access times of less than one-millionth of a second.

Memory hierarchies extend to a tertiary, or archival, level with capacity for trillions of bits of information. A 6-million-word encyclopedia such as this one contains about 288 million bits of information (6 million words × 6 characters per word × 8 bits per character). A trillion-bit storage can store about 3,500 times as much information as there is in such an encyclopedia, all of it directly accessible to the computer.

Common Storage Devices

Digital computers process information in the form of binary codes. Devices for storing the coded information include drums, discs, and tapes. For many years all three of these technologies have employed the property of magnetic material that allows particles to be oriented, or polarized, in one of two directions, corresponding to each of the values of binary code—zero or one. Strings of BINARY NUMBERS, referred to as bytes, are represented by arrays of magnetic particles. Other technologies are just beginning to replace magnetic devices.

Drums and discs are shaped differently but have many other properties in common. Drums are shaped like a drum, or cylinder, with the recording material wrapped around the outside. Information is recorded in individual tracks which form circles around the drum. Several hundred tracks lie adjacent to each other along its length. Discs are shaped like a disc, or phonograph record, with the recording material on the flat surfaces. Information is recorded in individual, concentric circle tracks. Several hundred tracks may be on each surface.

Both drums and discs have read/write heads similar to the play and record heads on tape recorders used for sound recording (see TAPE RECORDING). Rotation of the recording medium causes the information storage tracks to pass under the heads for both devices. Heads are positioned on selected tracks, to access selected information, by mechanical or electronic means. Both of these devices keep the recording surface in constant rotational motion when they are on-line (actively interfaced) to the computer. Both store information that needs to be readily accessible but that either exceeds the capacity of the computer's primary memory or is used infrequently enough not to merit being maintained there. Discs are by far the more predominant, especially in the form of the small, flexible "floppy" discs that are used with small computers and that can hold several hundred thousand characters (see COMPUTER, PERSONAL).

Magnetic tape units record digital signals on reels or cassettes of magnetic tape. Information is recorded in parallel tracks that run the length of the tape. Spinning the reels causes the tape to move from the supply reel, past the read/write heads, onto the take-up reel. Common tape drives have seven or nine parallel tracks across the tape. Storage capacity is determined by the total length of the tape and by the recording density in characters per inch. Typical values of length are 2,400 ft (230 m) with densities of 1,600 characters per in (630 characters per cm). Not all of the length is usable, however. Tapes may be dismounted from tape drives and stored in libraries, which may hold essentially unlimited amounts of information.

Information is recorded from the beginning of a tape toward the end in sequential fashion. This form of access is known as sequential access. To retrieve selected information it is necessary to wind or rewind the tape to the place where the information was recorded.

New Developments

Perhaps the most promising new information storage technology involves laser discs (also called COMPACT DISCS, or CDs)—round, metal discs on which digital information is stored in the form of pits and bumps. Information is retrieved from the disc by the reflection from the surface of a small laser beam as the disc rotates rapidly. Laser discs offer great storage capacity, retrieval speed, and durability.

Newer storage devices are also being developed out of electronic technology rather than the electromechanical technology of rotating or spinning devices. Bubble memories in which microscopic bubble patterns are formed on wafers of garnet crystals are available. These use the presence or absence of magnetic domains to represent the binary values zero and one. Similarly, CHARGE-COUPLED DEVICES (CCD) utilize the presence or absence of electronic charges to store information. Both devices are sometimes called electronic discs because they store information in patterns that make it accessible in a cyclic fashion, much like disc storage.

Another new technology is the electron beam accessed memory (EBAM). The EBAM stores information by using an electronic beam to charge a small area on a silicon dioxide plane.

Archival Storage

Archival storage is the third level in the memory hierarchy. Archival storage devices are intended to hold information that is infrequently accessed but extensive in quantity. The devices are slow but have great capacity. The most successful devices in this category use magnetic tape. A straightforward system is simply an automation of the conventional tape library. Reels of tape stored in racks are electromechanically selected, moved to one of several tape drives, and mounted.

Software Considerations

Information storage and retrieval involves more than hardware devices and storage media alone. To make the physical equipment readily usable it is necessary to provide software (see SOFTWARE, COMPUTER) routines or systems. If the information exists as a database, operations associated with it are to add information, to change existing information, to delete information, and to retrieve items of interest.

Large databases employ managers who maintain the database for users. The need for powerful retrieval methods while maintaining strict security against unauthorized access gives rise to the need for complex software. Users inevitably want to retrieve information in different ways from the way it is stored. For example, because of the way information is stored in a phone book, it is easy to find a phone number if the name is known. A complex software system without sufficient safeguards can make it equally easy to reverse the process and find the name if the phone number is known.

information theory   Information theory, also called the theory of communication, is a branch of PROBABILITY theory that has been developed to provide a measure of the flow of information from a source to a destination. It also supplies a measure of the channel capacity of a communications medium such as a telephone wire and shows the optimal coding procedures for communication. Although originally concerned with telephone networks, the theory has a wider application to any communication process. It may also be viewed as a branch of CYBERNETICS, the science of control and communication, and it has strong associations with control engineering, theories of learning, and the physiology of the nervous system.

Information theory was developed to a great extent at the Bell Telephone Company laboratories in New Jersey under the auspices of Claude SHANNON in the 1940s and '50s.

Principles. The principal features involved in information theory are a source of information that is encoded and transmitted on a channel to a receiver, where it is decoded.

There are two versions of information theory, one for continuous and the other for discrete information systems. The first theory is concerned with the wavelength, amplitude, and frequency of communications signals, and the second with the stochastic (random) processes associated with the theory of AUTOMATA. The discrete theory applies to a larger range of applications and was developed for both noiseless and noisy channels. A noisy channel contains unwanted signals and requires a filter to take a copy of the transmitted message and compare it to the message received.

Entropy—the Measure of Information. The Shannon-Weaver measure of information is given by the formula $H = -\Sigma P_i \log_2 P_i$, where the amount of information H is called the entropy (a term borrowed from thermodynamics, where it means a tendency toward randomness or disorder), P_i is the probability of the ith message being sent, and the minus sign and the LOGARITHM to base 2 are convenient in providing a simple and positive measure of information. The application of the formula can be illustrated by considering four message units $A, B, C,$ and D being sent that all have an equal chance of transmitting information. The application of the formula for H gives $H = \frac{1}{4} \log 4 + \frac{1}{4} \log 4 + \frac{1}{4} \log 4 + \frac{1}{4} \log 4$, which works as $\frac{1}{2} + \frac{1}{2} + \frac{1}{2} + \frac{1}{2}$, which equals 2, because $\log_2 4 = 2$. This result means that the average amount of information in this situation is worth 2 bits, where "bits" is a contraction of binary digits: 2 binary digits would be needed to encode the message "A transmitted information" where the conversion from the usual decimal code to BINARY NUMBER code is $0 = 0, 1 = 1, 2 = 10, 3 = 11, 4 = 100, 5 = 101, 6 = 110, 7 = 111, 8 = 1000,$ and so on. Thus the message unit A might be represented in binary code by 00, B by 01, C by 10, and D by 11.

Since the message units—for example, letters of the alphabet as used in English spelling—would not normally all have the same odds, the resultant value of H depends upon the actual odds, and the amount of information passed by any one message would depend upon the odds (the associated probability).

Channel Capacity. The measure of the channel capacity of an information system is best illustrated where the probabilities again are equal. Given a set of 16 message units $A, B, ..., P$, each carrying 4 bits of information, then the channel capacity is $4n$ bits per second, where the channel is capable of transmitting n symbols per second. The encoding of messages now requires a suitable procedure. It requires punctuation, as in the case of a "pause" in Morse code, or alternatively, all the words must be of fixed length. Furthermore, to achieve an optimal code, there are certain procedures that are all based on the principle that the most frequently occurring words (or letters) should be coded with the symbol of shortest duration.

Applications. More complicated theorems for continuous and discrete systems, with or without noise, make up the mathematical theory of information. The discrete theory can generate letter sequences and word sequences that can approximate ordinary English. A Markov net is a stochastic process that deals with conditional probabilities. Information theory is thus an important tool in the analysis of language or of any sequence of events—and its encoding, transmission, reception, and decoding.

infrared astronomy [in-fruh-red']   Infrared (IR) astronomy studies the radiation that arrives from celestial objects at infrared wavelengths. These wavelengths are longer than optical and shorter than radio wavelengths. The IR region of the electromagnetic spectrum (see ELECTROMAGNETIC RADIATION) is divided by astronomers into three smaller regions: the near, mid, and far infrared. These correspond, respectively, to wavelength ranges of 1 to 5, 5 to 25, and 25 to 350 microns. (One micron equals 10,000 angstroms, and one angstrom equals 10^{-10} m). These divisions relate to the varying ability of the Earth's atmosphere to transmit IR radiation and to the general types of celestial objects that can be observed. The near IR is mainly useful for star observation, the mid IR for warm interstellar dust, and the far IR for cool dust. Using IR detectors, astronomers can observe cooler celestial objects than they can with optical devices, and IR radiation is less dimmed by interstellar dust than is light.

Instruments. Prior to about 1960, astronomers could detect and photograph IR radiation only in the very near infrared, using conventional photographic plates (see ASTROPHOTOGRAPHY) and photoelectric photometers (see PHOTOMETRY). Objects in the near IR became available for study through the use of lead sulfide (PbS) photoconductive solid-state detectors, which were in widespread use as IR detectors by the late 1960s. These devices change their electrical conductivity proportional to the intensity of radiation, producing a change in electric current that can be measured.

To observe longer wavelengths, detectors are used that are composed of the SEMICONDUCTOR germanium, doped with other materials (see CHARGE-COUPLED DEVICE). Sensitivity to various wavelength regions depends on the doping material used. By combining many semiconductor sensors in a rectangular array, IR detectors can be made that provide images with resolutions comparable to those achieved in optical astronomy, particularly in the near and mid-IR ranges. This latter technology was developed for military systems and did not become more generally available until the late 1980s.

Observatories. Ground-based astronomers are faced with a serious problem because water and carbon dioxide molecules in the atmosphere strongly absorb IR radiation at many wavelengths. Thus they are able to observe only in the gaps between the molecular absorption bands, known as atmospheric windows. To optimize observing conditions, ground-based IR observatories are constructed at very high and dry locations. In 1983 the Dutch-U.S. Infrared Astronomy Satellite (IRAS) scanned nearly all of the celestial sphere and discovered about 250,000 new sources of IR emission. An advanced IR satellite called the Infrared Space Observatory (ISO) is planned for launch in the 1990s by the European Space Agency.

Infrared Objects. A large number of the IR sources found in early ground-based surveys are cool stars. Many of the remaining objects show an unexpectedly large amount of IR radiation, commonly referred to as IR excess. In surveying such objects, IRAS found regions where new stars are being formed, both in our galaxy and in neighboring galaxies. It also observed many more IR objects than ground-based astronomers are able to detect, including solid (possibly planetary) objects around nearby stars (see PLANETS AND PLANETARY SYSTEMS). IR observations within the solar system have also produced interesting results, including comet and asteroid discoveries by IRAS.

infrared radiation   Infrared radiation is the region of the electromagnetic spectrum between visible light and microwaves, containing radiation with wavelengths ranging from about 0.75 μ (1 micron equals 1 one-millionth of a meter) to about 1,000 μ (1 mm). These limits are arbitrary because the characteristics of the radiation are unchanged on either side of the limits. The discovery of infrared radiation is attributed to Sir William Herschel who, in 1800, dispersed sunlight into its component colors with a prism and showed that most of the heat in the beam fell in the spectral region beyond the red, where no visible light existed. In 1847, Armand Fizeau and Jean Foucault of France showed that infrared radiation, although invisible, behaved similarly to light in its ability to produce interference effects (see ELECTROMAGNETIC RADIATION).

Infrared radiation is generally associated with heat because heat is its most easily detected effect (see HEAT AND HEAT TRANSFER). Most materials, in fact, readily absorb infrared radiation in a wide range of wavelengths, which causes an increase in the temperatures of the materials. All objects with a temperature greater than absolute zero emit infrared energy, and even incandescent objects usually emit far more infrared energy than visible radiation; about 60% of the Sun's rays are infrared. Sources of infrared radiation other than hot, solid bodies include the emissions of electrical discharges in gases and the LASER, which can emit highly monochromatic (single-wavelength) infrared radiation.

Infrared radiation also has many temperature-sensing applications, such as in astronomy or in heat-seeking military missiles. Photographs taken by infrared radiation reveal information not detectable by visible light. In the laboratory infrared spectroscopy is an important method for identifying unknown chemicals.

Ingalik [ing'-guh-lik]   The Ingalik Indians, the westernmost Athabascan-speakers of interior Alaska, occupied territory along the lower Yukon and the upper Kuskokwim rivers. They borrowed a number of culture traits from their Eskimo neighbors, in spite of the traditional enmity between Athabascans and Eskimo.

The Ingalik occupied small winter villages composed of earth-covered semisubterranean lodges with elevated caches for winter stores, separate smokehouses, and drying racks for salmon. In summer they lived in houses made of cottonwood or spruce bark. The *kashim* was the center of various social activities. Fishing was the major activity from spring until summer. In spring muskrats provided both food and pelts that, stitched together, formed robes and parkas. Caribou, moose, and occasionally bears were hunted on snowshoes. Shamanism conformed to Western Eskimo patterns. POTLATCH festivals with feasts and gift giving, masked dances, ceremonials for animal souls, and memorials for the dead were popular events in traditional Ingalik society, demonstrating the tribe's thorough adaptation to Western Eskimo culture. The remaining Ingalik population today is largely assimilated into white society.

Inge, William [inj] A popular and respected playwright of the 1950s, William Motter Inge, b. Independence, Kans., May 3, 1913, d. June 10, 1973, graduated (1935) from the University of Kansas. Inge specialized in simple, well-crafted dramas describing the yearnings, frustrations, and failures experienced by small-town midwesterners. His most successful plays were *Come Back, Little Sheba* (1950; film, 1953), the Pulitzer Prize–winning *Picnic* (1953; film, 1956), *Bus Stop* (1955; film, 1956), and *The Dark at the Top of the Stairs* (1957; film, 1960). Inge wrote little after his 1959 Broadway failure, *A Loss of Roses* (filmed as *The Stripper*, 1963). He committed suicide.

Ingersoll, Robert Green [ing'-gur-sohl] Robert Green Ingersoll, b. Dresden, N.Y., Aug. 11, 1833, d. July 21, 1899, was an American orator known as the Great Agnostic. Self-educated, he was admitted to the Illinois bar in 1854. After serving in the Union army during the Civil War, he was attorney general of Illinois (1867–69) and became a vigorous campaigner for Republican candidates. His most famous political address was the speech in which he nominated James G. Blaine, whom he called a "plumed knight," for president. At the 1876 Republican convention, Ingersoll's own political ambitions were thwarted by public disapproval of his attacks on religion, which he delivered from lecterns all over the country. Ingersoll symbolized the intellectual ferment that buffeted orthodox religion in late-19th-century America.

Ingres, Jean Auguste Dominique [ang'-gruh]
The major French painters of the first half of the 19th century were Eugène Delacroix and Jean Auguste Dominique Ingres, b. Aug. 29, 1780, d. Jan. 14, 1867. The two were then seen as leaders of the opposed styles of romanticism and neoclassicism. The neoclassicism of Ingres's style was already apparent in the painting that won him the Prix de Rome, *The Ambassadors of Agamemnon Arriving at the Tent of Achilles* (1801; École des Beaux-Arts, Paris). Stress on line was an important part of this style. Although classical antiquity often inspired Ingres, his iconic portrait of Napoleon (1806; Musée de l'Armée, Paris) was influenced by Byzantine art and Jan van Eyck.

While in Italy Ingres sent paintings to Paris for exhibi-

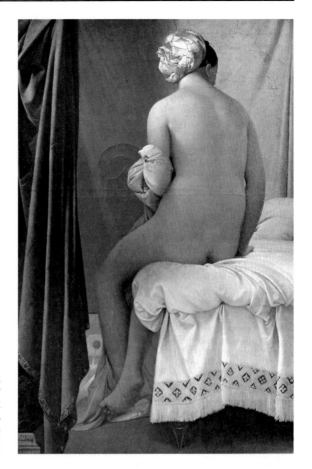

Woman Bathing, also known as La Grande Baigneuse, *painted by J. A. D. Ingres in 1808, reveals his training with Jacques Louis David in its austere linear composition and muted colors. (Louvre, Paris.)*

tion, but they were frequently attacked because of their unorthodox style. He rejected the influence of any artist after the 16th-century Italian painter Raphael, and vigorously defended his preference for classical art. In 1824 he returned to France to show his important religious painting *The Vow of Louis XIII* (1823; Montaubon Cathedral, France), which met with a triumphant success and appealed to both neoclassical and romantic tastes. Ingres became famous.

He painted historical and religious subjects throughout his career and was also drawn to exotic Levantine subjects, notably a series of bathers (begun 1807), of which the most famous are the *Turkish Bath* (1859–63; Louvre, Paris) and *The Grand Odalisque* (1814; Louvre). Ingres also executed commissions for portraits, in which his meticulous method of painting captured details and textures with astounding verisimilitude. The polemical distinction between romantic and neoclassic, which Ingres himself did much to enforce, cannot be applied to his work dogmatically. His enormous canvas *The Dream of Ossian* (1813; Musée Ingres, Montauban), originally intended to decorate a palace in which Napoleon was expected to stay while in Rome, is thoroughly romantic in subject and style. The nonclassical enthusiasms of his time are reflected in his taste for Eastern subjects and historical romances.

inheritance

The laws of inheritance regulate the disposition of private property after the owner's death. The ability of an owner to dispose freely of his or her property posthumously is embodied in the legal instrument of the WILL. Today in all Western countries and in many others, one may inherit under the provisions of a will or, if there is no will, of statutes called intestacy laws that designate the order and proportion by which relatives and spouses shall inherit.

Early Law. In many early legal systems PROPERTY belonged to the family, clan, or tribe, and within the family the father generally controlled its administration. Various provisions existed for distribution on the father's death. In Sparta the eldest son was entitled to all the father's property; in Athens the sons shared equally; in ancient Israel the eldest son was given a double share—a rule that was followed in parts of colonial New England.

The Right to Will Property. The right to make a will is a recognition of the right of private property rather than of family, clan, or tribal ownership. Perhaps the earliest wills were made in Athens where, under the reforms of Solon (*c.*639–559 BC), a childless man could will his property to anyone, whereas before that time his estate went to his clan.

In Anglo-Saxon England, wills of land could be made only with royal approval and could not be revoked. Early in the Norman period (*c.*1100), PRIMOGENITURE—the practice by which land devolved automatically on the eldest legitimate son—came into wide use. There were, however, pockets of contrary custom, where land went to the youngest son (borough English), or to all the sons equally (gavelkind). Only legitimate children could inherit. To make it impossible for the heir to sell his land, the unique English concept of the entailed estate was utilized. Land could be conveyed, for example, to "A and the heirs of his body." "A" did not fully own the land but merely had the right to its use during his lifetime. Upon the death of "A" the land went to his heir under the rules of primogeniture. The entailed estate was common in England until the 19th century.

Until 1540, when enactment of the Statute of Wills enabled landowners to will some or all of their lands as they chose, a landowner could achieve the effect of a will through the TRUST device, which allowed him to transfer property to one or more trustees on condition that he be permitted to use and profit from it until his death. The trustees would then convey it to the person or persons named in the trust. This trust device is still used today in both England and the United States to avoid the payment of inheritance taxes that would otherwise be levied at the owner's death.

Women as Heirs and Testators. In early Rome a male was always responsible for the care and support of the family's women, and the question of women as heirs was irrelevant. Mosaic law, however, permitted women to hold property, and a daughter could inherit if there were no sons. In English law, also, brotherless women could inherit, and a woman could own property and could will it to the same extent as a male. A wife, however, could not be her husband's heir because she was not of his bloodline. Nevertheless, under the right of dower, a widow could own one-third of her husband's lands for the duration of her life.

Today, in states of the United States that follow English common law, the right of dower has been replaced by the rule that a widow must receive a statutory portion of her husband's estate, ranging from one-third to one-half. In southwestern and far western states the system of community property, derived from Spanish and French law, provides that all property belonging to the married couple is shared half and half.

Contemporary Inheritance Practices. Within the Western world, and in countries whose legal systems are the legacy of a colonial power, inheritance practices are broadly the same: private property is, for the most part, freely available for its owner to will as he or she desires, with certain limitations on the disinheritance of children or spouses. PROBATE, the process by which a will is proved valid, and the administrative procedures of ESTATE settlement differ in detail from country to country (and, in the United States, from state to state).

inheritance tax

An inheritance tax is a tax levied on property when it is transferred from a deceased person to his or her heirs. The tax is assessed on each heir according to the amount of property received. An estate tax, on the other hand, levies taxes based on the value of the total estate before it is divided. Most U.S. states have inheritance taxes, estate taxes, or both. The federal government levies estate taxes and also taxes gifts of money, land, or other valuables given by the owner before his or her death. Such gifts are usually intended to reduce the tax burden for the heirs.

The most persistent rationale for the levying of such "death" taxes has been their effect in shrinking great concentrations of wealth as they pass from one generation to the next. In Great Britain and other countries that levy heavy death duties, these taxes have in fact worked to reduce large fortunes and estates. In the United States their effect has not been so pronounced, in part because the taxes are not so onerous, in part because various mechanisms, such as the philanthropic foundation, exist to siphon off much of the taxable funds in such enormous fortunes as those of the Ford and Rockefeller families.

inhibitor

A chemical substance that slows down or retards a chemical reaction is called an inhibitor. This type of substance, a form of catalyst, plays an important role in industrial chemistry or in chemical research. One important class of inhibitors is antioxidants, which are used to prevent organic compounds from deteriorating. For example, some spices are used as antioxidants to prevent the development of unpleasant tastes and odors in food. An inhibitor may also prevent a chemical CHAIN REACTION from taking place by combining with the chemical agents that perpetuate the chain. Tetraethyl lead was long added to gasoline to break the chain reaction known as "knocking" in automobile engines.

initiative   See REFERENDUM AND INITIATIVE

___

injunction   An injunction is a court decree granted by a judge requiring a person to act or to cease to act in a specific way. Injunctions are of two kinds: prohibitory and mandatory. Prohibitory injunctions forbid certain acts or activities; mandatory injunctions require that certain acts or activities be undertaken. A preliminary injunction remains in force until the issue has been settled by a court decision, or until a specified period of time has elapsed. A permanent, or final, injunction is granted at the conclusion of a lawsuit. If an injunction is defied, a judge may cite the offender for CONTEMPT.

Injunctions are governed by the common-law principles of EQUITY, which apply to situations in which legal remedies are deemed inadequate, as in labor-management disputes and issues involving governmental regulation. Because an injunction can be obtained quickly—as opposed to litigation, which is time-consuming—it is an effective way to enforce regulatory statutes. Injunctions were frequently used against labor unions until the Federal Anti-Injunction Act (Norris-LaGuardia Act) of 1932. The LABOR-MANAGEMENT RELATIONS ACT (Taft-Hartley Act) of 1947 and the LABOR-MANAGEMENT REPORTING AND DISCLOSURE ACT (Landrum-Griffin Act) of 1959 provided for the use of injunctions under certain conditions.

___

ink   Inks are paintlike fluids and pastes used for writing and printing. The use of colored fluids for drawing characters on parchment, hide, or cloth was common in ancient Egypt and China at least as early as 2000 BC. Ancient writings that are still preserved often used inks based on lampblack (carbon black), a finely ground pigment dispersed in water or oil. Modern India inks are similarly composed. Other inks were made from indigo; from the galls of oak and nut trees; from tannin; and from the inky fluids secreted by octopuses.

Writing Inks. Most fountain-pen inks employ solutions of water-soluble dyes. Soft-tip PENS also use soluble dyes, which are dissolved in alcohol solvents to prevent the tips from drying or clogging. Ball-point inks are considerably heavier in consistency and are mixtures of oils, polymers, dyes, and solvents; they are designed to provide a continuous delivery of ink and to dry instantaneously.

Printing Inks. Inks employed in PRINTING are prepared from natural and synthetic film-forming resins and generally use pigments rather than dyes to provide color. Modern letterpress inks must have sufficient consistency to adhere to the raised portion of the plate. The composition of resin, pigment or dye, and solvent depends on the method of drying the ink—whether by heat, absorption of solvents, or precipitating the ink through steam-removal of the solvent.

Lithographic, flexographic, and gravure inks are deposited from etched, molded, or raised printing plates. Since the lithography process (see OFFSET LITHOGRAPHY) uses water-saturated plates, the inks must not mix with water and are usually linseed-oil based. Flexographic printing deposits ink from molded rubber plates. Solvents in the inks evaporate or are absorbed into the surface. Gravure printing on high-speed presses uses inks that dry almost instantaneously. SILK-SCREEN PRINTING requires a relatively thick, viscous ink.

Industrial packaging requires inks that are resistant to scuffing or that have a high gloss. Fluorescent inks are available for use on labels and packages. Magnetic inks use pigments that can be magnetized so the characters can be read by computers.

See also: PAINT; VARNISH.

___

Inland Sea   The Inland Sea (Japanese: Seto-naikai) of Japan is a body of water surrounded by the major islands of Honshu, Kyushu, and Shikoku. Covering approximately 9,480 km^2 (3,660 mi^2), it is about 385 km (240 mi) long and ranges between 6 and 58 km (4 and 36 mi) in width. It is linked to the Pacific Ocean by the Akashi, Naruto, and Bungo straits, and to the Sea of Japan through the narrow Strait of Shimonoseki. The mountainous islands that enclose it offer protection from winds, making the waters unusually calm. The sea is shallow, and at no point does the depth exceed 150 m (492 ft). Dotting the waters are approximately 950 islands. The many natural harbors on the sea's shoreline include Hiroshima, Kobe, and Osaka. The shoreline is heavily industrialized, yet the area is noted for its scenic beauty.

___

Inn River   The Inn River, a major tributary of the Danube, is 515 km (320 mi) long. It rises in Lake Lughino in east central Switzerland and flows northeast along the Engadin Valley, through the Bavarian Alps of western Austria and southeastern Germany, to join the Danube River at Passau. It drains an area of about 25,900 km^2 (10,000 mi^2) and supplies much hydroelectric power. The river is part of the Austria-Germany border. Innsbruck is on its course.

___

innate ideas   Innate ideas are ideas or functions originating in the mind apart from sense experience. Different theories of innate ideas have appeared over the centuries. PLATO believed that people developed understanding in a previous life but were born into their present life in a condition resembling forgetfulness. All learning, according to this theory, is remembering what one once knew.

For the Stoics, all people have certain "common notions" that are the roots of science and morality prior to any sense experience. Saint AUGUSTINE adapted the Platonic remembrance theory and spoke of a nonsensory source of knowledge in a divine illumination. In the 17th century, René DESCARTES and others in the tradition of RATIONALISM taught that ideas such as God, the soul, and even geometrical axioms are innate, having been implanted by God.

For Immanuel KANT, space and time, "the categories" of understanding, and the "pure ideas" of God, the soul, and the world all derived from the structure of the knower prior to sensation. For Kant, as for others accepting innate ideas, morality is not rooted so much in experience as in common forms or rules possessed by everyone.

inner city   The inner city is the central portion of a CITY, comprising its business district and the areas of housing and industry that immediately surround it. Through much of the 19th and 20th centuries, the inner cities of the United States were dynamic and growing, fueled by the growth of business and industry and by the influx of immigrants. Beginning in the 1950s, however, cities began losing their white, middle-class populations to the suburbs, as the construction of new highways made large-scale automobile commuting feasible, and government programs—such as federally guaranteed home mortgages for World War II veterans—encouraged suburban home construction. Major inner-city stores followed their customers, relocating in suburban shopping malls. Urban factories were abandoned and new facilities built in the countryside. As the tax base—the taxable value of commerce and real estate—eroded, city revenues shrank. The populations remaining in the inner city were largely black and Hispanic, but the industrial jobs that had once supported these groups vanished along with the factories.

Attempts to reverse the degeneration of U.S. inner cities have ranged from large-scale federally funded urban-renewal programs to recent homesteading efforts aimed at rescuing abandoned housing. These programs have produced little positive effect. Most urban planners feel that without massive employment programs and such fundamental improvements as innovative mass transit the inner cities will remain conspicuous areas of decay on the American landscape.

See also: HOUSING; URBAN PLANNING.

Inner Mongolia   Inner Mongolia (Nei Monggol) is an autonomous region of northern China, bounded on the north by the Mongolian People's Republic and the USSR. The area is 1,177,500 km^2 (454,600 mi^2), and the population, in which Chinese outnumber the indigenous MONGOLS, is 20,536,000 (1988 est.). Hohhet is the capital. Inner Mongolia has long, cold winters and short, mild summers; most of the region is steppe or desert. The main occupation is livestock raising, but some farming (especially wheat) is possible in oases and areas irrigated with water from the Huang He (Yellow River), which flows through the region. The Inner Mongolian Autonomous Region was the first self-governing entity established by the Chinese communist government in 1947.

Inness, George [in'-is]   Widely regarded as the greatest American landscapist of the 19th century, George Inness, b. Newburgh, N.Y., May 1, 1825, d. Aug.

In The Lackawanna Valley *(1855) George Inness transformed a commission from a railroad into an original work of art by subordinating detail to a broad panoramic view. (National Gallery, Washington, D.C.)*

3, 1894, brought the influence of the French BARBIZON SCHOOL to the United States; later, he developed a style that was uniquely his own.

His early paintings were influenced by the HUDSON RIVER SCHOOL; *The Old Mill* (1849; Art Institute of Chicago) is typical. In 1854, during one of several visits to Europe, Inness studied the Barbizon painters—especially Jean COROT and Théodore ROUSSEAU, whom he imitated for a time—and the work of Claude Lorrain and Nicolas Poussin. His art began to show a breadth and grandeur that contrasted sharply with the literalism and "picturesqueness" plaguing the work of many of his contemporaries. *Peace and Plenty* (1968; Metropolitan Museum of Art, New York City) reflects this trend away from literal detail and toward more generalized form, a focus on atmosphere and color, and greater expressiveness.

During the middle period of his career (until *c.*1884), his paintings were characterized by a freer brushwork, an increasing interest in the possibilities of color, and less emphasis on detail, as seen in *Coming Storm* (*c.*1880; Addison Gallery of American Art, Andover, Mass.).

Inness's last period, from about 1884, is regarded by some as his finest; it was probably influenced by his immersion, about 1865, in Swedenborgian mysticism. The paintings of this period are semiabstract masses of color. The settings of such works as *Home of the Heron* (1893; Art Institute of Chicago) are intimate and undramatic, sometimes peopled by solitary, brooding figures, and reflect an intensely personal and mystical vision of nature.

Innocent III, Pope

Innocent III, b. *c.*1160, d. July 16, 1216, named Lotario de'Segni, was pope from 1198 to 1216; during his pontificate, the PAPACY reached the height of its political power. He was appointed cardinal in 1190 by his uncle, Pope Celestine III, and was elected pope on the very day that Celestine died.

From the beginning of his pontificate, Innocent was involved in imperial affairs. After Constance of Sicily, widow of Holy Roman Emperor HENRY VI, accepted papal sovereignty over Sicily, Innocent recognized (1198) her son, the future Holy Roman Emperor FREDERICK II, as king of Sicily. When Constance died the same year, Innocent became regent for the infant Frederick. Although he crowned OTTO IV emperor in 1209, he soon shifted his support to young Frederick, who became German king in 1212.

Innocent was equally successful in developing the claims of the papal authority over other nations. In England he intervened in the disputed appointment of the archbishop of Canterbury and procured the election of Stephen LANGTON. When King JOHN refused to allow the pope's appointee, Innocent placed (1208) England under interdict (in effect, banning church services). John finally yielded (1213) and became a papal vassal. In France, Innocent forced (1210) PHILIP II to obey canon law on the question of his divorce from his wife, Ingeborg of Denmark. The pope also made his authority felt in Spain, intervening in the marital affairs of Peter II of Aragon and Alfonso IX of León.

Innocent was instrumental in organizing the Fourth CRUSADE and also extended the crusade idea to the suppression of the ALBIGENSES. At the end of 1215 he called the Fourth LATERAN COUNCIL, the culminating event of his pontificate. Among his many works, *De contemptu mundi* (On Contempt for the World) was a popular ascetic treatise, written before he was elected pope.

Innocent IV, Pope

Innocent IV, b. *c.*1200, d. Dec. 7, 1254, was pope from 1243 to 1254. His name was Sinibaldo Fieschi. Because of his belief in the universal authority of the PAPACY, he was engaged in a constant struggle for power with Holy Roman Emperor FREDERICK II. Following his election, Innocent tried to negotiate with Frederick but was forced to flee (1244) to France. From 1244 to 1251 the papal court was at Lyon. In April 1245, Innocent condemned the emperor and summoned him to appear before the Council of Lyon. Since Frederick refused to appear, he was convicted in absentia and declared deposed; the pope then tried to secure the election of a new emperor. Innocent continued to interfere in the affairs of the empire under Frederick's successors. The papal bull *Ad extirpanda*, which he issued in 1252, justified the use of torture by the Inquisition.

Innocent XI, Pope

Innocent XI, b. May 19, 1611, d. Aug. 12, 1689, was pope from 1676 to 1689. His name was Benedetto Odescalchi. His pontificate was dominated by a constant struggle against LOUIS XIV of France, who had tried twice (in 1669 and again in 1676) to prevent his election. In 1682 a synod convoked by Louis issued the Gallican Articles (see GALLICANISM), which called for restrictions on papal authority. Innocent condemned the articles and refused to invest as bishops any of the clergy who supported them. He encouraged reforms in the church and was notable for his piety, generosity, and freedom from nepotism. He sympathized with JANSENISM but condemned QUIETISM in the bull *Coelestis Pastor* (1687). He was beatified by Pope Pius XII in 1956. Feast day: Aug. 13.

Innocent XII, Pope

Innocent XII, b. Mar. 13, 1615, d. Sept. 27, 1700, was pope from 1691 to 1700. His name was Antonio Pignatelli. He persuaded LOUIS XIV of France to disavow (1693) the Gallican Articles of 1682 (see GALLICANISM); in return he extended Louis's right to administer vacant French sees. Innocent's pontificate was noted for church reform.

Inns of Court

The Inns of Court, in London, are private associations that supervise legal education and control admission to the bar in Great Britain. The inns developed early in the 14th century in response to a growing interest in the teaching of common law. The four inns are the Inner Temple, Middle Temple, Lincoln's Inn, and Gray's Inn. Those seeking admittance to the bar must enroll in an inn for a period of "pupillage," as well as pass an examination. Similar but less important societies called Inns of Chancery went out of existence in the 1800s.

Innsbruck

Innsbruck [inz'-bruk] Innsbruck is the capital of TY-ROL province in western Austria. Its population is 117,011 (1986 est.). Located in the eastern Alps, it is an important tourist and winter-sports resort and hosted the 1964 and 1976 Winter Olympics. The city is also a rail and market center and manufactures textiles. The bridge over the River Inn, which gives the city its name, made Innsbruck an important point on the trade routes to Germany from Italy and Switzerland by the 12th century. Originally belonging to the counts of Andech, it passed to the Habsburgs in 1363, and became the ducal residence in 1420. Innsbruck has many notable medieval buildings, including the 16th-century Franciscan Hofkirche (church) and the Fürstenburg, a 15th-century castle with a copper-roofed balcony.

inoculation

inoculation see VACCINATION

İnönü, İsmet

İnönü, İsmet [ee-nu-noo', is-met'] The Turkish statesman and career military officer İsmet İnönü, b. Sept. 24, 1884, d. Dec. 25, 1973, became the principal lieutenant of Kemal ATATÜRK in the post-World War I struggle for Turkish independence. İnönü was the Turkish representative at the Lausanne Conference (see LAUSANNE, TREATY OF), which established the Turkish Republic in 1923. He was twice prime minister (1923–24, 1925–37) during Atatürk's presidency. As president (1938–50), İnönü kept Turkey neutral during World War II. İnönü's Republican People's party (RPP) lost in the elections of 1950, and İnönü then led the opposition to the Democratic party's regime until its overthrow by a coup in 1960. Prime minister again from 1964 to 1965, İnönü was ousted as RPP leader in 1972.

inorganic chemistry

inorganic chemistry Inorganic chemistry describes the properties and behavior of all ELEMENTS and their compounds except for the majority of the carbon compounds (compounds generally characterized by chains of connected carbon atoms), which are the domain of OR-GANIC CHEMISTRY. Chemists in the early 19th century sought to distinguish between organic compounds, which were thought to occur only in plants and animals, and inorganic compounds, which were thought to occur only in minerals and other nonliving matter. At the time, organic compounds were believed impossible to synthesize in the laboratory. Chemists theorized that a "vital force," present only in living things, was the catalyst behind the creation of organic compounds. Friedrich WÖHLER destroyed the distinction between organic and inorganic chemistry. In 1828 he synthesized the organic compound urea ($CO(NH_2)_2$) through a rearrangement of the inorganic compound ammonium cyanate (NH_4OCN). Although the name is no longer appropriate, inorganic chemistry has continued to exist as a specialty since the 1800s.

Early Work with Compounds. Inorganic chemists made wide-ranging discoveries during the late-18th and the 19th century. In the 1770s, Antoine LAVOISIER demonstrated that oxidation (see OXIDATION AND REDUCTION) is the process behind COMBUSTION, rusting (see CORROSION), and respiration (see METABOLISM). Lavoisier also incorrectly named oxygen as the necessary element in the formation of acids (see ACIDS AND BASES), but Humphrey Davy later proved that the key element is, in fact, hydrogen. Henry CAVENDISH established (1783) the composition of water; he was the first to chemically combine hydrogen and oxygen by means of an electric spark.

Inorganic chemists discovered and investigated many new compounds in the 1800s, including hydrides, halides, oxyacids, and metallic SALTS. Unusual compounds of sulfur, nitrogen, and phosphorus were synthesized. The chemistry of the metals uranium, vanadium, niobium, and tantalum was also developed. Henri Moissan investigated fluorine compounds and founded high-temperature chemistry with his development of the electric-arc furnace in the 1890s. With the furnace Moissan was able to synthesize many new compounds, including carbides, silicides, and borides. Seminal work on COORDINATION COMPOUNDS was also carried out in the 1890s, and the development of PHYSICAL CHEMISTRY during the same period led to improvements in laboratory techniques.

More Recent Developments. Theories of chemical bonding (see CHEMICAL BOND) had always proved difficult to formulate. Insights gained through the discovery (1895) of the ELECTRON and the development (1924–27) of QUANTUM MECHANICS led to a new understanding of the many ways in which atoms interact. It subsequently became easier for inorganic chemists to predict the outcome of chemical reactions.

In a more practical vein, the findings of inorganic chemists are crucial to almost every industry. Modern electronic components, textiles, pharmaceuticals, fertilizers, and explosives are just a few areas that benefit from inorganic-chemical research. Inorganic chemists are participating in the search for new superconductors (see SU-PERCONDUCTIVITY).

Inorganic chemists also have a new array of powerful tools with which to perform their work. These include computer programs and graphics that can accurately model complex chemical reactions, ELECTRON MICROSCOPES that can reveal the structure of a molecule, and pulsed lasers that can "freeze" a chemical reaction in process and provide a picture of various phases of the reaction. Chemists anticipate a time when molecules can be split apart and fused together with a laser.

See also: CHEMICAL INDUSTRY; CHEMISTRY; CHEMISTRY, HISTORY OF.

Inouye, Daniel K.

Inouye, Daniel K. [ee-noh'-way] Daniel Ken Inouye, b. Honolulu, Sept. 7, 1924, was first elected to the U.S. Senate as a Democrat from Hawaii in 1962. He was a member of the Senate select committee investigating the WATERGATE affair in 1973 and in 1987 chairman of the Senate panel inquiring into the IRAN-CONTRA AFFAIR. A lawyer, Inouye had previously served in the Hawaii legislature (1954–59) and the U.S. House of Representatives (1959–63).

input-output analysis   Input-output analysis is a system for comparing the flow of goods and services among different industries and sectors of an economy. The output of one industry, for example, coal, becomes the input of other industries, such as the steel and electric power industries; the outputs of these industries in turn become inputs for other industries. Input-output analysis is useful in determining how a change in the output of one industry will affect other industries. For example, before beginning a program of road building, a government would want to know how the program will affect key industries such as the cement, steel, and machinery industries and the industries that supply them. These effects can be determined from an input-output grid showing how each industry draws its inputs from the outputs of other industries. Input-output analysis was developed principally by Wassily Leontief of Harvard University, who received (1973) a Nobel Prize for economics for his work.

input-output devices   Devices that provide for the movement of information between the CENTRAL PROCESSING UNIT of a COMPUTER system and the external world are called input/output devices, or simply I/O devices. They are extremely important because every computer functions by accepting input and producing output. Input is the control information (programs and commands) that directs computing activities; it also includes the data information (digital numbers, characters, or pictures) that is manipulated by the computing activities. Output is information produced as a result of computing activities.

Because of the wide variety of forms of information, many types of I/O devices are used. They may be characterized according to the information medium, the hardware technology, the speed of information transfer, and the amount or capacity of information involved. Many devices support the movement of information between a storage medium and processor. Others support communication between the computer system and the external world of noncomputer devices.

Storage-oriented devices store information in computer-readable form. Nonstorage devices are used when it is not necessary to move the same information both into and out of the computer. Information is transformed from a computer-readable form to a form readable by a person or another machine.

Nonstorage-Oriented Devices. Typical devices that are not oriented toward machine-readable storage are computer terminals, printers, graphics and image displays, plotters, computer output microfilm (COM), optical scanners, and converters between analog and digital information.

COMPUTER TERMINALS may support the input of charac-

ter information via a keyboard or microphone. They may support the output of characters on paper or on a cathode ray tube (CRT) screen. Printers produce paper output of character information at high speed (see PRINTER, COMPUTER).

Graphics and image displays present pictorial information. The joystick, lightpen, mouse, and graphics tablet are common devices for input of graphic information. Graphs may be formed from dots or lines. Pictures are represented in a computer in a digitized form where a picture is composed of many small parts called picture elements, or pixels. Plotters and computer-output microfilm devices produce graphical output on paper or film.

Optical scanners are input devices that read intensities of reflected light. They are used commercially to read standard product code bars on retail merchandise for input to computers. The computer then computes sales price, updates inventory records, prepares purchase orders, and performs a variety of other tasks. ANALOG-TO-DIGITAL CONVERTERS, DIGITAL-TO-ANALOG CONVERTERS, and MODEMS enable communication between digital computers and analog devices.

Storage-Oriented Devices. Examples of storage-oriented devices include magnetic tapes, discs, and cylinders; COMPACT DISCS; bubble memories; and punched cards (see also INFORMATION STORAGE AND RETRIEVAL). Magnetic devices—the most popular type—employ the property of magnetic particles that allows them to be polarized in one of two directions, so that they can carry binary information. Compact-disc technology is developing rapidly and may eventually replace many magnetic devices. Bubble memories are a type of magnetic technology in which microscopic bubble patterns are formed on garnet crystals. Although potentially more powerful than the magnetic metal technologies, bubble memories have not been perfected.

Interfacing I/O Devices to Computers. To provide some standardization of interfaces for the many types of I/O devices and to increase efficiency of I/O operations, I/O channels have been developed. A channel exists between the computer and perhaps several devices so that the specializations of each device are isolated. Channels provide a direct path between various devices and the COMPUTER MEMORY. This feature is known as direct memory access. Channels are programmable and operate independently of the processor, once started, thus allowing I/O to take place simultaneously with computation.

The improvement of existing I/O devices in terms of speed, capacity, accuracy, and reliability makes I/O technology a fast-changing field. In addition, sophisticated forms of I/O, such as voice, visual, and tactile communication, have been developed and are being pursued.

inquest [in'-kwest]   An inquest is an inquiry made by a group of persons appointed by the law. The term usually applies to a jury conducting a legal investigation of evidence. Such investigations include those made by grand juries, CORONER's juries, and surrogate's courts. A GRAND JURY may initiate its own investigation or review indictments brought to it by a public prosecutor. A coroner's jury identifies victims of death by unnatural causes and decides how, where, and when the victim died. A surrogate's court inquires into the circumstances of a will offered for probate.

Inquisition [in-kwi-zish'-uhn]

The Inquisition was a medieval church court instituted to seek out and prosecute heretics. The term is applied to the institution itself, which was episcopal or papal, regional or local; to the personnel of the tribunal; and to the judicial procedure followed by the court.

Development and Institution. Problems with sects such as the ALBIGENSES (Cathari) and WALDENSES in the 12th century first led to the episcopal Inquisition. Often at the instigation of secular rulers, bishops were urged to investigate and deal locally with heretics, since heretics were seen as a threat to both the ecclesiastical and the social

This painting portrays the culminating ceremony of the Inquisition: the sermo generalis, *or auto-da-fé; the accused are seen being sentenced* (left), *awaiting punishment* (center), *and at the stake* (right). *(Prado, Madrid.)*

order. Papal documents as well as the Second, Third, and Fourth LATERAN COUNCILS (1139, 1179, 1215) prescribed imprisonment and confiscation of property as punishment for heresy and threatened to excommunicate princes who failed to punish heretics.

The papal Inquisition was formally instituted by Pope GREGORY IX in 1231. Following a law of Holy Roman Emperor FREDERICK II, enacted for Lombardy in 1224 and extended to the entire empire in 1232, Gregory ordered convicted heretics to be seized by the secular authorities and burned. He first appointed special inquisitors and later entrusted the task to members of the newly established DOMINICAN and FRANCISCAN orders of friars. The independent authority of the inquisitors was a frequent cause of friction with the local clergy and bishops.

Procedures. During the 13th century, the typical procedure began with the arrival of the inquisitors in a specific locality. A period of grace was proclaimed for penitent heretics, after which time denunciations were accepted from anyone, even criminals and other heretics. Two informants whose identity was unknown to the accused were usually sufficient for a charge. The court then summoned the suspect, conducted an interrogation, and tried to obtain the confession that was necessary for conviction. In order to do this, assisting secular authorities frequently applied physical torture.

At the beginning of the interrogation, which was recorded summarily in Latin by a clerk, suspects and witnesses had to swear under oath that they would reveal everything. Unwillingness to take the oath was interpreted as a sign of adherence to heresy. If a person confessed and was willing to submit, the judges prescribed minor penances such as flogging, fasts, prayers, pilgrimages, or fines. In more severe cases the wearing of a yellow "cross of infamy," with its resulting social ostracism, or imprisonment could be imposed. Denial of the charges without counterproof, obstinate refusal to confess, and persistence in the heresy resulted in the most severe punishments: life imprisonment or execution accompanied by total confiscation of property. Since the church was not permitted to shed blood, the sentenced heretic was surrendered to the secular authorities for execution, usually by burning at the stake. When the Inquisition had completed its investigations, the sentences were pronounced in a solemn ceremony, known as the *sermo generalis* ("general address") or, in Spain, as the *auto-da-fé* ("act of faith"), attended by local dignitaries, clergy, and townspeople.

The first inquisitors worked in central Europe (Germany, northern Italy, eastern France). Later centers of the Inquisition were established in the Mediterranean regions, especially southern France and Italy, Portugal, and Spain. The tribunal was used in England to suppress the LOLLARDS (followers of the 14th-century reformer John WYCLIFFE). Queen Mary I of England (r. 1553–58) used the tribunal in her effort to reverse the Protestant REFORMATION. The Inquisition's long survival can be attributed to the early inclusion of offenses other than heresy: sorcery, alchemy, blasphemy, sexual aberration, and infanticide. The number of witches and sorcerers burned after the late 15th century appears to have been far greater than that of heretics.

Spanish Inquisition. The Inquisition underwent special development in Portugal and Spain and their colonies. At the insistence of Ferdinand II of Aragon and Isabella I of Castile, Pope SIXTUS IV endorsed (1483) the creation of an independent Spanish Inquisition presided over by a high council and grand inquisitor. Legend has made the first grand inquisitor, Tomás de TORQUEMADA, a symbol of ultimate cruelty, bigotry, intolerance, and religious fanaticism. The truth is that the Spanish Inquisition was particularly severe, strict, and efficient because of its strong ties with the crown. Its major targets were the Marranos (converts from Judaism) and Moriscos (converts from Islam), many of whom were suspected of secretly adhering to their original faiths. During the 16th century, Protestants and Alumbrados (Spanish mystics) seemed to be the major targets. Often serving political ends, the inquisitors also exercised their dreaded functions among the converted Indian populations of the Spanish colonies in America. The Inquisition was finally suppressed in Spain in 1834 and in Portugal in 1821.

Roman Inquisition. At the time of the Reformation, Pope PAUL III created a cardinals' commission at the curia as the final court of appeal in matters of heresy. This Roman Inquisition was solidified (1588) by SIXTUS V into the Congregation of the Roman and Universal Inquisition, also known as the Holy Office, whose task was to watch over the correct doctrine of faith and morals for the whole Roman Catholic church. Reorganized in 1908 under the simpler title Congregation of the Holy Office, it was redefined by Pope PAUL VI in 1965 as the Congregation for the Doctrine of the Faith, with the more positive task of furthering right doctrine rather than censuring heresy.

—

insanity, legal   Insanity, in law, is a mental defect or disorder sufficient to prevent a person from knowing the difference between right and wrong conduct or from understanding the nature of his or her actions.

In criminal law, insanity is a defense against responsibility for a crime. Anglo-American common law has traditionally assumed that punishment for criminal behavior is applicable only to those who can make moral choices and who have the ability to conform their behavior to the dictates of law. The first modern test of insanity, still applicable in many jurisdictions, was the M'Naghten rule (1843). It held that a person was insane if he or she had such a defect of reason at the time of committing a criminal act that he or she did not know the nature and quality of the act or was unable to distinguish between right and wrong. Many jurisdictions have added the "irresistible impulse" test to the M'Naghten test. This labels as insane those who know the difference between right and wrong but cannot control their behavior because of mental disorder. The concept of legal insanity has been controversial; courtroom methods of establishing legal insanity, definitions of insanity, and ways of coping with those acquitted on grounds of insanity have been strongly criticized.

Another application of the concept of insanity in criminal law is the notion that a person must be sane to stand trial. Defendants must be able to understand the nature of the proceedings against them and to assist in their own defense.

—

inscription   Inscription is writing in the form of letters, words, or other conventional symbols cut into a permanent material for the purpose of conveying and preserving information. The earliest writings probably appeared in the form of inscription, which later gave rise to the related art of CALLIGRAPHY, or fine writing on perishable materials such as papyrus, parchment, and paper. The origins of writing and the evolution of alphabetic systems can be traced through epigraphy, the study of ancient inscriptions (see WRITING SYSTEMS, EVOLUTION OF).

Ancient inscriptions appear on diverse types of hard material, including marble, crystalline limestone, and other varieties of stone; metals such as bronze, gold, and silver; and bone, ivory, clay, and wood—although few examples of the last have survived. The inscribers' tools have varied, depending on the surface used; common implements include the chisel, often formed with a square blade; a stylus, with one end blunt and the other pointed, for impressing inscriptions into clay before firing; and a punch or pointed hammer.

Throughout history inscriptions have been executed on temples or churches, civic buildings, monuments, tombs, statues, vases, and coins; sometimes the text is accompanied by pictorial reliefs. Inscriptions have frequently been used for public announcements or administrative documents recording political and religious decrees, law codes, public and private contracts, treaties and other matters of state, dedications, benefactions, and honors. As such, they serve as an invaluable source of historical information, both social and political. Modern inscriptions are most often found on building facades, cornerstones, and tombstones, on which occurs the oldest continuous use of inscription.

Early Inscription. The history of Western inscription began in Mesopotamia, where in about 4000 BC the Sumerians developed CUNEIFORM. This writing system consists of characters made with wedge-shaped strokes impressed into clay, brick, or stone. By the 2d millennium BC an alphabet of 29 cuneiform signs was in use at ancient UGARIT; these signs closely resemble Hebrew and Phoenician letters. Cuneiform was also the system used by the HITTITES at Elam; Old Persian, the writing of the ACHAEMENIDS, was a revised form of cuneiform writing. The famous BEHISTUN inscriptions of Darius I, dated c.500 BC, exemplify Achaemenid script; with the conquest of these regions by Alexander the Great, Greek became the dominant inscribed language.

Egyptian inscriptions in the form of HIEROGLYPHIC writing date from the 1st dynasty (4th millennium BC). The system of inscription established then continued in use with only minor modifications until the time of the Romans. A fine example of the Egyptian style is preserved in the form of rock inscriptions at THEBES. Another renowned epigraphical monument is the ROSETTA STONE, discovered in 1799. This basalt tablet, dated 196 BC, was inscribed in three languages: ancient Egyptian hieroglyphs, demotic (an Egyptian cursive script), and Greek.

On the Aegean island of Crete an independent hieroglyphic system existed, replaced in the beginning of the Middle Minoan period (1750–1450 BC) by a linear script, read from left to right, which developed into the script known as Linear A; this in turn was followed by another script, designated LINEAR B.

Phoenician inscriptions date from *c.*1000 BC; the Phoenician alphabet, adapted and modified by the Greeks at an uncertain date, remained in use until the 3d century BC. The earliest Greek inscriptions date from the 7th century BC. At first each Greek state had its own alphabet, but in 403 BC, under the archon Euclides, the Ionian alphabet—still used for Greek capital letters—was officially adopted by Athens and soon spread throughout Greece. The art of inscription flourished, evidenced by the innumerable writings found on vases, coins, statues, votive offerings, and relief panels. An unusual example of early Greek inscription appears in the form of graffiti scratched (*c.*590 BC) by Greek mercenaries on the legs of the colossal statues of Abu Simbel in Egypt.

Latin Inscription. From the Greek alphabet were derived various local Italic alphabets, including that of the Etruscans and that of the Chalcidean colony of Cumae, on which the Roman alphabet was based. The Roman inscriptional style, in wide use from the 3d century BC, persists in essentially the same form to the present day. In Gaul, concurrent with Latin inscriptions of the late republic, a form of Celtic inscription appeared, based on Greek letters. Later, during the Christian period, Celtic inscriptions were written in ogham, one of the Irish runic languages. This writing was alphabetical and apparently an independent invention, based on arbitrary symbols much like a Morse code. The Germanic runes, much used in the same region, were derived from the Greek or Latin alphabets.

Non-Western Traditons. Important epigraphic traditions of the New World include the hieroglyphic inscriptions on stone monuments (stelae) of the AZTEC, MAYA, and TOLTEC cultures (see PRE-COLUMBIAN ART AND ARCHITECTURE) as well as the enigmatic rock inscriptions of EASTER ISLAND. In China the earliest known inscriptions were executed on bronze vessels and ORACLE BONES of the Shang dynasty (*c.*1600–1027 BC. After the Chinese invention of paper in about AD 100, inscription was relegated to a lesser role. At Harappa and Mohenjo-daro, two major sites of the INDUS CIVILIZATION, low-relief inscriptions made on steatite seals dated from *c.*2500 BC. An important inscription from the early Buddhist period in India is the Prakrit of ASOKA, dated 3d century BC.

insect Insects are members of the phylum Arthropoda (see ARTHROPOD), class Insecta, the largest and most diverse class in the animal kingdom. The number of described insect species is estimated to be 750,000, and the actual number of living species is perhaps 3 million. Even at 750,000 species, however, insects outnumber all other plant and animal groups.

Insects have three body divisions—head, thorax, and abdomen—and six legs borne as an adult. Many insects possess wings as adults. Because of their small size, ability to fly, rapid reproductive rate, and external skeleton (exoskeleton), insects are highly successful animals that have exploited every habitat except the polar ice caps. The exoskeleton is coated with a waxy layer that helps

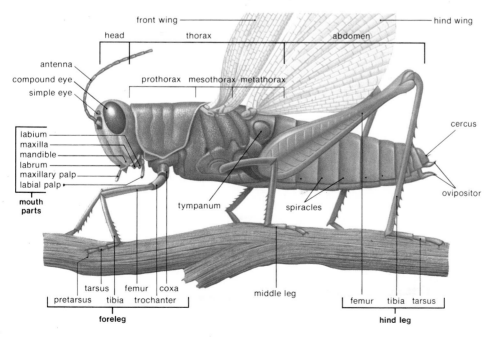

The external anatomy of a female grasshopper is representative of the majority of insects. The elongated body is bilaterally symmetrical, segmented, and covered by a hard exoskeleton; it is divided into three regions: head, thorax, and abdomen. The head bears both compound and simple eyes, antennae, and mouthparts. The thorax is divided into three segments; each bears a pair of jointed legs, and the last two each have a pair of wings. The abdomen has spiracles, or breathing pores, and the external parts of the reproductive organs. Some grasshoppers also have tympana—oval eardrums—located on the abdomen.

The internal structure of a female grasshopper, like that of most insects, includes a respiratory system (top) composed of spiracles, or breathing pores, and tracheae, a network of tubes that carry oxygen throughout the body. The circulatory system is open; blood is pumped from the heart to the aorta and then flows through the body back to the heart. The brain, ganglia, and nerve cords comprise the nervous system. Food enters the digestive system (bottom) through the mouth, mixes with saliva, and then passes into the esophagus, crop, and stomach; wastes are eliminated through the anus. Reproductive organs include two ovaries and a system of oviducts.

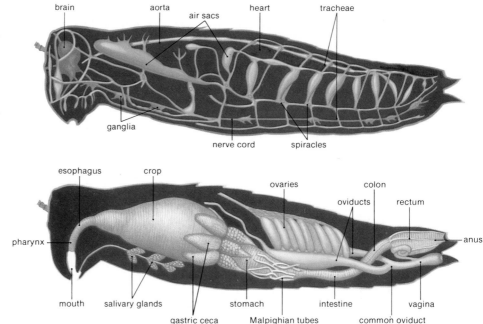

insects conserve body moisture. The small size of insects aids in their dispersal to more favorable habitats. Thrips and aphids are carried by frontal systems for long distances. Small insects have been collected by airplanes at 3,000 m (10,000 ft). Migratory butterflies and locusts may fly hundreds of kilometers in a few weeks.

Insects display almost every color, from drab, dull browns and black, to iridescent blues, reds, and purples, to the metallic greens, blues, yellows, and reds of some WASPS and BEES. Size varies from tiny mymarid wasps less than 1 mm (0.04 in) long to huge beetles or slender walking sticks up to 30 cm (12 in) long. Shape is equally variable. For example, legs may be adapted for walking, jumping, running, clinging to hairs, swimming, spinning silk, carrying pollen, hearing, or smelling, or they may be absent.

Structure and Function

Insects usually have a clearly defined head, thorax, and abdomen. The head bears antennae, eyes, and mouthparts; the thorax bears legs and wings; and the abdomen has various styli, cerci (antennalike sensory organs), and the genital apparatus. Most insects have a pair of relatively large compound eyes on the head as well as two or three simple eyes (ocelli). Food is chewed by the mandibles while it is held, sensed, and manipulated by the maxillae. In the true bugs (Hemiptera) the mouthparts are modified into piercing stylets, and juices of host plants or animals are sucked up.

The thorax, or middle body region, is divided into the prothorax, mesothorax, and metathorax. Each segment typically bears one pair of legs. The last two segments bear the wings. Insect legs are divided by joints into six segments. The legs often have secondary functions that may affect leg size and shape. A common secondary function of legs in males is that of holding the female during mating. Except when thickened and tough, insect wings often have veins, or hardened tubes that strengthen the wing.

The abdomen is composed of 11 or fewer segments. The last few abdominal segments are often associated with the external portions of the reproductive organs and with them are called the terminalia. The terminalia in female insects are often modified into an elaborate egg placer (ovipositor), which in the bees and wasps has been modified into a stinger.

The integument, or skin, is flexible, waterproof, and hard. The outermost layer of the integument is the cuticle, or exoskeleton, which also lines the fore and hind gut and which consists largely of protein and chitin. Cuticle is not extensible; growth is possible only until the wrinkles are smoothed out. Then, an insect must molt to resume growth.

Circulatory System and Breathing. The heart is a series of pumping chambers with an upper tube having openings along the side; the tube allows a colorless blood to be moved forward by a wave of contraction. Blood bathes the internal organs and is only partially enclosed by an upper diaphragm. Because insects are cold-blooded, pulse rate may range from 140 per minute in an active insect to 1 per hour in chilled insects. Insects usually breathe by taking in air through a series of holes (spiracles) along the thorax and abdomen. Leading from the spiracles are tubes (tracheae) that interconnect to form a tracheal system.

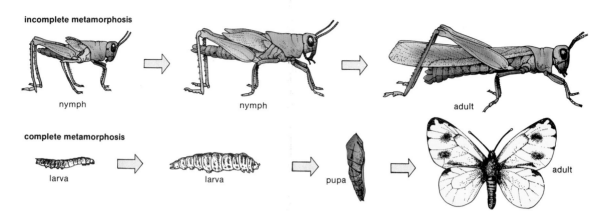

incomplete metamorphosis

nymph   nymph   adult

complete metamorphosis

larva   larva   pupa   adult

Most insects develop by metamorphosis, or changing form. Primitive insects, such as the grasshopper, undergo incomplete metamorphosis, in which changes are gradual. The nymph, or larva, resembles a wingless adult; it molts several times, emerging from the final molt as an adult. The large majority of insects, however, undergo complete metamorphosis. Higher insects such as the butterfly hatch into wormlike larvae that molt several times without change in form, then molt into pupae—a quiescent stage—and finally emerge as adults.

Feeding and Digestion. Insects obtain food by a variety of methods, including biting, lapping, and sucking. Carnivorous insects such as the praying mantis catch and chew their prey. Some wasps paralyze their prey with venomous stings, lay their eggs in the bodies, and provide a living food supply for their young. Termites are able to digest and receive nourishment from wood because tiny protozoans within their digestive system "predigest" the cellulose in the wood.

The digestive system is essentially a tube that begins with the mouth and is divided into a pharynx; esophagus; crop, stomach (midgut), and intestine (hindgut); colon; and rectum. The midgut has glandular outgrowths, the gastric ceca, which secrete digestive juices. The Malpighian tubes remove nitrogenous waste from the blood; the blind tubes empty into the hindgut.

Sense Organs and Nervous System

Insects orient to the environment by means of touch and stretch receptors in the integument. Auditory receptors are usually stretch-type receptors associated with an "eardrum" (tympanum). Unlike other animals, insects have light receptors, or eyes, that can neither be turned nor moved and are usually fitted together into a pair of compound eyes. A compound eye may contain a honeycomb of as many as 28,000 lenses. The images from each lens, or ommatidium, are somehow interpreted together in the insect's brain, but it is not known what the insect sees. Many insects also have two or three simple eyes, called ocelli, and these probably can only distinguish light from dark.

Most insects detect odors through olfactory receptors often found on the antennae and in the mouthparts and feet. Beetles that feed on carrion can scent a carcass for many kilometers, but if their antennae are damaged they cannot detect the carrion from a few meters away. Ants leave trails of odorous chemicals (pheromones) that can be recognized by others in the same colony, even when the scent leads through a maze of crossing trails left by ants of other colonies. The antennae are also sensitive to sound waves, or vibrations of air molecules, by means of special structures called Johnston's organs situated on the antennae. Katydids and crickets have ears in the form of sensitive hairs on the front legs.

The nervous system in insects primarily consists of paired nerve masses (ganglia) resembling a ladder lying on the lower inner surface of the body. In the head there is a ganglion (cluster of nerve cells). Nerves connect the cerebral ganglion with the ganglia in the body, which control muscles and direct the endocrine system to release hormones.

The stag beetles, family Lucanidae, are named for the elongated jaws, or mandibles, of the males, which resemble the antlers of a stag. The mandibles are used both in fighting and for holding the female during copulation.

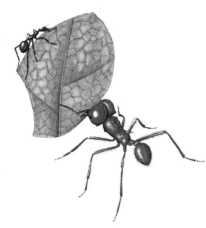

Leafcutting ants cut pieces of leaves and transport them to their nest, where they feed on fungi that grows on the leaves. The larger worker ant is carrying the leaf while the smaller worker guards against parasitic flies that may attempt to lay their eggs on the leaf's surface.

Growth and development in insects is largely regulated by hormones secreted by the brain. Hormones may be liberated in the blood to keep the insect actively growing or may be directed to specific endocrine glands via the connective nerve to control molting, heartbeat, sugar content of the blood, juvenile characteristics, and egg production.

Life Cycle

The reproduction system of insects consists of a pair of gonads (testes or ovaries) connected to a median duct, which opens at a gonopore. During copulation the male introduces sperm into a copulatory aperture, where it is stored in the female's spermatheca. As an egg matures, it slides into the median oviduct, where it is fertilized by the sperm.

Almost 85 percent of insect species develop by a process of complete METAMORPHOSIS, which is a series of

The bodies of stick insects and leaf insects mimic parts of the plants on which they live, providing an effective form of camouflage. During the day these insects hang motionless and are all but undetectable against their surroundings.

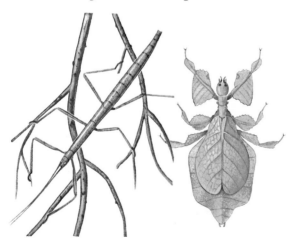

successive stages that do not resemble one another. The remainder, except for less than 1 percent, undergo incomplete metamorphosis, where changes are not extreme. The life cycle of an insect usually starts with the placement of an egg on a substrate, the development of an immature form through successive molts, and then the emergence of the adult stage at the last molt. Adult insects usually mate, feed, and then lay eggs. Some insects give birth to live young (an aphid may produce more than 175 young).

Immature insects are called nymphs, naiads, or larvae. Nymphs develop gradually and resemble their adult stage. Naiads develop gradually but are aquatic. Larvae generally do not resemble the adult stage, and they develop through a pupal stage, usually nonmotile, often in a cocoon. Larvae often live in a habitat different from that of the adult and feed on different resources. Larvae have been named on the basis of form and function. Caterpillars, grubs, and maggots are immature stages of moths, beetles, and flies, respectively. Pupae have also been catagorized by form (see PUPA).

Behavior

Insect behavior, for the most part, is hereditary, and responses to stimuli are mostly automatic or instinctive. Direct responses (moving toward or away from the stimuli) may be made in reaction to light, temperature, water, contact, gravity, or currents of air or water. Often a response to a stimulus can be modified by other stimuli, as well as by the insect's physiology, food, and state of development. Some behavior involves a series of different acts. Such complex behavior includes nest building and mating. While this behavior may appear intelligent, it is usually found to be instinctive. Because insects can be taught to modify their behavior, however, it is believed that they have a limited capacity to learn. Examples include the ant that can learn a maze and the honeybee that finds its way home by recognizing landmarks.

Social Behavior. Many insects occur in groups, each group differing in the factors that bring the individuals together. Often the aggregation results from a mutual attraction to the same stimulus, such as food supply. Ants, termites, and some bees live in more integrated groups, called societies. The insect society works as a unit despite the large number of individuals. One distinct feature is the division of labor.

Auditory Behavior. Sound plays an important role in insect behavior. Only a few sounds produced by insects are heard by humans, because these sounds are either too low or too high pitched. Sound is produced in several ways. Rubbing one body part against another, called stridulation, may involve almost any part of the body, in various species. Some insects vibrate special membranes called tymbols, as in the leafhoppers. A few insects will strike a part of their body on the substrate, for example, some grasshoppers use their feet. The principal role played by sound is in mating.

Defenses. Most insects try to escape when threatened and some insects "play dead." For example, some beetles fall to the ground after folding up their legs, giving the

The more than 750,000 species of insects are classified in 23 to 32 different orders (according to different authorities) on the basis of various characteristics that include presence or absence of wings, structure and position of mouthparts, type of wings and pattern of wing venation, and type of metamorphosis. Among the more primitive insects are the Collembola (springtails), wingless insects that do not metamorphose. The Odonata (dragonflies and damselflies) undergo incomplete metamorphosis and have wings that do not fold. Katydids and other Orthoptera have folding wings. The highest orders, including the Diptera (true flies) and Lepidoptera (butterflies and moths) have folding wings and undergo complete metamorphosis.

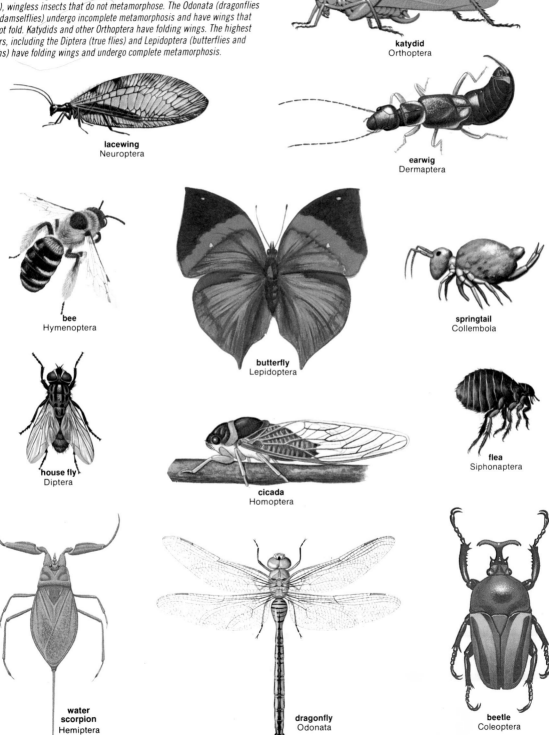

katydid
Orthoptera

lacewing
Neuroptera

earwig
Dermaptera

bee
Hymenoptera

butterfly
Lepidoptera

springtail
Collembola

house fly
Diptera

cicada
Homoptera

flea
Siphonaptera

**water
scorpion**
Hemiptera

dragonfly
Odonata

beetle
Coleoptera

appearance of a clump of dirt. Many insects use shelters ranging from burrows in the ground to elaborate shelters constructed of various materials. Insects also employ camouflage (see MIMICRY). Many are so colored that they blend into their background. Chemical defenses often involve distasteful body secretions, repellent secretions, or poisonous injection into an attacker. The use of the sting is probably the most effective and often a severe method. The only stinging insects are Hymenoptera (bees, wasps, and some ants).

Flight. Although most insects fly, their weight-to-wing ratio in theory is not advantageous to flight. They build up enough energy so that speed of the wing beat makes up for the theoretical lack of lifting power. The vibrating insect wing actually follows a figure eight or ellipsoid path. The effect is the same as a propeller going round and round, and the insect is drawn forward by a stream of air directed downward and backward.

Insects may vibrate their wings at speeds of up to 600 to 1,000 complete beats per second, which is about 20 times faster than the wing beats of any bird. Insects move their wings by a combination of forces: the action of the flight muscles, which attach the wings to the thorax, and the buildup of forces in the thorax itself, which acts as if it contained a spring. Each contraction of the wing muscles compresses the thoracic box, which then springs back and thus helps in powering the next wing stroke.

Evolution and Classification

In 1988 the oldest fossil insect found to date was determined to be more than 390 million years old. The fossil, which closely resembles modern insects, suggests that insects had evolved millions of years before this specimen existed. It has led experts to believe that the emergence of land animals may have occurred earlier than previously thought, at the same time as the appearance of the first land plants in the late Silurian period, 408 million years ago. Insects are generally thought to have evolved from a centipedelike class of terrestrial arthropods (class Symphyla). Some scientists believe that both the insects and the symphylans evolved from a common ancestral group called the Protosymphyla. All available evidence indicates that these first insects were wingless and not very different from those now included in the order Thysanura: the bristletails and silverfish common in houses. During the next 100 million years a great diversity of insects occurred over the land and winged insects appeared, representing the first animals to fly.

The known living species of insects may be divided into 23 to 32 orders, depending on the authority cited. The most convenient classification, however, may be according to evolutionary grades. At the lowest level are the primitive wingless insects such as silverfish and springtails (Collembola) and the proturans (Protura).

The higher orders of insects have wings and are divided into two major groups: Palaeoptera, or "ancient wings," and Neoptera, which are the greater number of present-day insects. Palaeoptera are the most primitive winged species and cannot fold the wings over the abdomen when at rest. They contain two surviving orders: dragonflies (Odonata) and may-flies (Ephemeroptera). Neoptera do possess a wing-flexing, or folding, mechanism and can crawl into small spaces. Many orders of Neoptera have this ability, including Orthoptera (CRICKETS and GRASSHOPPERS) and Isoptera (TERMITES).

The highest evolutionary grade includes those insects which undergo complete metamorphosis as well as fold their wings. Insects that undergo complete metamorphosis often emerge from the egg as wormlike larvae that change first into pupe, often encased in a cocoon, before emerging as adults. This group includes the most diverse and successful of all insects: beetles (Coleoptera); butterflies and moths (Lepidoptera); flies (Diptera); fleas (Siphonaptera, which have become wingless); and the bees, wasps, and ants (Hymenoptera).

Some bees and wasps and all ants have developed a highly organized social life, with differentiation of members of the community into castes with different duties. Evolution has also resulted in elaborate means of communication by pheromones or gestures (see ANIMAL COMMUNICATION) and highly engineered nest structures.

Insects and Humans

The science concerned with insects is called entomology, which involves the description, classification, and evolution of insects, and research studies such as insect metabolism, behavior, genetics, and ecology.

Pollination by insects is essential for many crops, especially fruit. Bees are the most important pollinators and also make honey, one of the oldest crops developed by humans. Other products derived from insects include beeswax, used in polishes, and silk from the cocoons of the silkworm moth.

Other insects, such as locusts and boll weevils, may destroy crops and stored products. The boll weevil, which is a tiny brown beetle, destroys millions of dollars worth of cotton annually in the United States. The gypsy moths defoliate a wide variety of orchard and forest trees. Much entomological research is directed at devising methods for controlling these pests.

Many insects carry diseases fatal to humans and livestock. Some of the diseases include sleeping sickness, bubonic plague, malaria, typhoid fever, dysentery, and cholera.

insecticide   SEE PESTICIDES AND PEST CONTROL

insectivore [in-sek'-ti-vor]   Insectivores are a group of small, insect-eating mammals classified in the order Insectivora. The most primitive of all living higher animals today, they include moles, tenrecs, hedgehogs, desmans, gymnures, and solenodons. The order comprises 8 living families, 63 genera, and about 400 species, of which about 300 are shrews. Savi's pygmy shrew, *Suncus etruscus*, is the smallest of all mammals, measuring only 60 mm (2.4 in) including the tail, and weighs as little as 1.5 g (0.005 oz). The largest insectivore has five clawed toes. The snout is long and narrow, useful for poking into insects' nests. The typical coat is short, thick fur, or sometimes spines. The eyes are extremely small and sometimes have no external opening. The ears are tiny. Insectivores inhabit all parts of the world with the exception of Antarctica, Greenland, Australia, and most of South America. They are useful to humans because of their great consumption of insects, most of which are considered pests. Many insectivores, especially hedgehogs, moles, and shrews, also eat invertebrates, such as worms, and some small vertebrates.

insomnia   see SLEEP

---

installment plan   The installment plan is a method of buying goods on credit and making payments for them over a period of time. In Great Britain the practice is called hire purchase. In the United States most durable goods can be bought this way. About one-fourth of all retail sales are made on the installment plan.

Installment buying is only one method of borrowing money and paying it back over a period of time. Other forms of credit include CREDIT CARDS, home MORTGAGES, bank loans, and charge accounts. In 1985 consumer installment credit in the United States was close to $490 billion.

A customer who buys on the installment plan does not usually gain title to the goods until they are paid for. If the buyer defaults on payments the seller can repossess the goods and sell them to someone else; the first buyer is entitled to receive his or her money back minus depreciation.

---

instinct   Instinct is inherited, essentially unlearned, and generally adaptive ANIMAL BEHAVIOR that is typical to each species. Instinct is prominent in aggression, courtship, and mating, and in various social behaviors, although learning, maturation, growth, or circumstance can modify the behavior. Human behavior is mostly a product of learning, whereas the behavior of a moth, a snail, or a bird depends mainly on instinct. A species can be characterized and perhaps identified by its behavior patterns as distinctively as by its anatomy. For example, almost all birds drink by scooping water into their bills and lifting their heads, letting the water trickle down their throats. Pigeons, however, which are anatomically like other birds, are among a few bird species that pump, not scoop, their drinking water. Different species of spiders can be identified by the webs they spin.

Instinctive Patterns. Behaviors that are most instinctive include reproduction, concealment, defense, escape, threats or warnings, and aggression, all of which are essential to the survival of the species.

A species' instinctive behaviors appear similar in form: chickens and turkeys seek a high place to roost at night, cats stalk prey in a characteristic manner, and dogs mark their territories in a species-specific method. Typical behavior patterns appear even in animals that are raised isolated from other members of their own species, a situation in which learning by observation, imitation, or instruction cannot occur. Many, but not all, birds sing the songs of their species even though they are removed from the nest before hatching and are raised in a quiet room.

The term *instinct* is usually restricted to relatively complex acts, depending on the capabilities of the animal, and excludes simple reflexes such as the eyeblink and knee jerk. An example of complex instinctive behavior is nest building, which involves a great many different motions. Specific instincts have probably evolved through countless generations, as they are characteristic of particular species.

Migration and Reproduction. ANIMAL MIGRATION and ANIMAL COURTSHIP AND MATING are instinctive behaviors. Many animals travel great distances to particular locations where they engage in courting, mating, or caring for their young. Salmon return to the river of their origin in order to reproduce; males and females of many mountain animals normally live in separate groups, but during mating season both sexes migrate to certain valleys and intermingle.

Mating rituals tend to be highly stylized for a given species. Because of this specificity, no mistakes are made in the meaning of the message or of the intent of the signaler. Moreover, messages announcing the receptivity of a female are usually interpretable only by members of the same species. Several kinds of fireflies can occupy the same yard without interbreeding, because each uses its own specific flashing pattern, and each responds only to its species' particular pattern.

Although the most dramatic instinctive behavior relates to reproduction, instincts have a role in other aspects of animal life. Nestlings gape when a parent bird arrives at the nest; the colored throat pattern is a stimulus for the parent to stuff food into the youngsters' beaks. Social organizations represent a kind of collective instinct that, although highly complex and adaptable, is similar enough for individuals of a species to act cooperatively, such as during hunting raids. Red-wing males rise to attack a crow that flies over their territory. Many species fly in formations, and some fishes school in characteristic arrangements.

Although instinctive behaviors are predictable, higher animals still can adapt to varying circumstances. Animals such as the fox hunt over great distances to seek widely dispersed prey. When confined to zoos, these animals develop trotting circuits about the cage, wearing down the ground in paths.

Institute for Advanced Study   Founded in 1930, the Institute for Advanced Study in Princeton, N.J., provides research facilities to approximately 150 visiting American and foreign scholars who spend a term or a year or more on advanced study and work on academic projects. A staff of 24 faculty members in four schools (mathematics, natural sciences, social science, and historical studies) work with the visiting members. The institute was endowed by Louis Bamberger, a department-store owner, and its first president was Abraham FLEXNER.

Institut de France [een-stee-tue' duh frahns] Established in Paris in 1795 to replace learned societies closed by the French Revolution, the Institut de France is the highest cultural center for science, learning, and the arts in France. After 19th-century reforms, it came to consist of five academies: The ACADÉMIE FRANÇAISE (1635, the French language academy), the ACADÉMIE DES SCIENCES (1666), the Académie des Inscriptions et Belles-Lettres (1663, for history and archaeology), the Académie des Beaux-Arts (1648), and the Académie des Sciences Morales et Politiques (1795). Membership in each academy is limited to a small, distinguished group of persons, and vacancies are filled by election.

insulating materials The principle of thermal insulation is central to the choice of materials in building construction. Materials that are poor conductors of heat are thermal insulators. They include mineral wool, vegetable fibers, glass fibers, cork, and foamed plastics. Metals, by contrast, are excellent conductors of heat. Concrete, brick, and stone have lower conductivities.

The transfer of heat by conduction (see HEAT AND HEAT TRANSFER) is resisted by all materials in direct proportion to their thickness, but construction techniques, weight factors, and economics limit the thickness of solid insulation employed in buildings. Moving air transfers heat by a process known as convection. Still air, however, is an excellent insulating medium. Materials of pressed fibrous materials have good insulating qualities because they entrap numerous pockets of still air.

Materials that reflect heat into adjacent air spaces insulate by a different principle. Polished aluminum foil will reflect up to 95% of the heat that reaches its surface. Such reflective insulation must be adjacent to a 2-cm (¾-in) air space to be effective. Cane fiber, wood fiber, mineral wool, or glass, pressed into boards, may be covered with aluminum foil to serve as both rigid insulating material and a reflective insulation. Loose fibers of mineral wool or glass fibers enclosed in a tough paper covering form flexible insulating batts or blankets. These same materials may be blown between framing members to form heat barriers. Foamed plastic boards formed of plastics such as polyurethane or polystyrene are also used as insulation.

The effectiveness of a given type and thickness of insulating material is expressed by its R-value. Building codes often specify certain minimum R-value standards for insulation in new construction.

insulator, electrical An electrical insulator is a substance that is a very poor conductor of electricity. A conductor has many free electrons (roughly one per atom), which are free to move throughout the material, while in an insulator essentially all the electrons are bound to the atoms. A material that is a poor conductor of heat generally is also a poor conductor of electricity since both phenomena largely depend on the transport of energy by electrons.

The distinction between conductors and insulators, although not absolute, is dramatic. It may be expressed in terms of the resistivity, which is the resistance in ohms of a piece of material 1 cm long, with a cross-sectional area of 1 cm. The difference between the resistivity of copper, an excellent conductor, and that of glass, a typical insulator, is more than 10^{20}, or 100 billion billion.

Intermediate between conductors and insulators are SEMICONDUCTORS, which can have resistivities of the order 1 ohm-cm. These include substances like germanium and silicon. Impurities strongly alter the conducting properties of such materials. For example, the addition of boron to pure silicon in the ratio of 1:100,000 increases the conductivity a thousandfold at room temperature.

insulin [in'-suh-lin] Insulin is a HORMONE produced in all vertebrates by beta cells of the islets of Langerhans in the PANCREAS. Insulin regulates the level and utilization of blood sugar and affects RNA and PROTEIN SYNTHESIS, as well as the METABOLISM and storage of fats. Specifically, it controls the absorption of glucose—an energy source—by cells. Low levels of insulin result in increased levels of blood sugar, which causes the disease DIABETES mellitus, characterized by excessive urination, acidosis, and vascular degeneration. High levels of insulin, or hyperinsulinism, result in lowered blood-sugar levels; the symptoms of this condition are dizziness, weakness, and coma.

Insulin is a protein consisting of 51 amino-acid residues. It was first isolated in 1921 by Frederick G. Banting and Charles H. Best, Canadian biochemists. It was the first protein to be characterized by its amino acid sequence—in research done in 1955 by Frederick Sanger, a British biochemist—and the entire structure was characterized in 1969. In 1966 insulin was synthesized independently by the American biochemist Michael Katsoyannis and by scientists in the People's Republic of China. Using recombinant-DNA techniques, scientists have created human insulin, which is artificially produced by gene-splicing methods in bacteria.

See also: ENDOCRINE SYSTEM; ENDOCRINE SYSTEM, DISEASES OF THE.

insurance Insurance, a mechanism for reducing financial risk and spreading financial loss, is a major social institution that is essential to the functioning of virtually any type of economy. In the United States, where one active company dates from before the Revolutionary War, some 6,000 insurance companies collect in excess of $200 billion in annual premiums, employ more than 2 million people, and hold assets of close to $800 billion.

Actuarial Theory

Insurance lends itself only to the treatment of pure risk. Pure risk involves uncertainty only as to loss (an automobile owner, for example, might or might not lose the automobile through a collision, fire, or other calamity), without affording any possibility of gain. Under the concept of indemnity, which is central to insurance, insurance is merely to cover a financial loss. The insured person is not to be placed in a better economic position than he or she occupied before the insured loss occurred.

An insurable pure risk must satisfy the following conditions: (1) the risk must have a sufficiently large number of homogeneous units of exposure (preferably thousands) to permit actuaries—the statisticians who work out insurance risks and costs mathematically—to predict the number and average size of insured losses for a given period; (2) a loss must be measurable—that is, the insurer must have standards against which to determine the monetary value of the loss; (3) the premium charged on the risk must be low enough to attract a sufficient number of insurees, yet high enough to support the numbers and size of probable losses; and (4) the risk must be free of any large-scale potential catastrophe. Insurers therefore try to avoid insuring groups that might be vulnerable to the same risk—for example, providing strike insurance for employers subject to industry-wide collective bargaining.

Basic Types of Insurance

One useful way of classifying insurance is by major categories: life, health, and property-liability (also called property-casualty). LIFE INSURANCE includes promises of the insurer to pay the policy proceeds when the insured dies or attains a given age. Life insurance also normally is deemed to include annuities, which are the promise of the insurer to make periodic payments to an individual for life or for a certain period. Health insurance carries the promise of the insurer to pay specified health-care costs, such as hospital charges or doctor bills, or to make periodic payments to an individual who meets the policy's definition of disability (see HEALTH-CARE SYSTEMS). Property-liability includes all other insurance, such as fire insurance, automobile insurance, ocean marine insurance, and legal liability insurance. (Another classification system divides insurance into group and individual policies. A group policy might be the contract purchased by an employer to provide health care to employees and their families. At least one-third of all insurance premiums relate to group insurance.) Within the three basic categories of insurance one can find several hundred different lines of insurance, with new lines being created and marketed each year, as the need for the new types of insurance arises. For example, insurance has recently been made available to cover the loss of communication satellites.

One type of financial contract sold by some insurers and often confused with insurance is a surety bond. Suretyship, unlike insurance, is a three-way relationship in which one party (the surety) agrees to reimburse another party (the obligee) for loss from the defaults of still a third party (the principal). Suretyship is used, for example, where a builder (the principal) is required to post a bond (obtained from a surety) whereby the surety agrees to pay up to a specified limit any losses the prospective building owner (the obligee) might suffer because of defaults of the builder.

The Insurance Industry

The two common types of insurer organizations are stock and mutual corporations. As the name implies, a stock company is owned by its stockholders. A mutual has no stockholders and is owned by its policyholders. Irrespective of the form of organization under which an insurer operates, several essential functions must be accomplished. One of these is pricing. By the use of prediction, probability theorems, and other tools, actuaries establish the prices at which units of the various types of insurance are to be sold. Because actual losses may exceed predicted losses, insurers for safety's sake often use participating policies, for which the unit price of the insurance is set a bit higher than strict cost accounting would dictate. If the predictions are borne out by the events during the policy period, the insurers return all or part of the excess premiums as dividends to policyholders. Both mutual and stock insurers use participating policies, especially in selling life insurance.

The growth of the insurance industry has been accompanied by a prodigious marketing effort, and marketing continues to be an essential insurance function. Still another essential function performed by insurers is the selection of applicants to insure, a process called underwriting. To prevent the predictions from going awry, insurers have to guard against the tendency of persons who sense an urgent and current need for insurance to be more aggressive in buying it than are other persons. This tendency is known as adverse selection; particular applicants—persons who are ill, for example, or people who plan to commit arson—tend to select adversely against the insurer.

Insurers normally collect premiums well in advance of payment of insured losses and related expenses, and they invest the funds until they are needed. With upward of $700 billion to invest, insurers rely principally on government and private-sector bonds and to a lesser extent on common stock and other equity types of investments. Insurers are heavy suppliers of investment funds. Because of the high degree of competition in the insurance industry, allowance is usually made in insurance pricing for the fact that insurance companies are likely to receive a substantial amount of investment income to supplement their premium income. As a result, premiums are significantly lower in each line of insurance than would otherwise be the case.

The insurance industry, like the banking industry, is highly regulated by government at both the federal and state levels. State regulation of insurance may include the licensing of insurers and agents, approval of unit prices for various types of insurance, specification of the accounting system to be used, control of investments, approval of the wording of insurance policies, and prohibition of various marketing and underwriting practices. Federal regulation applies to certain antitrust, investment, marketing, and related activities.

Government-Provided or -Subsidized Insurance

In the United States as well as in numerous other countries the role of the government as an insurer has increased dramatically in recent decades. The most conspicuous example of such growth in the United States is the SOCIAL SECURITY system, often referred to as social insurance. Social security includes life insurance (with annuities), health insurance sold in a compulsory, group plan by the federal government (see MEDICARE), other types of health and disability insurance, and several forms of special coverage for the very poor. The federal government also insures bank deposits (see FEDERAL DEPOSIT INSURANCE CORPORATION) and provides crop insurance for farmers. In cooperative arrangements with private insurance firms that market the policies, it offers flood insurance to homeowners and provides political risk insurance, protecting export businesses against losses from foreign credit defaults, expropriations, and the like. The government also subsidizes the rates at which homeowners insurance is offered to residents of central-city areas and requires that insurance carriers make such high-risk policies available.

See also: NEGLIGENCE; NO-FAULT INSURANCE.

intaglio   see GRAPHIC ARTS

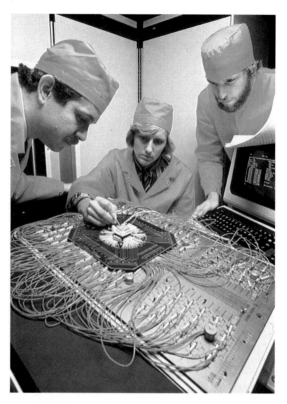

Technicians evaluate the operation of a very high speed integrated circuit (VHSIC) by connecting it to a computer.

integral calculus [in'-tuh-grul kal'-kue-luhs]   Integral calculus is a branch of CALCULUS in which a FUNCTION is discovered from a description of how the function changes. A classical example of a problem in integral calculus is that of finding the area of a quarter circle whose equation is $x^2 + y^2 = 1$ or $y = \sqrt{1 - x^2}$, where x is equal to or greater than 0 and less than or equal to 1. If the value of x is thought of as moving from 0 to 1, then the equation of the curve indicates how the area A changes at x—namely, by adding the segment of height $1 - x^2$ to the area already present. What is sought from the description of how the area changes is the area itself.

The basic problem of integral calculus is therefore the converse of the basic problem of DIFFERENTIAL CALCULUS, that of finding the rate of change (the derivative) of a given function. The discovery of integral calculus stems from the discovery that these problems are closely related.

integrated circuit   An integrated circuit is an organized assembly of interconnected electrode components contained within the upper layer of a small, flat SEMICONDUCTOR chip, usually made of silicon. Silicon is one of the few elements—germanium is another—that can be made to act as a semiconductor. In a pure form it will not conduct electricity, but if impurities are introduced, it becomes a conductor. The careful placing of impurities in a chip of silicon can produce a circuit of electronic components. Because the components are of microscopic size, millions can be placed on a single chip measuring less than a centimeter on a side and a few millimeters thick.

In fabrication, after the circuit to be integrated has been designed and tested, the entire circuit is drawn on a master transparency. The various components that require identical processing steps are then drawn on separate transparencies. The various overlays are then photographically reduced to the actual size of the integrated circuit chip, and arrays of up to a hundred or more patterns are formed on individual transparencies. The transparencies are then used to photographically reproduce a sequence of protective patterns on the surface of a circular wafer of silicon. This step is usually accomplished using visible light, but X-ray lithography techniques are being developed that will allow greater degrees of miniaturization.

A series of production steps such as etching, heating, and diffusion of impurities into the silicon is carried out simultaneously on the unprotected silicon surface. Finally, a network of aluminum interconnections is applied to interconnect the various components. The wafer is then separated into individual integrated circuits, which are tested and installed in protective plastic, ceramic, or metal packages.

Numerous kinds of integrated circuits have been developed by solid-state research laboratories. Most can be categorized as analog, digital, or analog-digital, according to their function.

Analog integrated circuits generally respond to a variable incoming voltage by producing a correspondingly variable output voltage. Many analog integrated circuits, particularly audio-frequency AMPLIFIERS and operational amplifiers, are designed to produce an output voltage that is an amplified but faithful copy of the input voltage. These are called linear.

Analog integrated circuits are also used to generate time delays, produce both simple and complex waveforms, compare the phase relationship of two different electrical signals, and synthesize audible tones and electronic music. Operational amplifiers are used in applications ranging from monitoring the faint electrical impulses produced by living organisms to comparing the magnitude of two signals and indicating which is larger. They are also used in electronic analog computers.

Digital integrated circuits are electronic logic circuits that count, compare, and otherwise process information in the form of on-off electrical pulses. This two-state operation means that the active components in a digital integrated circuit are either fully on or fully off at any given instant. The BINARY NUMBER system is used as a translator, or machine language, for this electrical activity. As the basis for data-processing devices, digital integrated-circuit chips are rated by range from 1 kilobyte (1,000 basic units of data) to 1 megabyte (1 million bytes) or more.

Very powerful and complex data-processing devices can be created by connecting many specialized integrated circuits, or microprocessors, thereby increasing the capacity to store and manipulate data (see PARALLEL PROCESSING). Manufacturers of chips (or microchips, as they are commonly called) have continued to increase the number of TRANSISTORS that can be incorporated in a single integrated circuit. State-of-the-art microprocessors in 1979 contained about 29,000 transistors linked together in an integrated circuit. By 1989, microprocessors containing more than 1 million transistors had been achieved.

See also: COMPUTER, PERSONAL; MICROELECTRONICS.

---

integration, racial Racial integration may be defined as a social situation in which a person's skin color has no important consequence. In a racially integrated society, people associate freely, regardless of race. Cultural differences may persist, but these do not diminish any group's access to jobs, housing, public services, or the ballot box. In such a society no systematic discrimination exists against members of a racial group.

A segregated society, by contrast, is one in which members of different races rarely, if ever, come into contact with one another as equals. All aspects of daily life are separated, and contact between the races is regulated so that one race is always in a superior position to the other. South Africa's extreme segregation is expressed in the official policy of apartness known as APARTHEID. Until recent decades, white-imposed segregation of blacks and whites was the prevailing practice in the United States. In the North, although not written into law, segregation was accomplished by informal custom, sometimes called de facto segregation. In the South, state laws (see JIM CROW LAWS) passed after the Reconstruction era actually decreed segregation of the races, or de jure segregation.

Societies are seldom completely segregated or completely integrated. In the United States today, for example, people of different races work or study side by side and ride buses together but often have little to do with one another in their private lives. In Brazil, on the other hand, social integration is a function of wealth, with most blacks remaining among the country's poor.

The Struggle against Segregation

Challenges to segregation in the United States have taken two forms. One was the insistence on equal treatment through integration. An early leader of the integrationist movement in the United States was W. E. B. DU BOIS, a founder (1909) of the NATIONAL ASSOCIATION FOR THE ADVANCEMENT OF COLORED PEOPLE (NAACP). The other major challenge came from those who urged the establishment of independent black states or nations that would not be subservient to white people. An early leader of the BLACK NATIONALISM movement was Marcus GARVEY, who founded the Universal Negro Improvement Association in 1914. Both positions are represented in black communities today.

The movement against de jure segregation in the South began to gather strength in the 1930s. Along with appeals to conscience, black leaders found economic leverage in all-black unions such as the Brotherhood of Sleeping Car Porters. At the beginning of World War II threats of strikes by black unions led President Franklin D. Roosevelt to order an end to racial discrimination in defense plants. Continuing pressure brought an end, in 1944, to all-white primary elections in the South and won the passage in 1947 of the Fair Employment Practices Act, which forbade discrimination in hiring on the basis of race or national origin. In 1948, President Harry S Truman ordered desegregation of the armed forces. In 1954 nearly three decades of grass-roots militancy and patient legal strategy culminated in the Supreme Court decision declaring separate schools for blacks and whites unconstitutional. In BROWN V. BOARD OF EDUCATION OF TOPEKA, KANSAS, the Court ruled that its 1896 decision in PLESSY V. FERGUSON upholding "separate but equal" facilities was invalid and that segregation necessarily meant inequality. Finally, with the passage of the 1964 Civil Rights Act, the 1965 Voting Rights Act, and the 1968 Fair Housing Act, all de jure segregation was declared unlawful.

The dismantling of de jure segregation required considerable agitation by both blacks and whites. An incident in Montgomery, Ala., in 1956 initiated one of the most important popular movements in U.S. history. Rosa Parks, a black working woman, refused to give up her seat in a bus and move to the section reserved for blacks. After the driver ordered her off the bus, the black community of Montgomery boycotted all public transportation. The boycott continued for months until Montgomery ended segregated seating on its buses. The protest spread to other cities and to other forms of segregation. Dr. Martin Luther KING, Jr., emerged as a leader of the movement against segregation and became, until his assassination in the spring of 1968, a powerful and charismatic figure in the fight for civil rights.

Thousands of boycotts, demonstrations, sit-ins, and marches occurred in those years as blacks and their sympathizers sought to overturn laws that protected racial segregation. Even though demonstrators were usually well disciplined and nonviolent, they often met bitter opposition, and reports and photographs of demonstrators being beaten by Southern law enforcement officers or attacked by police dogs and fire hoses had a strong impact on national opinion. The courts and the federal government began to respond to growing popular indignation.

As integration progressed in the South, attention shifted northward. Targets in the North, however, were more elusive. Segregation in northern cities rested on attitudes, customs, and economic relationships. These were more difficult to confront with the tactics of nonviolent protest. Frustration and resentment grew in the black ghettos. In 1965 the Watts area of Los Angeles erupted into a riot that lasted for several days and left 34 dead. For three successive summers outbursts of rebellion occurred in cities across the country. The most massive was the Detroit riot of 1967, which lasted nearly a week, took 40 lives, and destroyed property worth $250 million.

Progress and Prospects

By the end of the 1960s de jure segregation in all its aspects had been ended. The law was no longer an ally of those who believed that blacks were inferior to whites. The majority of whites said that they no longer subscribed to such racist notions, and support for integration steadily increased. With voting rights assured, blacks turned to the ballot box in large numbers, and by the late 1970s thousands of black elected officials were serving in municipal, county, state, and federal governments.

Many jobs traditionally reserved for whites became open to blacks. During the 1960s and '70s the proportions of blacks in the professions and in managerial positions increased dramatically. By the mid-1980s blacks were almost proportionately represented among the ranks of white-collar workers, even though they remained significantly underrepresented among professionals and managerial personnel. Educational differences between blacks and whites were also sharply reduced over the period 1960–85. For the growing numbers of black college graduates, at least, the prospect of a decent job and a good income was no longer a dream.

Serious problems still exist, however. Residential segregation in the North remains virtually intact. While the economic prospects of educated blacks improve, many blacks remain locked in a cycle of unemployment and poverty. The economic stagnation and high inflation of the 1970s and '80s, combined with the massive cuts in social spending that characterized the Reagan administration, have widened the unemployment gap between blacks and whites and increased the ranks of the black poor. Essentially, this has meant that progress along a broad front of economic and social indicators has slowed or stopped altogether.

There has also been a growing resistance on the part of many whites to programs that attempt to go beyond merely forbidding discrimination. The opposition to busing could be seen as one example of this resistance (see BUSING, SCHOOL). Another was the opposition that arose in the 1970s to the federal government's policy of AFFIRMATIVE ACTION in employment and education. This policy pressured employers and educators to seek out minority applicants and, wherever feasible, give them preference in hiring and promotion and in admission to higher education. Proponents of the policy saw it as necessary to compensate blacks and other minorities for the inequalities resulting from generations of segregation. Opponents argued that affirmative action was reverse discrimination and therefore in conflict with the principle of EQUAL OPPORTUNITY supposedly being upheld.

■

intelligence   Intelligence refers to the all-around effectiveness of an individual's mental processes, particularly his or her capabilities for comprehension, learning and recall, and thinking and reasoning. No consensus exists among psychologists on the definition of intelligence, or on the number of different factors of intelligence that can be tested.

Initially, intelligence was conceived of as innate brain power—that which distinguishes the more highly evolved animals from simpler organisms, and geniuses from average persons. Scientists now realize, however, that the development of intelligence, although partially determined by heredity, also depends on the stimulating or suppressing character of the environment in which an individual is reared.

Originally, intelligence was also conceived of as a unitary power or faculty of the mind. Experimental studies have shown, however, that intelligence includes numerous, partially distinguishable factors, such as verbal, spatial, memorizing, and reasoning abilities. Thus, it is preferable to think of intelligence as a collection of a large number of highly varied, although overlapping, skills, rather than as a single faculty.

The earliest tests of intelligence were the Binet-Simon (1908) and the Stanford-Binet scales (see STANFORD-BINET TEST). These consist of short tasks that provide samples of intelligent thinking. They are administered orally and individually, and a child's score consists of the mental age level of the tasks he or she can accomplish. The ratio of mental to chronological age gives the child's intelligence quotient, or IQ. The Wechsler scales are also widely used for testing adults and children.

Group tests, consisting of printed problems that can be given to a group of people simultaneously, came into use in the U.S. Army in 1917; many similar tests have since been devised for educational and occupational purposes. These, too, usually yield IQs, where the average person, regardless of age, obtains a score of 100; the mentally defective may range down to IQ 40 or below; and the extremely intelligent, up to 160 or above.

It is no longer claimed that the IQ remains constant over long periods of time. Tests of infant development are available; not until about age 5, however, do IQs begin to distinguish between those who are likely to show high, or low, intelligence as adults. From about age 12, measured intelligence is reasonably consistent with subsequent adult intelligence, although wide fluctuations with growth are still possible. Caution is necessary before using an IQ score to attempt to predict high or low achievement in school or daily life. School achievement depends at least as much on interest, home support, and the quality of instruction as it does on intelligence. Occupational success is even more a matter of personality,. opportunity, and specialized talents.

Intelligence tests are currently under heavy fire regarding the extent to which they measure genetic or inherited ability as opposed to reflecting the type of upbringing, social background, and education of a person. The tests were originally devised with a view to measuring potential ability, free from the influence of wealth or privilege. At present, however, some critics argue that intelligence tests have become instruments for discriminating against children of lower social class or minority groups. Careful research seems to support both points of view.

The reasonably close IQs of identical twins reared in different homes is taken to demonstrate genetic determinism. On the other hand, striking evidence indicates that children reared in highly deprived environments gain considerably when given more stimulating environments. The most effective type of stimulation seems to be provided by the mothers of such children through playing, talking, and interacting with their babies. Improvements in maternal and infant health and nutrition also play some part. This does not mean, however, that there is any easy recipe for training children to be more intelligent. Providing additional schooling, for example, may have no lasting effect; and coaching on intelligence tests may raise children's test scores without affecting their overall intellectual capabilities.

intelligence, artificial See ARTIFICIAL INTELLIGENCE

—

intelligence operations An intelligence operation is the process by which governments, military groups, businesses, and other organizations systematically collect and evaluate information for the purpose of discovering the capabilities and intentions of their rivals. With such information, or intelligence, an organization can both protect itself from its adversaries and exploit its adversaries' weaknesses.

Strategic or national intelligence is information about foreign nations that is collected by governmental intelligence agencies. Strategic intelligence commonly encompasses national-security, political, economic, and social trends in the target nation. Military intelligence is produced by specially trained military or civilian analysts and usually includes the strengths, weapons technology, and estimated military capabilities of actual or potential enemies. Industrial intelligence is information gathered by a business firm concerning its rivals in the marketplace. Political intelligence, as practiced in the United States, is usually concerned with ascertaining the campaign strategy of a political opponent. Political intelligence can also apply to the efforts of a ruler to uncover conspiracies. Counterintelligence embraces the wide variety of activities undertaken to forestall an adversary's intelligence efforts. This is accomplished by physically protecting one's own sensitive information and by penetrating and disrupting hostile intelligence organizations.

Covert operations are often undertaken by intelligence agencies, but these are distinct from intelligence operations whose purpose it is to gather information. Covert operations are activities aimed at the disruption of another nation's political process; they can include the dissemination of propaganda, the encouragement of dissidents, acts of sabotage, and even assassination.

Collection. Whether conducted by a governmental agency or a business firm, intelligence operations follow the same pattern. The first step in generating intelligence is always the collection of information. Overt collection is the acquisition of nonsecret "open source" material. To obtain highly sensitive information, however, it is usually necessary to resort to clandestine, or secret, collection.

Intelligence derived from clandestine collection generally falls into three categories: human intelligence, signals intelligence, and photographic intelligence. Human intelligence is simply information gathered by and from human agents. ESPIONAGE, or spying, is one time-honored method of obtaining human intelligence. Whereas other forms of clandestine collection often provide a greater volume of information, especially data of a technical nature, human intelligence is essential for uncovering the thinking, as opposed to the activity, of the adversary.

A second form of clandestine collection is known as signals intelligence—the interception of electronic communications and other emissions. Signals are intercepted by a variety of methods, including the tapping of telephone lines and the monitoring of radio transmissions. Messages intercepted in this manner are often in code. CRYPTOLOGY, the study of making and breaking codes, has become a science in itself over the years.

Another relatively new form of clandestine collection is photographic intelligence conducted from aircraft. Reconnaissance aircraft can also utilize thermography and advanced radars to reveal details indiscernible in visible light. Photo intelligence from aircraft is especially valuable for monitoring the movement of military forces on the ground and for spotting the construction of military facilities.

The advent of the reconnaissance satellite has revolutionized clandestine collection. In 1961 the United States first orbited its Satellite and Missile Observation System (see SAMOS), a photographic-reconnaissance satellite apparently designed for the express purpose of locating and monitoring Soviet intercontinental ballistic missile (ICBM) sites.

Evaluation and Utilization. The collection of raw intelligence is not an end in itself. Raw intelligence must be combined with related data, significant information must be identified, and extraneous material ("noise") deleted. This process of digesting raw intelligence, known as evaluation, yields a product that is usable by policymakers. It is up to the policymaker to utilize the intelligence that he or she receives in a timely and responsible manner.

Intelligence Organizations. Not until 1942, with the creation of the Office of Strategic Services (OSS), did the United States have a focal point for the collection and dissemination of strategic and military intelligence. Today the United States officially has two national intelligence organizations. The principal agency for intelligence activities and covert operations abroad is the CENTRAL INTELLIGENCE AGENCY (CIA). The NATIONAL SECURITY AGENCY (NSA) is responsible for collecting signals intelligence from all over the world and for overseeing the integrity of American secret communications. Some sources suggest that there is a third highly secret national intelligence agency responsible for satellite surveillance. Other members of the American intelligence community include the Defense Intelligence Agency (DIA), which provides military intelligence to the Department of Defense, and the FEDERAL BUREAU OF INVESTIGATION (FBI), which performs counterintelligence activities within the United States.

Whereas the United States is a relative newcomer to the field of national intelligence, Great Britain boasts an intelligence tradition dating from Queen Elizabeth I. Today the British intelligence community consists of two major branches. MI-5, the British equivalent of the FBI, is responsible for counterintelligence activities. MI-6, also known as the Secret Intelligence Service (SIS), is analogous to the CIA; it ran the famous "Ultra" program during World War II in which coded German radio messages, encrypted by the Germans' Enigma machine, were intercepted, broken, and translated, thereby aiding the Allies on the battlefield.

Perhaps no nation is more reliant on accurate intelligence for its survival than Israel. Consequently, Israel has developed an excellent intelligence apparatus in three parts. The Central Institute for Intelligence and Security (Mossad) conducts external espionage and also performs covert operations abroad. General Security Services (Shin Bet) is responsible for counterintelligence and internal security. The Intelligence Corps of the Defense Forces (Aman), largest of the three, focuses on military intelligence.

The Soviet Union is heavily dependent on its intelligence community as well, though for a different reason. Its premier intelligence agency, the Committee for State Security (KGB), doubles as a secret police force. Within the Soviet Union, the KGB controls the Soviet populace. Outside the Soviet Union, the KGB conducts espionage, spreads "disinformation" designed to discredit adversary nations, and attempts to influence the opinions and policies of other nations. A second Soviet intelligence agency, the Central Intelligence Office (GRU), provides military intelligence to the armed forces.

intelligence quotient   see INTELLIGENCE; PSYCHOLOGICAL MEASUREMENT

INTELSAT [in'-tel-sat]   The International Telecommunications Satellite Organization (INTELSAT) is a 110-nation consortium that manages international satellite communications. Its formation, on Aug. 24, 1964, developed from conferences held after U.S. president John F. Kennedy invited (1961) all nations to join the United States in forming a consortium to exploit the potential of COMMUNICATIONS SATELLITES. Ownership was apportioned on the basis of anticipated use. Permanent arrangements,

A giant Intelsat IV *communications satellite dwarfs technicians during the final stages of its assembly and testing. Seven* Intelsat IV *satellites were successfully placed in geosynchronous orbit at various points above the Atlantic, Pacific, and Indian oceans.*

opened for signing in 1971, went into force in February 1973.

INTELSAT has a board of governors (based on each nation's usage), an assembly of parties (one nation, one vote), a meeting of signatories, and an executive office with a director general. The U.S. member, the Communications Satellite Corporation (COMSAT), was established by the Communications Satellite Act of 1962 and incorporated as a private company on Feb. 1, 1963.

Satellites and a few ground stations are owned by INTELSAT; most of the latter, however, are owned by the member nations. The first satellite launched by INTELSAT was *Early Bird* (*Intelsat I*) in 1965. Since then the investment cost per circuit year has decreased as the series of satellites launched by INTELSAT have grown in size and capacity. *Intelsat I* could carry only 240 circuits or one television channel, while *Intelsat VI* can carry at least 33,000 simultaneous telephone calls plus four channels.

In 1984, INTELSAT revised its station-performance standards to enable a new service, Vista, to become available to areas otherwise without telecommunications capability. In 1985, after the U.S. Federal Communications Commission sanctioned private competition with INTELSAT, the organization replied by moving into direct competition with providers of satellite communications within the United States.

Inter-Parliamentary Union   The Inter-Parliamentary Union, founded in 1889, is an organization composed of members of parliaments throughout the world. Its purpose is to foster personal contacts among members of parliaments with the objective of promoting democratic institutions and international peace and cooperation. The Union holds an annual Inter-Parliamentary Conference open to all members and operates the International Centre for Parliamentary Documentation, which gathers information on legislative assemblies. Its headquarters are in Geneva, Switzerland.

interactions in physics see FUNDAMENTAL INTERACTIONS

Intercontinental Ballistic Missile see ROCKETS AND MISSILES

interest Interest is a sum of money paid for the use of another amount of money, called the principal. Banks and other financial institutions pay interest to savers for the use of money deposited in savings accounts; borrowers pay interest for the use of money loaned to them. Interest is usually stated as a yearly rate or percentage of the principal involved. Interest was regarded with disfavor in early times. Aristotle thought it evil, a view that persisted through the Middle Ages; religious and secular laws prohibited interest, or USURY as it was called. With the growth of commerce and the development of banks, usury came to be viewed merely as exorbitant interest, and governments began to set limits on interest rates.

Simple and Compound Interest

Interest is calculated in two different ways: as simple interest and as compound interest. Simple interest means that the interest payment for the year is the principal amount multiplied by the interest rate; for example, the interest on $1,000 is $60 if the interest rate is 6%. Most borrowing, lending, and saving use compound interest, however. When compound interest is computed, the basic one-year period is divided into smaller periods, and the interest earned in each shorter period is added to the principal amount. Because the principal amount becomes larger throughout the year, the total amount of interest paid for the entire year is larger under compound interest than it would be under simple interest.

Interest is usually compounded on a semiannual, quarterly, monthly, or daily basis, which means that earned interest is added to the principal at the end of every six months, every quarter, every month, or every day. For convenience, the interest rate is often stated as a nominal rate compounded at specified periods: 6% compounded monthly, for example. The effective rate, however, is higher than the nominal rate. The effective rate, or the rate actually paid, is illustrated in the following example using a $1,000 deposit that receives 6% interest (the nominal rate) compounded quarterly.

Principal (1st quarter)	$1,000.00	+ $15.00 interest (1st quarter)
Principal (2nd quarter)	$1,015.00	+ $15.23 interest (2nd quarter)
Principal (3rd quarter)	$1,030.23	+ $15.45 interest (3rd quarter)
Principal (4th quarter)	$1,045.68	+ $15.68 interest (4th quarter)
Principal (at the end of the year)	$1,061.36	$61.36 total interest for year = 6.136% of original ($1,000) principal.

The effective interest rate in this example is 6.136%. If the rate were 6% compounded *daily*, a principal sum of $1,000 would earn $61.83 in a year, and the effective rate would be 6.183%. The following formula may be used for calculating effective rate of interest:

$$E = \frac{P(1 + r)^n - P}{P} \times 100$$

where E = effective rate of interest; P = original principal; r = rate of interest per time period; and n = number of time periods. The effective rate, therefore, for $1,000 at 6% interest compounded quarterly is:

$$E = \frac{1000(1 + .015)^4 - 1000}{1000} \times 100 = 6.136\%$$

In some cases interest is discounted at the beginning of the loan period, meaning that it is deducted from the principal. On a discounted loan of $100 at 6%, the borrower receives only $94, thus paying $6 for the use of $94, or approximately 6.4% interest.

Government Regulation

Because interest rates influence the level of economic activity by affecting the ease with which money may be borrowed and the incentive for saving, governments frequently regulate interest rates. In the United States the federal government regulates interest rates indirectly through a variety of agencies. The most important of these, the FEDERAL RESERVE SYSTEM, influences interest rates by controlling the discount rate, which is the interest rate charged banks that borrow from the Federal Reserve banks; by setting reserve requirements, which fix the maximum ratio of loans to deposits for many commercial banks; and by controlling margin requirements, which stipulate the amounts that investors can borrow in order to buy or hold securities. Other federal agencies, or federally sponsored organizations, affect interest rates by buying and selling mortgages or by making funds available to savings and loan associations and various other lenders.

Interest and the Economy

The interest rate—the cost of borrowing money—has a profound effect on the performance of the economy and (in the case of U.S. interest rates) may also influence the well-being of foreign economies. High interest rates can reduce business investment, raise the cost of mortgages, and even help to push the economy into a recession. At the same time, foreign investors are drawn by the high rates. They buy dollars, pushing up the value of the dollar overseas, reducing the cost of imports, and engendering a balance-of-payments deficit. Domestic inflation is restrained by high interest rates, but other Western economies suffer because capital is being invested in the United States, and jobs are lost as more imported products are purchased.

interference

interference Interference is a phenomenon of LIGHT or any other type of wave in which two or more waves can combine to yield a resultant wave whose amplitude or intensity may be greater or less than the component waves. Interference has been demonstrated in all types of waves, including sound, microwaves, X rays, and water waves.

If two waves of the same type and the same frequency are combined so that the crest of one coincides with the trough of the other, they will completely cancel each other. This is destructive interference. Alternatively, the two waves could combine when their crests coincide; they would then interfere constructively, and the resultant amplitude would be equal to the sum of the separate amplitudes.

White light is a mixture of frequencies, each associated with a different COLOR. When two or more beams of white light interfere, certain frequencies are removed by destructive interference, and the resultant light is colored. This accounts for many of the striking natural-color displays, such as the colors of oil slicks and the iridescence of mother-of-pearl.

Interference is such a characteristic property of waves (as opposed to a stream of particles) that any beam that exhibits interference is considered a wave phenomenon or wavelike in nature. When Clinton Davisson and Lester Germer showed in the 1920s that two ELECTRON beams

Interference occurs when two or more wave disturbances travel in the same region of space. Two light waves (1, 2) of equal amplitude and wavelength with their peaks and troughs in phase, or in step, will combine to give a reinforced resultant wave (3) with double their amplitude (A). Two similar but slightly out-of-phase light waves (4, 5) will partially cancel each other and yield a resultant wave (6) of lower amplitude and brightness (B) than either original wave. Waves (7, 8) of opposite phase cancel each other, resulting in darkness (C).

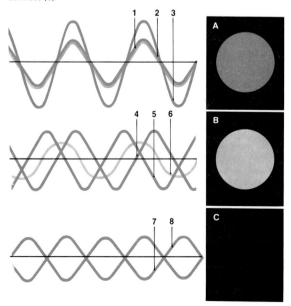

could be made to interfere, this was not considered a contradiction of the principle; rather, it was taken as evidence of the wavelike behavior of atomic particles.

Phase Difference. When two waves interfere, the resultant depends on the difference in *phase* between the two waves. Waves originating from the same source may travel different distances before they are recombined; the number of wavelengths in the path difference determines the phase difference. For example, if the path taken by one wave differs in length from the other by exactly 0, 1, 2, 3, wavelengths or any whole number of wavelengths, the waves will recombine *in phase*; that is, their peaks will coincide, and they will constructively interfere. The phase difference is zero. If the difference in path lengths is ½, 1½, 2½, ... wavelengths, the waves will be completely *out of phase* and will cancel each other. In this case the phase difference is half a wavelength. Intermediate values for phase differences will, of course, give resultants between these limits.

Newton's Rings. Although interference effects may be commonly observed in nature, it was not until the 17th century that they were studied under controlled conditions. Robert HOOKE examined the colors in thin, transparent films of mica, in soap bubbles, and in layers of air between two sheets of glass. Hooke is attributed with the discovery of Newton's rings, the colored circles that form in the air layer between a convex lens and a flat sheet of glass on which the lens rests. They are named for Isaac NEWTON because of his experiments on this effect.

Superposition Principle. Thomas YOUNG is generally considered the founder of the wave theory of light. Young discovered the interference principle in 1801 and calculated the wavelengths and frequencies of the visible spectrum. In 1802 he stated the important superposition principle that applies to all waves: when two waves travel simultaneously through the same medium, each behaves independently except at the region of crossing; there the waves are superimposed, and their effect may be greater or less than the effect of either alone.

Young demonstrated his theories with the now-famous double-slit experiment. (Although Young originally used sunlight passing through pinholes, the demonstration is best repeated by replacing the pinholes with slits and using a source of monochromatic light; that is, light of a single wavelength.) Light is allowed to pass through a narrow slit and then through a pair of closely spaced slits to form an image on a screen. The two sets of light waves emerging from the double slit will interfere with each other, and the image will consist of evenly spaced light and dark bands, or fringes. Young correctly traced the origin of the fringes to the differences in the path lengths of the two sets of waves, meaning that some would arrive in phase to create the bright fringes, and others would arrive out of phase, leaving dark bands on the screen.

Interference by Division of the Wave Front. Young's double-slit apparatus produced interference by recombining light in which the original wave front had been divided by the two slits. Other means were soon devised to accomplish this purpose. The biprism of Augustin FRESNEL is noteworthy because it answered the objections raised by

Young's experiment, that is, that the fringes were actually a result of the light being modified in some complicated way by the edges of the slit. Fresnel used (1818) a thin, double prism to refract light from a single source into two overlapping beams. Such a biprism can easily be made from a microscope slide by slightly beveling half of one of the faces. Using the results of this experiment and others, Fresnel was able to do what Young had not—to derive a detailed mathematical analysis of most known optical phenomena (see DIFFRACTION). There could now be no doubt that light is a wave.

Fresnel was also able to separate a single wave front into two by using two mirrors slightly inclined to each other, creating an interference pattern in the region where the beams overlap.

Coherent Light. Coherency is a necessary condition for obtaining a steady-state interference pattern. Two wave sources that emit identical frequencies and maintain a constant phase relationship are said to be coherent. For light waves, coherency is conveniently achieved by dividing the light from a single source.

Interference by Amplitude Division. In addition to wavefront splitting, a beam of light may be divided, for interference purposes, by partial reflection. If light is incident on a lightly silvered mirror, part of the light is reflected, while the remainder is transmitted. Each beam has a reduced amplitude. The two beams are sent in different directions and are then recombined with mirrors to give the interference. The INTERFEROMETER is an important example of a device that operates by amplitude division (see MICHELSON-MORLEY EXPERIMENT).

Interference by Multiple Reflections. Light incident on a thin, transparent medium, such as a soap film or an oil slick over water, can be reflected by both the upper and lower surfaces of the medium. In fact, light can be reflected several times within the medium before emerging. The interference of the reflected beams creates some of the most spectacular color effects seen in nature.

As noted earlier, the colors are the result of the nonreflection of certain components (frequencies) of white light according to the angle the surface makes with the observer's line of sight. Newton's rings are formed by this principle, as reflections from the lens-to-air surface interfere with those from the plate-to-air surface.

Nonreflecting Coatings. A simple and important application of interference principles is the coating of optical lenses and prisms used in cameras, binoculars, and other devices to render the surfaces nonreflective. This reduces both the loss of light that could be reflected from the surfaces and the stray light that could reach the image and cause a loss of contrast. A thin film of a transparent substance is deposited on the lens, so that the thickness of this coating is equal to one-quarter of the average wavelength of visible light. Light reflected from the film-lens surface travels through the film twice, so its path is half a wavelength longer than the light reflected from the air-film surface. The two reflected beams interfere destructively, and therefore there is no reflection. The light is not destroyed; it is added to the transmitted light.

See also: WAVES AND WAVE MOTION.

interferometer [in-tur-fuh-rahm'-uh-tur] An interferometer is an instrument that allows a variety of precise measurements to be made through the interference patterns of light, sound, or radio waves. In the laboratory the optical interferometer may be used to determine the thickness or refractive index of a material, and the acoustical interferometer can measure the velocity of sound in a gas or liquid. In optical astronomy the interferometer serves to determine the apparent diameter of stars. In RADIO ASTRONOMY the technique is used to obtain accurate measurements of the position of radio sources. The interferometer is also used in the study of stellar spectra.

The principle of the interferometer, first demonstrated by A. A. Michelson in 1881, is based on the phenomenon that waves can intensify or extinguish one another (see INTERFERENCE). If a beam of parallel rays is directed perpendicularly onto a plane, all the waves will be in phase on arrival. If the incoming rays at two different spots of the plane are converged to a single point along paths of equal length, the waves will intensify one another at that point. If the plane is not perpendicular to the beam, a phase difference is introduced through the difference in time of arrival, and an interference pattern is created at the focal point. Information can be extracted from this pattern.

In astronomy, for example, the interferometer can be used to distinguish the components of a very close double star or to measure the diameter of a single star whose light may be regarded as emanating from two halves of the star.

Modern interferometers can measure angles smaller than 0.001 second of arc. In addition, new techniques of interferometry are being applied to astronomy. Speckle interferometry, a technique that utilizes the pattern that emerges when light strikes—or originates from—a rough surface, has been particularly useful in studying phenomena that require high resolution. Because a star's surface also has irregular features that generate irregular light patterns, speckle interferometry reveals those features with more clarity than traditional methods. In Doppler imaging, a computer processes multiple images of the spectra of "hot" and "cool" regions on a rapidly rotating star. The computer is programmed to take into account the difference in light shift (see DOPPLER EFFECT) when the regions are rotating toward or away from the measuring instrument. Combining the images produces a distinct picture of the various regions.

interferon [in-tur-feer'-ahn] The protein interferon, produced by animal cells when they are invaded by viruses, is released into the bloodstream or intercellular fluid to induce healthy cells to manufacture an enzyme that counters the infection. Interferon is therefore considered a potential medical resource as a BIOPHARMACEUTICAL. For many years the supply of human interferon for research was limited by costly extraction techniques. In 1980, however, the protein became available in greater quantities through GENETIC ENGINEERING. Scientists also determined that the body makes three distinct classes of interferon, each perhaps with several members. These classes were first called leukocyte, fibroplast, and immune interferon after their supposed production sites, but it is now known that each particular class is not, after all, made by a single cell type. The classes are therefore now called, respectively, alpha, beta, and gamma interferon. Interferons were also first thought to be extremely species-specific, but it is now known that individual interferons may have different ranges of activity in other species.

Alpha interferon has been approved for therapeutic use against hairy-cell LEUKEMIA and HEPATITIS C. It has also been found effective against chronic hepatitis B, a major cause of liver cancer and cirrhosis, as well as for treatment of genital warts and some rarer cancers of blood and bone marrow. Nasal sprays containing alpha interferon provide some protection against colds caused by rhino-viruses.

Interior, United States Department of the

The U.S. Department of the Interior, described as "the custodian of the nation's natural resources," was created in 1849. A cabinet-level department, it administers conservation programs, manages fish and wildlife resources, operates national parks and historic sites, assesses mineral resources and directs their exploitation on federal lands, and looks after the interests of Indian and Alaskan native Americans and the inhabitants of Pacific island territories under U.S. administration. It is also responsible for the management of all federal lands not under the direct control of other federal agencies.

Perhaps the best-known agency of the department is the National Park Service, established in 1916 (see NATIONAL PARKS). The Bureau of Mines (1910) does research in mining technology and mineral resources. The Bureau of Land Management (1946) provides for the protection, development, and use of most federally owned land. The U.S. Fish and Wildlife Service (1940) guides the conservation and management of the country's wildlife populations. Other bureaus and offices include the UNITED STATES GEOLOGICAL SURVEY (1879) and the Bureau of INDIAN AFFAIRS (1824).

interior design

Interior design is the arrangement, decoration, and furnishing of the interior spaces in residential and nonresidential buildings and in such other enclosed structures as ships and aircraft. The term *interior decoration* has often been used interchangeably with *interior design*, although the former refers more specifically to the trades concerned with the ornamental aspects of interiors (wallpaper, upholstery, and so forth). Some U.S. states are now establishing licensing procedures and standards for professional interior designers.

Principles of Interior Design

The design of interiors is influenced by the related and overlapping professions of ARCHITECTURE, which deals with

all aspects of buildings, including their basic structure from the foundation up, and INDUSTRIAL DESIGN, which deals with the design of factory-made products, such as appliances; and by various specialized fields, such as FURNITURE design, lighting design, and textile design. The interior designer is concerned with the planning and layout of interior spaces not already fixed by the architect, including the selection of furniture and other appointments.

Functional and Aesthetic Considerations. Every project must begin with some consideration of the function of the space to be designed. An ordinary residential living room, for example, must accommodate a wide range of activities—from entertaining and visiting with friends and family members to reading, relaxing, listening to music, and watching television—each of which has its own requirements. The designer must tailor the space to fit its function within an allowable budget and make the atmosphere and character of the space "feel right" to its users—active or calm, formal or casual, cozy or spacious.

Once having ascertained the functions that an interior must serve, the designer turns to the vocabulary of expressive elements. The basic size and shape of a space—its proportions—are basic to defining its aesthetic qualities. More subtle is the concept of scale, or perceived size of spaces. Color and light, taken together, influence very powerfully the aesthetic impact of an interior space. Working with these elements—size, shape, light, and color—the designer creates an interior space.

The Design Process. The planning of an interior design usually begins with the designer's developing a written statement about the intended uses of the space and its specific requirements. This so-called programming stage is followed by the execution of sketches or preliminary plans showing proposed floor-plan layouts and rough perspective views. More formal perspective drawings, called renderings, and scale models may also be used. Next come color charts displaying actual samples of materials and illustrations depicting the furniture, light fixtures, and other appointments selected. Once all the design decisions have been made and approved, the designer develops working drawings to delineate the exact construction and placement of all elements. Lighting may require a special drawing, as may the plumbing and mechanical systems. The preparation of budgets, selection of contractors, placement of purchase orders, and supervision of all work follows. Selection and purchase of small accessories or even works of art may be part of the complete project.

History of Interior Design

The formalized design process described above is a recent development. Until modern times, most interiors were of the kind now called vernacular: that is, unplanned groupings of the normal everyday objects of the time.

Evidence from Ancient Times. Because furnishings and decorative elements are perishable, it is difficult to reconstruct the building interiors of antiquity. A partial exception is ancient Egypt, whose funerary customs included filling tombs with domestic and decorative objects (see EGYPTIAN ART AND ARCHITECTURE).

Modern knowledge of ancient Aegean and Greek domestic design is based chiefly on vase paintings, although remnants of brightly colored wall paintings survive from the elaborate palace at KNOSSOS (c.1700–1400 BC) in Crete and from other centers of AEGEAN CIVILIZATION. Greek vases dating from the Classical period (5th–4th century BC) depict refined and elegant furniture. During the Hellenistic period (late 4th–2d century BC) the Greeks perfected the art of MOSAIC, which was used to decorate the floors and walls of homes and public buildings. (See GREEK ARCHITECTURE; GREEK ART.)

Most fortunate for modern students of interior design was the preservation under layers of volcanic ash from Mount Vesuvius of nearly complete villas at POMPEII and HERCULANEUM. The elaborate wall paintings and floor and wall mosaics used to decorate these luxurious homes, which date from the 1st century AD, demonstrate the Roman adoption of Greek models. (See ROMAN ART AND ARCHITECTURE.)

Traditional Chinese buildings, executed almost exclusively in wood, featured roofs supported on columns, with walls independent of the main structure. Decorative details were concentrated on the richly carved and painted brackets between columns and roof beams; formally arranged furniture, although restricted to a few simple types (principally tables and chairs), was often elaborately carved. (See CHINESE ART AND ARCHITECTURE.) Japanese interior design diverged in the direction of austerity and simplicity. The traditional Japanese interior is based on the modular arrangement of floor mats (*tatami*); sliding screens (*shogi*) are used as walls, making possible a highly flexible interior. Furniture is minimal and portable. The simple, geometrically elegant Japanese interior influenced 20th-century modernism in the West. (See JAPANESE ART AND ARCHITECTURE.)

Medieval and Renaissance Europe. Early medieval Europe produced little of note in interior decoration. Most people lived in small, primitive dwellings; the CASTLES and manor houses (see HOUSE, in Western architecture) of the nobility were designed to facilitate defense rather than enhance comfort. The so-called great hall, the most important room in the castle, functioned as the kitchen, dining room, and even bedroom of the occupant. Aside from wall hangings and TAPESTRIES, which were introduced as a form of insulation in the Romanesque period (AD c.1050–1200), furnishings and accessories were few and simply designed.

During the late-medieval period (mid-12th to the 16th century), manor houses gradually became multiroom residences of increasing luxury and comfort. Wood paneling first appeared in late-medieval interiors.

In Renaissance Italy (c.1400–1600), palaces and villas, as in their Roman prototypes, were arranged symmetrically around a central courtyard. Moldings and other details of classical origin adorned doors, windows, fireplaces, cornices, and ceilings; mural paintings, tapestries, or stone inlay appeared on walls. The Medici Palace in Florence and the Farnese Palace in Rome exemplify the Italian Renaissance design style.

The great 16th-century CHÂTEAUX of France have interior spatial arrangements and decorative details quite similar to the Italian models of the previous century. In England the Renaissance era is identified with the TUDOR STYLE (1480–1540), the ELIZABETHAN STYLE (1558–1603), and the Jacobean style (1603–25), all of which incorporated Italian motifs into basically late-medieval forms.

Baroque to Neoclassical Periods. The rich elaboration, sumptuous decoration of walls and ceilings, and emphasis on complex spatial patterns characteristic of the baroque period (c.1600–1750; see BAROQUE ART AND ARCHI-

The Double Cube Room in Wilton House, Salisbury, is one of the finest examples of a baroque interior. Designed in the mid-17th century by Inigo Jones, one of England's greatest architects, the Double Cube Room is a classically proportioned setting for the earl of Pembroke's collection of portraits by Sir Anthony van Dyck. Jones introduced the Palladian style into England, initiating elegant and restrained interior and exterior architectural forms of classical proportion, design. and decoration.

Claude Nicolas Ledoux, one of the most gifted exponents of the neoclassical style in France, created (c.1780) this boudoir for Mme de Sérilly, a favorite of Marie Antoinette. The grace, symmetry, and quiet grandeur of this room are characteristic of both Ledoux's work and neoclassical style in general.

TECTURE) originated in such opulent interiors as the Pitti Palace in Florence. During the reign (1643–1715) of Louis XIV, the French designers Jules HARDOUIN-MANSART, Charles LE BRUN, and André LE NÔTRE adapted Italian baroque themes into an elegant, more austere style that in turn influenced 18th-century German and Austrian designers, whose principal monuments include the Schönbrunn Palace.

Under the guiding genius of Inigo JONES, 17th- and 18th-century English designers, such as Sir Christopher WREN and Sir John VANBRUGH, executed harmoniously proportioned interiors notable for their restrained and elegant decoration, including the fine woodcarving of Grinling GIBBONS.

During the reign (1715–74) of Louis XV, French designers and architects preferred smaller-scale rooms, lighter furniture, the use of free-curved forms, and a toned-down color scheme. This ROCOCO STYLE was influenced heavily by Chinese decorative motifs introduced through the importation of Chinese porcelain, lacquer, and other ornamental objects. Rococo artisans soon produced great numbers of objects in the fanciful style known as CHINOISERIE.

The rococo style was followed by the development, during the reign (1774–92) of Louis XVI, of French NEOCLASSICISM in art, characterized by a return to simplicity, the use of straight lines and semicircular curves, and a revival of the classical vocabulary of ornamentation. This is also apparent in the works of Robert ADAM in England. Allied to but significantly different from French neoclassicism was the GEORGIAN STYLE of 18th- and early-19th-

century Great Britain. This was also the age of the great furniture designers Thomas CHIPPENDALE, George HEPPLEWHITE, and Thomas SHERATON, as well as of the ceramics of Josiah WEDGWOOD. During the late Georgian period the neoclassical GREEK REVIVAL style and REGENCY STYLE dominated British design.

Origins of Modern Design. In the first half of the 19th century the utilitarian simplicity of colonial interiors (see COLONIAL STYLES IN NORTH AMERICA) gave way to the British-inspired neoclassicism of the FEDERAL STYLE and the furniture designs of Duncan PHYFE. Simultaneously, the eclectic and grandiose EMPIRE STYLE took hold in France under Napoleon I (r. 1804–15). German and Austrian designers preferred the solid, functional furniture and small-scale interiors of the BIEDERMEIER movement. The eclectic British VICTORIAN STYLE ranged from the romantic GOTHIC REVIVAL style to the crafts-oriented and individualistic ARTS AND CRAFTS MOVEMENT.

Toward the end of the 19th century, ART NOUVEAU emerged as the first concerted attempt to create a truly modern style of design. Characterized by rich, curvilinear forms and natural motifs, Art Nouveau was followed in the 1920s and '30s by ART DECO, a form of popular design that featured sleek, highly stylized geometric ornamentation.

Modern Design. After World War I the German BAUHAUS architects, along with Frank Lloyd WRIGHT in the United States and LE CORBUSIER in France, sought a design vocabulary free of reference to the historic past. They de-

The designs of the Shakers, an American religious community flourishing during the late 18th and the 19th century, are noted for an austere, functional style and economy of material and space. Cupboards and drawers built into the walls eliminated the need for bulky chests and sideboards; pegs on the walls provided storage space for unneeded furniture. The spare quality of a Shaker interior is emphasized by the simple, linear forms of their furniture.

signed light and simple furniture, usually geometric in form, meant to complement open, often asymmetrical interior spaces. This so-called INTERNATIONAL STYLE has dominated 20th-century design since the 1920s. In recent years architects and designers have experimented with postmodernism (see POSTMODERN ARCHITECTURE).

Interlaken [in'-tur-lah-ken]   Interlaken (1980 pop., 4,852) is a resort town in Bern canton, central Switzerland. Situated between Lakes Brienz and Thun in the first range of the Bernese Alps, Interlaken is near the JUNGFRAU peak. Tourism is the major industry. Originally the site of an Augustinian convent (founded 1130), Interlaken was virtually unknown until the 19th century, when interest in the Alps began to draw tourists.

interleukin   Interleukins are naturally occurring proteins that function importantly in the body's BLOOD-forming and immune systems (see IMMUNITY). Interleukin 1 (IL-1), produced by the white blood cells called macrophages, enhances the ability of the white blood cells called lymphocytes to respond to antigens. Once the lymphocytes called helper T cells are activated, IL-1 induces them to produce interleukin 2 (IL-2), which in turn stimulates production of more helper T cells and of cytotoxic T cells that destroy diseases or foreign cells. IL-2 is being tested as a therapeutic agent for cancer.
Interleukin 3 (IL-3) was isolated in 1986, along with the gene for the protein. IL-3 stimulates the production of almost all types of blood cells in the bone marrow.

Interlingua   see LANGUAGES, ARTIFICIAL

interlude   Interludes, from the Latin *interludium*, meaning "between the games," began in England as playlets of love and adultery that were performed by troupes of traveling actors at banquets and festivals. One of the earliest, the *Interludium de Clerico et Puella* (1290–1335), was a dialogue between a cleric and a girl. Similar playlets on the continent, called *entremeses* in Spain and *intermezzi* in Italy, were performed with music between the acts of plays or operas.
From at least 1493 to the time of Elizabeth, the Players of the King's Interludes, *Lusores Regis*, performed at the English court and at festivals. In a continuation of the medieval fabliau tradition, interludes at first treated contemporary life candidly, but about 1500 they became moralities, often historical and satirical, in the works of John Redford, John Rastell, John Heywood, David Lindsay, John Skelton, and John Bale. Some of their satire was so offensive that interludes were banned by proclamation in 1533, the more political having lost their lightness and their aristocratic audience. Later, some became debating dialogues. The interludes of Nicholas Udall, considered the first comedies, were classical in structure and theatrical in style. The plays of Marlowe,

Shakespeare, and Jonson were influenced by interludes, which they replaced in the Elizabethan theater.
See also: MEDIEVAL DRAMA.

intermezzo [in-tur-met'-soh]   The term *intermezzo* (literally, "placed between") has two meanings: a character piece, generally for piano, such as those composed by Brahms and Schumann (the term is also occasionally applied to short movements in orchestral and chamber works); a theater piece, usually humorous, placed between the acts of a serious work. In opera the insertion of intermezzi between acts of *opera seria* gave rise to a new form, *opera buffa*. The best-known intermezzo of this type is Pergolesi's *La Serva Padrona* (1733).

intermolecular forces [in-tur-muh-lek'-yoo-lur]   The three-dimensional shapes adopted by molecules, their ability to condense from gases to liquids, and their arrangement in solid crystal lattices are all controlled by weak intermolecular forces. These intermolecular interactions are termed *van der Waals forces*, in honor of Johannes van der Waals, and include hydrogen bonding, dipole-dipole attractions, and dispersion forces.
A very significant intermolecular force is the HYDROGEN BOND, which occurs between a hydrogen atom bound to an electronegative (or electron-attracting) atom and another such atom. Another intermolecular force is the dipole-dipole interaction that occurs between molecules having permanent DIPOLE moments. Intermolecular attractive interactions also occur between nonpolar molecules. Although these are more difficult to envision, they must occur to explain why a nonpolar gas such as chlorine, Cl_2, can exist as a liquid or, at sufficiently low temperatures, as a solid. The attractive interactions here are called dispersion, or London, forces (after Fritz London) and are caused by temporary polarizations of the electron cloud in a molecule that interacts with neighboring molecules undergoing a similar polarization.
Dispersion forces are weaker than dipole-dipole interactions and can occur between molecules that have a permanent dipole moment. They, like other intermolecular forces, are disrupted by raising the temperature and do not occur in gases in which molecular motion is essentially random. In addition to polarizability, dispersion forces are also related to molecular size and shape. Small, compact molecules are generally less polarizable than larger molecules, and the physical properties of matter consisting of small, compact molecules (low boiling and melting points) reflect weaker intermolecular forces. Dispersion forces are the most common and significant of the van der Waals forces.

internal-combustion engine   An internal-combustion ENGINE is a HEAT ENGINE that burns fuel and air inside a combustion chamber located within the engine proper. (Simply stated, a heat engine is an engine that converts heat energy to mechanical energy.) The internal-

A four-cylinder overhead valve engine is used in most European and Japanese cars, as well as in some small American cars. Fuel drawn from a gasoline tank by a fuel pump (1) is fed to a carburetor (2), where it is vaporized, mixed with air, and passed through an inlet valve (5) into a cylinder (10). The valve is kept closed by a spring (4) until opened by the action of a pushrod and rocker arm (3) controlled by a camshaft (12). The camshaft also turns a distributor (19), which feeds electricity from a coil to spark plugs that ignite the fuel in each cylinder in sequence. The burning gases expand and force each piston (7) downward, rotating a crankshaft. A pulley (13) on the crankshaft drives a generator (8), cooling fan (11), and water pump (9) by means of a belt. The crankshaft also spins the camshaft via a timing chain (14) and drives an oil pump that circulates oil through a filter (15) and around moving engine parts. Exhaust gases are forced out of the exhaust valve (6) when the piston moves upward. The engine is started by an electric motor (16) that turns the flywheel (17) after engaging the gear (18).

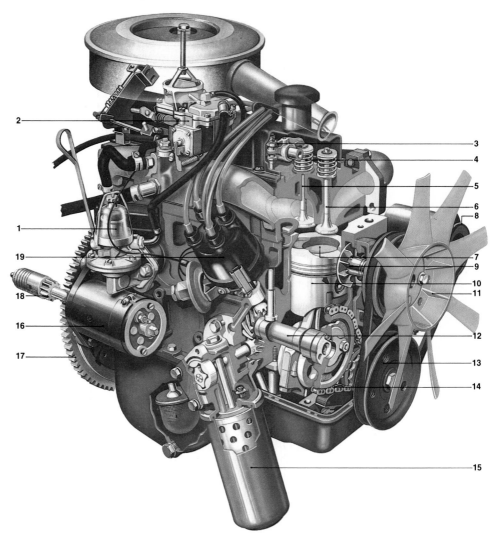

combustion engine should be distinguished from the external-combustion engine—for example, the STEAM ENGINE and the STIRLING ENGINE—which burns fuel outside the prime mover, that is, the device that actually produces mechanical motion. Both basic types produce hot, expanding gases, which may then be employed to move pistons, turn turbine rotors, or cause locomotion in accordance with the reaction principle as they escape through the nozzle.

Internal-combustion reciprocating engines are used to power most automobiles, boats, lawn mowers, and home generators. Based on the means of ignition, two types of internal-combustion reciprocating engines can be distinguished: spark-ignition engines and compression-ignition engines. In the former, a spark ignites a combustible mixture of air and fuel; in the latter, high compression raises the temperature of the air in the chamber and ig-

nites the injected fuel without a spark. The DIESEL ENGINE is a compression-ignition engine. This article emphasizes the spark-ignition engine.

History

The invention and early development of internal-combustion engines is usually credited to three Germans. Nikolaus OTTO patented and built (1876) the first such engine; Karl BENZ built the first automobile to be powered by such an engine (1885); and Gottlieb DAIMLER designed the first high-speed internal-combustion engine (1885) and carburetor. Rudolf Diesel invented a successful compression-ignition engine (the diesel engine) in 1892.

Operation

The operation of the internal-combustion reciprocating engine employs either a four-stroke cycle or a two-stroke

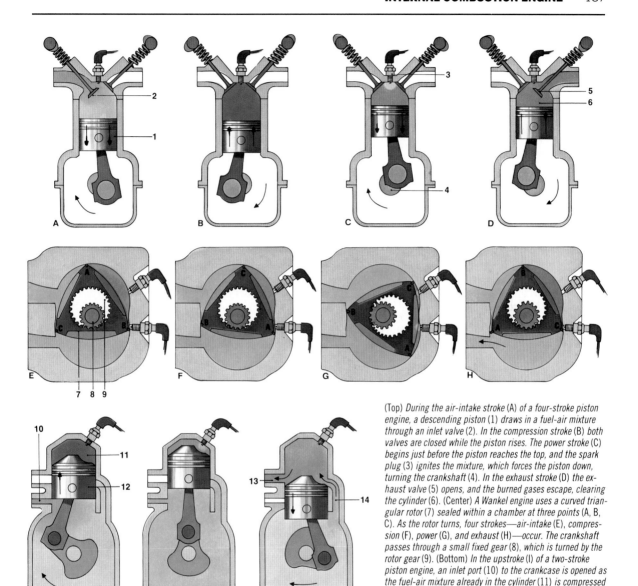

(Top) *During the air-intake stroke (A) of a four-stroke piston engine, a descending piston (1) draws in a fuel-air mixture through an inlet valve (2). In the compression stroke (B) both valves are closed while the piston rises. The power stroke (C) begins just before the piston reaches the top, and the spark plug (3) ignites the mixture, which forces the piston down, turning the crankshaft (4). In the exhaust stroke (D) the exhaust valve (5) opens, and the burned gases escape, clearing the cylinder (6). (Center) A Wankel engine uses a curved triangular rotor (7) sealed within a chamber at three points (A, B, C). As the rotor turns, four strokes—air-intake (E), compression (F), power (G), and exhaust (H)—occur. The crankshaft passes through a small fixed gear (8), which is turned by the rotor gear (9). (Bottom) In the upstroke (I) of a two-stroke piston engine, an inlet port (10) to the crankcase is opened as the fuel-air mixture already in the cylinder (11) is compressed by a piston (12). After combustion (J), the descending piston (K) first opens an exhaust port (13) and then a transfer port (14).*

cycle. (A stroke is one continuous movement of the piston within the cylinder.) In the four-stroke cycle, also known as the Otto cycle, the downward movement of a piston located within a cylinder creates a partial vacuum. Two VALVES located inside the combustion chamber are controlled by the motion of a camshaft connected to the crankshaft. The four strokes are called, in order of sequence, intake, compression, power, and exhaust. During the third stroke a compressed mixture of gas and air is ignited, and the heat produced by the combustion causes the gases to expand within the cylinder, thus forcing the piston downward. The piston's connecting rod transmits the power from the piston to the crankshaft. This assembly changes reciprocating—in other words, up-and-down or back-and-forth motion—to rotary motion.

Internal-combustion spark-ignition engines having a two-stroke cycle combine intake and compression in a single first stroke and power and exhaust in a second stroke.

The power capacity of an engine depends on a number of characteristics, including the volume of the combustion chamber. The volume can be increased by increasing the size of the piston and cylinder and by increasing the number of cylinders. The cylinder configuration, or arrangement of cylinders, can be straight, or in-line (one cylinder located behind the other); radial (cylinders located around a circle); in a V (cylinders located in a V configuration); or opposed (cylinders located opposite each other). Another type of internal-combustion engine, the WANKEL ENGINE, has no cylinders; it has a rotor that moves through a combustion chamber.

Engine Subsystems

The internal-combustion engine contains several subsystems.

Ignition System. The IGNITION SYSTEM of a spark-ignition engine consists of the sparking device (the spark plug); the connecting wire from the plug to the distributor; and the distributor, which distributes the spark to the proper cylinder at the proper time. Most ignition systems require an external electrical energy source in the form of a BATTERY or a magneto.

Fuel System. Spark-ignition engines require a means for mixing fuel and air. Generally, a device called the CARBURETOR is used for this purpose. The carburetor atomizes the fuel and air mixture. The mixture is then vaporized in the intake manifold before being drawn into the combustion chamber.

Starting System. Internal-combustion engines require some type of starting system. Small engines are generally started by pulling a starting rope or kicking a lever. Larger engines may use compressed air or an electric starting system. The latter includes a starter—a high-torque electric motor—to turn the crankshaft until the engine starts. Starting motors are extremely powerful for their size and are designed to utilize high currents (200 to 300 amperes). The large starting currents can cause a battery to drain rapidly; for this reason a heavy-duty battery is usually used. Interrupting this connection is an electrical switch called a SOLENOID, which is activated by the low-voltage starting switch. In this way the ignition switch can turn the starter on and off.

Cooling System. The cooling system is important because internal-combustion engines operate at high temperatures of combustion—spark-ignition engines at approximately 2,760° C (5,000° F) and diesel engines at even higher temperatures. If it were not for the cooling system, these high temperatures would damage and melt many parts of the engine. The cooling system essentially dissipates the heat of combustion in metal, water, or air and automatically regulates the temperature so that the engine can operate at its optimum temperature—about 93° C (200° F).

Air-cooled engines, popularly used to power small lawn mowers, chain saws, power generators, and motorcycles, as well as small cars and airplanes, often require no moving parts, and therefore little or no maintenance, for the cooling system. The head, or uppermost part, of the cylinder and the cylinder block have fins cast into them; these fins increase the surface exposed to the surrounding air, allowing more heat to be radiated. Usually a cover or shroud channels the air flow over the fins. A fan is sometimes included to increase air flow.

Water-cooled engines have water jackets built into the engine block. These jackets surround the cylinders. Usually a centrifugal water pump is used to circulate the wa-

ter continuously through the water jackets. In this way the high heat of combustion is drawn off the cylinder wall into the circulating water. The water must then be cooled in a radiator that transfers the heat energy of the water to the radiator's cooler surrounding fluid, which is usually air or water.

Exhaust System. Internal-combustion engines include an EXHAUST SYSTEM, which allows the hot exhaust gases to escape efficiently from the engine. In some small engines, if the noise is not too loud, the exhaust gases can exit directly into the atmosphere. Larger engines are noisier and require some type of muffler or sound deadener, usually a canister with an inner shell that breaks up the sound waves, dissipating their energy within the muffler.

Transmission. An internal-combustion engine must also have some kind of transmission (see TRANSMISSION, AUTOMOTIVE) system to control and direct the mechanical energy where it is needed; for example, in an automobile the energy must be directed to the driving wheels.

internal medicine   see MEDICINE

Internal Revenue Service   The U.S. government's tax collecting agency, the Internal Revenue Service (IRS), was created in 1862. However, it did not assume its present shape until the federal power to tax incomes was sanctioned by the 16th Amendment (1913) and revenues increased enormously after World War II. The IRS, a division of the Department of the Treasury, administers all of the internal revenue laws except those relating to alcohol, tobacco, firearms, and explosives; its most important assignments are to collect personal and corporate INCOME TAXES, social security taxes, and excise, estate, and gift taxes.

The IRS seeks to obtain voluntary compliance with the tax laws. To this end it stresses communication with taxpayers by providing assistance and information for those who need it. Most employees of the IRS work in field offices throughout the country. There are 7 regions, each headed by a regional commissioner, and 60 districts administered by district directors. Tax returns are processed in separate tax service centers. The national office in Washington, D.C., develops policies and supervises the field organization.

By the early 1980s the IRS was confronting increasing tax evasion and taxpayer resistance, fueled by perceptions that the tax laws were unfair and administered unfairly. Although the IRS is not responsible for writing the tax laws, it must interpret them through the regulations it issues. Its interpretations are often challenged in cases brought to the U.S. TAX COURT; and, in adjudication, IRS tax assessments are sometimes rejected. For businesses and individuals with the resources to pay for accountants and lawyers, it is often possible to negotiate settlements directly with the IRS. Another source of taxpayer unhappiness is the complexity of many of the tax forms.

In its efforts to discover tax evaders, the IRS has invested in computerized systems that will allow it to gather information from many different sources. Thus, the IRS can collect information from the 50 states on automobile and boat registration, professional licenses issued, and business activities that require state permits. It has also attempted to buy computerized lists from private marketing organizations. Such activities have raised questions relating to the issue of invasion of privacy. IRS information has been used by other state and government agencies. In most cases—the enforcement of child-support laws, for example, or the attempt to find those who have defaulted on student loans—the disclosure of information has been authorized by Congress.

International, Socialist Socialist Internationals were a series of organizations formed by socialists and communists in the 19th and 20th centuries to coordinate attempts to achieve SOCIALISM or COMMUNISM.

The International Workingmen's Association, known as the First International, was founded Sept. 28, 1864, in London, and Karl MARX became its leader. Annual congresses of the International were attended by workers' representatives from 13 European countries and the United States. Disputes between Marx and the anarchist Mikhail BAKUNIN over the structure of the International ended at the Hague Congress of 1872 with the expulsion of Bakunin. The First International was dissolved in 1876.

The Second International, established July 14, 1889, at Paris, was a loose federation of trade unions and socialist parties. The Socialist Bureau at Brussels under Emile Vandervelde coordinated its activities. Among the leaders were August BEBEL, Friedrich ENGELS, and Karl KAUTSKY of Germany, Jean JAURÈS of France, and Georgy PLEKHANOV of Russia. The Second International passed resolutions opposing support for capitalist governments and attacking colonialism and war. But the member parties supported their national governments at the outbreak of war in 1914, and the Second International dissolved. After World War I a Third International was formed (1919) under the leadership of Vladimir Ilich LENIN and the Soviet government in Moscow. It was known as the Communist International, or COMINTERN, and lasted until 1943. Moderate socialists reconstituted (1919) the Second International, which in 1923 became the Labor and Socialist International and in 1951 the Socialist International. In the mid-1980s, with headquarters in London, it had 58 member parties. A Fourth International was founded (1938) by Leon TROTSKY in opposition to the Third International. It broke up in 1953. The SOCIALIST WORKERS' PARTY in the United States was its only active offshoot.

International Atomic Energy Agency An autonomous intergovernmental agency of the United Nations, the International Atomic Energy Agency (IAEA) was founded in 1957 to promote the peaceful uses of atomic energy. The IAEA, headquartered in Vienna and consisting of a secretariat with a driector-general and a 34-member board of governors, meets annually in general conference to establish policy and organize programs for the exchange of information. It is authorized to buy and sell fissionable materials and to provide technical assistance to member states for use in agriculture, medicine, and other nonmilitary applications. The agency also sets standards and controls to ensure the peaceful use of atomic power. The agency provides technical assistance and training for countries interested in developing nuclear power.

The agency administers the Treaty on the Non-Proliferation of Nuclear Weapons (TNP), which took effect in 1970. Signatories to the treaty—countries that did not possess nuclear weapons prior to 1967—are required to agree to certain safeguards in order to receive assistance in planning and developing their own nuclear industries. The safeguards, which consist of inspections of nuclear plants by IAEA personnel, are designed to monitor the flow of weapons-grade nuclear fuel to insure that none is diverted to military uses. Most of the states that have signed the TNP have also agreed to safeguard inspections.

International Bank for Reconstruction and Development see WORLD BANK

International Bureau of Weights and Measures The International Bureau of Weights and Measures, founded in 1875, establishes measurement scales of physical quantities, verifies national and high-precision standards and measurement scales, and improves the international system of units (SI). (See METRIC SYSTEM.)

International Civil Aviation Organization
The International Civil Aviation Organization (ICAO) was established on Apr. 4, 1947. Its aims include the study of problems of international civil aviation and the establishment of international standards and regulations. ICAO encourages the use of safety measures, uniform regulations for operation, and simpler procedures at national borders. The organization has its headquarters in Montreal.

International Communications Agency see U.S. INFORMATION AGENCY

International Court of Justice The International Court of Justice—or the World Court, as it is also called—is the principal judicial organ of the United Nations (UN). It is designed to play a judicial role within the UN system as well as to decide disputes between states. Its seat is in The Hague.

From the time of ancient Greece leaders of states have agreed, on occasion, to submit a dispute for settlement on the basis of law. Often these adjudications have taken the form of court procedure; these tribunals, however, have been ad hoc courts existing only for the dispute for which they were created and without the power to require states in conflict to come before them.

In the 19th century a popular peace movement, based primarily in the United States, began to press for the creation of a real and permanent international court as a way of resolving international disputes and preventing war. At a widely attended conference at The Hague in 1899, the Permanent Court of Arbitration was formed. Despite its name, however, it scarcely differed from the traditional ad hoc tribunals. Under the Covenant of the League of Nations a Permanent Court of International Justice was established (1921). It operated until 1945, rendering 32 judgments and 27 advisory opinions.

The Charter of the United Nations (1945) created a successor court, the International Court of Justice. It has 15 judges, each with a 9-year term; decisions are taken by majority. Judges are elected in the United Nations, in simultaneous polling in the Security Council and the General Assembly. Candidates' names are submitted by groups of national experts who are selected by their governments. No state may have more than one judge on the court at any one time, and a state that appears in litigation has the right to appoint an ad hoc judge, who participates only in that particular case. Judges may sit in cases in which their states appear, but they are expected to remove themselves when they have a personal interest or connection with a case.

The International Court has two types of jurisdiction—contentious and advisory. Contentious jurisdiction is available to states for their disputes; when exercised it results in a decision that is binding upon the parties and is theoretically enforceable, if necessary, through the UN Security Council. Advisory jurisdiction is available to international organizations after authorization from the UN General Assembly; when exercised it results merely in an advisory opinion.

All UN members are automatically parties to the statute of the court. States not members of the United Nations may be permitted to sign the statute. States may sign an optional clause agreeing to submit all or certain types of disputes to the court, or they may agree to submit a specific dispute to the court. Except for these voluntary submissions, the court cannot compel a state to submit to its jurisdiction.

The court has pronounced on a wide variety of international legal issues. Though it supposedly only applies international law expressed in treaties, custom, and general principles, the World Court makes law as well.

international date line

The international date line is an imaginary line that runs approximately along the 180° meridian in the Pacific Ocean. By an 1884 international agreement, the earth day is considered to begin immediately west of the line and ends immediately east of it. Therefore, the TIME ZONES on each side are 24 hours apart. Those who cross the line from west to east repeat one day, while those traveling the reverse course omit one. In the few places where the 180° meridian crosses land the international date line deviates so as not to disrupt the pattern of life within a political union.

International Development Association

The International Development Association (IDA), instituted in September 1960, is an affiliated organization of the International Bank for Reconstruction and Development (WORLD BANK). Its members must also be members of the World Bank (total membership stands at 135 countries). The IDA extends credit to developing nations on terms that are easier and more flexible than those of the Bank.

International Falls

International Falls (1990 pop., 8,325) is a city and port of entry in northern Minnesota. Situated on the Rainy River, opposite Fort Frances, Ontario, it is the seat of Koochiching County. The economy is based on tourism and lumbering. The 11-m (35-ft) falls of the river, for which the city is named, are now concealed under a dam and a reservoir. International Falls was settled in 1881.

International Finance Corporation

The International Finance Corporation (IFC) is a specialized agency of the United Nations that is closely associated with the WORLD BANK. It was established in July 1956 to provide capital for private enterprise in its member countries, particularly less developed countries. The IFC invests in private enterprise when sufficient private capital is unavailable. It also serves as a clearinghouse to bring together investment opportunities, foreign and domestic private capital, and experienced management. It is authorized to borrow from the World Bank and to sell its own bonds to the public.

International Geophysical Year

The International Geophysical Year (1957–58) was an 18-month period of intense scientific exploration of the physical aspects of the Earth. Organized by the International Council of Scientific Unions, it coincided with a period of maximum solar activity (see SUNSPOTS). Thousands of scientists from 67 nations worked together, performing a variety of experiments and observations and sharing their results. During this period many new features of the Earth and its space environment were discovered. An early artificial satellite, the first of the EXPLORER series, was launched as part of this program and was responsible for discovery of the VAN ALLEN RADIATION BELTS.

See also: GEOPHYSICS; INTERNATIONAL YEARS OF THE QUIET SUN.

International Geosphere-Biosphere Program

The International Geosphere-Biosphere Program is a global research effort that has been urged for the 1990s by many scientific groups and governmental agencies. Scientists have long stressed that a comprehensive study of the interrelated processes of the atmosphere, hydrosphere, geosphere, and biosphere is required in order to understand and evaluate the effects of human activities on the environment. By the late 1980s the National Science Foundation and National Aeronautics and Space Administration were definitely committed to the effort, and the International Council of Scientific Unions had established a committee to coordinate the various planned and ongoing research programs of the countries that might be involved.

International Labor Organization

The International Labor Organization (ILO) was established on June 28, 1919, by the Treaty of Versailles for the purpose of improving labor conditions and living standards among the world's workers. Its headquarters is in Geneva, Switzerland. In 1946 it became the first specialized agency of the United Nations. The ILO recommends international standards for wages, hours of work, vacations, social insurance, and other issues affecting employees. It provides technical assistance in matters such as vocational training and management development. In 1969 the ILO was awarded the Nobel Peace Prize.

The supreme deliberative body of the ILO is the annual International Labor Conference. Each national delegation is composed of two government representatives, one employer representative, and one labor representative. The ILO's executive council is the Governing Body.

The United States rejoined the ILO in 1980. It had withdrawn from the organization in November 1977 after protesting political attacks made in ILO meetings against Israel and U.S. policies in the Middle East.

International Ladies' Garment Workers' Union

The International Ladies' Garment Workers' Union (ILGWU) is an industrial LABOR UNION representing workers in the women's garment industry. Established in 1900 in New York City, the ILGWU has been known for militancy and for progressive innovations such as developing (1910) a system of industrywide bargaining with the use of arbitration to settle disputes. Factionalism in the 1920s nearly destroyed the union, but under David DUBINSKY, its president from 1932 to 1966, membership grew from 45,000 to more than 450,000. The ILGWU was one of the first U.S. unions to include fringe benefits such as health insurance and pensions in its contracts with employers.

international law

International law has traditionally been defined as the body of rules governing relations between sovereign states. It is often called public international law to distinguish it from private international law, which concerns the transnational relations of individuals with one another and with states. Because of radical changes in the world, international lawyers have had to redefine international law as the institutions and processes governing matters of international concern and the norms or rules they produce. This definition allows for the law-creating part played by international organizations, multinational corporations, political parties, pressure groups, and even international gangs of terrorists, all of whose roles tend to erode the distinction between public and private international law. In addition, international law today is concerned with intranational matters—that is, those within states—such as HUMAN RIGHTS and investment by the citizens of one country in the economy of another.

In any community—local, national, or global—there is a constitutive process: a pattern of making decisions about how decisions will be made. Nationally, this process may produce a document—a constitution—or it may remain unwritten. Even when a document exists—be it the U.S. Constitution or the United Nations Charter—the process continues. The world constitutive process is one in which state elites, international officials of public and private organizations, corporate executives, interest- and pressure-group leaders, and individuals establish and maintain the basic structures for making key international decisions. The body of international law resulting from this constitutive process has to do with almost every area of international relations, including the recognition of states and their admission to international organizations; trade and foreign investment; diplomatic protection of nationals; nationality; war; human rights; boundaries; territorial acquisition; and the law of the oceans.

International law in the modern sense began to emerge with the growth of international trade and the development in the 14th and 15th centuries of the European state system. The increase in international trade contributed to growth and change in commercial and maritime laws. One of the first jurists to produce a systematic treatise on international law was the Dutch philosopher Hugo GROTIUS, whose *De jure belli ac pacis* (On the Laws of War and Peace, 1625) was a blend of natural law and Roman law applied to the practices of the new national states. Other important early theorists of international law were Baron Samuel von Pufendorf (1632–94), Francisco SUÁREZ, Christian WOLFF, Cornelis van Bynkershoek (1673–1743), Alberico Gentili (1552–1608), Emerich de Vattel (1714–67), and Richard Zouche (1590–1660).

During the 19th century the scope and ambition of international lawmakers began to broaden. In 1856 the Congress of Paris attempted the first significant codification of rules of maritime warfare. The Geneva and Hague Conferences of the late 19th and 20th centuries began to establish laws concerning the conduct of warfare. The League of Nations and the United Nations went further, attempting to outlaw military aggression. After World War II international law expanded into areas as diverse as war crimes, international economic cooperation and development, nuclear testing, deep-sea mining, and outer space.

Sources of International Law

Article 38 of the statute of the INTERNATIONAL COURT OF JUSTICE identifies three sources of international law: treaties, custom, and "general principles of law" common to civilized states.

Treaties and Resolutions. Treaties, or formal agreements between nations, are considered legally binding upon the parties concerned. To this formal means of lawmaking must now be added the work of international organizations, such as the United Nations (UN). Strictly speaking, these organizations have little or no formal lawmaking competence; in a number of leading decisions, however, the International Court of Justice has recognized the resolutions of the UN and other international organizations—as well as the decisions of international conferences—as important in the formation of international law.

Customary Law. Customary law consists of principles that are derived from actual behavior rather than from formal legislation, and the derivation can be subtle. For example, officials of State X may begin to police a belt of coastal waters that is 4 rather than 3 miles wide. Ships flying the flag of State Y defer to this new and hitherto unlawful assertion. Over time, a custom may form that State X is entitled to a 4-mile territorial sea. The custom may form even though officials of State Y protest the extension and direct their vessels not to honor it.

General Principles. The notion of "general principles" has caused controversy among legal writers. Although some principles have been widely recognized, such as *pacta sunt servanda* (agreements are to be honored by their signatories), some legal scholars feel that the use of "general principles" has been an invitation for courts to create law where none exists. In fact, the opinions of courts, together with the writings of legal scholars, are recognized as subsidiary sources of international law. They provide a basis for judicial decisions when no rules of customary law or treaty law apply.

The Effectiveness of International Law

International law tends to be most effective when governments share an obvious and continuing interest in its maintenance. When the contours of common interest are less clear, or when governments have no common interest, international norms that may have survived from earlier periods are usually ineffective, and matters are likely to be settled by power.

The law of boundaries and territorial acquisition has enjoyed wide support among nations at certain times. An international system based on national territorial units obviously demands that the territorial integrity and political independence of states be respected. With the advent of the principle of self-determination as the ultimate claim for title to territory, however, even this comparatively sedate area of international law has changed radically.

For more than 300 years the basic principles of the law of the seas were widely accepted and enforced. The oceans were considered a *res communis*, or common property, and not subject to appropriation. The freedoms of the oceans were available to all for reasonable use. With new technology and the growing demand for petroleum, minerals, and fish, the area of the *res communis* has decreased; more and more claims to certain parts of the oceans have been made and accepted, and the traditional public order of the oceans is being radically revised. (See SEA, LAW OF THE; SEAS, FREEDOM OF THE; TERRITORIAL WATERS.)

A basic function of the international system is maintaining minimum order. In the language of the UN Charter, "threats to the peace, breaches of the peace, and acts of aggression" are unlawful. In periods of world revolution, however, states will view differently what constitutes an acceptable system of minimum order. Since 1945 continuing violence has demonstrated, on the whole, the inability of international law to maintain minimum order; yet global war has been avoided.

---

international longshoremen's unions   The International Longshoremen's Association (ILA), founded in 1893, became the major trade union representing longshoremen on the Atlantic and Pacific coasts. Harry BRIDGES led (1937) the West Coast dockworkers out of the ILA, forming the International Longshoremen's and Warehousemen's Union (ILWU), which remains an unaffiliated union. In 1953 the ILA was expelled from the American Federation of Labor for corruption; it was readmitted in 1959 but has continued to be plagued by corruption. In 1971–72 the ILWU staged a 134-day dock strike along the West Coast, the longest in the nation's history.

International Monetary Fund   The International Monetary Fund (IMF), a creation of the BRETTON WOODS CONFERENCE (1944), was established on Dec. 27, 1945, to promote international monetary cooperation and exchange stability. A specialized agency of the United Nations, the IMF had 148 member countries in 1985. The IMF has a board of governors drawn from every member country, 22 executive directors, and a managing director. Its headquarters is in Washington, D.C.

Under the IMF's original rules, the members agreed not to alter the exchange value of their currencies beyond certain limits without prior consent by the IMF. Members who experienced BALANCE OF PAYMENTS difficulties could borrow foreign exchange from the IMF on condition that they follow approved antiinflationary and other policies to correct their difficulties. In the 1970s, however, the system of fixed EXCHANGE RATES gave way to floating rates, that is, to rates largely determined by supply and demand in international currency markets. In 1976 the IMF adopted new policies, which took effect in 1978, designed to help it control floating rates by exercising "firm surveillance" over exchange rates.

To enable members to overcome shortages of foreign exchange, the IMF in 1969 established currency reserve units called Special Drawing Rights (SDRs). Members are allocated SDRs in proportion to their quotas, or subscriptions. From 1974 to 1980 the value of SDRs was based not on gold but rather on a weighted average of the values of the currencies of the 16 leading trading nations. Since 1981 the SDR has been based on the currencies of the five largest exporting nations.

Member countries may borrow from the fund to cover financial emergencies, although strict conditions for these loans may include devaluation of the currency and limitations on government spending. Third World critics of IMF-imposed austerity measures, however, complain that these conditions strain internal political stability and amount to a new form of colonialism.

international relations   See FOREIGN POLICY

International Style The International Style of architecture, which became the dominant form of commercial and public buildings all over the world in the 1950s and 1960s, was first conceived in Germany during the 1920s. Its most characteristic expression appeared in buildings both of the Staatliche BAUHAUS in Dessau (1926) by Walter GROPIUS and of the Weissenhof Housing Exhibition of the Deutscher Werkbund in Stuttgart (1927) by a group of architects under the leadership of Ludwig MIES VAN DER ROHE. The theories that informed the style were published by Gropius in *Internationale Architecktur* (International Architecture, 1925), by Ludwig Hilberseimer in *Internationale neue Baukunst* (New International Architecture, 1927), and in 1932 by Henry-Russell Hitchcock and Philip JOHNSON in *The International Style* in conjunction with an exhibition at the Museum of Modern Art in New York City.

The influential characteristics of the International Style include asymmetrical composition, cubic interior spaces, steel girder and concrete construction, smooth exterior surfaces, and avoidance of applied ornament. Flat roofs and large glass windows arranged in horizontal bands are also preferred. For its originators, the style heralded the advent of a new social order, in which work and leisure could take place in well-lit, uncluttered surroundings. The work of LE CORBUSIER in France and of Alvar AALTO in Finland also played an important role in forming the style, which is now a commonplace of urban architecture. A typical New York City International Style structure is the Lever House office building (1950–52) by Skidmore, Owings, and Merrill.

international trade International trade is the exchange of goods and services among countries. Countries tend to specialize in the production and export of those goods and services which they can produce relatively cheaply and to import things that are produced more efficiently elsewhere.

Why Countries Trade

International trade enables countries to use their labor, capital, and other resources in the most productive way possible. The classical model of economics, however, holds that to realize the greatest possible gains from international specialization and trade, industries must be competitive, workers must be able to enter or leave occupations without difficulty, and government policies must encourage efficiency and promote competition.

The tendency of countries to specialize in the production and export of things that they can produce best and relatively cheaply is called by economists the principle of comparative advantage. It is sometimes difficult, however, to explain why countries specialize in some products and not in others. The major reasons involve differences in factor endowments and in technology.

Factor Endowments. A country's factor endowments include its stocks of physical capital, human capital, workers, and natural resources. Physical capital consists of machinery, factories, highways, railways, harbors, and other equipment and facilities used in production. Human capital represents investment in the labor and management force through education, on-the-job training, and work experience. To understand what determines the kinds of products that a nation exports or imports, a first step is to compare its factor endowments with those elsewhere. Great Britain, for example, although highly industrialized, is deficient in agricultural products and raw materials. It sells manufactured goods and machinery abroad in order to pay for the needed factor endowments.

Technology. Technology refers to the methods of producing goods and services that determine efficiency in production. New technology, for instance, is most readily available in the advanced industrialized countries. These countries also have highly trained scientific personnel and workers with considerable production skill and experience. Moreover, the markets for products in these countries are very large, and income levels are substantial. All these advantages encourage larger firms to expand their operations and to seek the economies of mass production (also called economies of scale), enabling them to compete with foreign producers who lack such advantages. Comparison of the technological characteristics of nations' major producing sectors, therefore, will aid in understanding differences among them in exports and imports. Many less-developed countries, for example, rich in natural-resource endowments, nevertheless need to import manufactured goods.

Protection

In addition to factor endowments and technology, government policies play an important role in shaping the structure of a country's trade. This is perhaps most obvious in the case of TARIFFS, import quotas, and other nontariff barriers to trade. The government may also encourage exporters by subsidizing them. Subsidies can be direct, as when the government makes up the difference between lower foreign and higher domestic prices, or indirect, as when the government supports research and development activities by private firms.

One reason why governments adopt such policies is to shield domestic producers from foreign competition. Other reasons why governments introduce policies that interfere with FREE TRADE are: to increase the wages of certain groups of workers and their share of the national income; to bring monopoly power to bear in trade with other countries; to offset difficulties in domestic markets, particularly those in which workers are unemployed; to increase national self-sufficiency in time of war or other emergency; and to protect young industries until they have had time to mature. Protectionist policies have also been invoked in the face of foreign government export subsidies and dumping by foreign exporting firms. Dumping occurs when a product is sold abroad at less than its domestic cost, especially when there is a glut in the home market. In order to counteract foreign competition, the United States may impose special customs duties on subsidized or dumped goods.

Economists have argued that restriction of trade may not be the best means to achieve the objectives listed above. This is because policies affecting trade may have unintended side effects. First, consumers may be made worse off by having to pay higher prices for imports. Second, by protecting inefficient industries the policies may discourage a more productive use of a country's factor endowments. Third, the restriction of imports may injure the economies of other countries by reducing their exports, especially countries that are relatively poor and less developed. As other countries then begin to experience unemployment and diminished incomes, they become increasingly unable to import goods, a situation that may have a deleterious effect on the protectionist country. Most countries nevertheless maintain varied protectionist policies (see PROTECTIONISM).

International Trade Agreements

The first half of the 20th century was a time of great disruption of world trade caused by World War I, the Depression of the 1930s, and World War II. In the 1930s in particular, the marked decline in national income and employment and the protectionist policies introduced in many countries were factors in the collapse of international trade. During World War II the BRETTON WOODS CONFERENCE (1944) was held to organize postwar international monetary and financial arrangements so that global commerce could be resumed cooperatively. The creation (1945) of the INTERNATIONAL MONETARY FUND and the WORLD BANK was a result of this conference. The GENERAL AGREEMENT ON TARIFFS AND TRADE was established in 1948 and meets regularly to negotiate tariff reductions on the basis of the MOST-FAVORED-NATION STATUS. Regional trade blocs—for example, the EUROPEAN COMMUNITY (EC), the EUROPEAN FREE TRADE ASSOCIATION, the COUNCIL FOR MUTUAL ECONOMIC ASSISTANCE, and the Latin American Integration Association—were established to promote international trade within certain areas of the world.

World Trade Patterns

In the late 1980s the United States, Canada, Western Europe, and Japan accounted for more than two-thirds of total world exports. The less-developed countries, which export mainly primary commodities, accounted for 20% of total world exports. More than two-thirds of their exports went to industrialized countries. Exports from the Eastern-bloc countries were less than 10% of the world total.

Shifts in comparative advantage—in labor-force proficiency, for example, or access to needed raw materials—constantly change competitive positions in international markets. The loss of a large portion of the U.S. automobile market to Japanese products is a notable case of a shift in comparative advantage. (There have been complaints against the Japanese, alleging that their government unfairly restricts imports and promotes exports of manufactured products.) Shifts in comparative advantage were reinforced by the strong dollar between 1980 and 1985, which encouraged imports into the United States and made U.S. exports more costly to foreign buyers. During the 1980s the United States took steps to limit the quantities of its imports of several manufactured goods by means of "voluntary export restraint" (VER) agreements negotiated with foreign exporters. A VER works much like an import quota in terms of its protectionist impact, but foreign exporters may capture the often substantial price differential between the export price and the higher price paid in the importing country.

A number of recent developments will influence world trade patterns during the 1990s. These include (1) the negotiation of a free trade agreement (1989) between the United States and Canada, and pending free trade negotiations between the United States and Mexico; (2) EC removal (1992) of remaining barriers to trade; (3) negotiated reductions in tariffs and nontariff barriers in the Uruguay Round (1990) of GATT negotiations; (4) the movement toward a market system in many Eastern-bloc countries; (5) the ongoing expansion of domestic manufacturing and exports in a number of East Asian countries; (6) continuing problems in coping with austerity and the servicing of foreign debt, especially in Latin America and Africa; and (7) problems created by increases in oil prices due to political turmoil in the Middle East.

International Trade Commission, U.S.   The U.S. International Trade Commission administers laws governing tariffs and international trade. It advises the president, Congress, and government agencies on tariff questions and on problems arising in trade negotiations with other countries. The commission also publishes tariff schedules and trade statistics. The commission is directed by six commissioners appointed by the president for terms of nine years. Established by an act of Congress in 1916, it was known as the U.S. Tariff Commission until 1974.

International Typographical Union   The International Typographical Union was established (1852) at a national convention of typographers in Cincinnati, Ohio, as the National Typographical Union. By 1886, when the ITU joined the American Federation of Labor, it had 30,000 members. The introduction of modern typesetting machines during the 1960s and 1970s was often resisted by the union, which feared for the job security of its members. In 1987 the union became the Printing, Publishing, and Media Workers Sector of the Communications Workers of America.

International Years of the Quiet Sun   During the International Years of the Quiet Sun, a 2-year period (1964–65) of minimum solar activity, scientists from 71 countries or research organizations studied solar radiation and its effects on the Earth and its atmosphere. About 1,000 stations studied meteorology, 265 geomagnetism, 109 the auroras, 58 airglow, 310 the ionosphere, 155 solar activity, and 117 cosmic radiation and geomagnetically trapped particles. Research ships made cruises, instrumented aircraft flew missions, and sounding rockets were launched. These studies were a sequel to those of the INTERNATIONAL GEOPHYSICAL YEAR, an 18-month period (1957–58) of maximum solar activity, and the 2-year period that followed.

Interpol [in'-tur-pohl]   Interpol (International Criminal Police Organization), founded in 1923, is a mutual-assistance organization of police forces. Day-to-day operations are handled at Interpol headquarters, which was located in Paris until 1989 when the organization moved to Lyons, France. Major policy decisions are made at annual meetings of the general assembly of all members.

Each member nation maintains a domestic clearinghouse that processes data on international criminals and their activities, especially smuggling, counterfeiting, and trade in narcotics. Members cooperate by detaining suspects within their borders and by providing information on criminals, missing property, and unidentified bodies. Interpol has its own agents, but they may not pass freely from one country to another; arrests and investigations are the responsibility of each country's own police force. Involvement in political, religious, military, or racial matters is strictly prohibited.

Interpretation of Dreams, The   *The Interpretation of Dreams* (1900; Eng. trans., 1909) is a theoretical interpretation of DREAMS AND DREAMING by Sigmund FREUD. Freud believed that dreams are expressions of unfulfilled wishes. Because such wishes often center on social taboos—particularly those concerning sex—their expression must be disguised; hence the frequent occurrence of symbols in dreams. In order to interpret such dream symbols, Freud described and analyzed the workings of the subconscious and unconscious mind and in so doing created the theory of PSYCHOANALYSIS. Many psychologists, including Freud himself, consider *The Interpretation of Dreams* his masterwork.

Interstate Commerce Commission   The U.S. Interstate Commerce Commission (ICC) regulates surface transportation among the states by trains, trucks, buses, water carriers, and companies that carry freight or parcels. Its duties are defined by the Interstate Commerce Act of Feb. 4, 1887, and other laws regulating transportation. The 5 commissioners are appointed for 5-year terms by the president (with Senate confirmation), who names one of them chairperson. The bulk of the ICC's work involves railroads, trucks, and buses, and centers on hearings and other proceedings concerning freight rates or operating rights.

Interstate Highway System   The U.S. Interstate Highway System, officially named the National System of Interstate and Defense Highways, is a network of multiple-lane, limited-access expressways. Authorized by the Federal-Aid Highway Act of 1944, a system not to exceed

40,000 mi (64,374 km) was planned. The highways were designed to carry one-fifth of the nation's motor traffic, connect all continental U.S. states, and reach 90% of all U.S. cities of 50,000 or more people. East-west routes were designated by even numbers and north-south routes by odd numbers. The federal government was to pay 90% of the system's total cost and the states 10%. Later highway acts increased the system's mileage several times. In 1990, with the system 99.2% complete, 42,400 mi (68,200 km) were open to traffic. Total cost is estimated at $124.9 billion. Although they constitute a little more than 1% of total highway mileage, the Interstates carry over 20% of all traffic.

interstellar matter   Interstellar matter is gas and dust existing between stars in a galaxy. Every atom that is not in a star in a particular galaxy can be considered as part of that galaxy's interstellar matter. The study of this matter is one of the most important branches of modern astrophysics.

Because interstellar matter is not as easy to see as stars, its existence was recognized only recently. By observing the spectrum of the Orion nebula, William Huggins found in 1864 that the nebula consists of luminous interstellar gas. In the early days of astronomical photography E. E. Barnard recognized the existence of dark matter, now called interstellar dust, by its effect in absorbing the light of stars behind it. In 1904, Johannes F. Hartmann found an absorption line in the spectrum of the star δ Orionis, showing the interfering presence of nonluminous interstellar gas. He recognized that this line, caused by ionized calcium (Ca^+), did not arise in the star, because it did not share the periodic changes in wavelength of all the other lines in the star's spectrum, caused by the changing velocity of its orbital motion. Large amounts of interstellar gas, composed mostly of atoms but also containing ions and molecules, are now known to be present in our galaxy. Interstellar dust also exists, although in a smaller amount, because hydrogen (H) and helium (He), the two most abundant elements in the universe, form only transparent gases; hydrogen can form dust particles only when combined with such elements as carbon (C), nitrogen (N), oxygen (O), magnesium (Mg), silicon (Si), and iron (Fe).

Interstellar Matter in Our Galaxy

Nearly all the information about interstellar matter is obtained from studying its interaction with radiation through the emission, absorption, or scattering of light at optical, ultraviolet, infrared, and radio wavelengths. Atoms, molecules, and ions emit and absorb radiation at discrete wavelengths, causing spectral lines, and dust particles with sizes ranging from 10^{-4} cm to 10^{-6} cm emit and absorb radiation at all wavelengths, resulting in a continuous spectrum. Considerably larger particles the size of baseballs could be present in interstellar matter, but because they are much less effective per unit mass in emitting or absorbing radiation, they would be essentially undetectable. On theoretical grounds, however, such large

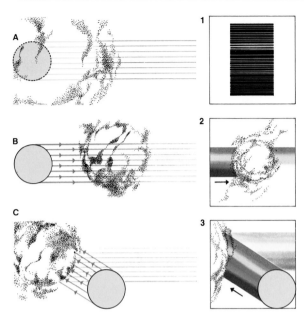

Large, visible clouds of gas and dust, called nebulae, are spread throughout the space between the stars. Nebulae are classified into three different types. An emission nebula (A) consists of gas near a very hot star that emits light as a result of fluorescence caused by ultraviolet radiation from the star. These emission neublae have bright-line spectra (1) that are characteristic of the elements present in the excited gases. A dark or absorption nebula (B) occurs when dust in the clouds blocks out all or most of the light from stars or emission nebulae beyond (2). A reflection nebula (C) results when a dust cloud either reflects or scatters starlight (3).

particles are thought not to exist.

The only indirect way of detecting the presence of interstellar matter, independently of its interaction with radiation, is by its gravitational effect on the motions of stars. Because all forms of mass have this effect, interstellar matter and low-luminosity stars are not easily distinguished by this method.

Atoms, Ions, and Molecules. Interstellar matter in cool regions of space can be observed by the absorption lines it causes in the spectra of distant hot stars. Interstellar absorption lines usually cannot be observed in the spectra of cooler stars, because absorption lines of atoms and ions in the stars' atmospheres blend with the interstellar lines. The strongest interstellar lines in the optical spectral region are those of sodium (Na) and Ca^+.

Interstellar matter also is observed by the radiation it emits if it is heated or ionized. Hot stars emit large amounts of high-energy ultraviolet radiation. If a hot star is located in a cloud of interstellar matter, its ultraviolet radiation ionizes the nearby interstellar gas and transfers energy to it, causing it to emit the characteristic emission-line spectrum of a galactic nebula with ionized hydrogen, known as an H II region.

Most abundant atoms and ions, such as H, O, O^+, C, and C^+, have their spectral lines in the ultraviolet spectral region. Ultraviolet radiation from hot stars can be mea-

sured using telescopes in rockets or artificial satellites above the Earth's atmospheres. The telescopes these orbiting observatories carry are small, and only a few of the brighter, nearer stars have been measured. These ultraviolet spectra, nevertheless, show the presence of many absorption lines including the interstellar absorption lines of molecular hydrogen (H_2). Previously, only the molecules CH, CN, and CH^+ were seen to have interstellar absorption lines in the ordinary optical region.

Even at the very low temperature (about 100 K) of typical neutral interstellar material, very low lying energy levels are collisionally excited and radiate. Neutral hydrogen (H) has an excited hyperfine-structure level close above its ground level, which causes an emission line with a wavelength of 21 cm, in the radio-frequency spectral region. Observations of this line have provided information on the distribution and amount of neutral interstellar gas in this galaxy.

Hydroxyl (OH) was the first interstellar molecule detected (1963, 1964), by several groups of radio astronomers, in the radio-frequency spectral region. It has four characteristic spectral lines with wavelengths near 18 cm. OH and CO, which has lines at 2.6 mm and 1.3 mm, are abundant interstellar molecules and are observed throughout our galaxy. They are found in dense clouds of interstellar matter because only in such clouds do the atoms collide frequently enough to form molecules. Sodium hydroxide has been revealed in clouds surrounding the galactic center by emission lines at 2.98 and 3.97 mm. In very dense interstellar clouds many more complicated molecules have been detected: water, ammonia, formaldehyde, methanol, ethanol, cyanoethyne, and many others, including molecules with 13 or more atoms. Perhaps half of the interstellar material in our Milky Way galaxy occurs within molecular clouds.

Dust Particles. Interstellar dust particles can be detected by the extinction of starlight. Extinction includes both absorption, in which light is actually destroyed by conversion into heat, and scattering, in which light's direction is changed, as by small water droplets. In both cases some light from a star shining through a cloud of interstellar particles does not reach the observer; for interstellar particles scattering is probably the more significant factor in the optical spectral region.

Very dense clouds of interstellar dust particles are seen as dark features silhouetted against the bright star field or nebula behind them. Examples are the dark nebulae discovered by Barnard, the "Gulf of Mexico" in the North American Nebula, and the dark Horsehead Nebula in Orion.

For small particles the extinction increases as the light's wavelength decreases, and light transmitted by a cloud of particles tends to have more long-wavelength radiation than incident light; that is, it tends to be redder. This causes the phenomenon known as interstellar reddening.

Interstellar matter in our galaxy is distributed so that most of it is in or very close to the galactic plane. To a first approximation, interstellar matter can be thought of as forming a layer about 700 light-years thick and

60,000 light-years in diameter. Interstellar matter is not uniformly distributed within this layer but tends to occur in various-sized clouds or condensations. In the inner part of the galaxy, closer to the galactic center, the clouds tend to be denser, and more of the interstellar matter is in the form of molecules. In the outer part of the galaxy more of it is in atomic form. Only a small fraction of interstellar gas is ionized.

Interstellar Matter in Other Galaxies

Interstellar matter can also be observed in other galaxies. The most direct method is the observation of individual galactic nebulae, or H II regions, which can be photographed in many nearby galaxies. The spectra of these nebulae show that they are identical with ionized interstellar-matter clouds in our galaxy. Dust can also be recognized by its extinction effects in other galaxies, particularly in spiral galaxies seen nearly edge on, because of the strong concentration of interstellar matter to the plane of the galaxy in which it is located. Radio measurements have detected the 21-cm emission line of interstellar hydrogen from many other galaxies.

Scientists are currently seeking causes for the unusual motions of galaxies and galaxy clusters in terms of the gravitational influences of unobserved matter—the so-called missing mass problem (see COSMOLOGY). These gravitational effects could be due to great amounts of cold, undetected interstellar matter or larger bodies. In fact, new forms of interstellar matter continued to be revealed, such as the galaxy-pervading clouds of very cold dust detected in 1983 by the Infrared Astronomy Satellite (IRAS) and since labeled infrared cirrus. Studies of distant quasars have also indicated the probable existence of many fairly compact masses of interstellar matter that diffract radio waves coming from the quasars. Some astronomers think these masses—the size of the Earth's orbital path around the Sun—may turn out to be up to 1,000 times as numerous as the stars are in our galaxy.

Interstellar Matter and Stellar Evolution

Interstellar matter is the material from which new stars form. Dense condensations in interstellar clouds are the nuclei that become gravitationally unstable and contract, forming a star or a group of stars (see STELLAR EVOLUTION). Young stars, such as high-luminosity O and B stars, are usually found in or close to interstellar matter. The only exceptions are high-velocity luminous stars, which have moved far from the interstellar gas clouds in which they formed.

At the end of their lifetimes most stars return some of their mass to interstellar space. For example, a star of approximately solar mass discards an outer shell, which briefly becomes a planetary nebula; the stellar remnant, after a short, high-luminosity episode, becomes a white

The Pleiades star cluster in the Taurus constellation is the best-known reflection nebula. Each bright star in the cluster is embedded in a blue nebulosity, a reflection of starlight by surrounding dust particles.

dwarf. A more massive star, at the end of its lifetime, becomes a supernova, consisting of a rapidly expanding shell of gas and a stellar remnant that probably becomes a neutron star. The planetary-nebula and supernova shells are slowed down by colliding with interstellar matter and merging with it. Probably other evolving stars, such as red giants, lose mass more gradually by "stellar winds," or flow of matter into space. Interstellar matter is a reservoir in which mass from evolving or evolved stars, often enriched in heavy elements by nuclear reactions, is captured and partly formed into new stars.

intertidal life [in-tur-ty'-dul]   Between the high and low tidemarks of marine coasts exists abundant and varied plant and animal life. Factors such as the type of

This illustration of a mixed rocky and sandy shore shows organisms from the Atlantic and Pacific coasts of North America. Fiddler crabs (1) burrow in sand along the Atlantic coast splash zone. Upper intertidal mollusks include the common periwinkle snail (2); Lister's keyhole limpet (4); Atlantic plate limpet (5); and, on the Pacific coast, the black tegula snail (3) and rough limpet (6). Barnacles (7) also inhabit this zone. Among the seaweeds, Fucus, or rockweed (9), often grows in rocky mid-intertidal areas; the red algae Gigartina (13) and Irish moss (12) typically form a zone between the rockweeds and the kelps, such as Laminaria (29; holdfast and stipe shown), which occupy the lowest intertidal zone. Seaweeds of the genera Ceramium (8), Codium (10); and Dasya (11) are usually found in lower intertidal and subtidal regions. The common sea star (16) preys on mollusks such as the blue mussel (15). Sea anemones (14, 19) occur in several zones. Lower intertidal animals include sea squirts (17) and sea grapes (20), both invertebrate chordates; sponges (18, 22); hermit crab (21), shown occupying a moon shell; rock crab (23); calico scallop (24), shown swimming; green sea urchin (25); sand dollar (26); blood star (27); and fanworm (28), a tube-dwelling polychaete worm.

rock, type of substrate, water temperature, protection from wave shock, and the interactions among organisms determine the basic features of an intertidal community.

North American Pacific Coast

Splash Zone and Upper Intertidal Zone. The rocky intertidal areas of temperate climates are easily visible. Regions such as the rocky shores of the North American Pacific coast can be subdivided into four broad zones: the splash zone, upper intertidal zone, mid-intertidal zone, and low intertidal zone. Highest above the waves, the splash zone is rarely covered by water for any length of time. Animals living in this zone, such as shore crabs and large isopods, are primarily adapted to terrestrial life.

Below this zone lies the upper intertidal, often covered by rough acorn barnacles and carnivorous snails, which prey on the barnacles, and a relatively sparse covering of leafy green and stubby brown seaweeds (algae). Periwinkle snails, turban snails, and limpets inhabit this zone and graze on the film of microscopic algae covering the hard rock substrate.

Mid-Intertidal Zone. Below these two zones, in the mid-intertidal zone, a broad band of mussels often forms a bed several inches thick. Many varieties of algae are common in this zone. The common starfish continually feeds on mussels, which would otherwise abound throughout all the available space. Within the mussel bed live many polychaete worms, snails, and crabs. Along headlands exposed to the roughest surf, gooseneck barnacles and sea palm algae sometimes replace mussels as the dominant life-forms.

Low Intertidal Zone. In the low intertidal zone both plant and animal life reach their greatest diversity. Algal species include red coralline algae and several types of large kelp. These plants form massive holdfasts, under which dwell many worms as well as snapping shrimp and porcelain crabs. Thick beds of sea urchins often abound. Their predator, the giant sunflower starfish, moves actively about, causing the sea urchins to loosen their grip. In moist and shady areas beneath overhanging rocks masses of sponge colonies, sea squirts, bryozoans, and hydroids cover the rocks. In protected areas deep tide pools often contain large sea anemones that capture food from the passing currents; hermit crabs compete for snail shells to occupy; and large crabs and small octopuses act as predators on many animals. Numerous fishes and small shrimp swim in the large tide pools.

Atlantic Coast

Along the rocky shores of New England the same intertidal zones occur as along the Pacific coast, but the diversity of life is much less. The Atlantic shores of North America largely consist of spacious sandy beaches that protect muddy bays and estuaries behind barrier islands. Sandy beaches of these coasts actually are deserts in terms of visible life. The few forms that survive are often quite abundant, however. Bean clams, mole crabs, and razor clams rapidly burrow in the shifting sands of the outgoing waves. Ghost crabs and beach-hopper amphipods help clear these beaches of the wrack that accumulates with the ebbing tide.

Marshes

Along both American coasts the quiet waters of bays and ESTUARIES are lined with marshes of pickleweed (genus *Salicornia*) or spartina grass. In these marshes dense populations of fiddler crabs undermine the banks with a honeycomb of burrows. Oyster banks often line the lower edge of the intertidal marsh and form hiding places for many crabs and snails as well as the only hard substrate available for sponges and the other encrusting forms. The mud flats appear sterile, but exploration with a shovel and sieve quickly uncovers the extensive burrow systems of large clams, mud shrimp, and many polychaete worms, as well as peanut worms and echiurans. Within the burrows small crabs, shrimp, and even a few species of small fishes often live as harmless guests.

---

intestine The intestine is the part of the DIGESTIVE SYSTEM in vertebrates that extends from the stomach to the anus and is divided into distinctive sections for handling the processes of digestion and absorption of food and the elimination of waste.

In the adult human the intestine is divided into the small and large intestines. The small intestine is a tightly coiled, hollow tube about 5 m (16.4 ft) in length and made up of the DUODENUM, the jejunum, and the ileum, in that order. The large intestine, which is also a coiled tube, is joined to the ileum at a region called the cecum, is about 1.5 m (5 ft) in length, and consists of the colon and the rectum. The length and internal features of intestines are adaptations that provide extensive surface areas for efficiently digesting foods and absorbing the products.

Small Intestine. The duodenum in mammals is notable for its role in the ENDOCRINE SYSTEM because it produces such HORMONES as the following: cholecystokinin, which causes the GALLBLADDER to release bile, a substance that aids in the digestion of fat; secretin, which stimulates the PANCREAS to release digestive enzymes; and enterogastrone, which inhibits the secretion of hydrochloric acid by the STOMACH after the stomach contents have passed into the duodenum.

At the end of the cecum is a small dead-end structure called the APPENDIX. In humans the cecum and appendix have no important function.

The intestine is surrounded by layers of smooth muscle. Contractions of the muscles propel the contents of the intestine from one segment to the next. The small intestine is the site of digestion and absorption of nutrients. Very few digestible substances reach the large intestine.

Large Intestine. The colon absorbs water and salts from the undigested residues and passes them into the bloodstream. A too-rapid passage of material through the colon does not permit adequate absorption of water and results in DIARRHEA. Unusually slow passage, on the other hand, may lead to excessive removal of water and cause CONSTIPATION.

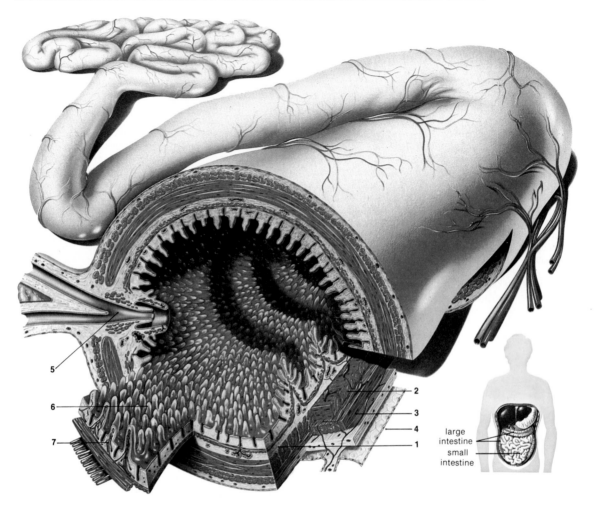

large
intestine
small
intestine

The small intestine completes the digestion of food delivered from the stomach and selectively absorbs the food into the blood and lymph vessels. About 5 m (16.4 ft) in length, the small intestine is folded and coiled into a compact mass within the abdominal cavity. The intestinal wall is lined with an inner mucosal layer (1), circular (2) and longitudinal (3) layers of smooth muscle, and an outer layer of connective tissue (4). The muscular layers contract in a wavelike motion (peristalsis), which pushes food forward in the intestines. Pancreatic juice and bile enter the small intestine from the hepatopancreatic duct (5) and break down food into simple components; the digested food then is absorbed by villi (6), fingerlike projections that carpet the inner surface of the intestines. Each villus contains a lacteal (7), which has blood and lymph vessels that carry digested food to the rest of the body. Waste matter with some digested food passes from the small intestine into the large intestine, where water and salts are absorbed and waste matter is excreted by way of the colon and rectum.

The normal bowel movement, or defecation, begins with the stimulation by feces of sensory nerve receptors in the rectum. The nerve receptors trigger a complex reflex action, which results in relaxation of the sphincter muscles at the junction of the rectum and anus, allowing defecation.

See also: DIGESTION, HUMAN.

Intolerable Acts   The Intolerable Acts was an American label for the laws sponsored by Lord NORTH's ministry and enacted by the British Parliament in 1774 in response to the BOSTON TEA PARTY. Also called the Coercive

Acts, they were a major factor contributing to the outbreak of the AMERICAN REVOLUTION.

The Boston Port Act (March 31) closed the harbor to commerce pending compensation by the city for the destroyed tea. The Massachusetts Government Act (May 20) made the upper house of the legislature appointive by the crown, increased the governor's patronage powers, provided that juries be summoned by sheriffs rather than elected, and banned all town meetings not authorized by law or gubernatorial approval. The Impartial Administration of Justice Act (May 20) made possible a change of venue to another colony or to England for crown officers charged with capital crimes while performing official duties. Two acts that were not specifically related to Massachusetts were also deemed "intolerable" by Americans. The Quartering Act (June 2) authorized civil officers to requisition houses and empty buildings to house royal troops where barracks were unavailable or unsuitable. The QUEBEC ACT (June 22) granted civil government and religious liberty to the Roman Catholic inhabitants of the former French colony and extended the Canadian boundary to the Ohio River.

Although intended primarily to prevent disorder in Massachusetts, the Intolerable Acts united Americans in a common cause and led to the First CONTINENTAL CONGRESS.

Intracoastal Waterway [in-truh-koh'-stul] The Intracoastal Waterway is a 4,800-km-long (3,000-mi) watercourse along the Atlantic and Gulf coasts of the United States; it utilizes the protected bays, inlets, and sounds of the ocean, rivers, and artificial channels. The Atlantic Intracoastal Waterway stretches about 3,000 km (1,900 mi) from Boston to Key West, Fla. The Chesapeake and Delaware Canal, Cape Cod Canal, and Albemarle and Delaware Canal are major components of the waterway, which passes Trenton, N.J., Norfolk, Va., and Miami, Fla.

The Gulf Intracoastal Waterway begins at Apalachee Bay on Florida's west coast and flows for 1,800 km (1,100 mi) to Brownsville, Texas (at the border with Mexico), passing Mobile, Ala., New Orleans, La., and the Texas port cities of Port Arthur, Galveston, and Corpus Christi.

introspection Introspection is the consideration of one's own inner experiences, or "seeing in." Systematic introspection, an organized system for reporting personal experiences under special conditions, was a research method of structural psychology, the dominant school of psychology from about 1880 to 1920. In modern investigations of human behavior, introspection is usually replaced or supplemented by observation of others.

introversion see EXTROVERSION-INTROVERSION

intrusive rock see IGNEOUS ROCK

intuition [in-too-ish'-uhn] Intuition is the knowledge of a concept, truth, or solution to a problem that is arrived at apparently spontaneously, without conscious steps of reasoning or inquiry. One explanation of intuition is that it is the result of a special faculty, or ability, or a special sympathy with the object known. Some philosophers and psychologists claim that human phenomena can be understood only by special intuition; many psychologists, however, attribute intuition to a thought process that occurs too fast for a person to be conscious of it. For instance, numerous minimal cues may be rapidly integrated, making possible identification of the present experience in relation to past experiences.

Inuit see ESKIMO

invention Invention is an act of creativity that results in a device, process, or technique novel enough to produce a significant change in the application of technology. The application is fundamental to invention. Credit for invention has frequently been claimed for someone who conceived an idea, but the inventor is the person who not only had the idea but worked out the method of putting it into practice. Thus LEONARDO DA VINCI conceived of flying machines and self-propelled vehicles and showed great ingenuity in working out possible designs, but he did not invent either the airplane or the automobile.

The element of novelty has various forms; it may be a new device or process, or even material, but it may also consist of a combination of existing knowledge in a manner not previously thought of. James WATT added a separate condensing chamber—a new device—to Thomas NEWCOMEN's atmospheric engine and created the steam engine; the basic patent of the Wright brothers (see WRIGHT, ORVILLE AND WILBUR) was their method of warping the wings in coordination with rudder movements in order to attain lateral stability, essentially a combination of existing techniques. Novelty is so difficult to define that in modern times it usually has to be determined in each specific case by patent offices and ultimately by courts of law.

The characteristics of inventiveness are as difficult to define as novelty. In modern times, when inventors have been identified, they usually appear to share the following qualities: an insatiable curiosity; determination in pursuit of their ideas, sometimes to the point of obsession; technical training or native technical skill; some familiarity with science; and the indefinable trait called creativity.

Theories of Invention. The two general theories of invention are the deterministic and the individualistic. The deterministic theory holds that when economic, technical, and cultural conditions are ripe, an invention will be made by one inventor or another; who does it is just historical accident. This theory has some support in the numerous instances of simultaneous and independent invention, such as the Bessemer-Kelly process of making steel (1857) and the Hall-Héroult process for reducing aluminum (1886). It also helps to explain the competing claims that emerged over the invention of the steamboat, the electric telegraph, the incandescent lamp, and the airplane. The theory is also plausible because timing is unquestionably important in invention. Leonardo had brilliant insights, but the Italy of his day lacked the level of technology or the economic structure required to make his ideas operative. Also, since inventors normally want reward or at least recognition, they are likely to focus on projects that are reasonably attainable and for which there is a recognizable need or demand.

Determinism, nevertheless, does not sufficiently account for invention. It does not explain the emergence of a creative genius who has the insight that others miss or of an inventor such as Oliver EVANS, whose automated gristmill (1785) run by water power and whose steam road vehicle (1805) were demonstrated in operation but were ahead of their time. These failures of the deterministic theory give rise to the individualistic theory of invention, which identifies the individual as the most important element in the inventive process.

Patents. Inventiveness can be found throughout history. The wheel and axle, definitely a conscious invention and not a technological accident, dates from about 3000 BC. Only within the last 500 years, however, has invention come to be recognized as an activity deserving encouragement by society. The first known PATENT was issued in Florence, Italy, in 1421, and Venice enacted the first general patent law in 1474. The general model for patent systems in the Western world was the English Statute of Patents and Monopolies (1623), which specifically gave the right of patent protection to the first inventor of a new device or technique. The Constitution of the United States followed the accepted pattern of the Western world.

Inventiveness in History. These patent systems came before the rise of modern industrialism, which they undoubtedly helped to bring about by stimulating inventiveness. For the first time in history inventors were recognized as individuals deserving social approval and entitled to reward.

Invention has also flourished in other periods. Medieval Europe showed great ingenuity in applying wind power and waterpower and developing gearing, and China in the same period had even greater technical achievements. But most technical progress during this period was in minor increments, which were kept closely guarded secrets by the craft guilds; even with the great breakthrough inventions like gunpowder, the magnetic compass, and papermaking, neither the name of the individual inventor nor the date of the invention is known.

Although no simple explanation can be made for the subsequent focusing of inventive leadership in western Europe, it seems clear that by the time of the Renaissance inventiveness had come to be more highly regarded in the West than in China. Continuing step-by-step advances in technology were important because successful invention requires an adequate background of technical competence. By the 18th century not only was invention encouraged, but also the level of European technology was capable of making the ideas work.

Both European and American patent systems have been based on the premise that invention is an individual act, and at the time the systems were created this assumption was accurate enough. The increasing complexity of modern technology, however, has inevitably affected the inventive process. Technological change had to become systematized, with organized effort directed to identified objectives. In the 20th century this process has become known as research and development (R & D).

Inverness (city) [in-vur-nes'] Inverness is a town in the Highland administrative region of northern Scotland. It has a population of 40,011 (1981). Located near Moray Firth on the River Ness, Inverness is the eastern terminus of the Caledonian Canal. A seaport and commercial center surrounded by rich farmland, Inverness is also a tourist site. The capital of the ancient kingdom of the Picts, Inverness became a chartered burgh in the 12th century and a royal burgh in the 13th century. Abertarff House, one of its many 16th- and 17th-century buildings, now contains a Gaelic museum.

Inverness (county) Inverness is a former county of northwestern Scotland that included many of the HEBRIDES. The burgh of Inverness was its county town. The mainland section of the county, part of the mountainous area known as the HIGHLAND, is bisected southwest to northeast by the Caledonian Canal and a series of lakes, including Loch NESS. BEN NEVIS, Great Britain's highest peak (1,343 m/4,406 ft), is in Inverness. First inhabited by the Picts, Inverness came under Scottish rule in 1078. The clans of the area figured prominently in the Jacobite uprisings of the 18th century. Inverness was divided between the administrative regions of Highland and Western Isles during the 1975 reorganization of local government in Scotland.

inversion [in-vur'-zhuhn] An inversion occurs whenever the normal decrease of atmospheric temperature or moisture or both with height changes anomalously over a relatively short vertical interval. Often inversions become sufficiently strong to produce a layer in the atmosphere where the temperature actually increases with height—that is, warm air covers cold air. Inversions, especially strong ones, limit the mixing upward of atmospheric pollutants, and thus they lower air quality if sources of contamination exist near the ground (see POLLUTION, ENVIRONMENTAL). Such strong inversions often form within stagnant HIGH-PRESSURE REGIONS in the middle and upper latitudes.

Nocturnal inversions are those which result from the night cooling of the lowest levels of the atmosphere. In the lower atmosphere a stable layer inversion caps the highly turbulent boundary layer that forms during sunny days over land, or when cold air blows over warmer ocean water. Over the TRADE WIND region of the tropics, this inversion is called the trade-wind inversion. A frontal inversion occurs when warmer air overrides a synoptic-scale cold AIR MASS.

At higher levels in the ATMOSPHERE the divisions between the troposphere and stratosphere (the TROPOPAUSE) and between the stratosphere and mesosphere (the stratopause) are also types of inversions.

invertebrate [in-vurt'-i-brayt] The invertebrate group is one of the two general categories of animals. The other group, vertebrates, includes those animals having backbones composed of a series of articulating vertebrae (fishes, amphibians, reptiles, birds, and mammals). Invertebrates lack vertebrae and include the remainder of the animal kingdom. The invertebrate group covers a wide range of organisms, from single-celled protozoans to those members of the phylum Chordata that lack a vertebral column.

Habitat

Invertebrates occupy all habitats. They live in all types of marine substrates, from soft oozes to rocky bottoms. Swimming forms may be found at all depths of the sea and include forms specialized to live in the nutrient-poor, perpetually cold and sunless waters of the deep sea as well as a species specialized to live under the surface film of the open ocean. Invertebrates occur over a wide range of aquatic habitats, being common in fresh, brackish, and fully marine environments. Some forms occur in hypersaline environments, where the salinity may greatly exceed that of full-strength seawater.

Terrestrial habitats, including subterranean locations, are universally occupied by invertebrate forms. Even the air has an invertebrate fauna in insects and spiders.

In all of these habitats invertebrates may occupy a wide range of temperatures, from near-freezing in the ocean depths to forms living in hot springs or HYDROTHERMAL VENTS. Invertebrates also range over a wide series of oxygen conditions, from richly oxygenated fresh water to oxygen-poor muds and oxygen-free parasitic environments.

The number of invertebrate species extant today is difficult to estimate. As many as 4.5 million species may exist, but only half have been named. Indeed, through habitat destruction, terrestrial species may be vanishing forever at a more rapid rate than scientists are discovering them.

Fossil Records

The study of the invertebrate fossil record is known as invertebrate paleontology. The oldest invertebrate fossils date to the Precambrian Period, more than 530 million years ago. Fossils from this period are few, and little is known of these life-forms. Fossil representatives of all major phyla with significant skeletal features have been found in the Cambrian Period (570–500 million years ago). The difference between the Precambrian and Cambrian periods may represent some unknown major event that led to the evolution of hardened skeletal structures for rapid movement (muscle attachments) or defense (armor). Controversy exists over the so-called EDIACARIAN FAUNA of the late Precambrian, which some theorists consider an evolutionary dead end rather than representing a transitional stage leading to forms existing today.

As geological time passed, certain organisms that now are extinct, or are a minor component, flourished. The trilobites (related to modern horseshoe crabs) were dominant members of the faunas of the Ordovician (500–425 million years ago) and Silurian (425–400 million years ago) periods but then declined and were extinct by the end of the Permian Period (280–230 million years ago). Nautiloids, shelled squidlike mollusks, were an important component of these early periods. Today only the beautiful coiled *Nautilus* still exists.

Although most groups are as ancient as the Cambrian, the first traces of a few groups do not appear in the fossil record until a much later date. Primitive crustaceans are first seen in the Ordovician. Scorpions become the first air-breathing terrestrial animals by the Silurian. Insects occur in the Devonian. Insects and arachnids (scorpions and related groups) have greatly increased and continue to be important today.

Classification

Protozoa. PROTOZOA are single-celled organisms. These individual cells are structurally much more complex, however, than any given cell in a multicellular organism. Protozoans (30,000 described species) are found in marine, freshwater, and terrestrial habitats and include many parasitic species.

Mesozoa. Mesozoans are a small group (about 50 species) and entirely parasitic, one branch of which occurs only in the kidneys of octopuses and squids. These parasites consist of a small number of cells of merely a few cell types.

Porifera. SPONGES (5,000 species) are simple, attached, filter-feeding organisms. They are common in marine habitats; a few species are found in fresh water.

Coelenterata. COELENTERATES (10,000 species) include the jellyfishes, hydroids, sea anemones, and colonial corals. All are marine except for a few freshwater forms (including the hydra, the common pond dweller). The COMB JELLIES (phylum Ctenophora, 80 species) are closely related to the coelenterates. All are marine, most being pelagic (deep-sea dwelling).

Platyhelminthes. FLATWORMS (nearly 13,000 species) are found in all habitats. This group includes the common planarian, as well as important parasitic groups, the flukes and tapeworms. Closely related are the RIBBON WORMS (phylum Nemertinea, 600 species), a mostly marine group with few freshwater, terrestrial, or parasitic members.

Pseudocoelomata. The pseudocoelomate phyla are mostly wormlike and are grouped together because they possess a few developmental similarities. SPINY-HEADED WORMS (phylum Acanthocephala, 300 species) are all parasitic. The adult worms are attached to vertebrate intestines. Life cycles are complex, involving two host species. The rotifers (1,500 species) are small freshwater organisms; a few are marine and parasitic. Gastrotrichs (phylum Gastrotricha, 150 species) are similar but are covered with bristles. They are inhabitants of fresh and marine water. The kinorhynchs (64 species) are all marine and are common in interstitial habitats, living in the fluid between the grains of mud or sand. The gnathostomulida (phylum Gnathostomata, 90 species) are small wormlike animals living in oxygen-poor marine sands in shallow water. The roundworms, or NEMATODES (phylum Nematoda, 10,000 species), are one of the most successful phyla. Parasitic members infect plants as well as every group of invertebrates and vertebrates (including humans). Additionally, many are free-living marine, freshwater, and terrestrial types. The gordian, or horsehair, worms (phylum Nematomorpha, 250 species), are free-living aquatic forms as adults; the juveniles are parasitic in the body cavities of arthropods.

Loricifera. The phylum LORICIFERA was established in 1983, and individual species are only beginning to be described. The tiny organisms, which dwell in marine sands and gravels, have a unique, flexible mouth cone surrounded by a mass of spines. This assemblage, along with the head, can be withdrawn into the body.

Bryozoa. BRYOZOANS (4,000 species) are small, colonial, and mostly marine, with a few freshwater representatives. They feed using a crescent-shaped crown of tentacles known as a lophophore. The small and structurally similar ENTOPROCTS (phylum Entoprocta) are sometimes included with the bryozoans, although they show embryological similarities to the pseudocoelomates. Two other phyla also feed with a lophophore. The phoronids are a small group (only 15 species) but are often found in marine muds, enclosed within a leathery or chitinous tube. The lamp shells, or BRACHIOPODS (phylum Brachiopoda, 260 species), are mostly deep-water inhabitants.

Mollusca. The MOLLUSKS are a major phylum (130,000 species), including the snails, bivalves (clams and oysters), chitons, cephalopods (squids and octopuses), as well as a few minor groups. Mollusks have invaded every major environment, being found in marine, freshwater (snails and bivalves only), and terrestrial (snails only) habitats. A few snails are also parasitic. Mollusks include some of the largest invertebrates (giant clam and giant squid).

Annelida. The ANNELID worms (8,800 species) encompass many marine (polychaetes), freshwater, and terrestrial (earthworms and other oligochaetes) types and an important group of parasites (leeches). They all have many-segmented bodies and well-developed musculature. Three small phyla, all marine, are sometimes treated as annelid allies, the spoonworms (phylum Echiura, 60 species), PEANUT WORMS (phylum Sipuncula, 275 species), and phylum Priapulida (8 species). All are burrowers, showing few remnants of their presumed former segmentation. The beardworms, (phylum Pogonophora, 80 species) are very elongate and dwell in deep-water sediments. They were recognized in the early 20th century, and recent evidence suggests that they are merely a type of polychaete annelid.

Onychophora. The onychophorans (65 species) are a curious "missing link" between the Annelida and Arthropoda. They are small forms living under leaf litter of tropical forests.

Arthropoda. The ARTHROPODS (about 900,000 species) are enormously diverse. Recent work suggests that some of the major branches are not closely related and should be relegated to separate phyla. Arthropods include the chelicerates (trilobites, horseshoe crabs, spiders, scorpions, ticks, and mites). Present-day representatives are mostly terrestrial, with ticks and mites representing important parasitic types. The crustaceans (fairy shrimp, ostracods, copepods, barnacles, shrimp, crabs, lobsters, pillbugs) are mostly marine, but also include important freshwater, terrestrial, and parasitic representatives. Millipedes and centipedes have only terrestrial representatives. The insects, however, include important freshwater and parasitic groups and a few marine forms. Insects dominate the terrestrial fauna. Among the parasitic insects are lice and fleas. Insects are also remarkable for their development of highly organized social colonies among the termites, ants, bees, and wasps.

Chaetagnatha. The ARROWWORMS (55 species) are a small group of transparent, unsegmented, pelagic predators. They feed on other marine planktonic animals.

Echinodermata. The ECHINODERMS (5,500 species) are the only major phylum limited solely to marine conditions. Included here are the sea lilies, sea cucumbers, sea urchins, sand dollars, starfish, and brittle stars. Acorn worms, or HEMICHORDATES (100 species), are also all marine.

Chordata. The final, partially invertebrate phylum encompasses three groups of seemingly dissimilar CHORDATES. Two are considered invertebrates, and the third and by far the largest is the vertebrates. All possess three distinctive features at some stage in their lives: a flexible stiffening notochord, a dorsal hollow nerve cord, and gill clefts. Of the two invertebrate groups, the urochordates (class Tunicata, 1,300 species) include the abundant, attached, filter-feeding sea squirts (tunicates) as well as some less well known planktonic forms. Like the urochordates, the cephalochordates are entirely marine. Cephalochordates, however, are active swimmers, filter-feeding while moving in and out of the sand along beaches.

Structure and Function

Because the invertebrates are such a diverse group of organisms, many different schemes have been advanced to classify them. Important features considered with regard to the body plan are changes in the basic symmetry of the organism, its gut structure, the development of body cavities, and the increase in cell types and their arrangement in organ systems.

Body Plan. The cells of sponges and mesozoans are differentiated into a few cell types, and these tend to be organized into tissues, groups of similar cells having a coordinated function. There is no gut in these organisms, although in sponges water does move through a series of channels. The coelenterates show the next series of advances. Here, symmetry is radial (biradial in the comb jellies), a gut is present with a mouth but usually lacks an anal opening, and tissues are grouped into primitive organ systems. All of the tissues tend to be arranged in outer and inner layers only.

In the flatworms the interior is filled with a solid mass of tissues and cells. Muscles tend to be extensively developed, and symmetry is now bilateral. With bilateral symmetry, the flatworms show the first signs of increasing cephalization, the tendency to group the sense organs and feeding structures at the anterior, or head, end. So situated, these features are now in a position to meet the environment. Ribbon worms are similar to flatworms, but the gut is complete, with an anus.

The pseudocoelomates have a primitive body cavity. It is not lined with a sheet of cells, like a peritoneum, and is thus not a true body cavity, or coelom. These phyla also have well-developed and complete digestive tracts.

The remaining phyla all have a coelom, although in some groups it is secondarily reduced. Because of the development of a coelomic body cavity, the higher invertebrates are able to attain life-styles possible to only a limited extent in the primitive phyla. Based on details of embryological development the higher invertebrates are grouped into two main branches: the protostomes and the deuterostomes. In protostomes the mouth develops from the blastopore in the embryonic gut. In deuterostomes the mouth develops an opening other than the blastopore, which becomes the anus.

At the base of this separation lie the lophophorates, united in having a lophophore and sharing characteristics of both main branches. Protostomes include the annelids, annelid allies, mollusks, and arthropods, all closely related. The mollusks appear to have developed from a presumed annelid ancestor before segmentation (the serially repeated arrangement of many organs, typical of the annelids) was well developed. Segmentation allows for specialization of different segments for different functions: sensory perception, food capture, and respiratory, locomotive, and reproductive activities.

Among the arthropods, this specialization is carried to an extreme. Certain segments are fused together, forming complex structures such as a head or an abdomen. The arthropod body cavity is greatly reduced; only small cavities associated with the gonads, kidneys, and heart remain. It is replaced by a hemocoel, a type of body cavity filled with blood. A further arthropodan elaboration is the sturdy exoskeleton. Arthropods also have a series of jointed appendages, which tend to serve specialized functions as mouthparts, walking legs, and swimming appendages.

Mollusks also show a reduction of their coelom in a manner similar to that of arthropods but have only traces of segmentation. In most groups a heavily calcified shell protects against predators and environmental stress. In cephalopod mollusks (squids and octopuses) the shell is greatly reduced or absent. Cephalopods have highly developed muscular and nervous systems and rely on speed, agility, and intelligence.

The deuterostomes include the arrowworms, echinoderms, acorn worms, and the lower chordates. Relations here are obscure except that the last two groups appear to be more closely related. The vertebrates, being chordates, also appear on this branch. Echinoderms present an unusual body plan, having reverted to radial symmetry. Certain echinoderm organ systems are without counterparts elsewhere in the animal kingdom. Hemichordates are closely related to the chordates. Both have a specialized anterior chamber with gill slits serving the dual functions of filter feeding and respiration.

The body plan of certain parasitic forms differs greatly from that of their closest free-living relatives. Tapeworms and spiny-headed worms entirely lack a digestive tract. Food is absorbed through the general body surface. Parasites also tend to have prominent holdfasts, arrangements of hooks and suckers, to adhere to the host. As a result of the difficulty in locating hosts, parasitic forms often have outstanding reproductive capacities compared with related free-living forms.

Body Covering. Body surfaces may either consist of a delicate tissue layer or be covered with a tough and sometimes hard skeleton. Only among the annelids and arthropods does one find terrestrial representatives; their external skeleton helps to prevent water loss, the chief stress produced by land environments. The integument of many invertebrates is often brilliantly colored, either providing camouflage or sometimes serving as a warning that the animal may be noxious. In the crustaceans, pigment granules occur in specialized cells, where they may be dispersed or contracted to permit gradual color change. In the cephalopod mollusks, pigment granules are found in little sacs operated by tiny sets of muscles; color change can be instantaneous.

Bioluminescence. Representatives of several invertebrate phyla possess a capability for BIOLUMINESCENCE. Organs located in the integument emit cold light and are used for species-recognition signals or camouflage. Some animals produce their own light, whereas others contain bacteria or fungi that actually synthesize luminescent substances.

Circulatory System. Circulatory systems are absent in small species of all invertebrate phyla, because substances can be moved throughout the body via simple diffusion. These forms have an open circulation system. Body-cavity fluids also serve this distributory function. Most higher invertebrates have at least a partially closed circulatory system where the fluid moves through well-defined blood vessels at least part of the time. In these animals, hearts, acting as muscular pumps, are necessary organs. A well-developed closed system is seen in annelid worms.

Respiratory System. Like circulatory systems, respiratory systems are also associated with large size. Oxygen can diffuse directly through the general body surface of small organisms. Large aquatic animals (mollusks, arthropods, annelids, annelid allies, and echinoderms) all have evolved gill-like structures with enormously expanded surface areas to increase the rate of gas exchange. These structures are closely associated with the circulatory system to distribute oxygen directly to cells and to remove waste gases. Terrestrial organisms have evolved more-protected respiratory structures, for exposed gills would quickly dry up on land. Land snails, scorpions, and spiders have evolved lunglike structures, called book lungs, and insects have a unique tracheal system of passageways leading from surface openings to the vicinity of every cell.

Excretory System. Excretory systems also tend to be most elaborately developed in large animals; simple diffusion suffices for small types. An excretory system basically involving a filtering structure leading to a duct that removes the wastes is found in most phyla above the coelenterates.

Nervous System. The nervous systems of invertebrates show a series of advances paralleling the evolution of the major vertebrate groups. Sponges have only a general sensitivity and no specialized sense organs. The coelenterates have a network of specialized nervous cells but are still capable of only general responses. Simple light receptors and balancing organs are also seen in this group. Flatworms have a well-defined nerve ladder and show coordinated responses to stimuli. Eyes are better developed but still only distinguish light from dark. Good images are formed only in mollusks, arthropods, and a few annelids, as compared to other invertebrates. The cephalopod eye is a remarkable parallel development to the vertebrate eye. A cornea, iris, lens, and associated musculature permit clear binocular images to be formed on the light-sensitive retina and carried thence to the well-developed brain for sensory processing. The nervous systems of these mollusks show other important advances. Giant nerve cells run the length of the body. Rapid conduction along these cells initiates the animal's rapid escape response.

Arthropods have a segmental nervous system with prominent nerve centers (fused ganglia) in each segment. Most crustaceans and insects possess compound eyes. Each eye is composed of many (sometimes hundreds) similar subunits. Compound eyes seem to be particularly well suited to recognize rapid changes in movement, or detection of light and shade, rather than for the formation of images. In crustaceans the compound eyes are on movable stalks.

Many invertebrates show a wide variety of touch receptors, chemical sensors, and balance detectors in addition to light receptors. Sound production and reception appears to be largely limited to insects and crustaceans.

Echinoderms, while an advanced phylum in many respects, show only modest sensory capabilities related to their return to radial symmetry and a sedentary life-style.

In addition to nervous conduction, messages may also be transmitted through slower systems involving hormonal effects. These are perhaps best seen in the insects and crustaceans where the cyclical shedding of the exoskeleton is induced by the increase in concentration of the substance ecdysone in the blood. Maturation in insects is controlled by the level of juvenile hormone.

Musculature. Sea anemones and higher invertebrates all have well-developed musculature. For worm-shaped organisms to be capable of subtle movements, locomotory muscles must be arranged in at least circular and longitudinal bands. The curious roundworms lack circular musculature. The whiplike movements imparted by antagonistic bands of only longitudinal muscles make this group readily identifiable.

Reproductive System. In addition to gonads, most invertebrates have a wide variety of accessory reproductive structures. Ducts and channels permit movement of reproductive products. Sperm may be stored in the male reproductive system in seminal vesicles or in the female system in seminal receptacles. Forms producing shelled eggs, including flatworms, mollusks, and arthropods, have accessory glands to produce the shells and a storage chamber (uterus) to hold the finished product. Although many groups have separate male and female individuals, most flatworms, some mollusks, and a few arthropods have both sexes combined in a single individual. Reproductive development of both sexes may be simultaneous or sequential with first the male and then the female system maturing. Sex may be determined genetically or, in a few forms, such as slipper shell snails, sex may be environmentally determined. Among several of the lower invertebrates the primary form of reproduction is asexual.

Regeneration. Most invertebrate phyla have excellent abilities to regenerate parts of the body if injured. The freshwater planarian flatworm can regenerate if cut into several pieces. More limited abilities typify other phyla.

Life Cycle. Many invertebrates have complicated life cycles. These developmental stages are often specialized for different functions. Many marine forms release numerous eggs that hatch as planktonic larvae, specialized for dispersal. Larval stages are followed by a habitat-selection stage, in which the organism attempts to settle in a habitat suitable for the development of the juvenile and adult forms. Between successive stages, these animals typically undergo complicated metamorphoses. Virtually every tissue and organ of a stage may be reorganized to form a new structure in the succeeding stage.

---

investiture controversy   In ecclesiastical tradition investiture is the conferring of symbols of higher office in the church to members of the church hierarchy, such as abbots of monasteries and bishops of dioceses. The question as to who should confer the symbols of office provoked a prolonged controversy during the High Middle Ages between the papacy and the secular rulers of Europe. When Christianity became the official state religion in the Roman Empire, the emperor approved and often nominated the higher clergy for office. In the medieval kingdoms, the secular rulers continued this practice; since bishops and abbots often held large estates (as feudatories of the crown) and performed secular as well as ecclesiastical functions, the monarchs had a crucial interest in maintaining control of their appointment. As papal power increased in the 11th and 12th centuries, the popes made a concerted effort to restore control of church offices and investiture to the hierarchy.

Pope GREGORY VII (r. 1073–85) battled for the freedom of the church from the secular powers. A synod of 1075 forbade all lay investiture of clergy, and from 1076 on Gregory fought all political control over the church. His chief opponent was Holy Roman Emperor HENRY IV, who could ill afford to have the German bishops become princes independent of the emperor. Henry attempted to depose Gregory, who responded (1076) by excommunicating Henry and declaring his office vacant. This action released all Henry's feudal vassals from their oaths of fealty. Faced with rebellion in Germany, Henry did penance before Gregory at Canossa (Jan. 25–28, 1077), forcing the pope to remove the ban of excommunication. The controversy continued, however, and effectively undermined the emperor's authority in Germany. Eventually Pope CALLISTUS II and Emperor HENRY V agreed to the compromise Concordat of Worms in 1122. The emperor guaranteed the free election of bishops and abbots and renounced the right to invest them with ring and staff, the symbols of their spiritual duties; within Germany (although not in Italy and Burgundy), however, the elections were to take place in the emperor's presence, and those elected were to pay homage to him as feudatories before consecration.

In England, King HENRY I (r. 1100–35) struggled with Saint ANSELM, archbishop of Canterbury, over the same issue. The later Middle Ages saw the secular rulers reasserting their power once again against the papacy.

investment   see SAVING AND INVESTMENT

investment banking   Investment banking is the distribution of new issues of STOCKS and BONDS to the investing public. An investment banking firm serves as an intermediary between the company or government agency issuing the securities and the investors who buy them. In effect a financial wholesaler, an investment banking firm buys a large block of securities from the issuer and sells it in smaller quantities to the public. Investment bankers may form a group or syndicate to market a large issue. In the process known as underwriting the bankers take responsibility for selling the securities at an agreed-upon price and establishing a permanent market for them. If they are unable to sell a security at the offering price listed, they may suffer a loss. Unlike the European system, where investment banking—also called merchant banking—is a function of commercial banks, in the United States it has no connection with the commercial or deposit BANKING SYSTEM. Investment banking enables the capital market system to function smoothly by making funds immediately available to businesses and by providing investment opportunities.

Invisible Man   see ELLISON, RALPH

Io [ee'-oh]   Io, a satellite of JUPITER, is the most geologically active body in the solar system. Its spewing volcanoes were first sighted by VOYAGER 2 in 1979, but some

The processes shaping Io's surface are not yet well understood. The plume rising from Pele, the volcano at center, can be seen against the blackness of space.

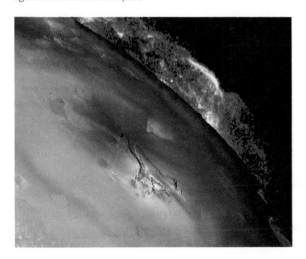

scientists had earlier predicted such activity. They theorized that tides raised in Io by the nearness of Jupiter would produce so much frictional heat that Io would be largely molten.

The satellite has an orangish, sulfurous crust with white and dark markings. Its several volcanoes send dust and gas high above the surface, leaving a trail of ions and molecules in the satellite's orbit. Calderas and flows of molten material are observed, as well as nonvolcanic mountains about 10 km (6 mi) high. No meteor craters exist, because the surface is constantly being renewed. Surface temperatures are in the range of –148° C (–235° F), but in the vicinity of eruptions they may reach 27° C (80° F).

Of the four moons of Jupiter discovered by Galileo, Io lies closest to the planet, at an average distance of about 421,600 km (261,970 mi) from its center, although four small satellites have since been found to lie inside Io's orbit. Io completes one revolution of Jupiter in about 42 hours 27 minutes. It is slightly smaller than Earth's Moon, with a diameter of 3,630 km (2,255 mi), and has a high density 3.55 times that of water.

iodine [y'-uh-dine]   Iodine, atomic number 53, symbol I, is a solid nonmetallic element of the HALOGEN family, Group VIIA in the periodic table, a group that includes FLUORINE, CHLORINE, and BROMINE. At room temperature iodine is a lustrous, blue black, crystalline solid of atomic weight 126.9045. Iodine is the least water-soluble halogen, but it dissolves readily in alcohol, chloroform, carbon tetrachloride, and benzene.

Iodine is poisonous, but as a trace element it is essential to plant and animal growth. In higher mammals it is concentrated in the THYROID GLAND and is involved in the synthesis of thyroxine and other biochemicals that govern metabolic activities. Besides affecting growth, iodine deficiency can also cause GOITER, so iodine salts are added to table salts in regions where iodine levels are low.

History

Iodine was first observed in 1811 by a French saltpeter manufacturer, Bernard Courtois, in the course of his work. Charles Bernard Desormes and Nicholas Clément confirmed its nature and announced the discovery of the new element. In 1813, Sir Humphry Davy's electrical experiments further confirmed the discovery; so did the experiments of Joseph Gay-Lussac, who named the element for the color of its vapor.

In 1819, Jean Baptiste Dumas provided proof that iodine existed in the sponges that had long been used to treat goiter. By 1820, data had been published linking kelp as a goiter treatment to the presence of iodine in this sea plant. Earlier, in 1814, J. J. Colin advanced microanalytical chemistry by the discovery that the starch reaction with iodine produced a blue coloration so intense that iodine could be detected in amounts as low as one part in 400,000.

Occurrence

Iodine is the 44th most abundant element in the cosmos, the 62d most abundant in the Earth's crust, and the 17th most abundant of those dissolved in seawater (gases excluded). Even though iodine is widely distributed in nature, no large deposits exist. Chilean nitrates in which it is an impurity serve as one important source. Several organisms in which it becomes concentrated are also important sources, such as the seaweeds known as KELP.

Chemical Properties

Like all members of the halogen family, iodine is very reactive, although it is somewhat less reactive than the other halogens. Both bromine and chlorine liberate free iodine from aqueous solutions of iodides by reactions similar to: $2NaI_{(aq)} + Br_{2(g)} \rightarrow 2NaBr_{(aq)} + I_{2(s)}$. Iodine vapor reacts directly with most metals to form metal iodides; for example, with nickel it forms NiI_2. Iodine also reacts with water to establish the equilibrium $I_2 + H_2O \rightleftharpoons H^+ + I^- + HOI$.

Iodine reacts with hydrogen sulfide (H_2S) to liberate sulfur. Its reactions with phosphorus, arsenic, and antimony are similar to that with bismuth: $3I_2 + 2Bi \rightarrow 2BiI_3$.

Iodine has several oxidation states: -1, $+1$, $+3$, $+5$, and $+7$. They help explain the compounds of halogens with halogens, such as ICl, ICl_3, IF_5, IF_7, $K(IF_6)$, IOF_3, and IO_2F, all of which are stable at room temperature. About half of all commercial iodine is produced from Chilean nitrate deposits, which contain about 0.2% calcium iodate ($Ca(IO_3)_2$). Iodine is recovered from solutions of the nitrate using sodium bisulfite ($NaHSO_3$) as a reducing agent. Other significant sources of iodine are underground brines, such as those found in Michigan. Seaweeds that are able to concentrate the element are now less important in the United States but are still major sources of iodine in some countries.

Uses

The principal use of iodine is in the health sciences. Almost from the year of its discovery it has been used to prevent goiter. An alcoholic solution of the element known as tincture of iodine has been used as a disinfectant, although iodine complexes now predominate in this application. Iodine complexed with surfactants are used in common sanitizers. Radioactive iodine, ^{131}I, has found important use in tracer studies, including studies of the thyroid gland. Iodine is also used in photographic papers, as a tracer in stereochemistry studies, in dyes, as a catalyst, as an INDICATOR in analytic chemistry, in engraving, in special soaps and lubricants, in rainmaking experiments (see WEATHER MODIFICATION), and as a measure of the degree of unsaturation of organic compounds.

---

ion and ionization   An ion is an atom or molecule bearing an electric charge as a result of having a number of negative electrons unequal to the number of positive protons in its nuclei. Ionization is the formation of ions from neutral atoms or molecules. This process may involve the removal or addition of one or more electrons un-

der high-energy conditions. It may arise by the splitting of a neutral molecule into a pair of oppositely charged ions. It may also arise through the transfer of a charged atom between two neutral molecules.

Types and Properties of Ions. Ions may be either positively charged, known as cations, or negatively charged, known as anions; double, triple, or even higher positive or negative charges are possible. Simple ions consist of a single charged atom; complex ions have a charged metal center that bears one or more covalently bonded atoms or groups (see COORDINATION COMPOUNDS); zwitterions contain an attached pair of groups bearing opposite charges; and polyelectrolytes are large molecules with many charged groups.

Ions differ markedly in their behavior from electrically neutral atoms and molecules; specifically, they can migrate in an electric field (see ELECTROCHEMISTRY), and they can bind strongly to such solvent molecules as water. Their unique properties directly result from the electrostatic force, whereby unlike charges attract each other, and like charges repel. The properties of ions are strongly influenced by their atomic or molecular structure, the localization of charge on this structure, and the nature of the atoms or molecules that surround them. Ions can exist in the solid state in ionic CRYSTALS, in the liquid state in solutions or molten salts, and in the gaseous state.

Initial studies of electrically conducting solutions, or electrolytes, by Michael FARADAY led him to postulate (1833) that ions are carriers of electrical currents (see ELECTROLYSIS). In 1884 the Swedish chemist Svante August ARRHENIUS suggested that free ions in solution are the principal species formed when salts, strong acids, or strong bases are dissolved in water. He found that the degree to which a dissolved substance undergoes DISSOCIATION into positive and negative ions influences the degree to which it affects the bulk properties of the solvent. Studying the migration of ions in an electric field, Peter DEBYE and Erich Hückel found (1923) that simple ions in solution are strongly associated with a mobile sphere of solvent molecules.

The crystalline properties of many SALTS—which contain oppositely charged ions in an exact proportion—may be explained in terms of ionic bonding, in which each ion interacts with other ions only by way of electrostatic forces (see CHEMICAL BOND). Most salts form stable ionic crystals, in which each ion is surrounded by ions of opposite charge in such a proportion that the net charge is zero. The resulting closely packed, three-dimensional lattice is held together by attractive forces among the ions, making the crystal stable.

Ionization. Ionization refers to either the direct formation of a pair of oppositely charged ions from one or more neutral molecules or the generation of an ion by the addition or removal of one or more electrons from a neutral molecule. The former process often occurs spontaneously in the liquid phase when such ion-stabilizing solvents as water are present; this process requires relatively little energy. The latter process may occur in any state of matter and requires a great deal of energy; this method typically is used to produce ions in the gaseous state that are difficult to generate in other ways. Various agents—including extremely high temperatures, electromagnetic radiation, and high-energy particles—are capable of dislodging an electron from a neutral molecule, leaving a positive ion. This process requires a specific amount of energy—the ionization potential—for a given atom or molecule. The extra electron may be picked up by a neutral molecule, forming a negative ion. A gaseous mixture of positive and negative ions, known as a plasma, may be formed in this way. This process of ionization has many applications in chemistry and physics, including measurement of radioactivity, determination of molecular weights, and the study of nuclear reactions.

ion exchange Ion exchange is a chemical REACTION that involves replacing one type of ion in a solution with another. This type of reaction has many industrial and scientific uses, including purification of such substances as water and sugar; extraction of gold and other valuable metals from ores; and separation of various molecules by means of thin-layer CHROMATOGRAPHY. Water-softening units (see WATER SOFTENER), which remove such ionic minerals as calcium from hard water, employ an ion-exchange reaction. These units usually contain zeolite minerals—natural clay mixtures of sodium aluminosilicates—which replace the ionic minerals in the water with sodium ions. Because many ion-exchange reactions are reversible, zeolite in which the sodium ions have been used up can be recharged by flushing it with a concentrated solution of sodium chloride. Deionized water can be prepared by another ion-exchange reaction in which water containing ionic minerals is passed through a cationic resin, which exchanges hydrogen ions for all the positively charged ions in the water, and then through an anionic resin, which exchanges hydroxide ions for the negatively charged ions.

ion propulsion see ROCKETS AND MISSILES

Ionesco, Eugène [ee-oh-nes'-koh, u-zhen'] The Romanian-born Eugène Ionesco, b. Nov. 26, 1912, is one of the foremost playwrights of the THEATER OF THE ABSURD. Ionesco came to playwriting almost by chance. Having decided to learn English, he was struck by the emptiness of the clichés of daily conversation that appeared in his phrase book. Out of such nonsensical sentences he constructed his first play, *The Bald Soprano* (1950; Eng. trans., 1958), which satirizes the deadliness and idiocy of the daily life of a bourgeois society frozen in meaningless formalities. Surprised by the success of the play, Ionesco embarked on a career as a writer of what he called antiplays, which characteristically combine a dream or nightmare atmosphere with grotesque, bizarre, and whimsical humor.

In *The Lesson* (1951; Eng. trans., 1958) a teacher gains domination over his pupil through his superior use of language and finally kills her. In *The Chairs* (1952; Eng. trans., 1958) an old couple attempt to pass on their life experience to humanity by inviting to a gathering a vast crowd of guests who never arrive but whose nonpresence is symbolized by a proliferation of empty chairs. Having convinced themselves that the crowd is assembled, the old people kill themselves, leaving their message to an orator they have engaged who turns out to be a feebleminded deaf-mute.

Ionesco's breakthrough into the English-speaking theater came with *Rhinoceros* (1959; Eng. trans., 1960), which depicts totalitarianism as a disease that turns humans into savage rhinoceroses. The hero, Bérenger, a simple sort of Everyman who is also a self-image of Ionesco, reappears in *The Killer* (1958; Eng. trans., 1960), *Exit the King* (1962; Eng. trans., 1963), *A Stroll in the Air* (1963; Eng. trans., 1965), and *Hunger and Thirst* (1964; Eng. trans., 1966).

Elected a member of the Académie Française in 1970, Ionesco has also published theoretical writings, *Notes and Counternotes* (1962; Eng. trans., 1964); *Fragments of a Journal* (1966; Eng. trans., 1968); and a novel, *Le Solitaire* (1973), on which his 1971 film *La Vase* (with Ionesco playing the lead) is based. *Man with Bags*, Ionesco's most recent play, was produced in 1977.

Ionia [y-ohn'-ee-uh] The term *Ionia* refers strictly to the central part of the west coast of ANATOLIA (western Turkey) where Ionic Greek was spoken, although the term is usually applied to the entire west coast. Many Mycenaean Greeks (see AEGEAN CIVILIZATION) emigrated to Ionia in order to escape the invading DORIANS (c.1100 BC). Their close contact with the more advanced civilizations of the East quickly raised the level of their culture. Trade and the arts and sciences flourished in Ionia, especially in MILETUS, which in the 7th century Hellenized the area around the Black Sea.

In the 6th century the Ionians were subjugated by CROESUS, ruler of LYDIA, to the north, and when CYRUS THE GREAT in turn conquered Croesus in 546 BC, the Ionians became subjects of the Persian Empire. They attempted a revolt against DARIUS I in 499–494, but they were defeated, and Miletus was destroyed. After the abortive invasion (480–479) of Greece by the Persian king XERXES I, the Ionians regained their freedom and became members of the DELIAN LEAGUE. They soon came under the domination of Athens. In the 4th century Ionia was at the center of a struggle between Greeks and Persians. When the collapse of the Athenian empire at the end of the 5th century BC created a power vacuum, the Persians once again extended their influence into the Aegean. ALEXANDER THE GREAT'S conquest of the Persian Empire (334–325) freed Ionia, but its cities soon became the prey of contending Hellenistic monarchs. When one of them, Attalus III of Pergamum, died in 133 BC, he bequeathed his kingdom to Rome. PERGAMUM then became the province of Asia and the Ionians Roman subjects.

Ionian Sea [y-ohn'-ee-uhn] The Ionian Sea is an arm of the MEDITERRANEAN SEA lying west of Greece and east of southern Italy. The Strait of Otranto, between Italy and Albania, is to its north. The Mediterranean's greatest depth, 4,846 m (15,900 ft), is found in the Ionian Sea.

ionic bonding   see CHEMICAL BOND

---

ionosphere [y-ahn'-uhs-feer]   The ionosphere is the part of the Earth's upper ATMOSPHERE where there are enough ions and electrons in the air to affect the propagation of radio waves. Such a region was first theorized in 1902 independently by the British physicist Oliver Heaviside (1850–1925) and by the American electrical engineer Arthur Edwin Kennelly (1861–1949), following Guglielmo MARCONI's success in sending a radio signal across the Atlantic Ocean on Dec. 12, 1901.

Origin and Description

The ionosphere originates from solar X rays and ultraviolet radiation ionizing, or splitting, electrically neutral atmospheric molecules and atoms into electrons and positive ions. The ionosphere is concentrated in a region approximately 80 to 400 km (50 to 240 mi) above the Earth's surface. Above this region few ionizable particles exist; below it ionospheric absorption prevents penetration by the solar X rays and ultraviolet radiation.

Electrons are produced only during the daytime; electron losses, on the other hand, occur continuously. Electrons may lose their free existence by either of two processes: recombination of an electron and a positive ion into an electrically neutral particle or attachment of an electron to a neutral particle. Electron concentrations of daytime are reduced 10 to 100 times at night.

The ionosphere has been subdivided into several regions. The D region, which disappears at night, is between 60 and 85 km (35 and 50 mi) of altitude. The E region, formerly the Kennelly-Heaviside layer, is between 85 and 140 km. The F_1 and F_2 regions occur above 140 km (85 mi) and merge at night; together they were formerly known as the Appleton layer. The D and E regions are sites of primarily molecular ionization; the F region is characterized primarily by atomic ionization, which produces equal numbers of electrons and positive ions.

Ionospheric recorders stationed at the Earth's surface yield data on the electron profile (the concentration of electrons as a function of height) of the lower ionospheric half. A surface recorder can provide no information on the upper half, because a surface signal is reflected either by a level below the maximum electron concentration or not at all. The upper half is now better known than the lower, however, due to the placing of ionospheric recorders on satellites, beginning with Canada's ALOUETTE.

Use

Most commercial broadcasts are transmitted first along a horizontal path, but the signal will eventually enter the ionosphere due to the Earth's curvature. Because transmission is not vertical, fewer electrons are needed to reflect the signal back to the Earth's surface.

AM broadcasts (0.53–1.65 MHz) have a reflection

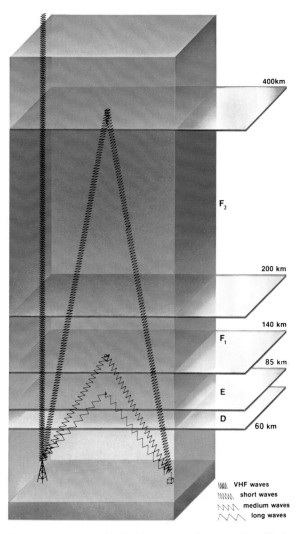

	400km
F_2	
	200 km
	140 km
F_1	
	85 km
E	
D	
	60 km

⩗⩗⩗ VHF waves
⩘⩘⩘ short waves
⩗⩗⩗ medium waves
⩗⩗⩗ long waves

The ionosphere, a region of the Earth's atmosphere from about 80 km (50 mi) to 400 km (250 mi) altitude, is composed of several different layers of ions and electrons. Long-distance radio transmission on Earth depends on these layers. Very short, or VHF, radio waves pass through all the layers into outer space, but successively longer waves are reflected to Earth by different, lower layers. Because the ionization of each layer results from the Sun's radiation, the reflection characteristics of the layers will vary with the time of day or night.

level within the D region, but this layer is at a height near 80 km (50 mi). Here the air is still so dense—it burns up meteors and satellites—that the signal's energy is transmitted via the electrons to the many surrounding air molecules. The signal loses its strength and is said to have been absorbed. Ionospheric reflection cannot occur; only the ground wave can be received. The reception of AM stations during daytime is therefore limited by the curvature of the earth to a radius of less than 200 km (120 mi). At night the D region disappears, and the electron concentration required for reflection is now found about

50 km (30 mi) higher, where atmospheric particles are so far apart that virtually no absorption takes place. A San Francisco station can thus be heard at night from Alaska to Baja California.

Long-distance ham-radio operators use a frequency of 3.75 MHz. Commercial short-wave transmissions have frequencies between 6 and 30 MHz. They are easily reflected by the E and F regions and then also by the Earth's surface, so that multiple hops are possible, connecting points on opposite sides of the globe. During the long polar winter night, however, electrons may become so rare that even short waves go through the skeleton ionosphere, and the result is a disruption—a polar-cap blackout—of long-distance communication. A radio fadeout may also occur under opposite circumstances. Charged particles from the Sun glide along the Earth's magnetic lines into the polar ionosphere, creating F-region-like electron concentrations in the D region; polar-cap absorption of signals results.

The ionosphere was first used for long-distance radio transmission in the years after World War I. In the 21st century, however, TELECOMMUNICATIONS will be mostly via COMMUNICATIONS SATELLITES using such high frequencies that no ionospheric interference can occur. The role of the ionosphere in the 21st century may be mainly scientific—its high vacuum is an excellent laboratory in which to explore exactly how solar radiation affects atmospheric atoms (see GEOPHYSICS).

Iowa   Iowa, an agricultural state located in the heart of the Midwest, is bordered by Wisconsin, Illinois, Missouri, Nebraska, South Dakota, and Minnesota. It represents a middle position economically, socially, and politically. Iowa even ranks in the middle (25th among the states) in size. One of the last of the midwestern states to be settled, it served as a bridge to the West. Its entrance into the Union (in 1846) as a free state was tied to the slavery question, and its people have reflected the changing mood of the nation—both in Civil War times and a century later—while not expressing extremes.

Land and Resources

Topography and Soils. Only about one-third of Iowa conforms to the popular stereotype of a flat landscape; most of the state is rolling to hilly land. Steep, rocky hills rise 100 to 115 m (330 to 380 ft) above the Mississippi River in the northeast, to an elevation of 335 m (1,100 ft), which is also the average elevation for the state. The lowest elevation, located along the Mississippi River in the southeast, is 146 m (480 ft); the maximum elevation is about 509 m (1,670 ft) in the northwest. Iowa's flatland is concentrated in the central portion north of Des Moines, where glacial deposits were left by the last retreating glacier.

Rich prairie soils cover most of the state and form the major resource base for agriculture. The rolling river valleys of the south and east have less fertile forest soils that are often severely eroded.

Rivers and Lakes. Numerous short rivers drain eastward into the Mississippi River or westward into the Missouri River. Those two large streams form the state's borders on the east and west, respectively. The Des Moines River (692 km/430 mi), the state's longest river, drains the centrally located Des Moines region, where the largest natural lakes and marshlands are found. The largest lake, Spirit Lake, is 6.4 km (4 mi) long and 5 km (3 mi) wide. Several large artificial reservoirs, including Rathbun, Red Rock, and Saylorville, have been constructed in recent years to aid in flood control.

Climate. Iowa's location deep in the continent's interior results in a climate characterized by temperature extremes and periodic droughts. Winter storms bring snowfalls that may total 61 cm (24 in) in the south to 100 cm (40 in) in the north, and occasional hazardous blizzards. Although average winter temperatures range from −10° C to −4° C (14° to 24° F), during storms temperatures may drop as low as about −34° C (−30° F). Summers are warm to hot and humid; temperatures average in the lower 20°s C (mid-70°s F), with daytime highs often in the high 30°s C (over 100° F).

Summer storms carry warm, moist air from the Gulf of Mexico, yielding much of the 865-mm (34-in) average annual precipitation of the southeast, which declines to 635 mm (25 in) in the northwest. Droughts may occur throughout the state but are most common and severe in the northwest. The warm, humid air also results in summer thunderstorms and tornadoes.

Vegetation and Animal Life. Most of Iowa was originally covered by prairie grasslands, but they have now been replaced chiefly by cropland and pastureland. Deciduous forests of oak-hickory and maple-basswood, found mainly in the hilly south and east, have shrunk to less than 10,100 km^2 (3,900 mi^2) as the land has been cleared for farming. White-tailed deer, game birds, and smaller forms of wildlife have adapted to dense agricultural settlement. Buffalo, cougars, and other large mammals, however, disappeared decades ago.

Resources. The bulk of Iowa's water resources comes from streams, most of which are too small to provide an adequate water supply during drought years. About one-fourth of the water supply comes from under ground. Some wells penetrate as deeply as 915 m (3,000 ft) into the Paleozoic marine sediments that underlie the drift. These sedimentary rocks also provide mineral resources. Gypsum and stone for construction are valuable resources, as are sand and gravel.

People

Iowa had a population of 2,787,424 in 1990, giving an average population density of just under 20 persons per km^2 (50 per mi^2). The rural and small-town population is exceptionally evenly distributed across the state. Most of the larger cities are in the eastern half; the largest city, DES MOINES, the capital, is quite near the center of the state. Only SIOUX CITY and COUNCIL BLUFFS (across the Missouri from Omaha, Nebr.) are located in the west. CEDAR RAPIDS, Waterloo, and IOWA CITY are the interior cities of the east; DAVENPORT, DUBUQUE, and several

AT A GLANCE

IOWA

Land: Area: 145,752 km² (56,275 mi²); rank: 25th. Capital and largest city: Des Moines (1990 pop., 193,187). Counties: 99. Elevations: highest—509 m (1,670 ft), in Osceola County; lowest—146 m (480 ft), at the Mississippi River.

People: Population (1990): 2,787,424; rank: 30th; density: 19.1 persons per km² (49.5 per mi²). Distribution (1988 est.): 43.4% metropolitan, 56.6% nonmetropolitan. Average annual change (1980–90): -0.4%.

Government (1991): Governor: Terry E. Branstad, Republican. U.S. Congress: Senate—1 Democrat, 1 Republican; House—2 Democrats, 4 Republicans. Electoral college votes: 8. State legislature: 50 senators, 100 representatives.

Economy: State personal income (1988): $41.6 billion; rank: 29th. Median family income (1979): $20,052; rank: 20th. Agriculture: income (1988)—$9.1 billion. Forestry: sawtimber volume (1987)—4.3 billion board feet. Mining: value (1987)—$317 million. Manufacturing: value added (1987)—$14.5 billion. Services: value (1987)—$8 billion.

Miscellany: Statehood: Dec 28th, 1846; the 29th state. Nickname: Hawkeye State; tree: oak; motto: Our liberties we prize and our rights we will maintain; song: "The Song of Iowa."

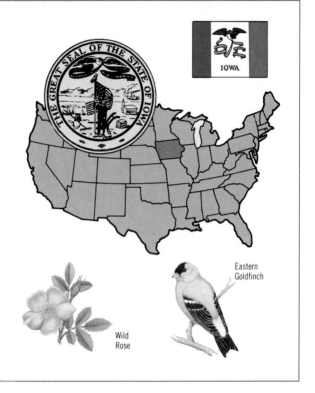

Eastern Goldfinch

Wild Rose

smaller cities line the banks of the Mississippi. Although 58.6% of the population are urban, small towns dominate; Iowa has almost 1,000 incorporated communities, most with fewer than 1,000 inhabitants.

Population growth was only 3.1% in 1970–80, and in 1980–90 the state registered a 4.3% decline, while the national population grew by 10.2%. The rural counties have lost population because of extensive out-migration, and some show a natural rate of decrease (an excess of deaths over births) due to an aging population; Iowa ranks high among the states in the proportion of population aged 65 and over.

The overwhelming majority of the population is native-born and of northwest European stock. Blacks (1.7% in 1990) are concentrated in the urban centers, particularly Des Moines and Waterloo. American Indians number over 7,000; most of them live either in Sioux City or in and around the Mesquakie Settlement near Tama. The majority of Iowa's population is Protestant, but Roman Catholics predominate in Dubuque and its surrounding area.

Education and Culture. The strength of Iowa's public educational system has resulted in the lowest illiteracy rate in the United States. Schools are consolidated in rural areas, but the declining number of pupils is creating pressures to close units in both rural and urban districts. Seventeen public and 37 private institutions of higher learning are located in the state. The University of Iowa (1847) in Iowa City has earned a national reputation in the fine arts; it includes the renowned Writer's Workshop. Iowa State University (1858) in Ames specializes in basic sciences and agriculture. The major libraries are located at the state universities and in the larger cities.

Des Moines and Iowa City have important art museums; presettlement and early white settlement are emphasized in museums in Cherokee and Decorah. The larger cities, notably Des Moines, Davenport, and Cedar Rapids, and the universities and colleges support theater, classical music, and dance. Because Iowa lacks large population concentrations, much of the population depends upon traveling artists and shows, a tradition that dates back to lecture circuits of the 19th-century and the CHAUTAUQUA movement (late 19th and early 20th centuries), providing education for adults.

Historical sites are associated largely with the settlement of the region and of the nation to the west. Noteworthy is the Herbert Hoover Presidential Library in West Branch, which includes not only official papers but also a preserved portion of the community, including the Hoover cabin, in which Iowa's only president was born (1874).

Communications. Iowa has approximately three dozen daily newspapers; the one with the largest circulation is the well-regarded *Des Moines Register*. A complete com-

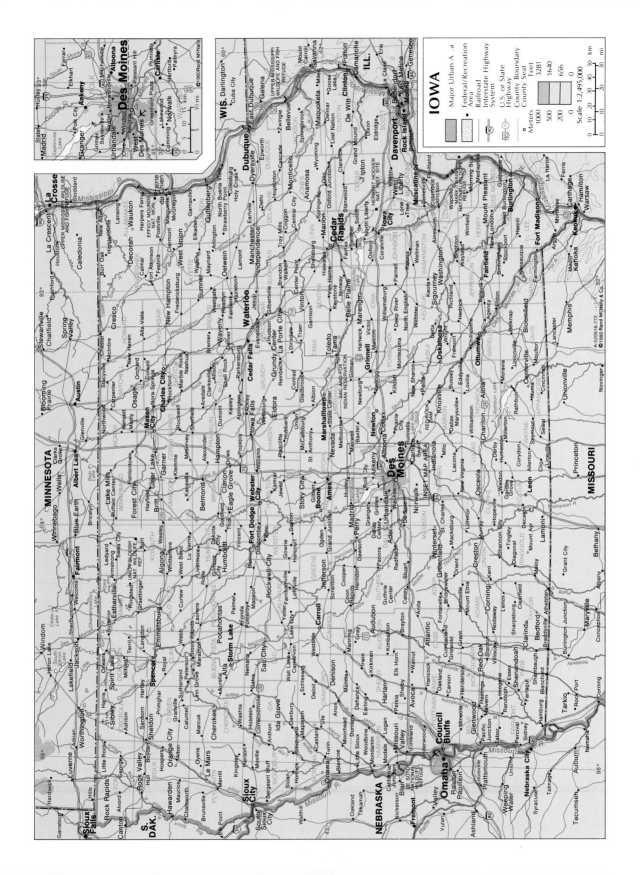

Des Moines, the capital and largest city of Iowa, is situated in the south central portion of the state at the junction of the Des Moines and Raccoon rivers. Originally established (1843) as a military garrison, Des Moines has become a regional center for banking, printing, and manufacturing.

munications network is provided by commercial and public television stations as well as by many radio stations.

Economic Activity

Iowa's economy is inextricably tied to the fortunes of farming. Although manufacturing now exceeds farming in employment and financial return, most industrial development is based upon the agricultural sector. As in most parts of the United States, however, employment in the trade and services sector exceeds that of either manufacturing or agriculture. The economy's growth rate has been steady, with per-capita income slightly below the U.S. average.

Agriculture. Iowa ranks second among the states in the value of agricultural production (California consistently leads the nation in agricultural receipts); Iowa maintains this position because of its corn, soybeans, cattle (both beef and dairy), and hogs. Livestock feeding within the state consumes most of the grain, but much is shipped to other states or is exported.

Manufacturing and Industry. Manufacturing is Iowa's single most important source of income. Processing of food products accounts for a large share of the total value of manufactured goods. The manufacturing of farm equipment and chemicals for farm use is significant, as are the manufacture of other machinery, electrical products, and rubber products and printing and publishing. Most mining is of stone or gypsum.

Tourism. Most tourists visit Iowa while in transit, as the state contains little spectacular scenery to slow their pace. Residents, however, use the outdoors heavily, with fishing, hunting, boating, and camping focused in the 91 state parks and on federal reservoirs. Because of the lack of large urban centers, professional sports are unimportant. Instead, organized sports at the high school and college levels are the centers of attention for many residents.

Transportation. A dense network of roads was constructed to serve the evenly scattered farms. With more than 180,000 km (112,000 mi) of roads and nearly 13,000 km (8,000 mi) of railroad track (both mileages rank high among the states), Iowa has a denser transport network than can be supported and maintained adequately, and the trend is to reduce this mileage. Barge traffic on the Mississippi and Missouri rivers is becoming increasingly important for transporting farm products.

Energy. Although much coal is located under southern Iowa, most of this has a high sulfur content and is found in relatively small and scattered deposits. Coal from outside the state and natural gas are far more important in providing energy. Nearly half the electrical power comes from nuclear-power plants.

Government and Politics

The Iowa constitution dates from 1857. The legislature is bicameral and consists of 50 senators who serve 4-year terms and 100 representatives who serve 2-year terms. The governor and other state executives are elected to 4-year terms. Counties and cities have separately elected officials and derive their authority from the state legislature.

Iowa has a long tradition of allegiance to the Republican party. In recent years, however, Democrats have gained more support and have occupied the governorship for five terms, elected three senators, and controlled both the congressional delegation and the state legislature for varying periods of time.

Despite the traditional dominance of the Republican party, Iowans tend to be moderate rather than conservative. Much of the credit for a liberal Republican position can be accorded to the influence of the *Des Moines Register*, a newspaper that is notable for its role in shaping public opinion on international as well as national issues.

History

Even as glacial ice was melting in central Iowa 13,000 years ago, it is believed that Paleo-Indians occupied the area. They hunted large, and now extinct, mammals such as mammoths and mastodons. The Woodland Indian tradition began in eastern Iowa about 500 BC and continued to about AD 1000. These Indians are best remembered for their complex burial mounds, such as those at Effigy Mounds National Monument (see MOUND BUILDERS). The small villages and incipient cultivation of the Woodland Indians gave way to post-Woodland cultures with larger settlements and a greater dependence upon cultivation.

European Exploration and Early Settlement. The first Europeans to see Iowa were the Frenchmen Louis JOLLIET and Jacques MARQUETTE, who traveled with their party down the Mississippi River in 1673. The first permanent white settler was Julien DUBUQUE, who mined lead along the Mississippi River, near the site of the city that bears his name, from 1788 to his death in 1810. After the LOUISIANA PURCHASE (1803) the land that was to become Iowa became part of the young United States, and the LEWIS AND CLARK EXPEDITION (1804–05) traveled the Missouri River en route to and from the Pacific. The SAUK and FOX (Mesquakie) tribes, forced into the Mississippi River valley from Wisconsin and Illinois by the oncoming pressure of white settlement, defeated the Iowa Indians and occupied their lands in the late 18th and early 19th centuries. Following the BLACK HAWK WAR of 1832, the resistance of these tribes to white settlers was broken, and the land was now open to pioneer settlement. The first legal settlement west of the Mississippi took place in 1833, and population growth was rapid. Successive purchases from the Indians led to settlement throughout the area of the state in the 1830s and 1840s—but not without some confrontations, the last being the Spirit Lake Massacre of 1857. Just before this event (in 1856) the Mesquakies, who had been forced to move to Kansas, convinced the Iowa legislature to permit their repurchase of land along the Iowa River near Tama. The Mesquakie Settlement now covers about 13 km^2 (5 mi^2).

Statehood and Settlement. The Territory of Iowa was created in 1838. Statehood was granted in 1846, with Southern congressional opposition an issue; unwritten practice tied the admission of a free state to that of a slave state, in order to maintain a balance of power. Iowa's "partner" was Florida, which had been waiting since 1838 for a Northern free territory to become eligible. Iowa thus became the 29th state, with its capital at Iowa City. The capital was moved to Des Moines in 1857.

By 1850 nearly 200,000 people lived in Iowa, and by 1860 roughly 600,000 made their homes there. The majority of settlers came from the eastern Midwest states of Ohio and Indiana. Thousands came from the border slave states; they primarily settled in southern Iowa.

The Civil War and Postwar Periods. In the pre-Civil War period Iowa was firmly Democratic. The war changed that, as antislavery forces finally coalesced into the new Republican party in 1856, turning Iowa into a virtual one-party state. With Republicans in the Senate, Iowa moved from isolationism on the slavery issue to a fervent antislavery position. John BROWN used Iowa and its Quaker communities as a base for his activities throughout the late 1850s, and six Iowans participated in his ill-fated attack at Harpers Ferry, W.Va., in 1859. During the Civil War, Iowa sent almost 80,000 soldiers to battle, a larger proportion of its population than any other Northern state. Following the war suffrage was extended to blacks, and integrated schools were instituted.

Immigration to Iowa continued during the latter half of the 19th century, mostly by settlers from northwestern Europe. Towns sprung up every few kilometers, evenly spaced on the physical landscape. From the outset farming was commercially rather than subsistence oriented, with corn rather than wheat the principal crop.

Because most agriculture was commercial, farmers needed railroads to get their produce to market. The railroads, however, which first arrived in 1867, established high freight rates. Regulation battles followed, and many farmers joined the Granger movement to fight the railroads. These problems were not the only ones to be faced. Pests, diseases, and droughts plagued the settlers' crops, and depressions plagued their finances. The productive land also created opportunities for utopian ideals, and a number of communes established on this basis were founded. Only one survived into the 20th century—the AMANA SOCIETY—with its seven villages along the Iowa River.

The Recent Period. Although Iowa has never been a leading industrial center, a number of enterprises became nationally successful as the need for a large farm population diminished. Laborers freed from the plow were me-

Corn, traditionally Iowa's most valuable cash crop, ripens in the south central portion of the state. Iowa is also a major producer of soybeans. Other inportant field crops include oats and hay.

chanically adept and had a tradition of hard work behind them. Innovation, particularly hybridization of corn, and mechanization paved the way for more efficient and productive farming. Surplus population moved off the land, and the numbers of rural Iowans declined. With the move to the cities came other social changes, and the long hold of the Republicans on the state political scene was broken. Today Iowa has a stable economy with a low growth rate, neither plunging to the depths with each new recession nor enjoying for long the dizzying heights of recovery. More than in most other parts of the nation, it holds a middle position, economically and socially, and this appears to be the role that Iowa is destined to play.

Iowa (Indian tribe)   The Pahodja ("dusty roses"), a Siouan-speaking tribe of North American Indians, received their better-known name, Iowa, or Ayuhwa ("sleepy ones"), from their Sioux enemies. Closely related to the OTO and MISSOURI, all descended from the WINNEBAGO, they are traditionally believed to have originated in the Great Lakes region. After leaving there, the three tribes lived in present-day Illinois before moving to the Lower Missouri and separating into dialect groups. They farmed maize, beans, and squash supplemented by hunting and lived in villages consisting of rectangular bark dwellings. The tepee was used on summer excursions into the Great Plains. Clans were grouped into summer and winter moieties (complementary subdivisions). Sons inherited leadership and clan membership from fathers. Religion was organized by special societies; the GHOST DANCE was adopted in the 1880s, and the use of peyote later became widespread.

In 1804, Lewis and Clark found the Iowa living on the Platte River in a single village of about 800. The Iowa did not resist white expansion and ceded their land in 1824, 1836, and 1854, accepting a reservation in northeast Kansas; they then numbered about 500. Some Iowa were persuaded to relocate in Indian Territory (present-day Oklahoma) in the 1880s. The Iowa who remained in Kansas now number more than 600, although only about 200 live on the reservation.

Iowa City   Iowa City lies along both banks of the Iowa River in eastern Iowa. With a population of 59,738 (1990), it is the seat of Johnson County. It is the commercial center of an agricultural region dominated by cattle, grain, hogs, and poultry production. Area industries produce urethane foam and toiletries. Founded in 1839 as the capital of the Iowa Territory, it remained the seat of government until 1857. The establishment (1847) of the University of Iowa and the arrival of the railroad in 1855 assured its growth.

ipecac [ip'-i-kak]   Ipecac, the dried roots and subterranean stems of one of several South American or Indian plants, contains a number of alkaloids. For medicinal uses the roots are ground into a powder from which a syr-up or tincture (alcohol solution) can be made. Ipecac is used as an emetic (induces vomiting) when poisonous material has been ingested, but its use should be avoided if the poison is a petroleum product, an acid, or an alkali. It is used in expectorant mixtures to treat bronchitis, because it can liquefy mucous secretions.

Iphigenia [if-uh-juh-ny'-uh]   In Greek mythology Iphigenia was the daughter of AGAMEMNON and CLYTEMNESTRA. When unfavorable winds detained the Greek army at Aulis from sailing for Troy, an oracle told Agamemnon that he must sacrifice Iphigenia to appease the anger of Artemis, whose sacred stag he had killed. Agamemnon accordingly had Iphigenia brought to Aulis, where he performed the sacrifice. In another version of the story, Artemis substituted a deer on the altar at the last moment and carried Iphigenia in a cloud to Tauris, where she became a priestess of Artemis. Many years later Iphigenia escaped with her brother Orestes to Attica, where she established a new temple to Artemis.

Ipiutak [ip-ee-oo'-tak]   Ipiutak, an archaeological site near Point Hope on the northwest coast of Alaska, is the name given a major prehistoric Eskimo culture of the first half of the first millennium AD. Excavations at the site have revealed the remains of more than 600 houses and a large burial ground. A great number of carefully worked arrows, harpoon heads, and other stone and antler implements were found in the open-hearthed, rectangular dwellings. Bows and arrows were important hunting tools. Neither blubber lamps nor pottery were known.

Ipiutak's remarkable cemetery consisted of wood coffins buried at depths of 0.5 to 1 m (1.5 to 3 ft), as well as burials in which the corpse was enclosed by logs placed directly on the surface of the tundra. The latter burials were especially rich in unusual grave goods, including ivory eyeballs, masks, animal figures, and bizarre openwork carvings. The style of these objects shows affinities with the OKVIK and Old Bering Sea cultures as well as with the so-called animal style art of the SCYTHIANS, suggesting links with Siberian cultural traditions. The Ipiutak site was discovered in 1939.

Iqbal, Muhammad [ik-bahl', muh-hahm'-uhd]   One of the greatest poets of the Indian subcontinent, Muhammad Iqbal, b. *c.*1877, was also a philosopher and Muslim political leader. He studied law and philosophy in Europe (1905–08) and, on his return to India, taught philosophy and literature, practiced law, and soon achieved fame as a poet. He wrote in both Persian and Urdu. The British knighted Iqbal in 1922 in recognition of his poetry. His works include *Asrar-e khudi* (1915; trans. as *The Secrets of the Self*, 1920, 1940), *Payam-e Mashrig* (The Message of the East, 1923), and *The Reconstruction of Religious Thought in Islam* (1934).

Iqbal also became active in Muslim politics, serving as a member of the Punjab Legislative Council (1926–30) and president of the Muslim League (1930). One of the first to advocate a separate Muslim state in India, he has been called the spiritual father of Pakistan, where the anniversary of his death (Apr. 21, 1938) is a national holiday.

IQ see INTELLIGENCE; PSYCHOLOGICAL MEASUREMENT

Iráklion [ee-rah'-klee-awn] Iráklion (Candia) is the largest city on Crete, with a population of 102,389 (1981). A seaport, it is the island's transportation, commercial, and tourism center. Wine, dried fruit, and grapes are major exports. Nearby are ruins of the Minoan city KNOSSOS. Iráklion's Archaeological Museum is famous for its collection of Minoan art and relics.

The modern city was founded by Arabs in the 9th century. Iráklion, called Kandaq by the Arabs, became part of the Byzantine Empire in the 10th century; in 1204 it was sold to the Venetians, who renamed it Candia. It was conquered by Turks in 1669 and served as the capital of Crete until 1841. When Crete was incorporated into Greece in 1913, the city was renamed Iráklion.

Iran [ir-an'] Iran is the largest and most populous country in southwest Asia. It shares a long land border with the USSR on the north, and its coastline commands navigation on the PERSIAN GULF, the Strait of HORMUZ, and the Gulf of Oman in the south (see OMAN, GULF OF). Iran also shares borders with Turkey and Iraq on the west and with Afghanistan and Pakistan on the east. The country was known to the West as Persia, from the ancient Greek name *Persis*, but in 1935 the Iranian government requested use of the older and correct name, Iran, meaning "Land of the Aryans." Iran was an independent monarchy for more than 2,500 years until 1979. In that year the shah of Iran, MUHAMMAD REZA SHAH PAHLAVI, was deposed and an Islamic republic declared.

Land and Resources

The topography of Iran consists mainly of a central plateau rimmed by high mountains; most of the country lies above 450 m (1,500 ft). The only extensive lowlands, all narrow, occur along the southern shores of the CASPIAN SEA and along the shores of the Gulf of Oman. About half the country is dominated by the arid central plateau, with elevations ranging from 600 to 900 m (about 2,000 to 3,000 ft). The mountain ranges encircling the plateau are the ELBURZ MOUNTAINS and their structural continuation in the Talish Mountains and the Koppeh Dagh on the north, the ZAGROS MOUNTAINS on the southwest, and the Makran Range on the south. The highest mountains are in the Elburz, where Mount Demavend rises to 5,671 m (18,606 ft), the highest point in Iran. One of the most extraordinary features of Iranian topography is an uninhabitable arid salt waste, the Dasht-e-Kavir, centered 485 km (300 mi) southeast of the capital, Tehran.

Soils. The soils used most extensively for farming are the rich brown forest soils found along the coastal regions of the Persian Gulf and the Caspian Sea. Elsewhere, soils suitable for farming are largely alluvial and limited to river valleys in mountainous areas and along the SHATT-AL-ARAB (the mouth of the Tigris-Euphrates). Water availability rather than soil quality is the determining factor for agriculture.

Climate. Iran has a varied continental type of climate marked by extremes in both temperature and precipitation. Summers are extremely hot along the Persian Gulf, where temperatures of 50° C (120° F) are not uncommon. In inland areas, daytime highs also occasionally exceed 50° C (120° F) but fall rapidly at night. Winters are generally cold, except along the milder Caspian and Persian Gulf shores, with temperatures reaching below 0° C (32° F) on the plateau. In Tehran the average January temperature is 2° C (36° F), and the average for July is 30° C (86° F). Precipitation ranges from more than 1,270 mm (50 in) in the northwestern Zagros and the Elburz mountains to less than 50 mm (2 in) in southeastern areas of the central plateau.

Drainage. The most important river in Iran is the Karun, the nation's only navigable river, which rises in the central Zagros and joins the Shatt-al-Arab at Khorramshahr. Three other rivers that maintain their flow all year are the Atrak in the northeast; the Safid, which flows through the Elburz to the south shore of the Caspian Sea; and the Araks in the northwest. *Qanats*, or long underground water tunnels, are widely used to bring water from the mountains into the plateau.

Vegetation and Animal Life. About 10% of Iran is covered with forest, most of it deciduous and located in the mountains bordering the Caspian Sea. A variety of trees and shrubs also covers parts of the Zagros Mountains. Drier parts of the country are generally devoid of vegetation, except in the oases. On the plateau the fauna include wild boars, foxes, jackals, and a few lions and tigers in the wilder areas; numerous smaller animals; and, in the drier areas, a variety of creatures adapted to arid conditions.

Resources. Iran is tremendously rich in minerals, especially petroleum and natural gas. It is estimated that the petroleum reserves will last for 40 years. Most oil fields are located in the southwest, especially in Khuzestan province; some are under the waters of the Persian Gulf; and extensive discoveries have been made in other parts of the country. Its natural gas reserves constitute the world's second largest (after the USSR). Much of the natural gas is exported by pipeline to the USSR. In the 1970s iron and coal deposits were developed for use in the new steel industry, and large deposits of chromite, copper, lead, zinc, and salt are only beginning to be exploited on a large scale.

People

The population of Iran is ethnically complex, and minority groups staunchly defend their provincial separatism and seek autonomy in local affairs. About two-thirds of the total population are descended from Aryan tribes who migrated to Iran from central Asia in the 17th century BC. The remaining one-third is composed mostly of Turks and Arabs, as well as small minorities of Armenians and Jews.

AT A GLANCE

ISLAMIC REPUBLIC OF IRAN

Land: Area: 1,648,000 km^2 (636,296 mi^2). Capital and largest city: Tehran (1986 est. pop., 6,042,584).

People: Population (1990 est.): 55,647,001. Density: 33.8 persons per km^2 (87.5 per mi^2). Distribution (1990 est.): 54% urban, 46% rural. Official language: Persian (Farsi). Major religions: Islam, Zoroastrianism, Christianity, Baha'i.

Government: Type: theocratic republic. Legislature: Islamic Consultative Assembly (Majlis). Political subdivisions: 24 provinces.

Economy: GNP (1989): $97.6 billion; $1,800 per capita. Labor distribution (1986): agriculture—28%; mining and manufacturing—10%; construction—12%; government and services—50%. Foreign trade (1988): imports—$12.0 billion; exports—$12.3 billion. Currency: 1 rial = 100 dinars.

Education and Health: Literacy (1986): 62% of adult population. Universities (1988): 21. Hospital beds (1986): 70,184. Physicians (1987): 16,918. Life expectancy (1990): women—63; men—62. Infant mortality (1990): 91 per 1,000 live births.

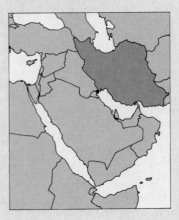

The largest Aryan group are Persians, or Farsi. Also of Aryan origin are the Gilani and Mazandarani. Many of Iran's important ethnic minorities (although also of Aryan descent) are nomadic and have strongly resisted culture change, with some even demanding separate nations; these groups include the KURDS, the BAKHTIARI, the Lurs, and the BALUCH. The largest Turkic-speaking group are the Azerbaijani. Arabs predominate in oil-rich Khuzestan province and along the Persian Gulf; Armenians and the few remaining Jews are concentrated in urban areas.

The official language is Persian, or Farsi, an INDO-EURO-PEAN language written in the Arabic script. Related to Persian but considered separate languages are Kurdish, Luri, and Baluchi. Azerbaijani is the most widely used of the Turkic languages, part of the URAL-ALTAIC LANGUAGE group.

About 98% of all Iranians are Muslims; 93% are SHI-ITES, or members of the Shia sect of Islam. Iran is the world's center of Shiite Islam, and it is the official state religion. Most of the ethnic minorities, however, including Kurds, Baluch, Turks, and Arabs, are SUNNITES, or members of the Sunni sect of Islam. Leadership of the Shiites rests with a priestly class of mullahs, whose leaders have great political influence and include about 400 ayatollahs, or "holy ones." Since the 1979 revolution, even the most secular Iranians have been forced to adhere to strict Islamic codes of behavior. The principal minority religions are BAHA'I, ZOROASTRIANISM, and Christianity (notably the NESTORIAN CHURCH). Baha'is have been severely persecuted by the government since the revolution.

Demography. Large areas of Iran are uninhabited. The population is concentrated along the southern shores of the Caspian Sea, the Atrek River valley in the northeast, the Karun River valley and Tigris-Euphrates delta in the southwest, and the mountain valleys of the northwest. The nation's largest urban center is TEHRAN, the capital. Other large urban centers are ISFAHAN, SHIRAZ, and TABRIZ. MASHHAD and QUM are important Shiite religious centers.

Education and Health. Education is free and compulsory for all children from age 6 to age 11. Since the revolution, many new schools have been built, textbooks have been rewritten to place greater emphasis on religion and traditional values, and classes have been segregated by sex. The country's universities, closed after the revolution, have gradually reopened since 1983; the largest is the University of Tehran (1934). Health care has improved since the 1960s but remains inadequate, particularly in rural areas.

The Arts. Iran has a rich indigenous culture. Poetry is traditionally the most important art form, and the 12th-century OMAR KHAYYAM is perhaps the most famous poet (see PERSIAN LITERATURE). Music and architecture are also historically important; traditional forms of both have been influenced by Western styles in recent decades (see PERSIAN ART AND ARCHITECTURE). Iran is famous for its crafts, including ceramics and silver and gold metalwork, but the traditional industry of carpetmaking seems to be in an irreversible decline.

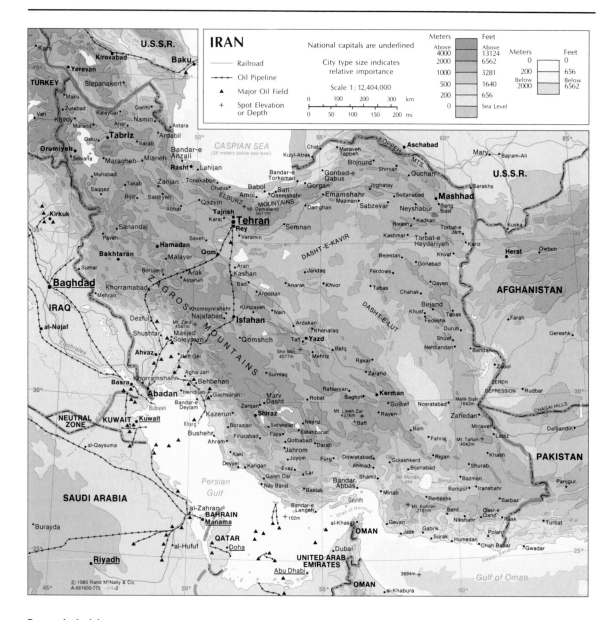

Economic Activity

During the 1960s and 1970s the shah attempted to transform Iran into a modern, industrial nation. Rapid economic growth created a prosperous middle class, but it also caused widespread social and cultural dislocation. After the 1979 revolution, Iran's revolutionary government emphasized self-sufficiency. Most industries (including oil, in 1981) were nationalized, and many large-scale projects were abandoned. Despite a worldwide oil glut and the damage to wells, refineries, and export terminals caused by the long IRAN-IRAQ WAR (1980–88), oil exports have been maintained at a relatively high level.

Manufacturing. Manufacturing now provides a larger share of the GNP than agriculture, although it employs fewer people. The principal industries are oil related and include refining and petrochemicals. The principal oil-processing center is ABADAN. Domestic steel is widely used in the production of automobiles, buses, trucks, tractors, refrigerators, and electrical machinery. The textile industry, Iran's oldest major industry, is centered mainly in Isfahan.

Agriculture and Fishing. About 12% of the land is suitable for agriculture; a dwindling percentage of the population are nomadic tribespeople raising sheep and goats.

Tehran, the capital and largest city of Iran, is situated on a plateau in the north central portion of the nation. An ancient city, much of its expansion has occured since the end of World War II.

In 1962 a major land-reform program redistributed much of the huge land holdings of absentee landlords to poor, landless peasants in an effort to raise the rural standard of living. Irrigation dams were also built, and the government attempted to establish huge, mechanized commercial farms. Most farms, however, remain small and inefficient. The government is attempting to reduce food imports and guarantee a minimum food security through rationing and food price supports. Commercial fishing is important along the Persian Gulf and in the Caspian Sea, the source of Iran's famous caviar.

Transportation. Railroads serve the major cities of Tehran, Mashhad, and Tabriz in the north and connect with lines serving Qum, Ahvaz, Bandar Khomeini, Khorramshahr, and Isfahan. The principal highway extends from the Turkish border to Herat, in Afghanistan. The leading ports are Khorramshahr, Bandar Abbas, Bandar Khomeini, and Bushehr. Kharg Island is the main terminus for oil exports.

Trade. More than 90% of Iranian exports consist of oil and oil products. Other exports include textiles, carpets, cotton, and dried and fresh fruit. In recent times all but the most essential imports have been tied to countertrade (oil for imports). The revolutionary government has repaid almost all of the nation's foreign debt, including claims by U.S. firms that lost assets after the shah's overthrow.

History and Government

Many dynasties and empires have ruled Persia, which at times has been at the center of vast empires extending through much of the Middle East (see PERSIA, ANCIENT). The modern Persian state traces its beginnings to CYRUS THE GREAT, who became the first of the ACHAEMENID emperors in 549 BC. In 330 BC, Persia became part of Alexander the Great's empire. It was subsequently part of the SELEUCID kingdom and then, beginning in 250 BC, of the Parthian empire (see PARTHIA). In AD c.224 the Parthian

Arsacid dynasty was overthrown by the SASSANIANS, a Persian dynasty that ruled until the Arab conquest, which was completed in 641. The Arabs introduced Islam and incorporated Persia into the dominions of the caliphs (see CALIPHATE). In the 11th and 12th centuries the country came under the rule of the SELJUK Turks, who laid down the administrative and economic structure that persisted until the 20th century. Persia was overrun by the MONGOLS under GENGHIS KHAN in the 13th century and by TIMUR in the late 14th century.

In the 16th century, after a long period of disunity, Shah Ismail (r. 1502–24) founded the SAFAVID dynasty, which restored Persia as a political entity and established Shiism as the national religion. The greatest Safavid ruler was Shah ABBAS I, who reconquered (1603–23) substantial territories from the Ottoman Empire. The Afghans overthrew the Safavids in 1722, but Persian independence was restored (1736) by the despotic Nadir Shah. His Afshar dynasty was followed (1750) by the Zand dynasty, which was overthrown in 1794 by the Qajars (Kajars), who held the throne until 1925.

The Anglo-Russian Entente of 1907 (see TRIPLE ENTENTE) divided the country into a Russian zone of influence, a British zone, and a neutral zone. In 1908 petroleum was discovered. The decadent Qajar dynasty was unable to save the country from a state of virtual civil war and from foreign domination until the emergence of REZA SHAH PAHLAVI, who was elevated to the throne by the Majlis (parliament) in 1925. He reorganized the army, restored internal order, broke the power of the reactionary Shiite clergy, and developed new industries.

In 1941 joint British-Soviet pressure forced the abdication of the allegedly pro-German Reza Shah. He was succeeded by his 22-year-old son, Muhammad Reza Shah Pahlavi. In the early 1950s the power of the new shah was challenged by the nationalist leader Muhammad MOSADDEQ, who tried to take over the government and nationalized the oil industry, previously controlled by foreign interests. The shah was forced to flee the country briefly in 1953, but he returned shortly with strong backing from the Western powers; Mosaddeq was subsequently convicted of treason. In 1954 a new arrangement with a consortium of Western oil companies was negotiated, giving Iran 50% of all profits (raised to 55% in 1970).

In 1963 the shah inaugurated an ambitious program of modernization (including land reform, emancipation of women, and rapid industrialization) known as the White Revolution. The reforms were too much for some and not enough for others and were accompanied by corruption and widespread social dislocation. As opposition grew, particularly among the clergy, order was kept by the army and the secret police, SAVAK.

During 1977 and 1978, however, tensions increased and opposition from both the left and right erupted into street rioting. In November 1978 the shah placed Iran under military rule. Opposition continued, however, led from Paris by the exiled Islamic fundamentalist Ayatollah Ruhollah KHOMEINI. On Jan. 6, 1979, the shah lifted military rule, and a few days later he left the country. Khomeini returned to a tumultuous welcome on February 1, and on February 12, Iran was proclaimed an Islamic republic. Hundreds of the shah's supporters and alleged members of SAVAK were arrested, tried, and executed. Khomeini initiated policies to reverse the Westernization of Iran, and a new constitution was approved at the end of the year, establishing a parliamentary form of government with an elected president and a unicameral parliament; the Sharia (Islamic law) as the basis of the legal system; and a council of guardians dominated by religious leaders. The constitution vested supreme authority in a *faqih* (supreme religious guide) and made Khomeini *faqih* for life.

The blue dome of the Masjid-i-Shah, or Royal Mosque, dominates the city of Isfahan, in central Iran. This outstanding example of Islamic architecture was constructed during the 17th century by command of Shah Abbas.

The new regime was antagonistic toward the United States because of the latter's long-time support of the shah. The seizure of the U.S. embassy in Tehran and its personnel by militant students in November 1979 precipitated a prolonged international crisis (see IRANIAN HOSTAGE CRISIS) that finally ended with the release of the hostages in January 1981. Meanwhile, in 1980, a border dispute with Iraq erupted into war (see IRAN-IRAQ WAR) when Iraqi troops invaded Iran. The war continued until 1988, when Iraq and Iran agreed to a cease-fire. Khomeini skillfully used both the hostage crisis and the war with Iraq to unify the country behind him.

Abolhassan BANI-SADR, a moderate who was elected president in January 1980, was dismissed in June 1981. His successor, Muhammad Ali Rajai, was assassinated later that year as the People's Mudjahedeen (a group of socialist Islamic guerrillas) and other opponents of the revolutionary government turned increasingly to violence. Hojatolislam Ali Khamenei was elected president in 1981 and reelected in 1985.

Iran's revolutionary government continued to enjoy widespread domestic support despite shortages of food and foreign exchange and political repression. It became increasingly isolated in the international community, however, partly due to its links to HEZBOLLAH and other terrorist groups, and its own terrorist-type activities in various countries. Signs of differences among the nation's political leaders emerged, particularly after the late 1986 revelations of U.S. arms sales to Iran in the so-called IRAN-CONTRA AFFAIR. In 1988, Khomeini reluctantly accepted a United Nations–mediated cease-fire in the Iran-Iraq war.

After Khomeini's death, on July 3, 1989, the Council of Experts elected Khamenei to succeed him as Iran's supreme religious leader. Hashemi RAFSANJANI, who had been speaker of parliament since 1980, became president after July 1989 elections in which voters also approved constitutional amendments abolishing the post of prime minister and strengthening the presidency. Soon after its August 1990 invasion of Kuwait, Iraq agreed to return to Iran all prisoners and territory taken during the Iran-Iraq war; the two nations reestablished diplomatic ties in September. Iran remained neutral during the brief 1991 GULF WAR, positioning itself, however, to play an influential role in shaping the postwar security structure of the region.

Iran-contra affair   The tangled U.S. foreign-policy scandal known as the Iran-contra affair came to light in November 1986 when President Ronald Reagan confirmed reports that the United States had secretly sold arms to Iran. He stated that the goal was to improve relations with Iran, not to obtain release of U.S. hostages held in the Middle East by terrorists (although he later acknowledged that the arrangement had in fact turned into an arms-for-hostages swap). Outcry against dealings with a hostile Iran was widespread. Later in November, Att. Gen. Edwin Meese discovered that some of the arms profits had been diverted to aid the Nicaraguan "contra" rebels—at a time when Congress had prohibited such aid. An independent special prosecutor, former federal judge Lawrence E. Walsh, was appointed to probe the activities of persons involved in the arms sale or contra aid or both, including marine Lt. Col. Oliver North of the NATIONAL SECURITY COUNCIL (NSC) staff.

Reagan appointed a review board headed by former Republican senator John Tower. The Tower Commission's report in February 1987 criticized the president's passive management style. Reagan accepted that judgment without serious disagreement as well as responsibility for the actions of his subordinates.

Select committees of the Senate and the House of Representatives conducted joint televised hearings from May to August. They heard evidence that a few members of the NSC staff set Iran and Nicaragua policies and carried them out with secret private operatives; that the few officials who knew about these policies lied to Congress and others; and that the contras received only a small part of the diverted money. Former national security advisor John Poindexter stated that he authorized the diversion of money and withheld that information from the president. William J. Casey, former director of the Central Intelligence Agency, who died in May 1987, was implicated in some testimony. These events shook the nation's faith in President Reagan and tarnished U.S. prestige abroad.

Special prosecutor Walsh continued his investigation. On Mar. 11, 1988, Poindexter's predecessor as national security advisor, Robert McFarlane, pleaded guilty to criminal charges of withholding information from Congress on secret aid to the contras. A year later McFarlane was fined and given two years' probation. On Mar. 16, 1988, a federal grand jury indicted North, Poindexter, and two other persons on a number of charges including conspiracy to defraud the U.S. government. In May 1989 a jury convicted North of 3 of the 12 criminal counts he was ultimately tried on, but these convictions were later set aside by a federal appeals court. On Apr. 7, 1990, Poindexter was convicted of deceiving congressional investigators and sentenced to 6 months in prison.

Iran-Iraq war   The Iran-Iraq war erupted on Sept. 22, 1980, when Iraq invaded Iran. The conflict had deep territorial, cultural, ethnic, and ideological roots and reflected a historic rivalry between Iraq and Iran for supremacy in the PERSIAN GULF area.

Iraq's stated war goal was to gain total control of the SHATT-AL-ARAB waterway dividing the two countries. However, Iraq's minority-based Sunnite government also feared the impact of Iran's 1979 Islamic revolution on its Shiite majority and hoped that Iran's military weakness and internal chaos would enable Iraq to reassert Arab claims to Iran's Khuzestan province and become the dominant power in the region. In June 1982, faced with strong Iranian resistance, Iraq withdrew its troops from most parts of Iran. Although Iran later launched several massive human wave attacks, the war essentially settled into a bloody stalemate with a death toll estimated at

more than 1 million. In 1984, Iraq began attacks on Gulf shipping as part of its economic warfare against Iran. This strategy also helped draw other countries into the conflict, increasing pressure on Iran to accept a negotiated settlement. In response, Iran attacked ships carrying war material to Iraq and those belonging to countries that helped Iraq.

From the beginning there was fear that the war would expand and possibly spark a superpower confrontation. Iraq purchased arms mainly from France and the USSR and received Western credits and massive financial aid from other Gulf Arab states. Iran, supported by Syria and Libya, purchased most of its arms in the black market. The United States, officially neutral, gave nonmilitary aid and intelligence information to Iraq but also, in 1985 and 1986, supplied a few arms to Iran (see IRAN-CONTRA AFFAIR). In May 1987, after the U.S. frigate *Stark* was hit by an Iraqi missile, apparently by accident, the United States increased its naval presence in the Gulf and allowed 11 Kuwaiti tankers to fly the U.S. flag. Other nations later joined the patrols. In July 1987, Iraq accepted a UN resolution designed to end the war. In July 1988, after Iraqi air attacks on Iranian cities, several Iraqi ground victories, and the accidental downing of a commercial Iranian airliner by the U.S. cruiser *Vincennes*, Iran also accepted the UN resolution. A cease-fire took effect on Aug. 20, 1988. In 1990, seeking Iranian support for its invasion of Kuwait, Iraq returned to Iran all Iraqi-occupied territory and prisoners of war. The two nations restored diplomatic ties in September.

Iranian hostage crisis   The Iranian hostage crisis was precipitated by the seizure of the U.S. embassy in Tehran by militant students on Nov. 4, 1979. The students took hostage 66 U.S. embassy employees and demanded the return of the shah (see MUHAMMAD REZA SHAH PAHLAVI) for trial. The Ayatollah KHOMEINI, who had taken power in February 1979 after the overthrow of the shah, warmly supported the students. On November 14, U.S. president Jimmy Carter ordered frozen all Iranian assets in U.S. banks. The release on November 19–20 of 13 hostages who were either black or female did little to alleviate the crisis, and although the shah left the United States in early December, the militants refused to release their hostages.

An unsuccessful U.S. attempt (Apr. 24, 1980) to rescue the hostages aggravated hostility between the two countries, and the death of the shah in July had no immediate effect on the hostages' status. In November, however, the Iranian parliament set four conditions for their release: no U.S. interference in Iran; the unfreezing of Iranian assets inside and outside the United States; the cancellation of all sanctions; and the return of the shah's property. Algeria was named mediator, and an agreement was finally signed in January 1981. On January 20, the day of Ronald Reagan's inauguration as president, the hostages were released. Former president Jimmy Carter went to West Germany as Reagan's special envoy to greet them.

AT A GLANCE

REPUBLIC OF IRAQ

Land: Area: 434,924 km² (167,952 mi²). Capital and largest city: Baghdad (1987 est. pop., 3,844,600).

People: Population (1990 est.): 18,781,770. Density: 43.2 persons per km² (111.8 per mi²). Distribution (1987): 70% urban, 30% rural. Official language: Arabic. Major religions: Islam, Christianity.

Government: Type: republic. Legislature: National Assembly. Political subdivisions: 18 provinces.

Economy: GNP (1989 est.): $35 billion; $1,940 per capita. Labor distribution (1987): agriculture—33%; services—39%; industry—28%. Foreign trade (1988): imports—$10.2 billion; exports—$12.5 billion. Currency: 1 Iraqi dinar = 100 fils.

Education and Health: Literacy (1989 est.): 55-65% of adult population. Universities (1989): 6. Hospital beds (1986): 32,166. Physicians (1986): 6,074. Life expectancy (1990): women—68; men—66. Infant mortality (1990): 67 per 1,000 live births.

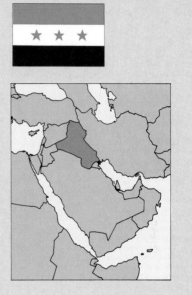

Iraq [ir-ak'] Iraq is a republic of southwest Asia, extending northwest from the head of the Persian Gulf. It is bounded on the south by the gulf, Kuwait, and Saudi Arabia; on the west by Jordan and Syria; on the north by Turkey; and on the east by Iran. Iraq is a major petroleum producer. Formerly called MESOPOTAMIA ("the land between the rivers"), Iraq is the site of one of the most ancient centers of civilization. In the 7th century AD it became part of the Arab world. Under Ottoman Turkish rule from the 17th century until World War I, it was then under British mandate until 1932. Iraq achieved independence as a monarchy, but a violent revolution brought the establishment of a socialist republic in 1958.

Land and Resources

The topography of Iraq has four main areas: lower Iraq, upper Iraq, the northeast mountain region (part of KURDISTAN), and the western desert. Lower Iraq extends from the ridge between al-Ramadi and BAGHDAD, the capital, southeastward for about 565 km (350 mi) to the Persian Gulf and encompasses the lower course of the TIGRIS and EUPHRATES river systems. Near the gulf the rivers unite in the SHATT-AL-ARAB, but they are independent rivers throughout most of their courses, separated by a strip of land that at some points is more than 160 km (100 mi) in width. The flat plain of lower Iraq never exceeds 90 m (300 ft) in altitude. The rivers run behind low levees to prevent flooding. Their waters are distributed for irrigation through extensive canals.

Upper Iraq is 215 to 365 m (700 to 1,200 ft) high,

composed primarily of rolling plains with fertile soil. The chief cities there are MOSUL and Kirkuk. Northeast of Kirkuk Mount Halgurd, the highest point in the country, rises to 3,728 m (12,230 ft). The western desert constitutes about 35% of the total area of Iraq and extends from Kuwait along the Saudi Arabian border to Jordan and Syria. It is composed of heavily eroded rock of ancient origin. The soils of Iraq are heavy alluvial deposits in the Tigris-Euphrates Basin and very light soil elsewhere.

Climate. Aridity and summer heat characterize the climate. In the lowlands, rainfall, occurring only between November and April, totals about 150 mm (6 in), whereas upper Iraq receives about 380–635 mm (15–25 in). Summer in the plains is dry and excessively hot, with a persistent northwest wind (the shamal). The July mean temperature in Baghdad is about 34° C (93° F). The January average is 10° C (50° F), although temperatures of up to 27° C (81° F) have been recorded. In the uplands temperatures are more moderate, and winters are cold.

Resources. Petroleum is the country's only substantial mineral resource. Four projects on the Tigris and Euphrates provide irrigation water, flood control, and hydroelectricity.

People

Iraq has undergone successive waves of conquest and immigration that have determined its ethnic diversity, but ARABS and Arabized elements of other ethnic strains make up nearly 80% of its present population. The largest, most visible minority is the KURDS, who live in the north-

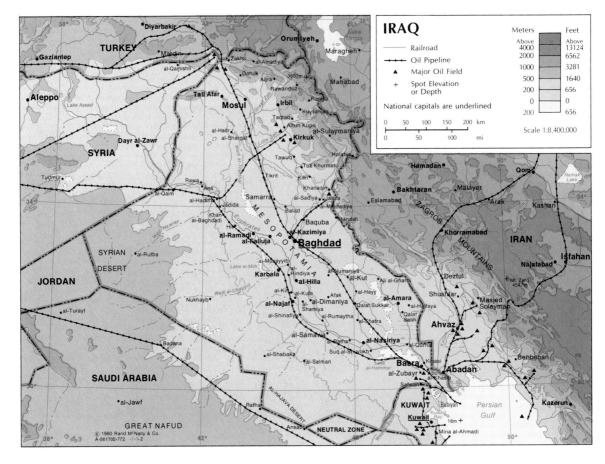

east, speak their own language, have a strong ethnic identity, and have demanded an autonomous Kurdish state. An important Iranian minority once lived within Iraq's borders, but almost all Iranians have left the country since the early 1970s.

Arabic is spoken almost universally, but Kurdish is commonly used in Kurdistan, and Persian is used along the Iranian border. The dominant religion is Islam, fairly evenly divided between the Sunnites and Shiites. Christians constitute about 3.5% of the population.

Vital statistics for Iraq lack reliability. Both emigration and immigration are low. The cities have grown rapidly since the 1950s as a result of rural-urban migration. The desert area is uninhabited except for Bedouin tribes.

A major expansion of educational facilities has taken place since 1958. Primary enrollment of children aged 6 to 11 reached 100% in 1978 but had fallen to 86% by 1985. Approximately 43% of children aged 12 to 17 attended secondary schools in 1986. Six universities have been established, all of them since 1957, and many Iraqis study abroad. The 1991 GULF WAR badly disrupted social services. Aerial bombardment destroyed water, electrical, and sewage systems, raising the threat of serious epidemic.

The traditional culture of Iraq developed from the broader Arab culture and is expressed in poetry and prose, dancing, and the design of rugs and artifacts. The Iraq Museum and the Museum of Arab antiquities in Baghdad house ancient relics. Ruins at Babylon were reconstructed in the 1980s.

Economic Activity

The economy of Iraq was almost exclusively agricultural until recent decades, when rising revenues from oil production reduced the importance of agriculture. During the IRAN-IRAQ WAR (1980–88), Iraqi oil shipments via the Persian Gulf were halted, although oil continued to be shipped by road and piped through Saudi Arabia and Turkey. The worldwide boycott imposed after the Aug. 2, 1990, Iraqi invasion of Kuwait, however, froze Iraqi assets abroad and instantly cut off Iraq's oil revenues (estimated at $10 billion per year). Later, allied bombing severely damaged more than two-thirds of the nation's oil export operations, including Iraqi links to the Saudi and Turkish pipelines. With a foreign debt of more than $70 billion from the Iran-Iraq war and demands that Iraq pay reparations for the damage done by the war, the money needed to rebuild the economy was unavailable.

Mining and Manufacturing. Petroleum is found in the north, northeast, and south; natural gas is also produced. Iraq's proven petroleum reserves in 1988 were estimated at 100 billion barrels, second only to those of Saudi Arabia. Before August 1990, production averaged 830 million barrels per year. The developer of the Iraqi oil industry was the British-dominated Iraq Petroleum Company. In 1972, Iraq's petroleum resources were nationalized. Iraq is a charter member of the ORGANIZATION OF PETROLEUM EXPORTING COUNTRIES (OPEC).

The 1990 boycott led to shortages of spare parts for Iraq's diversified industries, including petrochemicals, textiles, steel, sugar, and cement, which were later damaged by bombing.

Agriculture. The 1958 revolution led to the forced breakup of large estates. In 1990, in an effort to increase food production, land previously allocated to state and collective farms was opened to private farmers at nominal rents; food grain production was increased at the expense of livestock. Iraq is the world's leading date producer; wheat, barley, beans, and rice are major crops. Agriculture in the south relies on irrigation, and soil salinization is a severe problem.

Government

The overthrow of the monarchy in 1958 was followed by a succession of revolutionary socialist regimes that ruled the country under a provisional constitution. From the mid-1960s the Arab Socialist BAATH PARTY controlled the nation, forming a coalition known as the National Progressive Front in 1973. From 1979, Gen. Saddam HUSSEIN served as president, chairman of the small ruling junta (the Revolutionary Command Council, or RCC), commander of the armed forces, and secretary-general of the Baath party. The Kurdish area was granted limited autonomy in 1970. In 1980 the first elections for a new national assembly were held; a committee began preparing a new constitution in 1989. In March 1991, Hussein appointed a Shiite as prime minister and pledged to carry out earlier promises of reforms, including the creation of a multiparty system.

History

Iraq was one of the most ancient centers of urban civilization and settled cultivation. SUMER, AKKAD, ASSYRIA, and BABYLONIA all developed major civilizations in ancient Mesopotamia. In the early centuries AD, the area was part of various Persian empires. After the Arab conquest in the 7th century, Baghdad (founded in 762) became the seat of the CALIPHATE of the ABBASIDS. With the Mongol conquest by Hulagu in 1258, the country was virtually ruined.

In the 16th and 17th centuries control over Iraq was contested by the Ottoman and Persian empires. From 1638, however, Iraq was part of the Ottoman Empire, although often with some degree of autonomy. During World War I a British force occupied Iraq, and in 1920 it became a British mandate of the League of Nations, with FAISAL I of the Hashemite family as king. Following civil disturbances in the 1920s, the mandate was terminated in 1932, but the British maintained strong influence over Iraq until 1958.

Iraqi politics was dominated during the 1940s and '50s by the pro-Western leader Nuri es-Said, who initiated the modernization of Iraq. The country joined the CENTRAL TREATY ORGANIZATION in 1955, the only Arab state to do so. Radical nationalist forces created a ferment, however, that led to a military coup under Gen. Abdul Karim Kassem on July 14, 1958. A pro-Communist republic was proclaimed, and the royal family, along with Nuri es-Said, was murdered.

Since 1958 the history of Iraq has been marked by both extremism and violence. The Kassem regime collapsed in 1963. The government of Col. Abdul Salam

Baghdad, the capital and largest city of Iraq, is located along the flood plain of the Tigris River in the central portion of the country. Baghdad's importance as a center of Islamic culture dates from the 8th century.

Aref, which succeeded it, was replaced by that of the Baathist Ahmad Hassan al-Bakr in a 1968 coup. Saddam Hussein succeeded al-Bakr in 1979.

Consistently anti-Israel, Iraq participated in the Arab-Israeli War of 1973. Israel bombed (1981) a French-supplied Iraqi nuclear reactor because the Israelis feared it would be used to produce atomic weapons. Iraq signed a treaty of alliance with the USSR in 1972 and resumed diplomatic relations with the United States in 1984. Long-standing border and ideological differences between Iran and Iraq escalated into war in 1980, when Iraq invaded Iran. Although vastly outnumbered on the ground, Iraq was backed by most other Arab states and used its air superiority to attack Iranian economic targets and involve other nations in the conflict. After the two countries accepted a United Nations–mediated ceasefire in August, 1988, Iraq allegedly used chemical weapons to crush a Kurdish rebellion in the north.

In July 1990, Hussein accused Kuwait and the United Arab Emirates of exceeding their OPEC oil export quotas, thereby holding world oil prices down and reducing Iraqi revenues. He also charged that Kuwait had stolen Iraqi oil from the huge Rumelia oil field on the disputed border between the two countries and demanded that Kuwait and the other Arab Gulf states write off about $30 billion in loans they had granted Iraq during the Iran-Iraq war, which he contended he had fought for all Arabs. On August 2, when Hussein's demands were not met, Iraqi troops invaded and occupied Kuwait, formally annexing it on August 28.

International condemnation of this aggression was nearly universal. The United States immediately sent troops to Saudi Arabia; Britain, France, Egypt, Syria, and a number of other allied countries followed suit, and the hastily formed allied coalition set up a UN-authorized blockade aimed at forcing the Iraqis out of Kuwait. Meanwhile, Iraq tried to ease its isolation and neutralize a potentially vulnerable situation along its eastern flank by making peace concessions to Iran and restoring ties with its neighbor (September 1990). In December, as economic and diplomatic pressures increased, Hussein released Western hostages he had threatened to use as human shields against allied attacks, but he refused to withdraw from Kuwait by the UN deadline of Jan. 15, 1991.

On January 16 the GULF WAR began. For several weeks allied planes subjected Iraqi targets in Kuwait and Iraq itself to an intense aerial bombardment. Iraq launched missile attacks on Tel Aviv and other Israeli cities in an attempt to win support from other Arab nations by drawing Israel into the conflict, but Israel did not respond, and Hussein remained isolated, backed only by the PALESTINE LIBERATION ORGANIZATION. On February 23, U.S.-led troops moved against Iraqi positions on the ground. Iraq was swiftly and decisively defeated, agreeing to accept allied peace terms on February 27–28. After the war, revolts against Saddam Hussein's government among the Kurds in the north and disaffected Shiites south of Baghdad were crushed by the army, which remained loyal to its leader. An international relief effort was mounted to aid Kurdish refugees fleeing from Iraqi forces.

Iredell, James [ire'-dul]   James Iredell, b. England, Oct. 5, 1751, d. Oct. 20, 1799, was an American jurist and an associate justice of the U.S. Supreme Court. He played a leading role in North Carolina's ratification (1788) of the federal Constitution. In 1790, President George Washington appointed Iredell to the newly established U.S. Supreme Court, on which he served until his death.

Ireland   The Republic of Ireland (Eire) covers almost 85% of the island bearing its name. DUBLIN is its capital. The six northeastern counties form NORTHERN IRELAND, which is part of the United Kingdom. This partition dates from 1920–22, before which the whole island was under British rule. Ireland is separated from Great Britain by the IRISH SEA and otherwise surrounded by the Atlantic Ocean.

The Republic of Ireland is primarily suited to agricultural activities, although industry is increasing in importance. Recently discovered deposits of lead, silver, zinc, and copper are mined. The pleasant scenery, unspoiled countryside, and unhurried way of life attract many vacationers.

Land and Resources

Most of the country is a lowland less than 150 m (500 ft) above sea level and underlain by limestone rocks of Carboniferous age. The surface is covered by glacial drift, which has been shaped into distinctive landforms, as in long gravel ridges (eskers) of the midlands and hundreds of small hills (drumlins).

The central lowland is surrounded by a discontinuous rim of mountains. The oldest of these, in the north and west of the country, are the remnants of a mountain range that once was a chain extending from Ireland through Scotland to Scandinavia. Quartzite rocks give rise to rugged mountain scenery—Errigal (752 m/2,466 ft) in DONEGAL, Croagh Patrick (765 m/2,510 ft) in MAYO, and the Twelve Bens or Pins in County GALWAY.

In the south of Ireland a series of parallel ridges of Devonian sandstone are a continuation of the Hercynian structures of central Europe and Brittany. The ridges rise in elevation westward, culminating at Carrantuohill, the highest mountain in the country (1,041 m/3,413 ft). The Lakes of Killarney, famous for their scenic beauty, are situated in that area. A geologically recent depression of the land allowed the sea to enter the lower reaches of the river valleys, forming a deeply indented coastline with many natural harbors.

In the southeast of Ireland, granites of Devonian age form rounded uplands stretching for 129 km (80 mi) in a northeasterly direction through Counties WEXFORD and WICKLOW to the south shore of Dublin Bay. The eastern slopes of these uplands are penetrated by the deep, glacially modified valleys of Glendalough and Glenmalure.

Soils. Most Irish soils have been formed from glacial drift, and because limestone is the most common bedrock, some of them are slightly alkaline. The lowland soils are chiefly fertile brown and gray brown podzolics, but

REPUBLIC OF IRELAND

Land: Area: 70,284 km² (27,137 mi²). Capital and largest city: Dublin (1986 pop., 502,749).

People: Population (1990 est.): 3,500,000. Density: 50 persons per km² (129 per mi²). Distribution (1990): 56% urban, 44% rural. Official languages: Irish, English. Major religion: Roman Catholicism.

Government: Type: republic. Legislature: Oireachtas (National Parliament). Political subdivisions: 26 counties.

Economy: GNP (1988): $30.6 billion; $8,640 per capita. Labor distribution (1987): agriculture—12.7%; mining—0.7%; manufacturing—17.9%; construction—7.4%; public utilities—1.1%; transportation and communications—5.4%; trade—16.1%; services—22.6%; finance—6.4%; other—9.6%. Foreign trade (1989): imports—$17.4 billion; exports—$20.7 billion. Currency: 1 Irish pound = 100 new pence.

Education and Health: Literacy (1990): 99% of adult population. Universities (1989): 2. Hospital beds (1986): 27,634. Physicians (1988): 5,590. Life expectancy (1990): women—78; men—72. Infant mortality (1990): 6 per 1,000 live births.

some true podzols occur on the hills. Gleyed soils are common in the north central lowland. Raised bogs, which cover many thousands of hectares in the midlands, are an important source of peat fuel. Peat also blankets the higher hills and supports a heathland vegetation, which provides rough grazing for sheep.

Climate. All of Ireland has a cool maritime climate. July temperatures vary from 16° C (61° F) in the south to 14° C (57° F) in the north, while winters are relatively mild, with January temperatures ranging from 7° C (44° F) in Valentia to 4° C (40° F) in the northeast. Heaviest rainfalls of 1,524 to 2,540 mm (60 to 100 in) occur where the western winds first meet the western mountains. About 80% of the country has an annual rainfall of between 762 and 1,270 mm (30 and 50 in). The eastern coastal strip is relatively dry, with Dublin recording only 711 mm (28 in) annually. The annual rainfall distribution shows a minimum in late spring, a relatively dry fall, and heaviest rainfall occurring in August and December.

Drainage. Ireland has numerous rivers and lakes. Much of the central lowland is drained by the River SHANNON, which is 370 km (230 mi) long and navigable for most of its length. It expands into a number of lakes, notably Loughs Allen, Ree, and Derg. A few miles from LIMERICK, the Shannon's rapid fall to sea level is used to generate electricity. In the south of Ireland, rivers such as the Blackwater, Lee, and Bandon have unusual stream patterns in that their courses make right-angled bends, cutting southward through sandstone ridges to form narrow, steep-sided valleys.

Vegetation and Animal Life. Remnants of oak woodland, which once covered much of the country, survive only in KILLARNEY and in a few isolated mountain valleys. The peat bogs support heather, moss, and fern. Arctic-Alpine flora such as gentian are found near sea level at County CLARE, and a subtropical Mediterranean type of vegetation survives in the southwest because of the area's mild winters. Fauna is limited. The only reptile is a small lizard; larger mammals include deer, the pine marten, fox, badger, squirrel, and hare. Seabirds are numerous on the coastal fringes.

Resources. Agricultural land, Ireland's main resource, covers more than 70% of the country's surface. With less than 5% under tree cover, it is one of Europe's least forested countries.

The main mineral resources are the base metals lead, silver, and zinc. Coal is scarce and of poor quality, but peat is extensively used for fuel. Workable deposits of gypsum, dolomite, and barites have been found. Limestone, granite, sand, clay, and gravel are plentiful, and natural gas exists in modest quantities off the southern coast.

People

For more than 5,000 years successive waves of settlers arrived from the island of Great Britain or from the Continent. The Celtic element (see CELTS) remains dominant, but the east has been particularly influenced by the Anglo-Normans, who invaded Ireland in 1170. The first official language is Irish, but English is recognized as the

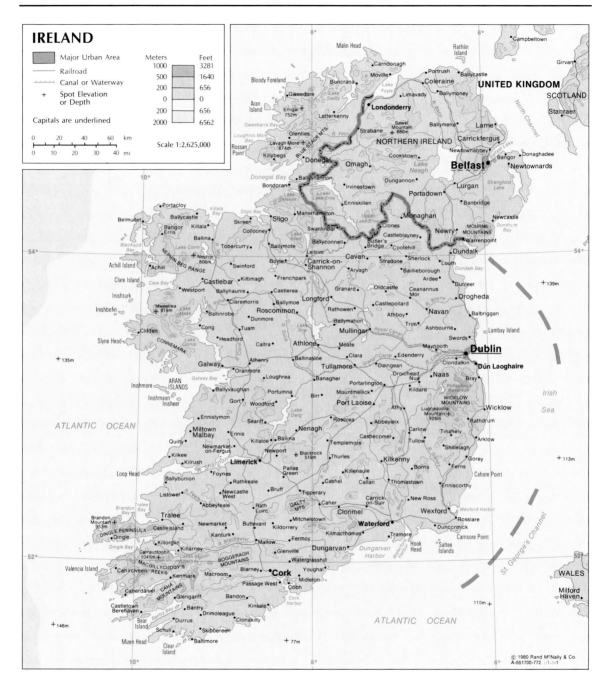

IRELAND

		Meters	Feet
	Major Urban Area	1000	3281
	Railroad	500	1640
	Canal or Waterway	200	656
+	Spot Elevation or Depth	0	0
		200	656
	Capitals are underlined	2000	6562

0   20   40   60 km
0   10   20   30   40 mi

Scale 1:2,625,000

© 1980 Rand McNally & Co.
A-551700-772 .-1-1-1

second official language (see CELTIC LANGUAGES). About 27% of the population know both Irish and English. In limited areas in the west Irish remains the first language of the people.

Religion. Freedom of conscience and free practice and profession of religion are guaranteed to every citizen under the constitution. Ninety-four percent of the people are Roman Catholics. The non–Roman Catholic population is composed largely of Anglicans, with a few Presbyterians and Methodists.

Demography. The population of Ireland, which expanded rapidly during the 18th and early 19th centuries, reached 8.1 million in 1841. The famine years, beginning in 1845, brought a sudden reversal of the population trend due to deaths and emigration. Migration to North America and Great Britain continued over the next hundred years; by 1930 the population numbered little more than half the 1845 figure. Since 1961 the population has been steadily increasing.

A distinctive feature of Ireland's rural population today is the low proportion to the total population of people in the 15-to-45-year age group. This low level results from the departure of working-age persons to seek employment in the cities or overseas. A considerable proportion of the population still lives in communities of fewer than 1,500 inhabitants. Dublin, together with its seaport of DÚN LAOGHAIRE, has more than one-fifth of the country's total population. Second in importance is the city of CORK, followed by Limerick, GALWAY, and WATERFORD, all port cities. The largest inland town is KILKENNY. The most urbanized areas of the country are the south and east; the population is increasing in these areas while densities elsewhere are declining. Migration has led to serious rural depopulation in the extreme west and in the LEITRIM and ROSCOMMON areas near Lough Allen.

Education. Elementary education is compulsory and free between the ages of 6 and 15 in schools financed by the state but managed by the religious denominations. Secondary education is provided by privately owned, state-subsidized schools and by state-owned comprehensive and vocational schools. On the next level there are five teacher-training colleges, nine regional technical colleges, a National Institute for Higher Education in Limerick, and two universities. The National University, founded in 1909, has constituent colleges in Dublin, Cork, Galway, and Maynooth. The latter is also a pontifical college. The University of Dublin was founded in 1592.

Health. Ireland has a comprehensive health service. Persons in the lower income groups and their dependents are entitled to general medical care, hospitalization, and specialized treatment at government expense. Ireland's crude birthrate ranks with that of Iceland as one of the two highest in Western Europe.

The Arts. A considerable body of literature written in the Irish language exists, dating from the 6th century; much of it is based on a rich oral tradition preserving the sagas of ancient Ireland. Gaelic literature continued to be common until the 17th century, when the use of English became more widespread. An Anglo-Irish writing style began with Jonathan SWIFT; in succeeding centuries many Irish writers and dramatists have become noteworthy, including Oliver GOLDSMITH, Richard Brinsley SHERIDAN, Oscar WILDE, James JOYCE, George Bernard SHAW, and Samuel BECKETT. The development of the ABBEY THEATRE as the National Theatre of Ireland is associated with the work of Lady GREGORY, William Butler YEATS, Sean O'CASEY, John Millington SYNGE, James STEPHENS, and many others who, even though they wrote in English, drew their inspiration from Gaelic traditions and Irish rural life. For additional information, see IRISH LITERATURE and IRISH LITERARY RENAISSANCE.

Ireland is noted for its early Christian art in both metalwork and illuminated manuscripts. An example of the former is the Ardagh Chalice and, of the latter, the BOOK OF KELLS; both date from the 8th century (see CELTIC ART). The most noteworthy architectural structures of the country are the round towers and early Celtic churches built between 700 and 1150. A few of the great castles constructed by the Anglo-Norman invaders dating from 1170 are still intact.

Economic Activity

Until recently Ireland was a predominantly agricultural country. Today farming is still important, but it employs only a minority of the work force. Most of the agricultural land is under pasture or hay. Dairying, usually by cooperatives, predominates in the south and in the north midlands; beef cattle are raised on the small farms in the

The neoclassical dome of the Four Courts (center, partially obscured), *headquarters of Ireland's judiciary, is one of the major architectural landmarks crowding the River Liffey in Dublin. Dublin is Ireland's capital, largest city, and cultural center.*

The limestone Cliffs of Moher border the Atlantic Ocean at the western extreme of County Clare. The area is sparsely populated because of its rugged terrain and poor access to the sea.

west and fattened on the larger farms of the east. Sheep graze on the uplands. The main crops are barley for feeding and for malting, oats, wheat, potatoes, and sugar beets.

Fishing employs a significant portion of the population. The chief fish caught are cod, whiting, plaice, sole, haddock, herring, and mackerel. Lobsters, prawns, periwinkles, and other shellfish abound along the rocky coasts.

In the 1930s the new state encouraged local industry, placing tariffs on imported goods so small-scale industries could develop to serve local needs. By 1950 this market had been saturated, and a decline in development necessitated a major change in government policy. Foreign-owned firms, especially those with export potential, were encouraged to locate in the country.

In 1959 a special industrial estate was established at Shannon, close to the international airport, where goods are imported and exported without customs restrictions. Dozens of factories, employing thousands of workers, are now located there. A government agency, the Industrial Development Authority (IDA), exists to promote the manufacturing sector and attract foreign investment. Ireland's dependence on foreign oil has decreased in recent years, largely because of the growth of domestic natural-gas production.

Ireland maintains an economy of both public and private enterprises. The electric-power network, along with the chemical, steel, and sugar industries, are state controlled. Unemployment is a serious problem—it was 17.7% in 1989; inflation, on the other hand, was reduced from 20% in 1981 to about 4% in 1989.

Ireland's public roads form a dense network throughout the country. Railroads radiate from Dublin and provide passenger and freight facilities to all the major towns; the roads, however, now carry a much greater volume of traffic. Dublin's seaport handles about two-thirds of the seaborne trade. Car ferries ply between British and Irish ports, and a direct ferry travels from Rosslare to Le Havre, France. International airports are located at Dublin, Cork, and Shannon. Public transportation is state owned, including Aer Lingus, the national airline.

A government corporation controls and operates the country's radio and television service. Irish-language radio stations broadcast from Kerry, Galway, and Donegal counties.

The United Kingdom is Ireland's chief trading partner, accounting for nearly 50% of external trade. Other major trade partners are the United States and Germany. More than one-third of all exports are agricultural products; machinery and woolen textiles are also exported. Imports are dominated by manufactured goods, petroleum, and coal. Tourism has become an important source of foreign currency.

Government

The modern independent state of Ireland dates from 1921 when, after a long and bitter struggle, the Irish Free State (Saorstat Éireann) was created. A new constitution was adopted on Dec. 29, 1937, making Ireland a member of the Commonwealth. The Free State was declared a republic and separated from the Commonwealth in 1949. The Republic of Ireland is a parliamentary democracy. Its constitution provides for a nonexecutive president elected by direct vote for a 7-year term. In December 1990, Mary Robinson became the first woman to be elected to the Irish presidency. The national parliament, the Oireachtas, consists of two houses, Dáil Éireann and Seanad Éireann. Dáil Éireann's 148 members are elected through a system of proportional representation. The voting age is 18.

The Seanad, or upper house, has 60 members, 11 of whom are nominated by the taoiseach, or prime minister. The remaining 49 are elected, 6 by the universities and 43 from panels of candidates selected on a vocational basis. The government is headed by the taoiseach, who is appointed by the president on the nomination of the Dáil Éireann. The taoiseach, in turn, nominates from 7 to 15 Dáil members to form his cabinet. The life of the Dáil is 5 years.

Ireland had 4 ancient provinces: CONNACHT, LEINSTER, MUNSTER, and ULSTER. Today the Republic of Ireland is divided politically into 27 county councils (TIPPERARY is divided for administrative purposes), 4 county borough corporations, 7 borough corporations, 49 urban district councils, and 28 town commissions. Local officials are elected for 5-year terms.

The two major political parties, both conservative in outlook, are FIANNA FÁIL, founded by Eamon DE VALERA in 1926, and FINE GAEL, formally established in 1933. Fianna Fáil, led in recent years by John LYNCH and Charles J. HAUGHEY, has dominated the government for much of the period since its foundation. Garret FITZGERALD of Fine Gael was premier from June 1981 to March 1982 and from December 1982 until February 1987, when he was replaced by Haughey.

Since joining the European Community (EC) in 1973, Ireland has benefited considerably from EC financial aid. The status of Northern Ireland, which the Irish have always considered part of their national territory, has remained an irritant in relations with Britain, as have the terrorist activities of the IRISH REPUBLICAN ARMY in the North. Tension was eased somewhat in 1985 by an agreement between the two countries in which the Irish government moderated its claims to Northern Ireland and in return was given a consultative voice in the affairs of the troubled province.

Ireland, history of

The first human settlements in Ireland, an island lying on the western fringe of Europe, were made relatively late in European prehistory, about 6000 BC.

Early Gaelic Ireland

Sometime between about 600 and 150 BC, Celtic peoples from western Europe, who came to be known as Gaels, invaded Ireland. The basic units of Gaelic society were the *tuatha*, or petty kingdoms, of which perhaps 150 existed in Ireland. The *tuatha* shared a common language, Gaelic (see CELTIC LANGUAGES), and a class of men called *brehons*, who were learned in customary law and helped to preserve throughout Ireland a remarkably uniform but archaic social system. The Romans never tried to conquer Ireland.

Medieval Ireland

One consequence of Ireland's isolation was the development of a distinctive Celtic type of Christianity. Saint PATRICK introduced mainstream Latin Christianity into the country in the 5th century AD, but the system of bishops with territorial dioceses did not take root; instead, the autonomous monastery became the basic unit of Celtic Christianity. During the 6th and 7th centuries the Irish monasteries sent out such missionaries as Saints COLUMBA and COLUMBAN to the rest of Europe. What was for most of Europe the Dark Ages was for Ireland the golden age. Religious art flourished alongside secular, even pagan, artistic achievements.

The Viking Invasions. In the late 8th century, VIKINGS began to raid Ireland. Other parts of Europe at about this time were responding to such pressures by developing the system of FEUDALISM, but the Gaelic society lacked the heritage of Roman law that provided the framework for feudal institutions elsewhere. Moreover, the elaborate kinship arrangements by which both property-holding and succession-to-leadership roles were regulated by *brehon* law may have impeded the exchange of land for military service, which is the fundamental bargain underlying the feudal system.

In 1014, King BRIAN BORU decisively defeated the Vikings at the Battle of Clontarf. Brian's tenure (1002–14) of the honorific title "high king of Ireland" is sometimes misunderstood as the seed time of a national monarchy. Actually, the high king's power throughout much of Ireland was insubstantial. Meanwhile, the Vikings had left their mark on the country by founding Ireland's first cities, including DUBLIN, LIMERICK, and WATERFORD.

The Anglo-Norman Conquest. In the late 12th century Ireland faced the challenge from the highly effective feudal monarchy founded in England by WILLIAM I. William's descendant HENRY II took advantage of an earlier letter from Pope ADRIAN IV authorizing Henry to make himself overlord of Ireland in order to bring the Irish church more into line with Roman standards. Several Anglo-Norman barons had already seized large parts of Ireland when Henry went to Ireland in 1171 with an army to receive the formal submission of those barons and of most of the Irish kings.

The Anglo-Norman barons established a feudal system like that which their ancestors had brought from Normandy to England, but the English monarchy, distracted by continental affairs, did not effectively subordinate to royal authority even the Anglo-Norman colony. In the late Middle Ages Ireland thus consisted of three concentric regions: (1) Dublin and its immediate hinterland (eventually called the PALE), the only area in which the English government really exercised authority; (2) a broad arc of territories beyond the Pale, which were the quasi-independent fiefs of the great Anglo-Norman lords; and (3) a further arc of territories along the western coast of Ireland that retained Gaelic customs and remained completely outside English rule.

The English colony in Ireland reached its greatest extent in the early 14th century, after which Gaelic society enjoyed considerable resurgence. As the Anglo-Normans intermarried with the Gaelic population and adopted the Gaelic language and customs, they gradually became "more Irish than the Irish." The Statutes of Kilkenny (1366) were an unsuccessful attempt to arrest this process.

The Anglo-Norman conquest brought the Irish church more into line with Roman standards. English legal practices and civil administration were introduced, and an Irish parliament modeled on the English one was created in the late 13th century. England's HENRY VII forced an Irish parliament of 1494–95 to adopt Poynings's Law, which gave the English Privy Council a veto over legislation proposed in future Irish parliaments.

ENGLISH PLANTATION (SETTLEMENT) OF IRELAND

Planted before the reign of Elizabeth

Planted during the reign of Elizabeth I, 1558-1603

Planted during the reign of James I, 1603-25

The plantations of Ireland, begun under Queen Mary I in the central plain and vigorously conducted under Elizabeth I in Munster (1584) and James I in Ulster (1608), saw the eviction and execution of thousands of native Irish.

In the 16th century the English monarchs HENRY VIII, MARY I, and ELIZABETH I tried to reconquer Ireland by military expeditions and by the establishment (or plantation) of colonies of English settlers. The English REFORMATION, however, complicated the reconquest. There was virtually no indigenous sympathy with the Protestant reformers among either the Gaelic Irish or the Anglo-Irish, and thus although the Church of Ireland was legally transformed into a Protestant church, it was rejected by the overwhelming majority of the population.

Modern Ireland

The most determined resistance to reconquest came from the Gaelic chieftains of Ulster (the northeastern quarter of the island), led by Hugh O'Neill, 2d earl of TYRONE, at the end of Elizabeth's reign. In suppressing their rebellion between 1595 and 1603, English forces devastated the Ulster countryside. Once these chieftains had submitted, however, King JAMES I of England was willing to let them live on their ancestral lands as English-style nobles, but not as petty kings within the old Gaelic social system. Dissatisfied with their new roles, the chieftains took ship to the Continent in 1607. This "flight of the earls" gave the English crown a pretext to confiscate their vast lands and sponsor scattered settlements of British Protestants throughout west and central Ulster (the Ulster Plantation). The crown's actions also encouraged large unsponsored migration of Presbyterian Scots to Ulster. The rebellion of the Gaelic Irish in Ulster against the British settlers in 1641 triggered the ENGLISH CIVIL WAR, which put an end to King CHARLES I's attempt to create an absolutist state (represented in Ireland by the policies of his lord deputy, Thomas Wentworth, 1st earl of STRAFFORD). When the Puritan party defeated Charles, their leader, Oliver CROMWELL, quickly imposed (1649–50) English authority on Ireland. Cromwell repaid his soldiers and investors in the war effort with land confiscated largely from the Anglo-Irish Catholics of the Irish midlands.

The Protestant Ascendancy. Hoping to recover their lands and political dominance in Ireland, Catholics took the side of the Catholic king JAMES II in England's GLORIOUS REVOLUTION of 1688 and thus shared in his defeat by WILLIAM III at the Battle of the Boyne in 1690. The Irish Protestant elite consolidated its victory by enacting a number of Penal Laws designed to exclude the Catholics from property and power. In 1782 a "Patriot" party led by Henry Grattan and backed by an army of Protestant volunteers persuaded the British government to amend Poynings's Law to give the Irish Parliament legislative independence, including the right to establish Ireland's own tariff policy.

The Revolutionary Era. The reforms of 1782 did not extend far enough in a democratic direction to satisfy such intellectuals as Wolfe TONE and many of the Presbyterian merchants and farmers of the north, who were prompted by the French Revolution to form the Society of UNITED IRISHMEN. A rebellion in 1798 was quickly put down, but it convinced the British government to end Ireland's sep-

The Battle of the Boyne (1690), portrayed by Jan Wyck, resulted in decisive victory for William III over Irish and French forces backing the deposed King James II. (National Museum of Ireland, Dublin.)

arate political institutions. The Act of Union (1800) provided for a single Parliament for the British Isles. Catholics, who had been granted the right to vote in 1793, were encouraged to believe that the united Parliament would grant them the right to hold parliamentary seats. Not until 1829, however, when faced by a menacing agitation for CATHOLIC EMANCIPATION led by Daniel O'CONNELL, did Parliament grant this right.

The Growth of Irish Nationalism. In the 1830s, when O'Connell started a new movement to repeal the Act of Union, he received practically no support from those northern Presbyterians whose fathers had been United Irishmen. Its growing prosperity as an outpost of industrializing Britain made the city of BELFAST increasingly committed to the legislative union with Britain. Meanwhile, those parts of Ireland where most Catholics lived lagged badly behind Britain and northeast Ulster in economic development. In the 1840s several successive failures of the potato crop produced a devastating famine. Between 1841 and 1851, Ireland's population fell from 8.2 million to 6.6 million through starvation, disease, and emigration—especially to the United States.

The long-term effect of the famine was to strengthen Irish nationalism. In rural Ireland the generation that came of age in the 1860s experienced modestly rising prosperity and a rapidly increasing awareness of the greater affluence enjoyed by British (and Ulster Protestant) beneficiaries of industrialization. A vigorous popular demand for national self-government was enthusiastically supported by the Irish emigrant community in the United States, some members of which had formed secret revolutionary society of FENIANS.

The Home-Rule Movement. The agricultural depression of the late 1870s and the resulting discontent was harnessed to emerging nationalist aspirations by Charles Stewart PARNELL. Parnell's Irish nationalist party, demanding home rule—a separate Irish parliament within the Union—and land reform, represented a solid bloc of votes. Under Parnell's successor, John REDMOND, the Irish party finally forced the enactment of a HOME RULE BILL—but it also evoked the Ulster Covenant, by which northern Protestants vowed to resist home rule by force. Enacted in 1914, home rule was suspended until the end of World War I, when it was understood that Ulster would receive some special treatment.

From the 1890s nationalism found expression in an IRISH LITERARY RENAISSANCE. The poet William Butler YEATS, the playwrights Sean O'CASEY and John Millington SYNGE, and others turned their attention to uniquely Irish subjects. This cultural revival also produced SINN FEIN, a political movement founded by Arthur GRIFFITH.

The Division of Ireland. Frustration arising from the postponement of home rule led to the 1916 EASTER RISING in Dublin. At the end of World War I, Sinn Fein candidates won all but six of the Catholic seats away from the more moderate Irish party and set themselves up as a revolutionary parliament, Dáil Éireann, in Dublin. While guerrilla warfare by the IRISH REPUBLICAN ARMY (IRA) and reprisals by crown forces were under way, the British government produced the 1920 Government of Ireland Act,
setting up separate parliaments for Northern Ireland and Southern Ireland.

Dáil Éireann refused to accept the new legislation, and in 1921 its representatives negotiated a treaty making the Irish Free State a self-governing dominion within the British COMMONWEALTH OF NATIONS and allowing the Northern Ireland Parliament to take the six northern counties out of the dominion. A civil war then broke out between protreaty and antitreaty factions, led respectively by Michael COLLINS and Eamon DE VALERA.

The Irish Free State; Eire; The Republic of Ireland

The three different names of the southern 26 of Ireland's 32 counties reflect the stages by which the goals of the defeated antitreaty side were eventually attained.

The Irish Free State. Under the 1922 constitution framed by the protreaty side, the first prime minister was William T. Cosgrave (1880–1965; see COSGRAVE family). De Valera's republican party first refused to sit in the Dáil because of the required oath of allegiance to the British crown, but in 1927, de Valera took the oath. After the 1932 election his FIANNA FÁIL party formed a government, and as prime minister until 1948, and again in 1951–54 and 1957–59, he consolidated his party's dominance over Cosgrave's party, FINE GAEL.

Eire. In 1937 a new constitution drafted by de Valera was adopted. The new state, Eire, a republic in all but name, remained formally within the British Commonwealth. During World War II de Valera followed a policy of neutrality.

The Republic of Ireland. In 1948, John A. Costello (1891–1976), a Fine Gael leader who succeeded de Valera as prime minister in a coalition government, introduced legislation by which the South became a republic outside the Commonwealth. In the 1950s the republic began to turn away from constitutional struggles and toward a greater concern with economic development. Under Fianna Fáil prime minister Sean Lemass (1959–66), the republic entered into a free-trade agreement with

Irish tenants evicted from their lands during the great famine of 1845 to 1849 crowd about the work house.

British soldiers and civilians under fire from the Irish Republican Army take cover in Belfast, Northern Ireland. The antagonism between Ulster's Catholic minority and Protestant majority erupted in violence in 1969, continuing into the 1990s.

Britain. His successor, John LYNCH, led (1973) the country into the EUROPEAN COMMUNITY. Lynch was displaced by Fine Gael's Liam Cosgrave in 1973. Fianna Fáil returned to power from 1977 to 1981, led first by Lynch and, from 1979, by Charles J. HAUGHEY. Fine Gael leader Garret FITZGERALD led a coalition government from 1982 to 1987, when Haughey again took over. After losses in the election of 1989, he formed a coalition with the Progressive Democrats.

Northern Ireland

Whereas the southern Irish state was born out of a positive nationalist demand, NORTHERN IRELAND arose out of a negative defensive reaction on the part of a people who never quite became nationalists of any sort. This difference helps in understanding why Northern Ireland failed, whereas the South of Ireland succeeded, at the enterprise of state building. Ulster Protestants assumed that conflict was inevitable and that constant vigilance was required on the part of the ORANGEMEN and the "Special Constabulary" into which their paramilitary force of 1912–14 had been transformed. This assumption dissuaded the Unionist governments elected by the Protestant majority from 1921 to the 1970s from even trying to win the allegiance of the Catholics. Members of that minority, however, were convinced by nationalist ideology that sooner or later Irish unity would be attained; they refused to face the fact that partition was a reality that would not go away. Thus in the North the assumptions of both Catholics and Protestants tended to inhibit reconciliation.

Several factors more conducive to rapprochement nevertheless appeared after World War II. The decline of Northern Ireland's traditional industries turned the government's attention to industrial development. Educated Protestants—notably Terence O'Neill (b. 1914), who served as prime minister (1963–69)—realized that better relations with the republic and with the North's Catholic minority were important to potential investors.

The postwar growth of the British welfare state gave many northern Catholics a practical reason for accepting the British connection. Unfortunately for O'Neill, such acceptance was expressed not so much in votes for him as in demonstrations for "British rights" led by Bernadette Devlin (b. 1947) and others beginning in 1968. In turning their attention from "Irish unity" to "British rights," northern Catholics were making an important, if hesitant, step toward rapprochement.

Some northern Protestants, however, represented by the Rev. Ian PAISLEY, were unwilling to accept the premise that Catholics might ever cease to be enemies. O'Neill's successor, James Chichester-Clark (b. 1923), requested British troops to keep the peace between civil rights demonstrators and extremist Protestant mobs. The state's inability to protect its Catholic citizens then led to the recrudescence of the IRA first as a community defense force and then as an assailant of the crumbling state. The decision of Brian FAULKNER, who became prime minister in 1971, to intern IRA suspects without trial led to increasing violence. The final dissolution of the Northern Irish state was recognized by the imposition of "direct rule" from London in March 1972.

An experimental "power-sharing" government of Protestants and Catholics was brought down by a Protestant general strike in 1974. In 1985, Britain and Ireland concluded an agreement that for the first time gave the Irish government an advisory role in Northern Irish affairs, but the agreement was denounced by extremists on both sides.

Ireland, Northern   see NORTHERN IRELAND

Irenaeus, Saint [y-ruh-nee'-uhs]   Saint Irenaeus, b. Anatolia, *c.*140–60, d. *c.*200, known as the father of Catholic theology, is the most important Christian theologian of the 2d century AD. His major efforts were spent in combating GNOSTICISM, and his great work, *Adversus haereses* (Against Heresies), was written for this purpose. He developed the doctrine of recapitulation (*anakephalaiosis*) of all things in Jesus Christ in opposition to the teachings of gnostics such as VALENTINUS and Basilides. A staunch defender of the apostolic tradition, Irenaeus was the first Father of the Church to systematize the religious and theological traditions of the church, so far as they existed. Feast day: June 28.

Irene, Byzantine Empress   Irene, b. *c.*752, d. Aug. 9, 803, was the first woman to rule (797–802) the Byzantine Empire. She married Leo IV in 768 and, on his death in 780, became regent and coemperor with her son Constantine VI. A strong opponent of ICONOCLASM, she convened the Seventh Ecumenical Council (787; see NICAEA, COUNCILS OF) which restored icon veneration. In 797, after having her son blinded, she began to rule. Military failures and rumors that she planned to marry Charlemagne aroused opposition, however, and Irene was deposed (802); Nicephorus I succeeded her as emperor (802–11). Irene is considered a saint by the Greek Orthodox church.

Irian Jaya [ir'-ee-uhn jah'-yuh]   Irian Jaya, formerly West New Guinea, West Irian, or Irian Barat, is an Indonesian province (1988 est. pop., 1,508,200) encompassing the western half of NEW GUINEA and bordering islands in the Arafura Sea, Ceram Sea, and Pacific Ocean. Its capital is Jayapura. The east-west trending Maoke Mountains, reaching 5,029 m (16,500 ft), divide the province. Most inhabitants are primitive Papuans, who subsist on fishing and hunting, and on taro, bananas, and sweet potatoes. The climate is tropical, with heavy rains during the monsoon. Formerly part of the Dutch East Indies, Irian Jaya was administered by Indonesia after 1963 under authority of the United Nations. After a 1969 plebiscite, Indonesia formally annexed the area. The Indonesian government is encouraging people from densely populated areas to resettle there.

iridium [ir-id'-ee-uhm]   Iridium is a dense, brittle, hard, silver white precious metal. It is a chemical element in Group VIII of the periodic table. Its symbol is Ir, its atomic number is 77, and its atomic weight is 192.22. The discovery of iridium was announced in 1804 by Smithson Tennant, who named the metal from the Latin *iris*, meaning "rainbow," because of its highly colored salts. Iridium is not found in nature in pure form but as osmiridium, an alloy with osmium and platinum. Many radioactive isotopes of iridium have been created in the laboratory. The pure metal cannot be dissolved by most acids, including aqua regia. Iridium is used in platinum alloys for jewelry and surgical pins; because of its resistance to corrosion, it is used in aircraft spark plugs.

iris   Irises comprise about 200 species of perennial herbs in the family Iridaceae, which also includes crocuses, freesias, and gladioli. Irises are mostly distributed in the northern temperate zone, the majority being native to Asia.

Structure. Irises are divided into two divisions, those arising from bulbs and those from horizontal underground rhizomes. They have grasslike or swordlike leaves, and large, showy flowers. There are three sepals, known as falls because they usually droop. The upper surface of each fall is usually bearded or crested. Three petals, called standards, alternate with the sepals and are upright. Three styles, which are petallike extensions of the ovary, arch over the base and midsection of each fall. Between each style and fall is a single stamen (male organ). The arrangement of the style and fall ensures cross-pollination of the flowers by insects. As an insect moves through the passageway between the style and fall, it deposits pollen from the previous flower on the stigma near the tip of the style. It then reaches the stamen, brushing against the flower's pollen and carrying it off to other flowers.

Varieties and Uses. Many horticulturally important species, hybrids, and cultivars are grown. The common garden irises of the United States are usually divided into

Irises are colorful, orchidlike flowers that have been cultivated into numerous hybrids, including (clockwise from left) the tall, bearded iris, which has prominent gold tufts at the base of its petals; the Siberian iris, which has upright petals and no beard; the Japanese iris, a beardless, fringed hybrid; and blue flag, a small, beardless, crested iris.

bearded, beardless, and crested irises, all of which are rhizomatous, and bulbous varieties. Bearded irises are by far the most popular. The Fleur-de-Lis, or German iris, *Iris germanica*, is the most commonly grown bearded iris. It is a source of orris root, used in perfumes and tooth powders. Although not as popular, many of the beardless irises are also cultivated. Bulbous irises are the florists' irises that are grown in greenhouses for cut flowers in winter. Very few crested irises are cultivated in the United States.

Irish art   see CELTIC ART

Irish Free State   see IRELAND, HISTORY OF

Irish Gaelic language   see CELTIC LANGUAGES

Irish Literary Renaissance   The Irish Literary Renaissance, also known as the Irish Revival and the Celtic Renaissance, was a literary movement sparked by a growing consciousness of a Celtic identity separate from English influence; it was bound up with Ireland's struggle for political independence. Beginning toward the end of the 19th century and continuing into the early decades of the 20th, it was inspired by the past glories of the Gaelic bards, Irish mythology and legends, and the simplicity of peasant folkways. Among its most gifted writers were the poets William Butler YEATS, George W. RUSSELL (pseudonym, Æ), and Padraic Colum; prose writers George MOORE and James Stephens; and dramatists John Millington SYNGE, Lady GREGORY, Lennox ROBINSON, and Sean O'CASEY.

William Butler Yeats, considered Ireland's greatest lyric poet, led the Irish Literary Renaissance with his efforts to reawaken Celtic traditions. (National Gallery, Dublin.)

The renaissance began when the Gaelic League was formed in 1893 to rekindle interest in Ireland's cultural past and particularly in Gaelic language and literature. Such works as *The Ballad Poetry of Ireland* (1845) by Charles Gavan Duffy (1816–1903), the seminal two-volume *History of Ireland* (1878 and 1880) by Standish James O'Grady (1846–1928), and *A Literary History of Ireland* (1892) by Douglas HYDE supplied a historical perspective for the movement. In 1888, Yeats collected and edited *Poems and Ballads of Young Ireland* and in 1891–92 was instrumental in founding the Irish Literary Society, which gave the movement a creative center. Yeats was the most prominent figure of the Irish Literary Renaissance. In mystical poems such as those in *The Wanderings of Oisin* (1889), in symbolic plays like *The Land of Heart's Desire* (1894), and in stirring essays he invoked the spirit of Irish myth and legend. In 1899, Yeats, Moore, Lady Gregory, and Edward Martyn (1859–1924) established the Irish Literary Theatre, a forerunner of the ABBEY THEATRE, where the plays of the movement were presented.

Irish literature   Irish literature encompasses literature in two languages: Irish, more exactly, Irish Gaelic, and English. The Early Irish Ulster cycle, which includes texts composed as early as the 7th century, comprises several heroic tales in verse and prose recounting the exploits of Cuchulain and the company of the Red Branch knights. The later Fenian cycle consists of heroic tales, mostly about Finn McCool and the *Fianna*—bands of warriors who lived outside the tribe, although they were recognized by the law. The language of the Ulster cycle is Old Irish; the Fenian cycle is in Middle and Modern Irish. Early Irish literature also comprises the writings of the Mythological cycle, about gods and goddesses of the Celtic pantheon; the works of the Historical cycles, which deal with recognizable figures; and tales described as voyages, such as "The Voyage of Mael Duin," adventures, such as "The Adventure of Bran, Son of Febal," or visions, such as "The Vision of Adamnan."

Modern Irish literature begins with Geoffrey Keating (*c*.1570–*c*.1650), whose *History of Ireland* may have been the last important work in Europe to circulate extensively in manuscript form as copies of it continued to be made until the 19th century. After Keating, Modern Irish literature has consisted primarily of poems. Two of the most important, written in the 18th century, are Michael Comyn's "Oisin in the Land of Youth," based on a Fenian theme, and Brian Merriman's "The Midnight Court," a masterpiece of contemporary satire dealing with a perennial problem in Ireland, the unwillingness of the men to take wives. By the mid-19th century, however, the Gaelic-speaking audience had been greatly reduced by centuries of English conquest and by the potato famine of the 1840s that decimated the rural population. A movement to revive the Irish language began at the end of the century, and today a small but distinctive body of literature continues to be written in Irish.

(Left) *James Joyce, one of the most influential writers of the 20th century, used such radical literary techniques as stream of consciousness in his explorations of Dublin.* (Center) *Sean O'Casey, a leading playwright of the Irish Literary Renaissance, achieved success at the Abbey Theatre with his tragicomic portraits of the Irish poor.* (Right) *Samuel Beckett, a member of Joyce's Paris circle, wrote of his Dublin experience before embracing the French language and existentialist thought.*

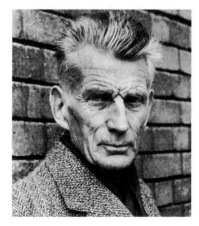

Although Irish authors such as the dramatists William CONGREVE and George FARQUHAR wrote within the mainstream of English literature during the 17th century, Irish literature in English—usually described as Anglo-Irish literature—begins in the 18th with Jonathan SWIFT, author of GULLIVER'S TRAVELS and *A Tale of a Tub*, and Oliver GOLDSMITH, author of the poem "The Deserted Village" and the novel *The Vicar of Wakefield*. In the 19th century, writing in English was limited largely to members of the ruling class, called the Ascendancy. These writers included novelists Maria EDGEWORTH and Charles Lever, poets Samuel Ferguson and William Allingham, and the dramatist Oscar WILDE. In contrast to these writers, Thomas Moore, the century's most widely read Irish writer and known as the national poet of Ireland, was the son of a Catholic grocer; and the novelists William Carleton and John and Michael Banim were of peasant stock. Gerald Griffin was Catholic but, like Moore, from a prosperous family.

With the Celtic revivalism of the second half of the 19th century, the literature in English began to take its inspiration from Irish tradition, a development culminating at the end of the century in the founding by William Butler YEATS and others of the IRISH LITERARY RENAISSANCE. In what might be called the manifesto of that movement Yeats asked, "Can we not build up a national literature which shall be none the less Irish in spirit from being English in language?" His answer was yes, by writing in an "English which shall have an indefinable Irish quality of rhythm and style," that is, English as spoken in Ireland. Because the Irish peasant of western Ireland still spoke Irish and was considered a direct link with the past and thus with Gaelic literary tradition, the dialect Yeats called for turned out to be largely a peasant dialect, especially as used in the plays of Lady GREGORY and John Millington SYNGE, produced at the ABBEY THEATRE in Dublin.

The Irish Literary Renaissance was successful not only because talented people responded to Yeats's appeal but also because the historical timing was propitious. Ireland, responding to the nationalist impetus that had swept Europe, was moving toward revolution and the establishment of its political independence. A small nation of only 4 million produced within a generation some of the foremost poets, dramatists, and novelists of this century in Yeats, Synge, Sean O'CASEY, James JOYCE, and Samuel BECKETT. Conor Cruise O'Brien could justly claim that for a time Dublin was the literary center of the English-speaking world.

Irish Republican Army   The Irish Republican Army (IRA) is a paramilitary force that opposes the connection of Northern Ireland to Great Britain and refuses to recognize the Irish government in Dublin. The name IRA was first applied to veterans of the 1916 EASTER RISING who fought a guerrilla war against British forces in support of Irish independence during 1919–21. In 1921, British and Irish political leaders negotiated a treaty that constituted 26 of Ireland's 32 counties as the Irish Free State: Northern Ireland, with its Protestant, pro-British majority, remained part of the United Kingdom.

Elements of the IRA who supported the treaty were organized into the army of the Irish Free State. Those units which, with Eamon DE VALERA, opposed the treaty and were defeated in the ensuing civil war of 1922–23 now came to be known as the IRA. However, when de Valera reentered political life and became prime minister, most republicans joined him in supporting the state, and the IRA was reduced to a tiny dissident element. In the 1950s the IRA turned its attention more to Northern Ireland, where it tried without much success to win support among the oppressed Roman Catholic minority.

The Northern Ireland crisis, precipitated in 1969 by Irish civil rights demonstrations, enabled the IRA to make a dramatic comeback. A new "Provisional" leadership that emphasized military confrontation seceded from the Marxist-oriented "Official" IRA. The Provisional IRA ("Provos") launched a campaign of terror and of direct attacks upon security forces that led to the collapse of the Northern Ireland government in 1972. The views of most northern Catholics in this period were represented by the moderate Catholic politicians of the Social Democratic and Labour party rather than by the IRA. As the conflict dragged on into the 1980s, however, there was evidence that the SDLP was losing support to the IRA and its political arm, Provisional SINN FEIN.

Irish Sea   The Irish Sea is a roughly circular arm of the North Atlantic Ocean bounded by Wales, England, and Scotland on the east and by Ireland to the west. About 210 km (130 mi) in diameter, the sea covers about 103,600 km^2 (40,000 mi^2) and has a mean depth of 60 m (200 ft). It joins the Atlantic through the North Channel, between Ireland and Scotland, in the north, and through the Saint George's Channel in the south. The ISLE OF MAN and Anglesey are its principal islands. The sea's largest ports are Dublin and Liverpool.

Irish setter   The Irish setter originated as a gun dog in Ireland before 1800 and was at that time primarily red

The Irish, or red, setter originally had a red and white coat. Bred for bird hunting in the early 19th century, the setter is today prized as a pet and a show dog

and white in color. Its solid red coat was developed in Ireland and England during the 1800s. The ancestry of the Irish setter is unknown, but speculation credits a variety of breeds as its progenitors: the Irish water spaniel, English setter, Gordon setter, springer spaniel, and pointer. The Irish setter stands approximately 63.5 to 68.5 cm (25 to 27 in) high at the shoulder and weighs about 27 kg (60 lb). It has a mahogany to rich chestnut red coat, which is thick, straight, and as free from curl as possible. Feathering is present on the ears, chest, legs, and tail. Although this feathering is desirable in a show dog, it is a handicap in the field.

Irish terrier   The Irish terrier is a rough-coated, generally reddish breed standing about 46 cm (18 in) high at the shoulder and weighing approximately 12 kg (27 lb). It has a long head, flattened skull, and small V-shaped ears that drop forward toward the eyes. Its tail is docked. Its wiry coat should be solid red, golden red, red wheaten, or wheaten (yellowish).

The Irish terrier has a curious history in that there is no definite mention of the breed prior to 1875, even though an Irish terrier club was founded in 1879 to promote the breed. It is obvious, therefore, that the breed or earlier variants of it were known in Ireland for many years previously. The Irish terrier has been used as a guard dog and as a hunter of small game and vermin.

The Irish terrier is a most versatile dog. In addition to being a pet and watchdog, it is adept at hunting large and small game and is an accomplished retriever. It was also used as a messenger and sentinel during both world wars.

Irish water spaniel   The Irish water spaniel, a curly-coated, large-sized dog, reaches about 60 cm (24 in) in height at the shoulder and 30 kg (65 lb) in weight. Its coat, always solid liver in color, is a dense mass of crisp ringlets. Its head is covered by a topknot, which consists of long, loose curls. The tail is thick near the root and bears dense curls along the first 5 to 8 cm (2 to 3 in), but from there to the tip it tapers to a fine point and is covered only with short, smooth hair. The Irish water spaniel originated in Ireland. The breed's fondness for water and its dense, oily coat, which protects it from the cold, make it ideally suited for duck retrieving.

The Irish wolfhound, originally bred to hunt wolves and deer, moves gracefully despite its massive size. Over short distances it can race as swiftly as a greyhound.

Irish wolfhound   The Irish wolfhound is the tallest of the breeds recognized by the American Kennel Club. Males must be at least 81 cm (32 in) in height at the shoulder and 54.5 kg (120 lb) in weight; females, 76 cm (30 in) and 47.5 kg (105 lb). Dogs of 91.5 cm (36 in) and even more and 68 kg (150 lb) are relatively common. The coat is wiry and of one color, with various shadings; it may be gray, brindle, red, black, white, or fawn. In recent times the Irish wolfhound has been used to hunt wolves, deer, and other large game. The origins of the modern breed of Irish wolfhound undoubtedly trace back to ancient times; large, greyhound-type hunting dogs were known in Ireland and Britain at least 2,000 years ago.

Irkutsk [ir-kootsk']   Irkutsk is the capital of Irkutsk oblast in the Russian republic of the USSR. It is situated in southern SIBERIA, on the Angara River, near its outlet from Lake BAIKAL. The city has a population of 626,000 (1989 est.). It is named for the small Irkut River, which enters the Angara here. Irkutsk is one of Siberia's largest cities, situated on the TRANS-SIBERIAN RAILROAD, and serves as a supply base for the development of Siberian resource areas to the north.

The city's industries produce transportation equipment and machinery for gold mining and other extractive industries and process mica mined in Siberia. A hydroelectric station was built there on the Angara River in 1956. The A. A. Zhdanov University (1918) and many research institutes train specialists for the development of Siberian resources.

During the Russian advance through Siberia, a fort was founded in Irkutsk in 1661. It became a major administrative and economic center in the 18th and 19th centuries. Its importance was enhanced after the railroad arrived in 1898.

iron [y'-urn] Iron, a silvery white solid metal, appears in Group VIII of the periodic table as a TRANSITION ELEMENT. Its atomic number is 26, and its atomic weight is 55.847. Its chemical symbol, Fe, is derived from *ferrum*, the Latin word for iron. Iron is notable among the elements in the abundance of its ores and the vast number of useful alloys that can be formulated with iron as the major constituent. Iron is also biologically important; it is the central atom in heme, the oxygen-carrying portion of HEMOGLOBIN found in blood.

Elemental iron has been known since prehistoric times. Although how humans first learned to extract the element from its ores is still debated, scientists are fairly certain that early, highly prized samples of iron were obtained from meteors. Several references to "the metal of heaven"—probably iron—have been found in ancient writings. By approximately 1200 BC iron was being obtained from its ores; this achievement marks the beginning of the IRON AGE. Iron and its alloys remain crucial in the economies of modern countries.

Occurrence

In its various compounds, iron is the fourth most abundant element (5.1%) in the Earth's crust. Evidence exists that the molten core of the Earth is primarily elemental iron. Iron occasionally occurs naturally in its pure or uncombined form but is abundant in combination with other elements, as oxides, sulfides, carbonates, and silicates. Many naturally occurring iron compounds are ores from which the metal can easily be recovered in significant quantity (see IRON AND STEEL INDUSTRY). Iron pyrite (FeS_2) is a yellow, crystalline mineral called fool's gold because of its goldlike appearance.

Physical Properties

In its pure form iron is rather soft and is malleable and ductile at room temperature. It melts at 1,535° C and boils at 3,000° C. At room temperature iron exhibits ferromagnetism, a strong magnetic behavior that the metal may retain even in the absence of an external, applied magnetic field (see MAGNETISM). Although pure iron does conduct electricity, compared with other metals used for that purpose, such as copper or aluminum, it is a poor conductor.

Chemical Properties

Easily oxidized, iron reacts directly with most common nonmetallic elements, forming compounds in which iron is in the +2 or +3 oxidation state: FeO, Fe_2O_3, FeF_3, $FeCl_3$, $FeBr_3$, FeI_2, and FeS. At high temperatures iron also absorbs hydrogen and nitrogen and forms phosphides, carbides, and silicides.

In the absence of water, and under various conditions, iron reacts with oxygen. Finely divided iron burns in air once it is ignited. Larger pieces of iron react with oxygen in dry air at temperatures above 150° C to form the mixed oxides Fe_2O_3 and Fe_3O_4. At temperatures above 575° C and at low concentrations of oxygen, FeO is formed.

Corrosion. Perhaps the most important chemical reaction of iron, at least from an economic standpoint, is the least desirable one: the reaction of iron, water, and oxygen to form hydrated iron oxide, or rust. The CORROSION of iron has been studied carefully, and the formation of rust is known to be an electrochemical reaction.

For rust to form at room temperature, three components in addition to iron must be present: oxygen, water, and an electrolyte (an ionic substance dissolved in the water). Iron that is partially immersed in salt or fresh water usually rusts more rapidly than does iron that is totally immersed. In the atmosphere the formation of rust begins when the relative humidity exceeds 50%. The presence of air pollutants, particularly the oxides of sulfur, greatly increases the rate at which rust forms. In the presence of air and water sulfur dioxide forms sulfuric acid that attacks and oxidizes the iron. Because rust on the surface of iron is porous, the metal beneath the rust also reacts.

The formation of rust may be inhibited by coating the surface of the metal with paint or certain other chemicals or by covering the metal with another metal such as zinc (galvanized iron) or tin (the derivation of "tin" cans).

Aqueous Solutions. The chemistry of iron in the +2 or the +3 oxidation state is complex; many oxidizing and reducing agents are capable of interconverting the various compounds of Fe^{2+} and Fe^{3+}. Solutions of iron ions exhibit various chemical and physical properties characteristic of many transition metals. When ferrous sulfate (iron in the +2 oxidation state is called ferrous iron) is dissolved in water, the pale-green $Fe(H_2O)_6^{2+}$ ion is formed. When ferric nitrate (iron in the +3 oxidation state is called ferric iron) is dissolved, the product is the pale-violet $Fe(H_2O)_6^{3+}$ ion, which differs from the former ion only by having one electron fewer. A seemingly endless number of chemical compounds, both ions and neutral molecules, can replace the water molecules associated with iron in solution. If cyanide ions (CN^-) are added to solutions of the ions mentioned above, the products are ferrocyanide ion, $Fe(CN)_6^{4-}$, and ferricyanide ion, $Fe(CN)_6^{3-}$, respectively. Iron in the +6 oxidation state can be made by reacting solutions of ferric ion with strong oxidizing agents to produce FeO_4^{2-}, a reddish-purple ion, which is also weakly paramagnetic.

Organometallic Compounds. Iron in its various oxidation states readily combines with many carbon compounds to form organometallic compounds. Finely divided iron reacts with carbon monoxide under pressure to form the yellow liquid iron pentacarbonyl, $Fe(CO)_5$. This transition metal carbonyl, like many others, contains the metal in a zero oxidation state. The compound is the starting material for thousands of iron compounds in unusually low oxidation states (including some that are formally negative). On decomposition, iron pentacarbonyl yields samples of very pure iron.

A new type of organometallic compound was discovered in 1951. If ferrous chloride, $FeCl_2$, is reacted with cyclopentadiene (C_5H_6) in the presence of a strong organic base, the orange crystalline compound ferrocene, $(C_5H_5)_2Fe$, is the product. This compound, which has a highly stable structure, is called a "sandwich" compound because the iron atom is strongly held between the two flat C_5H_5 rings. In this case it is not useful to attempt to assign an oxidation state to iron. The characterization of this compound has led to extensive transition metal organometallic chemistry.

Alloys

The desirable mechanical and magnetic properties of iron, as well as its resistance to corrosion, may be improved by mixing iron with other elements, frequently metals, to form ALLOYS, substances that may be simple mixtures of elements; solid solutions, in which the atoms of one substance occupy definite positions relative to the other substances; or intermetallic compounds.

Perhaps the most important alloy of iron is steel, which contains up to approximately 2% carbon. Steels that contain about 0.25% carbon are called mild steels; those with about 0.45% carbon are medium steels; and those with 0.60% to 2% carbon are high-carbon steels. Within this range the greater the carbon content, the greater the tensile strength of the steel. The hardness of steel may be substantially increased by heating the metal until it is red hot and then quickly cooling it, a process known as quench hardening. An important component of many steels is cementite, Fe_3C, a carbon-iron compound. Mild steels are ductile and are fabricated into sheets, wire, or pipe; the harder medium steels are used to make structural steel. High-carbon steels, which are extremely hard and brittle, are used in tools and cutting instruments.

At a carbon content below that of steel is wrought iron, which is nearly pure iron. Because of its low carbon content (usually below 0.035%), it is forgeable and nonbrittle. Iron of high carbon content (3 to 4%), obtained when pig iron is remelted and cooled, is called cast iron. If cast iron is cooled quickly, hard but brittle white cast iron is formed; if it is cooled slowly, soft but tough gray cast iron is formed. Because it expands while cooling, cast iron is used in molds.

The addition of other materials in alloys—for example, manganese or silicon—also increases the hardness of steel. The inclusion of tungsten permits high-speed drills and cutting tools to remain hard even when used at high temperatures. The inclusion of chromium and nickel improves the corrosion resistance of the steel and, within certain limits of composition, is called stainless steel. A common stainless steel contains 0.15% carbon, 18% chromium, and 8% nickel and is used in cooking utensils and food-processing equipment. The inclusion of silicon, ranging from 1% to 5%, results in an alloy that is hard and highly magnetic. An alloy with cobalt is used for permanent magnets.

Iron Age   The Iron Age marks the period of the development of TECHNOLOGY, when the working of iron came into general use, replacing bronze as the basic material for implements and weapons. It is the last stage of the archaeological sequence known as the three-age system (Stone Age, Bronze Age, and Iron Age).

Although iron is a commoner metal than copper or tin, the technique of iron smelting is more complicated than that with the other ores, requiring repeated hammering at red heat to expel slag impurities (primarily stone fragments) before wrought iron can be produced. Precisely when and where iron was first smelted remains unknown. Occasional objects of smelted iron are known from as early as 3000 BC in the ancient Near East and predynastic Egypt, but these objects were inferior in hardness to comparable objects produced in bronze.

True iron metallurgy began among the HITTITES in eastern Anatolia at some time between 1900 and 1400 BC. The art of iron smelting was perfected by the time of the fall of the Hittite empire (c.1200 BC), and by 1000 BC iron objects and the knowledge of iron metallurgy had spread throughout the Near East and the Mediterranean and westward into Europe. This development marked the end of the Near Eastern Bronze Age, although bronze working was still in use for various ritual or prestige objects.

After about 900 BC the widespread mass production of iron implements gave rise to large-scale folk migrations that extended widely over the continents of Asia and Europe. The beginning of the European Iron Age varied from place to place, depending upon available sources of raw materials. Outside of Greece, the earliest use of iron in Europe occurred about 800–750 BC in the late Urnfield culture of central Europe and northern Italy (see VILLANOVANS). Following the Urnfield culture came the HALLSTATT period (700–450 BC) of the European Iron Age. In about 500 BC the technique of forging iron tools and jewelry was introduced in Europe, a technique that remained virtually unchanged until the Middle Ages. The Celtic migration of about 450 BC, commonly referred to as the LA TÈNE phase of Celtic culture, marked the division between the Early and Late Iron Age in Europe. The end of the prehistoric Iron Age was heralded by the Roman expansion in the Alpine area as far as the Danube River (c.15 BC).

Elsewhere in the world, the Iron Age appeared in China by about 600 BC, spreading widely during the course of the Warring States period (403–222 BC). The Chinese developed superior blast furnaces and technical apparatus with which to produce cast iron, techniques not employed in Europe until the Middle Ages. In Africa, iron objects found in tombs of the ancient kingdom of MEROË date from the 6th century BC, although large-scale iron smelting did not occur there until the 4th century BC. Ironworking was unknown in the New World until the arrival of the Europeans.

Iron Curtain   The Iron Curtain refers to the economic, social, and military barriers that the Union of Soviet Socialist Republics and the Communist-dominated countries of Eastern Europe created against the West after World War II. The term first gained currency when Winston CHURCHILL said (Mar. 5, 1946), in a speech at Westminster College in Fulton, Mo., "From Stettin in the Baltic to Trieste in the Adriatic, an iron curtain has descended across the continent."

Iron Gate   The Iron Gate, the deepest gorge in Europe, is on the DANUBE RIVER on the Romania-Yugoslavia border. It is about 3 km (2 mi) long and 168 m (550 ft) wide. Cutting through the Carpathian and Balkan mountains, it has cliffs that rise more than 790 m (2,600 ft) above the river. In 1972 sluices to aid navigation and a hydroelectric plant were completed.

Iron Guard   The Iron Guard was a Fascist organization founded in Romania in 1927. A paramilitary group that used assassination freely, it was proscribed in 1933 but reemerged as a powerful force in the late 1930s despite the execution of its leaders by CAROL II in 1938. In 1940 the Iron Guard helped bring Ion ANTONESCU to power, but he suppressed the organization in 1941 and thousands of Guardists were killed. It never recovered.

iron lung   The iron lung was the first widely used mechanical device capable of artificial respiration. Invented by Philip Drinker of Harvard University during the 1930s, the iron lung was used initially to ventilate patients who could not breathe spontaneously. Many of these patients were victims of respiratory paralysis caused by poliomyelitis.

The iron lung consists of a large metal tank in which the patient's entire body is placed, with the exception of the head. A rubber collar fits tightly around the patient's neck, thus minimizing air leakage. As the pressure in the tank is increased, the chest is compressed; this forces air out of the lungs. When the pressure in the tank is decreased, the chest expands, and air is drawn into the lungs. Through the use of alternating high and low pressures in the tank, a patient can be artificially ventilated for prolonged periods of time.

See also: RESPIRATOR.

iron and steel industry   The iron and steel industry is made up of hundreds of large and small businesses, some of which are basic steel producers whereas others form steel into finished products.

Iron

IRON is one of the most widely distributed and abundant elements in the Earth's crust, constituting about 5% of the total. It is estimated that world supplies of iron ore are adequate for at least 100 years in spite of a projected increase in production that could double during the next quarter of a century.

Iron Ore. The development of present iron-ore deposits began millions of years ago when most of the world was under water. Immense quantities of sediment, some rich in iron, settled out through the ages. These age-old, iron-bearing marine sediments form the basis of the major usable iron deposits in the world today. After these deposits were incorporated into the crust of the Earth, they were gradually moved closer to the surface by the drift of the continents and the upheaval of sediment layers on the sea bottoms.

Iron ore reserves are found worldwide. Areas with more than 1 billion metric tons of reserves include, in order of decreasing amounts, Australia, Brazil, Canada, the United States, Venezuela, South Africa, India, the USSR, Gabon, France, Spain, Sweden, and Algeria.

North America has been fortunate in its ore deposits, which are found in commercially usable quantities in 22 states in the United States and in 6 Canadian provinces. In the United States the most abundant supplies, discovered in the early 1890s, are located in the Lake Superior region around the Mesabi Range. These deposits seemed inexhaustible in the 1930s. The tremendous demand for iron ore during World War II virtually tripled the output of the Mesabi Range and severely depleted its deposits of high-grade ore. A worldwide search for new deposits by U.S. companies yielded large deposits of rich ore, acceptable for blast furnace use, in Brazil, Australia, Canada, Venezuela, West Africa, and South Africa.

Two new upgrading techniques that have been developed are sintering and pelletizing. Sintering is used when ore is too fine to be charged directly into the furnace; the ore is agglomerated with a mixture of coal and coke breeze (a powder) so that it forms a clinkerlike substance. Sintering permits the passage of air through the blast furnace burden, whereas very fine particles of ore would make the air passage difficult. Pelletizing is used to increase the iron content of low-grade ores such as taconites and jaspers, which average from 20% to 30% iron in their natural form; after being crushed, screened, ground, and concentrated, the ore is formed into small pellets with an iron content of 60% or more.

Two methods are employed in mining iron ore (see MINING AND QUARRYING). Underground mining is the least economical and may take place at depths well in excess of 300 m (1,000 ft). The recent discoveries of iron ore made in the postwar period, however, involve reserves that are located close to the surface; the most widely used method of mining today is open-pit mining.

Ironmaking. Iron is made by refining iron ore to a point where it reaches 90% to 95% purity. Refining has been achieved in a number of ways through the centuries, dating back as far as the 2d millennium BC.

Iron production was at first extremely limited because of the slow and difficult methods used to refine ore. At first lumps of iron were heated in contact with charcoal, producing a pasty mass mixed with a great deal of slag. This was hammered into a semifinished bar and then further worked into finished products.

The current method of smelting iron is in the BLAST FURNACE, which was developed in a crude form during the Middle Ages. The furnace was a stone structure built in the form of a truncated pyramid into which iron ore, charcoal, and a fluxing material, usually limestone, were charged. Combustion was aided by a blast of cold air blown in at the base of the furnace. This operation changed little anywhere in the world until about 1840, when anthracite coal was used for fuel in place of charcoal, and the air blast was heated.

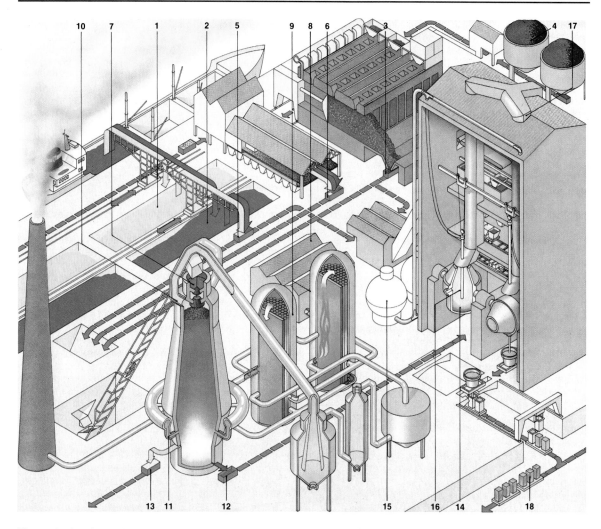

The production of steel, the most widely used of all the metals, is essentially a two-stage process. It involves the initial production of an impure form of iron from an ore composed primarily of iron oxide and varying amounts of silica and compounds of sulfur, phosphorus, and manganese. The extracted iron, called pig iron, is hard and brittle and contains several percent of carbon, as well as small amounts of silicon, manganese, sulfur, and phosphorus remaining from the original ore. A small amount of pig iron is made into different types of cast iron by remelting and cooling it under carefully controlled conditions. Most pig iron, however, is converted into steel by removing the impurities and later adding small but definite amounts of carbon and selected substances—particularly manganese, chromium, molybdenum, and vanadium—to produce alloys with specific properties that make them suitable for various uses. For reasons of economy, present iron and steel production facilities are generally combined in one large plant. Modern integrated iron and steel plants use such large amounts of coke that they are usually located near coal mines. Other raw materials, such as limestone (1) and iron ore (2) are brought in by train or ship. Before extraction of iron from the ore is begun, coke (3) is produced by controlled burning of coal (4). Specific amounts of correctly sized coke, ore, and limestone (5), and a sintered mixture of finely powdered ore, limestone, and coke (6) are then blended and charged into the top of a blast furnace (7). Air from a pumphouse (8) is preheated in heat exchangers (9) by hot gases (10) from the blast furnace and blown into the bottom of the furnace through tuyeres, or nozzles (11). A series of complicated reactions converts the ore into molten pig iron, which is tapped off (12) periodically at the bottom of the furnace into containers for further purification and conversion into steel. The limestone, which reacts with impurities to form a slag that floats on the liquid iron, is also removed (13). The pig iron, which still contains excessive impurities, is mixed with limestone and refined in a basic oxygen furnace (14) into which oxygen from a tank (15) is blown through a water-cooled metal tube, or lance (16). Some of the remaining impurities form a slag, which is withdrawn after a definite period of time. Carbon and other impurities are converted to gases, which are drawn off (17) and freed of pollutants before being discharged into the air. Predetermined amounts of carbon and alloying metals are added to the purified iron to form steel with specific properties. The final steel is poured into ladles and cast into ingots (18), which are shipped to manufacturers for rolling and forging into numerous products.

The construction of the furnace also changed at about that time. The short, square-based stone stack was replaced by a tall, cylindrical structure made of wrought-iron plates and lined with firebrick. These furnaces were larger and increased the production of iron considerably. In the 1870s and '80s anthracite was gradually replaced by COKE made from bituminous coal. Furnaces grew larger and by 1900 were capable of producing more than 200 tons of molten pig iron per day.

During the 20th century significant improvements in blast furnace structure and practice (but not in the basic process) have resulted in tremendous production increases. Facilities are also provided for handling and charging iron ore, coke, and limestone into the top of the vertical stack; as they descend they are met by a rising volume of hot gas formed by combustion of the coke with air preheated to 1,000° C (1,800° F) and blown in under pressure through openings called tuyères, which are located at the base of the stack. The carbon monoxide from the burning coke reduces the iron oxide to iron, while the limestone removes impurities from the ore. At the base of the furnace the molten iron is tapped into ladles capable of holding 300 tons.

The blast-furnace process operates 24 hours a day, 7 days a week. This continuity is essential to efficient operation; if the furnace is shut down, several days are often required before smooth operation is restored. The raw materials are constantly being charged into the top to replace the gasified carbon and the molten products that are removed from the furnace. The furnace is tapped about four times every day, at intervals of five or six hours.

Uses of Iron. Until 1870 the greatest use of iron was in railroad rails and railroad car wheels. Iron was used in construction to a limited extent. Iron also had significant uses in the form of nails and wire, and in sheets plated with tin, called tinplate, which were used for food containers.

With the advent of steel, most of the iron came to be used as raw material for the production of steel, and that remains its primary use.

Today the principal use of blast-furnace iron that is not turned into steel is for cast products. The iron is purchased by foundries in solid form and then melted together with scrap to make castings for a number of industries.

Steel Production

As it comes from the blast furnace, iron contains about 5% carbon and is too brittle for many applications. Most of this carbon must be removed along with small portions of other elements, such as phosphorus, silicon, and aluminum, to give the resultant material its strength and flexibility. In a number of instances, small amounts of other elements, such as manganese, molybdenum, chromium, and nickel, are added during the process.

Steel, which is the result of this refining process, can be defined as relatively pure iron containing less than 1.7% carbon. Although steel has been known for centuries, its production was extremely limited until the invention of the Bessemer process in the late 1850s.

The Bessemer Process. The Bessemer process, which gave birth to the modern steel industry, is a pneumatic process that forces air through a bath of molten iron in a pear-shaped vessel. The oxygen in the air is brought into contact with the carbon in the iron and reduces the carbon content to the desired level. The process was developed in the late 1850s by the Englishman Henry BESSEMER. At about the same time an American, William Kelly, developed a similar process.

The principal application of Bessemer steel in the last century was for railroad rails, since it had been discovered that rails made of steel were far more durable than those made of iron.

The Open-Hearth Process. The open-hearth process of steelmaking, referred to in Europe as the Siemens-Martin process, was first introduced into the United States in 1868. It makes use of a rectangular, boxlike structure lined with brick, forming a shallow basin, or hearth, into which materials are charged. The charge consists of large quantities of scrap and molten pig iron, and the fuel, either gas or oil, is introduced through openings at the ends of the furnace.

The new process was accepted slowly until 1895; its expansion in the next five years, however, was so rapid that by 1900 output of open-hearth steel had tripled.

Basic Oxygen Process. The basic oxygen process, one of the greatest technological breakthroughs in the steel industry during the 20th century, revolutionized the production of steel by reducing the time required in the normal open-hearth from an average of 8 or 9 hours to 45 minutes. This new method also required less investment and appreciably reduced operating costs. The process was developed in Austria after World War II and was installed in 1953 at the Voest plant in Linz. The vessel in which the steel is made is pear shaped, resembling the Bessemer converter. It is tilted to receive the charge, which consists of scrap and hot metal, and then brought to an upright position. An oxygen tube is lowered into the converter to a point about 2 m (6 ft) above the metal bath; from this position it blows 54 to 58 cubic m (1,700 to 1,800 cubic ft) of oxygen for each ton of steel produced.

The first vessels installed at Linz had a 30- to 35-ton capacity. Since that time the capacity of the vessels has increased tremendously; many operations throughout the world today are capable of producing between 300 and 350 tons at one time. The basic oxygen process has spread rapidly worldwide and now constitutes approximately 60% of world steel production.

Electric Furnace. The first commercial production of steel in an ELECTRIC FURNACE was recorded in France in 1900, and the initial installation of the process in the United States was in 1906 at the Halcomb Steel Company in Syracuse, N.Y. This furnace, tiny by comparison with today's units, had an output limited to 4 tons of steel per charge.

The electric-furnace process uses scrap iron almost exclusively as a raw material. The scrap is placed in the furnace—a round deep receptacle lined with refractory brick—while the roof is off. The roof is replaced, and electrodes are lowered through holes in the roof until they are in contact with the scrap charge. Once the power is turned on, tremendous heat is generated as arc temperatures reach 3,300° C (6,000° F). This heat melts the scrap into new steel in a matter of a few hours with an electric power consumption of approximately 500 kW h per ton of steel produced.

Acceptance of the process at first was confined to the production of alloy steels. Shortly before World War II a number of units were used to produce carbon steel with significant success, both physically and economically. This practice continued in the postwar period; electric furnaces were used to produce larger and larger tonnages of carbon steel.

In addition to the furnace, a considerable amount of electrical equipment, including a large transformer, is necessary to provide the electric power. Although the entire plant represents a sizable capital investment, the investment is small in comparison with the capital required for the basic oxygen process, which must be supported by blast furnaces and coke ovens. As the electric furnace uses scrap, which is gathered rather than produced, only a small investment is required for scrap processing and handling facilities.

Until recently, the largest electric-furnace plant had the capacity to produce 2 million tons annually; in 1979 a 4-million-ton electric-furnace plant opened in Venezuela. Electric furnaces have been installed in a number of developing countries throughout the world, where they provide a means for establishing a steel-making operation on a relatively small scale with a limited investment. Most of these operations consist of furnaces capable of producing 25 and 50 tons at one time, although some new electric arc furnaces can hold charges of up to 200 tons. The use of these "minimills" has soared in the United States. Because their basic material is steel scrap—rather than the coal, limestone, and iron ore needed in the giant, integrated steel plants—minimills are relatively inexpensive to build, and they can be efficiently sited near their markets instead of having to be built near sources of raw materials. In the 1980s, U.S. minimill production rose to well over 20% of total U.S. steel production.

A substitute for scrap, a material called sponge iron, was recently developed. It is made from iron ore combined with gas to reduce the ore's oxygen content and raise its iron content to better than 90%. This direct reduction process uses NATURAL GAS and, consequently, is employed only in those areas of the world where natural gas is abundant.

Steel Processing

Immediately after molten steel is poured from the furnace into a ladle at a temperature of about 1,600° C (3,000° F), it passes through one of two processes: ingot production or continuous casting.

Ingot Production. The molten steel can be discharged into ingot molds and allowed to solidify into ingots, which are tall, rectangular shapes weighing from less than a ton to 100 or more tons. After solidification, the molds are stripped off and the ingots are placed in a covered pit, called a soaking pit, where they are heated to an even temperature. Upon removal from the pit they pass through a primary rolling mill, which is a massive piece of equipment that can be powered by as much as 15,000 hp. This mill, called either a slabbing or blooming mill, reduces the ingots to a bloom or slab. A bloom is a square section usually more than 15 by 15 cm (6 by 6 in), varying in length up to 9 m (30 ft). A slab is a rectangular-shaped section that can vary in width from 50 to 200 cm (20 to 80 in) and in thickness from 5 to 30 cm (2 to 12 in). Blooms are further processed into smaller square sections, 13 by 13 cm (5 by 5 in) or less, called billets. These three classifications, blooms, billets, and slabs, constitute what is known as semifinished steel.

Continuous Casting. A recent technological breakthrough is continuous casting, a process in which the liquid steel is poured into a machine called a continuous caster, which produces a semifinished form without the intermediate ingot, soaking pit, and blooming or slabbing mill operations. A large number of units have been put in place throughout the world, and close to one-third of the steel made is now processed through continuous casting.

Semifinished steel made by either ingot or continuous casting is reheated to a temperature of about 1,200° C (2,300° F) and is then processed into many finished steel products on a variety of rolling mills. These include hot-strip and cold-strip sheet mills and plate, rail, pipe, rod, bar, and structural mills.

Hot-Strip Mill. The hot-strip mill consists of a series of consecutive stands each containing huge rolls that squeeze the slab successively until it is reduced in thickness from its original size (from 5 to 30 cm/2 to 12 in) to less than 3.175 mm (⅛ in). The strip is elongated from the original slab length of 4.5 to 10 m (15 to 33 ft) to over 900 m (3,000 ft).

Cold-Strip Mill. The product of the hot-strip mill, excluding that sold as hot-rolled sheets, is cleansed of its surface oxides by means of an acid bath in a process called pickling. The coil is then introduced at room temperatures into a cold-strip mill, which usually consists of five stands of rolls that reduce it to a thin sheet 1.588 mm (1⁄16 of an inch) or less thick. As the product comes off the cold mill in the form of a coil, it is usually too stiff for many uses and must be softened by a heat-treating process called ANNEALING. To restore some stiffness in the steel after this process is complete, the product is passed through another mill called the temper mill.

Plate Mills. Semifinished slabs are further processed into plates on a rolling mill, usually with one set of rolls having a reversible rotation. The slab is passed back and forth through the rolls until it reaches the desired thickness and length. Plates are produced in a variety of sizes, varying in thickness from 6.350 mm (¼ in) to 30 cm (12 in), and in width from 76 cm (30 in) to 535 cm (210 in).

Structural Mills. A number of blooms and, in some cases, ingots are rolled directly into structural shapes on rolling mills, which, unlike the flat rolls on a strip-and-plate mill, have rolls that are grooved and shaped to yield the structural shapes desired. A large variety of structural shapes are made.

Rail Mills. Rail mills take an ingot or a bloom and, through a series of rolls that are grooved and formed to shape the rail, produce railroad rails in lengths of 12 m (39 ft) and 24 m (78 ft). The rails are then processed further as they are hardened and straightened.

Bar Mills. The term *bar* encompasses a wide variety of steel products and shapes. Bars are produced by both large and small steelmakers and are put to many uses, including concrete reinforcing bars for construction and special cold-finished bars for the manufacture of machines and machine tools.

Wire and Wire Rod Mills. A semifinished section of bar steel, called a billet, can be rolled down through a series of as many as 20 consecutive stands into a round section about 13 mm (½ in) in diameter and more than 5,000 m (16,500 ft) in length. The section is now called a rod and comes from the mill in coil form. This material is then drawn through a die and formed into wire.

Seamless Pipe Mills. In this process the semifinished bloom is rolled into a round, solid section. It is then heated and its center pierced, so that a hollow is formed without a seam. The section is processed further to produce seamless pipe, which has a number of applications, particularly in oil-well drilling and as oil-well casing.

Uses of Steel

The steel industry's largest customer is the automobile industry. Other major steel consumers are the nonresidential construction industry, manufacturers of appliances, oilfield equipment, and machine tools, and railroads.

Alloy steels contain percentages of elements other than iron, which give them special properties to function in a variety of applications for which normal carbon steel would be inadequate. Alloy steels are called specialty steels by the industry and are usually divided into three categories—constructional alloy steels, STAINLESS STEEL, and tool steels. Outstanding properties of alloy steels include their resistance to heat, abrasion, and corrosion; they find many applications in sections of chemical plants, petroleum refineries, power plants, and jet engines.

The World Steel Industry

Throughout the 1980s the USSR was the world's largest steel producer, followed by the combined production of the European Community, Japan, and then the United States.

From the late 19th century until the years following World War II, the U.S. steel industry was the largest in the world. After World War II, however, both Europe and Japan rebuilt their steel plants from the ground up, replacing old furnaces with newer, more efficient technologies and operating their industries, often, with the help of government subsidies.

U.S. steelmakers, long accustomed to setting prices and selling their products with minimal competition, did little to meet the challenge of foreign steel. Steel-plant closings became common in the early 1980s, and by 1985 the industry had laid off over 150,000 workers and was operating at only about 50 percent of capacity.

The U.S. steel industry showed some signs of recovery in the late 1980s. The industry invested in plants for manufacturing such specialty products as high-strength, coated steel and rust-resistant electrogalvanized steel; also, to offset some advantages enjoyed by its subsidized foreign competition, import tariffs were implemented.

▬

ironweed Ironweed is any of a large number of widely distributed herbs, vines, shrubs, and small trees of the genus *Veronia*, family Compositae. Ironweeds have hard (ironlike) stems; purple, white, or pink disk florets; and lance-shaped, usually alternate and toothed leaves. The New York ironweed, *V. noveboracensis*, is native to eastern North America.

▬

irony Derived from the Greek *eironeia* ("simulated ignorance"), the term *irony* refers to a rhetorical device in which the intention is in sharp contrast with the literal meaning. Irony most likely originated with a character type in the Old Comedy, a seeming simpleton who asked questions and said less than he knew. In Socratic irony the speaker pretends to be naive and makes opponents expose their confused or false conceptions by asking them deceptively simple questions.

For a while irony was associated with a "dissembler" but soon came to be recognized as a habit of discourse, or conceit, serving a rhetorical purpose. For example, Jonathan Swift's *A Modest Proposal*, an attack on the attitudes of the English rulers, argues that to alleviate the famine in Ireland landlords should purchase and eat the children of the poor. In this respect irony is closely associated with SATIRE, being the method by which satire achieves its particular purpose.

Situational irony reveals a striking incongruity between what is expected and what results, as when a pickpocket discovers that his or her pocket has been picked. The concept of the twist of fate was long recognized but was not called irony until about the 19th century. Dramatic irony, a special instance of situational irony, occurs when a character is ignorant of a situation that is known to the spectators. When Oedipus, for example, prays that the unknown killer of Laius be eternally cursed, he is ironically cursing himself. Verbal irony admits of varying degrees. The New Critics have used the term for incongruities resulting from the special use of words. In the phrase "the short and simple annals of the poor," *annals* has an ironic ring because annals are usually long records of the rich and powerful.

▬

Iroquois League [ir'-uh-kwoy] The Iroquois League was a union of Iroquoian-speaking North American Indian peoples, originally composed of the SENECA, CAYUGA, ONONDAGA, ONEIDA, and MOHAWK Indians. The TUSCARORA became the sixth member of the league in the early 18th century. The tribes occupied a territory comprising what is now New York's Mohawk Valley and Finger Lakes region.

Although the precise date of the league's founding is unknown, some historians suggest that the confederacy was probably formed by the early 16th century. According to Iroquois legend, the league was founded by Deganawidah, a leader of divine status, who persuaded the original Five Nations to give up intertribal warfare marked by blood feud and cannibalism. Historians of Indian culture view its formation as a defensive response to warfare with neighboring Huron and other Algonquian-speaking tribes. The prophet HIAWATHA (fl. c.1550), Deganawidah's earthly spokesman, doggedly traveled among the five tribes in an attempt to unify them. His persistence succeeded, and the tribes united in what proved to be a nearly invulnerable political alliance until its eventual collapse during the American Revolution. Sporadic warfare and raiding against tribes outside the league afforded opportunities for young Iroquois warriors to earn prestige and honor. Initially, conquest and the gaining of economic and political advantages were of secondary importance. Eventually, however, in dealings with the British and French and, later, the British and the colonists, the league skillfully played off opposing parties against one another and subjugated neighboring tribes for both economic and territorial gains. Before its collapse in the late 18th century, the Iroquois League dominated lands as far west as the Mississippi River.

The league's Grand Council consisted of 50 life-appointed male sachems, or peace chiefs, who were nominated by the headwoman of certain sachem-producing lineages in each clan. The Onondaga had 14 sachems, the Cayuga 10, the Oneida and Mohawk 9 each, and the Seneca 8. After lengthy ratification procedures, the council members became responsible for keeping the internal peace, representing the body of tribes to outsiders, and coordinating tribal activities in unified warfare against nonmembers.

Major decisions were reached through unanimity, compensating for otherwise unequal tribal representation. An individual sachem could be deposed through impeachment proceedings initiated by his lineage's headwoman. Some historians claim that the highly democratic political organization of the Iroquois League may have served as a model for the compilers of the United States Constitution.

irradiation   see RADIATION THERAPY; RADIOLOGY.

irrational number   An irrational number is a NUMBER that is not a RATIONAL NUMBER—that is, not the quotient of two integers. Deciding whether or not a particular number is irrational is a problem that has perplexed mathematicians throughout the ages, starting with the Greeks in the 6th century BC. The Greeks proved that such numbers as $\sqrt{2}$ and $\sqrt{3}$ are irrational; it was not until 1761, however, that Johann Lambert proved that π (the number PI) is irrational. The irrational numbers themselves are divided into two classes: the algebraic numbers and those which are not algebraic, which are called TRANSCENDENTAL NUMBERS. The algebraic irrational numbers are defined as irrational numbers that are roots of polynomial EQUATIONS with integer coefficients, for example, $\sqrt{2}$ and $\sqrt[3]{5}$.

Irrawaddy River [ir-uh-wahd'-ee]   The Irrawaddy River (Iyawadi-Nmai), 2,095 km (1,300 mi) long, flows through central Burma. Its drainage basin covers more than 410,000 km² (158,000 mi²), and its delta is the rice bowl and population center of Burma. The river rises in the mountains of northern Burma as the headstreams Mali and Nmai, which join to the north of Myitkyina. Between Myitkyina and MANDALAY, a distance of 585 km (365 mi), the Irrawaddy passes through three deep gorges—one to the north and two to the south of Bhamo, an important river port. Just below Mandalay is the Ava Bridge. About 130 km (80 mi) below Mandalay the Chindwin River flows into the Irrawaddy. The river's enormous delta begins about 290 km (180 mi) from the Andaman Sea. The major delta city is RANGOON, Burma's capital.

irreversible processes   see REVERSIBLE AND IRREVERSIBLE PROCESSES

irrigation [ir-i-gay'-shuhn]   Irrigation is the practice of artificially supplying water to land to sustain the growth of crops. An ancient agricultural technique, irrigation may have been practiced as early as 5000 BC along the banks of such regularly flooding rivers as the Nile, by digging channels to extend the area covered by the flood, and by erecting dikes to trap water on the land after the river had subsided. The development of diversion dams and of water-lifting machines permitted the irrigation of lands lying above those normally reached by floodwaters. Ancient remnants of these structures have been found in Egypt, Babylonia, China, Phoenicia, Peru, Mexico, India, and the United States. Modern irrigation systems are still based on these two key engineering innovations.

Diversion Dams and Water-Lifting Machines

The diversion dam supplies water from a stream to a canal system at an elevation above the lands to be irrigated. Often a reservoir for storage is included in the system. The canals follow the natural land contours, so that water flows by gravity to the fields.

Water-lifting machines were developed to lift water directly from streams or from canals to irrigate higher-lying fields. The *shaduf* in Egypt, and its counterpart in many other early agricultures, is simply a bucket and a counterweight attached to the ends of a pivoted pole. The bucket is pulled down, filled by hand, and then lifted by the counterweight. ARCHIMEDES' SCREW, a large hand-turned screw within a wooden cylinder, lifts water on its wide threads from the end dipped in the stream. The Persian wheel consists of a chain of buckets that pass over a vertical wheel and dip into the water. This vertical wheel is turned by a horizontal wheel rotated by a draft animal. The filled buckets are tipped into a trough or canal leading to the fields.

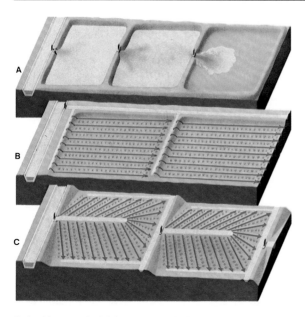

In the oldest, most basic irrigation method (A), fields are subdivided into basinlike sections, which are flooded as needed. In furrow irrigation, or infiltration (B), fields are divided into ridges and furrows, and controlled amounts of water are discharged into each furrow through a network of sluice gates or siphons. Irrigation by natural flow (C) requires that each field be built up into a gently sloping ridge. Water is then released from a channel that runs along the top of each ridge and percolates down the slope.

Modern Irrigation Systems

Water distribution systems are of two broad types: surface and closed-conduit distribution systems.

Surface Irrigation. In surface irrigation systems, the entire land surface may be covered with water (flood irrigation), or the water may be restricted to small ditches called furrows or rills (furrow irrigation). Both flood and furrow irrigation are used on naturally sloping, ungraded fields, although the effectiveness of water absorption by the soil is improved if the fields are graded to a uniform slope. Recently the practice of dead-level surface irrigation—grading fields to a zero slope—has been introduced to improve irrigation uniformity. This practice requires a water stream large enough to cover the field or to fill the furrows in a time period that is short compared to the time required for the water to infiltrate the soil. Dead-level surface irrigation is presently limited to arid climates, where waterlogging of the soil is not a potential problem.

Closed-Conduit Irrigation. Closed-conduit irrigation systems use pipes to distribute water over wide areas or to the ground area around each plant. These systems can apply water uniformly, and they permit frequent light irrigations that maintain the desired level of moisture in the soil. Sprinkler systems distribute water by pumping it through a network of pipes that are either laid on the ground or lifted above the field; often the pipes are on wheels or other devices that permit the network to be moved from field to field. Bubbler irrigation supplies water through a small pipe that periodically delivers equal quantities to small basins at each plant or group of plants. Drip, or trickle, irrigation uses narrow plastic tubes that deliver small quantities of water frequently, but at an extremely slow rate, to the soil around the roots of each plant. This type of irrigation, widely used in the United States, Australia, and Israel, has had spectacular results. Drip systems use less water than other closed-circuit systems, supplying the precise amount needed to replace transpired plant moisture and the water that is evaporated from the soil. They also reduce the problem of soil salinity and create impressive crop yields.

Problems Associated with Irrigation

Salt accumulation and waterlogging are the most severe problems caused by irrigation. Dissolved salts are present in small quantities in all irrigation water. As the water evaporates or is used by plants, the salt content of the water remaining in the soil increases. This remaining water may percolate down to the ground-water aquifer, which then becomes saltier. A few irrigated regions have sufficient natural drainage to prevent the water table from rising into the plant-root zone. But in many areas, the extra input to the aquifer as a result of percolation from irrigated fields and the seepage from unlined canals and reservoirs eventually exceeds the natural drainage capacity. Once the water table rises to within several feet of the

The furrow method of irrigation is commonly used in the cultivation of corn and other close-growing crops. Small, sloping furrows are plowed between the rows of corn and supplied with water from a ditch through siphon tubes. The water is absorbed into the soil as it flows down the slope.

Center-pivot irrigation systems use rotating sprinklers to spray water over circular fields. Such systems are effective where water supplies are limited.

surface the salty water moves to the ground surface by capillary action, and, as it evaporates, leaves behind a thin deposit of salt. Even if the aquifer itself does not become saline, the excess water in the root zone of the soil retards crop growth.

Historically, salt accumulation and the waterlogging caused by inadequate drainage have taken a huge toll where agriculture has been based on irrigation. Mesopotamia's once-productive farmlands now bear some of the world's lowest crop yields because the crops grow on waterlogged, salty fields. The world's largest irrigation enterprise, the Indus Basin in Pakistan, is in serious danger as water tables rise to the surface and salt accumulates. More than one-third of the world's irrigated land (including some of the lush cropland in California's Imperial Valley) is being undermined by salinity.

If irrigated lands in semiarid regions are to remain permanently productive, two steps are necessary. Water tables must be kept well below the surface by reducing the seepage of irrigation water and by installing artificial drainage. Irrigation must also be managed so that a small additional increment of water passes through the soil around plant roots to leach salts below the root zone.

Major Irrigation Systems of the World

Irrigation is now practiced on every continent. The world total is approximately 231 million irrigated ha (569 million acres), which represents about 15% of all farmed lands. Some irrigation is necessary for most agricultures, and it is crucial for nations like Egypt, where all farm-lands are irrigated. In addition, the production from irrigated agriculture supplies a far greater proportion of the world's food than its acreage represents. High-value crops such as vegetables, fruits, and nuts are often produced by irrigation, and the yield may be double the harvest from equally fertile but nonirrigated land. At present, five nations account for 71% of the world's total irrigated farmland: China, with the largest irrigated area; India; the United States; Pakistan; and the USSR.

Irtysh River [ir-tish'] The Irtysh River, a major waterway of central Asia, runs for 4,249 km (2,639 mi). It originates on the southwestern slopes of the ALTAI MOUNTAINS in Xinjiang province, China. From there it flows west as the Black Irtysh into Kazakhstan, USSR, where it broadens into Lake Zaisan. It then winds northwest into Soviet Siberia, where it joins the OB RIVER near Khanty-Mansiysk as the Ob's main tributary.

The Irtysh is navigable. Industrial cities along the river include OMSK, Khanty-Mansiysk, Tobolsk, Tara, Pavlodar, Semipalatinsk, and Ust-Kamenogorsk. Hydroelectric power stations along the Irtysh supply energy for the mining and smelting of the many minerals found along the upper river. Commercially important fish abound in its waters.

Irving, Edward Edward Irving, b. Aug. 4, 1792, d. Dec. 7, 1834, a Scottish minister, was one of the founders of the Catholic Apostolic church. After he came into contact with a group headed by Henry Drummond that was devoted to eschatological speculations, Irving began to preach the imminence of the SECOND COMING OF CHRIST. His writings on Christ, in which he deemed the human nature of Christ as sinful, led to his excommunication (1830) from the Church of Scotland and his expulsion (1833) from the ministry.

In 1832 he joined with others in forming the Catholic Apostolic church. The members, known for awhile as Irvingites, believed that the Second Coming was near and tried to restore the biblical organization of the church in preparation for Christ's return. The movement was somewhat influential in Britain until 1900; it then spread to Europe and the United States.

Irving, Sir Henry Actor, manager, and director Henry Irving (stage name of John Henry Brodribb, b. Feb. 6, 1838, d. Oct. 13, 1905) was the foremost theatrical figure on the London stage during the latter half of the 19th century. The role of Mathias in Leopold Lewis's melodrama *The Bells* at the Lyceum Theatre in 1871 made Irving famous, and in 1878 he took over the management of the theater, which during his tenure became the most notable in London.

Irving's repertoire consisted of Shakespearean works and conventional melodrama; he avoided new works. He was not handsome, and his voice lacked flexibility, but his interpretations were provocative, and he was a master of timing and byplay. His most noteworthy performances were in the roles of Hamlet (1874); Shylock (1878), to the Portia of his leading lady Ellen TERRY; Malvolio (1884) in *Twelfth Night*; the leads in Tennyson's *The Cup* (1881) and *Becket* (1893); and Iachimo (1896) in *Cymbeline*. He was knighted in 1895, the first actor to be accorded this honor.

Irving made many theatrical innovations; he was one of the first directors to abandon the grooves that for 200 years had been the usual method of shifting scenery on the stage, and he made an art of stage lighting; he was the first English producer to darken the auditorium during performances. He also paid careful attention to costumes, even those of extras. His greatest period was the decade between 1878 and 1888.

Irving, John   John Irving, b. Exeter, N.H., Mar. 2, 1942, is best known for his sprawling novel *The World According to Garp* (1978; film, 1982), the story of an eccentric feminist and her writer son. More recent fiction includes *The Hotel New Hampshire* (1981; film, 1984), *The Cider House Rules* (1985), and *A Prayer for Owen Meany* (1989). Irving, who also writes short stories, was writer-in-residence at the University of Iowa from 1972 to 1975 and today teaches English at Mount Holyoke College.

Irving, Washington   Washington Irving, b. New York City, Apr. 3, 1783, d. Nov. 28, 1859, was America's first successful professional writer. Although influenced by such English models as Joseph Addison, Oliver Goldsmith, and Sir Walter Scott, Irving won an international reputation as a distinctively American prose stylist.

Irving's youthful comic talents were best expressed in the sprightly *Salmagundi* papers (1807–08) and in *A History of New York* (1809), the latter purporting to be the work of Diedrich Knickerbocker. In 1815, Irving began a 17-year sojourn in Europe. *The Sketch-Book* (1819–20), under the pseudonym Geoffrey Crayon, was an immediate success. Its calculatedly miscellaneous contents included essays and sketches about the countryside and customs of England, two essays about the American Indian, and two American tales—RIP VAN WINKLE and "The Legend of Sleepy Hollow." Like its successors, *Bracebridge Hall* (1822) and *Tales of a Traveller* (1824), *The Sketch-Book* was light literature, mainly for amusement.

Seeking to broaden his reputation, Irving took up residence (1826) in Spain, where he wrote his *History of the Life and Voyages of Christopher Columbus* (1828) and *A Chronicle of Granada* (1829). This three-year interlude in Spain also bore fruit in *The Alhambra* (1832).

On his return (1832) to the United States, Irving contributed a series of distinctly indigenous works to the national literature: the autobiographical *A Tour on the Prairies* (1835); *Astoria* (1836), about John Jacob Astor's ill-fated commercial enterprise on the northwest Pacific Coast; *The Adventures of Captain Bonneville, U.S.A.*

Washington Irving was one of the first Americans to win international recognition as an author. Among the best known of his short stories are "Rip Van Winkle" and "The Legend of Sleepy Hollow."

(1837); and *The Life of George Washington*, published in five volumes between 1855 and 1859, which Irving regarded as the crowning achievement of his literary career.

Isaac   The biblical patriarch Isaac was the promised son of the aged ABRAHAM and SARAH and the father by Rebecca of the twins ESAU and JACOB. When Isaac was a boy, he was almost sacrificed by his obedient father, but God spared the boy. This story (Genesis 22) may illustrate ancient Israel's rejection of child sacrifice. Serving as a bridge in the patriarchal tradition, Isaac is also an important character in the Jacob story. According to Genesis 27, Jacob and his mother deceive the old and feeble Isaac into giving his final blessing to Jacob instead of the firstborn Esau. In the Bible, God is called the God of Abraham, Isaac, and Jacob.

Isaac II Angelus, Byzantine Emperor   Isaac II, b. c.1155, d. February 1204, was proclaimed emperor in 1185 by a mob rising up against the tyrant Andronicus I Comnenus. Isaac was deposed and blinded in 1195 by his elder brother Alexius III. In 1203 the Fourth CRUSADE restored him to the throne as coemperor with his son Alexius IV, but they were both overthrown in January 1204.

During his first reign Isaac fought successfully against invading Normans from Italy (1185), but he could not overcome the rebellious Walachians and Bulgarians nor prevent Holy Roman Emperor FREDERICK I from passing through his lands on the Third Crusade. In his second reign Isaac was senile, a helpless pawn of others.

Isabella I, Queen of Castile   (Isabella the Catholic)   Isabella, b. Apr. 22, 1451, d. Nov. 24, 1504, the daughter of King John II of Castile, laid the foundations for the unification of Spain into one kingdom by her marriage to FERDINAND II of Aragon. Despite intrigues against her during the troubled reign (1454–74) of her brother, Henry IV, Isabella was ultimately recognized as heir in

Isabella I, queen of Castile (1474–1504), laid the foundation of a unified Spanish state by her marriage to Ferdinand II of Aragon. Isabella sponsored the voyages of Christopher Columbus. (Royal Palace, Madrid.)

1468. On Oct. 19, 1469, she married Ferdinand, heir to the throne of Aragon, and on Dec. 13, 1474, she was crowned queen of Castile and León. Isabella and her husband were known as the Catholic kings.

Isabella's reign set the pattern of Spanish domestic policy for generations to come. Aided by her husband, who had few political rights in Castile, she enlisted the nobility in restoring order to the countryside and reformed both the court and the royal administration. Her deep religious convictions made her a guiding spirit behind the founding (1487) of the Spanish INQUISITION and the expulsion (1492) of the Jews, but they also led her to support Cardinal Francisco JIMÉNEZ DE CISNEROS in his efforts to reform the church. The queen inspired the conquest (1492) of GRANADA, the last Moorish stronghold in Spain. She also supported Christopher COLUMBUS, whose discoveries in the New World led to the establishment of a Spanish empire in America. As a patron of scholarship, Isabella helped introduce humanism to Spain. Few monarchs have been as popular in their own time or as venerated since.

Isabella's last years were clouded by the deaths of her son, her eldest daughter, and her infant grandson, and by increasing concern over the stability of her second daughter, JOAN THE MAD. At her death she left Castile to Joan, under the regency of Ferdinand. The Spanish kingdoms were finally united (1516) under Joan's son Charles I, who was to become Holy Roman Emperor CHARLES V.

Isabella II, Queen of Spain   Civil war and revolt marked the reign (1833–68) of Isabella II of Spain. Her conservative leanings and her personal life contributed to her eventual deposition.

Isabella, b. Oct. 10, 1830, d. Apr. 9, 1904, was the daughter of FERDINAND VII and his fourth wife, María Cristina. Isabella was proclaimed queen on Ferdinand's death (1833), but her succession was contested by her uncle Don Carlos. Civil war between her followers and his (the CARLISTS) lasted until 1839. In 1846, Isabella married her cousin Francisco de Asís de Borbón, but she did not live with him, preferring her lovers.

The many revolts during Isabella's reign were caused by demands for reform among army officers, the middle classes, and the urban poor. These demands were resisted, however, by the queen, most generals, and the wealthy. Isabella's most effective prime ministers were two generals, Ramón María Narváez (1800–1868) and Leopoldo O'Dónnell (1809–67). The queen was forced into exile in 1868 after an uprising of liberal officers led by Gen. Juan PRIM overthrew the government. In 1870 she abdicated in favor of her son Alfonso (later ALFONSO XII). Isabella died in Paris.

Isaiah, Book of [y-zay'-uh]   The Book of Isaiah is the first and longest of the books of the Major Prophets in the Old Testament of the BIBLE. It derives its name from the prophet Isaiah, who lived in Jerusalem, perhaps of aristocratic origin. His prophetic career spanned half a century, from about 742 BC to at least 701. The book, however, contains the work of more than one man. Scholars now generally agree that chapters 1 to 35, known as First Isaiah, can be ascribed either to Isaiah himself or to his disciples; chapters 36 to 39 have been taken directly from II Kings 18:13–20:18. Chapters 40 to 55, known as Second Isaiah, or Deutero-Isaiah, were the work of an anonymous prophet-poet during the latter part (c.545–540 BC) of the Babylonian exile. Chapters 56 to 66, known as Third Isaiah, or Trito-Isaiah, were written by authors unknown in detail but working approximately at the end of the 6th century (525–500 BC) or the beginning of the 5th (500–475 BC). Some of the material may be derived from a period even later than these times (c.375–250 BC).

First Isaiah falls roughly into four periods: (1) From 747 to 736 BC the prophet speaks about internal political and economic policy; (2) in 736–735 he addresses the crisis caused by the Syro-Ephraimite War, an attempt to force Jerusalem into an anti-Assyrian alliance; (3) after a period of silence, he speaks again, addressing himself to the attempt of King HEZEKIAH to free himself from status as a vassal to Assyria (716–711); (4) again after a time of silence, Isaiah speaks of Hezekiah's second attempt to establish political independence (705–701). The writings from these periods fall into seven collections of sayings on themes of sin, judgment, and deliverance from the judgment.

Second Isaiah comprises poems of various genres: oracles of deliverance, hymns, prophetic legal speech designed to show that the God of Israel alone is God, and discussion forms designed to repel opposition.

Third Isaiah includes 14 independent sayings concerning the operation of the restored Temple, with corresponding emphasis on the sabbath and cult.

Isère River [ee-zair']   The Isère River rises in the Alps of southeastern France at an elevation of 2,400 m (7,900 ft) above sea level. It flows west and then southwest for 290 km (180 mi), until it joins the RHÔNE RIVER above Valence. Its major tributaries are the Arly and the

Arc. GRENOBLE is the largest city along the Isère, and the river is important for hydroelectric power.

Isfahan

Isfahan [is-fah-hahn'] Isfahan (also Esfahan) is the second largest city of Iran and the capital of Isfahan province. The city is located on the north bank of the Zayandeh River about 320 km (200 mi) south of Tehran. The population is 986,753 (1986 est.).

Isfahan is a transportation center and has long been famous for its traditional handicrafts. The old art of tile making has been revived for use in restoring Isfahan's many historical monuments. A modern industrial complex manufactures steel and textiles. The University of Isfahan (1966) is located there.

First known as a city during the Sassanian period, Isfahan was conquered in 642 by the Arabs, who made it a provincial capital. During the mid-11th century the SELJUKS captured Isfahan and made it the capital of their vast empire in 1051. In 1387, TIMUR conquered the city and killed many of the inhabitants. Isfahan reached its zenith after 1598, when Shah ABBAS I chose the city as the capital of the Safavid dynasty. Abbas built many of the monuments that remain today. Isfahan fell into a long decline beginning in 1722 when it was captured by Afghans. In the reign of REZA SHAH PAHLAVI (1925–41) it was revived as an industrial center. Among Isfahan's many outstanding examples of medieval Islamic architecture are the Masjid-i-Imam (Imam Mosque) and Shayk Lutfulla mosque.

Isherwood, Christopher

Isherwood, Christopher [ish'-ur-wud] Christopher William Bradshaw-Isherwood, b. Cheshire, England, Aug. 26, 1904, d. Jan. 14, 1986, was a novelist and writer of nonfiction. While a schoolboy in Surrey he began a lifelong friendship with the poet W. H. AUDEN. Living off and on in Germany until 1933, Isherwood came to understand the social and political climate of pre-Hitler Germany, which he described in *Mr. Norris Changes Trains* (1935), *Sally Bowles* (1937), and *Goodbye to Berlin* (1939). The drama *I Am a Camera* (1951) and the musical *Cabaret* (1966) came from his writings on Germany.

In 1939, Isherwood settled in California, becoming a U.S. citizen in 1946. He also became a disciple of the California-based VEDANTA philosopher Swami Prabhavananda, with whom he collaborated on several Hindu religious works, as described in Isherwood's *My Guru and His Disciple* (1980).

Down There on a Visit (1962), perhaps his best novel, centers on Isherwood's life in Germany, Greece, England, and California. *Kathleen and Frank* (1971) is his effort to understand his early childhood. Homosexual love later became a central concern, as in *A Meeting by the River* (1967) and *Christopher and His Kind* (1976).

Ishmael

Ishmael [ish'-may-el] According to Genesis 16, Ishmael was the son of the patriarch ABRAHAM by the Egyptian handmaiden HAGAR. When Abraham's supposedly barren wife SARAH finally bore ISAAC, a rivalry developed between Sarah and Hagar and thus between the two half brothers, Isaac and Ishmael.

Cast out into the wilderness, Ishmael was the ancestor of the nomadic Arabian Ishmaelites, arranged, like the Israelites, into 12 tribes. Because Islam traces its lineage from Abraham through Ishmael, and Judaism and Christianity trace their lineages through Isaac, Muslims, Jews, and Christians are all spiritual "children of Abraham."

Ishtar

Ishtar [ish'-tahr] In Babylonian and Assyrian mythology, Ishtar was the principal goddess and the queen of heaven. She was worshiped by the Phoenicians as ASTARTE, by the Sumerians as Inanna, and by other peoples of the region under various names. A composite of many earlier goddesses, Ishtar was both the compassionate mother of all life, who brought fertility and relief from sickness, and the lustful goddess of sexual love and of war. These contrasting attributes are reflected in the story that she caused the great flood and then was sorry about it. The best-known legend about her is that of her imprisonment by Allatu, queen of the underworld, where Ishtar had gone to visit her lover, Tammuz, the god of vegetation. Ishtar was later identified with the Greek APHRODITE and the Roman VENUS.

Isidore of Seville, Saint

Isidore of Seville, Saint Isidore of Seville, b. *c.*560, d. Apr. 4, 636, was a Spanish churchman and encyclopedist who is generally regarded as the last of the western Fathers of the Church. Isidore exercised a wide influence throughout Spain, bringing about unity between Hispano-Romans and Visigoths. He fostered learning and culture, promoted the education of clergy, and preserved for the Middle Ages the intellectual riches of earlier centuries.

Isidore was a compiler rather than an original thinker. His encyclopedic writings covered all of the areas of knowledge of the time and were used as textbooks by students and as sources by authors during the Middle Ages. His best-known works are *Etymologiae* (Origins), a compendium of classical knowledge; and *Historia de Regibus Gothorum, Vandalorum et Suevorum* (History of the Kings of the Goths, Vandals, and Suevi), an important chronicle of the time. He was canonized in 1598. Feast day: Apr. 4.

Isis

Isis [y'-sis] In Egyptian mythology Isis was the mother goddess of fertility and nature. Her worship was combined with that of her brother and husband, OSIRIS, and her son HORUS. She is often depicted wearing on her head the horns of a cow, encircled by either a lunar or solar disk. Her worship originated in Egypt, and by Hellenistic times she had assimilated the attributes of the major Greek divinities DEMETER and APHRODITE. By the period of the Roman Empire she had become the most prominent deity of the Mediterranean basin, as her temple at Pompeii attests.

Although Isis's cult focused on the celebration of the mysteries associated with the death and resurrection of Osiris, she had many titles, including queen of heaven, earth, and the underworld, and mother of wheat.

During the early centuries AD the cult of Isis was a formidable contender with the newly founded Christian religion. Despite purges of the followers of Isis, her worship continued well into the 6th century AD.

—

Islam [iz'-luhm]   Islam is customarily defined in non-Islamic sources as the religion of those who follow the Prophet MUHAMMAD. Adherents of Islam are called Muslims (sometimes spelled Moslems). They number about 750 million worldwide.

Basis of Islam

The Name and Its Meaning. The Arabic word *al-islam* means the act of committing oneself unreservedly to God, and a Muslim is a person who makes this commitment. Widely used translations such as "resignation," "surrender," and "submission" fail to do justice to the positive aspects of the total commitment for which *al-islam* stands—a commitment in faith, obedience, and trust to the one and only God (ALLAH). All of these elements are implied in the name of this religion, which is characteristically described in the KORAN (Arabic, Qur'an; the sacred book of Islam) as "the religion of Abraham." In the Koran, ABRAHAM is the patriarch who turned away from idolatry, who "came to his Lord with an undivided heart" (37:84), who responded to God in total obedience when challenged to sacrifice his son (37:102–105), and who served God uncompromisingly.

Origin. Although Islam dates back to the lifetime (570–632) of the Prophet Muhammad and the years in which he received the divine revelations recorded in the Koran, most believers would stress that their religion is the restoration of the original religion of Abraham. They would also stress that Islam is a timeless religion, not just because of the "eternal truth" that it proclaims but also because it is "every person's religion," the natural religion in which every person is born.

Islam's Comprehensive Character. When applied to Islam, the word religion has a far more comprehensive meaning than it commonly has in the West. Islam encompasses personal faith and piety, the creed and worship of the community of believers, a way of life, a code of ethics, a culture, a system of laws, an understanding of the function of the state—in short, guidelines and rules for life in all its aspects and dimensions. While many Muslims see the SHARIA (the "way," denoting the sacred law governing the life of individuals as well as the structures of society) as fixed and immutable, others make a clear distinction between the unchangeable message of the Koran and the mutable laws and regulations for Muslim life and conduct. Throughout history, practices and opinions have differed with regard to the exact way in which Islam determines life in all its aspects, but the basic notion of Islam's comprehensive character is intrinsic to Muslim thought and feeling.

According to Muslim jurists, the *sharia* is derived from four sources—the Koran; the *sunna* ("customs") of the Prophet, which are embodied in the *hadith* ("tradition"); *qiyas* ("analogy"; the application of a decision of the past, or the principles on which it was based, to new questions); and *ijma* ("consensus"; the consensus of the community of believers, who, according to a saying of the Prophet, would not agree on any error).

History and Spread of Islam

The Prophet. Muhammad was born in 570 in MECCA, a trading center in western Arabia. About 610 he received the first of a series of revelations that convinced him that he had been chosen as God's messenger. He began to preach the message entrusted to him—that there is but one God, to whom all humankind must commit themselves. The polytheistic Meccans resented Muhammad's attacks on their gods, and finally he emigrated with a few followers to MEDINA. This migration, which is called the Hegira (Hijrah), took place in 622; Muslims adopted the beginning of that year as the first year of their lunar calendar (Anno Hegirae, or AH).

At Medina, Muhammad won acceptance as a religious and military leader. Within a few years he had gained control of the surrounding region, and in 630 he finally conquered Mecca. There, the KAABA, a shrine that had for some time housed the idols of the pagan Meccans, was rededicated to the worship of Allah, and it became the object of pilgrimage for all Muslims. By the time of his death in 632, Muhammad had won the allegiance of most Arab tribespeople to Islam. He had laid the foundation for a community (*umma*) ruled by the laws of God.

A Rapidly Growing Empire, 632–750. After the death of Muhammad, a successor (*khalifa*, or caliph; see IMAM) was chosen to rule in his place. The first caliph, the Prophet's father-in-law, ABU BAKR (r. 632–34), initiated an expansionist movement that was carried out most successfully by the next two caliphs, UMAR I (r. 634–44) and Uthman (r. 644–56). By 656 the CALIPHATE included the whole Arabian peninsula, Palestine and Syria, Egypt and Libya, Mesopotamia, and substantial parts of Armenia and Persia. Following the assassination of Uthman, the disagreements between those upholding the rights of the fourth caliph, ALI (r. 656–61), the Prophet's son-in-law, and his opponents led to a division in the Muslim community between the SHIITES and the SUNNITES that still exists today. When the governor of Syria, MUAWIYAH I, came to power after the murder of Ali, the Shiites refused to recognize him and his successors.

Muawiyah inaugurated an almost 90-year rule by the UMAYYADS (661–750), who made Damascus their capital. A second wave of expansion followed. After they conquered (670) Tunisia, Muslim troops reached the northwestern point of North Africa in 710. In 711 they crossed the Strait of Gibraltar, rapidly overran Spain, and penetrated well into France until they were turned back near Poitiers in 732. On the northern frontier Constantinople was besieged more than once (though without success), and in the east the Indus River was reached; the Islamic empire now bordered China and India.

Rival Dynasties and Competing Capitals (Baghdad, Córdoba, Cairo), 750–1258. In 750, Umayyad rule in Damascus was ended by the ABBASIDS, who moved the caliphate's capital to Baghdad. The succeeding period was marked more by an expansion of horizons of thought than by geographical expansion. In the fields of literature, the sciences, and philosophy, contributions by such Muslim scholars as al-KINDI, al-FARABI, and Ibn Sina (AVICENNA) far surpassed European accomplishments of that time.

Politically, the power of the Abbasids was challenged by a number of rival dynasties. These included an Umayyad dynasty in Córdoba, Spain (756–1031); the FATIMIDS, a dynasty connected with the ISMAILIS (a Shiite sect), who established (909) themselves in Tunisia and later (969–1171) ruled Egypt; the Almoravids and the Almohads, Muslim Berber dynasties that successively ruled North Africa and Spain from the mid-11th to the mid-13th century; the SELJUKS, a Muslim Turkish group that seized Baghdad in 1055 and whose defeat of the Byzantines in 1071 led indirectly to the Christian CRUSADES (1096–1254) against the Islamic world; and the Ayyubids, who displaced the Fatimids in Egypt and played an important role in the later years of the Crusades.

The Abbasids were finally overthrown (1258) in Baghdad by the MONGOLS, although a family member escaped to Egypt, where he was recognized as caliph. While the community of faith remained a reality, the political unity of the Muslim world was definitely broken.

Two Great Islamic Powers: The Ottomans and the Moguls, 15th–18th Century. The Ottoman Turkish dynasty, founded by Osman I (c.1300), became a major world power in the 15th century, and continued to play a significant role throughout the 16th and 17th centuries. The BYZANTINE EMPIRE, with which Muslim armies had been at war since the early days of Islam, came to an end in 1453 when Ottoman sultan MEHMED II conquered Constantinople.

That city then became the capital of the OTTOMAN EMPIRE.

In the first half of the 16th century, Ottoman power, already firmly established over all Anatolia and most of the Balkans, gained control over Syria, Egypt (the sultans assumed the title caliph after deposing the last Abbasid in Cairo), and the rest of North Africa. It also expanded significantly northwestward into Europe, besieging Vienna in 1529. The defeat of the Ottoman navy in the Battle of LEPANTO in 1571 was not, as many in Europe hoped, the beginning of a rapid disintegration of the Ottoman Empire; more than 100 years later, in 1683, Ottoman troops once again besieged Vienna. The decline of the empire became more visible from the late 17th century onward, but it survived through World War I. Turkey became a republic under Kemal ATATÜRK in 1923, and the caliphate was abolished in 1924.

The MOGULS were a Muslim dynasty of Turko-Mongol origin who conquered northern India in 1526. The Mogul Empire reached the climax of its power in the period from the late 16th century until the beginning of the 18th century. Under the emperors AKBAR, JAHANGIR, SHAH JAHAN, and AURANGZEB, Mogul rule was extended over most of the subcontinent, and Islamic culture (with a strong Persian flavor) was firmly implanted in certain areas. In the 18th century Mogul power began to decline. It survived, at least in name, however, until 1858, when the last sultan was dethroned by the British.

Two Examples of the Coming of Islam in Frontier Areas: Indonesia and West Africa. In the 13th century Islam established itself in Sumatra, where small Muslim states formed on the northeast coast. Islam spread to Java in the 16th century, and then expanded, generally in a peaceful manner, from the coastal areas inward to all parts of the Indonesian archipelago. By the 19th century it had reached to the northeast and extended into the Philippines.

Islam penetrated West Africa in three main phases.

The al-Haram, or Great Mosque, at Mecca contains the Kaaba (center), a square shrine housing the Black Stone, which Muslims believe to be one of the stones of paradise. According to the Koran, the Kaaba was built by Abraham and Ishmael. Revered as the place where heavenly power directly touches the Earth, it is the focus of the pilgrimage to Mecca.

Pilgrims at a mosque in Kano, Nigeria, attend a communal prayer gathering during Ramadan, the ninth month of the Muslim year, during which fasting is observed in the daylight hours. Through the activities of Arab and Berber caravan traders, Islam was established as a major religion in West Africa.

The first was that of contacts with Arab and Berber caravan traders, from the 10th century onward. Then followed a period of gradual Islamization of some rulers' courts, among them that of the famous MANSA MUSA (r. 1312–27) in Mali. Finally, in the 16th century the Sufi orders (brotherhoods of mystics; see SUFISM), especially the Qadiriyya, Tijaniyya, and Muridiyya, as well as individual saints and scholars, began to play an important role. In the 19th century more than one JIHAD (holy war) for the purification of Islam from pagan influences occurred, while later in the 19th century and in the first half of the 20th century, Muslims formed a significant element in the growing resistance to colonial powers. In the postcolonial period Islam played an important role in Nigeria, Senegal, Guinea, Mali, and Niger, and there are smaller Muslim communities in the other states in West Africa.

Islam in Modern History. Napoléon's invasion of Egypt in 1798, followed three years later by the expulsion of the French troops by the combined British-Ottoman forces, is often seen as the beginning of the modern period in the history of Islam. The coming to power of MUHAMMAD ALI (r. 1805–49) and the modernization of Egypt under his leadership was the beginning of a long struggle throughout the Muslim world to reestablish independence from the colonial powers and for Muslim countries to assume their place as autonomous states in the modern world. Resistance to foreign domination and an awareness of the need to restore the Muslim community to its proper place in world history are integral parts of the Pan-Islamic efforts of JAMAL AL-DIN AL-AFGHANI as well as the nationalist movements of the 20th century.

The political, social, and economic developments in the various countries with Muslim majorities show significant differences. For example, Turkey and many of the Arab countries have become secular republics, whereas Iran became an Islamic republic under the leadership of the Ayatollah KHOMEINI.

Islamic Doctrines

Islamic doctrines are commonly discussed and taught widely—often by means of a catechism, with questions and answers—under six headings: God, angels, Scriptures, messengers, the Last Day, and predestination. The Muslims' notion of God (Allah) is, in a sense, interrelated with all of the other points and will be referred to below. Some of the angels (all of whom are servants of God and subject to him) play a particularly important role in the daily life of many Muslims: the guardian angels; the recording angels (those who write down a person's deeds, for which he or she will have to account on Judgment Day); the angel of death; and the angels who question a person in the tomb. One of those mentioned by name in the Koran is Jibril (see GABRIEL, angel), who functioned in a special way as a transmitter of God's revelation to the Prophet.

The promise and threat of the Last Day, which occupy an important place in the Koran, continue to play a major role in Muslim thought and piety. On the Last Day, of which only God knows the hour, every soul will stand alone and will have to account for its deeds.

The last of the six articles, PREDESTINATION, is among the theocentric issues of Islam. Because the divine initiative is all-decisive in bringing humans to faith ("had God not guided us, we had surely never been guided," 7:43), many theologians concluded that God is not only responsible for guiding some but also for not guiding others, allowing them to go astray or even leading them astray. In the debate among later theologians, the antipredestinarians were concerned less with upholding the notion of human freedom and, therefore, of human dignity than with defending the honor of God. According to these thinkers—the Qadarites and the Mutazilites, of the 8th to the 10th century—the Koranic message of the justice of God "who does not wrong people" ("they wrong themselves," 43:76) excluded the notion of a God who would punish human beings for evil deeds and unbelief for which they themselves were not really responsible. The major concern of their opponents was to maintain, against any such reasoning, the doctrine of the sovereign freedom of God, upon whom no limits can be placed, not even the limit of "being bound to do what is best for his creatures." Two important theologians of the 10th century, al-Ashari (d. 935) and al-Maturidi (d. 944), formulated answers that would mark for the centuries to come the traditional (Sunni) position on these points. Although one's acts are willed and created by God, one has to appropriate them to make them one's own.

Around this concept of the unity of God another debate arose on the essence and attributes of God; it focused on the question whether the Koran—God's speech—was created or uncreated. Those who held that the Koran was created believed that the notion of an uncreated Koran implied another eternal reality alongside God, who alone is eternal and does not share his eternity with anyone or anything else. Their opponents felt that the notion of a created Koran detracted from its character as God's own speech. The Sunni position that emerged from these discussions was that the Koran as written down or recited is created, but that it is a manifestation of the eternal "inner speech" of God, which precedes any articulation in sounds and letters.

Theological issues often have political implications. For example, the Shiites were those who maintained that only "members of the family" (Hashimites, or, in the more restricted sense, descendants of the Prophet via his daughter, FATIMA and her husband Ali) had a right to the caliphate. Another group, the Kharijites (literally, "those who seceded"), broke away from Ali (who was murdered by one of their members) and from the Umayyads. They developed the doctrine that confession, or faith, alone did not make a person a believer and that anyone committing grave sins was an unbeliever destined to hell. They applied this argument to the leaders of the community, holding that caliphs who were grave sinners could not claim the allegiance of the faithful. While the mainstream of Muslims accepted the principle that faith and works

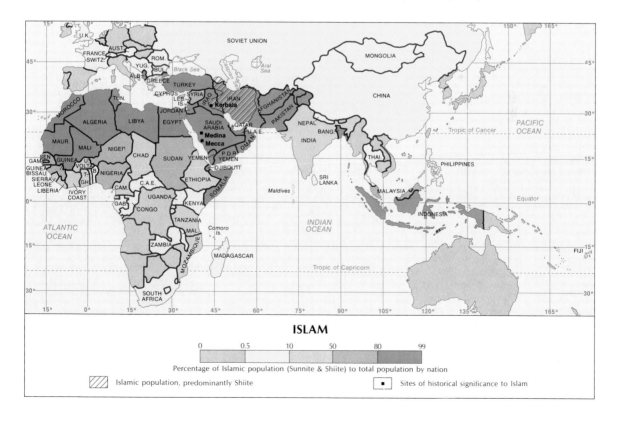

ISLAM

Percentage of Islamic population (Sunnite & Shiite) to total population by nation

0   0.5   10   50   80   99

Islamic population, predominantly Shiite

Sites of historical significance to Islam

must go together, they rejected the Kharijite ideal of establishing here on Earth a pure community of believers, insisting that the ultimate decision on whether a person is a believer or an unbeliever must be left to God.

Islamic Worship, Practices, and Duties

To what extent faith and works go together is evident from the traditional listing of the basic duties of any Muslim, the "five pillars" of Islam: *shahada*, the profession of faith in God and the apostleship of Muhammad; *salat*, the ritual prayer, performed five times a day facing Mecca; *zakat*, almsgiving; *sawm* (fasting), abstaining from food and drink during the daylight hours of the month of RAMADAN; and *hajj*, the pilgrimage to Mecca, incumbent on every believer who is financially and physically able to undertake it. The witness to God stands here side by side with the concern for the poor, reflected in almsgiving. The personal involvement of the individual believer, expressed most clearly in the formulation of the *shahada*, "*I* witness there is no God but God, and Muhammad is the messenger of God," is combined with a deep awareness of the strength that lies in the fellowship of faith and the community of all believers, significant dimensions of both the ritual prayer and the pilgrimage.

Muslim worship and devotion is not limited to the precisely prescribed words and gestures of the *salat* but finds expression also in a wealth of personal prayers, in the gathering of the congregation in the central mosque on Fridays, and in the celebration of the two main festivals: Id al-Fitr, the festival of the breaking of the fast at the end of Ramadan; and Id al-Adha, the festival of the sacrifice (in memory of Abraham's willingness to sacrifice his son). The latter, observed on the 10th day of the month of pilgrimage, is celebrated not only by the participants in the pilgrimage but also simultaneously by those who stay in their own locations. The interpretations of *jihad* (literally, "striving" in the way of God), sometimes added as an additional duty, vary from sacred war to striving to fulfill the ethical norms and principles expounded in the Koran.

Islam, Nation of   see BLACK MUSLIMS

Islam in the West, World Community of   see BLACK MUSLIMS

Islamabad [is-lum-uh'-bahd']   Islamabad, the capital city of Pakistan, is located in the northeastern part of the country, near the Himalayas. The city covers 65 km^2 (25 mi^2) and has a population of 201,000 (1981). Islamabad, whose name means City of Peace, is a new city, built between 1960 and 1975 to replace KARACHI as the capital. Nearby RAWALPINDI served as the interim capital (1959–67) until the new capital was completed. Islamabad is divided into eight districts; the government's administrative buildings make up the central district, which is surrounded by commercial, residential, and educational zones. Industrial and green zones encircle the city.

Islamic art and architecture   Islamic art and architecture refers to artistic achievements in those lands where, from the 7th century on, ISLAM became the dominant faith. The Islamic tradition encompasses the arts of the Middle East, North Africa, Spain, Anatolia and the Balkans, Central Asia, and northern and central India, from the time each of these areas became Muslim—as early as AD 622 in parts of Arabia and as late as the 15th century for Istanbul, parts of the Balkans, and central India. Generally excluded from consideration in this context are the arts of sub-Saharan and eastern Africa, Indonesia, Malaysia, the Philippines, and Muslim parts of China. These areas did not adopt Islam until relatively late, generally after the 16th century, and by that time the artistic creativity of the central Muslim lands had weakened; their arts tend to be closer to local traditions.

General Characteristics

During the most creative millennium in Islamic art (about 650–1650), certain key features emerged that came to characterize the Islamic style of art and architecture. These shared characteristics appeared despite the differences in environment ranging from Mediterranean Spain to arid Arabia, and despite the cultural diversity of such distant ethnic groups as Arabs, Berbers, Persians, Turks, and Indians. The developing Islamic tradition drew on complex artistic inheritances that included Late Roman art, Early Christian art of the Byzantines and the Copts, and Sassanian art of Persia, and on lesser influences from Mongol, Central Asian, and Indian sources.

Function of Art. From its inception Islamic art was an art created for the setting of daily life. Most religious architecture, notably the MOSQUE and the MINARET, was built less as a testimonial to Allah than as a place where people could best express their piety and learn the precepts

This 12th-century bronze incense burner from Gurgan, Iran, is representative of the highly decorative metalwork of the Seljuk period. (Archaeological Museum, Tehran.)

This relief tilework from a late-14th-century mausoleum at Fathabad, Uzbekistan, typifies the architectural inscription of the Timurid period. (Victoria and Albert Museum, London.)

of the faith. Islamic painting developed primarily in the form of book illustration and illumination, images created to explain or to enhance the text.

In the field of the decorative arts the Islamic style is distinguished by the quality of techniques used in the making of utilitarian objects: the application of lustrous glazes and rich colors in ceramics and glassware; intricate silver inlays that transform the surfaces of bronze metalwork; lavish molded stucco and carved wood wall panels; and endlessly varied motifs woven into textiles and rugs. In nearly all instances the objects decorated—whether ewers, candlesticks, or pen cases—served fundamentally practical purposes.

From Córdoba in Spain to Samarkand in Central Asia, the cities were the centers of Islamic learning and of mercantile wealth. The vast majority of surviving examples of Islamic art were made for the bourgeoisie of the cities.

Little has been preserved of the art created for kings and emperors. An exquisitely ornamented and rare rock-crystal ewer, preserved in the San Marco Museum, Venice, provides a hint of the richness of 10th- and 11th-century Fatimid art in Cairo; the countless treasures in the Topkapi Palace Museum, Istanbul, attest to the enormous wealth of the Turkish Ottomans.

Decorative Character of Art. A fundamental characteristic of much Islamic art is its powerfully decorative or ornamental quality. A variety of arbitrary geometric, floral, or other types of designs—such as the swirling, interlaced arabesque—tends to predominate over specific motifs taken from nature or from an idealized version of the natural world. In this decorative tendency Islamic art contrasts sharply with the representational art of the West, in which precise iconographic meanings are attached to most artistic forms.

Also characteristic of Islamic art is what is generally called its iconoclasm, or rejection of the representation of religious images and other living beings. Early Islamic art modified the art of previous centuries by tending to avoid the representation of humans and animals. Whether this reluctance was derived from a still undetected religious prohibition or from a search for a cultural identity distinct from the identities of other traditions remains a matter of scholarly debate.

Primacy of Calligraphy. The art of CALLIGRAPHY played a preeminent role throughout the world of Islam. Because of its association with the divine revelation, the Arabic alphabet became the vehicle for such diverse languages as Persian and Turkish. In addition, Islamic culture in general was highly verbal, therefore, unusual attention was given to the transformation of writing into a visually appealing expression of aesthetic forms. From the sharp angles of early Kufic to the flowing rhythms of later Persian *shekasteh* script or to the formal compositions of an Ottoman *tughra* (imperial emblem), many different systems of proportions between letters, relationships between parts of letters, and arrangements of words were developed. The impact of a fascination with writing appeared throughout the Islamic world: ceramics, metal objects, textiles, and architecture all acquired calligraphic forms as a universally appreciated means of decoration.

Historical Development

Although no universally accepted chronology of Islamic art and architecture exists, the following three major periods are generally recognized: the Formative period (650–1000), Middle period (1000–1250), and Late period (1250 on).

The Formative Period. From about 650 to 1000—under the Umayyad and early Abbasid CALIPHATES as well as the first local dynasties in Spain, Egypt, and eastern Iran—the Muslim world created its own identifying forms, from mosques to the abstract design known as the arabesque. Major monuments from this period include the mosques of Córdoba, Ibn Tulun in Cairo, Damascus, Samarra, and Dome of the Rock in Jerusalem; private palaces such as the Khirbat-al-Mafjar in Palestine; royal palaces such as Samarra's in Iraq; and the urban architecture of Baghdad. Peculiarly Islamic forms of decorative art were tin-glazed ceramics in Iraq, Egypt, and northeastern Iran; woodwork and rock-crystal carving in Egypt; and carved ivories in Spain. The most influential and perhaps most creative area was Iraq, which remained the center of the Muslim world until the early part of the 11th century.

The Middle Period. The year 1000 marks the beginning of the Middle period of Islamic art. During this brilliant period, cut short by the Mongol invasion during the early 13th century, a large number of local styles were formed. Eastern Iran, western Iran, Iraq, Egypt, Anatolia (newly conquered by the Seljuks), North Africa, and Spain all acquired their own stylistic and iconographic peculiarities. Cairo, Nishapur, Herat, Isfahan, and the Anatolian center of Konya rivaled the early Islamic capital city of Baghdad in cultural and artistic importance. Yet common threads were maintained in the art of these diverse centers. In almost all Islamic cities an architecture of citadels and city walls rather than of palaces reflected the new power of a military elite. Throughout the Muslim world a new emphasis was given to external forms of architecture (minarets, gates, and domes).

New or reinvented techniques in the decorative arts—minai, or enameling in ceramics, luster painting in glass, and silver inlays in metalwork—made it possible to increase the number and character of illustrated topics. Quite suddenly in the latter part of the 12th century, during this period of intense artistic creativity, books began to be illustrated. The proliferation of new forms of representation may in part reflect new contacts with other cultures (India and the Christian West), but it probably also reflected an internal need for more complex expressions of a richer culture. The Middle period was an era when mysticism began to affect all aspects of Muslim piety and when local cultural traditions, especially those in Iran, began to reassert themselves.

Late Period. After the devastating Mongol invasions of 1220–60 the Muslim world became more strictly divided both politically and culturally. West to east, the principal independent cultural areas were the Muslim West, the area comprising Egypt, Palestine, and Syria; the Ottoman Empire; Iran; and Muslim India.

In the Muslim West, Islam slowly disappeared from Spain, culminating in the fall of Granada in 1492, but was maintained in North Africa. Moorish art is distinguished primarily by brilliant geometrical ornamentation adorning mostly private, interiorized, architectural monuments. This striking decorative tradition was maintained by the Mudéjars, Moors remaining in Spain after its reconquest by the Christians, and exerted a strong influence on later Spanish styles of craftwork and architectural decoration. Except for the unique masterpiece of the 14th-century ALHAMBRA palace, however, most of western Islamic art tended to be conservative and repetitive, with limited novelties in the art of objects.

From 1258 to 1517 the area comprising Egypt, Palestine, and Syria was ruled by the unique system of military slaves known as the MAMELUKES. Its major artistic achievement was in architecture, as attested by the multitude of Mameluke monuments still extant in the cities of Cairo, Jerusalem, and to a lesser degree, Damascus and Aleppo. For complex economic and social reasons

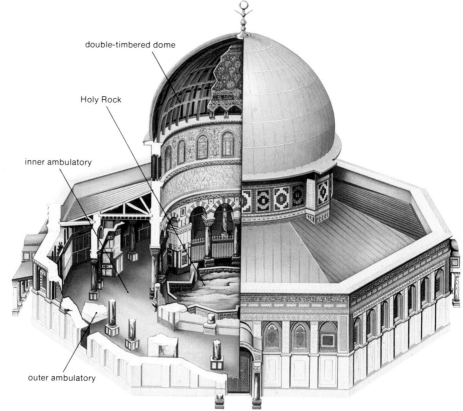

double-timbered dome

Holy Rock

inner ambulatory

outer ambulatory

The Qubbat al-Sakhra, or Dome of the Rock, Jerusalem, is one of the earliest and most important Islamic shrines. Constructed (691) by the Umayyad caliph Abd-al-Malik, the octagonal structure more closely resembles Christian architecture than it does Islamic. A double colonnade of Corinthian columns divides the interior into two concentric ambulatories focusing on the al-Sakhra, or Holy Rock, significant to Islamic, Judaic, and Christian tradition. The interior is lavishly decorated with quartered marble and naturalistic glass mosaics; the mosaics originally covering the exterior surfaces were replaced by ceramic decoration during the 16th century. The double-timbered dome is covered at present with sheets of gilded aluminum.

This miniature (1485), by the Herat calligrapher and artist Mirak Naqqash, illustrates a scene from the "Khusrau and Shirin" segment of Nezami's Khamseh, *a 12th-century dramatic poem. (Chester Beatty Library, Dublin.)*

the affluent classes invested in vast architectural projects that transformed these cities. The buildings are traditional in function, but their forms and techniques—superb stonework, brilliantly decorated gates and minarets, complex domes—display a level of sophistication and quality hitherto unknown in the Islamic world. A characteristic example, ranked among the masterpieces of world architecture, is the immense *madrasah* of Sultan Hasan in Cairo.

The Ottoman dynasty, having begun in western Anatolia, conquered the Balkans and took Constantinople in 1453 and nearly all Islamic lands around the Mediterranean by 1520. A strong, centralized state, the Ottoman Empire concentrated its creative energies on the development of a uniquely logical mosque architecture. As early as the 14th and 15th centuries, in Bursa and Iznik, the Ottomans chose to use the single dome as the focal compositional element of their monuments. This fascination with the cupola was in large part inspired by the Byzantine church of HAGIA SOPHIA (which was converted into a mosque) and culminated in the 16th-century masterpiece of the Suleiman (Süleymaniye) mosque in Istanbul. Ottoman decorative art, especially ceramic objects and tiles, and miniature painting are largely derivative of other traditions, although many examples are noteworthy for the exceptional precision of their execution.

Of all the Islamic lands, Iran was most strongly affected by the Mongol invasions, but this traumatic experience led to a rejuvenation of the arts, despite continuous political upheavals. Under the Ilkhanids (1280–1336), the Timurids (1370–1502), and Safavids (1502–1712), and several other minor dynasties, Persian architecture exhibited a whole gamut of styles ranging from the grandiloquent monumentality of the Sultaniyah mosque to the intense piety of Samarkand's mausoleums, to the colorful brilliance of the monuments around Isfahan's Masjid-i-Shah mosque. It was an imaginative, inventive, accretive tradition remarkably attuned to the composition of Persian religious thought. Especially impressive is the development of Persian painting. From the *Shah-Nama* (Book of Kings) to lyrical poems of Nizami, Persian literature was illuminated through a striking array of painting styles—rough and brutal in the early 14th century, poetically complex in the 15th century, and marked by precisely observed details of everyday life in later times. (See PERSIAN ART AND ARCHITECTURE.)

Farther east, after several centuries of rule by various military dynasties, Islamic India reached its apogee under the MOGULS (1526–1707). Their architecture was often inspired by Persia but rapidly acquired its own identity through the use of local materials and techniques. The Mogul achievements in architecture are most impressive in such celebrated buildings as the TAJ MAHAL or the urban complex of Fatehpur Sikri. The Persian influence was also strongly felt in painting in the early years, but soon Mogul art became uniquely inspired by the remarkable precision and human insights apparent in native Indian traditions of painting. (See MOGUL ART AND ARCHITECTURE.)

island   An island is most simply defined as any landmass that is smaller than the smallest continent and that is completely surrounded by water. Islands range in size from huge land-masses to tiny river islets, or aits. The world's ten largest islands, in descending order of size, are Greenland, New Guinea, Borneo, Madagascar, Baffin Island, Sumatra, Honshu, Great Britain, Ellesmere Island, and Canada's Victoria Island. Close island groupings are often called archipelagos.

Geologically, islands may be considered either continental or oceanic. Continental islands are part of neighboring continental masses, separated from them when the CONTINENTAL SHELF is flooded by rising sea levels (see ICE AGES). Examples include Greenland, Great Britain, and Newfoundland. Deposits of sediment may also form islands in lakes, rivers, and estuaries (see also BEACH AND COAST; RIVER DELTA).

Oceanic islands are generally volcanic in origin. They arise as repeated eruptions build up materials that eventually appear above the ocean surface. The Hawaiian Islands are an example. In addition, atolls may be formed by reef-building corals around the sites of eroded or submerged volcanoes (see CORAL REEF). Some large island groupings, such as those which constitute Indonesia, have a complex geological history combining both continental and oceanic origins.

Where volcanic islands occur in long, narrow, and usually curved chains, such as the Aleutians, they are known as island arcs. Such arcs occur where two plates of the Earth's crust converge (see PLATE TECTONICS). They are most common at boundaries between oceanic and continental plates; examples include the Aleutians, the islands of Japan, and the Kuril Islands (see also RING OF FIRE). Some, however, such as the Tonga, the Kermadec, and the Mariana islands, occur between convergent oceanic plates. At convergent boundaries, one plate is subducted beneath the other. The subduction zone is marked by a deep OCEANIC TRENCH located some distance oceanward of the island arc. Great EARTHQUAKES originate beneath the trench, at the contact of the two plates. The subducted plate descends and melts, forming MAGMA that erupts through the arc's VOLCANOES. Other volcanic islands, such as Iceland, form where crustal plates diverge, at MID-OCEANIC RIDGES.

Through various processes of buildup and erosion, island arcs may eventually be incorporated within a continental mass, forming mountains such as the South American Andes and the Cascade Range of western North America.

Isle of Man   The Isle of Man, a crown possession of the United Kingdom, lies in the Irish Sea 48 km (30 mi) west of England. A rocky, indented coast gives way to gentle hills that rise to a maximum height of 620 m (2,034 ft) at Snaefell. The island covers 572 km^2 (221 mi^2). The population is 64,282 (1986). Douglas, the capital, is the largest town (1986 pop., 20,368).

Agriculture (grains and root vegetables), dairying, and sheep raising are significant, but tourism forms the base of the island's economy. Although under the administration of the British Home Office, the island has its own bicameral legislature, the Court of Tynwald (979), the world's oldest continuous parliament. The Isle of Man has no income tax, and this has attracted many immigrants from Great Britain.

Inhabited from Neolithic times, the island became a refuge of Irish missionaries after the 5th century. Norsemen took it during the 9th century and sold it to Scotland in 1266. Since the 14th century it has been held by England. Manx, the indigenous Celtic language, is still spoken by a tiny minority.

Isle of Wight   The Isle of Wight is an island county off the southern coast of Hampshire, England. Newport is the administrative center. The area is 381 km^2 (147 mi^2), and the population is 129,800 (1988 est.). The Medina, Western Yar, and Eastern Yar rivers cut deeply into its chalk uplands, which reach their greatest height (240 m/ 787 ft) at Saint Boniface Down. A mild, sunny climate and arable lowlands aid agriculture. Agriculture, shipbuilding, aircraft manufacturing, and tourism are the economic mainstays. The island's points of interest include Bronze Age mounds, monoliths believed to be from the Neolithic period, Roman villas, Quarr Abbey, Carisbrooke Castle, where Charles I was imprisoned (1647–48), and Osborne House, Queen Victoria's seaside home. The resort town of Cowes is famous for its annual yachting regattas.

Ismail Pasha [is-mah-eel' pah'-shuh]   Ismail Pasha, b. Dec. 31, 1830, d. Mar. 2, 1895, ruled Egypt (1863–79) under the suzerainty of the Ottoman Empire, receiving the hereditary title of khedive (viceroy) in 1867. Ismail completed the SUEZ CANAL, extended Egyptian control over the Sudan, constructed irrigation facilities, and modernized education. His policies led to an enormous foreign debt, however, and in 1875, Ismail was forced to sell his interest in the Suez Canal to Great Britain. The Ottoman sultanate replaced him in 1879 with his son TAWFIQ PASHA. Ismail's policies had so weakened Egypt financially and politically that Britain was soon able to occupy the country (in 1882).

Ismailis [is-mah-eel'-eez]   The Ismailis are members of a sect of Muslim SHIITES who recognize Ismail as the seventh and last IMAM until the return of his son at the end of time. They are also called Sabiyah, or Seveners. The sect originated after the death (765) of the sixth Shiite imam, Jafar ibn Muhammad. Most Shiites accepted his younger son, Musa al-Kazim, as his successor; the Ismailis were those who supported his older, disinherited son, Ismail. The sect attained its greatest influence under the FATIMIDS, who claimed descent through Ismail's son from FATIMA, daughter of the Prophet Muhammad. This dynasty, established in Tunis in 908, ruled in Egypt from 969 to 1171. Late in the 11th century a split occurred between the Mustalis, who recognized al-Mustali as the caliph-imam (concentrated in Egypt, Yemen, and India), and the Nizaris, named for Mustali's brother Nizar, with strongholds in Iran and Syria. The latter, who became known as the ASSASSINS in Crusader stories, remained in power until the late 13th century. A subsection, under the AGA KHAN, moved to India in 1840.

In their interpretation of the Koran, the Ismailis distinguish between exoteric and esoteric knowledge, that is, between knowledge for the public and knowledge for the initiated. The same distinction finds organizational expression in the Ismaili hierarchy from the imam, who alone has perfect knowledge, by way of the *dais* (missionaries) to the believers at various levels of knowledge and insight.

See also: DRUZES; ISLAM.

isobar   see ISOGRAM

Isocrates [y-sahk'-ruh-teez]   Isocrates, 436–338 BC, was a Greek teacher of rhetoric and political philosophy. In Athens he opened (c.393 BC) the first permanent institution of higher education in the liberal arts. Isocrates' younger contemporaries, the philosophers Plato and Aristotle, regarded him as a superficial and misguided SOPHIST, but he trained many leaders of 4th-century BC Greece, including the general Timotheus and the historians Ephorus and Theopompus. He published a series of pamphlets in oratorical form, setting forth his moral and political ideas; these contributed to the definition of Hellenism, or Greek culture, and helped make the training of an orator the goal of ancient education. The *Panegyricus* (380 BC), in which he urged the Greeks to accept Athenian leadership in a campaign against Persia, is the most famous of his works. Later in the *Philippus* (346 BC) he urged Philip of Macedon to assume leadership in the continuing struggle against Persia. Of Isocrates' orations, 21 are extant.

isogram [y'-soh-gram] An isogram is a line drawn on a map or graph that connects points that are of equal value with regard to some variable (see MAPS AND MAPMAKING). Many isograms are familiar on weather maps: an isobar connects points having the same barometric pressure; an isohyet connects points receiving equal precipitation; an isotherm connects points having equal temperature (see WEATHER FORECASTING). An isochron is a line that connects points at which certain phenomena, such as wave reflection, occur simultaneously.

isolationism Isolationism is a foreign policy by which a nation deliberately makes no permanent alliances or commitments and tries to avoid all involvement beyond its borders. The term is most closely identified with the foreign policy of the United States from the American Revolution to World War II.

In an effort to secure independence from foreign intervention and to achieve a sense of national unity, the founders of the United States warned against the disruptive influences of attachments to European countries by U.S. citizens. The MONROE DOCTRINE (1823) reaffirmed America's intention not to interfere in European affairs and cautioned the nations of Europe not to intervene in the Western Hemisphere.

The United States could pursue an isolationist policy because of special circumstances that existed during the 19th century. An ocean was an effective barrier to the powerful nations of Europe, the British navy was interested in maintaining freedom of the seas, and the European powers were embroiled in their own affairs. The U.S. government, therefore, saw no contradiction between an isolationist policy toward Europe and a policy of expansion in the Western Hemisphere and even outward to Asia.

American isolationism was breached in 1898 by the Spanish-American War and again by World War I. After that war, the United States reverted to a policy of isolationism, only to have it shattered by World War II and its aftermath, when U.S. power and the changes that had occurred in the world situation made it difficult for the country to remain aloof from foreign commitments.

isomer [y'-suh-mur] In chemistry two molecules are isomers if they have identical chemical formulas but different atomic arrangements. Chain isomerism exists among the alkanes, or molecules possessing a chain of carbon atoms, because the chain may be straight or branched. For example, n-butane (CH_3–CH_2–CH_2–CH_3) is a straight chain, and isobutane [CH–(CH_3)$_3$] is a branched chain. Although the properties of isomers of a given formula are similar, the compounds are nonetheless distinct.

Position isomerism occurs because not all hydrogen atoms in a molecule are equivalent. The substitution of another element for one of these hydrogens or the loss of adjacent pairs to form multiple bonds at more than one possible location can give rise to isomeric structures. Thus, propyl alcohol (C_3H_7OH) can be either of two types, one with the hydroxyl group (OH) attached to a terminal carbon atom and the other in which it is attached to the middle carbon. A monosubstituted benzene ring, such as toluene ($C_6H_5CH_3$), can add another substituent to any of the other five carbon atoms; because two pairs are equivalent, there are only three possible isomers: ortho, meta, and para. The location of the double bond in ALKENES and the triple bond in ALKYNES determines another form of positional isomerism.

Functional group isomerism refers to compounds whose class cannot be determined from the formula alone. The formula C_3H_8O may be an ETHER or either of the two propyl alcohols. The same is true for formulas indicating an unsaturated hydrocarbon, which may represent an alkyne, a diene, an allene, or a cyclic compound.

Geometric isomerism refers to molecules in which the atoms are attached in the same order but have different spatial relationships. Cis-trans isomerism, common in alkenes, refers to asymmetry across the double bond. The important study of optical isomerism is discussed under STEREOCHEMISTRY.

isometric system [y-suh-met'-rik] CRYSTALS belong to the isometric system if they have 3 mutually perpendicular axes of equal length. Five symmetry classes exist in this system. Crystals in this system must have at least 4 threefold symmetry axes. The most symmetric class—the hexoctahedral—under this system contains a center of symmetry, 3 fourfold symmetry axes (coincident with the crystallographic axes), 4 threefold symmetry axes (body diagonals), and 6 twofold symmetry axes (between the centers of the cube edges).

Only crystals in the isometric system are isotropic; that is, their physical properties do not vary according to crystallographic direction. Isotropic minerals thus have a single index of REFRACTION and appear dark when viewed with crossed Nicols in the polarizing microscope (see POLARIZED LIGHT). Consequently, identification of isotropic minerals usually rests on their optical properties in reflected rather than transmitted light. Common minerals occurring in the isometric system include GARNET, HALITE (common salt), and PYRITE.

isometrics Isometrics is a method of exercise in which stress is created in stationary muscles. Isometrics may be performed by pushing or pulling an immovable object or by contracting or tightening opposing flexor and extensor muscles. Most exercises, such as calisthenics, running, or swimming, involve muscle tension through a range of movements, and they are called isotonics. The advantages of isometric exercise are that no specialized equipment is required and that only a few minutes each day are needed to produce noticeable results.

The benefits of isometric exercise are limited because each exercise only affects one specific point in the range of a muscle's movement; a regimen of isometrics fails to develop stamina, quickness, or flexibility. Some critics of isometrics contend that these exercises contribute to weight gain, muscle hypertrophy, and stiffness. In order to attain all-around physical fitness, isometrics should be combined with running, isotonic exercise, and other vigorous exercises.

isomorph [y'-soh-mohrf] Isomorphs are two or more crystalline substances that have similar chemical composition and atomic structures. Atoms of similar size can replace one another in the CRYSTAL structure, often forming a complete isomorphous, or solid-solution, series with a continuous chemical variation from one pure compound to the other. Notable examples of isomorphous MINERALS include the arsenate, FELDSPAR, and vanadate minerals, the aragonite and CALCITE groups of carbonate minerals, oxide minerals, and the APATITE group of phosphate minerals.

isopod [y'-suh-pahd] Isopods are members of the order Isopoda in the class Crustacea. The order includes about 4,000 species, most of which are marine, some of which live in fresh water, and some of which (pill bugs and wood lice) are the most successful of the few terrestrial crustaceans. Most isopods are 5 to 15 mm (0.2 to 0.6 in) long, but *Bathynomus giganteus* may exceed 36 cm (14 in). The body of an isopod is usually flat from top to bottom, with a shieldlike head region, unstalked eyes, and various paired appendages on the thorax and abdomen. These appendages are used for locomotion, respiration, and reproduction; the foremost pair is used for feeding.

The majority of isopods are free-swimming, omnivorous scavengers. Quite a few are parasitic and may be found in the gill chambers of shrimp, on the skin or in the mouths of fish, or in similar sites. Their mouthparts have been modified into piercing appendages for sucking blood and body fluids. Many terrestrial forms contain the enzyme cellulase or cellulose-digesting bacteria in their gut to aid in the digestion of wood and bark. They usually live in damp or protected habitats, such as beneath stones or in bark or leaf mold.

isoprene see RUBBER

Isoptera see TERMITE

isostasy [y-sahs'-tuh-see] Isostasy is a condition of balance that exists between different portions of the Earth's crust. The lighter rocks of the crust float on the heavier, plastic rocks of the mantle and either rise relatively higher or sink relatively lower, depending on their density and volume. Mountain chains, for example, are composed of large volumes of rocks of relatively low density that therefore rise to great heights. As this large volume is eroded away, the mountain chain continues to rise, at a progressively lower rate and to successively lesser heights, until both the root—the large volume of low-density rock below the land surface—and the mountain have been entirely consumed (see LANDFORM EVOLUTION).

Continents have formed because their crust is generally lighter and thicker than oceanic crust and therefore rises to a higher level. The weight of a large temporary mass of material, such as glacial ice, may cause a portion of continental crust to sink. When the mass is removed—by melting, for instance—the continent rises back up, or rebounds, as have most landmasses of the northern hemisphere that were covered by ice sheets during the last ICE AGE.

See also: EARTH, STRUCTURE AND COMPOSITION OF.

isotherm see ISOGRAM

isothermal process [y-soh-thurm'-ul] In thermodynamics, an isothermal process involves heat or energy transfer in which a system's temperature remains constant. A common isothermal process is the boiling of water, which occurs at 100° C (212° F). An ideal gas undergoing an isothermal process reacts according to Boyle's law, in which the product of the gas pressure and volume remains constant. In addition to isothermal processes, many other constant-property processes are important in thermodynamics. For example, isobaric processes occur at constant pressure, isochoric processes at constant volume, and isentropic processes at constant entropy.

isotope [y'-suh-tohp] The term *isotope* (from the Greek word meaning "same place") defines atoms that have the same number of protons but a different number of neutrons; that is, they are atoms of the same element that have different masses. Their atomic number (proton number) is the same, but their mass numbers (the total number of protons and neutrons in the nucleus) vary. Lighter elements tend to possess fewer isotopes (hydrogen has 3), while heavier elements tend to have more isotopes (polonium has 27). Several ways of denoting isotopes are used; ^3_1H, ^3H, H^3, and hydrogen-3 all symbolize TRITIUM, a radioactive isotope of hydrogen that has one proton and two neutrons. The superscript indicates the mass number; the subscript denotes the atomic number.

Types of Isotopes. There are two major types of isotopes, stable and unstable. Stable isotopes do not undergo radioactive decay but rather persist in nature. Unstable isotopes—radioisotopes or radionuclides—undergo radioactive decay toward a more energetically stable form.

Stable isotopes, of which there are approximately 280, make up most of the natural elements of the Earth. The major component of an element is usually one stable isotope accompanied by minor amounts of other stable and unstable isotopes. Sometimes an element, such as chlorine, is composed of more than one stable isotope in quantity; therefore, certain elements may have several atomic masses that differ greatly. Twenty-one elements have only one isotope and therefore consist of only one kind of atom.

Radioisotopes are of two major types, natural and artificial. Natural radioisotopes, of which there are only 25, were formed during the creation of the Earth; the only radioisotopes left from that time are those which decay very slowly. New radioisotopes are constantly being created; some are members of a decay series in which unstable isotopes decay to other unstable isotopes until a stable isotope is reached, and some are produced continuously in the Earth's atmosphere by cosmic-ray bombardment. The rate of decay of these types of isotopes has reached an equilibrium with their rate of formation. Tritium (^{3}H) is an example of a rapidly decaying isotope, while carbon 14 is an example of a more slowly decaying radioisotope produced in this fashion. Both are formed by the cosmic-ray bombardment of nitrogen-14.

Synthesis of Isotopes. Artificial production of radioisotopes was first achieved in 1934 when Frédéric and Irène Curie-Joliot converted aluminum-27 into phosphorus-30. More than 1,800 artificial radioisotopes have been produced since 1934 using several techniques based on the bombardment of stable nuclei with various particles. A new isotope is formed with an accompanying ejection of nuclear particles or the emission of electromagnetic radiation or both.

Applications. Many uses have been found for isotopes, both industrially and scientifically. Industrial applications include the synthesis of ethyl bromide from hydrogen bromide and ethylene using cobalt-60 gamma radiation, polymerization cross-linking with beta or gamma radiation, vulcanization of rubber, and curing or hardening of paint films. DEUTERIUM (^{2}H), a stable isotope of hydrogen, is used in the preparation of heavy water (deuterium oxide), which is used to moderate nuclear reactors. Other applications include liquid-flow monitoring, mechanical-wear analysis, X-ray analysis, age dating in water sources, thickness gauging, and food sterilization.

Research applications of isotopes are numerous, with ^{14}C, ^{13}C, ^{2}H, ^{3}H, ^{15}N, and others used in biological tracer experiments. Cobalt-60 is used in radiation therapy of tumors, and iodine-131 in hyperthyroid treatment as well as other medical uses. In analytical chemistry, activation analysis is performed by neutron irradiation of a sample, which converts a particular element in the sample to a known radioisotope.

See also: RADIOACTIVITY.

___

Isozaki Arata [ee-soh-zah'-kee ah-rah'-tah] The avant-garde architect Isozaki Arata, b. 1931, has demon-strated in a series of important Japanese public buildings his imaginative mastery and synthesis of various Western and Japanese influences. After working (1954–63) in Kenzo TANGE's office, Isozaki opened his own atelier in 1963. His early works (the Oita Prefectural Library, 1966, and the initial portion of the Oita Medical Center, 1960), executed in roughly cast coarse concrete, were composed of large-scale horizontal and vertical forms reminiscent of traditional Japanese timber-beam architecture. Subsequently, simple geometric volumes tended to dominate his designs. The sleek aluminum Gunma Prefectural Museum of Fine Arts (1974) in central Honshu is composed of a system of cubes. For the Museum of Contemporary Art in Los Angeles (opened 1986), Isozaki designed a reddish sandstone structure featuring curving lines and a main exhibition space under a skylighted courtyard.

___

Israel The State of Israel, an independent nation in southwest Asia, is located between the eastern shores of the Mediterranean Sea and the head of the Gulf of AQABA, an arm of the Red Sea. Israel was established on May 14, 1948, as a Jewish state on land that had been part of the British mandate for PALESTINE. Historically, it is considered the Holy Land for Christians, Jews, and Muslims.

Since 1948, Israel has fought several wars with its Arab neighbors. Despite a history dominated by hostilities, Israel has transformed its land and developed a modern, technologically advanced, and highly urbanized society.

Land

Israel extends for 420 km (260 mi) from the northern border with Lebanon and Syria in the Golan Heights to ELAT, the country's port on the Gulf of Aqaba in the south. The territory extends inland from the Mediterranean for 100 km (60 mi)—including the occupied WEST BANK—to the Rift Valley. The valley is a continuation of Africa's Great Rift Valley and is composed in part, from north to south, of the Hula Valley (Lake Hula was drained in the 1950s); the Sea of GALILEE, which lies 212 m (696 ft) below sea level; the JORDAN RIVER; and the DEAD SEA, with the world's lowest land elevation (-396 m/-1,300 ft).

The southern half of Israel west of the Rift Valley, mostly desert, is known as the NEGEV. North of the Negev, occupying most of Israel and the West Bank, is a mountainous region. The mountains rise to 1,208 m (3,963 ft) on Mount Meron, and are divided by the northwest-southeast trending Plain of ESDRAELON that extends from HAIFA to Beth Shean on the edge of the Rift Valley. North of Esdraelon are the hills of Galilee; to the south, partly in the West Bank area, are Samaria and Judea.

The principal lowland is a narrow coastal plain along the shores of the Mediterranean Sea. North of Haifa it is known as the Plain of Zebulun; between Haifa and TEL AVIV it forms the Plain of SHARON; and south of Tel Aviv, the Plain of Judea.

The steeper mountain slopes that cover much of Israel have been severely eroded and are mostly barren. Only

AT A GLANCE

STATE OF ISRAEL

Land: Area: 20,720 km² (8,000 mi²). Capital and largest city: Jerusalem (1986 est. pop., including East Jerusalem, 457,700).

People: Population (1990 est.): 4,409,218. Density: 213 persons per km² (551 per mi²). Distribution (1988): 90% urban, 10% rural. Official languages: Hebrew, Arabic. Major religions: Judaism, Islam, Christianity.

Government: Type: republic. Legislature: Knesset. Political subdivisions: 6 districts.

Economy: GNP (1989): $38 billion; $8,700 per capita. Labor distribution (1988): agriculture—4%; mining and manufacturing—21%; construction—5%; services—33%; trade—13%; finance—9%; transportation and communication—6%. Foreign trade (1989 est.): imports—$12.4 billion; exports—$10.4 billion. Currency: 1 shekel = 100 new agorot.

Education and Health: Literacy (1987): 95% of adult population. Universities (1988): 7. Hospital beds (1987): 27,500. Physicians (1986): 11,895. Life expectancy (1990): women—79; men—76. Infant mortality (1990): 9 per 1,000 live births.

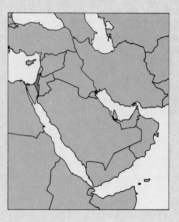

20% of the total land area is arable, and 40% of this is irrigated.

Climate. Israel's climate is Mediterranean in the north and arid in the south. In summer the entire area is dominated by a subtropical high that brings cloudless skies and no precipitation. In winter the northern half of the country receives moderate rainfall. Precipitation in the north averages 700 mm (28 in), falling primarily from October to March. Rainfall amounts diminish rapidly to the south. Beyond BEERSHEBA and GAZA desert conditions predominate.

Average summer temperatures range from 18° to 32° C (65° to 90° F) over most of the country. Winters are mild, with temperatures averaging 14° C (57° F) along the coast and 9° C (48° F) in the mountains. The Dead Sea area is one of the hottest regions in the world.

Drainage. Israel's most important river is the Jordan, 200 km (120 mi) long. Its principal tributary is the Yarmuk. Most other watercourses are usually dry except after heavy rainfall. The waters of the Sea of Galilee are fresh; those of the Dead Sea are saltier than the ocean and rich in minerals. In addition, Israel has large groundwater resources.

Vegetation and Wildlife. Little remains of Israel's natural vegetation and indigenous animal life. Recent reforestation of the uplands, promoted in the interest of soil and groundwater conservation, has created new forests consisting mainly of pine trees. Wildlife is being restored through protective laws and animal preserves.

Resources. Israel has no deposits of coal, only small deposits of petroleum and natural gas, and no rivers suitable for the generation of hydroelectric power. Israel's principal minerals are potash, produced by evaporation of Dead Sea water; phosphates; and limestone.

People

Israel was established in 1948 as a homeland for Jews, and the Jewish population now forms 82% of the total within the 1949 borders. Of these, Jews born in Israel, known as *Sabras*, account for 61%, and immigrants, *Olim*, 39%. The immigrants come from many different places, including Europe, North America, Asia, North Africa, and most recently, the USSR. Immigration generally exceeded emigration until the mid-1980s.

The non-Jewish population consists mainly of ARABS, who make up 13% of the total population, and DRUZES, who account for less than 2%. Both groups are concentrated in Galilee. In the territories occupied by Israel in the 1967 Arab-Israeli War, Arabs constitute by far the majority, although thousands of Jews have settled in the West Bank since 1979. Because of the high Arab birthrate, it is anticipated that Arabs will constitute nearly half of the total population of Israel and the occupied territories by the year 2000.

Language. The official languages of Israel are Hebrew and Arabic. The great majority of Jews speak Hebrew in public but in their homes use their native tongue. English is widely used as a second language.

Religion. Freedom of religion and the inviolability of the holy places and centers of worship for all religions are guaranteed by law. For the Jewish population, supreme religious authority is vested in the Chief Rabbinate. Small Jewish minorities that reject the rabbinic tradition and law include the Karaites and the Samaritans.

Israel's Arab minority is 77% Muslim and 13% Christian. Also followers of Islam are the Circassians, brought to the region in the 19th century from the Caucasus. The Druzes broke away from Islam in the 11th century and practice their own religion. Israel is also a center of the BAHA'I faith.

Demography. Israel has one of the highest population densities in the world, if the Negev is excluded. It is also one of the world's most highly urbanized nations. The three largest cities are JERUSALEM, Tel Aviv-Jaffa, and Haifa. Jewish rural settlers generally live in cooperative villages called moshavim or collective villages called kibbutzim (singular, KIBBUTZ) operated on a communal basis. In 1990 more than 1,670,000 Arabs and 180,000 Jews lived in the occupied GAZA STRIP and the West Bank area, including East Jerusalem. The natural rate of population growth among non-Jews is double that of Jews. Immigration was a factor in the rapid increase of the Jewish population before 1970. Because of a massive influx of Jews from the USSR since late 1989, expected to ultimately total 1 million, it was anticipated that European Jews would outnumber Jews from Asia and Africa again for the first time since the mid-1960s.

Education and Health. Israel ranks among the world's most highly developed nations in providing educational and health services. Education is free and compulsory between the ages of 5 and 15; parental income determines fees for children attending postprimary schools. Higher education is provided in the Technion-Israel Institute of Technology (1912) in Haifa and at six universities, including the Hebrew University of Jerusalem (1918). Health-care costs for the overwhelming majority of the population are covered by health-insurance programs.

The Arts. One of Israel's greatest cultural achievements is its revival of the HEBREW LANGUAGE, which has been adapted for modern use with the aid of Jerusalem's Academy for the Hebrew Language, founded in 1953. Modern Israeli literature is now written in Hebrew, and all plays performed are either translated into or originally written in Hebrew (see HEBREW AND YIDDISH LITERATURE). Israeli architects are working to develop a national style and design; the strongest influence is the style of the Israeli architect Moshe SAFDIE, creator of Habitat (in Montreal). The Israel Philharmonic Orchestra enjoys world renown. Five other orchestras and many choral and chamber music groups are active in the country. Archaeology is pursued not only by professionals but also by amateurs as a hobby. Many relics are housed in the nation's museums, especially the Israel Museum in Jerusalem.

Economic Activity

In the years immediately following independence, resources were scarce and rationing was imposed. Real

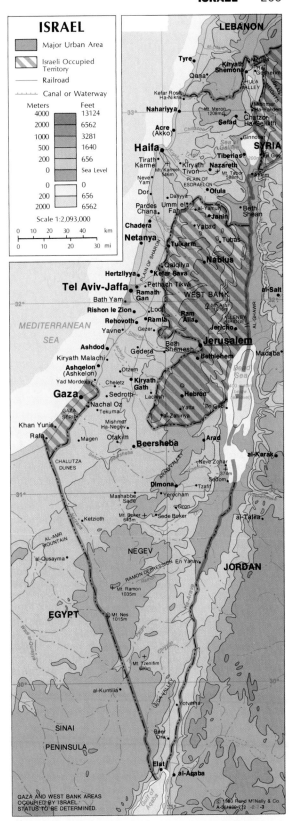

The Golan Heights, on the border between Syria and Israel, rise above the eastern edge of the Great Rift Valley, a geologic fault extending from the Middle East into East Africa. During the Six-Day War of 1967, Syrian artillery on the heights battered Israeli territory in the surrounding lowlands. Israel seized the strategic mountains in an armored assault and annexed them in 1981.

economic growth did not occur until the second half of the 1950s as overseas capital became available for investment. From that time until 1973 the gross national product grew at an annual rate of 10%. After 1973 its growth rate declined sharply, and the economy was adversely affected by inflation, currency devaluations, the world petroleum crisis, and military expenditures. Since the mid-1980s, faced with an inflation rate exceeding 100%, a huge foreign debt, and a severe balance-of-payments deficit, the government has introduced a series of economic austerity measures.

The Histadrut, Israel's labor federation, is the country's largest voluntary organization. A powerful political and economic force, it owns many economic enterprises and supervises health care.

Manufacturing, Mining, and Energy. Tel Aviv and Haifa are the principal manufacturing centers, but industrial facilities are dispersed throughout the nation. The major industries are food processing and the manufacture of textiles, chemicals, fertilizers, machinery, electrical goods, armaments, and electronic and precision equipment. Diamond cutting and polishing is the principal export-oriented industry.

Mining is not economically significant. Israel is totally dependent on petroleum for its energy needs. Except for the small domestic output, petroleum is imported, and it is refined in Haifa and Ashdod. In 1989 electricity production reached 17.5 billion kW h.

Agriculture, Forestry, and Fishing. The amount of land cultivated and irrigated has steadily increased since 1948, primarily through creation of new communal and collective settlements. Poultry and dairy farming have also expanded, along with increased output of citrus, olives, grapes, cotton, vegetables, and flowers. Citrus, especially Jaffa oranges, and early vegetables are important export items.

Transportation. All transportation facilities are state controlled. Rail transportation is poorly developed, and none of the country's waterways are navigable. Accordingly, most passenger and freight traffic moves by road. Israel's two ports on the Mediterranean are Haifa and Ashdod; Elat serves as the port for the Red Sea and Indian Ocean. El-Al, the Israeli airline, flies from Ben-Gurion Airport near Tel Aviv, the nation's principal international airport.

Communications. The Israeli government controls the radio and television broadcasting industry. Publishing is concentrated in Tel Aviv and Jerusalem, where all of the daily newspapers are printed. Most newspapers are in Hebrew, and many are subsidized by political parties or religious groups.

Trade. Israel's imports usually exceed exports in value. The deficit is made up in part by revenues from tourism, financial aid, and foreign investment. Diamonds are the leading export, followed by machinery, electronic equipment, fruit, and textiles. The principal imports are uncut diamonds from South Africa, fuel and lubricants, and consumer goods. Israel enjoys special trading privileges in the European Economic Community (EEC) and trades mostly with EEC members and the United States.

Government

Israel is a parliamentary democracy, with legislative powers vested in the Knesset, a unicameral parliament elected for four-year terms, pending dissolution. The cabinet,
which holds executive power, is chosen by the prime
minister. A draft constitution was released in 1987;
meanwhile, a number of basic laws serve together as the
fundamental law. All citizens of age 18 or over are eligible to vote. Votes are cast for national lists of candidates
submitted by each of the political parties. Usually about
10 parties win seats in an election, and the governments
are based on coalitions.

Until 1968 the Mapai party dominated Israeli politics,
led by David BEN-GURION, Moshe Sharett, and Levi ESH-
KOL. In 1968, Mapai merged with Rafi and Achdur Avoda
to form the Labor party, which remained dominant under
Golda MEIR and Yitzhak RABIN until 1977, when Likud, a
coalition of right-wing parties led by the Herut (Freedom)
party, came to power under Menachem BEGIN. He was
succeeded by Yitzhak SHAMIR in 1983. In a 1984 power-
sharing agreement, Labor leader Shimon PERES became
prime minister, with Shamir replacing him in 1986. In-
decisive results in the 1988 elections led to the formation of another Likud-Labor coalition, with Shamir as
prime minister. Disagreements over how to proceed with
the Middle East peace process led to the collapse of this
coalition on Mar. 15, 1990. On June 8, Shamir formed a
new right-wing coalition government with six small religious and nationalist parties. A president elected by the
Knesset for 5-year terms is head of state. Chaim Herzog
became Israel's sixth president in 1983.

History

The modern state of Israel was established in territory
that had been granted as a League of Nations mandate to
Great Britain following World War I. The creation of a
Jewish homeland was an objective of ZIONISM, a movement that developed politically in the 19th century. In
the BALFOUR DECLARATION of 1917 the British government
pledged its support for this goal, and the declaration was
incorporated into the terms of the mandate over Palestine, which took effect in 1922. Serious violence soon
arose between the Arabs and the Jews, and the British,
who had made promises to both groups, were unable to
satisfy either. Upheavals brought about by World War II
and the decimation of European Jewry stimulated action
toward the creation of a Jewish homeland. In 1947 the
United Nations voted to divide Palestine into Jewish and
Arab states. The British withdrew from the area on May
13, 1948, conceding failure to reconcile Arab and Jewish
goals. On May 14, Israel proclaimed its independence.
On May 15 the Arabs attacked, refusing to recognize both
the partition of Palestine and the new nation. Since the
partition Israel's boundaries have been redrawn along
truce lines established by cease-fire agreements following
the several ARAB-ISRAELI WARS.

During the first few years of Israel's existence, the
state's resources were strained by continued conflict with
the Arabs and by an influx of Jewish immigrants that

doubled the population from 650,000 in 1948 to
1,300,000 by 1952. Between 1953 and 1956 immigration slowed, and funds from overseas, plus restitution
money paid by West Germany for Nazi war crimes, financed Israel's planned development.

Following the Suez-Sinai War of 1956, Israel enjoyed
a period of consolidation and economic growth, although
the nation experienced repeated terrorist attacks mounted
by Palestinian guerrilla groups that were eventually consolidated under the control of the PALESTINE LIBERATION
ORGANIZATION (PLO). In the Six-Day War of 1967, Israel
occupied the SINAI Peninsula and the Gaza Strip as well
as the Golan Heights and the West Bank of Jordan, and it
refused to leave the occupied territories until permanent
peace treaties were signed. Another period of economic
expansion followed, with new growth in immigration, industry, and trade. Israel held off the surprise Arab attack
of October 1973 (the Yom Kippur War). In 1977 a right-
wing government under Menachem Begin assumed control. Its signing (Mar. 26, 1979) of a peace treaty with
Egypt led to the return of the Sinai to Egypt over a three-
year period and encouraged hopes for an end to the Arab-
Israeli conflict. Begin, however, formally proclaimed the
entire city of Jerusalem as Israel's capital in 1980, an-

*High-rise apartments ring the old city of Jerusalem, which Israel
has declared its "eternal capital." The city, which was partitioned
between Jordan and Israel from 1948 until 1967, is regarded as
holy by three faiths—Judaism, Christianity, and Islam.*

nexed the Golan Heights in 1981, and continued to promote Israeli settlement in the West Bank. In 1982, Israel invaded parts of Lebanon, which had become a base for PLO guerrillas. The Labor-Likud coalition that took office in 1984 withdrew most Israeli troops from Lebanon in 1985. In December 1987 the lack of progress in the Middle East peace process sparked an uprising by Palestinian Arabs in the West Bank and Gaza Strip that continued despite Israeli efforts to end it by military and administrative means. Negotiations over U.S. and Egyptian peace plans calling for elections in the occupied territories collapsed with the installation of a new right-wing government in June 1990.

Israel refrained from direct involvement in the 1991 GULF WAR, despite Iraqi Scud-missile attacks on Israeli civilian targets. After the war Israel faced increased pressure to negotiate a solution to the Palestinian problem, although it was even less willing than before to exchange land for peace or to engage in direct talks with the PLO, which had supported Iraq during the war. At home the already weak economy was further strained by the massive costs of resettling hundreds of thousands of Soviet Jews.

Israel, Kingdom of

The Kingdom of Israel was the name both of the united kingdom of the Israelites under Kings SAUL, DAVID, and SOLOMON (c.1020–c.922 BC) and of the political unit formed by the ten northernmost Israelite tribes when they revolted against the Davidic dynasty after the death of Solomon. The territory of the latter included what was left of the Davidic dynasty's holdings east of the Jordan River and extended south to a few kilometers north of Jerusalem, the capital of Judah, where the Davidic dynasty still held power. The northern kingdom's own capital moved several times until King Omri finally established it permanently at Samaria in c.875 BC.

The first king of Israel, the northern kingdom, was JEROBOAM, a former official of Solomon, but neither he nor any of his successors was able to establish a stable dynastic succession such as existed in Judah. Throughout its short history Israel was continually rocked by bloody dynastic changes. The small nation was constantly harassed by strong enemies and experienced only two brief periods of expansion in the 9th and 8th centuries BC before it was destroyed by Assyria in 722–721 BC.

Israeli-Arab Wars   see ARAB-ISRAELI WARS

Istanbul

[is-tan-bool'] Istanbul (1985 pop., 5,475,982) is Turkey's largest city, chief port, and industrial, commercial, and cultural center. The city, long known as Constantinople, occupies a strategic location at the entrance to the Black Sea on the traditional crossroads between Europe and Asia. The old city is located on a triangular peninsula jutting into the Sea of MARMARA. The Golden Horn inlet is to its north, the BOSPORUS to the east, and the Sea of Marmara to the south.

The city and surrounding province are administered by a mayor appointed by the president of Turkey. Industries

Istanbul's Galata Bridge, which spans the Golden Horn, links the historic quarter of Stamboul with the commercial district of Beyoglu. The Yeni Camii (right), or New Mosque, was constructed between 1597 and 1663.

include textiles, flour, tobacco, cement, glass, and soap.

The Palais de la Culture d'Istanbul is the home of the city's symphony orchestra and opera and an art gallery. Among the many museums are the Archaeological Museum of Istanbul, the Topkapi Palace Museum, and the Museum of Turkish and Islamic Art. Istanbul University was founded in 1453. The city's most famous monument is HAGIA SOPHIA (537), originally a Byzantine church, later a mosque, and now a museum. The Bosporus Bridge, linking the European and Asian parts of the city, opened in 1973.

Istanbul has been the capital of three states: the BYZANTINE EMPIRE, the OTTOMAN EMPIRE, and the Turkish Republic. It was founded (c.660 BC) as Byzantium by Greeks from Megara. The Persian king DARIUS I took the city in 512 BC. Sparta captured it in 479 BC, lost it to Athens, but regained it in 405 BC. For about 675 years Sparta, Macedonia, Rhodes, and Rome contended for the city. The Roman emperor Septimius SEVERUS virtually destroyed the city in AD 196, but rebuilt it. In 324, CONSTANTINE I, the Great, chose the city for the new capital of the entire Roman Empire. Named Constantinople for the emperor, the city was enlarged and walls were added for protection. As the capital of the Byzantine Empire, Constantinople became Europe's preeminent city, a position it held until the mid-11th century. It was subjected to attacks by the Persians (626), Arabs (673–77, 717–18), Bulgars (813, 924), Russians (860, 941, 1043), and Pechenegs (1090–91). None were successful, however, until the armies of the Fourth CRUSADE attacked and plundered the city in 1204.

The Crusaders established the Latin Empire of Constantinople (see CONSTANTINOPLE, LATIN EMPIRE OF). It lasted until 1261, when the Byzantines regained control. The fall of Constantinople to the Ottoman sultan MEHMED II in 1453 marked the end of the Byzantine state.

Constantinople then became the seat of government

for the Ottoman sultans. In the reign of SULEIMAN I (1520–66) the architect Mimar Sinan embellished the city with numerous mosques and other buildings.

The Ottoman Empire was dissolved in October 1918; by 1920, Turkey was forced to cede all its European territory except for Constantinople and its environs. The Allies held control of the city from the end of World War I until Turkish nationalists overthrew the sultan in 1922. Constantinople was officially renamed Istanbul in 1930.

Istria [is'-tree-uh]   Istria is a mountainous peninsula in northern Yugoslavia that penetrates the northern Adriatic Sea. It is about 96 km (60 mi) long and is bounded on the west by the Gulf of Venice and on the east by the Kvarner gulf. A coastal strip in the northwest that includes the city of TRIESTE belongs to Italy. Istria is 3,890–5,180 km² (1,500–2,000 mi²) in area; its highest elevation is 1,396 m (4,580 ft) at Mount Ucka. The coastline is irregular and rocky, with deep harbors and many offshore islands. Grape cultivation, forestry, fishing, and cattle raising are the major economic activities. Coal, quartz, and bauxite are mined. PULA is the major city and seaport.

Istria was ruled by the Illyrians until the 2d century BC, when it was taken over by the Romans. The Byzantines claimed the area until the 8th century AD. The peninsula was later divided between Austrian and Venetian control, but in 1797, Austria secured all of Istria. Italy was given sovereignty over Istria at the end of World War I. In 1947 control over most of the peninsula passed to Yugoslavia. The status of Trieste was settled in 1954.

Itagaki Taisuke [ee-tah'-gah-kee ty'-soo-kay]   Itagaki Taisuke, b. Apr. 17, 1837, d. July 1919, was a Japanese social reformer, educator, and statesman. Of noble birth, he advanced to military commander of the large Tosa feudal domain and was involved in the overthrow of the Tokugawa shogunate and the MEIJI RESTORATION in 1868. As an official in the new government, Itagaki called for broader representation. He participated in several cabinets but often resigned in protest. He founded the first political club, the first national organization with a wide following (Aikokusha, "Society of Patriots," 1875), a school, and the Jiyuto (1881), or Liberal party, of which he became the symbol.

Italian art and architecture   Italian art has its roots in the aesthetic traditions of classical Rome and in the pre-Roman cultures of the Italian peninsula, especially those of the Greeks and the ETRUSCANS (see ROMAN ART AND ARCHITECTURE). Such common elements as a shared classical heritage, Roman Catholicism, and the Italian language made possible a unified artistic style, technique, function, and content, despite the peninsula's political fragmentation, which lasted from the collapse of the Western Roman Empire in the 5th century AD until the establishment of the Italian nation in the mid-19th century. During that time Italy was divided politically and culturally into numerous continually changing states based on cultural regions, such as Tuscany or Lombardy, or cities, such as Venice and Rome. Italian art is thus made up of distinct local artistic styles or traditions called schools.

The Middle Ages

Italian art history begins in Rome during the 1st to 4th centuries with the emergence of a Christian religious iconography and architecture based on Roman prototypes (see EARLY CHRISTIAN ART AND ARCHITECTURE). The transfer of the Roman imperial capital to Byzantium in the 4th century meant that Constantinople, rather than Rome, would become the early medieval center of Mediterranean Christian culture. Ravenna in the 6th century and Venice and Sicily in the 11th and 12th centuries were the principal Italian locations for the orientalizing aesthetic of the Byzantines (see BYZANTINE ART AND ARCHITECTURE). Spatially impressive central plans, lavish materials, sumptuous color, mysterious lighting, and stylized iconic representation characterize the architecture and mosaics of Ravenna's SAN VITALE (6th century) and SAINT MARK'S BASILICA in Venice (begun 1063). Arab artisans resident in Sicily from the 9th to 12th centuries also introduced an oriental style of decorative magnificence, as evidenced by Palermo's Palatine Chapel (1132–40).

The Romanesque Period. Originating in 11th-century France, the Romanesque aesthetic quickly spread throughout western Europe. The Italian Romanesque was concentrated in Lombardy, Tuscany, and southern Italy. At Sant'Ambrogio in Milan (1088–1128), Lombard master brick masons constructed one of the earliest examples of rib groin vaults. The Lombard style, therefore, came to be characterized by large vaulted churches with elaborate exterior brickwork. In Tuscany, Pisan architects decorated facades by superimposing tiers of marble arcades, as in Pisa Cathedral (begun 1063). Cefalù (1131–48) and Monreale (1176–82) cathedrals in Sicily are representative of the southern Italian Romanesque.

Tuscan Romanesque architecture is represented by the Cathedral (begun 1063), baptistery (begun 1153), and famous Leaning Tower (1174–1372) of Pisa.

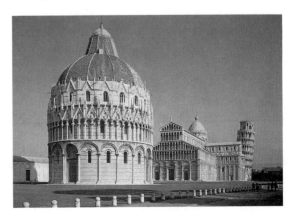

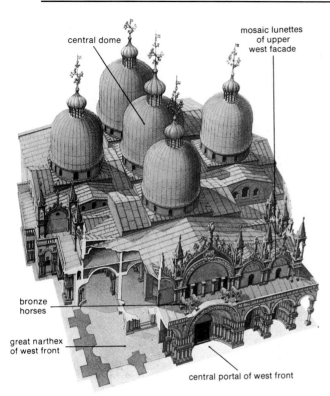

central dome

mosaic lunettes
of upper
west facade

bronze
horses

great narthex
of west front

central portal of west front

Saint Mark's Basilica (begun 1063) in Venice reflects the Byzantine influence on Venetian architecture. Constructed on the site of a 9th-century basilica, Saint Mark's features a five-domed Greek cross plan derived from the Church of the Apostles, Istanbul. Its interior decoration of glass mosaics and colored marble is typically Byzantine.

Northern Italian church facades were often richly decorated with stone sculpture exemplified by the work of Wiligelmo at Modena Cathedral (c.1099), or Benedetto Antelami's stone and bronze reliefs (1178–1223) in Parma's cathedral and baptistery.

From the 11th to the 14th century, Italian painting was in debted in form and imagery to Byzantine sources, although indigenous Latin humanism also invested the Byzantine-influenced paintings of CIMABUE and DUCCIO with a western gentleness and personal pertinence. The major innovation of the Italo-Byzantine school was the monumental painted crucifixes hung over the altars of Tuscan churches.

A classical Romanesque style developed principally in Rome and Tuscany. Florentine Romanesque exteriors, such as that of San Miniato al Monte (1018–62), were covered with Roman-derived geometric patterns in green and white marble. The most overt sculptural reference to the influence of antiquity was Nicola PISANO's Pisa baptistery pulpit (1259–60). (See ROMANESQUE ART AND ARCHITECTURE.)

The Gothic Style. Originating in the mid-12th century in France, the Gothic style was introduced into Italy dur-

ing the early 13th century. Italian Gothic architecture is characterized by a classical preference for width rather than medieval height. Italian churches such as San Francesco, Assisi (1228–53), or Santa Croce, Florence (begun 1294), appear massive, somber, and ornamentally chaste. Rather than vertical walls of stained glass, the Italians preferred horizontal surfaces for painting fresco murals. Sculpture was sparingly used to decorate Gothic buildings. Pulpits and doors, however, continued to be covered with narrative relief panels, as in Andrea Pisano's south doors (1330–35) of the Florence Baptistery.

Gothic painting turned from the symbolic to the natural. The Florentine GIOTTO DI BONDONE revolutionized European painting with telling observations of human events set in ordered, volumetric spaces such as the frescoes in the Arena Chapel, Padua (c.1304–13). The Sienese school was less classical; in addition to elegantly rendered religious subjects, Simone MARTINI and Pietro and Ambrogio Lorenzetti produced portraits and landscapes reflecting Gothic naturalism.

The elegant Gothic International Style permeated Italy from c.1375 to c.1425. The decorative anecdotal quality, intricate curvilinear forms, brilliant color, and lavish settings are seen in tempera panel paintings by GENTILE DA FABRIANO and Antonio PISANELLO, as well as in the north door reliefs of the Florence Baptistery (1403–24) by Lorenzo GHIBERTI.

The Renaissance

Patronized by leading banking families like the MEDICI, the classicizing Early Renaissance style was initiated in Florence during the 1420s by Filippo BRUNELLESCHI, DONATELLO, and MASACCIO. Their observations, coupled with the humanistic Tuscan intellectual climate, engendered an avant-garde aesthetic that replaced the Gothic in Italy by the end of the century.

Early Renaissance Architecture and Sculpture. Florentine architects determined the design standards for Early Renaissance buildings. The relationship of architectural proportion and human scale was a Renaissance concern first manifested in the works of Brunelleschi. Florentine buildings like the Pazzi Chapel achieve a serenity and clarity of design from the reductive organizational use of mathematics and the harmonious simplicity of materials and ornamentation. Leon Battista ALBERTI's formal and intellectual refinements of Brunelleschi's work influenced the next generation of Florentine architects.

Donatello was the most influential Early Renaissance sculptor. His *David* (c.1430–32; Bargello, Florence), the first free-standing bronze nude statue since antiquity, revived the classical compositional device of contrapposto, showed a concern for psychological interpretation, and displayed a scientific, as well as an erotic, interest in the human body. Poetic mood and lyrical line or contour typified the busts and reliefs of mid-century Florentines such as Luca Della Robbia (see DELLA ROBBIA family) and DESIDERIO DA SETTIGNANO. VERROCCHIO's anecdotal realism and Antonio Pollaiuolo's (see POLLAIUOLO family) energetic studies of the figure in motion were dominant in late-15th-century Florence.

Michelangelo, Leonardo da Vinci, and Raphael were among the most prominent figures of Italy's High Renaissance. Michelangelo's David *(1501–04; Accademia, Florence)* (left) *and Leonardo's* Mona Lisa *or* La Gioconda *(c.1503–05; Louvre, Paris)* (center) *show their creators' characteristic style; Raphael's* Sposalizio *or* Marriage of the Virgin *(1504; Brera, Milan)* (right) *is an early work, showing the influence of his teacher, Perugino.*

Painting. Masaccio's Brancacci Chapel frescoes in Santa Maria del Carmine, Florence (1427), are the initial and most influential statement of the Early Renaissance style in painting. He creates the illusion of three dimensions on a flat surface by using the system of linear perspective probably discovered in the 1420s by Brunelleschi. The heightened sculptural appearance of the figures results from his advancements in the use of chiaroscuro, or modeling in light and dark. The late Quattrocento (15th century) was dominated by the anecdotal bourgeois realism of GHIRLANDAIO and the decorative elegance and melancholic mood of BOTTICELLI, whose line and pattern had superseded Masaccio's mass and volume. ANTONELLO DA MESSINA, a Sicilian schooled in the Flemish tradition, introduced oil painting to Venice about 1475. The medium's luminosity attracted Giovanni Bellini (see BELLINI family), whose late works first fully manifested the Venetian school's preoccupation with color, light, and atmosphere.

The High Renaissance and Mannerism. During the High Renaissance (c.1495–1520), Rome succeeded Florence as the center for the artistic avant-garde. The patronage of MICHELANGELO, RAPHAEL, and BRAMANTE by Popes Julius II and Leo X engendered one of the most brilliant and influential periods in art history. Bramante and Michelangelo conceived an architecture of solemn splendor for a papacy wishing to construct a city that would rival and even surpass the imperial grandeur of ancient Rome.

In the early 16th century an aesthetic dichotomy arose between the intellectual classicism of the Florentine-Roman school and the sensual romanticism of the Venetians. Until the 20th century these differing aesthetics would polarize Western painting. The primary Florentine-Roman interest was drawing, or line, and sculptural modeling. Venetians, on the other hand, preferred atmospheric and textural paintings emphasizing the effects of light and richness of color. LEONARDO DA VINCI's *Last Supper* fresco in Santa Maria delle Grazie, Milan (c.1495–98), and Raphael's frescoes in the Vatican Palace's Stanza della Segnatura (1509) are visually and contextually ultimate Florentine-Roman statements, whereas the oil paintings of GIORGIONE and TITIAN are most representative of Venetian concerns. (See RENAISSANCE ART AND ARCHITECTURE.)

Although it began in Rome and Florence, MANNERISM was not identified with any particular locality. Artists moved to wherever there was opportunity and relative security. Many even left Italy, thereby spreading Mannerism throughout Europe and making it the first Italian international style since Roman antiquity.

Mannerist architects such as GIULIO ROMANO employed classical motifs in an eccentric way, designed bizarre ornamentation, and preferred ambiguous spatial relationships. Such painters as PONTORMO, PARMIGIANINO, and BRONZINO emphasized the unnatural and irrational. Compositions were elongated, compressed, asymmetrical, and entangled. The self-conscious works of CELLINI and Giovanni da BOLOGNA, with their improbable balance and neurotic agitation, are representative of Mannerist sculpture.

Venetian Mannerism was less extreme. PALLADIO's inventive extension of classical usage had a major impact on later English and American architecture, while TINTORETTO's dramatic use of light and the diagonal influenced the Italian baroque. VERONESE's decorative splen-

The classical grace of 16th-century sculpture was succeeded by the vigorous movement of the baroque style. Bernini's Apollo and Daphne *(1622–24; Galleria Borghese, Rome) illustrates his superb ability to evoke motion and feeling.*

dor elaborated the Venetian concern with opulent color and lavish setting.

The Baroque Period

Italian and foreign talent made Rome Europe's most artistically influential city from about 1600 until the 1660s, when it was supplanted by Paris and Versailles. The baroque popes rivaled their High Renaissance predecessors as art patrons in their determination to make Rome a visual symbol of the spiritual and secular power of a renewed Roman Catholic church.

Recently canonized saints, newly formed religious orders, and a growing population necessitated more ecclesiastical buildings. The elaborate Counter-Reformation liturgy, with its emphasis on emotional pageantry, further prompted remodeling or expanding older religious structures to make them suitably spacious and magnificent. Greater prosperity and an enlarged aristocracy prompted construction of luxurious palaces, villas, and gardens to accommodate the theatrical baroque life-style and, like the churches, served as emblems of an enhanced wealth and power. BERNINI in particular set the tone of the Italian baroque. The international prestige of Bernini's sculpture and architecture, as well as the painting of CARAVAGGIO and the CARRACCI, made the Italian baroque another internationally influential style, except in Protestant countries, where its exuberance and ostentation were often considered excessive and even immoral.

Bernini and BORROMINI in Rome, Guarino GUARINI in Turin, and Longhena in Venice were the geniuses of Italian baroque architecture. They achieved dynamism and

magnificence through complex plans with changing perspectives, undulating or curved walls, grandeur of scale, dramatic lighting, lavish materials, and exuberant ornamentation. Architecture, painting, and sculpture were all synthesized to create an overwhelming multimedia environment. Baroque architects were not just concerned with individual buildings, but were innovative town planners and landscape architects. Baroque sculpture was usually integrated into an urban or architectural setting as Bernini's *Fountain of the Four Rivers* in Rome's Piazza Navona (1648–51). Different materials such as bronze and various colored marbles were frequently combined to achieve a heightened richness or to simulate reality.

Two distinct Italian baroque schools of painting arose in the early 17th century. Caravaggio and followers like Orazio Gentileschi and his daughter Artemisia (see GENTILESCHI family) were uncompromising naturalists employing tenebrism, a type of spotlight illumination exploiting the drama of extreme contrast of light and dark. A classical counterpoint to the Caravaggio school was established in Bologna at the Academy founded in 1585 by the Carracci. Their classicizing "academic" synthesis of Michelangelo's energy, Raphael's idealization, and Titian's color influenced other Bolognese painters, such as Guido RENI and DOMENICHINO. (See BAROQUE ART AND ARCHITECTURE.)

The Eighteenth and Nineteenth Centuries

In the 18th century Italian influence declined as France, England, Austria, and Prussia became the political, economic, and artistic leaders of Europe. The Piedmont region produced the most innovative and influential Italian architecture of the 18th century. Filippo Juvarra designed churches and palaces of distinction and brought the Piedmont baroque style to Madrid and Lisbon.

During the final phase of its socioeconomic decline, Venice developed an era of cultural brilliance excelled only by the 16th century. Giambattista Tiepolo's (see TIEPOLO family) frescoes, noted for their effortless tech-

A further development in the representation of movement is seen in Umberto Boccioni's Unique Forms of Continuity in Space *(1913; Museum of Modern Art, New York City), a bronze by one of the progenitors of the futurist movement.*

nique and brilliant use of light and color, mark the end of the Italian mural painting tradition essentially begun by Giotto. The *veduta*, or Venetian scene paintings, of CANALETTO and Francesco GUARDI were popular souvenirs for the wealthy traveler.

The late baroque and rococo styles were fashionable in the first half of the century. By about 1750, however, interest in the excavations of Roman ruins at Pompeii and Herculaneum prompted a revived European interest in antiquity resulting in NEOCLASSICISM. Ironically, Italy did not excel in the new artistic style, except for the works of Antonio CANOVA, who became the most acclaimed neoclassical sculptor.

Aside from the Macchiaoli, a group of Florentine painters who produced Tuscan landscapes and genre scenes, Italian art remained generally derivative until the late 19th century, when new schools began to emerge. The symbolist paintings of Giovanni Segantini (1858–99) complemented the inventive decorative extravagance of the Stile Liberty or Floreale, a movement in architecture and the decorative arts paralleling France's Art Nouveau.

The Twentieth Century

From 1910 to 1920, Italy briefly emerged as a major contributor to the development of modern art through FUTURISM and metaphysical painting. Both movements originated in Milan, which has been the most important center of avant-garde 20th-century Italian art, architecture, and design. Umberto BOCCIONI's sculpture and the futurist paintings of Carlo CARRÀ, Giacomo BALLA, and Gino SEVERINI were primarily concerned with the phenomenon of movement. In 1915, Giorgio de CHIRICO founded metaphysical painting (pittura metafisica) both as a personal need and as a reaction against futurism.

Although related to some aspects of modernism, much Italian art in the first half of the 20th century was figurative and rooted in previous manifestations of Italian classicism. Drawn to French modernism, Amedeo MODIGLIANI produced portraits and nudes related to Florentine Renaissance linearism.

The pompous pretensions of fascist art and architecture dominated Italy in the 1920s and '30s. Mussolini's call for a new imperial Rome prompted the formation of the Novecento Group, which, opposing modernism, academically espoused a large-scale revival of ancient Roman and High Renaissance classicism. Also during the 1930s the foremost Italian architectural modernists, including Pier Luigi NERVI, began to design the office buildings and sports complexes that they perfected during the 1950s and '60s in Milan, Turin, and Rome.

Arte povera (poor art) was the name given in the late 1960s to Italian minimal art and conceptual art. During the 1980s the United States, Germany, and Italy became the principal centers for a postmodern avant-garde producing expressionistic figurative compositions with formal and contextual references to the past, as well as apocalyptic visions of the future.

Italian language   see ROMANCE LANGUAGES

Italian literature   A specifically Italian literature was late in developing primarily because Latin survived on the peninsula longer than elsewhere. The first Italian writers were members of the so-called Sicilian School. Flourishing at the court of Emperor Frederick II (r. 1208–50), these poets adapted the amatory substance of the Provençal troubadours to their lyrics. The idealized Lady of their verses was given philosophical and religious significance by their successors Guido Guinicelli and Guido Cavalcanti and achieved immortality in the Beatrice of DANTE ALIGHIERI and the Laura of PETRARCH.

After Frederick's death the Italian muse moved northward, and a wider range of themes—social, political, and religious—appears in the works of the Tuscan Guittone d'Arezzo (c.1230–c.1294) and Jacopone da Todi, whose devotional verse was popular in style. All these motifs were fused in Dante's DIVINE COMEDY, a perfect reflection of the 13th-century worldview and the greatest poem of the Middle Ages. Dante's use of his native Tuscan dialect ultimately established it as the literary language of Italy. Petrarch brought to his sonnets and songs, especially those of the *Canzoniere* (Song Book), a deep emotional commitment and an unsurpassed technical mastery. The bulk of his work, however, was written in Latin. A prime mover in the new HUMANISM, he was dedicated to a deeper appreciation of the classics, one of the principal facets of the RENAISSANCE. Giovanni BOCCACCIO, while chiefly celebrated for his DECAMERON (1351–53), also pioneered in a number of poetic genres widely imitated abroad. The lively *Novelle* (c.1378–c.1395), or short stories, of Franco Sacchetti (c.1332–1400) further developed the genre mastered by Boccaccio.

In the 15th century the versatile Leon Battista ALBERTI, better known as an architect, published a lengthy treatise, *On the Family* (1433–39). Toward the end of the century the Florentine tyrant Lorenzo de'Medici (1449–

Modigliani's Seated Nude *(c.1917) exemplifies the fluid line, elongated form, and tonally unified composition characteristic of his work. (Courtauld Institute, London.)*

Dante (right) *and Petrarch* (above) *were two of the greatest poets of the 14th century. Dante, reflecting the culmination of medieval thought, and Petrarch, anticipating that of the Renaissance, helped turn the vernacular into literary expression.*

92) and his protégé POLITIAN excelled in lyric, narrative, and satirical verse. The semipopular Carolingian epic was polished and exploited by Luigi Pulci in his comic *Morgante Maggiore* (1483) and by Matteo Maria Boiardo in *Orlando Innamorato* (left unfinished in 1487).

In 1532, Ludovico ARIOSTO finished his romantic epic, *Orlando Furioso*. Nicolò MACHIAVELLI's The PRINCE (1532), Baldassare CASTIGLIONE's *The Courtier* (1528), and Jacopo SANNAZARO's pastoral idyll *Arcadia* (1502) all exercised an important influence internationally. High Renaissance Italian writers also included Cardinal Pietro Bembo, who exemplified the Platonism of the times; Francesco GUICCIARDINI, the historian of the contemporary Italian Wars, as well as of his native Florence; the satirist Pietro ARETINO; the short-story writers Matteo Bandello and Giovanni Francesco Straparola; and MICHELANGELO, whose sonnets rival his paintings. Italy's golden age came to an end when most of the country fell under the domination of Spain. Intellectual freedom also suffocated as the Church attempted to contain the Protestant Reformation. The tensions of the times are evident in the writings of the philosopher Giordano BRUNO as well as in the last great poetic work of the century, Torquato TASSO's epic *Jerusalem Delivered* (1581). In *Aminta* (1573), Tasso contributed to the popularity of the pastoral play, a genre also represented by the *Pastor Fido* (1590) of Giovanni Battista GUARINI.

In the baroque twilight of the early 17th century, the flamboyant Neapolitan poet Giambattista Marini, alone among Italian writers, received international recognition. The mock-epic *The Rape of the Bucket* (1622) by Alessandro Tassoni (1565–1635), nevertheless, has a certain vivacity and may have influenced Alexander Pope's *The Rape of the Lock*; the poets Gabriello Chiabrera (1552–1638), Fulvio Testi (1593–1646), and Francesco Redi (1626–98) also show originality.

The early years of the 18th century produced three able dramatists: Pietro Metastasio, a deft composer of melodramas and librettos; Carlo GOLDONI, whose well-made comedies still hold their own on the stage; and Carlo GOZZI, who adapted the COMMEDIA DELL'ARTE to his own romantic uses.

Social concerns inspired the work of the economic reformer Pietro Verri (1728–97), of Giambattista VICO—the most powerful intellect of his century—whose cyclical interpretation of history helped establish the discipline on a modern, scientific basis, and of the satirical poet Giuseppe Parini.

Toward the end of the century, the plays of Vittorio ALFIERI, though classic in form, were already romantic in mood and informed by the nationalist spirit of the coming RISORGIMENTO. The era was perhaps best epitomized by the Venetian soldier-poet Ugo Foscolo in works that blend romantic emotion, classical discipline, and patriotic passion.

A strong element of Christian piety colors the work of Alessandro MANZONI, the leader of Italian romanticism, chiefly famous for his semirealistic, semiromantic historical novel *I promessi sposi* (1825–27; trans. as *The Betrothed*, 1828). The most lyrical voice of the century belonged to the poet Giacomo LEOPARDI, who employed traditional verse forms for his seductive blend of passionate spontaneity and linguistic precision. Other writers of note in the early 19th century include the historical novelists Tommaso Grossi (1790–1853) and Francesco Guerrazzi (1804–73). Because of Italy's growing struggle for independence and unification, the writings of such political theorists as Vincenzo Gioberti, Massimo D'Azeglio (1798–1866), and especially the great patriot Giuseppe MAZZINI also assumed significance.

Giosuè CARDUCCI, a poet of social commitment and also a distinguished critic, was the greatest lyrical talent to emerge in the second half of the century. Toward the end of the century the more personal verse of Giovanni Pascoli became popular. In the 1880s and '90s the Italian novel was ably represented by two great writers: the master of VERISMO, Giovanni VERGA, celebrated for his evocations of Sicilian life, and the subtle psychologist Italo Svevo.

Antonio Fogazzaro, author of *Piccolo Mondo Antico* (1896; trans. as *The Patriot*, 1906), and Matilde Serao (1856–1927), with her colorful observations of Neapolitan life, also wrote novels of note. By far the most versatile and certainly the most prominent of Italian writers during the period, however, was Gabriele D'ANNUNZIO, novelist, poet, and dramatist, as well as duelist, patriot, and dilettante. His soaring lyrics together with his flamboyant personal life and controversial activism kept his influence alive into the 1930s.

The early years of the 20th century witnessed the emergence of Luigi PIRANDELLO, already known for his novels, as one of modern drama's greatest innovators. Pirandello's work shows affinity with the "grotesque" theater of which Luigi Chiarelli, Pier Maria Rosso di San Secondo (1887–1956), and Massimo Bontempelli (1878–1959) were exponents. The symbolic dramas of Ugo Betti have also had an influence far beyond Italy.

In lyric poetry, three successive schools appeared: the crepuscolari, or "twilight" poets, of the early 20th century, chief among them Guido Gozzano (1883–1916), Sergio Corazzini (1887–1907), and Marino Moretti (1885–1979); the short-lived, clamorous futurists (see FUTURISM) captained by Filippo Tommaso MARINETTI; and the hermetics, whose origins may be found in the early verses of Giuseppe Ungaretti and who flourished unobtrusively during the Fascist era. Less easy to categorize are the original and irrational poetry of Dino Campana (1885–1932) and the sensitive, autobiographical verse of Umberto Saba (1883–1957).

The novel in the early part of the century was represented by the Sardinian regionalist Grazia DELEDDA, winner of the 1926 Nobel Prize for literature, and the Tuscan realist Federigo Tozzi. At the same time the writings of the great philosopher, critic, and historian Benedetto CROCE attracted an international audience, while the polemical essays and *Life of Christ* (1921; Eng. trans., 1923) of Giovanni Papini (1881–1956) also enjoyed a great if ephemeral vogue.

In spite of censorship during Mussolini's years in power (1922–43), many writers continued to express themselves with some degree of freedom. Overt criticism of the regime, however, was ventured mainly by such exiles as the socialist novelist Ignazio SILONE, author of *Bread and Wine* (1937; Eng. trans., 1962), and the critic and novelist Giuseppe Antonio Borgese; within Italy the social commentator Carlo Levi wrote his perceptive *Christ Stopped at Eboli* (1945; Eng. trans., 1947) from government-enforced exile in the south, while the novelist Elio VITTORINI, the father of NEOREALISM, was temporarily imprisoned (1943) for his Marxist-oriented writings. Many prominent figures espoused the regime—Pirandello,

Bontempelli, and Ungaretti among them. The discontent of such able novelists as Alberto MORAVIA, who in the postwar years became Italy's most prolific and popular novelist and who in *The Conformist* (1951; Eng. trans., 1952) exposed the suffocating destructiveness of the regime, and of Corrado Alvaro, author of *Revolt in Aspromonte* (1930; Eng. trans., 1962), was expressed only obliquely in the 1930s and early 1940s. Riccardo Bacchelli (1891–1985) turned to the historical novel, while the mischievous realism of Aldo Palazzeschi (1885–1974) had no political undertones.

The fall of fascism brought a new flowering. Reflecting Italian literature's traditional bias toward social concerns, the *Letters from Prison* (1947; selections trans., 1973) and *Prison Notebooks* (1948–51; selections trans., 1971) of Antonio Gramsci, prewar Italy's leading Marxist theoretician, became best-sellers a decade after his death and exerted a powerful influence on European intellectuals. Among neorealist novelists, Cesare Pavese and Vasco Pratolini came to the fore, joined by new recruits to neorealism, many, such as Giorgio BASSANI, the sensitive author of *The Garden of the Finzi-Continis* (1962; Eng. trans., 1965), and Natalia Ginzburg, in *A Light for Fools* (1952; Eng. trans., 1957), drawing on memories of the war and of the partisan resistance. The novel of fantasy was represented by Dino Buzzati and Italo CALVINO, while a sophisticated regionalism was cultivated by Carlo Cassola, the satirical Vitaliano Brancati, Michele Prisco, Leonardo Sciascia—perhaps the most talented writer of his generation—and Fulvio Tomizza. The novel of middle-class crises was given a new twist by Guido Piovene (1907–76), Mario Soldati (b. 1906), and Alba De Cespedes (b. 1911). Elsa MORANTE's sprawling novel *History* (1974; Eng. trans., 1977) takes place during World War II. Paradoxically, the two Italian novels that enjoyed the greatest international success in the postwar period were written by members of the older generation: *That Awful Mess in Via Merulana* (1958; Eng. trans., 1965), a riotous and multilevel detective story by Carlo Emilio Gadda, and *The Leopard* (1956; Eng. trans., 1960), a sad and disillusioned historical novel by Giuseppe di LAMPEDUSA, were both sui generis.

In poetry the older hermetics won worldwide recognition when Salvatore QUASIMODO in 1959 and Eugenio MONTALE in 1975 won the Nobel Prize for literature. In recent years a more "open" school of poets has come forth, among them Vittorio Sereni (1913–83) and Pier Paolo PASOLINI, the latter also a noted film director and Communist. A versatile writer of the era, the poet, novelist, and critic Edoardo Sanguineti (b. 1930), has assumed the role of spokesperson for the avant-garde in contemporary letters.

Since the 1950s a great deal of dramatic talent has been channeled into the renowned Italian film industry. Of popular works on the contemporary stage, the Neapolitan plays of Eduardo DE FILIPPO are staples of the Italian theater. The plays of Diego Fabbri (1911–80) reflect a Pirandellian influence. The plays of political satirist and actor Dario Fo likewise attract international interest.

Italian music No notated music from Roman times has been preserved. Therefore, the earliest known Italian music is bound up with the history of the Catholic church. The two great centers of liturgical and musical reform in Italy in the first millennium were Milan and Rome. Saint Ambrose (c.333–97), bishop of Milan, imported several musical practices from Syria, including the custom of antiphonal singing (see ANTIPHON). He was also the author of a number of HYMNS; Saint Augustine credits him with the introduction of hymn singing in the West.

Middle Ages

The most important sponsor of reformation and codification of musical ritual in the Church was Gregory the Great, pope from 590 to 604. The common custom of referring to all sacred chant as "Gregorian" is a tribute to his efforts. Another important figure for the orderly transmission of chant was the Benedictine monk Guido d'Arezzo.

Among the first pieces using vernacular Italian texts are the *laude spirituali*, the earliest of which date from the 13th century. The following century witnessed a flourishing of secular music, with advances in rhythmic notation and POLYPHONY. The principal forms were the MADRIGAL, the caccia (a piece dealing with the chase, or hunting), and the ballata. The outstanding composer of this period was Francesco LANDINI.

Renaissance

During the 15th and much of the 16th century Italy usually imported its musical talent. Toward the end of the 15th century, distinctively Italian secular music began to reappear at some of the Italian courts. In Florence, during the time of Lorenzo de'Medici (1448–92), carnival celebrations were enriched by *canti carnascialeschi* (carnival songs). In Mantua composers developed the *frottola*, a homophonic (chordal), clearly phrased, strophic piece. These forms preceded the 16th-century madrigal, one of the great flowerings of Italian musical art.

In the earlier part of the 16th century madrigals were written by French and Netherlandish composers as well as by Italians such as Costanzo Festa (1490–1545). The late madrigal, written in the last third of the century, was dominated by the Italians Luca Marenzio, Carlo GESUALDO, and Claudio MONTEVERDI. In sacred music the Roman school is epitomized in the works of Giovanni Pierluigi da PALESTRINA. Working under the influence of the Counter-Reformation, Palestrina wrote several hundred motets and 105 masses. The Venetian school had its founding father in the Flemish composer Adrian Willaert, who was director of music at Saint Mark's Cathedral from 1527 to 1562. Willaert, his student Andrea Gabrieli, and Andrea's nephew Giovanni Gabrieli (see GABRIELI family) developed a polychoral (multiple choruses) style of composition. Venice was also an important center of music printing from as early as the beginning of the 16th century.

Baroque

The period of Italy's greatest musical influence through-

Claudio Monteverdi, one of Italy's most acclaimed composers, was a major figure in the transition from the Renaissance tradition of polyphony to baroque drama and compositional innovation.

out Europe lasted from the end of the 16th to the middle of the 18th century. The Italian taste for passion and ornament dominated BAROQUE MUSIC through such genres as the opera, oratorio, cantata, concerto, and sinfonia.

The earliest operas that have survived complete are *Euridice* by Jacopo Peri and Giulio Caccini, performed in Florence in 1600, and *Rappresentazione di Anima e di Corpo* by Emilio de Cavalieri (c.1550–1602), performed in Rome in 1600. Peri, Caccini, and Cavalieri were all associated with a group of Florentine humanists called the Camerata, who hoped to achieve in their own time the great effects attributed to music by the ancient Greeks. To accomplish this goal they instituted a style of reciting in music, the *stile recitativo* (RECITATIVE), that allowed the text to be projected with clarity. The voice was accompanied by chords notated in a shorthand called FIGURED BASS. The full expressive possibilities of the new style were first demonstrated by Monteverdi in his opera *Orfeo* (1607).

Rome was a center of operatic composition from about 1620 until the late 1630s. In 1637 the first public opera house opened in Venice, and until the end of the 17th century, Venice was the operatic capital of Italy. Some of the finest Venetian operas were written by Monteverdi and his pupil Pier Francesco Cavalli. Other offspring of the new style were the cantata, similar to an operatic scene, and the oratorio, a musical presentation of a sacred subject.

One of the characteristics of baroque music was the development of an idiomatic style of writing for various instruments. The greatest keyboard composer at the turn of the 17th century was Girolamo FRESCOBALDI, organist at Saint Peter's in Rome.

Throughout the baroque era Italy was preeminent both in the manufacture of violins and in the composition and performance of music for them. Members of the AMATI, STRADIVARI, and GUARNERI families, all of whom worked in Cremona, are among the greatest violin makers of all time. Superb trio sonatas—music for two treble instruments, most often violins, and a melodic bass instrument such as the cello with a keyboard instrument filling in the harmonies—were written by Arcangelo CORELLI.

Orchestral music also had its origins in the baroque era. The term *concerto grosso* describes a piece built on the contrast between a larger and a smaller group of instruments; Corelli composed some of the best examples of the genre. The most important composers in the development of the solo concerto, which contrasts a single player with a group, were Giuseppe TORELLI, Tommaso ALBINONI, and Antonio VIVALDI.

The most important composer of operas at the turn of the century was Alessandro Scarlatti (see SCARLATTI family), who wrote more than 100. *Opera seria* (see OPERA) was cultivated by German composers as well as Italians such as Niccolò Jommelli and Tommaso Traetta. Comic opera made great advances in the hands of Giovanni PERGOLESI, Niccolò Piccinni, Giovanni PAISIELLO, and Domenico CIMAROSA.

In the second half of the 18th century, the Milanese composer Giovanni Battista SAMMARTINI won international fame for his symphonies. The concerto was cultivated by Giovanni Battista Viotti, an Italian working in France and England. Luigi BOCCHERINI, an Italian who spent much of his career in Spain, wrote a large quantity of chamber music.

Nineteenth Century

The most commanding figure in Italian opera at the beginning of the 19th century was Gioacchino ROSSINI. In two decades Rossini created nearly 40 operas, fairly evenly divided between the serious and the comic genres. He is best known for his comic masterpiece *The Barber of Seville* (1816).

After Rossini, the bel canto style flourished in the operas of Vincenzo BELLINI and Gaetano DONIZETTI. Bellini's art is one of refined and expressive lyricism, sometimes rising to high drama, as in *Norma* (1831). Donizetti's more robust temperament was at home both in comic works such as *Don Pasquale* (1843) and in tragic works

One of the most dramatic scenes in Giacomo Puccini's Tosca (1900), *Tosca's murder of Scarpia at the close of the second act, was used to illustrate this poster. Puccini is considered one of Italy's most successful operatic composers.*

such as *Lucia di Lammermoor* (1835).

For a half century, beginning in the 1840s, Italian opera was dominated by Giuseppe VERDI, the representative of the musical and the nationalistic aspirations of the Italian people. The best-known Verdi operas include *Rigoletto* (1851), *Il Trovatore* (1853), *La Traviata* (1853), *Aïda* (1871), and *Otello* (1887). Most of his works are tragic, but his final opera, *Falstaff* (1893), is a comedy.

The 1890s saw a new operatic style known as VERISMO (realism), which emphasized sordid settings and violent contrasts. Its landmark works are Pietro MASCAGNI's *Cavalleria rusticana* (1890) and Ruggero LEONCAVALLO's *I Pagliacci* (1892). Giacomo PUCCINI blended veristic elements with sentimentality in *La Bohème* (1896), with fancy costumes in *Tosca* (1900), and with exoticism in *Madama Butterfly* (1904).

Twentieth Century

Of the generation of composers who came to maturity at the turn of the 20th century, the most significant were Ottorino RESPIGHI, Alfredo Casella (1883–1947), Gian Francesco Malipiero, and Ildebrando Pizzetti, all of whom turned for inspiration to pre-19th-century Italian music. The most important representatives of the next generation, Luigi DALLAPICCOLA and Goffredo Petrassi, manifested in their works closer contacts with contemporary composers outside Italy. Petrassi was most influenced by Paul Hindemith and Igor Stravinsky. Dallapiccola, once he became acquainted with the works of Arnold Schoenberg and Anton Webern, incorporated 12-tone techniques into a distinct personal style.

Italian composers today are working in virtually all the current trends—SERIAL MUSIC, ELECTRONIC MUSIC, ALEATORY MUSIC, and collage techniques. Most prominent among the avant-garde composers are the late Bruno MADERNA, Luigi Nono, Luciano BERIO, and Sylvano Bussotti (b. 1931).

See also: RENAISSANCE MUSIC.

Verdi, one of the most brilliant composers of the 19th century, presented La Traviata, *a tragedy based on* La Dame aux camélias, *(1848) a novel by Alexandre Dumas fils. Verdi's operas include such other masterpieces as* Il Trovatore *(1853) and* Aïda *(1871).*

Italian Wars   Between 1494 and 1559, the HABSBURG rulers of Spain and the Holy Roman Empire fought the VALOIS kings of France for control of Italy in a series of conflicts known as the Italian Wars. These conflicts weakened Italy but helped to spread its RENAISSANCE culture to other areas of western Europe.

After the Peace of Lodi (1454), a precarious balance of power had been maintained among the chief Italian states: Florence, Milan, Naples, the papacy, and Venice. This equilibrium was upset when Ludovico Sforza (see SFORZA family) of Milan appealed to France for aid against a secret league of Florence and Naples. The French king CHARLES VIII descended (1494) into Italy with his army, expelled the Florentine ruler Piero de'Medici (see MEDICI family), and entered Naples in February 1495. Threatened by a coalition of Italian states allied with Emperor MAXIMILIAN I and King FERDINAND II of Aragon, Charles soon withdrew.

A period of intermittent warfare followed. The Spanish general Gonzalo FERNÁNDEZ DE CÓRDOBA conquered (1503–04) Naples, bringing southern Italy under Spanish control, and France dominated the northern half of the peninsula. Soon Venice seemed to pose a new threat, and in response France, the empire, the papacy, and Spain formed (1508) the League of Cambrai. Following its victory at Agnadello (1509), the league conquered all of Venice's mainland possessions. The league soon fell apart, however, and Venice recovered its empire. In 1512 the Habsburgs restored the Medici to Florence and in 1515 were defeated by the French at the battle of Marignano. By the Treaty of Noyon (1516) France received Milan but renounced its claim to Naples.

During the 1520s, France and the empire continued to fight over Lombardy, but the defeat of the French and the capture of their king, FRANCIS I, at Pavia (1525) doomed French influence in Italy. The League of Cognac, formed in May 1526, allied France, Florence, Milan, Venice, and the papacy against the Habsburgs in an attempt to reverse the effects of Pavia. Spanish pikemen quickly conquered Milan, however, and, in May 1527, sacked Rome.

France continued to meddle in Italian affairs until the Treaty of Cateau–Cambrésis (Apr. 3, 1559), by which all French claims in Italy, except in Savoy, were renounced. The Spanish Habsburgs were left free to dominate the severely weakened Italian peninsula until the early 18th century.

Italo-Turkish War   Italy's attempt to annex the Turkish North African provinces of Cyrenaica and Tripolitania (which constitute modern Libya) resulted in the Italo-Turkish War of 1911–12. Italian leaders, determined to build a colonial empire, declared war on the failing Ottoman (Turkish) Empire on Sept. 29, 1911. Italy landed troops in Libya and in November declared it to be Italian territory. While the fighting continued in Libya, where Turkish forces were backed by the Arab population, Italy widened the war to Rhodes and the other Dodecanese Is-

lands off the coast of Turkey. Faced with rebellion in the Balkans (see BALKAN WARS), Turkey conceded and signed the Treaty of Ouchy (or Treaty of Lausanne) on Oct. 18, 1912, making Libya an Italian protectorate. The Italo-Turkish War weakened the Ottoman Empire and upset the fragile balance of power in Europe, thus contributing to the outbreak of World War I in 1914.

Italy   Italy is an independent nation in southern Europe. It extends southward from the Alps to the Mediterranean Sea, forming a narrow, 1,100-km-long (700-mi), boot-shaped peninsula. The peninsula is bordered by the Ligurian Sea and the Tyrrhenian Sea on the west, the IONIAN SEA on the south, and the ADRIATIC SEA on the east. The national territory includes the two large islands of SARDINIA and SICILY; the smaller offshore islands of CAPRI, ELBA, and Ischia; the Lipari (Aeolian) Islands; the islands of Pantelleria, Linosa, Lampione, and Lampedusa in the Strait of Sicily; TRIESTE and the northern sections of ISTRIA. Located on the Italian peninsula are two small independent enclaves—VATICAN CITY, in Rome, and the Republic of SAN MARINO, near RIMINI. Italy is bordered on the northwest by France, on the north by Switzerland, on the northeast by Austria, and on the east by Yugoslavia. The capital is ROME.

The name *Italy* (*Italia*) came into the Latin language from the ancient Oscan tongue, which in turn may have taken it from a southern Greek dialect. Its etymology is linked to a Greek word meaning "calf," and according to a modern interpretation it is a reference to Calabria in southern Italy, where early inhabitants adopted the calf as their symbol.

The modern Italian state dates from 1861, when the title king of Italy was conferred on VICTOR EMMANUEL II, king of Sardinia. Before that time Italy consisted of separate states with a strong sense of regional identity. The nation has 20 administrative regions today. Eight of them are located in northern (or Upper) Italy: EMILIA-ROMAGNA, FRIULI–VENEZIA GIULIA, LIGURIA, LOMBARDY, PIEDMONT, TRENTINO–ALTO ADIGE, VALLE D'AOSTA, and VENETO. Six are in central Italy: ABRUZZI, LATIUM, MARCHE, TUSCANY, UMBRIA, and Molise. Southern Italy contains four: CALABRIA, CAMPANIA, Apulia, and Basilicata. The other two states are the island regions of Sardinia and Sicily.

Italy has been historically important since Roman times, and millions of tourists are attracted each year to its ancient cities and art treasures. Modern Italy is an important industrial nation and a leading member of the EUROPEAN COMMUNITY (EC). Italy's rapid growth since 1950 has been referred to as the "Italian miracle."

Land

Italy can be divided topographically into three parts—continental, peninsular, and insular Italy. Continental Italy, in the north, includes the triangular-shaped North Italian Plain—Italy's only large lowland—and the high mountains of the Alps, which curve along the northern border in a broad arc. These mountains extend from

ITALIAN REPUBLIC

Land: Area: 301,268 km^2 (116,320 mi^2). Capital and largest city: Rome (1988 est. pop., 2,816,474).

People: Population (1990 est.): 57,700,000. Density: 192 persons per km^2 (496 per mi^2). Distribution (1990): 72% urban, 28% rural. Official language: Italian. Major religion: Roman Catholicism.

Government: Type: republic. Legislature: Parliament. Political subdivisions: 20 regions.

Economy: GDP (1989): $803 billion; $14,000 per capita. Labor distribution (1988): agriculture—10%; industry and commerce—32%; services—58%. Foreign trade (1989): imports—$143.1 billion; exports—$141.6 billion. Currency: 1 Italian lira = 100 centesimi.

Education and Health: Literacy (1990): 93% of adult population. Universities (1987): 47. Hospital beds (1986): 450,377. Physicians (1986): 245,116. Life expectancy (1990): women—81; men—74. Infant mortality (1990): 6 per 1,000 live births.

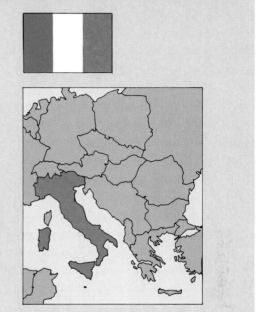

Savona, on the Ligurian coast, to near Trieste in the east. The highest peaks in the Alps are west of the SIMPLON PASS and include Gran Paradiso, south of Aosta; Mont Blanc (see BLANC, MONT), the highest mountain in Europe, on the border with France; the MATTERHORN, on the border with Switzerland; and Monte Rosa, Italy's highest point, which rises to 4,634 m (15,200 ft). The central Alps, located between the Simplon Pass on the west and the Resia Pass on the east, rise more than 3,300 m (10,800 ft) in the Lepontine Alps and to 4,049 m (13,284 ft) farther east in the Bernina Alps. Italy's eastern Alps include the Ötztal and Carnic Alps, on the border with Austria; the Dolomites, rising wholly within Italy; and the Julian Alps, located primarily in Yugoslavia.

Peninsular Italy stretches south of the North Italian Plain. The APENNINES form the backbone of the peninsula and reach their highest elevation in the central, or Abruzzi, Apennines. Broad lowlands, backed by the rolling hills of the pre-Apennines, border the Tyrrhenian coast in Tuscany and Latium. In the south, the highest mountains are close to the Tyrrhenian coast, which is rocky, steep, and indented south of Naples. VESUVIUS, Europe's only active mainland volcano, is near Naples.

Insular Italy includes Sardinia, Sicily, and many smaller islands. Sardinia covers an area of 23,812 km^2 (9,194 mi^2) and rises to a high point of 1,834 m (6,016 ft) in the ancient granite massif of Gennargentu. Sicily covers an area of 28,812 km^2 (11,124 mi^2) and rises to 3,262 m (10,703 ft) in Mount ETNA. Northern Sicily is traversed by high mountains geologically related to the

Apennines. This chain reappears across the Sicilian Channel as the ATLAS MOUNTAINS of northern Africa. Two active volcanoes—STROMBOLI and Vulcano—are located on islands off the north coast of Sicily.

Soils. The richest and most productive soils for agriculture are the alluvial soils of the North Italian Plain and the smaller river valleys of the peninsula. Well suited for forestry and pasture are the brown podzolic soils, which developed under an original forest cover and are found throughout the Apennines. Regosols have developed on the weathered volcanic deposits of Tuscany and Latium and on the lower slopes of active volcanoes. Red soils are common in Apulia and in other limestone areas in the south.

Climate. Except for the Alps, where the climate varies with altitude, Italy has a continental climate in the north and a Mediterranean climate in the south. Summer temperatures average 24° C (75° F) for July throughout the nation, but winter temperatures range from a January average of 1° C (33° F) at BOLZANO in the north to 7° C (45° F) at Rome, and 12° C (53° F) at Palermo on Sicily.

Precipitation ranges from 889 mm (35 in) at Trieste to 610 mm (24 in) in Palermo. It is concentrated during the winter in the south (typical of a Mediterranean climate) and during the warmer part of the year in the north.

Six climatic subregions may be distinguished. The Alpine zone is characterized by harsh winters, abundant precipitation, frequent snow, and cool summers. The North Italian Plain has harsh winters with long periods of frost, warm summers, precipitation concentrated in spring and fall, and intense fog in fall and winter. The

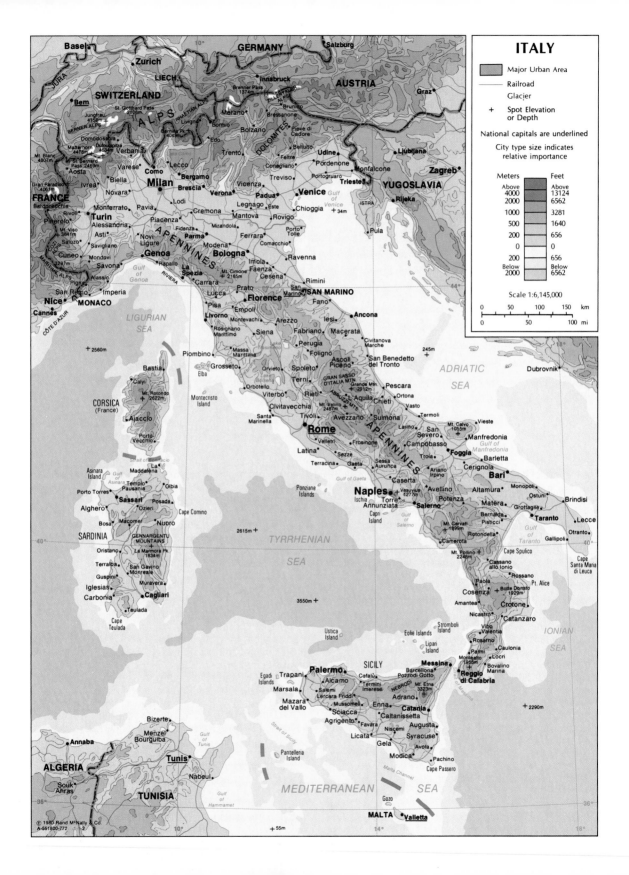

coastal Tyrrhenian region has mild winters and hot, dry summers. The climate of the Adriatic coast tends to be drier and colder in winter. The Apennines are climatically similar to the North Italian Plain. The islands have a typically Mediterranean climate, with hot, dry summers and mild winters.

Drainage. The principal Italian waterway is the 652-km-long (405-mi) Po RIVER, which drains most of the North Italian Plain and enters the Adriatic Sea south of Venice. The ADIGE RIVER, Italy's second longest, has a length of 410 km (255 mi) and flows into the Adriatic Sea north of the Po.

In peninsular Italy the 405-km-long (253-mi) TIBER RIVER flows from the Tuscan-Emilian Apennines through Rome and Ostia to the Tyrrhenian Sea. Also important is the 241-km-long (151-mi) ARNO RIVER, flowing through the cities of Florence and PISA before entering the Ligurian Sea.

The largest lakes in Italy, located in the Alps and pre-Alps and of glacial origin, include Lake GARDA, with an area of 370 km^2 (142 mi^2); Lake MAGGIORE; and Lake COMO. The largest lakes of the peninsula are Lake Trasimeno (Lake of Perugia) and Lake Bolsena.

Vegetation and Animal Life. About one-fifth of Italy is forested, with deciduous trees predominating in the North Italian Plain and needle-leaf trees predominating at higher altitudes. The typical lowland woodland is a mixture of holm oaks, cork trees, maritime pines, cypresses, oleasters (wild olive), carobs, laurels, and myrtles. Forests of chestnut and oak; beech trees, pines, and white fir; and larch, spruce, and pine are found in successive elevation zones in the mountains. Between the tree line (limit of tree growth) and the snow line stretch extensive alpine pastures. Heath is common on the North Italian Plain.

The principal large animals are the brown bear, in the Alps and the Abruzzi mountains; wolves, in the Apennines; wild boars, on Sardinia; red deer, chamois, roe deer, and Alpine ibex, in Gran Paradiso National Park; and fallow deer and mouflons, on Sardinia. The most numerous birds are larks, crows, and wrens; hawks, buzzards, and eagles can be seen in some upland areas.

Resources. Except for sulfur and mercury, Italy has only small deposits of minerals needed for industry. Minor coal deposits are located on Sardinia, and some lignite is mined in Tuscany, Umbria, and Basilicata. Petroleum and natural gas are found in Sicily, and a large natural-gas field underlies much of the North Italian Plain.

Abundant hydroelectric power is produced on rivers flowing from the Alps. This form of energy is increasingly important in the south as dams are built to regulate the flow of local rivers.

People

The Italian people are among the most ethnically homogenous in Europe. Nearly all are of Italian origin and speak Italian or related dialects and languages. Separate languages include Sardinian, spoken by about 1.2 million people on Sardinia; Friulian, a Rhaeto-Romanic language spoken by about 520,000 people in the northeastern district of Friuli; and Ladin, a Rhaeto-Romanic language

spoken in the mountains of the Alto Adige. The principal non-Italian minorities are about 260,000 German-Italians in the Alto Adige (formerly Austria's South TYROL), and 53,000 Slavic Italians, scattered in several areas in Friuli and Venezia-Giulia. Other isolated minority groups include Greek-speaking communities in Apulia and Calabria; Albanian colonies in Sicily and Calabria; and Serbo-Croatian communities in Molise. French is spoken in the Aosta valley.

Religion. Roman Catholicism was established as Italy's official religion by the Lateran Treaty between Vatican City and Italy on Feb. 11, 1929, but this status was abolished under a new concordat signed in 1984. There are about 180,000 Protestants and 35,000 Jews.

Demography. Italy has one of the highest population densities in Europe. The only sparsely populated areas are the Alpine uplands, parts of the Apennines in Liguria and Calabria; and the marshes of Tuscany and Latium.

Italy's current birthrate and death rate are slightly lower than the European average. Both rates have dropped dramatically in recent years. Generally the population of central and northern Italy has tended to grow faster than that of the Mezzogiorno (south), mostly because of an internal migration pattern in which people from the less developed south move northward in search of greater economic opportunities.

The Dolomites, a principal range of the eastern Alps, are located in northeast Italy, between the Adige and Piave river valleys.

The city of Venice, built on 118 islands in the Lagoon of Venice, is famous for its distinctive canals and bridges and its history as an Italian artistic center and European maritime power.

Just under three-quarters of the population live in urban areas, a figure close to the European average. Rome, the nation's capital, is also the largest city. MILAN, NAPLES, and TURIN each have more than 1 million inhabitants. Milan is Italy's chief commercial, financial, and industrial center. Other large cities include GENOA, PALERMO, BOLOGNA, FLORENCE, CATANIA, and VENICE.

Emigration has long been a feature of Italy's population. Between 1861 and 1965 an estimated 26.5 million Italians emigrated, primarily to the United States, Argentina, and Brazil. Only 6 million returned. Since World War II emigration has continued but mainly by workers leaving temporarily for employment in other European nations—particularly Germany and Switzerland.

Education and Health. Education is free and compulsory between the ages of 6 and 14. Children between the ages of 11 and 14 attend middle school, and those who graduate may continue their education in a classical or scientific high school, in a teacher training school, or in one of a variety of technical schools. Only a small number of students go on to study at a university. The principal universities are at Rome, Naples, Milan, Bologna, Turin, and Palermo. Italian education has made great progress in the 20th century. In the 1930s more than 20% of the population was illiterate. Today illiteracy has been virtually eliminated in northern Italy; the south, however, lags behind the rest of the country educationally as well as economically.

Health costs for most Italians are covered by compulsory insurance programs, but a shortage of medical facilities exists in rural areas. Many of the hospitals are run by Catholic religious orders.

Cultural Institutions. Academies are an important feature of intellectual life in Italy. Among the more prominent are the Accademia dei Lincei, founded in Rome in 1603; the National Academy of Saint Luke for fine arts,

founded in the 14th century; Florence's Accademia Nazionale della Crusca (1582) for philological, lexicographical, and grammatical studies; and the National Academy of Saint Cecilia for music, founded in Rome in 1566. The leading research institute for mathematics, physics, and natural sciences is the National Research Council of Italy (1923). Museums and art galleries can be found in all the larger towns. Among the most famous are the UFFIZI, Pitti Palace, and National Museum, in Florence; the Gallerio Borghese, Villa Giulia, Capitoline Museum, and National Gallery of Modern Art, in Rome; and the Accademia, in Venice.

Economic Activity

Modern industry developed in Italy at the beginning of the 20th century, about 100 years later than in other parts of Western Europe. This delay resulted in part from a lack of industrial raw materials, especially coal and other fuels, and also from the political fragmentation that hindered the development of a single national market. Early industrialization was concentrated mainly in the northwest, where industrial agglomeration in the iron-and-steel, shipbuilding, engineering, and textile industries continues. The rest of Italy remained industrially underdeveloped and primarily agricultural until the 1950s.

Governmental participation in industrial development continues. Through autonomous public organizations, an estimated one-third to one-half of all production by privately managed companies is directed by the state. In addition, programs such as the Southern Development Fund offer special financial incentives to companies locating in the south.

Manufacturing and Mining. In the late 1980s manufacturing contributed about 37% to the gross domestic product. Almost one-third of all industrial workers live in Lombardy. Italy's principal industries are the steel, automotive engineering, chemical, and textile industries. In 1988 steel output was 23.6 million metric tons (26 million U.S. tons), more than ten times the production at the end of World War II. The principal steel-making centers are TARANTO, Genoa, Naples-Bagnoli, and Piombino. The automobile industry is located in BRESCIA, MODENA, Milan, and Turin. Italy also exports sewing machines, typewriters, motor scooters, bicycles, mopeds, power tools, calculators, refrigerators, radios, and televisions. Airplanes are manufactured in Turin, and ships are built at ANCONA, LA SPEZIA, Genoa, Naples, Trieste, and Venice. The production of petrochemicals such as plastics, fertilizers, and synthetic rubber is concentrated in the natural-gas fields of the North Italian Plain and Sicily. The textile industry, important since the Middle Ages, was traditionally dependent on imported wool and cotton, but in recent decades a synthetic fiber and fabric industry has developed. Florence and Milan are leading textile and garment centers. Artisans play an important role in the Italian economy and receive assistance from the government. Glass, pottery, lace, carved marble, and gold and silver filigree work are among the most famous handcrafted products.

Local output of petroleum and natural gas supplies only a fraction of the nation's needs. Most petroleum is extracted in the Sicilian district of Ragusa. Natural gas underlies much of the North Italian Plain and parts of Sicily. Other minerals include marble, quarried as in Michelangelo's time at Carrara; lead and zinc, mined on Sardinia; sulfur, on Sicily; and bauxite, mined mainly in the south.

Energy. In 1989, Italy produced 201.4 billion kW h of electricity, most of it generated in thermal electric power plants, fueled by petroleum and natural gas. About 25% of electricity is provided by hydroelectric plants and 4% by nuclear reactors.

Agriculture. Agriculture contributed 5% to the gross domestic product in 1989. Slightly more than half of all land is used for farming, but productivity is low because only 29% of the land devoted to farming is in the fertile North Italian Plain; the rest is in the agriculturally marginal hill and mountain areas. Agricultural production is further limited by lack of investment capital for modern equipment, by a preponderance of tenant-farmed estates in the south, and by the small size of most farm units.

The principal crops include wheat, which is grown throughout the nation, and corn and rice, grown mainly in the North Italian Plain, where water is available in summer for irrigation of the rice crop. Olives, grapes, citrus fruits, peaches, and other tree crops are grown in the typically Mediterranean central and southern regions. Flowers are a specialty crop along the Ligurian coast. Livestock accounts for about 40% of all agricultural production by value, but Italy must import large quantities of meat, primarily from France and Germany. Dairy cattle dominate in the Alps and in the provinces of Emilia-Romagna, Lombardy, and Tuscany; and sheep and goats are raised in the hilly, drier areas of the south as well as on Sardinia and Sicily.

Fishing and Forestry. Many small fishing ports line Italy's long coast, but the Mediterranean is not abundant in fish. The 1987 catch of 554,464 metric tons (611,185 U.S. tons) was insufficient to meet the nation's needs. Some fishing fleets work in the Atlantic Ocean, but most fishers use small boats and outdated equipment. Forestry is of only minor importance.

Transportation. Road traffic is increasing as more Italians purchase automobiles; the highway (*autostrade*) system now covers 5,900 km (3,666 mi). The most important freeway is the 1,250-km-long (777-mi) highway linking Milan, Rome, Naples, and REGGIO DI CALABRIA, breaking the historic isolation of many southern communities. About half of the 20,085 km (12,480 mi) of railroad is electrified, and state-run lines provide fast, efficient service. International air traffic is centered on Rome, located on international air-traffic routes serving Europe and Asia. The Po River, navigable as far as CREMONA, is Italy's only natural inland water route.

Communications. The Italian Radio and Television System (RAI) is state owned; three other national TV networks and hundreds of local radio stations also exist. Most of the daily newspapers published in Italy have headquarters in either Rome or Milan.

Trade. Italy's imports are dominated by industrial raw materials, petroleum, meat, and cereal grains. The principal exports are manufactured goods and craft items, along with fruits and vegetables. Italy usually suffers a trade deficit, but the difference is offset by its large and profitable tourist industry and by money sent by Italian

Milan, Italy's second largest city and a major industrial center, has been a major financial and commercial center since the Middle Ages. The Galleria, a glass-roofed shopping arcade, also serves as a social meeting place.

(Right) *Montferrat is a historic area in the Piedmont region of northwestern Italy, where the fertile Po River valley yields grapes and cereals.* (Below) *The Umbria region in central Italy is divided into the provinces of Perugia and Terni. This fertile mountainous region is used extensively for crops and livestock.*

citizens working abroad. The main ports are Genoa, Trieste, Taranto, Venice, Savona, and Naples. Most of Italy's principal trading partners are members of the EC. Other major partners include the United States, and—for petroleum imports—Saudi Arabia, Iran, and Iraq.

Government

In a referendum vote held on June 2, 1946, Italy's monarchy was abolished and the Italian Republic established. According to the constitution, which took effect Jan. 1, 1948, executive power lies with the cabinet, and legislative powers are vested in a Parliament consisting of a 630-member chamber of deputies and a 315-member senate. Except for a few life members of the senate (including former presidents and five prominent citizens nominated by the president), both houses are elected directly by universal adult suffrage for 5-year terms. The president of the republic is head of state and is elected to a renewable 7-year term by a joint session of Parliament and three delegates from each of the regional legislatures. Executive power rests with the council of ministers (cabinet) headed by the prime minister appointed by the president. On July 22, 1985, Francesco Cossiga became president, and in July 1989, Giulio Andreotti was appointed prime minister.

Each of the 20 regions has an elected council, a president, and a *giunta regionale* that exercises executive power and is responsible to the regional council. The principal political party is the Christian Democratic party, which has led or participated in every government since 1945. The second largest party is the Communist party, which was excluded from the government from 1947 to 1977. Other parties include the Republican, Italian Socialist, and Social Democratic parties.

See also: ITALIAN ART AND ARCHITECTURE; ITALIAN LITERATURE; ITALIAN MUSIC.

Italy, history of   Since earliest times the history of Italy has been influenced by cultural and political divisions resulting from the peninsula's disparate geography and by circumstances that made Italy the scene of many important power struggles in Europe.

Early Italy

Recent excavations throughout Italy and Sicily have revealed evidence of human activity during the Paleolithic and Mesolithic periods. By the beginning of the Neolithic period (c.5000 BC), the small communities of hunters had been replaced by agricultural settlements. Painted vessels that seem to have been influenced by contemporary styles in Greece have been found at Castellaro Vecchio on the island of Lipari.

The Bronze Age. By 2000 BC new immigrants from the east had introduced metalworking into southern Italy and Sicily; the northern Italian Polada culture of the same period left evidence of strong links with cultures north of the Alps. During the Bronze Age (c.1800–1000 BC), much of central and southern Italy had a unified culture known as the Apennine, characterized by large agricultural and pastoral settlements; on the southeastern coast and in Sicily evidence indicates trading contacts with the Mycenaeans. After c.1500 BC, in the Po Valley to the north, the terramara culture—with its villages constructed on wooden piles, its advanced techniques of bronze working, and its cremation rites—rose to prominence. By the time of the introduction of iron into Italy (c.1000 BC), regional variations were well established.

The Etruscans. In the late 8th century BC, Greek colonizers arrived in the south and on Sicily, and the ETRUSCANS appeared in central Italy and the Po Valley. By the end of the 7th century BC, LATIUM and part of CAMPANIA had joined central Italy under Etruscan rule. As the Etruscans expanded their rule, many city-states were founded by various Italian peoples.

Roman Italy

According to later Roman historians, the city of ROME, founded in *c.*753—probably by local Latins and SABINES—was ruled by Etruscan kings from 616 BC. After the expulsion of the last of these kings, TARQUINIUS SUPERBUS in 510 BC, and the foundation of the Roman republic in 509, the power of the Etruscans declined as the Romans began the unification of Italy (see ROME, ANCIENT). This process reached its final stage in 89 BC, when the right of Roman citizenship was extended throughout Italy, with the consequent diffusion of Roman institutions and the Latin language and culture from the Alps to Sicily.

The Roman Empire. The Roman Empire began effectively with the defeat of Mark ANTONY and CLEOPATRA in 31 BC by the man who later became Emperor AUGUSTUS. During the following centuries the increasing extent of the Roman possessions outside Italy resulted in a decline in the importance of Italy itself, a process accelerated by the growing number of emperors elsewhere. The Edict of Caracalla (AD 212 or 213), which extended Roman citizenship to nearly all free provincials throughout the empire, further undermined Italy's special status. In 330, Emperor CONSTANTINE I transferred his capital from Rome to Constantinople. The loss of temporal power, however, was compensated for by the growing importance of Italy as a center of Christianity: starting in the 2d century AD several bishoprics were founded—in Milan, Ravenna, Naples, Benevento, and elsewhere—in addition to that of Rome.

After 476, when the Germanic chieftain ODOACER deposed the last Western emperor, Romulus Augustulus (r. 475–76), military control of Italy passed into barbarian hands. Under the Ostrogothic king, THEODORIC (r. 493–526; see GOTHS), Italian political and social ties were with the West, in spite of continuing theoretical ties with the BYZANTINE EMPIRE. By 553, however, internal feuds permitted the Byzantine emperor JUSTINIAN I to regain control. Peninsular Italy was administered from its capital at RAVENNA as merely one division of the empire.

The Middle Ages

Italian ties with the "New Rome" of the East (Constantinople) were loosened during a series of invasions from the west and north into Italy. The severing of ties with the East was confirmed by the eventual emergence of the PAPACY and the Italian cities as powers in their own right.

The Lombards. After the Ostrogoths, another Germanic people, the LOMBARDS, arrived in Italy—in 568; their control soon spread from the north to Tuscany and Umbria, although much of southern and eastern Italy remained in Byzantine hands. The Lombards were resisted chiefly by the popes—most notably GREGORY I (r. 590–604)—who acted as de facto political and military as well as ecclesiastical leaders and held a band of land stretching across the peninsula that later became the PAPAL STATES. By the end of the 7th century the Lombards consolidated their power in northern and central Italy. In 728, profiting from the unrest in the Byzantine centers in the south (which reflected the disturbances caused by ICONOCLASM), the Lombards extended their influence in spite of further papal attempts at intervention. During Liutprand's reign (712–44) many of the Lombards converted from ARIANISM to Roman Catholicism. By this time they were accepting many other elements of Roman culture, including the Latin language; their law and administration reflected both Roman and Germanic influences (see GERMANIC LAW).

The Franks. The success of the Lombards, however, was temporary. Under the pretense of restoring to the papacy its lost territories, Pope Stephen II (r. 752–57) invited the FRANKS, still another Germanic tribe, to invade Italy. In 774 the Franks expelled the Lombard rulers; Lombard territory passed into the hands of the Frankish ruler CHARLEMAGNE, who was crowned emperor in Rome on Dec. 25, 800.

The following century was characterized by continual feuding between Franks and Byzantines, the chief beneficiaries being the Saracens, newly arrived from North Africa. These Arabs originally came to assist rebels against the Byzantine Empire. The Saracens conquered (827–78) Sicily and established outposts in southern Italy; in 846 they launched an attack on Rome itself.

This 3rd-century AD relief portrays Roman legionaries in battle with Germans, with whom they came into conflict in securing the provinces of the Roman Empire bordering the Rhine and the Danube rivers. Subsequent barbarian invasions contributed to the final collapse of the empire in the 5th century AD.

The Ottonians. This constant alternation of power was temporarily ended by the arrival in Italy—once again by papal invitation—of the German king OTTO I, who was crowned Holy Roman emperor in 962 (see HOLY ROMAN EMPIRE). The Ottonian dynasty fell, however, shortly after 1000, leaving in the north a vacuum to be exploited by the small local landowners and town merchants. Meanwhile, local insurrections weakened the Saracens' hold on the southern coastal cities, although the Arabs remained strong in Sicily.

The Rise of the Italian City-States. In this climate of political and social fragmentation, individual Italian cities began to assert their autonomy, and many of them—especially FLORENCE, GENOA, MILAN, PISA, and VENICE—became powerful and independent CITY-STATES. Resisting the efforts of both the old landed nobles and the emperors to control them, these COMMUNES hastened the end of feudalism in northern Italy and spawned deeply rooted identification with the city as opposed to the larger region or country. The cities were often troubled by violent and divisive rivalries among their citizens, the most famous being the papal-imperial struggle—between the GUELPHS AND GHIBELLINES, the supporters respectively of the popes and the emperors.

The Kingdom of Sicily. Unlike the north, with its network of vigorously independent urban centers, southern Italy experienced a significant consolidation after its conquest by the NORMANS. Starting c.1046, Robert Guiscard and his successors expelled the Saracens and Byzantines and carved a powerful domain out of Apulia, Calabria, Campania, and Sicily. Although the Norman territories remained a fief of the papacy, papal overlordship became a mere formality in the 12th century—especially after 1127, when ROGER II united the southern part of the peninsula with Sicily; he assumed the title of king of Sicily in 1130 (see NAPLES, KINGDOM OF; SICILY).

Meanwhile, the papacy and the Holy Roman Empire continued their struggle for dominance in northern and central Italy. In 1077, Pope GREGORY VII humbled Holy Roman Emperor HENRY IV at Canossa during the INVESTITURE CONTROVERSY. Later, Pope ALEXANDER III successfully supported an alliance of northern cities known as the Lombard League against the efforts of Emperor FREDERICK I (Barbarossa; r. 1152–90) of the HOHENSTAUFEN dynasty to impose imperial authority over them. Early in the 13th century the Hohenstaufen FREDERICK II succeeded in uniting the thrones of German and Norman Sicily. Although Pope INNOCENT III (r. 1198–1216) opposed the emperor, Frederick established one of the most powerful states in Europe, centering on his brilliant court at PALERMO.

The papal-imperial conflict culminated in 1262 with a papal invitation to Charles of Anjou, brother of King Louis IX of France, to conquer Sicily. Charles, the founder of the ANGEVIN dynasty of Naples, ruled from 1266 as CHARLES I, king of Naples and Sicily. In 1282 a successful revolt against the unpopular French rule (the SICILIAN VESPERS) resulted in the separation of Sicily from the mainland. PETER III of Aragon was made king of Sicily, while the former Norman domains on the mainland remained under Angevin rule as the Kingdom of Naples. In the 15th century both

kingdoms became Spanish possessions and were reunited under the title Kingdom of the TWO SICILIES.

The Italian Renaissance and Foreign Domination

After 1300 both the papacy and the Holy Roman Empire turned their attention away from Italy. The emperors concentrated on German affairs, while the popes, for much of the 14th century, resided outside Italy—at Avignon, in southern France.

The weakening of papal and imperial authority accompanied great intellectual changes in Italy. An intellectual revival gave rise to the humanist attitudes and ideas (see HUMANISM) that formed the basis of the RENAISSANCE. About the same time, many of the communal governments of the city-states fell under the rule of dictators called *signori*, who curbed their factionalism and became hereditary rulers. In Milan the VISCONTI family rose to power in the 13th century, to be succeeded by the SFORZA family in the mid-15th century—a few decades after the MEDICI family had seized control of Florence. Meanwhile, the ESTE family ruled Ferrara from the 13th through the 16th century. The *signori* (who became known as *principi*, with royal titles) were instrumental in advancing the cultural and civic life of Renaissance Italy. During the 14th and 15th centuries Italian thought and style influenced all Europe.

As the larger cities expanded into the surrounding countryside, they involved themselves in complex inter-

Rivalries among the Italian city-states, which began to emerge in the 11th century, led to wars and fragmentation. In 1494, Charles VIII of France invaded Italy, beginning the Italian Wars (1494–1559) and long periods of foreign occupation.

ITALY c.1494

The city of Naples, a commercial and cultural center of southern Italy, is depicted in this 15th-century painting. The city, then the capital of the kingdom of Naples, was seized from the Angevins by Alfonso V of Aragon in 1442.

national politics. The frequent wars between city-states brought to Italy the mercenary leaders known as the CONDOTTIERI and ultimately resulted in foreign intervention. In 1494, CHARLES VIII of France invaded Italy (see ITALIAN WARS), signaling the beginning of a period of foreign occupation that lasted until the 19th century. By 1550 almost all Italy had been subjugated by the Habsburg ruler CHARLES V, who was both Holy Roman emperor and king of Spain; when Charles abdicated in 1555–56, dividing the Habsburg territories between his brother Emperor FERDINAND I and his son PHILIP II of Spain, Italy was part of the latter's inheritance. Spain remained the dominant power in Italy until Austria replaced it after the War of the SPANISH SUCCESSION (1701–14).

In the 18th century some areas of Italy achieved independence. SAVOY (the Kingdom of Sardinia after 1720) annexed SARDINIA and portions of LOMBARDY (see SARDINIA, KINGDOM OF); in 1735 the Kingdom of the Two Sicilies became an independent monarchy under the junior branch of the Spanish Bourbon dynasty.

Italian Unification

In the 18th century intellectual changes began to break down traditional values and institutions. ENLIGHTENMENT ideas from France and Britain spread rapidly, and from 1789 the French Revolution excited liberal Italians.

The Napoleonic Era in Italy. Between 1796, when troops under General Napoléon Bonaparte (see NAPOLEON I) invaded Italy, and 1814, when they withdrew, the entire peninsula was under French domination (see FRENCH REVOLUTIONARY WARS; NAPOLEONIC WARS). After two decades of Napoleon's modern but often harsh rule, many Italians began to see the possibilities of forging a united country free of foreign control. Following the restoration of European peace in 1815, Italy consisted of the Kingdom of Sardinia (Piedmont, Sardinia, Savoy, and Genoa); the Kingdom of the Two Sicilies (including Naples and Sicily); the Papal States; and TUSCANY and a series of smaller duchies in north central Italy. Lombardy and Venetia were now controlled by the Austrians.

The Risorgimento. The repressive policies imposed on Italy by the Austrian leader METTERNICH and the Congress of Vienna (see VIENNA, CONGRESS OF) stimulated intense antiforeign sentiment. These conditions gave rise to the Italian unification movement known as the RISORGIMENTO. Revolutionaries and patriots, especially Giuseppe MAZZINI, began to work actively for unity and independence. A series of unsuccessful revolts led in the 1820s by the Carbonari, a conspiratorial nationalist organization, and in the 1830s by Mazzini's Young Italy group, provided the background for the REVOLUTIONS OF 1848. Charles Albert, king of Sardinia (1831–49), declared war on Austria; but both the war of liberation and the revolutionary republics set up in Rome, Venice, and Tuscany were crushed by Austria in 1849. Charles Albert abdicated in favor of his son, VICTOR EMMANUEL II.

Unity. Under the leadership of Camillo Benso, conte di CAVOUR, Sardinia led Italy to unification. In 1859, after gaining the support of France and England, Cavour, in alliance with the French emperor NAPOLEON III, seized Lombardy; in 1860 almost all of Italy north of the Papal States was added to Sardinia. Giuseppe GARIBALDI, a popular guerrilla leader, led an expedition of 1,000 "Red Shirts" to Sicily in the same year and subsequently seized the southern part of peninsular Italy, which with Sicily

The Italian patriot and hero of the Risorgimento, Giuseppe Garibaldi, is portrayed leading his volunteer army of Red Shirts in his Sicilian campaign (1860).

constituted the Kingdom of the Two Sicilies. Garibaldi turned his conquests over to Victor Emmanuel, and in 1861 the Kingdom of Italy was proclaimed. Only Venetia and Rome were not included in the new state (the former was added in 1866 and the latter in 1870).

The Kingdom of Italy

The new nation faced serious problems. A large debt, few natural resources, and almost no industry or transportation facilities combined with extreme poverty, a high illiteracy rate, and an uneven tax structure. Only a fraction of the citizens had the right to vote. To make matters worse, the pope, angered over the loss of Rome and the papal lands, refused to recognize the Italian state. In the countryside, banditry and peasant anarchism resulted in government repression. Parliament did little to resolve these problems: throughout this so-called Liberal Period (1870–1915), the nation was governed by a series of coalitions of liberals to the left and right of center who were unable to form a clear-

The unification of Italy began with the Sardinian seizure of Lombardy from Austria in 1859. The Kingdom of Italy was proclaimed in 1861, and Venetia and Rome were included in 1866 and 1870, respectively.

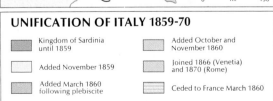

UNIFICATION OF ITALY 1859-70

- Kingdom of Sardinia until 1859
- Added November 1859
- Added March 1860 following plebiscite
- Added October and November 1860
- Joined 1866 (Venetia) and 1870 (Rome)
- Ceded to France March 1860

cut majority. (The most notable leaders of the period were Francesco CRISPI and Giovanni GIOLITTI.) Despite some economic and social progress, Italy before World War I was a dissatisfied and crisis-ridden nation.

In an attempt to increase its international influence and prestige, Italy joined Germany and Austria in the TRIPLE ALLIANCE in 1882; in the 1890s, Italy unsuccessfully tried to conquer Ethiopia; and in 1911 it declared war on Turkey to obtain the North African territory of Libya (see ITALO-TURKISH WAR). After the outbreak of WORLD WAR I in 1914, Italy remained neutral for almost a year while the government negotiated with both sides. In 1915, Italy finally joined the Allies, after having been promised territories that it regarded as *Italia irredenta* (unliberated Italy). The country was unprepared for a major war, however; aside from a few victories in 1918, Italy suffered serious losses of men, materièl, and morale. Moreover, despite the efforts of Vittorio Emanuele ORLANDO at the PARIS PEACE CONFERENCE, the treaties that followed the war gave Italy only Trentino and Trieste—a small part of the territories it had expected.

The Fascist Period

Italy was plunged into deep social and political crisis by the war. Veterans, unemployed workers, desperate peasants, and a frightened middle class demanded changes, and the 1919 elections suddenly made the Socialist and the new Popular (Catholic) parties the largest in parliament.

The Rise of Fascism. In 1919, in the midst of these unsettled conditions, Benito MUSSOLINI, a former revolutionary socialist, founded a new movement called FASCISM. Through a combination of shrewd political maneuvering and widespread violence perpetrated by Mussolini's BLACKSHIRT squads, the Fascists gained increasing support. In October 1922, after the Fascists had marched on Rome, King VICTOR EMMANUEL III named Mussolini prime minister. Within four years, Mussolini had become a dictator, imposing a totalitarian regime on the country by means of terror and constitutional subversion. Public-works projects, propaganda, and the appearance of order gained Mussolini considerable prestige, and the Lateran Treaty with the papacy in 1929 gave the *duce* (as he was called) wide popularity.

Fascist Expansionism. Mussolini's foreign policy moved Italy closer to war during the 1930s. In 1935–36 the Italian army invaded and conquered ETHIOPIA, and in 1936, Italy sent troops to support Francisco Franco in the SPANISH CIVIL WAR. Later that year Mussolini and Adolf HITLER, the National Socialist dictator of Germany, established the Rome-Berlin Axis; in 1939, Italy took Albania, and the two dictators then concluded a military alliance known as the Pact of Steel. In June 1940, nine months after the outbreak of WORLD WAR II in Europe, Italy entered the conflict on Germany's side.

World War II. Mussolini's war effort met with setbacks and defeats on all fronts; in July 1943 the Allies invaded Sicily. The Fascist leadership turned against Mussolini, and the king forced him to resign. Rescued by German paratroopers, Mussolini escaped to Salò in northern Italy,

Benito Mussolini, known as Il Duce, was the Fascist dictator of Italy from 1922 to 1943. He is shown leading his Blackshirt brigade in their march on Rome in 1922.

where he established a puppet government (the Italian Social Republic) under German protection. In the south the king and his new prime minister, Pietro Badoglio, surrendered to the Allies in September and then joined in the war against Germany. The Allies pushed the German armies out of Italy with great difficulty, and in April 1945 the partisans captured and executed Mussolini.

Postwar Italy

Between 1945 and 1948 a new Italian nation emerged from the disaster of fascism and war. In June 1946 a popular election abolished the monarchy in favor of a republic; a new constitution was adopted the next year. The Christian Democrats, the Communists, and the Socialists became the strongest political parties in the country. The largest of these parties, the Christian Democrats, first under the leadership of Alcide DE GASPERI, dominated the Italian government after 1948. De Gasperi stressed industrial growth, agricultural reform, and close cooperation with the United States and the Vatican. With massive U.S. aid, Italy underwent a remarkable economic recovery that saw rapid industrial expansion and a sharp increase in the standard of living. Italy joined the NORTH ATLANTIC TREATY ORGANIZATION in 1949, the European Coal and Steel Community (see EUROPEAN COMMUNITY) in 1951, and the Common Market in 1958.

The 1960s were marked by continued prosperity and a lessening of tensions between the Right and the Left. In the early 1970s the Italian Communists, led by Enrico Berlinguer, became prominent advocates of Eurocommunism, a doctrine stressing independence from the USSR. In the late 1970s and early 1980s labor unrest, frequent government scandals, and the violence of extremist groups (especially the left-wing Red Brigades terrorists, who kidnapped and murdered former premier Aldo MORO in 1978), all contributed to a volatile political situation.

In 1981 the Christian Democrats relinquished the premiership for the first time since World War II, when a Republican, Giovanni Spadolini, became prime minister. The economy, which had suffered during the turbulent 1970s, experienced a new resurgence under the leadership (1983–87) of Socialist Bettino CRAXI, a strong premier who remained in office longer than any of his postwar predecessors. The Craxi government was succeeded by a short-lived coalition under Christian Democrat Giovanni Goria, who in 1988 was replaced by another Christian Democrat, Ciriaco De Mita.

Ithaca (Greece) [ith'-uh-kuh]   Ithaca (Greek: Itháki), a mountainous island in the Ionian Sea, forms, with nearby Cephalonia, a *nome* (department) of Greece. Ithaca has an area of 96 km^2 (37 mi^2) and a population of 4,150 (1981). Olives, grapes, and currants are grown; fishing is a major industry. Ithaca has been traditionally associated with Odysseus of Homer's *Odyssey*.

Ithaca (New York)   Ithaca (1990 pop., 29,541) is the seat of Tompkins County, N.Y. Located at the southern tip of Cayuga Lake in the Finger Lakes region, it is the southern terminus of the New York State Barge Canal system. It is an agricultural center for the area's dairy and poultry farms; industries in the city manufacture business machines and research instruments. It was settled about 1790 and was incorporated as a city in 1888. Ithaca is the site of CORNELL UNIVERSITY (1865), a member of the Ivy League, and of Ithaca College (1892).

Ito Hirobumi [ee'-toh hee-roh'-boo-mee]   Ito Hirobumi, b. October 1841, d. Oct. 26, 1909, was a leading Japanese statesman after the MEIJI RESTORATION. Ito was an aide to Kido Takayoshi, one of the organizers of the Satsuma-Choshu alliance that overthrew the shogunate in 1868. He held several important posts in the new Meiji government and helped lead the movement to modernize Japan.

In 1878, after the powerful Okubo Toshimichi was assassinated, Ito succeeded him as home minister. In 1881 he persuaded his rival OKUMA SHIGENOBU to resign and exacted from the oligarchic government a promise to adopt a more representative form of government. In preparation for drafting the Meiji Constitution of 1889, Ito headed a mission (1882–83) to Europe to study European governments. He then helped reorganize the peerage and created a cabinet system.

Ito served as Japan's first prime minister under the new cabinet system (1885–88) and headed the privy council that ratified (1889) the constitution. He was prime minister again in 1892–96, 1898, and 1900–01. In 1900 he founded the Seiyukai party in the Diet. After the RUSSO-JAPANESE WAR of 1904–05, Ito became resident general in Korea, which had become a protectorate of Japan. Despite Ito's moderate policies he was assassinated by a Korean nationalist, an act that precipitated the Japanese annexation of Korea.

Iturbi, José [ee-toor'-bee]   The pianist and conductor José Iturbi, b. Valencia, Spain, Nov. 28, 1895, d. June 28, 1980, was best known for his interpretations of Spanish music and for his appearances in several American musical films during the 1940s. He studied at the Paris Conservatory, and after a successful concert career in Europe he made his U.S. debut in 1928, touring the country. He again toured the United States in 1930, giving recitals and performing with leading symphony orchestras, and from 1936 to 1944 he was conductor of the Rochester (N.Y.) Philharmonic. He frequently performed with his pianist sister, Amparo Iturbi (1898–1969), in duo-piano concerts.

Iturbide, Agustín de [ee-toor-bee'-day, ah-goos-teen' day]   Agustín de Iturbide, b. Sept. 27, 1783, d. July 19, 1824, was an army officer who declared Mexican independence from Spain and who for a short time served (1822–23) as emperor of Mexico. From an upper-class background, Iturbide briefly attended the seminary but then dedicated himself to a military career. When rebellion against Spain, led by Miguel HIDALGO Y COSTILLA and José María MORELOS Y PAVÓN, broke out in 1810, Iturbide, like most other aristocratic Mexicans, supported the Spanish government, and for more than ten years he fought to quell the independence movement.

In 1820, Iturbide was appointed to lead an army against Vicente Guerrero's insurgent band in southern Mexico. Because he and the Mexican elite feared that Spain would introduce liberal reforms, however, Iturbide instead came to terms with the insurgents in 1821, overthrew the viceroy, and, on Sept. 27, 1821, proclaimed Mexico an independent constitutional monarchy according to the conservative Plan de Iguala (Feb. 24, 1821). In the following year he proclaimed himself emperor of Mexico, but he was overthrown in March 1823 by the revolutionary forces led by Antonio López de SANTA ANNA and went into exile in Italy. In 1824, Iturbide tried to reestablish himself in power, but he was arrested, tried, and executed as a traitor.

Ivan III, Grand Duke of Moscow (Ivan the Great)   Ivan III, b. Jan. 22, 1440, d. Oct. 27, 1505, was grand duke of Moscow from 1462 until 1505. Known as Ivan the Great, he began the centralization of the Russian lands under Moscow. After a tumultuous childhood and youth, Ivan succeeded his father, Vasily II. During Ivan's reign the declining Khanate of the GOLDEN HORDE made several attempts to reimpose its rule on Russia; in 1480, Ivan, repelling a Tatar invasion, finally freed Moscow from domination by the TATARS. During the 1470s and '80s, Ivan absorbed Moscow's old rivals in the north, Novgorod and Tver, and established a unified rule over what had been a divided Russia. He also fought Lithuania (1492–94 and 1500–03) in an attempt to reconquer Ukraine. During Ivan's reign, Moscow was the site of an impressive building campaign directed by Italian artists and artisans.

After the death (1467) of his first wife, Ivan married (1472) Sophia, a Byzantine princess and niece of the last Byzantine emperor. Following the marriage Ivan developed a complicated court ceremonial based on the Byzantine model and began to use the title of *tsar* (a variation of the word *caesar*). Ivan was succeeded by his eldest son by Sophia, who became VASILY III.

Ivan IV, Grand Duke of Moscow and Tsar of Russia (Ivan the Terrible)   Ivan IV, known as the Terrible, b. Aug. 25, 1530, d. Mar. 18, 1584, was the first Russian ruler to be crowned tsar. He centralized the administration of Russia and expanded the boundaries of the Russian empire. His father, VASILY III, grand duke of Moscow, died in 1533. Ivan's mother, Yelena Glinskaya, who was from a leading boyar, or noble, family, established a regency, but it soon degenerated into intrigue, denunciation, and wild violence between rival boyars.

Ivan, who suffered from poor health, was largely ignored, his education neglected. Yelena died in 1538, and in 1547, Ivan was crowned tsar. In the same year, he married Anastasia Romanov; the ROMANOV dynasty, which ruled Russia from 1613 to 1917, traces its claim to the throne from their union—through Anastasia's brother, Nikitu.

The years 1547 through 1560 are usually considered the constructive period of Ivan's reign, although the exact date that he assumed de facto control from the aristocracy is in dispute. He appointed an advisory council, founded (1549) a national assembly, enacted reforms in local government, drew up (1550) a new law code, and standardized the responsibilities and duties of the aristocracy. Ivan annexed Kazan (1552) and Astrakhan (1556), the first non-Slavic states in the empire, thus ensuring Russian control of the Volga River and access to the Caspian Sea. Expansion to the east, beyond the Ural Mountains, also began during this period. In addition, trade contacts with the English, French, and Dutch were begun.

Anastasia's death in 1560 marked the end of Ivan's constructive policies. Increasingly powerful, Ivan turned against his advisors—convinced that they, backed by the boyars, had caused her death. Threatening to abdicate unless the boyars were punished for their treachery, Ivan abandoned Moscow in 1564, settling in the village of Aleksandrovsk. Confused and frightened, the people of Moscow begged Ivan to return. He eventually agreed to do so on two conditions: he was to have the right to punish traitors and wrongdoers; and a political and territorial subdivision—the *oprichnina*—was to be established, managed entirely at the discretion of the tsar.

The *oprichnina* included most of the wealthy towns, trade routes, and cultivated areas of Russia and was, therefore, a stronghold of wealthy old boyar families. Ivan's select bodyguard, the *oprichniki*, then set about to destroy many of these great lords. Contemporary estimates of the number killed are from 400 to as high as 10,000. Only a few of the old boyar families survived. Ivan controlled this personal territory until 1572.

In foreign affairs, too, turmoil and disaster marked the

latter part of Ivan's reign. Russia attempted, unsuccessfully, to gain access to the Baltic Sea in the Livonian War (1557–82) with Poland-Lithuania. The transition from Ivan to his son and successor, Fyodor I, was relatively easy and quiet, but Moscow was on the verge of anarchy as a result of Ivan's policies.

Ivanhoe [y'-vuhn-hoh]   Set in 12th-century England, *Ivanhoe* is the first of Sir Walter Scott's novels set outside Scotland. Scott's principal concern in *Ivanhoe* is to show the noble idealism of chivalry along with its often cruel and impractical consequences. The work also introduces some of Scott's most memorable characters: Richard the Lion-Hearted, the Jewess Rebecca, the Knight Templar Sir Brian de Bois-Guilbert. Long one of Scott's most popular novels, *Ivanhoe* colorfully depicts a medieval panoply in the age of the Third Crusade and offers narrative excitement in such episodes as the tournament at Ashby-de-la-Zouche and the siege of Torquilstone.

Ivanov, Lev Ivanovich   Lev Ivanovich Ivanov, b. Feb. 18 (N.S.), 1834, d. Dec. 11 (N.S.), 1901, was a dancer and choreographer in the Imperial Theaters of Saint Petersburg (now Leningrad). In 1852 he became a member of the Imperial Ballet but did not gain promotion to premier danseur until 1869. His most significant contribution to ballet history was his choreography, which in the classical purity of its symphonic form influenced later choreographers like George Balanchine. Always working under the shadow of the dictatorial Marius Petipa, Ivanov created the Polovetsian Dances for Aleksandr Borodin's opera *Prince Igor* (1890). Ivanov was also responsible for portions of Petipa's *Nutcracker* (1892) and *Swan Lake* (1895).

Ives, Burl [yvz]   Folksinger and actor Burl Icle Ivanhoe Ives, b. Jasper County, Ill., June 14, 1909, began to learn his art as a child from his folksinging family. As a youth, he hoboed around the country, reaching New York in 1937. A series of bit acting parts and nightclub stints as an increasingly popular singer led in 1940 to his own radio show, "The Wayfaring Stranger," to a number of successful recordings, and, from 1945, to a career in Hollywood. Ives starred in the New York production of Tennessee Williams's *Cat on a Hot Tin Roof* (1955) and in the film version (1958) of the play. He won an Academy Award for his role in *The Big Country* (1958).

Ives, Charles   Considered by many to have been America's greatest composer, Charles Edward Ives, b. Danbury, Conn., Oct. 20, 1874, d. May 19, 1954, typified in his life and music much of the New England tradition. Ives studied with his father, George, a Civil War band director with an inquiring mind, and with Horatio Parker at Yale University (1894–98). Ives was also deeply influenced by the writings of Ralph Waldo Emerson,

Charles Ives, a 20th-century American composer, was among the first to use the innovative devices of polytonality and polyrhythm that dominate later musical composition. He often used traditional American melodies in his compositions.

Nathaniel Hawthorne, the Alcotts, and Henry David Thoreau, which inspired his remarkable *Second Piano Sonata: Concord, Mass., 1840–60* (1909–15).

Ives frequently quoted hymns and popular, patriotic, and ragtime music in his compositions, but he adapted these borrowings to new formal and sound contexts that were either misunderstood by tradition-minded listeners or regarded as curiosities. At a surprisingly early date he employed or created many of the important 20th-century composing techniques that are still used, notably polytonality and polyrhythmic textures. To earn a living, he founded (1907) the firm of Ives and Myrick, which became a famous insurance agency in New York City. A heart attack in 1921 and a diabetic condition forced Ives to virtually cease composing; he retired from business in 1930.

In the 30 or so years of his creative activity (about 1890–1921), Ives composed more than 500 works, about a third of which were left incomplete. He produced nearly 70 instrumental pieces for large ensembles; the most significant of these are his four numbered symphonies, three orchestral sets (sometimes called symphonies), including *Three Places in New England* (1903–14), and two overtures (*Emerson* and *Browning*). He also wrote music for chamber or theater orchestra; string quartets and other chamber groups; band; organ; piano; chorus; and more than 200 solo songs with piano accompaniment. The wide variety of his songs alone gives a broad overview of Ives's shorter forms and the techniques of composition that spanned his entire creative career. Scholarly editions of Ives's works are in the process of being published, under the sponsorship of the Charles Ives Society.

Ivory Coast   Ivory Coast (Côte d'Ivoire) is a West African nation, located on the Gulf of Guinea. It is bordered by Ghana on the east, Burkina Faso (Upper Volta) and Mali on the north, and Guinea and Liberia on the west. Formerly a territory within French West Africa, it achieved independence on Aug. 7, 1960.

REPUBLIC OF CÔTE D'IVOIRE

Land: Area: 322,463 km² (124,504 mi²). Official capital: Yamoussoukro (1984 est. pop., 120,000); acting capital and largest city: Abidjan (1984 est. pop., 1,850,000).

People: Population (1990 est.): 12,478,024. Density: 38.7 persons per km² (100.2 per mi²). Distribution (1986): 53% rural, 47% urban. Annual growth (1989): 3.8%. Official language: French. Major religions: traditional religions, Islam, Roman Catholicism.

Government: Type: republic. Legislature: National Assembly. Political subdivisions: 49 departments.

Economy: GNP (1988): $10.0 billion; $900 per capita. Labor distribution (1985): agriculture—61%; manufacturing, construction, and mining—10%; government and services—29%. Foreign trade (1988): imports—$1.3 billion; exports—$2.2 billion. Currency: 1 C.F.A. franc = 100 centimes.

Education and Health: Literacy (1985): 57% of adult population. Universities (1989): 1. Hospital beds (1982): 10,062. Physicians (1982): 502. Life expectancy (1990): women—56; men—52. Infant mortality (1990): 100 per 1,000 live births.

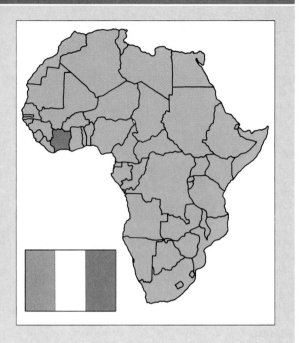

Land and People

The terrain of Ivory Coast rises gradually from the Gulf of GUINEA northward in four east-west zones: the littoral strip, rain forest, savanna, and tableland. The littoral strip, reaching as far as 50 km (30 mi) inland, is characterized by lagoons separated from the ocean by long sandbars. North of these lagoons, a cross-country rain-forest belt some 300 km (185 mi) wide gives way to wooded savanna. Tablelands in the northernmost areas approach elevations of about 400 m (1,300 ft), with occasional peaks rising more than 900 m (2,950 ft). The highest altitudes are found near the Guinea-Liberia border, including Mount Nimba, the highest point in Ivory Coast, which rises to 1,752 m (5,747 ft). The country's four main rivers are the Komoé, Bandama, Sassandra, and Cavally.

The climatic zones of the country vary with topography. The subequatorial south is characterized by high humidity and a temperature range of 26°–28° C (79°–82° F). Precipitation averages 2,000 to 3,000 mm (80 to 120 in) annually, occurring primarily from April to November. The forest zone has lower humidity, temperature variations from 15° to 40° C (59° to 104° F), and rainfall of 1,000 to 2,500 mm (40 to 100 in), which decreases to the north. Temperatures drop with increasing elevations in the north, but a hot, dry wind from the Sahara desert prevails in the winter.

Wildlife includes antelope, giraffes, hyenas, lions, elephants, monkeys, hippopotamuses, crocodiles, and snakes, as well as numerous species of birds. Forests constitute the country's greatest resource other than agricultural lands, and there are deposits of petroleum, diamonds, and iron ore.

The country's more than 60 ethnic groups form seven main divisions: the Akan, mainly in the southeast; the Kru, in the southwest; the Lagoon or Kwa, along the littoral; the Mande, nuclear and peripheral, and the Senufo throughout the north; and the Lobi in the central regions. About 2,000,000 non-Ivorian Africans live in the country, particularly immigrants from Burkina Faso, Mali, and Guinea, as well as French and Lebanese. Bouaké is the only large city other than ABIDJAN.

Although stress has been placed on education, literacy remains low. The university at Abidjan was established in 1964.

Economic Activity

Ivory Coast has one of Africa's most diversified economies. It is the world's largest producer of cacao and third-largest producer of coffee; together with hardwoods, these crops account for 75% of all export earnings. Serious depletion of the country's forests has led to a decline in timber exports and encouraged reforestation efforts. A variety of other export crops—sugarcane, pineapples, oil palms, rubber, cotton, and bananas—are of growing importance. Petroleum from offshore deposits in the Gulf of Guinea is the chief mineral product. Diamonds are also mined. Light manufacturing industries process the raw materials of the country.

Machinery, vehicles, iron and steel, and electrical equipment are major imports. Ivory Coast retains close ties to France, its leading trade partner. Heavy borrowing for development projects, however, has created a large foreign debt. The country's rate of economic growth, once one of the highest in Africa, slowed in the 1980s, due partly to falling prices for exports, forcing economic austerity measures.

History and Government

Little is known of Ivory Coast's history before European involvement in the ivory and slave trades. French missionary contact in Ivory Coast began as early as 1637, but an official French protectorate was not established until 1843–45, when treaties were concluded with local chiefs. Ivory Coast became a French colony in 1893 and was a constituent of French West Africa from 1904 until 1958. It was made an overseas territory in 1946, and its inhabitants were given French citizenship. Ivory Coast was proclaimed a republic within the French Community in 1958; in 1960 it became independent.

Ivory Coast is a republic, with a president elected for a 5-year term, an appointed cabinet, and a unicameral national assembly whose members are popularly elected for 5-year terms. Although voters had been offered a choice of legislative candidates within the ruling party since 1980, the country was a de facto one-party state from 1960 until 1990, when unprecedented popular protests led the government to legalize multiple political parties. Despite calls for his resignation, Félix HOUPHOUËT-BOIGNY, president since independence, won a seventh term, and his party retained its legislative majority in multiparty elections held later that year.

ivory and ivory carving Ivory is the smooth, solid, usually white material that makes up the tusks of elephants and the tusks and teeth of walruses, sperm whales, narwhals, hippopotamuses, and wild boars. Ivory is actually modified dentine. The elephant tusk is built up of layers of ivory; in cross section it shows the distinctive pattern of hair-thin curving lines that gives ivory its fine grain and elasticity. A large proportion of the tusk is buried in the bone socket of the skull and is hollow for part of its length, narrowing to thread diameter toward the point of the tusk. A very dense material, ivory has close, compact pores filled with a gelatinous substance that produces a glowing finish when the ivory surface is polished. Ivory has been used for thousands of years in jewelry, art objects, and ornamental carvings.

Types of Ivory. The most widely used ivory has been that of African elephants. High demand led to soaring prices in recent decades and to a dramatic decline in elephant populations. In Kenya, for example, the number of elephants declined from 130,000 in 1973 to about 17,000 by the end of the 1980s. Following a worldwide campaign by environmentalists to save the elephants from extinction, the Convention on International Trade in Endangered Species voted in 1989 to ban trade in elephant ivory. Countries such as South Africa that have flourishing populations of elephants may, however, receive permission to sell ivory from a certain number of elephants culled from their herds.

Ancient mammoth and elephant ivory found in frozen riverbeds and along the Arctic Ocean was once used in great quantity. Parcels of Siberian mammoth ivory weighing from 10 to 20 metric tons were common in the ivory markets of the 1890s. Today what little fossil ivory remains comes from Alaska. Walrus ivory was used for centuries by European ivory carvers, and the north European walrus herds were hunted to the point of extinction by ivory traders in the late Middle Ages. Walrus ivory is less dense than elephant ivory, and the tusk is hollow for much of its length. Ancient Egyptian ivory carvers often used the extremely hard hippopotamus ivory, which must first be steeped in acid to remove its outer casing of enamel. Because of its hardness, dentists in ancient Rome used hippopotamus ivory to make dentures. Ivory obtained from the teeth of the sperm whale has limited attraction for carvers because the teeth are relatively

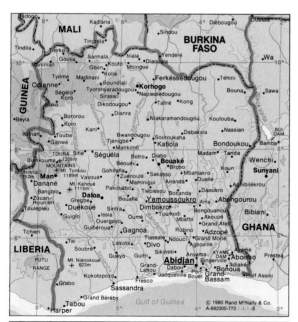

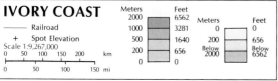

IVORY COAST

——— Railroad
  +   Spot Elevation
Scale 1:9,267,000
0   50   100 150 200   km
0   50   100   150 mi

Meters	Feet
2000	6562
1000	3281
500	1640
200	656
0	0

Meters	Feet
0	0
200	656
Below 2000	Below 6562

The Byzantine diptych of the consul Anastasius (c.517), a hinged writing tablet, embodies the boldly carved, balanced design typical of ivories produced at Constantinople from the 4th to the 6th century. (Cabinet des Médailles, Paris.)

Byzantine times ivory came to be appreciated for its own inherent qualities, and the painting or staining of ivory carvings began to lose importance.

Ivory carving rose to a very high level in Europe, particularly in the Early Christian, Byzantine, and Carolingian eras. The ivory carvings of the Byzantine period inspired the stone Romanesque sculptures of France. The Gothic style produced a wealth of carvings, especially in the form of relief plaques on caskets, altarpieces, and reliquaries.

In the Orient ivory carving is a very ancient art. Early Chinese ivories from the Shang dynasty (c.1558–1027 BC) include ornamental plaques and pieces of inlay. Ivory was valued as much as gold or jade. Japanese carvers of the 8th century AD created superlative ivories, but surviving examples are extremely rare, and the ivory art of Japan is usually assessed from work dating from the 18th century to the present (SEE NETSUKE). India, the Near East, and most southern Asian countries retain a deeply rooted ivory-carving tradition.

In North America, Eskimo ivory carving dates back at least 2,000 years. Ivory, bone, antler, and tooth were all used to create utilitarian and shamanistic objects.

African ivory art is rooted in the remote past, particularly in the Ivory Coast and Congo regions, where carvings ranged from elaborate knife handles to entire elephant tusks.

See also: SCRIMSHAW.

ivy Trailing plants that belong to the genus *Hedera*, family Araliaceae, are usually known as ivies. The English ivy, *H. helix*, native to Eurasia, is an evergreen vine with handsome, glossy leaves. It is a hardy, dependable climber that clings to walls or the ground by means of aerial roots. Varieties of *H. helix* include 'Baltica,' a very

The Canary Island ivy (left) *has large leaves that are edged in white. Two varieties of the common ivy are* H. helix *"Caenwoodiana"* (center) *and* H. helix *"Manda's Crested"* (right).

small. The single large tusk of the Arctic narwhal, sometimes 2.5 m (8 ft) long, is of good color and texture, but its spiral groove and a deep cavity running almost its entire length makes working it difficult. Nevertheless, narwhal ivory is widely used in Japan.

Various substitutes for ivory are in common use. The most important is vegetable ivory, made from the fruit of the South American ivory nut palm, *Phytelephas macrocarpa*. In present-day Japan, vegetable ivory is often carved and stained to simulate mellow old ivory. Celluloid and plastics also serve as substitutes for ivory and have largely replaced genuine ivory for such uses as buttons, billiard balls, and piano keys.

Ivory Carving. Prehistoric peoples fashioned sculptured or incised designs from bone or ivory. By 4000 BC the Egyptians had achieved a highly developed art of ivory carving, which included freestanding objects, incised designs on flat surfaces, mosaics, inlay, and ivory panels with designs carved in relief. The colossal statues of gods made by the ancient Greeks were fashioned of hammered gold, with painted ivory faces, hands, and feet of a composite material called chryselephantine. In Roman and

hardy plant; 'Conglomerata,' a slow-growing dwarf variety; 'Hahn's Self-branching,' used as ground cover because of its very dense growth; and 'Minima,' which has small leaves and is used primarily for decorative purposes indoors. Algerian ivy, or Canary Island ivy, *H. canariensis*, is an attractive ivy from the Canary Islands that thrives in gardens of the southeastern United States.

Other species with ivylike leaves and growth habits are American ivy or five-leaved ivy, *Parthenocissus quinquefolia*; Boston or Japanese ivy, *P. tricuspidata*; Cape ivy, *Senecio macroglossus*; German ivy, *S. mikanioides*; ground ivy, *Glechoma hederacea*; poison ivy, *Rhus toxicodendron*; and ivy geranium, *Pelargonium peltatum*.

Ivy League   The Ivy League is a group of seven universities and one college in the northeastern United States: Brown, Columbia, Cornell, Dartmouth, Harvard, Pennsylvania, Princeton, and Yale. All but Cornell were established before the American Revolution, and all have very selective admissions standards. Social and athletic competition among the colleges dates from the late 19th century. The concept of the league began when policies for athletic competition were set down in 1956. Ivy League college presidents, directors of athletics, and other officers meet periodically to discuss common problems of admissions, financial aid, and administration.

See also: articles on each of these institutions.

Iwo Jima [ee'-woh jee'-muh]   Iwo Jima is the largest of three islands that make up Japan's Volcano group. Located about 1,210 km (750 mi) south of Tokyo, it has an area of 21 km^2 (8 mi^2) and a maximum elevation, on Mount Suribachi, of 166 m (546 ft). About 1,000 Japanese live on the island. Volcanic in origin, Iwo Jima has soil suitable for growing sugarcane, making a sugar refining industry possible. Sulfur mining is a major activity.

Japan annexed the Volcano Islands in 1887 and used them as a major military base during World War II. In February 1945, U.S. Marines launched a costly battle to capture Iwo Jima; a photograph of the American flag being raised on Suribachi was the basis for the famous sculpture in Arlington National Cemetery. The U.S. Navy controlled Iwo Jima until its return to Japan in 1968.

IWW   see INDUSTRIAL WORKERS OF THE WORLD

Ixion [iks'-ee-ahn]   In Greek mythology Ixion, king of the Lapiths, was traditionally considered the first murderer of a kinsman. He refused to pay his father-in-law, Eioneus, the promised price for his bride, Dia, and finally murdered him by throwing him into a fiery pit. To purify Ixion of this sin, ZEUS invited him to Olympus; there Ixion tried to violate HERA, but she was transformed into a cloud. From Ixion's union with the cloud was born either the CENTAURS or their father, Centaurus, depending on the version of the legend. In punishment, Ixion was bound to a fiery, eternally revolving wheel.

Ixtacihuatl [ees-tah-see'-wah-tul]   Ixtacihuatl, Mexico's third-highest mountain, is located about 55 km (35 mi) southeast of Mexico City in the SIERRA MADRES. One of its three volcanic cones rises 5,386 m (17,671 ft) above sea level. The pinnacles suggest a reclining figure, thus its popular name, "sleeping woman." It last erupted in 1868.

Izapa [ee-sahp'-ah]   Izapa, an archaeological site located east of Tapachula in the southeastern Chiapas state, Mexico, contains important remains of pre-Columbian civilization. A ceremonial center in Early Formative times (1500–800 BC), it is composed of more than 80 scattered earthen temple mounds faced with cobblestones. Located in its labyrinth of courts and plazas are elaborately carved stone monuments (steles) dating mainly from the Late Formative (300 BC–AD 150) and Proto-Classic (AD 150–300) eras.

The Izapa art style is thought to represent a cultural link between the OLMEC (1000–300 BC) and the Classical MAYA (AD 300–900) civilizations. Prominent features include complex depictions of various secular activities and distinctive representations of deities, notably the large-lipped god of rain and lightning, an adaptation of the Olmec were-jaguar and a forerunner of the long-nosed Mayan rain god.

İzmir [iz-mir']   İzmir (formerly Smyrna) is a port city in west central Turkey on the Aegean Sea at the eastern end of the Gulf of İzmir. The population is 1,489,772 (1985). Textile, cigarette, soap, and food processing plants are found there. Agricultural products and carpets are major exports. The city is the home of Aegean University (1955) and an archaeological museum. The agora (marketplace), the ancient aqueducts, and splendid beaches attract tourists to the city.

İzmir, first settled about 3000 BC, was an Aeolian, then an IONIAN, colony in the 11th century BC. Destroyed by about 600 BC, it was refounded in the 4th century BC by Alexander the Great's successors ANTIGONUS I and LYSIMACHUS. It came under Roman rule late in the 1st century BC. Attacked by the Arabs in the 7th century, the city fell to the Seljuks in the late 11th century. From 1204 to 1261 it was part of the Byzantine state of NICAEA. In 1424 it was incorporated into the OTTOMAN EMPIRE. At the end of World War I, İzmir was occupied by Greek forces, and the Treaty of Sèvres (1920) awarded the city and its surrounds to Greece. Turkish nationalist forces captured the city in September 1922, and the Treaty of Lausanne (1923; see LAUSANNE, TREATY OF) gave İzmir to the new Turkish republic.

Izvestia [iz-ves'-tee-uh]   The official newspaper of the USSR since the Russian Revolution, *Izvestia* (English, "news") is published by the Supreme Soviet Presidium, the legislative branch of the Soviet government. The other major newspaper in the USSR is PRAVDA.

Jj

GERMAN-GOTHIC	CLASSICAL LATIN	EARLY LATIN	ETRUSCAN	CLASSICAL GREEK	EARLY GREEK	EARLY ARAMAIC	EARLY HEBREW	PHOENICIAN

J *J/j*, the tenth letter of the English alphabet, is one of the few relatively modern additions to the Semitic-Greek-Etruscan-Latin line of development that gave rise to the alphabet. The letter *J/j* was derived from the letter *I/i* by the addition of a curved stroke at the bottom.

J/j occurs as early as the 14th century AD, but its early use was ornamental, created by lengthening *I/i*, especially in initial or final position. Eventually *J/j* came to contrast with *I/i* to distinguish the consonant *y* from the vowel *i*, both represented by the letter *I/i* in Latin. This differentiation was not fully established in English until the 17th century.

Because of early French influence, the letter *J/j* has the pronunciation *dzh* in modern English speech, as in *jet* and *jury*. This sound is partly shared by the letter *G/g* and is the voiced counterpart of *ch* (*tsh*). In German *J/j* has only the sound of consonantal *y*, a sound found in a few English words, such as *hallelujah*.

Jabbar, Kareem Abdul   see ABDUL-JABBAR, KAREEM

Jabotinsky, Vladimir [yab-uh-tin-skee']   Vladimir Jabotinsky, b. Russia, Oct. 18 (N.S.), 1880, d. Aug. 3, 1940, was a militant Zionist leader in Palestine during the British mandate period. In 1920 he helped organize the Haganah, the Jewish self-defense movement. He formed (1925) the World Union of Zionist Revisionists, which advocated the creation of a Jewish state on both sides of the Jordan by force, if necessary. In the 1930s some of Jabotinsky's followers founded the Irgun Zvai Leumi, a group that made terrorist attacks on the British and the Arabs.

jacana [jak'-uh-nuh]   The jacanas are seven species of pantropical, ploverlike birds (family Jacanidae) with greatly elongated toes that enable them to walk, and sometimes even nest, on floating vegetation. They are polyandrous—large, dominant females lay several clutches of eggs, and a different male incubates each clutch and raises the young. The American jacana, *Jacana spinosa*, which ranges from Mexico to Argentina, measures 20 to 25 cm (8 to 10 in) in length and has cinnamon red coloration with bright green wing patches.

jack   A jack is a type of mechanism that is used to press against an object, moving it if it is free, or exerting pressure on the object if it is fixed. Common types of jacks are the lever jack, the screw jack, and the hydraulic jack; all three produce a sizable mechanical advantage, so that the applied force of a person is multiplied, resulting in a larger force being exerted on a heavy body. The lever jack is essentially a LEVER combined with a ratchet device that prevents the object from slipping back down during the reverse motion of the lever. The object is thus raised a small amount each stroke. In the screw jack, or jackscrew, the turning of a screw (by the use of a lever) causes the screw, which is fitted into a threaded base, to move upward as it rotates. A hydraulic jack makes use of the properties of an enclosed liquid to exert a large force on a piston in a large cylinder by applying a smaller force to the piston of a smaller cylinder (see HYDRAULIC SYSTEMS).

jack-o'-lantern   One species of poisonous mushroom, *Clitocybe illudens*, is known as the jack-o'-lantern fungus. The name is derived from its gills, which become luminescent during active growth periods. The plant is characterized by crowded, narrow gills and the lack of a veil. It fruits during late summer and early fall. The jack-o'-lantern fungus is distributed throughout eastern North America to the southern United States and to the Pacific coast; it also occurs in southern Europe.

jack-in-the-pulpit   *Arisaema triphyllum*, family Araceae, is a plant species most commonly referred to as

Jack-in-the-pulpit derives its name from the way the flower looks, like a clergyman giving a sermon in his pulpit. In fall, a cluster of bright-red berries appear, which are unpleasantly bitter and hot to the taste.

jack-in-the-pulpit. This herbaceous perennial grows in damp or shady places. The inflorescence is a densely flowered spadix surrounded by a large bract known as the spathe. In the fall, red berries are borne in a dense, egg-shaped cluster. The plants are monoecious; each season, however, flowers of just one sex are produced. For about two years staminate flowers are formed; in subsequent seasons pistillate flowers are produced.

Calcium oxalate crystals accumulate in the rhizome and, if taken into the mouth by a human, will cause irritation and a burning sensation. Pawnee Indians pulverized and dried the roots and dusted the powder on their temples to relieve headaches. The roots are also a source of flour, but they must be processed first in order to dispel the "acrid principle."

Jack the Ripper   Jack the Ripper was the name popularly given to a London murderer who killed seven prostitutes in the East End between Aug. 7 and Nov. 10, 1888. The murderer's identity has never been discovered, although some have suggested that he was the duke of Clarence, Queen Victoria's grandson, or the royal family's physician. The name *Jack the Ripper* came from letters received by the police that were presumed to have been written by the killer. He struck at night while his victim was walking the street, cutting her throat and then mutilating her body with the skill of a surgeon.

Jack the Ripper became a staple theme of mysteries and horror stories. One such novel, *The Lodger* (1913), by Marie Belloc Lowndes, has been filmed three times.

jackal [jak'-ul]   Jackal is the name applied to several carnivorous mammals in the genus *Canis* of the dog family, Canidae, which includes the dog and the wolf. They inhabit brush country, deserts, and grasslands. Jackals are about 90 cm (3 ft) long, including the bushy 35-cm (14-in) tail, and weigh about 10.8 kg (24 lb). They have erect ears, fairly long legs, and a slinking gait. The Asiatic, or golden, jackal, *C. aureus*, is found from Turkestan through the Near East and North Africa. The black-

The golden jackal resembles a small wolf. It feeds on plants, insects, and other small animals and carrion left by the larger predators.

backed jackal, *C. mesomelas*, and the side-striped jackal, *C. adustus*, inhabit eastern and southern Africa. Night hunters, jackals kill small mammals and poultry and often eat carrion. They hide in brush or in a hole during the day and howl in the evening, like a coyote. Litters consist of two to seven pups.

jacks   Jacks, or jackstones, is a children's game using 6 to 12 six-pointed jacks and a rubber ball. A player throws the ball in the air and tries to pick up increasing numbers of jacks with each toss. Jacks is of prehistoric origin and is played worldwide. Games similar to jacks are depicted in ancient Greek art, and in pre-Christian Rome jacks was a gambling game. In other parts of the world, seeds, stones, bones, or filled bags are used by adults and children of both sexes to play games similar to jacks. Only in the United States and Canada is jacks considered a girl's game.

Jackson (Michigan)   Jackson is a city on the Grand River in southern Michigan. The seat of Jackson County, it has a population of 37,446 (1990). Manufactures include auto and aircraft components. The city, settled in 1829 and named for President Andrew Jackson, was the site of the founding of the Republican party in 1854.

Jackson (Mississippi)   Jackson, the capital and largest city of Mississippi, is situated on the Pearl River. It is one of two seats of Hinds County (the other is Raymond) and has a population of 196,637 (1990) in the city proper and 395,396 in the metropolitan area. Jackson is a railroad and distribution center; manufactures include textiles, glass, and electronic equipment. Established as a trading post in 1792, the town was selected for the state capital in 1821 and named for Andrew Jackson. In the mid-1800s the city served as an important rail junction, but it was nearly destroyed by Gen. William Sherman's forces during the Civil War. The capitol building survived and is now a museum. A new capitol was completed in 1903. Growth was spurred in the 20th century by the convergence of new rail lines on Jackson and the opening of natural-gas fields in the 1930s. In 1979 heavy rains caused severe flooding of the Pearl River in Jackson.

Jackson, Alexander Young   A member of the GROUP OF SEVEN, the Canadian landscape painter Alexander Young Jackson, b. Montreal, Oct. 3, 1882, d. 1973, specialized in scenes of the rugged Canadian wilderness. After studying at the Art Institute of Chicago and in Europe, Jackson settled (1913) in Toronto, where he joined (1920) the Group of Seven. Jackson seldom used human figures in his work, and when they do appear—Indians, Eskimos, and fishermen—they are insignificant when compared to the power and majesty of nature. *Valley of the Gouffre River* (1933; McMichael Canadian Collection, Kleinburg, Ontario) is a typical example of his work.

ANDREW JACKSON
7th President of the United States (1829–37)

Nickname: "Old Hickory"

Born: Mar. 15, 1767, Waxhaw area, on N.C.-S.C. border

Professions: Lawyer, Soldier

Religious Affiliation: Presbyterian

Marriage: August 1791 (2d ceremony, Jan. 17, 1794), to Rachel Donelson Robards (1767–1828)

Children: None

Political Affiliation: Democrat

Writings: *Correspondence of Andrew Jackson* (7 vols., 1926–35), ed. by J. S. Bassett and J. F. Jameson

Died: June 8, 1845, Nashville, Tenn.

Buried: The Hermitage, Nashville, Tenn.

Vice-Presidents: John C. Calhoun (1829–32); Martin Van Buren (1822–37)

Jackson, Andrew   Andrew Jackson, a frontier general and Indian fighter, was elected seventh president of the United States on a platform that proclaimed him the champion of democracy and of the common man. Jackson served two terms (1829–37), marked by bitter controversies over state rights, nullification, the tariff, the spoils system, Indian removal, and banking policies.

Early Political and Military Career

Born Mar. 15, 1767, in the Waxhaw settlement on the border of North Carolina and South Carolina, Jackson was orphaned at the age of 14. After reading law and gaining admission to the bar in North Carolina, he migrated to Nashville, Tenn. In 1791, Jackson married Rachel Donelson Robards; both he and Rachel mistakenly believed that she and her first husband had received a legal divorce. When they discovered their error, they remarried (1794).

Jackson served as a delegate to the Tennessee constitutional convention in 1796 and as congressman from Tennessee (1796–97). He was elected U.S. senator in 1797, but financial problems forced his resignation and return to Tennessee in less than a year. After serving (1798–1804) as a Tennessee superior court judge, he retired from the bench to devote all his energies to business ventures and to his plantation, the Hermitage, near Nashville. His political career seemed to be over.

The WAR OF 1812 dramatically changed Jackson's political fortunes. In 1814, Jackson, a major general in the Tennessee militia, was ordered to march against the pro-British faction of the CREEK Indians. Assisted by pro-American Indian allies, he crushed Creek resistance at Horseshoe Bend (March 1814). He then forced all the Indians of the region, friends and foes alike, to surrender enormous tracts of land in both Alabama and Georgia. Impressed by his stunning victory, the federal government placed Jackson in command of the defense of New Orleans. Old Hickory, as Jackson was known to his admirers, organized the defense of the city and on Jan. 8, 1815, decimated an invading British army. Coming at the end of a war marked by military ineptness and humiliating defeats, Jackson's victory was seized upon by a public hungry for vindication of national honor. The Battle of New Orleans made Andrew Jackson a legend and a symbol of American virtue.

Jackson was called into action in 1817 against the Seminole Indians. In the spring of 1818 (in the First Seminole War) he pursued the Indians into Spanish Florida and then proceeded to depose the Spanish authorities there. These actions helped lead to the U.S. acquisition of Spanish Florida in 1819. Jackson resigned his army commission in 1821 and served briefly as territorial governor of Florida in the same year.

Return to Politics

In 1822 the Tennessee legislature nominated Jackson for the presidency; the following year it elected him to the U.S. Senate. He soon became involved in the presidential campaign of 1824. He almost won the presidency, but the election of 1824 was bitterly contested. The demise of the FEDERALIST PARTY, discredited by its opposition to the War of 1812, had left the nation with a one-party system. The Democratic-Republicans were unable, however, to agree on a common presidential candidate. The congressional caucus nominated Georgia's William H. CRAWFORD. Local party organizations and state legislatures, however, in addition to Jackson, placed in candidacy John Quincy ADAMS of Massachusetts, Henry CLAY of Kentucky, and John C. CALHOUN of South Carolina, who soon withdrew to seek the vice-presidency. No candidate received a majority, and although Jackson led in both tallies, the House of Representatives chose John Quincy Adams as president. Jackson's supporters charged that Adams's election was the result of a "corrupt bargain" with Henry Clay, whom Adams named secretary of state.

During the Adams administration, Jackson's supporters, aided by Vice-President Calhoun and Sen. Martin VAN BUREN, built a powerful political machine dedicated to Jackson's election in 1828. That machine became the nucleus of the DEMOCRATIC PARTY. Critical of Adams's nationalist policies and lack of concern for STATE RIGHTS, the Jackson organization represented Old Hickory as champion of the common man. They attacked Adams and Clay for the "corrupt bargain" that, they alleged, revealed the aristocratic principles of Adams and Clay and their contempt for democracy. Adams's supporters in turn attacked Jackson for the irregularity of the first years of his marriage and portrayed him as an ignorant and uncouth barbarian. Jackson defeated Adams in his bid for a second term.

The Presidency

During his presidency Jackson relied more heavily on his KITCHEN CABINET, a group of unofficial advisors, than on his official cabinet.

Rotation in Office. President Jackson sought to make government more sensitive to the will of the people through his principle of "rotation in office." Proclaiming that no person should regard officeholding as a right, Jackson declared all intelligent citizens equally qualified to serve and announced his intention to protect the nation from a permanent aristocratic officeholding clique by removing long-term officeholders. Although only a minority of federal officials (estimated at no more than ten percent) were actually removed by Jackson, his political foes charged him with seeking to corrupt the civil service for political reasons and dubbed his principle of "rotation in office" the "spoils system" (see PATRONAGE).

State Rights. Although Jackson declared his belief in state rights and in limitations on the activities of the federal government, he was inconsistent in applying these principles. In 1830 he vetoed a bill appropriating funds to construct a road between Maysville and Lexington entirely within Kentucky, the state of his rival Henry Clay. Since many of Jackson's supporters in Western states favored internal improvements at federal expense, however, his administration increased rather than limited federal spending for road, canal, and harbor construction.

In another case, that of the CHEROKEE Indians of Geor-

gia, Jackson effectively supported a state-rights position (and asserted his independence of the Supreme Court). Despite two U.S. Supreme Court decisions (1831 and 1832) upholding the rights of the Cherokee nation against the state of Georgia, which was attempting to destroy Cherokee sovereignty and take the Indians' land, Jackson refused to intervene on behalf of the Indians. Many tribes were resettled west of the Mississippi while he was in office.

The Tariff Question and Nullification. Jackson's followers were divided on the tariff question. Southerners were generally opposed to a protective tariff and had supported Jackson in the belief that he would lower duties drastically from the levels established in 1828; but Jacksonians in other areas tended to be protectionists. In 1832 his administration approved only modest reductions in duties (see TARIFF ACTS). On Nov. 24, 1832, however, South Carolina, acting on the doctrine of NULLIFICATION espoused by Vice-President Calhoun, declared the federal tariff laws of 1828 and 1832 null and void and prohibited the collection of tariffs in South Carolina after Feb. 1, 1833. Jackson, in his Nullification Proclamation of Dec. 10, 1832, declared his intent to enforce the law but also promised to seek further downward adjustment of the tariff. In 1833, Congress passed both a force bill, empowering Jackson to coerce South Carolina, and a compromise tariff. The threat of disunion was averted.

Economic Policy. Although Jackson had not made the Second BANK OF THE UNITED STATES an issue in the 1828 election, he soon announced his belief that the bank had failed to provide a stable currency, had favored the privileged few at the expense of the common people in its financial operations, and had received its federal charter in violation of the Constitution. The bank's charter was not due to expire until 1836, but in July 1832 the president of the bank, Nicholas BIDDLE, encouraged by Jackson's political enemies—particularly Henry Clay and Daniel WEBSTER—pushed a bill through Congress granting recharter. Jackson quickly vetoed the bill. The bank recharter was a major issue in the 1832 presidential election, in which Jackson (with Martin Van Buren as his running mate) overwhelmingly defeated Clay.

Jackson's war against the Bank of the United States extended throughout his second term of office. Angered by Biddle's use of bank funds to support anti-Jacksonian candidates, Jackson ordered federal deposits withdrawn from the bank in 1833.

Although Jackson destroyed the Second Bank of the United States by withdrawing government money, his administration failed to develop a coherent national banking policy. In many states, especially in the South and West, state-chartered banks engaged in irresponsible and speculative issuance of paper currency—a policy that Jackson and other hard-money advocates opposed. (The federal government issued no paper legal tender prior to the Civil War.) Thus during the mid-1830s the United States was swept by a land boom. Sales of federal lands soared, helping to wipe out the national debt and creating a large federal surplus. By 1836, however, the boom was becoming increasingly speculative. Alarmed and determined to curb extensive use of paper currency issued by private state-chartered banks, Jackson, in the Specie Circular of 1836, forbade further purchases of federal land or payment of federal debts in any currency except federally issued coins. His actions, which created a demand for specie that led to many bank failures, were opposed by conservatives in the business community; they charged him with responsibility for disrupting the economy and blamed him for the ensuing Panic of 1837.

Last Years and Influence

Even after his retirement, Jackson was a powerful force, continuing to shape both an important concept—that of mass democracy—and a powerful political organization, the Democratic party. He died at the Hermitage on June 8, 1845.

Jackson, Glenda The English actress Glenda Jackson, b. May 9, 1936, made her stage reputation as the demented Charlotte Corday in Peter Weiss's *Marat/Sade* (1964; film, 1966), directed by Peter Brook. In 1971 she scored notable successes as the brittle divorcee in the film *Sunday, Bloody Sunday* and as Queen Elizabeth I in the BBC-TV production of *Elizabeth R*. Her performances have earned her two Academy Awards as best actress, for *Women in Love* (1969) and *A Touch of Class* (1972).

Jackson, Henry M. Henry Martin "Scoop" Jackson, b. Everett, Wash., May 31, 1912, d. Sept. 1, 1983, was a Democratic senator from the state of Washington for 20 years. First elected in 1952, he was reelected for the last time a year before his death. A liberal in domestic policy, he supported larger defense expenditures and advocated an unyielding policy toward the USSR. In 1972 and 1976 he campaigned unsuccessfully for the Democratic presidential nomination. Jackson practiced law before being elected to the U.S. House of Representatives in 1940, where he served six terms.

Jackson, Jesse L. Jesse Louis Jackson, b. Greenville, S.C., Oct. 8, 1941, cemented his position as a national—as well as a black—leader in the race for the Democratic presidential nomination in 1988. A Baptist minister, he was active in the Southern black protest movement with Martin Luther King, Jr., in the early 1960s. Jackson directed the Chicago branch of Operation Breadbasket (1966–77), a group dedicated to eliminating racial discrimination in employment and business dealings, and founded PUSH (People United to Save Humanity) to advance the interests of African Americans and other disadvantaged groups. He made a strong bid for the 1984 presidential nomination. In 1988, however, calling for "economic justice," he had striking success. He was runner-up, with about 30% of the delegates and many more white votes than in 1984, to the victor, Michael Dukakis. Jackson's autobiography is *A Time to Speak* (1988).

Jesse Jackson began his public career in the 1960s as a civil-rights activist and subsequently broadened his involvement until, in 1988, he came closer than any black person had ever come to winning a major political party's presidential nomination.

Jackson, Mahalia Mahalia Jackson, b. New Orleans, Oct. 26, 1911, d. Jan. 27, 1972, was the most famous gospel singer of her time. Like many other African-American singers, Jackson began by singing in a church choir; but unlike those who moved into the pop-music field, she continued to sing GOSPEL MUSIC throughout her career. She first attracted national attention with recordings made in 1945; at the time of her death she had sung in countries as far removed from the gospel idiom as Japan and India. Her voice was as magnificent as Bessie Smith's, and although her music is sacred and Smith's is mostly secular, their vocal techniques were similar.

Jackson, Michael The world-famous singer-dancer Michael Joe Jackson, b. Gary, Ind., Aug. 29, 1958, formed the Jackson Five with his older brothers in the early 1960s and, beginning in 1968, gained fame through their MOTOWN recordings and television appearances with Michael as the boy soprano. In 1978, Michael produced his new persona. He was no longer a child, but now a child-man—delicate, frail, with a tremulous, often girlish voice; yet he was a powerful performer. His solo album *Off the Wall* (1978) catapulted him back into fame. *Thriller* (1982), boosted by Jackson's videos, broke sales records worldwide. *Bad* (1987) was also a big seller.

Jackson, Reggie Baseball player Reginald Martinez Jackson, b. Wyncote, Pa., May 18, 1946, became one of his sport's most talented and publicized players in the 1970s. During his long American League career with the Kansas City, then Oakland, Athletics (1967–75), Baltimore Orioles (1976), New York Yankees (1977–81), California Angels (1982–86), and, again, Oakland (1987), Jackson seemed to generate as many headlines with his cantankerous personality as with his prowess on the field. Nicknamed "Mr. October" for his ability to hit dramatically well during World Series play, the outfielder led his teams to 5 championships (Oakland, 1972–74, and New York, 1977–78) and set a Series record in 1977 with 5 home runs (3 in one game). Although a prodigious home-run hitter—he had 563 in his career, 6th on the all-time list—Jackson also set a major league record for strikeouts—2,597.

Jackson, Robert Houghwout   Robert Houghwout Jackson, b. Spring Creek, Pa., Feb. 13, 1892, d. Oct. 9, 1954, was U.S. solicitor general (1938–40) and attorney general (1940–41) under President Franklin D. Roosevelt and served as an associate justice of the U.S. Supreme Court from 1941 to 1954. He was also U.S. chief counsel at the Nuremberg War Crimes Trials (1945–46). A Jamestown, N.Y., lawyer, Jackson became prominent in New York State's Democratic party during Roosevelt's governorship (1928–32) and after Roosevelt became president was appointed to a series of posts in the federal government. During his term on the Supreme Court, Jackson was a defender of civil liberties and an advocate of judicial restraint. His books include *The Case against the Nazi War Criminals* (1945) and *The Supreme Court in the American System of Government* (1955).

Jackson, Shirley   Shirley Jackson, b. San Francisco, Dec. 14, 1919, d. Aug. 8, 1965, was an American short-story writer and novelist. Innovatively mixing the conventions of the gothic tale with sophisticated psychology, she produced stories of chilling evil, which she perceived under the surfaces of everyday life. Her short story "The Lottery" caused a sensation when it appeared in the *New Yorker* in 1948 and remains a classic of civilized horror. Her best-known novels are *The Haunting of Hill House* (1959) and *We Have Always Lived in the Castle* (1962). More of her work appeared in *Come along with Me* (1968).

Jackson, Stonewall   Thomas Jonathan "Stonewall" Jackson, b. Clarksburg, Va., now W.Va., Jan. 21, 1824, d. 1863, a Confederate general in the Civil War, is held second only to Robert E. LEE in the affection and esteem of Southerners. He was left an orphan at an early age but later graduated (1846) from West Point. He fought with distinction in the Mexican War and resigned from the army to teach at the Virginia Military Institute.

During his ten years of teaching (1851–61), Jackson's first wife died and he remarried. He became a zealous Presbyterian and was sometimes called "Deacon Jackson." Austere in personal habits, he also became something of an eccentric. Imagining one side of his body to weigh more than the other, he often walked or rode with one arm raised to restore his balance. He stood while eating to straighten his intestinal tract and thus aid digestion.

Thomas "Stonewall" Jackson, a military officer who first distinguished himself during the Mexican War, became one of the finest Confederate field commanders of the Civil War. Jackson is best remembered for his tactically brilliant Shenandoah Valley campaign of 1862.

In 1861, Jackson joined the Confederate army. In July, at the first battle of BULL RUN, he won his famous nickname. As the Confederates fell back before a Northern attack, Jackson and his brigade stood firm—"like a stone wall," according to Gen. Barnard Bee.

In the spring of 1862, Jackson commanded a Confederate army in the Shenandoah Valley. By a brilliant campaign of hard marching and hard fighting, he defeated Federal generals whose combined strength was several times his own. He then joined Robert E. Lee, who was trying to drive another Northern army away from Richmond. In the Seven Days battles (June 1862; see PENINSULAR CAMPAIGN), however, Jackson was physically exhausted, and his performance was slow and ineffective. Later, at the Second Bull Run (August) and at ANTIETAM (September) and FREDERICKSBURG (December), he contributed greatly to a remarkable string of Southern victories.

At CHANCELLORSVILLE the following spring, Jackson fought his last and greatest battle: on May 2, 1863, with more than half the available Confederate troops under his command, he made a crushing attack on the exposed flank of the Federal army. As he returned from a night reconnaisance, however, he was shot by some of his own men who mistook him for an enemy. Pneumonia developed as a result of his wounds, and he died on May 10, 1863. A brilliant tactician, Jackson was the ablest of Lee's generals; his loss was a great blow to the Confederacy. Lee wrote, "I know not how to replace him."

Jackson Hole   Jackson Hole is a valley in Grand Teton National Park, northwestern Wyoming. A long, narrow valley, about 80 km (50 mi) long and 10 to 13 km (6 to 8 mi) wide, it lies east of the Teton Mountains and west of the Wind River Range, at an elevation of 2,134 m (7,000 ft). Jackson Hole is watered by the Snake River, which meets Jackson Lake to the north. The area was settled in the late 1880s and named for David Jackson, an American trapper. It is noted for abundant wildlife—an enormous elk herd winters there.

Jacksonville Jacksonville is a major transportation and commercial center in northeast Florida. Located on the St. Johns River, 35 km (22 mi) from the Atlantic coast, it has a population of 672,971 (1990) in the city proper and 906,727 in the metropolitan area. Jacksonville and Duval County merged in 1968, creating the nation's fourth largest city in area, 1,984 km^2 (766 mi^2).

The leading deep-water port on the southern U.S. Atlantic coast, Jacksonville is a major coffee and automobile importing center. Industrial products include lumber, paper, chemicals, and processed food. Jacksonville is also a rail hub and a finance and insurance center. The city's institutions of higher education include Jacksonville University (1934). The Gator Bowl (a major football stadium), the Cummer Gallery of Art, and Jacksonville Art Museum are much visited.

In 1564, French Huguenots led by René Goulaine de LAUDONNIÈRE established Fort Caroline on the St. Johns River. The city of Jacksonville was laid out in 1822, after the United States had acquired the area from Spain, and named for Florida's first territorial governor, Andrew Jackson. In 1870–90, Jacksonville developed into a resort and experienced its first building boom.

Jacob In the Bible Jacob was the grandson of Abraham and Sarah, the son of ISAAC and REBECCA, and the traditional ancestor of all Israel. Jacob obtained his prominence in the line of Abraham by tricking his elder twin brother ESAU out of both his birthright and his paternal blessing (Gen. 25:29–34; 27:1–41). As he fled from the enraged Esau, Jacob had a dream at Bethel of angels ascending and descending a ladder to heaven (Gen. 28:10–22). He married his cousins RACHEL and Leah and worked 20 years for their father, Laban, in Haran. He later wrestled with an angel, who gave him the name Israel (Gen. 32:22–32), and was reconciled with Esau. Jacob's 12 sons were the ancestors of the 12 tribes of Israel; Jacob's favorite was JOSEPH.

Jacob, François [zhah-kohb'] François Jacob, a French biologist, b. June 17, 1920, contributed to the knowledge of how genes function and was awarded, along with French biologists Jacques Monod and André Lwoff, the 1965 Nobel Prize for physiology or medicine. At the Pasteur Institute in 1958, Jacob and Monod proposed that molecules of ribonucleic acid (RNA) carry the genetic message from the deoxyribonucleic acid (DNA) in the nucleus to the ribosomes, or sites of protein synthesis in cells. They also found that some genes, which they called operator genes, regulate the activity of other, protein-synthesizing genes.

Jacobean literature [jak-uh-bee'-uhn] *Jacobean literature* is the term used for the corpus of English writings produced during the reign (1603–25) of James I ("Jacobus" in Latin). A strikingly restless, pained, and analytical literary age, it witnessed a high point in dramatic development. SHAKESPEARE during this time wrote three of his great tragedies—*Othello, King Lear*, and *Macbeth*—and vied with Francis Beaumont and John Fletcher (see BEAUMONT, FRANCIS, AND FLETCHER, JOHN) in romantic comedy. Ben JONSON was the master of satire and, with John DONNE, dominated the age's nondramatic poetry. Jonson's polished classical verse linked the previous Elizabethans to the later CAVALIER POETS, and Donne's witty and theatrical metaphysical style (see METAPHYSICAL POETRY) generated a new poetic mode. English prose was evolving into the "plain style" heralded by Francis BACON's *Essays* and the King James translation of the Bible.

Jacobi, Friedrich Heinrich [yah'-kohb-ee] The German philosopher Friedrich Heinrich Jacobi, b. Jan. 25, 1743, d. Mar. 19, 1819, known during his life primarily as an opponent of German idealism, is now considered a precursor of EXISTENTIALISM. Jacobi advocated the romantic view that God dwells within humans and reveals himself through humans' feelings, not reason. Stressing feeling and faith over reason, he became a strong critic of Enlightenment views, deism, and especially of the then-current idealism.

Jacobins [jak'-uh-binz] During the FRENCH REVOLUTION the Jacobins were members of the Society of the Friends of the Constitution, a political group that met from 1790 to 1794 in a former Dominican, or Jacobin, monastery in Paris. Members of the many local affiliated societies throughout France were also called Jacobins. A struggle (1792) in the Paris group between moderate supporters of the GIRONDISTS and the radical followers of Maximilien ROBESPIERRE ended in a victory for the radicals. During the Reign of Terror (1793–94) the middle-class Jacobins, allied with the *sans-culottes* (Parisian republicans of the artisan class) were the dominant party in France. After the execution of Robespierre and his colleagues in the Thermidorian Reaction (1794), the Jacobin clubs were closed down. Revived under the DIRECTORY but shorn of their former power, they were permanently suppressed by Napoléon Bonaparte in 1799.

Jacobite church [jak'-uh-byt] A body of Monophysite Christians, living primarily in Syria, Iraq, and India, the Jacobite church takes its name from Jacob (James) Baradai (d. 578), bishop of Edessa, who organized a separate church, opposed to the Orthodox episcopate of Eastern Christendom. Together with the Copts of Egypt, the Armenians, and the Ethiopians, the Jacobites reject the doctrine of the Council of Chalcedon (451; see CHALCEDON, COUNCIL OF) on the "two natures in one person" of Christ and prefer to define Christ's person as "one nature" (see MONOPHYSITISM). Modern historians generally consider that their doctrine, as elaborated in the 6th century by Severus of Antioch and Philoxenus of Mabbug, is not essentially different from that of Saint CYRIL OF AL-

EXANDRIA, whom Orthodox, Roman Catholics, and Monophysites equally venerate as a Father of the Church. The MALABAR CHRISTIANS of India, also often designated as "Jacobites," have established their own patriarchate.

Jacobites

Jacobites [jak'-uh-byts]   After Britain's GLORIOUS REVOLUTION of 1688 the adherents of the exiled STUART king JAMES II and his Roman Catholic descendants were known as Jacobites. The major support for their cause was in Scotland and Ireland, where the Jacobites continued to resist after the accession to the throne of WILLIAM III and MARY II in 1689. William, however, defeated the Scottish Jacobites under Viscount DUNDEE at Killiecrankie (1689) and the Irish Jacobites in the Battle of Boyne (1690).

When James II died in 1701, his son, James Edward (known as the Old Pretender; see STUART, JAMES FRANCIS EDWARD), was recognized as king of England and Scotland by Spain and France. His first attempted invasion of Scotland in 1708 was a total fiasco. More serious was the Jacobite rising of 1715, after the accession of the Hanoverian GEORGE I, which had support in England as well as Scotland. The Scottish Jacobites were defeated, nonetheless, at Preston in Lancashire on November 13, and by the time James Edward landed in Scotland on Dec. 22, 1715, the cause was lost.

In 1745 his son, Charles Edward (Bonnie Prince Charlie or the Young Pretender), sailed to Scotland and raised certain Highland clans. He defeated Sir John Cope at Prestonpans on Sept. 21, 1745, but was later routed at Culloden Moor on Apr. 16, 1746. Charles Edward fled, and with him went the last of the Jacobite hopes.

Jacob's ladder

Jacob's ladder   Jacob's ladder is the common name for approximately 25 species of annual or perennial plants constituting the genus *Polemonium* in the phlox family, Polemoniaceae. These plants have reclining stems or underground rhizomes and bear blue, purple, yellow, or white funnel-shaped flowers. A Eurasian perennial grown as an ornamental and now also found wild in eastern North America is *P. caeruleum*, which grows to 1 m (3 ft) high and bears clusters of typically bright blue flowers with yellow stamens.

Jacob's Pillow Dance Festival

Jacob's Pillow Dance Festival   The Jacob's Pillow Dance Festival is a summer performance series at Jacob's Pillow, the former Ted SHAWN retreat in Lee, Mass., which developed out of informal performances by Shawn and his Men Dancers beginning in 1933. The festival itself was organized in 1940; at first it was directed by others, but Shawn eventually gained complete control. Programs at the Pillow were noted for their diverse content, including ballet, modern, and ethnic dance, and for the many companies given important exposure there. The festival declined in quality near the end of Shawn's life but has been revived and continued since his death.

See also: DANCE; DENISHAWN; MODERN DANCE; ST. DENIS, RUTH.

Jacob's staff

Jacob's staff   The Jacob's staff, also known as the forestaff and later as the cross-staff, was an instrument used by early astronomers and navigators to measure angles and the altitude of the Sun and other stars. The staff, of square cross section, was held against the navigator's cheekbone; a crosspiece was moved along the staff until the ends of the crossbar appeared to touch the horizon and the Sun or another star simultaneously.

Jacobsen, Arne

Jacobsen, Arne [yah'-kohp-sen, ar'-neh]   The Danish architect Arne Jacobsen, b. Feb. 11, 1902, d. Mar. 21, 1971, produced some of the most elegant and meticulous buildings of modern Scandinavia. Initially influenced by Erik Gunnar ASPLUND, Jacobsen began as an architect of private houses and later turned to public commissions. He produced three distinguished town halls: Aarhus (1939–42), Søllerød (1940–42), and Rødovre (1955). The SAS Royal Hotel and Air Terminal (1958–60), a particularly smooth and sophisticated application of INTERNATIONAL STYLE technique, was Copenhagen's first skyscraper. The tradition of Scandinavian craftsmanship evident in the details of Jacobsen's buildings is also apparent in his designs for furniture and household articles of the 1950s.

Jacquard, Joseph Marie

Jacquard, Joseph Marie [zhah-kar']   The French inventor Joseph Marie Jacquard, b. July 7, 1752, d. Aug. 7, 1834, built the first successful LOOM for automatically weaving patterned fabrics. This loom, which used a system of punched cards to produce a pattern, was a forerunner of the computer. Several inventors had improved the draw, or pattern, loom when Jacquard undertook his work about 1800. His creation gave impetus to the development of the textile industry and paved the way for the fully automatic loom. Jacquard's loom was demonstrated to Napoleon I and patented in 1804. It won for its inventor both royalties and a pension. Although Jacquard and his invention were opposed by silk workers, the loom was gradually accepted and became used worldwide. The punched cards used in it were adopted (1835) by the British inventor Charles BABBAGE for his calculator and by Herman HOLLERITH for use in tabulating the 1890 U.S. census.

See also: SPINNING; WEAVING.

Jacqueline of Hainaut

Jacqueline of Hainaut [jak'-wuh-leen, en-oh']   Jacqueline of Hainaut, b. July 25, 1401, d. Oct. 9, 1436, countess of Holland, Zeeland, and Hainaut, surrendered control of her three counties to her cousin PHILIP THE GOOD, duke of Burgundy, in 1428 and thus contributed to the Burgundian domination of the Low Countries. Before inheriting (1417) the counties from her father, Jacqueline married (1415) Jean de Touraine, second son of Charles VI of France. Later she married John IV, duke of Brabant (1418), and Humphrey, duke of Gloucester (1422; see GLOUCESTER, HUMPHREY, DUKE OF) in order to protect her territories from Philip. Abandoned by Humphrey, she was forced to sign over her lands to Philip by the Treaty of Delft (1428). Jacqueline remained titular countess until 1433, when Philip forced her abdication.

Jacquerie

Jacquerie [zhahk-uh-ree'] The Jacquerie was a French peasant insurrection in 1358. During the HUNDRED YEARS' WAR the French peasants suffered in the extensive pillaging of the countryside by English soldiers and were further victimized by the financial exactions of their own nobles. On May 21, 1358, an uprising began near Compiègne, northeast of Paris. Led by Guillaume Cale, or Carle, the peasants destroyed castles and slew their occupants. They joined forces with another rebel group from Paris, led by Étienne Marcel, but both groups were routed on June 9 and 10. Savage reprisals followed.

jade

jade Jade, a translucent ornamental material, has been carved since ancient times. Jade carving has flourished in China since 2000 BC, notably during the Zhou dynasty and the Qianlong era of the Qing dynasties. The Chinese have ascribed to this GEM many human virtues. The Han scholar Xu Shen, for example, asserted that its bright yet warm luster typified charity; its translucency, revealing inner color and markings, represented rectitude; its pure and penetrating note when struck displayed wisdom; its ability to break but not bend exemplified courage; and its sharp edges, not intended for violence, symbolized equity. Jade ornaments and tools have also been carved by the Mesoamerican Maya and Aztec, the Maori of New Zealand, and the Alaskan Eskimo, as well as by inhabitants of India since the 17th century.

Jade consists of two separate SILICATE MINERAL species: nephrite, and the less common but harder, more valued jadeite. Nephrite has a splintery fracture, vitreous or silky luster, and dark-colored inclusions. A calcium and ferro-magnesian silicate ($Ca_2(Mg, Fe)_5Si_8O_{22}(OH,F)_2$), nephrite is the massive form of actinolite and tremolite (see AMPHIBOLE).

Jadeite has a granular fracture, a glassy or pearly luster, and a pitted or polished surface. A PYROXENE mineral, jadeite is a sodium aluminosilicate ($NaAlSi_2O_6$). It occurs as transparent-to-opaque compact lenses, veins, or nodules that vary in color due to impurities: the white through emerald green or apple green, red, blue, and brown varieties contain calcium; the dark green to blackish varieties contain iron.

Jade has been carved into ornaments and tools by various cultures. This carved ornament is typical of the intricate shapes and designs for which Chinese artisans have long been noted.

jadeite   see JADE

Jadwiga, Queen of Poland

Jadwiga, Queen of Poland [yahd-vee'-gah]   Jadwiga, b. *c.*1373, d. July 17, 1399, reigned as queen of Poland from 1384 to 1399. The younger daughter of the Hungarian King LOUIS I, who ruled Poland from 1370 to 1382, she was elected queen by the Polish nobles in order to separate Poland from Hungary, which was inherited by her older sister, Maria. In 1386 the young Jadwiga married Jogaillo, grand duke of Lithuania, who was baptized a Christian and crowned king of Poland as Władysław II (or V). This marriage eventually brought the unification of Poland and Lithuania (see JAGELLO dynasty). Jadwiga restored the University of Kraków and is venerated as a saint in Poland.

Jaffa   see TEL AVIV–JAFFA

Jagello

Jagello (dynasty) [yah-gel'-loh]   The dynasty of Jagello (Polish: Jagiełło; Lithuanian: Jogaillo) ruled Poland and Lithuania (1386–1572), Hungary (1440–44, 1490–1526), and Bohemia (1471–1526). It took its name from Jogaillo (*c.*1350–1434), grand duke of Lithuania, who in 1386 married JADWIGA, queen of Poland. The marriage led to the Christian conversion of Lithuania and the eventual union of Poland and Lithuania.

Jogaillo, who became King Władysław II (or V) of Poland, was succeeded by his oldest son, Władysław III (or VI), who also reigned as king of Hungary (1440–44) and then, after a brief interregnum, by his younger son, CASIMIR IV (r. 1447–92). Casimir was followed by his three sons in succession: John I (r. 1492–1501), Alexander I (r. 1501–06), and SIGISMUND I (r. 1506–48). The last Jagello ruler of Poland was SIGISMUND II (r. 1548–72). Another son of Casimir's became king of Bohemia (1471) and then Hungary (1490) as Ladislas II. He was succeeded in both countries by his son, LOUIS II (r. 1516–26).

Under the Jagello rulers the Poles and Lithuanians overwhelmed the TEUTONIC KNIGHTS (1410, 1466) and fought against Muscovite Russia. By the Union of Lublin in 1569 the two nations merged in the Polish-Lithuanian Commonwealth, with one king and a common parliament. The great age of the commonwealth was the 16th century, when it enjoyed peace, prosperity, and cultural flowering.

jaguar

jaguar [jag'-war]   The jaguar is the largest member of the cat family, Felidae, found in either North or South America. Formerly designated either *Leo onca* or *Felis onca*, the jaguar is now classified as *Panthera onca*. In Latin America it is commonly called a *tigre*; the term *jaguar* is derived from its native Indian name.

A male jaguar may reach 1.8 m (6 ft) in length (head and body) with a 75-cm-long (2.5-ft) tail, and may weigh nearly 180 kg (400 lb). Its coat ranges from grayish to

The jaguar, the largest cat found in the Americas, looks like a leopard but is more heavily built. The solitary jaguar establishes its own territory, and males and females disregard each other except during mating season.

reddish tan and is spotted like that of a leopard, with body spots grouped into small circles, or rosettes; unlike the leopard, the jaguar's rosettes surround one or more solid spots. The jaguar is also more stoutly built, with a larger, broader head.

Jaguars are found from the southwestern United States to Patagonia in southern Argentina. They inhabit marshes, scrub brush areas, and both temperate and tropical forests. They feed on a wide variety of large and small animals and also occasionally prey on domestic animals; very rarely, they have become man-eaters. Jaguars breed once a year. After a gestation period of about 14 weeks, usually one to four young are born.

Jahangir, Mogul Emperor of India [juh-huhn-geer'] Jahangir, or Jehangir, b. Aug. 31, 1569, d. Oct. 28, 1627, the fourth Mogul emperor of India, ruled from 1605 to 1627. He was the son of AKBAR and the father of SHAH JAHAN. Although he rebelled against his father in 1599, Jahangir continued Akbar's expansionist policies after his succession; he fought long wars in the Deccan but won little new territory.

Like his father, Jahangir was a patron of the arts, especially painting and poetry. Otherwise, however, he was a cruel tyrant. Pursuing his private pleasures, he left the running of his empire mostly to his Persian wife, Nur Jahan, who became the strong-willed dispenser of imperial justice. Jahangir's last years were troubled by frequent rebellions by his son, Prince Khurram (later Shah Jahan).

Jahn, Friedrich Ludwig [yahn] Friedrich Ludwig Jahn, b. Aug. 11, 1778, d. Oct. 15, 1852, was a German nationalist educator and the father of GYMNASTICS. In 1811, as an anti-Napoleonic move, he organized group outdoor exercises to strengthen German youth and to raise national morale. Jahn introduced new gymnastic apparatuses such as the horizontal bar, the side horse, the balance beam, and the parallel bars. After the fall of Napoleon the reac-

tionary government of Prussia suppressed the movement and arrested Jahn. Much later, Jahn was elected to the revolutionary German parliament of 1848.

jai alai [hy'-ly] Jai alai is a form of handball for singles or doubles competition played on a court (cancha) with three walls in an arena (fronton). Players use a curved wicker basket (cesta) for catching and throwing the ball. The game is played most seriously in the United States (Connecticut, Florida, and Rhode Island), Spain, and France, and on a less competitive level in Mexico, Latin America, and elsewhere in Europe. The players are professionals, and wagering is common.

Jai alai is derived from either the Aztecs or a Basque variation of handball. It developed in Spain, was imported to Cuba in 1900, and arrived in Miami, Fla., in 1924.

The ball (pelota) is made of hard, wound rubber covered by nylon thread and two layers of goatskin; it is about 2 in. (5 cm) in diameter and travels at speeds up to 273 km/h (170 mph). The rules are similar to those of handball, except the court is much larger—176 ft (53.7 m) long. The format for U.S. play is called quiniella, wherein each game is played to 7 points. Eight teams of 2 players each or 8 individuals compete in a game. In team competition 4 players are always on the court; in singles, 2. The pelota, once thrown against the front wall, must be caught on the fly or on one bounce. The players or teams appear on the court in a specified, rotating order, with the winner of each point remaining on the floor. During the first complete round, 1 point is awarded for each rally; during all subsequent rounds, 2 points. Wagers, as in horse racing, are on win, place, and show.

Jainism [jy'-nizm] Jainism is a religious faith of India that is usually said to have originated with Mahavira, a contemporary of the Buddha (6th century BC). Jains, however, count Mahavira as the last of 24 founders, or Tirthamkaras, the first being Rishabha.

The major distinction within Jainism is between the Digambara and Svetambara sects, a schism that appears to date from about the 1st century AD. The major difference between them is that whereas the Svetambaras wear white clothes, the Digambaras traditionally go naked.

The most notable feature of Jain ethics is its insistence on noninjury to all forms of life. Jain philosophy finds that every kind of thing has a soul; therefore, strict observance of this precept of nonviolence (*ahimsa*) requires extreme caution in all activity. Jain monks frequently wear cloths over their mouths to avoid unwittingly killing anything by breathing it in, and Jain floors are kept meticulously clean to avert the danger of stepping on a living being. Jains regard the intentional taking of life, or even violent thoughts, however, as much more serious. Jain philosophy posits a gradation of beings, from those with five senses down to those with only one sense. Ordinary householders cannot help harming the latter, although they should strive to limit themselves in this regard by refraining from eating meat, certain fruits, or honey or from drinking wine. In addition Jain householders are expected to practice other virtues, similar to those in HINDUISM. The vows taken by the Jain monks are more severe. They eventually involve elements of ASCETICISM: fasting, peripatetic begging, learning to endure bodily discomfort, and various internal austerities constituting a Jain variety of YOGA. Jainism is unique in allowing the very spiritually advanced to hasten their own death by certain practices (principally fasting) and under specified circumstances.

Jain philosophy is based on a fundamental distinction between living and nonliving matter. Living souls are divided into bound and liberated; the living souls are found in both mobile and immobile loci. Nonliving matter is composed of *karman*, or very fine particles that enter a soul and produce changes in it, thus causing its bondage. This influx of *karman* is induced by activity and has to be burned off by experience. A soul, which is thought of as having the same size as its body, at liberation has lost the matter that weights it down and thus ascends to the top of the universe, where it remains forever.

Jaipur [jy'-pur] Jaipur, the capital and largest city of Rajasthan state in western India, is located about 300 km (190 mi) southwest of Delhi. The city has an area of approximately 206 km^2 (80 mi^2) and a population of 966,677 (1981). Jaipur, which lies at an altitude of about 427 m (1,400 ft), occupies a strategic position on the eastern flanks of the Aravalli Range on the trade routes from Gujarat to Agra and Delhi. Jaipur is noted for its jewelry, printed cloth, and enamelware. Rajasthan University was established there in 1947.

Jaipur was planned and founded in 1727 by Maharaja Sawaii Jai Singh II. Although his plan was not followed completely, Jaipur's regular layout is unusual for an Indian city of its size. Jaipur is called the pink city because most of its buildings are of light red sandstone. Landmarks include the city palace, which contains Chandra

Mahal and the Jantar Mantar, an 18th-century astronomical observatory with masonry instruments; and the Hawa Mahal, or Hall of Winds.

Jakarta [juh-kart'-uh] Jakarta (Djakarta), the capital of Indonesia, has a population of 7,829,000 (1985 est.), the largest of any urban center in Southeast Asia and one of the largest in the world. It is located on the alluvial plain of the Liwung River in northwestern Java. The city is coextensive with its metropolitan area, Djakarta Raya, covering 592 km^2 (229 mi^2) and forming a special capital region. The city has expanded from the Kota, or Old City, and now includes the modern port of Tanjung Priok, 10 km (6 mi) to the east.

Jakarta is the major industrial and commercial center in Indonesia, with textiles and food processing among its industries. Jakarta's port is the nation's center for waterborne international trade. Jakarta is also the cultural center of Indonesia. The Museum of Indonesian Culture (1778) houses both ancient and modern works of art. The University of Indonesia (1950) is among its universities.

Jakarta was settled as a trading center by Hindus and Buddhists from India about the 5th century. Originally called Sunda Kelapa, the town was renamed Jakarta, meaning "victory," by the sultan of Bantam, who won a battle against the Portuguese there. In 1619 the Dutch under Jan Pieterszoon Coen captured the city, fortified it, and named it Batavia. The city became the capital of the Dutch East Indies. For a time during the Napoleonic Wars British rule prevailed. The Netherlands again controlled the area from 1815 until 1949, when the Dutch recognized Indonesian independence and Jakarta was chosen as the national capital.

Jakobson, Roman [yah'-kub-suhn, roh'-mahn] The linguist Roman Jakobson, b. Moscow, Oct. 11 (N.S.), 1896, d. July 18, 1982, contributed to virtually every aspect of language study. His early books and articles dealt with aphasia and language acquisition. As a member of the Prague school, Jakobson wrote on the relation of language to literature and culture. His publications include *Main Trends in the Science of Language* (1973), six volumes of selected writings (1962–78), and *Framework of Language* (1980).

Jalapa [hah-lah'-pah] Jalapa (Jalapa Enríquez), the capital of Veracruz state in east central Mexico, is situated in the Sierra Madre Oriental. Its population is 212,769 (1980). The city is a tourist center and a market for the region's coffee and tobacco crops. During the Spanish colonial era Jalapa was a trading center. Veracruzana University was founded there in 1944.

Jalisco [hah-lees'-koh] Jalisco, a state in west central Mexico, has an area of 80,836 km^2 (31,211 mi^2) and a population of 5,269,826 (1989 est.). Its capital is GUADALAJARA. The narrow coastal plain on the Pacific Ocean gives way to a high plateau with numerous volcanic peaks. Lake Chapala, on the border with Mihoacán state, is Mexico's largest lake. Jalisco has large silver and gold deposits. Corn, wheat, beans, tobacco, and citrus fruits are grown; stock raising is also important. Jalisco was conquered by the Spanish in 1529. In the 1820s it was an important stronghold during the independence movement.

jam and jelly Jam is a confection made by cooking fruit and sugar in order to achieve a mixture with a fairly thick consistency. Jellies are fruit juices cooked with sugar to form a firm gel, using the PECTIN of the fruit itself or added pectin to aid the gelling process. Fruit preserves are whole or sectioned fruits cooked in a thick, clear, sugar syrup. Citrus preserves are called marmalades. The smooth, semisolid fruit butters and the thick-to-solid fruit pastes are made of fruit pulp and sugar.

In addition to the fruit and sugar, federal standards permit the use of citric, tartaric, or other food-derived acids to improve gelling and to stabilize color and flavor. Other sweeteners include corn syrup and dextrose. No artificial flavors or colors are permitted except in mint and cinnamon jellies.

In the commercial manufacture of preserves and jellies the fruits or juices, pectin, and sugar are blended and heated. The mixture is then pumped to a vacuum pan, where rapid boiling at 60° C (140° F) protects the fruit's color and flavor as the water content evaporates. When the mixture reaches the required degree of thickness, a food-acid mix is added. The finished product is immediately packed into jars, sterilized, cooled in a water spray, labeled, and cartoned.

Jamaica [juh-may'-kuh] Jamaica, a nation in the West Indies, occupies the third largest island in the Caribbean Sea. Located south of Cuba and west of Hispaniola, Jamaica is slightly larger than the island of Hawaii. KINGSTON is its capital.

Land

Jamaica, about 235 km (146 mi) long and 82 km (51 mi) at its widest point, is bisected by highlands that cover 80% of the island. The highest elevations are in the Blue Mountains to the east. The coastal plains are widest and most arid to the south. Most of the soil of the island, particularly in the central section, contains a high percentage of limestone, making cultivation difficult. Rainwater percolates through the limestone soil to unusable depths. The island has few large rivers; only the Black

AT A GLANCE

JAMAICA

Land: Area: 10,990 km² (4,243 mi²). Capital and largest city: Kingston (1982 est. pop., 104,041).
People: Population (1990 est.): 2,441,396. Density: 222 persons per km² (575 per mi²). Distribution (1989): 49% urban, 51% rural. Languages: English, Creole. Major religions: Anglicanism, Protestantism, Roman Catholicism.
Government: Type: independent state within the Commonwealth. Legislature: Parliament. Political subdivisions: 12 parishes and the Kingston–St. Andrew corporate area.
Economy: GNP (1988): $2.6 billion; $1,080 per capita. Labor distribution (1988): agriculture—24.3%; manufacturing and mining—12.8%; finance, real estate, and services—15.6%; trade—12.6%; public administration and defense—6.9%; public utilities, transportation, and communications—3.8%; construction—4.5%; other, including unemployed—19.5%. Foreign trade (1989): imports—$1.6 billion; exports—$948 million. Currency: 1 Jamaican dollar = 100 cents.
Education and Health: Literacy (1990): 74% of adult population. Universities (1989): 1. Hospital beds (1988): 5,698. Physicians (1988, government employed only): 367. Life expectancy (1990): women—79; men—75. Infant mortality (1990): 16 per 1,000 live births.

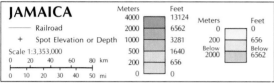

JAMAICA	Meters	Feet		
—— Railroad	4000	13124	Meters	Feet
+ Spot Elevation or Depth	2000	6562	0	0
	1000	3281	200	656
Scale 1:3,353,000	500	1640	Below 2000	Below 6562
0 20 40 60 80 km	200	656		
0 10 20 30 40 50 mi	0	0		

River is navigable. The mean annual temperature is about 27° C (80° F) on the coast. Annual rainfall averages 1,955 mm (77 in), but it reaches 5,080 mm (200 in) in some mountainous regions. Jamaica has a great diversity of vegetation, although many areas have been cleared for agriculture.

People

The population of Jamaica consists mostly of descendants of African blacks. There are also several small East Indian, Chinese, and European minorities. The official language is English, but most of the rural population speak a Creole dialect. Population is concentrated on the coastal plains; the highlands are mostly uninhabited. A high birthrate and low death rate have resulted in high population densities in recent years. Anglicans and Baptists are the largest religious groups. Approximately 5% of the population are Roman Catholics. The RASTAFARIANS are a small but highly visible sect. The administrative center for the University of the West Indies (1948) is near Kingston. The Institute of Jamaica (1879), in Kingston, has a library and museum of Jamaican history, art, and natural history.

Economic Activity

Agriculture and the mining industry are dominant factors in Jamaica's economy. Sugar, tropical fruits, coffee, cacao, and spices are grown for export through the ports of Kingston and Montego Bay. Jamaica has recently developed a profitable mining industry. It ranks among the world's top nations in the production of bauxite and alumina, which are exported to Canada, Norway, and the United States. A petroleum refinery operates in Kingston. Other industries include sugar processing, textiles, printing, and chemicals.

The lack of indigenous energy sources has slowed industrial development. In the mid-1980s reduced world demand for bauxite hurt Jamaica, and political unrest damaged the important tourist industry. The 1989 foreign debt of $4 billion was one of the largest in the world in proportion to population.

Government

Jamaica became an independent member of the Commonwealth of Nations in 1962. Executive power within Jamaica's government lies with a cabinet headed by a prime minister responsible to the parliament.

History

Jamaica was discovered by Christopher Columbus on May 4, 1494, and was subsequently settled by the Spanish, who ruled the island until 1655, when it was captured by the British.

ARAWAK Indians, who inhabited the island at the time of Columbus's arrival, had died out, so African slaves were imported to work the sugarcane fields. With the abolition of slavery in Jamaica in 1833 the plantations declined, and the former slaves took to peasant farming. In 1958, Jamaica formed the West Indies Federation with nine other British possessions, but it withdrew in 1961, a move that led to the eventual collapse of the federation. Jamaica's withdrawal was urged by Sir Alexander BUSTAMANTE, a labor leader who became prime minister when Jamaica achieved full independence in 1962. Michael Manley (see MANLEY family), leader of the People's National party (PNP), became prime minister in 1972 and instituted wide-ranging socialist reforms. The resulting trade deficit brought Jamaica near bankruptcy by 1980, forcing new elections that brought the conservative Labour party, led by Edward P. G. SEAGA, to power. Reelected in 1983, Seaga was defeated by Manley in the 1989 elections after his economic-austerity programs grew unpopular. Hurricane Gilbert, the powerful storm that struck Jamaica in 1988, also added to the nation's economic woes.

Jamal al-Din al-Afghani   The Muslim teacher and political activist Jamal al-Din al-Afghani, b. 1839, d. Mar. 9, 1897, sought to promote Pan-Islamism as a force to combat European domination of the Muslim world. Advocating a liberal theology and democratic socialism, he gathered a group of followers in Cairo but was deported in 1879. In Paris (1883–86) he coedited a Pan-Islamic journal with his disciple Muhammad 'Abduh. After a period of travel he returned to Persia in 1889, but his attempts to achieve legal and social reform brought him into conflict with the shah, Nasir al-Din. He ended his career in Istanbul, from where he was accused of instigating the assassination (1896) of Nasir al-Din.

James, Saint (the "brother" of Jesus Christ)   In the Bible James is listed first among the "brothers of Jesus," a relationship often posited as that of stepbrothers or cousins, but was not a follower of Jesus during his early ministry (Matt. 3:31–35, 12:36–50; John 7:5). He became a believer after the resurrected Christ appeared to him (1 Cor. 15:7), and was regarded as an apostle (Gal. 1:19). Later he became a leader in the Jerusalem church (Gal. 1:19, 2:9; Acts 15:13–29), and tradition describes him as Jerusalem's first bishop. Roman Catholic tradition identifies him with Saint James the Lesser, and he is possibly the author of the Epistle of James. According to the historian Josephus, James was stoned to death in AD 62.

James, Saint (James the Great) Together with his brother Saint JOHN, Saint James was among the first disciples called by Jesus (Matt. 4:21). These sons of Zebedee, called the Boanerges ("Sons of Thunder"), joined the brothers PETER and ANDREW, also fishermen by trade, in a close inner circle around Jesus. James, Peter, and John were the only disciples present, for example, at the TRANSFIGURATION (Luke 9) and near Jesus in the Garden of Gethsemane. James was martyred under Herod Agrippa I (Acts 12). According to legend, his bones were taken to Spain, and his shrine at Santiago de Compostela was one of the most important pilgrimage centers in the Middle Ages. Feast day: Apr. 30 (Eastern); July 25 (Western).

James, Saint (James the Lesser) Saint James the Lesser was the Apostle James, son of Alphaeus and disciple of Jesus (Mark 3:18). His mother, Mary, was one of the women at the crucifixion and at the tomb (Matt. 10:3, 27:56; Mark 15:40, 16:1; Acts 1:13). This James is sometimes identified with James the "brother of Jesus," although this and other identifications are unproven. Feast day: Oct. 9 (Eastern); May 3 (Western, since 1969).

James, Epistle of The Epistle of James, the first of the general letters (Catholic epistles) of the New Testament of the BIBLE, is an exhortation to Christian patience and obedience. The book, more a sermon than a letter, uses 54 imperatives in 108 verses to call its readers to responsible living that accords with what they profess. Traditionally, JAMES, "the Lord's brother," has been accepted as the author, which would date the book between AD 45 and 50 and would account for its primitive Christology.

Although accepted by the church from the 2d century, James was reluctantly admitted into the Protestant New Testament canon. Martin Luther rejected the book as "a right strawy epistle," because he thought that James contradicted Saint Paul's view of justification by faith alone. Paul, however, was emphasizing the inappropriateness of works for salvation, whereas James spoke of works that issue from faith. For both, the essentials are the same, and both were probably dealing independently with a traditional topic of Jewish belief.

James, Henry An influential force in the development of literary realism, the American novelist, short-story writer, travel essayist, and critic Henry James, b. New York City, Apr. 15, 1843, d. London, Feb. 28, 1916, enjoyed a long, productive career during which he achieved international stature. He wrote 22 novels, 113 tales, 15 plays, the equivalent of 10 books of criticism, 7 travel books, 3 autobiographical volumes, and 2 biographies. Approximately 15,000 of his letters are extant.

James's parents—Henry James, Sr., a rich, eccentric philosopher, and Mary Walsh James, loving and practical—had four other children, including psychologist-philosopher William JAMES. By 1861 young Henry had crossed the Atlantic Ocean six times with his purposely rootless parents; lived in France, England, Switzerland, Germany, and New England; and studied literature and languages, including French, which he spoke flawlessly. James stayed out of the Civil War because of a back injury and soon became a celibate, detached observer of the international social scene.

James's long apprenticeship may be dated from 1864 to 1875. At the age of 21 he published his first works, an anonymous short story and an unsigned book review. He wrote more reviews and easily found magazine outlets for his early short fiction. In 1869 he took his first European trip as an adult, going from England to Switzerland and then to Italy, which ultimately became his favorite country. In 1872, James escorted an aunt and a sister to Europe but stayed on alone, writing and roaming for two years. A winter in New York was productive but mainly helped him decide to live permanently abroad. After publishing his first two books (short stories and travel essays, both 1875) and completing his first mature novel (*Roderick Hudson*, 1876), he set sail for Paris.

From this time through 1881, James was highly popular. In Paris he met Ivan Turgenev, Gustave Flaubert, Guy de Maupassant, and Émile Zola. During this phase of his career James wrote *The American* (1877), about a man whose Yankee dollars fail to buy him admission to French society. Feeling unwelcome in Paris, James moved (1876) to London, where he soon met Alfred Lord Tennyson, Robert Browning, George Eliot, William Morris, and Leslie Stephen. He gained notoriety with his short novel *Daisy Miller* (1878), about an innocent, socially naive American girl destroyed by European mores. He also published (1879) the first book-length treatment of

The American writer Henry James, one of the most influential figures in the development of the modern novel, appears here in a portrait by John Singer Sargent.

Nathaniel Hawthorne and began his first masterpiece, *The Portrait of a Lady* (1881).

Between 1882 and 1895, James published several experimental short stories and three long novels but was unsuccessful in his attempts to write popular drama. The tales include "The Liar," "The Lesson of the Master," "The Pupil," "The Real Thing," and "The Middle Years." The novels, all political in subject, are *The Bostonians* (1886), about the feminist movement in post–Civil War New England; *The Princess Casamassima* (1886), featuring international anarchists in and out of London; and *The Tragic Muse* (1890), which contrasts art (painting and acting) with politics (including diplomacy). When these books failed commercially James tried to conquer the London stage, but his most ambitious play, *Guy Domville* (1895), was also a failure.

From 1896 until World War I, when the Anglo-French cultural community he revered was shattered, James was extremely active. He bought an 18th-century house south of London and wrote and entertained there. He produced streams of fiction, a two-volume biography (1903) of the American expatriate sculptor William Wetmore Story, autobiographical material, and *The American Scene* (1907). His short fiction of the period includes *The Turn of the Screw* (1898), "The Beast in the Jungle" (possibly James's finest tale), "The Birthplace," and "The Jolly Corner."

Three long novels of this major phase of his career would alone ensure the author's fame. *The Wings of the Dove* (1902) contrasts a rich young American with European fortune hunters who are ultimately shamed by the dying heroine's charity. *The Ambassadors* (1903), which James called "the best, 'all round,' of my productions," describes the initiation of an aging American into the relativistic ethics of the Old World in "huge iridescent" Paris. *The Golden Bowl* (1904) verbosely analyzes father-daughter and adulterous relations, all symbolized by the glittering, flawed bowl.

James next revised about half of his fiction for a sumptuous edition (1907–09), complete with 18 profound critical prefaces. *The American Scene* (1907), reflecting his first visit to the United States since the death of his parents in 1882, is one of the subtlest travel books ever written.

James, Jesse   Jesse James, b. Clay County, Mo., Sept. 5, 1847, d. Apr. 3, 1882, one of the most famous outlaws of the American West, acquired a Robin Hood reputation among the people of his region. At the age of 15, during the Civil War, he joined a band of pro-Confederate guerrillas led by William C. Quantrill. After the war he formed a gang with his brother, Frank, and several other men. They held up banks, stagecoaches, and trains until 1876, when the gang was decimated trying to rob a bank in Northfield, Minn. The two brothers escaped and formed a new gang. Jesse was shot and killed by a fellow gang member for a reward. Frank later surrendered; he was tried and acquitted twice.

James, P. D.   P. D. James is the pen name of Phyllis Dorothy James White, b. Aug. 3, 1920, an English civil servant and detective novelist. Her books, many featuring Adam Dalgliesh of the C. I. D. (Criminal Investigation Department of Scotland Yard), have won consistently high praise. In such novels as *Cover Her Face* (1962), *Shroud for a Nightingale* (1971), and *Death of an Expert Witness* (1977), James uses medical backgrounds and seems as concerned with the spiritual condition of her characters as with their guilt or innocence. Later novels include the dark-toned *Innocent Blood* (1980), *The Skull beneath the Skin* (1982)—featuring female detective Cordelia Gray—*A Taste for Death* (1986), and *Devices and Desires* (1989).

James, Thomas   Thomas James, *c*.1593–*c*.1635, was an English navigator whose account of his journey in search of the NORTHWEST PASSAGE probably inspired Samuel Taylor Coleridge's poem The RIME OF THE ANCIENT MARINER. Sailing on the *Henrietta Maria*, James set out from Bristol in May 1631 and returned in October 1632 after visiting Greenland and the southern extension of Hudson Bay (named James Bay in his honor). His *Strange and Dangerous Voyage* was published in 1633.

James, William   The American philosopher and psychologist William James, b. New York City, Jan. 11, 1842, d. Aug. 26, 1910, was one of the founders and leading proponents of PRAGMATISM. He was the brother of novelist Henry JAMES. At Harvard College he was a member of "The Metaphysical Club," an informal group that met to discuss philosophy and included Charles PEIRCE, Oliver Wendell HOLMES, Jr., and Chaunsey Wright, all of whom were to become well known in the pragmatist movement.

In his famous work *The Principles of Psychology* (1890), James developed the view, in opposition to the more traditional ASSOCIATIONISM, that consciousness functions in an active, purposeful way to relate and organize thoughts, giving them a streamlike continuity.

In the history of psychology, James's theory of mind is called functionalism. James had established an international reputation in psychology before his main focus turned to philosophy, and many of his philosophical views have their roots in his psychological studies.

James considered pragmatism to be both a method for analyzing philosophic problems and a theory of truth. He also saw it as an extension of the empiricist attitude (see EMPIRICISM) in that it turned away from abstract theory and fixed or absolute principles and toward concrete facts, actions, and relative principles.

James considered philosophies to be expressions of personal temperament and developed a correlation between "tough-minded" and "tender-minded" temperaments and empiricist and rationalist positions in philosophy. Theories, he felt, are "instruments" that humans

William James, a leading American philosopher and psychologist and the brother of novelist Henry James, established pragmatism as an influential American philosophy.

use to solve problems and should be judged in terms of their "cash value" or practical consequences for human conduct.

He developed the notion of truth as a "leading" that is useful: it can change as human experience changes. The morality, as well as the truth, of an idea or action should be judged, according to James, in a similar way—in terms of its outcome in human experience.

In *The Will to Believe* (1897) and *The Varieties of Religious Experience* (1902), James examined the problem of belief in cases in which no immediate evidence exists on which to base one's belief. He concluded that in the area of religious commitment, belief can create its own truth through the effects created in the experience of the believer by his "willing nature." Belief in God is thus pragmatically justified if it makes a positive difference in the experience of the believer.

In *A Pluralistic Universe* (1909) and *Essays in Radical Empiricism* (1912), James developed his metaphysical position: there is no fixed external world to be discovered by one's mind but instead a "humming-buzzing confusion" that one organizes through experience. The universe, as well as one's knowledge of it, is continuously evolving.

James Bay   James Bay is the southern extension of HUDSON BAY situated between the provinces of Quebec and Ontario, Canada. The shallow bay is 445 km (275 mi) long and 217 km (135 mi) wide. Numerous rivers (including the La Grande, Moose, Nottaway, Albany, and Attawapiskat rivers) enter the bay. The largest of the many islands in the bay is Akimiski. Settlements include Fort George, Nouveau-Comptoir, Eastmain, and Fort-Rupert. The bay was discovered in 1610 by Henry Hudson and was named for Capt. Thomas James, who explored it in 1631.

James River   The James River is formed in west central Virginia by the confluence of the Jackson and Cow-pasture rivers. It zigzags eastward 547 km (340 mi) through the Blue Ridge Mountains and enters Chesapeake Bay through the 8-km-wide (5-mi) estuary of HAMPTON ROADS. The river is navigable by ocean vessels to Richmond, about 160 km (100 mi) upstream. In 1607, Jamestown Island in the lower river was the site of the first permanent English settlement in America.

James I, King of Aragon (James the Conqueror) James I, b. Feb. 2, 1208, d. July 27, 1276, ruled the Spanish kingdom of Aragon from 1213 and greatly expanded his dominions. After a turbulent minority, James, the son of Peter II (r. 1196–1213), undertook the conquest of the Muslim kingdom of Majorca in 1229. This campaign was the first stage in the extension of Aragonese power into the western Mediterranean. When he completed the conquest of the Muslim kingdom of Valencia in 1238, he had brought the kingdom of Aragon (Aragon, Catalonia, Valencia) to the limits it would retain in the peninsula for the rest of the Middle Ages. His son PETER III succeeded him to the Aragonese throne.

James II, King of Aragon   James II (called James the Just), b. 1264, d. Nov. 2, 1327, was king of Aragon (1291–1327) and king of Sicily (1285–95). His father, PETER III, seized Sicily from CHARLES I of Naples in 1282 during the revolt known as the SICILIAN VESPERS. After Peter's death (1285), James's older brother, Alfonso III, became king of Aragon, and James became king of Sicily. On Alfonso's death (1291), James became king of Aragon. He continued to rule Sicily until 1295, when he signed an agreement with Pope BONIFACE VIII and Charles II of Naples exchanging Sicily for Corsica and Sardinia, ending French claims in Aragon, and arranging a marriage with Charles's daughter Bianca.

James I, King of England   James I, b. June 19, 1566, d. Mar. 27, 1625, the only child of MARY, QUEEN OF SCOTS, was the first king to rule both England and Scotland, the latter as James VI. James was only 15 months old when he succeeded his mother to the Scottish throne. He received an excellent education from tutors, such as George BUCHANAN, and in 1583 began his personal rule of Scotland. Being eager to succeed the childless ELIZABETH I to the English throne, he merely protested when his mother was executed for treason against Elizabeth in 1587. James married Anne of Denmark, who bore him several children but annoyed him by becoming a Roman Catholic.

In 1603, James became the first STUART king of England, and he devoted himself almost entirely to English affairs thereafter. Although raised as a Presbyterian, he immediately antagonized the rising Puritan movement (see PURITANISM) by rejecting a petition for reform of the Church of England at the Hampton Court Conference (1604). Roman Catholic hostility, manifested in the at-

James I, the first Stuart king of England, offended his subjects by his arrogant disregard of Parliament, his policy of conciliation with Catholic Spain, and his excessive reliance on court favorites.

(Right) James II, the last Stuart king of England, succeeded his brother, Charles II, in 1685 despite efforts to exclude him from the throne for his openly Catholic faith. He so alienated his subjects that he was forced to flee the country in the bloodless Glorious Revolution of 1688.

tempt (1605) by Guy FAWKES to blow up both king and Parliament, did not dissolve the English suspicion that James was pro-Catholic because he had concluded peace with Spain in 1604.

Initially guided by Robert Cecil, 1st earl of SALISBURY, an able chief minister, James subsequently allowed his court favorites—first Robert Carr, earl of Somerset, and later George Villiers, 1st duke of BUCKINGHAM—effective control. These ministers complicated James's stormy relations with Parliament. That body's conception of its rights, especially in financial matters, clashed with the king's view of the royal prerogative.

Confident in his own wisdom and experience, James avoided hard work, preferring to hunt. He was fortunate in having the services of Lionel Cranfield, earl of Middlesex, a former merchant, who looked after the royal finances until he was impeached (1624) for corruption at the behest of Buckingham. Parliament also impeached (1621) another able minister, Francis BACON, and blocked James in his attempts to arrange a formal Anglo-Scottish union and to exchange his rights to feudal dues for a permanent grant of revenue from Parliament.

James wrote books about kingship, theology, witchcraft, and tobacco and commissioned the Authorized (King James) Version of the Bible. Before his death he warned his son and heir, CHARLES I, of future dangers to the monarchy from Parliament.

James II, King of England   James II, b. Oct. 4, 1633, d. Sept. 5, 1701, the second son of CHARLES I, reigned as king of England, Scotland, and Ireland from 1685 to 1688, when he was overthrown by the GLORIOUS REVOLUTION. In Scotland he was known as James VII.

James, a Stuart (see STUART family), was in exile from 1648 in the aftermath of the ENGLISH CIVIL WAR. After his brother, CHARLES II, was restored to the throne in 1660, James fought bravely as lord high admiral in the ANGLO-DUTCH WARS. James's conversion (about 1671) to Roman Catholicism caused the House of Commons to attempt, unsuccessfully, to exclude him from the throne. He suc-

ceeded Charles unopposed, however, on Feb. 6, 1685.

In 1687 and 1688, James issued two declarations of indulgence, which alienated the Church of England. He also evaded the TEST ACT of 1673 by promoting Catholics to high office and military commissions. In 1688 he put seven bishops on trial for refusing to order his declarations to be read in all the churches, but the bishops were acquitted. All of these actions contributed to his overthrow, which was precipitated by the birth of his son in June 1688. The prospect of a Catholic succession led the Protestant opposition to invite James's Dutch Protestant nephew and son-in-law, William of Orange, to come to England. He assumed the crown as WILLIAM III, and his wife, James's older daughter, became MARY II.

Although James's opponents saw him as a tyrant, acting as a tool of the expansionist Catholic LOUIS XIV of France, it was not tyranny but stupidity and cowardice that brought his downfall. In 1689 he assembled an Irish-French army in an attempt to restore himself, but in 1690 his army was defeated by William at the Battle of the Boyne in Ireland. James spent his last years in France, hoping that his renunciation of the throne would merit him eternal salvation.

James I, King of Scotland   James I, b. July 1394, d. Feb. 20, 1437, became titular king of Scotland in 1406. His father, Robert III, shortly before his death (1406), had sent James to France for safety, but the young prince was captured en route by the English, who detained him until 1424. During James's absence Scotland was governed by his uncle, Robert Stuart, 1st duke of Albany (d. 1420), and later by Albany's son, Murdoch. In his last year of captivity James married Joan Beaufort, a cousin of Henry V of England.

After James's return (1424) to Scotland, he quickly subdued the powerful nobility, executing many, including Murdoch (1425). He also reorganized Scotland's financial administration and improved the judicial system. James's assassination at Perth was apparently instigated by rival claimants to the throne, but he was succeeded by his son James II. James I is generally considered the author of *The Kingis Quair* ("The King's Book"; rev. ed. by John Norton-Smith, 1971), a long poem about his captivity and about his romance with Joan.

James IV, King of Scotland

James IV, b. Mar. 17, 1473, d. Sept. 9, 1513, one of the most energetic of Scotland's Stuart monarchs, personified the ideal of the Renaissance king. A patron of the arts and education, he encouraged alchemy, architecture, and printing. James, who succeeded his father, James III, in 1488, raised Scotland's status in European politics.

Continuing Scotland's pro-French diplomacy, James, beginning in 1495, supported Perkin Warbeck's claims to the English throne. In 1497, however, Scotland and England signed a seven-year truce, which was strengthened in 1503 when James married Margaret Tudor, the daughter of HENRY VII of England. This union prepared the way for the ultimate succession of a Stuart to the English throne (see JAMES I, KING OF ENGLAND). In 1512, however, Scotland renewed its French alliance, and when HENRY VIII invaded France in 1513, James marched into northern England. He was killed in the Battle of Flodden and was succeeded by his son, James V.

James V, King of Scotland

James V, b. Apr. 10, 1512, d. Dec. 14, 1542, was the seventh Stuart king of Scotland (1513–42), the son of James IV. In 1514, James V's mother, Margaret Tudor, married Archibald Douglas, 6th earl of Angus (see DOUGLAS family). John Stuart, duke of Albany, became regent, and a power struggle ensued among factions controlled by Albany, Angus, and Margaret. For a time Angus, a leader of the pro-English faction, held James prisoner (1526–28).

When James reached his majority, he sided with Scotland's pro-French party against the English. On Jan. 1, 1537, he married Madeleine, the daughter of Francis I of France. She died the following July, and James married (1538) Mary of Guise (see GUISE family). His aggressive, vindictive policies lost him the support of the nobility, weakening his army and contributing to his defeat by the English at Solway Moss in 1542. Soon after this battle, he died at Falkland Palace, leaving a week-old daughter, MARY, QUEEN OF SCOTS, to succeed him.

James VI, King of Scotland   see JAMES I, KING OF ENGLAND

Jameson, Sir Leander Starr

Sir Leander Starr Jameson, b. Feb. 9, 1853, d. Nov. 26, 1917, a British colonial administrator in Africa, led a disastrous raid into the Boer Republic of the Transvaal in 1895. The Jameson Raid intensified the hostility between the Boers and British that led to the SOUTH AFRICAN WAR (1899–1902).

A physician, Jameson immigrated to South Africa in 1878, became a close friend of Cecil RHODES, and in 1891 assumed office as administrator of Mashonaland,

now part of Zimbabwe. On Dec. 29, 1895, Jameson led a raiding party into the Transvaal, hoping to overthrow the government of President Paul KRUGER. Although the raid was not approved by the British government, Rhodes was clearly implicated and forced to resign as prime minister of Cape Colony; British colonial secretary Joseph CHAMBERLAIN was cleared of charges of involvement, but he probably knew of the conspiracy. After a prison term in Britain, Jameson served as prime minister of the Cape Colony from 1904 to 1908.

Jamestown

Jamestown, the first permanent English settlement in North America, financed by the London Company, was situated on a marshy peninsula (now Jamestown Island) in the James River of Virginia. About 100 men, under the leadership of Capt. Christopher Newport, settled there on May 14, 1607. In the first seven months they were nearly wiped out by disease and famine, but Capt. John SMITH revived the settlement in 1608. After the severe winter of 1609–10 (the "starving time"), the settlement was saved by the arrival in June of the governor, Lord De La Warr, with supplies and more men.

In time, the settlers discovered that the land was suited to the cultivation of an important cash crop, tobacco. Unfortunately, though, they managed to turn the Indians of the POWHATAN Confederacy against them—despite the marriage (1614) of John ROLFE to POCAHONTAS, the daughter of Chief Powhatan. On Mar. 22, 1622, the Indians massacred 347 people. Charging mismanagement, the crown recalled the London Company's charter in 1624, and Jamestown, with the entire colony of Virginia, came under royal control.

A representative assembly, the House of Burgesses, had been established at Jamestown in 1619. The settlement was burned to the ground on Sept. 19, 1676, during BACON'S REBELLION, but Jamestown remained Virginia's capital until 1699.

Jamison, Judith

Judith Jamison, b. Philadelphia, May 10, 1944, is a dancer and choreographer who in 1989, following the death of Alvin AILEY, became director of his American Dance Theater. Primarily associated with Ailey's modern-dance company, she performed nearly exclusively with the troupe from 1965 until 1980, when she left for a two-year run on Broadway in *Sophisticated Ladies*. Her first choreographed work, *Divining* (1984), was for Ailey's company. In 1988 she created her own company, the Jamison Project, and planned to bring several of its dancers and some of the repertory to the Ailey company.

Jammu and Kashmir   see KASHMIR

Janáček, Leoš

[yahn'-ah-chek, lay'-ohsh] Leoš Janáček, b. July 3, 1854, d. Aug. 12, 1928, is generally considered the greatest Czech-Moravian composer since Antonín Dvořák and among the most original of the post-romantics. He was born in Moravia, the son of a school-master and organist. Trained as a choirboy, he was directing choirs by the age of 16. He studied composition in Prague (1875) and in Leipzig and Vienna (1879–80). From 1881 to 1919 he worked in Brno as a teacher and conductor, his compositions attracting little attention. He also studied Czech folk music and developed theories on projecting the rhythms and inflections of the Czech language in music.

Throughout his career Janáček composed numerous orchestral, chamber, piano, vocal, and choral works, culminating in his two surviving string quartets (1923, 1928); a wind sextet, *Mládí* (1924); a symphonic poem, *Taras Bulba* (1915–18); the spectacular *Sinfonietta* (1926); and the nationalistic *Glagolitic Mass* (1926). His vocal works, especially the operas, are perhaps Janáček's most original productions. The opera *Jenůfa* (1894–1903) is a compelling treatment of human character. A pair of one-act comedies, *Mr. Brouček's Excursions* (1908–17), was followed, after the dramatic song cycle *The Diary of One Who Vanished* (1917–19), by another masterpiece, *Kátya Kabanová* (1919–21). His last three operas were the whimsical *The Cunning Little Vixen* (1921–23), the gloomy *Makropulos Affair* (1923–25), and the grimly powerful *From the House of the Dead* (1927–28). Only in 1916, with the Prague production of *Jenůfa*, did Janáček at last win recognition from his fellow Czechs, including a professorship in Prague (1919–25). His reputation has grown steadily since his death, particularly through recordings of his works.

Jane Eyre see BRONTË (family)

Janissaries [jan'-i-sair-eez] The Janissaries, an elite infantry corps in the army of the OTTOMAN EMPIRE, was established by Sultan MURAD I in the late 14th century. The corps, made up of Christian slaves who were forced to convert to Islam, became the most powerful part of the army. The Janissaries were subject to severe discipline, could not marry, and had to reside in barracks. Starting in the 17th century, however, discipline and effectiveness declined. Members married, abandoned their training, and occupied most of their time as merchants and artisans. The corps continued to play an active role in politics, however, making and breaking sultans, extorting payments from town and country alike, and blocking reform efforts. Its members were massacred, and the corps was abolished by MAHMUD II in 1826.

Jannings, Emil [yahn'-ings] A distinguished German actor best known for the pathos he brought to his portrayals of defeated, broken men, Emil Jannings, originally named Theodor Friedrich Emil Janenz, was born in Brooklyn, N.Y., July 26, 1886, but grew up in Europe, where he died Jan. 2, 1950, his reputation tarnished because of his wartime cooperation with the Nazis. Jannings briefly enjoyed success at the end of the silent era in Hol-lywood, where he won an Academy Award (the first given) for his role in *The Way of All Flesh* (1927). His greatest parts were in such German-language films as F. W. Murnau's *The Last Laugh* (1924) and *Faust* (1926), E. A. Dupont's *Variety* (1925), and Josef von Sternberg's *Blue Angel* (1930), opposite Marlene Dietrich.

Jansenism [jan'-sen-izm] The theological position known as Jansenism was probably the single most divisive issue within the Roman Catholic church between the Protestant Reformation and the French Revolution. The doctrine took its name from the Flemish theologian and bishop of Ypres, Cornelius Jansen (1585–1638), who argued in favor of absolute PREDESTINATION, in which humans are perceived as incapable of doing good without God's unsolicited grace and only a chosen few are believed to receive salvation. As Jansenism was elaborated in France, especially by Jansen's friend Jean Duvergier de Hauranne, the Abbé de SAINT-CYRAN, and by the latter's protégé Antoine ARNAULD, it also entailed an austere form of piety and a rigorously puritanical morality. From the 1640s, the spiritual center of Jansenism became the convent of Port-Royal-des-Champs (near Paris), where numerous nobles, parlementarians, and intellectuals favorable to the movement made religious retreats.

Almost from the beginning, the Jansenists aroused the hostility both of the Jesuits, who opposed the theology and moral teachings of the group, and of the French royal government, who associated the Jansenists with the opposition. In 1713, under intense pressure from King Louis XIV, Pope CLEMENT XI issued the bull *Unigenitus* condemning 101 propositions in a treatise by the Jansenist Pasquier Quesnel (1634–1719). The French king closed Port-Royal-des-Champs in 1709 and had it razed to the ground in 1710.

During the 18th century, Jansenism acquired a much broader following among the lower French clergy and spread to other areas of Europe, notably Spain and Italy. The Jansenists increasingly allied themselves with the Gallicans in the French parlements in an effort to force the calling of an ecclesiastical council to reconsider the pope's condemnation (see GALLICANISM). The greatest triumph of the Jansenists came in the 1760s when the parlements forced the suppression of the Jesuits in France. Thereafter, however, the movement declined in importance.

Jansky, Karl [jan'-skee] The American radio engineer Karl Guthe Jansky, b. Norman, Okla., Oct. 22, 1905, d. Feb. 14, 1950, was the first to detect radio waves from an extraterrestrial source—a discovery that initiated the science of RADIO ASTRONOMY. After graduating with a degree in physics from the University of Wisconsin, he joined the staff of the Bell Telephone Laboratories in Holmdel, N.J., in 1928. Assigned to identify the sources of atmospheric static that interfered with ship-to-shore and transatlantic communication, Jansky built a linear directional antenna and with it detected (1931) a type of

JAPAN

Land: Area: 377,801 km^2 (145,870 mi^2). Capital and largest city: Tokyo (1988 est. pop., 8,155,781).

People: Population (1990 est.): 123,642,461. Density: 327.2 persons per km^2 (847.3 per mi^2). Distribution (1990): 77% urban, 23% rural. Official language: Japanese. Major religions: Buddhism, Shinto.

Government: Type: constitutional monarchy. Legislature: Diet. Political subdivisions: 47 prefectures.

Economy: GNP (1989): $2,920 billion; $23,730 per capita. Labor distribution (1990): commerce and services—55%; manufacturing—24%; construction—8%; agriculture—9%; government and public services—3%. Foreign trade (1989): imports—$210,847 million; exports—$275,175 million. Currency: 1 yen = 100 sen.

Education and Health: Literacy (1990): virtually100% of adult population. Universities (1990): more than 400. Hospital beds (1987): 1,582,000. Physicians (1987): 183,129. Life expectancy (1990): women—82; men—76. Infant mortality (1990): 5 per 1,000 live births.

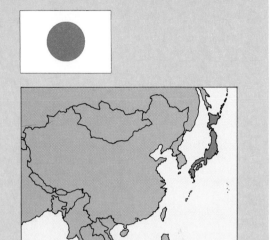

interference that moved around the sky each day. Jansky perceived that this third source was extraterrestrial and later determined that its direction was nearly identical with that of the center of the Galaxy in the constellation of Sagittarius.

Janus [jayn'-uhs]   In Roman mythology Janus was the doorkeeper of heaven and the god of beginnings and endings. He was originally a supreme deity and in later mythology was second only to Jupiter. His blessing was asked at the beginning of every day, month, and year, and the first month of the year, January (Latin, *Januarius*), was named for him. He also presided over the sowing of crops. Roman commanders departed to war through the doors of his temple in the Forum, which were closed only in time of peace.

Japan   Japan is one of the world's leading industrial and trading nations and the first Asian nation to develop a technologically advanced industrial economy. It is small compared with such nations as the United States but is larger than all major European nations except Sweden, France, and Spain.

Before World War II, Japan was the center of an empire that at times included Taiwan, Korea, Manchuria, much of eastern China, southern Sakhalin island, and the Marshall and Mariana islands. Today, following concessions of territory at the end of the war, Japan, greatly reduced in size, consists of four main islands and hundreds

of lesser islands that stretch in a series of arcs for nearly 3,000 km (1,875 mi) along the eastern edge of the Asian mainland. Japan's closest neighbor is the USSR (Sakhalin island). The nearest mainland neighbor is South Korea. To the southwest is Taiwan; and to the north, the mainland of the USSR. The name *Japan* is the romanized version of the Japanese name *Nihon* or *Nippon*, which means "land of the rising sun."

Land and Resources

Japan's four main islands, which together constitute 98% of the total area, are HOKKAIDO, in the north; HONSHU, the largest and most populous, located in the center; and the southern islands of KYUSHU and SHIKOKU. The two southern islands are separated from the main island of Honshu by the protected waters of the INLAND SEA, which has been Japan's core for over 2,000 years. Also integral parts of Japan are more than 3,000 islands and islets, including Iki and Tsushima, located in the narrow Korea Strait; Awaji, located in the Inland Sea between Shikoku and Honshu; and Sado, located off the northwest coast of Honshu. OKINAWA, one of the RYUKYU ISLANDS, an island chain located southwest of Kyushu, was administered by the United States after World War II but was restored to Japan in 1972. Located approximately 600 km (375 mi) away in the Pacific Ocean are the Marcus, Bonin, and Volcano (including IWO JIMA) island groups, which were placed under U.S. administration after World War II and were returned to Japan in 1968. Japan disputes the claim by the USSR to some of the KURIL ISLANDS, which stretch northeastward from Hokkaido, and also the claim

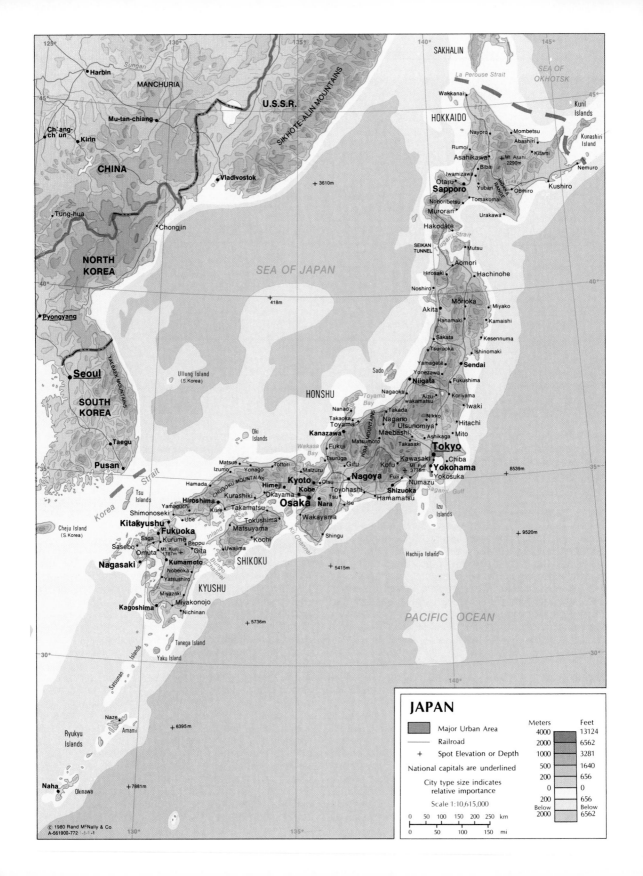

JAPAN

Harbin

MANCHURIA

U.S.S.R.

SIKHOTE-ALIN MOUNTAINS

SAKHALIN

La Perouse Strait

SEA OF
OKHOTSK

Wakkanai

Mu-tan-chiang

Ch'ang-
ch'un · Kirin

CHINA

Vladivostok

Tung-hua

Chongjin

NORTH
KOREA

Pyongyang

TAEBAEK MOUNTAINS

Seoul

SOUTH
KOREA

Taegu

Pusan

+ 3610m

Ullung Island
(S.Korea)

SEA OF JAPAN

+ 418m

Oki
Islands

HOKKAIDO

Nayoro
Rumoi
Asahikawa
Iwamizawa
Otaru
Sapporo
Noboribetsu
Muroran
Hakodate

SEIKAN
TUNNEL

Mombetsu
Abashiri
Kitami
Bibai
Mt Asahi
2290m
Yubari
Obihiro
Tomakomai
Urakawa

Kunashiri
Island

Nemuro

Kushiro

Tsugaru Strait

Mutsu

Hirosaki

Aomori

Hachinohe

Noshiro

Akita

Morioka
Hanamaki

Miyako

Kamaishi
Kesennuma

Sakata

Tsuruoka

Ishinomaki

HONSHU

Sado

Yamagata
Yonezawa
Nagaoka

Niigata

Toyama Bay

Nanao

Takaoka
Toyama

Takada

Nagano

Fukushima
Aizu-
wakamatsu
Koriyama

Iwaki

Nikko

Hitachi

Utsunomiya
Takasaki
Ashikaga

Mito

Maebashi

Takaoka

Kanazawa

Fukui

Matsumoto

Matsue
Izumo
Yonago

Tottori

Hamada

CHUGOKU MOUNTAINS

Himeji

Kyoto

Nagoya

Tokyo

Kawasaki

Chiba

Yokohama

Yokosuka

Kofu
Mt Fuji
3776m
Fuji

Numazu

Shizuoka

Hamamatsu

Izu
Islands

+ 8539m

Tsuruga

Gifu

Otsu

Kobe

Nara

Tsu

Ise

Osaka

Wakayama

+ 9520m

Matsuyama

Kochi

SHIKOKU

Shingu

Kii Channel

Hachijo Island

Okayama

Kurashiki

Takamatsu

Tokushima

Hiroshima

Kure

Yamaguchi

Shimonoseki

Kitakyushu

Fukuoka

Saga
Kurume

Omuta

Mt Kuju
1787m +

Beppu
Oita

Uwajima

Sasebo

Nagasaki

Kumamoto

Nobeoka
Yatsushiro

Miyazaki

KYUSHU

Miyakonojo

Nichinan

Kagoshima

Tsu
Islands

Korea Strait

Cheju Island
(S.Korea)

Ube

Inland Sea

Uwa

Bungo Channel

+ 5415m

+ 5736m

PACIFIC OCEAN

Tanega Island

Yaku Island

Satsunan Islands

Ryukyu
Islands

Naze

Amami

+ 6395m

+ 7881m

Naha

Okinawa

© 1980 Rand McNally & Co.
A-561900-772 -1-1-1

	Major Urban Area
	Railroad
+	Spot Elevation or Depth

National capitals are underlined

City type size indicates
relative importance

Scale 1:10,615,000

0 50 100 150 200 250 km

0   50   100   150 mi

Meters	Feet
4000	13124
2000	6562
1000	3281
500	1640
200	656
0	0
200 Below 2000	656 Below 6562

by Taiwan to the uninhabited Senkaku Islands located 344 km (213 mi) southwest of Okinawa.

Japan's islands constitute part of the Circum-Pacific Ring—a tectonically unstable zone of volcanic activity and continuing mountain building that rims the Pacific Ocean. The islands that constitute Japan are actually the peaks of otherwise submerged mountain ranges. About 50 active volcanoes are known in Japan; every year about 1,500 minor earthquakes occur; and hot springs and other features of crustal instability are found. The most famous volcanic area is the Fuji-Hakone-Izu area, located near Tokyo. It is dominated by Mount FUJI, a dormant volcano and Japan's highest mountain, rising to 3,776 m (12,388 ft).

About 75% of Japan's land is mountainous and too steep for easy cultivation and settlement. The principal mountain ranges follow fault lines of great geologic complexity. Where two or more of these arcs intersect are knots of rugged mountains. One such node occurs in central Hokkaido (the Hokkaido Node), where the north-south arc from Sakhalin intersects a northeast-southwest-trending arc that forms the Kuril Islands. A second mountain node (the Chubu Node) occurs in central Honshu and west of this is an east-west arc broken into two parallel faults between which the Inland Sea is located. The northern fault passes through western Honshu, and the southern fault is traceable through the Kii Peninsula of Honshu, the island of Shikoku and into Kyushu. A third (Kyushu) node is located in north-central Kyushu, from which run the Ryukyu Archipelago to the southwest and the aforementioned arcs to the northeast. Faults also line the sides of the Fossa Magna, a great rift valley that cuts across the core of the Chubu Node from northwest to southeast. To the north of the rift valley are the rugged Japan Alps, where several peaks rise to more than 3,050 m (10,000 ft).

Lowlands constitute only about 16% of the islands and are generally small, discontinuous, and found mostly in coastal areas. The largest is the Kanto Plain, where Tokyo and surrounding cities are located.

Soils. The most productive soils are developed on alluvium that has accumulated to considerable depths in all of the lowlands. For nearly 2,000 years these coastal soils have been carefully managed and enriched. The soils in the rest of Japan, as in many mountain areas, tend to be thin.

Climate. Japan has a range of climates typical of middle latitudes and similar to that of the east coast of most of North America. Hokkaido and the interior of northeastern Honshu have a humid continental climate, characterized by short, cool summers and long, cold, and often snowy winters. Summers become warmer and longer, and winters become shorter and milder toward the south, where subtropical conditions prevail. Demonstrating this latitudinal change in climate, Sapporo, on Hokkaido, has a January mean temperature of –6° C (21° F) and a July temperature of only 19° C (67° F); and Nagasaki, in the southwest, averages 6° C (42° F) in January and 26° C (79° F) in July.

Wind and rainfall patterns are primarily influenced by the monsoon system typical of East Asia. Coasts facing the Pacific receive the most precipitation from mid-June to mid-July, while the northeast coast receives heavy winter precipitation from the northwest monsoon, much of it in the form of snow. Average annual precipitation for most of Japan is 1,270 mm (50 in), with some mountain areas receiving up to 2,540 mm (100 in). The Inland Sea area is somewhat drier because it is protected by surrounding mountain chains.

Japan's climate is also strongly influenced by two ocean currents and occasional storms and typhoons. The Japan Current (or Kuro Shio), a warm ocean current, flows northward through the islands; its warm waters moderate winter temperatures along the entire southern coast. By contrast, the cold Okhotsk Current originates in polar waters and flows southward along Hokkaido, contributing to the harsh climate of that island. Typhoons occur from late August to early October.

Drainage. Japan's rivers are short, swift, and shallow. Only 10 are more than 200 km (125 mi) long; thus navigation is limited to short stretches, usually near the sea. Drainage is mostly toward the Pacific and Inland Sea coastal regions.

Vegetation and Animal Life. Forests cover about 70% of the total land area and more than 60% of each of the four main islands. Conifers, including fir, spruce, and larch, predominate on Hokkaido and the mountainous interior of northern Honshu. Mixed forest, with conifers such as cy-

The snowcapped cone of Mount Fuji, which rises to an elevation of 3,776 m (12,388 ft), is the highest point in Japan. The peak is considered sacred and is a traditional goal for Buddhist pilgrims.

Residents are frequently seen in Western clothing throughout Tokyo. Increased contact with the West has resulted in the adoption of many Western practices; however, traditional values are still an integral part of Japanese culture.

press and hemlock and deciduous trees including oak, maple, birch, and ash, predominate in the warmer parts of Honshu. Subtropical evergreen vegetation predominates in the southwest and warmer parts of Kyushu and Shikoku. Natural vegetation is also widely interspersed with exotics (introduced species) including bamboo, giant *cryptomeria*, and camphor. Reforested areas account for one-third of the total wooded area.

The most common large animals are deer, bears, and boars. Native monkeys are widely found, as are many introduced smaller animals. Reptiles include snakes and lizards. The bird population includes the crown eagle, other birds of prey, and more than 400 additional species.

Resources. Japan produces a wide range of metallic minerals, including chromite, zinc, manganese, copper, lead, molybdenum, and gold. Extensive deposits of low-grade coal are located on northwestern Kyushu and western Hokkaido. Domestic production accounts for only 0.3% of total petroleum consumption. Hydroelectric power resources are abundant. Nonmetallic minerals include clay and gypsum.

People

The dominant ethnic group is the Japanese, a Mongoloid people. The Japanese have developed a culture that was strongly influenced between the 3d and 10th century by contact with the Chinese and Koreans, contact with the West during the 16th century, isolation during the Tokugawa period (1603–1868), and renewed contact with the West and the rest of the world after 1854.

The largest minority group is the approximately 600,000 Koreans, who began settling in Japan mostly during the 1920s and have retained their language and culture. A smaller minority is the Ainu, a remnant of an indigenous people who live mostly in Hokkaido. The *Buramkumin* (or *Eta*) are ethnically Japanese but are often considered a separate group because they are descended from an ancient order of social outcasts; although they were given legal parity in 1868, they are often discriminated against, work in low-paying positions if their origins are known, and live in segregated communities. Okinawans, or inhabitants of the Ryukyu Islands, consider themselves Japanese, but they have some unique cultural elements, including language.

Spoken Japanese was long considered a unique language but is now known to bear a strong association with Korean. Written Japanese is complex, being derived from Chinese with the addition of parallel *Kana* (sets of phonetic syllabaries of 48 characters each) used to supplement Chinese characters or to bridge the gap between the two languages. The Kanto dialect, spoken in the Tokyo area, is considered standard spoken Japanese. (See JAPANESE LANGUAGE.)

BUDDHISM, introduced from China during the 6th century, is followed by about 75% of the population. SHINTO, the ancient Japanese and former state religion, is a parallel faith for most Japanese Buddhists. CONFUCIANISM, introduced during the 4th century, is also influential. About 1% of the population are officially listed as Christians.

Demography. About 80% of the total population live on Honshu, 12% on Kyushu, 5% on Hokkaido, and 3% on Shikoku. The population is predominantly urban. The largest urban concentration is the Tokaido megalopolis. This urban core on Honshu is an almost continuously inhabited and built-up area along the Pacific corridor from Tokyo in the east to Kobe in the west, with extensions growing westward onto northern Kyushu and along the shores of the Inland Sea and to the east of Tokyo. Only 11 of Japan's 47 prefectures (the largest unit of government below the national level) are located in the urban core, but 45% of the total population live in the region. Japan's 6 largest cities—in order of population TOKYO, YOKOHAMA, OSAKA, NAGOYA, KYOTO, and SAPPORO—dominate the area. Other large cities include KOBE and KAWASAKI, on Honshu; and FUKUOKA and KITAKYUSHU, on Kyushu. All of these cities have more than 1 million inhabitants. Most urban growth has occurred since the 1920s, but many cities have existed since the early years of the Tokugawa period. Edo (modern Tokyo), the seat of government under the Tokugawa dynasty, had approximately 1 million inhabitants in 1721.

Japan's population is now more than four times what it was in 1868 (30 million) and more than twice as large as in 1920 (56 million). Since about 1952, however, the growth rate has slowed dramatically; the current rate is one of the lowest in Asia and similar to rates in other economically developed nations. As a result, the average age of the population is increasing rapidly.

Japan has one of the highest overall population densities in the world. Almost the entire population crowded onto the 16% of land that is level enough for cultivation and settlement. As a result congestion of living space, highways, railways, and industrial and agricultural space is a characteristic feature of Japanese life. The supply of adequate housing falls far short of demand, despite prodigious building programs by government and industry. Alleviating environmental pollution resulting from such concentrated development is a source of concern for the Japanese.

Education and Health. Virtually the entire population is literate, and education is free and compulsory for all children between the ages of 6 and 15. Education after the age of 15 is a matter of choice, but more than 90% of all students, male and female, continue to high school, and about one-third of all students attend an institution of higher education. Universities in Japan were established as early as the 8th century. Today the higher-education system includes more than 450 universities and graduate schools and more than 400 junior colleges and technical schools. Nearly three-fourths of Japan's top civil servants are graduates of the University of Tokyo, founded in 1877. Although higher education has been transformed since 1950 from an elitist system to one that enables young people from diverse social backgrounds to consider further education, the competition to enter the University of Tokyo and other prestigious universities is so severe that a large number of *juki* (extra-hour schools) operate to prepare students for the entrance examination.

Medical facilities and training are highly developed in urban areas but are often limited elsewhere. Life expectancy is among the highest in the world, and infant mortality rates have declined dramatically since the 1930s, when they were about 124 per 1,000 live births.

The Arts. During the 6th century, when Buddhism was adopted from China, Japanese literature, architecture, painting, sculpture, theater, and other art forms were greatly influenced by contact with that culture. The Chinese impact remained strong, except perhaps in literature, until the end of the 16th century. During the isolated Tokugawa period, distinctly Japanese art forms developed, including the UKIYO-E (wood block print), KABUKI and other theater, and unique forms of architecture and exquisite landscape design. In later years, as art forms from many cultures including the West were adopted, an unmistakably Japanese touch was added to the imports. The rich artistic heritage of Japan's past continues to be reflected in modern machine-made ceramics and textiles and in the continuation of such ancient practices as the tea ceremony and Japanese flower-arranging. (See JAPANESE ART AND ARCHITECTURE; JAPANESE LITERATURE; JAPANESE MUSIC.)

Economic Activity

From the 13th to the 16th century the Japanese became known as skillful navigators, traders, and pirates. In the 15th and 16th centuries, the Japanese conducted lively trade with Asia and the West. Foreign trade was halted during the Tokugawa period, but small Japanese industries continued to produce clothing, utensils, food products, guns, and other military hardware for the domestic market. At the same time, progress was made in the organization of a national system of marketing, management, trade, and finance. Thus, when seclusion ended, Japan already possessed the infrastructure on which to build a modern system of industry, banking, and commerce.

Textiles became the leading industry during the Tokugawa era, with some other light industries. Heavy industry was slow to develop because of the lack of adequate iron ore and coking coal but was stimulated by Japan's involvement in a series of wars beginning with the Sino-Japanese War of 1894–95 and culminating in World War II. After the defeat of Japan in World War II, the economy was directed away from military needs. Japan overcame its deficiency of industrial raw materials to create one of the world's most productive modern economic systems. Despite industrial modernization, traditional industries have continued as family enterprises.

Manufacturing. Industry expanded rapidly after the 1950s, with a heavy emphasis on export items, and now

Graceful horizontal lines impart an air of serenity to these Buddhist temples in Kyoto. The capital of Japan from 794 until 1868, Kyoto is still one of the country's most important cultural and religious centers.

employs about 25% of the labor force. Industry is concentrated in Japan's urban core, from Tokyo in the east through the coastal areas along the Inland Sea in the west to northern Kyushu. Japan ranks high as a world producer of manufactured goods and commands a large share of the world market for ships; iron and steel; automobiles, bicycles, mopeds, and other transportation equipment; machinery; chemicals; ceramics; cameras, precision goods, and optical equipment; and televisions, radios, and other electronic items. Much of manufacturing is concentrated in the hands of a relatively small number of large diversified concerns—including the giant Mitsubishi, Mitsui, Sumitomo, Toyota, and Nissan groups.

Power. In 1989, 700 billion kW h of electricity were produced in Japan. Imported petroleum, natural gas, and coal, most of which is also imported, account for 85% of all electricity generated. Waterpower accounts for 5% and nuclear plants for 10%.

Agriculture. Most Japanese farms consist of a number of small and scattered fields that add up to an average size of less than 1.2 ha (3 acres); many are so small that they are run on a part-time basis by women and children, while men commute to other jobs in nearby urban areas. Three crops a year are possible on lands in the warmer areas of Kyushu, Shikoku, and southwestern Honshu; two crops on most of southern Honshu; and only one on northern Honshu and Hokkaido. Irrigation, terracing, fertilizers, and other intensive cultivation methods are widely employed, giving Japan some of the highest crop yields per cultivated area in the world. Rice, whose production is subsidized by the government, is the chief summer crop. Animal husbandry is of minor importance, and little land is used as pasture. Chief commercial crops are mulberry bushes—the leaves are fed to silkworms—and tea, both grown in upland areas. The silkworm-raising industry has declined due to competition from synthetic textiles. Computer-monitored hydroponic farming of vegetables and fruit has become large scale.

Forestry and Fishing. Only about one-fourth of Japan's forest cover is accessible for cutting, and Japan currently imports more than one-half of its wood, much of it from Indonesia, India, and the Philippines. Since the 1950s fishing has become a large-scale industry, and Japanese fishing fleets now operate in all the world's oceans. Japan leads the world in total quantity of fish caught and in 1987 landed 12.5 million metric tons (13.8 million U.S. tons) of fish—one-eighth of the world's total fish catch.

Transportation. Railroads link all of Japan's major cities and the four main islands; most are publicly owned and operated. A 1,069-km-long (664-mi) high-speed rail line, with trains able to travel at 249 km/h (155 mph), links Tokyo with other cities in the urban core, including Yokohama, Nagoya, Kyoto, Osaka, Okayama, and Hiroshima. Despite major new construction, the railroads are continuing to lose traffic; a highway culture threatens to dominate the future landscape of the nation.

Japan Air Lines, partially government operated, is the principal airline, and international airports are located at Tokyo, Osaka, and Narita. Japan's merchant fleet is the second largest in the world (after Liberia) and includes the world's second largest fleet of oil tankers and ore carriers. Yokohama, Kobe, and Nagasaki are the leading ports.

Trade. Trade is central to the Japanese economy because of the scarcity of agricultural land and of industrial raw materials and fuel. Japan accounts for about 6.6% of all world imports by value and for 8% of all world exports. The principal imports are metal ores, petroleum, coal, chemicals, machine equipment, and food. Exports include machinery, textiles, iron and steel, optical instruments, automobiles, and electronic items. The export trade has become so successful that balance-of-payments problems have arisen with trading partners with competitive industries. This situation is especially true of the United States, Japan's single largest trading partner, which in 1988 imported 213% more by value from Japan than it exported. Other leading trade areas are East Asia (especially South Korea, Taiwan, and China), which provides more than 16% of all Japanese imports and absorbs about 20% of the exports; Western Europe, which provides about 18% of the imports and takes 23% of Japan's exports; Saudi Arabia; Australia; Canada; and Indonesia.

Government

Japan is a constitutional monarchy, with a hereditary emperor and a parliamentary system of government. The present constitution was adopted on Oct. 7, 1946, and became effective on May 3, 1947. The emperor is ceremonial head of state with little governmental power; Emperor HIROHITO reigned from 1926 until his death in 1989; he was succeeded by his son AKIHITO. Legislative power is vested in the Diet, a bicameral body composed of a House of Representatives, with 512 members elected to 4-year terms, and a House of Councillors, whose 252 members serve 6-year terms. Executive power rests with the cabinet, which is headed by a prime minister, who heads the majority party in the Diet. Since 1955 the majority political party has been the Liberal-Democratic party (LDP), a generally conservative organization with strong agrarian roots. In July 1989, after scandals and unpopular LDP policies on agriculture and tax reform threatened the party's dominance, the LDP lost its majority in the upper house of the Diet—the first time it had not controlled both houses since 1955. KAIFU TOSHIKI, who became prime minister in August, sought to restore the LDP's reputation. In February 1990 elections for the lower house of the Diet, the LDP made a strong showing, capturing 275 of 512 seats. The principal opposition party, the Socialist party, captured 136 seats.

Judicial powers rest with the supreme court, consisting of a chief justice and 14 other justices who are appointed by the government but who are subject to review in public referendums. Local government is by the 47 prefectures, each with its own elected governor and assembly. All citizens over the age of 20 are eligible to vote.

Japan, history of Although the date of the first human habitation of the Japanese archipelago is not known, anthropologists have identified one of the earliest cul-

(Above) Burning of the Sanjo Palace, *an illustration from the 13th-century saga* Heiji Monogatari *(Tales of Heiji), portrays a decisive event during the Heiji Wars (1159) (Museum of Fine Arts, Boston.)*
(Left) *Minamoto Yoritomo, depicted in this 12th-century portrait, conquered the Taira in 1185 and established the Kamakura shogunate (Jingoji, Kyoto.)*

tures in Japan as the Jomon culture, which dates from about 8000 BC. A hunting and gathering culture, it used stone and bone tools and made pottery of distinctive design. In the 3d century BC, Jomon culture was disrupted by a new people, known as Yayoi, who probably emigrated from continental Asia. They introduced rice cultivation, primitive weaving, wheel-made pottery, domesticated horses and cows, and simple iron tools. Yayoi culture overlaid and fused with the earlier Jomon culture.

Early Historical Period

The earliest written Japanese histories, the *Kojiki* (Record of Ancient Matters, 712) and the *Nihon shoki* (Chronicles of Japan, 720), include legends about the origins of the Japanese and attribute the foundation of the state to a mythological emperor Jimmu in 660 BC. Another legend concerns the empress JINGO (AD *c.*169–269), who allegedly conquered Korea.

Yamato Period. Beginning in the 3d or 4th century AD a new culture appeared—either from within Yayoi society or from the Asian mainland. Its leaders left massive tombs with evidence that they were mounted warriors. From this culture emerged rulers from the Yamato plain in the southern part of the main Japanese island of Honshu; they claimed descent from the sun goddess and achieved

political unity—apparently in the mid-4th century. By placing the sun goddess at the head of the SHINTO deities the hereditary Yamato emperor reinforced his leadership position. Other tribal chieftains were gradually subordinated by a system of court ranking, a development influenced by Chinese concepts of statecraft learned through Japan's military endeavors in Korea. Japan also adopted Chinese script, and BUDDHISM was introduced from Korea about 538.

In the 6th century the centralized control of the Yamato court began to break down. At the end of the century, however, the regent Prince SHOTOKU TAISHI reasserted court authority. He promulgated (604) a 17-article constitution based on the Chinese political theory of centralized imperial government. Imperial authority was further asserted by the Taika reforms of 646, by which all land was claimed by the emperor and an elaborate taxation system was initiated.

Nara Period. The first permanent capital was built at NARA in 710. In the following century tribal elites were replaced by a hereditary court aristocracy. Court patronage made Buddhism a major force, which in turn reinforced state power. Buddhist priestly intrusion in state affairs provoked a reaction, however. Finally, Emperor Kammu (r. 781–806) asserted imperial independence and established a new capital at Heian (modern KYOTO) in 794.

Heian and the Fujiwaras. In Heian, safe from Buddhist interference, imperial authority increased; however, the simplification of government that accompanied the move to Heian allowed the Fujiwara family to assert great influence. Many emperors were married to Fujiwara women or were their sons. Fujiwara men proved capable administrators, and they used their family ties to dominate the government. In 858, Fujiwara Yoshifusa (804–72) had his grandson, the infant Emperor Seiwa, placed on the throne and made himself regent. Until the end of the 11th century the Fujiwara used the position of regent to dominate the emperors.

Under imperial patronage two new Buddhist sects emerged in Heian. Tendai and Shingon, more Japanese in spirit than earlier Buddhist sects, ended the monopoly of the Nara Buddhist establishment. A reassertion of tribal, or clan, authority also accompanied the move to Heian, and land increasingly fell into private hands. Private armies were created, and a class of rural warriors (SAMU-RAI) emerged.

Notable among the samurai class were the Taira and Minamoto families. In 1156 they applied military force to settle a court dispute, and a war in 1159–60 left the Taira as the effective rulers. In 1180, Taira Kiyomori placed his grandson Antoku on the throne, briefly reviving the use of the regency to dominate the government.

The Shogunates

In 1180 the Minamoto revolted against the Taira and in the Gempei War (1180–85) defeated them and established the Kamakura shogunate, the first of the military governments that would rule Japan until 1868. (See SHOGUN.)

Kamakura Period. The shogun Minamoto YORITOMO (r. 1192–99) assigned military governors and military land stewards to supplement the civil governors and estate officials. Although Yoritomo established military authority, his sons were first dominated, then eliminated, by the Hojo clan. The Hojo upheld the military virtues on which the shogunate had been founded and proved apt successors to Yoritomo.

In 1274 and 1281 the shogunate was tested by two Mongol invasions (see MONGOLS), but the Japanese warriors drove away the invaders. The Kamakura period was also one of spiritual awakening. Buddhism was simplified, and new sects—PURE LAND BUDDHISM, True Pure Land, and Lotus (see NICHIREN)—guaranteed salvation to all believers.

By the early 14th century, however, political and social stability were breaking down. In 1334 the Kamakura shogunate was destroyed when Emperor Go-Daigo reasserted imperial authority (the Kemmu Restoration). In 1336, driven from Kyoto and replaced by another puppet emperor, Go-Daigo established a rival court in Yoshino. For 56 years there were two imperial courts.

Ashikaga Period. In 1338, Ashikaga Takauji was made shogun. The Ashikaga reached the height of their power under the third shogun, Yoshimitsu (r. 1368–94), who ended (1392) the schism within the imperial house.

The shogunate rested on an alliance with local military leaders (*shugo*), who gradually became powerful regional rulers. The great *shugo*, however, became increasingly involved in the politics of the shogunate, and by the mid-15th century many had lost control of their provincial bases. Their weakness became apparent in the Onin War of 1467–77. Beginning as a dispute over the shogunal succession, it turned into a general civil war in which the provinces eventually fell under the control of new lords called *daimyo*. The war effectively destroyed Ashikaga authority. The shogun Yoshimasa (r. 1440–73) simply turned his back on the troubles; he retired (1473) to his estate on the outskirts of Kyoto, where he built the Silver Pavilion (*Ginkaku*) and became the patron of a remarkable artistic flowering.

The Onin War marked the beginning of a century of warfare called the "Epoch of the Warring Country." In the provinces new feudal lords, the *daimyo*, independent of imperial or shogunal authority, concentrated their vassals in castle towns and left the villagers to administer them-

Under the Tokugawa shogunate Japan entered a period of isolation, which lasted until U.S. Commodore Matthew Perry arrived in 1853.

selves and pay taxes. The castle towns became market and handicraft centers, and a new style of urban life began to develop.

This was the Japan found by the Europeans who began to visit the country after 1543. The Portuguese began trade in 1545, and in 1549 the Jesuit missionary Saint FRANCIS XAVIER introduced Roman Catholicism. Christianity conflicted with feudal loyalties and was completely banned after 1639. All Europeans, except the Dutch, were also excluded from Japan.

Period of Unification. Between 1560 and 1600, Japan was reunified by a succession of three great *daimyo*: Oda NOBUNAGA, Toyotomi HIDEYOSHI, and Tokugawa IEYASU. By 1568, Nobunaga had extended his influence to Kyoto, where he set up a puppet shogun and established control over central Japan. Eight years after his death (1582), Hideyoshi completed the military unification of the country. The use of firearms (supplied initially by the Europeans), the construction of fortified castles, the disarmament of the peasants, and a major land survey were the chief tools of pacification. When Hideyoshi died in 1598, centralized authority was secure.

The third great unifier, Tokugawa Ieyasu, emerged as the guarantor of Hideyoshi's young heir, Hideyori. In 1600, Ieyasu defeated his military rivals at Sekigahara. He was appointed shogun in 1603, but in 1605 he turned that office over to his son and devoted the rest of his life to consolidating Tokugawa control. In 1615, Hideyori was finally eliminated, and when Ieyasu died in 1616, the Tokugawa held unchallenged feudal supremacy over the whole country.

Tokugawa Period. From their castle town of Edo (modern TOKYO), the TOKUGAWA ruled Japan as shoguns until 1867. A careful distribution of land ensured their control of the major cities—Kyoto, OSAKA, and NAGASAKI—and the chief mines. Thus they controlled the main economic centers and strategic military points, while unrelated *daimyo* administered some 250 autonomous domains. The *daimyo* spent half their time in Edo attending the shogun.

The Tokugawa period saw the flowering of urban culture and a monetized commodity economy. The samurai stood at the top of a legally established four-class system as military bureaucrats who served both the shogunal and *daimyo* governments. Below them were the peasants, artisans, and merchants. Although despised, merchants became essential to urban life. A national market system developed for textiles, food products, handicrafts, books, and other goods. Osaka was the center of the national rice market. After 1639 the Tokugawa pursued a policy of almost total seclusion from the outside world. Nagasaki, where the Chinese and the Dutch had trading quarters (the Dutch on an offshore island), was the only point of foreign contact.

By the 19th century peasant uprisings had become commonplace, and the samurai and even the *daimyo* were badly indebted to the merchant class. Thus the old socioeconomic system had virtually collapsed, while the shogunal government displayed increasing extravagance and inefficiency. In the early 1840s the national government attempted a series of reforms to improve economic conditions, but they were largely ineffectual. The shogunate, therefore, was already in a discredited position when U.S. Commodore Matthew PERRY forced Japan to abandon its seclusionist policy in 1854.

With the arrival of Perry's ships the Tokugawa shogun turned to the *daimyo* for advice, and the imperial house, long excluded from politics, was drawn into the controversy. In 1858 the shogun signed disadvantageous commercial treaties with the United States and several European countries. By 1864 most activists realized that the foreigners' military power prevented their exclusion, and they turned against the Tokugawa instead. Samurai from the domains of Satsuma, Choshu, Tosa, and Hizen played major roles forcing the resignation (1867) of the shogun, and imperial government was restored under the young Meiji emperor in 1868 (see MEIJI RESTORATION).

Modern Japan

The Meiji Period. In less than half a century Japan was transformed from a secluded feudal society into an industrialized world power. During the Meiji period, corresponding to the reign (1868–1912) of Emperor Meiji,

Under Emperor Meiji (1868–1912), Japan was transformed from a secluded feudal society into a military and industrial world power. Rapid modernization occured during the Meiji Restoration.

centralized bureaucracy replaced the balance of power between the Tokugawa and the autonomous domains. A conscript army replaced the military authority of the samurai. Restrictions on residence and employment were abolished, and people flocked to Edo, now renamed Tokyo and adopted as the imperial capital. The government imported foreign advisors and technology, and official missions were sent to examine modern Western societies.

Japan was determined to gain a position of equality with the West, and government stability was crucial to this objective. In 1873 a new tax system provided a secure revenue base and abolished the feudal land system. In 1877 the conscript army defeated a major samurai revolt led by SAIGO TAKAMORI, a leading figure in the restoration. Inflation reduced the value of government revenues, and between 1881 and 1885 a rigorous deflation policy initiated by Matsukata Masayoshi stabilized the currency. Education was basic to Japan's emergence. The Meiji government required primary education for all children and established (1872) a centralized school system.

In 1881 domestic political pressure forced the oligarchical government to promise a constitution by 1889 and representative government by 1890. The statesman ITO HIROBUMI took charge of drafting the new constitution. A cabinet was established in 1885, a peerage was created, and in 1889 the constitution was promulgated as a gift from the emperor.

Japan thus became a constitutional monarchy, with a bicameral legislature (Diet) composed of a house of peers and an elected lower house. Suffrage was very limited, however, and the prime minister and cabinet were responsible only to the emperor, who was still regarded as a divine figure.

During the SINO-JAPANESE WAR of 1894–95, Japan displayed its military superiority over the Chinese and secured control of Korea. In 1902, Japan concluded an alliance with Britain as an equal power. In 1904–05, Japan and Russia fought over Manchuria and Korea. Victorious in this RUSSO-JAPANESE WAR, the Japanese added southern Sakhalin to their empire of Taiwan and the Ryukyu Islands; and in 1910 they formally annexed Korea. By 1905, therefore, Japan was a major military power in East Asia and an industrialized nation. When Japan entered World War I as an ally of Britain, the strains of industrialization were apparent in Japanese society.

World War I and the Interwar Years. During World War I, Japan seized several of the German holdings in East Asia, including Chinese territory on the Shandong peninsula. When the Chinese demanded its return, the Japanese government responded with the Twenty-one Demands of January 1915, forcing Chinese acceptance of extended Japanese influence in China. In 1917, Japan extracted further concessions of rights in Manchuria and Inner Mongolia, setting the stage for its later open aggression against China.

In 1918, HARA TAKASHI became prime minister in the first cabinet based on a party majority in the Diet. Although the political parties were essentially controlled by the major business interests—called the zaibatsu—they were a major step toward more democratic forms of gov-

Kamikaze ("divine wind") forces were used during the last year of World War II as a new strategy for the failing Japanese military. Kamikaze pilots crashed their explosive-laden planes into enemy targets.

ernment, a trend that was continued by the expansion of the electorate in 1925. The party governments of the 1920s and after attempted modest reforms and pursued a less-aggressive foreign policy than that of prewar Japan. At the WASHINGTON CONFERENCE of 1921–22, Japan signed a naval arms limitation treaty that replaced the Anglo-Japanese alliance and established a balance of power in the Pacific. In 1930 further naval limitations were agreed to at the London Naval Conference.

The Japanese military felt, however, that the politicians were compromising the nation's security and the emperor's right to supreme command. As the World Depression of the 1930s set in, the discontented began to rally around the militarists. Right-wing terrorism increased (3 of Japan's 11 prime ministers between 1918 and 1932 were assassinated), and in 1931, Japanese officers in Manchuria acted without government authorization in precipitating the Mukden Incident and occupying Manchuria. Unable to stop the army, the civilian government accepted the establishment of the puppet state of Manchukuo in February 1932. From May 1932 until August 1945, the succession of cabinets and the young emperor HIROHITO, who had succeeded to the throne in 1926, were essentially the tools of the military extremists.

World War II. Japanese economic and political penetration of northern China proceeded against minimal Chinese resistance until 1937. In July 1937, however, the Second Sino-Japanese War began. By 1940 the Japanese controlled eastern China and had established a puppet regime at Nanjing. In the same year Japan allied with the Axis powers of Germany and Italy, which were already at war in Europe.

Having occupied the northern part of French Indochi-

na in 1940, Japanese troops moved into southern Indochina in July 1941. The United States and Britain imposed a total trade embargo on Japan, which then had the choice of withdrawing or continuing its expansion in order to secure oil supplies from the Dutch East Indies. The latter alternative would mean war with the United States, and Prime Minister KONOE FUMIMARO negotiated to avoid that contingency. In October 1941, however, Konoe was replaced by the more militant Gen. TOJO HIDEKI. On Dec. 7, 1941, Japanese forces launched simultaneous attacks on PEARL HARBOR in Hawaii, the Philippines, Hong Kong, and Malaya. The United States immediately declared war, and WORLD WAR II entered its worldwide phase.

At first the Japanese forces achieved great success, conquering the Philippines, the Dutch East Indies, Malaya and Singapore, and Burma. The tide turned in June 1942, however, with the defeat of a Japanese fleet by the U.S. Navy at Midway Island in the Pacific. The atomic bombing of HIROSHIMA and Nagasaki on August 6 and 9 and the Soviet declaration of war on Aug. 8, 1945, were the final blows. Emperor Hirohito intervened and ordered the army to surrender unconditionally on Aug. 14, 1945.

Postwar Japan. The Allied occupation, under the command of U.S. Gen. Douglas MACARTHUR, lasted from 1945 to 1952 and resulted in political, social, and economic reforms. The emperor was placed in a symbolic role, government was democratized, and a new constitution with a bill of rights went into effect in 1947. Article 9 of the constitution renounced the right to use force in foreign policy.

As millions of soldiers and civilians were repatriated from overseas, the government under YOSHIDA SHIGERU worked to implement reforms and achieve economic recovery. The outbreak of the Korean War (1950–53) aided that recovery by increasing Japanese exports. It also prompted the United States to press for rapid conclusion of a Japanese peace treaty. In 1951, Japan signed not only a peace treaty but a mutual defense treaty with the United States. It resumed full sovereignty in 1952 but remained under U.S. protection.

From 1954 until 1972 the Japanese economy expanded rapidly. Building on its prewar industrial base, Japan imported modern technology and machinery and made economic development the main focus of national policy. Central planning helped the government control the structure of the economy, placing labor, resources, and capital where the growth potential was greatest.

The 1972 return to Japan of Okinawa, which had been under U.S. occupation since 1945, signaled the end of Japanese subordination to the United States. Japan handled the U.S. rapprochement with Communist China by establishing its own diplomatic ties with that long-time enemy in 1972.

The Liberal-Democrats, the conservative party that has dominated Japanese politics since 1954, has emphasized economic growth. Scandals led to the resignations of prime ministers TANAKA KAKUEI (in 1974) and TAKESHITA NOBURU and Uno Sosuki (in 1989). The party lost its majority in the upper house of parliament in July 1989, although it regained control in February 1990 elections under Prime Minister KAIFU TOSHIKI. In January 1989 the death of long-reigning Hirohito marked the end of an era; he was succeeded by his son AKIHITO.

In the 1980s Japan played an increasingly visible role in global affairs, becoming the world's largest provider of development aid in 1988. It has been the world's leading exporter of manufactured goods since 1985 and remains closely linked to the United States and Western Europe. Because Japan is more dependent on oil imports from the Middle East than any other country, it was criticized for its relatively moderate financial contribution to the allied effort in the 1991 GULF WAR.

Japan, Sea of   The Sea of Japan (Japanese: Nihon-Kai) separates the Japanese islands from the Asian mainland. It is about 1,600 km (1,000 mi) long, has an area of 1,000,000 km^2 (389,000 mi^2), and reaches a maximum depth of 3,750 m (12,300 ft). The Tsushima archipelago and the shallow Korea Strait form its southwestern boundary. To the west are South and North Korea, and to the northwest, the USSR. The main Japanese island, Honshu, is to the east. The sea's most important port is the Soviet city of Vladivostok. The sea is extensively fished.

Japanese art and architecture   The art and architecture of Japan bears the imprint of that country's unusual geographic location, separated from Korea by about 160 km (100 mi) and from China by about 800 km (500 mi). This location has both protected Japan from foreign invasion and enabled its rulers to close or open the doors to contacts with other nations almost at will. Thus, during periods of cultural extroversion such as the 7th and 8th centuries, the 14th and 15th centuries, and, more recently, from 1868 to the present day, Japan has seen the massive influx of foreign culture. During such periods the arts produced in Japan have exemplified the adulation of foreign culture, whereas during the intervening periods of cultural introversion imported modes have become transformed into what can be considered to be typically Japanese art forms.

Early Cultures: Jomon, Yayoi, and Tumulus Periods. Evidence of Stone Age culture in Japan dates back at least to 70,000 BC. However, the earliest ceramic culture, known by its cord-pattern wares as Jomon, is now dated from about 7500 to 300 BC. Jomon wares vary from the early conical and cylindrical types found in northeastern Japan and Hokkaido to the elaborately decorated, sculpturesque wares from the 4th and 3d millennia BC that are found principally in central Japan. From this period onward a number of small clay figurines are also found, which may be associated with fertility and mortuary rites.

The culture of the Yayoi people (c.300 BC–AD 300) is more recognizably Japanese in character. Wet-rice cultivation and bronze technology appear to have been introduced from Korea by way of Kyushu. As opposed to the robust vigor of Jomon wares, Yayoi ceramics are made with finer clay, are turned on a wheel, and are generally more utilitarian in character. Bronze weapons, mirrors, and bells, originally close to their Asian prototypes, were evidently used in rituals that led to the exaggeration of their forms.

During the Tumulus period, lasting from the 4th through the 6th century, the increasing concentration of power in the hands of the great clans of central Japan culminated in the unification of the nation under the imperial clan. The later tombs contain equestrian trappings and weaponry suggestive of invasion or infiltration by a warlike Mongoloid people from northeast Asia. The culture of the later Tumulus period is most vividly represented in the *haniwa* clay figures that were set around the center and later the borders of the great tombs. These lively, mass-produced grave guardians include figures of shamans, crowned figures, soldiers, court ladies, dancers, houses, ships, and animals; they provide very literal images of the daily life of this period and, in addition, seem to indicate a much changed attitude toward the afterlife.

Mid-6th to Early 8th Century. In the mid-6th century, Buddhism and Chinese learning reached Japan in the form of official emissaries and gifts from the Korean kingdom of Paekche, heralding 200 years of regular contact with the Asian mainland. Monasteries were furnished with bronze images of Buddhas made by immigrant Korean artisans such as the Tori group. Other statues from the first half of the 7th century preserved in the Horyuji include the painted wooden statues of the *Kudara Kwannon* and the *Yumedono Kwannon*, a popular deity of compassion and mercy, and the *Four Celestial Kings*, guardians of the four directions and protectors of the state.

In the latter half of the 7th and the early 8th century contact with China became more frequent, and the more refined sculptural styles of early-7th-century China are reflected in works such as the *Tachibana Shrine* (c.710; Horyuji, Nara).

The 7th-century Gojunoto, or five-storied pagoda, of the Horyuji temple and monastery compound, is typical of the Buddhist-inspired Chinese architecture of the Tang dynasty.

The delicate beauty of the Hoodo, or Phoenix Hall, of the Byodoin temple at Uji, near Kyoto, built during the 11th century, reflects the "Pure Land" aesthetic of the Heian period. The Hoodo evokes the serenity and refinement of the Western Paradise.

Nara Period (710–784). With the establishment in 710 of the new capital of NARA, modeled after Chang'an, the Chinese capital during the Tang dynasty (618–907), the building of temple-monasteries reached a peak. Older temples such as the Yakushiji were rebuilt on the new site; the Horyuji, burned in 670 and rebuilt shortly afterward, was equipped with huge mural paintings in its Golden Hall, and many new temples were constructed. Dominant among them was the great Todaiji, whose colossal *Great Buddha*, or *Daibutsu*, a cast bronze image more than 16 m (53 ft) high, was completed in a grand opening ceremony in 752.

By contrast with the more introspective design of 7th-century temples, in which a five-storied PAGODA had often occupied the central place, the centerpiece in the Todaiji is the great Golden Buddha Hall, now flanked by twin pagodas. Buddhist sculptures in such buildings, executed in bronze, painted clay, and dry lacquer, closely reflect Chinese prototypes in their vigorous blend of ideal and real forms; this is especially notable in the statues of guardian deities that often surrounded the central images on the altar.

Early Heian Period (784–897). The early Heian period, named after the new capital at Heian-kyo (KYOTO), was strongly influenced by the introduction of esoteric Buddhism, or *Mikkyo*. MANDALA paintings were executed on huge silk hangings, either drawn in gold and silver line or painted in a rich variety of colors. Groups of deities derived from the mandalas were represented in sculptural form. Sculpture tended to be made from a single block of wood and became heavier and more sensuous in appearance, emphasizing solemnity and spiritual force. Among the deities favored for individual paintings, the images of the ferocious Fudo and the Five Mighty Bodhisattvas were worshiped individually or in groups of five.

Late Heian Period (897–1185). During the late Heian period, also called the Fujiwara period, PURE LAND BUDDHISM arose. Paintings centered attention on the wel-

coming figure of Amida and his heavenly troupe of music-making bodhisattvas coming to carry the believer to paradise at the moment of death. The same group was represented in sculptural form, now using a multiblock technique in wood that allowed for greater refinement of execution. The Hoodo, or Phoenix Hall, of the Byodoin temple at Uji, completed (1053) with sculpture by Jocho and his studio, is a fine example of a Heian villa garden.

The greatest achievement of the late Heian period may be said to lie in the development of native traditions in secular painting and CALLIGRAPHY. During this period the term *yamato-e* ("paintings of Japanese themes") is recorded in connection with paintings of famous places and themes from Japanese poetry, as opposed to *kara-e* ("paintings of Chinese themes"). Although works from the 9th and 10th centuries are all lost, an 11th-century landscape painting on a folding screen from the Jingo-ji, Kyoto (now in the Kyoto National Museum), reveals an early blend of the two modes.

Abbreviation of the cumbersome usage of Chinese characters as phonetic symbols led to the emergence of the phonetic kana script. This distinctive form of Japanese calligraphy developed at the hands of Heian noblewomen into a respectable mode for poems, diaries, and romances. The ability to compose short Japanese poems, written in a cultivated hand, became a requirement in social exchanges, resulting in the emergence in the 11th century of major masters of the kana script, such as Fujiwara no Yukinari. Thereafter, classical Japanese poems came to be rendered on increasingly finely decorated paper, as seen in the famous *Thirty-Six Poets* anthology (c.1120; Tokyo National Museum).

Heian noblewomen also appear to have originated a subtle style for illustrating their courtly romances. The horizontal hand-scroll illustrations (now widely dispersed) of Lady Murasaki's epic *Tale of Genji* (c.1010), produced by a team of painters and calligraphers working in the early 12th century, is the finest surviving example of the onna-e (ladies'-style painting). In largely interior scenes with the roofs removed, action is centered on the affairs of the heart. A symphonic array of human emotions, with a pervasive pathos, is conveyed by the carefully chosen postures and masklike facial expressions of the main characters.

In contrast to the delicate, emotive style of the Genji scrolls is the racy narrative style of otoko-e (gentlemen's-style painting), in which action is as lively as the humor of the caricature. This tradition, seen in works such as the Legends of Mt. Shigi scroll (late 12th century; Chogoson-shiji, Nara), developed from the style of painting that appeared in 8th-century Buddhist propaganda scrolls. Another highly developed tradition of Buddhist scroll painting during the Heian period is that of the animal cartoons, in which frolicking animals parody the popular human entertainments of the day.

Kamakura Period (1185–1333). The reign of Minamoto YORITOMO, who gained the title of shogun (generalissimo) in 1192, marked the start of seven centuries of rule by military dictators. The rebuilding of the Nara temples of Todaiji and Kofukuji (destroyed by fire in 1180) included the recasting of the colossal bronze Great Buddha (1182–85), under the direction of technicians from Song China, and the rebuilding of the Great Buddha Hall and the Great South Gate in a new Song Chinese-inspired style known as Tenjikuyo.

The Nara-based school of sculptors descended from Jocho gained ascendancy in the competition for contracts during this period of rebuilding in Nara. The new style represented a blending of the naturalistic vigor derived from Nara-period antecedents with a humanistic realism that evidently suited the pragmatic tenor of warrior-dominated society. A fine example is seen in Unkei's Nio (1203), one of the colossal wooden guardian figures standing at the Great South Gate of the Todaiji. Song influence is also evident in Kamakura sculpture, notably in the works of Kaikei.

In paintings as in sculpture, the trends toward greater realism and humanism favored the emergence of a lively tradition of realistic portraiture. The personalities of great generals such as Yoritomo, members of the aristocracy,

The Daibutsu, or Great Buddha (1252) of the Kotoku temple at Kamakura is a heroic representation of the Amida Buddha.

and even the emperor were fully expressed in the new form of painting called nise-e ("likeness paintings") that emerged during the Kamakura period. New developments in narrative hand scrolls included a focus on the vigorous portrayal of military history, on the vivid and sometimes bizarre depiction of Buddhist hell scenes, and on the biographies of famous evangelist priests.

The transmission of ZEN BUDDHISM from China to Japan in the early 13th century created a significant new impetus in religious painting. The pragmatic, fundamentalist doctrines of Zen, stressing meditation as the most reliable path to realization of Buddhahood, appealed to the warrior class, with the result that Chinese monks were invited to head the newly built Kenchoji (1253) and Enkakuji (1282) monasteries in Kamakura. With such figures came Song monastic architectural style and a variety of painting styles associated with the Zen sect, notably the highly personalized portraits of Zen masters (chinso). By the early 14th century, Japanese monk-painters such as Mokuan (d. 1343) went to China for extended periods, becoming the direct inheritors of Chan (Zen) painting traditions in China. Prominent among such works were paintings of the free and uncommitted saints, eccentrics

The decorative style which developed during the Momoyama period is exemplified by Pine Trees and Eagle, a screen attributed to Kano Eitoku. Such works are characterized by bold, horizontal patterns and brilliant colors against a gold-leaf background. (Academy of Art, Tokyo.)

such as Putai, Hanshan, and Shide. With the advent of Chinese literati monks such as Yishan Yining (d. Japan, 1317), scholasticism began to flourish in Zen circles, resulting in literati-oriented paintings of orchids and bamboo by monks such as Tesshu (d. 1366) and Bonpo (1348–c.1420).

Muromachi (or Ashikaga) Period (1338–1573). The Ashikaga shoguns relied on Zen monks as intermediaries in foreign relations and were equally influenced by their tastes in literature and art. Collecting Chinese paintings and art objects became a passion with the shogun Yoshimitsu (1358–1408), who indulged in elaborate ceremonial displays of his collection, setting a pattern for later shoguns. The priest-painters Josetsu, Shubun, and their associates in the first half of the 15th century formulated a national style based on Chinese styles of the Southern Song painting academy. A notable example is Shubun's *Studio of the Three Worthies*—pine, bamboo, and plum (1418; Seikado Foundation, Tokyo). This 15th-century tradition of "poem paintings," usually symbols of seclusion in the form of rustic huts, surmounted by numerous eulogies in Chinese verse, gradually gave way to an increasing interest in landscape painting for its own sake. Nature themes such as the popular *Eight Views of the Xiao and Xiang Rivers*, as well as other paintings of landscape and of bird-and-flower motifs, tended to be arranged within a four-seasons format reflecting native Japanese tastes. One of the greatest masters of landscape painting was SESSHU, who founded an influential school of monochrome painting in Yamaguchi. Kenko Shokei, headed a school in Kamakura. Soga-school painters descended from Shubun's line worked for the Asakura clan in Echizen, and the Kano school, headed by MOTONOBU, developed a widely patronized decorative orthodoxy. The works of the 16th-century master Sesson, as exemplified in his boldly painted *Hawk on a Pine Tree* (Tokyo National Museum), presage trends toward more martial styles favored by the warring daimyos (great lords) of the succeeding Momoyama period.

Momoyama Period (1573–1614). In 1576 the warlord NOBUNAGA commissioned Kano EITOKU to decorate his Azuchi castle. Although pillaged in 1582, Nobunaga's castle set a pattern of ostentatious decoration that was followed by his successor Hideyoshi in the decoration of Osaka castle (1582), the Jurakudai castle-palace (1587), and the Momoyama castle near Fushimi (1594). Eitoku and his pupils developed the *konpeki* style, using rich mineral colors over thick gold leaf to produce dazzling images of flowering trees, birds and flowers, and animals. Murals and screens in this bold, polychrome style were generally reserved for grand reception halls; monochrome ink paintings in a vigorous decorative mode were often preferred for more private rooms.

The drinking of green tea, introduced from China in the 12th century, was initially practiced by Zen monks to prevent drowsiness; by the Muromachi period the practice had become an elite form of secular gathering, known as the tea ceremony, at which imported art objects were often displayed. A simple, mat-covered room in a rustic yet elegant hut within the confines of a small garden became a favored environment for appreciation of the tea-drinking ceremony and the few chosen art objects being displayed. The secluded, highly restrained Tai-an in Kyoto, designed by the great tea master Rikyu (1520–91), is a classic example of teahouse architecture. Increasing demand for tea wares led to the development of the native Japanese *Seto* and *Mino* wares. The organic, deliberately rough-textured *raku* wares of Kyoto are considered the epitome of the quality of *wabi* (quiet simplicity) that was inextricably linked with the cult of tea.

Early Edo Period (1615–88). During the early years of the Edo (or Tokugawa) period (1615–1868), a renaissance and transformation of Heian aristocratic traditions was achieved by the school of decorative art and painting called Rimpa. A curious artistic alliance between courtly and upper bourgeois tastes appeared in the work of KOETSU, SOTATSU, and others. Honnami Koetsu presided over an artistic colony in Kyoto that produced decorated paper, lacquer ware, brushes, and ceramics. Koetsu's raku tea-bowls are considered among the most powerful and evocative ever produced.

Sotatsu, master of the Tawaraya painting shop in Kyoto, produced paper for calligraphy and fans richly decorated with paintings evoking themes from Heian poetic

Ogata Korin illuminated the decorative style of the early Edo period with richly dramatic lacquer work and screens such as Irises, *one of a pair of screens considered his masterpiece. (Nezu Museum, Tokyo.)*

The bold coloring and imaginative compositions that distinguish the work of Hokusai are seen in "Mount Fuji on a Clear Day" (c.1825), one of a series of prints contained in Thirty-Six Views of Mount Fuji *(c.1823–29). Hokusai is considered one of the most brilliant representatives of the Ukiyo-e school of the early 19th century. (Musée Guimet, Paris.)*

romances. His innovative ink wash techniques (*tarashikomi*) opened new directions for emotive expression. In the *Deer Scroll* (early 17th century; Seattle Art Museum), classical poems are inscribed by Koetsu on paper richly decorated with gold and silver renderings of deer herds by Sotatsu; in its bold approach to traditional subject matter, this collaborative work well exemplifies the early Edo-period rejuvenation of classical Japanese tastes. Ogata KORIN, a major heir of this traditon, executed sumptuously decorated gold screens and lacquered objects characteristic of the extravagant tastes of the rich merchant class of his time. His brother Ogata KENZAN produced ceramics that combined dramatic designs with the conventions of calligraphy and lyrical painting.

The Tosho-gu mausoleum of Tokugawa Ieyasu at Nikko, built in 1617–19 and expanded (1634–36) by the third Tokugawa shogun, was designed with the express purpose of deifying in perpetuity the founder of the Tokugawa regime. Its extraordinarily ornate decoration with elaborate relief work and lavish use of gold, lacquer, and rich colors provides an overwhelming statement of shogunal power. A marked contrast is found in the classical elegance and restraint of the imperial villas of the period. The Katsura villa of Prince Hachijo Toshihito, built in the 1620s, is the earliest, combining an exquisite classical garden with rustic teahouses and dignified simplicity in the main residence.

Later Edo Period: Genroku Era (1688–1703) to 1868.
The tradition of genre paintings featuring popular life and festivals, typified by screen compositions of life in and around Kyoto, was patronized by both the feudal establishment and the urban bourgeoisie in the 16th and 17th centuries. Out of this tradition emerged the yet more popular art of UKIYO-E ("pictures of the floating world"). During the Genroku era, the heyday of popular entertainment, hand-colored woodblock prints began to appear celebrating the pleasures of the Yoshiwara or gay quarter of Edo. Thereafter, prints of individual courtesans and of popular theater, or KABUKI scenes, were produced in great

numbers. Rudimentary color printing prevailed until Suzuki HARUNOBU's polychrome prints of 1765 elevated the medium to new levels of artistic expression. His lyrical, idealized female figures were later surpassed by the statuesque geisha type of Torii KIYONAGA. During this period Kitagawa UTAMARO perfected the languid sensuousness of his prints of beautiful women, and the greatest actor prints were produced, notably in the incisive, satirical work of Toshusai SHARAKU.

Sumptuary edicts prohibiting "licentious material" and restrictions on travel in the 18th century contributed to the rise of landscape prints; the prodigious genius of Katsushika HOKUSAI was expressed in such brilliantly innovative landscape series as the *Thirty-six Views of Mount Fuji* (c.1823–29), while Ando HIROSHIGE gave rein to a lyrical mode in works such as his *Fifty-three Stations of the Tokaido* (1833).

With the spread in Japan of Chinese painting manuals such as the *Mustard Seed Garden*, the presence of Chinese painters in Nagasaki, and the influence of erudite Chinese monks at monasteries near Kyoto, the literati movement gained momentum among the urban bourgeoisie as a sanctioned alternative to the academic traditions of the KANO school. Ike no TAIGA's eclectic blend of Chinese and native Rimpa traditions served to define the nature of the "southern school" (*nanga*) in Japan. The personal spirit of the modern age began to assert itself in the evocative works of Uragami Gyokudo (1745–1820) and the uninhibited style of Mokubei (1767–1833). In Edo the passion for Western learning sparked the Western influence on *nanga* seen in the works of Tani Buncho (1764–1840) and Kazan (1793–1841).

Modern Period (1868 to the Present).
The determined modernization of Japan during the Meiji period (1868–1912) was accompanied by the rapid introduction of an enormous variety of European forms of art and architecture. Palatial buildings, such as Tokyo's Akasaka palace, modeled (1909) after Versailles, appeared in many large cities. Increasingly national adaptations of Western forms

of architecture emerged as Japan approached World War II. Sculpture revealed a similar hybrid variety of Western-oriented forms, closely reflecting rapid social and political changes. In painting the most lasting of the hybrid forms emerged, in part through the encouragement of the American scholar Ernest FENOLLOSA. In this tradition, called *nihonga* ("Japanese painting"), traditional pigments and an instinct for emotive design are combined with techniques of Western realism. The works of painting masters such as Yokoyama Taikan (1868–1958), Kobayashi Kokei (1883–1957), and Maeda Seison (1885–1977) preserve most clearly the cultural identity of Japan through a period of extraordinary change and diversity.

Japanese beetle   Japanese beetles, *Popillia japonica*, are small, shiny beetles that were accidentally brought into the United States from Japan in the early 1900s and are now serious pests to many agricultural and ornamental plants. The beetles range in color from metallic green to bronze or copper.

Japanese chin   The Japanese chin was registered with the American Kennel Club as the Japanese spaniel until 1977, when its name was officially changed to Japanese chin. There is little doubt that the Japanese chin, the Pekingese, and several other related breeds are of ancient Chinese origin and that the Japanese chin reached Japan long ago. The Japanese chin is a small, long-legged, long-coated breed. It has a short muzzle, prominent eyes, a large forehead, and a plumed tail carried over its back. The Japanese chin may reach 25 cm (10 in) in height at the shoulder and 4 kg (9 lb) in weight. Its coat color is white with reddish or black markings.

Japanese giant salamander   The Japanese giant salamander, *Andrias japonicus*, of the family Cryptobranchidae, is the world's largest salamander, reaching a length of 1.6 m (5.25 ft). It is long-lived; the first living specimen ever sent to Europe was maintained for 52 years. This salamander is found only on the southern end of the Japanese island of Honshu, in cold mountain streams. The skin of this species contains many blood vessels and is apparently used in respiration, absorbing oxygen from the water. The Japanese giant salamander retains certain larval features. Fertilization is external.

Japanese language   Japanese, one of the branches of the URAL-ALTAIC family, is the language of nearly 115 million people living mainly on the four home islands of Japan—Honshu, Kyushu, Shikoku, and Hokkaido—as well as on Okinawa and many other smaller islands. The earliest written records of Japanese consist of a few names appearing in late-5th-century inscriptions; the first substantial texts date from the 8th century. The language of the earliest texts is called Old Japanese. Middle Japanese extends to the end of the 16th century. Old Japa-

nese differed from both Middle and modern Japanese in many ways. Its sound system, for example, had eight vowels, while the present-day language of Tokyo has only five. Old Japanese, however, lacked the contrast between long and short vowels so important to modern Japanese.

Old Japanese made a sharp distinction between the standard, prestige language of the court at Nara and what were already designated the Eastern dialects. Similar distinctions have been important in Japanese ever since. The many surviving dialects of modern Japan are classified as those of Eastern Japan, with Tokyo as the focal point; those of Western Japan, in the area of Osaka and Kyoto; and those of the island of Kyushu. Since the middle of the last century, however, the language of an educated elite in Tokyo has been used as the official standard in schools, for most writing, and more recently, on radio and television.

Since earliest times Japanese has been written with characters borrowed from China. Phonetic signs were later added to this script by altering and simplifying a few of the borrowed Chinese characters; today both the original Chinese characters and the Japanese phonetic signs are used together in the most complex writing system of any developed nation. Minimal basic literacy for the modern language requires mastery of at least 1,850 characters.

Japanese literature   The major work of classical Japanese literature is the early-11th-century novel *Tale of Genji* (Eng. trans., 1925–33), considered by many the first true novel of psychological depth and complexity written anywhere in the world. The style of NO DRAMA, or Noh drama—restrained dance drama with lyrical, poetic texts and masked actors—has influenced Ezra Pound and W. B. Yeats; the 17-syllable poetic form, the HAIKU, has become well known outside Japan through its influence on symbolist poets; and the works of many modern Japanese novelists have found a wide Western audience through translation.

The Heian period (794–1185), which takes its name from the establishment of the capital at Heian-kyo, was the high point of indigenous prose fiction. Poetry in the classical 31-syllable *waka* form flourished between the 10th and 14th centuries, the most famous anthologies of which are the *Kokinshu* of 905 (Eng. trans., 1922) and the *Shinkokinshu* of 1205. The great dramatic works of No date from the 14th and 15th centuries, while the 17th and 18th centuries were the peak for the BUNRAKU and KABUKI theaters.

Beginnings. The origins of Japanese literature lie in oral poetry and mythology, and the earliest surviving work, the *Kojiki* (Record of Ancient Matters), explains the cosmology of the Japanese and justifies the legitimacy of the ruling house as descendants of the sun goddess. The mid-8th-century *Man'yoshu* (Collection of Ten Thousand Leaves) is a compendium of some 4,500 poems in several forms, including both *waka* and longer poems.

By the 9th century the development of *kana*, a syllabic writing system, helped foster prose. The early-10th-century *Tales of Ise* (Eng. trans., 1968) is a collection of poems with long prose contexts; *The Tosa Diary* (936; Eng. trans., 1912) is a travel diary by Ki no Tsurayuki, who maintained the ruse of being a woman writer. In fact, the greatest prose works of the period were produced by women, including *The Tale of Genji* by MURASAKI SHIKIBU and *The Pillow Book* (*c.*1000; Eng. trans., 1967) by Sei Shonagon (b. *c.*966).

A Period of Instability. The Gempei wars of 1180–85 are the subject of Japan's major epic, the *Tale of the Heike* (Eng. trans., 1975). A few 14th-century works continued the classical literary style, notably *The Confessions of Lady Nijo* (1306; Eng. trans., 1973) by the imperial consort Lady Nijo and *Essays in Idleness* (*c.*1340; Eng. trans., 1967) by the Buddhist monk Yoshida Kenko. Under government patronage, and largely through the writings of Zeami Motokiyo (1363–1443), No drama was transformed from rural folk entertainment into a highly literary, dramatic art.

The Tokugawa Period. Some of the most notable works of the Tokugawa period (named after the shogun Tokugawa Iyeyasu and his successors of 1600–1867) include the haiku and poetic travel accounts of BASHO; the plays of CHIKAMATSU MONZAEMON, and the witty fiction of IHARA SAIKAKU. Later Tokugawa fiction is best represented by Ueda Akinari (1734–1809) and Takizawa Bakin (1767–1848), whose work was influenced by Kabuki theater.

The Modern Period. TSUBOUCHI SHOYO published a critical monograph, *Shosetsu Shinzui* (The Essence of the Novel, 1886), which introduced many ideas from Victorian literary criticism as standards for creating a modern literature for Japan. Among well-known modern authors, Mori Ogai wrote heavily romantic novels based on his experiences in Germany; the naturalist Shimazaki Toson is best known for *The Broken Commandment* (1906; Eng. trans., 1974), dealing with discrimination; NATSUME SOSEKI wrote enduring introspective, philosophical novels; and Abe Kobo has produced surrealistic fiction and drama influenced by Western avant-garde literature. Both TANIZAKI JUNICHIRO and the Nobel Prize–winning KAWABATA YASUNARI, have been extensively translated into English. The works of MISHIMA YUKIO—whose life of right-wing political activity and eventual public suicide electrified the nation—have also found an enthusiastic foreign audience.

Japanese music The history of Japanese music begins in the 8th century. Music styles in Japan, like those of the West, have changed frequently in the last thousand years. Common characteristics found throughout this period, however, are as follows: (1) scales with five-tone (pentatonic) cores plus two auxiliary tones; (2) a chamber-music sound ideal in which instruments can be heard separately rather than merged, as in Western orchestras; (3) a maximum effect from a minimum amount of sound material; (4) music closely allied to verbal expression; (5) aural learning with limited use of detailed notations; (6) through-composed forms rather than forms that repeat or return to previous themes or sections; (7) an emphasis on melodic or rhythmic tension, with little harmony in the Western sense; (8) the use of melodic or rhythmic stereotyped patterns that tend to move in progressions, producing a sense of forward motion like that created in Western music by chords; and (9) a greater interest in the combination of standard materials than in "originality."

The *ryo* and *ritsu* scales are derived from Buddhist chant (*shomyo*) and court music (*gagaku*), the first known sources of Japanese music. They originally came from Korea and China and gradually became "Japanized." *Ryo*, like the *yo* scale of Japanese folk music, is close to Chinese models; *ritsu* is more Japanese in character. Although *gagaku* orchestras include wind, string, and percussion instruments, their sound is similar to chamber music. The melody is played by flutes (*ryuteki* or *komabue*) and oboes (*hichiriki*). The mouth organ (*sho*) plays tone clusters to create another texture. The 13-stringed zither (*koto*) and the pear-shaped lute (*biwa*) play stereotyped patterns that mark off musical phrases, as do the sounds of the large hanging drum (*tsuri-daiko*), a small gong (*shoko*), and a horizontal drum struck on two heads (the *kakko* or the *san-no tsuzumi*).

Maximum effect from minimum material is illustrated by the 14th- and 15th-century NO DRAMA. It uses few actors plus a unison chorus (*ji*) and an ensemble (*hayashi*) of flute (*nokan*), shoulder drum (*ko tsuzumi*), hip drum (*o tsuzumi*), and, in dance sections, a stick drum (*taiko*). No music, like most Japanese forms, is totally set and without improvisation.

A classical Japanese gagaku *orchestra is arranged in playing position, with percussion, wind, and string instruments. Gagaku was the official court music of Japan during the Nara (710–84) and Heian (794–1185) periods. Numbered parts include: three* ryuteki (1), *three* hichiriki (2), *three* sho *pipes (3), two* biwa (4), *one* shoko (5), *one* tsuridaiko (6), *one* kakko (7), *two* gaku-so (8).

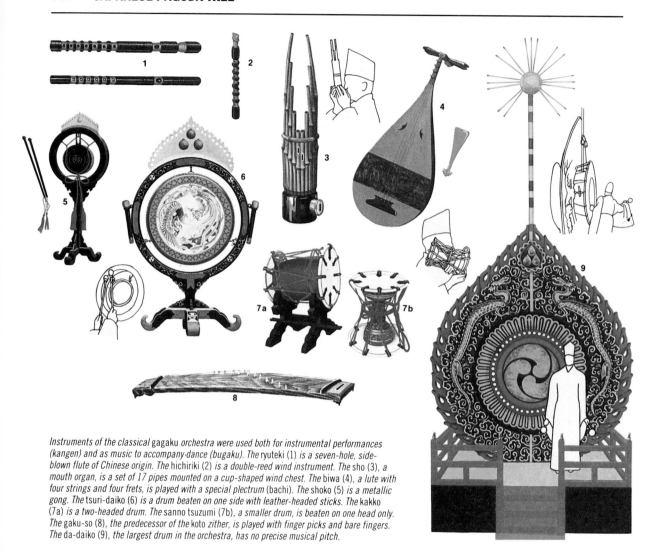

Instruments of the classical gagaku orchestra were used both for instrumental performances (kangen) and as music to accompany dance (bugaku). The ryuteki (1) is a seven-hole, side-blown flute of Chinese origin. The hichiriki (2) is a double-reed wind instrument. The sho (3), a mouth organ, is a set of 17 pipes mounted on a cup-shaped wind chest. The biwa (4), a lute with four strings and four frets, is played with a special plectrum (bachi). The shoko (5) is a metallic gong. The tsuri-daiko (6) is a drum beaten on one side with leather-headed sticks. The kakko (7a) is a two-headed drum. The sanno tsuzumi (7b), a smaller drum, is beaten on one head only. The gaku-so (8), the predecessor of the koto zither, is played with finger picks and bare fingers. The da-daiko (9), the largest drum in the orchestra, has no precise musical pitch.

The *yo* and *in* scales appear frequently after 1500, as do solo instrumental pieces for the *shakuhachi* (end-blown flute) and the koto. *Sankyoku*, a genre of chamber music, is played by the koto combined with a plucked three-stringed samisen (or shamisen) and a *shakuhachi* or a bowed lute (*kokyu*). In the puppet theater (*bunraku*) a narrative shamisen music is essential, whereas the KABU-KI theater contains both narrative and lyrical genres, particularly *kiyomoto* and *nagauta*.

Since 1868, Western and traditional music (*hogaku*) have existed together in Japan. Public school music is primarily Western-oriented, although interest in traditional styles has increased since the mid-20th century.

Japanese pagoda tree   Despite its name, the Japanese pagoda tree, *Sophora japonica*, is native to China and Korea. It is a member of the pea family, Legumino-

sae, and grows to 24 m (80 ft) high. Its pinnate leaves are shed in the fall. From July to September the tree bears yellowish white flowers in long clusters. The seedpods are about 8 cm (3 in) long and are narrowed between the seeds, giving them a necklacelike appearance.

Jarmo [jar'-moh]   Jarmo is an archaeological site named for the Kurdish village of Qallat Jarmo in the foothills of northern Iraq, about 55 km (35 mi) east of Kirkuk. It was excavated by the American archaeologist Robert Braidwood in 1948–55. Dated *c.*6750 BC, this early Neolithic settlement is important for its evidences of early plant and animal domestication. Two kinds of domesticated wheat were found, and domesticated sheep and goats were identified. Braidwood hypothesized that plant domestication and early farming in the Near East originated in the hilly flanks of northern Iraq's Zagros Mountains.

Jarrell, Randall [jair'-ul] One of the most accomplished of a gifted generation of American poets, Randall Jarrell, b. Nashville, Tenn., May 16, 1914, d. Oct. 15, 1965 (possibly a suicide), published his first book of poetry, *Blood from a Stranger*, in 1942. He then enlisted in the U.S. Air Force, serving for the remainder of World War II as a pilot or pilot trainer. The war loomed large in his second and third collections, *Little Friend, Little Friend* (1945) and *Losses* (1948). His two final volumes, *The Woman at the Washington Zoo* (1960) and *The Lost World* (1965), turned to a world of children and of pained adults overwhelmed by their social destinies and mental struggles. Two of Jarrell's collections of essays, *Poetry and the Age* (1953) and *A Sad Heart at the Supermarket* (1962), were widely applauded, and a posthumous volume, *The Third Book of Criticism* (1969), contains many valuable insights. He was also a gifted translator of German poetry. *The Complete Poems* of Randall Jarrell was published in 1969.

Jarry, Alfred [zhah-ree', ahl-fred'] Alfred Jarry, b. Sept. 8, 1873, d. Nov. 15, 1907, was a highly eccentric French dramatist, poet, and humorist who invented a pseudophilosophical system called "pataphysics," or the science of imaginary solutions. He is best known for his series of Ubu plays that include *King Ubu* (1896; Eng. trans., 1953), *Ubu in Chains* (1900; Eng. trans., 1953); and *Ubu the Cuckold* (1944; Eng. trans., 1953). A cruel, cowardly, and absurd figure, Ubu caricatured the ineptitude of the bourgeois and expressed Jarry's own hostility toward the established order. The novels *L'Amour Absolu* (Absolute Love, 1899), *The Supermale* (1902; Eng. trans., 1977), and *The Gestures and Opinions of Doctor Faustroll* (1911; Eng. trans., 1965) contain a mixture of poetry and black comedy. Jarry is considered a precursor of DADA and SURREALISM for his idiosyncrasies and strange literary creations.

Jaruzelski, Wojciech [yah-roo-zhel'-skee, voy'-chek] Wojciech Witold Jaruzelski, b. July 6, 1923, is a Polish military commander who, as first secretary of the United Workers' (Communist) party, dominated Poland from 1981 to 1989. Jaruzelski became prime minister and party chief in 1981, when the implementation of liberal reforms inspired by the SOLIDARITY labor movement was causing alarm in the USSR. In December 1981 he declared martial law, banned Solidarity, and arrested its leaders. Martial law was ended in 1983. In the spring of 1989, influenced by the liberal *glasnost* policy of Soviet leader Mikhail Gorbachev, he legalized Solidarity and permitted free elections. He served in the new post of president from July 1989 to December 1990.

jasmine [jaz'-min] Jasmine is the common name given to a large number of plants, many of them unrelated. The poet's, or common, jasmine, *Jasminum officinale*, of

Common white jasmine is a tropical and subtropical climbing shrub easily cultivated both outdoors (in warm climates) and in greenhouses. Its fragrant white flowers contain an essential oil used in making perfumes.

the olive family, is a tropical and subtropical plant that probably originated in the Middle East and is now cultivated principally in France, Morocco, and Italy. The fragrant jasmine odor can be extracted (see ESSENTIAL OILS) and is one of the most widely used scents in the making of perfume. The flowers of Arabian jasmine, *J. sambac*, are used to scent and flavor tea. The nectar of the fragrant flowers of Carolina jasmine, *Gelsemium sempervirens*, is poisonous, although the dried roots are used in medicinal preparations as a sedative.

Jason [jay'-suhn] In Greek mythology Jason was the leader of the Argonauts, who sought the GOLDEN FLEECE. After Pelias, his uncle, usurped the throne of Iolcus, the young Jason was taken to the centaur CHIRON, who reared him on Mount Pelion. When, as a man, Jason claimed his kingdom, Pelias gave him the task of bringing to him the Golden Fleece. Jason ordered the construction of a 50-oared ship called the *Argo*, for which he assembled a crew including HERCULES, ORPHEUS, THESEUS, and other heroes. After many adventures, they reached Colchis, the land of the Golden Fleece.

At Colchis, Jason yoked fire-breathing bulls, sowed the dragon's teeth of CADMUS, vanquished champions, and seized the fleece with the help of the princess MEDEA, with whom he returned home. They brought about the murder of Pelias but were expelled from the city by Pelias's son. Jason and Medea went to Corinth, where they lived as man and wife for many years. When Jason wished to marry Creusa (or Glauce), daughter of King Creon, Medea revenged herself by using her knowledge of magic and sorcery to burn to death both the father and daughter. For breaking his vow to Medea, Jason was condemned to wander the earth until his death.

jasper [jas'-pur] Jasper is an opaque and fine-grained QUARTZ. Colored red, yellow, brown, or off-white to gray by impurities, jasper has long been used as an ornamental stone because it takes a fine polish. The color of a streak made on a black jasper touchstone will give a good indication of the gold content of gold ores.

Jaspers, Karl [yahs'-purs]

Karl Jaspers, b. Feb. 23, 1883, d. Feb. 26, 1969, was a leading exponent of German EXISTENTIALISM. He became a professor of psychology at Heidelberg in 1916 and of philosophy there in 1921. During the Nazi regime he was relieved of his duties, but after the war in 1945 he was reinstated. It was as a psychiatrist that Jaspers first studied philosophy, and all his later thought reflects this. His existential philosophy was influenced primarily by Friedrich NIETZSCHE and Søren KIERKEGAARD and only incidentally by Martin HEIDEGGER and Jean Paul SARTRE, who wrote most of their works after Jaspers had already published a good deal.

Jaspers's thought rests on the distinction between two states of being—Dasein and Existenz. Dasein (not to be confused with the meaning Heidegger gives it) refers to existence in an ordinary and minimal sense. It is concerned with the practical management of everyday life and known through objective scientific investigation. Existenz refers to the richness of authentic being. Jaspers defines it as the authentic self and as the experience of total freedom, of infinite possibility, and of loneliness. It is concerned with personal choice and known through individual insight or intuition. Existenz is inaccessible to traditional philosophic investigation, which quests for certainty. Only when such quests have been "shipwrecked" upon the limitations of Existenz can true philosophizing begin. Jaspers calls these limitations "boundary situations." They include death, suffering, guilt, chance, and conflict. Of these boundaries, the most important is death because the anticipation of death is the source not only of such negative emotions as dread but also of true relish for life. Experiences with such boundary situations force us to recognize the shallowness of Dasein and provide an introduction, says Jaspers, "to that shaking up of thought from which Existenzphilosophie must spring." Jaspers's examination of boundary situations constitutes an existentialist statement of the problem of evil.

In both outlook and method Jaspers was a strong subjectivist. Asserting that personal experience is the individual's only source of information about reality, he used his own experiences as the basis for philosophic generalization. Although Jaspers understood human Existenz as an individual state, he also believed that subjectivity was essentially social. One can discover one's authentic self only through reflection in someone else's authentic self. In fact, philosophy is the disclosure of oneself through communication. Such communication requires what Jaspers called "philosophic faith," which involves a belief in personal freedom, the inadequacy of a person alone, and the transcendence of the ordinary world.

Jaspers was a religious existentialist. Like Kierkegaard, he believed the "leap of faith" to be essentially absurd, in that nothing logically demonstrates that one should take this leap.

jaundice [jawn'-dis]

Jaundice, a disorder symptomatic of several BLOOD and LIVER diseases, is characterized by yellowing of the skin and mucous membranes, particularly the white of the eyes. It is caused by the excess production or inadequate excretion of bilirubin, which is a yellow bile pigment formed from hemoglobin breakdown products after red blood cells decompose.

Because red blood cells continually wear out and break down, bilirubin is usually present, in small amounts, in blood plasma. It is excreted from the liver into the intestines through the bile ducts. Hemolytic jaundice occurs when red blood cells are destroyed excessively, as in some forms of anemia or sepsis (an infection of the bloodstream) or after the transfusion of an incompatible blood type. Hepatogenous jaundice is caused by liver damage, particularly hepatitis, the ingestion or inhalation of toxic chemicals, or cirrhosis. Obstructive jaundice results from blockage of the bile ducts, usually by gallstones or tumors.

Newborn infants frequently develop mild hemolytic jaundice, which lasts several days until a normal excess of red blood cells is destroyed. Erythroblastosis fetalis, a serious form of jaundice in infants, generally is due to an RH FACTOR incompatibility. Adolescents and young adults who have a viral inflammation of the liver often develop jaundice; jaundice in middle-aged adults is commonly due to gallstones. In older adults jaundice may signal cancer of the liver or the bile ducts. It is often the first symptom of liver damage in alcoholics.

Jaurès, Jean [zhoh-res']

Jean Joseph Marie Auguste Jaurès, b. Sept. 3, 1859, d. July 31, 1914, an eminent French socialist, helped bring the various socialist factions of France into a single party. He taught philosophy at Toulouse before entering the Chamber of Deputies in 1885. As a leading supporter of Alfred Dreyfus in the prolonged DREYFUS AFFAIR, Jaurès won many converts to socialism, but he was attacked by doctrinaire Marxists for supporting the bourgeois government of René WALDECK-ROUSSEAU. In 1905, Jaurès brought together the five different schools of French socialists in the Section française de l'internationale ouvrière (French section of the worker's international). In that year, however, the Second International (see INTERNATIONAL, SOCIALIST), which had facilitated the union, rejected the participation in bourgeois politics.

In 1904, Jaurès founded L'Humanité, a leading left-wing newspaper. He was assassinated by a fanatical nationalist in Paris on the eve of World War I. Jaurès wrote a notable history of the French Revolution, Histoire socialiste de la Révolution française (1901–07).

Java [jah'-vuh]

Java, the most important island of Indonesia, is located south of Borneo and Sumatra. The island is about 1,000 km (620 mi) long and has a maximum width of about 200 km (125 mi). Its area is 125,740 km^2 (48,550 mi^2), and it has a population of

105,560,200 (1988 est.). The island is divided into three provinces and two districts; JAKARTA, the capital of Java and Indonesia, is on the northwestern coast.

Java is made up of longitudinal belts of limestone platforms, eroded volcanic mountains, volcanoes (35 of which are active), and alluvial valleys. Volcanic ash has created fertile soils.

Java is one of the most densely populated areas in the world. The Javanese, who occupy the central and eastern two-thirds of the island, constitute about 45% of all Indonesians. Although the Javanese converted to Islam beginning in the 13th century, many indigenous and Hindu-Buddhist practices are retained today. Javanese dances, music (gamelan orchestra), dramas (shadow and puppet plays), woodcarvings, paintings, and textile decorations are world famous.

Most Javanese are farmers who tend the rice terraces that make up 40% of Java's cultivated land; large numbers of landless Javanese are being resettled on less populous islands. Java's commercial crops include rubber, coffee, tea, tobacco, cacao, and timber; petroleum, coal, tin, gold, and silver are mined. Most of Indonesia's heavy industry is in Jakarta and SURABAYA, and BANDUNG is a textile center.

By AD 700, Java had been conquered by Indian princes. Indian influence reached its height with the Majapahit Empire (founded 1293). Expanding Muslim influence led to the destruction of the empire in the early 16th century. The Dutch East India Company gradually gained control of the island in the early 17th century. It passed to the Dutch government in 1799, which retained it, except for occupations by the British (1811–16) and Japanese (1942–45), until Indonesian independence in 1950.

Java man   The remains of Java man, the first known fossils of the extinct species HOMO ERECTUS, were discovered (1891–93) by a young Dutch anatomist, Eugène Dubois, in a bank of the Solo River, at Trinil, Java. Dubois's finds consisted of a low, thick-boned, primitive-looking skullcap, with prominent brow ridges and a brain size only half that of modern humans, and a thighbone, which in contrast appeared entirely human in form. Dubois named his creature *Pithecanthropus erectus*, meaning "erect apeman." This name was later changed to *Homo erectus*.

Subsequent finds in Africa of an earlier creature, AUSTRALOPITHECUS, more primitive still than *Pithecanthropus* but also clearly a hominid—and discoveries of additional fossils in Java dated between about 700,000 and 1.5 million years ago—helped settle the debate. Java man is now recognized as belonging to the category *Homo erectus*, along with fossils from China, Europe, and Africa; on an evolutionary scale this species lies between the earlier *Australopithecus* and the later species *Homo sapiens*.

Java Sea   The Java Sea is the part of the western Pacific Ocean between the islands of Borneo on the north and Java on the south. It covers 433,000 km^2 (167,000 mi^2) and is shallow, with a mean depth of only 46 m (151 ft). The Makasar Strait connects it with Celebes Sea.

Javanese language   see MALAYO-POLYNESIAN LANGUAGES

javelin   see TRACK AND FIELD

Javits, Jacob K. [jav'-its]   Jacob Koppel Javits, b. New York City, May 18, 1904, d. Mar. 7, 1986, was U.S. senator from New York from 1957 to 1981. A liberal Republican, Javits also served in the House of Representatives (1947–55) and as attorney general of New York (1955–57). He focused on legislation concerning foreign affairs, urban development, civil rights, organized labor, and big business. He was instrumental in gaining passage (1973) of the War Powers Act, limiting the ability of the president to make war without the consent of Congress. Javits was a strong supporter of Israel. His last book was *Javits: The Autobiography of a Public Man* (with Rafael Steinberg, 1981).

Jaworski, Leon [juh-wor'-skee]   Leon Jaworski, b. Waco, Tex., Sept. 19, 1905, d. Dec. 9, 1982, was a prominent Texas lawyer who led the last phase of the WATERGATE investigation that culminated in the resignation of President Richard M. NIXON in August 1974. Jaworski, named special prosecutor in November 1973, presented evidence to a federal grand jury that led to the indictment of seven important figures in the Nixon administration. He also successfully challenged Nixon's attempt to withhold White House tape recordings from use as evidence, in United States v. Richard M. Nixon. Jaworski wrote *The Right and the Power* (1976) and *Crossroads* (with Dick Schneider, 1981).

jay   The 35 species of jays, classified in the avian family Corvidae, are distributed throughout the Northern Hemisphere and South America. They measure 20 to 76 cm (8 to 30 in) in length and are usually crested and colorful; some species have very long tails. Jays eat a wide variety of

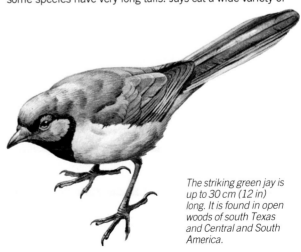

The striking green jay is up to 30 cm (12 in) long. It is found in open woods of south Texas and Central and South America.

foods, from seeds to eggs and young birds. Many jays give harsh, noisy calls; some can mimic other birds.

Only two species inhabit the Old World: the widespread common jay, *Garrulus glandarius*; and the Siberian jay, *Perisoreus infaustus*. The common jay, which has a distinctive brownish plumage and wing bands of black, blue, and white, is considered beneficial in dispersing tree seeds. Two well-known species that occur in North America are the gray jay, *P. canadensis*, which is found in northern and mountainous coniferous forests, and the blue jay, *Cyanocitta cristata*, which inhabits oak and pine regions of eastern and central North America. Most species occur in the tropics.

Jay, John   The American statesman John Jay, b. New York City, Dec. 12, 1745, d. May 17, 1829, was the first chief justice of the U.S. Supreme Court. Embodying the best of the moderate reform tradition, he initially favored limited resistance to Great Britain but supported the American Revolution after the signing of the Declaration of Independence. A seeker of social stability, he advocated a strong federal government and close ties to Britain during the early national period.

Jay grew up in a comfortable home, graduated from King's College (now Columbia University) in 1764, and four years later joined the bar. He began a brilliant career as a lawyer and soon became absorbed in public life. In prerevolutionary New York politics and as a delegate to the First and Second CONTINENTAL CONGRESS, he was a leading spokesperson and strategist for the moderate faction. Once the Declaration of Independence had been adopted, however, Jay accepted it and worked earnestly in Congress and in New York City for the success of the American Revolution. New York's first state constitution (1777) was largely his work, and he took office under it as the state's chief justice in 1777.

Continuing to serve in Congress, Jay was elected its president in 1778. The next year he was appointed minister to Spain, embarking on fruitless negotiations to win Spanish recognition of American independence. In 1782,

John Jay, one of the leading figures of the early years of the American republic, was appointed as the first chief justice of the Supreme Court in 1789 and established procedures still observed by that body. Jay was sent on a mission to London in 1794, where he negotiated the treaty that bears his name.

Jay went to Paris as one of the American peace commissioners. There, with Benjamin FRANKLIN and John ADAMS, he negotiated the peace treaty of 1783, which ended the Revolution.

He returned home in 1784 to serve as foreign secretary under the Articles of Confederation. He worked actively for adoption of the Constitution of 1787, most notably as one of the authors of The FEDERALIST. He became (1789) the first chief justice of the Supreme Court under the new Constitution, but his most important national service thereafter was to negotiate JAY'S TREATY (1794). In the early 1790s he became a staunch Federalist (see FEDERALIST PARTY), favoring a strong national government sympathetic to the growth of commerce and industry. He resigned as chief justice to serve as governor of New York (1795–1801) and then refused further public office.

Jaycees International   [jay'-seez]   An association of young businesspeople, the Jaycees meet in local chapters and participate in programs of civic service and business education. The international organization, founded in 1944, has about 75 national groups and a membership exceeding 400,000. The U.S. Jaycees, with about 240,000 members from ages 21 to 40, was founded in St. Louis, Mo., in 1915. It has had several names. From 1918 it was the Junior Chamber of Commerce. It took its present name in 1965.

Jay's Treaty   On Nov. 19, 1794, U.S. Chief Justice John JAY, acting in his capacity as special envoy, signed a treaty with Great Britain. It proved advantageous to the new American nation, although it raised a storm of controversy. By averting the threat of war, Jay's Treaty ensured Anglo-American trade and thus provided revenues to the U.S. customs.

Friction between Great Britain and its former colony had arisen from various sources. Despite the Treaty of Paris (1783), which had ended the American Revolution, the British government had refused to evacuate the frontier forts in the Old Northwest (see NORTHWEST TERRITORY), and Americans believed that the British were encouraging the Indians to attack local settlers. The British maintained that Americans had refused to pay prerevolutionary debts owed British creditors. Anglo-American relations were further aggravated when Britain began seizing American ships and impressing American sailors into British service in its war against France.

Jay's Treaty secured the British evacuation of the frontier forts. It also referred the debt question and the settlement of boundary disputes to joint commissions, but it made no provision for settlement of the Indian issue or the impressment question. The treaty passed through the Senate in June 1795.

jazz   Jazz is the only indigenous American musical form to have exerted an influence on musical development throughout the Western world. Created by obscure black musicians in the late 19th century, jazz at first synthesized Western harmonic language and forms with the rhythms and melodic inflections of Africa. Black vocal music—SPIRITUALS, the work song, the field holler, and BLUES—provided the structure through which popular tunes were transmuted into jazz. The music was characterized by improvisation; by syncopation, where rhythmic stress is placed on the normally weak beats of the musical measure; and by intonation that would be considered out of tune in Western classical music.

The black marching bands of New Orleans, which often accompanied funeral processions, played traditional slow hymns on the way to the cemetery; for the procession back to town, they broke into jazzed-up versions of the same hymns, RAGTIME tunes, or syncopated renditions of popular marches. The instruments in the marching band—a cornet or a trumpet to carry the melody, with a clarinet and trombone to fill in, and a rhythm section of drums or a string bass—formed the nucleus of the first jazz bands, which usually added only a piano, guitar, or banjo.

Dixieland

The earliest recordings identified as jazz were made in 1917 in New York by the Original Dixieland Jazz Band, a group of white musicians from New Orleans under the leadership of Nick La Rocca. When jazz bands traveled to Chicago and New York City, the music became available nationwide through recordings released by the major record companies. The first important recordings by black musicians were made in 1923, by King OLIVER's Creole Jazz Band, a group that included some of the foremost New Orleans musicians then performing in Chicago: Louis ARMSTRONG, Johnny and "Baby" Dodds, and Honore Dutrey.

Many white groups in Chicago and elsewhere adopted the style, among them the New Orleans Rhythm Kings and the Wolverines, led by Bix BEIDERBECKE. The characteristics of this early style, known as Dixieland, included a relatively complex interweaving of melodic lines among the cornet (or trumpet), clarinet, and trombone and a

Duke Ellington, a seminal figure in the history of jazz, introduced the "big band" sound to jazz with the brilliant compositions and arrangements performed by his 10-member band.

Bessie Smith, known as the Empress of the Blues, is considered by many the greatest blues singer in history.

steady chomp-chomp beat from the rhythm instruments (piano, bass, drums). Most bands used no written notation, preferring "head" arrangements agreed on verbally; improvisation was a must.

During the 1920s all sections of the country were caught up in the dances associated with jazz. The period itself became known as the Jazz Age.

In Chicago the most influential artists were members of small bands like the Wolverines. In New York, on the other hand, the trend was toward larger groups with two or more trumpets, one or two trombones, three or four reeds, plus a rhythm section. The larger groups played in revues and vaudeville shows and in large dance halls and theaters.

New York Jazz

As the decade progressed, the performance styles in all groups featured more written arrangements and placed increasing emphasis on solo performance. Representative of the many players who led the outburst of jazz virtuosity that marked the 1920s were Sidney Bechet, Jelly Roll MORTON, Coleman HAWKINS, Armstrong, and James P. Johnson. Among the leaders in establishing the sound of the new big bands were Fletcher HENDERSON (with Don Redman, his arranger) and Duke ELLINGTON. It was Henderson who developed the performance style that became known as SWING, featuring call-and-response patterns between brass and reeds, extensive use of the riff—the repetition of a motif—for ensemble work and as accompaniment for soloists, elaborate written arrangements, and the frequent insertion of improvised solos. Ellington extended the role of bandleader beyond mere arranging and into the area of composition, principally because of his need to provide music for the Cotton Club revues in Harlem. Many of his compositions have become standards for jazz players.

Around this time, vocal blues recordings were produced in New York and marketed principally to blacks. The unique form of the blues allowed many of the best jazz performers to play as backup artists and insert instrumental "comments" between the sung phrases. The most definitive singer of the period was Bessie SMITH,

Tommy Potter, Charlie Parker, Dizzy Gillespie, and John Coltrane are seen in performance (c. 1950). The Parker-Gillespie combination produced some of the finest bop of the 1940s and early '50s.

whose 1920s recordings are considered landmarks of vocal blues.

Swing

The dominant idiom of the 1930s and much of the 1940s was swing. Utilized almost exclusively for dancing, the music of the big bands borrowed heavily from the techniques introduced by Henderson. Among the most popular bands were those led by Benny GOODMAN, Glenn MILLER, Woody Herman, Jimmy and Tommy DORSEY, and Artie Shaw. A Kansas City swing style developed under the influence of Count BASIE and Bennie Moten that emphasized a blues vocabulary and form as well as tempos of breakneck speed and an overwhelming use of riffs. Among the outstanding soloists associated with Kansas City was Lester YOUNG of the Basie band.

The Jazz Revolution: Bebop

In the early 1940s a rejection of the restrictive arrangements required by big-band style spread among jazz musicians. Under the leadership of Charlie PARKER, Dizzy GILLESPIE, Thelonious MONK, and others, a style known as bop, or BEBOP, emerged on the New York scene.

It represented a return to the small group concept of Dixieland, with one instrument of a kind rather than the sections used by swing groups. Emphasizing solos rather than ensembles, bop players developed an astounding degree of virtuosity. Bop was extremely complex rhythmically; it used extensions of the usual harmonic structures and featured speed and irregular phrasing. It demanded great listening skill, and its erratic rhythms made it unsuitable for dancing. Because of its sophistication, bop resulted in the first breakaway of jazz from the popular-music mainstream. The style was adopted by many performers during the 1940s and '50s; others still preferred the more conservative techniques of swing.

Cool. One of the most important new jazz styles of the 1950s was known as "cool." Inaugurated by a group of highly trained academic performers under the leadership of Miles DAVIS, cool was a return to the carefully organized and scored principles of swing but without the latter's emphasis on call-and-response and riffing. The ensembles played frequently as an entire unit and included a number of new instruments in jazz: French horn, flute, baritone sax, flügelhorn, and others. The players rejected the emotional emphasis of bop as well as its exploitation of range and virtuosity. They preferred to play in the middle register, utilizing a smooth attack, little vibrato, and largely on-beat phrasing.

Third Stream. Closely allied to cool jazz was third stream, a style that attempted to combine modern classical forms with jazz techniques. It used improvisational segments interwoven with compositions scored for symphony orchestras and chamber groups, including string quartets. Musical forms identified with classical tradition were utilized—fugue, rondo, symphonic development. Polyphony became an important texture, best exemplified by the jazz fugues played by the MODERN JAZZ QUARTET.

Jazz Extremes: The 1960s

The jazz of the 1960s was in many ways a mirroring of the social ferment of that decade. Much of the performance was characterized by a search for freedom from melodic, harmonic, and rhythmic restraints. One of the leaders was Ornette Coleman, whose 1960 album, *Free Jazz*, set the tone of the decade. It featured eight musicians improvising individually and collectively without predetermined thematic material of any kind. The ultimate result was a breakdown in the traditional framework for improvisation, which had relied for decades on melodic variations based normally on a stated tune or harmonic progression. Cecil TAYLOR and others moved even farther away from traditional jazz practice and used atonality and other dissonances.

The leading figure of the decade was John COLTRANE. In many of his performances he abandoned tonality completely and improvised at length within a single-scale structure or over a single chord or mode. His many fol-

Herbie Hancock was influenced by Miles Davis's avant-garde jazz. Hancock played in Davis's quartet in the 1960s and formed his own sextet in the '70s.

lowers cultivated an almost totally emotional style, extending the expressive range of their instruments to screaming, moaning, and piercing outbursts of passionate sound. As a result, the audience for jazz decreased dramatically and many critics expressed the fear that the art was doomed.

The 1970s Jazz Revival

The decade of the 1970s brought renewed interest in jazz. The popularity of big bands, using many of the devices of swing, spread to high school and college campuses. Thad Jones, Mel Lewis, Woody Herman, and Count Basie provided the leadership for this renaissance of big-band style.

Many leading musicians, on the other hand, turned toward a fusion of ROCK MUSIC and jazz, trading on the overwhelming popularity of the 1960s rock innovations. Among the leaders in the fusion movement were Miles Davis, Herbie Hancock, Chick COREA, Wayne Shorter, and George Benson. Their music placed great emphasis on the use of electronic instruments, enlarged percussion sections, repeated melodic and rhythmic figures, and relatively long segments performed without any significant harmonic change. Other leading players such as McCoy Tyner experimented extensively with modal themes and drone effects, reflecting the African-American identification with Eastern religions and spiritualism. Large-scale dissonant compositions for jazz groups gained in popularity under the influence of men like Anthony Braxton and Sun Ra. At the same time, more traditional performers like the New Orleans Preservation Hall Jazz Band found enthusiastic audiences.

The 1980s were years of eclectic additions to jazz language. African music began to penetrate and color the jazz picture, just as in Africa the new "Afro-Pop" combined jazz influences with African sounds and rhythms. Latin American music—Brazilian music, especially—added another new strain to jazz. More jazz musicians were classically trained, and many of them, like the Marsalis brothers (see MARSALIS family), were technical perfectionists. In contrast to a music that was becoming more difficult and complex, interest was nonetheless reviving in improvisation, the heart of jazz before the electronic age.

▬

jeep   The jeep is a small, 1¼-ton open-topped military car, first used by the U.S. Army in 1941. The name is derived from the Army's designation, General Purpose vehicle, or GP. The army jeep has a 71-hp engine, a top speed of 105 km/h (65 mph), and, with its 4-wheel drive and high ground clearance, the capacity to travel over roads that might be impassable to ordinary vehicles.

The jeep was designed as a small, light, reconnaissance and command vehicle, but during World War II it was used in several roles. In addition to hauling supplies and acting as an emergency ambulance, it became an antiaircraft vehicle when heavy machine guns on steel mounts were added; a field-kitchen transporter; and a gun tractor for moving antitank guns. With the addition of waterproof hulls, some models were used as small, amphibious landing craft.

The jeep was made by several automobile companies during World War II. It is produced today only by a division of the Chrysler Corporation, which uses the capitalized name as its trademark.

▬

Jeffers, Robinson   The American poet John Robinson Jeffers, b. Pittsburgh, Pa., Jan. 10, 1887, d. Jan. 20, 1962, became closely associated with the rugged Pacific Coast, which provided the setting for many of his poems, and noted for his adaptations of Greek and biblical myths.

His first book, *Flagons and Apples* (1912), is an undistinguished collection of love poems. The following year he moved to Carmel, Calif., where he deepened his knowledge of the classics and meditated on humanity's place in the universe. Under the influence of modern psychology he began to adapt old stories to modern themes. He derived "The Tower Beyond Tragedy" (1924) from the *Oresteia*, "Solstice" (1935) and "Medea" (1937) from the Medea story, and "Tamar" (1924) and "Dear Judas" (1929) from biblical themes.

Jefferson, Territory of   see COLORADO

▬

Jefferson, Thomas   Thomas Jefferson wished to be remembered for three achievements in his public life. He had served as governor of Virginia, as U.S. minister to France, as secretary of state under George WASHINGTON, as vice-president in the administration of John ADAMS, and as president of the United States from 1801 to 1809. On his tombstone, however, which he designed and for which he wrote the inscription, there is no mention of these offices. Rather, it reads that Thomas Jefferson was "author of the Declaration of American Independence, of the Statute of Virginia for religious freedom, and Father of the University of Virginia" and, as he requested, "not a word more." Historians might want to add other accomplishments—for example, his distinction as an architect, naturalist, and linguist—but in the main they would concur with his own assessment.

Early Life. Jefferson was born at Shadwell in what is now Albemarle County, Va., on Apr. 13, 1743. He attended (1760–62) the College of William and Mary and then studied law with George WYTHE. In 1769 he began six years of service as a representative in the Virginia House of Burgesses. The following year he began building MONTICELLO on land inherited from his father. The mansion, which he designed in every detail, took years to complete, but part of it was ready for occupancy when he married Martha Wayles Skelton on Jan. 1, 1772. They had six children, two of whom survived into adulthood.

Jefferson's reputation began to reach beyond Virginia in 1774, when he wrote a political pamphlet, *A Summary View of the Rights of British America*. Arguing on the basis of natural-rights theory, Jefferson claimed that colonial allegiance to the king was voluntary. "The God who gave us life," he wrote, "gave us liberty at the same time:

AT A GLANCE

THOMAS JEFFERSON
3d President of the United States (1801–09)

Nicknames: "Man of the People"; "Sage of Monticello"
Born: Apr. 13, 1743, Shadwell plantation, Goochland (now in
    Albemarle) County, Va.
Education: College of William and Mary (graduated 1762)
Professions: Lawyer, Planter
Religious Affiliation: None
Marriage: Jan.1, 1772, to Martha Wayles Skelton (1748–82)
Children: Martha Washington Jefferson (1772–1836); Jane
    Randolph Jefferson (1774–75); infant son (1777); Mary
    Jefferson (1778–1804); Lucy Elizabeth Jefferson (1780–
    81); Lucy Elizabeth Jefferson (1782–84)
Political Affiliation: Democratic-Republican
Writings: *Writings* (10 vols. 1892–99), ed. by Paul L. Ford;
    The Papers of Thomas Jefferson (1950–   ), ed. by Julian
    P. Boyd, et al.; *Notes on the State of Virginia 1781* (1955),
    ed. by William Peden; *Autobiography* (1959), ed. by Du-
    mas Malone
Died: July 4, 1826, Monticello, near Charlottesville, Va.
Buried: Monticello, near Charlottesville, Va.
Vice-Presidents: Aaron Burr (1801–05); George Clinton
    (1805–09)

the hand of force may destroy, but cannot disjoin them."

Declaration of Independence. Elected to the Second CONTINENTAL CONGRESS, meeting in Philadelphia, Jefferson was appointed on June 11, 1776, to head a committee of five in preparing the DECLARATION OF INDEPENDENCE. He was its primary author, although his initial draft was amended after consultation with Benjamin FRANKLIN and John Adams and altered both stylistically and substantively by Congress. Based on the same natural-rights theory contained in *A Summary View*, to which it bears a strong resemblance, the Declaration of Independence made Jefferson internationally famous.

Revolutionary Legislator. Returning to Virginia late in 1776, Jefferson served until 1779 in the House of Delegates, one of the two houses of the General Assembly of Virginia—established in 1776 by the state's new constitution. While the AMERICAN REVOLUTION continued, Jefferson sought to liberalize Virginia's laws. Joined by his old law teacher, George Wythe, and by James MADISON and George MASON, Jefferson introduced a number of bills that were resisted fiercely by those representing the conservative planter class. In 1776 he succeeded in obtaining the abolition of entail; his proposal to abolish primogeniture became law in 1785. Jefferson proudly noted that "these laws, drawn by myself, laid the ax to the foot of pseudoaristocracy."

In June 1779 the introduction of Jefferson's bill on religious liberty touched off a quarrel that caused turmoil in Virginia for eight years. The bill was significant, for no other state—indeed, no other nation—provided for complete religious liberty at that time. Jefferson's bill stated "that all men shall be free to profess, and by argument to maintain, their opinions on matters of religion, and that the same shall in no wise diminish, enlarge, or affect their civil capacities." Many Virginians regarded the bill as an attack on Christianity. It did not pass until 1786, and then mainly through the perseverance of James Madison. Jefferson, by then in France, congratulated Madison, adding that "it is honorable for us to have produced the first legislature who had the courage to declare that the reason of man may be trusted with the formation of his own opinions."

Wartime Governor of Virginia. In June 1779, Jefferson was elected governor of Virginia. His political enemies criticized his performance as war governor mercilessly. He was charged with failure to provide for the adequate defense of Richmond in 1780–81, although he knew a British invasion was imminent, and of cowardice and "pusillanimous conduct" when he fled the capital during the moment of crisis. In June 1781 he retired from the governorship. The Virginia assembly subsequently voted that "an inquiry be made into the conduct of the executive of this state." Jefferson was exonerated: in fact, the assembly unanimously voted a resolution of appreciation of his conduct. The episode left Jefferson bitter, however, about the rewards of public service.

Money and the Ordinance of 1784. The death of his wife, on Sept. 6, 1782, added to Jefferson's problems, but by the following year he was again seated in Congress. There he made two contributions of enduring importance to the nation. In April 1784 he submitted *Notes on the Establishment of a Money Unit and of a Coinage for the United States* in which he advised the use of a decimal system. This report led to the adoption (1792) of the dollar, rather than the pound, as the basic monetary unit in the United States.

As chairman of the committee dealing with the government of western lands, Jefferson submitted proposals so liberal and farsighted as to constitute, when enacted, the most progressive colonial policy of any nation in modern history. The proposed ordinance of 1784 reflected Jefferson's belief that the western territories should be self-governing and, when they reached a certain stage of growth, should be admitted to the Union as full partners with the original 13 states. Jefferson also proposed that slavery should be excluded from all of the American western territories after 1800. Although he himself was a slave owner, he believed that slavery was an evil that should not be permitted to spread. In 1784 the provision banning slavery was narrowly defeated. Congress approved the proposed ordinance of 1784, but it was never put into effect; its main features were incorporated, however, in the Ordinance of 1787, which established the NORTHWEST TERRITORY. Moreover, slavery was prohibited in the Northwest Territory.

Minister to France. From 1784 to 1789, Jefferson lived outside the United States. He was sent to Paris initially as a commissioner to help negotiate commercial treaties; then in 1785 he succeeded Benjamin Franklin as minister to France. Most European countries, however, were indifferent to American economic overtures. "They seemed, in fact," Jefferson wrote, "to know little about us. They were ignorant of our commerce, and of the exchange of articles it might offer advantageously to both parties." Only one country, Prussia, signed a pact based on a model treaty drafted by Jefferson.

During these years Jefferson followed events in the United States with understandable interest. He advised against any harsh punishment of those responsible for SHAY'S REBELLION (1786–87) in Massachusetts. He worried particularly that the new CONSTITUTION OF THE UNITED STATES lacked a bill of rights and failed to limit the number of terms for the presidency.

Secretary of State. When Jefferson left Paris on Sept. 26, 1789, he expected to return to his post. On that date and unknown to him, however, Congress confirmed his appointment as secretary of state in the first administration of George Washington. Jefferson accepted the position with some reluctance and largely because of Washington's insistence.

Jefferson came to distrust both the proposals and the motives of his fellow cabinet member Secretary of the Treasury Alexander HAMILTON. He thought Hamilton's financial programs both unwise and unconstitutional, flowing "from principles adverse to liberty." On the issue of federal assumption of state debts, Jefferson struck a bargain with Hamilton permitting assumption to pass—a concession that he later regretted. He attempted, unsuccessfully, to persuade Washington to veto the bill incorporating a BANK OF THE UNITED STATES—recommended by Hamilton. As time passed, the more Washington sided with Hamilton, the more Jefferson became dissatisfied with his minority position within the cabinet. Finally, after being twice dissuaded from resigning, Jefferson did so on Dec. 31, 1793.

Brief Retirement. At home for the next three years, Jefferson devoted himself to farm and family. He experimented with a new plow and other ingenious inventions, built a nail factory, commenced the rebuilding of Monticello, set out a thousand peach trees, received distinguished guests from abroad, and welcomed the visits of his grandchildren. He also followed national and international developments with a mounting sense of foreboding. Jefferson thought Washington's expedition to suppress the WHISKEY REBELLION (1794) an unnecessary use of military force. He deplored Washington's denunciation of the Democratic societies and considered JAY'S TREATY (1794) with Britain a "monument of folly and venality."

Vice-President. Thus Jefferson welcomed Washington's decision not to run for a third term in 1796. Jefferson became the reluctant presidential candidate of the Democratic-Republican party, and he seemed genuinely relieved when the Federalist party candidate, John Adams, gained a narrow electoral college victory (71 to 68). As the runner-up, however, Jefferson became vice-president under the system then in effect.

Jefferson hoped that he could work with Adams, as of old, especially since both men shared an anti-Hamilton bias. Those hopes were soon dashed, however. Relations with France deteriorated. In 1798, in the wake of the XYZ AFFAIR, the so-called Quasi-War began. New taxes were imposed and the ALIEN AND SEDITION ACTS (1798) threatened the freedom of Americans. Jefferson, laboring to check the authoritarian drift of the national government, secretly authored the Kentucky Resolution (see KENTUCKY AND VIRGINIA RESOLUTIONS). More important, he provided his party with principles and strategy, aiming to win the election of 1800.

President. Jefferson's triumph was delayed temporarily as a result of a tie in electoral ballots with his running mate, Aaron BURR, which shifted the election to the House of Representatives. There Hamilton's influence helped Jefferson to prevail, although most Federalists supported Burr as the lesser evil. In his inaugural speech Jefferson held out an olive branch to his political enemies, inviting them to bury the partisanship of the past decade, to unite as Americans.

Federalist leaders remained adamantly opposed to Jefferson, but the people approved of his policies. Internal taxes were reduced; the military budget was cut; the Alien and Sedition Acts were permitted to lapse; and plans were made to extinguish the public debt. Simplicity and frugality became the hallmarks of Jefferson's administration. The Louisiana Purchase (1803) capped his achievements. In the election of 1804, Jefferson swept every state except two—Connecticut and Delaware.

Jefferson's second administration began with a minor success—the favorable settlement concluding the Tripolitan War (1801–05), in which the newly created U.S. Navy fought its first engagements. The following year the Lewis and Clark Expedition, which the president had dispatched to explore the Louisiana Territory, returned triumphantly after crossing the continent.

Jefferson's main concern in his second administration was foreign affairs, in which he experienced a notable failure. In the course of the Napoleonic Wars Britain and France repeatedly violated American sovereignty in incidents such as the Chesapeake affair (1807). Jefferson attempted to avoid a policy of either appeasement or war by the use of economic pressure.

The Embargo Act (Dec. 22, 1807), which prohibited virtually all exports and most imports and was supplemented by enforcing legislation, was designed to coerce British and French recognition of American rights. Although it failed, it did rouse many northerners, who suffered economically, to a state of defiance of national authority. The Federalist party experienced a rebirth of popularity. In 1809, shortly before he retired from the presidency, Jefferson signed the act repealing the embargo, which had been in effect for 15 months.

Later Life. In the final 17 years of his life, Jefferson's major accomplishment was the founding (1819) of the University of Virginia at Charlottesville. He conceived it, planned it, designed it, and supervised both its construction and the hiring of faculty.

The university was the last of three contributions by which Jefferson wished to be remembered; they constituted a trilogy of interrelated causes: freedom from Britain, freedom of conscience, and freedom maintained through education. On July 4, 1826, the 50th anniversary of the Declaration of Independence, Jefferson died at Monticello.

Jefferson Airplane

The rock music group Jefferson Airplane came out of San Francisco's Haight-Ashbury during that area's heyday as the center of the counterculture movement. Founded in early 1965 by singer Marty Balin (b. Cincinnati, Ohio, Jan. 30, 1943) and singer-guitarist Paul Kantner (b. San Francisco, Mar. 12, 1942), the band gained a large following after singer Grace Slick (b. Chicago, Oct. 30, 1939) joined the group in late 1966, bringing with her two popular American songs, "Somebody to Love" and "White Rabbit" (both released in 1967). From 1970 rifts between members caused a gradual disbanding, but in 1974 the group reformed under the name Jefferson Starship, released their extraordinarily successful album *Red Octopus* in 1975, and have continued to play concerts and record.

Jefferson City

Jefferson City, in central Missouri on the Missouri River, is the capital of the state and seat of Cole County. It has a population of 35,481 (1990). Jefferson City is the center of trade for an agricultural region that grows grain and fruit and raises livestock. Manufactured goods include clothing, steel products, and processed food. The state and local governments are important employers.

The capitol contains murals by painters N. C. Wyeth and Thomas Hart Benton and houses two museums. Lincoln University (1866), a state penitentiary, and a national cemetery are also located there.

A small river settlement when chosen as state capital in 1821, Jefferson City was laid out (1822) by Daniel M. Boone, son of the frontiersman, and developed slowly with railroad and river commerce. During the Civil War, because of its divided loyalties, the city was occupied by Union troops.

Jeffords, Thomas

[jef'-urdz] Thomas Jeffords, b. Chautauqua County, N.Y., 1832, d. 1914, a U.S. Army scout and stagecoach driver in Arizona, became a friend and agent of the Chiracahua Apaches. In 1872, Jeffords took part with Gen. Oliver O. Howard in negotiations with the Chiracahua chief, Cochise, that helped secure for the Chiracahua a reservation in their southeastern Arizona homeland. At Cochise's request, Jeffords was named the reservation's agent, a post he held until the Chiracahua were transferred (1876) to another reservation.

Jeffries, James J.

James J. Jeffries, b. Carroll, Ohio, Apr. 15, 1875, d. Mar. 3, 1953, was an American heavyweight boxing champion who won the title in 1899 and defended it successfully 6 times, retaining it until he retired undefeated in 1905. A strong, intelligent boxer who made the defensive crouch popular, Jeffries knocked out Bob Fitzsimmons to earn the title. His defenses of the title included 2 victories over James J. Corbett and 1 over Fitzsimmons. His only loss against 20 wins and 2 draws was to Jack Johnson during a comeback attempt in 1910; Johnson knocked out Jeffries in the 15th round.

Jehoshaphat, King of Judah

[jee-hahsh'-uh-fat] Jehoshaphat, son and successor of Asa, was king of Judah, the southern kingdom of the ancient Israelites, from 873 to 849 BC. He became an ally of Ahab, king of Israel, and his successors, and during Jehoshaphat's reign, Judah and Israel agreed upon a treaty, ending the warfare dating from King Solomon. He was succeeded by his son Jehoram.

Jehovah   see God

Jehovah's Witnesses

[juh-hoh'-vuhz] Jehovah's Witnesses are a society of Christians who promote home study of the Bible, which they hold to be the complete Word of God. They believe that God's kingdom is an actual government now ruling in heaven that will soon restore the Earth to its original paradisaic condition. They expect an early end to the present world system in a "great tribulation" from God that will rid the Earth of wickedness and suffering. Following Armageddon will come a millennial reign over the Earth by Jesus. The gaining of eternal life depends on complete obedience to Jehovah God and faith in the provision of Jesus Christ's ransom sacrifice. The Witnesses encourage adherence to the Bible's moral standards. Because of their neutrality as to affairs of secular government, their refusal to salute any flag, and their rejection of the practice of blood transfusion (which they believe is forbidden by the Bible), the Witnesses have been the subject of controversy.

The activities of Jehovah's Witnesses are coordinated by a governing body at international headquarters in Brooklyn, N.Y. Elders, male members meeting certain scriptural qualifications, preside as a body over individual congregations. Instruction and training are provided for all at five meetings a week, held primarily in "Kingdom Halls." The Watchtower Bible and Tract Society of Pennsylvania, and the Watchtower Bible and Tract Society of New York, Inc., are the legal agencies of Jehovah's Witnesses. They print and distribute the Bible. Their principal periodical, *The Watchtower*, is distributed in more than 100 languages.

The Witnesses acknowledge Jehovah God as their founder. The modern movement was organized in the 1870s by Charles Taze RUSSELL.

Jehu, King of Israel [jee'-hyoo] Jehu reigned as king of ancient Israel from 842 to 815 BC. He was anointed king by the prophet ELISHA, who instructed him to overthrow the wicked King AHAB (2 Kings 9–10). With the army's support Jehu slaughtered the entire royal family and purged Israel of the idolatrous BAAL worship.

jellyfish A jellyfish is a free-swimming, sexually reproductive stage (medusa) found in the life cycle of certain species of COELENTERATES (phylum Cnidaria). It typically is shaped like a bell or inverted bowl from 3 mm to 2 m (0.12 in to 6.5 ft) in diameter. The bell's margin contains small sense organs that respond to light and gravity; the margin also bears tentacles, the length and position of which vary considerably from species to species. The mouth is at the end of a projection called the manubrium, which hangs down within the center of the bell; the corners of the manubrium, in some species, extend into four or more oral arms. Much of the animal is composed of a firm, gelatinous middle layer (mesoglea), from which the common name *jellyfish* is derived.

Jellyfish feed on organisms ranging from plankton and fish to other jellyfish. They catch their prey by using nematocysts, small stinging organs present in the tentacles and oral arms. Rhythmic contractions of the bell's margin expel water from within the bell, and the animal moves forward by jet propulsion. Some species are strong swimmers, whereas others drift with the currents.

Jellyfish are of separate sexes and thus produce eggs

A jellyfish propels itself easily through the ocean by shooting water from its gelatinous, bell-like body. The jellyfish stings and paralyzes prey that wander into its curtain of tentacles.

or sperm. The fertilized egg develops into a planktonic larva. Eventually the larva develops into a sedentary polyp, which reproduces asexually, forming new medusae.

Jellyfish often become abundant in coastal areas. The nematocysts of some species, such as sea nettles, can penetrate human skin, causing stings and rashes. The most dangerous are certain boxlike jellyfish of the order Cubomedusae, found from the Philippines to tropical Australia; their stings have caused a number of fatalities.

The PORTUGUESE MAN-OF-WAR, sometimes mistakenly called a jellyfish, is a colony of polyplike and medusalike individuals that are attached to a gas-filled, floating membrane.

Jemison, Mary [jem'-ih-suhn] Mary Jemison, b. 1743, d. Sept. 19, 1833, was taken from her parents' frontier farm in Pennsylvania by an Indian raiding party in 1758. Known as the White Woman of the Genesee, she lived the rest of her life with the Seneca on the Genesee River in New York State, marrying two Seneca men. Her life story appears in J. E. Seaver's *Narrative of the Life of Mrs. Jemison* (1824; repr. 1967).

Jena [yay'-nah] Jena (1987 est. pop., 107,678) is a city in east central Germany, on the Saale River. The site of the famous Schott and Zeiss glass plants, it is noted for optical instruments, lenses, astronomical equipment, and chemicals.

First mentioned in 9th-century documents, Jena was chartered in 1230 and flourished during the Middle Ages. Some of the city's medieval fortifications, Saint Michael's Church (begun 1390), and the 14th-century town hall remain. The Friedrich Schiller University (1548) attracted Germany's most liberal philosophers and writers during the late 18th and early 19th centuries. Napoleon defeated the Prussian and Saxon armies on the outskirts of the city on Oct. 14, 1806.

Jenkins, Charles Francis   The inventor Charles Francis Jenkins, b. near Dayton, Ohio, Aug. 22, 1867, d. June 6, 1934, was a pioneer in the fields of CINEMATOGRAPHY and TELEVISION. He invented the phantascope, one of the earliest successful motion-picture projectors. He also designed (1925) an experimental television system based on a mechanical scene-scanning method, invented by Paul Nipkow. Jenkins was awarded more than 400 patents and was the founder and first president (1916) of the Society of Motion Picture Engineers, which later became the Society of Motion Picture and Television Engineers (SMPTE).

Jenkins, Roy   The British politician Roy Harris Jenkins, b. Nov. 11, 1920, cofounded (1981) the new Social Democratic party and was elected its first leader in 1982. Jenkins attended Oxford University and was first elected to Parliament in 1948 as a Labourite. He was minister of aviation (1964–65), home secretary (1965–67, 1974–76), and chancellor of the exchequer (1967–70) in Harold Wilson's Labour governments. From 1977 to 1981 Jenkins served as president of the Commission of the European Community. He was reelected to Parliament as an SDP member in 1982.

Jenner, Bruce   Bruce Jenner, b. Mount Kisco, N.Y., Oct. 28, 1949, was an American track and field star who won the decathlon in the 1976 Olympic Games at Montreal with a record 8,618 points. It was the 3d time he had broken the world record in two years. As a youth he played football, ran track, and was a champion water-skier. Jenner first competed in a decathlon in 1970 and his rapid progress earned him a place on the 1972 U.S. Olympic team. In the years between Olympics he won 12 of the 13 decathlons that he participated in. After his Olympic victory, he parlayed his athletic success and good looks into an entertainment career, mainly in television.

Jenner, Edward   The English physician Edward Jenner, b. May 17, 1749, d. Jan. 26, 1823, was responsible for a practical vaccination against SMALLPOX. While practicing medicine in Berkeley, England, Jenner noticed that dairy maids who had contracted the relatively mild disease cowpox did not later contract smallpox. In 1796 he inoculated an 8-year-old boy with material taken from cowpox pustules, and the boy developed cowpox. Several weeks later Jenner inoculated the boy with smallpox, but the disease failed to develop.

In 1798, Jenner published *An Inquiry into the Causes and Effects of the Variolae Vaccinae* and later promoted smallpox vaccinations, the practice of which spread throughout the world, apparently eliminating this disease by the late 1970s.

Jenney, William LeBaron   William LeBaron Jenney, b. Fairhaven, Mass., Sept. 25, 1832, d. May 14, 1907, was an influential American engineer and architect credited with developing a load-bearing frame of metal that made possible the development of the skyscraper. His Home Insurance Building (1883–85; demolished 1931) in Chicago is considered the first tall building in which a frame, or skeleton, of metal columns and beams replaced load-bearing walls. While this building was under construction, structural steel first became available in quantity and at reasonable prices so that Jenney was able to add a second innovation by making the upper portions of his structural skeleton of steel rather than of the weaker and more common cast iron.

Jenney also had an important role in training architects who later rose to great prominence in Chicago, including Daniel Hudson BURNHAM, Louis SULLIVAN, William Holabird, and Martin Roche.

Jensen, Arthur   Arthur Robert Jensen, b. San Diego, Calif., Aug. 24, 1923, is an American educational psychologist whose article "How Much Can We Boost IQ and Scholarly Achievement?" (1969) in the *Harvard Educational Review* aroused widespread controversy. "Compensatory education has been tried and it apparently has failed," Jensen claimed in the article. He attributed this failure largely to severe genetic limits to what educational intervention can achieve.

Jensen claimed that the observed gap in IQs between children of disadvantaged backgrounds and of more privileged backgrounds and between black and white children is largely due to genetic factors. His article met with a severely critical reception from many scholars.

See also: INTELLIGENCE.

---

jerboa [jur-boh'-uh]   Jerboas are jumping rodents of the family Dipodidae. There are 25 species, grouped into 10 genera, found in open, usually arid areas from northern Africa to northern China. Their hind legs are at least four times as long as their forelegs, and some species are capable of covering 2.5 m (8 ft) in a single leap. Jerboas range from 38 mm to 20 cm (1.5 to 8 in) in length; their tails may be 6 to 25 cm (2.5 to 10 in) long.

Jeremiah, Book of [jair-uh-my'-uh]   The Book of Jeremiah, second of the Major Prophets or longer books of the prophetic collection of the Old Testament of the Bible, derives its name from the prophet Jeremiah who lived in Anathoth, on the outskirts of Jerusalem. His prophetic career ranged from about 626 BC, during the reign of Josiah, at least to the fall of Jerusalem (586 BC) and the deportation of the population; at this time Jeremiah was taken by the remaining Jewish community to Egypt, where he died. The career of Jeremiah embraced the period of Josiah's reformation (626–622 BC); the years of resurgent Judaic nationalism (608–597 BC); the period leading to the final demise of Judah (597–586 BC); and the time in Egypt.

The message of Jeremiah was a call to moral reform to establish a personal relationship between God and humankind. He advocated resignation in the face of political and religious crisis and denounced sin as a perversion of creation. He called urgently for repentance so that turning to God might lead to a new creation; he thus prefigured the New Testament notion of the "new covenant."

The first 25 chapters of the Book of Jeremiah consist of a collection of prophecies against Jerusalem and Judah, along with some autobiographical passages known as the "confessions of Jeremiah." The "confessions" reveal Jeremiah's inner struggle to surrender himself to God, and they show a strong affinity with later biblical writings, especially the complaint or lamentation Psalms. In addition, the book contains biographical narratives concerning Jeremiah (chapters 26–45), as dictated to the scribe Baruch, and prophecies against foreign nations (46–51). It ends with a description of the destruction of Jerusalem by the Babylonians (52).

Jerez de la Frontera [hah'-rayth day lah frohntay'-rah]   Jerez de la Frontera is a city in southwestern Spain, 23 km (14 mi) northeast of Cádiz. Its population is 179,349 (1987 est.). The city is famous for its sherry wines (the word *sherry* is derived from the city's name), brandies, and Jerez horses. Originally a Roman colony, Jerez was held by the Moors from the early 8th century until its recapture by Alfonso X of Castile in 1264. A notable landmark is the Moorish Alcázar, an 11th-century palace rebuilt in the 14th century.

Jericho [jair'-ih-koh]   Excavations at ancient Jericho, identified as Tell al-Sultan, 10 km (6 mi) north of the Dead Sea in Israeli-occupied Jordan, have revealed remains of the oldest city yet discovered by archaeologists. The earliest occupation of the site, dating from the 10th millennium BC, consists of remains of the Natufian culture and includes what may have been a shrine. During the 8th millennium BC the site was greatly expanded under a culture known as the Aceramic, or Prepottery Neolithic A, and a wall 5.2 m (17 ft) high was erected around it. Following a break the next city was populated by a culture known as the Prepottery Neolithic B (7th–6th millennium BC). That the two cultures represent different groups is shown by significant changes both in the architectural tradition and in the flint tools.

In the ceramic stage of the Neolithic (6th–4th millennium BC) the dwellers lived in pits and produced a characteristic painted pottery. Early Bronze Age occupation

(3100–2100 BC) was extensive and consisted of large, well-built homes. Following the destruction of the Early Bronze Age settlement, occupation was resumed by people who have been identified with the Amorites. They did not build a permanent settlement and buried their dead in shaft tombs.

During the Middle Bronze Age (c.1900–1550 BC) houses consisting of small irregularly shaped rooms were built, and the city was fortified by an earthen rampart faced with plaster, surmounted by city walls. Mass burials were excavated in a cemetery off the mound in shaft graves. The city was destroyed about 1560 BC by the Egyptians during their campaigns against the Hyksos. The remains of the Late Bronze Age and later periods were almost totally eroded away, and nothing remained of the walls that Joshua is alleged to have demolished (see JOSHUA, BOOK OF).

Jeritza, Maria [yuh-rits'-uh]   A Czech dramatic soprano, Maria Jeritza (or Jedlitzka), b. Oct. 6, 1887, d. July 12, 1982, had a brilliant voice and powerful stage magnetism. She made her debut (1910) as Elsa in Wagner's *Lohengrin* at Olomouc. From 1912 to 1935 she was prima donna of the Vienna State Opera, and from 1921 to 1932 she appeared at the Metropolitan Opera. She sang in the USSR and at all the great opera houses of Europe, often in roles created for her by composers. She was outstanding as Ariadne in Strauss's *Ariadne auf Naxos* (1912), as Janáček's *Jenůfa* (1918), as the empress in Strauss's *Frau ohne Schatten* (1919), and as Marietta in Korngold's *Die tote Stadt* (1921).

Jerne, Niels K.   British-born Danish immunologist Niels Kai Jerne, b. Dec. 23, 1911, laid the theoretical foundation for the cellular basis of immunology and made other major contributions to theory and methodology. He received his Ph.D. from the University of Copenhagen and worked in the United States and West Germany before becoming (1969) director of the Basel Institute of Technology, which he helped to found. He retired in 1980. Jerne shared the 1984 Nobel Prize for physiology or medicine with the Argentinian-born Cesar Milstein and the German J. F. Kohler for their work in immunology.

Jeroboam I, King of Israel [jair-uh-boh'-uhm]
When ancient Israel split into two kingdoms after Solomon's death, Jeroboam was the first king of the ten northern tribes, from about 922 to 901 BC. Initially a trusted aide, Jeroboam led a revolt against SOLOMON and fled from his sudden wrath to Egypt. When the northern tribes refused allegiance to Solomon's son REHOBOAM, Jeroboam was named king; war resulted between the northern kingdom of Israel and the southern kingdom of Judah. Jeroboam fortified Shechem and waged continuous war on Judah. Choosing Dan and Bethel as alternative shrines to the south's Jerusalem, Jeroboam set up the

golden calves there; the Bible (1 Kings 12) interpreted this as idolatry. He was succeeded by his son Nadab.

Jerome, Saint   Jerome (Eusebius Hieronymus), c.347–420, was a Father of the Church and Doctor of the Roman Catholic church, whose great work was the translation of the Bible into Latin, the edition known as the Vulgate.

About 373, after pursuing studies in Gaul and Italy, Jerome set out on a pilgrimage to the East. In Antioch he had a profound spiritual experience, dreaming that he was accused of being "a Ciceronian, not a Christian." Accordingly, he determined to devote himself exclusively to the Bible and theology, although the translator Rufinus (345–410), Jerome's close friend, suggested later that the vow was not strictly kept. Jerome moved to the desert of Chalcis and, while practicing more rigorous austerities, pursued his studies, including the learning of Hebrew.

When Jerome returned to Rome, Pope Damasus I appointed him confidential secretary and librarian and commissioned him to begin his work of rendering the Bible into Latin. After the death (384) of Damasus, however, Jerome fell out of favor and again decided to go to the East. He made brief visits to Antioch, Egypt, and Palestine. In 386, Jerome settled at Bethlehem in a monastery established for him by Paula, one of a group of wealthy Roman women to whom he had been spiritual advisor and who remained his lifelong friend. There he began his most productive literary period, remaining for 34 years, until his death. From this period come his major biblical commentaries and the bulk of his work on the Latin Bible.

The writings of Jerome express a scholarship unsurpassed in the early church and helped to create the cultural tradition of the Middle Ages. He developed the use of philological and geographical material in his exegeses and recognized the scientific importance of archaeology. In his interpretation of the Bible he used both the allegorical method of the Alexandrian and the realism of the Antiochene schools. Feast day: Sept. 30 (Western).

Jerome of Prague   Jerome of Prague, b. c.1370, d. May 30, 1416, a Bohemian church reformer and associate of John Huss, led the life of a wandering scholar. An advocate of John Wycliffe's views, he acquainted (1401) Huss with these metaphysical and theological opinions. Brilliant in debate, Jerome became (1407) a spokesman for the Bohemian reform party in the university at Prague. Although he was persuaded to renounce Wycliffe and Huss, he later withdrew his recantation and was burned at the stake for heresy.

Jersey   Jersey, with an area of 117 km² (45 mi²) and a population of 80,212 (1986), is the largest and southernmost of the Channel Islands, a British dependency. It is located in the English Channel about 24 km (15 mi) west of the Normandy coast of France. Its capital is Saint Helier. Known for Jersey cattle, the island also supports

the growing of potatoes, tomatoes, and greenhouse flowers for export and is a popular tourist resort. French is the official language.

jersey   Jersey is a general term for a variety of knitted fabrics made of wool, cotton, silk, or synthetic fibers. Weft-knitted jerseys, in which the yarn loopings run across the fabric, stretch both vertically and horizontally and are used for hosiery, gloves, nightgowns, and T-shirts. Warp-knitted jerseys stretch only along the width and are usually less elastic and more tightly woven than weft knits. Warp knits are used for dresses, shirts, and lingerie. The fabric name is derived from the island of Jersey in the English Channel, where the knitting of woolen cloth for fishers is an old cottage industry. In Britain sweaters are commonly called jerseys.

Jersey cattle   see CATTLE AND CATTLE RAISING

Jersey City   Located in northeastern New Jersey on the Hudson River opposite lower Manhattan, Jersey City is the seat of Hudson County and the state's second largest city, with a population of 228,537 (1990). This busy port city (part of the Port of New York) has one of the most comprehensive transportation complexes on the Atlantic seaboard, making it a leading commercial and industrial center in the state (surpassed only by Newark). Chemicals, transportation equipment, clothing manufacturing, and petroleum refining are the major products of Jersey City's diversified industries. Jersey City has several colleges and a huge medical center.

First settled in 1618 by Dutch trappers, the area was acquired by Michiel Paux about 1629. About 1660 the stockaded village of Bergen was laid out. The site came under British rule in 1664. In the American Revolution the British-held fort at Paulus Hook was attacked and captured (1779) by Light-Horse Harry Lee. Jersey City, incorporated in 1820, was later expanded to include the former communities of Hudson City, Bergen, and Greenville. In 1916 a munitions warehouse on the Black Tom docks exploded, causing extensive damage; the incident was attributed to German saboteurs. Political boss Frank Hague was mayor of the city from 1917 to 1947.

Jerusalem   [juh-roo′-suh-lem]   Jerusalem (Hebrew: Yerushalayim; Arabic: Bayt al-Muqaddas), the capital of Israel, is a holy city of Judaism, Christianity, and Islam. It is situated in the Judaean Hills, 55 km (35 mi) from the Mediterranean Sea. The population of the city is 457,700 (1986 est.), and that of the Jerusalem District, which includes the suburbs, is 532,500 persons (1988 est.). The growth of the city may be attributed to its location along an ancient trade route and to its religious importance. For Jews, Jerusalem is the site of their ancient Temple and their historical capital; for Christians the city is the site of many of the events in the life of Jesus Christ; for Muslims the city is their third-holiest as the site from which Muhammad is said to have risen to heaven. Jerusalem's religious status has made control of the city a very volatile issue. In 1949, Jerusalem was partitioned between Israel and Jordan. Israel took control of the entire city in 1967 and officially proclaimed all of Jerusalem the capital of Israel in 1980. These actions were bitterly resented by Arabs, and most nations refuse to recognize the Israeli claim to sovereignty over all of Jerusalem.

Contemporary City. Jews have constituted a majority of Jerusalem's population since about 1876; today they make up about 75% of its residents. Both Hebrew and Arabic are spoken.

Jerusalem is divided into the Old City, New City (West Jerusalem), and East Jerusalem. The walled Old City, in the center, contains Muslim, Jewish, Christian, and Armenian quarters. Many of Jerusalem's religious landmarks are located in the Old City. The Western Wall (or Wailing Wall) is a small remaining portion of the original wall of Solomon's Temple. After the Jews were banished from the Temple Mount, the Western Wall became the most sacred place of Judaism. Atop the Temple Mount are the gold-domed Dome of the Rock (begun AD 661) and the silver-domed al-Aqsa (begun AD 710) mosques. The street called the Via Dolorosa is believed to be the site of the original Stations of the Cross. The Church of the Holy Sepulcher was begun in the 4th century AD and was rebuilt by the Crusaders beginning in 1099.

The New City, built mostly by Jews, was under Israeli control during the period of partition and is the site of many government buildings. To the south are the Israel Museum and the Shrine of the Book, where the DEAD SEA SCROLLS are located. East Jerusalem, located just north of the Old City, is the modern Arab section. Although primarily a residential area, it is also the site of the Rockefeller Museum. Since 1967 a ring of Israeli settlements has been built around the entire city.

Tourism is the major industry of the city, along with the government-related functions. Industries include diamond cutting and polishing, home appliances, furniture, pharmaceuticals, chemicals, shoes, plastics, textiles and clothing, printing and publishing, and jewelry. The city is connected by rail and bus to Tel Aviv. Jerusalem is governed by a municipal council of members elected to 4-year terms by proportional representation.

History. About 2500 BC, the Canaanites inhabited the city. Later, Jerusalem became a Jebusite citadel. When DAVID captured the city (c.1000 BC), the Jebusites were absorbed into the Jewish people. David made Jerusalem his capital, and SOLOMON built the first Temple to house the Ark of the Covenant. In 586 BC, the Babylonian NEBUCHADNEZZAR II destroyed Jerusalem and the Temple and exiled the Jews to Babylonia. In 537 BC, CYRUS THE GREAT of Persia conquered Babylonia and permitted the Jews to return to Jerusalem and rebuild their Temple. Persia held the city until 333 BC, when ALEXANDER THE GREAT added Palestine to his empire. In 323 BC, PTOLEMY I of Egypt took Palestine into his kingdom.

About 198 BC, the Seleucid king ANTIOCHUS III conquered Judaea, making it tributary to Syria. The Jews later revolted under the leadership of Maccabees (see MAC-

Jerusalem is held sacred by three religions. Jews meet in prayer at the Wailing Wall, which contains stones from the original Temple built by King Solomon. Above the wall is the Dome of the Rock, believed by Muslims to mark the point from which Muhammad ascended to heaven. The Mount of Olives, in the background, is important in Christianity as the site of Gethsemane.

CABEES family) and defeated the Syrians. The Temple was reconsecrated in 165 BC, and the Maccabean, or Hasmonean, dynasty ruled until Rome took the city in 63 BC. The Romans set up a local dynasty, the house of HEROD to rule most of Palestine; Herod the Great (r. 40–4 BC) rebuilt much of Jerusalem, including the Temple. Roman governors, however, retained ultimate control; one of them, Pontius Pilate, authorized the execution of Jesus Christ. While suppressing a major Jewish revolt, the Romans destroyed the Second Temple in AD 70. In 135, after the failure of the BAR KOCHBA revolt, Jews were banished from Jerusalem. From the early 4th century, when Christianity became legal in the Roman Empire, Jerusalem developed as a center of Christian pilgrimage. The Church of the Holy Sepulcher and many other Christian shrines were erected. Except for a brief period of Persian rule (614–28) the city remained under Roman (later, Byzantine) control until 638, when the Muslim Arabs took it. The Arabs built (688–91) the Dome of the Rock mosque on the site of the Temple.

In the 11th century, Muslim toleration of both Jews and Christians gave way to persecution under the FATIMID caliph al-Hakim (r. 996–1021) and under the SELJUKS, who seized Jerusalem in 1071. European Christendom responded by launching the CRUSADES. The Crusaders conquered Jerusalem in 1099 and established a Crusader state (see JERUSALEM, LATIN KINGDOM OF). SALADIN recaptured the city for the Muslims in 1187, and the Ayyubid and Mameluke dynasties ruled until 1517, when the Ottoman Empire took control.

In 1917 the British occupied Jerusalem, and it became the capital of mandated PALESTINE from 1923 until 1948. The 1948 United Nations partition plan for Palestine called for the internationalization of the city. The Arabs rejected this resolution, and Jerusalem was divided into an Israeli and a Jordanian sector from 1949 to 1967. Today the Israeli government guarantees religious freedom and protection of all holy places, but the question of who will ultimately control Jerusalem remains a major obstacle to any lasting peace settlement in the Middle East.

Jerusalem, Latin Kingdom of   The Latin Kingdom of Jerusalem was created in 1099 by the leaders of the First CRUSADE; it fell to the Muslims in 1291. At its greatest extent (c.1140) it included Palestine from the Gulf of Aqaba to Beirut and claimed sovereignty over the other Crusader states to the north, the principality of Antioch and the counties of Tripoli and Edessa.

During its first phase (1099–1187) the kingdom had its capital at Jerusalem. The Crusaders initially chose GODFREY OF BOUILLON as ruler (1099–1100). Although he took only the title of Defender of the Holy Sepulcher, his successors, beginning with his brother Baldwin I (r. 1100–18), used the royal title. They set out to capture the coastal towns, a task that they accomplished with naval help from Venice, Genoa, and Pisa.

After 1128 the Arab states were gradually unified by outstanding leaders, the greatest being SALADIN, who became the ruler of Egypt in 1169. Launching a holy war in 1187, he defeated the Crusaders at Hattin, regained Jerusalem for the Muslims, and besieged the remaining Crusaders in Tyre, Tripoli, and Antioch.

The Third Crusade (1189) and later expeditions succeeded only in retaking the coastal towns. Thus, from 1191 the capital of the Latin Kingdom was at Acre. The kingdom thereafter was torn by conflicts between barons and their rulers; among the Venetian, Genoese, and Pisan colonists; and between the HOSPITALERS and the TEMPLARS. The knights of these military orders provided the only reliable armed force. The fall of Acre to the Egyptian MAMELUKES in 1291 marked the end of the kingdom.

The kingship of Jerusalem was held by various dynasties, including the ANGEVINS and HOHENSTAUFENS (notably Holy Roman Emperor FREDERICK II) and the house of Lusignan, which also ruled Cyprus and Lesser Armenia.

LATIN KINGDOM OF JERUSALEM c.1140

☐ Kingdom of Jerusalem   ◼ Other crusader states

Jerusalem artichoke   Jerusalem artichoke is the common name for *Helianthus tuberosus*, a member of the sunflower family, Compositae. It is a perennial herb with edible potatolike roots. The plant is a native of North America and was cultivated by the Indians. The tubers store inulin, which forms fructose and can be used in the diet of diabetics.

Jespersen, Otto [yes'-pur-sen]   The noted Danish linguist Jens Otto Jespersen, b. July 16, 1860, d. Apr. 30, 1943, devoted the first part of his career to reforming his native language. While professor of English at the University of Copenhagen from 1893 until his retirement in 1925, he produced a series of influential and highly original works on linguistics, notably *The Growth and Structure of the English Language* (1905), *A Modern English Grammar on Historical Principles* (7 vols., 1909–49), *Language: Its Nature and Development* (1922), and *The Philosophy of Grammar* (1924). Early on he advanced the view that a word's meaning can affect the development of its pronunciation.

Jesuit Martyrs of North America   The Jesuit Martyrs of North America—Saints Jean de BRÉBEUF, Noël Chabanel (1613–49), Antoine Daniel (1601–48), Charles Garnier (1606?–1649), Isaac JOGUES, and Gabriel Lalemant (1610–49), all priests; and René Goupil (1608–42) and Jean de Lalande (d. 1646), laymen—were French missionaries who were killed by Indians in the 1640s. All of them worked among the HURON Indians, and all but one were put to death by the Hurons' enemies, the Iroquois (see IROQUOIS LEAGUE); Chabanel was killed by a Huron hostile to Christianity. The eight martyrs were canonized as a group (1930). Feast day: Oct. 19 (formerly Sept. 16).

Jesuits The Society of Jesus, the largest Roman Catholic religious order, whose members are called Jesuits, was founded by Saint IGNATIUS LOYOLA. Noted for its discipline, based on the *Spiritual Exercises* of Ignatius, and for its lengthy training period of as much as 15 years, the society is governed by a general who lives in Rome. Jesuits do not wear a special habit and are not subject to local ecclesiastical authority. Professed members are bound by a vow of obedience to the pope.

The Jesuits began as a group of seven men who as students in Paris took (1534) vows of poverty and chastity. Ordained as priests, they placed themselves at the disposal of the pope, PAUL III, who gave formal approval to the society in 1540. Ignatius became (1541) its first general. The order grew so rapidly that at Ignatius's death (1556) the little band had expanded to nearly a thousand persons.

From the first, the Jesuits concentrated on foreign missions, education, and scholarship. Saint FRANCIS XAVIER, one of the original seven, was the first Jesuit to open the East to missionaries; Matteo RICCI and others followed at the court of China. Jesuits established missions throughout Latin America and founded a model commune for Paraguayan Indians.

When the COUNTER-REFORMATION was launched, the Jesuit order was its driving force. During the Council of TRENT, several Jesuits, notably Diego Laínez, served as theologians. The English mission, a bold attempt to reclaim England for Catholicism during the reign (1558–1603) of Elizabeth I, was led by Edmund CAMPION and included the poet Robert SOUTHWELL. Jesuits established schools in almost every important European city and were leaders in education until the 18th century. Members of the society taught the sons of leading families and served as spiritual advisors to kings.

Because of the extent of the Jesuits' influence, powerful forces opposed them—forces composed of such unlikely allies as Blaise PASCAL and the Jansenists, VOLTAIRE, the Bourbon monarchs of France and Spain, and certain cardinals at the Vatican. These forces were instrumental in bringing about the suppression (1773) of the society by Pope CLEMENT XIV. Among the members of the order at that time was John Carroll, who later became the first Roman Catholic bishop in the United States.

The Jesuit order was reestablished (1814) by Pope PIUS VII and resumed its work. Jesuit schools and universities, such as Georgetown, Fordham, and St. Louis in the United States, were opened. In Europe, Jesuit traditions of learning were continued by the Bollandists, who were charged with compiling the lives of the saints; the Jesuits also published several periodicals and journals.

Jesus Christ Jesus of Nazareth, a 1st-century Jewish teacher who was crucified by the Romans, is believed by

Jesus is shown preaching the Sermon on the Mount in this fresco by Fra Angelico. (Monastery of San Marco, Florence.)

Christians to be the Christ or MESSIAH through whom God revealed himself to the world and whose death reconciles the world to God.

Knowledge of Jesus (Yeshua or Joshua) as a historical person is provided mainly by the New Testament of the BIBLE (especially the Gospels). Jesus was born in Roman-ruled Palestine during the reign of the Roman emperor Augustus (27 BC–AD 14) and grew up in the Galilean village of Nazareth. Associated early in his career with JOHN THE BAPTIST, he gathered around him a group of disciples attracted by his interpretation of Jewish law and his MIRACLES, especially his exorcisms and healing of the sick. Jesus' criticisms of Jewish religious leaders, coupled with the political rhetoric he used in announcing that God's rule was about to replace human rule, led to mounting opposition toward him in both the Jewish and Roman establishments. Arrested in Jerusalem, he was tried, condemned, and executed as a claimant to Jewish kingship. This death by CRUCIFIXION—a form of execution used by the Romans to punish non-Roman citizens who threatened Roman authority—took place when Pontius PILATE was Roman governor of Judea (AD 26–36). Jesus' followers subsequently claimed that God had raised him from the dead, and CHRISTIANITY, the movement launched in his name, quickly spread throughout the Mediterranean world.

Jesus in the Gospels

The Gospel accounts vary in the information they provide about Jesus. The Gospels according to MARK and JOHN concentrate on the story of his public activity and teachings. The Gospels of MATTHEW and LUKE furnish accounts of his birth and childhood.

The Infancy Narratives. Matthew begins his Gospel by tracing the genealogy of Jesus back to two central figures in the history of Israel: Abraham, the father of the Jewish people, and David, their most illustrious king. Luke gives a somewhat different line of descent, tracing it back to Adam and thereby emphasizing the significance of Jesus for the whole human race. Both Matthew and Luke report the birth of Jesus as taking place in Bethlehem, the ancestral city of David, giving the name of his mother as MARY and of her husband as JOSEPH. They describe his conception as a miraculous event—Mary being a virgin—and tell of signs and prophecies pointing to his importance as the fulfillment of the hopes of Israel and of God's redemptive purpose for the world. In Matthew, Herod, king of Judea, tries to kill the child, forcing Mary and Joseph to take him to Egypt for safety. The birth of Jesus is commemorated at CHRISTMAS.

The Ministry of Jesus. Jesus' ministry began when he was baptized by John the Baptist, and all the Gospels report that at the moment of his baptism a divine voice was heard assuring him of his unique relationship with God. After this experience he saw himself as empowered and commissioned to announce the coming of the Kingdom of God foretold by the prophets. As God's messenger, he summoned into the service of the kingdom those willing to leave home, family, and livelihood and devote themselves to calling people to prepare for the new age that was to be established on Earth. Chief among his followers were a group of men referred to in the Gospels as the APOSTLES or the Twelve. The apostles mentioned most frequently are the fishermen Simon Peter, Andrew, James, and John.

Of special significance among Jesus' miracles were his exorcisms. In his time it was widely believed by both Jews and pagans that those who exhibited strange or pathological behavior were possessed by demons (agents of SATAN). Others claimed the power to expel these demons, but Jesus' interpretation of his own exorcisms was unique. He declared that he performed these feats by divine power ("by the finger of God," Luke 11:20) and that these instances of God's triumph over the powers of evil were signs that his reign was already breaking into the present.

The Gospels also emphasize Jesus' attitude toward Jewish law. The law forbade the eating of certain foods, but Jesus taught that people are defiled by their words and deeds rather than by what they eat. He performed forbidden activities on the SABBATH when it was necessary to serve human needs and did not hesitate to eat and drink with those regarded as sinners. At a time when observance of purity laws at the meals eaten by family and friends was the most important means of establishing Jewish identity, he not only accepted invitations to eat with the ritually impure, but invited himself to their meals.

Jesus taught his disciples both directly by precepts and indirectly by means of stories or PARABLES. Matt. 5–7 contains a summary of his ethical teachings, known as the Sermon on the Mount. Two of his dominant themes were the command to love one's neighbor and the assurance that God's purpose is achieved through the suffering of the righteous. Jesus refused to allow his followers to take up arms and advised his questioners to pay taxes to the Roman state. In contrast to his followers' hopes for a conquering Messiah, he repeatedly told them that he would be rejected by the authorities, suffer, and die in fulfillment of his messianic role. They could not accept this, even though some of them shared in a visionary experience on a mountain—the TRANSFIGURATION—that was meant to assure them that beyond his sacrificial death was a day of triumphant vindication. He was to be raised up from the dead and exalted as God's chosen instrument.

Death and Resurrection. According to the Gospels, Jesus took the initiative in bringing things to a head by entering the great temple of Jerusalem and denouncing the commercial operations that were carried on there in the selling of animals and other materials for sacrifices. He predicted the destruction of the temple and of Jerusalem, but this was to be a sign that God would act in history in a climactic way to restore and vindicate his true peo-

PALESTINE IN THE TIME OF JESUS

——— Political boundaries AD 6–34

——— Principal roads

• Cities or towns

• Cities or towns visited by Jesus

→ Journeys of Jesus during his ministry

▢ Principal regions of the ministry of Jesus

△ Significant historical mounts

0   10   30   50 km
0   10   20   30   mi

The Crucifixion scene from Andrea Mantegna's San Zeno Altarpiece (1456–59) shows Jesus on the cross. To his right are the women who remained with him to the end and one of the two thieves who were crucified with him (Mark 15:27). (Louvre, Paris).

ple. The remembrance of Jesus' own suffering and death was to be perpetuated in the community through the solemn meal of the New COVENANT, the Communion or EUCHARIST, which Jesus shared as his LAST SUPPER with the Apostles. He was betrayed by JUDAS ISCARIOT, one of the Twelve, and the others abandoned him when he was seized by the authorities in the Garden of GETHSEMANE. A handful of faithful women remained with him when he died at CALVARY. The women returned to his tomb on the third day after his death and were astonished to find it empty. An angel told them that Jesus was alive and that the fellowship they had enjoyed with him would be renewed. This day of Jesus' RESURRECTION is celebrated by Christians on EASTER Sunday.

The Gospels describe in varying detail Jesus' subsequent appearances to his disciples, reviving their faith in him. At the end of Luke and in the first chapter of the ACTS OF THE APOSTLES are reports of his ASCENSION into heaven and the outpouring of the HOLY SPIRIT on the faithful community at PENTECOST.

Historicity of the Traditional Account

Early in the 2d century, only a short time after the last of the Gospels was written, people began to be troubled by the fact that the Gospels differ among themselves in certain details. For example, in the first three Gospels, Jesus cleanses the temple at the end of his career; in John he does it near the beginning. In Matthew, Joseph and Mary live in Bethlehem at the time of his birth, while in Luke they live in Nazareth and go to Bethlehem only because a Roman census requires them to return to their ancestral home. Tatian, a Christian scholar of the later 2d century,

set about resolving these difficulties by weaving the accounts into one harmonious whole, smoothing out the differences in his *Diatessaron* (literally, "Through the Four" [Gospels]). Even though some leaders of the church opposed what he had done, the practice of harmonizing the Gospels has continued down to the present day.

In the 17th and 18th centuries, however, European scholars, especially in Germany, began to reexamine the Gospel stories and to raise questions about their accuracy. Hermann Samuel REIMARUS (1694–1768) attacked them as the deceitful work of Jesus' followers, who, after he had failed to establish a Jewish state along nationalist lines, created accounts depicting him as a spiritual savior of humanity. Heinrich Paulus (1761–1851) adopted another approach, offering ingenious natural explanations of Jesus' supposed miracles. David Friedrich Strauss (1808–74) classified the Gospel stories as myths, meaning that the authors had expressed enduringly important ideas and principles in stories that surrounded spiritual truths with the appearance of history.

In reaction to these mythical and symbolic interpretations of the Gospel stories, historians began to reconstruct what they called "objective" historical accounts of Jesus. This undertaking was launched by Ferdinand Christian BAUR (1792–1860) and reached its climax in the work of Heinrich Holtzmann (1832–1910).

Following World War I, scholarly attention turned to an assessment of the Gospels as literature, and particularly to the question of oral and written sources on which the writers might have drawn. This began with the effort to sort out the evidence as to which Gospel was the first. The clear consensus was that Mark was the first Gospel and that it served as both source and model for the other Gospel writers, who adopted much of his material but also adapted it, adding sayings and narrative from other sources.

Questions about the authenticity of the sayings and historicity of the narratives were raised and answered in a variety of ways. Some scholars considered all the sayings to be authentic, and all the accounts historical, assuming that if the reports differed, they were derived from different events or situations. At the other extreme were those who found almost all the sayings and stories to be the product of the later church, especially after Christianity had moved away from Judaism into the wider Gentile world. Most scholars, however, sought to discern a basic core of authentic material, while acknowledging that all the Jesus tradition was transmitted and recorded by persons who shared the belief in Jesus as Risen Lord and who wanted to address the needs of the particular segment of Christianity for which their Gospel was written.

Christology

In addition to the title Messiah, or Christ, tradition records that Jesus was acclaimed as Son of God, Son of Man, Son of David, the Prophet who is to come, King of Israel, Savior, and Servant. In each case the messianic title implied a special relationship to God. As Son of Man, his future rule over the creation was to be achieved through obedience, suffering, and death. Similarly, as king and as Son of David, his rule was to be extended over all humanity, not primarily over Israel. As Son of God, he was the one destined to exercise power in God's name, even though the achievement of that goal required his apparent abandonment by God (Mark 15:34). As the future prophet announced by Moses (Deut. 18:15, 18), he is the one through whom all human beings have the possibility of hearing the word of God.

Beyond the evidence of the Gospels, it is clear that the early Christians, especially those reared or educated in Gentile territory, used other images to describe what God had done through Jesus for the redemption of the world. Building on the idea expressed in both Jewish and pagan sources that God created the world and sustains its order through his Word (LOGOS) or Wisdom personified, several New Testament writers speak of Jesus as "the Word become flesh," or assuming human form (John 1:14); as the one through whom everything was created (Col. 1:15–17); as the one through whom God has spoken his ultimate word (Heb. 1:1–3); or as "our wisdom, our righteousness, our sanctification and redemption" (1 Cor. 1:30).

By the time the later Gospels were written, Jesus was identified as being one with God (John 1:1, 14; 10:30; Matt. 28:19). In the 2d century, controversy arose as to whether Jesus had two natures, one human and one divine. The Jewish tradition of the oneness of God appeared to be in conflict with the Christian sense of Jesus' unique kinship with God. Some insisted that there was only one ultimate principle in the universe, so that God was one. Others tried to distinguish between God as the source of power and Jesus as the manifestation of it, as did JUSTIN MARTYR with his teaching of the Logos as distinct from God. Others declared that God and Jesus were merely two different names for the one God, or that the same spirit dwelt in both God and Jesus. At the end of the 2d century TERTULLIAN asserted that God was of one substance consisting in three persons. Although the proponents of ARIANISM wanted to differentiate the Son from the eternal substance that was the First Cause of creation, the language—and with it the ambiguity—of Tertullian's formula prevailed. It became the official creed of the church—backed by the power of the newly Christian Roman emperor Constantine at the Council of Nicea in 325—that the Son is of one substance with the Father. Later efforts to resolve this controversy led to the continuing use of this creedal formulation in the western churches, while in the eastern churches other ways of describing the relationship of Jesus to God were adopted. No matter how deep were the disagreements on detail, the place of Jesus within the TRINITY became a nearly universal feature of Christian faith.

jet   Jet, a black gemstone formed by the submersion of driftwood in seafloor mud, is a dense variety of lignite coal. Used since ancient times to make carved talismans, it has also been used as gems for mourning and for religious ceremonies, but it has been largely replaced by the harder black tourmaline and black onyx.

jet propulsion   Jet propulsion is a type of propulsion in which the thrust is produced by generating a high-velocity jet of hot gases inside an engine and expelling it through a suitably shaped nozzle in the rear. The reaction produced is based on the third of Newton's laws of motion, which states that every action has an equal and opposite reaction. The mass of gases rushing out the rear propels the engine forward.

Types of Jet Propulsion

Two types of engines based on jet propulsion are generally distinguished. The true rocket engine carries with it, in addition to its fuel, a supply of oxygen to burn that fuel (see ROCKETS AND MISSILES). The other type, called a jet engine, obtains its supply of oxygen from atmospheric air that it must take in. Its use is thus restricted to within the Earth's atmosphere. The jet engine itself can be divided into a number of types. The simplest jet engine is the RAMJET, in which the forward motion of the engine compresses the incoming air, fuel is injected and ignited in a combustion chamber, and the hot exhaust gases rush out the nozzle at the rear. In the turbojet, a turbine within the engine is driven by the high-speed gases; this turbine runs a compressor to compress the incoming air. The gases, after they pass the turbine, continue out the nozzle to supply the propulsion. In the turboprop (turbo-propeller) engine, the turbine drives a propeller as well as the compressor. The propeller supplies most of the engine's thrust, although the exhaust gases provide a small contribution.

History

The first examples of jet propulsion were Hero of Alexandria's Aeolipile (AD c.70)—an elementary turbine driven by steam jets—and medieval Chinese rockets used as missiles against Kublai Khan. In the 19th century many jet engines were patented, but practical achievement awaited technological advances, notably heat-resisting metal alloys. No single person can be credited with the invention of jet propulsion. Among the pioneers are: for the rocket, Robert GODDARD of the United States, Hermann OBERTH and Wernher VON BRAUN of Germany, and Sergei Korolev and Konstantin TSIOLKOVSKY of the USSR; for the ramjet, René Leduc of France and Eugen Sänger and Otto Pabst of Germany; and for the turbojet, Sir Frank Whittle of Britain, Hans von Ohain and Max Adolf Müller of Germany, and Secondo Campini of Italy.

The first jet-propelled airplane to fly was a rocket-propelled tail-first glider flown in Germany on June 11, 1928; in the tail-first configuration, stabilizing fins are situated ahead of the wing. Two German research airplanes were built by Ernst Heinkel in 1939; the He 176 was flown on rocket power in June (precise date not recorded), and the He 178 was flown on turbojet power on August 24 (a short hop) and August 27 (the first full flight). The first jet fighter to fly was the He 280 on Apr. 5, 1941, and the first to enter service was Britain's Gloster Meteor in July 1944, though the German Messerschmitt Me 262 was the first to engage an enemy and was built in larger numbers than other jets of World War

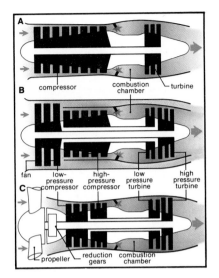

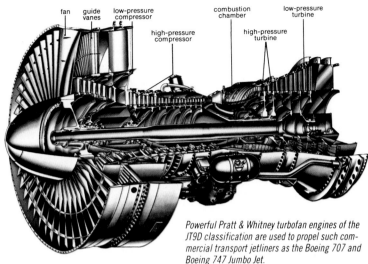

Powerful Pratt & Whitney turbofan engines of the JT9D classification are used to propel such commercial transport jetliners as the Boeing 707 and Boeing 747 Jumbo Jet.

In a turbojet engine (A), thrust is provided by hot exhaust gases (red) produced by burning fuel with compressed air in a combustion chamber. Part of the gas flow powers a turbine that drives the compressor for the incoming air (blue). A turbofan engine (B) has an additional low-pressure turbine and compressor-fan combination to bypass part of the incoming air through ducts around the engine to provide extra thrust. In a turboprop engine (C), thrust is also obtained from a conventional propeller driven by the low-pressure turbine through reduction gears.

II. The first jet transport was the British de Havilland Comet, flown on July 27, 1949, and in regular passenger service beginning May 2, 1952.

Today nearly all combat airplanes are jet propelled, as are virtually all large civil transports. The favored type of engine is the turbofan, a turbojet with an oversized low-pressure compressor.

Jet Propulsion Laboratory The Jet Propulsion Laboratory (JPL), founded in 1936 and given its present name in 1944, is a government contract research facility that has been operated for the National Aeronautics and Space Administration by the California Institute of Technology since 1958. It is located in Pasadena, Calif., and has a staff of 4,200, of whom 1,700 are scientists. In the 1930s the laboratory helped carry out the early rocket work of Robert GODDARD. During World War II, JPL became a large research and development establishment. Since 1958, JPL has concentrated on work with unpiloted scientific missions to the Moon and the planets, as well as on research in physics, propulsion, electronics, and related subjects.

jet stream A jet stream is a narrow, elongated core of air characterized by strong vertical and horizontal gradients of speed. It is often thousands of kilometers long, hundreds of kilometers wide, and a few kilometers deep. Jet streams vary in intensity—with the strongest having speeds surpassing 300 km/h (180 mph)—and in geographic location. Jet streams can be grouped roughly as tropospheric westerly, tropospheric easterly (particularly

in the Eastern Hemisphere), and mesospheric.

Geographical and Temporal Variations. Jet streams may be highly variable in space and time. The mesospheric jet stream is strong and westerly (that is, blowing from the west) during winter, but it reverses to an easterly jet of comparable strength during summer. The altitude of its core is about 50 km (30 mi) in mid-latitudes. The tropical easterly jet stream, which occurs during summer, originates in the upper troposphere near Burma and extends to the west of Africa, some 10,000 km (6,000 mi) to the west. A weaker counterpart exists to the north of Australia during the Southern Hemisphere summer. Both are fairly constant in position and strength.

In both hemispheres a fairly continuous band of strong WESTERLIES extends around the globe, with the most intense encountered usually on the eastern margins of continents. The tropospheric westerly jet streams achieve maximum strength at about 15 km (9 mi) altitude in winter, when the jets move to within 30° of the equator. The weaker summer westerlies lie some 15° further poleward. A second class of jet stream is attached to the migratory weather systems that lie poleward of the winter westerly jet stream. Such systems are highly transient and are generally smaller in spatial extent than the basic westerly jet streams to which they are intimately related.

Causes. WIND velocities are determined by the distribution of horizontal pressure differences, which in turn are governed by the temperature distribution. Consequently, regions of intense temperature gradients should be expected wherever winds occur in narrow bands. Such regions exist in a number of locations.

In middle and high latitudes, frontal zones demark the boundaries between AIR MASSES of differing character. At such interfaces of warm and cold air (regions of strong pressure gradient and, because of geostrophic considerations, of strong wind), jet streams develop with the same rapid variations in form as the fronts or weather systems to which they are attached.

A marked temperature gradient also exists between the equator and the pole. The resulting pressure gradient drives a meridional circulation called the Hadley cell (see ATMOSPHERE). A flow of air from the equator to high latitudes moves along the upper branch of the cell. As the air slows down relative to the rotating Earth, weak easterly winds develop. The decreasing distance of the Hadley cell current to the rotational axis, together with the right-deviating effect of the Coriolis force (see CORIOLIS EFFECT), however, causes increasingly strong westerlies as the air parcels move poleward, resulting in a band of intense winds. The differentially heated continents and oceans, however, cause another form of temperature gradient that interferes and produces local concentrations of the temperature gradient. A wavelike structure of the westerly band results with centers of intense wind on the eastern side of the continents.

jetty   see COASTAL PROTECTION

———

jewelry   Jewelry, one of the oldest decorative arts, is a collective term for objects of personal adornment, prized both for their craftsmanship and for the intrinsic value of their precious materials. The earliest jewelry was probably amuletic, protecting its wearer from hostile forces, but as soon as social order developed, jewelry was used to denote rank.

The Ancient World

Virtually all modern kinds of jewelry—necklaces, earrings, rings, bracelets, and their ornaments—were in use as early as 2500 BC in the Sumerian civilization (see MESOPOTAMIA). Sumerian goldsmiths used advanced metalworking techniques of coldhammering, casting, smelting, soldering, filigree, granulation, cloisonné, inlay, and lapidary work. Jewelry had begun to play an important role in Egyptian civilization by about 3000 BC; the tomb of TUTANKHAMEN (r. 14th century BC) contained numerous pieces of fine gold jewelry embedded with precious stones.

The art of fashioning gold jewelry reached the Mediterranean island of Crete from western Asia about 2400 BC. Diadems, hair ornaments, beads, bracelets, and complex chains have been found in Minoan tombs (see MINOAN ART).

Metalworking techniques reached northern Europe by about 2000 BC, and the earliest jewelry found there dates from between 1800 and 1400 BC. These artifacts include lunulae—spectacular, crescent-shaped neck ornaments of beaten gold—most of which were found in graves in Ireland, where gold was once plentiful (see CELTIC ART). There is evidence that the Celtic and early British people were trading with the eastern Mediterranean races by this time, exchanging gold for faïence beads.

By 1200 BC jewelry making was flourishing in central

and western Europe, where bronze as well as gold was frequently used to make jewelry, and the spiral was the most common motif of decoration. Twisted gold torcs, the characteristic ornament of the chiefs of the Celtic race, were made in the British Isles and northern France from the 5th to the 1st century BC.

By the 7th century BC the ETRUSCANS of central Italy were also making fine gold jewelry. They brought to perfection the difficult technique of granulation, whereby the surface of the metal is covered with tiny gold grains.

Gold was plentiful in Greece during the Hellenistic Age (323–30 BC), and Greek jewelry of this period is characterized by its great variety of forms and fine workmanship in gold. In the 3d century BC polychrome effects were achieved in gold jewelry by the use of colored stones and glass. At first garnets, chalcedonies, and carnelians were used and later emeralds, amethysts, and pearls. The engraving of CAMEOS also began at this time.

Jewelry continued to be made in Greek styles during the early Roman Empire, when the chief centers of production were Alexandria, Antioch, and Rome, to which Greek craftsmen had migrated. For the first time the hardest stones were used—uncut but polished diamonds, sapphires, and, notably, emeralds from newly discovered Egyptian mines. Colorful jewelry was a striking characteristic of the Migration period (4th to 8th centuries AD), which followed the collapse of the Roman Empire. From the 9th to the 13th century the technique of cloisonné enameling

Ancient Egyptian jewelry served religious and royal purposes, as well as being used for decoration. Gold was the primary material in jewelry making, and it was usually ornamented with filigree designs. Semiprecious stones, such as carnelian, turquoise, and lapis lazuli, were widely used and magical significance was attributed to specific gems. This selection of Egyptian jewelry includes: rebus pectoral (1); faience collar (2); hinged bracelet (3); signet ring (4); bezel ring (5); shell pendant (6); and a pair of gold earrings (7).

Representative styles of Greek jewelry popular during the 4th century BC were: a bracelet of chased gold with filigree ornamentation (1); a gold ring carved in intaglio (2); a gold ring carved with a woman's profile (3); a gold spiral-shaped earring ending in a lion's head (4); and an elaborate gold earring with a filigree rosette and suspended pieces (5). The period of detailed gold work began in Greece about 800 BC and reached its height during the classical period from 475 to 330 BC. In later developments, glass and colored stones were used as insets.

on gold was widespread, the finest pieces emanating from the workshops at Constantinople, the capital of the Byzantine Empire (see BYZANTINE ART AND ARCHITECTURE).

The Middle Ages and the Renaissance

After the creation of Charlemagne's empire in AD 800 (followed by the Holy Roman Empire in 962) there was a fusion of northern and Mediterranean cultures, and the principal patrons of the arts were the emperor and the church. Jewelry design was based on the setting in gold of precious stones and pearls in colorful patterns. Precious stones, which were polished but still used in their natural form, were credited with talismanic powers; for instance, the sapphire, symbolic of chastity and spiritual peace, was used for papal rings. European jewelry had been produced mainly in imperial and monastic workshops, but by the 13th century a system of independent guilds of goldsmiths had become established.

Gothic jewelry reflects the chivalrous ethic of aristocratic society in its symbolism and frequent use of amatory inscriptions. The ring brooch, or fermail, which had originated in Anglo-Saxon times, became very popular; pendants were occasionally used as RELIQUARIES. The use of earrings ceased entirely, because women wore elaborate jeweled headdresses that concealed the ears. About 1300, French jewelers began to use translucent enamels over engraved silver or gold.

In the 14th and 15th centuries jewelry was an important feature of both male and female attire. The affluence of the Spanish court during the 16th century, which was based on gold from colonies in the New World, set a standard for the other princely courts of Europe. The most fa-

mous artist-goldsmith of this period was Benvenuto CELLINI, who worked first in his native Italy and later for Francis I of France.

From the Seventeenth Century to the Present Day

Figurative designs became less fashionable in the 17th century, when there was a shift of interest to formal designs using faceted gems and pearls. The uncut, or cabochon, gem is rarely found in jewelry after 1640. The Golconda diamond mines were opened in India during the 17th century, and Dutch merchants supplied diamonds for the European market. Consequently, Amsterdam became the center for the trading and cutting of gems and has remained so. By the middle of the 17th century the new, many-faceted "rose" style of cutting had superseded the old, square "table" cut. Since this time diamonds have tended to dominate jewelry.

Gilles Légaré (fl. c.1660), court jeweler to Louis XIV of France, was responsible for some of the finest designs of the late 17th century. Black-enameled mourning jewelry and the memento mori jewel, a reminder of human mortality, reflected the somber Counter-Reformation mentality of the period.

Eighteenth-century fashions were lighter and more frivolous. Diamonds were cut in the new "brilliant" style, invented in Venice between the end of the 17th and the beginning of the 18th century. Other innovations included the informal spray of flowers entirely formed of stones, a type of jewel that required the utmost skill of the jeweler, and parures, matched sets of jewels consisting of necklace, earrings, and brooches or clasps of various sizes. There was a large demand for imitation, or paste, diamonds.

The Renaissance pieces illustrated here exemplify the elaborate jewelry created by European artisans during the 16th century. This enameled gold pendant, set with rubies, emeralds, and pearls, represents Spanish goldwork (1). This English gem-studded enameled portrait bust of Elizabeth I was known as an Armada jewel (2). Pendants in unusual forms became popular during this time, typified by this fanciful Venetian ship pendant (3).

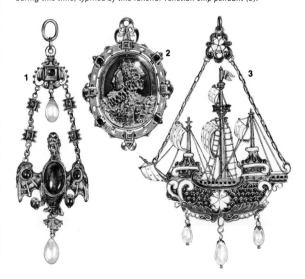

The eclectic taste of the Victorian era asserted itself in jewelry design as it did in all other arts. The setting of diamonds, which had become more abundant owing to the discovery of South African mines, reached a new height of technical perfection and highly stylized forms prevailed. This selection of 19th-century Victorian jewelry includes: a gold brooch set with turquoises, diamonds and other gems (1); a jet and gold pin (2); a gold, cameo and enamel earring (3); and an enameled gold brooch set with precious stones (4).

The jewelry of the period immediately following the First Empire (1804–14) of Napoleon I was bourgeois in character, as was every other decorative art. The fashion was for light filigree, or mechanically stamped-out gold jewelry, set with pale-colored semiprecious stones that produced a rich effect at a comparatively low cost. This style originated in Britain. Much Victorian jewelry was sentimental in feeling and low in intrinsic value. The Victorian enthusiasm for keepsakes led to a curious fashion for wearing jewelry made of woven human hair.

During the brief period of the Second Empire of Napoleon III (1852–70), the Parisian jewelers again rose to great heights of achievement. Diamond setting reached a peak of technical virtuosity in the late 1860s with the monture illusion, an elaborate gem-encrusted framework associated with the jeweler Oscar Massin (b. 1829).

South African diamonds were first brought to Europe in 1869 and supplied an enormous market for jewelry among the newly rich of the United States and South America. Large and valuable stones were often set *en solitaire* or as necklaces of single stones, called rivières. A somewhat mechanical technical excellence prevailed, and jewelry making became increasingly industrialized. Large commercial establishments that produced jewelry of superb craftsmanship included those of Peter Carl FABERGÉ, which originated in Saint Petersburg, Russia, and of Charles Lewis TIFFANY in New York.

A movement devoted to reforming the applied arts began to affect jewelry about 1895. Although this development originated in the British ARTS AND CRAFTS MOVEMENT, the most progressive jeweler was the Frenchman René LALIQUE. The profession of the artist-jeweler has become firmly established in the 20th century.

See also: ENAMEL; GEM CUTTING.

Jewett, Sarah Orne [joo'-et, orn] An American writer who lived her entire life in South Berwick, Maine, Sarah Orne Jewett, b. Sept. 3, 1849, d. June 24, 1909, built her reputation on fiction that is usually set in the impoverished land and seascape of rural Maine. Her best short stories are contained in her first major book, *Deephaven* (1877), and in the better-known collection *A White Heron and Other Stories* (1886). Her most ambitious work, *The Country of the Pointed Firs* (1896), is a novel dealing with the lives of isolated people.

Jewish Defense League Founded under the leadership of Rabbi Meir Kahane in 1968, the Jewish Defense League is a militant organization centered in New York City that uses radical tactics in the name of combating anti-Semitism and protecting Jews. The league was especially active in protesting the USSR's treatment of Jews and its restrictions on Jewish emigration to Israel. More moderate Jewish leaders have been critical of the organization's violent methods. Kahane was assassinated in November 1990.

Jewish Theological Seminary of America
Established in 1886, the Jewish Theological Seminary of America provides undergraduate and graduate training for men and women for the Conservative rabbinate. The seminary, located in New York City and affiliated with the University of Judaism in Los Angeles, permits students to supplement their undergraduate work with courses at Columbia University.

Jews The Jews are a people who trace their descent from the biblical Israelites and who are united by the religion called JUDAISM. They are not a race; Jewish identity is a mixture of ethnic, national, and religious elements. An individual may become part of the Jewish people by conversion to Judaism; but a born Jew who rejects Judaism or adopts another religion does not entirely lose his Jewish identity.

The word *Jew* is derived from the kingdom of Judah, which included 2 of the 12 Israelite tribes. The name *Israel* referred to the people as a whole and especially to the northern kingdom of 10 tribes. Today it is used as a collective name for all Jewry and since 1948 for the Jewish state. (Citizens of the State of ISRAEL are called Israelis; not all of them are Jews.) In the Bible, *Hebrew* is used by foreign peoples as a name for the Israelites; today it is applied only to the HEBREW LANGUAGE.

Biblical Period

The origin of the Jews is recounted in the Hebrew BIBLE. According to the Book of GENESIS, God ordered the patriarch ABRAHAM to leave his home in Mesopotamia and travel to a new land, which he promised to Abraham's descendants as a perpetual inheritance. Although the historicity of Abraham, his son ISAAC, and his grandson JACOB is uncer-

Moses leads the Jews across the Red Sea in this illustration from a prayer book (1427). According to biblical tradition, God parted the Red Sea to allow the Jews safe passage. Pursuing Egyptians drowned when the waters closed.

tain, the Israelite tribes certainly came to Canaan (later Palestine) from Mesopotamia. Later they, or some of them, settled in Egypt, where they were reduced to slavery; they finally fled to freedom under the leadership of an extraordinary man named MOSES, probably about 1200 BC. After a period of desert wandering, the tribes invaded Canaan at different points, and over a lengthy period of time they gained control over parts of the country.

Formation of a National Kingdom. For a century or more the tribes, loosely united and sometimes feuding among themselves, were hard pressed by Canaanite forces based in fortified strongholds and by marauders from outside. But when the PHILISTINES threatened the very existence of the Israelites, the tribes formed a kingdom under the rule (1020–1000 BC) of SAUL. Saul died fighting the Philistines and was succeeded by DAVID.

David crushed the Philistine power and established a modest empire. He conquered the fortress city of JERUSALEM, which up to that time had been controlled by a Canaanite tribe, and made it his capital. His son SOLOMON assumed the trappings of a potentate and erected the Temple in Jerusalem, which became the central sanctuary of the distinctive monotheistic Israelite religion and ultimately the spiritual center of world Jewry.

Division, Conquest, and Exile. The national union effected by David was shaky. The economically and culturally advanced tribes of the north resented the rule of kings from pastoral Judah, and after Solomon's death the

kingdom was divided (see ISRAEL, KINGDOM OF; JUDAH, KINGDOM OF). Assyria was the dominant empire during the period of the divided kingdom. When Israel, with Egyptian encouragement, tried to throw off Assyrian rule, it was destroyed and a large number of its inhabitants were deported (722 BC). Judah managed to outlive the Assyrian Empire (destroyed *c.*610), but the Chaldean (Neo-Babylonian) Empire that replaced it also insisted on control of Judah. When a new revolt broke out under Egyptian influence, the Chaldeans under NEBUCHADNEZZAR II destroyed Jerusalem and burned the Temple (587 or 586 BC); the royalty, nobility, and skilled craftsmen were deported to Babylonia (see BABYLONIAN CAPTIVITY; DIASPORA).

Return to Palestine. CYRUS THE GREAT of Persia conquered Babylonia in 536 BC. Subsequently he permitted the exiles to return to Judah and rebuild the Temple. (Many chose, however, to remain in Mesopotamia, where the Jewish community existed without interruption for more than 2,500 years.) Returning exiles rebuilt the walls of Jerusalem and consolidated spiritual life by a public ceremony of allegiance to the TORAH (Law of Moses) and by stringent rules against mixed marriage. In the following centuries leadership was provided mainly by priests, who claimed descent from Moses' brother AARON.

Hellenistic and Roman Periods

Hellenistic influences penetrated Jewish life deeply, but when the Seleucid king of Syria, ANTIOCHUS IV, tried to impose the worship of Greek gods upon the Jews, a rebellion ensued (168 BC).

The Maccabees. The popular revolt was led by the MACCABEES, a provincial priestly family (also called Hasmoneans). By 165 BC they recaptured the Temple, which had been converted into a pagan shrine, and rededicated it to the God of Israel. Hostilities with Syria continued; but Simon, the last of the Maccabean brothers, consolidated his power and was formally recognized in 131 BC as ruler and high priest. His successors took the title of king

This detail from the arch built by the Emperor Titus to commemorate his conquest of Palestine in AD 70, which still stands in Rome, shows the looting of Jerusalem's Temple by Roman soldiers.

and for about a century ruled an independent commonwealth. Dynastic quarrels, however, gave the Roman general POMPEY THE GREAT an excuse to intervene and make himself master of the country in 63 BC.

The Herodians. With Roman help, the HEROD dynasty ruled Judea (as Judah was then known) until, in 6 BC, the Romans put the country formally under the control of their own officials, known as procurators.

New spiritual forces emerged during the Maccabean and Herodian periods. The leadership of hereditary priests was contested by laymen distinguished for their learning and piety, who won the respect and support of the people. The priestly conservatives came to be known as SADDUCEES, the more progressive lay party as the PHARISEES. The latter came to dominate the SANHEDRIN, which was the highest religious and legal authority of the nation.

Burdened by excessive taxation and outraged by acts of brutality, the Judeans became more and more restive under Roman rule. Revolutionary groups such as the ZEALOTS emerged calling for armed revolt. The Sadducees were inclined to collaborate with the Romans; the Pharisees advocated passive resistance but sought to avoid open war.

The Era of Revolts and the Mishnah and Talmud

The Great Revolts. In AD 66 the moderates could no longer control the desperate populace, and rebellion against Roman tyranny broke out. After bitter fighting the Romans captured Jerusalem and burned the Temple in 70; at MASADA the Zealots held out until 73, when most of the 1,000 surviving defenders killed themselves to defy capture by the Romans. As a result of the revolt thousands of Jews were sold into slavery and thus were scattered widely in the Roman world. The last vestiges of national autonomy were obliterated.

The Pharisaic leaders, shortly thereafter given the title of RABBI (Hebrew, "my teacher"), rallied the people for a new undertaking—the reconstruction of religious and social life. Using the institution of the SYNAGOGUE as a center of worship and education, they adapted religious practice to new conditions. Their assembly, the Sanhedrin, was reconvened at Jabneh, and its head was recognized by the Romans and given the title of patriarch; the Diaspora Jews accepted his authority and that of the Sanhedrin in matters of Jewish law.

Palestinian Jewry, led by BAR KOCHBA, revolted against Rome in 132; the revolt was put down after three years of savage fighting. For a time thereafter observance of basic Jewish practices was made a capital crime, and Jews were banned from Jerusalem. Under the Antonine emperors (138–92), however, milder policies were restored, and the work of the scholars was resumed, particularly in Galilee, which became the seat of the patriarchate until its abolition (c.429) by the Romans. There the sages called tannaim completed the redaction of the MISHNAH (oral law) under the direction of JUDAH HA-NASI.

Babylonian Community. In the 3d and 4th centuries the Babylonian TALMUD became the standard legal work for Jews everywhere. Babylonian Jewry enjoyed peace and prosperity under the Parthian and Sassanian rulers, with only occasional episodes of persecution. In addition to the heads of the academies, the Jews had a secular ruler, the exilarch.

This situation was not significantly changed by the Muslim conquest of the Persian empire. At the end of the 6th century, the heads of the academies had adopted the title of gaon (Hebrew, "excellency"), and the next four centuries are known as the gaonic period; communities throughout the world turned to the Babylonian leaders for help in understanding the Talmud and applying it to new problems. About 770 the sect of KARAITES, biblical literalists who rejected the Talmud, appeared in Babylonia. Despite the vigorous opposition of the great SAADIA BEN JOSEPH GAON and other leaders, the Karaites continued to flourish for centuries in various lands; today the sect has only a few small remnants.

The Middle Ages

The Sephardim. The last influential gaon died in 1038, but as the eastern center was declining, creative forces emerged in North Africa and especially in Muslim Spain. The Christian Visigoths had all but exterminated the Spanish Jewish communities dating from Roman times, but the tolerant Arab rulers who conquered southern Spain were generally reasonable in their treatment of the Jews. (The Jews of Spain, Portugal, and the Middle Eastern countries and their descendants are known as SEPHARDIM. They differ somewhat in their rituals, customs, and life-style and in their pronunciation of Hebrew from the ASHKENAZIM, Jews of other European countries and their descendants.) Jews participated in the Arab cultural renaissance. This golden age was not entirely without problems, however. Muslim religious leaders and many of the common people resented the authority entrusted by their monarchs to Jewish statesmen and bankers. In the 12th century the Almohads, a fanatical sect from North Africa, took control of Muslim Spain, and the Jews had to choose between Islam, martyrdom, and flight. Many found a precarious refuge in northern Spain, where Christian rulers found Jews useful to them in their effort to reconquer the peninsula.

Fanaticism continually stirred the Spanish mobs. In 1391 thousands of Jews were massacred and thousands more were converted by force or accepted baptism to save their lives. These "new Christians" (also known as Marranos, Spanish for "swine") were suspected of practicing Judaism in secret; it was largely to ferret out these Marranos that the INQUISITION was introduced. Many Marranos rose to high posts in the court and in the church, but they were constantly spied on, and many perished in the autos-da-fé, festive celebrations in which heretics were burned at the stake. Such tragic events stimulated the spread among Spanish Jews of the mystical doctrines of KABBALAH.

Once the last Muslim rulers were driven out and Spain was united under FERDINAND II and ISABELLA I, all professing Jews had to choose between baptism and expulsion. In August 1492 most of them left Spain in search of new homes. Under Spanish pressure, Portugal expelled its Jews in 1498. The exiles found refuge in North Africa, Italy, and especially in the Ottoman Empire, including the Balkans.

In 1665, Nathan of Gaza hailed the Jewish ascetic Sabbatai Zevi as Messiah. The Sabbatian movement grew rapidly, attracting adherents all over Europe. This German engraving (1666) depicts a multitude of Jews being led from exile to the Holy Land.

The Ashkenazim. Jews had lived in Italy, Germany, France, and the Low Countries since Roman times and in England since the Norman Conquest (1066). They were generally secure during the early Middle Ages, and because they had ties with other Jews in distant lands, they played a considerable role in international trade. Conditions changed drastically, however, during the CRUSADES (beginning in 1096), when whole communities in France and Germany were massacred. During the Black Death (1347–51; see BUBONIC PLAGUE), Jews were accused of poisoning wells; further violence was roused by accusations of ritual murder and of desecrating the Eucharist.

Nevertheless, Jews were needed in the very countries that persecuted them. Medieval Christian doctrine forbade Christians to take interest on loans; as a result, Jews were required to engage in money lending. The royal treasuries took a large part of the profits, and the Jews bore the popular resentment against usurers. In general, they were excluded from ownership of land and from the guilds that controlled the skilled trades.

When Christian money lenders learned to collect interest under other names, Jews were no longer needed. They were expelled from England in 1290 and, after several earlier bans, finally from the kingdom of France in 1394. In the German states, life for Jews was difficult and uncertain. Many moved eastward into Poland, which lacked a middle class with the financial and commercial skills Jews could provide.

Early Modern Period

The Ghetto. Jews had long been accustomed to living in neighborhoods of their own, for security and for ready access to a synagogue. From the 16th century, however, they were systematically compelled to live in walled enclosures, to be locked in at night and on Christian holidays, and to wear a distinguishing badge when outside the walls. The Jewish quarter of Venice (established 1516) was called the GHETTO, and this local name became a general term for such segregated areas. Cut off from normal relations with non-Jews, few Jews had any idea of the cultural revival of the Renaissance (except in Italy).

In Poland and Lithuania, social conditions also had a segregatory effect. The Jews continued to speak a German dialect, mixed with many Hebrew words and with borrowings from Slavic languages—now known as Yiddish (see GERMANIC LANGUAGES; HEBREW AND YIDDISH LITERATURE). Intellectual life was focused on study of the Talmud.

Persecutions became more frequent, however, inspired by competition from the growing Christian merchant class and by overly zealous churchmen. In 1648 a rebellion of Cossacks and Tatars in the Ukraine—then under Polish rule—led to an invasion of Poland, in which hundreds of thousands of Jews were massacred.

Sectarian Responses to Persecution. In 1665 a Turkish Jew named SABBATAI ZEVI proclaimed himself MESSIAH. Throughout the years there had been a number of such messianic claimants, but none had received more than local support. Sabbatai's announcement, however, evoked an unheard-of response; thousands of Jews from all over Europe and the Middle East sold their belongings and went to join Sabbatai in Palestine. Under threat of death Sabbatai adopted Islam, and the movement collapsed.

Poland was also the birthplace of HASIDISM, the mystical sect founded by BAAL SHEM TOV. Although it was condemned by the rabbinic leadership, most notably by ELIJAH BEN SOLOMON, it established deep roots and became a significant social factor in the life of East European Jewry.

Toward Emancipation

The successful revolt of the Netherlands against Spain during the 16th century encouraged a number of Marranos to flee Spain and Portugal and to settle in Amsterdam, where they formally returned to Judaism. Members of this Sephardic group later founded Jewish communities in England, even before they were formally readmitted in 1656, and the New World; they were soon followed by larger numbers of Ashkenazim.

Western Developments. Some 18th-century liberals began to advocate an improvement of Jewish status; at the same time Moses MENDELSSOHN and a few other Jews were urging their coreligionists to acquire secular education and prepare themselves to participate in the national life of their countries. Such trends were intensified by the French Revolution. The French National Assembly granted (1791) Jews citizenship, and Napoleon I, although not free from prejudice, extended these rights to Jews in the countries he conquered, and the ghettos were abolished.

Equal rights were achieved in the Netherlands, and more slowly in Great Britain. Germany and Austria, even after 1870, discriminated against Jews in military and academic appointments; in these countries much popular hostility continued, now called ANTI-SEMITISM and supposedly justified on racial rather than religious grounds. In the American colonies the Jews had suffered relatively minor disabilities; with the founding of the United States, Jews became full citizens—although in a few states discriminatory laws had to be fought.

This portrait of Theodor Herzl was painted in 1903, one year before the great Zionist leader died. Herzl outlined his plan for establishing a homeland for the Jews in a pamphlet, The Jewish State, published in 1897.

Persecution in Russia. In Russia hopes of improvement were soon abandoned; the government engaged in open war against Jews. Under Nicholas I (r. 1825–55), 12-year-old Jewish boys were drafted into the army for terms of more than 30 years (whereas other Russians were drafted at 18 for 25 years); and Jewish conscripts were treated with the utmost brutality to make them convert to Christianity.

After 1804, Jews were allowed to reside only in Poland, Lithuania, and the Ukraine; Russia proper was closed to them. This PALE of Settlement was later made smaller. From 1881 on, anti-Jewish riots (POGROMS), tolerated and sometimes instigated by the government, sent thousands fleeing to Western Europe and the Americas. Because Russia refused to honor the passports of American Jews, the United States abrogated a trade treaty in 1913.

In response to these policies, new trends appeared in Russian Jewry. A movement of Jewish nationalism expressed itself in a revival of Hebrew as a secular language and in a few attempts at colonization in Palestine. A Jewish socialist movement, the Bund, appeared in urban centers, stressing the Yiddish language and folk culture.

The Twentieth Century

Zionism and Palestine. The violent outburst of hatred that accompanied the DREYFUS AFFAIR in France inspired Theodor HERZL to launch the movement of ZIONISM, which sought to establish a Jewish state. Its chief support came from East European Jews; elsewhere Herzl's proposals were considered impractical and a threat to newly won civil status.

During World War I, East European Jews suffered heavily from troops on both sides. American Jewry now found itself for the first time the leading element in the world Jewish community, bearing the major responsibility for relief and reconstruction of the ravaged centers. The peace treaties guaranteed equal rights to minorities in the newly constituted or reconstituted countries, but these agreements were not consistently upheld with regard to Jewish minorities, and colonization in Palestine expanded considerably.

In the BALFOUR DECLARATION of 1917, Great Britain announced its support for a Jewish national home; this purpose, approved by the Allied governments, was embodied in the mandate for PALESTINE that Britain assumed after the war. British agents had secretly made contradictory promises to Arab leaders, however, and growing Arab nationalism expressed itself in anti-Jewish riots in Palestine in 1920–21 and 1929.

Soviet and Nazi Anti-Semitism. The Communist Revolution of 1917 did not end the sufferings of the Jewish population in Russia. Much of the fighting in the Civil War of 1918–20 took place in the Ukraine, where the White Russian armies conducted savage pogroms in which thousands of Jews were massacred. Although discriminatory decrees were abolished and anti-Semitism was banned as counterrevolutionary under the Soviet system, Judaism suffered the same disabilities as other religious groups. After the fall of Leon TROTSKY, the old anti-Semitism was revived as a government policy.

In Germany the Weimar Republic for the first time abolished all official discrimination against Jews. The republic was unpopular, however, and anti-Semitism was popular. Calculated use of anti-Semitism as an instrument was a major factor in Adolf HITLER's rise to power in 1933, whereupon the German Jews were immediately disfranchised, robbed of possessions, deprived of employment, barred from the schools, and subjected to physical violence and constant humiliation. Once World War II occupied the attention of the democracies, Hitler and his supporters attempted "the final solution," the complete extermination of the Jews (see HOLOCAUST).

On May 14, 1948, in Tel Aviv, the Jewish National Council established the new State of Israel, with Chaim Weizmann as president and David Ben Gurion (reading) as prime minister. In the background is a portrait of Theodor Herzl.

About 6 million Jews—almost a third of their total number—were massacred, starved, or systematically gassed in CONCENTRATION CAMPS.

Establishment of Israel. The Western democracies all but closed their doors to refugees. Britain meanwhile had gradually abandoned the Balfour Declaration. The United Nations adopted a resolution calling for the partition of Palestine into Jewish and Arab areas.

On May 14, 1948, the State of Israel was proclaimed. Since then Israel has fought four wars against Arab coalitions to establish and preserve its independence (see ARAB-ISRAELI WARS). A peace treaty (Mar. 26, 1979) between Israel and Egypt was not accepted by the other Arab states.

The Diaspora since World War II. Although the USSR voted for the UN partition resolution in 1947, it later became markedly anti-Israel in its policies. A resurgence of Jewish self-consciousness, however, occurred within Soviet Jewry despite deprivation of religious education and other discriminations.

Since World War II the Jews of the United States have achieved a degree of acceptance without parallel in Jewish history, and Jews play a significant role in intellectual and cultural life. The elimination of social barriers has led to a high rate of mixed marriage. During the same period there has been a growth in synagogue affiliation and fervid support for the State of Israel.

Jew's harp   The Jew's harp (its name possibly corrupted from jaw's harp) is a simple metal percussion instrument (bamboo in Oceania). The clothespin- or horseshoe-shaped frame is held between the teeth, a strip of metal (or bamboo) is vibrated by strumming with a finger, and various overtones are produced by changes in the oral cavity. Found in many parts of the world, the instrument has ancient roots and was introduced into Europe from Asia about 1350.

Jezebel [jez'-uh-bel]   Jezebel, d. c.843 BC, was a Phoenician princess and wife of AHAB, the king of ancient Israel. According to 1 Kings 18 and 19, Jezebel fostered the worship of the Phoenician god BAAL and supported 450 prophets of Baal. When ELIJAH opposed her and stirred up popular sentiment against the pagan prophets, she decreed his death, forcing him to flee. Jezebel was killed when her eunuchs threw her from a palace window at the order of King JEHU; her body was eaten by dogs, as Elijah had prophesied.

Jhabvala, R. Prawer [jahb-vah'-lah, prah'-wur]   The novelist Ruth Prawer Jhabvala, b. Germany, May 7, 1927, went to England as a refugee in 1939. In 1951 she married an Indian architect and moved to Delhi. Her novels set in India include *To Whom She Will* (1955; U.S. title, *Amrita*, 1956), *The Householder* (1960), and *A New Dominion* (1972; U.S. title, *Travelers*, 1973). Jhabvala has also written numerous screenplays. Among the most suc-

cessful are *Shakespeare Wallah* (1966); *Bombay Talkie* (1970); *Heat and Dust* (1983, from Jhabvala's 1975 novel), *The Bostonians* (1984, from the Henry James novel), and *A Room with a View* (1986). Her novel *In Search of Love and Beauty* (1983) explores the lives of German refugees in New York City from the 1930s.

Jiang Qing (Chiang Ch'ing) [jee-ahng'jing]   Jiang Qing, b. 1914, d. May 14, 1991, was the fourth wife of the Chinese leader MAO ZEDONG. She was an actress when she married Mao in 1939. She joined the Communist party and held some minor posts but remained in political obscurity until the 1960s, when she became a leader of the CULTURAL REVOLUTION. Jiang Qing was named to the party politburo in 1969. After Mao's death, however, she was arrested as a member of the radical GANG OF FOUR for crimes against the state and in 1981 was sentenced to death. In 1983 her sentence was commuted to life imprisonment; she was released in 1987.

Jiang Zemin (Chiang Tse-min) [jee-ahng' dzuh-meen']   Jiang Zemin, b. Jiangsu province, July 1926, became general secretary of the Chinese Communist party and a member of the Politburo standing committee on June 24, 1989. He succeeded ZHAO ZIYANG (Chao Tzuyang), a backer of the prodemocracy movement. An engineer who joined the party in 1946, he went to Moscow for futher training in the mid-1950s. He served on the party central committee (1982–) and Politburo (1987–) and was mayor of Shanghai (1985–88) and head of the Shanghai party organization (1988–89) before becoming party chief. DENG XIAOPING (Teng Hsiao-ping) later designated Jiang as China's next paramount leader.

Jiangsu (Kiangsu) [jyang'-soo']   Jiangsu is a province on the Yellow Sea coast in eastern China. Most of the region's 102,300-km^2 (39,500-mi^2) area lies on a low fertile alluvial plain crossed by the CHANG JIANG (Yangtze River), the Huai He, the GRAND CANAL, and an intricate network of lakes, canals, and streams. The capital is NANJING. The population, consisting entirely of Han Chinese, is 63,480,000 (1988 est.). Modern SHANGHAI, the largest urban center in China, lies within the province but is administered by the central government in Beijing.

Major crops include rice, wheat, barley, corn, cotton, and sweet potatoes. The growing of silkworms and raising of fish are also important. Jiangsu was part of Nanjing province under the Ming dynasty (1368–1644); during the 18th century under the Qing, it became a separate province. Jiangsu was the center of the Taiping Rebellion (1850–64). During the Japanese occupation in 1937–45, the province was greatly damaged, but it has since recovered.

Jiangxi (Kiangsi) [jyang'-see']   Jiangxi is a landlocked province in south central China. It has an area of

164,700 km^2 (63,600 mi^2) and a population of 35,590,000 (1988 est.). The capital is Nanzhang. The Gan River provides a natural north-south corridor through many mountain ranges before emptying into Poyang Hu, the second largest lake in China.

A fertile province, Jiangxi produces two crops of rice every year. Other crops include tea, sugarcane, cotton, fruit, and ramie fiber. Its mines yield tungsten, coal, tin, and manganese. The most notable provincial product, however, is Jiangxi porcelain, made since the 11th century from high-quality kaolin from the banks of Poyang Hu. From the early Chou dynasty (770–453 BC) to the Long March of the Communists in the 1930s, the Gan River valley has provided an important route for migration, commerce, and military conquest.

Jidda [jid'-uh]   Jidda (1983 est. pop., 1,500,000) is a port city on the Red Sea in the HEJAZ region of western Saudi Arabia. It is Saudi Arabia's leading business and diplomatic center. Steel, petroleum, cement, clothing, and pottery are the city's major industries. Because of its location, 72 km (45 mi) west of MECCA, it is the port of entry for millions of Muslims on pilgrimage to Mecca; tourism is therefore an important industry. King 'Ahd al-Aziz Private University (1967) is there.

Old Jidda was founded by Caliph Uthman about 646. Present-day Jidda, north of the original site, is about 300 years old. Ruled by Turkey until 1916, it was briefly part of the Kingdom of Hejaz. King IBN SAUD conquered the area in 1925.

jig   The jig, a folk dance that was often a part of European peasant celebrations of the 16th century, is today most closely associated with Ireland. Performing to lively fiddle or bagpipe music, the dancer keeps an erect torso while executing rapid, springy steps. Jig tempos and forms were the basis of the gigue, a movement in the instrumental SUITE of the 17th century.

jigsaw puzzle   A jigsaw puzzle is a collection of interlocking pieces that can be joined together to form a picture. Simple puzzles, made for children, consist of a few large pieces; more complex puzzles, made for more sophisticated solvers, may consist of 1,000 or more pieces. Most puzzles contain from 300 to 750 pieces. The ease or difficulty of solving a puzzle depends on the number of pieces, their shapes and shadings, and the design of the picture. Modern jigsaw puzzles are manufactured in two layers; the top is a reproduction of a painting or color photograph, and the bottom is a backing of wood or cardboard. The puzzle is cut into pieces.

Jigsaws are not used to make modern puzzles; instead, a die press stamps out the pattern, after which the pieces are separated and packaged. With the exception of custom-made puzzles, most jigsaw puzzles are mass-produced.

jihad [jih-hahd']   In Islam, the duty of each Muslim to spread his religious beliefs is termed *jihad*. Although the word is widely understood to mean a "holy war" against nonbelievers, jihad may also be fulfilled by a personal battle against evil inclinations, the righting of wrongs, and the supporting of what is good.

Jim Crow laws   Jim Crow laws, named for an antebellum minstrel-show character, were late-19th-century statutes passed by the legislatures of the Southern states that created a racial caste system in the American South. Although slavery had been abolished, many whites at this time believed that nonwhites were inherently inferior and to support this belief sought rationalizations through religion and science. The U.S. Supreme Court was inclined to agree with the white-supremacist judgment and in 1883 began to strike down the foundations of the post–Civil War RECONSTRUCTION, declaring the CIVIL RIGHTS ACT of 1875 unconstitutional. In 1896 it legitimized the principle of "separate but equal" in its ruling PLESSY V. FERGUSON.

The high-court rulings led to a profusion of Jim Crow laws. By 1914 every Southern state had passed laws that created two separate societies—one black, the other white. This artificial structure was maintained by denying the franchise to African Americans through the use of devices such as GRANDFATHER CLAUSES, poll taxes, and literacy tests. It was further strengthened by the creation of separate facilities in every part of society, including schools, restaurants, streetcars, health-care institutions, and cemeteries.

The first major blow against the Jim Crow system of racial segregation was struck in 1954 by the Supreme Court's decision in BROWN V. BOARD OF EDUCATION OF TOPEKA, KANSAS, which declared segregation in the public schools unconstitutional. In the following decade the system slowly crumbled under the onslaught of the civil rights movement. The legal structure of segregation was finally ended by the civil rights legislation of 1964–68.

See also: INTEGRATION, RACIAL.

Jiménez, Juan Ramón [hee-may'-nayth, hwahn rah-mohn']   Juan Ramón Jiménez, b. Dec. 24, 1881, d. May 29, 1958, was one of the most influential Spanish poets of the 20th century. After studying in Cádiz and Seville he went to Madrid in 1900, where he produced several volumes of verse that identified him with the Spanish modernist movement. In *Almas de Violeta* (Violet Souls, 1900), *Ninfeas* (Water Lilies, 1900), and *Arias tristes* (Sad Airs, 1903) he displayed the preoccupation with love, natural beauty, and death that haunted all his later work.

A sojourn (1905–11) in his native Andalusia inspired the ornate *Elejías* (Elegies, 1908) as well as his famous prose poem collection *Platero and I* (1914–17; Eng. trans., 1957). The *Diario de un poeta recién casado* (Diary of a Recently Married Poet, 1917) signaled the beginning of his experiments with free verse and the spare style of his later poetry.

Jiménez's subsequent volumes, illustrating both this denuded style and a growing mysticism, include *Eternidades* (Eternities, 1918), *Piedra y cielo* (Stone and Sky, 1919), *La estación total* (All Seasons in One, 1946), and *Animal de fondo* (Animal of the Depths, 1949). He also wrote the personal sketches collected in *Españoles de tres mundos* (Spaniards of Three Worlds, 1942) and translated Blake, Eliot, and (with his American-born wife) Rabindranath Tagore. In 1956 he received the Nobel Prize for literature.

Jiménez de Cisneros, Francisco [hee-may'-nayth day thees-nay'-rohs, frahn-thees'-koh]

The Spanish cardinal, statesman, and grand inquisitor Francisco Jiménez (or Ximenes) de Cisneros, b. 1436, d. Nov. 8, 1517, initiated important reforms of the Spanish clergy that helped to eradicate much of the kind of corruption later criticized in Germany by Martin Luther during the REFORMATION.

In 1499, Jiménez began a ruthless campaign of converting the Moors, burning a million priceless Arabic manuscripts and provoking the Muslim revolt of 1499–1500. Appointed cardinal and head of the INQUISITION in Castile by Isabella's widower, FERDINAND II of Aragon, in 1507, Jiménez financed and led the conquest (1509) of Moorish Oran. In 1508 he founded the university at Alcalá de Henares. After Ferdinand's death in 1516, Jiménez, as regent of Castile, managed the accession of Charles I (later Holy Roman Emperor CHARLES V) to the Spanish throne.

Jiménez de Quesada, Gonzalo [hee-may'-nayth day kay-sah'-dah, gohn-zahl'-oh]

Gonzalo Jiménez de Quesada, b. *c.*1496, d. Feb. 16, 1579, a Spanish conquistador, founded the city of BOGOTÁ. He arrived on the northern coast of South America in 1535 as chief magistrate of the colony of Santa Marta. The following year he headed an expedition that went inland in search of the legendary city of gold, EL DORADO. Finally penetrating the central plain of Colombia in 1537, Jiménez conquered the kingdom of the CHIBCHA Indians and discovered great mineral wealth. He founded the city of Santa Fé de Bogotá in 1538.

Jiménez then went to Spain to claim the territory he had discovered, which he called NEW GRANADA, but he was rebuffed by the Spanish crown. Returning to South America, Jiménez struck out from Bogotá in search of El Dorado again in 1569. He spent three futile years in the plains crossed by the Orinoco River (in present-day Venezuela) before returning to Bogotá bankrupt and ill. He died, a leper, a few years later. Jiménez is thought by some to have been the model for Cervantes's Don Quixote.

jimsonweed [jim'-suhn-weed]

Jimsonweed, or common thorn apple, *Datura stramonium*, family Solanaceae, is a widespread annual weed common to roadsides and pastures. It grows up to 1.6 m (5.3 ft) tall, and the white to violet flowers are funnel shaped. The jimsonweed contains poisonous alkaloids and is a source of the drug stramonium, which is used for relaxing bronchial muscles in the treatment of asthma and bronchial complaints. Seed and plant extracts have been used in Europe to treat a number of disorders, including rheumatism and epilepsy.

Jin (Chin) [jin]

Jin was the name of several dynasties in the early history of China. The first Jin dynasty (AD 265–420) was founded by a Wei prince from the Three Kingdoms period, Sima Yen (reigned as Wu Di, 265–89), who brought a semblance of unity to the empire. The dynasty weakened and in 317 was driven south of the Chang Jiang (Yangtze River) by the Huns; it ruled there from Nanjing until eliminated in 420. Some historians refer to the dynasty as the Western Jin before 317 and the Eastern Jin thereafter.

A second Jin dynasty (936–46) appeared in the period of Five Dynasties, when a series of contenders held power following the end of the TANG dynasty. The founder, a Turk with the Chinese name Shi Jingtang, tried to preserve his throne by concessions to the northern Khitan empire but was swept aside when the Khitan invaded China.

The third dynasty called Jin (1115–1234) was established by the Jurzhen, another tribal league from the north, which defeated the Khitan. The Jurzhen invasion forced the SONG (Sung) dynasty southward in 1127, but both empires eventually fell to the MONGOLS, who conquered all of China. Many of the Jurzhen people returned to Manchuria; they reappeared later in Chinese history as the Manchus.

Jinan (Tsinan) [jee'-nahnn]

Jinan, the capital of Shandong province in eastern China, lies just south of the Huang He (Yellow River), 370 km (230 mi) south of Beijing. The city (1988 est. pop., 2,140,000) is a commercial, educational, and transportation center for the province. Industries include food processing, textiles, iron and steel, electrical parts, machine tools, paper, and chemicals. Archaeological remains indicate that Jinan was settled during the Shang dynasty (*c.*1600–*c.*1207 BC). The Venetian traveler Marco Polo visited the city in the 13th century. Occupied by the Japanese from 1937 to 1945, it was taken by the Communists after a major battle in 1948.

Jingde Zhen (Ching-te-chen) [jing-duh-jun]

The city of Jingde Zhen (1982 pop., 400,000) is on the Chang River in northeast Jiangxi province, China. With rich clay beds located nearby, it has been associated from the 6th century AD with fine ceramic production. Especially famous are the imperial household porcelains supplied to the SONG dynasty emperors, from one of whom (the Jingde emperor, r. 1004–07) the city's name derives. Jingde

Zhen's widely exported underglaze blue-and-whites were produced from the 1400s. During the Taiping Rebellion (1850–64) the Jingde Zhen kilns were destroyed. Large-scale production was not resumed until the 1950s.

Jingo   Jingo (Jingu Kogo), c.169–c.269, was the semilegendary empress of Japan during the period of Japanese expansion into southern Korea. She is supposed to have been the wife of Chuai (r. 192–200) and regent for her son Ojin. Although most of her attributes—such as her ability to control tides—are legendary, historians believe that Japanese women exerted a powerful influence on politics in that period and that some parts of Jingo's history are probably based on fact.

Jinnah, Muhammad Ali [jin-uh, muh-hahm'-ud ah'-lee]   Muhammad Ali Jinnah, b. Dec. 25, 1876, d. Sept. 11, 1948, led the Indian Muslims in the years before independence and founded the state of Pakistan. A brilliant, prosperous, westernized lawyer, Jinnah began his political activities in the 1906 session of the INDIAN NATIONAL CONGRESS party. In 1913 he joined the All-India MUSLIM LEAGUE. He left the Congress party in 1920 because of differences with its leader Mahatma GANDHI, who opposed the Muslim demand for a separate communal electorate and advocated policies of noncooperation. Thereafter Jinnah used the Muslim League to propagate his views and to demand political equality for India's large Muslim minority.

By the late 1930s, converting the poetic concept of the word Pakistan—meaning "land of the pure"—into a political slogan, Jinnah was advocating the idea of a separate independent state for the Indian Muslims. His struggle bore fruit in 1947 when the Indian subcontinent was partitioned into two states: Muslim Pakistan and Hindu India. Jinnah became the first governor-general of Pakistan.

jinni [jin'-ee]   In Arab and Muslim folklore a jinni (often anglicized as *genie*) is a desert or wilderness spirit that can assume human or animal form and exercise supernatural powers. Often, as in the tale of ALADDIN's lamp in the *Arabian Nights*, it serves a summoner who knows the correct magical words or gesture. Most jinn are ugly, evil demons, but some are beautiful and good. Their ruler is Suleiman, or Solomon, and the foremost of them is Iblis, the prince of darkness.

jitterbug   The jitterbug, an uninhibited, acrobatic dance, reached the height of its popularity during the SWING era of the 1930s and '40s. A dance for couples, it could range from a sedate series of steps—including variations of the lindy hop, the shag, and the black bottom—to a wild improvisation using swings, lifts, and turns. Jitterbugging was also called jiving, and jitterbug music, jive.

Jívaro [hee'-vah-roh]   The Jívaro are a South American Indian people who inhabit the *montaña* region of Ecuador. Of uncertain linguistic affiliation, the Jívaro have never been conquered. Throughout their history they have fought among themselves in intercommunity blood feuds; they are popularly known for their practice of shrinking the heads of their enemies (see HEADHUNTING). Their population numbers approximately 8,000.

A typical community consists of a single, large, elliptically shaped house containing a man, his wives, and their children. The community is usually abandoned after about five years, as the residents move to cultivate new, fertile areas.

Jívaro religion is animistic and involves shamanism, witchcraft, and the use of hallucinogens. The Jívaro are thought to believe in a supreme deity and a creation myth involving Sun, Moon, and flood.

Joachim, Joseph [yoh'-ah-kim, yoh'-sef]   The Hungarian violinist and composer Joseph Joachim, b. June 28, 1831, d. Aug. 15, 1907, was an influential musician and a close friend of Johannes Brahms. After early years in Hungary and Vienna he lived in Germany and studied for a time with Ferdinand David in Leipzig. His wide-ranging concertizing included numerous visits to England, where he was especially popular. In 1869 he organized the celebrated Joachim Quartet. Brahms, who greatly valued Joachim's musical advice, dedicated his violin concerto to him, as did Dvořák. Joachim's compositions include three violin concertos, of which the *Hungarian Concerto* (1857) is the best known.

Joan, Pope   Pope Joan was a legendary female pope who supposedly ruled the church as John VIII from 855 to 858, between the pontificates of Leo IV (847–55) and Benedict III (855–58). Another version of the story places her election at about the year 1100. According to the legend, a learned woman in male disguise became the papal notary and was eventually elected pope. Her sex was discovered when she gave birth during a papal procession. Some variations of the story record her name as Agnes or Gilberta. Although the legend was widely believed during the Middle Ages, it has since been totally discredited. A literary treatment of the subject is Lawrence Durrell's *Pope Joan* (1960; adapted from a Greek work by Emmanuel Royidis).

Joan of Arc, Saint   Joan of Arc (French, Jeanne d'Arc), b. c.1412, was a French peasant girl who led the French army against the English during the HUNDRED YEARS' WAR. Called the Maid of Orléans, she is a French national heroine and patron saint.

When Joan was about 13 years old she began to hear "voices" (which she later identified as those of Saint Catherine, Saint Margaret, and Saint Michael) that gave her the mission of liberating France from English domi-

The French visionary Joan of Arc, here portrayed (1854) by J. A. D. Ingres, revived the hopes of French troops when she led them to victory over the English during the Hundred Years' War. Captured in 1430, she refused to deny her claim to divine inspiration and was burned as a heretic. (Louvre, Paris.)

nation. In 1429 she left her home in Domrémy, Champagne, to travel with an escort to the court of the dauphin, later King CHARLES VII, who had been deprived of his rights as heir to the French throne by the Treaty of Troyes of 1420. Charles was persuaded to reassemble his troops and place them under Joan's command in an expedition to relieve Orléans. In eight days during May 1429, she lifted the siege that had lain on the city for eight months. In June 1429, Joan and her troops were able to break through to Reims, where she persuaded Charles to hold his coronation.

In May 1430, while attempting to relieve Compiègne, Joan was captured by the Burgundians, who sold her to the English. The latter turned her over to a church court in Rouen, where she was tried on charges of heresy and witchcraft, and the judges declared her visions diabolical. After months of interrogation, Joan was tricked into an admission of guilt. She soon retracted her confession, however, and was condemned as a relapsed heretic. On May 30, 1431, she was burned at the stake in Rouen. When French fortunes were finally restored, Joan was rehabilitated in a formal trial (1456) called for by Charles VII, who had done nothing to save her while she was alive. She was canonized in 1920. Feast day: May 30.

Joan the Mad, Queen of Castile Joan the Mad, or Juana la Loca, b. Nov. 6, 1479, d. Apr. 11, 1555, was the daughter of the Spanish monarchs FERDINAND II of Aragon and ISABELLA I of Castile. She was already insane when she succeeded (1504) to her mother's throne, and a regency was set up by her father. Her husband, the Habsburg PHILIP I of Castile, whom she had married in 1496, reigned briefly in 1506. On Philip's death, Ferdinand resumed control until his own death in 1516, when Joan's son, later Holy Roman Emperor CHARLES V, became joint ruler with Joan. She lived most of her life in seclusion at Tordesillas castle.

Joan I, Queen of Naples Joan I, b. 1326, d. May 22, 1382, succeeded her grandfather King Robert I on the Neapolitan throne in 1343. She was involved in the murder (1345) of her cousin and husband, Andrew, and thus earned the enmity of his brother, King LOUIS I of Hungary, who drove her out of Naples in 1348. She returned in 1352, but the remainder of her reign was troubled by intrigues and by struggles between Louis of Anjou and Charles of Durazzo to secure her throne. Deposed by Pope URBAN VI in 1380, she was murdered on the orders of Charles, who succeeded her as CHARLES III.

Job, Book of [johb] The Book of Job, in the Old Testament of the BIBLE, is a complex wisdom writing that uses a blend of prose and poetry in dramatic form to explore the perennial problem of innocent suffering and God's justice. The principal figure of the book is Job, a pious Jew afflicted with disease and stripped of all his goods. The free and imaginative transformations of the Job figure are literarily and intellectually comparable to Shakespeare's treatment of Hamlet and Goethe's use of Faust. The identity of the author, usually dated 600–400 BC, is completely unknown.

Throughout the drama, Job asserts his innocence of wrong, thereby rejecting the traditional view that suffering is the result of sin. The humble and patient Job who bears his sufferings as proofs of piety, however, becomes the raging and insistent Job pressing relentlessly for divine vindication in the dialogue that forms the main part of the book (chaps. 3–31). The argument is pursued through three cycles of speeches in which Job's three friends—Eliphaz, Bilbad, and Zophar—chide the hero and he, in answering them, challenges God. Job's final self-defense and call upon the deity is answered by God's speech from a whirlwind in which Job is invited to trust in the divine omniscience and power. This direct experience of the mysteries of God leaves Job at peace with himself. Although no final solution to the problem is offered, the author clearly rejects traditional explanations of suffering. It is a moot point whether he offers a positive answer to questions about suffering and divine justice.

Job Corps The Job Corps is a U.S. government agency that provides vocational training, remedial education, health care, and personal counseling to disadvantaged youth in order to enable them to find work. It is managed by the Employment and Training Administration of the Department of Labor and was established by the Economic Opportunity Act of 1964 as part of the Johnson administration's WAR ON POVERTY program. From 1973 to 1982 the Job Corps was funded under the Comprehensive Employment and Training Act (CETA). Since then it has operated under the Job Training Partnership Act, open-ended authorizing legislation that was passed in 1982.

Drawing on the experience of the CIVILIAN CONSERVATION CORPS—which provided public works employment for 2.6 million young men between 1933 and 1942—the

Job Corps houses, educates, and trains young men and women from 16 to 21 years of age at 106 centers across the country. The centers are run by private companies under federal contract. Training lasts from 6 to 24 months.

Jochum, Eugen

Jochum, Eugen [yoh'-kuhm, oy'-guhn] The distinguished German conductor Eugen Jochum, b. Nov. 1, 1902, d. Mar. 26, 1987, was known as one of the foremost interpreters of Mozart and Bruckner. After working as a conductor in various German cities, Jochum became the general musical director of the Philharmonic Orchestra in Hamburg (1934–49) and of the Bavarian Radio Symphony Orchestra (1949–60). He was coconductor (1961–64) of the Concertgebouw Orchestra in Amsterdam and was a guest conductor of most of the leading European and American orchestras, touring with several. From 1971 to 1977 he was chief conductor of the Bamberg Symphony.

Joel, Book of

Joel, Book of [joh'-ul] The Book of Joel, a prophetic book of the Old Testament of the Bible, derives its name from the prophet Joel. Nothing other than his name is known about the prophet. The date of composition was probably between 400 and 350 BC, although some scholars place it much earlier (9th–7th century BC). The book falls into two sections. The first (1:1–2:17) gives an account of a plague of locusts and a drought that ravaged Judah as a symbol of divine judgment. The second (2:18–3:21) promises the gift of the spirit of the Lord for the entire population and declares final judgment on all nations, with protection and fertility for Judah and Jerusalem. The passage on the outpouring of God's Spirit (2:28–32) is cited in Saint Peter's Pentecost sermon in Acts 2:17–21.

Joffre, Joseph Jacques Césaire

Joffre, Joseph Jacques Césaire [zhawf, zhoh-zef' zhahk say-zair'] Joseph Jacques Césaire Joffre, b. Jan. 12, 1852, d. Jan. 3, 1931, was commander in chief of the French Army at the outbreak of World War I. He had received that post in 1911, as one of a new group of republican officers elevated in response to the Dreyfus Affair.

When war broke out in August 1914, Joffre's plan for a French offensive into Alsace-Lorraine was frustrated by the speed of the German advance through Belgium into northeastern France. An orderly retreat enabled the Allies to regroup and counterattack, however, in the First Battle of the Marne in September (see MARNE, BATTLES OF THE). For this victory, Joffre was hailed as the savior of France. Joffre's failure to provide further victories led to increasing criticism, however. After the costly battles of Verdun and the SOMME in 1916, Joffre was transferred to an advisory position. On Dec. 26, 1916, he was made a marshal of France.

Joffrey Ballet

Joffrey Ballet [jahf'-ree] The Joffrey Ballet, a New York City–based ensemble without stars, performs an eclectic repertory. The company was founded by Robert Joffrey (1930–88), who served as artistic director until his death. From 1954 to 1962, Joffrey presented mainly his own choreography, using several company names for a constantly growing group of dancers. After a well-received season at the City Center Theater in 1966, they were invited to become the official resident ballet company. Joffrey expanded the repertory with revivals of important works, including Kurt Jooss's *Green Table* (1967), Leonid Massine's *Parade* (1973), Frederick Ashton's *A Wedding Bouquet* (1978), and Vaslav Nijinsky's *L'Après-midi d'un faune* (1979). Gerald Arpino, longtime chief choreographer and associate director, is the current artistic director. His ballets include *Olympics* (1966) and *Trinity* (1968), to rock music. Other choreographers who have worked with the Joffrey include Anna Sokolow, Eliot Feld, Twyla Tharp—*Deuce Coupe* and *As Time Goes By* (both 1973)—and Laura Dean—*Fire* (1982) and *Force Field* (1986).

In 1970, Joffrey II was formed, an apprentice group for young dancers serving as an intermediate stage between the American Dance Center, the company's school, and the parent company. The Joffrey gained a second official residency, at the Los Angeles Music Center, in 1983.

jogging

jogging see RUNNING AND JOGGING

Jogues, Saint Isaac

Jogues, Saint Isaac [johg] Isaac Jogues, b. Jan. 10, 1607, d. Oct. 18, 1646, was a French Jesuit missionary to the North American Indians. Sent to preach among the HURONS in the Georgian Bay area, he was entrusted with the construction of Fort Sainte Marie I. In 1642, when returning from a visit to Quebec, Jogues was captured and mutilated by Mohawk warriors. On a peace mission to the Mohawk country in the late spring of 1646, he appeared to be succeeding; but after he had returned there in the autumn, he was slain by a hostile warrior near present-day Amsterdam, N.Y. He was canonized in 1930 as one of the JESUIT MARTYRS OF NORTH AMERICA. Feast day: Sept. 26.

Johanan ben Zakkai

Johanan ben Zakkai [joh-han'-uhn ben za-ky'] Johanan ben Zakkai, fl. 1st century AD, was a Jewish leader who contributed to the reconstitution of Jewish communal life in Palestine after the destruction (AD 70) of the Second Temple. Johanan reconvened the SANHEDRIN at Jabneh, where it became both an executive organ and an academy for the study of the Torah. He was succeeded as head of the Sanhedrin by GAMALIEL OF JABNEH.

Johannesburg

Johannesburg [joh-han'-es-burg] Johannesburg is the third-largest city in South Africa. It is situated on the Witwatersrand, a ridge of gold-bearing hills in the southern Transvaal, about 160 km (100 mi) southwest of Pretoria. The population of the city proper is 632,369 (1985), and that of its metropolitan area is 1,609,408. Johannesburg is the administrative headquarters of

Johannesburg, founded in 1886 as a gold-mining camp, is South Africa's financial center as well as one of its largest cities. During the 1970s and 1980s Soweto, one of the black townships of Johannesburg, was the scene of violent racial disturbances resulting from South Africa's apartheid policies.

many mining, banking, industrial, and commercial concerns and is the home of the South African Stock Exchange (1887). Its industries (metallurgical, engineering, printing, food processing) contribute one-fifth of the nation's total output. Gold production is declining, but gold-related industries and general manufacturing are expanding. The city has numerous branch offices of governmental institutions and consular offices. Johannesburg forms the hub of South Africa's major urban-industrial region called the Rand. Landlocked, it has road, rail, and air service with all major cities, and the nearby Jan Smuts Airport is South Africa's main port of entry. Johannesburg is home of the English-language University of the Witwatersrand (1903), the Rand Afrikaans University (1966), and the Witwatersrand College for Advanced Technical Education (1925).

Johannesburg was settled when gold mining began there in 1886. As a mining and gold-processing center, it grew rapidly. Originally part of the Boer-controlled Transvaal, it passed to the British after the SOUTH AFRICAN WAR (1899–1902).

John, Saint   Saint John, a Galilean fisherman and the son of Zebedee, was one of the Twelve Apostles. John and his brother, Saint JAMES (the Great), were called Boanerges, or Sons of Thunder, by Christ. Several passages in the Bible imply that this describes their intense loyalty and aggressive zeal (Mark 9:38; Luke 9:49, 54). John was one of the inner circle among the Twelve. Saint Peter, James, and John witnessed the Transfiguration (Matt. 17:1; Mark 9:2; Luke 9:28) and went to Gethsemane

with Jesus (Matt. 26:37; Mark 14:33).

Many people believe that John was the beloved disciple referred to in the fourth gospel. If so, he was beside Jesus at the Last Supper (John 13:23); was asked to care for Jesus' mother, Mary (John 19:26); and was the first to comprehend Jesus' resurrection (John 20:2–9). John had a prominent role in the early church (Acts 1:13, 8:14). Traditionally, five New Testament books are ascribed to him: the fourth gospel, three Epistles, and the Book of REVELATION. Feast day: Dec. 27 (Western); Sept. 26 (Eastern).

John, Augustus   The British portraitist Augustus John, b. Jan. 4, 1878, d. Oct. 31, 1961, was one of a number of brilliant students from the Slade School of Art, London, which he attended from 1894 to 1898, who changed the direction of British art in the 20th century. His early work was in the Slade tradition of figure compositions and fine drawing. Later, in association with J. D. Innes, his style became freer and more colorful. He lived a bohemian life, touring in a horse-drawn caravan, and became the epitome of the modern artist, exhibiting at the New English Art Club and in the ARMORY SHOW (1913) in New York City.

After service as a war artist in World War I, John found fashionable success with his portraits of famous people such as *George Bernard Shaw* (1915; Fitzwilliam Museum, Cambridge), *T. E. Lawrence* (1919; Tate Gallery, London), *Thomas Hardy* (1923; Fitzwilliam Museum), and *Tallulah Bankhead* (1930; National Portrait Gallery, Washington, D.C.).

John, Elton   Singer-pianist-composer Elton Hercules John, b. Reginald Kenneth Dwight in England on Mar. 25, 1947, is one of rock music's durable performers. For most of his career he has worked with lyricist Bernie Taupin. The albums *Elton John* and *Tumbleweed Connection* (both 1970) were his first successes, and throughout the 1970s his popularity, bolstered by lavishly staged and exuberant performances, was high. From 1972 to 1975 he recorded seven consecutive number-one albums; his rendition of the song "Pinball Wizard" in the rock opera *Tommy* (1975) was quintessential Elton John. In 1979 he became the first Western pop star to tour the Soviet Union. John maintained his visibility—though at a somewhat lower level—throughout the 1980s and into the early 1990s. Few singers have sold as many records as John.

John, Epistles of   The Epistles of John are three letters in the New Testament of the Bible traditionally ascribed to Saint JOHN, the Apostle. They are classed with the General, or Catholic, Epistles because they are addressed to a general readership rather than to specified churches or individuals. The first epistle bears no clue to its authorship, but in the other two epistles the author calls himself "the elder." The three letters were probably written in the Roman province of Asia (western Anatolia) toward the end of the 1st century.

The first epistle should probably be understood as a general pamphlet written to churches in Anatolia. Its message is about life, meaning eternal life, life in fellowship with God through faith in JESUS CHRIST. The book was written to give a series of standards by which people can know that they possess eternal life. Two features stand out in the series of tests. First, the validity of the INCARNATION is affirmed against those who claimed special knowledge (see DOCETISM; GNOSTICISM) and denied that Christ came in the flesh (1 John 4:2–3). The second feature of the test is love. The true follower of Christ is to love as Christ loved (1 John 2:6; 4:7–12, 19).

The second epistle, the shortest book of the Bible, is a note to a church addressed as the "elect lady." In this letter the message of 1 John is applied to a local church situation. The people are warned about teachers with special knowledge. They are encouraged to be hospitable toward one another. The third epistle is a personal word to Gaius, a follower of the truth. He is encouraged to show kindness to traveling believers who pass his way.

John, Gospel According to   The Gospel According to John is the fourth book of the New Testament of the Bible. In style, language, and content, it differs dramatically from the Gospels of Matthew, Mark, and Luke—called the synoptic Gospels. Unlike these Gospels, the fourth Gospel opens with a philosophical prologue (John 1:1–18). It identifies the LOGOS, or Word, with Christ and introduces the themes to be developed in the Gospel. Further comparisons show that the synoptic Gospels describe the ministry of Christ mainly in Galilee, with reference to only one Passover; but John situates most of the events in Judea and refers to three Passovers. Thus, it is from John's Gospel that one concludes that Jesus' ministry lasted three years. In the synoptic Gospels, parables are Jesus' vehicle for teaching; in John, long discourses are used. Although John omits significant events such as the Temptation of Christ and the Transfiguration, he relates a number of events in Jesus' life not found in the synoptic Gospels.

By the time the fourth Gospel was written, in the latter half of the 1st century, Christianity had shifted from Jerusalem to the Aegean world. The thought of the day was directed more to universal truths than to historical facts. With the development of GNOSTICISM, the idea of the spirit was stressed, and the idea of the material was de-emphasized. Weaving into his message concepts such as truth, light, life, spirit, and word, John aimed to teach that God's eternal truth had become incarnated for the SALVATION of humankind in events that happened once for all. He could not overlook historical events, because he believed that in Christ the eternal had become flesh and dwelt among humankind. For John, the true meaning of the eternal could be understood only through the revelation of God in the historical person JESUS CHRIST.

According to a tradition dating from the second half of the 2d century, the author of the Gospel was Saint JOHN, the Apostle. Many theologians are still convinced of the tradition's accuracy. Others, while acknowledging that John the Apostle is the source behind the Gospel, refer to John the Elder, a disciple of John, as the author.

John of Austria, Don   Don John of Austria, b. Feb. 24, 1547, d. Oct. 1, 1578, was the illegitimate son of Holy Roman Emperor CHARLES V and the half brother of King Philip II of Spain. After fighting against the Moriscos in Granada (1569), he commanded the naval force of Spain, Venice, and the papacy that crushed the Turkish fleet in the Battle of LEPANTO on Oct. 7, 1571. Appointed Spanish governor of the Low Countries in 1576, Don John could not subdue the DUTCH REVOLT either by concessions or by war. He was succeeded at death by Alessandro Farnese.

John the Baptist, Saint   Saint John the Baptist, a Jewish prophet, is believed by Christians to be the forerunner of Jesus Christ. John achieved recognition as a prophet in the region of the lower Jordan Valley, where he attracted disciples. His public ministry began with the proclamation of a baptism of repentance in preparation for the Messiah. Throngs came to be baptized, among them his cousin Jesus of Nazareth, whom John recognized as the Messiah.

When John spoke against the marriage of Herod Antipas (see HEROD dynasty) to Herodias, his brother's wife, Herod imprisoned John. John was executed after Herodias had instructed her daughter, traditionally identified as SALOME, to request his head as a reward for her dancing

(Mark 6:17–29). Herod later believed that Jesus was John the Baptist risen from the dead (Mark 6:14–16; 8:27, 28). Feast day: June 24.

John Baptist de La Salle, Saint [duh-lah-sahl']

Saint John Baptist de La Salle, b. Apr. 30, 1651, d. Apr. 7, 1719, was a French educator and the founder of the Institute of the Brothers of Christian Schools, popularly known as Christian Brothers. In 1684 he founded a religious order devoted to teaching. Distinguished as a pioneer of training colleges for teachers and in the use of the vernacular in teaching, he ranks among the outstanding educators of modern times. Canonized in 1900, he is the patron saint of schoolteachers. Feast day: Apr. 7.

John Birch Society

The John Birch Society, an ultraconservative, anticommunist organization founded in 1958 by Robert Welch, Jr., a retired Boston candy manufacturer, actively campaigns for U.S. withdrawal from the United Nations, for repeal of the income tax and social-security laws, and for withdrawal of U.S. recognition of the USSR. It is named for John Birch, a Baptist missionary and an intelligence officer in the U.S. Army, who was killed by Chinese Communists on Aug. 25, 1945. Society members honor Birch as the first American casualty of the cold war. The end of the cold war entailed no policy changes for the society, now headquartered in Appleton, Wis.

John Bull (locomotive)   see LOCOMOTIVE

John Bull (personification)   see BULL, JOHN

John of the Cross, Saint

Saint John of the Cross, b. June 24, 1542, d. Dec. 14, 1591, was a Spanish mystic (see MYSTICISM) and one of Spain's finest lyric poets. He entered a CARMELITE monastery in 1563 and was ordained a priest in 1567. Dissatisfied with the laxity of the order, he began to work for the reform of the Carmelites. With Saint TERESA OF ÁVILA, he founded the Discalced Carmelites.

Saint John combined the imagination and sensitivity of a poet with the precision and depth of a theologian and philosopher trained in the tradition of Saint Thomas AQUINAS, making his writings powerfully descriptive and analytical of the mystical experience. His poems deal with the purification of the soul—through detachment and suffering—in its mystical journey toward God and give a detailed description of three stages of mystical union: purgation, illumination, and union. Saint John was canonized in 1726 and declared a Doctor of the Church in 1926. Feast day: Dec. 14.

John Damascene, Saint [dam'-uh-seen]

Saint John Damascene, b. c.675, d. Dec. 4, 749, was a Syrian Christian theologian who synthesized the doctrines of the Eastern FATHERS OF THE CHURCH. When Byzantine Emperor LEO III issued (726–730) edicts against the cult of images, John became a leading figure in the defense of icons in the iconoclastic controversy (see ICONOCLASM).

Among his many writings the *Fountain of Knowledge* is the main work. It is divided into three parts—a study of Greek philosophy, a history of heresies, and an exposition of the teaching of the Eastern Fathers on the central Christian doctrines. John is a Doctor of the Church. Feast day: Dec. 4.

John Dory

The John Dory, *Zeus faber*, or the European John Dory, is a solitary, midwater marine fish of the family Zeidae found in the temperate waters from the British Isles southward to the African coasts and into the Mediterranean Sea. It is distinguished by a large, eyelike spot—black circled by a yellow ring—located in the center of its body. Another identifying feature is the presence of short spines along the bases of the anal and dorsal fins, as well as commonly found along the belly midline. Older fish develop long filaments on the first eight to ten spiny rays of the dorsal fin. The John Dory may attain a weight of up to 20 kg (44 lb). *Z. japonicus* (Indo-Pacific water), *Z. nebulosa* (Japanese water), and the American John Dory, *Zenopsis ocellata* (Atlantic coast of North America), are other species in the dory family.

John the Fearless, Duke of Burgundy

John the Fearless, b. May 28, 1371, d. Sept. 10, 1419, was the oldest son of PHILIP THE BOLD and the first cousin of King CHARLES VI of France. In 1396 he was a leader of a crusade against the Turks that ended disastrously at Nicopolis (now in Bulgaria). John succeeded his father as duke of Burgundy in 1404 and became count of Flanders on his mother's death (1405); he was thus the leading prince of the Low Countries. He also struggled with his cousin Louis of Orléans (see ORLÉANS family) for control of the resources of the French government. Virtually excluded from power in Paris, he had Louis murdered in 1407, provoking a disastrous civil war. After a period of dominance in France (1408–13), he was again excluded from power until 1418. In that year he took advantage of French defeats by the English in the HUNDRED YEARS' WAR to seize Paris. The following year, however, he was assassinated while negotiating with the dauphin (the future CHARLES VII).

John of Gaunt, Duke of Lancaster [gawnt, lang'-kuhs-tur]

John of Gaunt, b. March 1340, d. Feb. 3, 1399, was the fourth son of King EDWARD III of England. Through marriage (1359) to Blanche, heiress of Lancaster, he secured her large holdings and became duke of Lancaster. After Blanche's death he married (1371) Constance, heiress of PETER I of Castile, and claimed the Castilian crown. He was a leading English magnate under his nephew RICHARD II, but his military campaigns in Europe kept him out of the major domestic conflicts of that reign. Gaunt supported John WYCLIFFE for a time and patronized Geoffrey CHAUCER. In 1386 he invaded Castile, but he surrendered his claim in 1388. In 1396, Gaunt married his mistress Catherine Swynford and legitimized his children by her (see BEAUFORT family). Gaunt's son by Blanche became King HENRY IV and thus founded the royal house of Lancaster (see LANCASTER dynasty).

John Henry   The legend about the African-American railroad worker John Henry, who died from exertion after successfully competing with a hammer and steel bit against an automated steam hammer, originated about 1870, soon after steam hammers were introduced on railroad construction sites in the Allegheny Mountains. John Henry's legend, which may have some factual basis, is celebrated in stories and songs.

John Maurice of Nassau [mor'-is, nas'-aw]   John Maurice, count of Nassau-Siegen, b. June 17, 1604, d. Dec. 20, 1679, was called "the Brazilian" because he governed the Dutch colony in Brazil at the height of its power and prosperity. He was a cousin of the Dutch stadtholders MAURICE OF NASSAU and FREDERICK HENRY, PRINCE OF ORANGE, under whose command he served in the Dutch army from 1621 until 1636. In the latter year he was named governor of Brazil, newly conquered from the Portuguese. His ambitious plans for the development of the colony proved too costly for the Dutch West India Company, which recalled him in 1644. His residence at The Hague, known as Mauritshuis ("Maurice's House"), later became a world-famous museum.

John Nepomucene, Saint [ne-poh-muh-seen']   Saint John Nepomucene, b. c.1345, d. Mar. 20, 1393, was a Bohemian martyr who is the patron saint of the Czechs. As vicar general to the archbishop of Prague, he opposed the attempts of King Wenceslas IV of Bohemia to create a new bishopric for one of the king's favorites. The king had him tortured and drowned. According to a tradition declared unfounded in 1961, Saint John was put to death for refusing to reveal the confessional secrets of Wenceslas's wife. He was canonized in 1729. Feast day: May 16.

John Paul II, Pope   John Paul II, b. May 18, 1920, was elected pope on Oct. 16, 1978, succeeding John Paul I. His name was Karol Josef Wojtyla. John Paul II is the first Polish pope and the first non-Italian pope since the 16th century; he is also the first pope to come from a Communist country, and during his pontificate he has traveled more extensively than any of his predecessors, preaching to millions of people on six continents and in more than 50 nations.

The son of a Polish army officer, Karol Wojtyla was born in Wadowice, Poland. He attended an underground seminary during the World War II German occupation and

was ordained a priest in 1946. After studying in Rome and at the University of Kraków, he was appointed (1956) professor of ethics at the University of Lublin, where he published the first of many articles and books on philosophical and theological themes. Consecrated bishop in 1958, he served first as auxiliary bishop of Kraków and in 1964 became archbishop of Kraków. He was made a cardinal in 1967.

John Paul II's pontificate has revealed two principal goals. The first is his vigorous commitment to justice and peace. He has consistently encouraged nations to construct a social order that fosters human dignity. He has criticized the injustices of both Communism and capitalism. The pope has presented his ideas on social justice and other theological themes in the encyclicals *Redemptor hominis* (1979), *Dives in misericordia* (1980), *Laborem exercens* (1981), *Slavorum apostolorum* (1985), *Dominum et vivificantem* (1986), and *Redemptoris mater* (1987).

John Paul's second goal is to affirm the unambiguous identity of Roman Catholicism by implementing the directives of the Second Vatican Council (1962–65). Uneasy with dissent, he has attempted to enforce the church's disciplinary rules and to resist uncontrolled innovations. He has, for example, condemned some aspects of LIBERATION THEOLOGY; censured such theologians as Hans KÜNG, Edward Schillebeeckx, Leonardo Boff, and Charles Curran; and opposed the ordination of women to the priesthood. Through the congregations of the Roman Curia, he has exercised strong control over theology, moral behavior, liturgy, and catechetics. The Congregation for the Doctrine of the Faith, for example, issued with his approval documents condemning homosexuality (1986) and on the ethical implications of new medical technologies dealing with human reproduction (1987). John Paul has followed the practice introduced by John XXIII and Paul VI of meeting with leaders of other Christian church-

Pope John Paul II, the first non-Italian pontiff in 456 years, has won worldwide admiration by his personal charm. His pontificate has combined unprecedented globe-trotting and informality with staunch conservatism on doctrinal and disciplinary issues.

es. In 1983 he promulgated a revised Code of Canon Law. He has continued to convene the Synod of Bishops, a consultative body established by Paul VI.

John Paul II has been an active and forceful pontiff whose public exposure has made him a spiritual leader throughout the world. He has survived two assassination attempts: one in Saint Peter's Square in 1981 in which he was seriously wounded, and another, without injury, in Portugal in 1982.

John I Tzimisces, Byzantine Emperor [zi-mi'-sees]

John I Tzimisces, b. 924, d. Jan. 10, 976, was an able military commander and diplomat who greatly increased Byzantine prestige during his brief reign. An Armenian by birth, John Tzimisces succeeded Nicephorus II Phocas in 969. He drove (971) the Russians out of Bulgaria, established ties with the West by arranging (972) a marriage between a Byzantine princess and the German king Otto II, and led (974–75) successful campaigns against the Fatimids in Syria and Palestine.

John II Comnenus, Byzantine Emperor [kuhm-nee'-nuhs]

John II Comnenus, b. 1088, d. Apr. 8, 1143, succeeded his father, Alexius I, as ruler of the Byzantine Empire in 1118. He reestablished imperial authority in the Balkans by defeating the Pechenegs in 1122, controlling the Serbs, and checking Hungarian expansion. His alliance with Holy Roman Emperor Lothair II countered the threat from the NORMANS in southern Italy. In the East John conquered the Armenian state of Cilicia in 1137 and forced the Latin principality of Antioch to acknowledge his suzerainty.

John, King of England

The youngest son of HENRY II and ELEANOR OF AQUITAINE, John, b. Dec. 24, 1167, d. Oct. 18–19, 1216, succeeded his brother Richard I as king on May 27, 1199. John's reign is notable for his conflicts with the church and the barons, the latter resulting in the MAGNA CARTA.

John was hedonistic, mercurial, unstable, and unforgiving, but he was also highly intelligent, well versed in law and government, efficient, and sophisticated. His greatest shortcoming, in view of his contemporaries, was that he was no warrior. Moreover, John's difficulties stemmed largely from the policies of his father and brother. Richard had bequeathed financial bankruptcy and a ruinously expensive war in France. John also bore the brunt of baronial reaction to the centralization of government, a policy initiated by his predecessors.

Early in his reign John lost most of the English possessions in France; by 1206, PHILIP II of France had conquered Anjou, Normandy, and Brittany. In that year John also became embroiled in a quarrel with the church by refusing to accept the election of Stephen LANGTON as archbishop of Canterbury. The pope placed England under interdict (in effect, closing the churches) until John abandoned the fight in 1213 and accepted papal vassalage.

King John's arbitrary policies so antagonized the English barons that they mustered an army to force him to yield to their demands, embodied in the Magna Carta (1215), which he is shown signing.

The king took this step to strengthen his hand against the barons, with whom trouble had been building since 1208. The failure of John's expedition to Poitou in 1214, however, coupled with the defeat of his ally, Holy Roman Emperor OTTO IV, in the Battle of Bouvines, gave the English barons their excuse for rebellion. In June 1215 the barons forced the king to accede to their demands for the restoration of feudal rights in the famous document called Magna Carta. The civil war was resumed soon after, however, and continued at the time of John's death. John was succeeded by his young son, HENRY III.

John II, King of France (John the Good)

John II, b. Apr. 16, 1319, d. Apr. 8, 1364, the elder son of PHILIP VI, assumed a major role in French government by 1348 and became king in 1350. John waged war against both England (see HUNDRED YEARS' WAR) and domestic rebels led by his son-in-law, Charles the Bad, king of Navarre. He was criticized for his lowborn and corrupt advisors. In September 1356, John was captured by EDWARD, THE BLACK PRINCE in the Battle of Poitiers. To ransom him from the English under the terms of the Treaty of Bretigny (1360), the French paid the first regular peacetime taxes in their history. When his hostage son broke parole, John returned to England late in 1363 and died there.

John I, King of Hungary (John Zápolya)

John Zápolya, b. 1487, d. July 22, 1540, was one of the two rival kings of HUNGARY in the period following the Battle of Mohács (1526). In the chaos after the death (1490) of MATTHIAS CORVINUS, John became the leader of the so-called national party of the Hungarian nobility. He was governor of TRANSYLVANIA from 1511 to 1526, but he failed to appear at the Battle of Mohács, where Turkish victory ended Hungary's unity and independence for centuries.

Although elected king by his supporters in 1526, John was never able to consolidate his rule against his rival, the future Holy Roman emperor FERDINAND I. In the Treaty of Várad (1538) he agreed to leave his section of Hungary to

Ferdinand, but Turkish pressure and the birth (1540) of his son, John Sigismund (John II), made him change just before his death. John I was a weak and vacillating ruler whose policies contributed to Hungary's prolonged division.

John II, King of Hungary (John Sigismund Zápolya)

John Sigismund Zápolya, b. July 7, 1540, d. Mar. 14, 1571, was titular king of Hungary, as John II, from 1540 to 1570 and the first prince of Transylvania from 1556 until his death. Although elected king immediately after the death (1540) of his father, John I, he never ruled more than the eastern section of Hungary, and that only under Turkish protection. In 1570, John gave up the royal Hungarian title. Under his rule Transylvania became largely Calvinist and was separated from Hungary—a separation that lasted for a century and a half.

John II, King of Poland (John Casimir)

John II, b. Mar. 21, 1609, d. Dec. 16, 1672, ruled Poland from 1648 to 1668. The younger son of SIGISMUND III, John Casimir pursued a military career before becoming a Jesuit novice (1646) and a cardinal (1647). He gave up his cardinal's hat, however, to succeed his brother, Władysław IV, as king.

John's reign was marked by constant wars with Sweden, Russia, Prussia, and the Ottoman Empire. He was a pretender to the Swedish throne, and this fact gave Sweden's King CHARLES X a formal pretext for invading Poland. John rallied popular support against the Swedes in 1655–60, but his country was devastated and the crown bankrupted. John recognized Brandenburg's sovereignty over East Prussia in .1657 and lost eastern Ukraine to Russia in 1667. Forced to abdicate in 1668, John lived his last years in Nevers, France, supported by Louis XIV.

John III, King of Poland (John Sobieski)

John Sobieski, b. Aug. 17, 1629, d. June 17, 1696, ruled Poland as King John III from 1674 to 1696. He is best known for saving Vienna from the Turks on Sept. 12, 1683.

A Polish noble, John studied at Kraków and toured Europe in 1646–48. He married (1655) Marie Casimiere d'Arguien and was devoted to her to the end of his life; his collected letters to her are a classic of Polish literature. As commander of the Polish army, he defeated the Turks at Chocim (Khotin) in 1673, and this feat led to his election the following year as successor to King Michael (Wisniowiecki). After defeating the Turks before Vienna, John tried to build an anti-Turkish league, but this attempt failed. John was a patron of the arts, and his palace at Wilanów is a monument of baroque art and architecture.

John I, King of Portugal (John the Great)

John I, b. Apr. 11, 1357, d. Aug. 14, 1433, ruled Portugal from 1385 to 1433, a period when Portugal began its overseas expansion. The illegitimate son of PETER I, John came to the throne in a revolt against the regency established by

the widow of his half brother, Ferdinand I (see FERDINAND I, KING OF PORTUGAL), on behalf of Ferdinand's daughter Beatrice, the wife of John I of Castile. John's defeat of the Castilians in 1385 assured Portuguese independence, although a formal peace was not concluded until 1411. In 1387, John married Philippa of Lancaster, daughter of JOHN OF GAUNT.

John strengthened the powers of the monarchy and of the merchants and lesser nobles at the expense of the higher aristocracy, and he encouraged shipbuilding and overseas trade. In 1415 a major expedition seized the strategic harbor and trading city of Ceuta on the coast of Morocco, and in the 1420s the Portuguese began to settle the Madeira Islands. John was succeeded as king by his eldest son, Edward I; John's sons, especially HENRY THE NAVIGATOR, continued Portuguese patronage of overseas exploration.

John II, King of Portugal (John the Perfect)

John II, b. May 3, 1455, d. Oct. 25, 1495, who ruled Portugal from 1481 to 1495, earned the nickname "the Perfect" for his assertion of power over the aristocracy and for his patronage of the arts and of overseas expeditions. His father, Alfonso V, placed him in charge of explorations in 1474. John sent Bartolomeu DIAS around the Cape of Good Hope to the Indian Ocean (1487–88), but he rebuffed the Genoese Christopher COLUMBUS in 1484. In 1492, John admitted into Portugal thousands of Jews after their expulsion from Spain, and in 1494 he agreed to the Treaty of TORDESILLAS, which divided the New World between the Spanish and the Portuguese. He was succeeded by his brother-in-law and cousin, MANUEL I.

John III, King of Portugal (John the Pious)

John III, b. June 6, 1502, d. June 11, 1557, succeeded his father, MANUEL I, to the Portuguese throne in 1521. In 1525 he married Catherine, sister of Holy Roman Emperor Charles V. A strong Roman Catholic, sometimes called "the Pious," John allowed the establishment of the INQUISITION (1536) and the Jesuits (1540) in Portugal and encouraged the arts and literature. During his reign Lisbon became one of the largest, richest, and most cosmopolitan cities of Europe. John was succeeded by his young grandson, SEBASTIAN.

John IV, King of Portugal

John IV, b. Mar. 18, 1604, d. Nov. 6, 1656, became king of Portugal in 1640 as a result of the revolution against Spanish rule that reestablished Portuguese independence. John, as duke of BRAGANÇA, was the most powerful aristocrat in Portugal. In December 1640, after the successful national revolt against PHILIP IV of Spain, he was crowned king. Victory over the Spanish at Montijo (1644) confirmed Portuguese independence, but Spain did not recognize Portugal's independence until 1668. During John's reign Portugal regained Angola and Brazil but lost its Asian colonies to the Dutch. John was succeeded by his son Alfonso VI.

John VI, King of Portugal   John VI, b. May 13, 1767, d. Mar. 10, 1826, was king of Portugal from 1816 to his death. When his mother, Queen Maria I, became insane in 1792, John took over her duties, becoming regent in 1799. Portugal long remained untouched by the Napoleonic Wars, but in 1807, as a French Army advanced across Spain, the royal family and court fled to Brazil, where John succeeded to the throne on Maria's death (1816). In 1820 a liberal revolt broke out in Portugal. The following year John was persuaded to return to Portugal, leaving his son Pedro (later Emperor PEDRO I) as regent of Brazil. John's indulgent, irresolute personality encouraged ambitious conspirators to use the monarchy for their own ends. After his death, his daughter Maria Isabel became regent for Pedro, who ruled Portugal briefly as Peter IV.

John XXII, Pope   John XXII, b. *c.*1245, d. Dec. 4, 1334, was pope from 1316 to 1334. He was a Frenchman named Jacques Duèse. After his election he established the papal residence at Avignon, where he remained until his death. John's pontificate was filled with conflicts, both theological and political. The FRANCISCANS were divided over the interpretation of poverty; a radical group, called Spiritual Franciscans, held that the practice of evangelical poverty was absolute and could not be modified. When John condemned the rigid view of the Spirituals, they sought the help of the pope's enemy, Holy Roman Emperor LOUIS IV, who in 1328 set up as antipope a Spiritual Franciscan, Pietro Rainalducci, under the name of Nicholas V. In 1329, John excommunicated and imprisoned Nicholas.

John XXIII, Pope   John XXIII, b. Nov. 25, 1881, d. June 3, 1963, was pope from 1958 to 1963. His name was Angelo Giuseppe Roncalli. He began his long career in the Vatican diplomatic corps when he was appointed (1925), with the title of archbishop, to be the apostolic visitor to Bulgaria. Pope PIUS XI named him apostolic delegate to Turkey and Greece in 1935. As nuncio to France (1944–53), Roncalli dealt with the delicate controversies concerning the hated VICHY GOVERNMENT and problems between conservatives and liberals. He was also Vatican observer at UNESCO (1946–53). In 1953 he was made a cardinal and named patriarch of Venice. His energetic half decade there ended in his 77th year.

When he was elected pope, Roncalli seemed to be a compromise candidate because of his advanced years. His reign was full of surprises. John XXIII left the Vatican often to visit Italian churches, hospitals, and prisons. His common touch and jovial warmth inspired great popular affection. The Second VATICAN COUNCIL, announced in 1959, initiated an *aggiornamento*, or modernization, of the church. Even before Vatican II began, John steered the Roman Catholic church toward the eventual goal of reunion with other Christians, creating (1960) the Secretariat for Christian Unity. During the council, which began in October 1962 with 2,600 prelates present, three doz-

John XXIII's reign (1958–63) as the 261st pope of the Roman Catholic church was liberal and innovative. He sought to depoliticize and reinvigorate the church and in 1962, convened Vatican II, the first ecumenical council in almost 100 years.

en Protestant and Orthodox representatives were observers. Curialists and other conservatives were unable to thwart revision of formulas and discipline that had been established 400 years earlier at the Council of Trent.

John XXIII supported use of the vernacular in the LITURGY and other progressive reforms discussed during the council. During his pontificate, he sought rapprochement with Communist governments. He also enlarged the College of CARDINALS and promoted the development of regular native hierarchies in former European colonies. Among his encyclicals, *Mater et Magistra* (1961) dealt with economic problems and social reforms, and *Pacem in Terris* (1963) discussed peace among nations based on justice, freedom, and the right organization of society. The process of his beatification, the first step toward canonization, was begun in 1965.

John XXIII, "Antipope"   During the Great SCHISM of the West, John XXIII, b. *c.*1370, d. Nov. 22, 1419, the second pope of the Pisan line, named Baldassare Cossa, reigned (1410–15) in competition with the rival claimants of the Roman (Gregory XII) and the Avignon (BENEDICT XIII) lines. While he was endeavoring to end the schism, he was elected pope himself in May 1410. He summoned the Council of Constance, which deposed (May 1415) him and secured the removal of the other papal claimants, thus bringing to an end the Great Schism that had divided the Western church for almost 40 years. The legitimacy of John's original claim to the papal office has remained a disputed question to the present day; Angelo Roncalli adopted the name John XXIII on election to the papacy in 1958.

Johns, Jasper   Jasper Johns, b. Allendale, S.C., May 15, 1930, is a major modern artist who changed the course of ABSTRACT EXPRESSIONISM and reexamined the relation between works of art and physical objects. Three paintings from his first one-man show in 1958, including

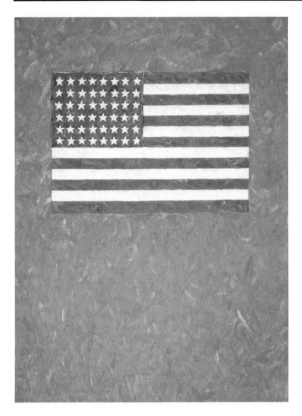

The American artist Jasper Johns's Flag on an Orange Field *(1957) represented a transition from abstract expressionism to the representationalism of Pop art and other modern trends. (Wallraf-Richartz Museum, Cologne.)*

Target with Four Faces (1955), were purchased by the Museum of Modern Art, New York City. Johns's early paintings contained much of the imagery for which he later became famous: the American flag, in its familiar or in unfamiliar colors; the map of the United States; and the target.

Johns also incorporated "found" objects in his work, selecting flat materials to place on flat canvas, thus removing the conventional distinction between the surface of a painting and the object represented. Johns put the short, active strokes of abstract expressionism to quite a different purpose: to contrast the craft of painting with mechanically reproduced images, such as maps, targets, and stenciled numbers. In the 1960s, he began making prints, such as his series of numerals, rendered singly and in patterns. Johns's sculpture *Painted Bronze* (1964; Leo Castelli Gallery, New York City)—two beer cans, one manufactured, the other a plaster and bronze facsimile—also plays with the ambiguous relation between reality and the illusions of art.

Johns Hopkins University, The   Established in 1876, The Johns Hopkins University is a private coedu-

cational institution in Baltimore, Md., and the first in the United States to be formed as a university, offering graduate study and research. Qualified students may pursue graduate degrees before completing their undergraduate work. Associated with the university are a hospital (1889) and a medical school (1893), The Peabody Institute of Music (1857), and the School of Advanced International Studies, which is located in Washington, D.C., with a campus in Bologna, Italy. The Johns Hopkins University Press (1878) is America's oldest university press in continuous operation.

Johnson, Andrew   Andrew Johnson became the 17th president of the United States after the assassination of Abraham LINCOLN, on Apr. 15, 1865. As president he was the focal point of a struggle over how to restore the Union after the Civil War. The contest over RECONSTRUCTION became so bitter that he was impeached by the House of Representatives and tried before the U.S. Senate, which ultimately found him not guilty of the charges.

Early Life. Johnson was born in Raleigh, N.C., on Dec. 29, 1808. His family, already poor, was left destitute by the death of his father four years later. When he was 14 his mother apprenticed him to a tailor. Johnson never received a formal education; he learned the rudiments of reading and writing from the manager in his place of work. In 1826, Johnson and his family moved to eastern Tennessee, and a year later he opened his own tailor shop in Greeneville. On May 17, 1827, Johnson married Eliza McCardle, the daughter of a shoemaker. She furthered his education, teaching him arithmetic and improving his reading and writing.

Attracted by Andrew JACKSON's antiaristocratic rhetoric, Johnson had become an important figure in Tennessee Democratic politics by the 1830s. Representing the mostly non-slave-owning small farmers of the eastern Tennessee hill country, he successfully challenged the western Tennessee cotton planters who usually controlled the party. Having served as alderman (1829–30) and then mayor (1831–33) of Greeneville, he became a state representative (1835–37, 1839–41) and senator (1841–42). Johnson then served as U.S. congressman (1843–53), governor (1853–57), and finally U.S. senator (1857–62).

Johnson believed passionately that government at every level should interfere as little as possible in people's lives, no matter how desirable the benefits of government action might seem. Moreover, he was convinced that the U.S. Constitution imposed such limitations on the national government.

As a Southerner Johnson defended SLAVERY in the conflicts of the 1840s and '50s, taking the strong STATE RIGHTS position that Congress could not prevent its spread to territories of the United States. Accordingly, in 1860 he supported the proslavery Democratic presidential candidate, John C. BRECKINRIDGE. When the Southern states began to secede after the victory of the antislavery Republican candidate, Abraham Lincoln, however, Johnson denied that secession could be undertaken legally. He

ANDREW JOHNSON
17th President of the United States (1865–69)

Born: Dec. 29, 1808, Raleigh, N.C.

Professions: Tailor; Public Official

Religious Affiliation: None

Marriage: May 17, 1827, to Eliza McCardle (1810–1876)

Children: Martha Johnson (1828–1901); Charles Johnson (1830–63); Mary Johnson (1832–83); Robert Johnson (1834–69); Andrew Johnson (1852–79)

Political Affiliation: Democrat; Unionist

Writings: *Papers of Andrew Johnson* (1967), ed. by L. P. Graf and R. W. Haskins

Died: July 31, 1875, Carter's Station, Tenn.

Buried: Greeneville, Tenn.

Vice-President: None

therefore fought unsuccessfully to keep Tennessee in the Union and refused to resign his place in Congress—the only Southern senator to remain loyal to the United States. When Union forces occupied part of Tennessee in 1862, Lincoln appointed Johnson military governor there.

In 1864 the Republicans, seeking to balance the UNION PARTY ticket with a prowar Southern Democrat, chose Johnson to be Lincoln's running mate. Thus in 1865, Johnson became vice-president of the United States.

Presidency. Succeeding to the presidency after Lincoln's assassination, Johnson tried to restore the Union with as little change as possible beyond the abolition of slavery. Following Lincoln's Reconstruction plan, he pardoned nearly all Southerners for their parts in the rebellion and let them reorganize their state governments, urging Congress to permit representatives who passed tests of loyalty to take their old seats. When Congress refused to agree, Johnson broke with the Republican party.

Like most white Southerners of his time, Johnson was a racist who believed whites should have firm control over society and government. As a believer in state rights, he also thought that Congress had no power to interfere in the Southern states' internal affairs. He therefore opposed Republican legislation to protect the rights of ex-slaves in the South and tried unsuccessfully to prevent Congress from replacing the Southern state governments he had authorized with new ones. In 1868 the struggle between Johnson and Congress came to a head. In defiance of the TENURE OF OFFICE ACT, which Congress had passed over presidential veto in 1867, Johnson attempted to fire his secretary of war, Edwin M. STANTON. Con-

gress responded by impeaching the president for "high crimes and misdemeanors." After a trial lasting a few months (March–May 1868), the Senate found Johnson not guilty. Johnson's power had been broken, however, and he spent the remainder of his term in impotent frustration. Foreign-affairs achievements, such as Secretary of State William H. SEWARD's purchase (1867) of Alaska, had been overshadowed by Johnson's domestic troubles.

Later Life. When his term ended in 1869, Johnson returned to Tennessee. After several unsuccessful candidacies for Congress, he was again elected to the U.S. Senate in 1875. He died shortly afterward, however, on July 31, 1875.

Johnson, Eastman   Jonathan Eastman Johnson, b. Lovell, Maine, July 29, 1824, d. Apr. 5, 1906, was an important American painter of portraits and scenes of country life. He spent nine years as a successful crayon portraitist before studying in Europe. From 1851 to 1855 he resided at The Hague, imitating the naturalism of the 17th-century Dutch masters so effectively that he would be called the American Rembrandt.

On his return to the United States his first major successes were *The Old Kentucky Home* (1859; New-York Historical Society, New York City) and *Corn Husking* (1860; Everson Museum, Syracuse, N.Y.). In the 1860s he painted in a freer style a series of subjects dealing with maple sugaring in Maine, followed in the 1870s by a series dealing with cranberry picking in Nantucket, Mass. In their integration of figures with landscape, atmospheric light and color, and sincerity of feeling, these paintings constitute Johnson's best work and represent a major achievement in American art. An excellent example is *The Cranberry Harvest* (1880; Timkin Art Gallery, San Diego, Calif.). A decline in the sales of his genre subjects made Johnson turn almost exclusively to portraiture in the mid-1880s.

Johnson, Edward The Canadian operatic tenor Edward Johnson, b. Guelph, Ontario, Aug. 22, 1881, d. Apr. 20, 1959, was general manager of the Metropolitan Opera from 1935 to 1950. He made his operatic debut in 1912 in Padua, Italy, and two years later joined La Scala, where, under Arturo Toscanini, he sang the first performance in Italian (1914) of Wagner's *Parsifal.* From 1919 to 1922 he sang with the Chicago Opera, after which he became a member of the Metropolitan Opera, where he remained until his retirement as manager in 1950. Johnson sang the traditional tenor repertoire and created such roles as Deems Taylor's *Peter Ibbetson.* He became a U.S. citizen in 1922.

Johnson, Emily Pauline Emily Pauline Johnson, b. Mar. 10, 1862, d. Mar. 7, 1913, also called *Tekahionwake,* or "the Mohawk Princess," was a Mohawk Indian poet. Born and educated at the Six Nations Reserve in Ontario, she was a great-granddaughter of the British colonial leader Sir William JOHNSON and Molly Brant. She began writing early and in 1895 published her first volume of verse, *White Wampum.* Her collected poems were published under the title *Flint and Feather* (1912).

Johnson, Eyvind A prolific Swedish novelist, Eyvind Johnson, b. July 29, 1900, d. Aug. 15, 1976, was, like some other writers of his generation such as Harry Edmund Martinson and Vilhelm Moberg, largely self-educated. His early life in northern Sweden provided the material for a renowned series of novels, including *Nu var det 1914* (1934; trans. as *1914*, 1970). Johnson's postwar fiction explores a wide range of historical periods—ancient Greece in *Strändernas svall* (1946; trans. as *Return to Ithaca*, 1952), 17th-century France in *Drömmar om rosor och eld* (Dreams about Roses and Fire, 1949), and the age of Charlemagne in *Hans nådes tid* (1960; trans. as *The Days of His Grace,* 1965). Johnson was made a member of the Swedish Academy in 1957 and in 1974 shared the Nobel Prize for literature with Harry Martinson.

Johnson, Fenton The reputation of the American poet Fenton Johnson, b. Chicago, May 7, 1888, d. Sept. 17, 1958, rests on a small number of widely anthologized poems. In the years just before the HARLEM RENAISSANCE, Johnson, in such poems as "The Scarlet Woman," "The Minister," and "Tired," voiced scathing bitterness at the plight of African Americans. His *Visions of the Dusk* (1915; repr. 1971) and *Songs of the Soil* (1916; repr. 1969) have recently been reissued.

Johnson, Hiram Warren Hiram Warren Johnson, b. Sacramento, Calif., Sept. 2, 1866, d. Aug. 6, 1945, was a U.S. progressive Republican political leader and one of the founders of the BULL MOOSE PARTY. He served (1910–17) as governor of California and then entered the U.S. Senate, serving there until his death. As governor, Johnson effected broad social and economic reforms, including women's suffrage, and broke the political power of the Southern Pacific Railroad.

After helping to found the Progressive, or Bull Moose, party, Johnson was chosen as Theodore ROOSEVELT's running mate in the latter's unsuccessful bid for the presidency in 1912. In 1916, Johnson refused to support the Republican presidential candidate, Charles Evans HUGHES. As a result, Hughes lost California, and hence the election, to the Democratic candidate, Woodrow Wilson.

Johnson supported Franklin D. Roosevelt and the Democrats in the 1932 election and generally favored the NEW DEAL domestic programs. He was a lifelong isolationist who opposed U.S. participation in the League of Nations and entry into World War II.

Johnson, Jack John Arthur Johnson, b. Galveston, Tex., Mar. 31, 1878, d. June 10, 1946, was an American heavyweight boxer who became the first African American to hold the world title. Because he was black, flamboyant, and outspoken, Johnson incurred much hostility when he won the title by defeating Tommy Burns in Australia in 1908. He was convicted in 1913 for violating the Mann Act and took sanctuary in Europe. Meanwhile, the white-controlled boxing world began its search for a "great white hope" to regain the title from the champion. In desperate need of money, Johnson fought 2 m–1 cm (6 ft–7 in) Jess Willard in Havana in 1915, losing the title when he was knocked out in the 26th round. The ex-champion later claimed that the fight was fixed. Johnson fought in exhibitions almost up to the time of his death. He had a career record of 80 victories, 7 losses, 14 draws, and 13 no-decisions in 114 bouts.

Johnson, James Weldon James Weldon Johnson, b. Jacksonville, Fla., June 17, 1871, d. June 26, 1938, was an author, editor, social reformer, and a leader of the HARLEM RENAISSANCE. He graduated from Atlanta University in 1894 and became principal of a school for blacks in his hometown and the first African American admitted (1897) to the Florida bar. From 1906 to 1912 he was a consul in Venezuela and Nicaragua. He later became executive secretary of the National Association for the Advancement of Colored People. From 1930 until his death he was professor of creative literature at Fisk University in Nashville, Tenn. He published the novel *Autobiography of an Ex-Coloured Man* (1912), an autobiography, and several books of verse.

Johnson, John Harold   John Harold Johnson, b. Arkansas City, Ark., Jan. 19, 1918, founded *Ebony* and other magazines for black American readers. His family moved from Arkansas to Chicago's South Side in 1933. After high school he went to work as an office boy for a black-owned life insurance company, eventually becoming chairman of the board. In the meantime he founded *Negro Digest* in 1942 (later called *Black World*), *Ebony* in 1945, *Tan* in 1950 (later *Black Stars*), *Jet* in 1951, and *Ebony, Jr.* in 1973. In 1987 the combined circulation of the surviving and thriving *Ebony* and *Jet* was approximately 2,500,000. Johnson has collected numerous honorary degrees and has served as a director on the boards of several national companies.

Johnson, John Rosamond   The American composer and bass singer John Rosamond Johnson, b. Jacksonville, Fla., Aug. 11, 1873, d. Nov. 11, 1954, wrote with his brother, the poet James Weldon Johnson, "Lift Every Voice and Sing" (1900), known as the Negro national anthem. He sang in music halls and in operas in London, and toured (1930–32) Europe and the United States in programs of Negro spirituals. He also sang the role of Lawyer Frazier in early productions of George Gershwin's *Porgy and Bess*. Johnson's compositions include a ballet, *African Drum Dance*, and much vocal music. In 1937 he published *Rolling Along in Song*, a history of black music.

Johnson, Lyndon B.   Lyndon Baines Johnson became the 36th president of the United States on the assassination of John F. KENNEDY in November 1963. A skilled promoter of liberal domestic legislation, he was also a staunch believer in the use of military force to help achieve the country's foreign-policy objectives. His escalation of American involvement in the VIETNAM WAR eroded his popular standing and led to his decision not to run for reelection to the presidency in 1968.

Early Life. Johnson was born on Aug. 27, 1908, near Johnson City, Tex., the eldest son of Sam Ealy Johnson, Jr., and Rebekah Baines Johnson. He received a B.S. degree from Southwest Texas State Teachers College in San Marcos and taught for a year in Houston. In 1931 he went to Washington as secretary to a Democratic Texas congressman, Richard M. Kleberg.

During the next four years Johnson developed a wide network of political contacts in Washington, D.C. On Nov. 17, 1934, he married Claudia Alta Taylor, known as "Lady Bird."

In 1935, President Franklin D. ROOSEVELT named Johnson, at age 27, to head the National Youth Administration in Texas. This job entailed helping young people obtain employment and schooling. It confirmed John-

AT A GLANCE

LYNDON BAINES JOHNSON
36th President of the United States (1963–69)

Nickname: "LBJ"

Born: Aug. 27, 1908, near Johnson City, Tex.

Education: Southwest Texas Teachers College (graduated 1930)

Professions: Teacher, Public Official

Religious Affiliation: Disciples of Christ

Marriage: Nov. 17, 1934, to Claudia Alta ("Lady Bird") Taylor (1912–   )

Children: Lynda Bird Johnson (1944–   ); Luci Baines Johnson (1947–   )

Political Affiliation: Democrat

Writings: *The Vantage Point* (1971)

Died: Jan. 22, 1973, near Johnson City, Tex.

Buried: Near Johnson City, Tex.

Vice-President: Hubert H. Humphrey (1965–69)

son's faith in the positive potential of government and won for him a coterie of supporters in Texas.

In 1937, Johnson sought and won a Texas seat in Congress, where he championed public works, reclamation, and public power programs. When war came to Europe he backed Roosevelt's efforts to aid the Allies. During World War II he served a brief tour of active duty with the U.S. Navy in the Pacific (1941–42) but returned to Capitol Hill when Roosevelt recalled members of Congress from active duty.

During the 1940s, Johnson and his wife developed profitable business ventures, including a radio station, in Texas. In 1948 he ran for the U.S. Senate, winning the Democratic party primary by only 87 votes. The opposition accused him of fraud and derisively tagged him "Landslide Lyndon." Although unsuccessfully challenged in the courts, he took office in 1949.

Senator and Vice-President. Johnson moved quickly into the Senate hierarchy. In 1953 he won the job of Senate Democratic leader. The next year he became majority leader, a post he held for the next six years, despite a serious heart attack in 1955.

In the late 1950s, Johnson began to think seriously of running for the presidency in 1960. His record had been fairly conservative, however. Many Democratic liberals resented his friendly association with the Republican president, Dwight D. Eisenhower; others considered him a tool of wealthy Southwestern gas and oil interests. Either to soften this image as a conservative or in response to inner conviction, Johnson moved slightly to the Left on some domestic issues, especially on civil rights laws, which he supported in 1957 and 1960. Although these laws proved ineffective, Johnson had demonstrated that he was a resourceful Senate leader.

To many northern Democrats, however, Johnson remained a sectional candidate. The presidential nomination of 1960 went to Senator John F. Kennedy of Massachusetts. Kennedy, a northern Roman Catholic, then selected Johnson as his running mate to balance the ticket. In November 1960 the Democrats defeated the Republican candidates, Richard M. Nixon and Henry Cabot Lodge, by a narrow margin.

Kennedy appointed Johnson to head the President's Committee on Equal Employment Opportunities, which enabled him to work on behalf of African Americans and other minorities. As vice-president, he also undertook some missions abroad, which offered him limited insights into international problems.

Presidency. The assassination of President Kennedy on November 22, 1963, elevated Johnson to the White House, where he quickly proved a masterful, reassuring leader in the realm of domestic affairs. In 1964, Congress passed a tax-reduction law that promised to promote economic growth and the Economic Opportunity Act, which launched the program called the WAR ON POVERTY. Johnson was especially skillful in securing a strong CIVIL RIGHTS ACT in 1964. It became a vital source of legal authority against racial and sexual discrimination.

In 1964 the Republicans nominated Sen. Barry M. GOLDWATER of Arizona for president. Goldwater was a con-

servative in domestic policy and an advocate of strong military action to protect U.S. interests in Vietnam. Johnson had increased the number of U.S. military personnel there from 16,000 at the time of Kennedy's assassination to nearly 25,000 a year later. Compared with Goldwater, however, he seemed a model of restraint. Johnson, with Hubert H. HUMPHREY as running mate, ran a low-key campaign and overwhelmed Goldwater, who won only his home state and five others in the Deep South.

Johnson's triumph in 1964 gave him a mandate for the Great Society, as he called his domestic program. Congress responded by passing the MEDICARE program, approving federal aid to elementary and secondary education, supplementing the War on Poverty, and creating the Department of Housing and Urban Development. It also passed another important civil rights law—the Voting Rights Act of 1965.

At this point Johnson began the rapid deepening of U.S. involvement in Vietnam; as early as February 1965, U.S. planes began to bomb North Vietnam. American troop strength in Vietnam increased to more than 180,000 by the end of the year and to 500,000 by 1968.

While the nation became deeply involved in Vietnam, racial tension sharpened at home, culminating in widespread urban RACE RIOTS between 1965 and 1968. The breakdown of the interracial civil rights movement, together with the imperfections of some of Johnson's Great Society programs, resulted in Republican gains in the 1966 elections, thus thwarting Johnson's hopes for further congressional cooperation.

It was the policy of military escalation in Vietnam, however, that proved to be Johnson's undoing as president. It deflected attention from domestic concerns, resulted in sharp inflation, and prompted rising criticism, especially among young, draft-age people. Escalation also failed to win the war. The drawn-out struggle made Johnson even more secretive, dogmatic, and hypersensitive to criticism.

The New Hampshire presidential primary of 1968, in which the antiwar candidate Eugene McCARTHY made a strong showing, revealed the dwindling of Johnson's support. Some of Johnson's closest advisors now counseled deescalation in Vietnam. Confronted by mounting opposition, Johnson made two surprise announcements on Mar. 31, 1968: he would stop the bombing in most of North Vietnam and seek a negotiated end to the war, and he would not run for reelection.

Johnson's influence thereafter remained strong enough to dictate the nomination of Vice-President Humphrey, who had supported the war, as the Democratic presidential candidate in 1968. Although Johnson stopped all bombing of the North on November 1, he failed to make real concessions at the peace table, and the war dragged on. Humphrey lost in a close race with the Republican candidate, Richard M. Nixon.

Retirement. After stepping down from the presidency in January 1969, Johnson returned to his ranch in Texas. He died on Jan. 22, 1973, five days before the conclusion of the treaty by which the United States withdrew from Vietnam.

Johnson, Magic   Earvin "Magic" Johnson, b. Lansing, Mich., Aug. 14, 1959, was, along with Michael Jordan, professional basketball's premier guard in the 1980s and early 1990s. Johnson rose to fame as a Michigan State University sophomore, leading his team to the 1979 national title. He then joined the Los Angeles Lakers of the National Basketball Association, and immediately spurred them—with his superb passing and enthusiasm—to the first of 5 NBA championships (1980, 1982, 1985, 1987–88). The 6-ft 9-in (2-m 5-cm) Johnson has won 3 Most Valuable Player awards (1987, 1989–90)—more than any guard in NBA history—and has per-game career averages of about 20 points, 7½ rebounds, and 11 assists. During the 1990-91 season he broke Oscar Robertson's NBA career record (9,887) for assists.

Johnson, Philip   Architect Philip Cortelyou Johnson, b. Cleveland, Ohio, July 8, 1906, has been profoundly influential as critic, historian, and designer. After graduating (1927) from Harvard College, where he studied philosophy and Greek, Johnson became director of the architecture department of the newly founded Museum of Modern Art in New York City. There he and architectural historian Henry-Russell Hitchcock introduced (1932) the American public to the achievements of recent European design through a seminal exhibition and its accompanying book, *The International Style: Architecture since 1922* (see INTERNATIONAL STYLE).

After returning to Harvard to study architecture, he designed a number of notable houses that showed the pervasive influence of Ludwig Mies van der Rohe. The outstanding example is his own residence, the Glass House (1949) in New Canaan, Conn., a single room entirely walled in glass and set in parklike surroundings. In such designs as the Amon Carter Museum (1961) in Fort Worth, Tex., and the Sheldon Art Gallery (1963) in Lincoln, Neb., Johnson experimented with classical elements including templelike facades. His more recent buildings are no longer neutral, glazed containers; Yale's Kline Science Center (1965) in New Haven, Conn., has a massive masonry tower set in an arcaded court; Pennzoil Place (1976) in Houston, Tex., has a sharp, picturesque roof silhouette recalling earlier American skyscrapers. His

design (1978), with his partner John Burgee, for the new New York City headquarters of American Telephone & Telegraph Company—a 60-story, pink granite office tower set on a gigantic colonnade and topped with a colossal broken pediment—aroused a storm of controversy and has been seen by critics as a total rejection of the International Style.

See also: POSTMODERN ARCHITECTURE.

Johnson, Rafer   Rafer Lewis Johnson, b. Hillsboro, Tex., Aug. 18, 1935, was an American track and field star who was considered one of the greatest decathlon competitors of all time. At age 19 he won the decathlon in the Pan American Games, and the following year he placed second in the event in the 1956 Olympic Games. He proceeded to dominate decathlons during the next 4 years, culminating his success by setting a world record in 1960 and the Olympic record that same year in Rome. A student leader as well as an athlete at the University of California, Los Angeles, Johnson retired from sports in 1960 and devoted himself to public service.

Johnson, Reverdy   The U.S. statesman Reverdy Johnson, b. Annapolis, Md., May 21, 1796, d. Feb. 10, 1876, was reputed to be one of the ablest constitutional lawyers of his time. He served most notably as counsel for the slave-owning defendant in the DRED SCOTT V. SANDFORD case. Johnson was U.S. attorney general (1849–50) and served twice as U.S. senator from Maryland (1845–49, 1863–68). He backed Andrew Johnson's RECONSTRUCTION program and was instrumental in persuading the Senate to vote against the president's impeachment. In 1868–69, Reverdy Johnson served as minister to Great Britain; in that capacity he negotiated the Johnson-Clarendon Treaty in settlement of the Alabama Claims. The Senate rejected the treaty, however, largely for partisan reasons.

Johnson, Richard M.   Richard Mentor Johnson, b. near what is now Louisville, Ky., Oct. 17, 1780, d. Nov. 19, 1850, was vice-president of the United States (1837–41) under Martin VAN BUREN. He was admitted to the bar in his native Kentucky in 1802. Johnson served in

Philip Johnson's "glass house" (1949–50) in New Canaan, Conn., exemplifies the International Style of architecture.

the U.S. House of Representatives (as a Democratic-Re-publican, 1807–19, and as a Democrat, 1829–37) and in the Senate (1819–29). His career was aided by his claim that he had killed the Indian chieftain TECUMSEH at the Battle of the Thames (1813).

A man of rough frontier manners and unconventional habits, Johnson won Andrew JACKSON's support as the vice-presidential nominee in 1836. His candidacy was unacceptable to Southerners, however, who were offend-ed by his efforts to introduce his mulatto daughters into polite society. Despite Van Buren's decisive majority, Johnson received only a plurality of the electoral vote and was chosen vice-president by the U.S. Senate. His vice-presidential career was undistinguished. In 1840 he was denied renomination by the Democratic Convention, which chose no vice-presidential candidate.

Samuel Johnson, poet, critic, and es-sayist, is considered one of the greatest figures of 18th-cen-tury England. John-son is known for his biography of Bos-well, as well as his Dictionary of the English Language (1755), the 1765 edition of Shake-speare, and his Lives of the Poets (1779–81).

Johnson, Samuel (philosopher)   Samuel Johnson, b. Oct. 14, 1696, d. Jan. 6, 1772, was an American phi-losopher and clergyman. A Congregationalist minister, he was converted (1722) to Anglicanism. He was one of the founders of King's College (later Columbia University), New York City, and its first president (1754–63). A friend of George BERKELEY, he became the leading exponent of Berkeley's IDEALISM in America. With Berkeley, Johnson held that the sensible world is made up of the ideas peo-ple receive from God and that what is commonly thought to be matter is actually in the mind as passive ideas.

Johnson, Samuel (writer)   Samuel Johnson, b. Lich-field, England, Sept. 18, 1709, d. Dec. 13, 1784, was an eminent lexicographer, essayist, poet, and critic. In recog-nition of his role as the leading English writer of the second half of the 18th century, this period is called the Age of Johnson. Johnson developed the first English dictionary based on historical principles, produced the first editorially intelligent edition of Shakespeare's plays, and wrote literary criticism that ranks among the finest in English. He is also admired as a moralist. Thanks to James BOSWELL's mas-sive, brilliant LIFE OF SAMUEL JOHNSON (1791), Johnson's personality and conversational powers have entertained thousands who have never read his writings.

Though constitutionally robust, Johnson suffered throughout life from bodily afflictions. To these were add-ed poverty—which compelled him to leave Oxford without a degree—and mental disturbance. At 21 he suffered the first of two mental breakdowns, which left him with a lifelong dread of insanity, death, and religious damnation.

He tried teaching school but hated it, was attracted to law but lacked the necessary diploma, and settled for writing because writing was what he could do. His first book, a translation (1735) of A Voyage to Abyssinia by a Portuguese Jesuit, was typical of the literary hackwork Johnson produced to support himself for 20 years. In 1738 he joined the staff of The Gentleman's Magazine, for which he wrote poetry—in both Latin and English—and essays. As occasion required he also produced pref-aces, reviews, encyclopedia articles, and biographies; one

of the latter, his life of the notorious minor poet Richard Savage (1744), achieved considerable popularity. His talents so impressed the London publishers that in 1747 they commissioned him to write A Dictionary of the En-glish Language (1755). While working on this mammoth project he also wrote his chief poem, The Vanity of Hu-man Wishes (1749), a satire in imitation of the Roman poet Juvenal; saw his tragedy Irene produced (1749); and composed a powerful series of periodical essays, The Rambler (1750–52).

In 1756, Johnson turned to editing Shakespeare. By the time The Plays of William Shakespeare appeared (1765), he had also produced a second series of essays, The Idler (1758–60), and a comic romance, Rasselas (1759), his finest satire on the human propensity to hopeful self-delusion. He had also experienced a second breakdown (1766), been awarded a government pension (1762), and made two friends who were to become his principal biographers: James Boswell and Hester Thrale. With Thrale he found domestic comforts his life had not hitherto afforded. (His wife of 17 years had died in 1752.) With Boswell he made a tour (1773) of the Hebrides that produced the travel book A Journey to the Western Islands of Scotland (1775).

Johnson's last and greatest work was again the result of a publisher's commission. Paid to supply prefaces to an edition of 52 English poets from Abraham Cowley to Tho-mas Gray, he wrote a massive set of biographies and criti-cisms, The Lives of the Poets (1779–81). The 10-volume work sums up Johnson's two main interests as a writer: people and literature. His biographies treat the poets as tragicomic representatives of human aspiration and its ul-timate defeat. His criticism of their works is an extraordi-narily honest, sometimes withering, estimate of their value; its impact on readers is indicated by the controversy John-son's judgments have provoked for two centuries.

Johnson cultivated a literary style of sonorous distinc-tion. He became a master of the personified generality: his sentences give life to terms like envy, hope, and mal-ice. This style confers on his moral writings an air of ex-ceptional authority. His conversation, if Boswell's and others' famous renderings are accurate, was distinguished by a similar power and also by such epigrammatic brilliance that many of his recorded sayings have become proverbial.

Johnson, Uwe [yohn'-zohn, oo'-vay]   One of Germany's leading novelists, Uwe Johnson, b. July 20, 1934, d. Mar. 13, 1984, was raised in East Germany and moved to West Germany when he had trouble publishing his first novel, *Speculations about Jacob* (1959; Eng. trans., 1963). That novel, *The Third Book about Achim* (1961; Eng. trans., 1967), and *Two Views* (1965; Eng. trans., 1966) all focused on the lack of communication between East and West. Johnson's greatest achievement is a series of novels entitled *Anniversaries* (1970–74; Eng. trans., 1975), tracing the wanderings of a young German woman who eventually emigrates to America.

Johnson, Walter Perry   Walter Perry Johnson, b. Humboldt, Kans., Nov. 6, 1887, d. Dec. 10, 1946, was an American professional baseball player whose pitching record is one of the most impressive in the sport's history. Johnson won 20 or more games in 12 of his 21 major league seasons—his best years were 1912, when he won 32 games, and 1913, when he won 36 games—and set an as yet unapproached record for shutouts (113) and an only recently surpassed total for strikeouts (3,508). He also led the American League in strikeouts 12 times, and he pitched 416 career victories (with 279 losses), 2d in history. All of his major league pitching (1907–27) was for the Washington Senators. Johnson was one of the five original members of the Baseball Hall of Fame.

Johnson, Sir William   Sir William Johnson, b. Ireland 1715, d. July 11, 1774, an American colonial fur trader, land speculator, soldier, and Indian agent, exerted crucial influence on the IROQUOIS LEAGUE during the last two FRENCH AND INDIAN WARS (1744–63). About 1738, Johnson emigrated to New York, settling in the lower Mohawk Valley. He soon became involved in trading and negotiating with the Indians. Appointed to the New York provincial council in 1750, Johnson participated in the ALBANY CONGRESS in 1754.

During King George's War (1744–48), Johnson had organized Indian war parties against the French. In August 1755 he defeated an invading French force under Ludwig August, Baron Dieskau, at Lake George. For that achievement he was made a baronet and was soon appointed (1756) superintendent for northern Indian affairs.

Johnson was also involved in the taking of Fort Niagara (1759) and in Gen. Jeffrey AMHERST's successful campaign against Montreal (1760). Subsequently he played a constructive role in several important negotiations with Indians, most notably during PONTIAC'S REBELLION (1763-66) and in concluding the Treaty of Fort Stanwix (1768), by which the Iroquois ceded extensive territory to the British.

Johnson, William Samuel   William Samuel Johnson, b. Stratford, Conn., Oct. 7, 1727, d. Nov. 14, 1819, was one of the framers of the U.S. Constitution and president (1787–1800) of Columbia College (later Columbia University). He was the son of Samuel Johnson, the first president of Columbia, originally called King's College. A Connecticut lawyer, he served on the governor's council, as the colony's agent in London (1767–71), and as judge of the superior court (1772). During the American Revolution, Johnson was suspected of pro-British sympathies, but he eventually accepted the break with England. He played an influential role at the Constitutional Convention in 1787 and was one of the two Connecticut signers of the Constitution. While president of Columbia, Johnson also served as U.S. senator from Connecticut (1789–91).

Johnson Space Center   The Lyndon B. Johnson Space Center, Houston, Tex., is the development, training, and operations center for U.S. manned space missions. It was named in 1973 by act of Congress, in remembrance of President Johnson's support for space research. The installation began as the Space Task Group, an autonomous unit of the Goddard Space Flight Center at Langley Research Center, Hampton, Va. The group was then assigned with development of the one-man MERCURY spacecraft. Following President John F. Kennedy's commitment in 1961 to land a man on the Moon, plans were announced to build a manned-spacecraft center responsible for manned space missions, including the design, development, and testing of manned spacecraft, the training of astronauts, the coordination of tracking stations, and mission control. The APOLLO, GEMINI, and SKYLAB missions were directed from mission control, and beginning in 1974 it was modified to support the SPACE SHUTTLE program.

Johnston, Albert Sidney   Albert Sidney Johnston, b. Washington, Ky., Feb. 2, 1803, d. Apr. 6, 1862, was a Confederate general in the U.S. Civil War. He graduated from West Point in 1826 but in 1834 left the U.S. Army to go to Texas. He served as commander of the Texan army (1837–38) and then as secretary of war (1838–40) of the Texas republic. Johnston was recommissioned into the U.S. Army in 1849. In 1861 he joined the Confederacy and was given the impossible task of defending the area between the Appalachian Mountains and the Mississippi River. He was killed at the Battle of SHILOH.

Johnston, Franz   The Canadian landscape painter Franz (Frank) Johnston, b. 1888, d. July 9, 1949, was a founding member of the GROUP OF SEVEN. Johnston's restrained renderings of northern Ontario, in particular the Algoma region, display his exceptional drawing abilities. Frequently, however, his landscapes are simply decorative and anecdotal. During World War I, he documented the role of the Canadian armed forces in Europe. He resigned from the Group of Seven in 1924 but continued as a successful painter for the rest of his life.

Johnston, Joseph E.

Joseph Eggleston Johnston, b. Prince Edward County, Va., Feb. 3, 1807, d. Mar. 21, 1891, was a Confederate general in the U.S. Civil War. After graduating from West Point in 1829, he served with distinction in the Second Seminole War and in the Mexican War. In April 1861 he resigned from the U.S. Army and joined the Confederacy. After coming to the aid of P. G. T. BEAUREGARD at the First Battle of BULL RUN (July 1861), Johnston became commander of the Army of Northern Virginia. He was wounded (May 1862) during the PENINSULAR CAMPAIGN and replaced by Robert E. LEE. By then Johnston and President Jefferson DAVIS had quarreled bitterly over Johnston's rank in the army and over matters of strategy.

In 1863, Johnston assumed command of the Department of the West, but he was unable to prevent the fall of Vicksburg in July. In December he succeeded Braxton BRAGG as commander of the Army of Tennessee. Outnumbered and constantly outmaneuvered by the Federals under Gen. William Tecumseh SHERMAN in the ATLANTA CAMPAIGN, he fell back to Atlanta, exposing important areas of the Confederacy to invasion. In July 1864, Davis replaced him with John B. HOOD. After Lee became general in chief in February 1865, he restored Johnston to his command; Johnston surrendered to Sherman in April.

Gen. Joseph E. Johnston is regarded, after Robert E. Lee, as the most able military strategist of the Confederacy. Johnston conducted a masterful series of engagements against the numerically superior Union army of William T. Sherman.

Johnston, Samuel

Samuel Johnston, b. Dundee, Scotland, Dec. 15, 1733, d. Aug. 17, 1816, was a political leader of North Carolina during the American Revolution and the early national period. A lawyer, he served in the colonial assembly and in 1770 drafted the so-called Bloody Act under which Gov. William Tryon suppressed the REGULATORS' revolt. Johnston supported the rebellion against British rule, but he was a conservative force in North Carolina's four provincial Congresses (1774–76).

He represented North Carolina in the Continental Congress (1781–82) and served as governor of the state (1787–89), U.S. senator (1789–93), and superior-court judge (1800–03).

Johnstown

Johnstown, a city in southwestern Pennsylvania, is located in a deep valley at the confluence of the Conemaugh River and Stony Creek. Its population is 28,134 with 241,247 in the metropolitan area (1990). Johnstown is a major center for the mining of bituminous coal and the manufacture of iron, steel, and metal products. It is the site of the University of Pittsburgh at Johnstown.

Johnstown was laid out in 1800. In 1831–34, Johnstown grew as the terminus of the Allegheny Portage Railroad, which hauled canal barges piggyback for 58 km (36 mi) on railroad cars. During the second half of the 19th century, it was the nation's leading steel manufacturing center. Johnstown has often suffered from disastrous floods, most notably in 1889 (when 2,200 people died), 1936, and 1977.

JOIDES

The Joint Oceanographic Institutions for Deep Earth Sampling, or JOIDES, is an organization that was established in early 1964 by the Lamont-Doherty Geological Observatory of Columbia University, the Rosenstiel School of Marine and Atmospheric Science of the University of Miami, the Scripps Institution of Oceanography of the University of California, and the Woods Hole Oceanographic Institution. These institutions were later joined by the departments of oceanography at the University of Rhode Island, the University of Washington, Oregon State University, and Texas A & M and by the Institute of Geophysics at the University of Hawaii. JOIDES drilled (1965) a line of six geological exploratory wells as deep as 1 km (0.6 mi) in the Blake Plateau, a broad flat-bottom feature extending several hundred kilometers east off the CONTINENTAL SHELF bordering Florida.

See also: DEEP-SEA DRILLING PROJECT; OCEAN DRILLING PROGRAM.

joint

(in anatomy)   Any union between adjacent BONES is a joint, whether or not movement of the bones relative to one another is possible. The many joints in the human body differ from each other in shape and in structure and are classified into three main types: fibrous, cartilaginous, and synovial.

Joint classifications are based on the manner in which the adjacent bones are attached to each other. In fibrous joints the bones are held together only by LIGAMENTS, a type of fibrous connective tissue. Cartilaginous joints are those in which the bones are attached to each other by CARTILAGE, a different and special type of connective tissue. The synovial joints are freely movable. The ends of bones are covered by cartilage, but there is a space, the joint cavity, between them. The entire area is enclosed by a capsule made up of a tough, fibrous outer layer and a

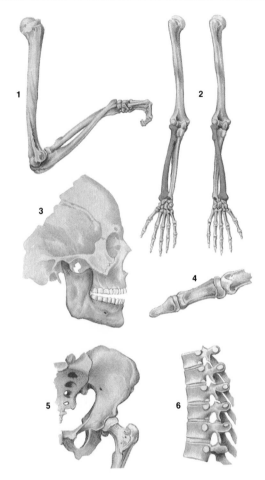

ment or membrane is found between the bony processes. In sutures there can be very little or no movement.

Cartilaginous Joints. Cartilaginous joints are also subdivided into two subtypes. A primary (temporary) joint is present between the end and the shaft of a growing long bone such as the humerus. Normally this cartilage ossifies into bone by the time the bone reaches its adult size. A secondary (permanent) cartilaginous joint occurs between the bodies of the vertebrae; the ends of the articulating bones are covered by hyaline cartilage and are held together by softer, more pliable, fibrocartilage and reinforced by ligaments.

Synovial Joints. The synovial joints are more freely movable and are more variable in structure than other joints. Classification depends on the shapes of the articulating surfaces and also on the kind of movements permitted. Some of these joints, including the knee, have a fibrocartilaginous disk, or meniscus, that partially or completely divides the joint cavity into two cavities. Movements in these joints may occur around one or more axes, or without regard to any axis.

When movement occurs around a single axis, or is limited to a single plane, it is a uniaxial joint. One type of uniaxial joint is the hinge joint. The humeroulnar articulation in the elbow illustrates movement around a single axis,

The knee is the largest and most complicated joint in the human body. The femur (1) and tibia (2) are joined at the back and sides by the capsular ligament (3), which is continuous with the periosteum (4), or outer membrane, of the bones. In front, the patellar ligament (5) and tendon of the quadriceps muscle (6) attach to the patella (7), or knee cap. The bursae (8, 9) and articular cavity (10), filled with synovial, or lubricating fluid, increase mobility of the joint, as does the cartilage (11), which covers the articulating surfaces of the bones. The menisci (12) and ligaments lend stability to the knee. The biceps muscle (13) controls flexion and lateral rotation of the knee; the gastrocnemius muscle (14) controls ankle flexion.

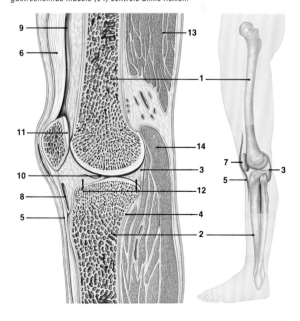

Classification of joint articulations is based on the kind of movement they permit. The elbow (1) is essentially a hinge joint, or ginglymus, allowing movement in a single transverse axis. The pivot, or trochoid, joint found at the upper end of the ulna and radius (2) permits motion around a longitudinal axis. It is shown here in two different positions. A condyloid joint, such as the articulation between the jaw and the skull (3), and a saddle joint, such as the thumb (4), are biaxial joints. The hip (5), a ball and socket joint, can move in an indefinite number of axes. The articulating surfaces of the vertebrae (6), or spinal column, provide examples of gliding, or nonaxial, joints.

thinner, more delicate inner layer known as the synovial membrane. The cavity is filled with a slightly viscous fluid, the synovial fluid.

Fibrous Joints. There are two subtypes of fibrous joints: syndesmoses and sutures. In syndesmoses the bones are attached by an interosseous (between bones) membrane or ligament, and some movement of the bones is possible. The union between spinous processes of the vertebrae is one example.

Sutures occur between bones of the skull. The roots of teeth fitting into alveoli (sockets) of the jawbone are also sutures. The articuloli ends of bones have bony processes that interlock with each other, and a sutural liga-

although some side-to-side motion is possible as well.

The pivot (trochoid) joint may be illustrated by the articulation between the upper end of the radius and the ulna in the elbow. Here the head of the radius rotates within a ring formed by a ringlike ligament and a groove in the ulna bone.

When movement is permitted around two transverse axes set at right angles to each other, the joint is said to be biaxial. The joint between the mandible (lower jaw bone) and the temporal bone of the skull is a biaxial joint. The joint between the metacarpal bone of the thumb and a carpal bone of the wrist is of the saddle-joint type. Here the articulating surfaces are shaped somewhat like the surfaces of a saddle and fit together reciprocally.

Ball-and-socket joints, such as the hip joint, are polyaxial; motion may occur around an indefinite number of axes. A globular-shaped process on one bone fits into a cuplike cavity in the other. Motion is limited only by the cavity's contours and by soft tissues such as ligaments and muscles.

In nonaxial joints a plane or slightly convex surface on one bone lies in contact with another plane or slightly concave surface on another bone. Movement is a sliding or gliding action. Examples include joints between carpal bones in the wrist and those between tarsal bones in the foot.

Injury and Disease. All joints are vulnerable to injury (see FRACTURE) and to damage by diseases such as ARTHRITIS and OSTEOPOROSIS (see also BONE DISEASES). The diagnosis of joint injuries has been greatly facilitated by the arthroscope, a fiber-optics device that can be inserted into a joint, where it functions somewhat like a telescope. Using modified arthroscopes, doctors can perform microsurgery on joints through very small incisions. When joints are too badly diseased or injured for surgical remedy, they can often be replaced by prosthetic devices; replacements for the hip, knee, and finger joints have been particularly successful.

joint (in geology)   A joint is a fracture in rock along which little or no FAULT displacement has occurred. The term derives from mining jargon in Britain, where miners once regarded rocks as being "joined" along fractures. Mining or quarrying would not be possible without the joints present in exposed rocks.

The pattern and distribution of joints determine directions of weakness in rocks, and they may control the movement of GROUNDWATER, petroleum, and mineralizing solutions. Joints are commonly classified according to their relation to other structures, such as bedding, FOLDS, or ore bodies. Where rock cleavage is present, joints tend to form parallel to cleavage planes.

Cooling of some volcanic rocks produces extension joints arranged in hexagonal prisms; such columnar jointing is especially evident at Devil's Tower, in Wyoming.

Joint Chiefs of Staff   see DEFENSE, U.S. DEPARTMENT OF

joint-stock company   A joint-stock company is a type of partnership having many of the attributes of a corporation. Like a corporation, a joint-stock company has shares that may be transferred from one owner to another. Also, as in a corporation, management is centralized in a board of directors who are elected by the partners (shareholders). A joint-stock company differs from a corporation in that the former's shareholders are personally liable for the company's debts. Historically, many of the famous chartered companies—the British EAST INDIA COMPANY, for example—were joint-stock companies. In recent times, because statutes in most of the United States have made it relatively easy to form corporations, the joint-stock company has not been widely used as a form of business organization.

jojoba [huh-hoh'-buh]   The jojoba, a shrub that is native to the Sonoran desert of the United States and Mexico, is under development as a potentially important crop plant for semiarid lands. The shrub, *Simmondsia chinensis*, of the box family, Buxaceae, grows to an adult plant about 6 m (20 ft) high in 3 to 4 years.

The jojoba is valued for its seeds, which consist of about 50 percent oil by weight. The oil resembles sperm whale oil and is notably resistant to degradation by bacteria. Thus far it has been used mainly by the cosmetic industry for making shampoos and lotions, but it is edible and does not grow rancid and could become a substitute for vegetable oil. It could also be used as a lubricant and for other industrial purposes.

Joliot-Curie, Frédéric and Irène [zhol-yoh'-kooree']   The French physicists Jean Frédéric Joliot, b. Mar. 19, 1900, d. Aug. 14, 1958, and Irène Curie, b. Sept. 12, 1897, d. Mar. 17, 1956, are known for their pioneering work in RADIOACTIVITY and nuclear science. They adopted the name Joliot-Curie when they married in 1926.

Irène was the daughter of Marie and Pierre CURIE, the discoverers of radium. She began her career as an assistant at the Radium Institute of the Sorbonne in Paris, where she studied the ejection of alpha rays from polonium. There she met and married Frédéric, who later received (1930) his doctorate from the University of Paris. Working together, the two scientists obtained results that were instrumental in the discovery (1932) of the neutron by the Englih physicist James Chadwick. Continuing their work with the alpha particles emitted by plutonium, they discovered (1934) that the irradiation of aluminum by these particles produces a new, unstable isotope of phosphorus. For this first instance of artificial radioactivity, the Joliot-Curies were awarded the 1935 Nobel Prize for chemistry.

In 1937, Irène was appointed professor at the Sorbonne. The next year she and P. P. Savic, a Yugoslav physicist, showed that the irradiation of uranium with slow protons produces a new radioisotope. This work led

Otto HAHN and Fritz Strassmann to publish (1939) data showing that the impact of a neutron can cause the nucleus of a uranium atom to split into two nuclei of comparable mass. Within a few days Frédéric obtained decisive proof of this phenomenon of nuclear FISSION and showed that a chain reaction releasing enormous amounts of energy was possible among uranium atoms.

Jolliet, Louis [joh-lee-et']   Louis Jolliet, 1645–1700, was a French-Canadian explorer who, with Father Jacques MARQUETTE, opened the Great Lakes and Mississippi Valley to European influence. Originally intending to become a Jesuit, he attended the Jesuit seminary in Quebec but then studied hydrography in France. He became (1669) a fur trader in the Lake Superior region.

In 1672 the Comte de FRONTENAC commissioned Jolliet to find the "great western river" described by Indians. With Marquette, he left Michilimackinac in May 1673 and followed the Fox and Wisconsin rivers to the Mississippi, which Marquette and Jolliet canoed down as far as the Arkansas River. Jolliet's subsequent explorations of the lower St. Lawrence, Labrador, and Hudson Bay persuaded his superiors to appoint him royal hydrographer for Canada in 1697. He executed many notable charts of the area.

Jolson, Al [johl'-suhn]   The singer Al Jolson, b. Asa Yoelson in Lithuania, c.1886, d. Oct. 23, 1950, emigrated with his family to Washington, D.C., about 1895. After a long apprenticeship as a singer in burlesque, minstrel shows, and vaudeville, he won (1911) his first important role in the Broadway show *La Belle Paree*. Jolson's voice was rich and strong; in style he was notable for his vigorous delivery, blatant sentimentality, and occasional use of blackface—a leftover convention from the moribund minstrel show. His work—especially his film roles, beginning with *The Jazz Singer* (1927), the first major sound picture—won him a large audience.

Jonah, Book of   The Book of Jonah, in the Old Testament of the BIBLE, is one of the works of the Minor Prophets. Unlike the other prophetic books, it is not a book written by a prophet but is a narrative about a prophet. Jonah seems to be the prophet mentioned in 2 Kings 14:25 who lived during the reign of Jeroboam II (c.785 BC). The book is anonymous and was probably composed during the 4th century BC.

A short novella, the book describes how Jonah sought to evade God's command to go to Nineveh, the capital of Assyria, to preach repentance. He booked passage on a ship to Tarshish, only to have his flight brought to an end by a divinely ordained storm. Thrown overboard and swallowed by a great fish, Jonah was vomited up on shore after three days and nights. He then obeyed God's command and preached in Nineveh. When the population responded to his preaching and repented, God changed his

plan to destroy the city. Divine mercy was thus shown to possess a distinctly universal dimension. The purpose of the book, then, was primarily didactic, dramatizing God's care for Jews and Gentiles alike. It was a polemic against the exclusivism that was beginning to dominate Judaic theology, depicted so clearly by Jonah himself.

Jonathan   Jonathan was the eldest son of King SAUL and a respected warrior who captured a Philistine outpost single-handedly. He was killed during Saul's last campaign against the Philistines (1 Sam. 13–31). Jonathan and the future king DAVID became close friends when David entered the service of Saul.

Jones, Anson   Anson Jones, b. near Great Barrington, Mass., Jan. 20, 1798, d. Jan. 9, 1858, was the last president of the Texas Republic. He fought in the Texas Revolution and served (1837–41) in the House and Senate of the Texas Congress before becoming the republic's secretary of state under President Sam HOUSTON. He was elected to succeed Houston in 1844. Jones resigned (February 1846) after the formal annexation of Texas by the United States.

Jones, Bobby   Robert Tyre Jones, Jr., b. Atlanta, Ga., Mar. 17, 1902, d. Dec. 18, 1971, was the greatest amateur golfer and perhaps the greatest golfer ever. He entered the U.S. Amateur tournament in 1916 at the age of 14 but did not win a major tournament until 1923, when he won the U.S. Open. In the ensuing years Jones won a succession of championships. He won the U.S. Open again in 1926 and 1929; the U.S. Amateur in 1924, 1925, 1927, and 1928; and the British Open in 1926 and 1927. He was the first golfer to win both the U.S. Open and the British Open in the same year (1926). In 1930 he achieved the first and never-repeated Grand Slam of golf by winning the British Amateur, British

Bobby Jones hits a fairway shot on his way to winning the 1926 British Open. Jones retired after his most successful season, 1930, when he won the Amateur and Open championships of both the United States and Great Britain.

Open, U.S. Open, and U.S. Amateur tournaments all in the same year. In eight years Jones won 13 of the 27 major tournaments that he entered. He never became a professional golfer and retired from tournament play in 1930 to practice law. He entered business with his father for a time, and he later, in cooperation with investment banker Cliff Roberts, designed a new golf course in Augusta, Ga. The course, now known as the Augusta National Golf Club, has been since 1934 the site of the Masters tournament, one of the most prestigious events on the professional golf tour.

Jones, Casey   "Casey," or John Luther, Jones, b. Fulton County, Ky., Mar. 14, 1864, d. Apr. 30, 1900, an engineer for the Illinois Central Railroad, became a hero of American railroad workers and was immortalized in song after his death in a collision near Vaughan, Miss. According to tradition, he saved the lives of his passengers by remaining at the throttle to brake his train.

Jones, George   A crusading publisher of the *New York Times*, George Jones, b. Poultney, Vt., Aug. 16, 1811, d. Aug. 12, 1891, began planning with Henry Jarvis Raymond the "ideal daily" newspaper in the early 1840s when the two were employed at Horace Greeley's newly founded *New York Tribune*. By 1851 they had managed to purchase the *Times*, called until 1857 the *New York Daily Times*. After Raymond's death, Jones's *Times* exposed "Boss" Tweed and the scandalous Tammany Hall maneuverings.

Jones, Inigo   [in'-ig-oh]   The buildings and designs of Inigo Jones, baptized July 19, 1573, d. June 21, 1652, established in England the principles of ancient classical architecture as interpreted during the Italian Renaissance by Andrea PALLADIO.

Jones traveled extensively in Italy, acquiring a knowledge of Mannerist painting and an enthusiasm for ancient classical architecture, which he knew both firsthand and through study of the buildings and writings of Palladio. From 1604 to 1611 he designed costumes and sets for court masques. From 1615 to 1642 he was surveyor of the king's works, first under James I and then Charles I. His earliest surviving structure, the Queen's House at Greenwich, is the first strictly classical English building. Jones's greatest monument is the Banqueting Hall (1619–22), all that remains of his additions to the Palace of Whitehall, London. He planned the first town square in London in Covent Garden (1631–35) and worked on numerous other projects, which included country houses and the restoration of Saint Paul's Cathedral (1634–42, destroyed in the great London fire of 1666). As advisor in the remodeling of Wilton House, Wiltshire, he left the imprint of his style on the work of his nephew and assistant, John Webb, who executed the building and its interior design (c.1650).

Jones was captured by Cromwell's forces in 1645 and released after paying a heavy fine. Immediately after his death his example was emulated only by Webb, but his later influence on English architecture was profound. The Palladian principles of design that Jones imported to England reached fruition in the work of Sir Christopher Wren and the designs of William Kent.

Jones, James   James Jones, b. Robinson, Ill., Nov. 6, 1921, d. May 9, 1977, one of the most notable novelists of the World War II generation, became famous overnight with *From Here to Eternity* (1951; film, 1953), a powerful, often shocking picture of the lives of Hawaii-based U.S. Army personnel in the days preceding the attack on Pearl Harbor. Winner of a National Book Award, it was written in a style that, although seldom graceful, had the force of absolute fidelity to its subject. Two later Jones novels form part of a war trilogy: *The Thin Red Line* (1962; film, 1964) and *Whistle* (1978). *Some Came Running* (1957; film, 1958), about post–World War II small-town life, was his most successful novel. Other works include *The Pistol* (1958), *Go to the Widow-Maker* (1967), *The Merry Month of May* (1971), and *A Touch of Danger* (1973).

Jones, James Earl   The actor James Earl Jones, b. Arkabutla, Miss., Jan. 17, 1931, played numerous Shakespearean roles before earning acclaim—and a Tony Award—as the black boxing champion Jack Jefferson in *The Great White Hope* (1968; film, 1970). As a member of the New York Shakespeare Festival, he has appeared as Caliban in *The Tempest* (1962), as Othello (1964), and as Lear (1973). He has also done television work and several movies.

Jones, John Paul   John Paul Jones, originally John Paul, b. Scotland, July 6, 1747, d. July 18, 1792, became an American naval hero during the AMERICAN REVOLUTION. At the age of 12 he entered the British merchant marine, receiving his first command in 1769. In 1773, however, he murdered a mutinous crewman at Tobago in the West Indies and fled to North America, adopting the name Jones. In 1775, Jones obtained a lieutenant's commission in the Continental navy and later became captain of the sloop *Providence*.

Sailing to France aboard the 18-gun *Ranger* in 1778, Jones received from the French the first salute given to the new American flag by a foreign warship. During the spring he terrorized the coastal population of Scotland and England by making daring raids ashore.

The French government gave Jones a converted French merchant ship, which he renamed *Bonhomme Richard* ("poor Richard") in honor of Benjamin Franklin. Setting sail at the head of a small squadron on Aug. 14, 1779, Jones captured 17 merchant ships off the British coast and on September 23 fell in with a convoy of British merchant vessels escorted by H.M.S. *Serapis* and *Countess of Scarborough*. Challenging the *Serapis*, Jones deftly maneuvered the *Bonhomme Richard* alongside the larger British

John Paul Jones, an American naval hero of the Revolutionary War, stands ready for battle in this contemporary engraving.

vessel and lashed the two ships together. With the muzzles of their guns touching, the two warships fired into each other's insides. Although his smaller vessel was on fire and sinking, Jones rejected the British demand for surrender; "I have not yet begun to fight," he replied. More than three hours after the bloody battle began, the *Serapis* surrendered, and Jones took command of it.

In 1788, Russian empress CATHERINE II appointed Jones rear admiral in the Russian navy, and he served in the Black Sea until political intrigue resulted in his discharge (1790). Jones lived quietly in Paris until his death.

Jones, LeRoi   see BARAKA, IMAMU AMIRI

Jones, Margo   Margo Jones, b. Livingston, Tex., 1913, d. July 24, 1955, was an American theatrical producer and director who in 1947 established in Dallas the country's first professional theater-in-the-round. Its work was described by Jones in her book *Theatre-in-the-Round* (1951).

A champion of regional, repertory, and experimental theater, Jones also worked in New York, most notably as a codirector of Tennessee Williams's first Broadway production, *The Glass Menagerie* (1944).

Jones, Mother   The small, black-bonneted figure of Mother (Mary Harris) Jones, b. Cork, Ireland, May 1, 1830, d. Nov. 30, 1930, was a familiar sight at strikes all over the United States for almost 60 years. A widowed dressmaker who lost her possessions in the Chicago Fire (1871), she committed herself to the labor movement during the 1870s and began to travel the country organizing unions. She was in the thick of some of the most violent disputes of the period, including that at the Rockefeller-owned coal mines in Colorado (1913–14), and was an effective publicist of labor's cause. Active until her death, she published her autobiography in 1925.

Jones, Robert Edmond   Robert Edmond Jones, b. Milton, N.H., Dec. 12, 1887, d. Nov. 26, 1954, was one of the major forces in American theatrical design in the first half of the 20th century. His sets for Anatole France's *The Man Who Married a Dumb Wife* (1915) had a revolutionary effect on U.S. stagecraft and began a movement away from realism toward suggestion and mood. He designed sets for many of the plays of Eugene O'Neill and, together with O'Neill and Kenneth Macgowan, managed the Provincetown Playhouse and the Greenwich Village Theatre after 1923. He was the first American to design for the Ballets Russes de Serge Diaghilev (1916), and he began to work in color films in 1933.

Jones, Rufus Matthew   Rufus Matthew Jones, b. South China, Maine, Jan. 25, 1863, d. June 16, 1948, was an American Quaker philosopher and social reformer. Attempting to emancipate Quakers from what he defined as a parochial evangelism, Jones argued that the Society of Friends (Quakers) combined mysticism and social reform. He served (1893–1912) as editor of the *Friends' Review* (renamed *American Friend*), wrote 4 volumes of the 7-volume Rowntree series on the history of the Society of Friends, and helped found (1917) and later served as chairman of the AMERICAN FRIENDS SERVICE COMMITTEE. Jones wrote more than 50 books, many of them about the Quakers and mysticism.

Jones, Spike   The bandleader and composer Lindley "Spike" Jones, b. Long Beach, Calif., Dec. 14, 1911, d. May 1, 1964, was a drummer with several Hollywood-based bands before organizing his own group, The City Slickers, in 1942. Specializing in bizarre antics and corny humor, the band used sound effects as well as their instruments to create musical mayhem. Their wartime recording of "Der Fuehrer's Face," which featured a derisive Bronx cheer, and their lunatic renditions of romantic ballads ("Chloe," for example) were instant hits during the 1940s and '50s.

Jones, Sir William   The English linguist and jurist Sir William Jones, b. Sept. 28, 1746, d. Apr. 27, 1794, revolutionized the study of language when he argued that Sanskrit, Greek, Latin, and several other languages all descend from an earlier, extinct tongue—INDO-EUROPEAN. Jones had already mastered 10 languages when he turned his attention to law, publishing the widely used *An Essay on the Law of Bailments* in 1781. He went to Calcutta as a Supreme Court judge in 1783 and had learned 20 more languages by the time of his death.

Jonestown   Jonestown, an agricultural commune in northwestern Guyana, was the site of the 1978 mass suicide of more than 900 members of an American religious cult called the People's Temple, led by James Warren "Jim" Jones (1931–78). A native of Indiana, Jones founded his church in Indianapolis, Ind., in the late 1950s and in 1965 moved with his followers to California. He preached a gospel of social and racial equality to his integrated congregation.

After allegations that Jones exercised a sinister power over his followers, extorting money from them, encouraging sexual promiscuity, and enforcing discipline by beatings and blackmail, Jones and 800 faithful fled to Guyana. In November 1978, California congressman Leo Ryan visited the commune to investigate the charges against Jones. On November 18, Ryan and several of his party were murdered, after which Jones ordered his followers to commit suicide with him by drinking a mixture of a powdered fruit drink and cyanide. Although some were forced to do so, many apparently followed the order without question.

Jong, Erica [jawng]   The novelist, poet, and feminist Erica Mann Jong, b. New York City, Mar. 26, 1942, won overnight success with her candidly erotic novel *Fear of Flying* (1973). The further sexual misadventures of Jong's heroine, Isadora Wing, and her eventual satisfying relationship with a younger man form the basis of a second novel, *How to Save Your Own Life* (1977). Jong's poetry includes the volumes *Fruit and Vegetables* (1971), *Loveroot* (1975), *At the Edge of the Body* (1979), and *Ordinary Miracles: New Poems* (1983). Recent fiction includes *Parachutes and Kisses* (1984), *Serenissima: A Novel of Venice* (1987), and *Any Woman's Blues* (1990).

Jongkind, Johan Barthold [yawng'-kint, yoh'-hahn bar'-tohlt]   The Dutch landscape painter, watercolorist, and graphic artist Johann Barthold Jongkind, b. June 3, 1819, d. Feb. 27, 1891, was a precursor of French impressionism. Jongkind admired the artists of the Barbizon school, but his own style was derived more from the 17th-century Dutch landscapists. He painted the flat, low-lying countryside and the rivers and seacoasts of the Netherlands and France in an increasingly free manner, as in *Moulins à Rotterdam* (1870; Musée des Beaux-Arts, Reims, France). His creation of the effects of light and his loose, colorful brush strokes greatly influenced the impressionists, especially Claude Monet.

Jonson, Ben   Ben Jonson, b. June 11?, 1572, d. Aug. 6, 1637, one of the outstanding English poets of the 17th century and one of the greatest comic dramatists ever, had a lasting impact on both English poetry and stage comedy. His comic masterpieces VOLPONE and *The Alchemist* show a parade of rogues and fools verging on monomania, each character exhibiting one or two traits—greed, jealousy, religious fanaticism—developed to an abnormal degree.

Jonson was educated at Westminster School, and after a brief, unwilling apprenticeship to his bricklayer stepfather and military service in Flanders, he gravitated toward

Ben Jonson, an English satirist, is considered, after Shakespeare, the most influential dramatist of the Elizabethan stage.

the theater. He first tried his hand as an actor, then became a playwright. His career was embattled at every point, and he was imprisoned (1597) for his part in a lost satiric comedy declared seditious by the authorities.

Jonson pioneered in a form of corrective comedy known later as the "comedy of humors," a term derived from his own first significant venture in the form, *Every Man In His Humour* (1598). His classical tragedy *Sejanus* (1603), based on Roman history, offered a powerful picture of dictatorship but embroiled Jonson anew with the authorities. In three of the four great comedies that followed—*Volpone, or the Fox* (1606), *Epicene, or The Silent Woman* (1609), and *The Alchemist* (1610), the fourth being *Bartholomew Fair* (1614)—Jonson used the conspiracy to expose human baseness and the lengths to which self-destructive folly could go. His last plays (1616–33), however, suggest he was losing touch with his playhouse audiences. During these years, however, he continued to compose brilliant court masques.

Jonson also wrote much nondramatic poetry, chiefly satiric epigrams in the manner of Martial and verse epistles addressed to friends and patrons. His notebook of critical comments, collected after his death under the title *Timber, Or Discoveries* (1640), did much to cement Jonson's reputation as the first "literary dictator" in English.

Jonson's conversion to Roman Catholicism brought him briefly into the orbit of government espionage at the time of the Gunpowder Plot (1605), an experience he seems to have commemorated in his second classical tragedy, *Catiline* (1611). Although the play failed in the theater, later in the century it held readers spellbound with its veiled analogy between the ancient Roman conspiracies and the intrigues of the Jesuits in 17th-century England.

The accession of Charles I to the throne in 1625 brought Jonson on evil days. The new king preferred to entrust the production of court masques to Jonson's rival, the architect and stage designer Inigo Jones. The theatergoing public hissed his comedy *The New Inn* in 1629, by which time Jonson had suffered a paralytic stroke from which he never fully recovered. Although he continued to read and write, he spent his last years bedridden, visited by the coterie of younger admirers known as the "Sons of Ben." When he died he was buried in Westminster Abbey under the inscription, "O Rare Ben Jonson."

Jooss, Kurt [yohs, koort] Kurt Jooss, b. Jan. 12, 1901, d. May 22, 1979, was an important figure in the world of German dance, not only because of his long career as a leading choreographer, teacher, and artistic director but also because of his early and enduring resistance to totalitarianism from the moment the Nazis seized power in 1933. Outside of Germany, his fame is largely based on a single work, *The Green Table* (1932), which remains after nearly 50 years a chilling indictment of war.

Jooss, who studied with Rudolf von LABAN and subsequently became his assistant, acquired international renown in 1932, when *The Green Table* won first prize at a choreographic competition in Paris. In 1933 the Jooss Dance Company, originally called the Essen Dance Theater, was established in England and toured Europe and the Americas. During most of World War II the company was confined to Britain, and it disbanded in 1947. Returning to Essen in 1949, Jooss formed another company—which lasted until 1953—and established a school, from whose direction he retired in 1968. He also briefly took charge (1954–55) of the ballet in Düsseldorf. Jooss's works remain in the repertoire of several companies, including the Joffrey Ballet.

Joplin, Janis [jahp'-lin] The rock singer Janis Joplin, b. Port Arthur, Tex., Jan. 19, 1943, d. Oct. 4, 1970, overwhelmed audiences with the anger, passion, and sexual intensity of her singing, a unique rock interpretation of blues styles. As lead singer with the rock group Big Brother and the Holding Company, she gained instant fame at the 1967 Monterey Pop Festival, and her recordings, especially the song "Me and Bobby McGee," were widely popular. She died of a heroin overdose.

Joplin, Scott Scott Joplin, b. Texas—possibly in Texarkana, where he was raised—Nov. 24, 1868, d. Apr. 1, 1917, was the most celebrated composer of instrumental RAGTIME. Although his family was poor—his parents had been slaves—the young Joplin studied classical piano as a child; he later worked as a dance musician, and at about the age of 20 he became an itinerant pianist, traveling throughout the Midwest. He published his first composition, the song "Please Say You Will," in 1895; other sentimental songs and marches followed. His "Maple Leaf Rag" (1899) became the most popular piano rag of the period, securing for Joplin a modest lifetime income from royalties and the title "King of Ragtime." Altogether, he published about 60 compositions, of which 41 are piano rags; the balance consists of songs, marches, and the opera *Treemonisha* (1911), produced unsuccessfully in concert form in 1915 but revived successfully 57 years later. During his lifetime, Joplin was never acknowledged as a serious composer. Recognition came posthumously, however, with the republication (1972) of his music, a Pulitzer Prize (1976), and popular and scholarly acclaim.

Jordaens, Jacob [yor'-dahns, yoh'-kohp] The baroque artist Jacob Jordaens, b. May 19, 1593, d. Oct. 18, 1678, has been called the quintessential painter of 17th-century Flemish life. His lusty figure style took shape under the impact of Michelangelo Caravaggio as well as his two great Flemish contemporaries, Peter Paul Rubens and Sir Anthony van Dyck. Unlike Rubens and van Dyck, whose art reflected their lives as courtiers, Jordaens was the painter of burgher and peasant life. A homelier, down-to-earth spirit predominates even in his mythological paintings, such as *Triumph of Bacchus* (late 1640s; Staatlich Gemäldegalerie, Kassel, Germany), and in religious works, such as *Christ Driving the Money Changers from the Temple* (c.1657; Louvre, Paris). Among his most famous works is the warm and hearty *The King Drinks* (c.1638–40; Musée Royaux des Beaux-Arts, Brussels). Jordaens also designed numerous tapestries and decorative cycles.

Jordan The Hashemite Kingdom of Jordan is an Arab nation in southwest Asia at the northwest corner of the Arabian Peninsula. A small country, Jordan is bounded on the west by Israel and the Israeli-occupied WEST BANK (whose final status is yet to be determined), on the north by Syria, and on the east by Iraq and Saudi Arabia. Only a 19-km (12-mi) southern coastline on the Gulf of AQABA, a northern arm of the Red Sea, prevents the country from being completely landlocked. AMMAN, the capital and dominant city, is located about 40 km (25 mi) east of the Jordan River. Since the creation (1948) of the state of Israel, Jordan has experienced a large influx of Palestinian refugees, straining the nation's meager resource base and involving it in the issue of Palestinian autonomy.

Jordan's former official area of 97,740 km² (37,738 mi²) included the West Bank and East Jerusalem, with an area of 5,878 km² (2,270 mi²). This area, which had been designated as Arab by the United Nations when it voted in 1947 to divide PALESTINE into Arab and Jewish states, was occupied by Jordanian forces during the first of the ARAB-ISRAELI WARS and was formally annexed by Jordan in 1950. The Jordanian annexation, however, was not recognized by the United Nations or by any nation except Great Britain

The American composer Scott Joplin helped develop the syncopation and rhythmic diversity characteristic of the musical genre known as ragtime. He was posthumously awarded the 1976 Pulitzer Prize in music.

THE HASHEMITE KINGDOM OF JORDAN

Land: Area: 91,862 km^2 (35,468 mi^2). Capital and largest city: Amman (1988 est. pop., 900,000).

People: Population (1990 est.): 3,064,508. Density: 33.4 persons per km^2 (86.4 per mi^2). Distribution (1988): 59% urban, 41% rural. Official language: Arabic. Major religions: Islam, Christianity.

Government: Type: Constitutional monarchy. Legislature: National Assembly. Political subdivisions: 8 governorates.

Economy: GNP (1989): $5.2 billion; $1,760 per capita. Labor distribution (1987): manufacturing and mining—20%; agriculture—20%; other—60%. Foreign trade (1989 est.): imports— $1.7 billion; exports—$910 million. Currency: 1 Jordanian dinar = 100 fils.

Education and Health: Literacy (1986): 79.4% of adult population. Universities (1989): 3. Hospital beds (1986): 5,246. Physicians (1986): 3,144. Life expectancy (1990): women—71; men—68. Infant mortality (1990): 55 per 1,000 live births.

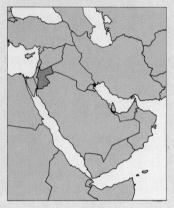

and Pakistan, and the area has been occupied by Israel since the Arab-Israeli War of 1967. Jordan implicitly renounced its West Bank claims at a 1974 Arab summit meeting when it signed the Rabat resolution, which declared the PALESTINE LIBERATION ORGANIZATION (PLO) the sole legitimate representative of the Palestinian people. On July 31, 1988, Jordan announced that it was officially severing all legal and administrative ties to the West Bank and surrendering its claims to the PLO.

Land

More than 90% of Jordan's area is desert. Jordan is composed of two major landform regions: the Jordan Valley and the Transjordan Plateau. The flat-floored valley of the Jordan River is part of the GREAT RIFT VALLEY. The DEAD SEA occupies the lowest portion of this depression. Only 108 km (67 mi) separate the Sea of Galilee (see GALILEE, SEA OF) in the north from the Dead Sea in the south, but the Jordan River, connecting the two lakes, meanders to such a degree that its course is twice that distance.

Most of Jordan is part of the Transjordan Plateau, a great upthrust block that is part of the Arabian Plateau. Its western edge forms a 610–915-m (2,000–3,000-ft) escarpment above the Jordan River. It rises to a maximum height of 1,754 m (7,755 ft) at Mount Ramm, near Aqaba. The SYRIAN DESERT covers most of the northeast.

Climate. A Mediterranean climate characterizes much of Jordan. The summers are long, hot, and dry, and the winters mild with periods of precipitation. Northern Jordan receives more moisture than the deserts of southern and eastern Jordan, which receive as little as 50 mm (2

in) of rainfall annually. Temperatures there are more extreme than in the north, where yearly precipitation averages 400 mm (16 in). In the Jordan Valley, summer daytime temperatures reach 32° C (90° F), and winter nighttime temperatures drop below freezing.

Drainage. The Jordan River is the heart of the country's drainage system. The Transjordan Plateau is dissected by the deep valleys of intermittent streams draining into the Jordan River. The largest tributary entering from the east is the Yarmuk, a permanent river that follows part of the border between Syria and Jordan. Wells provide additional water for much of the country, but underground aquifers are being rapidly depleted as the population outstrips available water supplies.

Vegetation and Wildlife. Much of Jordan is dry, and the ground is generally rocky with sparse vegetation. Willow, oleander, and tamarisk grow along the lower Jordan River valley. Low shrubs, thorny bushes, and seasonal grasses dot the semiarid regions and the desert margins. Wild boars, ibex, foxes, jackals, wildcats, hyenas, wolves, hare, and some panthers can be found in isolated gorges, particularly south of the Sea of Galilee. Birds are plentiful.

People

More than 90% of all Jordanians are Arabs. In 1987, 845,542 Palestinian refugees were registered in Jordan with the United Nations Relief and Works Agency for Palestinian Refugees (UNRWA). The remainder of the population is largely descended from BEDOUIN Arabs. Arabic is the official language, and Islam is the state religion. Sunni Muslims vastly outnumber both Shiite Muslims and

Christians; most of the latter are members of the Eastern Orthodox Church. Palestinian refugees live in camps administered by the UNRWA. Most other Jordanians live in towns and villages, although nomadic and seminomadic Bedouins inhabit the deserts and steppes.

The vast majority of all 6- to 11-year-olds are enrolled in free elementary schools. Compulsory schooling lasts for 9 years. The University of Jordan (1962) is located in Amman, but many students study abroad. The government provides medical and welfare assistance. Palestinian refugee children are educated by the UNRWA, which also maintains its own hospitals and a refugee welfare program.

Economic Activity

When Jordan annexed the West Bank and East Jerusalem in 1950, it more than doubled its population, greatly increased its productive agricultural land, and added numerous tourist attractions. The Israeli occupation of the West Bank swelled the Palestinian refugee population in Jordan proper and hampered development efforts. Largely due to foreign aid from Arab oil-producing countries

and remittances from Jordanians working abroad, however, the country experienced steady economic growth from 1974 to 1980. Both of these sources of income declined in the 1980s, as did the world price for phosphate, its leading export. After the signing of the 1979 Egyptian-Israeli peace treaty, Iraq and Kuwait had replaced Egypt as Jordan's leading trade partners. Trade links with Egypt were restored in 1983, but Jordan was economically devastated by the boycott imposed following the August 1990 Iraqi invasion of Kuwait and further burdened by an influx of refugees from Kuwait and Iraq. By the end of the 1991 GULF WAR, Jordan's gross national product had declined by as much as 70%, and its pro-Iraqi stance during the conflict had cost it substantial foreign aid.

Manufacturing. Although Jordan produces cement, refined petroleum, cigarettes, olive oil, soap, leather, and clay, most industry has not developed far beyond the handicraft stage. Obstacles to industrial development include the paucity of natural resources, the limited local market, prohibitive transport costs, and lack of energy resources such as hydroelectric power and petroleum reserves. Imported petroleum supplies most of Jordan's energy; oil supplies were disrupted by the Gulf crisis of 1990–91. In addition to phosphate, salt, potash, limestone, gypsum, and marble are extracted.

Agriculture. Wheat, barley, lentils, vegetables, melons, and citrus fruits are the chief crops, but corn (maize), sesame, tobacco, olives, dates, and nuts are also grown. Goats and sheep are the most important livestock. Many farmers are small landowners, although tenancy is still common. In 1967, Jordan completed the East Gher Canal Project that uses water from the Yarmuk River for irrigation. Subsequent land reform, along with improved water management and cultivation practices, vastly strengthened Jordan's agricultural base.

Transportation. Paved and gravel roads link most of Jordan's villages and towns, and a railroad runs northward from just to the south of Ma'an through Amman to the Syrian border. The Trans-Arabian oil pipeline runs through Jordan en route from Saudi Arabia to the Mediterranean coast of Lebanon.

Trade. In international trade, Jordan's imports habitually exceed exports. Agricultural crops, particularly vegetables, and phosphates are the primary exports. Imports include foods, machinery, textiles, and military equipment.

Government

Jordan is a constitutional monarchy. Its constitution, adopted in 1952, provides for a prime minister appointed by the king. A cabinet is named by the prime minister. The king also selects the 30 members of the Senate for 8-year terms. The House of Representatives—which included members representing the West Bank until 1988, when Jordan severed its links to the Israeli-occupied territories—was expanded from 60 to 80 seats in 1989. The first national elections since 1967 (and the first in which women could vote) also were held in 1989. The judges of the separate Muslim and Christian religious courts are appointed by the king. Jordan is divided into 8 governorates, each headed by a centrally appointed governor.

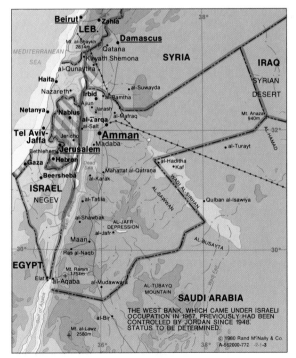

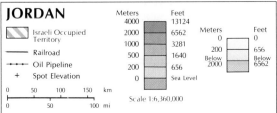

JORDAN

	Meters	Feet
	4000	13124
▨ Israeli Occupied Territory	2000	6562
—— Railroad	1000	3281
•–•– Oil Pipeline	500	1640
+ Spot Elevation	200	656
	0	0

	Meters	Feet
	0	0
	200	656
	Below 2000	Below 6562
	Sea Level	

0   50   100   150   km
0   50   100   mi

Scale 1:6,360,000

Amman, known in the Bible as Rabbath Ammon, capital of the Ammonites, had declined to little more than a village when Emir Abdullah made it the capital of Transjordan in 1921. Today Amman is the capital and largest city in Jordan and is an industrial and commercial center.

History

Village life in Jordan dates from at least 8000 BC at JERICHO. Hebrew states developed west of the Jordan River, while the small states of EDOM, GILEAD, MOAB, and Ammon were settled east of the Jordan River. The area was frequently invaded by Assyrians, Egyptians, Babylonians, and Persians.

In the 4th century BC the northern area was incorporated into the kingdom of the SELEUCIDS, but the south was ruled by the Arab tribe of Nabataeans, with their capital at PETRA. The Romans displaced the Seleucids in the 1st century BC, but Petra did not fall to Rome until AD 106. Muslim Arabs dominated from the 7th century until the 16th century, except for an interlude of Crusader control (see JERUSALEM, LATIN KINGDOM OF). The Ottoman Turks conquered the area in 1517.

After the Turkish defeat in World War I, the territory of Jordan became part of the short-lived Syrian kingdom of FAISAL I (later king of Iraq). After Faisal's defeat by French forces in 1920, Transjordan was incorporated into Britain's League of Nations' mandate of PALESTINE. Transjordan was treated separately from Palestine, however, and its residents were assured that it would not be affected by the establishment of a Jewish homeland in the future. ABDULLAH, Faisal's brother, was chosen to rule Transjordan in 1921. He cooperated closely with the British, who helped create the Arab Legion, a small army later commanded by Sir John GLUBB. In 1928 a treaty with Britain made Transjordan a constitutional monarchy. A second treaty with the British on Mar. 22, 1946, created the Hashemite Kingdom of Transjordan.

Transjordan opposed the partition of Palestine and joined the other ARAB LEAGUE nations in fighting the new Israeli state in 1948 (see ARAB-ISRAELI WARS). By the end of the war it occupied a section of West Bank territory designated for the Arabs in the United Nations partition plan. The country's name was changed to Jordan in 1949, and in 1950 it formally annexed the West Bank territory, including Old Jerusalem.

Abdullah was assassinated in 1951, and a year later his son Talal was forced to abdicate in favor of Talal's son HUSSEIN I. Hussein established greater independence from Britain, especially after 1956, but his relations with the other Arab countries were somewhat strained.

In the Six-Day War of June 1967, Jordan's forces were routed by the Israelis, who then occupied the West Bank territories. As a result Jordan, which already had many Palestinian refugees, received a new influx. Guerrilla groups among the refugees challenged Hussein's authority and made Jordan a target for Israeli attacks. In 1970 civil war erupted between government and guerrilla forces; in 1971, Hussein succeeded in destroying the guerrilla bases in Jordan. Jordan, like other Arab states, condemned the 1979 Egyptian-Israeli peace treaty, breaking diplomatic ties with Egypt from 1979 to 1984. In 1988, Hussein formally severed all links between Jordan and the West Bank in favor of the PLO. Legislative elections were held in 1989, and martial law (imposed in 1967) was gradually eased.

Many Jordanians supported the August 1990 Iraqi invasion of Kuwait. Hussein initially tried to remain neutral, advocating a negotiated Arab solution to the crisis and the withdrawal of foreign troops from the area. His rhetoric became increasingly pro-Iraqi, although Jordan did not enter the Gulf war. By the end of the war the nation faced economic collapse; Hussein's future regional role was unclear.

Jordan, Barbara Noted for her eloquent speaking style, Barbara Jordan, b. Houston, Tex., Feb. 21, 1936, was a Democratic representative from Texas to the U.S. House of Representatives from 1973 to 1979. Jordan graduated from Texas Southern University (1956) and was the first black student at Boston University Law School (1956–59). She served as the only woman and the only black in the Texas state senate (1966–72) and was consulted by President Lyndon B. Johnson on civil rights legislation. She did not run for reelection to Congress in 1978 and later taught at the University of Texas. Her autobiography, *Barbara Jordan: A Self-Portrait*, was published in 1979.

Jordan, Michael An exciting basketball player with great leaping ability, Michael Jeffrey Jordan, b. Brooklyn, N.Y., Feb. 17, 1963, was college basketball's Player of the Year in 1984 before joining the Chicago Bulls of the National Basketball Association. The 6-ft 6-in (2-m 1-cm) guard led the NBA in scoring in 5 straight years (1987–91) and was its Most Valuable Player twice (1988, 1991) and Defensive Player of the Year in 1988.

Jordan, Vernon Vernon Eulion Jordan, Jr., b. Atlanta, Ga., Aug. 15, 1935, an attorney and civil rights leader, became executive director of the National URBAN LEAGUE in 1972. After graduating from DePauw University in 1957, Jordan studied law at Howard University and entered private practice as a civil rights lawyer. He served as director of the Southern Regional Council's Voter Education Project (1964–68) and of the National Negro College Fund (1970–71). At the Urban League, Jordan was an advocate of full employment, of affirmative action, and of national health and housing programs. Wounded by a sniper in Fort Wayne, Ind., in 1980, he resigned his Urban League post in 1981 to enter private law practice.

Jordan River The Jordan River (Hebrew: Iha-Yarden; Arabic: Nahr al-Urdunn), the longest river of Israel and Jordan, meanders for 359 km (223 mi) from Mount HERMON to the DEAD SEA. It drains an area of 16,000 km² (6,000 mi²). The headwaters of the Jordan descend from the Anti-Lebanon Mountains and join in the Hula Basin. The river flows along the west side of the Golan Heights to the Sea of GALILEE (Lake Tiberias) at 209 m (686 ft) below sea level. Following the 1967 Arab-Israeli War, the river formed the border between Jordan and Israel and the Israeli-occupied WEST BANK. After receiving its main tributary, the Yarmuk, it winds through the Ghor depression to the north end of the Dead Sea, where it empties.

Shallow and tortuous, the Jordan is not used for navigation but is very important for irrigation. Diversion of the Jordan's waters for irrigation and power remains a matter of dispute between Israel and Jordan. The main crossing is the Allenby Bridge on the road from Jerusalem to Amman.

Joseph Joseph, the eleventh son of JACOB and the first son of Jacob's favorite wife, RACHEL, is the biblical hero in the drama of Genesis 37–50. Joseph's favored status and

his coat of many colors, a gift from his father, caused his brothers to be jealous, and they staged his accidental "death." Joseph was actually taken to Egypt, where his ability to interpret dreams brought him into favor with the pharaoh. Joseph became a high Egyptian official. When, during a famine, his unsuspecting brothers sought grain in Egypt, the forgiving Joseph—whom his brothers did not at first recognize—arranged a family reunion. Thus, the whole family of Jacob moved to Egypt and lived there until the Exodus.

Joseph, Chief Chief Joseph, c.1840–1904, was a chief of the NEZ PERCÉ Indian tribe. He is remembered principally for his leadership during the hostilities that broke out between the U.S. Army and the Nez Percé in 1877. Under the terms of the Stevens Treaty of 1855, the Nez Percé agreed to cede much of their land to the U.S. government in return for the guarantee of a large reservation in Oregon and Idaho. When gold was discovered (1863) in Oregon, however, the government demanded that the Nez Percé relinquish this part of the reservation also. Chief Joseph resisted but later agreed to move peacefully with his people to the Lapwai Reservation in Idaho.

Fighting broke out in 1877 when young Nez Percé warriors retaliated for what they considered outrageous acts by the white settlers. In the war that followed, Joseph showed remarkable skill in military tactics. On Sept. 30, 1877, however, federal troops overtook the Nez Percé only 48 km (30 mi) from the Canadian border. Because most of his warriors were dead or wounded and his people were starving, Chief Joseph surrendered, saying, "I will fight no more forever." Sent to Indian Territory in Oklahoma, the Nez Percé were allowed to return to Idaho in 1883–84. Chief Joseph died on the Colville Indian Reservation in the state of Washington.

Joseph, Saint Saint Joseph was the husband of MARY, the mother of Jesus Christ. Given prominent attention in the first two chapters of Matthew and Luke in the Christian Bible, Joseph is portrayed as a carpenter in Nazareth, a righteous descendant of Bethlehem's David, and a kind husband and father. Although little else is known of his life, Joseph's faithful cooperation in the birth of Christ earned him sainthood. He is venerated by Orthodox and by Roman Catholics, who consider him the patron saint of workers. Feast day: May 1 (Western); first Sunday after Christmas (Eastern).

Joseph Andrews see FIELDING, HENRY

Joseph of Arimathea [ar-ih-muh-thee'-uh] In the New Testament, Joseph of Arimathea was a rich, devout member of the Sanhedrin who would not consent to that body's decision to put Jesus Christ to death (Matt. 27:57; Mark 15:43; Luke 23:50, 51). After the crucifixion of Jesus, Joseph asked the Roman procurator Pontius Pilate for Jesus' body and, with the assistance of Nicodemus, buried the body in a garden tomb near Golgotha (John 19:38–42; Matt. 25:57–60). Joseph became a popular figure in apocalyptic literature. Medieval legends connect Joseph with the Holy Grail (see GRAIL, HOLY) and with Glastonbury, England, where his staff was believed to have taken root and grown into a thorn tree that flowered every Christmas Eve.

Joseph I, Holy Roman Emperor   Joseph I, b. July 26, 1678, d. Apr. 17, 1711, king of Hungary from 1687, succeeded his father, LEOPOLD I, as emperor in 1705. The War of the SPANISH SUCCESSION continued throughout his reign, and the imperial armies under EUGENE OF SAVOY won victories in Italy, Germany, and Flanders. Joseph's death, without male issue, and the succession of his brother CHARLES VI, however, altered the course of the war. The allies who had earlier supported Charles's claim to the Spanish throne abandoned him, fearing a united Spain and Austria. During Joseph's reign the Hungarian revolt led by Ferenc II Rákóczy was finally suppressed in 1711.

Joseph II, Holy Roman Emperor   Joseph II, b. Mar. 13, 1741, d. Feb. 20, 1790, became emperor and coregent of the Habsburg monarchy with his mother, MARIA THERESA, after the death of his father, FRANCIS I, in 1765. When his mother died in 1780, he inherited the crowns of Bohemia and Hungary. Joseph's policy of centralization and reform enhanced the power of his state and the welfare of his subjects. With his curious blend of humanitarian ideals and autocratic methods, Joseph II exemplified the characteristics of 18th-century enlightened despotism.

Joseph's reform program included the abolition of serfdom, freedom of the press, the elimination of torture and the death penalty, and an attempt to establish equality before the law. He introduced a single tax based on land, granted official toleration to Protestants and Jews, and dissolved the monasteries of contemplative Catholic orders. In his efforts to unify the administrative structure of his monarchy, Joseph sought to diminish the influence of provincial diets (legislatures) and the special privileges of the aristocracy.

Fourteen years before the French Revolution, Joseph warned his sister MARIE ANTOINETTE, queen of France: "The revolution, if you fail to avert it, will be an atrocious one." His own actions, however, provoked mounting unrest in his Austrian and Bohemian lands and open revolt in Hungary and the Low Countries. While some of his reforms survived, many were revoked by his brother and successor, LEOPOLD II.

Josephine   Josephine, b. June 23, 1763, d. May 29, 1814, became empress of France as the consort of NAPOLEON I. Born in Martinique, she was originally named Marie Josèphe Rose Tascher de La Pagerie. She married Alexandre, vicomte de Beauharnais in 1779 and had two children by him, Eugène and Hortense.

After Beauharnais was guillotined (1794), Josephine became a leading figure in the salon society of Paris. She met Napoléon Bonaparte and married him on Mar. 9, 1796. She soon became involved in numerous affairs, scandalizing the Bonaparte clan.

Josephine was crowned empress by Napoleon in 1804, but her failure to bear him a male heir led to the annulment of their marriage in 1810. She withdrew to Malmaison and lived in imperial style until her death. Josephine contributed to Napoleon's success by serving as a link with the French bourgeoisie.

Josephson effect   The Josephson effect is the flow of electrons across an insulating barrier placed between two superconducting materials (see SUPERCONDUCTIVITY). The flow of electrons across a barrier between nonsuperconducting materials was predicted by QUANTUM MECHANICS and has been known since the 1950s; it is called the TUNNEL EFFECT. Superconductive tunneling, however, involves electron pairs called Cooper pairs and was first predicted (1962) by English physicist Brian Josephson, who shared the 1973 Nobel Prize for physics for his work. The currents involved in the Josephson effect are very sensitive to magnetic fields and are useful in observing basic physical phenomena. So-called Josephson junctions, involving use of the effect, are also being explored for use in high-speed computers.

Josephus, Flavius   [joh-see'-fuhs, flay'-vee-uhs] Flavius Josephus, b. AD 37, d. after 93, was a Jewish historian whose works are invaluable sources for the history of the Jews under Roman domination. A Pharisee, originally named Joseph ben Matthias, he reluctantly joined the revolt against Rome in AD 66 and served as commander in Galilee until captured by the Romans in 67. Through the patronage of Vespasian, he later became a Roman citizen. Josephus's *The Jewish War* (75–79), a description of the tragic events of the revolt, is based to a large extent on his firsthand knowledge. His *Jewish Antiquities* (93), covering the history of the Jews from the Creation on, gives a particularly full account of the Maccabees and the dynasty of Herod. Though criticized for his subservience to the Romans, he was a passionate defender of Jewish religion and culture, as shown in his apologia entitled *Against Apion* and in his historical works.

Joshua, Book of   [jahsh'-oo-uh]   Joshua is the sixth book of the Old Testament of the Bible. It is named for the leader who succeeded Moses and led Israel in the successful conquest of Canaan, the Promised Land. The book is divided into three parts: the conquest of Canaan during Joshua's three major campaigns (chaps. 1–12); the division of Canaan by tribes (chaps. 13–22); and Joshua's farewell speeches and death (chaps. 23–24).

The Book of Joshua forms part of the Deuteronomistic History, the collective name given by scholars to the books of DEUTERONOMY, Joshua, JUDGES, 1 and 2 SAMUEL, and 1 and 2 KINGS, all of which appear to have been compiled by the same editor or editors. This history was recorded during the time of Josiah (c.640–609 BC) and revised around 550 BC. Joshua is based on earlier sources, however; some parts of the text date from the premonarchial period. The book was edited almost 600 years after the conquest of Canaan (c.1225 BC).

Joshua tree   The Joshua tree, *Yucca brevifolia*, a yucca plant belonging to the family Agavaceae, is found in North American desert and semidesert areas. It has bayonetlike leaves (stiff with long points) and showy white flowers, which are fragrant at night. The flowers are borne on a tall stalk.

The Joshua tree, with its unusually shaped branches and spiked leaves, adds beauty to the deserts of southern California.

Josiah, King of Judah   [joh-sy'-uh]   Josiah was the king of Judah, ancient Israel's southern kingdom, from c.640 to 609 BC. According to 2 Kings 22 and 23, his reign was noted for religious reforms. A book of the law, the core of the biblical book of DEUTERONOMY, was discovered in the Temple during repair work. This law prohibited all altars outside Jerusalem and thus made the worship of Baal and other foreign gods practically impossible. Josiah died at Megiddo in a battle with Egypt. His attempts to restore the kingdom of David were unsuccessful.

Josquin des Prez   [zhohs-kan' day pray']   Josquin des Prez, b. c.1440, d. Aug. 27, 1521, was a celebrated composer of the Renaissance and one of the most influential figures in the history of Western music. Born in the region of Hainaut (in present-day Belgium), he probably received his musical training at Cambrai, France. In 1459 he became a singer at the cathedral in Milan and was employed there until the end of 1472.

He served at the courts of two members of the Sforza family until September 1486, when he became a papal singer in Rome. After a period in France (1501) and then in Italy (1503–04) at the court of Ferrara, Josquin returned to Hainaut in May 1504, where he served as provost of the local church at Condé until his death.

Josquin's mastery of every important musical genre of his time is evidenced by his surviving works, which include 19 masses, about 100 motets, approximately 70 French chansons, and a handful of instrumental pieces and Italian frottole (part songs). These were published widely both during his lifetime and long after his death. In many of his works the contrapuntal artifices of the Franco-Netherlanders and the chordal, harmonically controlled style of the Italians are fused into a rich and expressive musical language that has as its primary goal the perfect union of words and music. These works set a standard for composers of the later Renaissance that was often emulated but never surpassed.

Jotunheimen   [yoh'-tun-hay-men]   The Jotunheimen (Norwegian for "home of the giants"), the highest mountain group in Scandinavia, is located in south central Norway. It extends for about 110 km (70 mi) from the Jostedalsbreen ice cap and is surrounded by lakes. Glittertind is the tallest peak, rising to 2,481 m (8,104 ft). The setting for many Scandinavian legends, the sparsely populated Jotunheimen is now a tourist center.

joule   [jool]   The joule is the unit of energy or work in the mks (meter-kilogram-second) system of units. It is the WORK done when a force of 1 newton acts through a distance of 1 meter and is thus synonymous with a newton-meter of work. One joule is equivalent to 1 watt-second, 10^7 ergs, 0.7376 foot-pounds, and 9.48×10^{-4} Btu.

Joule, James Prescott   The British physicist James Prescott Joule, b. Dec. 24, 1818, d. Oct. 11, 1889, is known for his contributions to the science of thermodynamics. In his first major publication (1840), Joule stated that the amount of heat produced by an electric current is proportional to the product of the resistance of the wire and the square of the current. In his study of electrical, chemical, and mechanical energy, Joule observed that the amount of heat produced by each form of energy is proportional to the energy expended. In 1843 he determined a value for the coefficient of equivalence, the amount of energy needed to produce a unit of heat. During the period 1852–62, Joule and William Thomson (Lord KELVIN) observed that when a gas expands without performing work, its temperature falls. This Joule-Thomson effect was later applied to refrigeration, air-conditioning, and air-liquefaction technology.

Joule-Thomson effect   see JOULE, JAMES PRESCOTT

journalism   The broad term *journalism* can be defined as those mass-communication activities which per-tain to the collection and publishing of news-related material for general and specialized segments of society. The linkage with *news* is what keeps ADVERTISING or PUBLIC RELATIONS, for example, from falling under the rubric.

Journalism is big business, heavily dependent on advancing communications technology—and on persons expert in technological fields. At the heart of the enterprise, however, are individual *journalists*: reporters, columnists, editors in various capacities, editorial writers, editorial cartoonists, feature writers, photojournalists, correspondents, commentators, news directors, newscasters, and newswriters. In fact, journalists have been called the FOURTH ESTATE, serving as a cement for society, providing the citizenry with essential (and much nonessential) information for the efficient running of social institutions.

Two types of media, each with two subcategories, have played significant roles in the history of journalism: the print media—NEWSPAPERS and PERIODICALS—and the broadcast, or electronic, media—RADIO AND TELEVISION (see also RADIO AND TELEVISION BROADCASTING).

Newspapers. The invention (c.1450) by Johann GUTENBERG of printing by movable type made possible the development of modern journalism. From crude European newsletters of the 17th and 18th centuries came the sophisticated news journals of the 19th and 20th centuries, including PHOTOJOURNALISM. From the small sheets published by printers came newspapers with diverse content, veering away from mere notices to in-depth stories and news analyses.

An important development came in the 18th century—political pamphlets. People such as John DICKINSON, Thomas PAINE, and Samuel ADAMS in the American colonies entered into political journalism with a vengeance. Subsequently, in the 1800s, the so-called Penny Press developed, providing journalism, written and edited for the ordinary person at a low price. Representative of the flamboyant Penny Press were James Gordon BENNETT's *New York Herald*, founded in 1835, the *Baltimore Sun*, and three other New York newspapers—the *Sun*, the *Evening Post*, and the *Tribune*. The editorial page, which expressed opinion, was becoming a basic newspaper department, with Horace GREELEY of the *Tribune* especially influential in its development.

Following the Civil War came the period known as the New Journalism, exemplified by Joseph PULITZER. The newspaper took on its modern form, and circulations grew rapidly. Men such as Pulitzer and William Randolph HEARST emphasized the news function of journalism, although some overemphasized sensationalism, or YELLOW JOURNALISM—especially at the time of the Spanish-American War. Other outstanding New Journalism editors were E. W. SCRIPPS in Cleveland, Charles Dana in New York, Melville Stone in Chicago, William Rockhill Nelson in Kansas City, and Henry W. Grady in Atlanta.

A significant 19th-century development in Europe and the United States was the formation of PRESS AGENCIES AND SYNDICATES. These were able to supply subscribing newspapers with news (and later, feature material) that otherwise would have been beyond the individual newspaper's resources to obtain.

At the turn of the century a debate began concerning the training of newspaper journalists—one view holding that on-the-job training in a newspaper office was most appropriate, another holding that special courses of study in a school of journalism constituted the best preparation. The first school of journalism was founded at the University of Missouri in 1908. In 1903, Joseph Pulitzer had agreed to give Columbia University $2 million for another pioneering school of journalism, which opened in 1912.

Newspapers in the late 20th century exhibit a wide range in subject matter and format. The expression of personal opinion is still important in the op-ed (opposite-editorial) pages and in various personal columns, reviews, and analyses; distinguished columnists include Walter LIPPMANN and James RESTON. In the 1960s the term *New Journalism* was reapplied to a new style of "nonfiction reportage" (appearing in magazines as well as some newspapers). Practitioners of New Journalism include Jimmy BRESLIN and Tom WOLFE. The tradition of investigative reporting was vigorously pursued by Carl Bernstein and Bob Woodward (see BERNSTEIN, CARL, AND WOODWARD, BOB) in the Watergate affair. The traits of yellow journalism persist here and there in popular general newspapers and in gossip-oriented newspapers such as the *National Enquirer*, a national supermarket-based tabloid. Serious news-and-analysis newspapers survive in such journals as the NEW YORK TIMES, the *Louisville Courier-Journal*, and the *Los Angeles Times*. Specialized papers are represented by the WALL STREET JOURNAL, and a national mass-appeal paper was inaugurated in the early 1980s with *USA Today*.

Magazines. Magazine journalism started in the 19th century, although journals with a little more than 500 subscribers and a life span of five to eight years were around prior to the 1800s. In 1800 there were only a dozen magazines in the United States. By the end of the first quarter of the 19th century there were still fewer than 100, but circulations were growing. By the mid-19th century about 600 magazines were published, but the majority were not significantly concerned with "news."

After the Civil War, magazines grew from about 700 in 1865 to approximately 5,000 at the turn of the century. By the late 1980s more than 10,000 magazines were being published in the United States for almost every interest imaginable. The movement toward more emphasis on public affairs was stimulated by *Harper's* and later by the *Atlantic Monthly*. In the early 1900s the factual reports (and the fiction) of the MUCKRAKERS, often published in such popular magazines as *McClure's*, constituted sensational exposés of corrupt practices in business and politics. Muckraking writers such as Edwin Markham, Ida M. TARBELL, and David Graham PHILLIPS attracted support for the reforms of the PROGRESSIVE ERA. Subsequently, magazine readers' interest in public affairs was heightened, and satisfied, by newsmagazines such as TIME, followed by *Newsweek* and *U.S. News and World Report*. Political commentary was added to the range of magazines by such journals as the *Nation*, *New Republic*, *Progressive*, *Commonweal*, *Commentary*, and *National Review*.

Radio. Radio appeared in the United States early in the 20th century. The first U.S. radio news item is attributed to Lee DE FOREST, who in 1916 broadcast the brief news-related prediction that Charles Evans Hughes would be the next president of the United States. Although in succeeding years there was some interest in news, radio's pioneers were mainly interested in providing entertainment. Radio's great boom period began in the 1920s; network radio started then with the founding of the National Broadcasting Company (NBC) and the Columbia Broadcasting System (CBS).

It was really with World War II that radio became a significant news medium, and *broadcast journalism* entered the vocabulary. Especially prominent radio journalists in World War II were Edward R. MURROW, Elmer DAVIS, Gabriel Heatter, and H. V. Kaltenborn. Also important in the early journalistic development of radio broadcasting were Walter WINCHELL, Lowell THOMAS, and Eric Severeid.

Television. Although experimental television has existed since the 1920s, it was not until the middle of the 20th century that TV found a significant place among the journalistic media. Television grew rapidly, and many of the established radio journalists transferred to the new medium. News on television at first consisted of newsreels from outside suppliers. Then there were on-the-spot broadcasts of major events, along with some documentaries and public-affairs reports. In the early 1950s television gained respect covering the inauguration of President Dwight Eisenhower and the live Army-McCarthy hearings (see McCARTHY, JOSEPH R.).

In the 1960s with the American involvement in Vietnam; the assassinations of President John F. Kennedy, Martin Luther King, Jr., and Sen. Robert F. Kennedy; and the fiery Democratic convention in Chicago (1968), TV was well established as a journalistic medium. CBS personalities such as Walter CRONKITE, Eric Severeid, Mike Wallace, Dan Rather, Lesley Stahl, Charles Kuralt, Diane Sawyer, Bruce Morton, and Marvin Kalb have made their mark on television journalism—some of them shifting from one network to another.

For NBC there have been such notables as Chet Huntley and David BRINKLEY, John CHANCELLOR, Barbara WALTERS, Frank McGee, Tom Brokaw, Tom Pettit, and Judy Woodruff. The American Broadcasting Company (ABC) has added to the roster of outstanding journalists with Howard K. SMITH, Frank Reynolds, Harry Reasoner, Peter Jennings, Sam Donaldson, and Tom Jarriel. Outstanding journalists on the Public Broadcasting Service (PBS) include Robert MacNeil and Jim Lehrer.

In the 1960s satellite news distribution provided a big boost to television news. The first transmission between Europe and the United States occurred in 1962. Increasingly since then news events have been transmitted worldwide via satellite. Such events as summit conferences, papal visits, Olympic and other sports festivals, terrorist episodes, and various international crises have been flashed live globally.

By the mid-1980s cable television had 6,000 systems in operation serving 16,000 U.S. communities. Cable TV has provided the viewing public with many more channels and much clearer pictures. The news emphasis of much cable TV, especially Ted TURNER's CNN (Cable News Net-

work), adds a new journalistic dimension to television and stresses continuous news and commentary—as seen in the coverage of the GULF WAR.

Issues in Modern Journalism. The journalist is part of an enterprise that is challenged by a multiplicity of problems and issues. Because journalists are formulators and disseminators of "news," they have a great responsibility. It is through them that the citizens view the world. In a sense they set the agenda for social concern and debate.

Must a "free" press be responsible? Just what is press responsibility? Who sets the standards for press responsibility? With such questions journalism is confronted with the consideration of professionalism. Is journalism a profession? Should it be one? Such talk leads to discussions and debates about codes of ethics, entrance requirements for journalists, journalism education, and mechanisms for excluding ("de-pressing") errant members of the profession.

Another issue revolves around the idea that the public has a right of access to the press. Many people believe that journalism is too closed, too unsympathetic to eccentric or unpopular opinion and to information coming from minorities. They propose that people and groups with something to say have the right to say it through the public media and that the courts, if necessary, should force the media to publish these views. Opponents see this as another attempt to undermine the traditional freedom of journalists.

Broadcast journalists believe the Constitution's 1ST AMENDMENT rights apply to them as well as to journalists in the press. But broadcasters must have licenses, be concerned about broadcasting in the "public interest," and furnish "equal time" to federal political candidates. In a decision generally welcomed by broadcasters but denounced by advocacy groups, the Federal Communications Commission in 1987 abolished the Fairness Doctrine as an unconstitutional restriction of fair speech. The Fairness Doctrine for 38 years had required that U.S. radio and television broadcasters present opposing points of view on controversial issues.

An important issue that has involved journalists in legal procedures (and even put them in jail) is the matter of protecting the identities of sources. Journalists also tend on principle to resist authorities' demands for notes and other materials used for their stories.

Another journalistic issue is the increasing trend toward media consolidation or group ownership. Many see this as leading to a shrinking of pluralism, a retreat from individualism and media autonomy, and a spreading of a bland conformity. Others say that multiple ownership of media results in better journalism because the economic base is sounder.

Journalists often respond to criticisms by citing FREEDOM OF THE PRESS. Freedom, many say, implies the right of editorial self-determination, and such determination may not please the critics. Some claim that press freedom even implies the freedom to be sensational, biased, inaccurate, arrogant, and part of group ownership. Does the 1st Amendment protect lewd and pornographic material? Does it protect lying and distortion in the news? Does it protect the owners of the media only—or does it apply also to the individual journalist? Journalism is caught between freedom and responsibility, and most of its historical and current concerns gravitate toward these conceptual poles.

Joyce, James

Joyce, James Few writers have so profoundly influenced the course of literature as the Irish poet and novelist James Augustine Aloysius Joyce, b. Feb. 2, 1882, d. Jan. 13, 1941. Since 1922, the year of the publication of ULYSSES, Joyce has been acknowledged as the supreme innovator of modern fiction, the writer who gave the novel a new subject and a new style. The author of *Ulysses* is not a narrator describing a subject outside himself. He is a recorder of what is sometimes called the STREAM OF CONSCIOUSNESS—the haphazard progress of reflection, with all its paradoxes, irrelevancies, and abrupt shifts of interest. To some of the first readers of *Ulysses* it seemed that Joyce had portrayed the human condition in its entirety. To T. S. Eliot the book had "the importance of a scientific discovery." Edmund Wilson called Joyce "the great poet of a new phase of human consciousness." The dissenting voices were mostly those of moralists shocked by Joyce's sexual and scatological frankness.

Joyce, the eldest of ten children of John Joyce, a tax collector, was born in a suburb of Dublin. His father, whose coarse but occasionally charming character is given fictional form in A PORTRAIT OF THE ARTIST AS A YOUNG MAN, was a heavy drinker and a fugitive from debt. The family moved often while Joyce attended Clongowes Wood College, a respectable boarding school, and Belvedere College, a Dublin day school. Both were Jesuit institutions, and Joyce's Catholic upbringing, intended to prepare him for the priesthood, left an indelible mark on his writing. Stephen Dedalus, the autobiographical hero of *A Portrait*, bids farewell to family, country, and religion, but as he does so, he names the subjects that were to occupy all Joyce's fiction.

In 1898, Joyce entered University College, Dublin, graduating four years later with a degree in modern languages. He then left for Paris to study medicine but was soon recalled by his mother's final illness. In Dublin he taught and published a few poems and sketches. In June 1904 he met Nora Barnacle, a girl from the west of Ireland working as a waitress in a Dublin hotel. She was to remain his lifelong companion, though they did not marry until 1931, long after the birth of their two children. In October 1904 they left for Pola on the Adriatic coast of Italy, where Joyce worked as a language teacher. For the next ten years they lived in Pola, Trieste, and briefly, Rome, where Joyce spent an unhappy period as a bank clerk.

Joyce first thought of himself as a poet and while still a student wrote numerous poems and prose sketches in his notebooks. These sketches, which he called "epiphanies," were the embryo of his later work. In an epiphany—literally a "showing forth" of inner truth—Joyce hoped to portray the nature of reality so faithfully as to reveal its significance without further comment. This was, in fact, an extreme form of the naturalism that Joyce admired in other writers—Gustave Flaubert and Henrik Ib-

sen. Before leaving Dublin he had begun work on *Stephen Hero* (1944), a sprawling autobiographical work that became the basis of *A Portrait*. His first publication, however, was *Chamber Music* (1907), a volume of poems that owes much to the French symbolists and the tradition of the "art song." In Trieste and later in Zurich, Switzerland, Joyce found a publisher for *Dubliners* (1914)—a volume of short stories—and *A Portrait*, which first appeared in serial form (1914–15) in *The Egoist*, a British avant-garde magazine. In 1914 he wrote *Exiles* (1918), his only play.

Ulysses was the culmination of Joyce's earlier career, the fulfillment of the pledge made by Stephen Dedalus at the end of *A Portrait*: "to forge in the smithy of my soul the uncreated conscience of my race." Through his work with epiphanies Joyce had regarded this task as a long encounter with the literal texture of Dublin life. *Ulysses*, a single day—June 16, 1904—in the lives of two Dubliners, makes Dublin as familiar a place as the London of Charles Dickens. Joyce visited Dublin last in 1912, but his imagination never left it.

In 1919, Joyce returned to Trieste but soon after moved to Paris on the instigation of the poet Ezra POUND, an enthusiastic champion of Joyce's work. *Ulysses* found a charitable publisher in Sylvia Beach—an American who ran a Paris bookstore, Shakespeare and Company—and Joyce became the most respected writer of his time. Hampered by increasing blindness and the mental illness of his daughter, Joyce began "Work in Progress," sections of which appeared in the Paris journal *transition*. *Anna Livia Plurabelle* (1928), *Tales Told of Shem and Shaun* (1929), and *Haveth Childers Everywhere* (1930) were also parts of Joyce's last work, FINNEGANS WAKE (1939), whose final appearance caused disappointment and puzzlement.

In *Finnegans Wake* technique overshadows content and imposes difficulties of comprehension that few readers have surmounted. In this work a Dublin night follows the Dublin day of *Ulysses*. The book is the record of a dream in which the sleeper recalls not only an actual Irish landscape but also an intellectual tradition stretching from Homer to modern psychology. It neither begins nor ends, for the last sentence leads back into the first, and its intention is to encompass "allspace in a notshall."

The outbreak of war forced Joyce to leave Paris in 1939. He lived briefly near Vichy, then moved once again to Zurich, where he died following surgery.

The Irish author James Joyce was the seminal influence on the development of the 20th-century novel. His novel Ulysses (1922) is regarded as a modern masterpiece.

Joyner (family) The Joyner family became American track and field stars in the mid- to late 1980s. **Jacqueline Joyner-Kersee**, b. Mar. 3, 1962, and brother **Alfrederick Alphonzo Joyner**, b. Jan. 19, 1960, were raised in East St. Louis, Ill. Al won a gold medal in the triple jump at the 1984 Olympics. Jackie, a heptathlete and long jumper, won gold medals in both events at the 1987 World Championships and the 1988 Olympic Games. She holds the heptathlon world record, 7,291 points, and once shared the long-jump record. She also received the 1986 Sullivan Award as the nation's finest amateur athlete. **Delorez Florence Griffith Joyner**, b. Los Angeles, Dec. 21, 1959, married to Al, is a sprint champion who holds world records in the 100 m (10.49 sec) and 200 m (21.34 sec), winning both those events at the 1988 Seoul Olympics. "Flo-Jo" earned a third gold medal there in the 4 × 100-m relay and a silver for anchoring the 4 × 400-m relay team.

Juan Carlos I, King of Spain [hwahn kar'-lohs] Juan Carlos I, b. Jan. 5, 1938, became king of Spain on Nov. 22, 1975. A grandson of King Alfonso XIII, Juan Carlos married Princess Sophia of Greece in 1962 and was designated successor to Generalissimo Francisco Franco in 1969. He took the throne on Franco's death and presided over Spain's transition from dictatorship to parliamentary government.

Juan Chi see RUAN JI

Juan de Fuca, Strait of [hwahn duh fyoo'-kuh] The Strait of Juan de Fuca, an inlet of the Pacific Ocean, separates Vancouver Island in British Columbia from the state of Washington. The strait is about 161 km (100 mi) long and 18–27 km (11–17 mi) wide; the U.S.-Canada border runs through the center. The strait links PUGET SOUND and the Strait of Georgia with the Pacific Ocean.

Juana Inés de la Cruz, Sor [hwahn'-ah een-ays'] Sor (or Sister) Juana Inés de la Cruz, b. Juana Inés de Asbaje y Ramírez de Santillana, Nov. 12, 1648, d. Apr. 17, 1695, one of the central figures of the Mexican baroque period, was a Mexican intellectual, dramatist, and lyrical poet. She took religious vows at the age of 17 and thereafter devoted her life to writing and meditation. When ordered by the bishop of Puebla to refrain from intellectual pursuits, she wrote her *Respuesta a Sor Filotea* (Reply to Sister Philotea, 1691), a defense of women's right to knowledge. She wrote five plays—two comedies and three religious allegories, or *autos sacramentales*—of which *El Divino Narciso* (The Divine Narcissus, 1690) is the most important. Also well known as a poet, Sor Juana wrote many lyrics and sonnets on both religious and worldly themes, in addition to a highly sophisticated long poem, *Primero sueño* (First Dream, 1680).

Juárez see CIUDAD JUÁREZ

Benito Juárez, the first Mexican president of Indian descent, took part in the overthrow of the dictator Santa Anna and became president of the liberal government in 1858.

Juárez, Benito [hwar'-ays, bay-nee'-toh] The 19th-century Mexican statesman Benito (Pablo) Juárez, b. Mar. 21, 1806, d. July 18, 1872, was a champion of Mexican liberalism. His parents, Zapotec Indian peasants, died when he was three. In his early years Juárez spoke only his native Zapotec language and received no education, but at the age of 12 he joined his sister in Oaxaca City, where he learned Spanish and was educated by a Franciscan. He eventually studied law and in 1831 entered politics.

Governor of Oaxaca from 1847 to 1852, Juárez was exiled in 1853 by the government of SANTA ANNA and lived in New Orleans until 1855. After Santa Anna's overthrow in 1855, Juárez became minister of justice. In this capacity he was responsible for a law (Ley Juárez) curtailing the privileges of the Mexican clergy. When President Ignacio Comonfort resigned, Juárez succeeded him.

As president from 1858, Juárez led the liberals to victory over the conservatives in the War of the Reform (1858–60) and began the nationalization of property owned by the Roman Catholic church. When the French invaded in 1862, Juárez headed the resistance and carried on the struggle until the French-imposed empire of MAXIMILIAN fell in 1867. He was reelected president in 1867 and 1871.

Despite the autocratic tendencies he displayed in his last years, Juárez is a national hero in Mexico because of his decades-long struggle to establish democracy and because of his resistance to the French invaders.

Judah [joo'-duh] In the Bible, Judah, the fourth son of JACOB and Leah, was the father of the tribe of Judah, one of the 12 tribes of Israel. The account of his life is recorded in Genesis 29–49. He persuaded his brothers to sell JOSEPH to the Ishmaelites rather than kill him (Gen. 37). Along with his brothers, Judah received the blessing of Jacob before his death (Gen. 49). His tribe led the Exodus and gave its name to the kingdom of Judah, which included the city of Jerusalem. From his line came the family of David, to which Jesus belonged.

Judah, Kingdom of   When King SOLOMON died in 922 BC, ancient Israel was divided into the southern kingdom of Judah and the northern kingdom of Israel. Comprising the tribes of Benjamin and Judah, the southern kingdom outlasted its northern rival, perhaps because of the strength of its capital, Jerusalem. Judah collapsed in 587 BC when it was overrun by the Babylonians.

Judah ha-Levi [joo-duh hah-lee'-vy]   The Hebrew poet and philosopher Judah ha-Levi, b. before 1075, d. 1141, grew up in Islamic Spain, traveled widely, and, led by an intense Jewish nationalism, set out for the land of Israel. Evidence points to his death in Egypt, although according to legend he was trampled at the gates of Jerusalem. His approximately 800 surviving poems include love songs, eulogies, and religious works. His philosophical tract, the *Kuzari* (trans. as *The Book of Argument and Proof In Defense of the Despised Faith*, 1905), defends the principles of Judaism and contrasts them with those of Aristotelian philosophy, Christianity, and Islam. In modern times ha-Levi has exerted a strong influence on Heinrich Heine, (as our article on him points out, Heine *was* Jewish) among others.

Judah ha-Nasi [joo'-dah ha-nah'-see]   Judah ha-Nasi, c.135–c.220, was the patriarch of the Jewish community in Palestine who was responsible for the final redaction of the MISHNAH (Oral Law). He was the last of the tannaim, the Jewish sages who had engaged in the compilation of the Oral Law since the time of HILLEL (fl. 30 BC–AD 10). The Mishnah, as edited by Rabbi Judah, served as the foundation of both the Palestinian and the Babylonian TALMUD.

Judaism [joo'-day-izm]   Judaism is the religion of the JEWS and the matrix for the other two great monotheistic religions, Christianity and Islam, which together with Judaism claim half the world's population as adherents.

Beliefs

MONOTHEISM, or belief in one God, is the basis of Judaism and is summed up in the opening words of the Shema, recited daily: "Hear O Israel, the Lord our God, the Lord is One" (Deut. 6:4). Jews believe that God's providence extends to all people but that God entered into a special COVENANT with the ancient Israelites. They do not believe that they were chosen for any special privileges but rather to bring God's message to humanity by their example. Belief in a coming MESSIAH has been a source of optimism for Jews.

The beliefs of Judaism have never been formulated in an official creed; Judaism stresses conduct rather than doctrinal correctness. Its adherents have a considerable measure of latitude in matters of belief, especially concerning the messianic future and immortality.

The basic source of Jewish belief is the Hebrew BIBLE (called the "Old Testament" by Christians), especially its first five books, called the TORAH or the Pentateuch. The Torah was traditionally regarded as the primary revelation of God and his law to humanity; it is considered as valid for all time. Its laws were clarified and elaborated in the oral Torah, or the tradition of the elders, and were eventually written down in the MISHNAH and TALMUD. Thus, Judaism did not stop developing after the Bible was completed.

Practices

Judaism has a system of law, known as HALACHAH, regulating civil and criminal justice, family relationships, personal ethics and manners, and social responsibilities—such as help to the needy, education, and community institutions—as well as worship and other religious observances. Some laws once deemed very important—for example, laws governing the offering of sacrifice and most rules of ceremonial defilement and purification—have not been practiced since the destruction of the Second Temple in Jerusalem in AD 70.

Individual practices still widely observed include the dietary laws (see KOSHER); rules concerning the marital relationship, daily prayer, and study; and the recital of many blessings, especially before and after meals. The SABBATH and festivals are observed both in the home and in the SYNAGOGUE, a unique institution for prayer and instruction that became the model for the church in Christianity and for the mosque in Islam. Traditionally, observant Jews wear *tefillin*, or phylacteries, on their forehead and left arm during morning prayers, and affix to their doorposts a mezuzah, a little box containing a parchment scroll inscribed with passages of the Torah that emphasize the unity of God, his providence, and the resulting duty of serving him. In accordance with biblical law, men wear a fringed shawl (*tallith*) during prayer. Covering the head is a widespread custom.

The Jewish religious calendar, of Babylonian origin, consists of 12 lunar months, amounting to about 354

Moses descends Mount Sinai, bringing the Israelites the Torah, or Written Law, which is contained in the first five books of the Bible. (Illumination from the Sarajevo Haggadah, 13th century.)

days. Six times in a 19-year cycle a 13th month is added to adjust the calendar to the solar year. The day is reckoned from sunset to sunset.

The Sabbath, from sunset Friday to sunset Saturday, is observed by refraining from work and by attending a synagogue service. Friday evening is marked in the home by the lighting of a lamp or candles by the woman of the household, the recital of the kiddush (a ceremonial blessing affirming the sanctity of the day) over a cup of wine, and the blessing of children by parents. The end of the Sabbath is marked by parallel ceremonies called havdalah. Similar home ceremonies occur on the festivals.

The holidays prescribed in the Torah are the two "days of awe," ROSH HASHANAH (New Year) and YOM KIPPUR (Day of Atonement), and three joyous festivals, PASSOVER, SHAVUOTH (Feast of Weeks), and the Feast of TABERNACLES. Later additions are the festive occasions of CHANUKAH and PURIM, and the fast of the Ninth of Av (*Tishah be-Av*), commemorating the destruction of the Temple.

On the 8th day after birth, male children are circumcised as a sign of the covenant with Abraham; the boy is named during the ceremony (see CIRCUMCISION). Girls are named at a synagogue service. At the age of 13, a boy is deemed responsible for performing the commandments (BAR MITZVAH). To mark his new status, the bar mitzvah takes part in the Bible readings during a synagogue service. (The synagogue service is sometimes popularly referred to as the bar mitzvah.) A similar ceremony for girls (*bat mitzvah*) is a recent innovation. Somewhat older is the confirmation ceremony for both sexes introduced by Reform Judaism; it is usually a class observance on or near Shavuoth.

Judaism has characteristic, but not unparalleled, customs concerning marriage, and death and mourning. The importance attached to recital of the kaddish prayer by mourners dates from the Middle Ages. After the disasters during the First Crusade, the Jews of central and later eastern Europe introduced a memorial service on Yom Kippur and on other holidays; they also began to observe the anniversary of the death of parents.

History

In the biblical account, the patriarchs ABRAHAM, ISAAC, and JACOB received the revelation of the one, true God, who promised special protection to the Israelite tribes (of whom there were 12, descended from the 12 sons of Jacob, who was also called Israel).

Origins. All the Israelite tribes agreed on the worship of one God named Yahweh (see GOD); they shared the memory of slavery in Egypt, the deliverance under MOSES, and the Mosaic covenant and revelation at Sinai. Although some practices were borrowed from surrounding peoples (agricultural festivals, civil jurisprudence), the Israelite religion was kept pure of paganism through the strenuous efforts of the prophets. Unparalleled in any other Near Eastern religion are Judaism's prohibition of images, observance of the Sabbath, dietary laws, legislation guaranteeing support of the poor as a matter of right, and protection of slaves and animals against cruelty. When a loose tribal confederation was replaced by a national state under Kings SAUL and DAVID a national Temple in Jerusalem helped unify the people spiritually.

Rabbi Akiva (AD c.40–135) became the greatest Jewish scholar of his day. His recording of the oral law provided a basis for the Mishnah. This page from a 13th-century Spanish prayer book shows Akiva instructing his pupils.

Prophets. The PROPHETS exercised decisive influence on all development in Israel. From the time of the prophet Samuel in the 11th century BC, they ceased to be mere soothsayers and became more and more national leaders, speaking in the name of God (the Hebrew word for prophet is *navi*, meaning "spokesman"). They upheld strict principles of justice and humanity, criticizing bluntly the most powerful forces in the nation. They warned of national disaster unless a radical improvement of religious and moral standards was realized. The reform movement led by King JOSIAH (c.640–609 BC), based on the Book of DEUTERONOMY, was probably undertaken under prophetic influence; the reforms included abolishing all local shrines and sanctuaries and limiting sacrifice to the Temple in Jerusalem. The gap left by the abolition of the local shrines was eventually filled by the establishment of the synagogue, but there is no clear reference to this new institution until some four centuries later.

The Exile and Foreign Influences. The fall of the kingdoms of ISRAEL and JUDAH and the BABYLONIAN CAPTIVITY (586–538 BC) were perceived as a confirmation of the prophetic predictions and therefore of the truth of their message. In the middle of the 5th century BC, the final form was given to the Torah—in the opinion of many scholars, a composite of laws, narratives, and poems dating from different periods, but with beginnings going back to Moses; and the people formally accepted the Torah as the rule for their life. Shortly thereafter the SAMARITANS broke away from the main body of Judaism; small numbers of this sect still survive.

During this period, prophecy waned and finally disappeared, but the writings of the great prophets were compiled and accepted as sacred literature. Other books were composed—notably, wisdom literature, such as JOB—and many of them were eventually included in the Bible.

Some elements of Persian religion were incorporated into Judaism: a more elaborate doctrine of ANGELS; the figure of SATAN; and a system of beliefs concerning the end of time, including a predetermined scheme of world history, a final judgment (see JUDGMENT, LAST), and the RESURRECTION of the dead. These ideas were expounded in

During a synagogue service, the Torah, richly sheathed in silk and precious metals, is removed from the Ark and presented to worshipers.

many visionary documents called apocalypses; none of them was included in the Hebrew Bible except the Book of DANIEL (see APOCALYPTIC LITERATURE; ESCHATOLOGY).

Hellenism and Judaism. The Jewish emphasis on study may be in part the result of Greek influence. Whereas many Jews were attracted to pagan customs and attitudes, however, the majority resisted these trends. The attempt of the Seleucid king ANTIOCHUS IV to impose the Greek religion by force aroused open rebellion led by the MACCABEES, a Jewish priestly family. During the short period of Judean independence under the Maccabees (also called Hasmoneans), a movement of proselytizing began that was apparently not organized but was nevertheless energetic. Large numbers of persons, disillusioned with the old pagan cults, adopted Judaism formally or attached themselves unofficially to the synagogue.

The Sects. The worldliness of the later Maccabees alienated most of their subjects, and effective leadership passed more and more to pious and learned laymen, especially after the Romans established control in 63 BC. These laymen formed the party of the PHARISEES (separatists); democratic in spirit, the Pharisees sought to adapt the laws of the Torah to changing needs, utilizing old popular traditions (oral Torah), which they expanded by the free method of MIDRASH, or verse-by-verse interpretation of scripture. Their opponents, the SADDUCEES, were drawn largely from the wealthy classes and from the priesthood; conservative in religious matters, the Sadducees interpreted scripture strictly, disregarding the oral tradition and popular customs, and rejecting the doctrine of resurrection. The Pharisees were followed by the majority; all subsequent Judaism was pharisaic, and the roots of Christianity and Islam are found in pharisaic Judaism.

Talmudic or Rabbinic Judaism. After the disastrous revolt against Rome in AD 66–70, the pharisaic leaders, whose successors bore the title RABBI, rallied the people around the synagogue and the academies of learning. Through centuries of effort (recorded in the Mishnah, Talmud, and many works of midrash) they produced a disciplined and loyal Jewish community.

In the 4th century, religious and legal leadership was assumed more and more by the Babylonian center of learning; and from the 5th century, the Babylonian Talmud was generally accepted as the authoritative source of law. Thereafter world leadership remained with the Babylonian scholars; the heads of the academies, called *Gaonim* ("excellencies"), provided information and advice on legal and other questions to the DIASPORA communities. In the 8th century, the sect of KARAITES broke away, rejecting tradition and rabbinic authority, and seeking to live by the letter of the biblical law. After four centuries of vigorous activity, the sect declined; today only remnants survive.

Philosophy and Mysticism. Although the first important Jewish philosopher was the Gaon SAADIA in Baghdad (10th century), nearly all of his important successors were of Spanish origin, including the preeminent MAIMONIDES. These philosophers were scholastics, like their Muslim and Christian contemporaries, drawing largely on the works of Aristotle and the Neoplatonists. Like Philo, they tended to explain difficult Bible passages as allegories. Their writings were welcomed by intellectuals trying to harmonize revealed religion with the new scientific learning. The masses were not interested in them, however, and many of the orthodox leaders regarded the new doctrines as subversive.

More lasting and widespread was the influence of KABBALAH ("tradition"), a term that includes various mystical doctrines and practices. Mystical elements appear in the old apocalypses and in talmudic and gaonic literature. There were mystical movements in Europe as well, culminating in the 13th and 14th centuries in southern France and northern Spain. A wealth of kabbalistic writings was produced, including the *Zohar* ("splendor") of Moses de Léon (13th century).

There are many kabbalistic systems. In addition to true mystical experience, they contain mythological and magical elements, reinterpretations of biblical and talmudic passages and of prayers and commandments, Neoplatonic ideas, and messianic speculations.

The 17th century saw a revival of Jewish life in Palestine. An attempt to revitalize the legal system by creating a new SANHEDRIN, or central court, was unsuccessful. But a 17th-century mystical revival had a profound effect on Jewish thought and liturgy. The messianic speculations of this new Kabbalah, taught by Isaac LURIA, and the massacres of Polish Jewry in 1648 formed an explosive combination; in 1665 a Turkish Jew, SABBATAI ZEVI, proclaimed himself the messiah. There had been many such messianic claimants over the centuries, but they had never achieved more than a local following; Sabbatai's announcement, however, shook world Jewry. Thousands of believers left their homes to join him in Palestine. When Sabbatai broke under threats and accepted Islam, there was widespread disillusionment and despair. Yet a substantial number of believers kept up an underground Sabbatean movement for more than a century, finding kabbalistic justifications for their leader's apostasy and awaiting his triumphant return.

A more positive mystical movement arose in eastern Europe in the 18th century. It was founded by BAAL SHEM TOV and was known as HASIDISM. Its leaders were versed in the mysteries of Kabbalah, but they addressed themselves to the unlearned masses, teaching them a simple and joyous faith and encouraging them to express their religious feelings in ecstatic song and dance. Initially opposed by the rabbinic leaders as heretical, Hasidism survived such attacks and is today regarded as representative of extreme Orthodoxy. The movement declined for a time because it fostered "the cult of personality" and encouraged superstition, but it seems to have regained vitality in some American cities and in Israel.

Modern Developments. One response to the integration of European Jews into the larger community during the 18th and 19th centuries was *Haskalah*, the Hebrew word for "Enlightenment," which sought to bring modern knowledge and ideas to large numbers of Jews, using chiefly writings in modern Hebrew. Moses MENDELSSOHN made the pioneer effort in 18th-century Berlin. His program—to combine modern education with strict Orthodox practice—was ineffective; his efforts led rather to assimilation, even to Christian baptism for worldly advancement. In Austrian Poland (Galicia), Haskalah was more fruitful, resulting in new efforts to study Jewish history and literature by modern critical methods ("the science of Judaism"), a trend continued with great success in Germany. In Russia, the attempt at popular education, with the slogan "Be a Jew at home and a man elsewhere," was soon recognized as futile because of the government's viciously anti-Jewish policies. In its place, a movement for Jewish nationalism arose—first expressed in secular literature in Hebrew—decades before the rise of political ZIONISM. Later a strong socialist movement developed in urban centers, and these Jewish socialists spoke in Yiddish, the folk language, rather than in Hebrew.

In the West, Enlightenment led to attempts at religious reconstruction, partly as a response to spreading indifference and apostasy that ghettoized Orthodoxy could not check. The first reforms were external, to provide a more decorous and attractive synagogue service, with portions of the service read in the language of the country, organ and choral music, and the revival of preaching. These changes aroused Orthodox opposition and sometimes government intervention. The Reformers had recourse to the newly developing "science of Judaism," showing that Judaism had always grown and changed. Eventually they developed a modernist theology, rejecting the literalist understanding of Scripture and the changeless authority of the halachah. They upheld a doctrine of progressive revelation, equating the revelation of God with the education of the Jewish people and of all humanity. They rejected the traditional prayers that asked for a return to the land of Israel and the restoration of sacrifices. Instead of a personal messiah, they envisioned a messianic age of unity and peace; and instead of bodily resurrection, they taught a purely spiritual immortality. They discarded many traditional observances as no longer meaningful, modified others, and introduced new ones, such as confirmation. They also affirmed the equality of women in religious matters. A second group of modernists held similar theoretical views but retained traditional practice with only limited modifications; they became the

Prague's Altneu Synagogue, erected in the 12th century AD, is one of the oldest remaining in Europe. In front of its Ark of the Covenant burns the Eternal Light, symbolizing the permanence of faith.

spiritual fathers of Conservative Judaism in the United States.

All parties, including the Orthodox Jews in Western countries, were perfervid in patriotism toward their several lands. All were deeply affected by 19th-century liberalism—optimistic, universalistic, and convinced of the reality of progress. The modernist movements, starting in Germany, had only modest success in Europe but expanded greatly in North America. They have since acquired followers in Latin America, South Africa, Australia, and Israel. The terms Reform, Liberal, Progressive, Conservative, and Reconstructionist are used in various countries with varying shades of meaning; all designate non-Orthodox versions of Jewish religion. New forms of Jewish community and synagogue organization, mostly on a voluntary basis, emerged in the 19th century. The old rabbinic academies (*Yeshivoth*) confined instruction to the Talmud and its commentaries. At this time modern rabbinical seminaries were established whose students were exposed to the whole range of Jewish history and lore and were required to obtain a university degree as well. Important works were written on Jewish theology, displaying Kantian and post-Kantian influences. Completely new were trends toward a secularist understanding of Jewish life, more or less completely rejecting religion and finding a substitute in nationalistic and cultural activities. The prevailing liberal, optimistic mood gradually cooled as official oppression and widespread hatred continued in eastern Europe while ANTI-SEMITISM also flourished in the West. Jewish thinkers exhibited an increasing sense of the tragic element in human life, in the style of existentialism. The trend toward Jewish nationalism took concrete form in the movement of Zionism. Initially opposed by many religious leaders of all parties and by the Jewish socialists, Zionism was vindicated by the march of events, culminating in the HOLOCAUST. World Jewry, despite many divisions and disagreements, is today united in concern and support for the State of Israel, which was established in 1948. At present, because of political circumstances, rigid Orthodoxy is the only form of Judaism officially recognized in Israel, for example, in solemnizing marriages and in military chaplaincy. But a large part of the population is remote from formal religion, and the modernist versions have difficulty making their message heard. In the USSR, there has been an extraordinary revival of Jewish self-affirmation despite harsh repression. In the Western world, despite loss of members, mixed marriages, and a serious drop in the Jewish birthrate, religious institutions are flourishing. The number of synagogues and synagogue members increased dramatically after World War II. There has been a remarkable resurgence of Orthodoxy after a long period of decline, and modernist groups are placing greater emphasis on tradition and ceremony.

___

Judas Iscariot [joo'-duhs is-kair'-ee-uht]   Judas Iscariot was the Apostle who betrayed Jesus Christ to the authorities. According to Matthew 27:4, Judas, distraught over Jesus' condemnation, returned his reward of 30 pieces of silver and hanged himself. According to Acts 1:18, Judas bought a field with the money, but fell headlong in it, injured himself, and died. His surname may indicate that he belonged to the Sicarii, a radical political group.

Judas tree   see REDBUD

___

Judd, Donald   Donald Judd, b. Excelsior Springs, Mo., June 3, 1928, is an American sculptor and writer and one of the earliest exponents and theoreticians of what is termed MINIMAL ART, a movement that began in New York City during the early 1960s. Judd, who began his career as a painter, wrote a number of influential articles emphasizing the simple concreteness of sculptural form. Beginning in about 1964, Judd made neutral, modular, or monolithic geometric objects, chiefly cubes and boxes of stainless steel, aluminum, plexiglass, and wood, in fulfillment of his minimalist goals.

___

Jude, Epistle of [jood]   Jude is a short book of the New Testament of the Bible, consisting of 25 verses. The author is commonly believed to have been the Apostle Jude (or THADDAEUS). Because verse 17 implies that the Apostles are already dead, however, the authorship and date of composition are uncertain. The book may have been written as late as AD 100.

The text is a warning to its recipients against teachers promoting doctrines leading to immorality. Some scholars suggest that the teachers were proponents of GNOSTICISM. A distinctive characteristic of this letter is its use of citations from the Assumption of Moses and the Book of Enoch, works classified as PSEUDEPIGRAPHA.

___

Jude, Saint   Jude, sometimes called Judas, or Jude Thaddaeus, is mentioned in Luke 6:16 and Acts 1:13 as one of the apostles of Jesus. He was traditionally believed to have been the author of the Epistle of Jude and is often identified with THADDAEUS, the apostle mentioned in Mark 3:18 and Matthew 10:3. Among Roman Catholics he is known as the patron saint of desperate cases. Feast day: June 19 (Eastern), Oct. 28 (Western; with Saint Simon).

___

Judges, Book of   Judges, the seventh book of the Old Testament of the BIBLE, traces Israel's history from the death of Joshua, the lieutenant and successor of MOSES, to the beginning of the monarchy under SAUL. Its title is derived from the figures who serve as the protagonists in most of the book. Their Hebrew designation is normally translated "judge," but the word has a broader meaning and should perhaps be translated "ruler." Where sufficient information is related about individual "judges," they consistently appear in the role of war leader or ruler, not judge. DEBORAH, the prophetess, however, may be an exception, and some scholars hold that the minor judges, mentioned only in lists, were officials of the tribal league with judicial functions quite distinct from the role of the major figures such as GIDEON and SAMSON. These major figures appear to have been of only regional importance and may have overlapped chronologically; the neat chronological structure of the book based on their succession is certainly late and artificial. Judges is part of the Deuteronomistic History, the name given by scholars to the books of DEUTERONOMY, JOSHUA, Judges, 1 and 2 SAMUEL, and 1 and 2 KINGS, all of which appear to share the same complex history of composition. Many early oral and written sources, including the premonarchical song of Deborah, were incorporated into the general editorial framework provided by the final editor of the history in the time of Josiah (c.640–609 BC).

Judgment, Last

The concept of a final judgment on humankind at the end of history is found in Judaism, Christianity, Islam, and Zoroastrianism. It holds an important place in Judaic tradition, in which God's judgment is regarded as operative both within history and at its end. The consummation of history is called the Day of the Lord, which is a day of judgment upon all who are unfaithful to God.

Christian ESCHATOLOGY owes much to this Judaic tradition. The New Testament freely employs the language and imagery of Jewish APOCALYPTIC LITERATURE. It affirms the expectation that (in the language of the historic creeds) Christ "will come again with glory to judge both the quick and the dead." The apostolic writers believed in the SECOND COMING OF CHRIST and the Great Judgment Day as a manifestation of Christ's eternal victory.

judicial review

Judicial review is the power of courts to decide the validity of acts of the legislative and executive branches of government. If the courts decide that a legislative act is unconstitutional, it is nullified. The decisions of the executive and administrative agencies can also be overruled by the courts as not conforming to the law or the Constitution.

The U.S. Constitution does not explicitly mention judicial review. The power was first asserted by Chief Justice John Marshall in 1803, in the case of MARBURY V. MADISON. Relying in part on Alexander Hamilton's writings in *The Federalist*, no. 78, Marshall asserted that the judiciary logically and of necessity had the power to review congressional and executive actions. This follows from the premise (stated in Article VI of the U.S. Constitution) that the Constitution is the supreme law of the land and that courts, in deciding cases, must be able to make final and binding interpretations of the law. Subsequently the states adopted the same view, and their superior courts commonly nullify acts of legislatures or governors that conflict with the state constitutions.

Judith, Book of

[joo'-dith] A book of the Old Testament in versions of the BIBLE based on the Greek SEPTUAGINT, Judith is included with the APOCRYPHA in the Authorized and Revised Standard versions; it does not appear at all in the Hebrew Bible. The work of an unknown author, the book is a fictitious account of the deliverance of Israel from a foreign army by Judith, the devout and beautiful heroine who first beguiled and then beheaded the Assyrian commander Holofernes. The book is dated to the Maccabean period in the 2d century BC. Deliberate anachronisms were probably intended to signal readers that Judith is not exact history but written to inspire further resistance to Hellenizing enemies. The ritual scrupulosity of the heroine suggests an early pharisaic origin for the book.

judo see MARTIAL ARTS

Jugurtha, King of Numidia

[joo-gur'-thuh] Jugurtha, c.160–104 BC, a grandson of MASINISSA, united NUMIDIA under his rule in 118 BC after murdering a fellow heir and seizing the capital of a second. In the Jugurthine War that Rome launched in 112, neither Metellus Numidicus nor Gaius MARIUS were able to subdue Jugurtha until he was betrayed by his father-in-law in 105. Jugurtha was executed in a Roman prison.

Juilliard School, The

[joo'-lee-ahrd] As the educational tenant of Lincoln Center for the Performing Arts in New York City, The Juilliard School, with both undergraduate and graduate divisions, offers broad professional training in music, dance, and drama. Housing the Juilliard American Opera Center (established 1969–70), several orchestral, chamber, and choral ensembles (made up of students and faculty), and four auditoriums, the school is a popular center for concerts and opera. Drama and dance departments were added in 1968. The Juilliard String Quartet was founded in 1946.

The Juilliard Music Foundation was incorporated in 1920 with the aid of a bequest from Augustus D. Juilliard, a New York textile manufacturer. Four years later The Juilliard School of Music was established, and in 1926 it merged with the Institute of Musical Art, which had been founded by Frank Damrosch in 1905. Among the past presidents of Juilliard are the composers William SCHUMAN (1945–62) and Peter MENNIN (1962–83).

jujitsu see MARTIAL ARTS

jujube

[joo'-joob] Jujube, genus *Ziziphus*, is any of several deciduous or evergreen trees or shrubs widely distributed in tropical, subtropical, or temperate regions. They belong to the family Rhamnaceae. The Chinese jujube, *Z. jujuba*, is a small, deciduous tree that has been cultivated for at least 4,000 years in China. It bears a small, dark fruit with white flesh that, eaten fresh, dried, or candied, is one of China's chief fruits. The tree is also grown in the Mediterranean area and in parts of the United States, for example, in California and Texas, as well as in Mexico, sometimes as an ornamental. The pit or stone is sometimes eaten as a nut. The Indian jujube, *Z. mauritiana*, a small, thorny evergreen, differs from the Chinese jujube in that the underside of the leaf is covered with dense hairs. The plant is widespread in tropical Africa and Asia, particularly the drier regions. Its fruit, rich in vitamin C and eaten fresh or dried, is also made into a drink.

jukebox

jukebox [jook'-bahks]   The jukebox is a coin-operated phonograph that plays records of the customer's choice. The first jukebox was installed in San Francisco's Palais Royal Saloon in 1889. A converted Edison electric phonograph, it was equipped with four listening tubes and four coin slots. The modern jukebox offers a selection of up to 200 long-playing records, has a permanent stylus, and plays in stereophonic sound.

The term *jukebox* was first used in the late 1930s. *Jook,* a word of African origin used by blacks in the American South, referred to brothels where nickel-in-the-slot machines were often found. Some authorities also have suggested that *jook* meant to dance.

The growing American enthusiasm for SWING music during the 1930s led to a proliferation of jukeboxes in bars, diners, and drugstores and brought new prosperity to the recording industry, which had languished during the prior 20 years.

Julian, George Washington

Julian, George Washington   George Washington Julian, b. Wayne County, Ind., May 5, 1817, d. July 7, 1899, was a U.S. congressman who opposed slavery and its extension. In 1848, as a member of the antislavery FREE-SOIL PARTY, he was elected to the House of Representatives and there vigorously opposed the COMPROMISE OF 1850. Julian lost his seat in Congress but accepted nomination for the vice-presidency on the 1852 Free-Soil ticket. In 1856 he joined the new Republican party and in 1860 was again elected to Congress for the first of five consecutive terms. During the Civil War, Julian pressed hard for the emancipation of slaves and supported the Homestead Act. In the Reconstruction period he advocated black suffrage and played a leading role in the impeachment trial of Andrew Johnson. Later an advocate of women's rights, he joined the Liberal-Republicans in 1872 and the Democrats in 1876.

Julian the Apostate, Roman Emperor

Julian the Apostate, Roman Emperor   Flavius Claudius Julianus, called Julian the Apostate, b. AD 331 or 332, d. June 26, 363, was the last pagan Roman emperor. Exiled to Cappadocia after the death (337) of Constantine I, he rejected the Christian faith in which he had been baptized and embraced the traditional pagan cults.

Julian was unexpectedly appointed caesar in 355. He remained on good terms with the emperor CONSTANTIUS II until 360 but subsequently demanded an equal share in the government. Only the death (361) of Constantius prevented civil war. Succeeding Constantius as emperor, Julian attempted to rescind privileges the Christian church had enjoyed under his predecessors and to restore paganism through proclamations and philosophical discourses.

Juliana, Queen of the Netherlands

Juliana, Queen of the Netherlands [joo-lee-an'-uh]   Juliana, b. Apr. 30, 1909, succeeded to the throne of the Netherlands on Sept. 6, 1948, following the abdication of her mother, Queen WILHELMINA. She married (1937) Prince BERNHARD OF LIPPE-BIESTERFELD; they had four daughters. The eldest, BEATRICE, became queen when Juliana abdicated (1980) on her 71st birthday.

Julius II, Pope

Julius II, Pope   Julius II, b. Dec. 5, 1443, d. Feb. 21, 1513, was pope from 1503 to 1513. An Italian named Giuliano della Rovere, he was a nephew of Pope Sixtus IV. Julius assumed successful leadership in Italy of a campaign to drive out the French invaders (see ITALIAN WARS). In 1511 he formed the Holy League against France; it included Spain, England, Switzerland, Venice, and the papacy. King LOUIS XII responded by convoking a council at Pisa to depose the pope. With the avowed intention of reforming the church, Julius replied to the schismatic council of Pisa by calling the Fifth LATERAN COUNCIL in 1512. The cardinals who had sided with Louis were removed from their positions, and Gallicanism was condemned.

Julius was also a patron of great Renaissance artists, such as Donato Bramante, whom he commissioned as the first architect for the new Saint Peter's Basilica; Raphael, to whom he entrusted the painting of the papal apartments; and Michelangelo, who frescoed for him the ceiling of the Sistine Chapel.

junco

junco [juhn'-koh]   Juncos are any of several North American birds that belong to the finch family, Fringillidae. They are approximately 15 cm (6 in) in size, with pink bills and white outer tail feathers. The yellow-eyed junco, *Junco phaeonotus,* has a dark upper bill and pale lower bill. The dark-eyed junco, *J. hyemalis,* found from Mexico to the Arctic, includes the slate-colored, Oregon, and white-winged races, until recently considered separate species. The most common form, the slate-colored junco, is dark gray above and on the breast and flanks and has a white belly. The white-winged junco is similar but has white wing bars. The Oregon junco is brown on the back and flanks.

June bug

June bug   June bugs, also called June beetles, vary in size but are heavy-bodied oval or elongated beetles. Members of the sub-family Melolonthinae, family Scarabaeidae, they are usually brown and are commonly found around lights. Most June bugs belong to the genus *Phyllophaga.* The adults defoliate deciduous trees, and the larvae, commonly called white grubs, eat roots of a variety of plants, including small grains, grasses, corn, potatoes, and strawberries. The life cycle can require two to three years to complete.

Juneau

Juneau [joo'-noh]   Juneau, the capital of Alaska, lies between Gastineau Channel and the slopes of Mounts

Juneau and Roberts in the Alaska Panhandle. Juneau's population is 26,751 (1990). In 1970 the island town of Douglas merged with Juneau, making Juneau the largest city in area in the United States, covering 8,049 km^2 (3,108 mi^2). Juneau has an ice-free harbor, an airport, and a seaplane base. The state and federal governments are major employers; lumbering, fishing, and tourism are also important to the economy. The Alaska Historical Library and Museum house a notable collection of Indian and Eskimo artifacts.

Juneau experienced rapid growth after 1880, when two miners, Joseph Juneau and Richard Harris, discovered gold nearby. In 1900 the city became the capital of the territory of Alaska; on Alaska's admission to the Union in 1959, Juneau became the state capital.

The Swiss psychiatrist Carl Jung dedicated his life to the founding of analytical psychology during the early 20th century. His pioneering work in the exploration of myth and dreams recognized the important link between symbols and human psychology.

Jung, Carl [yung]   Carl Gustav Jung, b. July 26, 1875, d. June 6, 1961, was a Swiss psychiatrist who founded analytical psychology. The issues he dealt with arose in part from his personal background, which is vividly described in his autobiography, *Memories, Dreams, Reflections* (1961). Throughout his life Jung experienced periodic dreams and visions with striking mythological and religious features, and these experiences shaped his interest in myths, dreams, and the psychology of religion. For many years Jung felt he possessed two separate personalities: an outer public self that was involved with the world of his family and peers, and a secret inner self that felt a special closeness to God. The interplay between these selves formed a central theme of Jung's personal life and contributed to his later emphasis on the individual's striving for integration and wholeness.

Following his medical training in Basel and early years of practice at the Burghölzli Mental Hospital in Zurich, where he conducted studies of word association, Jung was deeply influenced by Sigmund Freud's writings on mental illness and dreams. From 1907 to 1913, Jung maintained close ties to Freud, and in 1911, Jung became the first president of the Internationale Psychoanalytische Gesellschaft (International Psychoanalytic Association). Theoretical disputes, chiefly concerned with the significance of sexuality in human life, finally led to Jung's breaking off the relationship with Freud.

Theory of Motivation and Personality. Jung felt that the emphasis of psychoanalysis on erotic factors led to a one-sided, reductionistic view of human motivation and behavior. He proposed that motivation be understood in terms of a general creative life energy—the libido—capable of being invested in different directions and assuming a variety of different forms. The two principal directions of the libido are known as extroversion (outward into the world of other people and objects) and introversion (inward into the realm of images, ideas, and the unconscious). Persons in whom the former directional tendency predominates are extroverts, while those in whom the latter is strongest are introverts. Jung also proposed that people could be grouped according to which of four psychological functions is most highly developed: thinking, feeling, sensation, or intuition. Transformations of libido

from one sphere of expression to another—for example, from sexuality to religion—are accomplished by symbols that are generated during personality change.

Theory of Symbols. Jung viewed symbol creation as central to understanding human nature, and he explored the correspondences between symbols arising from the life struggles of individuals and the symbolic images underlying religious, mythological, and magical systems of many cultures and eras. To account for the many striking similarities between independently originating symbols in individuals and across cultures, he suggested the existence of two layers of the unconscious psyche: the personal and the collective. The personal unconscious comprises mental contents acquired during the individual's life that have been forgotten or repressed, whereas the collective unconscious is an inherited structure common to all humankind and composed of the archetypes—innate predispositions to experience and symbolizing universal human situations in distinctively human ways. There are archetypes corresponding to such situations as having parents, finding a mate, having children, and confronting death, and highly elaborated derivatives of these archetypes populate all the great mythological and religious systems. Toward the end of his life Jung also suggested that the deepest layers of the unconscious function independently of the laws of space, time, and causality, giving rise to paranormal phenomena, such as clairvoyance and precognition.

Therapy. In Jungian therapy, which deals extensively with dreams and fantasies, a dialogue is set up between the conscious mind and the contents of the unconscious. Patients are made aware of both the personal and collective (archetypal) meanings inherent in their symptoms and difficulties. Under favorable conditions they may enter into the individuation process: a lengthy series of psychological transformations culminating in the integration of opposite tendencies and functions and the achievement of personal wholeness.

Jungfrau [yung'-frow]   The Jungfrau is a famous peak in the Bernese ALPS, on the border of the Bern and Valais cantons of Switzerland. Noted for its graceful contours and the dazzling whiteness of its snow cover, it rises to a height of 4,158 m (13,642 ft). Aletsch Glacier, on its south side, was first ascended in 1927. The eastern side was climbed in 1811.

Jungle, The   see SINCLAIR, UPTON

---

jungle and rain forest

Jungle and *rain forest* are terms that are often used synonymously but with little precision. The more meaningful and restrictive of these terms is *rain forest*, which refers to the climax or primary forest in regions with high rainfall (greater than 1.8 m/70 in per year), chiefly but not exclusively found in the tropics. Rain forests are significant for their valuable timber resources, and in the tropics they afford sites for commercial crops such as rubber, tea, coffee, and bananas.

The term *jungle* originally referred to the tangled, brushy vegetation of lowlands in India, but it has come to be used for any type of tropical forest or woodland. The word is more meaningful if limited to the dense, scrubby vegetation that develops when primary rain forest has been degraded by destructive forms of logging or cultivation.

Types of Rain Forest. Rain forests may be grouped into two major types: tropical and temperate. Tropical rain forest is characterized by broad-leaved evergreen trees that form a closed canopy, below which is found a zone of vines and epiphytes (plants growing on the trees), a relatively open forest floor, and a very large number of species of both plant and animal life. The largest trees have buttressed trunks and emerge above the continuous canopy, while smaller trees commonly form a layer of more shade-tolerant species beneath the upper canopy. The maximum height of the upper canopy of tropical rain forests is generally about 30 to 50 m (100 to 165 ft), with some individual trees rising as high as 60 m (200 ft).

The largest areas of tropical rain forest are in the Amazon basin of South America, in the Congo basin and other lowland equatorial regions of Africa, and on both the mainland and the islands off Southeast Asia. Small areas are found in Central America and along Australia's Queensland coast.

Temperate rain forests, growing in higher-latitude regions having wet, maritime climates, are less extensive than those of the tropics but include some of the most valuable timber in the world. Notable forests in this category are those on the northwest coast of North America, in southern Chile, in Tasmania, and in parts of southeastern Australia and New Zealand. These forests contain trees

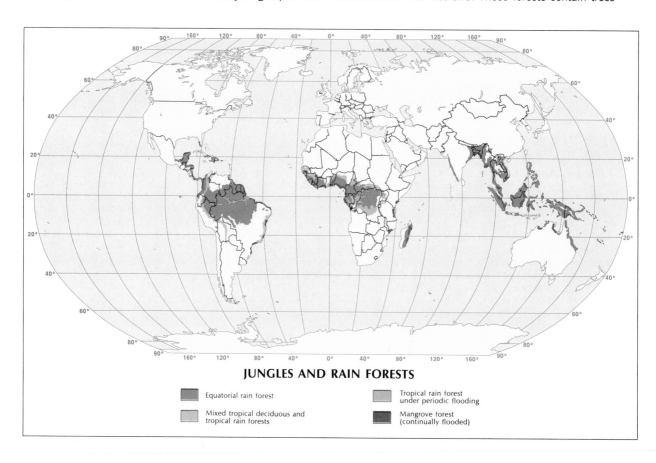

JUNGLES AND RAIN FORESTS

Equatorial rain forest

Mixed tropical deciduous and tropical rain forests

Tropical rain forest under periodic flooding

Mangrove forest (continually flooded)

that may exceed in height those of tropical rain forests, but there is less diversity of species. Conifers such as REDWOOD and Sitka spruce tend to predominate in North America, whereas their counterparts in the Southern Hemisphere include various species of EUCALYPTUS, *Araucaria*, and *Nothofagus* (Antarctic beech).

Ecology. Rain forests cover less than 6 percent of the Earth's total land surface, but they are the home for up to three-fourths of all known species of plants and animals; undoubtedly they also contain many more species as yet undiscovered. Despite their appearance of fertile abundance, rain forests are fragile ecosystems. Their soils can quickly lose the ability to support most forms of vegetation once the forest cover is removed. The effect of forest removal on local climates is also often profound.

Humans and Rain Forests. Throughout history, human beings have encroached on rain forests for living space, timber, and agricultural purposes. In vast portions of upland tropical forests, for example, the practice of "shifting cultivation" has caused deterioration of the primary forest. In this primitive system of agriculture, trees are killed in small plots that are cropped for two or three seasons and then abandoned; if the plots are again cultivated before primary vegetation has reestablished itself, the result is a progressive deterioration of the forest, leading to coarse grass or jungle. Lowland forests are similarly being reduced in many areas. These incursions on rain forests have grown rapidly, and numerous organizations are now attempting to reduce the rate of the loss.

junior colleges   see COMMUNITY AND JUNIOR COLLEGES

junior high school   see MIDDLE SCHOOLS AND JUNIOR HIGH SCHOOLS

juniper [joon'-ih-pur]   Junipers, genus *Juniperus*, are evergreen trees or SHRUBS belonging to the cypress fami-

ly, Cupressceae. They include approximately 35 species found throughout the Northern Hemisphere from the Arctic Circle to Mexico and the West Indies, Azores, Canary Islands, North Africa, Abyssinia, the mountains of tropical East Africa, the Himalayas, China, and Formosa.

Juniper bark is usually thin and scales off in longitudinal strips. Leaves are awl-shaped, closely pressed, and scalelike. The wood is fragrant, usually highly colored, reddish brown, and very durable. An essential oil is distilled from the wood and used for perfume and, sometimes, in medicine. Juniper leaves have powerful diuretic properties, and the characteristic taste of gin is derived from juniper berries. The common juniper, *J. communis*, is a small tree that is found in the colder northern areas of the Northern Hemisphere, and many are grown as landscape plants. Red "cedar," *J. virginiana*, is the most important juniper native to the United States. Its wood is the main source of "cedar" lining used to mothproof closets.

Junius [joon'-ee-uhs]   Junius was the pseudonym of the author of a series of political lampoons published in the *London Public Advertiser* between Jan. 21, 1769, and Jan. 21, 1772, denouncing the government of King George III and many of its officials, including the prime minister Lord NORTH. Dozens of writers have been identified as Junius, but Sir Philip Francis, a clerk in the war office, is considered the likeliest candidate.

junk   By the late Middle Ages the ancient Chinese sailing SHIP had evolved into the junk, one of the world's strongest and most seaworthy ships. (The term probably is derived from the Chinese *Chuan*, "boat," via Malay *djong*.) The junk is notable for two innovations in SHIPBUILDING, the construction of the hull and the rigging of the sails. Lacking three components—the keel as well as the stemposts and sternposts (upright beams at the bow and the stern)—that

The juniper is a small, coniferous tree that has scaly leaves and berrylike cones, each of which contains one to six seeds. The western juniper (left) is found in the Sierra Nevada mountains of California. The common juniper (right) is found throughout temperate and cold northern climates.

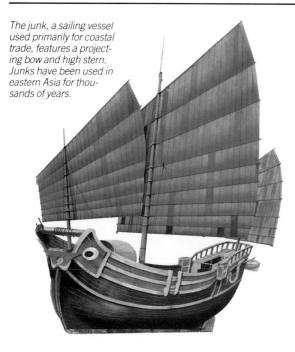

The junk, a sailing vessel used primarily for coastal trade, features a projecting bow and high stern. Junks have been used in eastern Asia for thousands of years.

are basic to other types of ships, the junk has a hull that is partitioned off by solid plank walls, or bulkheads, running both lengthwise and crosswise, dividing the junk into watertight compartments and giving it structural rigidity. (Crosswise bulkheads were not adopted in the West until the 19th century.) The lack of a keel is compensated for by using a deep, heavy rudder mounted so that it can be raised and lowered. The sails, made of narrow, horizontal sheets of linen or of matting panels, are carried on masts numbering from one to five. Each panel has its own sheet, or line; the numerous lines help distribute the wind's force, and each sail can be quickly spread or closed.

By the 9th century, Chinese junks were carrying merchants to Indonesia and India. Marco Polo, in his *Travels* (1298), describes such a junk and praises its system of bulkheads. By the 15th century, junks had sailed as far as eastern Africa, and in 1848 a junk sailed from China by way of Cape Horn to Boston, New York City, and London.

Junkers [yunk'-urz] The name *Junker*, derived from a German term meaning "young lord," was applied to the aristocracy of Prussia, which became the ruling elite of the German Empire created in 1871. The Junkers, descendants of the medieval German knights who conquered the territory east of the Elbe River, owned huge feudal estates in eastern Germany. When the rulers of Brandenburg-Prussia began to centralize government in the 17th century, the Junkers received a monopoly on the military and administrative services. After the unification of Germany under the Prussian monarchy, the Junker values of extreme conservatism and militarism permeated

the German government. Junker hostility helped undermine the Weimar Republic (1918–33) and thus contributed to the rise of Adolf Hitler.

Juno (mythology) In Roman mythology Juno, the wife and sister of JUPITER, was the queen of heaven. Like HERA, her Greek counterpart, she was the goddess of marriage and the protectress of women. She presided over the finances of the Roman state, and the mint was located in her temple on the Capitoline Hill. A festival, the Matronalia, was celebrated in her honor on March 1.

Juno (rocket) see JUPITER (rocket)

Junot, Andoche [zhoo-noh', ahn-dohsh'] Andoche Junot, b. Oct. 23, 1771, d. July 29, 1813, was a French general during the Napoleonic Wars. He rose through the ranks and served as aide-de-camp to Napoléon Bonaparte (later Napoleon I) in Italy and Egypt. In 1807, Junot opened the Peninsular War by invading Portugal and was rewarded for his entry into Lisbon with the title duc d'Abrantès. Defeated in 1808 by the future duke of Wellington, however, he had to evacuate Portugal. Despite later military service in Spain, Austria, and Russia, Junot never regained his reputation. He became mentally unstable and committed suicide.

junta [hun'-tuh] *Junta*, a Spanish word meaning council or committee, is the name given to a small group of people who rule a country, usually after a revolution or coup d'état. Juntas usually count among their members high-ranking military officers and tend to advocate a conservative or moderate approach. Juntas either govern by decree or form governments that will carry out their wishes. Although juntas have most commonly been associated with Spanish-speaking countries of the New World, the term *junta* has international application.

Jupiter (mythology) In Roman mythology Jupiter was the king of the gods and the lord of life and death. He was also called Jove. Jupiter was the son of SATURN and Rhea, the husband of JUNO, and the father of MINERVA. The Romans identified him with the Greek god ZEUS, but he retained to some degree his own distinctive character. Unlike Zeus, for example, he never came to visit humankind on earth. Jupiter was usually represented in art sitting on an ivory throne and holding a sheaf of thunderbolts. The eagle and the ox were sacred to him. His most celebrated temple was on the CAPITOLINE HILL in Rome.

Jupiter (planet) Jupiter, the fifth planet from the Sun, is by far the most massive planet. Its mass represents more than two-thirds of the total mass of all the planets, or 318 times the mass of the Earth. If Jupiter had been several times more massive, it would have been a star, because the pressure and temperature at its center would have been great enough to set off nuclear fusion. Because Jupiter's density (1.3 g/cm^3, or 82 lb/ft^3) is relatively low, it has the volume of 1,000 Earths. Jupiter is 1,000 times smaller than the Sun. The planet's fast axial rotation—once every 9 hr 55.5 min—causes it to be considerably flattened: the equatorial diameter is 142,800 km (88,700 mi), but the distance from the North to the South Pole is only 133,500 km (83,000 mi). Jupiter orbits the Sun in 11.9 years at a distance of 778.3 million km (483.3 million mi), or 5.2 times the Earth's distance from the Sun.

Origin, Structure, Composition, and Weather

Jupiter may have formed, like the Sun, by gravitational

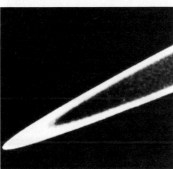

(Above) The winds of Jupiter, moving parallel to the planet's equator, produce a pattern of cloud bands. (Left) Although Jupiter is larger than Saturn, its ring system is smaller. This thin ring, viewed by the Voyager 2 probe in 1979, is invisible from Earth.

collapse of part of the primeval solar nebula. Alternatively, if the nebula was less massive, dust particles that condensed as the nebula cooled would have coalesced due to collisions. Once Jupiter's "embryo" (now its rocky core, with a mass several times that of Earth's) became large enough, its gravity pulled together a surrounding envelope of gas from the nebula. Like the Sun and the primeval nebula, Jupiter is primarily composed of hydrogen and helium. Because the temperature is sufficiently warm, there is no solid surface under the atmosphere, only a gradual transition from gas to liquid. About one-fourth of the way into the planet the pressure and temperature are so high that the liquid becomes metallic, by which physicists mean that the molecules are stripped of their outer electrons.

Jupiter's atmosphere also contains trace amounts of water, ammonia, methane, and other organic (carbon) compounds. Astronomers theorize that three layers of clouds exist, separated by about 30 km (19 mi) in altitude. The lowest are made of water ice or droplets, the next are crystals of a compound of ammonia and hydrogen sulfide, and the highest are ammonia ice. Of the observed clouds, the blue ones are warmest and therefore at the lowest altitude. Browns, whites, and reds lie increasingly higher, in that order. These shades are believed to be caused by chemical disequilibrium, which allows sulfur, phosphorus, and organic compounds to color the clouds. This disequilibrium may be due to impact by charged particles, rapid vertical motion through changing temperature levels, or lightning. The two VOYAGER spacecraft that flew past Jupiter in 1979 observed lightning as well as AURORAS on Jupiter's night side.

The winds on Jupiter move in jets parallel to the equator. The speeds—some eastward, some westward, and varying with latitude, or distance from the equator—are tens to a hundred meters per second relative to the rotating interior. The latitudes of the zonal jets correlate well with positions of broad, alternately colored bands of orange brown and whitish clouds seen by Earth-based telescopes. The differences in cloud coloration may be due to gas rising in some bands and descending in others.

Weather on Jupiter is still not well understood. Eddies and storms form and dissipate, some lasting only a few days, others much longer. Some get caught between regions of different east-west wind speeds and are sheared apart. Larger eddies, such as long-lived white spots and the Earth-sized Great Red Spot, are able to survive by rolling like ball bearings between zones.

Magnetic Field, Satellites, and Rings

Rotation and currents within the metallic hydrogen interior of Jupiter generate a magnetic field, much as the molten iron core of the Earth does. Jupiter's field is 4,000 times stronger than the Earth's, and extends at least 20 Jovian radii away from the planet.

Although Jupiter was not large enough to begin nuclear burning, the compression of its own gravity generated a tremendous amount of heat when the planet formed. Even now, 4.6 billion years later, Jupiter radiates nearly

The turbulent, complex nature of Jupiter's cloud-top is illustrated in this photograph of the region near the Great Red Spot taken by the Voyager 2 spacecraft. The Great Red Spot is a gigantic, permanent hurricane system that rotates counterclockwise with one revolution every 6 days.

twice as much heat as it receives from the Sun. Early on, when satellites were forming around Jupiter, heat radiating from the planet was much greater. Hence the satellites that formed are rockier near Jupiter and icier farther away. This trend is evident among the four large satellites discovered by Galileo in 1610 and called the Galilean moons. The regular, circular, equatorial orbits of these satellites suggest that they did indeed form from a cloud of small particles circling the planet. The satellites, named Callisto, Ganymede, Europa, and Io, are described in separate entries.

In addition to the Galilean moons, Jupiter has several smaller satellites and rings. Amalthea, the largest satellite interior to Io's orbit, is irregularly shaped, about 265 km

(165 mi) long and 150 km (93 mi) wide. Its surface is dark and red and is continually bombarded by the energetic particles of Jupiter's magnetosphere. *Voyager 1* photographed (1979) a narrow ring orbiting the planet about halfway from the surface out to Amalthea. A fainter ring was found to extend from the bright ring right down to the planet. Unlike the bright ring, it also extends away from the equatorial plane to form a cloud of particles surrounding the planet.

Jupiter's rings are very diffuse. The ring particles must generally be about as big as the wavelength of light, that is, only a few microns. The bright ring may contain particles of a wide range of sizes, with two satellites found by the Voyager spacecraft near the ring's outer edge being

SATELLITES OF JUPITER

Name	Discoverer	Year of Discovery	Average Distance from Center of Jupiter km	mi	Period of Revolution (days)	Diameter km	mi	Orbital Inclination (degrees)	Orbital Eccentricity
Metis	Stephen Synnott	1980	128,000	79,500	0.295	~40	~25	?	?
Adrastea	G. E. Danielson, D. Jewitt	1979	128,700	80,000	0.297	24	15	?	?
Amalthea	Edward Barnard	1892	181,300	112,700	0.489	260×150	162×93	0.455	0.003
Thebe	Stephen Synnott	1980	221,900	137,900	0.675	80	50	1.25	?
Io	Galileo, Simon Mayr	1610	421,600	262,000	1.769	3,632	2,256	0.027	0.004
Europa	Galileo, Simon Mayr	1610	670,900	416,900	3.551	3,126	1,942	0.468	0.01
Ganymede	Galileo, Simon Mayr	1610	1,070,000	665,000	7.155	5,276	3,278	0.183	0.001
Callisto	Galileo, Simon Mayr	1610	1,880,000	1,168,000	16.689	4,820	2,995	0.253	0.01
Leda	Charles Kowal	1974	11,110,000	6,904,000	240	20	12	27	0.146
Himalia	Charles Perrine	1904	11,470,000	7,127,000	250.6	170	105	28	0.158
Lysithea	Seth Nicholson	1938	11,710,000	7,277,000	260	30	19	29	0.130
Elara	Charles Perrine	1905	11,740,000	7,295,000	260.1	80	50	25	0.207
Ananke	Seth Nicholson	1951	20,700,000	12,850,000	617	30	19	147	0.169
Carme	Seth Nicholson	1938	22,350,000	13,900,000	692	40	25	164	0.207
Pasiphae	P. J. Mellote	1908	23,300,000	14,500,000	735	50	31	145	0.40
Sinope	Seth Nicholson	1914	23,700,000	14,750,000	758	40	25	153	0.275

SOURCE: Adapted from table in J. Kelly Beatty et al., eds., *The New Solar System* (Sky Publishing Corp. and Cambridge Univ. Press, 1981), p. 220.

the largest. Voyager also found another tiny satellite between the orbits of Amalthea and Io.

The eight outer satellites of Jupiter are small, dark, stony objects that closely resemble the Trojan asteroids. This evidence, combined with their highly eccentric and inclined orbits near the limit of Jupiter's gravitational sphere of influence, suggests that the outer satellites were captured from interplanetary orbits. No satisfactory explanation has been offered for their clustering at two distinct distances from Jupiter or for the retrograde (opposite Jupiter's rotation) motion of the outer four satellites.

Jupiter (rocket) *Jupiter* is the name given to two different rockets. One (Jupiter C) was the basis for the Juno I satellite launches. The other was an intermediate-range ballistic missile (IRBM) later developed into Juno II. Both were under the control of the U.S. Army Ballistic Missile Agency.

The Jupiter C, first launched on Sept. 20, 1956, to test nose-cone materials for the Jupiter IRBM, was a REDSTONE rocket lengthened to a total of 20 m (65.6 ft). Its original LO_2/ethyl alcohol propellants were changed to liquid oxygen and Hydyne, a mixture of 60% unsymmetrical dimethylhydrazine and 40% diethylene triamine. Two solid-propellant stages were clustered in a spinning "tub" on the separable nose. Stage 2 had an outer ring of 11 solid-propellant rocket motors; stage 3 had 3 of these motors (Baby Sergeants) inside.

Juno I consisted of a fourth-stage Baby Sergeant motor added to the Jupiter C. This allowed the rocket to achieve orbital velocity. The 29,000-kg (64,000-lb) four-stage rocket, which stood 21.7 m (71.2 ft) tall and had a liftoff thrust of about 369,000 newtons, or 37,600 kg (83,000 lb), placed the first U.S. artificial satellite, EXPLORER I, into orbit in 1958.

The Jupiter IRBM, first test-launched at Cape Canaveral on Mar. 1, 1957, was a liquid-propellant (LO_2/kerosene) rocket. It stood 18.4 m (60.3 ft) tall and had a launch weight of approximately 49,900 kg (110,000 lb). Maximum design range was 2,575 km (1,600 mi). The later development of lightweight thermonuclear warheads and the desire to place missiles in nuclear submarines resulted in the more compact solid-propellant Polaris missile, and Jupiter production was terminated.

Juno II, a four-stage launcher, was a Jupiter IRBM lengthened by 0.9 m (3 ft) to allow enough propellant for 20 seconds of extra burning. It carried an arrangement of Baby Sergeant upper stages similar to the Jupiter IRBM. The weight was about 55,340 kg (122,000 lb).

See also: ROCKETS AND MISSILES.

Jura [jur'-uh] The Jura, a mountain range of the Alpine system (see ALPS), forms a natural boundary between France and Switzerland. The range extends 200 km (125 mi) from the Rhône River gorge near Geneva, north to the Rhine River near Basel. The narrow, parallel ridges reach a maximum width of 65 km (40 mi). Average elevation is about 860 m (2,800 ft); the maximum is 1,723 m (5,650 ft) at Crêt de la Neige, in France.

The Jura was formed in two stages: during the Early Tertiary Period when the Alps originated and during the Jurassic Period (the latter period is named for the mountains). The ridges and furrows of fossiliferous limestone conceal many underground rivers and caverns. Principal aboveground rivers include the Ain, the Doubs, and the Loire. The slopes are heavily forested.

Jurassic Period see EARTH, GEOLOGICAL HISTORY OF

jurisdiction see COURT

jurisprudence see LAW

jury A jury is a body of lay men and women randomly selected to determine facts and to provide a decision in a legal proceeding. The jury is of Frankish origin, beginning with Charlemagne's *inquisitio*, which had an accusatory and interrogatory function. Trial by jury was brought to England by the Normans in 1066. Jurors were witnesses summoned from the vicinity of the crime, and they were used as part of the proof of innocence or guilt. In the 14th century the role of the jury finally became that of judgment of evidence. By the 15th century trial by jury became the dominant mode of resolving a legal issue. It replaced such primitive forms of resolution as trial by ordeal, in which a person could prove innocence by enduring a test by fire or boiling water.

English influence and settlers brought the custom of jury trial to America. Deprivation of the "benefits of trial by jury" was a specific complaint mentioned in the American Declaration of Independence, and the right to a jury in federal courts was established in the U.S. Constitution. Article III provides for trial by jury in federal criminal cases; the 5th Amendment, the 6th Amendment, and the 7th Amendment provide respectively for the rights to presentment or indictment of a GRAND JURY, to trial in criminal prosecutions by an impartial jury of the state in which the crime has been committed, and to trial by jury in COMMON LAW suits where the value in controversy exceeds twenty dollars. The Supreme Court in *Duncan* v. *Louisiana* (1968) declared through the 14TH AMENDMENT that the jury trial is a constitutional right applicable to all criminal trials—state or federal—in which the punishment may exceed six months.

The mechanics of the American jury system vary with each state, but its function does not. Once selected and sworn, the juror is questioned by the attorneys, the judge, or both as to background or possible bias. This is known as a *voir dire* examination. If an attorney believes there is a reason a juror should not sit on a particular jury, that juror can be challenged "for cause" and replaced by another juror. The attorneys have additional challenges, for which no reason must be given. These are called "peremptory challenges." Use of these limited "peremptory challenges" and the selection of the jury are important parts of each trial.

The jury always deliberates in private and is not compelled to reveal its reasons for a decision. Occasionally a jury will be "sequestered," or separated from society so that its members are protected from being influenced by publicity concerning a case to which they have been assigned. If the jury cannot agree on a decision, a "hung" jury results. The case must then be retried before a different jury.

In a civil case, such as a personal injury action, the jury determines liability and the amount of the award. In most criminal cases the jury renders a verdict of innocence or guilt, but the judge sentences the defendant. In some states, juries may determine punishment in capital cases.

See also: COURT; LEGAL PROCEDURE.

Justice, U.S. Department of   The U.S. Department of Justice, established in 1870, is the federal government's legal office. It is headed by the cabinet-rank ATTORNEY GENERAL, who is responsible for the enforcement of federal laws, represents the government in all legal matters, and gives advice and opinions to the president and the heads of the executive departments. The Justice Department also includes the FEDERAL BUREAU OF INVESTIGATION and a number of other bureaus and agencies.

Assisting the attorney general are the deputy attorney general, the associate attorney general, and the solicitor general. The last handles government cases in the Supreme Court. The department has six divisions, each headed by an assistant attorney general, that are devoted primarily to legal affairs. The Antitrust Division is responsible for enforcing the federal antitrust laws. The Civil Division represents the government in civil lawsuits arising from the commercial and governmental activities of federal agencies. The Criminal Division is responsible for enforcing about 900 federal criminal statutes. Other legal divisions are the Civil Rights Division, the Land and Natural Resources Division, and the Tax Division.

The department also contains the Federal Bureau of Prisons, the Parole Commission, the Immigration and Naturalization Service, the Board of Immigration Appeals, the Drug Enforcement Administration, and the agencies established by the Justice System Improvement Act (1979), which assist local governments in law enforcement, largely through research and statistics.

justice of the peace   A justice of the peace is a local magistrate with limited judicial power. Justices of the peace are usually elected officials in the United States, although in some states they are appointed. They usually have the power to try minor criminal cases and civil cases involving small amounts of money. Their other duties include issuing arrest and search warrants, holding preliminary hearings in criminal cases, holding inquests, and performing marriage ceremonies. The office was created in 14th-century England, where subsequent justices of the peace were powerful agents of the king, responsible for keeping the peace in each county. By the end of the 19th century they had lost their administrative (but not judicial) authority.

Justin Martyr, Saint   Saint Justin Martyr, c.100–c.165, is recognized as one of the most important early Christian writers. Justin tried to make a reasoned defense of Christianity to outsiders. He went to Rome and opened a school of philosophy. Justin is the reputed author of a vast number of treatises, but the only authentic remaining works are two *Apologies*, his *Dialogue with Trypho the Jew*, and fragments of *On the Resurrection*. Justin was beheaded, probably in 165. Feast day: June 1.

Justine   see SADE, MARQUIS DE

Justinian Code   [juhs-tin'-ee-uhn]   The Justinian Code was part of a collection of ROMAN LAW, known as the *Corpus Juris Civilis* ("Body of Civil Law"), prepared during the reign of the Byzantine emperor Justinian I (r. 527–65). In the 6th century AD the mass of Roman legal material that had accumulated in 1,000 years of development was generally unavailable to those who needed it, and it frequently contained contradictions. Early in his reign Justinian established three committees, under the general chairmanship of his chief legal advisor, Tribonian, to gather and edit the legal material.

One committee collected all the laws that had emanated from the emperors themselves. These form the *Code*, which appeared in 12 books in 529 and contains mainly public, administrative, and criminal law. Another committee collated and removed contradictions from the writings of the foremost Roman legal experts to form the *Digest*. A third committee prepared a textbook, the *Institutes*, for beginning students. It is still used and has been a model for later texts.

Justinian I, Byzantine Emperor   (Justinian the Great)   Justinian I, or Justinian the Great, b. c.482, d. Nov. 15, 565, ruled the BYZANTINE EMPIRE from 527 to 565 as one of its greatest emperors. Born near Scupi (the modern Skopje, Yugoslavia), he was originally named Petrus Sabbatius. He was educated in Constantinople by his uncle Justin, an army officer, who became emperor as Justin I in 518. Justinian married (525) THEODORA and in 527 succeeded Justin to the throne.

Justinian's aim was the reconquest of Roman areas lost to the Germanic tribes. With the help of his general BELISARIUS, he regained North Africa from the VANDALS (533–34) and, after a lengthy war (535–54), Italy from the Ostrogoths (see GOTHS). Justinian also acquired southeastern Spain. Repeated wars with the SASSANIAN Persians, however, usually ended with the Byzantines buying peace; and the Slavs occupied much of the Balkan Peninsula.

To finance his wars, Justinian extorted heavy taxes from his subjects. He also improved the system of justice by the codification of Roman law in the celebrated Justinianic Code. After the great Nika riot and fire in Constantinople (532), he rebuilt HAGIA SOPHIA with extraordinary magnificence. He intervened repeatedly in theological quarrels to reconcile Eastern Monophysites (see

MONOPHYSITISM) and Western Catholics, but without success (see CONSTANTINOPLE, COUNCILS OF). His contemporary PROCOPIUS OF CAESAREA wrote the history of the reign.

jute [joot]

Jute is the fiber from the inner bark of *Corchorus capsularis*, a tall, annual, Asiatic plant cultivated almost exclusively in India and Pakistan. Its cultivation has not yet been mechanized; therefore, substantial hand labor is required to prepare the fiber.

Jute is one of the cheapest natural textile fibers and is second only to cotton in world consumption. (Other important woody fibers are flax and hemp.) The plant grows to a height of 0.6–3.6 m (2–12 ft); the stalks will produce up to five times more fiber than the flax plant.

The yellowish jute fibers, which may reach a length of 3 m (10 ft), are thick, brittle, and harsh to the touch. Coarser grades of jute are made into gunny sacking, scrim, or rope and twine. Finer grades are woven into carpets, shirting, and coat linings. Jute threads are used as backing and binding for carpets. Burlap, a coarse, plain-weave fabric, is also made of jute.

Because jute does not bleach or dye well, will disintegrate with prolonged exposure to moisture, and is one of the weakest of the plant fibers, its use is limited.

Jutland [juht'-luhnd]

Jutland (Danish: Jylland) is the peninsula on which mainland Denmark is located; it is bounded on the west by the North Sea, on the north by the SKAGERRAK, and on the east by the Kattegat and the Lille Baelt. The southern portion of the peninsula is part of the German state Schleswig-Holstein, but the term *Jutland* usually refers only to the Danish section. Danish Jutland, including several offshore islands, is low-lying and covers an area of 29,766 km^2 (11,493 mi^2).

The World War I Battle of Jutland (1916) between British and German fleets was fought off Jutland's North Sea coast.

Jutland, Battle of   see WORLD WAR I

Juvenal [joo'-vuh-nul]

The Roman poet Decimus Iunius Iuvenalis, AD *c.*60–130, known in English as Juvenal, was the last great satirist of LATIN LITERATURE. In his first SATIRE Juvenal claims that moral indignation forces him to write, but for fear of his own safety he will speak only of the dead. After Domitian's death (96) Juvenal published a series of poems that lashed out at the corruption, vices, and follies of imperial Rome, masking his concern with the contemporary city by explicit allusions to the dead emperor. Whether Juvenal was successful cannot be known, for only MARTIAL alludes to him, in epigrams that antedate Juvenal's earliest publication. Writing over a period of 30 years, growing older in a Rome that fared variously under Domitian, Nerva (96–98), Trajan (98–117), and Hadrian (117–138), Juvenal moderated his themes in later satires. This can be seen by comparing his two most famous poems: in "Satire 3" he attacks contemporary Rome, measuring its citizens against the moral standards established during the early years of the Roman republic, but in "Satire 10" he discourses on the vanity of all human wishes regardless of place or time.

juvenile delinquency

Juvenile delinquency is law-breaking by nonadult persons. It includes such crimes as murder or robbery, as well as some offenses, such as truancy or certain sexual acts, that are illegal only when committed by juveniles. The definition of *juvenile* varies from state to state, but the term most commonly refers to someone under 18 years of age.

Causes of Delinquency. Criminologists who study juvenile delinquency attempt to explain it in several ways. One theory is that children from the poorest part of society lack opportunities to develop in socially acceptable ways and turn to delinquency as a substitute. Another theory is that delinquency is learned behavior, acquired by associating with people who have little respect for the law. A third explanation is that juveniles who are caught and labeled delinquent by the authorities are likely to continue to break the law because that label makes it harder for them to be law-abiding. Other explanations stress biological or psychological causes.

Juvenile Justice. Police departments often employ special officers who handle many juvenile cases informally, without making arrests. Once arrested, a juvenile normally appears before a juvenile court. Because juvenile courts have been traditionally less concerned with legal guilt or innocence than with helping the offender, they have been more informal than adult criminal courts. The court may assign a probation officer, who tries to provide guidance for the young offender and to encourage more acceptable social behavior.

If the judge feels that the case is serious enough, the offender may be sentenced to a correctional institution. Juvenile correctional institutions usually offer work training and try to instill a sense of social responsibility. Although most juveniles who come into contact with the juvenile justice system do not become adult criminals, a large proportion do commit further violations.

Juvenile rights in the United States have become increasingly defined in recent years. The U.S. Supreme Court has held, for example, that the due process clause of the 14th Amendment requires that juveniles accused of criminal offenses have the right to counsel, to confront and cross-examine witnesses, and to protection against self-incrimination (In re *Gault*, 1967). The Court has also held that conviction must be by "proof beyond a reasonable doubt" (In re *Winship*, 1970). At the same time, the standards of the juvenile justice system have also become more severe. The Supreme Court has held that due process does not assure the right of trial by jury in a state juvenile court proceeding (*McKeiver* v. *Pennsylvania*, 1971) and that states can hold juvenile criminal suspects in preventive detention before bringing them to trial (*Schall* v. *Martin*, 1984).

juvenile hormone   see METAMORPHOSIS

ILLUSTRATION CREDITS

6 Brown Brothers
10 Focus on Sports
13 Focus on Sports/Tony Duffy
14 Duomo/Paul Sutton; Sports Illustrated/Bill Eppridge
15 Uniphoto, Washington, D.C./Paul Robert Perry
17 Rand McNally & Company; Camera Press Ltd./Charbonniere
19 Snark International
20 Scala, Florence
23 Nassau Mauritshuis
25 Rand McNally & Company
26 Photo Researchers/Margaret Durrance
27 Photo Researchers/Jack Fields; Photo Researchers/Russ Kinne
30 Scala, Florence
32 Courtesy Wyoming Travel Commission
38 Rand McNally & Company
39 ROLOC; Courtesy Illinois Office of Tourism
40 ROLOC
42 The British Library
46 All pictures—Woods Hole Oceanographic Institute/Ben Dawson
47 All pictures—Woods Hole Oceanographic Institute
52 CDC/Atlanta, Ga.
55 Mary Evans Picture Library
60 LIFE NATURE LIBRARY: Animal Behavior Photographs by Nina Leen © 1965 Time-Life Books, Inc.
62 Museo Historico Regional de Cuzco/ Calle Heirderos, Peru
63 Picturepoint, London; Courtesy Museum of the American Indian, Heye Foundation
69 Photo Researchers/Harold Kinne
71 Rand McNally & Company
72 Gamma/Liaison/Karen Rubin
73 Superstock/Shostal/Manley; Superstock/Shostal/Manley
74 Superstock/Shostal/Streichan
75 Photo Researchers/Diane Rawson; Servizio Editoriale Fotografico
76 Agence De Presse Photografique Rapho; ANP-Foto/CTK
78 Scala, Florence
81 Cauboue; The Bettmann Archive
83 Photo Researchers/Mathias Oppersdorff
84 Scala, Florence; A. F. Kersting
85 Scala, Florence
92 Librarie Hachette, Paris
94 The Bettmann Archive
97 Rand McNally & Company

98 Photo Researchers/Van Bucher
99 Photo Researchers/Van Bucher
100 Photo Researchers/William Carter
101 Stedelijk Museum, Amsterdam
102 The British Museum, London; Aldus Archives; Smithsonian Institution, Washington, D.C.: United States National Museum, on deposit with the National Collection of Fine Arts
103 The Thomas Gilcrease Institute of American History and Art, Tulsa, Okla.; The British Museum, London
104 The British Museum, London
105 Smithsonian Institution, Washington, D.C.: National Collection of Fine Arts; Photo Researchers/Calvin Larsen; Courtesy Glenbow Foundation, Calgary, Alberta
106 Photo Researchers/George Holton; Smithsonian Institution, Washington, D.C.: National Collection of Fine Arts; Michael Holford Library
107 Courtesy Royal Ontario Museum, Toronto, Canada
108 Smithsonian Institution, Washington, D.C.: National Collection of Fine Arts
111 Aldus Archives; Courtesy Royal Ontario Museum, Toronto, Canada
112 Pitt-Rivers Museum, Oxford, England; Smithsonian Institution, Washington, D.C.: National Collection of Fine Arts
113 Smithsonian Institution, Washington, D.C.: National Collection of Fine Arts; National Archives, Washington, D.C.
114 Musée du Seminaire de Quebec; The British Museum, London
118 Metropolitan Museum of Art, New York, The Michael C. Rockefeller Memorial Collection of Primitive Art, Bequest of Nelson A. Rockefeller; Paul C. Pet
119 Reproduced from "Historia Fisicia y Politica de Chile," 1854, by Claude Gay; Aldus Archives
120 The British Museum, London; Yale University Library, Courtesy of the Western Americana Collection
121 The Bettmann Archive
122 Paolo Koch
123 Tom Prescott; Shostal Associates
124 Shostal Associates; Milwaukee Public Museum, Wisconsin
125 Shostal Associates
126 Smithsonian Institution, Washington, D.C.: National Collection of Fine Arts
127 Photo Researchers/F. B. Grunzweig

131 Rand McNally & Company
132 Paul C. Pet
133 Photo Researchers/David Barnes
135 Rand McNally & Company
137 Pakistan Council
138 Smithsonian Institution, Washington, D.C.; The Granger Collection; Ettore Sottass/Memphis/Milano, photo courtesy Daniel Saxon
141 Metropolitan Museum of Art, New York, Gift of Lyman G. Bloomingdale, 1901
163 Scala, Florence
174 © TRW, Inc.
178 Courtesy Josef Charyk
197 California Institute of Technology
207 U.S. Geological Survey/Alfred S. McEwen
213 Rand McNally & Company
214 Photo Researchers/Porterfield-Chickering
215 Uniphoto/Washington, D.C.
219 Rand McNally & Company
220 Photo Researchers/Paolo Koch
221 Taurus Photos/Richardson
224 Rand McNally & Company
225 Photo Researchers/Georg Gerster
228 Rand McNally & Company
229 Photo Researchers/Farrell Grehan
230 Photo Researchers/Louis Goldman
232 National Gallery of Ireland, Dublin
233 The Bettmann Archive
234 Camera Press/O'Brien
236 National Gallery of Ireland, Dublin; Brown Brothers; Brown Brothers; Jerry Baues
247 Grant Heilman Photography/John Colwell
248 Grant Heilman Photography/John Colwell
249 Brown Brothers
250 Culver Pictures
253 Photo Researchers/Mehmet Biber
254 AAA-Photo
257 Victoria and Albert Museum, London
265 Rand McNally & Company
266 AGE/World Photo Service
267 Agence De Presse Photografique Rapho/Goldman
268 Photo Researchers/Farrell Grehan
269 Art Resource/Scala
272 Scala, Florence
274 The Bettmann Archive; Art Resource/ Scala
276 Scala, Florence
277 The Bettmann Archive; The Bettmann Archive
280 Rand McNally & Company
281 Photo Researchers/R. G. Everts
282 Photo Researchers/Porterfield-Chickering
283 Paolo Koch
284 Magnum/Dennis Stock; Bavaria-Verlag Bildagentur/Pedone
285 Art Resource/Scala
286 Lothar Roth and Associates

287 Art Resource/Scala; The Bettmann Archive
288 Lothar Roth and Associates
289 The Bettmann Archive
291 Culver Pictures
293 Rand McNally & Company
298 White House Historical Society
300 Gamma/Liaison/Diana Walker
301 The Bettmann Archive
304 Photo Researchers/Russ Kinne
308 Rand McNally & Company
309 National Portrait Gallery, London
311 National Portrait Gallery, London
312 National Portrait Gallery, London; The Bettmann Archive
316 Rand McNally & Company
317 Photo Researchers/Paolo Koch
318 Photo Researchers/Paolo Koch
319 AAA-Photo
321 Courtesy Museum of Fine Arts, Boston: Fenollosa-Weld Collection
322 Sem Presser
323 BBC—Hulton Picture Library
324 Het Spectrum
325 Mireïlle Vautier
326 Shashinka Photo Library
336 Brown Brothers
337 The Bettmann Archive; The Bettmann Archive
338 The Bettmann Archive; Retna Ltd./ Ben DeSoto
340 Corcoran Gallery of Art
347 Photo Researchers/William Katz
349 Scala/Monastery of San Marco, Florence
351 Scala, Florence
353 Courtesy Pratt and Whitney Aircraft
357 Staats und Universitäts Bibliothek, Hamburg; Art Resource/Scala
359 Kunstsammlungen der Veste, Coburg
360 Courtesy Haifa Publishing Company, Ltd.; The Bettmann Archive
365 The Bettmann Archive
367 Photo Researchers/Georg Gerster
370 Gamma/Liaison/Diana Walker
371 Picturepoint, London
373 UPI/Bettmann Newsphotos
375 White House Historical Society
377 White House Historical Society
379 Philip Johnson
380 Brown Brothers
382 The Bettmann Archive
385 Central Press
387 The Bettmann Archive
388 National Portrait Gallery, London
389 The Bettmann Archive
391 Rand McNally & Company
392 Photo Researchers/Paolo Koch
398 The Bettmann Archive
399 The Bettmann Archive
400 Zemaljski Museum, Sarajevo
401 Sasson Library/Letchworth, England
402 Sem Presser
403 Keter Publishing House
407 © Karsh Ottawa
411 NASA; NASA
412 NASA